UNITED NATIONS CONFERENCE ON TRADE AND DEVELOPMENT
CONFÉRENCE DES NATIONS UNIES SUR LE COMMERCE ET LE DÉVELOPPEMENT

CNUCED

UNCTAD

UNCTAD
HANDBOOK
OF STATISTICS

MANUEL
DE STATISTIQUES
DE LA CNUCED

2013

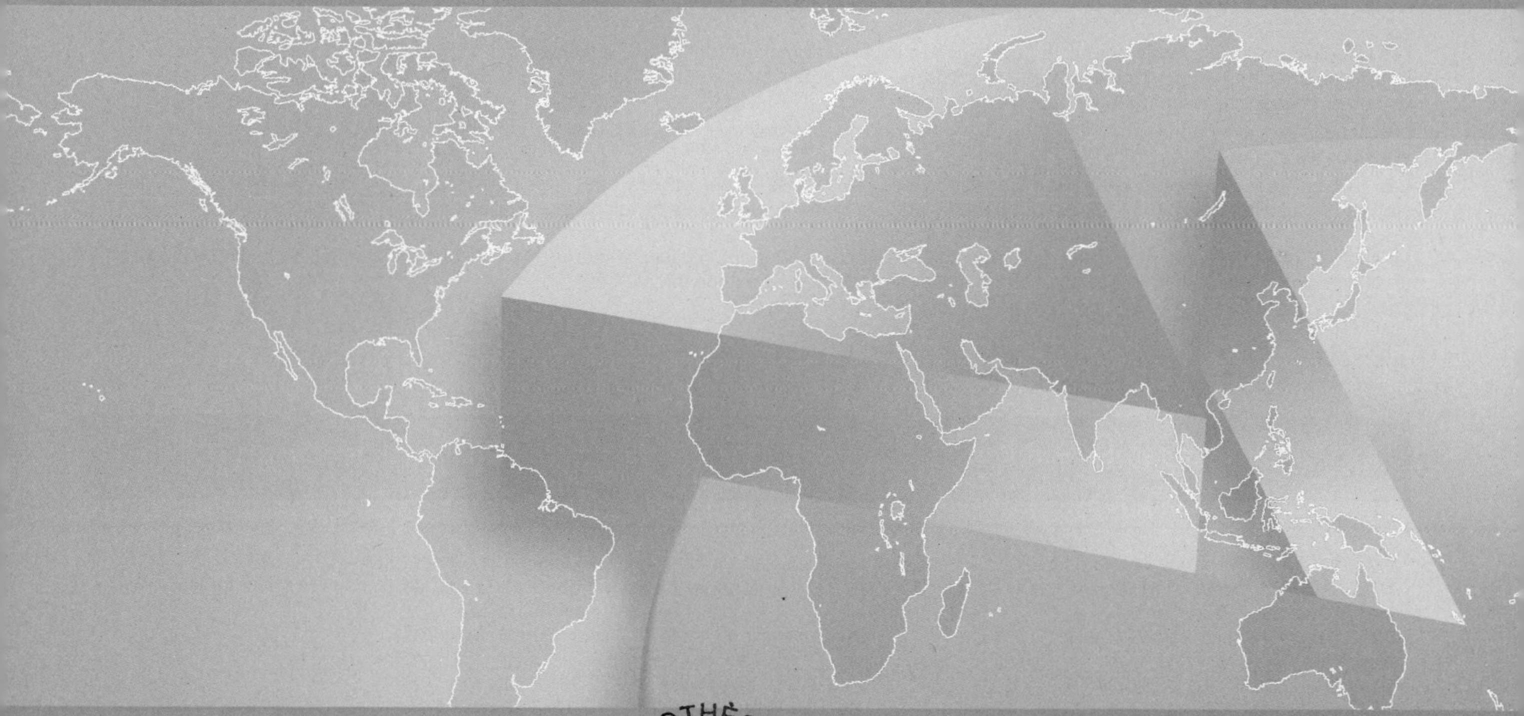

UNITED NATIONS
New York and Geneva

2013

NATIONS UNIES
New York et Genève

NOTE

Symbols of United Nations documents are composed of capital letters combined with figures. Mention of such a symbol indicates a reference to a United Nations document.

General disclaimer

The designations employed and the presentation of the material in this publication do not imply the expression of any opinion whatsoever on the part of the secretariat of the United Nations concerning the legal status of any country, territory, city or area, or of its authorities, or concerning the delimitation of its frontiers or boundaries.

Where the designations "economy" or "country or area" appear in tables, they cover countries, territories, cities and areas.

The designations "developing", "transition" and "developed" are intended for statistical convenience and do not necessarily express a judgement about the stage reached by a particular country or area in the development process.

Material in this publication may be freely quoted or reprinted, but acknowledgement is obligatory, together with a reference to the document number (TD/STAT.38). A copy of the publication containing the quotation or reprint should be sent to the UNCTAD secretariat.

*
* *

La cote des documents de l'Organisation des Nations Unies se compose de lettres majuscules et de chiffres. La mention d'une telle cote indique qu'il est fait référence à un document de l'Organisation.

Déni de responsabilité

Les appellations employées dans cette publication et la présentation des données qui y figurent n'impliquent, de la part du secrétariat de l'Organisation des Nations Unies, aucune prise de position quant au statut juridique des pays, territoires, villes ou zones, ou de leurs autorités, ni quant au tracé de leurs frontières ou limites.

Les appellations «économie» ou «pays ou zone» figurant dans certaines rubriques des tableaux désignent des pays, des territoires, des villes ou des zones.

Les termes «en développement», «en transition» et «développés» sont utilisés pour plus de commodité dans la présentation des statistiques et n'impliquent pas nécessairement un jugement quant au stade de développement atteint par un pays ou une zone donnée.

Le contenu de la présente publication peut être cité ou reproduit sans autorisation, sous réserve qu'il soit fait mention de ladite publication et de sa cote (TD/STAT.38) et qu'un justificatif soit adressé au secrétariat de la CNUCED.

How to order the *Handbook*   Comment commander le *Manuel*

To order the print version of the
UNCTAD Handbook of Statistics, please contact:
United Nations Publications
300 East 42nd Street, Room IN-919
New York, NY 10017, USA
Telephone: 1-212-963-8302
Toll free: 1-800-253-9646
Fax: 1-212-963-3489
Internet: https://unp.un.org

Pour commander la version imprimée du
Manuel de Statistiques de la CNUCED, veuillez vous adresser à :
Publications des Nations Unies
300 East 42nd Street, Bureau IN-919
New York, NY 10017, USA
Téléphone : 1-212-963-8302
Numéro vert : 1-800-253-9646
Fax : 1-212-963-3489
Internet : https://unp.un.org

TD/STAT. 38
UNITED NATIONS PUBLICATION – PUBLICATION DES NATIONS UNIES
Sales number / Numéro de vente : B.13.II.D.4
ISBN 978-92-1-012076-0
e-ISBN 978-92-1-056200-3
ISSN 1992-8408

The **UNCTAD Handbook of Statistics** provides essential data for analysing and measuring world trade, investment, international financial flows and development. Reliable statistical information is often considered as the first step during the preparation of recommendations or decisions that will commit countries for many years as they strive to integrate into the world economy and improve the living standards of their citizens. Whether it is for research, consultation or technical cooperation, UNCTAD needs comparable, often detailed economic, demographic and social data, over several decades and for as many countries as possible.

In addition to facilitating the work of the secretariat's economists, the **UNCTAD Handbook of Statistics** also enables other users, such as policymakers, research specialists, academics, officials from national governments or international organizations, executive managers or members of non-governmental organizations (NGOs) from developing, transition or developed countries to have access to this rich statistical information. The **Handbook** further offers journalists comprehensive information in a presentation that meets their needs.

This publication is available in printed copy and DVD. Moreover, the underlying data of the **Handbook** are available online at *UNCTADstat* (http://unctadstat.unctad.org). Unlike the **Handbook**, which captures statistics at one point of time, *UNCTADstat* is continuously updated, enriched and provides users with the latest available data. In this regard, users should use caution when comparing data between the **Handbook** and *UNCTADstat,* as the date of update may differ.

The list of the country groupings presented in the DVD version of this new edition of the **Handbook** has been aligned with the list of groupings included in the *UNCTADstat* database.

To help us provide better and more relevant statistics to users, you are invited to send your comments to **statistics@unctad.org**.

Le but du **Manuel de statistiques de la CNUCED** est de fournir les données statistiques essentielles à l'analyse du commerce mondial, de l'investissement, des flux financiers internationaux et du développement. Une information statistique fiable est souvent le préalable à la formulation de recommandations et à la prise de décisions qui engageront les pays pour de longues années dans leur processus d'intégration dans l'économie mondiale et l'amélioration des conditions de leurs peuples. Que ce soit pour la recherche, la concertation ou la coopération technique, la CNUCED a besoin de données économiques, démographiques et sociales comparables et souvent détaillées, disponibles si possible sur plusieurs décennies et pour un maximum de pays.

Au-delà de la mobilisation et de la vérification des données, du calcul d'indicateurs dérivés qui alimentent les travaux des économistes du secrétariat, le **Manuel de statistiques de la CNUCED** est l'occasion de partager une base statistique riche avec les décideurs et les chercheurs, qu'ils soient universitaires, fonctionnaires d'administrations nationales ou d'organisations internationales, cadres d'entreprises ou membres d'organisations non gouvernementales de pays en développement, en transition ou développés. Les journalistes trouvent aussi dans ce manuel une information synthétique dans une présentation bien adaptée à leurs préoccupations.

Le **Manuel** est disponible en version imprimée et DVD. Les données présentées dans le **Manuel** sont disponibles en ligne, dans *UNCTADstat* (http://unctadstat.unctad.org). À la différence du **Manuel** qui présente des statistiques figées à un moment donné, *UNCTADstat* est actualisé et enrichi régulièrement pour mettre à la disposition des utilisateurs les données les plus récentes. À cet égard, il est important de signaler que les données d'*UNCTADstat* et du **Manuel** ne pourront être comparées systématiquement en raison de la différence de date de leur mise à jour et de publication.

Dans la version DVD de cette nouvelle édition du **Manuel**, la liste des groupements de pays a été étendue pour correspondre à la liste des groupements présentés dans la base de données *UNCTADstat*.

Pour mieux nous adapter aux besoins de nos utilisateurs et mettre à leur disposition des statistiques pertinentes, vous pouvez nous faire part de vos commentaires en nous écrivant à **statistics@unctad.org**.

TABLE OF CONTENTS

TABLE DES MATIÈRES

PART ONE
International merchandise trade

PREMIÈRE PARTIE
Commerce international des marchandises

EXPLANATION OF SYMBOLS	**SIGNIFICATION DES SYMBOLES**

0   Zero means that the amount is nil or negligible.

_   The symbol underscore indicates that the item is not applicable.

..   Two dots indicate that the data are not available or are not separately reported.

-   The use of a hyphen on data area of individual countries means that data is estimated and included in the aggregation but not to be shown; on data area of country aggregates, it signifies non-publishable estimates.
A hyphen between years (e.g. 1985-1990) signifies the full period involved, including the initial and final years.

(b)   Break in the series
(e)   Estimate
(f)   Forecast
(p)   Provisional data
(r)   Revised data
(u)   Preliminary estimate

Some exceptions are indicated in footnotes.

0   Un zéro signifie que le montant est nul ou négligeable.

_   Un tiret signifie que la rubrique est sans objet.

..   Deux points signifient que les données ne sont pas disponibles ou ne sont pas communiquées séparément.

-   Le trait d'union dans le champ de données des pays individuels indique que le chiffre est estimé et inclus dans l'agrégation mais n'est pas publié; dans le champ de données des agrégats de pays, il indique que le chiffre estimé n'est pas publiable.
Le trait d'union entre deux millésimes (par exemple 1985-1990) indique qu'il s'agit de la période tout entière, y compris la première et la dernière année mentionnées.

(b)   Interruption de la série
(e)   Estimation
(f)   Prévision
(p)   Donnée provisoire
(r)   Donnée révisée
(u)   Estimation préliminaire

Les exceptions sont indiquées dans les notes en bas de page.

These notes summarize the content of each part of the *Handbook* according to the revised Table of Contents of the present issue of the *Handbook of Statistics*.

The tables included in this book represent analytical summaries of the full time series contained in the **UNCTAD Handbook of Statistics 2013** on DVD.

PART ONE
International merchandise trade

Table **1.1** shows the value of total exports (f.o.b.) and imports (c.i.f.), expressed in millions of dollars and percentages of the world total, of individual countries and geographical regions (1.1.1), economic groupings (1.1.2), and trade groups (1.1.3). The trade flows shown in table 1.1.1 refer to the General Trade System except for the countries which employ the Special Trade System and which are marked with an asterisk. The General Trade System is used when the statistical territory of a compiling country coincides with its economic territory. Consequently, imports include all goods entering the economic territory of a compiling country and exports include all goods leaving the economic territory of the compiling country. The Special Trade System is used when the statistical territory comprises only a particular part of the economic territory within which "goods may be disposed of without customs restriction". In such a case, imports include all goods entering the free circulation area of the compiling country, which means cleared through customs for home use, and exports include all goods leaving the free circulation area of a compiling country.

Average annual growth rates of international trade derived from table 1.1 are presented in table **1.2**.

Table **1.3** contains trade balances (exports f.o.b. minus imports c.i.f.) and these balances as a percentage of imports of individual countries, geographical regions and economic groupings.

Table **1.4** shows the relative importance of trade among group members as compared to the regional or total trade of that group.

PART TWO
International merchandise trade by region

Table **2.1** shows the export and import structure of individual countries by main regions of origin and destination. Data are presented for as many individual countries as possible, while trade partners are grouped in 14 major clusters.

Table **2.2** (**A to L**) presents the structure of exports by destination and imports by origin by major commodity groups for 12 selected country groups. The table provides detailed information on the world trade network for 19 regions of origin and destination and six commodity groups.

Totals of international merchandise trade presented in the tables found in parts one and two are not strictly comparable due to complementary but different sources and remaining unallocated trade flows, despite efforts to distribute trade flows by destination, origin and commodity group.

Exports by destination may differ considerably in some cases from data on imports as reported by countries of destination for a variety of factors, among which the following may be of particular importance:
- Most import data are reported on a c.i.f. rather than an f.o.b. basis;
- There is a time lag between the date on which goods are recorded as exports and their arrival at their destination;
- There may be considerable differences between the recorded destination of exports and the actual destination as shown in import statistics.

PART THREE
International merchandise trade by product

Table **3.1** shows the export and import structure of individual economies by commodity groups for selected years for nine commodity groups (total, all food items, agricultural raw materials, fuels, ores and metals, manufactured goods, including chemical products, machinery and transport equipment and other manufactured goods).

Table **3.2** (**A**, **B** and **C**, respectively) presents the structure of exports for the world, for developing and developed economies, by product, at the SITC group (Revision 3, 3-digit) level. Each product share of world exports is calculated for each economic grouping as well as the average annual growth rate and the latter's deviation in relation to the world growth rate.

Table **3.2D** establishes for each economy the list of main products exported (SITC group, Revision 3, 3-digit level). Each product's share of total exports of individual countries, geographical regions and the world is also indicated.

Table **3.2E** lists major exporters of 70 leading products among developing economies at the SITC group (Revision 3, 3-digit) level as well as corresponding shares in world trade.

Table **3.3** provides concentration indices and structural change indices for exports and imports by product group at SITC (Revision 3, 3-digit) level. The first indicator shows how a product market is concentrated in a few countries or homogeneously distributed among several countries. The structural change indicator shows whether the market share for a given product among export countries has changed significantly when compared with a reference year.

Totals of international merchandise trade presented in the tables of this third part may also differ from the data contained in the first part for the above reasons, to which must be added margins of exports and imports not distributed by commodity group or the use of different product nomenclatures by the exporting and importing countries.

PART FOUR
International merchandise trade indicators

Table **4.1** includes calculation results of concentration and diversification indices for individual countries, geographical regions and economic groupings. This concentration index specifically shows how exports and imports of individual countries or country groupings are concentrated on several products or otherwise distributed in a more homogeneous manner among a series of products. The diversification indicator signals whether the structure of exports or imports by product of a given country or country grouping differs from the structure by product shown for the world.

Table **4.2** contains volume indices of exports and imports, rounding out trade value available in tables 1.1 and 1.2, unit value indices of exports and imports and derived terms of trade and purchasing power of exports. They are all presented at the level of individual countries and geographical regions (4.2.1) and economic groupings (4.2.2).

To improve data coverage, especially for the latest periods, the following procedure was used in the calculation of unit value indices:
- A set of average prices indices at SITC (Revision 3, 3-digit) group level was constructed using *UNCTADstat* Commodity Price Statistics, international and national sources and UNCTAD secretariat estimates;
- At the country level, unit value indices were calculated using current year's trade values as weights at the SITC (Revision 3, 3-digit) level. Trade values are available in table 3.2.

In some instances these indices may differ from the estimates published in official sources, since the main aim is to provide tentative estimates for most developing countries on a comparable basis.

Table **4.3** presents average applied import MFN tariff rates for major categories of non-agricultural and non-fuel products by individual markets.

PART FIVE
International trade in services

Tables **5.1.1**, **5.1.2** and **5.1.3** present exports and imports of total trade in services by individual country, geographical region, economic grouping and trade group. The statistics shown are a result of the common work of UNCTAD and World Trade Organization (WTO) and they correspond to the definitions of the IMF *Balance of Payments Manual (BPM5, 1993)*. The aggregate data from tables 5.1 include estimates of missing values that are not shown separately. Services are defined as the economic output of intangible commodities that may be produced, transferred and consumed at the same time. However, services cover a heterogeneous range of intangible products and activities that are difficult to capture within a single definition and are sometimes hard to separate from goods. Services are outputs produced to order, and they typically include changes in the condition of the consumers realized through the activities of the producers at the demand of customers. By the time production of a service is completed, it must have been provided to a consumer.

Table **5.2** presents statistics on international trade in services by category of service for selected country groups and for major individual economy exporters and importers among developing and transition economies, as well as among developed countries. The data shown are a result of the common work of UNCTAD and WTO and they correspond to the definitions of the IMF *Balance of Payments Manual (BPM5, 1993)*. The following services categories are included: transport, travel, communication, construction, computer and information services, insurance, financial services, royalties and licence fees, other business services, and personal, cultural and recreational services.

To the extent possible, the inter-agency Task Force on Statistics of International Trade in Services aims to explain and reduce the divergences noticed in statistics for trade in services published by different international organizations. An overview of existing databases covering statistics on international trade in services is described at

http://unstats.un.org/unsd/tradeserv/TFSITS/matrix.htm.

Table **5.3** describes international maritime transport. It contains data on the size of the world merchant fleet by flag of registration and by type of ship by region and economy. The table incorporates consolidated time series from various issues of the *UNCTAD Review of Maritime Transport*. The *Review* reports on the worldwide evolution of shipping, ports and multimodal transport related to the major traffics of liquid bulk, dry bulk and containers.

PART SIX
Commodities

Table **6.1** includes aggregated price indices for primary commodity groups such as food, tropical beverages, vegetable oilseeds and oils, agricultural raw materials and minerals, ores and metals, as well as an all groups price index in current United States dollars. Also included are the annual and quarterly free-market price indices for selected commodities exported by developing economies. The weight of price indices for the above mentioned commodity groups (2000=100) are based on the value of exports of developing countries from 1999 to 2001.

Table **6.2** presents instability indices and trends in free-market prices for selected primary commodities that are of particular interest to developing economies.

PART SEVEN
International finance

Tables **7.1.1**, **7.1.2** and **7.1.3** present values of the current account net in millions of dollars and as percentages of GDP for individual countries, geographical regions, and trade and economic groupings. Balance-of-payments current account data cover all transactions between residents and non-residents of a reporting economy. In general, the current account balance describes the difference between current receipts and expenditures for internationally traded goods, services and income payments. At the same time, from a national perspective, the current account balance would equal the gap between national savings and domestic investment.

Tables **7.2.1**, **7.2.2** and **7.2.3** contain information on foreign direct investment (FDI) inflows and outflows by individual country, geographical region, economic grouping and trade group. These figures correspond to the Statistical Annexes of the UNCTAD *World Investment Report 2013*. FDI is defined as an investment involving a long-term relationship and reflecting a lasting interest in and control by a resident entity in one economy (foreign direct investor or parent enterprise) of an enterprise resident in a different economy (FDI enterprise or affiliate enterprise or foreign affiliate). Such investment involves both the initial transaction between the two entities and all subsequent transactions between them and among foreign affiliates. A direct investment enterprise is defined as an incorporated or unincorporated enterprise in which the direct investor, resident in another economy, owns 10 percent or more of the ordinary shares or voting power (or the equivalent).

Tables **7.3.1** and **7.3.2** present values of receipts (credits) of total migrants' remittances, in millions of dollars, for individual economies and regional and economic groupings. They also show total remittances receipts as percentage of GDP and international trade. Migrants' remittances are the sum of workers' remittances, compensation of employees and migrants' transfers.

Tables **7.4.1** and **7.4.2** include data on payments (debits) of total migrants' remittances, based on the same approach used for tables 7.3.1 and 7.3.2.

Tables **7.5.1** and **7.5.2** present statistics on total international reserves (including gold) of developing countries by country, region and economic grouping, in millions of dollars. Other calculations included show months of imports that these reserves could finance at current import levels, as well as the annual change in total reserves. According to the IMF definition, International reserves consist of the sum of the country's foreign exchange, its reserve position in the IMF, the monetary gold reserves, and the United States dollar value of SDR holdings by its monetary authorities.

Tables **7.6** give a summary of official financial flows by type of flow, country, region and economic grouping. Flows from bilateral and multilateral sources are shown, as recorded by the Organization for Economic Cooperation and Development (OECD) Development Assistance Committee (DAC).

Tables **7.7** present time series on the external long-term indebtedness of developing economies. They also provide a detailed breakdown of public and publicly guaranteed debt by source of lending. External debt data in this table are based on the Debtor Reporting System (DRS) maintained by the World Bank.

PART EIGHT
Development indicators

Table **8.1** provides information on total and per capita nominal gross domestic product (GDP) (in United States dollars) by individual country, geographical region and economic grouping. The GDP figures in dollars are derived from GDP data provided in national currencies. The prevailing annual average market exchange rates, as reported by IMF, have been used for the conversion from national currencies to dollars.

Table **8.2** contains annual average growth rates of total and per capita real GDP by individual country, geographical region and economic grouping. The growth rates are based on GDP in United States dollars at constant 2005 prices.

Table **8.3** provides data on GDP by type of expenditure and kind of economic activity by country, geographical region and economic grouping.

Tables **8.4.1** and **8.4.2** provide some estimates on population and labour force: total population, urban population (as a percentage of total population), total labour force, female labour force (as a percentage of total labour force), total agriculture labour force and female labour force (as a percentage of total agriculture labour force). The figures for certain groups may be different from those published by the sources cited when the UNCTAD definitions for those groups are different.

OTHER NOTES

Unless otherwise specified, country aggregates are the sums of the relevant country data by group. Calculations of aggregates may in some cases include data estimated by the UNCTAD secretariat that are not necessarily all reported separately. When there are not enough representative reported or estimated data points within a country aggregate, no aggregation is undertaken and symbol (-) is assigned.

Because of rounding, details and percentages in tables do not necessarily add up to totals.

Data were checked to ensure that they matched the geographical coverage of the countries, as described at the beginning of the *Handbook*. However, some gaps could not be avoided due to data unavailability and are described in the notes at the end of tables.

Unless otherwise stated, dollars ($) refer to United States dollars and data in dollars are expressed in current United States dollars of the year to which they refer.

Average annual growth rates are defined as the coefficient b in the exponential trend function $y = ae^{bt}$ where t stands for time. This method takes all observations in a period into account. Therefore, the resulting growth rates reflect trends that are not unduly influenced by exceptional values.

The country distributions presented are for statistical convenience only and follow those used by the Statistics Division, Department of Economic and Social Affairs (DESA), of the United Nations. They are grouped by economic criteria or by adhesion to commercial agreements for the purpose of statistical analysis and research.

The term "economies", as used in this publication, refers to regions, countries and territories. In case of change in the statistical coverage of a country, it is identified by adding an end year after the country name. For example, Indonesia (...2002) indicates that the statistical coverage of Indonesia, including Timor-Leste, was valid until 2002.

The composition of country groupings presented in the *Handbook* is evolving in order to provide relevant statistics for research and analysis. In this regard, UNCTAD reviews and updates the definition and composition of groups every year. User should be aware that the changes may impact significantly the figures from one given release to the other. The changes in the groups are thoroughly outlined in the section Methodology and Classifications under 'Useful links' at *UNCTADstat* website.

1. Developing, transition and developed economies

There is no established convention for the designation of "developed" and "developing" countries or areas in the United Nations system. In common practice, Israel and Japan in Asia, Bermuda, Canada, Greenland, Saint Pierre et Miquelon, and the United States in North America, Australia and New Zealand in Oceania, and Europe are considered "developed" regions or areas. This section includes all countries and territories divided into three major categories: developing countries, transition economies and developed economies. Each category is further divided into geographical regions.

1) Developing economies

This category includes countries and territories in America, Africa, Asia and Oceania not specified below. The geographical regions are further subdivided into subregions in order to present more detailed statistics. Exceptions are specified in table footnotes.

2) Transition economies

This group includes countries in transition from centrally planned to market economies.

3) Developed economies

This category is subdivided into four geographical regions: America, Asia, Europe and Oceania.

World' total represents the sum of the figures of the three above-mentioned groups plus the figures of a group of territories and partners not elsewhere classified, whose composition is detailed below. Data of these territories are included in the world total if they have been reported but are not presented individually or in any group..

The composition of the group "not elsewhere classified" is as follows:

- Territories: Antarctica, Bouvet Island, British Antarctic Territory, British Indian Ocean Territory, Christmas Island, Cocos (Keeling) Islands, French Southern Territories, Heard and McDonald Islands, Norfolk Island, Pitcairn, Saint Barthélemy, Saint Martin (French part), South Georgia and South Sandwich Islands, United States Minor Outlying Islands, and United States Miscellaneous Pacific Islands.

- Partners: "Confidential information and differences", "Neutral zone", "Free zones", "Bunkers", and "Ship stores". These specific partners are only used in the merchandise trade tables.

The total of each group presented in the *Handbook* is also completed, should the case arise, with data that have not been allocated to the different elements composing the group.

2. Economic groupings of developing countries

The *Handbook* includes numerous and varied groups of countries and territories in order to provide easy access to the statistics necessary for socio-economic analysis and development research.

Developing economies are presented at three levels of aggregation: the total group, the group excluding China (referring to continental China) and the group excluding the least developed countries.

The category of heavily indebted poor countries includes those economies benefiting from the HIPC debt reduction initiative of the World Bank and the International Monetary Fund.

LDCs and landlocked developing countries (LLDCs) are recognized by the United Nations as categories that require special attention from the international community.

Since 1994, the United Nations has recognized the particular problems of the Small Island Developing States (SIDS), even though the criteria for drawing up an official list of SIDS were never determined. The unofficial list is used by UNCTAD for analytical purposes only.

The developing economies are also categorized into three subgroups according to their average 2004-2006 per capita GDP: high-income (above $4,500), middle-income (between $1,000 and $4,500) and low-income (below $1,000).

The group of major petroleum and gas exporters consists of countries whose share of petroleum and gas (SITC code 33 plus 34) was not less than 50 per cent of their total exports, and whose exports of these products amounted to at least 1 per cent of petroleum and gas world share for the period 2004–2006. This group is divided into three geographical zones: Africa, America and Asia.

The group of major manufactured goods exporters consists of economies whose share of manufactured products (SITC 5 to 8, excluding 667 and 68) was not less than 50 per cent of their total exports, and whose exports of these products amounted to at least 1 per cent of manufactured goods world share for the period 2004–2006. The group comprises countries in America and Asia.

The composition of the groups of emerging economies (in America and Asia) and newly industrialized Asian economies (composed of first and second tier) corresponds to UNCTAD's *Trade and Development Report*.

The different geographical regions are also presented at various levels of aggregation:- Africa: Northern Africa excluding Sudan, sub-Saharan Africa, including Sudan, including and excluding South Africa.

- America: Central America and Greater Caribbean Islands excluding Puerto Rico, including and excluding Mexico, South America and Central America, and South America excluding Brazil.

- Asia: Eastern and South-Eastern Asia excluding China, and Southern Asia excluding India.

3. Trade groups and interregional groupings

Statistics of trade groups with special analytic interest are presented according to their pertinence. These groupings include all relevant economies and are sub-classified by geographical regions, with the exception of the following interregional groups: African, Caribbean and Pacific Group of States; Asia–Pacific Economic Cooperation; Black Sea Economic Cooperation; and Commonwealth of Independent States.

DISTRIBUTION OF COUNTRIES AND TERRITORIES

DEVELOPING ECONOMIES

AFRICA

Eastern Africa

Burundi	Malawi	Uganda
Comoros	Mauritius	United Republic of Tanzania
Djibouti	Mozambique	Zambia
Eritrea	Rwanda	Zimbabwe
Ethiopia	Seychelles	
Kenya	Somalia	
Madagascar	South Sudan	

Middle Africa

Angola	Congo	Sao Tome and Principe
Cameroon	Democratic Republic of the Congo	
Central African Republic	Equatorial Guinea	
Chad	Gabon	

Northern Africa

Algeria	Morocco	Western Sahara
Egypt	Sudan	
Libya	Tunisia	

Southern Africa

Botswana	Namibia	Swaziland
Lesotho	South Africa	

Western Africa

Benin	Guinea	Nigeria
Burkina Faso	Guinea-Bissau	Saint Helena
Cape Verde	Liberia	Senegal
Côte d'Ivoire	Mali	Sierra Leone
Gambia	Mauritania	Togo
Ghana	Niger	

AMERICA

Caribbean islands

Greater Caribbean

Cuba	
Dominican Republic	
Haiti	
Jamaica	

Small Caribbean islands

Anguilla	Dominica
Antigua and Barbuda	Grenada
Aruba	Montserrat
Bahamas	Saint Kitts and Nevis
Barbados	Saint Lucia
Bonaire, Sint Eustatius and Saba	Saint Vincent and the Grenadines
British Virgin Islands	Sint Maarten (Dutch part)
Cayman Islands	Trinidad and Tobago
Curaçao	Turks and Caicos Islands

Central America

Belize	Guatemala	Nicaragua
Costa Rica	Honduras	Panama
El Salvador	Mexico	

DEVELOPING ECONOMIES (concluded)

AMERICA (concluded)

South America

Argentina	Ecuador	Suriname
Bolivia (Plurinational State of)	Falkland Islands (Malvinas)	Uruguay
Brazil	Guyana	Venezuela (Bolivarian Republic of)
Chile	Paraguay	
Colombia	Peru	

ASIA

Eastern Asia

China	Macao, Special Administrative	
Democratic People's Republic	Region of China	
of Korea	Mongolia	
Hong Kong, Special Administrative	Republic of Korea	
Region of China	Taiwan Province of China	

Southern Asia

Afghanistan	India	Nepal
Bangladesh	Iran (Islamic Republic of)	Pakistan
Bhutan	Maldives	Sri Lanka

South-Eastern Asia

Brunei Darussalam	Malaysia	Thailand
Cambodia	Myanmar	Timor-Leste
Indonesia	Philippines	Viet Nam
Lao People's Democratic Republic	Singapore	

Western Asia

Bahrain	Oman	Turkey
Iraq	Qatar	United Arab Emirates
Jordan	Saudi Arabia	Yemen
Kuwait	State of Palestine	
Lebanon	Syrian Arab Republic	

OCEANIA

American Samoa	Micronesia (Federated States of)	Samoa
Cook Islands	Nauru	Solomon Islands
Fiji	New Caledonia	Tokelau
French Polynesia	Niue	Tonga
Guam	Northern Mariana Islands	Tuvalu
Kiribati	Palau	Vanuatu
Marshall Islands	Papua New Guinea	Wallis and Futuna Islands

DISTRIBUTION OF COUNTRIES AND TERRITORIES

TRANSITION ECONOMIES

Albania
Armenia
Azerbaijan
Belarus
Bosnia and Herzegovina
Croatia
Georgia
Kazakhstan

Kyrgyzstan
Montenegro
Republic of Moldova
Russian Federation
Serbia
Tajikistan
The former Yugoslav Republic
    of Macedonia

Turkmenistan
Ukraine
Uzbekistan

DEVELOPED ECONOMIES

AMERICA

Bermuda
Canada
Greenland
Saint Pierre and Miquelon

United States of America
    including Puerto Rico and
    United States Virgin Islands

ASIA

Israel
Japan

EUROPE

Andorra
Austria
Belgium
Bulgaria
Cyprus
Czech Republic
Denmark
Estonia
Faeroe Islands
Finland including Åland Islands
France including French Guyana,
    Guadeloupe, Martinique, Mayotte*,
    Monaco and Réunion
Germany

Gibraltar
Greece
Holy See
Hungary
Iceland
Ireland
Italy
Latvia
Lithuania
Luxembourg
Malta
Netherlands
Norway including Svalbard
    and Jan Mayen

Poland
Portugal
Romania
San Marino
Slovakia
Slovenia
Spain
Sweden
Switzerland including Liechtenstein
United Kingdom of Great Britain and
    Northern Ireland including Channel
    Islands and Isle of Man

* Since 2012, Mayotte has been included in the statistical territory of France

OCEANIA

Australia
New Zealand

DISTRIBUTION OF DEVELOPING ECONOMIES BY ECONOMIC GROUPING

Heavily indebted poor countries (39)

Afghanistan	Ethiopia	Mozambique
Benin	Gambia	Nicaragua
Bolivia (Plurinational State of)	Ghana	Niger
Burkina Faso	Guinea	Rwanda
Burundi	Guinea-Bissau	Sao Tome and Principe
Cameroon	Guyana	Senegal
Central African Republic	Haiti	Sierra Leone
Chad	Honduras	Somalia
Comoros	Liberia	Sudan
Congo	Madagascar	Togo
Côte d'Ivoire	Malawi	Uganda
Democratic Republic of the Congo	Mali	United Republic of Tanzania
Eritrea	Mauritania	Zambia

Landlocked developing countries (32)

Afghanistan	Kazakhstan*	Rwanda
Armenia*	Kyrgyzstan*	South Sudan
Azerbaijan*	Lao People's Democratic Republic	Swaziland
Bhutan	Lesotho	Tajikistan*
Bolivia (Plurinational State of)	Malawi	The former Yugoslav Republic
Botswana	Mali	of Macedonia*
Burkina Faso	Mongolia	Turkmenistan*
Burundi	Nepal	Uganda
Central African Republic	Niger	Uzbekistan*
Chad	Paraguay	Zambia
Ethiopia	Republic of Moldova*	Zimbabwe

* These countries are classified as economies in transition (neither developed nor developing).
  However, as they are landlocked States, they are also members of this group.

Small island developing States (29)

Antigua and Barbuda	Maldives	Samoa
Bahamas	Marshall Islands	Sao Tome and Principe
Barbados	Mauritius	Seychelles
Cape Verde	Micronesia (Federated States of)	Solomon Islands
Comoros	Nauru	Timor-Leste
Dominica	Palau	Tonga
Fiji	Papua New Guinea	Trinidad and Tobago
Grenada	Saint Kitts and Nevis	Tuvalu
Jamaica	Saint Lucia	Vanuatu
Kiribati	Saint Vincent and the Grenadines	

Least developed countries (49)

Africa and Haiti	Year of inclusion in the group		Year of inclusion in the group	Asia	Year of inclusion in the group
Angola	1994	Mali	1971	Afghanistan	1971
Benin	1971	Mauritania	1986	Bangladesh	1975
Burkina Faso	1971	Mozambique	1988	Bhutan	1971
Burundi	1971	Niger	1971	Cambodia	1991
Central African Republic	1975	Rwanda	1971	Lao People's Democratic Republic	1971
Chad	1971	Senegal	2000	Myanmar	1987
Democratic Republic of the Congo	1991	Sierra Leone	1982	Nepal	1971
Djibouti	1982	Somalia	1971	Yemen	1971
Equatorial Guinea	1982	South Sudan	2012		
Eritrea	1994	Sudan	1971	Islands	
Ethiopia	1971	Togo	1982	Comoros	1977
Gambia	1975	Uganda	1971	Kiribati	1986
Guinea	1971	United Republic of Tanzania	1971	Samoa	1971
Guinea-Bissau	1981	Zambia	1991	Sao Tome and Principe	1982
Haiti	1971			Solomon Islands	1991
Lesotho	1971			Timor-Leste	2003
Liberia	1990			Tuvalu	1986
Madagascar	1991			Vanuatu	1985
Malawi	1971				

DISTRIBUTION OF DEVELOPING ECONOMIES BY ECONOMIC GROUPING

UNCTAD ECONOMIC GROUPINGS

2004-2006 average per capita current GDP above $4 500: High-income (57)

American Samoa
Anguilla
Antigua and Barbuda
Argentina
Aruba
Bahamas
Bahrain
Barbados
Bonaire, Sint Eustatius and Saba
Botswana
Brazil
British Virgin Islands
Brunei Darussalam
Cayman Islands
Chile
Cook Islands
Costa Rica
Curaçao
Dominica
Equatorial Guinea

Falkland Islands (Malvinas)
French Polynesia
Gabon
Grenada
Guam
Hong Kong, Special Administrative
    Region of China
Kuwait
Lebanon
Libya
Macao, Special Administrative
    Region of China
Malaysia
Mauritius
Mexico
Montserrat
New Caledonia
Niue
Northern Mariana Islands
Oman

Palau
Panama
Qatar
Republic of Korea
Saint Kitts and Nevis
Saint Lucia
Saint Vincent and the Grenadines
Saudi Arabia
Seychelles
Singapore
Sint Maarten (Dutch part)
South Africa
Taiwan Province of China
Trinidad and Tobago
Turkey
Turks and Caicos Islands
United Arab Emirates
Uruguay
Venezuela (Bolivarian Republic of)

2004-2006 average per capita current GDP between $1 000 and $4 500: Middle-income (47)

Algeria
Angola
Belize
Bolivia (Plurinational State of)
Bhutan
Cape Verde
China
Colombia
Congo
Cuba
Dominican Republic
Ecuador
Egypt
El Salvador
Fiji
Guatemala

Guyana
Honduras
Indonesia
Iran (Islamic Republic of)
Jamaica
Jordan
Kiribati
Maldives
Marshall Islands
Micronesia (Federated States of)
Mongolia
Morocco
Namibia
Nauru
Paraguay
Peru

Philippines
Saint Helena
Samoa
Sri Lanka
State of Palestine
Suriname
Swaziland
Syrian Arab Republic
Thailand
Tokelau
Tonga
Tunisia
Tuvalu
Vanuatu
Wallis and Futuna Islands

2004-2006 average per capita current GDP below $1 000: Low-income (55)

Afghanistan
Bangladesh
Benin
Burkina Faso
Burundi
Cambodia
Cameroon
Central African Republic
Chad
Comoros
Côte d'Ivoire
Democratic People's Republic of Korea
Democratic Republic of the Congo
Djibouti
Eritrea
Ethiopia
Gambia
Ghana
Guinea

Guinea-Bissau
Haiti
India
Iraq
Kenya
Lao People's Democratic Republic
Lesotho
Liberia
Madagascar
Malawi
Mali
Mauritania
Mozambique
Myanmar
Nepal
Nicaragua
Niger
Nigeria
Pakistan

Papua New Guinea
Rwanda
Sao Tome and Principe
Senegal
Sierra Leone
Solomon Islands
Somalia
South Sudan
Sudan
Timor-Leste
Togo
Uganda
United Republic of Tanzania
Viet Nam
Yemen
Zambia
Zimbabwe

DISTRIBUTION OF DEVELOPING ECONOMIES BY ECONOMIC GROUPING

Major petroleum and gas exporters (12)

Africa	**America**	**Asia**
Algeria	Venezuela (Bolivarian Republic of)	Iran (Islamic Republic of)
Angola		Iraq
Libya		Kuwait
Nigeria		Oman
		Qatar
		Saudi Arabia
		United Arab Emirates

Major manufactured goods exporters (8)

America	**Asia**
Mexico	China
	Hong Kong, Special Administrative Region of China
	Malaysia
	Republic of Korea
	Singapore
	Taiwan Province of China
	Thailand

Emerging economies (10)

America	**Asia**
Argentina	Malaysia
Brazil	Republic of Korea
Chile	Singapore
Mexico	Taiwan Province of China
Peru	Thailand

Newly industrialized Asian economies (8)

First tier	**Second tier**
Hong Kong, Special Administrative Region of China	Indonesia
Republic of Korea	Malaysia
Singapore	Philippines
Taiwan Province of China	Thailand

DISTRIBUTION OF ECONOMIES BY TRADE GROUP

AFRICA

	Year of accession
Arab Maghreb Union (5) - UMA	
Algeria	1989
Libya	1989
Mauritania	1989
Morocco	1989
Tunisia	1989
Common Market for Eastern and Southern Africa (19) - COMESA	
Burundi	1994
Comoros	1994
Democratic Republic of the Congo	1994
Djibouti	1994
Egypt	1994
Eritrea	1994
Ethiopia	1994
Kenya	1994
Libya	2005
Madagascar	1994
Malawi	1994
Mauritius	1994
Rwanda	1994
Seychelles	1994
Sudan	1994
Swaziland	1994
Uganda	1994
Zambia	1994
Zimbabwe	1994
East African Community (5) - EAC	
Burundi	2007
Kenya	2001
Rwanda	2007
Uganda	2001
United Republic of Tanzania	2001

	Year of accession
Economic Community of Central African States (10) - ECCAS	
Angola	1999
Burundi	1983
Cameroon	1983
Central African Republic	1983
Chad	1983
Congo	1983
Democratic Republic of the Congo	1983
Equatorial Guinea	1983
Gabon	1983
Sao Tome and Principe	1983
Economic Community of the Great Lakes Countries (3) - CEPGL	
Burundi	1976
Democratic Republic of the Congo	1976
Rwanda	1976
Economic Community of West African States (15) - ECOWAS	
Benin	1975
Burkina Faso	1975
Cape Verde	1977
Côte d'Ivoire	1975
Gambia	1975
Ghana	1975
Guinea	1975
Guinea-Bissau	1975
Liberia	1975
Mali	1975
Niger	1975
Nigeria	1975
Senegal	1975
Sierra Leone	1975
Togo	1975

	Year of accession
Economic and Monetary Community of Central Africa (6) - CEMAC	
Cameroon	1994
Central African Republic	1994
Chad	1994
Congo	1994
Equatorial Guinea	1994
Gabon	1994
Mano River Union (4) - MRU	
Côte d'Ivoire	2008
Guinea	1980
Liberia	1973
Sierra Leone	1973
Southern African Development Community (15) - SADC	
Angola	1992
Botswana	1992
Democratic Republic of the Congo	1992
Lesotho	1992
Madagascar	2005
Malawi	1992
Mauritius	1992
Mozambique	1992
Namibia	1992
Seychelles	2007
South Africa	1994
Swaziland	1992
United Republic of Tanzania	1992
Zambia	1992
Zimbabwe	1992
West African Economic and Monetary Union (8) - UEMOA	
Benin	1994
Burkina Faso	1994
Côte d'Ivoire	1994
Guinea-Bissau	1997
Mali	1994
Niger	1994
Senegal	1994
Togo	1994

AMERICA

	Year of accession
Andean Community (4) - ANCOM	
Bolivia (Plurinational State of)	1996
Colombia	1996
Ecuador	1996
Peru	1996
Caribbean Community (15) - CARICOM	
Antigua and Barbuda	1974
Bahamas	1983
Barbados	1973
Belize	1974
Dominica	1974
Grenada	1974
Guyana	1973
Haiti	2002
Jamaica	1973
Montserrat	1974
Saint Kitts and Nevis	1974
Saint Lucia	1974
Saint Vincent and the Grenadines	1974
Suriname	1995
Trinidad and Tobago	1973

	Year of accession
Central American Common Market (5) - CACM	
Costa Rica	1962
El Salvador	1961
Guatemala	1961
Honduras	1961
Nicaragua	1961
Free Trade Area of the Americas (34) - FTAA	
Antigua and Barbuda	1994
Argentina	1994
Bahamas	1994
Barbados	1994
Belize	1994
Bolivia (Plurinational State of)	1994
Brazil	1994
Canada	1994
Chile	1994
Colombia	1994
Costa Rica	1994
Dominica	1994

	Year of accession
Dominican Republic	1994
Ecuador	1994
El Salvador	1994
Grenada	1994
Guatemala	1994
Guyana	1994
Haiti	1994
Honduras	1994
Jamaica	1994
Mexico	1994
Nicaragua	1994
Panama	1994
Paraguay	1994
Peru	1994
Saint Kitts and Nevis	1994
Saint Lucia	1994
Saint Vincent & the Grenadines	1994
Suriname	1994
Trinidad and Tobago	1994
United States of America	1994
Uruguay	1994
Venezuela (Bolivarian Rep. of)	1994

DISTRIBUTION OF ECONOMIES BY TRADE GROUP

AMERICA (concluded)

Latin American Integration Association (13) - LAIA

	Year of accession
Argentina	1980
Bolivia (Plurinational State of)	1980
Brazil	1980
Chile	1980
Colombia	1980
Cuba	1999
Ecuador	1980
Mexico	1980
Panama	2012
Paraguay	1980
Peru	1980
Uruguay	1980
Venezuela (Bolivarian Rep. of)	1980

Mercado Común del Sur (6) - MERCOSUR

	Year of accession
Argentina	1994
Bolivia	2012
Brazil	1994
Paraguay	1994
Uruguay	1994
Venezuela (Bolivarian Rep. of)	2012

North American Free Trade Agreement (3) - NAFTA

	Year of accession
Canada	1994
Mexico	1994
United States of America	1994

Organization of American States (35) - OAS

	Year of accession
Antigua and Barbuda	1981
Argentina	1948
Bahamas	1982
Barbados	1967
Belize	1991
Bolivia (Plurinational State of)	1948
Brazil	1948
Canada	1990
Chile	1948
Colombia	1948
Costa Rica	1948
Cuba	2009
Dominica	1979
Dominican Republic	1948
Ecuador	1948
El Salvador	1948
Grenada	1975
Guatemala	1948
Guyana	1948
Haiti	1948
Honduras	1948
Jamaica	1969
Mexico	1948
Nicaragua	1948
Panama	1948
Paraguay	1948
Peru	1951
Saint Kitts and Nevis	1984
Saint Lucia	1979
Saint Vincent & the Grenadines	1981
Suriname	1977
Trinidad and Tobago	1967
United States of America	1951
Uruguay	1951
Venezuela (Bolivarian Rep. of)	1951

Organization of Eastern Caribbean States (9) - OECS

	Year of accession
Anguilla	1995
Antigua and Barbuda	1981
British Virgin Islands	1984
Dominica	1981
Grenada	1981
Montserrat	1981
Saint Kitts and Nevis	1981
Saint Lucia	1981
Saint Vincent & the Grenadines	1981

ASIA

Asia–Pacific Trade Agreement (6) - APTA

	Year of accession
Bangladesh	1975
China	2001
India	1975
Lao People's Democratic Republic	1975
Republic of Korea	1975
Sri Lanka	1975

Association of South-East Asian Nations (10) - ASEAN

	Year of accession
Brunei Darussalam	1984
Cambodia	1999
Indonesia	1967
Lao People's Democratic Republic	1997
Malaysia	1967
Myanmar	1997
Philippines	1967
Singapore	1967
Thailand	1967
Viet Nam	1995

Economic Cooperation Organization (10) - ECO

	Year of accession
Afghanistan	1992
Azerbaijan	1992
Iran (Islamic Republic of)	1985
Kazakhstan	1992
Kyrgyzstan	1992
Pakistan	1985
Tajikistan	1992
Turkey	1985
Turkmenistan	1992
Uzbekistan	1992

Gulf Cooperation Council (6) - GCC

	Year of accession
Bahrain	1981
Kuwait	1981
Oman	1981
Qatar	1981
Saudi Arabia	1981
United Arab Emirates	1981

South Asian Association for Regional Cooperation (8) - SAARC

	Year of accession
Afghanistan	2007
Bangladesh	1985
Bhutan	1985
India	1985
Maldives	1985
Nepal	1985
Pakistan	1985
Sri Lanka	1985

EUROPE

European Free Trade Association (3) - EFTA

	Year of accession
Iceland	1970
Norway	1960
Switzerland	1960

European Union (27) - EU

	Year of accession
Austria	1995
Belgium	1957
Bulgaria	2008
Cyprus	2004
Czech Republic	2004
Denmark	1973
Estonia	2004
Finland	1995
France	1957
Germany	1957
Greece	1981
Hungary	2004
Ireland	1973
Italy	1957
Latvia	2004
Lithuania	2004
Luxembourg	1957
Malta	2004
Netherlands	1957
Poland	2004
Portugal	1986
Romania	2008
Slovakia	2004
Slovenia	2004
Spain	1986
Sweden	1995
United Kingdom	1973

Euro area (17)

	Year of accession
Austria	2002
Belgium	2002
Cyprus	2008
Estonia	2011
Finland	2002
France	2002
Germany	2002
Greece	2002
Ireland	2002
Italy	2002
Luxembourg	2002
Malta	2008
Netherlands	2002
Portugal	2002
Slovakia	2009
Slovenia	2007
Spain	2002

DISTRIBUTION OF ECONOMIES BY TRADE GROUP

OCEANIA

Year of accession

Melanesia Spearhead Group (4) - MSG

Fiji	1998
Papua New Guinea	1993
Solomon Islands	1993
Vanuatu	1993

DISTRIBUTION OF ECONOMIES BY INTERREGIONAL GROUPING

African, Caribbean and Pacific Group of States (79) - ACP

Angola	Gambia	Rwanda
Antigua and Barbuda	Ghana	Saint Kitts and Nevis
Bahamas	Grenada	Saint Lucia
Barbados	Guinea	Saint Vincent and the Grenadines
Belize	Guinea-Bissau	Samoa
Benin	Guyana	Sao Tome and Principe
Botswana	Haiti	Senegal
Burkina Faso	Jamaica	Seychelles
Burundi	Kenya	Sierra Leone
Cameroon	Kiribati	Solomon Islands
Cape Verde	Lesotho	Somalia
Central African Republic	Liberia	South Africa
Chad	Madagascar	Sudan
Comoros	Malawi	Suriname
Congo	Mali	Swaziland
Cook Islands	Marshall Islands	Timor-Leste
Côte d'Ivoire	Mauritania	Togo
Cuba	Mauritius	Tonga
Democratic Republic of the Congo	Micronesia (Federated States of)	Trinidad and Tobago
Djibouti	Mozambique	Tuvalu
Dominica	Namibia	Uganda
Dominican Republic	Nauru	United Republic of Tanzania
Equatorial Guinea	Niger	Vanuatu
Eritrea	Nigeria	Zambia
Ethiopia	Niue	Zimbabwe
Fiji	Palau	
Gabon	Papua New Guinea	

Year of accession   *Year of accession*   *Year of accession*

Asia-Pacific Economic Cooperation (21) - APEC		Black Sea Economic Cooperation (12) - BSEC		Commonwealth of Independent States (11) - CIS	
Australia	1989	Albania	1992	Armenia	1991
Brunei Darussalam	1989	Armenia	1992	Azerbaijan	1991
Canada	1989	Azerbaijan	1992	Belarus	1991
Chile	1994	Bulgaria	1992	Kazakhstan	1991
China	1991	Georgia	1992	Kyrgyzstan	1991
Hong Kong, Special Administrative Region of China	1991	Greece	1992	Republic of Moldova	1991
Indonesia	1989	Republic of Moldova	1992	Russian Federation	1991
Japan	1989	Romania	1992	Tajikistan	1991
Malaysia	1989	Russian Federation	1992	Turkmenistan	1991
Mexico	1993	Serbia	2004	Ukraine	1991
New Zealand	1989	Turkey	1992	Uzbekistan	1991
Papua New Guinea	1993	Ukraine	1992		
Peru	1998				
Philippines	1989				
Republic of Korea	1989				
Russian Federation	1998				
Singapore	1989				
Taiwan Province of China	1991				
Thailand	1989				
United States of America	1989				
Viet Nam	1998				

ACP	African, Caribbean and Pacific Group of States
ANCOM	Andean Community
APEC	Asia–Pacific Economic Cooperation
APTA	Asia-Pacific Trade Agreement (former Bangkok Agreement)
ASEAN	Association of South-East Asian Nations
BPM	*Balance of Payments Manual* (IMF)
BSEC	Black Sea Economic Cooperation
CACM	Central American Common Market
CARICOM	Caribbean Community
CCSA	Committee for the Coordination of Statistical Activities
CEMAC	Economic and Monetary Community of Central Africa
CEPGL	Economic Community of the Great Lakes Countries
c.i.f.	cost, insurance and freight
CIS	Commonwealth of Independent States
COMESA	Common Market for Eastern and Southern Africa
DAC	Development Assistance Committee (of OECD)
DRS	Debtor Reporting System
EAC	East African Community
ECCAS	Economic Community of Central African States
ECE	Economic Commission for Europe
ECLAC	Economic Commission for Latin America and the Caribbean
ECO	Economic Cooperation Organization
ECOWAS	Economic Community of West African States
EFTA	European Free Trade Association
EIU	Economic Intelligence Unit
ESCAP	Economic and Social Commission for Asia and the Pacific
ESCWA	Economic and Social Commission for Western Asia
EU	European Union
excl.	excluding
FAO	Food and Agriculture Organization of the United Nations
FDI	foreign direct investment
f.o.b.	free on board
FTAA	Free Trade Area of the Americas
GATS	General Agreement on Trade in Services
GCC	Gulf Cooperation Council
GDP	gross domestic product
GFCF	gross fixed capital formation
GNP	gross national product
HIPC	heavily indebted poor countries
HS	Harmonized System
ILO	International Labour Organization
IMF	International Monetary Fund
LAIA	Latin American Integration Association
LDC	least developed country
LME	London Metal Exchange
MERCOSUR	Mercado Común del Sur
MFN	most favoured nation
MRU	Mano River Union
MSG	Melanesia Spearhead Group
NAFTA	North American Free Trade Agreement
n.e.s.	not elsewhere specified
NIE	newly industrialized economies
n.i.e.	not included elsewhere
NPISHs	non-profit institutions serving households
OA	official aid
OAS	Organization of American States
ODA	official development assistance
OECD	Organization for Economic Cooperation and Development
OECS	Organization of Eastern Caribbean States
OOF	other official flows
OPEC	Organization of the Petroleum Exporting Countries
SAARC	South Asian Association for Regional Cooperation
SADC	Southern African Development Community
SAR	Special Administrative Region
SDR	special drawing right
SFR	Socialist Federative Republic of Yugoslavia (former)
SIDS	Small Island Developing States
SITC	Standard International Trade Classification
TFYR	The former Yugoslav Republic of Macedonia
TNC	transnational corporation
TRAINS	Trade Analysis and Information System
UMA	Arab Maghreb Union
UN/DESA/SD	United Nations Department of Economic and Social Affairs, Statistics Division
UNDP	United Nations Development Programme
UNESCO	United Nations Educational, Scientific and Cultural Organization
UNICEF	United Nations Children's Fund
USSR	Union of Soviet Socialist Republics
WAEMU	West African Economic and Monetary Union
WITS	World Integrated Trade Solution
WTO	World Trade Organization

Ces notes générales présentent le contenu de chaque tableau du *Manuel de statistiques* ainsi que les modifications introduites dans cette nouvelle édition, s'il y a lieu.

Les tableaux inclus dans cette publication constituent un résumé analytique des séries chronologiques complètes publiées dans le *Manuel de statistiques 2013 de la CNUCED* sur DVD.

PREMIÈRE PARTIE
Commerce international des marchandises

Les tableaux **1.1** donnent la valeur des exportations (f.a.b.) et des importations (c.a.f.) totales de marchandises, exprimée en millions de dollars et en pourcentage du monde, des pays et régions géographiques (1.1.1), groupements économiques (1.1.2) et groupements commerciaux (1.1.3). Les flux du commerce présentés dans le tableau 1.1.1 se réfèrent au Système du Commerce Général, à l'exception des pays et territoires qui utilisent le Système du Commerce Spécial et qui sont munis d'un astérisque. Le Système du Commerce Général est utilisé lorsque le territoire statistique d'un pays coïncide avec son territoire économique, et en conséquence, les importations comprennent tous les biens admis sur le territoire du pays déclarant et les exportations tous les biens qui le quittent. Le Système du Commerce Spécial est utilisé lorsque le territoire statistique ne comprend qu'une partie du territoire économique à l'intérieur de laquelle « les biens peuvent être écoulés librement sans restriction douanière ». Dans ce cas, les importations comprennent tous les biens qui entrent dans la zone de libre circulation du pays déclarant, c'est-à-dire qui ont été dédouanés pour mise à la consommation et les exportations comprennent tous les biens qui quittent la zone de libre circulation du pays déclarant.

Les taux d'évolution annuels moyens du commerce international des marchandises, calculés à partir des valeurs des tableaux 1.1, figurent dans les tableaux **1. 2**.

Les tableaux **1.3** présentent les balances commerciales (exportations f.a.b. moins importations c.a.f.), ainsi que ces mêmes balances en pourcentage des importations des pays, régions géographiques et groupements économiques.

Le tableau **1.4** indique l'importance des échanges entre pays membres de groupements commerciaux par rapport aux exportations régionales et totales de ces groupements.

DEUXIÈME PARTIE
Commerce international des marchandises par régions

Le tableau **2.1** présente la structure des exportations et des importations des pays par régions de destination et d'origine. Le plus grand nombre possible de pays en développement sont inclus tandis que les partenaires commerciaux sont regroupés en 14 groupes considérés comme particulièrement importants pour l'analyse du commerce international.

Les tableaux **2.2** (**A** à **L**) indiquent la structure des exportations par destination ainsi que des importations par origine et par groupes de produits pour le monde et une sélection de 12 groupements de pays. Le tableau fournit une information détaillée sur le réseau du commerce international avec le monde, 19 régions d'origine et de destination, et pour six différents groupes de produits.

Les totaux du commerce international des marchandises présentés dans les tableaux des première et deuxième parties ne sont pas strictement comparables en raison de sources complémentaires mais différentes et d'une marge d'exportations et d'importations non distribuées, en dépit des efforts déployés pour répartir les flux commerciaux par destinations et origines.

Les exportations ventilées par destinations peuvent accuser un écart parfois considérable par rapport aux importations déclarées par les pays destinataires en raison de divers facteurs dont les plus importants sont les suivants :

- Les importations sont déclarées en principe "valeur c.a.f." plutôt que "valeur f.a.b".;

- Les importations de marchandises peuvent arriver à destination et être enregistrées longtemps après la date de leur enregistrement à l'exportation ;

- D'importantes différences peuvent exister entre la destination des exportations déclarée par les pays exportateurs et la destination réelle telle qu'indiquée dans les statistiques d'importation.

TROISIÈME PARTIE
Commerce international des marchandises par produits

Le tableau **3.1** fournit la structure des exportations et des importations des pays par produits classés en 9 groupes (total, produits alimentaires, matières premières d'origine agricole, combustibles, minerais et métaux, produits manufacturés, dont produits chimiques, machines et matériel de transport, articles manufacturés divers) pour plusieurs années.

Les tableaux **3.2A**, **B** et **C** présentent respectivement les exportations par produits du monde, des économies en développement et développées, à un niveau très détaillé (CTCI révision 3, position à trois chiffres). Les parts que représente chaque produit dans les exportations du monde et de la région, sont calculées pour chaque groupe d'économies, ainsi que le taux annuel de croissance et l'écart de ce dernier par rapport au taux de croissance mondial.

Le tableau **3.2D** établit, pour chaque économie, la liste des principaux produits qu'elle exporte (CTCI révision 3, position à trois chiffres). La part de chaque produit dans le total des exportations du pays, de la région et du monde est également indiquée.

Le tableau **3.2E** liste les plus gros exportateurs de 70 produits parmi les produits les plus exportés par les économies en développement (CTCI révision 3, position à trois chiffres), ainsi que les parts correspondantes dans le commerce mondial.

Le tableau **3.3** fournit les indices de concentration et de changements structurels des exportations et des importations des produits au niveau de la CTCI (révision 3, position à trois chiffres). Le premier indicateur a vocation à montrer comment le marché d'un produit est concentré sur quelques pays ou réparti de façon plus homogène entre les pays. L'indicateur de changement structurel indique si la répartition du commerce d'un produit entre les pays exportateurs ou importateurs a connu une évolution importante par rapport à une année de référence.

Les totaux du commerce international des marchandises présentés dans les tableaux de cette troisième partie peuvent aussi être différents des données de la première partie pour les raisons précédemment citées, auxquelles il convient d'ajouter des marges d'exportations et d'importations non distribuées par groupes de produits ou l'utilisation de nomenclatures différentes de produits par le pays exportateur et le pays importateur.

QUATRIÈME PARTIE
Indicateurs du commerce international des marchandises

Les tableaux **4.1** contiennent les résultats du calcul des indices de concentration et de diversification des pays, régions géographiques et groupements économiques. Cet indice de concentration a vocation à montrer comment les exportations et importations d'un pays ou groupe de pays sont concentrées sur quelques produits ou réparties de façon plus homogène sur une gamme de produits. L'indicateur de diversification indique si la structure par produits des exportations ou importations d'un pays ou groupe de pays diverge de la structure par produits observée au niveau du monde.

Les tableaux **4.2** fournissent les indices de volume des exportations et des importations complétant ainsi l'information en valeur disponible dans les tableaux 1.1 et 1.2, les indices de la valeur unitaire des exportations et importations ainsi que les indices de termes de l'échange et le pouvoir d'achat des exportations dérivés des indices de valeur unitaire. Ces indices sont calculés au niveau des pays et régions géographiques (4.2.1) et des groupements économiques (4.2.2).

Afin d'améliorer la couverture des données et spécialement pour les années récentes, la méthode suivante a été utilisée pour le calcul des valeurs unitaires :

- Un ensemble d'indices de prix moyens au niveau des groupes de la CTCI (révision 3, position à 3 chiffres) a été construit en utilisant des données provenant de *UNCTADstat* Statistiques des produits de base, des sources internationales et nationales ainsi que des estimations du secrétariat de la CNUCED.

- Au niveau des pays individuels, les indices de la valeur unitaire ont été calculés en utilisant comme pondération les valeurs des exportations et des importations de l'année courante disponibles dans la table 3.2 au niveau de la CTCI (révision 3, position à 3 chiffres).

Dans certains cas ces indices peuvent différer des estimations publiées dans les sources officielles, le but principal étant de fournir des estimations approximatives et comparables pour la plupart des pays en développement.

Le tableau **4.3** contient les données sur les droits de douane NPF moyens appliqués à l'importation des principales catégories de produits non-agricoles et non-pétroliers, par marchés individuels.

CINQUIÈME PARTIE
Commerce international des services

Les tableaux **5.1.1**, **5.1.2** et **5.1.3** présentent les exportations et les importations totales des services par pays, par régions géographiques, groupements économiques et groupements commerciaux. Les statistiques comprises sont le résultat d'un travail commun entre la CNUCED et l'Organisation mondiale du commerce (OMC) et elles correspondent aux définitions du *Manuel de la balance des paiements* du FMI (*MBP5, 1993*). Les agrégats inclus dans le tableau 5.1 comprennent les valeurs estimées qui ne sont pas présentées séparément. Les services sont définis comme rendements économiques de produits intangibles qui peuvent être produits, transférés et consommés au même moment. Cependant, les services recouvrent un groupe large et hétérogène de produits et d'activités que l'on peut difficilement englober dans une définition. Parfois, la démarcation entre services et marchandises n'est pas aisée. Les services sont produits sur commande et ont généralement pour résultat un changement des conditions des consommateurs qui ont demandé ces services. Pour que la production d'un service soit terminée, il doit être fourni au consommateur.

Le tableau **5.2** présente les statistiques sur le commerce international des services par catégories de services pour une sélection de groupements de pays, ainsi que pour les principaux exportateurs et importateurs parmi les économies en développement et en transition, et parmi les pays développés. Ces statistiques sont le résultat d'un travail commun entre la CNUCED et l'OMC et elles correspondent aux définitions du *Manuel de la balance des paiements* du FMI (*MBP5, 1993*). Le tableau présente des données pour les catégories de services suivantes: les transports; les voyages; les services de communications; les services du bâtiment et des travaux publics; les services d'assurance; les services financiers; les services informatiques et d'information; les redevances et droits de licence; les autres services aux entreprises; et les services personnels, culturels et relatifs aux loisirs.

Dans la mesure du possible, le but du groupe de travail inter-agences sur les statistiques du commerce international de services est d'expliquer et réduire les divergences relevées dans les statistiques sur les services publiées par différentes organisations internationales. Un aperçu des bases de données couvrant les statistiques du commerce international des services est disponible sur

http://unstats.un.org/unsd/tradeserv/TFSITS/matrix.htm.

Le tableau **5.3** concerne le transport maritime international. Il contient des données sur la flotte marchande mondiale par pavillons d'immatriculation et par types de navires. Le tableau incorpore les informations consolidées provenant des différentes éditions de la publication *Review of Maritime Transport* de la CNUCED. Elle rend compte de l'évolution du transport multimodal, portuaire et maritime concernant les principaux trafics de vrac liquide, de vrac sec et de conteneurs.

SIXIÈME PARTIE
Produits de base

Le tableau **6.1** donne les indices annuels et trimestriels de prix en dollars courants sur le marché libre d'une sélection de produits de base exportés par les économies en développement. Ces indices sont aussi disponibles au niveau des groupes de produits de base suivants : produits alimentaires, boissons tropicales, huiles et graines oléagineuses, matières premières d'origine agricole, minéraux, minerais et métaux ainsi qu'un indice de l'ensemble. Les pondérations ont été calculées à partir de la valeur des exportations des pays en développement de 1999 à 2001 et les indices en utilisant 2000=100 comme année de base.

Le tableau **6.2** complète l'information sur les prix des produits de base par les indices d'instabilité et les tendances de prix sur le marché libre d'une sélection de produits de base ayant une importance particulière pour les économies en développement.

SEPTIÈME PARTIE
Finance internationale

Les tableaux **7.1.1**, **7.1.2** et **7.1.3** fournissent les valeurs de compte courant net par pays, par régions et par groupements économiques et commerciaux. Les chiffres sont présentés en millions de dollars, ainsi qu'en pourcentage du produit intérieur brut. Le compte des transactions courantes de la balance des paiements recouvre toutes les transactions entre entités résidentes et non-résidentes de l'économie déclarante. En général, la balance du compte courant indique la différence entre les recettes et les paiements pour les biens, les services et les revenus faisant partie des transactions internationales. De même, de la perspective nationale, la balance du compte courant représente l'écart entre les épargnes nationales et l'investissement intérieur.

Les tableaux **7.2.1**, **7.2.2** et **7.2.3** sont consacrés aux investissements directs en provenance de l'étranger (IED). Ils représentent les flux entrants et sortants de l'IED par pays et régions géographiques, groupements économiques et groupements commerciaux. Les chiffres correspondent aux données contenues dans l'Annexe statistique du *Rapport sur l'investissement dans le monde 2013* de la CNUCED. L'investissement étranger direct (IED) est un investissement impliquant une relation à long terme et témoignant de l'intérêt durable d'une entité résidant dans un pays (investisseur étranger direct ou société mère) à l'égard d'une entreprise résidant dans un autre pays (entreprise bénéficiaire, entreprise affiliée, ou encore filiale étrangère). Cet investissement englobe à la fois la transaction initiale entre les deux entités et toutes les transactions ultérieures entre elles et entre filiales étrangères, qu'elles soient constituées ou non en sociétés. L'entreprise d'investissement direct est définie comme une entreprise dotée ou non de la personnalité morale, dans laquelle un investisseur direct qui est résident d'une autre économie détient au moins 10% des actions ordinaires ou des droits de vote (ou l'équivalent).

Les tableaux **7.3.1** et **7.3.2** fournissent les informations sur les recettes (crédits) des envois de fonds des migrants - en millions de dollars - par pays, par régions et par groupements économiques. Ces données sont également communiquées en pourcentage du PIB et du commerce international. Les envois de fonds des migrants est la somme des envois de fonds des travailleurs, de la rémunération des salariés et des transferts des migrants.

Les tableaux **7.4.1** et **7.4.2** font apparaître les statistiques sur les paiements (débits) des envois des travailleurs et migrants, suivant la même approche utilisée dans les tableaux 7.3.1 et 7.3.2.

Les tableaux **7.5.1** et **7.5.2** incluent les données relatives aux réserves internationales (y compris l'or) des économies en développement par pays, par régions et par groupements économiques. Les mois d'importation que ces réserves peuvent financer, dans la situation actuelle du commerce international du pays, sont également indiqués, ainsi que la variation annuelle des réserves totales. Selon la définition du FMI, les réserves totales représentent la somme des avoirs du pays en devises, la position de ses réserves au FMI, les réserves de l'or monétaire, et la valeur en dollars des États-Unis des avoirs en DTS de ses autorités monétaires.

Les flux financiers publics sont présentés dans les tableaux **7.6** par catégories de flux, pays, régions géographiques et groupements économiques. La définition des flux bilatéraux et multilatéraux est conforme aux publications du Comité d'aide au développement (CAD) de l'OCDE.

Les tableaux **7.7** contiennent les données sur la dette extérieure à long terme des principaux groupes d'économies en développement, en particulier la ventilation détaillée de la dette publique ou garantie par l'État par sources d'emprunt. Les données de la dette extérieure présentées dans ces tableaux se basent sur le Système de notification des pays débiteurs (SNPD), géré par la Banque mondiale.

HUITIÈME PARTIE
Indicateurs du développement

Les tableaux **8.1** fournissent le produit intérieur brut (PIB) nominal total et par habitant des pays, régions géographiques et groupements économiques. Les données de PIB en dollars ont été obtenues à partir des valeurs de PIB exprimées à l'origine en monnaies nationales. Les taux de change moyens annuels sur le marché libre, obtenus des séries statistiques du FMI, ont été utilisés pour la plupart des pays lors de la conversion en dollars.

Les taux annuels moyens de variation du PIB réel total et du PIB réel par habitant des pays, régions géographiques et groupements économiques sont disponibles dans les tableaux **8.2**. Les taux de croissance se basent sur le PIB aux prix constants en dollars de l'année 2005.

Le PIB total est décomposé par catégories de dépenses et la valeur ajoutée totale par branches d'activité économique dans les tableaux **8.3** pour les pays, régions géographiques et groupements économiques.

Les tableaux **8.4.1** et **8.4.2** présentent des estimations sur la population et la main-d'œuvre : population totale, population urbaine (en pourcentage de la population totale), main-d'œuvre totale, main-d'œuvre féminine (en pourcentage de la main-d'œuvre totale), main-d'œuvre dans l'agriculture, main-d'œuvre féminine (en pourcentage de la main-d'œuvre totale dans l'agriculture). Les chiffres pour certains groupes peuvent être différents de ceux publiés par la Division de la population lorsque les définitions de la CNUCED de ces groupes sont différentes.

AUTRES NOTES

Sauf indication contraire, les agrégats de pays sont obtenus en sommant les données des pays composant le groupe. Les calculs d'agrégats peuvent dans certains cas inclure des données estimées par le secrétariat de la CNUCED qui ne sont pas nécessairement toutes rapportées séparément. Les agrégats ne sont calculés que lorsqu'il y a assez de données significatives, rapportées ou estimées. Dans le cas contraire, l'agrégation ne sera pas calculée et la valeur sera remplacée par le symbole (-).

Par ailleurs, la somme des chiffres et des pourcentages indiqués dans les tableaux ne correspond pas nécessairement aux totaux en raison des arrondis.

Les données ont été collectées et vérifiées pour qu'elles correspondent à la couverture géographique des pays, telle qu'elle est décrite en début de *Manuel*. Toutefois certains écarts n'ont pu être évités en fonction de la disponibilité des données. Ils sont alors décrits dans les notes de fin de tableau.

Sauf indication contraire, le terme «dollar» s'entend du dollar des États-Unis d'Amérique et les données en dollars sont exprimées en dollars courants de l'année à laquelle elles se réfèrent.

Les taux moyens d'évolution annuelle sont définis par le coefficient b de la fonction exponentielle de tendance $y = ae^{bt}$, où t représente le temps. Cette méthode permet de prendre en compte toutes les observations concernant une période donnée sans que le taux de croissance obtenu ne soit trop affecté par des valeurs exceptionnelles.

Les pays et territoires sont présentés suivant des critères géographiques conformes à ceux de la Division de statistique, Département des affaires économiques et sociales (DAES) de l'ONU. Les pays et territoires sont aussi regroupés suivant des critères économiques ou d'adhésion à des accords commerciaux à des fins d'analyse statistique et de recherche.

Dans cette publication, le terme «économie» couvre les régions, les pays et les territoires. Une année ajoutée au nom d'un pays indique un changement de la couverture statistique de ce pays. Par exemple, Indonésie (...2002) indique que la couverture statistique de l'Indonésie incluant le Timor-Leste était valide jusqu'à la fin 2002.

La composition des groupements de pays présentée dans le **Manuel** évolue constamment pour mettre des statistiques pertinentes à la disposition de la recherche et de l'analyse. C'est pourquoi la CNUCED révise et met à jour la définition et la composition des groupes chaque année. Ces changements peuvent affecter de manière significative les chiffres d'une année de publication à l'autre. Le détail des changements est disponible dans la rubrique 'Méthodologie et classifications' sous 'Liens utiles' sur le site web d'*UNCTADstat.*

1. Économies en développement, économies en transition et économies développées

La distinction entre pays ou régions "développés" et "en développement" ne correspond à aucune nomenclature officielle à l'échelle du système des Nations Unies. Dans la pratique, on considère généralement comme développés Israël et Japon pour l'Asie, Bermudes, Canada, États-Unis, Groenland et Saint-Pierre-et-Miquelon pour l'Amérique septentrionale, Australie et Nouvelle-Zélande pour l'Océanie et l'Europe. Les pays et territoires sont répartis en trois grandes catégories, les économies en développement, les économies en transition et les économies développées, elles-mêmes subdivisées suivant des critères géographiques.

1) Économies en développement
Ces économies sont réparties entre quatre grandes régions géographiques : Afrique, Amérique, Asie et Océanie elles-mêmes subdivisées en sous-régions pour permettre la présentation de statistiques plus détaillées. Les exceptions à ce classement que l'on retrouve dans certains tableaux sont indiquées dans des notes.

2) Économies en transition
Il s'agit des pays opérant la transition d'une économie planifiée à une économie de marché.

3) Économies développées
Ces économies sont réparties entre quatre grandes régions géographiques : Amérique, Asie, Europe et Océanie.

Le total 'Monde' inclut la somme des données de ces trois groupes à laquelle s'ajoutent les données d'un groupement 'Autres territoires' (territoires ou partenaires non classés ailleurs), dont la composition est détaillée ci-dessous. Lorsqu'elles sont rapportées, les données relatives à ces territoires ne sont pas présentées individuellement.

La composition du groupement 'Autres territoires' est la suivante :

-Territoires non-classés ailleurs : Antarctique, île Bouvet, Territoire britannique de l'Antarctique, Territoire britannique de l'océan Indien, île Christmas, îles des Cocos (Keeling), Terres australes et antarctiques françaises, îles Heard et McDonald, île Norfolk, Pitcairn, Saint-Barthélemy, Saint-Martin (partie française), Géorgie du Sud et îles Sandwich méridionales, îles mineures éloignées des États-Unis et îles du Pacifique sous administration des États-Unis.

- Partenaires non classés ailleurs : 'combustibles de soute et provisions de bord', 'informations confidentielles et différences', 'zone neutre', 'zones franches' qui sont utilisés exclusivement dans les tableaux du commerce de marchandises.
Les statistiques présentées au niveau de chacun des groupements précédemment décrits sont calculées à partir des valeurs des économies qui entrent dans la composition du groupement et complétées le cas échéant par un reliquat qu'il n'a pas été possible de répartir entre les éléments du groupement.

2. Groupements économiques des économies en développement

Dans le *Manuel de statistiques de la CNUCED*, les regroupements des pays et territoires en développement sont nombreux et variés afin de disposer facilement des données statistiques nécessaires à l'analyse socio-économique et aux recherches sur le développement.

Les économies en développement sont présentées à trois niveaux d'agrégation : le groupe dans son intégralité, puis sans la Chine continentale et enfin sans les pays les moins avancés.

Le groupe des pays très pauvres très endettés inclut les pays bénéficiant de l'initiative de désendettement de la Banque mondiale et du Fonds monétaire international.

Les PMA et les pays en développement sans littoral sont des groupes de pays qui requièrent une attention particulière de la communauté internationale.

Depuis 1994, les Nations Unies ont également pris en compte les problèmes particuliers des petits États insulaires en développement mais n'ont jamais établi de liste officielle de ces États. La liste non officielle présentée dans le *Manuel de statistiques* est utilisée par la CNUCED à des fins analytiques uniquement.

Les économies en développement sont également réparties en trois groupes de revenu en fonction du PIB par habitant pour la moyenne des années de 2004 à 2006 : revenu élevé (supérieur à 4 500 dollars), revenu intermédiaire (compris entre 1 000 et 4 500 dollars) et revenu faible (inférieur à 1 000 dollars).

Le groupement des principaux exportateurs de pétrole et de gaz comprend les pays, dont la part de pétrole et de gaz (CTCI codes 33 plus 34), ne représentait 1) pas moins de 50 % de leurs exportations totales, et les exportations de ces produits s'élevaient à 2) au moins 1% de la part mondiale pour la période 2004-2006. Les pays composant ce groupement sont répartis en trois zones géographiques : Afrique, Amérique et Asie.

Le groupement des principaux exportateurs d'articles manufacturés (CTCI 5 à 8 moins 667 et 68), répartis entre Amérique et Asie, comprend les économies dont la part d'articles manufacturés ne représentait 1) pas moins de 50 % de leurs exportations totales, et 2) leurs exportations d'articles manufacturés représentait au moins 1% de la part mondiale pour la période 2004-2006.

La composition des groupements des économies émergentes (réparties entre Amérique et Asie) et des économies nouvellement industrialisées d'Asie (première et deuxième génération) correspond à celle utilisée dans le *Rapport sur le commerce et le développement* de la CNUCED.

Les différentes régions géographiques sont également présentées à différents niveaux d'agrégation :
- Afrique : Afrique septentrionale sans le Soudan, Afrique subsaharienne, Soudan compris, avec et sans l'Afrique du Sud.
- Amérique : Amérique centrale et Grandes Antilles sans Porto Rico, avec et sans le Mexique, Amérique du Sud et centrale, Amérique du Sud sans le Brésil.
- Asie : Asie orientale et du Sud-Est sans la Chine et Asie méridionale sans l'Inde.

3. Groupements commerciaux et interrégionaux

Les statistiques des groupements régionaux et commerciaux sont présentées dès lors qu'elles sont pertinentes et présentent un intérêt analytique. Ces groupements englobent toutes les économies concernées et sont classés selon les grandes régions géographiques utilisées précédemment, à l'exception des groupements interrégionaux suivants : le groupe des États d'Afrique, des Caraïbes et du Pacifique, le groupe de Coopération économique de l'Asie et du Pacifique, le groupe de Coopération économique de la mer Noire et la Communauté des États indépendants.

RÉPARTITION DES PAYS ET TERRITOIRES

ÉCONOMIES EN DÉVELOPPEMENT

AFRIQUE

Afrique orientale

Burundi	Malawi	Somalie
Comores	Maurice	Soudan du Sud
Djibouti	Mozambique	Zambie
Érythrée	Ouganda	Zimbabwe
Éthiopie	République-Unie de Tanzanie	
Kenya	Rwanda	
Madagascar	Seychelles	

Afrique centrale

Angola	Gabon	République démocratique du Congo
Cameroun	Guinée équatoriale	Sao Tomé-et-Principe
Congo	République centrafricaine	Tchad

Afrique septentrionale

Algérie	Maroc	Tunisie
Égypte	Sahara occidental	
Libye	Soudan	

Afrique australe

Afrique du Sud	Lesotho	Swaziland
Botswana	Namibie	

Afrique occidentale

Bénin	Guinée	Nigéria
Burkina Faso	Guinée-Bissau	Sainte-Hélène
Cap-Vert	Libéria	Sénégal
Côte d'Ivoire	Mali	Sierra Leone
Gambie	Mauritanie	Togo
Ghana	Niger	

AMÉRIQUE

Amérique centrale

Belize	Guatemala	Nicaragua
Costa Rica	Honduras	Panama
El Salvador	Mexique	

Amérique du Sud

Argentine	Équateur	Suriname
Bolivie (État plurinational de)	Guyana	Uruguay
Brésil	Îles Falkland (Malvinas)	Venezuela (République bolivarienne du)
Chili	Paraguay	
Colombie	Pérou	

RÉPARTITION DES PAYS ET TERRITOIRES

ÉCONOMIES EN DÉVELOPPEMENT (fin)

AMÉRIQUE (fin)

Caraïbes

Grandes Antilles

Cuba
Haïti
Jamaïque
République dominicaine

Petites Antilles

Anguilla	Îles Caïmanes
Antigua-et-Barbuda	Îles Turques et Caïques
Aruba	Îles Vierges britanniques
Bahamas	Montserrat
Barbade	Sainte-Lucie
Bonaire, Saint-Eustache et Saba	Saint-Kitts-et-Nevis
Curaçao	Saint-Martin (partie néerlandaise)
Dominique	Saint-Vincent-et-les Grenadines
Grenade	Trinité-et-Tobago

ASIE

Asie orientale

Chine	Mongolie
Hong Kong, région administrative spéciale de Chine	Province chinoise de Taiwan
	République de Corée
Macao, région administrative spéciale de Chine	République populaire démocratique de Corée

Asie méridionale

Afghanistan	Inde	Népal
Bangladesh	Iran (République islamique d')	Pakistan
Bhoutan	Maldives	Sri Lanka

Asie du Sud-Est

Brunéi Darussalam	Myanmar	Thaïlande
Cambodge	Philippines	Timor-Leste
Indonésie	République démocratique populaire lao	Viet Nam
Malaisie	Singapour	

Asie occidentale

Arabie saoudite	Jordanie	République arabe syrienne
Bahreïn	Koweït	Turquie
Émirats arabes unis	Liban	Yémen
État de Palestine	Oman	
Iraq	Qatar	

OCÉANIE

Fidji	Kiribati	Polynésie française
Guam	Micronésie (États fédérés de)	Samoa
Îles Cook	Nauru	Samoa américaines
Îles Mariannes septentrionales	Nioué	Tokélaou
Îles Marshall	Nouvelle-Calédonie	Tonga
Îles Salomon	Palaos	Tuvalu
Îles Wallis-et-Futuna	Papouasie-Nouvelle-Guinée	Vanuatu

RÉPARTITION DES PAYS ET TERRITOIRES

ÉCONOMIES EN TRANSITION

Albanie
Arménie
Azerbaïdjan
Bélarus
Bosnie-Herzégovine
Croatie
ex-République yougoslave
   de Macédoine

Fédération de Russie
Géorgie
Kazakhstan
Kirghizistan
Monténégro
Ouzbékistan
République de Moldova
Serbie

Tadjikistan
Turkménistan
Ukraine

ÉCONOMIES DÉVELOPÉES

AMÉRIQUE

Bermudes
Canada

États-Unis d'Amérique, y compris
   Porto Rico et les îles Vierges
   américaines

Groenland
Saint-Pierre-et-Miquelon

ASIE

Israël
Japon

EUROPE

Allemagne
Andorre
Autriche
Belgique
Bulgarie
Chypre
Danemark
Espagne
Estonie
Finlande, y compris les îles d'Åland
France, y compris la Guadeloupe,
   la Guyane française, la Martinique,
   Mayotte*, Monaco et la Réunion
Gibraltar

Grèce
Hongrie
Îles Féroé
Irlande
Islande
Italie
Lettonie
Lituanie
Luxembourg
Malte
Norvège, y compris les îles Svalbard
   et Jan Mayen
Pays-Bas
Pologne

Portugal
République tchèque
Roumanie
Royaume Uni de Grande-Bretagne et
   d'Irlande du Nord, y compris les îles
   Anglo-Normandes et l'île de Man
Saint-Marin
Saint-Siège
Slovaquie
Slovénie
Suède
Suisse, y compris le Liechtenstein

* Depuis 2012, Mayotte est inclus dans le territoire statistique de la France

OCÉANIE

Australie
Nouvelle-Zélande

RÉPARTITION DES ÉCONOMIES EN DÉVELOPPEMENT PAR GROUPEMENTS ÉCONOMIQUES

Pays pauvres très endettés (39)

Afghanistan	Guinée	Ouganda
Bénin	Guinée-Bissau	République centrafricaine
Bolivie (État plurinational de)	Guyana	République démocratique du Congo
Burkina Faso	Haïti	République-Unie de Tanzanie
Burundi	Honduras	Rwanda
Cameroun	Libéria	Sao Tomé-et-Principe
Comores	Madagascar	Sénégal
Congo	Malawi	Sierra Leone
Côte d'Ivoire	Mali	Somalie
Érythrée	Mauritanie	Soudan
Éthiopie	Mozambique	Tchad
Gambie	Nicaragua	Togo
Ghana	Niger	Zambie

Pays en développement sans littoral (32)

Afghanistan	Kirghizistan*	République démocratique populaire lao
Arménie*	Lesotho	République de Moldova*
Azerbaïdjan*	Malawi	Rwanda
Bhoutan	Mali	Soudan du Sud
Bolivie (État plurinational de)	Mongolie	Swaziland
Botswana	Népal	Tadjikistan*
Burkina Faso	Niger	Tchad
Burundi	Ouganda	Turkménistan*
Éthiopie	Ouzbékistan*	Zambie
ex-République yougoslave de Macédoine*	Paraguay	Zimbabwe
Kazakhstan*	République centrafricaine	

* Ces pays font partie du groupement des économies en transition (ni développées ni en développement). Cependant, comme ce sont des pays sans littoral, ils appartiennent aussi à ce groupement.

Petits États insulaires en développement (29)

Antigua-et-Barbuda	Jamaïque	Saint-Vincent-et-les Grenadines
Bahamas	Kiribati	Samoa
Barbade	Maldives	Sao Tomé-et-Principe
Cap-Vert	Maurice	Seychelles
Comores	Micronésie (États fédérés de)	Timor-Leste
Dominique	Nauru	Tonga
Fidji	Palaos	Trinité-et-Tobago
Grenade	Papouasie-Nouvelle-Guinée	Tuvalu
Îles Marshall	Sainte-Lucie	Vanuatu
Îles Salomon	Saint-Kitts-et-Nevis	

Pays les moins avancés (49)

Afrique et Haïti	Année d'inclusion dans le groupe		Année d'inclusion dans le groupe	*Asie*	Année d'inclusion dans le groupe
Angola	1994	Niger	1971	Afghanistan	1971
Bénin	1971	Ouganda	1971	Bangladesh	1975
Burkina Faso	1971	République centrafricaine	1975	Bhoutan	1971
Burundi	1971	République démocratique du		Cambodge	1991
Djibouti	1982	Congo	1991	Myanmar	1987
Érythrée	1994	République-Unie de Tanzanie	1971	Népal	1971
Éthiopie	1971	Rwanda	1971	République démocratique populaire lao	1971
Gambie	1975	Sénégal	2000	Yémen	1971
Guinée	1971	Sierra Leone	1982		
Guinée-Bissau	1981	Somalie	1971	*Îles*	
Guinée Équatoriale	1982	Soudan	1971	Comores	1977
Haïti	1971	Soudan du Sud	2012	Îles Salomon	1991
Lesotho	1971	Tchad	1971	Kiribati	1986
Libéria	1990	Togo	1982	Samoa	1971
Madagascar	1991	Zambie	1991	Sao Tomé-et-Principe	1982
Malawi	1971			Timor-Leste	2003
Mali	1971			Tuvalu	1986
Mauritanie	1986			Vanuatu	1985
Mozambique	1988				

RÉPARTITION DES ÉCONOMIES EN DÉVELOPPEMENT PAR GROUPEMENTS ÉCONOMIQUES

GROUPEMENTS ÉCONOMIQUES DE LA CNUCED

PIB courant par habitant supérieur à 4 500 dollars pour la moyenne 2004-2006 : Revenu élevé (57)

Afrique du Sud
Anguilla
Antigua-et-Barbuda
Arabie saoudite
Argentine
Aruba
Bahamas
Bahreïn
Barbade
Bonaire, Saba et Saint-Eustache
Botswana
Brésil
Brunéi Darussalam
Chili
Costa Rica
Curaçao
Dominique
Émirats arabes unis
Gabon
Grenade

Guam
Guinée équatoriale
Hong-Kong, région administrative
    spéciale de Chine
Îles Caïmanes
Iles Cook
Îles Falkland (Malvinas)
Îles Mariannes du Nord
Îles Turques et Caïques
Îles Vierges britanniques
Koweït
Liban
Libye
Macao, région administrative
    spéciale de Chine
Malaisie
Maurice
Mexique
Montserrat
Nioué

Nouvelle-Calédonie
Oman
Palaos
Panama
Polynésie française
Province chinoise de Taiwan
Qatar
République de Corée
Sainte-Lucie
Saint-Kitts-et-Nevis
Saint-Martin (partie holandaise)
Saint-Vincent-et-les Grenadines
Samoa américaines
Seychelles
Singapour
Trinité-et-Tobago
Turquie
Uruguay
Venezuela (République bolivarienne du)

PIB courant par habitant compris entre 1 000 et 4 500 dollars pour la moyenne 2004-2006 : Revenu intermédiaire (47)

Algérie
Angola
Belize
Bhoutan
Bolivie (État plurinational de)
Cap-Vert
Chine
Colombie
Congo
Cuba
Égypte
El Salvador
Équateur
État de Palestine
Fidji
Guatemala

Guyana
Honduras
Îles Marshall
Îles Wallis-et-Futuna
Indonésie
Iran (République islamique d')
Jamaïque
Jordanie
Kiribati
Maldives
Maroc
Micronésie (États fédérés de)
Mongolie
Namibie
Nauru
Paraguay

Pérou
Philippines
République arabe syrienne
République dominicaine
Sainte-Hélène
Samoa
Sri Lanka
Suriname
Swaziland
Thaïlande
Tokélaou
Tonga
Tunisie
Tuvalu
Vanuatu

PIB courant par habitant inférieur à 1 000 dollars pour la moyenne 2004-2006 : Revenu faible (55)

Afghanistan
Bangladesh
Bénin
Burkina Faso
Burundi
Cambodge
Cameroun
Comores
Côte d'Ivoire
Djibouti
Érythrée
Éthiopie
Gambie
Ghana
Guinée
Guinée-Bissau
Haïti
Îles Salomon
Inde

Iraq
Kenya
Lesotho
Libéria
Madagascar
Malawi
Mali
Mauritanie
Mozambique
Myanmar
Népal
Nicaragua
Niger
Nigéria
Ouganda
République centrafricaine
République démocratique du Congo
République populaire démocratique
    de Corée

République démocratique populaire lao
Pakistan
Papouasie-Nouvelle-Guinée
République-Unie de Tanzanie
Rwanda
Sao Tomé-et-Principe
Sénégal
Sierra Leone
Somalie
Soudan
Soudan du Sud
Tchad
Timor-Leste
Togo
Viet Nam
Yémen
Zambie
Zimbabwe

RÉPARTITION DES ÉCONOMIES EN DÉVELOPPEMENT PAR GROUPEMENTS ÉCONOMIQUES

Principaux pays exportateurs de pétrole et de gaz (12)

Afrique
Algérie
Angola
Libye
Nigéria

Amérique
Venezuela
(République bolivarienne du)

Asie
Arabie saoudite
Émirats arabes unis
Iran (République islamique d')
Iraq
Koweït
Oman
Qatar

Principaux pays exportateurs d'articles manufacturés (8)

Amérique
Mexique

Asie
Chine
Hong Kong, région administrative
   spéciale de Chine
Malaisie
Province chinoise de Taiwan
République de Corée
Singapour
Thaïlande

Économies émergentes (10)

Amérique
Argentine
Brésil
Chili
Mexique
Pérou

Asie
Malaisie
Province chinoise de Taiwan
République de Corée
Singapour
Thaïlande

Économies nouvellement industrialisées d'Asie (8)

Première génération
Hong Kong, région administrative
   spéciale de Chine
Province chinoise de Taiwan
République de Corée
Singapour

Deuxième génération
Indonésie
Malaisie
Philippines
Thaïlande

RÉPARTITION DES ÉCONOMIES PAR GROUPEMENTS COMMERCIAUX

AFRIQUE

Communauté de l'Afrique de l'Est (5) - CAE

	Année d'adhésion
Burundi	2007
Kenya	2001
Ouganda	2001
République-Unie de Tanzanie	2001
Rwanda	2007

Communauté de développement de l'Afrique australe (15) - CDAA

Afrique du Sud	1994
Angola	1992
Botswana	1992
Lesotho	1992
Madagascar	2005
Malawi	1992
Maurice	1992
Mozambique	1992
Namibie	1992
République démocratique du Congo	1992
République-Unie de Tanzanie	1992
Seychelles	2007
Swaziland	1992
Zambie	1992
Zimbabwe	1994

Communauté économique des États de l'Afrique centrale (10) - CEEAC

Angola	1999
Burundi	1983
Cameroun	1983
Congo	1983
Gabon	1983
Guinée équatoriale	1983
République centrafricaine	1983
République démocratique du Congo	1983
Sao Tomé-et-Principe	1983
Tchad	1983

Communauté économique et monétaire de l'Afrique centrale (6) - CEMAC

	Année d'adhésion
Cameroun	1994
Congo	1994
Gabon	1994
Guinée équatoriale	1994
République centrafricaine	1994
Tchad	1994

Communauté économique des États de l'Afrique de l'Ouest (15) - CEDEAO

Bénin	1975
Burkina Faso	1975
Cap-Vert	1977
Côte d'Ivoire	1975
Gambie	1975
Ghana	1975
Guinée	1975
Guinée-Bissau	1975
Libéria	1975
Mali	1975
Niger	1975
Nigéria	1975
Sénégal	1975
Sierra Leone	1975
Togo	1975

Communauté économique des pays des Grands Lacs (3) - CEPGL

Burundi	1976
République démocratique du Congo	1976
Rwanda	1976

Marché commun des États de l'Afrique de l'Est et du Sud (19) - COMESA

Burundi	1994
Comores	1994
Djibouti	1994
Égypte	1994
Érythrée	1994
Éthiopie	1994
Kenya	1994
Libye	2005
Madagascar	1994
Malawi	1994
Maurice	1994
Ouganda	1994
République démocratique du Congo	1994
Rwanda	1994
Seychelles	1994
Soudan	1994
Swaziland	1994
Zambie	1994
Zimbabwe	1994

Union du fleuve Mano (4) - UFM

Côte d'Ivoire	2008
Guinée	1980
Libéria	1973
Sierra Leone	1973

Union du Maghreb arabe (5) - UMA

Algérie	1989
Libye	1989
Maroc	1989
Mauritanie	1989
Tunisie	1989

Union économique et monétaire Ouest-africaine (8) - UEMOA

Bénin	1994
Burkina Faso	1994
Côte d'Ivoire	1994
Guinée-Bissau	1997
Mali	1994
Niger	1994
Sénégal	1994
Togo	1994

AMÉRIQUE

Accord de libre-échange nord-américain (3) - ALENA

	Année d'adhésion
Canada	1994
États-Unis d'Amérique	1994
Mexique	1994

Association latino-américaine d'intégration (13) - ALADI

Argentine	1980
Bolivie (État plurinational de)	1980
Brésil	1980
Chili	1980
Colombie	1980
Cuba	1999
Équateur	1980
Mexique	1980
Panama	2012
Paraguay	1980
Pérou	1980
Uruguay	1980
Venezuela (République bolivarienne du)	1980

Communauté andine (4) - ANCOM

	Année d'adhésion
Bolivie (État plurinational de)	1996
Colombie	1996
Équateur	1996
Pérou	1996

Communauté des Caraïbes (15) - CARICOM

Antigua-et-Barbuda	1974
Bahamas	1983
Barbade	1973
Belize	1974
Dominique	1974
Grenade	1974
Guyana	1973
Haïti	2002
Jamaïque	1973
Montserrat	1974
Sainte Lucie	1974
Saint-Kitts-et-Nevis	1974
Saint-Vincent-et-les- Grenadines	1974
Suriname	1995
Trinité-et-Tobago	1973

Marché commun d'Amérique centrale (5) - MCAC

	Année d'adhésion
Costa Rica	1962
El Salvador	1961
Guatemala	1961
Honduras	1961
Nicaragua	1961

Marché commun sud-américain (6) - MERCOSUR

Argentine	1994
Bolivie	2012
Brésil	1994
Paraguay	1994
Uruguay	1994
Venezuela (République bolivarienne du)	2012

RÉPARTITION DES ÉCONOMIES PAR GROUPEMENTS COMMERCIAUX

AMÉRIQUE (fin)

	Année d'adhésion		Année d'adhésion		Année d'adhésion
Organisation des États américains (35) - OEA		République dominicaine	1948	Brésil	1994
Antigua-et-Barbuda	1981	Sainte-Lucie	1979	Canada	1994
Argentine	1948	Saint-Kitts-et-Nevis	1984	Chili	1994
Bahamas	1982	Saint-Vincent-et-les Grenadines	1981	Colombie	1994
Barbade	1967	Suriname	1977	Costa Rica	1994
Belize	1991	Trinité-et-Tobago	1967	Dominique	1994
Bolivie (État plurinational de)	1948	Uruguay	1948	El Salvador	1994
Brésil	1948	Venezuela (Rép. Bolivarienne du)	1948	Équateur	1994
Canada	1990			États-Unis d'Amérique	1994
Chili	1948	**Organisation des États des Caraïbes orientales (9) - OECO**		Grenade	1994
Colombie	1948			Guatemala	1994
Costa Rica	1948	Anguilla	1995	Guyana	1994
Cuba	2009	Antigua-et-Barbuda	1981	Haïti	1994
Dominique	1979	Dominique	1981	Honduras	1994
El Salvador	1948	Grenade	1981	Jamaïque	1994
Équateur	1948	Îles Vierges britanniques	1984	Mexique	1994
États-Unis d'Amérique	1948	Montserrat	1981	Nicaragua	1994
Grenade	1975	Sainte-Lucie	1981	Panama	1994
Guatemala	1948	Saint-Kitts-et-Nevis	1981	Paraguay	1994
Guyana	1948	Saint-Vincent-et-les Grenadines	1981	Pérou	1994
Haïti	1948			République dominicaine	1994
Honduras	1948	**Zone de libre-échange des Amériques (34) - ZLEA**		Sainte-Lucie	1994
Jamaïque	1969			Saint-Kitts-et-Nevis	1994
Mexique	1948	Antigua-et-Barbuda	1994	Saint-Vincent-et-les Grenadines	1994
Nicaragua	1948	Argentine	1994	Suriname	1994
Panama	1948	Bahamas	1994	Trinité-et-Tobago	1994
Paraguay	1948	Barbade	1994	Uruguay	1994
Pérou	1948	Belize	1994	Venezuela (Rép. bolivarienne du)	1994
		Bolivie (État plurinational de)	1994		

ASIE

	Année d'adhésion		Année d'adhésion		Année d'adhésion
Accord commercial de l'Asie et du Pacifique (6) - ACAP		**Association des nations de l'Asie du Sud-Est (10) - ANASE**		Oman	1981
				Qatar	1981
Bangladesh	1975	Brunéi Darussalam	1984		
Chine	2001	Cambodge	1999	**Organisation de coopération économique (10) - ECO**	
Inde	1975	Indonésie	1967		
République de Corée	1975	Malaisie	1967	Afghanistan	1992
République démocratique populaire lao	1975	Myanmar	1997	Azerbaïdjan	1992
		Philippines	1967	Iran (République islamique d')	1985
Sri Lanka	1975	République démocratique populaire lao	1997	Kazakhstan	1992
		Singapour	1967	Kirghizistan	1992
Association de l'Asie du Sud pour la coopération régionale (8) - SAARC		Thaïlande	1967	Ouzbékistan	1992
		Viet Nam	1995	Pakistan	1985
Afghanistan	2007			Tadjikistan	1992
Bangladesh	1985	**Conseil de coopération du Golfe (6) - CCG**		Turkménistan	1992
Bhoutan	1985			Turquie	1985
Inde	1985	Arabie saoudite	1981		
Maldives	1985	Bahreïn	1981		
Népal	1985	Émirats arabes unis	1981		
Pakistan	1985	Koweït	1981		
Sri Lanka	1985				

EUROPE

	Année d'adhésion		Année d'adhésion		Année d'adhésion
Association européenne de libre-échange (3) - AELE		Hongrie	2004	**Zone euro (17)**	
		Irlande	1973	Allemagne	2002
Islande	1970	Italie	1957	Autriche	2002
Norvège	1960	Lettonie	2004	Belgique	2002
Suisse	1960	Lituanie	2004	Chypre	2008
		Luxembourg	1957	Espagne	2002
Union européenne (27) - EU		Malte	2004	Estonie	2011
Allemagne	1957	Pays-Bas	1957	Finlande	2002
Autriche	1995	Pologne	2004	France	2002
Belgique	1957	Portugal	1986	Grèce	2002
Bulgarie	2008	République tchèque	2004	Irlande	2002
Chypre	2004	Roumanie	2008	Italie	2002
Danemark	1973	Royaume-Uni	1973	Luxembourg	2002
Espagne	1986	Slovaquie	2004	Malte	2008
Estonie	2004	Slovénie	2004	Pays-Bas	2002
Finlande	1995	Suède	1995	Portugal	2002
France	1957			Slovaquie	2009
Grèce	1981			Slovénie	2007

RÉPARTITION DES ÉCONOMIES PAR GROUPEMENTS COMMERCIAUX

OCÉANIE

Année d'adhésion

Groupe Fer de lance mélanésien (4)

Fidji	1998
Îles Salomon	1993
Papouasie-Nouvelle-Guinée	1993
Vanuatu	1993

RÉPARTITION DES ÉCONOMIES PAR GROUPEMENTS INTERRÉGIONAUX

Groupe des États d'Afrique, des Caraïbes et du Pacifique (79) - ACP

Afrique du Sud	Guinée équatoriale	République démocratique du Congo
Angola	Guyana	République dominicaine
Antigua-et-Barbuda	Haïti	République-Unie de Tanzanie
Bahamas	Îles Cook	Rwanda
Barbade	Îles Marshall	Sainte-Lucie
Belize	Îles Salomon	Saint-Kitts-et-Nevis
Bénin	Jamaïque	Saint-Vincent-et-les Grenadines
Botswana	Kenya	Samoa
Burkina Faso	Kiribati	Sao Tomé-et-Principe
Burundi	Lesotho	Sénégal
Cameroun	Libéria	Seychelles
Cap-Vert	Madagascar	Sierra Leone
Comores	Malawi	Somalie
Congo	Mali	Soudan
Côte d'Ivoire	Maurice	Suriname
Cuba	Mauritanie	Swaziland
Djibouti	Micronésie (États fédérés de)	Tchad
Dominique	Mozambique	Timor-Leste
Érythrée	Namibie	Togo
Éthiopie	Nauru	Tonga
Fidji	Niger	Trinité-et-Tobago
Gabon	Nigéria	Tuvalu
Gambie	Nioué	Vanuatu
Ghana	Ouganda	Zambie
Grenade	Palaos	Zimbabwe
Guinée	Papouasie-Nouvelle-Guinée	
Guinée-Bissau	République centrafricaine	

Coopération économique de l'Asie et du Pacifique (21) - CEAP	Année d'adhésion	Coopération économique de la mer Noire (12) - CEMN	Année d'adhésion	Communauté des États indépendants (11) - CEI	Année d'adhésion
Australie	1989	Albanie	1992	Arménie	1991
Brunéi Darussalam	1989	Arménie	1992	Azerbaïdjan	1991
Canada	1989	Azerbaïdjan	1992	Bélarus	1991
Chili	1994	Bulgarie	1992	Fédération de Russie	1991
Chine	1991	Fédération de Russie	1992	Kazakhstan	1991
États-Unis d'Amérique	1989	Géorgie	1992	Kirghizistan	1991
Fédération de Russie	1998	Grèce	1992	Ouzbékistan	1991
Hong Kong, région administrative spéciale	1991	République de Moldova	1992	République de Moldova	1991
Indonésie	1989	Roumanie	1992	Tadjikistan	1991
Japon	1989	Serbie	2004	Turkménistan	1991
Malaisie	1989	Turquie	1992	Ukraine	1991
Mexique	1993	Ukraine	1992		
Nouvelle-Zélande	1989	Grèce	1992		
Papouasie-Nouvelle-Guinée	1993				
Pérou	1998				
Philippines	1989				
Province chinoise de Taiwan	1991				
République de Corée	1989				
Singapour	1989				
Thaïlande	1989				
Viet Nam	1998				

ABRÉVIATIONS ET ACRONYMES

AASP	autres apports du secteur public
ACAP	Accord commercial de l'Asie et du Pacifique (ex-Accord de Bangkok)
ACP	Groupe des États d'Afrique, des Caraïbes et du Pacifique
AELE	Association européenne de libre-échange
AGCS	Accord général sur le commerce des services
ALADI	Association latino-américaine d'intégration
ALENA	Accord de libre-échange nord-américain
ANASE	Association des nations de l'Asie du Sud-Est
ANCOM	Communauté andine
anc.	ancien, ancienne, anciennement
AP	aide publique
APD	aide publique au développement
BML	Bourse des métaux de Londres
CAD	Comité d'aide au développement (OCDE)
CARICOM	Communauté des Caraïbes
CCG	Conseil de coopération du Golfe
CCSA	Comité de coordination des activités statistiques
CAE	Communauté de l'Afrique de l'Est
CDAA	Communauté de développement de l'Afrique australe
CEAP	Coopération économique de l'Asie et du Pacifique
CEDEAO	Communauté économique des États de l'Afrique de l'Ouest
CEE	Commission économique pour l'Europe
CEEAC	Communauté économique des États de l'Afrique centrale
CEI	Communauté des États indépendants
CEMAC	Communauté économique et monétaire de l'Afrique centrale
CEMN	Coopération économique de la mer Noire
CEPALC	Commission économique pour l'Amérique Latine et les Caraïbes
CEPGL	Communauté économique des pays des Grands Lacs
CESAP	Commission économique et sociale pour l'Asie et le Pacifique
CESAO	Commission économique et sociale pour l'Asie occidentale
c.a.f.	coût, assurance, fret
COMESA	Marché commun d'Afrique de l'Est et du Sud
CTCI	Classification type pour le commerce international
DTS	droit de tirage spécial
EIU	Economic Intelligence Unit
f.a.b.	franco à bord
FAO	Organisation des Nations Unies pour l'alimentation et l'agriculture
FBCF	formation brute de capital fixe
FMI	Fonds monétaire international
IED	Investissement étranger direct
ISBLM	institutions sans but lucratif au service des ménages
LERY	L'ex-République yougoslave de Macédoine
MBP	Manuel de la balance des paiements (FMI)
MCAC	Marché commun d'Amérique centrale
MERCOSUR	Marché commun sud-américain
MSG	Groupe Fer de lance mélanésien
n.c.a.	non classé ailleurs
n.d.a.	non dénommé ailleurs
NEI	nouvelles économies industrialisées
NPF	nation la plus favorisée
OCDE	Organisation de coopération et de développement économiques
OCE	Organisation de coopération économique
OEA	Organisation des États américains
OECO	Organisation des États des Caraïbes orientales
OIT	Organisation internationale du travail
OMC	Organisation mondiale du commerce
ONU/DAES/DS	Organisation des Nations Unies, Département des affaires économiques et sociales, Division de statistique
OPEP	Organisation des pays exportateurs de pétrole
PIB	produit intérieur brut
PMA	pays les moins avancés
PNB	produit national brut
PNUD	Programme des Nations Unies pour le développement
PPTE	pays pauvres très endettés
RAS	région administrative spéciale
RSF	République socialiste fédérative de Yougoslavie (anc.)
SAARC	Association de l'Asie du Sud pour la coopération régionale
SH	Système harmonisé
SNPD	Système de notification des pays débiteurs
STN	société transnationale
UE	Union européenne
UEMOA	Union économique et monétaire des États de l'Afrique de l'Ouest
UFM	Union du fleuve Mano
UMA	Union du Maghreb arabe
UNESCO	Organisation des Nations Unies pour l'éducation, la science et la culture
UNICEF	Fonds des Nations Unies pour l'enfance
URSS	Union des Républiques socialistes soviétiques
ZLEA	Zone de libre-échange des Amériques

The *Handbook of Statistics* refers to the Standard International Trade Classification (SITC) Revision 3 detailed below.

Depending on the table, nomenclature of statistics is detailed at the 3-digit level or by broad product groupings as follows:

Le *Manuel de statistiques* se réfère à la Classification type pour le commerce international (CTCI) révision 3 détaillée ci-dessous.

Selon les tableaux, les statistiques sont présentées, au niveau détaillé de la nomenclature (position à trois chiffres) ou par groupements de produits dont la composition est la suivante :

SITC Codes – Codes CTCI	Product groupings	Groupements de produits
0 to 9 – 0 à 9	All products	Total tous produits
0 + 1 + 22 + 4	All food items	Produits alimentaires
2 - (22 + 27 + 28)	Agricultural raw materials	Matières premières d'origine agricole
27 + 28 + 68 + 667 + 971	Ores, metals, precious stones and non-monetary gold	Minerais, métaux, pierres précieuses et or à usage non monétaire
3	Fuels	Combustibles
5 + 6 + 7+ 8 - (667 + 68)	Manufactured goods:	Articles manufacturés :
5	- Chemical products	- Produits chimiques
7	- Machinery and transport equipment	- Machines et matériel de transport
6 + 8 - (667 + 68)	- Other manufactured goods	- Articles manufacturés divers

Codes	Standard International Trade Classification (SITC) Revision 3 (1 to 3 digits)	Classification type pour le commerce international (CTCI) Révision 3 (positions de un à trois chiffres)
0	**Food and live animals**	**Produits alimentaires et animaux vivants**
00	**Live animals other than animals of division 03**	**Animaux vivants autres que ceux figurant dans la division 03**
001	Live animals other than animals of division 03	Animaux vivants autres que ceux figurant dans la division 03
01	**Meat and meat preparations**	**Viandes et préparations de viande**
011	Meat of bovine animals, fresh, chilled or frozen	Viande des animaux de l'espèce bovine, fraîche, réfrigérée/congelée
012	Other meat and edible meat offal	Autres viandes et abats comestibles
016	Meat, edible meat offal, salted, dried; flours, meals	Viandes et abats comestibles salés, fumés; farines et poudres
017	Meat, edible meat offal, prepared, preserved, n.e.s.	Préparations de viandes et d'abats, n.d.a.
02	**Dairy products and birds' eggs**	**Produits laitiers et oeufs d'oiseaux**
022	Milk, cream and milk products (excluding butter, cheese)	Lait et produits laitiers (sauf beurre, fromages)
023	Butter and other fats and oils derived from milk	Beurre et autres matières grasses du lait
024	Cheese and curd	Fromages et caillebotte
025	Birds' eggs, and eggs' yolks; egg albumin	Oeufs d'oiseaux et jaunes d'oeufs frais, blanc d'oeuf
03	**Fish (not marine mammals), crustaceans, molluscs and aquatic invertebrates and preparations thereof**	**Poissons (sauf mammifères marins), crustacés, mollusques et autres invertébrés aquatiques et préparations**
034	Fish, fresh (live or dead), chilled or frozen	Poissons frais, vivants ou morts, réfrigérés ou congelés
035	Fish, dried, salted or in brine; smoked fish	Poissons séchés, salés, fumés
036	Crustaceans, molluscs and aquatic invertebrates	Crustacés, mollusques et invertébrés aquatiques
037	Fish, aqua. invertebrates, prepared, preserved, n.e.s.	Poissons, crustacés, mollusques, préparés ou conservés, n.d.a.
04	**Cereals and cereal preparations**	**Céréales et préparations à base de céréales**
041	Wheat (including spelt) and meslin, unmilled	Froment (dont épeautre) et méteil non moulus
042	Rice	Riz
043	Barley, unmilled	Orge non mondée
044	Maize (not including sweet corn), unmilled	Maïs non moulu
045	Cereals, unmilled (excluding wheat, rice, barley, maize)	Céréales non moulues (sauf froment, riz, orge, maïs)
046	Meal and flour of wheat and flour of meslin	Semoules et farines de froment et farines de méteil
047	Other cereal meals and flour	Autres semoules et farines de céréales
048	Cereal preparations, flour of fruits or vegetables	Préparations à base de céréales, de farines, de fécules
05	**Vegetables and fruit**	**Légumes et fruits**
054	Vegetables, fresh, chilled, frozen or simply preserved; roots tubers and other edible vegetable products, n.e.s. fresh, dried	Légumes et plantes potagères, frais, réfrigérés, congelés ou simplement conservés; autres produits végétaux n.d.a. frais, séchés
056	Vegetables, roots, tubers, prepared, preserved, n.e.s.	Préparations ou conserves de légumes, n.d.a.
057	Fruits and nuts (excluding oil nuts), fresh or dried	Fruits (sauf oléagineux), frais ou secs
058	Fruit, preserved, and fruit preparations (no juice)	Préparations et conserves de fruits (sauf jus)
059	Fruit and vegetable juices, unfermented, no spirit	Jus de fruits, non fermentés, sans alcool
06	**Sugars, sugar preparations and honey**	**Sucres, préparations à base de sucre et miel**
061	Sugars, molasses and honey	Sucres, mélasses et miel
062	Sugar confectionery	Sucreries
07	**Coffee, tea, cocoa, spices and manufactures thereof**	**Café, thé, cacao, épices, et produits dérivés**
071	Coffee and coffee substitutes	Café et succédanés du café
072	Cocoa	Cacao
073	Chocolate, food preparations with cocoa, n.e.s.	Chocolat et autres préparations du cacao, n.d.a.
074	Tea and mate	Thé et maté
075	Spices	Épices

08	**Feeding stuff for animals (excluding unmilled cereals)**	**Nourriture destinée aux animaux (sauf céréales non moulues)**
081	Feeding stuff for animals (excluding unmilled cereals)	Nourriture destinée aux animaux (sauf céréales non moulues)
09	**Miscellaneous edible products and preparations**	**Produits et préparations alimentaires divers**
091	Margarine and shortening	Margarine et graisses culinaires
098	Edible products and preparations, n.e.s.	Produits et préparations alimentaires, n.d.a.
1	**Beverages and tobacco**	**Boissons et tabacs**
11	**Beverages**	**Boissons**
111	Non-alcoholic beverages, n.e.s.	Boissons non alcooliques, n.d.a.
112	Alcoholic beverages	Boissons alcooliques
12	**Tobacco and tobacco manufactures**	**Tabacs bruts et fabriqués**
121	Tobacco, unmanufactured; tobacco refuse	Tabacs bruts ou non fabriqués; déchets de tabac
122	Tobacco, manufactured (whether or not containing tobacco substitutes)	Tabacs fabriqués (même contenant des succédanés de tabac)
2	**Crude materials, inedible, except fuels**	**Matières brutes non comestibles, sauf carburants**
21	**Hides, skins and furskins, raw**	**Cuirs, peaux et pelleteries, bruts**
211	Hides and skins (except furskins), raw	Cuirs et peaux (sauf pelleteries), bruts
212	Furskins, raw, other than hides and skins of group 211	Pelleteries brutes autres que ceux du groupe 211
22	**Oil seeds and oleaginous fruits**	**Graines et fruits oléagineux**
222	Oil seeds and oleaginous fruits (excluding flour) of a kind used for the extraction of "soft" fixed vegetable oils	Graines et fruits oléagineux (sauf farines) servant normalement à l'extraction d'huiles végétales fixes douces
223	Oil seeds and oleaginous fruits (incl. flour, n.e.s.) of a kind used for the extraction of other fixed vegetable oils	Graines et fruits oléagineux (y compris les farines) servant normalement à l'extraction d'autres huiles végétales fixes
23	**Crude rubber (including synthetic and reclaimed)**	**Caoutchouc brut (y compris synthétique et régénéré)**
231	Natural rubber, balata, gutta percha, guayule, chicle and similar natural gums, in primary forms	Caoutchouc naturel, balata, gutta-percha, guayule, chicle et gommes naturelles analogues sous formes primaires
232	Synthetic rubber; reclaimed rubber; waste and scrap	Caoutchouc synthétique; caoutchouc régénéré; déchets et débris
24	**Cork and wood**	**Liège et bois**
244	Cork, natural, raw and waste (incl. blocks, sheets)	Liège naturel brut et déchets (dont blocs, feuilles)
245	Fuel wood (excluding wood waste) and wood charcoal	Bois de chauffage (sauf déchets), charbon de bois
246	Wood in chips or particles and wood waste	Bois en plaquettes, particules, déchets de bois
247	Wood in the rough or roughly squared	Bois bruts ou équarris
248	Wood, simply worked, and railway sleepers of wood	Bois simplement travaillés, traverses de bois pour voies ferrées
25	**Pulp and waste paper**	**Pâtes à papier et déchets de papier**
251	Pulp and waste paper	Pâtes à papier et déchets de papier
26	**Textiles fibres and their wastes**	**Fibres textiles et leurs déchets**
261	Silk	Soie
263	Cotton	Coton
264	Jute and other textile bast fibre, n.e.s., not spun; tow, waste	Jute et autres fibres textiles libériennes, n.d.a.; déchets
265	Vegetable textile fibres, not spun; waste of them	Fibres textiles végétales (sauf coton, jute); déchets
266	Synthetic fibres suitable for spinning	Fibres synthétiques discontinues, pour filature
267	Other man-made fibres suitable for spinning and waste	Autres fibres synthétiques/artificielles pouvant être filées; déchets
268	Wool and other animal hair (including wool tops)	Laines et autres poils (dont rubans de laine)
269	Worn clothing and other worn textile articles, rags	Friperie, drilles et chiffons
27	**Crude fertilizers, other than those of division 56, & crude minerals (excluding coal, petroleum & precious stones)**	**Engrais bruts, autres que ceux de la division 56 et minéraux bruts (à l'exclusion du charbon, pétrole et pierres précieuses)**
272	Crude fertilizers (excluding those of division 56)	Engrais bruts (sauf ceux de la division 56)
273	Stone, sand and gravel	Pierres, sables et graviers
274	Sulphur and unroasted iron pyrites	Soufre et pyrites de fer non grillées
277	Natural abrasives, n.e.s. (including industrial diamonds)	Abrasifs naturels, n.d.a. (dont diamants industriels)
278	Other crude minerals	Autres minéraux bruts
28	**Metalliferous ores and metal scrap**	**Minerais métallifères et déchets de métaux**
281	Iron ore and concentrates	Minerais de fer et leurs concentrés
282	Ferrous waste and scrap; remelting ingots, iron, steel	Déchets et débris de fer, fonte, acier; lingots
283	Copper ores & concentrates; copper mattes, cement copper	Minerais de cuivre, concentrés; mattes de cuivre; cuivre de cément
284	Nickel ores and concentrates; nickel mattes, etc.	Minerais de nickel et concentrés; mattes, etc.
285	Aluminium ores and concentrates (including alumina)	Minerais d'aluminium et concentrés (dont alumine)
286	Ores and concentrates of uranium or thorium	Minerais d'uranium ou de thorium et concentrés
287	Ores and concentrates of base metals, n.e.s.	Minerais de métaux communs et concentrés, n.d.a.
288	Non-ferrous base metal waste and scrap, n.e.s.	Déchets et débris de métaux communs non ferreux, n.d.a.

	PRODUCT CLASSIFICATION FOR INTERNATIONAL TRADE	CLASSIFICATION DES PRODUITS POUR LE COMMERCE INTERNATIONAL
289	Ores and concentrates of precious metals; waste, scrap	Minerais de métaux précieux et concentrés; débris et déchets
29	**Crude animal and vegetable materials, n.e.s.**	**Matières brutes d'origine animale ou végétale, n.d.a.**
291	Crude animal materials, n.e.s.	Matières brutes d'origine animale, n.d.a.
292	Crude vegetable materials, n.e.s.	Matières brutes d'origine végétale, n.d.a.
3	**Mineral fuels, lubricants and related materials**	**Combustibles minéraux, lubrifiants et produits connexes**
32	**Coal, coke and briquettes**	**Houilles, cokes et briquettes**
321	Coal, whether or not pulverized, not agglomerated	Houilles, même pulvérisées, mais non agglomérées
322	Briquettes, lignite and peat	Briquettes, lignite et tourbe
325	Coke and semi-cokes of coal, lignite or peat; retort carbon	Cokes, semi-cokes de houille, lignite ou tourbe; charbon de cornue
33	**Petroleum, petroleum products and related materials**	**Pétrole et produits dérivés du pétrole et produits connexes**
333	Petroleum oils, oils from bituminous materials, crude	Huiles brutes de pétrole ou de minéraux bitumineux
334	Petroleum oils or bituminous minerals > 70 % oil	Huiles de pétrole ou minéraux bitumineux > 70% huile
335	Residual petroleum products, n.e.s., related materials	Produits résiduels du pétrole, n.d.a.; produits connexes
34	**Gas, natural and manufactured**	**Gaz naturel et gaz manufacturé**
342	Liquefied propane and butane	Propane et butane liquéfiés
343	Natural gas, whether or not liquefied	Gaz naturel, même liquéfié
344	Petroleum gases, other gaseous hydrocarbons, n.e.s.	Gaz de pétrole et autres hydrocarbures gazeux, n.d.a.
345	Coal gas, water gas and similar gases (excl. hydrocarbons)	Gaz de houille, pauvre et similaires (sauf hydrocarbures)
35	**Electric current**	**Énergie électrique**
351	Electric current	Énergie électrique
4	**Animal and vegetable oils, fats and waxes**	**Huiles, graisses et cires d'origine animale ou végétale**
41	**Animal oils and fats**	**Huiles et graisses d'origine animale**
411	Animal oils and fats	Huiles et graisses d'origine animale
42	**Fixed vegetable fats and oils, crude, refined or fractionated**	**Graisses et huiles végétales fixes, brutes, raffinées ou fractionnées**
421	Fixed vegetable oils & fats, 'soft', crude, refined or fractionated	Huiles végétales fixes, douces, brutes, épurées ou raffinées
422	Fixed vegetable fats and oils, crude, refined, fractionated, other than 'soft'	Huiles végétales fixes, brutes, épurées ou raffineés, autres que douces
43	**Animal and vegetable fats and oils, processed; waxes of animal or vegetable origin; inedible mixtures**	**Huiles et graisses animales ou végétales, préparées ; cires d'origine animale et végétale; mélanges non alimentaires**
431	Animal or veg. oils and fats, processed, n.e.s.; waxes, mixt.	Huiles et graisses animales ou végétales, préparées, n.d.a.; cires
5	**Chemicals and related products, n.e.s.**	**Produits chimiques et produits connexes, n.d.a.**
51	**Organic chemicals**	**Produits chimiques organiques**
511	Hydrocarbons, n.e.s., and halogenated, nitr. derivatives	Hydrocarbures, n.d.a., dérivés halogènes, nitrosés, sulfonés, nitrés
512	Alcohols, phenols, and their derivatives	Alcools, phénols, et leurs dérivés halogénés
513	Carboxylic acids, anhydrides, halides, peroxides; derivatives	Acides carboxyliques, anhydrides, halogénures, péroxydes; dérivés
514	Nitrogen-function compounds	Composés à fonctions azotées
515	Organo-inorganic, heterocyclic compounds, nucl. acids	Composés organo-inorganiques et composés hétérocycliques; sels
516	Other organic chemicals	Autres produits chimiques organiques
52	**Inorganic chemicals**	**Produits chimiques inorganiques**
522	Inorganic chemical elements, oxides and halogen salts	Produits chimiques inorganiques : éléments, oxydes, sels
523	Metallic salts and peroxysalts, of inorganic acids	Sels et persels métalliques des acides inorganiques
524	Other inorganic chemicals; organic and inorganic compounds of precious metals	Autres produits chimiques inorganiques, composés organiques ou inorganiques de métaux précieux
525	Radioactive and associated materials	Matières radioactives et produits associés
53	**Dyeing, tanning and colouring materials**	**Produits pour teinture et tannage et colorants**
531	Synthetic organic colouring matter and colouring lakes	Matières colorantes organiques synthétiques; préparations, laques
532	Dyeing and tanning extracts, synthetic tanning materials	Extraits pour teinture et tannage
533	Pigments, paints, varnishes and related materials	Pigments, peintures, vernis et produits connexes
54	**Medical and pharmaceutical products**	**Produits médicinaux et pharmaceutiques**
541	Medicinal and pharmaceutical products, excluding 542	Produits médicinaux et pharmaceutiques (sauf 542)
542	Medicaments (including veterinary medicaments)	Médicaments pour médecine humaine ou vétérinaire
55	**Essential oils and resinoids and perfume materials; toilet, polishing and cleaning preparations**	**Huiles essentielles, résinoïdes et produits de parfumerie; préparations pour la toilette; produits d'entretien et détersifs**
551	Essential oils, perfume and flavour materials	Huiles essentielles, produits utilisés en parfumerie et en confiserie
553	Perfumery, cosmetics or toilet preparations (excluding soaps)	Produits de parfumerie ou de toilette préparés et préparations cosmétiques (à l'exclusion des savons)
554	Soaps, cleansing and polishing preparations	Savons, produits d'entretien et détersifs
56	**Fertilizers (other than those of group 272)**	**Engrais (autres que ceux du groupe 272)**

562	Fertilizers (other than those of group 272)	Engrais (autres que ceux du groupe 272)
57	**Plastics in primary forms**	**Matières plastiques sous formes primaires**
571	Polymers of ethylene, in primary forms	Polymères de l'éthylène, sous formes primaires
572	Polymers of styrene, in primary forms	Polymères du styrène, sous formes primaires
573	Polymers of vinyl chloride or of halogenated olefins	Polymères du chlorure de vinyle ou d'autres oléfines halogènes
574	Polyacetals, other polyethers and epoxide resins, polyesters	Polyacétals, autres polyéthers et résines époxydes, polyesters
575	Other plastics, in primary forms	Autres matières plastiques, sous formes primaires
579	Waste, parings and scrap, of plastics	Déchets, rognures et débris de matières plastiques
58	**Plastics in non-primary forms**	**Matières plastiques sous formes autres que primaires**
581	Tubes, pipes and hoses of plastics	Tubes et tuyaux en matières plastiques
582	Plates, sheets, films, foil and strip, of plastics	Plaques, feuilles, rubans en matières plastiques
583	Monofilament, cross-sectional dimension > 1 mm, rods, sticks, profile shapes, of plastics	Monofilaments, coupe transversale > 1mm (monofils), joncs, bâtons et profiles, en matières plastiques
59	**Chemical materials and products, n.e.s.**	**Matières et produits chimiques, n.d.a.**
591	Insecticides and similar products, for retail sale	Insecticides, produits similaires, pour la vente au détail
592	Starches, wheat gluten; albuminoidal substances; glues	Amidons, fécules, gluten de froment; matières albuminoïdes; colles
593	Explosives and pyrotechnic products	Explosifs et articles de pyrotechnie
597	Prepared additives for mineral oils; lubricating preparations;	Additifs pour huiles minérales
598	Miscellaneous chemical products, n.e.s.	Produits chimiques divers, n.d.a.
6	**Manufactured goods classified chiefly by material**	**Articles manufacturés classés principalement d'après la matière première**
61	**Leather, leather manufactures, n.e.s. and dressed furskins**	**Cuirs et peaux, préparés et ouvrages en cuir, n.d.a.; et pelleteries apprêtées**
611	Leather	Cuirs et peaux préparés
612	Manufactures of leather, n.e.s.; saddlery and harness	Ouvrages en cuir, n.d.a.; articles de bourrellerie ou de sellerie
613	Furskins, tanned or dressed, excluding those of 8483	Pelleteries tannées ou apprêtées (sauf 8483)
62	**Rubber manufactures, n.e.s.**	**Caoutchouc manufacturé, n.d.a.**
621	Materials of rubber (e.g. pastes, plates, sheets, bods, etc.)	Produits en caoutchouc (pâtes, plaques, feuilles, fils, tubes, etc.)
625	Rubber tyres, interchangeable tyre treads, tyre flaps and inner tubes for wheels of all kinds	Pneumatiques, en caoutchouc; bandes de roulement amovibles pour pneumatiques, "flaps" et chambres à air pour tous types de roues
629	Articles of rubber, n.e.s.	Ouvrages en caoutchouc, n.d.a.
63	**Cork and wood manufactures (excluding furniture)**	**Ouvrages en liège et en bois (à l'exclusion des meubles)**
633	Cork manufactures	Ouvrages en liège
634	Veneers, plywood, and other wood, worked, n.e.s.	Placage, contre-plaqué et autres bois travaillés, n.d.a.
635	Wood manufacture, n.e.s.	Ouvrages en bois, n.d.a.
64	**Paper, paperboard, aricles of paper pulp, of paper, or of paperboard**	**Papiers, cartons et ouvrages en pâte de cellulose, en papier ou en carton**
641	Paper and paperboard	Papiers et cartons
642	Paper and paperboard, cut to shape or size, and articles of paper or paperboard	Papiers et cartons découpés en vue d'un usage déterminé; ouvrages en papier ou carton
65	**Textile yarn, fabrics, made-up articles, n.e.s., and related products**	**Fils, tissus, articles textiles façonnés, n.d.a. et produits connexes**
651	Textile yarn	Fils textiles
652	Cotton fabrics, woven (excluded narrow or special fabrics)	Tissus de coton (sauf petites largeurs ou spéciaux)
653	Fabrics, woven, of man-made fabrics	Tissus en matières textiles synthétiques ou artificielles
654	Other textile fabrics, woven	Autres tissus
655	Knitted or crocheted fabrics, n.e.s.	Étoffes de bonneterie (dont velours), n.d.a.
656	Tulles, trimmings, lace, ribbons and other small wares	Tulles, dentelles et autres articles de mercerie
657	Special yarn, special textile fabrics and related	Fils spéciaux, tissus spéciaux et produits connexes
658	Made-up articles, wholly or chiefly of textile materials, n.e.s	Articles confectionnés entièrement ou principalement en matières textiles, n.d.a.
659	Floor coverings, etc.	Revêtements de sols, etc.
66	**Non metallic mineral manufactures, n.e.s.**	**Articles minéraux non métalliques manufacturés, n.d.a.**
661	Lime, cement and fabricated construction materials (excluding glass and clay materials)	Chaux, ciments et matériaux de construction fabriqués (sauf argile et verre)
662	Clay construction and refractory construction materials	Matériaux de construction réfractaires, en argile
663	Mineral manufactures, n.e.s.	Articles minéraux manufacturés, n.d.a.
664	Glass	Verre
665	Glassware	Ouvrages en verre
666	Pottery	Poterie

667	Pearls, precious and semi-precious stones	Perles fines ou de culture, pierres gemmes et similaires
67	**Iron and steel**	**Fer et acier**
671	Pig iron and spiegeleisen, sponge iron, powder and granules	Fonte, fer spongieux, poudres de fer et d'acier
672	Ingots, primary forms, of iron or steel; semi-finished products	Lingots et autres formes primaires en fer ou acier;
673	Flat-rolled prod., iron, non-alloy steel, not coated	Produits laminés plats, en fer ou aciers non alliés
674	Flat-rolled prod., iron, non-alloy steel, coated, clad	Produits laminés plats, fer, aciers non alliés, zingués
675	Flat-rolled products of alloy steel	Produits laminés plats, en aciers alliés
676	Iron and steel bars, rods, angles, shapes and sections	Barres et profilés en fer ou acier (y compris les palplanches)
677	Rails and railway track construction mat., iron, steel	Rails et autres éléments de voies ferrées, en fonte, fer ou acier
078	Wire of iron or steel	Fils de fer ou d'acier
679	Tubes, pipes and hollow profiles, fittings, iron, steel	Tubes, profilés creux et accessoires, fer ou acier
68	**Non-ferrous metals**	**Métaux non ferreux**
681	Silver, platinum, other metals of the platinum group	Argent, platine et métaux de la mine du platine
682	Copper	Cuivre
683	Nickel	Nickel
684	Aluminium	Aluminium
685	Lead	Plomb
686	Zinc	Zinc
687	Tin	Étain
689	Miscellaneous non-ferrous base metals for metallurgy	Autres métaux communs non ferreux utilisés en métallurgie
69	**Manufactures of metal, n.e.s.**	**Articles manufacturés en métal, n.d.a.**
691	Structures and parts, n.e.s., of iron, steel, aluminium	Constructions et parties, n.d.a. en fonte, fer, acier ou aluminium
692	Metal containers for storage or transport	Récipients métalliques pour le stockage ou le transport
693	Wire products (excluding electrical) and fencing grills	Ouvrages en fils métalliques (sauf électriques), grillages
694	Nails, screws, nuts, bolts, rivets and the like, of iron, steel, copper or aluminium	Pointes, clous, vis, écrous, boulons, rondelles, rivets et articles similaires, en fer, en acier, en cuivre ou en aluminium
695	Tools for use in the hand or in machine	Outils à main et outils pour machines
696	Cutlery	Coutellerie
697	Household equipment of base metal, n.e.s.	Articles d'économie domestique en métaux communs, n.d.a.
699	Manufactures of base metal, n.e.s.	Articles manufacturés en métaux communs, n.d.a.
7	**Machinery and transport equipment**	**Machines et matériel de transport**
71	**Power generating machinery and equipment**	**Machines génératrices, moteurs et leur équipement**
711	Steam or other vapour generating boilers, super-heated water boilers and auxiliary plant for use therewith; parts	Chaudières à vapeur, chaudières dites "à eau surchauffée", et leurs appareils auxiliaires, leurs parties et pièces détachées
712	Steam turbines and other vapour turbines, parts thereof, n.e.s.	Turbines à vapeur, leurs parties et pièces détachées, n.d.a.
713	Internal combustion piston engines and parts thereof, n.e.s.	Moteurs à explosion ou à combustion interne, n.d.a.
714	Engines and motors, non-electric; parts, n.e.s.	Moteurs et machines motrices, non électrique; leurs parties n.d.a.
716	Rotating electric plant and parts thereof, n.e.s.	Appareils électriques rotatifs, leurs pièces détachées, n.d.a.
718	Other power generating machinery and parts thereof, n.e.s.	Moteurs et machines motrices, leurs parties et pièces, n.d.a.
72	**Machinery specialized for particular industries**	**Machines et appareils spécialisés pour industries particulières**
721	Agricultural machinery (excluding tractors) and parts	Machines agricoles (sauf tracteurs), parties, pièces
722	Tractors (excluding those of 71414 and 74415)	Tracteurs (sauf 74414 et 74415)
723	Civil engineering and contractors' plant and equipment	Appareils et matériel de génie civil et de construction; parties
724	Textile and leather machinery, and parts thereof, n.e.s.	Machines pour l'industrie textile, cuir et peaux, n.d.a.
725	Paper mill and pulp mill machinery; paper cutting machines and other machinery; parts thereof	Machines et appareils pour la fabrication de la pâte à papier et du papier; coupeuses et autres appareils; leurs parties et pièces
726	Printing and bookbinding machinery, and parts thereof	Machines pour imprimerie, brochage, reliure; parties
727	Food-processing machines (excluding domestic)	Machines pour industrie alimentaire (appareils ménagers exclus)
728	Other machinery and equipment specialized for particular industries, and parts thereof, n.e.s.	Autres machines et appareils spécialisées pour industries particulières, et leurs parties et pièces détachées, n.d.a.
73	**Metal working machinery**	**Machines et appareils pour le travail des métaux**
731	Machine-tools working by removing metal or other material	Machines-outils travaillant par enlèvement de métal/autres matières
733	Machine.-tools for working metal (without removing material)	Machines pour travail des métaux (sans enlèvement de matière)
735	Parts, n.e.s., and accessories for machines of 731, 733	Pièces et accessoires, n.d.a., des machines des groupes 731, 733
737	Metalworking machinery (excluding machine tools) and parts	Machines pour travail des métaux, n.d.a.; pièces détachées
74	**General industrial machinery and equipment, n.e.s. and machine parts, n.e.s.**	**Machines et appareils industriels d'application générale, n.d.a.; parties et pièces détachées de machines, d'appareils, d'engins**
741	Heating and cooling equipment and parts thereof, n.e.s.	Appareils de chauffage et de réfrigération, n.d.a.; pièces détachées

742	Pumps for liquids; liquid elevators; parts for such pumps	Pompes pour liquides; élévateurs à liquides; parties et pièces
743	Pumps (excluding liquid), air and gas compressors, and fans; centrifuges; filtering or purifying apparatus; parts	Pompes (sauf pour liquides), compresseurs; ventilateurs; hottes aspirantes; centrifugeuses; appareils pour la filtration, l'épuration
744	Mechanical handling equipment, and parts, n.e.s.	Équipement mécanique de manutention, pièces, n.d.a.
745	Other non-electrical machinery, tools and mechanical apparatus, and parts thereof, n.e.s.	Machines, appareils et outils non électriques et leurs parties et pièces détachées, n.d.a.
746	Ball or roller bearings	Roulements à billes, à galets, à rouleaux ou à aiguilles
747	Taps, cocks, valves and similar appliances, for pipes, boiler shells, tanks, vats and the like	Articles de robinetterie, organes similaires pour tuyauteries, chaudières, réservoirs, cubes ou contenants similaires
748	Transmission shafts and cranks; bearings housings; gears and gearing; flywheels and pulleys; clutches, shaft couplings	Arbres de transmission et manivelles; engrenages et roues de friction; volants et poulies; embrayages, organes d'accouplement
749	Non-electric parts and accessories. of machinery, n.e.s.	Parties, non électriques d'appareils mécaniques, n.d.a.
75	**Office machines and automatic data processing machines**	**Machines et appareils de bureau ou pour le traitement automatique de l'information**
751	Office machines	Machines et appareils de bureau
752	Automatic data processing machines and units thereof; magnetic or optical readers	Machines automatiques de traitement de l'information et leurs unités; lecteurs magnétiques ou optiques
759	Parts, accessories for machines of groups 751, 752	Parties et pièces détachées pour groupes 751, 752
76	**Telecommunications and sound recording apparatus and reproducing apparatus and equipment**	**Appareils et équipements de télécommunication et pour l'enregistrement et la reproduction du son**
761	Television receivers, whether or not combined	Téléviseurs, même combinés à d'autres appareils
762	Radio-broadcast receivers, whether or not combined	Appareils de radiodiffusion, même combinés à d'autres appareils
763	Sound recorders or reproducers; television image and sound recorders or reproducers, prepared unrecorded media	Appareils d'enregistrement ou de reproduction du son; appareils d'enregistrement/reproduction de l'image et du son en télévision
764	Telecommunication equipment, n.e.s.; and parts, n.e.s.	Équipements de télécommunication, n.d.a. et parties
77	**Electrical machinery, apparatus and appliances, n.e.s. and electrical parts thereof**	**Machines et appareils électriques, n.d.a.; et leurs parties et pièces détachées électriques**
771	Electric power machinery, and parts thereof	Appareils pour production, transformation de l'électricité
772	Apparatus for switching or protecting electrical circuits or for making connections; switchboard, control panels	Appareils pour la coupure, la protection, le branchement la connexion des circuits électriques; tableaux de commande
773	Equipment for distributing electricity, n.e.s.	Équipement pour la distribution d'électricité, n.d.a.
774	Electro-diagnostic apparatus for medical or veterinary sciences and radiological apparatus	Appareils d'électrodiagnostic à usage médical ou vétérinaire et appareils de radiologie
775	Household type, electrical and non-electrical equipment, n.e.s.	Machines et appareils, électriques ou non, à usage domestique, n.d.a.
776	Thermionic, cold cathode or photo-cathode valves and tubes; diodes, transistors and similar;	Lampes, tubes, valves électroniques à cathode chaude, froide ou à photocathode; diodes, transistors et dispositifs similaires
778	Electrical machinery and apparatus, n.e.s.	Machines et appareils électriques, n.d.a.
78	**Road vehicles (including air-cushion vehicles)**	**Véhicules routiers (y compris les véhicules à coussin d'air)**
781	Motor cars and other motor vehicles principally designed for the transport of persons	Véhicules de tourisme et autres véhicules automobiles principalement conçus pour le transport de personnes
782	Motor vehicles for the transport of goods and special purposes	Véhicules automobiles pour le transport de marchandises et pour usages spéciaux
783	Road motor vehicles, n.e.s.	Véhicules routiers, n.d.a.
784	Parts and accessories of the motor vehicles of groups 722, 781, 782, and 783	Parties, pièces détachées et accessoires des véhicules automobiles des groupes 722, 781, 782 et 783
785	Motorcycles and cycles, motorized or not; invalid carriages	Motocycles et cycles, avec ou sans moteur; fauteuils roulants
786	Trailers and semi-trailers; other vehicles, not mechanically propelled; specially designed & equiped transport containers	Remorques et semi-remorques; autres véhicules non automobiles; cadres et conteneurs conçus et équipés pour le transport
79	**Other transport equipment**	**Autres matériels de transport**
791	Railway vehicles and associated equipment	Véhicules et matériel pour chemin de fer
792	Aircraft and associated equipment; spacecraft and spacecraft launch vehicles, parts thereof	Aéronefs et matériels connexes; véhicules spatiaux et leurs véhicules lanceurs; leurs parties et pièces détachées
793	Ships, boats (including hovercrafts) and floating structures	Navires, bateaux (y compris les aéroglisseurs) et engins flottants
8	**Miscellaneous manufactured articles**	**Articles manufacturés divers**
81	**Prefabricated buildings, sanitary plumbing, heating and lighting fixtures and fittings, n.e.s.**	**Constructions préfabriquées, appareils sanitaires et appareillage de plomberie, de chauffage et d'éclairage, n.d.a.**
811	Prefabricated buildings	Constructions préfabriquées
812	Sanitary, plumbing and heating fixtures, and fittings, n.e.s.	Appareils sanitaires et appareillage de plomberie, chauffage, n.d.a.
813	Lighting fixtures and fittings, n.e.s.	Appareillages d'éclairage, n.d.a.
82	**Furniture and parts thereof; bedding, mattresses,**	**Meubles et leurs parties; articles de literie; matelas, sommiers**

	mattress supports, cushions and similar stuffed furnishings	coussins, articles similaires rembourrés/garnis intérieurement
821	Furniture and parts thereof; bedding, mattresses, mattress supports, cushions and similar stuffed furnishings	Meubles et leurs parties; articles de literie; matelas, sommiers, coussins et articles similaires rembourrés ou garnis intérieurement
83	**Travel goods, handbags and similar containers**	**Articles de voyage, sacs à mains et contenants similaires**
831	Travel goods, handbags and similar containers	Articles de voyage, sacs à mains et contenants similaires
84	**Articles of apparel, and clothing accessories**	**Vêtements et accessoires du vêtement**
841	Men's or boy's clothing of textile fabrics, not knitted or crocheted	Articles d'habillement en matières textiles pour hommes et garçonnets, autres que de bonneterie
842	Women's and girl's clothing, of textile fabrics, not knitted or crocheted	Articles d'habillement en matières textiles pour femmes ou fillettes, autres que de bonneterie
843	Men's or boy's clothing, of textile, knitted, crocheted	Articles d'habillement, en bonneterie pour hommes et garçonnets
844	Women's and girl's clothing, of textile, knitted or crocheted	Articles d'habillement, en bonneterie pour femmes ou fillettes
845	Articles of apparel, of textile fabrics, n.e.s.	Vêtements en matières textiles, même en bonneterie, n.d.a.
846	Clothing accessories, of textile fabrics	Accessoires du vêtement en matières textiles
848	Articles of apparel, clothing access., excluding textile	Vêtements et accessoires en matières non textiles
85	**Footwear**	**Chaussures**
851	Footwear	Chaussures
87	**Professional, scientific, and controlling instruments and apparatus, n.e.s.**	**Instruments et appareils professionnels, scientifiques et de contrôle, n.d.a.**
871	Optical instruments and apparatus, n.e.s.	Appareils et instruments d'optique, n.d.a.
872	Instruments and appliances, n.e.s., for medical, surgical, dental or veterinary purposes	Instruments et appareils, n.d.a. pour la médecine, la chirurgie, l'art dentaire ou l'art vétérinaire
873	Meters and counters, n.e.s.	Compteurs et instruments de mesure, n.d.a.
874	Measuring, checking, analysing and controlling instruements and apparatus, n.e.s.	Appareils et instruments de mesure, de vérification, d'analyse et de contrôle, n.d.a.
88	**Photographic apparatus, equipment and supplies and optical goods, n.e.s.; watches and clocks**	**Appareils et fournitures de photographie et d'optique, n.d.a.; montres et horloges**
881	Photographic apparatus and equipment, n.e.s.	Appareils et équipement photographiques, n.d.a.
882	Cinematographic and photographic supplies	Fournitures cinématographiques et photographiques
883	Cinematograph films, exposed and developed, whether or not incorporating sound track	Films cinématographiques, impressionnés, développés, comportant ou non l'enregistrement du son
884	Optical goods, n.e.s.	Éléments d'optique et articles de lunetterie, n.d.a.
885	Watches and clocks	Horlogerie
89	**Miscellaneous manufactured articles, n.e.s.**	**Articles manufacturés divers, n.d.a.**
891	Arms and ammunition	Armes et munitions
892	Printed matter	Imprimés
893	Articles, n.e.s., of plastics	Ouvrages, n.d.a. en matières plastiques
894	Baby carriages, toys, games and sporting goods	Voitures pour le transport des enfants, jouets, jeux et articles pour divertissements et pour sports
895	Office and stationery supplies, n.e.s.	Articles de papeterie et fournitures de bureau, n.d.a.
896	Works of art, collectors' pieces and antiques	Objets d'art, de collection et d'antiquité
897	Jewellery and articles of precious material., n.e.s.	Articles de bijouterie et d'orfèvrerie, n.d.a.
898	Musical instruments, parts and accessories therof; records, tapes and other sound or similar recordings	Instruments de musique et leurs parties; disques, bandes et autres supports pour l'enregistrement du son
899	Miscellaneous manufactured articles, n.e.s.	Autres articles manufacturés divers
9	**Commodities and transactions, not classified elsewhere in the SITC**	**Articles et transactions, non classés ailleurs dans la CTCI**
91	**Postal packages not classified according to kind**	**Colis postaux non classés par catégorie**
911	Postal packages not classified according to kind	Colis postaux non classés par catégorie
93	**Special transactions and commodities not classified according to kind**	**Transactions spéciales et articles spéciaux non classés par catégorie**
931	Special transactions and commodities not classified according to kind	Transactions spéciales et articles spéciaux non classés par catégorie
96	**Coin (other than gold coin), not being legal tender**	**Monnaies (autres que les pièces d'or) n'ayant pas cours légal**
961	Coin (other than gold coin), not being legal tender	Monnaies (autres que les pièces d'or) n'ayant pas cours légal
97	**Gold, non-monetary (excluding ores and concentrates)**	**Or, à usage non monétaire (sauf minerais et concentrés d'or)**
971	Gold, non-monetary (excluding gold ores and concentrates)	Or, à usage non monétaire (sauf minerais et concentrés d'or)

1 INTERNATIONAL **MERCHANDISE** TRADE

COMMERCE INTERNATIONAL DES **MARCHANDISES**

Region, country or territory	Exports (f.o.b.) - Exportations (f.a.b.) Millions of dollars							
	1980	1990	2000	2005	2009	2010	2011	2012
WORLD	2 049 407	3 495 585	6 448 851	10 499 521	12 554 774	15 283 481	18 320 316	18 402 184
DEVELOPING ECONOMIES	607 605	842 977	2 055 742	3 804 984	5 005 193	6 425 928	7 882 841	8 208 324
TRANSITION ECONOMIES	85 478	118 378	154 008	362 644	477 271	620 989	827 266	840 551
DEVELOPED ECONOMIES	1 356 325	2 534 230	4 239 101	6 331 892	7 072 309	8 236 564	9 610 210	9 353 309
Developing economies: Africa	121 378	104 923	147 656	311 127	393 529	510 730	598 315	630 023
Eastern Africa	*7 013*	*7 322*	*9 870*	*16 599*	*24 774*	*32 333*	*39 331*	*41 250*
Burundi*(1)	65	75	50	58	67	101	123	134
Comoros*	11	18	14	12	15	21	25	19
Djibouti (2)	13	25	32	40	77	85	93	(e)95
Eritrea (3)	_	_	37	11	(e)11	(e)12	(e)400	(e)480
Ethiopia (...1991)	425	298						
Ethiopia	_	_	486	903	1 618	2 330	2 875	(e)3 000
Kenya	1 245	1 032	1 734	3 420	4 463	5 169	5 756	6 127
Madagascar*	401	319	824	855	1 052	1 071	(e)1 590	(e)1 500
Malawi	295	417	379	509	1 188	1 066	1 425	1 184
Mauritius	435	1 194	1 557	2 143	1 939	2 261	2 565	2 673
Mozambique	281	126	364	1 783	2 147	(e)3 000	3 604	(e)4 100
Rwanda	121	109	53	125	235	297	464	591
Seychelles	21	57	194	340	395	400	483	497
Somalia (4)	141	(e)150	(e)193	(e)250	435	450	520	510
Uganda	345	152	403	813	1 568	1 619	2 159	2 357
United Republic of Tanzania	511	331	734	1 679	2 982	4 051	4 735	(e)5 500
Zambia (5)	1 305	1 309	892	1 810	4 312	7 200	9 001	(e)8 600
Zimbabwe	1 396	1 711	1 925	(e)1 850	2 269	3 199	3 512	3 884
Middle Africa	*8 837*	*11 844*	*17 092*	*49 463*	*71 364*	*91 410*	*118 094*	*125 286*
Angola*(6)	1 883	3 910	7 921	24 109	40 828	50 595	67 310	(e)74 000
Cameroon*(7)	1 384	2 002	1 833	2 861	3 552	3 878	4 517	(e)4 500
Central African Republic*(7)	116	120	161	128	(e)120	(e)140	(e)190	(e)210
Chad*(6)	71	234	183	3 081	(e)2 800	(e)3 500	(e)4 600	(e)4 400
Congo*(7)	911	981	2 489	4 745	(e)6 100	(e)9 300	(e)11 600	(e)10 700
Dem. Rep. of the Congo*	2 269	2 326	807	2 403	(e)3 500	(e)5 300	(e)6 600	(e)6 300
Equatorial Guinea (6)	14	62	1 097	7 064	(e)9 100	(e)10 000	(e)13 500	(e)15 500
Gabon*(8)	2 173	2 204	2 598	5 065	5 356	8 686	9 766	9 665
Sao Tome and Principe*	17	4	3	7	8	11	11	(e)11
Northern Africa	*44 042*	*36 856*	*54 874*	*116 780*	*141 943*	*177 764*	*173 245*	*205 260*
Algeria*	13 871	12 880	22 031	46 002	45 174	57 053	73 489	71 866
Egypt	3 046	2 585	5 276	12 912	23 062	26 438	31 570	29 385
Libya	21 910	13 225	12 725	31 358	36 951	48 673	18 996	62 216
Morocco*	2 441	4 265	7 185	11 190	14 054	17 771	21 654	21 417
Sudan (...2011) (9)	543	374	1 807	4 824	8 257	11 404	9 689	_
Sudan	_	_	_	_	_	_	_	3 368
Tunisia (10)	2 231	3 527	5 850	10 494	14 445	16 427	17 847	17 008
Southern Africa	*27 919*	*27 038*	*35 113*	*60 542*	*70 673*	*92 289*	*111 418*	*100 262*
Botswana*	504	1 785	2 675	4 425	3 456	4 693	5 882	5 971
Lesotho	58	62	221	651	734	878	1 172	(e)1 100
Namibia	1 459	1 086	1 320	2 070	3 146	4 026	4 407	4 034
South Africa	25 525	23 549	29 983	51 626	61 677	80 892	98 047	87 256
Swaziland	373	557	914	(e)1 770	(e)1 660	(e)1 800	(e)1 910	(e)1 900
Western Africa	*33 567*	*21 863*	*30 707*	*67 744*	*84 775*	*116 934*	*156 228*	*157 965*
Benin*	63	288	392	578	1 225	1 282	(e)1 410	(e)1 400
Burkina Faso	90	152	209	468	900	1 585	2 352	2 183
Cape Verde (11)	5	6	11	18	35	44	69	53
Côte d'Ivoire*	3 135	3 072	3 888	7 697	11 327	11 555	12 542	(e)12 350
Gambia (12)	31	31	15	(e)8	66	35	95	(e)100
Ghana	1 258	897	1 671	2 802	5 840	7 960	12 785	(e)13 000
Guinea*	401	671	666	853	1 050	1 471	1 433	(e)1 300
Guinea-Bissau	11	19	62	89	122	127	(e)230	(e)130
Liberia*	600	(e)868	(e)329	131	149	222	367	459
Mali*	205	359	545	1 101	1 774	1 996	2 391	2 164
Mauritania*	194	447	355	625	1 364	2 074	2 776	2 641
Niger*	566	283	283	489	(e)1 000	(e)1 150	(e)1 250	(e)1 500
Nigeria	25 968	13 596	20 975	50 467	56 742	(e)84 000	(e)114 500	(e)116 000
Saint Helena	(e)1	(e)7	(e)9	(e)20	(e)31	(e)31	(e)37	(e)44
Senegal (13)	477	762	920	1 578	2 017	2 161	2 542	2 532
Sierra Leone*	224	138	13	158	231	341	349	1 109
Togo*	338	268	364	660	903	(e)900	(e)1 100	(e)1 000

For sources and notes, see end of table 1.1.1.

	Imports (c.i.f.) - Importations (c.a.f.) Millions de dollars								Régions, pays ou territoires
	1980	1990	2000	2005	2009	2010	2011	2012	
	2 085 939	3 607 430	6 656 939	10 777 308	12 689 566	15 414 304	18 414 014	18 512 495	MONDE
	497 382	797 814	1 915 851	3 423 910	4 647 590	6 016 837	7 339 305	7 671 570	ÉCONOMIES EN DÉVELOPPEMENT
	83 591	140 131	104 136	258 721	391 273	473 499	609 947	632 646	ÉCONOMIES EN TRANSITION
	1 504 966	2 669 485	4 636 951	7 094 677	7 650 703	8 923 968	10 464 763	10 208 279	ÉCONOMIES DÉVELOPPÉES
	96 490	94 658	129 967	256 561	411 263	476 083	566 020	609 855	Économies en développement : Afrique
	10 542	12 833	16 938	31 493	52 483	60 864	74 310	83 346	Afrique orientale
	168	231	148	269	402	509	752	751	Burundi*(1)
	29	52	43	99	210	233	277	273	Comores*
	213	215	207	277	451	374	511	(e)580	Djibouti (2)
			471	(e)490	(e)590	(e)690	(e)890	(e)1 000	Érythrée (3)
	722	1 081	–	–	–	–	–	–	Éthiopie (...1991)
			1 260	4 095	7 668	8 602	8 896	12 656	Éthiopie
	2 125	2 223	3 105	5 846	10 202	12 093	14 782	16 290	Kenya
	600	651	1 097	1 706	3 199	2 525	2 906	(e)3 050	Madagascar*
	439	575	532	1 165	2 022	2 173	2 428	2 724	Malawi
	614	1 618	2 207	3 157	3 733	4 386	5 149	5 354	Maurice
	800	878	1 158	2 408	3 764	(e)4 600	6 306	(e)6 800	Mozambique
	262	287	213	430	1 308	1 431	1 776	2 408	Rwanda
	99	187	342	675	794	(e)650	(e)750	(e)800	Seychelles
	435	(e)95	(e)343	(e)626	750	940	880	670	Somalie (4)
	293	288	1 536	2 054	4 247	4 664	5 631	6 044	Ouganda
	1 258	1 364	1 524	3 287	6 411	7 874	10 799	11 346	République-Unie de Tanzanie
	1 088	1 255	888	2 558	3 832	5 321	7 178	(e)8 200	Zambie (5)
	1 396	1 833	1 863	(e)2 350	(e)2 900	(e)3 800	(e)4 400	(e)4 400	Zimbabwe
	5 884	6 991	7 589	19 038	43 976	41 295	51 036	56 982	Afrique centrale
	1 328	1 578	3 040	8 353	22 660	16 667	20 229	(e)24 000	Angola*(6)
	1 602	1 400	1 484	2 735	4 442	5 133	6 800	(e)7 300	Cameroun*(7)
	81	154	117	175	(e)270	(e)300	(e)310	(e)320	République centrafricaine*(7)
	74	499	317	950	(e)2 000	(e)2 400	(c)2 700	(c)2 800	Tchad*(6)
	562	621	465	1 304	(e)2 900	(e)4 000	(e)5 200	(e)5 200	Congo*(7)
	1 519	1 739	683	2 690	(e)3 900	(e)4 500	(e)5 500	(e)6 100	Rép. dém. du Congo*
	26	61	504	1 310	(e)5 200	(e)5 200	(e)6 500	(e)7 500	Guinée équatoriale (6)
	674	918	950	1 471	2 501	2 983	3 665	3 631	Gabon*(8)
	19	21	30	50	103	112	132	131	Sao Tomé-et-Principe*
	31 552	37 374	49 135	89 609	158 767	178 712	194 952	218 441	Afrique septentrionale
	10 558	9 770	9 171	20 357	39 294	40 473	47 247	47 490	Algérie*
	4 860	9 216	14 578	22 449	44 946	52 923	62 245	69 254	Égypte
	6 777	5 336	3 732	6 079	12 859	17 674	(e)8 000	(e)23 000	Libye
	4 255	6 922	11 534	20 790	32 881	35 381	44 272	44 776	Maroc*
	1 576	619	1 553	6 757	9 691	10 045	9 236	–	Soudan (...2011) (9)
	–	–	–	–	–	–	–	9 475	Soudan
	3 526	5 513	8 567	13 177	19 096	22 215	23 952	24 447	Tunisie (10)
	22 499	22 846	35 187	71 353	87 392	109 713	139 688	143 280	Afrique australe
	693	1 947	2 081	3 161	4 728	5 657	7 272	8 025	Botswana*
	427	673	809	1 410	(e)1 850	(e)2 300	(e)2 500	(e)2 600	Lesotho
	1 156	1 163	1 550	2 577	(e)4 980	(e)5 570	(e)6 360	(e)6 420	Namibie
	19 598	18 399	29 695	62 304	74 054	94 226	121 606	124 245	Afrique du Sud
	625	664	1 052	(e)1 900	(e)1 780	(e)1 960	(e)1 950	(e)1 990	Swaziland
	26 013	14 613	21 118	45 068	68 645	85 499	106 035	107 805	Afrique occidentale
	331	265	613	1 018	2 064	2 054	(e)2 200	(e)2 200	Bénin*
	359	536	611	(e)1 260	1 870	2 048	2 406	(e)3 150	Burkina Faso
	68	136	230	438	709	742	947	765	Cap-Vert (11)
	2 991	2 098	2 482	5 865	6 960	7 849	6 720	9 777	Côte d'Ivoire*
	165	188	187	260	304	285	344	(e)380	Gambie (12)
	1 129	1 205	2 976	5 347	8 046	10 922	15 968	(e)18 000	Ghana
	360	723	612	(e)820	1 060	1 405	2 106	(e)2 300	Guinée*
	55	86	60	123	202	197	(e)260	(e)250	Guinée-Bissau
	535	(e)570	(e)668	310	551	710	1 044	1 066	Libéria*
	439	602	806	1 544	2 486	3 428	3 390	2 941	Mali*
	286	220	454	1 428	1 498	1 935	2 467	3 170	Mauritanie*
	594	389	395	943	(e)2 200	2 476	(e)2 700	(e)2 900	Niger*
	16 660	5 627	8 721	20 754	33 906	44 235	(e)56 000	(e)51 000	Nigéria
	(e)13	(e)19	(e)39	(e)56	(e)46	(e)61	56	(e)51	Sainte-Hélène
	1 052	1 220	1 553	3 498	4 713	4 782	5 909	6 434	Sénégal (13)
	427	149	149	345	520	770	1 717	1 572	Sierra Leone*
	551	581	562	1 060	1 509	1 599	(e)1 800	(e)1 850	Togo*

Pour les sources et les notes, se reporter à la fin du tableau 1.1.1.

Region, country or territory	Exports (f.o.b.) - Exportations (f.a.b.) Millions of dollars							
	1980	1990	2000	2005	2009	2010	2011	2012
Developing economies: America	111 503	145 626	366 452	584 117	703 820	889 689	1 109 130	1 120 507
Caribbean	*22 627*	*13 317*	*19 016*	*26 756*	*23 914*	*27 239*	*40 395*	*35 524*
Anguilla	..	..	4	15	23	13	16	(e)21
Antigua and Barbuda	26	21	52	83	51	46	56	(e)60
Aruba (14)	'	..	2 524	4 416	1 952	264	5 179	(e)1 850
Bahamas (15)	5 009	238	576	549	711	702	834	984
Barbados	228	215	272	359	379	429	475	565
Bonaire, Sint Eustatius and Saba	—	—	—	—	—	—	(e)6	(e)4
British Virgin Islands (4)	(e)1	(e)3	(e)27	(e)35	37	38	39	40
Cayman Islands (4)	(e)3	(e)18	(e)19	(e)59	(e)19	(e)13	(e)22	(e)20
Cuba*	5 577	5 100	1 676	2 319	3 092	4 914	6 440	5 972
Curaçao	—	—	—	—	—	—	928	948
Dominica*	10	55	54	42	33	37	30	(e)35
Dominican Republic (16)	1 217	2 170	5 737	6 145	5 483	6 754	8 612	9 079
Grenada*	17	26	48	28	29	25	29	(e)35
Haiti	226	160	318	470	576	579	767	815
Jamaica	963	1 158	1 295	1 532	1 316	1 328	1 624	1 708
Montserrat*	1	2	1	1	3	1	2	(e)2
Netherlands Antilles*(17)	5 162	1 790	2 009	608	810	811		
Saint Kitts and Nevis*	24	28	33	34	38	32	45	(e)45
Saint Lucia*	70	134	43	64	166	215	161	(e)160
Saint Vincent and the Grenadines*	15	83	47	40	49	42	38	(e)43
Sint Maarten (Dutch part)	—	—	—	—	—	—	127	131
Trinidad and Tobago*	4 077	1 960	4 274	9 942	9 126	10 982	14 944	12 981
Turks and Caicos Islands	..	..	9	15	21	16	(e)20	(e)25
Central America	*23 271*	*45 641*	*182 934*	*243 204*	*266 766*	*339 968*	*400 681*	*424 820*
Belize	111	133	218	208	253	304	376	(e)390
Costa Rica*	1 002	1 448	5 850	7 026	8 784	9 448	10 408	11 453
El Salvador (18)	967	582	2 941	3 418	3 866	4 499	5 308	5 339
Guatemala (19)	1 520	1 163	2 711	5 381	7 214	8 463	10 401	9 983
Honduras (20)	829	934	3 343	5 048	4 827	6 111	7 800	7 931
Mexico	18 031	40 711	166 368	214 207	229 712	298 305	349 569	370 827
Nicaragua (21)	451	331	643	866	1 394	1 851	2 264	2 677
Panama, excl. Canal Zone	361							
Panama*(22)	—	340	859	7 050	10 717	10 987	14 555	(e)16 220
South America	*65 605*	*86 668*	*164 502*	*314 157*	*413 140*	*522 482*	*668 054*	*660 162*
Argentina*	8 021	12 353	26 341	40 351	55 672	68 133	83 950	80 927
Bolivia (Plurinational State of)	942	926	1 230	2 827	4 960	6 402	8 348	11 107
Brazil	20 132	31 414	55 119	118 529	152 995	201 915	256 040	242 580
Chile*	4 705	8 373	19 210	41 267	55 463	71 109	81 455	78 277
Colombia	3 924	6 721	13 043	21 190	32 853	39 820	57 420	60 274
Ecuador	2 481	2 714	4 927	10 100	13 863	17 490	22 322	23 847
Falkland Islands (Malvinas) (4)	(e)8	(e)17	(e)87	(e)150	140	170	180	200
Guyana*	389	251	502	553	763	880	1 116	1.393
Paraguay	310	959	869	1 688	5 061	6 505	7 764	7 271
Peru*	3 898	3 280	6 955	17 368	26 962	35 565	46 268	45 639
Suriname	514	472	396	997	1 402	2 026	2 467	2 563
Uruguay	1 059	1 693	2 295	3 422	5 405	6 724	7 912	8 743
Venezuela (Bolivarian Rep. of)	19 221	17 497	33 529	55 716	57 603	65 745	92 811	97 340
Developing economies: Asia	372 473	589 649	1 536 462	2 903 030	3 900 786	5 016 456	6 164 547	6 447 694
Eastern Asia	*77 692*	*280 961*	*779 294*	*1 541 802*	*2 103 101*	*2 725 754*	*3 226 817*	*3 399 828*
China	18 099	62 091	249 203	761 953	1 201 612	1 577 754	1 898 381	2 048 714
China, Hong Kong SAR	20 323	82 390	202 683	292 119	329 422	400 692	455 573	492 907
China, Macao SAR	613	1 701	2 539	2 476	961	870	869	1 021
China, Taiwan Province of	19 842	67 245	151 357	198 432	203 675	274 601	308 257	301 181
Korea, Dem. People's Rep. of	(e)900	(e)1 857	(e)708	(e)1 338	(e)1 995	(e)2 555	(e)3 705	(e)3 750
Korea, Republic of (23)	17 512	65 016	172 268	284 419	363 534	466 384	555 214	547 870
Mongolia	403	661	536	1 065	1 903	2 899	4 818	4 385
Southern Asia	*26 137*	*47 005*	*93 119*	*189 230*	*285 581*	*378 955*	*497 279*	*459 423*
Afghanistan	670	235	137	384	403	388	376	(e)370
Bangladesh	759	1 671	6 389	9 297	15 083	19 194	24 439	25 113
Bhutan	17	70	103	258	496	641	675	(e)610
India (24)	8 586	17 969	42 379	99 616	164 909	226 350	302 905	294 158
Iran (Islamic Rep. of)*	12 338	19 305	28 739	56 252	78 830	101 316	(e)132 000	(e)104 000
Maldives	8	78	109	162	169	198	346	314
Nepal	80	175	804	863	823	856	919	911
Pakistan	2 618	5 589	9 028	16 051	17 523	21 410	25 383	24 567
Sri Lanka	1 062	1 912	5 430	6 347	7 345	8 602	10 236	9 380

For sources and notes, see end of table 1.1.1.

Imports (c.i.f.) - Importations (c.a.f.) Millions de dollars								Régions, pays ou territoires
1980	1990	2000	2005	2009	2010	2011	2012	
123 809	124 886	388 890	537 496	693 825	895 315	1 095 622	1 135 721	Économies en développement : Amérique
27 504	16 955	33 316	43 888	49 046	53 993	68 268	65 174	Caraïbes
..	..	95	130	169	158	153	(e)149	Anguilla
88	255	407	506	534	501	471	(e)530	Antigua-et-Barbuda
..	581	2 582	4 288	2 449	1 378	5 891	(e)2 600	Aruba (14)
7 546	1 112	2 074	2 312	2 535	2 591	2 966	3 386	Bahamas (15)
525	704	1 156	1 604	1 449	1 569	1 805	1 780	Barbade
						(e)55	(e)60	Bonaire, Saint-Eustache et Saba
(e)40	(e)115	(e)237	(e)280	290	300	320	310	Îles Vierges britanniques (4)
(e)101	(e)288	(e)665	(e)1 214	(e)893	(e)828	(e)911	(e)910	Îles Caïmanes (4)
0 505	4 000	4 043	0 004	0 610	11 406	11 213	13 710	Cuba*
						2 130	2 254	Curaçao
48	118	148	165	225	224	226	(e)200	Dominique*
1 964	3 006	9 479	9 869	12 296	15 489	17 436	17 758	République dominicaine (16)
50	105	239	328	282	318	330	(e)335	Grenade*
375	332	1 036	1 454	2 124	3 146	3 020	3 170	Haïti
1 171	1 928	3 301	4 739	5 064	5 225	6 439	6 585	Jamaïque
12	44	22	30	30	29	33	(e)37	Montserrat*
5 676	2 141	2 862	1 950	2 607	2 687			Antilles néerlandaises*(17)
45	110	196	210	296	270	247	(e)230	Saint-Kitts-et-Nevis*
124	271	355	486	520	662	700	(e)660	Sainte-Lucie*
57	136	163	240	333	338	332	(e)360	Saint-Vincent-et-les Grenadines*
						734	768	Saint-Martin (partie néerlandaise)
3 178	1 109	3 308	5 694	6 955	6 480	9 511	9 065	Trinité-et-Tobago*
..	..	149	304	375	302	(e)316	(e)309	Îles Turques et Caïques
29 743	51 774	205 667	274 614	297 172	376 552	442 695	466 621	Amérique centrale
150	211	524	593	669	706	831	882	Belize
1 540	1 990	6 389	9 824	11 395	13 570	16 220	17 578	Costa Rica*
966	1 263	4 947	6 690	7 325	8 416	9 965	10 270	El Salvador (18)
1 598	1 649	5 171	10 499	11 531	13 838	16 613	16 994	Guatemala (19)
1 009	938	3 988	6 545	7 372	8 907	10 994	11 179	Honduras (20)
22 144	43 548	179 464	228 240	241 515	310 205	361 068	380 477	Mexique
887	637	1 805	2 623	3 489	4 173	5 204	5 851	Nicaragua (21)
1 449								Panama, sans la zone du canal
	1 539	3 379	9 600	13 877	16 737	21 802	(e)23 390	Panama*(22)
66 562	56 157	149 906	218 995	347 607	464 770	584 659	603 926	Amérique du Sud
10 545	4 078	25 154	28 689	38 786	56 502	73 938	68 508	Argentine*
665	687	1 830	2 431	4 545	5 590	7 664	8 269	Bolivie (État plurinational de)
24 961	22 522	58 643	77 628	133 677	191 537	236 946	233 372	Brésil
5 797	7 940	18 507	32 735	42 806	59 288	75 230	79 468	Chili*
4 739	5 589	11 539	21 204	32 898	40 683	54 675	59 111	Colombie
2 253	1 862	3 721	10 287	15 090	20 591	24 286	25 197	Équateur
(e)6	(e)32	(e)59	(e)60	55	100	180	130	Îles Falkland (Malvinas) (4)
396	311	573	788	1 161	1 397	1 763	1 974	Guyana*
615	1 352	2 260	3 715	6 940	10 033	12 366	11 555	Paraguay
2 573	2 634	7 415	12 502	21 814	30 030	37 747	42 545	Pérou*
504	472	526	1 050	1 390	1 398	1 638	1 782	Suriname
1 680	1 343	3 466	3 879	6 907	8 622	10 726	11 614	Uruguay
11 827	7 335	16 213	24 027	41 540	(e)39 000	(e)47 500	(e)60 400	Venezuela (Rép. bolivarienne du)
273 525	573 173	1 390 798	2 620 099	3 530 457	4 631 216	5 661 278	5 909 702	Économies en développement : Asie
87 273	268 089	745 115	1 412 382	1 865 596	2 526 502	3 079 045	3 182 420	Asie orientale
19 941	53 345	225 024	659 953	1 005 923	1 396 247	1 743 484	1 818 405	Chine
22 994	84 725	214 042	300 160	352 241	441 369	510 855	553 486	Chine (RAS de Hong Kong)
544	1 539	2 625	4 514	4 751	5 629	7 927	8 982	Chine (RAS de Macao)
19 754	54 782	140 642	182 614	174 371	251 236	281 438	270 473	Province chinoise de Taiwan
(e)1 200	(e)2 930	(e)1 686	(e)2 718	(e)3 095	(e)3 530	(e)4 330	(e)4 750	Corée, Rép. populaire dém. de
22 292	69 844	160 481	261 238	323 085	425 212	524 413	519 584	Corée, République de (23)
548	924	615	1 184	2 131	3 278	6 598	6 739	Mongolie
38 359	57 368	94 762	236 876	380 733	507 010	641 399	658 438	Asie méridionale
841	936	1 176	2 471	3 336	5 154	6 390	(e)5 500	Afghanistan
2 599	3 618	8 883	13 889	21 833	27 821	36 214	34 131	Bangladesh
50	81	175	386	529	854	1 052	(e)1 090	Bhoutan
14 864	23 580	51 523	142 870	257 202	350 234	464 463	489 668	Inde (24)
12 246	18 330	13 898	40 041	50 768	65 404	61 760	57 092	Iran (Rép. islamique d')*
29	137	389	745	963	1 091	1 465	1 554	Maldives
342	624	1 573	2 283	4 384	5 133	5 774	6 063	Népal
5 350	7 376	10 864	25 357	31 668	37 807	44 012	44 157	Pakistan
2 037	2 685	6 281	8 834	10 049	13 512	20 269	19 183	Sri Lanka

Pour les sources et les notes, se reporter à la fin du tableau 1.1.1.

Region, country or territory	Exports (f.o.b.) - Exportations (f.a.b.) Millions of dollars							
	1980	1990	2000	2005	2009	2010	2011	2012
South-Eastern Asia	*71 915*	*144 148*	*429 845*	*655 973*	*813 985*	*1 050 067*	*1 237 070*	*1 252 683*
Brunei Darussalam*	4 581	2 213	3 903	6 249	7 200	8 907	12 440	12 982
Cambodia (6)	16	86	1 389	3 092	4 196	5 143	(e)7 000	(e)8 200
Indonesia (...2002)	21 909	25 674	65 403					
Indonesia	–	–	–	86 996	119 646	158 074	200 788	188 496
Lao People's Dem. Rep.*	28	79	330	553	1 053	1 746	2 216	2 269
Malaysia (25)	12 945	29 452	98 229	140 980	157 433	198 612	228 086	227 388
Myanmar	477	325	1 620	3 813	6 662	8 661	9 238	8 900
Philippines	5 741	8 117	37 757	41 255	38 436	51 496	48 305	51 995
Singapore (26)	19 375	52 730	137 804	229 649	269 832	351 867	409 503	408 393
Thailand*	6 505	23 068	68 963	110 936	152 422	193 306	222 576	229 519
Timor-Leste (27)	–	–	–	8	8	17	12	(e)12
Viet Nam	338	2 404	14 447	32 442	57 096	72 237	96 906	114 529
Western Asia	*196 729*	*117 536*	*234 205*	*516 025*	*698 120*	*861 680*	*1 203 381*	*1 335 760*
Bahrain (6)	3 606	3 761	6 194	10 242	11 874	14 971	19 650	19 768
Iraq*	26 349	10 314	18 743	23 697	41 929	52 483	(e)83 300	(e)94 400
Jordan	574	1 064	1 899	4 302	6 375	7 028	8 006	7 885
Kuwait*	19 663	7 042	19 436	44 869	54 008	69 978	102 168	118 546
Lebanon (28)	955	494	715	2 337	4 187	5 021	5 664	5 615
Oman	3 748	5 508	11 319	18 692	27 651	36 601	47 092	52 138
Qatar*	5 680	3 529	11 594	25 762	48 007	74 800	114 299	132 968
Saudi Arabia*(29)	109 083	44 417	77 583	180 711	192 314	251 143	364 735	388 370
State of Palestine	..	..	401	335	518	576	759	(e)1 001
Syrian Arab Republic*	2 108	4 212	4 633	8 708	10 855	12 796	(e)10 000	(e)4 000
Turkey*	2 910	12 959	27 775	73 476	102 143	113 883	134 907	152 469
United Arab Emirates	(e)21 970	23 544	49 835	117 287	(e)192 000	(e)214 000	(e)302 000	(e)350 000
Yemen, Arab Republic	23							
Yemen, Democratic	60							
Yemen*	–	692	4 079	5 608	6 259	(e)8 400	(e)10 800	(e)8 600
Developing economies: Oceania	*2 251*	*2 778*	*5 172*	*6 710*	*7 057*	*9 053*	*10 848*	*10 099*
American Samoa*(30)	127	311	346	374	(e)470	(e)300	(e)280	(e)420
Cook Islands	4	5	9	5	3	5	3	(e)3
Fiji	377	497	585	701	630	841	1 070	1 224
French Polynesia*	30	111	221	217	148	153	168	139
Guam (4)	61	(e)82	74	52	51	46	43	46
Kiribati	3	3	4	4	6	4	9	6
Marshall Islands	–	3	9	25	21	32	(e)35	(e)35
Micronesia (Federated States of)	–	4	22	19	25	(e)25	(e)28	(e)35
Nauru (4)	65	60	(e)29	(e)3	25	50	70	90
New Caledonia*	418	449	606	1 093	993	1 493	1 661	1 321
Niue	0	0	0	0	(e)0	(e)0	(e)0	(e)0
Northern Mariana Islands (4)	–	..	(e)1 017	(e)691	(e)9	(e)5	(e)2	(e)4
Palau (4)	–	..	12	13	(e)6	(e)6	(e)6	(e)8
Papua New Guinea	1 031	1 144	2 070	3 273	4 394	5 742	6 908	6 128
Samoa (28)	17	9	65	87	46	70	66	76
Solomon Islands*	74	70	69	103	165	224	415	493
Tokelau (4)	..	..	..	(e)0	(e)0	(e)0	(e)0	(e)0
Tonga	7	11	9	10	8	8	14	16
Tuvalu	0	0	0	0	(e)0	(e)0	(e)0	(e)0
Vanuatu	36	19	26	38	57	49	67	55
Wallis and Futuna Islands (4)	..	..	(e)0	(e)0	(e)0	(e)0	(e)0	(e)0
Transition economies	*85 478*	*118 378*	*154 008*	*362 644*	*477 271*	*620 989*	*827 266*	*840 551*
Albania	..	230	261	658	1 091	1 545	1 951	1 968
Armenia*	–	–	294	974	710	1 041	1 334	1 428
Azerbaijan (31)	–	–	1 745	7 649	21 097	26 476	34 495	32 634
Belarus	–	–	7 326	15 979	21 304	25 284	41 419	45 991
Bosnia and Herzegovina*(32)	–	–	1 069	2 400	3 954	4 803	5 850	5 162
Croatia*	–	–	4 432	8 773	10 474	11 811	13 364	12 344
Georgia (33)	–	–	323	865	1 134	1 677	2 189	2 377
Kazakhstan*(34)	–	–	8 812	27 849	43 196	59 971	87 603	92 286
Kyrgyzstan	–	–	511	672	1 673	1 760	1 972	1 894
Montenegro	–	–	–	–	388	437	632	472
Republic of Moldova	–	–	472	1 091	1 283	1 541	2 217	2 162
Russian Federation (35)	–	–	105 036	243 798	303 388	400 630	522 011	529 255
Serbia and Montenegro*	–	–	1 723	(e)5 065				
Serbia	–	–	–	–	8 345	9 795	11 779	11 353
SFR of Yugoslavia	8 978	14 308						
Tajikistan (33)	–	–	785	909	1 010	1 195	1 257	1 358
TFYR of Macedonia*	–	–	1 323	2 041	2 708	3 351	4 478	4 002

For sources and notes, see end of table 1.1.1.

		Imports (c.i.f.) - Importations (c.a.f.) Millions de dollars						Régions, pays ou territoires
1980	1990	2000	2005	2009	2010	2011	2012	
65 640	*162 346*	*380 641*	*603 159*	*727 321*	*953 435*	*1 153 360*	*1 220 072*	**Asie du Sud-Est**
572	1 001	1 107	1 491	2 449	2 562	3 629	3 582	Brunéi Darussalam*
180	164	1 936	3 927	5 830	6 791	(e)9 300	(e)11 000	Cambodge (6)
10 834	21 768	43 595						Indonésie (...2002)
–	–	–	75 725	93 786	135 323	176 201	190 383	Indonésie
92	185	535	882	1 461	2 060	2 398	2 467	Rép. dém. populaire lao*
10 779	29 258	81 963	114 625	123 832	164 622	187 473	196 615	Malaisie (25)
357	270	2 371	1 927	4 348	4 760	9 019	9 201	Myanmar
8 291	13 004	37 027	49 487	45 878	58 468	63 693	65 350	Philippines
24 007	60 899	134 545	200 047	245 785	310 791	365 770	379 723	Singapour (26)
9 214	33 045	61 923	118 178	133 709	182 921	228 787	247 590	Thaïlande*
			109	295	298	340	(e)380	Timor-Leste (27)
1 314	2 752	15 638	36 761	69 949	84 839	106 750	113 780	Viet Nam
82 253	*85 370*	*170 281*	*367 682*	*556 806*	*644 269*	*787 475*	*848 772*	**Asie occidentale**
3 483	3 712	4 633	9 393	(e)10 100	(e)12 260	(e)12 730	(e)13 920	Bahreïn (6)
8 707	6 526	11 009	23 532	38 437	43 915	(e)49 000	(e)57 000	Iraq*
2 402	2 600	4 597	10 498	14 236	15 564	18 930	20 691	Jordanie
6 530	3 972	7 157	15 801	19 892	22 675	25 405	25 880	Koweït*
3 650	2 525	6 230	9 633	16 574	18 460	20 750	21 945	Liban (28)
1 732	2 798	5 131	8 971	17 936	19 973	24 019	(e)28 600	Oman
1 423	1 695	3 252	10 061	24 922	23 240	29 888	(e)34 200	Qatar*
30 166	24 069	30 238	59 459	95 552	106 863	131 586	155 593	Arabie saoudite*(29)
..	..	2 383	2 667	3 601	3 959	4 492	(e)5 097	État de Palestine
4 124	2 400	3 815	10 862	15 443	17 562	(e)16 800	(e)7 300	République arabe syrienne*
7 910	22 303	54 503	116 774	140 928	185 544	240 842	236 545	Turquie*
8 746	11 199	35 009	84 654	(e)150 000	(e)165 000	(e)203 000	(e)230 000	Émirats arabes unis
1 853	–	–	–	–	–	–	–	Yémen, République arabe du
1 527	–	–	–	–	–	–	–	Yémen, Démocratique
–	1 571	2 324	5 378	9 185	9 255	10 034	(e)12 000	Yémen*
3 558	*5 097*	*6 197*	*9 754*	*12 045*	*14 223*	*16 384*	*16 292*	**Économies en développement : Océanie**
95	360	506	520	(e)600	(e)550	(e)700	(e)690	Samoa américaines*(30)
23	52	51	81	72	81	110	(e)120	Îles Cook
562	754	830	1 607	1 440	1 808	2 182	2 253	Fidji
547	930	971	1 723	1 717	1 726	1 796	1 706	Polynésie française*
400	(e)461	(e)421	533	850	950	1 100	1 200	Guam (4)
17	27	40	74	67	73	92	109	Kiribati
–	56	55	(e)94	(e)105	(e)135	(e)140	(e)140	Îles Marshall
–	84	107	130	172	(e)170	(e)180	(e)210	Micronésie (États fédérés de)
12	34	(e)26	(e)25	30	20	30	40	Nauru (4)
456	883	922	1 774	2 574	3 312	3 698	3 245	Nouvelle-Calédonie*
3	4	2	(e)10	6	(e)6	(e)8	(e)7	Nioué
–	..	(e)607	(e)591	(e)70	(e)87	(e)71	(e)67	Îles Mariannes du Nord (4)
–	..	127	105	(e)130	(e)120	(e)120	(e)140	Palaos (4)
1 176	1 118	1 151	1 729	(e)3 210	(e)3 950	(e)4 760	(e)4 940	Papouasie-Nouvelle-Guinée
63	81	90	239	231	310	346	346	Samoa (28)
89	91	92	185	268	404	466	(e)495	Îles Salomon*
..	..	1	(e)0	(e)0	(e)0	(e)0	(e)0	Tokélaou (4)
38	62	69	121	145	159	193	199	Tonga
4	5	5	13	(e)14	(e)16	(e)25	(e)25	Tuvalu
73	96	87	149	294	285	304	297	Vanuatu
..	..	37	51	(e)51	(e)60	(e)63	(e)65	Îles Wallis-et-Futuna (4)
83 591	*140 131*	*104 136*	*258 721*	*391 273*	*473 499*	*609 947*	*632 646*	**Économies en transition**
..	380	1 091	2 618	4 550	4 406	5 396	4 882	Albanie
		882	1 802	3 321	3 749	4 145	4 267	Arménie*
–	–	1 172	4 350	6 514	6 746	10 167	10 417	Azerbaïdjan (31)
–	–	8 646	16 708	28 569	34 884	45 771	46 404	Bélarus
–	–	3 107	7 070	8 773	9 223	11 051	10 024	Bosnie-Herzégovine*(32)
–	–	7 887	18 560	21 203	20 067	22 715	20 762	Croatie*
–	–	709	2 490	4 500	5 257	7 058	7 842	Géorgie (33)
–	–	5 040	17 353	28 409	31 107	37 056	44 539	Kazakhstan*(34)
–	–	558	1 102	3 040	3 223	4 261	5 374	Kirghizistan
–	–			2 313	2 182	2 544	2 337	Monténégro
–	–	777	2 292	3 278	3 855	5 191	5 213	République de Moldova
–	–	49 348	125 434	191 803	248 634	323 831	335 446	Fédération de Russie (35)
–	–	3 711	(e)11 635	–	–	–	–	Serbie-et-Monténégro*
–	–	–	–	16 047	16 735	19 862	19 013	Serbie
15 076	18 871							RSF de Yougoslavie
–	–	675	1 330	2 570	2 657	3 206	3 778	Tadjikistan (33)
–	–	2 094	3 228	5 073	5 474	7 027	6 511	LERY de Macédoine*

Pour les sources et les notes, se reporter à la fin du tableau 1.1.1.

Region, country or territory	Exports (f.o.b.) - Exportations (f.a.b.) Millions of dollars							
	1980	1990	2000	2005	2009	2010	2011	2012
Turkmenistan (33)	–	–	2 506	4 944	(e)5 000	(e)6 500	(e)13 000	(e)16 500
Ukraine (33)	–	–	14 573	34 228	39 782	51 478	68 460	68 530
USSR	76 500	(e)103 840	–	–	–	–	–	–
Uzbekistan (33)	–	–	2 817	4 749	10 735	11 695	13 254	10 836
Developed economies: America	**293 524**	**521 759**	**1 058 865**	**1 262 021**	**1 372 531**	**1 666 377**	**1 932 915**	**2 000 995**
Bermuda (6)	37	60	51	49	29	15	13	12
Canada	67 734	127 629	276 617	360 475	316 094	387 481	452 131	454 794
Greenland	186	452	273	402	360	380	475	474
Saint Pierre and Miquelon (4)	1	26	(e)6	(e)12	(e)6	(e)6	(e)6	(e)6
United States (36)	225 566	393 592	781 918	901 082	1 056 043	1 278 495	1 480 290	1 545 709
Developed economies: Asia	**135 979**	**299 660**	**510 700**	**637 711**	**628 654**	**828 252**	**890 980**	**861 708**
Israel*	5 538	12 080	31 404	42 770	47 935	58 413	67 796	63 141
Japan	130 441	287 580	479 296	594 941	580 719	769 839	823 184	798 568
Developed economies: Europe	**899 457**	**1 663 665**	**2 591 787**	**4 304 333**	**4 891 860**	**5 497 904**	**6 478 259**	**6 196 621**
Andorra*	..	..	45	142	63	54	77	(e)110
Austria*	17 489	41 135	67 543	125 182	136 989	152 560	177 428	166 439
Belgium*	64 540	117 703	187 906	334 400	370 125	407 700	476 109	446 529
Bulgaria*	10 390	5 030	4 852	11 739	16 318	20 630	28 208	26 715
Cyprus*	532	957	951	1 465	1 257	1 402	1 818	1 737
Czechoslovakia (37)	14 930	11 880						
Czech Republic*(38)	–	–	29 094	78 110	112 955	132 982	162 939	156 569
Denmark*(39)	16 749	36 870	51 166	85 121	93 984	96 440	111 864	105 594
Estonia*(33)	–	–	3 830	7 716	9 048	11 591	16 723	16 124
Faeroe Islands	178	418	474	599	762	839	1 008	948
Finland*	14 150	26 571	45 989	65 498	62 854	69 518	79 142	73 012
France*	116 423	217 262	326 802	463 428	484 781	523 767	596 473	568 920
Germany, Democratic Republic of	18 590	–	–	–	–	–	–	–
Germany, Federal Republic of	192 860	–	–	–	–	–	–	–
Germany*	–	421 100	550 447	970 914	1 120 041	1 258 924	1 473 985	1 407 082
Gibraltar (40)	10	83	127	(e)200	264	258	246	240
Greece*	5 153	8 105	11 722	17 278	20 469	21 713	33 899	35 479
Hungary*(41)	8 610	(e)10 000	28 192	62 936	83 008	95 483	112 312	103 927
Iceland	918	1 592	1 901	3 091	4 057	4 604	5 347	5 064
Ireland*	8 398	23 747	77 222	109 657	115 928	116 497	125 740	117 227
Italy*	78 104	170 304	240 518	373 135	406 909	447 301	523 258	500 719
Latvia*	–	–	1 868	5 161	7 702	9 532	13 130	14 094
Lithuania*(33)	–	–	3 548	11 807	16 454	20 748	28 050	29 640
Luxembourg*	3 005	6 305	8 357	18 797	21 339	19 748	21 866	19 447
Malta	483	1 130	2 453	2 399	2 857	3 586	4 386	4 250
Netherlands*	84 948	131 775	232 554	406 372	497 891	574 251	667 101	655 700
Norway	18 543	34 047	60 058	103 759	116 778	130 669	160 305	161 026
Poland*	17 020	(e)14 320	31 747	89 437	136 503	159 724	188 696	183 420
Portugal*	4 640	16 422	24 303	38 150	44 211	49 406	59 675	58 328
Romania*	11 400	(e)4 960	10 412	27 688	40 567	49 579	63 012	57 824
Slovakia*	–	–	11 832	31 889	56 082	64 664	79 830	81 497
Slovenia*			8 770	19 248	26 177	29 200	34 756	32 173
Spain*	20 720	55 521	114 966	192 644	227 338	254 418	306 551	293 939
Sweden*	30 906	57 538	86 917	130 962	130 781	158 549	186 963	172 424
Switzerland*	29 632	63 784	80 500	130 930	172 474	195 609	234 819	225 949
United Kingdom*	110 137	185 107	284 720	384 477	354 893	415 959	502 540	474 476
Developed economies: Oceania	**27 365**	**49 146**	**77 749**	**127 827**	**179 264**	**244 031**	**308 055**	**293 984**
Australia	21 944	39 752	63 870	106 097	154 331	212 634	270 387	256 680
New Zealand	5 421	9 394	13 879	21 730	24 933	31 396	37 669	37 305

For sources and notes, see end of table 1.1.1.

1.1.1   Exportations et importations des pays
et des régions géographiques
Valeur

1

Imports (c.i.f.) - Importations (c.a.f.) Millions de dollars								Régions, pays ou territoires
1980	1990	2000	2005	2009	2010	2011	2012	
–	–	1 786	2 947	(e)6 800	(e)5 700	(e)7 600	(e)9 900	Turkménistan (33)
–	–	13 956	36 136	45 487	60 911	82 594	84 639	Ukraine (33)
68 515	120 880	–	–	–	–	–	–	URSS
–	–	2 697	3 666	9 023	8 689	10 472	11 296	Ouzbékistan (33)
320 179	641 357	1 505 232	2 056 765	1 937 237	2 373 870	2 731 319	2 812 400	Économies développées : Amérique
312	595	719	985	1 064	988	900	900	Bermudes (6)
62 544	123 244	244 778	322 411	329 907	402 690	463 410	474 920	Canada
328	445	365	593	742	808	915	854	Groenland
10	86	(e)70	(e)70	(e)228	(e)200	(e)200	(e)190	Saint-Pierre-et-Miquelon (4)
256 985	516 987	1 259 300	1 732 706	1 605 296	1 969 184	2 265 894	2 335 537	États-Unis (36)
151 000	252 162	417 196	563 000	601 259	755 268	931 210	961 236	Économies développées : Asie
9 784	16 794	37 686	47 142	49 278	61 209	75 830	75 392	Israël*
141 296	235 368	379 510	515 866	551 981	694 059	855 380	885 843	Japon
1 005 836	1 724 480	2 628 760	4 323 404	4 921 162	5 562 574	6 521 427	6 135 448	Économies développées : Europe
..	..	1 019	1 802	1 581	1 514	1 597	(e)1 685	Andorre*
24 444	49 088	72 215	127 327	143 063	159 009	191 417	178 416	Autriche*
71 860	119 702	177 073	318 700	353 364	391 204	466 625	437 246	Belgique*
9 670	5 100	6 544	18 163	23 539	25 513	32 582	32 742	Bulgarie*
1 202	2 568	3 846	6 316	7 835	8 569	8 678	7 293	Chypre*
15 180	12 460							Tchécoslovaquie (37)
		31 974	76 512	105 048	126 652	152 125	140 736	République tchèque*(38)
19 340	33 333	45 445	75 581	83 133	83 052	95 663	91 971	Danemark*(39)
–	–	5 052	10 238	10 140	12 287	17 708	17 681	Estonie*(33)
223	338	533	743	783	780	987	1 149	Îles Féroé
15 635	27 001	34 358	58 766	60 889	68 803	84 264	76 240	Finlande*
137 532	240 803	338 103	504 124	560 873	611 070	720 028	673 794	France*
19 080	–	–	–	–	–	–	–	Allemagne, Rép. dém. d'
188 002	–	–	–	–	–	–	–	Allemagne, Rép. fédérale d'
	355 686	495 970	777 073	926 347	1 054 814	1 254 869	1 167 236	Allemagne*
110	362	482	(e)551	747	746	867	860	Gibraltar (40)
10 548	19 777	33 397	54 436	69 448	63 793	67 394	63 164	Grèce*
9 190	(e)10 340	32 172	66 552	77 761	88 178	102 440	95 316	Hongrie*(41)
999	1 680	2 589	4 979	3 604	3 920	4 841	4 772	Islande
11 153	20 682	50 915	68 565	62 704	60 276	66 606	62 768	Irlande*
100 741	181 968	238 757	384 790	415 105	487 049	558 787	486 630	Italie*
–	–	3 202	8 697	9 811	11 691	16 290	17 198	Lettonie*
–	–	5 219	15 548	18 304	23 403	31 773	32 216	Lituanie*(33)
3 612	7 596	11 250	21 893	25 330	25 092	29 318	27 555	Luxembourg*
938	1 961	3 413	3 681	4 478	5 062	6 293	6 598	Malte
88 419	126 475	217 728	363 822	443 153	516 409	599 035	591 198	Pays-Bas*
16 926	27 231	34 391	55 488	68 970	77 326	90 787	87 316	Norvège
19 120	(e)11 570	49 029	101 639	149 459	178 049	210 597	196 021	Pologne*
9 309	25 264	39 854	61 184	71 663	77 749	82 466	72 216	Portugal*
13 200	(e)7 600	13 148	40 518	54 324	62 109	76 475	70 183	Roumanie*
–	–	12 760	34 649	55 650	65 026	79 842	78 206	Slovaquie*
–	–	10 147	20 337	26 507	30 094	35 527	32 009	Slovénie*
34 078	87 554	155 757	288 786	293 218	327 016	376 606	334 790	Espagne*
33 438	54 245	72 700	111 697	119 876	148 946	177 026	162 528	Suède*
36 341	69 681	82 521	126 574	155 378	176 281	208 220	197 787	Suisse*
115 545	224 416	347 198	513 673	519 078	591 095	673 691	689 927	Royaume-Uni*
27 871	51 486	85 763	151 500	191 045	232 256	280 806	299 196	Économies développées : Océanie
22 399	41 985	71 529	125 281	165 471	201 639	243 701	260 942	Australie
5 472	9 501	14 235	26 219	25 574	30 617	37 105	38 254	Nouvelle-Zélande

Pour les sources et les notes, se reporter à la fin du tableau 1.1.1.

Region, country or territory	Exports (f.o.b.) - Exportations (f.a.b.) Percentage - En pourcentage										
	1980	1990	1995	2000	2005	2007	2008	2009	2010	2011	2012
WORLD	100	100	100	100	100	100	100	100	100	100	100
DEVELOPING ECONOMIES	29.648	24.115	27.704	31.878	36.240	37.805	39.018	39.867	42.045	43.028	44.605
TRANSITION ECONOMIES	4.171	3.387	2.322	2.388	3.454	3.931	4.575	3.802	4.063	4.516	4.568
DEVELOPED ECONOMIES	66.181	72.498	69.974	65.734	60.306	58.264	56.407	56.332	53.892	52.457	50.827
Developing economies: Africa	5.923	3.002	2.157	2.290	2.963	3.115	3.483	3.134	3.342	3.266	3.424
Eastern Africa	*0.342*	*0.209*	*0.188*	*0.153*	*0.158*	*0.169*	*0.169*	*0.197*	*0.212*	*0.215*	*0.224*
Burundi*(1)	0.003	0.002	0.002	0.001	0.001	0.000	0.000	0.001	0.001	0.001	0.001
Comoros*	0.001	0.001	0.000	0.000	0.000	0.000	0.000	0.000	0.000	0.000	0.000
Djibouti (2)	0.001	0.001	0.000	0.000	0.000	0.000	0.000	0.001	0.001	0.001	(e)0.001
Eritrea (3)	_	_	0.002	0.001	0.000	0.000	(e)0.000	(e)0.000	(e)0.000	(e)0.002	(e)0.003
Ethiopia (...1991)	0.021	0.009									
Ethiopia	_	_	0.008	0.008	0.009	0.009	0.010	0.013	0.015	0.016	(e)0.016
Kenya	0.061	0.030	0.036	0.027	0.033	0.029	0.031	0.036	0.034	0.031	0.033
Madagascar*	0.020	0.009	0.010	0.013	0.008	0.009	0.008	0.008	0.007	(e)0.009	(e)0.008
Malawi	0.014	0.012	0.008	0.006	0.005	0.006	0.005	0.009	0.007	0.008	0.006
Mauritius	0.021	0.034	0.030	0.024	0.020	0.016	0.015	0.015	0.015	0.014	0.015
Mozambique	0.014	0.004	0.003	0.006	0.017	0.017	0.016	0.017	(e)0.020	0.020	(e)0.022
Rwanda	0.006	0.003	0.001	0.001	0.001	0.001	0.002	0.002	0.002	0.003	0.003
Seychelles	0.001	0.002	0.001	0.003	0.003	0.003	0.003	0.003	0.003	0.003	0.003
Somalia (4)	0.007	(e)0.004	(e)0.003	(e)0.003	(e)0.002	(e)0.002	(e)0.003	0.003	0.003	0.003	0.003
Uganda	0.017	0.004	0.009	0.006	0.008	0.010	0.011	0.012	0.011	0.012	0.013
United Republic of Tanzania	0.025	0.009	0.013	0.011	0.016	0.016	0.019	0.024	0.027	0.026	(e)0.030
Zambia (5)	0.064	0.037	0.020	0.014	0.017	0.033	0.032	0.034	0.047	0.049	(e)0.047
Zimbabwe	0.068	0.049	0.041	0.030	(e)0.018	(e)0.017	(e)0.014	0.018	0.021	0.019	0.021
Middle Africa	*0.431*	*0.339*	*0.217*	*0.265*	*0.471*	*0.554*	*0.687*	*0.568*	*0.598*	*0.645*	*0.681*
Angola*(6)	0.092	0.112	0.070	0.123	0.230	0.317	0.396	0.325	0.331	0.367	(e)0.402
Cameroon*(7)	0.068	0.057	0.032	0.028	0.027	0.030	0.032	0.028	0.025	0.025	(e)0.024
Central African Republic*(7)	0.006	0.003	0.003	0.002	0.001	0.001	(e)0.001	(e)0.001	(e)0.001	(e)0.001	(e)0.001
Chad*(6)	0.003	0.007	0.005	0.003	0.029	0.026	0.026	(e)0.022	(e)0.023	(e)0.025	(e)0.024
Congo*(7)	0.044	0.028	0.023	0.039	0.045	0.040	0.052	(e)0.049	(e)0.061	(e)0.063	(e)0.058
Dem. Rep. of the Congo*	0.111	0.067	0.030	0.013	0.023	(e)0.022	(e)0.027	(e)0.028	(e)0.035	(e)0.036	(e)0.034
Equatorial Guinea (6)	0.001	0.002	0.002	0.017	0.067	0.073	0.094	(e)0.072	(e)0.065	(e)0.074	(e)0.084
Gabon*(8)	0.106	0.063	0.052	0.040	0.048	0.045	0.059	0.043	0.057	0.053	0.053
Sao Tome and Principe*	0.001	0.000	0.000	0.000	0.000	0.000	0.000	0.000	0.000	0.000	(e)0.000
Northern Africa	*2.149*	*1.054*	*0.688*	*0.851*	*1.112*	*1.182*	*1.356*	*1.131*	*1.163*	*0.946*	*1.115*
Algeria*	0.677	0.368	0.198	0.342	0.438	0.429	0.491	0.360	0.373	0.401	0.391
Egypt	0.149	0.074	0.066	0.082	0.123	0.137	0.162	0.184	0.173	0.172	0.160
Libya	1.069	0.378	0.173	0.197	0.299	0.335	0.385	0.294	0.318	0.104	0.338
Morocco*	0.119	0.122	0.133	0.111	0.107	0.109	0.126	0.112	0.116	0.118	0.116
Sudan (...2011) (9)	0.026	0.011	0.011	0.028	0.046	0.063	0.072	0.066	0.075	0.053	_
Sudan	_	_	_	_	_	_	_	_	_	_	0.018
Tunisia (10)	0.109	0.101	0.106	0.091	0.100	0.108	0.120	0.115	0.107	0.097	0.092
Southern Africa	*1.362*	*0.773*	*0.627*	*0.544*	*0.577*	*0.574*	*0.566*	*0.563*	*0.604*	*0.608*	*0.545*
Botswana*	0.025	0.051	0.041	0.041	0.042	0.037	0.031	0.028	0.031	0.032	0.032
Lesotho	0.003	0.002	0.003	0.003	0.006	0.005	0.005	0.006	0.006	0.006	(e)0.006
Namibia	0.071	0.031	0.027	0.020	0.020	0.021	0.019	0.025	0.026	0.024	0.022
South Africa	1.245	0.674	0.538	0.465	0.492	0.498	0.500	0.491	0.529	0.535	0.474
Swaziland	0.018	0.016	0.017	0.014	(e)0.017	(e)0.013	(e)0.011	(e)0.013	(e)0.012	(e)0.010	(e)0.010
Western Africa	*1.638*	*0.625*	*0.439*	*0.476*	*0.645*	*0.635*	*0.704*	*0.675*	*0.765*	*0.853*	*0.858*
Benin*	0.003	0.008	0.008	0.006	0.006	0.007	0.008	0.010	0.008	(e)0.008	(e)0.008
Burkina Faso	0.004	0.004	0.005	0.003	0.004	0.004	0.004	0.007	0.010	0.013	0.012
Cape Verde (11)	0.000	0.000	0.000	0.000	0.000	0.000	0.000	0.000	0.000	0.000	0.000
Côte d'Ivoire*	0.153	0.088	0.072	0.060	0.073	0.062	0.064	0.090	0.076	0.068	(e)0.067
Gambia (12)	0.002	0.001	0.000	0.000	(e)0.000	0.000	0.000	0.001	0.000	0.001	(e)0.001
Ghana	0.061	0.026	0.033	0.026	0.027	0.030	0.033	0.047	0.052	0.070	(e)0.071
Guinea*	0.020	0.019	0.014	0.010	0.008	0.009	0.008	0.008	0.010	0.008	(e)0.007
Guinea-Bissau	0.001	0.001	0.000	0.001	0.001	0.001	0.001	0.001	0.001	(e)0.001	(e)0.001
Liberia*	0.029	(e)0.025	(e)0.016	(e)0.005	0.001	0.001	0.002	0.001	0.001	0.002	0.002
Mali*	0.010	0.010	0.009	0.008	0.010	0.011	0.013	0.014	0.013	0.013	0.012
Mauritania*	0.009	0.013	0.009	0.005	0.006	0.010	0.011	0.011	0.014	0.015	0.014
Niger*	0.028	0.008	0.006	0.004	0.005	0.005	(e)0.006	(e)0.008	(e)0.008	(e)0.007	(e)0.008
Nigeria	1.267	0.389	0.238	0.325	0.481	0.475	0.534	0.452	(e)0.550	(e)0.625	(e)0.630
Saint Helena	(e)0.000	(e)0.000	(e)0.000	(e)0.000	(e)0.000	(e)0.000	(e)0.000	(e)0.000	(e)0.000	(e)0.000	(e)0.000
Senegal (13)	0.023	0.022	0.019	0.014	0.015	0.012	0.013	0.016	0.014	0.014	0.014
Sierra Leone*	0.011	0.004	0.001	0.000	0.002	0.002	0.001	0.002	0.002	0.002	0.006
Togo*	0.016	0.008	0.007	0.006	0.006	0.005	0.005	0.007	(e)0.006	(e)0.006	(e)0.005

For sources and notes, see end of table.

Imports (c.i.f.) - Importations (c.a.f.) Percentage - En pourcentage											Régions, pays ou territoires
1980	1990	1995	2000	2005	2007	2008	2009	2010	2011	2012	
100	100	100	100	100	100	100	100	100	100	100	**MONDE**
23.844	22.116	28.787	28.780	31.770	33.165	34.926	36.625	39.034	39.857	41.440	ÉCONOMIES EN DÉVELOPPEMENT
4.007	3.885	2.051	1.564	2.401	3.132	3.542	3.083	3.072	3.312	3.417	ÉCONOMIES EN TRANSITION
72.148	74.000	69.163	69.656	65.830	63.703	61.532	60.291	57.894	56.830	55.143	ÉCONOMIES DÉVELOPPÉES
4.626	2.624	2.369	1.952	2.381	2.636	2.925	3.241	3.089	3.074	3.294	**Économies en développement : Afrique**
0.505	*0.356*	*0.299*	*0.254*	*0.292*	*0.317*	*0.359*	*0.414*	*0.395*	*0.404*	*0.450*	*Afrique orientale*
0.008	0.006	0.004	0.002	0.002	0.002	0.002	0.003	0.003	0.004	0.004	Burundi*(1)
0.001	0.001	0.001	0.001	0.001	0.001	0.001	0.002	0.002	0.002	0.001	Comores*
0.010	0.006	0.003	0.003	0.003	0.003	0.003	0.004	0.002	0.003	(e)0.003	Djibouti (2)
		0.009	0.007	(e)0.005	(e)0.004	(e)0.004	(e)0.005	(e)0.004	(e)0.005	(e)0.005	Érythrée (3)
0.035	0.030	–	–	–	–	–	–	–	–	–	Éthiopie (…1991)
–	–	0.022	0.019	0.038	0.041	0.050	0.060	0.056	0.048	0.068	Éthiopie
0.102	0.062	0.057	0.047	0.054	0.063	0.068	0.080	0.078	0.080	0.088	Kenya
0.029	0.018	0.012	0.016	0.016	0.019	0.023	0.025	0.016	0.016	(e)0.016	Madagascar*
0.021	0.016	0.009	0.008	0.011	0.010	0.013	0.016	0.014	0.013	0.015	Malawi
0.029	0.045	0.038	0.033	0.029	0.027	0.028	0.029	0.028	0.028	0.029	Maurice
0.038	0.024	0.013	0.017	0.022	0.021	0.024	0.030	(e)0.030	0.034	(e)0.037	Mozambique
0.013	0.008	0.005	0.003	0.004	0.005	0.007	0.010	0.009	0.010	0.013	Rwanda
0.005	0.005	0.004	0.005	0.006	0.006	0.007	0.006	(e)0.004	(e)0.004	(e)0.004	Seychelles
0.021	(e)0.003	(e)0.005	(e)0.005	(e)0.006	(e)0.006	(e)0.005	0.006	0.006	0.005	0.004	Somalie (4)
0.014	0.008	0.020	0.023	0.019	0.025	0.027	0.033	0.030	0.031	0.033	Ouganda
0.060	0.038	0.032	0.023	0.030	0.038	(e)0.047	0.051	0.051	0.059	0.061	République-Unie de Tanzanie
0.052	0.035	0.013	0.013	0.024	0.028	0.031	0.030	0.035	0.039	(e)0.044	Zambie (5)
0.067	0.051	0.051	0.028	(e)0.022	(e)0.018	(e)0.018	(e)0.023	(e)0.025	(e)0.024	(e)0.024	Zimbabwe
0.282	*0.194*	*0.113*	*0.114*	*0.177*	*0.220*	*0.261*	*0.347*	*0.268*	*0.277*	*0.308*	*Afrique centrale*
0.064	0.044	0.028	0.046	0.078	0.096	0.127	0.179	0.108	0.110	(e)0.130	Angola*(6)
0.077	0.039	0.023	0.022	0.025	0.033	0.035	0.035	0.033	0.037	(e)0.039	Cameroun*(7)
0.004	0.004	0.003	0.002	0.002	0.002	(e)0.002	(e)0.002	(e)0.002	(e)0.002	(e)0.002	République centrafricaine*(7)
0.004	0.014	0.009	0.005	0.009	(e)0.013	(e)0.012	(e)0.016	(e)0.016	(e)0.015	(e)0.015	Tchad*(6)
0.027	0.017	0.013	0.007	0.012	(e)0.018	(e)0.019	(e)0.023	(e)0.026	(e)0.028	(e)0.028	Congo*(7)
0.073	0.048	0.017	0.010	0.025	(e)0.024	(e)0.026	(e)0.031	(e)0.029	(e)0.030	(e)0.033	Rép. dém. du Congo*
0.001	0.002	0.002	0.008	0.012	0.019	(e)0.024	(e)0.041	(e)0.034	(e)0.035	(e)0.041	Guinée équatoriale (6)
0.032	0.025	0.017	0.014	0.014	0.015	0.016	0.020	0.019	0.020	0.020	Gabon*(8)
0.001	0.001	0.001	0.000	0.000	0.001	0.001	0.001	0.001	0.001	0.001	Sao Tomé-et-Principe*
1.513	*1.036*	*0.886*	*0.738*	*0.831*	*0.923*	*1.053*	*1.251*	*1.159*	*1.059*	*1.180*	*Afrique septentrionale*
0.506	0.271	0.193	0.138	0.189	0.194	0.240	0.310	0.263	0.257	0.257	Algérie*
0.233	0.255	0.224	0.219	0.208	(e)0.261	0.294	0.354	0.343	0.338	0.374	Égypte
0.325	0.148	0.103	0.056	0.056	0.047	0.056	0.101	0.115	(e)0.043	(e)0.124	Libye
0.204	0.192	0.191	0.173	0.193	0.225	0.257	0.259	0.230	0.240	0.242	Maroc*
0.076	0.017	0.023	0.023	0.063	0.062	0.057	0.076	0.065	0.050	–	Soudan (…2011) (9)
										0.051	Soudan
0.169	0.153	0.151	0.129	0.122	0.134	0.150	0.150	0.144	0.130	0.132	Tunisie (10)
1.079	*0.633*	*0.691*	*0.529*	*0.662*	*0.700*	*0.696*	*0.689*	*0.712*	*0.759*	*0.774*	*Afrique australe*
0.033	0.054	0.037	0.031	0.029	0.029	0.032	0.037	0.037	0.039	0.043	Botswana*
0.020	0.019	0.021	0.012	0.013	0.012	(e)0.011	(e)0.015	(e)0.015	(e)0.014	(e)0.014	Lesotho
0.055	0.032	0.031	0.023	0.024	(e)0.025	(e)0.026	(e)0.039	(e)0.036	(e)0.035	(e)0.035	Namibie
0.940	0.510	0.583	0.446	0.578	0.622	0.617	0.584	0.611	0.660	0.671	Afrique du Sud
0.030	0.018	0.019	0.016	(e)0.018	(e)0.013	(e)0.010	(e)0.014	(e)0.013	(e)0.011	(e)0.011	Swaziland
1.247	*0.405*	*0.380*	*0.317*	*0.418*	*0.476*	*0.556*	*0.541*	*0.555*	*0.576*	*0.582*	*Afrique occidentale*
0.016	0.007	0.014	0.009	0.009	0.014	0.014	0.016	0.013	(e)0.012	(e)0.012	Bénin*
0.017	0.015	0.009	0.009	(e)0.012	0.012	0.012	0.015	0.013	0.013	(e)0.017	Burkina Faso
0.003	0.004	0.005	0.003	0.004	0.005	0.005	0.006	0.005	0.005	0.004	Cap-Vert (11)
0.143	0.058	0.056	0.037	0.054	0.047	0.048	0.055	0.051	0.036	0.053	Côte d'Ivoire*
0.008	0.005	0.003	0.003	0.002	0.002	0.002	0.002	0.002	0.002	(e)0.002	Gambie (12)
0.054	0.033	0.036	0.045	0.050	0.057	0.062	0.063	0.071	0.087	(e)0.097	Ghana
0.017	0.020	0.016	0.009	(e)0.008	0.009	0.008	0.008	0.009	0.011	(e)0.012	Guinée*
0.003	0.002	0.003	0.001	0.001	0.001	0.001	0.002	0.001	(e)0.001	(e)0.001	Guinée-Bissau
0.026	(e)0.016	(e)0.010	(e)0.010	0.003	0.004	0.005	0.004	0.005	0.006	0.006	Libéria*
0.021	0.017	0.015	0.012	0.014	0.015	0.020	0.020	0.022	0.018	0.016	Mali*
0.014	0.006	0.008	0.007	0.013	0.010	0.012	0.012	0.013	0.013	0.017	Mauritanie*
0.028	0.011	0.007	0.006	0.009	0.008	0.010	(e)0.017	0.016	(e)0.015	(e)0.016	Niger*
0.799	0.156	0.157	0.131	0.193	0.245	0.303	0.267	0.287	(e)0.304	(e)0.275	Nigéria
(e)0.001	(e)0.001	(e)0.000	(e)0.001	0.001	(e)0.001	(e)0.000	(e)0.000	0.000	0.000	(e)0.000	Sainte-Hélène
0.050	0.034	0.027	0.023	0.032	0.034	0.040	0.037	0.031	0.032	0.035	Sénégal (13)
0.020	0.004	0.003	0.002	0.003	0.003	0.003	0.004	0.004	0.009	0.008	Sierra Leone*
0.026	0.016	0.011	0.008	0.010	0.009	0.009	0.012	0.010	(e)0.010	(e)0.010	Togo*

Pour les sources et les notes, se reporter à la fin du tableau.

Region, country or territory	Exports (f.o.b.) - Exportations (f.a.b.) Percentage - En pourcentage										
	1980	1990	1995	2000	2005	2007	2008	2009	2010	2011	2012
Developing economies: America	5.441	4.166	4.437	5.682	5.563	5.592	5.613	5.606	5.821	6.054	6.089
Caribbean	*1.104*	*0.381*	*0.251*	*0.295*	*0.255*	*0.249*	*0.252*	*0.190*	*0.178*	*0.220*	*0.193*
Anguilla	..	..	0.000	0.000	0.000	0.000	0.000	0.000	0.000	0.000	(e)0.000
Antigua and Barbuda	0.001	0.001	0.001	0.001	0.001	0.000	0.000	0.000	0.000	0.000	(e)0.000
Aruba (14)	..	0.004	0.026	0.039	0.042	0.037	0.034	0.016	0.002	0.028	(e)0.010
Bahamas (15)	0.244	0.007	0.003	0.009	0.005	0.006	0.006	0.006	0.005	0.005	0.005
Barbados	0.011	0.006	0.005	0.004	0.003	0.004	0.003	0.003	0.003	0.003	0.003
Bonaire, Sint Eustatius and Saba	–	–	–	–	–	–	–	–	–	(e)0.000	(e)0.000
British Virgin Islands (4)	(e)0.000	(e)0.000	(e)0.000	(e)0.000	(e)0.000	(e)0.000	(e)0.000	0.000	0.000	0.000	0.000
Cayman Islands (4)	(e)0.000	(e)0.001	(e)0.000	(e)0.000	(e)0.001	(e)0.000	(e)0.000	(e)0.000	(e)0.000	(e)0.000	(e)0.000
Cuba*	0.272	0.146	0.031	0.026	0.022	0.028	0.025	0.025	0.032	0.035	0.032
Curaçao	–	–	–	–	–	–	–	–	–	0.005	0.005
Dominica*	0.000	0.002	0.001	0.001	0.000	0.000	0.000	0.000	0.000	0.000	(e)0.000
Dominican Republic (16)	0.059	0.062	0.073	0.089	0.059	0.051	0.042	0.044	0.044	0.047	0.049
Grenada*	0.001	0.001	0.000	0.001	0.000	0.000	0.000	0.000	0.000	0.000	(e)0.000
Haiti	0.011	0.005	0.002	0.005	0.004	0.004	0.003	0.005	0.004	0.004	0.004
Jamaica	0.047	0.033	0.028	0.020	0.015	0.016	0.015	0.010	0.009	0.009	0.009
Montserrat*	0.000	0.000	0.000	0.000	0.000	0.000	0.000	0.000	0.000	0.000	(e)0.000
Netherlands Antilles*(17)	0.252	0.051	0.029	0.031	0.006	0.005	0.007	0.006	0.005		
Saint Kitts and Nevis*	0.001	0.001	0.000	0.001	0.000	0.000	0.000	0.000	0.000	0.000	(e)0.000
Saint Lucia*	0.003	0.004	0.002	0.001	0.001	(e)0.001	0.001	0.001	0.001	0.001	(e)0.001
Saint Vincent and the Grenadines*	0.001	0.002	0.001	0.001	0.000	0.000	0.000	0.000	0.000	0.000	(e)0.000
Sint Maarten (Dutch part)	–	–	–	–	–	–	–	–	–	0.001	0.001
Trinidad and Tobago*	0.199	0.056	0.047	0.066	0.095	0.096	0.116	0.073	0.072	0.082	0.071
Turks and Caicos Islands	..	..	..	0.000	0.000	0.000	0.000	0.000	0.000	(e)0.000	(e)0.000
Central America	*1.135*	*1.306*	*1.733*	*2.837*	*2.316*	*2.198*	*2.050*	*2.125*	*2.224*	*2.187*	*2.309*
Belize	0.005	0.004	0.003	0.003	0.002	0.002	0.002	0.002	0.002	0.002	(e)0.002
Costa Rica*	0.049	0.041	0.067	0.091	0.067	0.067	0.059	0.070	0.062	0.057	0.062
El Salvador (18)	0.047	0.017	0.032	0.046	0.033	0.029	0.029	0.031	0.029	0.029	0.029
Guatemala (19)	0.074	0.033	0.038	0.042	0.051	0.049	0.048	0.057	0.055	0.057	0.054
Honduras (20)	0.040	0.027	0.034	0.052	0.048	0.041	0.038	0.038	0.040	0.043	0.043
Mexico	0.880	1.165	1.537	2.580	2.040	1.939	1.804	1.830	1.952	1.908	2.015
Nicaragua (21)	0.022	0.009	0.009	0.010	0.008	0.009	0.009	0.011	0.012	0.012	0.015
Panama, excl. Canal Zone	0.018	–	–	–	–	–	–	–	–	–	–
Panama*(22)	–	0.010	0.012	0.013	0.067	0.063	0.061	0.085	0.072	0.079	(e)0.088
South America	*3.201*	*2.479*	*2.454*	*2.551*	*2.992*	*3.145*	*3.311*	*3.291*	*3.419*	*3.647*	*3.587*
Argentina*	0.391	0.353	0.405	0.408	0.384	0.398	0.434	0.443	0.446	0.458	0.440
Bolivia (Plurinational State of)	0.046	0.026	0.021	0.019	0.027	0.032	0.040	0.040	0.042	0.046	0.060
Brazil	0.982	0.899	0.899	0.855	1.129	1.146	1.226	1.219	1.321	1.398	1.318
Chile*	0.230	0.240	0.310	0.298	0.393	0.485	0.400	0.442	0.465	0.445	0.425
Colombia	0.191	0.192	0.196	0.202	0.202	0.214	0.233	0.262	0.261	0.313	0.328
Ecuador	0.121	0.078	0.083	0.076	0.096	0.102	0.117	0.110	0.114	0.122	0.130
Falkland Islands (Malvinas) (4)	(e)0.000	(e)0.000	(e)0.001	(e)0.001	(e)0.001	(e)0.001	(e)0.001	0.001	0.001	0.001	0.001
Guyana*	0.019	0.007	0.009	0.008	0.005	0.005	0.005	0.006	0.006	0.006	0.008
Paraguay	0.015	0.027	0.018	0.013	0.016	0.020	0.028	0.040	0.043	0.042	0.040
Peru*	0.190	0.094	0.106	0.108	0.165	0.200	0.192	0.215	0.233	0.253	0.248
Suriname	0.025	0.014	0.009	0.006	0.009	0.010	0.011	0.011	0.013	0.013	0.014
Uruguay	0.052	0.048	0.041	0.036	0.033	0.032	0.037	0.043	0.044	0.043	0.048
Venezuela (Bolivarian Rep. of)	0.938	0.501	0.357	0.520	0.531	0.499	0.589	0.459	0.430	0.507	0.529
Developing economies: Asia	18.175	16.868	21.010	23.825	27.649	29.033	29.863	31.070	32.823	33.649	35.038
Eastern Asia	*3.791*	*8.038*	*10.902*	*12.084*	*14.684*	*15.652*	*15.392*	*16.751*	*17.835*	*17.613*	*18.475*
China	0.883	1.776	2.875	3.864	7.257	8.706	8.861	9.571	10.323	10.362	11.133
China, Hong Kong SAR	0.992	2.357	3.360	3.143	2.782	2.492	2.293	2.624	2.622	2.487	2.679
China, Macao SAR	0.030	0.049	0.039	0.039	0.024	0.018	0.012	0.008	0.006	0.005	0.006
China, Taiwan Province of	0.968	1.924	2.184	2.347	1.890	1.760	1.583	1.622	1.797	1.683	1.637
Korea, Dem. People's Rep. of	(e)0.044	(e)0.053	(e)0.019	(e)0.011	(e)0.013	(e)0.012	(e)0.013	(e)0.016	(e)0.017	(e)0.020	(e)0.020
Korea, Republic of (23)	0.854	1.860	2.417	2.671	2.709	2.650	2.614	2.896	3.052	3.031	2.977
Mongolia	0.020	0.019	0.009	0.008	0.010	0.013	0.016	0.015	0.019	0.026	0.024
Southern Asia	*1.275*	*1.345*	*1.256*	*1.444*	*1.802*	*1.992*	*2.199*	*2.275*	*2.480*	*2.714*	*2.497*
Afghanistan	0.033	0.007	0.003	0.002	0.004	0.004	0.003	0.003	0.003	0.002	(e)0.002
Bangladesh	0.037	0.048	0.068	0.099	0.089	0.089	0.095	0.120	0.126	0.133	0.136
Bhutan	0.001	0.002	0.002	0.002	0.002	0.005	0.003	0.004	0.004	0.004	(e)0.003
India (24)	0.419	0.514	0.592	0.657	0.949	1.071	1.207	1.314	1.481	1.653	1.598
Iran (Islamic Rep. of)*	0.602	0.552	0.355	0.446	0.536	0.633	0.704	0.628	0.663	(e)0.721	(e)0.565
Maldives	0.000	0.002	0.002	0.002	0.002	0.002	0.002	0.001	0.001	0.002	0.002
Nepal	0.004	0.005	0.007	0.012	0.008	0.006	0.006	0.007	0.006	0.005	0.005
Pakistan	0.128	0.160	0.154	0.140	0.153	0.127	0.126	0.140	0.140	0.139	0.134
Sri Lanka	0.052	0.055	0.073	0.084	0.060	0.055	0.052	0.059	0.056	0.056	0.051

For sources and notes, see end of table.

			Imports (c.i.f.) - Importations (c.a.f.) Percentage - En pourcentage								Régions, pays ou territoires
1980	1990	1995	2000	2005	2007	2008	2009	2010	2011	2012	
5.935	3.462	4.739	5.842	4.987	5.333	5.629	5.468	5.808	5.950	6.135	Économies en développement : Amérique
1.319	0.470	0.390	0.500	0.407	0.406	0.431	0.387	0.350	0.371	0.352	Caraïbes
..	..	0.001	0.001	0.001	0.002	0.002	0.001	0.001	0.001	(e)0.001	Anguilla
0.004	0.007	0.007	0.006	0.005	0.005	0.005	0.004	0.003	0.003	(e)0.003	Antigua-et-Barbuda
..	0.016	0.031	0.039	0.040	0.036	0.037	0.019	0.009	0.032	(e)0.014	Aruba (14)
0.362	0.031	0.024	0.031	0.021	0.021	0.019	0.020	0.017	0.016	0.018	Bahamas (15)
0.025	0.020	0.015	0.017	0.015	0.012	0.012	0.011	0.010	0.010	0.010	Barbade
–	–	–	–	–	–	–	–	–	(e)0.000	(e)0.000	Bonaire, Saint-Eustache et Saba
(e)0.002	(e)0.003	(e)0.002	(e)0.004	(e)0.003	(e)0.002	(e)0.002	0.002	0.002	0.002	0.002	Îles Vierges britanniques (4)
(e)0.005	(e)0.008	(e)0.008	(e)0.010	(e)0.011	(e)0.007	(e)0.007	(e)0.007	(e)0.005	(e)0.005	(e)0.005	Îles Caïmanes (4)
0.312	0.128	0.054	0.073	0.075	0.077	0.093	0.076	0.075	0.077	0.074	Cuba*
									0.012	0.012	Curaçao
0.002	0.003	0.002	0.002	0.002	0.001	0.002	0.002	0.001	0.001	(e)0.001	Dominique*
0.094	0.083	0.099	0.142	0.092	0.096	0.097	0.097	0.100	0.095	0.096	République dominicaine (16)
0.002	0.003	0.002	0.004	0.003	0.003	0.002	0.002	0.002	0.002	(e)0.002	Grenade*
0.018	0.009	0.012	0.016	0.013	0.012	0.014	0.017	0.020	0.016	0.017	Haïti
0.056	0.053	0.054	0.050	0.044	0.048	0.051	0.040	0.034	0.035	0.036	Jamaïque
0.001	0.001	0.001	0.000	0.000	0.000	0.000	0.000	0.000	0.000	(e)0.000	Montserrat*
0.272	0.059	0.035	0.043	0.018	0.018	0.019	0.021	0.017	–	–	Antilles néerlandaises*(17)
0.002	0.003	0.003	0.003	0.002	0.002	0.002	0.002	0.002	0.001	(e)0.001	Saint-Kitts-et-Nevis*
0.006	0.008	0.006	0.005	0.005	0.004	0.004	0.004	0.004	0.004	(e)0.004	Sainte-Lucie*
0.003	0.004	0.003	0.002	0.002	0.002	0.002	0.003	0.002	0.002	(e)0.002	Saint-Vincent-et-les Grenadines*
									0.004	0.004	Saint-Martin (partie néerlandaise)
0.152	0.031	0.033	0.050	0.053	0.054	0.058	0.055	0.042	0.052	0.049	Trinité-et-Tobago*
..	..	..	0.002	0.003	0.004	0.004	0.003	0.002	(e)0.002	(e)0.002	Îles Turques et Caïques
1.426	1.435	1.734	3.090	2.548	2.474	2.365	2.342	2.443	2.404	2.521	Amérique centrale
0.007	0.006	0.005	0.008	0.006	0.005	0.005	0.005	0.005	0.005	0.005	Belize
0.074	0.055	0.078	0.096	0.091	0.091	0.093	0.090	0.088	0.088	0.095	Costa Rica*
0.046	0.035	0.064	0.074	0.062	0.062	0.060	0.058	0.055	0.054	0.055	El Salvador (18)
0.077	0.046	0.063	0.078	0.097	0.095	0.088	0.091	0.090	0.090	0.092	Guatemala (19)
0.048	0.026	0.036	0.060	0.061	0.062	0.063	0.058	0.058	0.060	0.060	Honduras (20)
1.062	1.207	1.422	2.696	2.118	2.040	1.933	1.903	2.012	1.961	2.055	Mexique
0.043	0.018	0.019	0.027	0.024	0.025	0.026	0.027	0.027	0.028	0.032	Nicaragua (21)
0.069											Panama, sans la zone du canal
–	0.043	0.048	0.051	0.089	0.093	0.096	0.109	0.109	0.118	(e)0.126	Panama*(22)
3.191	1.557	2.616	2.252	2.032	2.453	2.833	2.739	3.015	3.175	3.262	Amérique du Sud
0.506	0.113	0.383	0.378	0.266	0.314	0.349	0.306	0.367	0.402	0.370	Argentine*
0.032	0.019	0.027	0.027	0.023	0.025	0.031	0.036	0.036	0.042	0.045	Bolivie (État plurinational de)
1.197	0.624	1.034	0.881	0.720	0.890	1.108	1.053	1.243	1.287	1.261	Brésil
0.278	0.220	0.304	0.278	0.304	0.331	0.381	0.337	0.385	0.409	0.429	Chili*
0.227	0.155	0.265	0.173	0.197	0.231	0.241	0.259	0.264	0.297	0.319	Colombie
0.108	0.052	0.080	0.056	0.095	0.098	0.114	0.119	0.134	0.132	0.136	Équateur
(e)0.000	(e)0.001	(e)0.001	(e)0.001	(e)0.001	(e)0.001	(e)0.000	0.000	0.001	0.001	0.001	Îles Falkland (Malvinas) (4)
0.019	0.009	0.010	0.009	0.007	0.007	0.008	0.009	0.009	0.010	0.011	Guyana*
0.029	0.037	0.060	0.034	0.034	0.041	0.055	0.055	0.065	0.067	0.062	Paraguay
0.123	0.073	0.145	0.111	0.116	0.143	0.182	0.172	0.195	0.205	0.230	Pérou*
0.024	0.013	0.011	0.008	0.010	0.007	0.008	0.011	0.009	0.009	0.010	Suriname
0.081	0.037	0.055	0.052	0.036	0.040	0.055	0.054	0.056	0.058	0.063	Uruguay
0.567	0.203	0.242	0.244	0.223	0.324	0.301	0.327	(e)0.253	(e)0.258	(e)0.326	Venezuela (Rép. bolivarienne du)
13.113	15.889	21.560	20.892	24.311	25.107	26.285	27.822	30.045	30.744	31.923	Économies en développement : Asie
4.184	7.432	10.901	11.193	13.105	13.448	13.447	14.702	16.391	16.721	17.191	Asie orientale
0.956	1.479	2.523	3.380	6.124	6.719	6.878	7.927	9.058	9.468	9.823	Chine
1.102	2.349	3.745	3.215	2.785	2.601	2.386	2.776	2.863	2.774	2.990	Chine (RAS de Hong Kong)
0.026	0.043	0.039	0.039	0.042	0.042	0.036	0.037	0.037	0.043	0.049	Chine (RAS de Macao)
0.947	1.519	1.978	2.113	1.694	1.541	1.460	1.374	1.630	1.528	1.461	Province chinoise de Taiwan
(e)0.058	(e)0.081	(e)0.026	(e)0.025	(e)0.025	(e)0.021	(e)0.022	(e)0.024	(e)0.023	(e)0.024	(e)0.026	Corée, Rép. populaire dém. de
1.069	1.936	2.581	2.411	2.424	2.508	2.643	2.546	2.759	2.848	2.807	Corée, République de (23)
0.026	0.026	0.008	0.009	0.011	0.015	0.022	0.017	0.021	0.036	0.036	Mongolie
1.839	1.590	1.414	1.424	2.198	2.420	2.837	3.000	3.289	3.483	3.557	Asie méridionale
0.040	0.026	0.007	0.018	0.023	0.020	0.018	0.026	0.033	0.035	(e)0.030	Afghanistan
0.125	0.100	0.128	0.133	0.129	0.131	0.145	0.172	0.180	0.197	0.184	Bangladesh
0.002	0.002	0.002	0.003	0.004	0.004	0.003	0.004	0.006	0.006	(e)0.006	Bhoutan
0.713	0.654	0.663	0.774	1.326	1.612	1.950	2.027	2.272	2.522	2.645	Inde (24)
0.587	0.508	0.265	0.209	0.372	0.316	0.349	0.400	0.424	0.335	0.308	Iran (Rép. islamique d')*
0.001	0.004	0.005	0.006	0.007	0.008	0.008	0.008	0.007	0.008	0.008	Maldives
0.016	0.017	0.025	0.024	0.021	0.022	0.022	0.035	0.033	0.031	0.033	Népal
0.256	0.204	0.219	0.163	0.235	0.229	0.257	0.250	0.245	0.239	0.239	Pakistan
0.098	0.074	0.099	0.094	0.082	0.079	0.085	0.079	0.088	0.110	0.104	Sri Lanka

Pour les sources et les notes, se reporter à la fin du tableau.

Region, country or territory	Exports (f.o.b.) - Exportations (f.a.b.) Percentage - En pourcentage										
	1980	1990	1995	2000	2005	2007	2008	2009	2010	2011	2012
South-Eastern Asia	*3.509*	*4.124*	*6.211*	*6.665*	*6.248*	*6.174*	*6.131*	*6.483*	*6.871*	*6.752*	*6.807*
Brunei Darussalam*	0.224	0.063	0.046	0.061	0.060	0.055	0.064	0.057	0.058	0.068	0.071
Cambodia (6)	0.001	0.002	0.017	0.022	0.029	0.029	0.029	0.033	0.034	(e)0.038	(e)0.045
Indonesia (...2002)	1.069	0.734	0.878	1.014							
Indonesia	–	–	–	–	0.829	0.842	0.865	0.953	1.034	1.096	1.024
Lao People's Dem. Rep.*	0.001	0.002	0.006	0.005	0.005	0.007	0.007	0.008	0.011	0.012	0.012
Malaysia (25)	0.632	0.843	1.428	1.523	1.343	1.257	1.236	1.254	1.300	1.245	1.236
Myanmar	0.023	0.009	0.016	0.025	0.036	0.045	0.043	0.053	0.057	0.050	0.048
Philippines	0.280	0.232	0.338	0.585	0.393	0.360	0.304	0.306	0.337	0.264	0.283
Singapore (26)	0.945	1.508	2.285	2.137	2.187	2.135	2.094	2.149	2.302	2.235	2.219
Thailand*	0.317	0.660	1.091	1.069	1.057	1.098	1.101	1.214	1.265	1.215	1.247
Timor-Leste (27)	–	–	–	–	0.000	0.000	0.000	0.000	0.000	0.000	(e)0.000
Viet Nam	0.016	0.069	0.105	0.224	0.309	0.346	0.388	0.455	0.473	0.529	0.622
Western Asia	*9.599*	*3.362*	*2.642*	*3.632*	*4.915*	*5.216*	*6.142*	*5.561*	*5.638*	*6.569*	*7.259*
Bahrain (6)	0.176	0.108	0.079	0.096	0.098	0.097	0.107	0.095	0.098	0.107	0.107
Iraq*	1.286	0.295	0.038	0.291	0.226	0.294	0.379	0.334	0.343	(e)0.455	(e)0.513
Jordan	0.028	0.030	0.034	0.029	0.041	0.041	0.049	0.051	0.046	0.044	0.043
Kuwait*	0.959	0.201	0.247	0.301	0.427	0.447	0.542	0.430	0.458	0.558	0.644
Lebanon (28)	0.047	0.014	0.013	0.011	0.022	0.025	0.028	0.033	0.033	0.031	0.031
Oman	0.183	0.158	0.117	0.176	0.178	0.176	0.234	0.220	0.239	0.257	0.283
Qatar*	0.277	0.101	0.067	0.180	0.245	0.300	0.417	0.382	0.489	0.624	0.723
Saudi Arabia*(29)	5.323	1.271	0.967	1.203	1.721	1.664	1.941	1.532	1.643	1.991	2.110
State of Palestine	..	..	0.008	0.006	0.003	0.004	0.003	0.004	0.004	0.004	(e)0.005
Syrian Arab Republic*	0.103	0.120	0.069	0.072	0.083	0.082	0.095	0.086	0.084	(e)0.055	(e)0.022
Turkey*	0.142	0.371	0.417	0.431	0.700	0.765	0.818	0.814	0.745	0.736	0.829
United Arab Emirates	(e)1.072	0.674	0.548	0.773	1.117	1.274	1.482	(e)1.529	(e)1.400	(e)1.648	(e)1.902
Yemen, Arab Republic	0.001										
Yemen, Democratic	0.003										
Yemen*	–	0.020	0.038	0.063	0.053	0.045	0.047	0.050	(e)0.055	(e)0.059	(e)0.047
Developing economies: Oceania	*0.110*	*0.079*	*0.099*	*0.080*	*0.064*	*0.064*	*0.059*	*0.056*	*0.059*	*0.059*	*0.055*
American Samoa*(30)	0.006	0.009	0.005	0.005	0.004	(e)0.003	(e)0.004	(e)0.004	(e)0.002	(e)0.002	(e)0.002
Cook Islands	0.000	0.000	0.000	0.000	0.000	0.000	0.000	0.000	0.000	0.000	(e)0.000
Fiji	0.018	0.014	0.012	0.009	0.007	0.005	0.006	0.005	0.006	0.006	0.007
French Polynesia*	0.001	0.003	0.004	0.003	0.002	0.001	0.001	0.001	0.001	0.001	0.001
Guam (4)	0.003	(e)0.002	0.002	0.001	0.000	0.001	0.001	0.000	0.000	0.000	0.000
Kiribati	0.000	0.000	0.000	0.000	0.000	0.000	(e)0.000	0.000	0.000	0.000	0.000
Marshall Islands	–	0.000	0.000	0.000	0.000	0.000	0.000	0.000	0.000	(e)0.000	(e)0.000
Micronesia (Federated States of)	–	0.000	0.000	0.000	0.000	0.000	0.000	0.000	(e)0.000	(e)0.000	(e)0.000
Nauru (4)	0.003	0.002	(e)0.001	(e)0.000	(e)0.000	(e)0.000	(e)0.001	0.000	0.000	0.000	0.000
New Caledonia*	0.020	0.013	0.011	0.009	0.010	0.015	0.008	0.008	0.010	0.009	0.007
Niue	0.000	0.000	0.000	0.000	0.000	0.000	0.000	(e)0.000	(e)0.000	(e)0.000	(e)0.000
Northern Mariana Islands (4)	–	..	(e)0.008	(e)0.016	(e)0.007	(e)0.002	(e)0.001	(e)0.000	(e)0.000	(e)0.000	(e)0.000
Palau (4)	–	..	(e)0.000	0.000	0.000	(e)0.000	(e)0.000	(e)0.000	(e)0.000	(e)0.000	(e)0.000
Papua New Guinea	0.050	0.033	0.051	0.032	0.031	0.033	0.035	0.035	0.038	0.038	0.033
Samoa (28)	0.001	0.000	0.000	0.001	0.001	0.001	0.000	0.000	0.000	0.000	0.000
Solomon Islands*	0.004	0.002	0.003	0.001	0.001	0.001	0.001	0.001	0.001	0.002	0.003
Tokelau (4)	..	..	..	..	(e)0.000	(e)0.000	(e)0.000	(e)0.000	(e)0.000	(e)0.000	(e)0.000
Tonga	0.000	0.000	0.000	0.000	0.000	0.000	0.000	0.000	0.000	0.000	0.000
Tuvalu	0.000	0.000	0.000	0.000	0.000	0.000	(e)0.000	(e)0.000	(e)0.000	(e)0.000	(e)0.000
Vanuatu	0.002	0.001	0.001	0.000	0.000	0.000	0.000	0.000	0.000	0.000	0.000
Wallis and Futuna Islands (4)	..	..	..	(e)0.000	(e)0.000	(e)0.000	(e)0.000	(e)0.000	(e)0.000	(e)0.000	(e)0.000
Transition economies	*4.171*	*3.387*	*2.322*	*2.388*	*3.454*	*3.931*	*4.575*	*3.802*	*4.063*	*4.516*	*4.568*
Albania	..	0.007	0.004	0.004	0.006	0.008	0.008	0.009	0.010	0.011	0.011
Armenia*	–	–	0.005	0.005	0.009	0.008	0.007	0.006	0.007	0.007	0.008
Azerbaijan (31)	–	–	0.012	0.027	0.073	0.152	0.189	0.168	0.173	0.188	0.177
Belarus	–	–	0.093	0.114	0.152	0.173	0.202	0.170	0.165	0.226	0.250
Bosnia and Herzegovina*(32)	–	–	(e)0.003	0.017	0.023	0.030	0.031	0.031	0.031	0.032	0.028
Croatia*	–	–	0.087	0.069	0.084	0.088	0.087	0.083	0.077	0.073	0.067
Georgia (33)	–	–	0.003	0.005	0.008	0.009	0.009	0.009	0.011	0.012	0.013
Kazakhstan*(34)	–	–	0.101	0.137	0.265	0.341	0.441	0.344	0.392	0.478	0.501
Kyrgyzstan	–	–	0.008	0.008	0.006	0.009	0.011	0.013	0.012	0.011	0.010
Montenegro	–	–	–	–	–	–	0.004	0.003	0.003	0.003	0.003
Republic of Moldova	–	–	0.014	0.007	0.010	0.010	0.010	0.010	0.010	0.012	0.012
Russian Federation (35)	–	–	1.567	1.629	2.322	2.528	2.921	2.417	2.621	2.849	2.876
Serbia and Montenegro*	–	–	0.030	0.027	(e)0.048	0.069					
Serbia	–	–	–	–	–	–	0.068	0.066	0.064	0.064	0.062
SFR of Yugoslavia	0.438	0.409									
Tajikistan (33)	–	–	0.014	0.012	0.009	0.010	0.009	0.008	0.008	0.007	0.007
TFYR of Macedonia*	–	–	0.023	0.021	0.019	0.024	0.025	0.022	0.022	0.024	0.022

For sources and notes, see end of table.

14

Imports (c.i.f.) - Importations (c.a.f.) Percentage - En pourcentage											Régions, pays ou territoires
1980	1990	1995	2000	2005	2007	2008	2009	2010	2011	2012	
3.147	*4.500*	*6.787*	*5.718*	*5.597*	*5.453*	*5.706*	*5.732*	*6.185*	*6.263*	*6.591*	**Asie du Sud-Est**
0.027	0.028	0.040	0.017	0.014	0.015	0.016	0.019	0.017	0.020	0.019	Brunéi Darussalam*
0.009	0.005	0.023	0.029	0.036	0.038	0.040	0.046	0.044	(e)0.051	(e)0.059	Cambodge (6)
0.519	0.603	0.776	0.655								Indonésie (...2002)
–	–	–	–	0.703	0.654	0.775	0.739	0.878	0.957	1.028	Indonésie
0.004	0.005	0.011	0.008	0.008	0.007	0.009	0.012	0.013	0.013	0.013	Rép. dém. populaire lao*
0.517	0.811	1.484	1.231	1.064	1.033	0.953	0.976	1.068	1.018	1.062	Malaisie (25)
0.017	0.007	0.025	0.036	0.018	0.023	0.026	0.034	0.031	0.049	0.050	Myanmar
0.397	0.360	0.541	0.556	0.459	0.408	0.367	0.362	0.379	0.346	0.353	Philippines
1.151	1.688	2.378	2.021	1.856	1.849	1.942	1.937	2.016	1.986	2.051	Singapour (26)
0.442	0.916	1.352	0.930	1.097	0.984	1.088	1.054	1.187	1.242	1.337	Thaïlande*
				0.001	0.001	0.002	0.002	0.002	0.002	(e)0.002	Timor-Leste (27)
0.063	0.076	0.156	0.235	0.341	0.440	0.490	0.551	0.550	0.580	0.615	Viet Nam
3.943	*2.367*	*2.458*	*2.558*	*3.412*	*3.787*	*4.295*	*4.388*	*4.180*	*4.276*	*4.585*	**Asie occidentale**
0.167	0.103	0.071	0.070	0.087	0.081	(e)0.091	(e)0.080	(e)0.080	(e)0.069	(e)0.075	Bahreïn (6)
0.417	0.181	0.055	0.165	0.218	0.151	(e)0.200	0.303	0.285	(e)0.266	(e)0.308	Iraq*
0.115	0.072	0.071	0.069	0.097	0.096	0.103	0.112	0.101	0.103	0.112	Jordanie
0.313	0.110	0.149	0.108	0.147	0.150	0.151	0.157	0.147	0.138	0.140	Koweït*
0.175	0.070	0.139	0.094	0.089	0.086	0.102	0.131	0.120	0.113	0.119	Liban (28)
0.083	0.078	0.084	0.077	0.083	0.113	0.141	0.141	0.130	0.130	(e)0.154	Oman
0.068	0.047	0.065	0.049	0.093	0.165	0.169	0.196	0.151	0.162	(e)0.185	Qatar*
1.446	0.667	0.537	0.454	0.552	0.634	0.699	0.753	0.693	0.715	0.840	Arabie saoudite*(29)
..	..	0.032	0.036	0.025	0.022	0.022	0.028	0.026	0.024	(e)0.028	État de Palestine
0.198	0.067	0.090	0.057	0.101	0.103	0.110	0.122	0.114	(e)0.091	(e)0.039	République arabe syrienne*
0.379	0.618	0.682	0.819	1.084	1.195	1.226	1.111	1.204	1.308	1.278	Turquie*
0.419	0.310	0.454	0.526	0.785	(e)0.931	1.216	(e)1.182	(e)1.070	(e)1.102	(e)1.242	Émirats arabes unis
0.089											Yémen, République arabe du
0.073	–	–	–	–	–	–	–	–	–	–	Yémen, Démocratique
–	0.044	0.030	0.035	0.050	0.060	0.064	0.072	0.060	0.054	(e)0.065	Yémen*
0.171	*0.141*	*0.118*	*0.093*	*0.091*	*0.089*	*0.088*	*0.095*	*0.092*	*0.089*	*0.088*	**Économies en développement : Océanie**
0.005	0.010	0.008	0.008	0.005	(e)0.005	(e)0.004	(e)0.005	(e)0.004	(e)0.004	(e)0.004	Samoa américaines*(30)
0.001	0.001	0.001	0.001	0.001	0.001	0.001	0.001	0.001	0.001	(e)0.001	Îles Cook
0.027	0.021	0.017	0.012	0.015	0.013	0.014	0.011	0.012	0.012	0.012	Fidji
0.026	0.026	0.019	0.015	0.016	0.013	0.013	0.014	0.011	0.010	0.009	Polynésie française*
0.019	(e)0.013	(e)0.008	(e)0.006	0.005	0.005	0.004	0.007	0.006	0.006	0.006	Guam (4)
0.001	0.001	0.001	0.001	0.001	0.000	(e)0.000	0.001	0.000	0.000	0.001	Kiribati
–	0.002	0.001	0.001	(e)0.001	0.001	(e)0.001	(e)0.001	(e)0.001	(e)0.001	(e)0.001	Îles Marshall
–	0.002	0.002	0.002	0.001	0.001	0.001	0.001	(e)0.001	(e)0.001	(e)0.001	Micronésie (États fédérés de)
0.001	0.001	(e)0.001	(e)0.000	(e)0.000	0.000	(e)0.001	0.000	0.000	0.000	0.000	Nauru (4)
0.022	0.024	0.018	0.014	0.016	0.020	0.020	0.020	0.021	0.020	0.018	Nouvelle-Calédonie*
0.000	0.000	(e)0.000	0.000	(e)0.000	0.000	0.000	0.000	(e)0.000	(e)0.000	(e)0.000	Nioué
–	..	(e)0.005	(e)0.009	(e)0.005	(e)0.002	(e)0.001	(e)0.001	(e)0.001	(e)0.000	(e)0.000	Îles Mariannes du Nord (4)
–	..	(e)0.001	0.002	0.001	(e)0.001	(e)0.001	(e)0.001	(e)0.001	(e)0.001	(e)0.001	Palaos (4)
0.056	0.031	0.028	0.017	0.016	0.021	(e)0.021	(e)0.025	(e)0.026	(e)0.026	(e)0.027	Papouasie-Nouvelle-Guinée
0.003	0.002	0.002	0.001	0.002	0.002	0.002	0.002	0.002	0.002	0.002	Samoa (28)
0.004	0.003	0.003	0.001	0.002	0.002	0.002	0.002	0.002	0.003	(e)0.003	Îles Salomon*
..	..	..	0.000	(e)0.000	(e)0.000	(e)0.000	(e)0.000	(e)0.000	(e)0.000	(e)0.000	Tokélaou (4)
0.002	0.002	0.001	0.001	0.001	0.001	0.001	0.001	0.001	0.001	0.001	Tonga
0.000	0.000	0.000	0.000	0.000	0.000	0.000	(e)0.000	(e)0.000	(e)0.000	(e)0.000	Tuvalu
0.003	0.003	0.002	0.001	0.001	0.002	0.002	0.002	0.002	0.002	0.002	Vanuatu
..	..	..	0.001	0.000	(e)0.000	(e)0.000	(e)0.000	(e)0.000	(e)0.000	(e)0.000	Îles Wallis-et-Futuna (4)
4.007	*3.885*	*2.051*	*1.564*	*2.401*	*3.132*	*3.542*	*3.083*	*3.072*	*3.312*	*3.417*	**Économies en transition**
..	0.011	0.014	0.016	0.024	0.029	0.032	0.036	0.029	0.029	0.026	Albanie
–	–	0.013	0.013	0.017	0.023	0.027	0.026	0.024	0.023	0.023	Arménie*
–	–	0.013	0.018	0.040	0.042	0.046	0.051	0.044	0.055	0.056	Azerbaïdjan (31)
–	–	0.106	0.130	0.155	0.202	0.239	0.225	0.226	0.249	0.251	Bélarus
–	–	(e)0.021	0.047	0.066	0.068	0.074	0.069	0.060	0.060	0.054	Bosnie-Herzégovine*(32)
–	–	0.140	0.118	0.172	0.182	0.187	0.167	0.130	0.123	0.112	Croatie*
–	–	0.007	0.011	0.023	0.037	0.038	0.035	0.034	0.038	0.042	Géorgie (33)
–	–	0.073	0.076	0.161	0.230	0.230	0.224	0.202	0.201	0.241	Kazakhstan*(34)
–	–	0.010	0.008	0.010	0.020	0.025	0.024	0.021	0.023	0.029	Kirghizistan
–	–					0.023	0.018	0.014	0.014	0.013	Monténégro
–	–	0.016	0.012	0.021	0.026	0.030	0.026	0.025	0.028	0.028	République de Moldova
–	–	1.164	0.741	1.164	1.571	1.772	1.512	1.613	1.759	1.812	Fédération de Russie (35)
–	–	0.051	0.056	(e)0.108	0.153						Serbie-et-Monténégro*
–	–					0.148	0.126	0.109	0.108	0.103	Serbie
0.723	0.523	–	–	–	–	–	–	–	–	–	RSF de Yougoslavie
–	–	0.015	0.010	0.012	0.017	0.020	0.020	0.017	0.017	0.020	Tadjikistan (33)
–	–	0.033	0.031	0.030	0.037	0.042	0.040	0.036	0.038	0.035	LERY de Macédoine*

Pour les sources et les notes, se reporter à la fin du tableau.

Region, country or territory	Exports (f.o.b.) - Exportations (f.a.b.) Percentage - En pourcentage										
	1980	1990	1995	2000	2005	2007	2008	2009	2010	2011	2012
Turkmenistan (33)	–	–	0.036	0.039	0.047	0.064	0.074	(e)0.040	(e)0.043	(e)0.071	(e)0.090
Ukraine (33)	–	–	0.254	0.226	0.326	0.352	0.415	0.317	0.337	0.374	0.372
USSR	3.733	(e)2.971	–	–	–	–	–	–	–	–	–
Uzbekistan (33)	–	–	0.066	0.044	0.045	0.057	0.064	0.086	0.077	0.072	0.059
Developed economies: America	**14.322**	**14.926**	**15.021**	**16.419**	**12.020**	**11.195**	**10.804**	**10.932**	**10.903**	**10.551**	**10.874**
Bermuda (6)	0.002	0.002	0.001	0.001	0.000	0.000	0.000	0.000	0.000	0.000	0.000
Canada	3.305	3.651	3.714	4.289	3.433	3.001	2.827	2.518	2.535	2.468	2.471
Greenland	0.009	0.013	0.007	0.004	0.004	0.003	0.003	0.003	0.002	0.003	0.003
Saint Pierre and Miquelon (4)	0.000	0.001	(e)0.000	(e)0.000	(e)0.000	(e)0.000	(e)0.000	(e)0.000	(e)0.000	(e)0.000	(e)0.000
United States (36)	11.006	11.260	11.299	12.125	8.582	8.191	7.974	8.411	8.365	8.080	8.400
Developed economies: Asia	**6.635**	**8.573**	**8.930**	**7.919**	**6.074**	**5.482**	**5.220**	**5.007**	**5.419**	**4.863**	**4.683**
Israel*	0.270	0.346	0.368	0.487	0.407	0.386	0.380	0.382	0.382	0.370	0.343
Japan	6.365	8.227	8.562	7.432	5.666	5.096	4.840	4.625	5.037	4.493	4.340
Developed economies: Europe	**43.889**	**47.593**	**44.732**	**40.190**	**40.996**	**40.386**	**39.035**	**38.964**	**35.973**	**35.361**	**33.673**
Andorra*	..	..	0.001	0.001	0.001	0.001	0.001	0.001	0.000	0.000	(e)0.001
Austria*	0.853	1.177	1.116	1.047	1.192	1.167	1.123	1.091	0.998	0.968	0.904
Belgium*	3.149	3.367	3.445	2.914	3.185	3.074	2.922	2.948	2.668	2.599	2.427
Bulgaria*	0.507	0.144	0.103	0.075	0.112	0.132	0.138	0.130	0.135	0.154	0.145
Cyprus*	0.026	0.027	0.024	0.015	0.014	0.010	0.010	0.010	0.009	0.010	0.009
Czechoslovakia (37)	0.729	0.340									
Czech Republic*(38)	–	–	0.419	0.451	0.744	0.874	0.909	0.900	0.870	0.889	0.851
Denmark*(39)	0.817	1.055	0.984	0.793	0.811	0.736	0.724	0.749	0.631	0.611	0.574
Estonia*(33)	–	–	0.036	0.059	0.073	0.079	0.077	0.072	0.076	0.091	0.088
Faeroe Islands	0.009	0.012	0.007	0.007	0.006	0.005	0.005	0.006	0.005	0.006	0.005
Finland*	0.690	0.760	0.783	0.713	0.624	0.642	0.597	0.501	0.455	0.432	0.397
France*	5.681	6.215	5.834	5.068	4.414	3.992	3.817	3.861	3.427	3.256	3.092
Germany, Democratic Republic of	0.907										
Germany, Federal Republic of	9.411	–	–	–	–	–	–	–	–	–	–
Germany*	–	12.047	10.116	8.536	9.247	9.425	8.957	8.921	8.237	8.046	7.646
Gibraltar (40)	0.000	0.002	0.002	0.002	(e)0.002	(e)0.002	(e)0.002	0.002	0.002	0.001	0.001
Greece*	0.251	0.232	0.214	0.182	0.165	0.168	0.163	0.163	0.142	0.185	0.193
Hungary*(41)	0.420	(e)0.286	0.249	0.437	0.599	0.681	0.672	0.661	0.625	0.613	0.565
Iceland	0.045	0.046	0.035	0.029	0.029	0.034	0.033	0.032	0.030	0.029	0.028
Ireland*	0.410	0.679	0.864	1.197	1.044	0.867	0.779	0.923	0.762	0.686	0.637
Italy*	3.811	4.872	4.517	3.730	3.554	3.566	3.361	3.241	2.927	2.856	2.721
Latvia*	–	–	0.025	0.029	0.049	0.059	0.063	0.061	0.062	0.072	0.077
Lithuania*(33)	–	–	0.052	0.055	0.112	0.122	0.146	0.131	0.136	0.153	0.161
Luxembourg*	0.147	0.180	0.150	0.130	0.179	0.160	0.159	0.170	0.129	0.119	0.106
Malta	0.024	0.032	0.037	0.038	0.023	0.022	0.022	0.023	0.023	0.024	0.023
Netherlands*	4.145	3.770	3.926	3.606	3.870	3.929	3.951	3.966	3.757	3.641	3.563
Norway	0.905	0.974	0.811	0.931	0.988	0.973	1.064	0.930	0.855	0.875	0.875
Poland*	0.830	(e)0.410	0.442	0.492	0.852	1.000	1.056	1.087	1.045	1.030	0.997
Portugal*	0.226	0.470	0.440	0.377	0.363	0.375	0.354	0.352	0.323	0.326	0.317
Romania*	0.556	(e)0.142	0.153	0.161	0.264	0.289	0.307	0.323	0.324	0.344	0.314
Slovakia*	–	–	0.166	0.183	0.304	0.417	0.441	0.447	0.423	0.436	0.443
Slovenia*	–	–	0.161	0.136	0.183	0.215	0.211	0.209	0.191	0.190	0.175
Spain*	1.011	1.588	1.891	1.783	1.835	1.807	1.743	1.811	1.665	1.673	1.597
Sweden*	1.508	1.646	1.555	1.348	1.247	1.204	1.135	1.042	1.037	1.021	0.937
Switzerland*	1.446	1.825	1.578	1.248	1.247	1.228	1.243	1.374	1.280	1.282	1.228
United Kingdom*	5.374	5.295	4.598	4.415	3.662	3.132	2.848	2.827	2.722	2.743	2.578
Developed economies: Oceania	**1.335**	**1.406**	**1.290**	**1.206**	**1.217**	**1.201**	**1.349**	**1.428**	**1.597**	**1.681**	**1.598**
Australia	1.071	1.137	1.026	0.990	1.010	1.008	1.160	1.229	1.391	1.476	1.395
New Zealand	0.265	0.269	0.264	0.215	0.207	0.192	0.189	0.199	0.205	0.206	0.203

For sources and notes, see next page.

1.1.1 Exportations et importations des pays
et des régions géographiques
Part

1

Imports (c.i.f.) - Importations (c.a.f.) Percentage - En pourcentage											Régions, pays ou territoires
1980	1990	1995	2000	2005	2007	2008	2009	2010	2011	2012	
–	–	0.026	0.027	0.027	0.025	(e)0.034	(e)0.054	(e)0.037	(e)0.041	(e)0.053	Turkménistan (33)
–	–	0.296	0.210	0.335	0.426	0.519	0.358	0.395	0.449	0.457	Ukraine (33)
3.285	3.351										URSS
–	–	0.053	0.041	0.034	0.045	0.056	0.071	0.056	0.057	0.061	Ouzbékistan (33)
15.349	**17.779**	**17.955**	**22.611**	**19.084**	**16.955**	**15.733**	**15.266**	**15.400**	**14.833**	**15.192**	**Économies développées : Amérique**
0.015	0.016	0.011	0.011	0.009	0.008	0.007	0.008	0.006	0.005	0.005	Bermudes (6)
2.998	3.416	3.210	3.677	2.992	2.742	2.545	2.600	2.612	2.517	2.565	Canada
0.016	0.012	0.008	0.005	0.005	0.005	0.005	0.006	0.005	0.005	0.005	Groenland
0.000	0.002	(e)0.001	(e)0.001	(e)0.001	(e)0.001	(e)0.001	(e)0.002	(e)0.001	(e)0.001	(e)0.001	Saint-Pierre-et-Miquelon (4)
12.320	14.331	14.725	18.917	16.077	14.198	13.175	12.651	12.775	12.305	12.616	États-Unis (36)
7.243	**6.990**	**6.981**	**6.267**	**5.224**	**4.788**	**5.042**	**4.738**	**4.900**	**5.057**	**5.192**	**Économies développées : Asie**
0.469	0.466	0.565	0.566	0.437	0.415	0.411	0.388	0.397	0.412	0.407	Israël*
6.774	6.525	6.416	5.701	4.787	4.373	4.631	4.350	4.503	4.645	4.785	Japon
48.220	**47.804**	**42.789**	**39.489**	**40.116**	**40.581**	**39.333**	**38.781**	**36.087**	**35.416**	**33.142**	**Économies développées : Europe**
..	..	0.020	0.015	0.017	0.013	0.012	0.012	0.010	0.009	(e)0.009	Andorre*
1.172	1.361	1.265	1.085	1.181	1.146	1.119	1.127	1.032	1.040	0.964	Autriche*
3.445	3.318	3.151	2.660	2.957	2.892	2.832	2.785	2.538	2.534	2.362	Belgique*
0.464	0.141	0.108	0.098	0.169	0.211	0.224	0.185	0.166	0.177	0.177	Bulgarie*
0.058	0.071	0.071	0.058	0.059	0.061	0.065	0.062	0.056	0.047	0.039	Chypre*
0.728	0.345										Tchécoslovaquie (37)
–	–	0.479	0.480	0.710	0.830	0.863	0.828	0.822	0.826	0.760	République tchèque*(38)
0.927	0.924	0.878	0.683	0.701	0.689	0.664	0.655	0.539	0.520	0.497	Danemark*(39)
–	–	0.049	0.076	0.095	0.110	0.097	0.080	0.080	0.096	0.096	Estonie*(33)
0.011	0.009	0.006	0.008	0.007	0.007	0.006	0.006	0.005	0.005	0.006	Îles Féroé
0.750	0.748	0.563	0.516	0.545	0.574	0.557	0.480	0.446	0.458	0.412	Finlande*
6.593	6.675	5.668	5.079	4.678	4.433	4.353	4.420	3.964	3.910	3.640	France*
0.915	–	–	–	–	–	–	–	–	–	–	Allemagne, Rép. dém. d'
9.013	–	–	–	–	–	–	–	–	–	–	Allemagne, Rép. fédérale d'
–	9.860	8.862	7.450	7.210	7.414	7.197	7.300	6.843	6.815	6.305	Allemagne*
0.005	0.010	0.008	0.007	(e)0.005	(e)0.006	(e)0.005	0.006	0.005	0.005	0.005	Gibraltar (40)
0.506	0.548	0.495	0.502	0.505	0.552	0.562	0.547	0.414	0.366	0.341	Grèce*
0.441	(e)0.287	0.295	0.483	0.618	0.672	0.662	0.613	0.572	0.556	0.515	Hongrie*(41)
0.048	0.047	0.034	0.039	0.046	0.047	0.038	0.028	0.025	0.026	0.026	Islande
0.535	0.573	0.618	0.765	0.636	0.589	0.510	0.494	0.391	0.362	0.339	Irlande*
4.830	5.044	3.935	3.587	3.570	3.596	3.412	3.271	3.160	3.035	2.629	Italie*
–	–	0.035	0.048	0.081	0.108	0.098	0.077	0.076	0.088	0.093	Lettonie*
–	–	0.070	0.078	0.144	0.172	0.189	0.144	0.152	0.173	0.174	Lituanie*(33)
0.173	0.211	0.186	0.169	0.203	0.194	0.195	0.200	0.163	0.159	0.149	Luxembourg*
0.045	0.054	0.056	0.051	0.034	0.033	0.032	0.035	0.033	0.034	0.036	Malte
4.239	3.506	3.538	3.271	3.376	3.462	3.528	3.492	3.350	3.253	3.194	Pays-Bas*
0.811	0.755	0.630	0.517	0.515	0.564	0.548	0.544	0.502	0.493	0.472	Norvège
0.917	(e)0.321	0.555	0.737	0.943	1.165	1.268	1.178	1.155	1.144	1.059	Pologne*
0.446	0.700	0.623	0.599	0.568	0.577	0.573	0.565	0.504	0.448	0.390	Portugal*
0.633	(e)0.211	0.196	0.198	0.376	0.494	0.510	0.428	0.403	0.415	0.379	Roumanie*
–	–	0.168	0.192	0.322	0.426	0.449	0.439	0.422	0.434	0.422	Slovaquie*
–	–	0.181	0.152	0.189	0.222	0.225	0.209	0.195	0.193	0.173	Slovénie*
1.634	2.427	2.169	2.340	2.680	2.736	2.555	2.311	2.122	2.045	1.808	Espagne*
1.603	1.504	1.242	1.092	1.036	1.077	1.023	0.945	0.966	0.961	0.878	Suède*
1.742	1.932	1.531	1.240	1.174	1.133	1.115	1.224	1.144	1.131	1.068	Suisse*
5.539	6.221	5.105	5.216	4.766	4.378	3.846	4.091	3.835	3.659	3.727	Royaume-Uni*
1.336	**1.427**	**1.437**	**1.288**	**1.406**	**1.379**	**1.425**	**1.506**	**1.507**	**1.525**	**1.616**	**Économies développées : Océanie**
1.074	1.164	1.171	1.074	1.162	1.162	1.216	1.304	1.308	1.323	1.410	Australie
0.262	0.263	0.267	0.214	0.243	0.217	0.209	0.202	0.199	0.202	0.207	Nouvelle-Zélande

Pour les sources et les notes, se reporter à la page suivante.

Sources:

UNCTAD secretariat calculations, based on:

- UN DESA Statistics Division, *Yearbook of International Trade Statistics*
- UN DESA Statistics Division, *Monthly Bulletin of Statistics*
- UN DESA Statistics Division, *UN COMTRADE*
- IMF, *International Financial Statistics*
- IMF, *Direction of Trade Statistics*
- IMF, *Balance of Payments Statistics*
  WTO, *Statistics database*
- Eurostat, *Comext*
- World Bank, *World Development Indicators*
- OECD, *OECD.Stat Extracts*
- OPEC, *Annual Statistical Bulletin*
- Economist Intelligence Unit, *Country Data*
- Other international and national sources

Notes:

(*)   Special Trade System.

(1)   Excluding exports of gold.

(2)   From 1996 onward, imports f.o.b.

(3)   From 2011 onwards, commercial mining is included.

(4)   Estimates based on UN *Comtrade* mirror structure.

(5)   Prior to 2008, special trade.

(6)   Imports f.o.b.

(7)   Trade with other member countries of CEMAC is excluded. Imports f.o.b.

(8)   Trade with other member countries of CEMAC is excluded.

(9)   Prior to 1995, data refer to fiscal year ending June.

(10) Prior to 1974, special trade.

(11) Excluding re-exports (oil for bunkering).

(12) Prior to 2009, re-exports are excluded.

(13) Prior to 2005, special trade.

(14) Prior to 1986, included in Netherlands Antilles. Including exports and imports of crude oil and oil products. Prior to 2000, free zone trade is excluded. Imports f.o.b.

(15) From 1990 onwards, trade statistics exclude certain oil and chemical products. Imports f.o.b.

(16) Prior to 1993, excluding free trade processing zones. Imports f.o.b.

(17) Prior to 1986, including Aruba.

(18) Prior to 1992, excluding free trade processing zones.

(19) Prior to 2002, special trade.

(20) From 1990 onward, including goods for processing. Imports f.o.b.

(21) Excluding free trade processing zones.

(22) Prior to 2005, excluding customs free zones.

(23) Excluding imports of goods financed through foreign aid.

(24) Excluding military goods, fissionable materials, bunkers, ships and aircraft.

(25) Inter-trade between the States of Malaysia included. From 1965 onwards, excluding military imports and offshore installations of petroleum industry.

(26) Including trans-shipments to and from Peninsular Malaysia.

(27) Excluding exports of oil and gas.

(28) Prior to 2001, special trade.

(29) Excluding defense imports.

(30) Data refer to fiscal year ending September.

(31) Excluding military goods, precious metals and goods procured in foreign ports.

(32) Prior to 1998, data refer to the Federation of Bosnia and Herzegovina only. The other entity of Bosnia and Herzegovina, Republika Srpska, is not included.

(33) Prior to 1994, covers only trade with countries outside the CIS.

(34) Prior to 1994, covers only trade with countries outside the CIS. As of 2011, adjusted to include bilateral trade with Russian Federation.

(35) Prior to 1994, excluding trade with independent states which succeeded from the former USSR.

(36) Prior to 1975, excludes non-monetary gold.

(37) From 1985 onwards, data are not comparable to those shown for prior periods due to revisions of the koruna-to-US dollar exchange rate.

(38) From 1995 onward, including goods for processing.

(39) Prior to 1988, excluding ships.

(40) Excluding petroleum products. Estimates based on UN *Comtrade* mirror structure.

(41) Prior to 1996, excluding customs free zones.

Sources :

Calculs du secrétariat de la CNUCED, basés sur :

- ONU DAES Division de statistique, *Annuaire statistique du commerce international*
- ONU DAES Division de statistique, *Bulletin mensuel de statistique*
- ONU DAES Division de statistique, *ONU COMTRADE*
- FMI, *Statistiques financières internationales*
- FMI, *Direction of Trade Statistics*
- FMI, *Statistiques de la balance des paiements*
- OMC, *Base de données statistiques*
- Eurostat, *Comext*
- Banque mondiale, *Indicateurs du développement dans le monde*
- OCDE, *OECD.Stat Extracts*
- OPEP, *Bulletin statistique annuel*
- Economist Intelligence Unit, *Country Data*
- Autres sources internationales et nationales

Notes :

(*) Système du commerce spécial.

(1) Non-compris les exportations d'or.

(2) À partir de 1996, importations f.a.b.

(3) À partir de 2011, l'exploitation minière commerciale est incluse.

(4) Estimations basées sur la structure des données miroirs de UN *Comtrade*.

(5) Avant 2008, commerce spécial.

(6) Importations f.a.b.

(7) Non-compris le commerce avec les autres pays membres de la CEMAC. Importations f.a.b.

(8) Non-compris le commerce avec les autres pays membres de la CEMAC.

(9) Avant 1995, les données se rapportent à l'exercice budgétaire finissant juin.

(10) Avant 1974, commerce spécial.

(11) Non-compris les réexportations (huile pour mise en soute).

(12) Avant 2009, non-compris les réexportations.

(13) Avant 2005, commerce spécial.

(14) Avant 1986 compris dans Antilles néerlandaises. Les données comprennent les exportations et importations de pétrole brut et produits dérivés. Avant 2000, non-compris les zones franches douanières. Importations f.a.b.

(15) À partir de 1990, certains produits pétroliers et chimiques ne sont plus inclus dans les statistiques du commerce. Importations f.a.b.

(16) Avant 1993, non-compris les zones franches douanières. Importations f.a.b.

(17) Avant 1986, y compris Aruba.

(18) Avant 1992, non-compris les zones franches douanières.

(19) Avant 2002, commerce spécial.

(20) À partir de 1990, y compris les biens destinés à subir des transformations. Importations f.a.b.

(21) Non-compris les zones franches douanières.

(22) Avant 2005, non-compris les zones franches douanières.

(23) Non-compris les biens d'importation financés par l'aide à l'étranger.

(24) Non-compris les biens à usage militaire, le matériel fissile, le combustible de soute et l'avitaillement des navires et aéronefs.

(25) Y compris le commerce entre les États de la Malaisie. Non-compris les importations militaires et l'installation près des côtes de l'industrie pétrolière.

(26) Y compris les transbordements vers et en provenance de la Malaisie péninsulaire.

(27) Non-compris les exportations de pétrole et de gaz.

(28) Avant 2001, commerce spécial.

(29) Non-compris les importations de la défense.

(30) Les données se rapportent à l'exercice budgétaire finissant septembre.

(31) Non-compris les biens à usage militaire, les métaux précieux et les biens fournis dans les ports étrangers.

(32) Avant 1998, les données se réfèrent uniquement à la Fédération de la Bosnie-Herzégovine. L'autre entité de la Bosnie-Herzégovine, Republika Srpska, n'est pas incluse.

(33) Avant 1994, concerne seulement le commerce avec les pays extérieurs à la CEI.

(34) Avant 1994, concerne seulement le commerce avec les pays extérieurs à la CEI. A partir de 2011, y compris le commerce bilatéral avec la Fédération de Russie.

(35) Avant 1994, non-compris le commerce avec les républiques indépendantes de l'ancienne URSS.

(36) Avant 1975, non-compris l'or industriel.

(37) À partir de 1985, les chiffres ne sont pas comparables à ceux des années antérieures à cause des révisions du taux de change de la couronne par rapport au dollar des États-Unis.

(38) À partir de 1995, y compris les biens destinés à subir des transformations.

(39) Avant 1988, non-compris les navires.

(40) Non-compris les produits pétroliers. Estimations basées sur la structure des données miroirs de UN *Comtrade*.

(41) Avant 1996, non-compris les zones franches douanières.

Economic grouping	Exports (f.o.b.) - Exportations (f.a.b.) Millions of dollars							
	1980	1990	2000	2005	2009	2010	2011	2012
DEVELOPING ECONOMIES	607 605	842 977	2 055 742	3 804 984	5 005 193	6 425 928	7 882 841	8 208 324
Developing economies excluding China	589 506	780 886	1 806 539	3 043 031	3 803 581	4 848 174	5 984 460	6 159 610
Developing economies excluding LDCs	593 035	824 677	2 019 596	3 722 553	4 877 505	6 263 481	7 679 459	8 002 416
High-income developing economies	401 211	503 008	1 345 990	2 230 175	2 074 731	3 386 144	4 131 603	4 321 852
Middle-income developing economies	119 133	203 223	562 772	1 271 558	1 879 874	2 440 308	2 954 410	3 074 741
Low-income developing economies	87 260	76 146	146 974	297 252	450 588	599 476	796 738	811 731
Heavily indebted poor countries (IMF)	20 313	20 435	27 595	54 243	80 858	103 821	126 423	123 626
Landlocked developing countries	8 386	10 726	32 653	76 696	125 812	164 524	224 034	229 200
Small island developing States	12 547	7 096	11 479	19 639	19 850	23 840	30 438	28 361
Least developed countries	*14 570*	*18 300*	*36 146*	*82 431*	*127 688*	*162 448*	*203 382*	*205 907*
Africa and Haiti	12 283	14 843	21 113	58 303	92 409	117 022	147 113	150 262
Asia	2 129	3 334	14 852	23 868	34 974	45 031	55 663	54 973
Islands	158	123	180	260	306	395	606	672
Major petroleum and gas exporters	*281 684*	*174 767*	*314 430*	*674 922*	*872 037*	*1 106 386*	*1 512 700*	*1 661 844*
Africa	63 632	43 611	63 653	151 936	179 695	240 320	274 295	324 082
America	19 221	17 497	33 529	55 716	57 603	65 745	92 811	97 340
Asia	198 831	113 659	217 248	467 269	634 740	800 321	1 145 594	1 240 422
Major exporters of manufactured goods	*132 633*	*422 703*	*1 246 874*	*2 232 695*	*2 907 642*	*3 761 520*	*4 427 160*	*4 626 799*
America	18 031	40 711	166 368	214 207	229 712	298 305	349 569	370 827
Asia	114 602	381 992	1 080 506	2 018 488	2 677 930	3 463 215	4 077 591	4 255 972
Emerging economies	*130 967*	*333 641*	*902 613*	*1 396 138*	*1 667 699*	*2 159 796*	*2 540 919*	*2 532 601*
America	54 788	96 130	273 993	431 722	520 804	675 027	817 283	818 250
Asia	76 179	237 511	628 620	964 416	1 146 896	1 484 769	1 723 636	1 714 350
Newly industrialized Asian economies	*124 153*	*353 692*	*934 463*	*1 384 786*	*1 634 400*	*2 095 032*	*2 428 302*	*2 447 749*
First tier	77 052	267 381	664 112	1 004 619	1 166 462	1 493 543	1 728 548	1 750 351
Second tier	47 100	86 311	270 351	380 167	467 937	601 488	699 754	697 398
Developing economies: Africa	121 378	104 923	147 656	311 127	393 529	510 730	598 315	630 023
Northern Africa excluding Sudan	43 500	36 482	53 067	111 956	133 686	166 360	163 556	201 892
Sub-Saharan Africa	77 878	68 441	94 589	199 172	259 843	344 370	434 759	428 131
Sub-Saharan Africa excluding South Africa	52 353	44 892	64 606	147 546	198 166	263 478	336 712	340 875
Developing economies: America	111 503	145 626	366 452	584 117	703 820	889 689	1 109 130	1 120 507
Central America and Greater Caribbean Islands excluding Puerto Rico	31 254	54 230	191 959	253 669	277 234	353 542	418 124	442 395
Central America and Greater Caribbean Islands excluding Mexico and Puerto Rico	13 223	13 519	25 591	39 462	47 521	55 237	68 555	71 568
South America and Central America	88 876	132 309	347 436	557 361	679 907	862 450	1 068 735	1 084 983
South America excluding Brazil	45 473	55 254	109 383	195 628	260 146	320 567	412 014	417 582
Developing economies: Asia	372 473	589 649	1 536 462	2 903 030	3 900 786	5 016 456	6 164 547	6 447 694
Eastern and South-Eastern Asia excluding China	131 508	363 017	959 935	1 435 822	1 715 474	2 198 067	2 565 506	2 603 797
Southern Asia excluding India	17 552	29 035	50 739	89 614	120 672	152 605	194 374	165 265

Source: Data in this table are based on trade figures in table 1.1.1.

Imports (c.i.f.) - Importations (c.a.f.) Millions de dollars								Groupements économiques
1980	1990	2000	2005	2009	2010	2011	2012	
497 382	797 814	1 915 851	3 423 910	4 647 590	6 016 837	7 339 305	7 671 570	ÉCONOMIES EN DÉVELOPPEMENT
477 440	744 469	1 690 827	2 763 957	3 641 667	4 620 590	5 595 821	5 853 165	Économies en développement sans la Chine
472 409	771 888	1 872 385	3 336 777	4 493 884	5 847 328	7 131 853	7 447 656	Économies en développement sans les PMA
292 025	502 892	1 250 607	1 897 353	2 362 804	3 007 241	3 601 007	3 757 737	Économies en développement à revenu élevé
122 543	211 620	511 412	1 171 460	1 686 568	2 251 011	2 776 204	2 896 372	Économies en développement à revenu intermédiaire
82 814	83 302	153 833	355 097	598 218	758 586	962 093	1 017 461	Économies en développement à revenu faible
24 973	24 483	36 398	73 980	113 720	134 880	162 662	179 181	Pays pauvres très endettés (FMI)
10 813	15 905	36 473	75 686	130 919	150 372	185 658	204 889	Pays en développement sans littoral
15 722	10 405	17 267	26 029	31 107	33 141	40 924	41 582	Petits États insulaires en développement
24 972	*25 926*	*43 466*	*87 134*	*153 706*	*169 509*	*207 451*	*223 914*	*Pays les moins avancés*
16 838	18 103	24 106	55 074	101 316	105 949	125 289	140 406	Afrique et Haïti
7 841	7 450	18 973	31 143	50 907	61 829	80 181	81 453	Asie
294	373	387	917	1 483	1 731	1 982	2 055	Îles
116 700	*98 235*	*146 571*	*322 089*	*547 767*	*605 119*	*703 633*	*794 255*	*Principaux exportateurs de pétrole et de gaz*
35 323	22 311	24 664	55 543	108 720	119 050	131 476	145 490	Afrique
11 827	7 335	16 213	24 027	41 540	39 000	47 500	60 400	Amérique
69 550	68 589	105 693	242 519	397 507	447 070	524 658	588 365	Asie
151 125	*429 447*	*1 198 084*	*2 065 055*	*2 600 459*	*3 482 604*	*4 203 287*	*4 366 354*	*Principaux exportateurs d'articles manufacturés*
22 144	43 548	179 464	228 240	241 515	310 205	361 068	380 477	Amérique
128 981	385 898	1 018 620	1 836 815	2 358 944	3 172 399	3 842 219	3 985 877	Asie
152 066	*328 550*	*868 738*	*1 256 496*	*1 479 377*	*1 982 344*	*2 372 809*	*2 418 356*	*Économies émergentes*
66 020	80 722	289 184	379 794	478 597	647 562	784 929	804 370	Amérique
86 046	247 828	579 554	876 702	1 000 780	1 334 783	1 587 880	1 613 986	Asie
128 166	*367 325*	*874 219*	*1 302 074*	*1 492 685*	*1 969 943*	*2 338 629*	*2 423 205*	*Économies nouvellement industrialisées d'Asie*
89 047	270 250	649 710	944 059	1 095 481	1 428 609	1 682 475	1 723 267	Première génération
39 118	97 075	224 509	358 015	397 204	541 334	656 154	699 939	Deuxième génération
96 490	94 658	129 967	256 561	411 263	476 083	566 020	609 855	Économies en développement : Afrique
29 976	36 756	47 582	82 852	149 076	168 667	185 716	208 966	Afrique septentrionale sans le Soudan
66 514	57 902	82 385	173 709	262 187	307 416	380 305	400 889	Afrique subsaharienne
46 916	39 503	52 690	111 405	188 133	213 190	258 699	276 644	Afrique subsaharienne sans l'Afrique du Sud
123 809	124 886	388 890	537 496	693 825	895 315	1 095 622	1 135 721	Économies en développement : Amérique
39 759	61 640	224 327	298 760	326 275	411 909	483 833	507 852	Amérique centrale et Grandes Antilles sans Porto Rico
17 615	18 092	44 863	70 520	84 760	101 703	122 765	127 375	Amérique centrale et Grandes Antilles sans le Mexique et Porto Rico
96 305	107 931	355 574	493 609	644 779	841 322	1 027 355	1 070 547	Amérique du Sud et Amérique centrale
41 601	33 635	91 263	141 367	213 930	273 233	347 714	370 554	Amérique du Sud sans le Brésil
273 525	573 173	1 390 798	2 620 099	3 530 457	4 631 216	5 661 278	5 909 702	Économies en développement : Asie
132 972	377 090	900 731	1 355 588	1 586 994	2 083 690	2 488 920	2 584 087	Asie orientale et Asie du Sud-Est sans la Chine
23 494	33 788	43 239	94 006	123 531	156 776	176 936	168 771	Asie méridionale sans l'Inde

Source : Les données dans ce tableau ont été calculées d'après les chiffres du tableau 1.1.1.

Economic grouping	Exports (f.o.b.) - Exportations (f.a.b.) Percentage										
	1980	1990	1995	2000	2005	2007	2008	2009	2010	2011	2012
DEVELOPING ECONOMIES	**29.65**	**24.12**	**27.70**	**31.88**	**36.24**	**37.80**	**39.02**	**39.87**	**42.04**	**43.03**	**44.61**
Developing economies excluding China	28.76	22.34	24.83	28.01	28.98	29.10	30.16	30.30	31.72	32.67	33.47
Developing economies excluding LDCs	28.94	23.59	27.24	31.32	35.45	36.89	37.98	38.85	40.98	41.92	43.49
High-income developing economies	19.58	16.12	18.83	20.87	21.30	20.93	21.34	21.30	22.16	22.55	23.49
Middle-income developing economies	5.81	5.81	7.07	8.73	12.11	13.82	14.26	14.97	15.97	16.13	16.71
Low-income developing economies	4.26	2.18	1.81	2.28	2.83	3.06	3.41	3.59	3.92	4.35	4.41
Heavily indebted poor countries (IMF)	0.99	0.58	0.46	0.43	0.52	0.54	0.59	0.64	0.68	0.69	0.67
Landlocked developing countries	0.41	0.31	0.53	0.51	0.73	0.94	1.10	1.00	1.08	1.22	1.25
Small island developing States	0.61	0.20	0.19	0.18	0.19	0.19	0.21	0.16	0.16	0.17	0.15
Least developed countries	*0.71*	*0.52*	*0.46*	*0.56*	*0.79*	*0.92*	*1.04*	*1.02*	*1.06*	*1.11*	*1.12*
Africa and Haiti	0.60	0.42	0.30	0.33	0.56	0.68	0.80	0.74	0.77	0.80	0.82
Asia	0.10	0.10	0.16	0.23	0.23	0.23	0.23	0.28	0.29	0.30	0.30
Islands	0.01	0.00	0.00	0.00	0.00	0.00	0.00	0.00	0.00	0.00	0.00
Major petroleum and gas exporters	*13.74*	*5.00*	*3.38*	*4.88*	*6.43*	*6.84*	*8.09*	*6.95*	*7.24*	*8.26*	*9.03*
Africa	3.10	1.25	0.68	0.99	1.45	1.56	1.81	1.43	1.57	1.50	1.76
America	0.94	0.50	0.36	0.52	0.53	0.50	0.59	0.46	0.43	0.51	0.53
Asia	9.70	3.25	2.34	3.37	4.45	4.79	5.70	5.06	5.24	6.25	6.74
Major exporters of manufactured goods	*6.47*	*12.09*	*17.18*	*19.33*	*21.26*	*22.04*	*21.59*	*23.16*	*24.61*	*24.17*	*25.14*
America	0.88	1.16	1.54	2.58	2.04	1.94	1.80	1.83	1.95	1.91	2.02
Asia	5.59	10.93	15.64	16.76	19.22	20.10	19.78	21.33	22.66	22.26	23.13
Emerging economies	*6.39*	*9.54*	*12.66*	*14.00*	*13.30*	*13.07*	*12.68*	*13.28*	*14.13*	*13.87*	*13.76*
America	2.67	2.75	3.26	4.25	4.11	4.17	4.06	4.15	4.42	4.46	4.45
Asia	3.72	6.79	9.41	9.75	9.19	8.90	8.63	9.14	9.71	9.41	9.32
Newly industrialized Asian economies	*6.06*	*10.12*	*13.98*	*14.49*	*13.19*	*12.59*	*12.09*	*13.02*	*13.71*	*13.25*	*13.30*
First tier	3.76	7.65	10.25	10.30	9.57	9.04	8.58	9.29	9.77	9.44	9.51
Second tier	2.30	2.47	3.73	4.19	3.62	3.56	3.51	3.73	3.94	3.82	3.79
Developing economies: Africa	5.92	3.00	2.16	2.29	2.96	3.12	3.48	3.13	3.34	3.27	3.42
Northern Africa excluding Sudan	2.12	1.04	0.68	0.82	1.07	1.12	1.28	1.06	1.09	0.89	1.10
Sub-Saharan Africa	3.80	1.96	1.48	1.47	1.90	2.00	2.20	2.07	2.25	2.37	2.33
Sub-Saharan Africa excluding South Africa	2.55	1.28	0.94	1.00	1.41	1.50	1.70	1.58	1.72	1.84	1.85
Developing economies: America	5.44	4.17	4.44	5.68	5.56	5.59	5.61	5.61	5.82	6.05	6.09
Central America and Greater Caribbean Islands excluding Puerto Rico	1.53	1.55	1.87	2.98	2.42	2.30	2.13	2.21	2.31	2.28	2.40
Central America and Greater Caribbean Islands excluding Mexico and Puerto Rico	0.65	0.39	0.33	0.40	0.38	0.36	0.33	0.38	0.36	0.37	0.39
South America and Central America	4.34	3.79	4.19	5.39	5.31	5.34	5.36	5.42	5.64	5.83	5.90
South America excluding Brazil	2.22	1.58	1.55	1.70	1.86	2.00	2.09	2.07	2.10	2.25	2.27
Developing economies: Asia	18.17	16.87	21.01	23.83	27.65	29.03	29.86	31.07	32.82	33.65	35.04
Eastern and South-Eastern Asia excluding China	6.42	10.39	14.24	14.89	13.68	13.12	12.66	13.66	14.38	14.00	14.15
Southern Asia excluding India	0.86	0.83	0.66	0.79	0.85	0.92	0.99	0.96	1.00	1.06	0.90

Source: Data in this table are based on trade figures in table 1.1.1.

				Imports (c.i.f.) - Importations (c.a.f.) En pourcentage							Groupements économiques
1980	1990	1995	2000	2005	2007	2008	2009	2010	2011	2012	
23.84	22.12	28.79	28.78	31.77	33.17	34.93	36.63	39.03	39.86	41.44	ÉCONOMIES EN DÉVELOPPEMENT
22.89	20.64	26.26	25.40	25.65	26.45	28.05	28.70	29.98	30.39	31.62	Économies en développement sans la Chine
22.65	21.40	28.14	28.13	30.96	32.29	33.94	35.41	37.93	38.73	40.23	Économies en développement sans les PMA
14.00	13.94	19.01	18.79	17.61	18.05	18.54	18.62	19.51	19.56	20.30	Économies en développement à revenu élevé
5.87	5.87	7.62	7.68	10.87	11.40	12.06	13.29	14.60	15.08	15.65	Économies en développement à revenu intermédiaire
3.97	2.31	2.16	2.31	3.29	3.72	4.33	4.71	4.92	5.22	5.50	Économies en développement à revenu faible
1.20	0.68	0.56	0.55	0.69	0.73	0.79	0.90	0.88	0.88	0.97	Pays pauvres très endettés (FMI)
0.52	0.44	0.64	0.55	0.70	0.83	0.93	1.03	0.98	1.01	1.11	Pays en développement sans littoral
0.75	0.29	0.26	0.26	0.24	0.25	0.25	0.25	0.21	0.22	0.22	Petits États insulaires en développement
1.20	0.72	0.65	0.65	0.81	0.88	0.98	1.21	1.10	1.13	1.21	*Pays les moins avancés*
0.81	0.50	0.39	0.36	0.51	0.56	0.65	0.80	0.69	0.68	0.76	Afrique et Haïti
0.38	0.21	0.25	0.29	0.29	0.30	0.33	0.40	0.40	0.44	0.44	Asie
0.01	0.01	0.01	0.01	0.01	0.01	0.01	0.01	0.01	0.01	0.01	Îles
5.59	2.72	2.33	2.20	2.99	3.37	3.95	4.32	3.93	3.82	4.29	*Principaux exportateurs de pétrole et de gaz*
1.69	0.62	0.48	0.37	0.52	0.58	0.73	0.86	0.77	0.71	0.79	Afrique
0.57	0.20	0.24	0.24	0.22	0.32	0.30	0.33	0.25	0.26	0.33	Amérique
3.33	1.90	1.61	1.59	2.25	2.46	2.93	3.13	2.90	2.85	3.18	Asie
7.24	11.90	17.46	18.00	19.16	19.27	19.28	20.49	22.59	22.83	23.59	*Principaux exportateurs d'articles manufacturés*
1.06	1.21	1.42	2.70	2.12	2.04	1.93	1.90	2.01	1.96	2.06	Amérique
6.18	10.70	16.04	15.30	17.04	17.23	17.35	18.59	20.58	20.87	21.53	Asie
7.29	9.11	13.06	13.05	11.66	11.63	12.04	11.66	12.86	12.89	13.06	*Économies émergentes*
3.17	2.24	3.29	4.34	3.52	3.72	3.95	3.77	4.20	4.26	4.35	Amérique
4.13	6.87	9.77	8.71	8.13	7.91	8.09	7.89	8.66	8.62	8.72	Asie
6.14	10.18	14.84	13.13	12.08	11.58	11.61	11.76	12.78	12.70	13.09	*Économies nouvellement industrialisées d'Asie*
4.27	7.49	10.68	9.76	8.76	8.50	8.43	8.63	9.27	9.14	9.31	Première génération
1.88	2.69	4.15	3.37	3.32	3.08	3.18	3.13	3.51	3.56	3.78	Deuxième génération
4.63	2.62	2.37	1.95	2.38	2.64	2.92	3.24	3.09	3.07	3.29	Économies en développement : Afrique
1.44	1.02	0.86	0.71	0.77	0.86	1.00	1.17	1.09	1.01	1.13	Afrique septentrionale sans le Soudan
3.19	1.61	1.51	1.24	1.61	1.77	1.93	2.07	1.99	2.07	2.17	Afrique subsaharienne
2.25	1.10	0.92	0.79	1.03	1.15	1.31	1.48	1.38	1.40	1.49	Afrique subsaharienne sans l'Afrique du Sud
5.94	3.46	4.74	5.84	4.99	5.33	5.63	5.47	5.81	5.95	6.13	Économies en développement : Amérique
1.91	1.71	1.95	3.37	2.77	2.71	2.62	2.57	2.67	2.63	2.74	Amérique centrale et Grandes Antilles sans Porto Rico
0.84	0.50	0.53	0.67	0.65	0.67	0.69	0.67	0.66	0.67	0.69	Amérique centrale et Grandes Antilles sans le Mexique et Porto Rico
4.62	2.99	4.35	5.34	4.58	4.93	5.20	5.08	5.46	5.58	5.78	Amérique du Sud et Amérique centrale
1.99	0.93	1.58	1.37	1.31	1.56	1.73	1.69	1.77	1.89	2.00	Amérique du Sud sans le Brésil
13.11	15.89	21.56	20.89	24.31	25.11	26.28	27.82	30.04	30.74	31.92	Économies en développement : Asie
6.37	10.45	15.17	13.53	12.58	12.18	12.28	12.51	13.52	13.52	13.96	Asie orientale et Asie du Sud-Est sans la Chine
1.13	0.94	0.75	0.65	0.87	0.81	0.89	0.97	1.02	0.96	0.91	Asie méridionale sans l'Inde

Source : Les données dans ce tableau ont été calculées d'après les chiffres du tableau 1.1.1.

Trade group	Exports (f.o.b) - Exportations (f.a.b.) Millions of dollars							
	1980	1990	2000	2005	2009	2010	2011	2012
AFRICA								
CEMAC	4 668	5 604	8 361	22 944	27 028	35 504	44 173	44 975
CEPGL	2 455	2 510	910	2 585	3 802	5 698	7 188	7 024
COMESA	34 220	25 782	30 108	66 154	92 639	118 447	99 237	134 310
EAC	2 288	1 699	2 973	6 094	9 316	11 237	13 237	14 709
ECCAS	9 023	12 028	17 195	49 645	71 667	91 809	118 681	126 010
ECOWAS	33 372	21 409	30 344	67 099	83 380	114 830	153 415	155 280
MRU	4 360	4 749	4 896	8 840	12 756	13 589	14 691	15 218
SADC	36 718	38 738	50 710	98 022	131 285	170 433	212 243	208 499
UMA	40 648	34 344	48 146	99 669	111 988	141 996	134 762	175 148
WAEMU	4 884	5 202	6 664	12 661	19 268	20 756	23 817	23 259
AMERICA								
ANCOM	11 246	13 641	26 154	51 484	78 638	99 276	134 359	140 867
CACM	4 769	4 458	15 488	21 739	26 084	30 372	36 181	37 383
CARICOM	11 681	4 936	8 128	14 902	14 895	17 626	22 965	21 781
FTAA	394 051	659 762	1 418 632	1 838 056	2 069 860	2 549 425	3 028 592	3 111 796
LAIA	88 663	132 079	332 421	536 033	654 357	833 612	1 034 854	1 049 025
MERCOSUR	49 685	64 841	119 382	222 532	281 695	355 424	456 824	447 969
NAFTA	311 331	561 932	1 224 903	1 475 764	1 601 849	1 964 281	2 281 990	2 371 330
OAS	399 628	664 862	1 420 308	1 840 374	2 072 952	2 554 339	3 035 032	3 117 768
OECS	165	352	308	342	429	447	417	442
ASIA								
APTA	46 045	148 738	476 000	1 162 185	1 753 535	2 300 031	2 793 391	2 927 504
ASEAN	71 915	144 148	429 845	655 965	813 976	1 050 050	1 237 058	1 252 671
ECO	18 537	38 088	82 855	192 935	281 610	344 594	444 246	436 914
GCC	163 750	87 801	175 961	397 562	525 855	661 493	949 944	1 061 790
SAARC	13 799	27 700	64 380	132 978	206 751	277 639	365 279	355 423
EUROPE								
EFTA	49 093	99 423	142 459	237 780	293 309	330 883	400 472	392 038
EU27	850 176	1 563 742	2 448 682	4 065 612	4 597 462	5 165 870	6 076 456	5 803 284
Euro area	630 035	1 238 037	1 916 165	3 178 173	3 604 297	4 006 244	4 678 741	4 478 600
OCEANIA								
MSG	1 518	1 730	2 750	4 116	5 245	6 856	8 461	7 900
INTERREGIONAL								
ACP	97 966	82 464	113 027	226 806	288 672	380 704	481 442	473 097
APEC	625 943	1 331 855	3 117 235	4 689 668	5 652 346	7 245 126	8 505 901	8 747 154
BSEC	29 853	31 284	177 464	419 444	556 327	699 988	904 463	922 195
CIS	–	–	144 877	342 842	449 178	587 571	787 022	802 874

Source: Data in this table are based on trade figures in table 1.1.1.

			Imports (c.i.f.) - Importations (c.a.f.) Millions de dollars					Groupements commerciaux
1980	1990	2000	2005	2009	2010	2011	2012	
								AFRIQUE
3 018	3 653	3 837	7 945	17 313	20 016	25 175	26 751	CEMAC
1 949	2 256	1 044	3 390	5 611	6 440	8 028	9 259	CEPGL
23 406	28 069	35 511	65 047	114 734	134 552	143 256	174 349	COMESA
4 106	4 392	6 526	11 887	22 571	26 571	33 741	36 839	CAE
6 315	7 509	7 950	19 737	45 686	43 235	53 564	60 141	CEEAC
25 714	14 373	20 626	43 584	67 102	83 503	103 511	104 584	CEDEAO
4 312	3 539	3 912	7 340	9 091	10 734	11 586	14 714	UFM
31 640	34 525	48 521	99 703	140 605	162 208	205 332	216 054	SADC
25 401	27 761	33 458	61 831	105 628	117 680	125 939	142 883	UMA
6 371	5 777	7 082	15 311	22 004	24 433	25 385	29 501	UEMOA
								AMÉRIQUE
10 230	10 772	24 504	46 424	74 346	96 894	124 372	135 122	ANCOM
6 001	6 476	22 300	36 180	41 112	48 904	58 995	61 872	MCAC
14 268	7 218	14 029	20 200	23 568	24 854	30 311	30 975	CARICOM
430 998	757 315	1 881 455	2 576 274	2 612 541	3 249 909	3 799 960	3 924 931	ZLEA
95 754	105 028	336 434	463 021	610 011	800 314	978 191	1 017 625	ALADI
50 294	37 317	107 566	140 369	232 394	311 284	389 141	393 718	MERCOSUR
341 673	683 779	1 683 542	2 283 357	2 176 718	2 682 079	3 090 372	3 190 934	ALENA
437 503	761 915	1 886 298	2 584 358	2 622 160	3 261 406	3 814 203	3 938 650	OEA
464	1 154	1 861	2 376	2 679	2 801	2 812	2 811	OECO
								ASIE
61 826	153 257	452 727	1 087 666	1 619 553	2 215 086	2 791 241	2 883 438	ACAP
65 640	162 346	380 641	603 050	727 026	953 137	1 153 020	1 219 692	ANASE
26 347	48 945	92 369	215 391	283 057	352 031	425 766	428 599	ECO
52 080	47 445	85 420	188 339	318 402	350 010	426 628	488 193	CCG
26 113	39 038	80 864	196 835	329 965	441 606	579 639	601 346	SAARC
								EUROPE
54 266	98 592	119 501	187 041	227 952	257 526	303 849	289 875	AELE
951 237	1 625 188	2 507 225	4 133 268	4 690 099	5 302 009	6 214 127	5 841 878	UE27
716 554	1 266 124	1 900 595	3 104 687	3 529 767	3 963 321	4 645 464	4 313 040	Zone euro
								OCÉANIE
1 901	2 059	2 160	3 670	5 212	6 448	7 713	7 985	MSG
								INTERRÉGIONAUX
91 286	75 125	113 408	216 448	314 071	367 000	451 501	472 953	ACP
670 379	1 406 748	3 341 224	5 123 403	5 750 381	7 403 887	8 860 618	9 197 344	CEAP
41 328	55 160	175 527	405 013	563 740	687 252	875 537	874 354	CEMN
_	_	85 537	213 120	328 814	410 155	534 294	561 274	CEI

Source : Les données dans ce tableau ont été calculées d'après les chiffres du tableau 1.1.1.

Trade group	Exports (f.o.b) - Exportations (f.a.b.) Percentage										
	1980	1990	1995	2000	2005	2007	2008	2009	2010	2011	2012
AFRICA											
CEMAC	0.23	0.16	0.12	0.13	0.22	0.22	0.26	0.22	0.23	0.24	0.24
CEPGL	0.12	0.07	0.03	0.01	0.02	0.02	0.03	0.03	0.04	0.04	0.04
COMESA	1.67	0.74	0.47	0.47	0.63	0.70	0.79	0.74	0.77	0.54	0.73
EAC	0.11	0.05	0.06	0.05	0.06	0.06	0.06	0.07	0.07	0.07	0.08
ECCAS	0.44	0.34	0.22	0.27	0.47	0.56	0.69	0.57	0.60	0.65	0.68
ECOWAS	1.63	0.61	0.43	0.47	0.64	0.62	0.69	0.66	0.75	0.84	0.84
MRU	0.21	0.14	0.10	0.08	0.08	0.07	0.08	0.10	0.09	0.08	0.08
SADC	1.79	1.11	0.85	0.79	0.93	1.03	1.10	1.05	1.12	1.16	1.13
UMA	1.98	0.98	0.62	0.75	0.95	0.99	1.13	0.89	0.93	0.74	0.95
WAEMU	0.24	0.15	0.13	0.10	0.12	0.11	0.11	0.15	0.14	0.13	0.13
AMERICA											
ANCOM	0.55	0.39	0.41	0.41	0.49	0.55	0.58	0.63	0.65	0.73	0.77
CACM	0.23	0.13	0.18	0.24	0.21	0.19	0.18	0.21	0.20	0.20	0.20
CARICOM	0.57	0.14	0.11	0.13	0.14	0.14	0.16	0.12	0.12	0.13	0.12
FTAA	19.23	18.87	19.36	22.00	17.51	16.71	16.35	16.49	16.68	16.53	16.91
LAIA	4.33	3.78	4.01	5.15	5.11	5.16	5.18	5.21	5.45	5.65	5.70
MERCOSUR	2.42	1.85	1.74	1.85	2.12	2.13	2.35	2.24	2.33	2.49	2.43
NAFTA	15.19	16.08	16.55	18.99	14.06	13.13	12.60	12.76	12.85	12.46	12.89
OAS	19.50	19.02	19.39	22.02	17.53	16.74	16.37	16.51	16.71	16.57	16.94
OECS	0.01	0.01	0.01	0.00	0.00	0.00	0.00	0.00	0.00	0.00	0.00
ASIA											
APTA	2.25	4.26	6.03	7.38	11.07	12.58	12.84	13.97	15.05	15.25	15.91
ASEAN	3.51	4.12	6.21	6.67	6.25	6.17	6.13	6.48	6.87	6.75	6.81
ECO	0.90	1.09	1.17	1.28	1.84	2.16	2.44	2.24	2.25	2.42	2.37
GCC	7.99	2.51	2.03	2.73	3.79	3.96	4.72	4.19	4.33	5.19	5.77
SAARC	0.67	0.79	0.90	1.00	1.27	1.36	1.49	1.65	1.82	1.99	1.93
EUROPE											
EFTA	2.40	2.84	2.42	2.21	2.26	2.23	2.34	2.34	2.16	2.19	2.13
EU27	41.48	44.73	42.30	37.97	38.72	38.14	36.69	36.62	33.80	33.17	31.54
Euro area	30.74	35.42	33.72	29.71	30.27	29.91	28.69	28.71	26.21	25.54	24.34
OCEANIA											
MSG	0.07	0.05	0.07	0.04	0.04	0.04	0.04	0.04	0.04	0.05	0.04
INTERREGIONAL											
ACP	4.78	2.36	1.77	1.75	2.16	2.26	2.47	2.30	2.49	2.63	2.57
APEC	30.54	38.10	45.44	48.34	44.67	44.38	43.74	45.02	47.40	46.43	47.53
BSEC	1.46	0.89	2.75	2.75	3.99	4.42	5.05	4.43	4.58	4.94	5.01
CIS	–	–	2.17	2.25	3.27	3.70	4.34	3.58	3.84	4.30	4.36

Source: Data in this table are based on trade figures in table 1.1.1.

Imports (c.i.f.) - Importations (c.a.f.) En pourcentage											Groupements commerciaux
1980	1990	1995	2000	2005	2007	2008	2009	2010	2011	2012	
											AFRIQUE
0.14	0.10	0.07	0.06	0.07	0.10	0.11	0.14	0.13	0.14	0.14	CEMAC
0.09	0.06	0.03	0.02	0.03	0.03	0.04	0.04	0.04	0.04	0.05	CEPGL
1.12	0.78	0.63	0.53	0.60	0.66	0.72	0.90	0.87	0.78	0.94	COMESA
0.20	0.12	0.12	0.10	0.11	0.13	0.15	0.18	0.17	0.18	0.20	CAE
0.30	0.21	0.12	0.12	0.18	0.23	0.27	0.36	0.28	0.29	0.32	CEEAC
1.23	0.40	0.37	0.31	0.40	0.46	0.54	0.53	0.54	0.56	0.56	CEDEAO
0.21	0.10	0.08	0.06	0.07	0.06	0.06	0.07	0.07	0.06	0.08	UFM
1.52	0.96	0.91	0.73	0.93	0.99	1.04	1.11	1.05	1.12	1.17	SADC
1.22	0.77	0.65	0.50	0.57	0.61	0.71	0.83	0.76	0.68	0.77	UMA
0.31	0.16	0.14	0.11	0.14	0.14	0.15	0.17	0.16	0.14	0.16	UEMOA
											AMÉRIQUE
0.49	0.30	0.52	0.37	0.43	0.50	0.57	0.59	0.63	0.68	0.73	ANCOM
0.29	0.18	0.26	0.33	0.34	0.34	0.33	0.32	0.32	0.32	0.33	MCAC
0.68	0.20	0.19	0.21	0.19	0.18	0.19	0.19	0.16	0.16	0.17	CARICOM
20.66	20.99	22.54	28.26	23.90	22.13	21.19	20.59	21.08	20.64	21.20	ZLEA
4.59	2.91	4.12	5.05	4.30	4.65	4.94	4.81	5.19	5.31	5.50	ALADI
2.41	1.03	1.80	1.62	1.30	1.63	1.90	1.83	2.02	2.11	2.13	MERCOSUR
16.38	18.95	19.36	25.29	21.19	18.98	17.65	17.15	17.40	16.78	17.24	ALENA
20.97	21.12	22.60	28.34	23.98	22.20	21.28	20.66	21.16	20.71	21.28	OEA
0.02	0.03	0.03	0.03	0.02	0.02	0.02	0.02	0.02	0.02	0.02	OECO
											ASIE
2.96	4.25	6.01	6.80	10.09	11.06	11.71	12.76	14.37	15.16	15.58	ACAP
3.15	4.50	6.79	5.72	5.60	5.45	5.70	5.73	6.18	6.26	6.59	ANASE
1.26	1.36	1.36	1.39	2.00	2.14	2.26	2.23	2.28	2.31	2.32	ECO
2.50	1.32	1.36	1.28	1.75	2.07	2.47	2.51	2.27	2.32	2.64	CCG
1.25	1.08	1.15	1.21	1.83	2.10	2.49	2.60	2.86	3.15	3.25	SAARC
											EUROPE
2.60	2.73	2.19	1.80	1.74	1.74	1.70	1.80	1.67	1.65	1.57	AELE
45.60	45.05	40.56	37.66	38.35	38.81	37.61	36.96	34.40	33.75	31.56	UE27
34.35	35.10	31.60	28.55	28.81	29.02	28.26	27.82	25.71	25.23	23.30	Zone euro
											OCÉANIE
0.09	0.06	0.05	0.03	0.03	0.04	0.04	0.04	0.04	0.04	0.04	MSG
											INTERRÉGIONAUX
4.38	2.08	1.90	1.70	2.01	2.18	2.36	2.48	2.38	2.45	2.55	ACP
32.14	39.00	46.41	50.19	47.54	45.55	45.06	45.32	48.03	48.12	49.68	CEAP
1.98	1.53	3.00	2.64	3.76	4.61	5.14	4.44	4.46	4.75	4.72	CEMN
_	_	1.78	1.28	1.98	2.63	3.00	2.59	2.66	2.90	3.03	CEI

Source : Les données dans ce tableau ont été calculées d'après les chiffres du tableau 1.1.1.

Region, country or territory	Exports (f.o.b) - Exportations (f.a.b.) Percentage										
	80-00	90-00	00-10	04-07	05-12	08-12	2005	2009	2010	2011	2012
WORLD	7.1	6.7	10.9	15.0	7.4	6.6	13.9	-22.2	21.7	19.9	0.4
DEVELOPING ECONOMIES	7.6	9.1	14.4	19.3	10.6	10.3	21.8	-20.6	28.4	22.7	4.1
TRANSITION ECONOMIES	1.5	5.6	18.3	25.1	11.0	8.4	28.8	-35.4	30.1	33.2	1.6
DEVELOPED ECONOMIES	7.2	5.8	8.5	12.0	4.9	3.7	8.9	-22.3	16.5	16.7	-2.7
Developing economies: Africa	1.9	3.2	16.4	21.9	9.3	6.7	29.9	-30.0	29.8	17.1	5.3
Eastern Africa	3.3	4.7	13.3	18.1	13.3	13.8	13.6	-9.0	30.5	21.6	4.9
Burundi*(1)	-2.1	-4.3	8.3	7.1	14.5	25.8	23.7	17.3	50.2	22.0	8.1
Comoros*	-3.1	-10.9	-3.2	-10.3	12.4	30.2	-35.5	129.4	37.8	22.1	-25.1
Djibouti (2)	4.2	7.1	11.2	17.4	(e)12.6	(e)8.6	4.0	12.5	10.0	8.9	(e)2.5
Eritrea (3)	_	_	(e)-9.5	5.6	(e)67.5	(e)203.7	0.1	(e)-1.8	(e)9.1	(e)3 233.3	(e)20.0
Ethiopia	_	_	18.7	22.7	(e)20.0	(e)20.1	33.1	1.0	44.0	23.4	(e)4.3
Kenya	3.8	6.3	12.2	13.7	8.9	6.8	27.4	-10.7	15.8	11.3	6.5
Madagascar*	3.8	9.0	5.1	8.4	(e)7.0	(e)7.1	-13.8	-19.7	1.8	(e)48.4	(e)-5.7
Malawi	3.4	0.9	12.2	22.5	13.5	8.1	5.3	35.1	-10.2	33.7	-16.9
Mauritius	9.4	3.6	3.6	4.4	2.2	5.2	7.5	-18.7	16.7	13.4	4.2
Mozambique	2.5	9.6	(e)20.7	18.6	(e)10.4	(e)14.9	18.6	-19.1	(e)39.7	(e)20.1	(e)13.8
Rwanda	-5.2	-3.8	19.2	21.3	24.0	25.4	27.0	-12.2	26.5	56.2	27.3
Seychelles	12.6	15.5	8.3	7.8	5.0	5.0	16.8	-8.1	1.2	20.7	2.8
Somalia (4)	(e)3.8	(e)6.5	(e)7.9	(e)23.9	(e)10.9	(e)5.8	(e)38.9	(e)3.6	3.4	15.6	-1.9
Uganda	1.8	14.7	17.9.	26.1	15.3	9.9	24.4	-9.1	3.3	33.4	9.2
United Republic of Tanzania	3.3	7.8	18.3	14.6	(e)18.9	(e)17.3	13.5	-4.4	35.8	16.9	(e)16.2
Zambia (5)	(e)0.3	(e)-0.8	25.9	48.6	(e)21.6	(e)19.5	14.9	-15.4	67.0	25.0	(e)-4.5
Zimbabwe	3.1	3.5	(e)5.7	(e)8.3	(e)11.2	(e)17.0	(e)-2.0	(e)3.1	41.0	9.8	10.6
Middle Africa	3.4	3.2	23.2	33.4	12.4	7.7	54.8	-35.7	28.1	29.2	6.1
Angola*(6)	6.8	5.7	27.4	47.0	(e)14.7	(e)8.3	78.9	-36.1	23.9	33.0	(e)9.9
Cameroon*(7)	3.7	-1.3	10.9	20.1	(e)4.5	(e)-0.6	15.5	-32.2	9.2	16.5	(e)-0.4
Central African Republic*(7)	3.4	3.6	(e)-0.4	11.2	(e)4.2	(e)12.0	-4.4	(e)-20.0	(e)16.7	(e)35.7	(e)10.5
Chad*(6)	7.1	0.3	(e)42.5	17.7	(e)4.3	(e)6.2	40.6	(e)-32.8	(e)25.0	(e)31.4	(e)-4.3
Congo*(7)	3.7	7.5	(e)16.6	18.9	(e)12.8	(e)12.1	38.2	(e)-26.7	(e)52.5	(e)24.7	(e)-7.8
Dem. Rep. of the Congo*	-3.3	-6.2	(e)21.0	(e)16.9	(e)16.2	(e)14.5	25.3	(e)-20.5	(e)51.4	(e)24.5	(e)-4.5
Equatorial Guinea (6)	23.6	41.2	(e)27.5	29.0	(e)9.2	(e)4.4	53.6	(e)-40.2	(e)9.9	(e)35.0	(e)14.8
Gabon*(8)	1.9	1.5	(e)14.6	(e)18.0	(e)9.8	6.4	35.9	-44.0	62.2	12.4	-1.0
Sao Tome and Principe*	-5.8	-5.6	13.3	8.5	(e)7.7	(e)3.7	25.9	-23.7	34.3	0.0	(e)0.9
Northern Africa	0.9	2.9	16.5	24.7	5.8	0.7	37.8	-35.2	25.2	-2.5	18.5
Algeria*	0.4	3.1	14.6	23.8	4.7	2.9	47.0	-43.0	26.3	28.8	-2.2
Egypt	0.8	3.7	21.5	26.1	12.3	5.6	33.6	-12.1	14.6	19.4	-6.9
Libya	-2.7	-2.1	20.0	31.7	0.8	-6.4	53.6	-40.5	31.7	-61.0	227.5
Morocco*	7.5	7.8	11.0	15.4	9.0	5.5	12.7	-30.9	26.4	21.9	-1.1
Sudan (...2011) (9)	2.1	14.0	24.2	31.3	_	_	27.7	-29.2	38.1	-15.0	_
Tunisia (10)	7.1	6.0	12.4	15.6	6.7	-0.4	8.4	-25.2	13.7	8.6	-4.7
Southern Africa	2.8	2.8	11.7	13.9	7.6	6.6	11.8	-22.7	30.6	20.7	-10.0
Botswana*	9.5	4.9	7.3	12.6	3.3	9.5	26.0	-30.2	35.8	25.3	1.5
Lesotho	11.5	12.4	14.0	3.2	(e)8.1	(e)9.5	-8.1	-17.0	19.5	33.6	(e)-6.2
Namibia	2.0	0.9	14.4	18.0	10.2	8.7	13.3	0.2	27.9	9.5	-8.5
South Africa	2.4	2.5	12.0	14.6	8.0	6.4	11.9	-23.7	31.2	21.2	-11.0
Swaziland	7.6	6.0	(e)6.5	(e)-1.0	(e)0.8	(e)3.7	(e)-9.2	(e)-2.4	(e)8.4	(e)6.1	(e)-0.5
Western Africa	1.2	3.7	17.0	17.9	12.4	13.5	25.2	-25.5	37.9	33.6	1.1
Benin*	13.5	3.3	15.0	23.0	(e)12.6	(e)3.2	1.7	-4.5	4.6	(e)10.0	(e)-0.7
Burkina Faso	7.2	12.7	20.3	10.7	28.1	38.5	-2.4	29.9	76.1	48.4	-7.2
Cape Verde (11)	6.5	10.8	16.2	9.2	21.5	18.3	16.7	9.8	26.7	54.2	-22.6
Côte d'Ivoire*	2.6	5.4	12.2	8.0	(e)7.7	(e)4.6	11.2	9.0	2.0	8.5	(e)-1.5
Gambia (12)	-4.7	-12.6	(e)12.8	(e)10.9	(e)47.9	(e)54.4	(e)-20.0	383.0	-47.0	170.8	(e)5.6
Ghana	(e)3.9	(e)9.0	(e)17.2	(e)20.9	(e)25.3	(e)29.6	(e)14.4	10.8	36.3	60.6	(e)1.7
Guinea*	(e)2.4	1.1	8.5	17.7	(e)6.1	(e)2.5	14.6	-21.8	40.1	-2.6	(e)-9.3
Guinea-Bissau	8.5	13.6	9.3	8.7	(e)11.0	(e)6.9	17.7	-5.2	4.1	(e)81.7	(e)-43.5
Liberia*	(e)-0.3	(e)-3.3	(e)1.1	24.0	16.5	24.4	26.5	-38.6	49.2	65.3	25.2
Mali*	8.1	6.1	13.8	19.0	9.3	3.7	12.7	-15.4	12.6	19.8	-9.5
Mauritania*	2.8	-1.8	23.7	54.8	18.7	16.1	42.2	-23.7	52.0	33.9	-4.9
Niger*	-1.4	0.0	(e)16.9	13.8	(e)18.3	(e)13.0	11.9	(e)9.9	(e)15.0	(e)8.7	(e)20.0
Nigeria	0.4	3.2	(e)18.5	19.6	(e)11.9	(e)13.8	30.6	-34.2	(e)48.0	(e)36.3	(e)1.3
Saint Helena	(e)15.2	(e)2.6	(e)11.9	(e)5.0	(e)11.2	(e)7.1	(e)-5.4	(e)-10.8	(e)0.5	(e)19.7	(e)19.7
Senegal (13)	3.6	4.0	9.3	3.3	7.8	5.5	4.6	-7.1	7.1	17.6	-0.4
Sierra Leone*	-12.8	-29.5	33.2	23.2	22.1	44.6	14.4	7.0	47.9	2.3	217.4
Togo*	3.8	6.7	(e)10.1	3.2	(e)8.2	(e)5.3	9.8	5.9	(e)-0.3	(e)22.2	(e)-9.1

For sources and notes, see end of table.

1.2.1 Taux d'évolution annuels moyens des exportations et importations des pays et des régions géographiques

Imports (c.i.f.) - Importations (c.a.f.) En pourcentage											Régions, pays ou territoires
80-00	90-00	00-10	04-07	05-12	08-12	2005	2009	2010	2011	2012	
7.0	6.6	10.6	14.5	7.1	6.3	13.7	-22.9	21.5	19.5	0.5	**MONDE**
8.1	8.6	14.1	17.5	11.6	10.9	18.1	-19.2	29.5	22.0	4.5	ÉCONOMIES EN DÉVELOPPEMENT
0.8	2.9	19.4	28.0	11.4	6.3	21.8	-32.9	21.0	28.8	3.7	ÉCONOMIES EN TRANSITION
6.9	6.1	8.6	12.6	4.3	3.3	11.5	-24.5	16.6	17.3	-2.5	ÉCONOMIES DÉVELOPPÉES
2.2	4.3	16.4	20.6	12.3	8.2	20.7	-14.6	15.8	18.9	7.7	**Économies en développement : Afrique**
4.1	4.3	15.9	20.0	14.0	10.9	20.9	-11.3	16.0	22.1	12.2	*Afrique orientale*
-1.3	-6.9	15.8	25.2	14.5	20.6	52.8	-0.1	26.5	47.9	-0.2	Burundi*(1)
3.0	-1.7	19.3	17.3	17.1	11.8	15.3	17.2	10.6	18.9	-1.2	Comores*
-0.8	-1.3	10.6	21.8	(e)7.8	(e)1.5	6.1	-21.4	-17.0	36.6	(e)13.6	Djibouti (2)
_	_	(e)3.6	(e)1.9	(e)11.1	(e)15.3	(e)2.1	(e)-1.9	(e)16.9	(e)29.0	(e)12.4	Érythrée (3)
_	_	22.6	26.5	14.9	10.5	42.5	-7.4	12.2	3.4	42.3	Éthiopie
3.6	6.0	17.1	25.3	14.7	12.0	28.4	-8.3	18.5	22.2	10.2	Kenya
3.5	6.1	14.9	15.1	(e)7.6	(e)-5.1	1.6	-15.4	-21.1	15.1	(e)5.0	Madagascar*
4.2	-0.6	16.7	12.8	13.6	6.3	25.0	-8.3	7.5	11.7	12.2	Malawi
9.6	4.1	9.0	12.3	6.9	6.2	13.9	-19.8	17.5	17.4	4.0	Maurice
2.1	1.2	(e)15.9	14.9	(e)15.9	(e)17.0	18.4	-6.1	(e)22.2	(e)37.1	(e)7.8	Mozambique
-1.1	-1.6	23.5	38.3	26.7	19.0	51.7	11.5	9.4	24.1	35.6	Rwanda
8.8	9.6	(e)9.5	19.2	(e)0.0	(e)-6.5	35.9	-26.9	(e)-18.1	(e)15.4	(e)6.7	Seychelles
(e)0.7	(e)18.3	(e)10.0	(e)14.6	(e)1.2	(e)-4.0	(e)2.6	(e)-15.7	25.3	-6.4	-23.9	Somalie (4)
8.5	21.3	15.8	26.3	15.8	9.0	19.0	-6.2	9.8	20.7	7.3	Ouganda
3.0	0.1	(e)20.4	25.5	(e)18.6	(e)13.8	20.6	(e)-16.7	22.8	37.1	5.1	République-Unie de Tanzanie
0.2	-1.0	20.8	22.7	(e)16.7	(e)17.3	18.9	-24.3	38.9	34.9	(e)14.2	Zambie (5)
4.7	2.3	(e)7.6	(e)4.3	(e)11.1	(e)12.9	(e)6.6	(e)-1.7	(e)31.0	(e)15.8	(e)0.0	Zimbabwe
1.5	3.1	21.1	27.0	16.3	7.4	28.3	2.5	-6.1	23.6	11.7	*Afrique centrale*
4.4	7.8	24.1	29.7	(e)15.7	(e)1.6	43.2	8.0	-26.4	21.4	(e)18.6	Angola*(6)
-0.2	1.9	14.5	23.6	(e)13.7	(e)9.7	13.7	-21.9	15.6	32.5	(e)7.3	Cameroun*(7)
2.0	0.2	(e)12.5	17.8	(e)8.4	(e)2.7	15.7	(e)-10.0	(e)11.1	(e)3.3	(e)3.2	République centrafricaine*(7)
9.0	-1.3	(e)16.7	(e)25.3	(e)15.2	(e)10.2	-0.3	(e)0.0	(e)20.0	(e)12.5	(e)3.7	Tchad*(6)
1.0	2.8	(e)24.4	(e)39.3	(e)20.6	(e)18.0	34.5	(e)-4.9	(e)37.9	(e)30.0	(e)0.0	Congo*(7)
-3.9	-5.8	(e)22.1	(e)17.2	(e)12.2	(e)11.0	31.1	(e)-9.3	(e)15.4	(e)22.2	(e)10.9	Rép. dém. du Congo*
16.5	29.7	(e)29.1	37.9	(e)27.3	(e)16.5	20.0	(e)33.0	(e)0.0	(e)25.0	(e)15.4	Guinée équatoriale (6)
1.3	2.2	12.8	17.0	14.0	11.4	9.2	-2.4	19.3	22.9	-0.9	Gabon*(8)
4.3	-0.7	17.3	25.9	13.8	5.4	20.3	-9.4	8.6	17.3	-0.2	Sao Tomé-et-Principe*
2.0	4.3	16.3	19.8	13.1	6.9	19.2	-8.4	12.6	9.1	12.0	*Afrique septentrionale*
-0.7	0.6	18.1	14.0	14.0	5.7	12.0	-0.5	3.0	16.7	0.5	Algérie*
2.5	7.9	(e)17.7	(e)31.4	(e)16.7	11.0	40.7	-7.1	17.7	17.6	11.3	Égypte
-1.7	-1.9	14.7	1.8	(e)18.1	(e)14.7	-3.9	40.5	37.4	(e)-54.7	(e)187.5	Libye
6.3	5.5	15.3	20.9	10.6	4.2	16.7	-22.4	7.6	25.1	1.1	Maroc*
1.0	9.8	22.9	28.1	_	_	65.8	3.6	3.7	-8.1	_	Soudan (…2011) (9)
6.3	5.2	11.2	14.2	8.5	2.1	2.8	-22.5	16.3	7.8	2.1	Tunisie (10)
3.7	5.3	14.6	17.5	9.0	9.6	14.2	-23.7	25.5	27.3	2.6	*Afrique australe*
7.0	1.9	12.5	6.9	14.9	13.8	-2.2	-9.3	19.6	28.6	10.4	Botswana*
5.6	2.0	(e)11.7	6.5	(e)9.6	(e)10.9	-2.1	(e)2.8	(e)24.3	(e)8.7	(e)4.0	Lesotho
3.3	3.9	(e)15.3	(e)13.5	(e)15.2	(e)10.8	(e)7.6	(e)14.7	(e)11.8	(e)14.2	(e)0.9	Namibie
3.5	5.8	15.0	19.1	8.5	9.4	16.5	-27.1	27.2	29.1	2.2	Afrique du Sud
5.1	5.1	(e)6.4	(e)-1.2	(e)0.8	(e)5.4	(e)-1.3	(e)11.2	(e)10.1	(e)-0.5	(e)2.1	Swaziland
0.1	3.6	17.8	25.0	12.6	7.9	32.5	-25.0	24.6	24.0	1.7	*Afrique occidentale*
4.0	9.7	15.9	30.5	(e)10.3	(e)-0.2	13.9	-9.8	-0.5	(e)7.1	(e)0.0	Bénin*
4.0	3.6	(e)14.2	(e)10.6	(e)11.7	(e)12.1	(e)-0.8	-7.3	9.5	17.5	(e)30.9	Burkina Faso
7.9	6.0	15.0	20.6	8.1	1.4	1.6	-14.1	4.7	27.6	-19.2	Cap-Vert (11)
1.5	3.5	14.3	10.9	5.7	4.0	24.4	-11.7	12.8	-14.4	45.5	Côte d'Ivoire*
4.3	0.2	8.6	10.7	(e)4.5	(e)4.6	13.4	-5.7	-6.2	20.6	(e)10.6	Gambie (12)
(e)7.1	(e)9.1	16.3	25.6	(e)17.4	(e)19.8	31.3	-21.6	35.7	46.2	(e)12.7	Ghana
3.9	-3.0	(e)9.6	(e)16.1	(e)14.5	(e)18.9	(e)5.1	-22.4	32.5	49.9	(e)9.2	Guinée*
2.4	-4.1	17.2	30.6	(e)9.8	(e)4.6	48.4	-10.8	-2.8	(e)32.3	(e)-3.8	Guinée-Bissau
(e)2.0	(e)3.2	(e)10.5	22.0	17.2	12.5	5.0	-32.3	28.8	47.1	2.0	Libéria*
5.2	4.7	15.8	17.1	10.9	0.6	13.2	-25.5	37.9	-1.1	-13.3	Mali*
3.8	3.1	18.4	11.8	12.6	16.0	54.7	-22.8	29.2	27.5	28.5	Mauritanie*
-0.2	0.8	(e)21.3	(e)13.7	(e)20.5	(e)13.6	(e)25.7	(e)29.7	(e)12.5	(e)9.1	(e)7.4	Niger*
-2.5	3.1	21.1	34.2	(e)13.1	(e)5.6	46.5	-32.1	30.5	(e)26.6	(e)-8.9	Nigéria
(e)5.2	(e)8.8	(e)7.3	(e)39.1	(e)-4.8	(e)1.1	(e)40.6	(e)-14.1	(e)33.3	(e)-8.6	(e)-8.6	Sainte-Hélène
2.3	3.9	14.5	18.2	7.7	2.0	23.2	-27.8	1.5	23.6	8.9	Sénégal (13)
-4.4	-4.2	15.2	15.5	26.4	39.8	20.3	-2.6	48.0	122.9	-8.4	Sierra Leone*
2.2	5.5	(e)12.7	(e)11.0	(e)8.9	(e)6.0	(e)20.5	-0.1	6.0	(e)12.5	(e)2.8	Togo*

Pour les sources et les notes, se reporter à la fin du tableau.

Region, country or territory	Exports (f.o.b) - Exportations (f.a.b.) Percentage										
	80-00	90-00	00-10	04-07	05-12	08-12	2005	2009	2010	2011	2012
Developing economies: America	6.4	10.5	11.3	18.0	8.7	9.2	21.9	-22.3	26.4	24.7	1.0
Caribbean	-2.1	4.0	6.9	18.0	2.0	2.5	23.6	-41.3	13.9	48.3	-12.1
Anguilla	-	(e)26.6	18.6	11.3	(e)6.8	(e)9.3	149.2	100.6	-45.1	29.5	(e)29.5
Antigua and Barbuda	4.8	0.6	2.4	0.1	(e)-5.4	(e)-0.7	45.6	-22.4	-10.0	22.8	(e)6.9
Aruba (14)	(e)35.1	16.6	-5.4	14.0	(e)-16.9	(e)-11.2	28.6	-64.2	-86.5	1859.3	(e)-64.3
Bahamas (15)	-17.3	8.5	6.6	19.6	5.3	2.2	15.1	-25.6	-1.2	18.7	18.1
Barbados	-0.2	3.9	7.5	25.2	2.4	5.4	29.2	-22.4	13.3	10.8	18.9
Bonaire, Sint Eustatius and Saba	–	–	–	–	–	–	–	–	–	–	(e)-25.3
British Virgin Islands (4)	(e)19.2	(e)15.1	(e)3.8	(e)5.5	(e)1.4	(e)1.0	(e)9.0	(e)-4.9	2.4	1.9	3.9
Cayman Islands (4)	(e)16.2	(e)1.8	(e)0.2	(e)-6.5	(e)-11.1	(e)7.1	(e)147.1	(e)29.0	(e)-30.6	(e)63.1	(e)-9.4
Cuba*	(e)-8.8	(e)-5.9	12.5	21.1	13.4	16.8	-0.6	-21.9	58.9	31.1	-7.3
Curaçao											2.1
Dominica*	6.1	0.6	-3.0	-3.9	(e)-3.5	(e)-3.7	-0.5	-16.3	10.0	-18.2	(e)16.2
Dominican Republic (16)	9.5	9.9	2.2	6.6	4.5	11.0	3.5	-18.7	23.2	27.5	5.4
Grenada*	2.5	6.3	-5.4	0.8	(e)1.7	(e)2.7	-12.4	-4.4	-14.4	16.6	(e)20.2
Haiti	0.4	12.2	8.2	9.9	7.9	14.4	20.2	20.1	0.5	32.4	6.3
Jamaica	3.6	2.1	4.1	18.1	-2.8	-4.9	9.2	-46.0	0.9	22.3	5.2
Montserrat*	3.9	-2.4	8.2	-13.5	(e)4.1	(e)-13.0	-66.0	-22.5	-65.1	121.4	(e)-5.5
Netherlands Antilles*(17)	.-5.4	-0.4	-9.4	9.6	–	–	16.6	-25.6	0.1		
Saint Kitts and Nevis*	2.1	1.8	1.0	-3.2	(e)2.4	(e)-0.8	-14.8	-26.4	-15.0	40.2	(e)0.3
Saint Lucia*	0.7	-11.1	(e)18.2	(e)10.5	(e)14.6	(e)-0.8	-19.5	1.2	29.3	-24.7	(e)-0.9
Saint Vincent and the Grenadines*	2.4	-5.3	1.4	7.8	(e)0.1	(e)-6.1	8.9	-6.0	-15.4	-7.4	(e)11.9
Sint Maarten (Dutch part)	–	–	–	–	–	–	–	–	–	–	3.0
Trinidad and Tobago*	-0.1	6.8	14.7	28.6	1.0	-2.3	52.5	-51.1	20.3	36.1	-13.1
Turks and Caicos Islands	-	-	11.2	10.9	(e)5.0	(e)-0.2	20.5	-16.2	-22.9	(e)25.0	(e)25.0
Central America	10.5	16.0	7.5	14.0	7.1	9.5	16.3	-19.4	27.4	17.9	6.0
Belize	4.3	5.0	5.4	10.0	(e)7.7	(e)9.3	-2.6	-16.7	20.1	23.5	(e)3.8
Costa Rica*	(b)11.2	(b)17.0	7.1	14.3	5.6	5.6	11.5	-7.6	7.6	10.2	10.0
El Salvador (18)	7.3	19.2	4.9	6.9	6.2	6.2	3.4	-16.7	16.4	18.0	0.6
Guatemala (19)	4.5	10.2	12.4	11.1	9.5	9.2	6.8	-6.8	17.3	22.9	-4.0
Honduras (20)	8.2	15.3	6.5	8.1	6.2	10.2	11.3	-22.1	26.6	27.6	1.7
Mexico	11.0	16.1	7.0	13.4	6.8	9.4	14.0	-21.1	29.9	17.2	6.1
Nicaragua (21)	1.7	10.3	12.9	17.8	16.6	18.3	14.6	-5.5	32.8	22.3	18.3
Panama*(22)	_	9.4	39.7	98.1	(e)12.0	(e)14.0	647.1	9.2	2.5	32.5	(e)11.4
South America	5.5	7.2	15.0	21.1	10.3	9.4	26.4	-22.7	26.5	27.9	-1.2
Argentina*	7.6	10.1	11.8	17.1	10.2	7.3	16.7	-20.5	22.4	23.2	-3.6
Bolivia (Plurinational State of)	2.3	4.3	21.2	28.8	18.3	17.2	30.5	-24.0	29.1	30.4	33.0
Brazil	5.4	5.9	15.5	18.2	10.7	9.7	22.6	-22.7	32.0	26.8	-5.3
Chile*	10.0	9.4	17.4	29.2	7.5	8.0	26.9	-14.0	28.2	14.6	-3.9
Colombia	8.1	7.4	14.6	21.9	15.8	16.2	30.6	-12.7	21.2	44.2	5.0
Ecuador	4.3	6.8	16.5	23.0	11.5	10.0	30.3	-26.3	26.2	27.6	6.8
Falkland Islands (Malvinas) (4)	(e)15.3	(e)27.1	(e)7.6	(e)7.5	(e)4.4	(e)5.9	(e)25.0	(e)-17.6	21.4	5.9	11.1
Guyana*	4.7	8.7	6.3	4.8	13.2	16.2	-6.7	-4.0	15.4	26.9	24.8
Paraguay	7.7	1.7	23.2	18.6	27.2	15.1	3.8	13.4	28.5	19.4	-6.3
Peru*	4.2	8.7	20.6	30.6	13.5	14.0	35.6	-13.1	31.9	30.1	-1.4
Suriname	(e)-0.1	(e)0.4	18.7	16.1	14.4	14.3	14.1	-19.6	44.5	21.8	3.9
Uruguay	5.5	5.2	14.0	.15.6	14.1	12.2	16.7	-9.0	24.4	17.7	10.5
Venezuela (Bolivarian Rep. of)	2.3	6.1	12.2	20.5	6.1	5.4	40.5	-39.4	14.1	41.2	4.9
Developing economies: Asia	8.9	9.5	14.8	19.3	11.1	10.9	20.9	-19.1	28.6	22.9	4.6
Eastern Asia	13.0	10.0	15.3	19.1	11.1	11.1	18.6	-15.4	29.6	18.4	5.4
China	14.7	14.5	22.4	27.2	13.8	12.5	28.4	-16.0	31.3	20.3	7.9
China, Hong Kong SAR	14.4	8.3	8.0	9.7	7.0	9.4	10.0	-11.0	21.6	13.7	8.2
China, Macao SAR	7.1	3.8	-8.2	-2.7	-16.9	-13.4	-11.9	-51.9	-9.5	0.0	17.5
China, Taiwan Province of	10.9	7.4	7.6	10.8	5.6	7.7	8.8	-20.3	34.8	12.3	-2.3
Korea, Dem. People's Rep. of	(e)-2.3	(e)-9.2	(e)12.7	(e)9.6	(e)16.8	(e)19.9	(e)4.7	(e)-3.2	(e)28.1	(e)45.0	(e)1.2
Korea, Republic of (23)	12.2	10.1	12.5	13.6	9.7	9.9	12.0	-13.9	28.3	19.0	-1.3
Mongolia	-1.4	1.5	21.2	31.0	21.8	22.4	22.5	-25.1	52.4	66.2	-9.0
Southern Asia	6.4	6.5	17.4	23.9	13.5	11.3	28.5	-19.5	32.7	31.2	-7.6
Afghanistan	-9.8	-2.0	20.1	16.5	(e)-2.0	(e)-7.9	25.9	-25.3	-3.7	-3.3	(e)-1.6
Bangladesh	12.5	15.7	12.9	15.6	15.2	15.8	11.9	-1.9	27.3	27.3	2.8
Bhutan	11.5	7.0	24.4	55.1	(e)10.3	(e)6.4	41.1	-4.9	29.3	5.2	(e)-9.6
India (24)	9.4	9.5	20.1	24.8	17.0	15.4	30.0	-15.4	37.3	33.8	-2.9
Iran (Islamic Rep. of)*	2.5	1.3	17.3	29.4	(e)8.7	(e)3.4	34.9	-30.6	28.5	(e)30.3	(e)-21.2
Maldives	14.1	4.4	8.0	10.8	7.0	6.3	-10.7	-49.0	16.9	75.4	-9.2
Nepal	10.7	13.1	2.7	3.3	0.8	0.5	11.8	-12.4	4.0	7.4	-0.9
Pakistan	7.9	4.3	9.6	9.6	6.6	7.8	20.0	-13.8	22.2	18.6	-3.2
Sri Lanka	9.6	11.3	6.3	10.2	6.0	5.6	10.2	-13.1	17.1	19.0	-8.4

For sources and notes, see end of table.

Imports (c.i.f.) - Importations (c.a.f.) En pourcentage											Régions, pays ou territoires
80-00	90-00	00-10	04-07	05-12	08-12	2005	2009	2010	2011	2012	
7.8	12.1	10.8	19.1	10.2	9.0	19.8	-25.1	29.0	22.4	3.7	**Économies en développement : Amérique**
0.2	8.2	7.7	17.8	4.3	1.6	24.2	-30.9	10.1	26.4	-4.5	*Caraïbes*
-	(e)13.0	12.4	37.6	(e)-3.2	(e)-12.2	26.7	-37.8	-6.5	-2.9	(e)-2.9	Anguilla
7.8	4.4	5.2	17.7	(e)-3.0	(e)-7.7	11.5	-28.1	-6.1	-6.0	(e)12.5	Antigua-et-Barbuda
(e)18.7	10.0	1.9	12.4	(e)-8.3	(e)-7.7	19.5	-59.3	-43.7	327.4	(e)-55.9	Aruba (14)
-8.0	7.7	5.1	16.0	3.0	2.7	21.3	-20.7	2.2	14.5	14.2	Bahamas (15)
3.3	7.2	5.1	7.2	0.5	0.7	13.6	-24.5	8.3	15.0	-1.4	Barbade
										(e)9.2	Bonaire, Saint-Eustache et Saba
(e)7.4	(e)7.8	(e)5.2	(e)5.2	(e)1.2	(e)-0.3	(e)5.7	(e)-12.1	3.4	6.7	-3.1	Îles Vierges britanniques (4)
(e)9.3	(e)8.7	(e)5.2	(e)5.3	(e)-4.2	(e)-3.1	(e)46.2	(e)-17.2	(e)-7.3	(e)10.0	(e)-0.1	Îles Caïmanes (4)
(e)-5.1	(e)7.4	12.8	24.9	6.2	1.7	44.0	-37.4	19.5	23.9	-3.7	Cuba*
										5.9	Curaçao
6.5	3.5	7.0	9.7	(e)3.8	(e)-4.1	14.5	-8.8	-0.7	1.0	(e)-11.5	Dominique*
9.4	12.0	6.7	20.2	7.5	5.7	25.1	-23.1	26.0	12.6	1.8	République dominicaine (16)
7.7	8.5	5.0	13.3	(e)0.0	(e)0.0	40.6	-22.4	12.8	3.8	(e)1.5	Grenade*
3.7	14.4	11.1	9.0	13.1	10.3	11.3	-8.3	48.1	-4.0	5.0	Haïti
5.8	7.1	7.7	20.4	1.9	-2.6	20.3	-40.2	3.2	23.2	2.3	Jamaïque
4.0	-6.3	4.2	1.1	(e)2.1	(e)0.6	3.6	-22.1	-0.9	13.9	(e)10.7	Montserrat*
-3.6	1.3	0.4	13.9			13.2	-15.3	3.1			Antilles néerlandaises*(17)
7.8	5.7	5.4	14.6	(e)0.5	(e)-8.4	15.2	-9.0	-8.8	-8.6	(e)-6.8	Saint-Kitts-et-Nevis*
6.6	2.3	7.6	14.2	(e)3.6	(e)3.1	15.2	-20.6	27.3	5.6	(e)-5.7	Sainte-Lucie*
6.1	3.9	8.9	13.1	(e)4.7	(e)-0.8	6.6	-10.6	1.3	-1.8	(e)8.5	Saint-Vincent-et-les Grenadines*
										4.7	Saint-Martin (partie néerlandaise)
0.0	12.1	10.1	16.2	5.3	2.0	17.2	-27.5	-6.8	46.8	-4.7	Trinité-et-Tobago*
-	-	13.5	40.5	(e)-5.3	(e)-13.7	37.7	-36.5	-19.6	(e)4.6	(e)-2.1	Îles Turques et Caïques
12.1	13.9	7.5	14.0	6.5	7.9	15.1	-23.7	26.7	17.6	5.4	*Amérique centrale*
6.3	5.9	4.3	9.8	4.6	3.3	14.1	-20.1	5.5	17.8	6.1	Belize
(b)10.9	(b)13.9	9.2	16.3	6.9	6.4	18.8	-25.9	19.1	19.5	8.4	Costa Rica*
9.9	14.0	6.7	12.0	4.7	4.1	5.7	-25.4	14.9	18.4	3.1	El Salvador (18)
7.6	11.6	10.5	12.8	6.0	7.0	10.8	-20.7	20.0	20.1	2.3	Guatemala (19)
8.0	16.8	9.9	14.8	6.7	5.5	12.3	-29.5	20.8	23.4	1.7	Honduras (20)
13.2	14.1	6.7	13.1	6.2	7.9	12.8	-24.1	28.4	16.4	5.4	Mexique
3.1	11.6	10.7	17.5	10.7	10.6	18.6	-19.2	19.6	24.7	12.4	Nicaragua (21)
	8.7	23.5	49.7	(e)13.1	(e)13.3	167.1	-11.8	20.6	30.3	(e)7.3	Panama*(22)
7.1	11.1	15.1	25.6	14.7	10.9	25.1	-25.5	33.7	25.8	3.3	*Amérique du Sud*
10.3	16.9	14.6	25.1	13.0	10.5	27.8	-32.5	45.7	30.9	-7.3	Argentine*
6.8	9.7	14.3	23.7	19.0	16.1	29.5	-10.6	23.0	37.1	7.9	Bolivie (État plurinational de)
7.2	12.6	14.9	23.9	17.0	11.2	16.9	-26.7	43.3	23.7	-1.5	Brésil
9.9	10.2	15.2	23.2	12.5	10.9	32.0	-31.8	38.5	26.9	5.6	Chili*
6.9	9.6	15.3	25.1	14.4	13.9	26.6	-17.1	23.7	34.4	8.1	Colombie
5.0	7.7	17.5	19.0	13.6	11.1	25.0	-20.0	36.5	17.9	3.7	Équateur
(e)12.1	(e)8.0	(e)3.1	(e)0.0	(e)14.4	(e)31.4	(e)-25.9	(e)-8.3	81.8	80.0	-27.8	Îles Falkland (Malvinas) (4)
4.5	5.8	10.8	17.1	13.4	13.1	21.0	-11.5	20.4	26.2	12.0	Guyana*
10.8	7.0	19.4	24.1	18.3	11.3	20.0	-23.2	44.6	23.2	-6.6	Paraguay
7.6	12.2	17.5	25.9	18.0	13.3	23.8	-27.2	37.7	25.7	12.7	Pérou*
1.5	0.9	12.9	10.4	8.7	8.2	41.4	6.6	0.5	17.2	8.8	Suriname
7.9	10.1	14.3	22.0	16.3	9.8	24.6	-23.8	24.8	24.4	8.3	Uruguay
2.2	5.3	(e)15.0	40.3	(e)9.3	(e)5.4	44.1	-16.3	(e)-6.1	(e)21.8	(e)27.2	Venezuela (Rép. bolivarienne du)
9.4	8.3	14.7	16.9	11.8	11.6	17.5	-18.4	31.2	22.2	4.4	**Économies en développement : Asie**
12.5	9.2	14.5	15.8	11.9	13.0	14.3	-15.7	35.4	21.9	3.4	*Asie orientale*
13.0	13.0	20.9	19.5	15.4	16.1	17.6	-11.2	38.8	24.9	4.3	Chine
14.2	8.5	8.4	10.8	8.4	11.1	10.0	-10.4	25.3	15.7	8.3	Chine (RAS de Hong Kong)
7.7	2.9	8.9	14.1	8.0	14.6	10.3	-19.2	18.5	40.8	13.3	Chine (RAS de Macao)
11.9	8.6	7.9	9.2	5.5	7.4	7.9	-27.5	44.1	12.0	-3.9	Province chinoise de Taiwan
(e)-1.3	(e)-7.0	(e)8.2	(e)9.8	(e)7.7	(e)9.4	(e)19.3	(e)-13.5	(e)14.1	(e)22.7	(e)9.7	Corée, Rép. populaire dém. de
11.1	7.1	12.6	16.9	9.6	8.7	16.4	-25.8	31.6	23.3	-0.9	Corée, République de (23)
-4.3	0.8	20.5	27.3	27.5	26.8	16.0	-41.1	53.8	101.3	2.1	Mongolie
4.9	5.2	20.7	24.7	15.7	12.8	35.5	-18.5	33.2	26.5	2.7	*Asie méridionale*
-3.2	5.5	11.0	8.5	(e)15.4	(e)20.3	13.5	10.5	54.5	24.0	(e)-13.9	Afghanistan
7.3	11.3	13.3	15.6	14.7	13.0	15.4	-8.5	27.4	30.2	-5.8	Bangladesh
4.8	7.9	16.3	8.6	(e)17.1	(e)23.1	-6.0	-2.6	61.3	23.2	(e)3.6	Bhoutan
6.9	10.1	24.6	31.3	18.8	15.4	43.2	-19.9	36.2	32.6	5.4	Inde (24)
0.6	-5.2	16.4	11.0	6.8	1.9	25.2	-11.6	28.8	-5.6	-7.6	Iran (Rép. islamique d')*
15.1	11.8	14.2	20.0	8.8	6.7	16.1	-30.6	13.3	34.3	6.1	Maldives
8.5	10.7	14.1	16.4	16.4	14.2	17.8	22.1	17.1	12.5	5.0	Népal
4.5	3.1	16.8	21.6	7.4	4.2	41.3	-25.2	19.4	16.4	0.3	Pakistan
7.8	8.9	9.2	12.7	11.4	14.3	10.8	-28.0	34.5	50.0	-5.4	Sri Lanka

Pour les sources et les notes, se reporter à la fin du tableau.

Region, country or territory	Exports (f.o.b) - Exportations (f.a.b.) Percentage										
	80-00	90-00	00-10	04-07	05-12	08-12	2005	2009	2010	2011	2012
South-Eastern Asia	**11.2**	**11.1**	**11.1**	**15.2**	**9.1**	**9.3**	**15.3**	**-17.8**	**29.0**	**17.8**	**1.3**
Brunei Darussalam*	-1.7	2.4	11.0	15.6	9.5	10.6	23.6	-30.2	23.7	39.7	4.3
Cambodia (6)	32.1	26.8	14.5	14.1	(e)13.4	(e)17.6	10.5	-10.9	22.6	(e)36.1	(e)17.1
Indonesia (...2002)	6.5	8.7	–	–	–	–	–	–	–	–	–
Indonesia	–	–	–	18.6	11.9	11.8	22.9	-14.3	32.1	27.0	-6.1
Lao People's Dem. Rep.*	16.1	15.4	19.8	38.6	21.5	24.7	52.2	-3.6	65.9	26.9	2.4
Malaysia (25)	12.7	12.2	8.9	11.9	6.4	6.5	11.4	-21.1	26.2	14.8	-0.3
Myanmar	7.3	14.4	17.2	36.7	13.1	8.6	60.2	-4.0	30.0	6.7	-3.7
Philippines	11.4	18.6	3.7	9.0	1.8	3.5	4.0	-21.7	34.0	-6.2	7.6
Singapore (26)	12.2	9.9	12.0	15.0	7.8	8.3	15.6	-20.2	30.4	16.4	-0.3
Thailand*	15.2	10.5	12.6	16.9	10.4	9.3	15.3	-14.3	26.8	15.1	3.1
Timor-Leste (27)	–	–	–	4.5	(e)7.6	(e)1.9	10.2	-34.7	96.3	-28.0	(e)0.0
Viet Nam	21.0	22.7	19.4	22.4	18.7	18.9	22.5	-8.9	26.5	34.2	18.2
Western Asia	**1.8**	**6.6**	**17.7**	**23.6**	**12.8**	**12.1**	**34.4**	**-29.6**	**23.4**	**39.7**	**11.0**
Bahrain (6)	2.0	3.5	12.2	21.5	8.5	8.0	35.5	-31.4	26.1	31.3	0.6
Iraq*	-6.4	33.9	17.9	31.5	(e)19.9	(e)16.8	33.1	-31.6	25.2	(e)58.7	(e)13.3
Jordan	6.5	6.6	14.9	14.5	8.4	2.2	10.8	-19.7	10.2	13.9	-1.5
Kuwait*	0.0	16.5	19.2	29.4	12.2	13.3	56.9	-38.2	29.6	46.0	16.0
Lebanon (28)	-0.3	4.1	20.6	17.9	13.4	8.0	6.3	-6.0	19.9	12.8	-0.9
Oman	3.9	5.8	14.8	22.0	15.3	12.5	40.1	-26.7	32.4	28.7	10.7
Qatar*	2.0	10.3	23.9	31.1	25.3	25.0	37.9	-28.7	55.8	52.8	16.3
Saudi Arabia*(29)	-0.3	3.1	16.5	22.2	9.8	11.3	43.4	-38.6	30.6	45.2	6.5
State of Palestine	–	(e)1.1	7.6	17.0	(e)14.8	(e)16.7	7.3	-7.2	11.0	31.9	(e)31.9
Syrian Arab Republic*	4.8	0.9	11.9	17.0	(e)-6.8	(e)-24.3	18.0	-29.6	17.9	(e)-21.9	(e)-60.0
Turkey*	10.8	9.1	17.4	19.0	9.1	5.8	16.3	-22.6	11.5	18.5	13.0
United Arab Emirates	(e)5.1	7.1	(e)19.7	25.1	(e)14.8	(e)12.9	28.9	(e)-19.7	(e)11.5	(e)41.1	(e)15.9
Yemen*	–	20.6	(e)9.6	15.9	(e)7.5	(e)8.3	37.7	-17.5	(e)34.2	(e)28.6	(e)-20.4
Developing economies: Oceania	**6.3**	**6.2**	**7.7**	**14.0**	**5.2**	**5.8**	**9.9**	**-25.4**	**28.3**	**19.8**	**-6.9**
American Samoa*(30)	4.3	1.4	(e)1.8	(e)1.9	(e)-3.3	(e)-10.7	-16.1	(e)-17.5	(e)-36.2	(e)-6.7	(e)50.0
Cook Islands	0.4	0.4	-7.7	-13.0	(e)-5.6	(e)-4.9	-27.6	-32.5	86.3	-39.3	(e)-4.3
Fiji	3.5	3.1	4.1	2.5	7.4	11.6	1.2	-31.7	33.6	27.2	14.4
French Polynesia*	13.8	9.2	-1.9	0.4	-6.7	-5.4	9.1	-24.2	3.3	9.7	-17.3
Guam (4)	(e)3.8	(e)-0.5	0.6	18.1	-5.3	-16.5	-1.8	-51.1	-11.1	-4.9	6.4
Kiribati	3.6	4.2	(e)9.0	57.0	(e)0.0	(e)-14.6	74.5	(e)-58.2	-38.0	120.8	-32.4
Marshall Islands	–	4.1	9.1	-5.7	(e)9.1	(e)17.6	28.2	3.0	55.3	(e)8.4	(e)0.0
Micronesia (Federated States of)	–	9.8	(e)0.0	5.9	(e)8.9	(e)6.3	5.7	-8.8	(e)0.4	(e)12.0	(e)25.0
Nauru (4)	(e)-6.2	(e)-5.2	(e)9.6	(e)7.4	(e)61.5	(e)6.5	(e)-76.9	(e)-77.3	100.0	40.0	28.6
New Caledonia*	4.1	2.4	12.4	26.4	1.3	5.6	5.8	-23.6	50.3	11.3	-20.5
Niue	(e)-5.1	9.9	(e)-13.2	174.6	(e)-45.6	(e)1.0	13.7	(e)5.3	(e)0.0	(e)0.0	(e)0.0
Northern Mariana Islands (4)	–	(e)19.7	(e)-38.5	(e)-26.4	(e)-60.9	(e)-56.1	(e)-16.3	(e)-92.2	(e)-44.4	(e)-60.0	(e)100.0
Palau (4)	–	(e)-4.6	(e)-7.1	(e)20.8	(e)-11.3	(e)-4.4	128.1	(e)-40.0	(e)0.0	(e)0.0	(e)33.3
Papua New Guinea	6.2	3.6	14.0	22.9	9.0	6.1	28.3	-23.1	30.7	20.3	-11.3
Samoa (28)	0.4	20.0	-0.8	1.0	-2.7	4.9	2.0	-36.1	52.8	-5.7	14.8
Solomon Islands*	4.1	2.3	16.3	19.0	23.5	30.1	6.4	-21.5	35.8	85.6	18.8
Tokelau (4)	..	..	(e)-24.0	(e)-12.9	(e)-10.8	(e)4.4	(e)36.4	(e)57.8	(e)-40.0	(e)60.7	(e)-16.9
Tonga	3.3	-3.8	-2.6	-16.0	6.0	17.8	-33.3	-15.6	5.2	74.3	8.4
Tuvalu	(e)-15.3	-15.3	(e)30.0	-12.5	(e)32.7	(e)8.4	-53.0	(e)50.0	(e)0.0	(e)0.0	14.0
Vanuatu	-0.1	4.8	11.5	11.9	5.1	1.0	1.3	0.0	-14.0	38.1	-18.7
Wallis and Futuna Islands (4)	..	..	(e)-10.3	(e)-14.0	(e)0.6	(e)2.0	(e)-19.1	(e)-30.0	(e)50.0	(e)-35.7	(e)66.7
Transition economies	**1.5**	**5.6**	**18.3**	**25.1**	**11.0**	**8.4**	**28.8**	**-35.4**	**30.1**	**33.2**	**1.6**
Albania	(e)1.4	7.9	20.1	21.2	16.7	14.2	8.7	-19.5	41.6	26.3	0.9
Armenia*	–	–	12.3	15.1	4.2	13.1	34.7	-32.8	46.6	28.2	7.0
Azerbaijan (31)	–	–	38.6	79.5	20.0	6.4	111.6	-31.0	25.5	30.3	-5.4
Belarus	–	–	16.4	21.1	13.7	14.5	16.0	-34.6	18.7	63.8	11.0
Bosnia and Herzegovina*(32)	–	–	20.6	32.9	10.5	4.6	33.9	-21.3	21.5	21.8	-11.8
Croatia*	–	–	12.5	15.8	3.9	-0.2	9.3	-25.8	12.8	13.1	-7.6
Georgia (33)	–	–	20.0	22.3	15.3	17.2	33.7	-24.2	47.9	30.5	8.6
Kazakhstan*(34)	–	–	25.8	33.8	16.3	13.1	38.6	-39.3	38.8	46.1	5.3
Kyrgyzstan	–	–	16.8	23.5	15.3	2.1	-6.5	-9.8	5.2	12.1	-4.0
Montenegro	–	–	–	–	-0.5	–	–	-37.2	12.7	44.7	-25.4
Republic of Moldova	–	–	12.6	9.3	10.9	12.3	10.7	-19.4	20.1	43.8	-2.5
Russian Federation (35)	–	–	17.7	24.6	10.1	8.0	33.1	-35.7	32.1	30.3	1.4
Serbia and Montenegro*	–	–	–	(e)35.1	–	–	(e)27.3	–	–	–	–
Serbia	–	–	–	–	–	4.2	–	-23.9	17.4	20.3	-3.6
Tajikistan (33)	–	–	7.0	20.3	1.6	1.5	-0.6	-28.3	18.3	5.1	8.1
TFYR of Macedonia*	–	–	13.6	25.6	9.2	5.2	21.8	-32.1	23.7	33.6	-10.6
Turkmenistan (33)	–	–	(e)13.5	33.4	(e)12.1	(e)17.4	27.8	(e)-58.1	(e)30.0	(e)100.0	(e)26.9
Ukraine (33)	–	–	15.1	14.4	9.2	6.1	4.8	-40.6	29.4	33.0	0.1
Uzbekistan (33)	–	–	18.8	22.8	14.3	3.2	11.0	4.2	8.9	13.3	-18.2

For sources and notes, see end of table.

Imports (c.i.f.) - Importations (c.a.f.) En pourcentage											Régions, pays ou territoires
80-00	90-00	00-10	04-07	05-12	08-12	2005	2009	2010	2011	2012	
11.0	*8.2*	*11.5*	*14.7*	*9.8*	*10.3*	*17.4*	*-22.6*	*31.1*	*21.0*	*5.8*	*Asie du Sud-Est*
6.9	1.6	9.3	13.7	13.4	11.1	4.9	-4.8	4.6	41.6	-1.3	Brunéi Darussalam*
14.8	25.2	15.0	19.6	(e)14.1	(e)16.4	23.0	-10.4	16.5	(e)37.0	(e)18.3	Cambodge (6)
7.9	6.3	–	–	–	–	–	–	–	–	–	Indonésie (...2002)
–	–	–	17.9	14.2	15.4	38.0	-26.5	44.3	30.2	8.0	Indonésie
10.3	12.7	16.1	15.0	17.2	17.6	23.7	4.1	41.0	16.4	2.9	Rép. dém. populaire lao*
12.9	9.5	8.5	12.0	7.0	9.0	8.9	-21.1	32.9	13.9	4.9	Malaisie (25)
12.8	22.6	7.6	16.4	24.4	25.3	-12.3	1.4	9.5	89.5	2.0	Myanmar
10.5	12.5	4.9	8.1	3.0	5.0	7.3	-24.1	27.4	8.9	2.6	Philippines
10.6	7.7	11.4	15.3	8.5	7.7	15.2	-23.1	26.4	17.7	3.8	Singapour (26)
12.9	5.0	12.6	13.5	10.7	12.6	25.2	-25.4	36.8	25.1	8.2	Thaïlande*
		–	6.1	(e)21.5	(e)8.7	-25.3	9.9	1.0	14.1	(e)11.8	Timor-Leste (27)
13.6	22.9	20.7	24.9	16.7	11.7	15.0	-13.3	21.3	25.8	6.6	Viet Nam
3.4	*7.1*	*17.4*	*20.3*	*11.6*	*7.4*	*20.3*	*-21.3*	*15.7*	*22.2*	*7.8*	*Asie occidentale*
1.2	0.3	(e)12.9	15.5	(e)4.3	(e)0.9	27.2	(e)-32.6	(e)21.4	(e)3.8	(e)9.3	Bahreïn (6)
-8.5	27.7	(e)16.1	-0.9	(e)16.4	(e)14.3	10.5	(e)16.5	14.3	(e)11.6	(e)16.3	Iraq*
2.4	5.1	15.8	17.8	9.2	7.0	28.3	-16.2	9.3	21.6	9.3	Jordanie
0.9	5.5	13.7	18.1	6.6	3.3	25.1	-19.9	14.0	12.0	1.9	Koweït*
5.5	8.7	12.1	7.6	13.7	7.9	0.2	-1.1	11.4	12.4	5.8	Liban (28)
4.9	5.8	16.8	22.2	(e)15.9	(e)7.4	2.0	-22.5	11.4	20.3	(e)19.1	Oman
5.2	7.4	28.2	58.0	(e)14.6	(e)6.1	67.6	-10.7	-6.7	28.6	(e)14.4	Qatar*
-0.5	0.8	16.2	23.3	12.9	9.7	25.5	-17.0	11.8	23.1	18.2	Arabie saoudite*(29)
-	(e)9.2	8.2	9.1	(e)9.6	(e)9.8	12.4	0.9	9.9	13.5	(e)13.5	État de Palestine
0.4	3.6	18.8	18.8	(e)-0.6	(e)-15.9	29.1	-14.7	13.7	(e)-4.3	(e)-56.5	République arabe syrienne*
10.7	10.3	17.0	20.3	9.4	8.9	19.7	-30.2	31.7	29.8	-1.8	Turquie*
9.5	11.7	(e)20.1	(e)22.1	(e)13.9	(e)6.0	17.4	(e)-25.1	(e)10.0	(e)23.0	(e)13.3	Émirats arabes unis
–	0.6	17.9	27.1	(e)10.3	(e)3.5	34.9	-12.9	0.8	8.4	(e)19.6	Yémen*
4.2	*2.2*	*9.6*	*12.0*	*6.8*	*5.6*	*6.6*	*-16.9*	*18.1*	*15.2*	*-0.6*	*Économies en développement : Océanie*
5.9	3.0	(e)1.8	(e)3.3	(e)2.8	(e)1.9	-13.9	(e)-11.8	(e)-8.3	(e)27.3	(e)-1.4	Samoa américaines*(30)
4.6	-1.3	7.2	13.1	(e)2.3	(e)6.0	6.4	-35.2	12.8	35.5	(e)9.5	Îles Cook
3.7	2.7	9.1	8.0	3.5	4.1	11.1	-36.4	25.6	20.7	3.3	Fidji
3.7	0.9	6.4	6.3	-0.2	-4.3	14.9	-20.8	0.5	4.1	-5.1	Polynésie française*
(e)3.5	(e)-0.8	(e)8.2	(e)18.1	(e)8.6	16.1	5.8	31.1	11.8	15.8	9.1	Guam (4)
6.1	4.1	(e)6.5	3.5	(e)5.6	(e)11.4	24.7	(e)-9.3	9.1	25.5	18.3	Kiribati
–	0.9	(e)8.4	(e)5.1	(e)7.3	(e)10.1	(e)12.1	(e)5.0	(e)28.6	(e)3.7	(e)0.0	Îles Marshall
–	1.3	(e)5.2	2.5	(e)6.6	(e)6.7	-1.9	10.6	(e)-1.0	(e)5.9	(e)16.7	Micronésie (États fédérés de)
(e)2.4	(e)-9.8	(e)5.0	(e)45.1	(e)-1.5	(e)-15.0	(e)38.9	(e)-66.7	-33.3	50.0	33.3	Nauru (4)
6.3	1.1	15.0	19.7	9.1	3.8	8.4	-20.4	28.7	11.6	-12.3	Nouvelle-Calédonie*
(e)0.9	(e)-6.6	(e)19.4	(e)-13.7	(e)1.0	(e)1.2	(e)27.2	-24.2	(e)2.6	(e)33.3	(e)-12.5	Nioué
–	(e)18.7	(e)-19.6	(e)-22.7	(e)-29.6	(e)-16.0	(e)-11.0	(e)-56.2	(e)24.2	(e)-18.6	(e)-6.0	Îles Mariannes du Nord (4)
–	(e)16.5	(e)1.8	(e)1.7	(e)3.1	(e)2.3	-2.0	(e)8.3	(e)-7.7	(e)0.0	(e)16.7	Palaos (4)
1.2	-0.8	(e)15.4	21.6	(e)15.2	(e)11.4	2.9	(e)-8.5	(e)23.1	(e)20.5	(e)3.8	Papouasie-Nouvelle-Guinée
4.3	0.9	11.6	8.9	4.8	8.0	13.7	-19.9	34.4	11.6	-0.1	Samoa (28)
3.1	0.7	19.1	32.4	(e)14.7	(e)15.9	52.4	-14.1	50.8	15.3	(e)6.2	Îles Salomon*
-	-	(e)-28.6	(e)-58.4	(e)-21.3	(e)-12.0	(e)-39.5	(e)-24.0	(e)-24.6	(e)2.3	(e)2.3	Tokélaou (4)
4.0	1.9	9.3	9.3	7.7	6.5	15.2	-13.7	9.7	21.5	3.2	Tonga
5.0	4.2	(e)14.9	9.9	(e)9.2	(e)4.8	13.3	(e)-47.0	(e)14.3	(e)56.2	(e)0.0	Tuvalu
2.5	0.9	16.2	23.7	8.8	-0.8	16.6	-6.2	-3.1	6.7	-2.5	Vanuatu
..	..	(e)6.5	(e)5.2	(e)2.3	(e)0.5	-3.5	(e)-28.1	(e)18.3	(e)5.0	(e)3.2	Îles Wallis-et-Futuna (4)
0.8	*2.9*	*19.4*	*28.0*	*11.4*	*6.3*	*21.8*	*-32.9*	*21.0*	*28.8*	*3.7*	*Économies en transition*
(e)10.6	10.7	17.3	21.4	9.0	0.2	13.4	-13.3	-3.2	22.5	-9.5	Albanie
–	–	19.3	32.9	11.8	1.5	33.4	-25.0	12.9	10.6	2.9	Arménie*
–	–	21.5	19.9	12.1	11.4	23.7	-14.0	3.6	50.7	2.5	Azerbaïdjan (31)
–	–	18.3	21.6	14.0	8.3	1.3	-27.5	22.1	31.2	1.4	Bélarus
–	–	14.4	16.5	4.9	-1.6	19.5	-28.0	5.1	19.8	-9.3	Bosnie-Herzégovine*(32)
–	–	12.2	15.9	-0.1	-6.9	11.9	-31.0	-5.4	13.2	-8.6	Croatie*
–	–	27.9	42.0	14.0	9.3	34.9	-28.6	16.8	34.3	11.1	Géorgie (33)
–	–	24.0	36.8	10.5	6.1	35.8	-25.0	9.5	19.1	20.2	Kazakhstan*(34)
–	–	26.1	46.5	19.8	9.3	17.1	-25.3	6.0	32.2	26.1	Kirghizistan
–	–	–	–	-8.1	–	–	-38.0	-5.7	16.6	-8.1	Monténégro
–	–	20.2	26.7	11.0	6.0	29.6	-33.1	17.6	34.7	0.4	République de Moldova
–	–	20.5	31.8	12.9	8.4	28.8	-34.3	29.6	30.2	3.6	Fédération de Russie (35)
–	–	–	(e)23.4	–	–	(e)-1.0	–	–	–	–	Serbie-et-Monténégro*
–	–	–	–	–	-2.8	–	-34.0	4.3	18.7	-4.3	Serbie
–	–	18.9	27.5	13.2	5.2	11.6	-21.5	3.4	20.7	17.8	Tadjikistan (33)
–	–	14.4	21.1	9.8	2.2	10.1	-26.3	7.9	28.4	-7.3	LERY de Macédoine*
–	–	(e)13.2	1.2	(e)20.2	(e)13.3	-11.2	(e)21.4	(e)-16.2	(e)33.3	(e)30.3	Turkménistan (33)
–	–	18.7	27.5	10.5	5.9	24.6	-46.8	33.9	35.6	2.5	Ukraine (33)
–	–	16.2	22.8	17.0	5.6	8.1	-2.7	-3.7	20.5	7.9	Ouzbékistan (33)

Pour les sources et les notes, se reporter à la fin du tableau.

Region, country or territory	Exports (f.o.b) - Exportations (f.a.b.) Percentage										
	80-00	90-00	00-10	04-07	05-12	08-12	2005	2009	2010	2011	2012
Developed economies: America	**7.5**	**7.5**	**6.1**	**11.6**	**5.8**	**6.4**	**11.5**	**-21.3**	**21.4**	**16.0**	**3.5**
Bermuda (6)	3.9	-0.7	-10.3	-30.1	-16.3	-19.3	-32.9	19.5	-48.8	-8.1	-11.0
Canada	7.2	8.3	5.0	9.7	2.1	3.6	13.8	-30.8	22.6	16.7	0.6
Greenland	2.9	-3.6	4.4	3.6	1.6	2.2	5.5	-26.1	5.6	24.9	-0.1
Saint Pierre and Miquelon (4)	(e)7.7	(e)-18.2	(e)7.0	(e)46.4	(e)-18.3	(e)-11.7	(e)50.0	(e)-50.0	(e)-6.3	(e)11.2	(e)0.8
United States (36)	7.6	7.2	6.5	12.3	7.1	7.3	10.6	-18.0	21.1	15.8	4.4
Developed economies: Asia	**7.1**	**4.4**	**6.4**	**8.4**	**4.0**	**4.0**	**5.5**	**-25.4**	**31.8**	**7.6**	**-3.3**
Israel*	9.7	10.9	8.1	11.6	5.6	4.1	10.8	-21.9	21.9	16.1	-6.9
Japan	7.0	4.1	6.3	8.1	3.9	4.0	5.2	-25.7	32.6	6.9	-3.0
Developed economies: Europe	**7.1**	**5.5**	**9.5**	**12.6**	**4.4**	**2.5**	**8.4**	**-22.4**	**12.4**	**17.8**	**-4.3**
Andorra*	-	(e)1.2	3.6	1.9	(e)-9.2	(e)4.8	17.4	-34.0	-14.6	42.7	(e)42.7
Austria*	8.9	6.1	9.9	11.2	3.4	0.9	5.7	-24.4	11.4	16.3	-6.2
Belgium*	7.8	5.7	9.6	11.8	3.5	1.4	9.0	-21.6	10.2	16.8	-6.2
Bulgaria*	(e)-6.9	(e)1.3	18.0	23.6	11.2	9.5	18.2	-27.0	26.4	36.7	-5.3
Cyprus*	5.1	1.3	5.7	11.2	3.0	5.0	54.6	-23.0	11.5	29.7	-4.4
Czech Republic*(38)	–	–	18.5	21.1	9.4	5.1	13,2	-23.1	17.7	22.5	-3.9
Denmark*(39)	7.5	3.7	8.3	10.1	2.5	-0.3	10.4	-19.6	2.6	16.0	-5.6
Estonia*(33)	–	–	13.4	23.2	9.6	12.0	30.1	-27.4	28.1	44.3	-3.6
Faeroe Islands	5.9	1.4	5.9	6.8	6.9	5.1	-2.8	-10.6	10.1	20.1	-5.9
Finland*	7.4	8.0	6.7	14.0	-0.4	-3.2	6.5	-34.8	10.6	13.8	-7.7
France*	7.4	5.0	6.2	7.3	2.3	0.5	2.5	-21.3	8.0	13.9	-4.6
Germany*	–	3.7	10.2	13.3	4.4	2.2	6.7	-22.6	12.4	17.1	-4.5
Gibraltar (40)	16.5	10.0	(e)9.8	(e)15.8	(e)1.0	(e)-3.9	(e)0.7	(e)-6.7	-2.2	-4.6	-2.6
Greece*	6.0	3.6	9.2	15.9	8.7	11.6	12.9	-22.4	6.1	56.1	4.7
Hungary*(41)	(e)5.4	(e)12.5	15.1	19.7	6.4	2.2	13.3	-23.5	15.0	17.6	-7.5
Iceland	5.4	3.1	11.0	18.2	6.4	1.6	8.9	-24.6	13.5	16.1	-5.3
Ireland*	13.2	13.8	4.7	4.5	1.2	-0.6	4.6	-7.8	0.5	7.9	-6.8
Italy*	7.7	4.6	8.1	12.2	3.1	0.9	5.5	-25.0	9.9	17.0	-4.3
Latvia*	–	–	20.5	26.6	13.9	12.7	28.7	-24.1	23.8	37.7	7.3
Lithuania*(33)	–	–	20.5	22.3	12.7	10.4	26.9	-30.4	26.1	35.2	5.7
Luxembourg*	7.4	3.3	11.1	12.3	-0.7	-5.2	15.7	-17.0	-7.5	10.7	-11.1
Malta	10.6	6.3	5.7	7.9	8.1	8.6	-4.7	-17.9	25.5	22.3	-3.1
Netherlands*	6.7	7.0	11.5	15.4	6.2	3.5	13.7	-22.0	15.3	16.2	-1.7
Norway	6.4	5.2	11.1	18.2	4.8	1.9	25.7	-32.0	11.9	22.7	0.4
Poland*	(e)4.7	(e)9.8	19.9	23.2	9.8	4.8	19.2	-19.9	17.0	18.1	-2.8
Portugal*	11.1	5.3	9.1	13.6	5.0	3.5	6.6	-22.6	11.8	20.8	-2.3
Romania*	(e)-2.1	(e)9.1	18.5	19.5	11.2	7.8	17.6	-18.1	22.2	27.1	-8.2
Slovakia*	–	–	21.7	28.5	12.5	6.4	14.9	-21.2	15.3	23.5	2.1
Slovenia*	–	–	15.5	22.3	6.5	1.7	17.6	-23.3	11.5	19.0	-7.4
Spain*	11.0	8.3	9.7	11.5	5.6	3.9	5.5	-19.2	11.9	20.5	-4.1
Sweden*	6.9	5.9	8.3	11.2	3.1	2.4	6.2	-28.7	21.2	17.9	-7.8
Switzerland*	7.1	3.0	10.5	12.0	7.9	5.6	6.6	-14.1	13.4	20.0	-3.8
United Kingdom*	6.6	5.5	5.0	8.9	1.9	4.2	10.6	-22.8	17.2	20.8	-5.6
Developed economies: Oceania	**6.6**	**4.8**	**13.3**	**16.1**	**13.3**	**12.1**	**19.6**	**-17.7**	**36.1**	**26.2**	**-4.6**
Australia	6.7	5.0	14.1	17.6	14.2	12.7	22.6	-17.6	37.8	27.2	-5.1
New Zealand	5.9	4.2	9.3	9.1	8.2	8.4	6.8	-18.5	25.9	20.0	-1.0

For sources and notes, see next page.

Imports (c.i.f.) - Importations (c.a.f.) En pourcentage											Régions, pays ou territoires
80-00	90-00	00-10	04-07	05-12	08-12	2005	2009	2010	2011	2012	
7.9	**9.1**	**6.0**	**10.2**	**3.3**	**5.2**	**13.8**	**-25.2**	**22.5**	**15.1**	**3.0**	**Économies développées : Amérique**
3.8	2.7	4.9	6.2	-2.6	-6.5	-0.3	-8.2	-7.1	-8.9	0.0	Bermudes (6)
7.3	7.5	6.6	11.7	4.7	6.1	15.2	-21.3	22.1	15.1	2.5	Canada
1.8	-0.7	10.5	11.5	5.1	1.2	8.5	-17.0	8.9	13.2	-6.7	Groenland
(e)14.7	(e)1.4	(e)14.0	(e)4.4	(e)19.3	(e)1.0	(e)-12.5	(e)34.9	(e)-12.3	(e)0.0	(e)-5.0	Saint-Pierre-et-Miquelon (4)
8.1	9.5	5.9	9.9	3.1	5.0	13.6	-26.0	22.7	15.1	3.1	États-Unis (36)
6.2	**4.9**	**7.9**	**11.1**	**7.0**	**7.6**	**13.2**	**-27.6**	**25.6**	**23.3**	**3.2**	**Économies développées : Asie**
7.9	8.6	6.4	10.8	6.3	6.7	10.0	-27.2	24.2	23.9	-0.6	Israël*
6.1	4.6	8.0	11.2	7.1	7.7	13.5	-27.6	25.7	23.2	3.6	Japon
6.6	**4.0**	**0.8**	**13.8**	**4.2**	**1.7**	**10.1**	**-24.0**	**13.0**	**17.2**	**-5.9**	**Économies développées : Europe**
-	(e)3.1	5.2	2.7	(e)-2.2	(e)-2.6	3.4	-18.2	-4.2	5.5	(e)5.5	Andorre*
8.0	4.5	9.8	10.5	4.5	2.3	6.2	-22.4	11.1	20.4	-6.8	Autriche*
6.7	4.7	10.1	12.7	3.9	1.5	11.6	-24.2	10.7	19.3	-6.3	Belgique*
(e)-5.8	(e)3.1	18.4	27.6	6.0	0.9	25.7	-36.2	8.4	27.7	0.5	Bulgarie*
7.6	4.3	10.7	15.5	2.2	-6.3	14.8	-26.4	9.4	1.3	-15.9	Chypre*
_	_	16.5	19.4	8.2	3.6	9.4	-26.0	20.6	20.1	-7.5	République tchèque*(38)
6.2	4.1	8.6	12.9	1.4	-2.0	10.9	-24.0	-0.1	15.2	-3.9	Danemark*(39)
_	_	11.5	24.2	4.9	7.8	22.8	-36.7	21.2	44.1	-0.2	Estonie*(33)
3.0	5.5	6.2	16.2	3.8	5.5	18.3	-20.7	-0.4	26.6	16.4	Îles Féroé
5.3	5.1	10.0	16.8	2.2	-0.5	14.2	-33.7	13.0	22.5	-9.5	Finlande*
6.3	3.8	8.0	10.0	3.8	1.3	7.0	-21.8	8.9	17.8	-6.4	France*
_	3.3	9.9	14.1	5.2	2.8	8.6	-21.8	13.9	19.0	-7.0	Allemagne*
11.5	1.7	(e)7.6	(e)17.3	(e)4.7	(e)2.3	(e)3.0	(e)-9.7	-0.2	16.3	-0.8	Gibraltar (40)
7.5	5.1	10.4	14.4	0.5	-7.6	3.2	-25.0	-8.1	5.6	-6.3	Grèce*
(e)6.5	(e)12.6	12.8	16.6	4.0	0.1	9.9	-28.6	13.4	16.2	-7.0	Hongrie*(41)
5.5	5.5	8.7	22.8	-4.3	-2.3	36.7	-41.9	8.8	23.5	-1.4	Islande
9.4	10.7	3.9	10.3	-2.8	-5.1	10.9	-25.3	-3.9	10.5	-5.8	Irlande*
5.8	3.2	9.1	13.1	2.8	0.1	8.3	-26.1	17.3	14.7	-12.9	Italie*
_	_	17.1	29.6	6.4	6.5	22.6	-39.2	19.2	39.3	5.6	Lettonie*
_	_	18.0	25.3	8.6	6.4	25.5	-41.1	27.9	35.8	1.4	Lituanie*(33)
8.2	4.2	10.6	12.2	1.9	-1.6	9.2	-21.2	-0.9	16.8	-6.0	Luxembourg*
8.7	4.5	6.8	10.1	7.4	8.1	1.1	-15.5	13.1	24.3	4.9	Malte
6.4	6.7	11.3	15.4	6.2	3.4	13.8	-23.7	16.5	16.0	-1.3	Pays-Bas*
5.2	4.1	11.1	18.0	5.5	2.1	14.3	-23.6	12.1	17.4	-3.8	Norvège
(e)8.0	(e)15.3	16.6	22.9	8.7	2.2	13.3	-28.4	19.1	18.3	-6.9	Pologne*
9.8	5.3	9.1	13.8	2.1	-3.9	11.3	-24.1	8.5	6.1	-12.4	Portugal*
(e)0.8	(e)8.1	19.9	28.8	6.2	-0.2	23.9	-35.4	14.3	23.1	-8.2	Roumanie*
_	_	20.3	26.9	10.6	4.9	16.0	-24.7	16.8	22.8	-2.0	Slovaquie*
_	_	14.5	20.9	5.7	0.0	14.5	-28.4	13.5	18.1	-9.9	Slovénie*
9.7	6.0	10.1	14.6	1.0	-2.0	11.8	-30.3	11.5	15.2	-11.1	Espagne*
5.5	4.4	9.9	15.0	4.7	3.2	11.2	-28.9	24.2	18.9	-8.2	Suède*
6.1	2.5	9.2	11.7	6.3	4.5	9.3	-15.4	13.5	18.1	-5.0	Suisse*
7.1	5.6	6.7	10.5	2.7	4.4	9.1	-18.0	13.9	14.0	2.4	Royaume-Uni*
6.5	**6.3**	**12.5**	**13.5**	**9.6**	**9.1**	**14.3**	**-18.6**	**21.6**	**20.9**	**6.5**	**Économies développées : Océanie**
6.7	6.4	13.1	14.4	10.4	9.6	14.5	-17.4	21.9	20.9	7.1	Australie
6.0	5.9	9.6	9.1	4.9	6.0	13.0	-25.6	19.7	21.2	3.1	Nouvelle-Zélande

Pour les sources et les notes, se reporter à la page suivante.

Sources:

UNCTAD secretariat calculations, based on:

- UN DESA Statistics Division, *Yearbook of International Trade Statistics*
- UN DESA Statistics Division, *Monthly Bulletin of Statistics*
- UN DESA Statistics Division, *UN COMTRADE*
- IMF, *International Financial Statistics*
- IMF, *Direction of Trade Statistics*
- IMF, *Balance of Payments Statistics*
- WTO, *Statistics database*
- Eurostat, *Comext*
- World Bank, *World Development Indicators*
- OECD, *OECD.Stat Extracts*
- OPEC, *Annual Statistical Bulletin*
- Economist Intelligence Unit, *Country Data*
- Other international and national sources

Notes:

(*)   Special Trade System.

(1)   Excluding exports of gold.

(2)   From 1996 onward, imports f.o.b.

(3)   From 2011 onwards, commercial mining is included.

(4)   Estimates based on UN *Comtrade* mirror structure.

(5)   Prior to 2008, special trade.

(6)   Imports f.o.b.

(7)   Trade with other member countries of CEMAC is excluded. Imports f.o.b.

(8)   Trade with other member countries of CEMAC is excluded.

(9)   Prior to 1995, data refer to fiscal year ending June.

(10)   Prior to 1974, special trade.

(11)   Excluding re-exports (oil for bunkering).

(12)   Prior to 2009, re-exports are excluded.

(13)   Prior to 2005, special trade.

(14)   Prior to 1986, included in Netherlands Antilles. Including exports and imports of crude oil and oil products. Prior to 2000, free zone trade is excluded. Imports f.o.b.

(15)   From 1990 onwards, trade statistics exclude certain oil and chemical products. Imports f.o.b.

(16)   Prior to 1993, excluding free trade processing zones. Imports f.o.b.

(17)   Prior to 1986, including Aruba.

(18)   Prior to 1992, excluding free trade processing zones.

(19)   Prior to 2002, special trade.

(20)   From 1990 onward, including goods for processing. Imports f.o.b.

(21)   Excluding free trade processing zones.

(22)   Prior to 2005, excluding customs free zones.

(23)   Excluding imports of goods financed through foreign aid.

(24)   Excluding military goods, fissionable materials, bunkers, ships and aircraft.

(25)   Inter-trade between the States of Malaysia included. From 1965 onwards, excluding military imports and offshore installations of petroleum industry.

(26)   Including trans-shipments to and from Peninsular Malaysia.

(27)   Excluding exports of oil and gas.

(28)   Prior to 2001, special trade.

(29)   Excluding defense imports.

(30)   Data refer to fiscal year ending September.

(31)   Excluding military goods, precious metals and goods procured in foreign ports.

(32)   Prior to 1998, data refer to the Federation of Bosnia and Herzegovina only. The other entity of Bosnia and Herzegovina, Republika Srpska, is not included.

(33)   Prior to 1994, covers only trade with countries outside the CIS.

(34)   Prior to 1994, covers only trade with countries outside the CIS. As of 2011, adjusted to include bilateral trade with Russian Federation.

(35)   Prior to 1994, excluding trade with independent states which succeeded from the former USSR.

(36)   Prior to 1975, excludes non-monetary gold.

(37)   From 1985 onwards, data are not comparable to those shown for prior periods due to revisions of the koruna-to-US dollar exchange rate.

(38)   From 1995 onward, including goods for processing.

(39)   Prior to 1988, excluding ships.

(40)   Excluding petroleum products. Estimates based on UN. *Comtrade* mirror structure.

(41)   Prior to 1996, excluding customs free zones.

Sources :

Calculs du secrétariat de la CNUCED, basés sur :

- ONU DAES Division de statistique, *Annuaire statistique du commerce international*
- ONU DAES Division de statistique, *Bulletin mensuel de statistique*
- ONU DAES Division de statistique, *ONU COMTRADE*
- FMI, *Statistiques financières internationales*
- FMI, *Direction of Trade Statistics*
- FMI, *Statistiques de la balance des paiements*
- OMC, *Base de données statistiques*
- Eurostat, *Comext*
- Banque mondiale, *Indicateurs du développement dans le monde*
- OCDE, *OECD.Stat Extracts*
- OPEP, *Bulletin statistique annuel*
- Economist Intelligence Unit, *Country Data*
- Autres sources internationales et nationales

Notes :

(*)   Système du commerce spécial.

(1)   Non-compris les exportations d'or.

(2)   À partir de 1996, importations f.a.b.

(3)   À partir de 2011, l'exploitation minière commerciale est incluse.

(4)   Estimations basées sur la structure des données miroirs de UN *Comtrade*.

(5)   Avant 2008, commerce spécial.

(6)   Importations f.a.b.

(7)   Non-compris le commerce avec les autres pays membres de la CEMAC. Importations f.a.b.

(8)   Non-compris le commerce avec les autres pays membres de la CEMAC.

(9)   Avant 1995, les données se rapportent à l'exercice budgétaire finissant juin.

(10) Avant 1974, commerce spécial.

(11) Non-compris les réexportations (huile pour mise en soute).

(12) Avant 2009, non-compris les réexportations.

(13) Avant 2005, commerce spécial.

(14) Avant 1986 compris dans Antilles néerlandaises. Les données comprennent les exportations et importations de pétrole brut et produits dérivés. Avant 2000, non-compris les zones franches douanières. Importations f.a.b.

(15) À partir de 1990, certains produits pétroliers et chimiques ne sont plus inclus dans les statistiques du commerce. Importations f.a.b.

(16) Avant 1993, non-compris les zones franches douanières. Importations f.a.b.

(17) Avant 1986, y compris Aruba.

(18) Avant 1992, non-compris les zones franches douanières.

(19) Avant 2002, commerce spécial.

(20) À partir de 1990, y compris les biens destinés à subir des transformations. Importations f.a.b.

(21) Non-compris les zones franches douanières.

(22) Avant 2005, non-compris les zones franches douanières.

(23) Non-compris les biens d'importation financés par l'aide à l'étranger.

(24) Non-compris les biens à usage militaire, le matériel fissile, le combustible de soute et l'avitaillement des navires et aéronefs.

(25) Y compris le commerce entre les États de la Malaisie. Non-compris les importations militaires et l'installation près des côtes de l'industrie pétrolière.

(26) Y compris les transbordements vers et en provenance de la Malaisie péninsulaire.

(27) Non-compris les exportations de pétrole et de gaz.

(28) Avant 2001, commerce spécial.

(29) Non-compris les importations de la défense.

(30) Les données se rapportent à l'exercice budgétaire finissant septembre.

(31) Non-compris les biens à usage militaire, les métaux précieux et les biens fournis dans les ports étrangers.

(32) Avant 1998, les données se réfèrent uniquement à la Fédération de la Bosnie-Herzégovine. L'autre entité de la Bosnie-Herzégovine, Republika Srpska, n'est pas incluse.

(33) Avant 1994, concerne seulement le commerce avec les pays extérieurs à la CEI.

(34) Avant 1994, concerne seulement le commerce avec les pays extérieurs à la CEI. A partir de 2011, y compris le commerce bilatéral avec la Fédération de Russie.

(35) Avant 1994, non-compris le commerce avec les républiques indépendantes de l'ancienne URSS.

(36) Avant 1975, non-compris l'or industriel.

(37) À partir de 1985, les chiffres ne sont pas comparables à ceux des années antérieures à cause des révisions du taux de change de la couronne par rapport au dollar des États-Unis.

(38) À partir de 1995, y compris les biens destinés à subir des transformations.

(39) Avant 1988, non-compris les navires.

(40) Non-compris les produits pétroliers. Estimations basées sur la structure des données miroirs de UN *Comtrade*.

(41) Avant 1996, non-compris les zones franches douanières.

Economic grouping	Exports (f.o.b.) - Exportations (f.a.b.) Percentage										
	80-00	90-00	00-10	04-07	05-12	08-12	2005	2009	2010	2011	2012
DEVELOPING ECONOMIES	7.6	9.1	14.4	19.3	10.6	10.3	21.8	-20.6	28.4	22.7	4.1
Developing economies excluding China	7.1	8.5	12.6	17.3	9.7	9.7	20.2	-21.9	27.5	23.4	2.9
Developing economies excluding LDCs	7.7	9.1	14.3	19.1	10.6	10.4	21.5	-20.5	28.4	22.6	4.2
High-income developing economies	7.6	8.7	11.9	16.0	8.8	9.3	18.8	-22.4	26.6	22.0	4.6
Middle-income developing economies	8.8	10.4	18.2	24.4	12.3	10.8	26.2	-18.4	29.8	21.1	4.1
Low-income developing economies	4.2	8.1	17.5	21.8	15.1	14.4	25.9	-18.2	33.0	32.9	1.9
Heavily indebted poor countries (IMF)	2.4	4.7	15.7	18.6	12.4	10.3	18.3	-14.5	28.4	21.8	-2.2
Landlocked developing countries	9.2	11.3	21.3	31.1	15.2	11.4	30.1	-29.3	30.8	36.2	2.3
Small island developing States	-0.3	4.2	11.0	21.1	3.2	1.1	30.8	-40.4	20.1	27.7	-6.8
Least developed countries	5.0	7.8	19.4	28.2	12.9	9.1	36.4	-24.0	27.2	25.2	1.2
Africa and Haiti	3.0	4.3	22.6	32.1	13.1	7.9	42.1	-28.8	26.6	25.7	2.1
Asia	11.0	16.4	13.0	19.2	12.6	13.0	24.5	-7.2	28.8	23.6	-1.2
Islands	2.3	3.5	9.4	10.5	13.8	19.8	2.3	-20.4	29.3	53.3	10.9
Major petroleum and gas exporters	0.8	4.8	17.8	25.6	11.8	10.9	40.4	-33.3	26.9	36.7	9.9
Africa	0.0	2.1	19.1	27.5	8.8	6.5	46.3	-38.4	33.7	14.1	18.2
America	2.3	6.1	12.2	20.5	6.1	5.4	40.5	-39.4	14.1	41.2	4.9
Asia	1.0	5.5	18.1	25.5	13.2	12.6	38.6	-31.0	26.1	43.1	8.3
Major exporters of manufactured goods	12.8	10.9	13.5	17.6	10.1	10.4	17.2	-16.6	29.4	17.7	4.5
America	11.0	16.1	7.0	13.4	6.8	9.4	14.0	-21.1	29.9	17.2	6.1
Asia	13.1	10.3	14.3	18.1	10.4	10.5	17.6	-16.2	29.3	17.7	4.4
Emerging economies	10.9	10.3	10.9	14.7	8.3	8.8	14.2	-18.6	29.5	17.6	-0.3
America	8.5	11.8	11.0	17.3	8.7	9.4	18.4	-20.5	29.6	21.1	0.1
Asia	12.2	9.7	10.8	13.5	8.1	8.6	12.4	-17.7	29.5	16.1	-0.5
Newly industrialized Asian economies	12.0	9.6	10.0	12.9	8.0	8.9	12.2	-16.3	28.2	15.9	0.8
First tier	12.5	8.8	10.0	12.2	7.8	9.0	11.6	-15.8	28.0	15.7	1.3
Second tier	10.9	11.5	9.9	14.5	8.6	8.5	14.1	-17.3	28.5	16.3	-0.3
Developing economies: Africa	1.9	3.2	16.4	21.9	9.3	6.7	29.9	-30.0	29.8	17.1	5.3
Northern Africa excluding Sudan	0.8	2.8	16.1	24.3	5.9	1.5	38.2	-35.5	24.4	-1.7	23.4
Sub-Saharan Africa	2.4	3.5	16.5	20.5	11.0	9.3	25.6	-26.8	32.5	26.2	-1.5
Sub-Saharan Africa excluding South Africa	2.4	4.0	18.2	22.8	11.9	10.1	31.2	-27.8	33.0	27.8	1.2
Developing economies: America	6.4	10.5	11.3	18.0	8.7	9.2	21.9	-22.3	26.4	24.7	1.0
Central America and Greater Caribbean Islands excluding Puerto Rico	9.1	14.8	7.4	13.9	7.0	9.5	15.8	-19.5	27.5	18.3	5.8
Central America and Greater Caribbean Islands excluding Mexico and Puerto Rico	3.3	9.1	9.8	16.9	8.0	10.0	26.7	-10.8	16.2	24.1	4.4
South America and Central America	7.4	10.9	11.5	18.0	9.0	9.5	21.8	-21.4	26.8	23.9	1.5
South America excluding Brazil	5.5	8.0	14.7	22.8	10.1	9.3	28.8	-22.7	23.2	28.5	1.4
Developing economies: Asia	8.9	9.5	14.8	19.3	11.1	10.9	20.9	-19.1	28.6	22.9	4.6
Eastern and South-Eastern Asia excluding China	11.8	9.6	10.2	13.1	8.4	9.3	12.6	-16.1	28.1	16.7	1.5
Southern Asia excluding India	4.6	4.4	14.4	22.8	8.9	5.5	27.0	-24.6	26.5	27.4	-15.0

Source: Data in this table are based on trade figures in table 1.1.1.

Imports (c.i.f.) - Importations (c.a.f.) En pourcentage											Groupements économiques
80-00	90-00	00-10	04-07	05-12	08-12	2005	2009	2010	2011	2012	
8.1	8.6	14.1	17.5	11.6	10.9	18.1	-19.2	29.5	22.0	4.5	**ÉCONOMIES EN DÉVELOPPEMENT**
7.8	8.2	12.7	17.1	10.5	9.5	18.2	-21.2	26.9	21.1	4.6	Économies en développement sans la Chine
8.3	8.7	14.0	17.5	11.5	10.9	17.9	-19.6	30.1	22.0	4.4	Économies en développement sans les PMA
9.2	8.8	11.4	16.0	9.2	8.7	15.0	-22.6	27.3	19.7	4.4	Économies en développement à revenu élevé
7.9	8.5	17.3	18.2	13.6	13.4	19.9	-15.0	33.5	23.3	4.3	Économies en développement à revenu intermédiaire
3.0	7.7	19.9	24.2	15.9	12.6	30.3	-16.0	26.8	26.8	5.8	Économies en développement à revenu faible
2.8	5.3	15.7	19.6	12.7	10.4	23.6	-13.1	18.6	20.6	10.2	Pays pauvres très endettés (FMI)
8.3	9.3	17.7	22.7	14.1	9.8	18.5	-14.3	14.9	23.5	10.4	Pays en développement sans littoral
1.1	5.9	9.2	15.8	5.3	2.7	15.7	-25.6	6.5	23.5	1.6	Petits États insulaires en développement
3.5	*6.3*	*16.6*	*20.2*	*14.1*	*9.9*	*22.9*	*-5.2*	*10.3*	*22.4*	*7.9*	*Pays les moins avancés*
2.8	4.1	18.6	21.9	13.6	7.9	26.8	-5.1	4.6	18.3	12.1	Afrique et Haïti
4.8	10.4	13.6	17.4	15.0	13.7	16.9	-5.3	21.5	29.7	1.6	Asie
3.5	0.7	17.6	16.7	12.1	8.6	14.2	-5.9	16.8	14.4	3.7	Îles
0.9	*3.4*	*18.0*	*21.7*	*12.7*	*6.7*	*23.2*	*-15.8*	*10.5*	*16.3*	*12.9*	*Principaux exportateurs de pétrole et de gaz*
-1.3	1.5	19.6	22.0	14.6	6.0	24.8	-9.1	9.5	10.4	10.7	Afrique
2.2	5.3	15.0	40.3	9.3	5.4	44.1	-16.3	-6.1	21.8	27.2	Amérique
1.5	3.7	18.0	19.8	12.6	7.0	21.2	-17.5	12.5	17.4	12.1	Asie
12.4	*9.5*	*12.8*	*15.1*	*10.7*	*11.8*	*14.5*	*-18.1*	*33.9*	*20.7*	*3.9*	*Principaux exportateurs d'articles manufacturés*
13.2	14.1	6.7	13.1	6.2	7.9	12.8	-24.1	28.4	16.4	5.4	Amérique
12.4	8.8	13.6	15.4	11.2	12.2	14.7	-17.4	34.5	21.1	3.7	Asie
11.2	*9.4*	*10.6*	*15.0*	*9.0*	*9.1*	*15.0*	*-25.4*	*34.0*	*19.7*	*1.9*	*Économies émergentes*
10.5	13.6	10.2	17.5	10.5	9.6	16.5	-26.5	35.3	21.2	2.5	Amérique
11.6	7.7	10.8	13.8	8.4	8.8	14.3	-24.8	33.4	19.0	1.6	Asie
11.8	*8.0*	*10.2*	*13.1*	*8.6*	*9.7*	*14.1*	*-22.0*	*32.0*	*18.7*	*3.6*	*Économies nouvellement industrialisées d'Asie*
12.1	8.1	10.1	13.1	8.3	9.0	12.4	-21.1	30.4	17.8	2.4	Première génération
11.2	7.9	10.5	13.0	9.5	11.4	19.1	-24.2	36.3	21.2	6.7	Deuxième génération
2.2	4.3	16.4	20.6	12.3	8.2	20.7	-14.6	15.8	18.9	7.7	**Économies en développement : Afrique**
2.0	4.1	15.9	19.2	13.7	7.3	16.6	-9.1	13.1	10.1	12.5	Afrique septentrionale sans le Soudan
2.4	4.5	16.7	21.2	11.6	8.7	22.8	-17.4	17.3	23.7	5.4	Afrique subsaharienne
1.8	3.8	17.5	22.5	13.2	8.5	26.6	-12.9	13.3	21.3	6.9	Afrique subsaharienne sans l'Afrique du Sud
7.8	12.1	10.8	19.1	10.2	9.0	19.8	-25.1	29.0	22.4	3.7	**Économies en développement : Amérique**
10.2	13.3	7.6	14.5	6.5	7.5	16.1	-24.4	26.2	17.5	5.0	Amérique centrale et Grandes Antilles sans Porto Rico
4.6	11.0	10.5	19.7	7.5	6.2	28.3	-25.1	20.0	20.7	3.8	Amérique centrale et Grandes Antilles sans le Mexique et Porto Rico
9.2	12.5	11.0	19.2	10.6	9.6	19.4	-24.7	30.5	22.1	4.2	Amérique du Sud et Amérique centrale
7.0	10.3	15.2	26.6	13.4	10.7	30.2	-24.7	27.7	27.3	6.6	Amérique du Sud sans le Brésil
9.4	8.3	14.7	16.9	11.8	11.6	17.5	-18.4	31.2	22.2	4.4	**Économies en développement : Asie**
11.7	8.1	10.5	13.5	9.0	9.9	14.1	-21.5	31.3	19.4	3.8	Asie orientale et Asie du Sud-Est sans la Chine
3.4	1.3	14.8	14.7	9.4	6.7	25.2	-15.4	26.9	12.9	-4.6	Asie méridionale sans l'Inde

Source : Les données dans ce tableau ont été calculées d'après les chiffres du tableau 1.1.1.

Trade group	Exports (f.o.b) - Exportations (f.a.b.) Percentage										
	80-00	90-00	00-10	04-07	05-12	08-12	2005	2009	2010	2011	2012
AFRICA											
CEMAC	3.5	3.4	18.9	21.7	9.0	6.1	38.5	-36.7	31.4	24.4	1.8
CEPGL	-3.3	-6.0	20.5	16.9	16.6	15.4	25.4	-19.5	49.9	26.1	-2.3
COMESA	-0.2	1.3	18.4	26.1	7.5	1.8	34.6	-27.1	27.9	-16.2	35.3
EAC	2.8	6.9	14.9	15.8	13.5	11.5	22.8	-8.4	20.6	17.8	11.1
ECCAS	3.3	3.2	23.2	33.3	12.4	7.8	54.6	-35.6	28.1	29.3	6.2
ECOWAS	1.2	3.8	16.9	17.6	12.3	13.5	25.0	-25.5	37.7	33.6	1.2
MRU	2.0	3.3	11.7	9.5	8.2	6.0	11.8	4.6	6.5	8.1	3.6
SADC	3.0	2.9	15.5	21.6	10.6	8.3	22.9	-26.2	29.8	24.5	-1.8
UMA	0.9	2.6	15.4	24.3	5.0	1.0	38.9	-38.8	26.8	-5.1	30.0
WAEMU	3.3	5.1	12.6	9.4	9.8	6.9	9.5	4.0	7.7	14.8	-2.3
AMERICA											
ANCOM	5.7	7.4	17.2	25.5	14.4	14.4	32.2	-16.3	26.2	35.3	4.8
CACM	7.6	15.1	8.0	11.1	7.4	8.3	9.1	-11.7	16.4	19.1	3.3
CARICOM	-2.7	5.1	12.1	23.4	2.8	0.6	35.0	-43.3	18.3	30.3	-5.2
FTAA	7.4	8.2	7.7	13.5	6.8	7.4	14.6	-21.6	23.2	18.8	2.7
LAIA	7.0	10.5	11.7	18.3	9.1	9.5	22.3	-21.8	27.4	24.1	1.4
MERCOSUR	4.9	6.8	14.1	18.6	9.9	8.5	25.3	-25.9	26.2	28.5	-1.9
NAFTA	7.8	8.3	6.3	11.8	5.9	6.8	11.8	-21.3	22.6	16.2	3.9
OAS	7.3	8.2	7.7	13.6	6.8	7.4	14.5	-21.6	23.2	18.8	2.7
OECS	3.3	-2.5	5.2	3.2	3.7	-1.0	3.9	-6.2	4.2	-6.6	5.8
ASIA											
APTA	12.9	12.2	19.3	23.4	13.2	12.3	23.9	-15.4	31.2	21.5	4.8
ASEAN	11.2	11.1	11.1	15.2	9.1	9.3	15.3	-17.8	29.0	17.8	1.3
ECO	7.3	7.1	18.5	26.0	10.9	6.9	26.9	-28.5	22.4	28.9	-1.7
GCC	1.3	5.5	18.2	24.5	13.2	13.4	39.4	-31.0	25.8	43.6	11.8
SAARC	9.0	9.1	17.4	21.6	15.4	14.4	26.0	-14.3	34.3	31.6	-2.7
EUROPE											
EFTA	6.8	3.8	10.7	14.6	6.5	3.9	14.2	-22.4	12.8	21.0	-2.1
EU27	7.1	5.6	9.4	12.5	4.3	2.4	8.1	-22.4	12.4	17.6	-4.5
Euro area	7.5	5.5	9.3	12.2	4.1	2.0	7.1	-22.2	11.2	16.8	-4.3
OCEANIA											
MSG	5.3	3.4	12.3	19.0	9.3	7.8	21.8	-24.0	30.7	23.4	-6.6
INTERREGIONAL											
ACP	1.7	3.5	15.6	20.3	10.3	8.9	25.0	-27.7	31.9	26.5	-1.7
APEC	9.3	8.4	10.6	15.2	8.5	8.7	14.9	-20.0	28.2	17.4	2.8
BSEC	10.7	16.7	17.7	22.8	10.4	7.6	25.4	-31.8	25.8	29.2	2.0
CIS	_	_	18.4	25.2	11.2	8.7	29.4	-35.9	30.8	33.9	2.0

Source: Data in this table are based on trade figures in table 1.1.1.

Imports (c.i.f.) - Importations (c.a.f.) En pourcentage											Groupements commerciaux
80-00	90-00	00-10	04-07	05-12	08-12	2005	2009	2010	2011	2012	
											AFRIQUE
1.7	3.0	18.3	27.4	18.0	13.0	14.8	-1.1	15.6	25.8	6.3	CEMAC
-3.0	-5.3	21.7	20.6	15.0	13.5	35.0	-4.5	14.8	24.7	15.3	CEPGL
2.0	4.7	16.7	21.9	14.2	10.3	27.5	-3.9	17.3	6.5	21.7	COMESA
3.7	5.2	17.9	26.0	16.6	12.6	25.6	-9.5	17.7	27.0	9.2	CAE
1.3	2.7	21.1	27.2	16.6	7.9	29.0	2.7	-5.4	23.9	12.3	CEEAC
0.0	3.7	17.8	25.4	12.6	7.7	31.9	-25.1	24.4	24.0	1.0	CEDEAO
1.6	2.0	13.1	12.4	9.2	9.4	20.8	-14.2	18.1	7.9	27.0	UFM
3.6	4.5	15.7	18.2	10.5	8.8	16.8	-17.9	15.4	26.6	5.2	SADC
2.1	2.7	15.3	15.1	12.3	5.8	10.3	-10.2	11.4	7.0	13.5	UMA
2.3	3.9	15.1	15.1	9.1	4.4	19.7	-13.7	11.0	3.9	16.2	UEMOA
											AMÉRIQUE
6.7	10.0	16.3	23.9	15.5	13.3	25.6	-20.5	30.3	28.4	8.6	ANCOM
8.4	13.6	9.3	14.3	6.5	6.3	12.7	-24.6	19.0	20.6	4.9	MCAC
-0.1	7.7	8.3	15.4	4.8	2.1	18.6	-25.6	5.5	22.0	2.2	CARICOM
8.0	9.7	7.1	12.0	5.0	6.3	14.9	-25.1	24.4	16.9	3.3	ZLEA
8.6	12.4	11.2	19.7	10.9	9.6	20.3	-25.0	31.2	22.2	4.0	ALADI
6.9	11.6	14.9	26.8	15.0	10.3	23.5	-25.7	33.9	25.0	1.2	MERCOSUR
8.3	9.5	6.1	10.5	3.7	5.5	13.7	-25.1	23.2	15.2	3.3	ALENA
7.9	9.7	7.1	12.1	5.0	6.3	15.0	-25.2	24.4	16.9	3.3	OEA
7.3	5.1	6.6	14.6	0.9	-3.0	15.5	-19.9	4.5	0.4	0.0	OECO
											ASIE
11.0	10.1	18.9	20.2	14.6	14.4	20.0	-16.0	36.8	26.0	3.3	ACAP
11.0	8.2	11.5	14.7	9.8	10.3	17.4	-22.6	31.1	21.0	5.8	ANASE
7.0	5.6	17.4	20.0	9.5	7.1	23.2	-24.0	24.4	20.9	0.7	ECO
2.7	5.2	18.3	23.7	12.8	6.8	22.1	-21.6	9.9	21.9	14.4	CCG
6.4	8.8	21.5	27.4	17.0	14.2	37.7	-19.5	33.8	31.3	3.7	SAARC
											EUROPE
5.8	3.1	9.7	13.8	5.9	3.6	11.3	-18.6	13.0	18.0	-4.6	AELE
6.6	5.0	9.8	13.8	4.1	1.7	10.0	-24.3	13.0	17.2	-6.0	UE27
6.8	4.6	9.7	13.4	4.0	1.2	9.6	-24.2	12.3	17.2	-7.2	Zone euro
											OCÉANIE
2.1	0.5	13.4	16.6	10.7	8.7	8.7	-18.6	23.7	19.6	3.5	MSG
											INTERRÉGIONAUX
1.9	5.2	15.1	20.6	10.7	7.9	22.8	-19.1	16.9	23.0	4.8	ACP
9.1	8.7	9.8	13.3	7.8	9.0	14.8	-22.5	28.8	19.7	3.8	CEAP
9.9	12.1	18.1	25.0	9.8	5.2	21.0	-33.3	21.9	27.4	-0.1	CEMN
–	–	20.1	29.7	12.6	7.7	24.5	-33.4	24.7	30.3	5.0	CEI

Source : Les données dans ce tableau ont été calculées d'après les chiffres du tableau 1.1.1.

Region, country or territory	Trade balance (1) - Balance commerciale (1) Millions of dollars - Millions de dollars								
	1989-91	1994-96	1999-01	2005-07	2006-08	2007-09	2008-10	2009-11	2010-12
WORLD	-113 412	-69 485	-188 161	-239 939	-254 335	-222 449	-195 530	-119 771	-111 611
DEVELOPING ECONOMIES	17 268	-62 796	103 772	504 144	559 980	495 482	438 426	436 744	496 460
TRANSITION ECONOMIES	-8 958	10 294	37 277	111 303	128 463	115 597	129 631	150 269	190 905
DEVELOPED ECONOMIES	-121 723	-16 983	-329 210	-855 385	-942 779	-833 527	-763 588	-706 784	-798 976
Developing economies: Africa	2 843	-6 996	3 098	61 329	70 060	41 558	32 557	16 403	29 036
Eastern Africa	*-4 763*	*-6 063*	*-7 308*	*-17 785*	*-23 473*	*-27 013*	*-29 399*	*-30 406*	*-35 202*
Burundi*(2)	-143	-106	-87	-281	-326	-313	-363	-457	-551
Comoros*	-30	-48	-37	-105	-134	-164	-194	-220	-239
Djibouti (3)	-186	-164	-168	-311	-400	-431	-389	-360	-397
Eritrea (4)	_	-411	-443	-486	-523	-555	-616	-582	-563
Ethiopia (...1991)	-526								
Ethiopia	_	-789	-1 067	-3 963	-5 124	-5 752	-6 332	-6 114	-7 316
Kenya	-1 080	-832	-1 235	-3 689	-4 922	-5 591	-6 263	-7 230	-8 705
Madagascar*	-155	-112	-207	-1 023	-1 562	-2 005	-2 024	-1 639	-1 440
Malawi	-211	-121	-163	-568	-791	-889	-1 088	-981	-1 216
Mauritius	-376	-503	-556	-1 322	-1 740	-1 906	-2 062	-2 167	-2 463
Mozambique	-731	-647	-677	-584	-827	-1 203	-1 524	-1 973	-2 334
Rwanda	-209	-158	-183	-433	-634	-858	-1 038	-1 173	-1 421
Seychelles	-128	-191	-232	-404	-511	-518	-435	-305	-273
Somalia (5)	31	-113	-154	-472	-503	-441	-425	-388	-337
Uganda	-43	-555	-1 033	-1 664	-2 184	-2 546	-2 842	-3 066	-3 401
United Republic of Tanzania	-954	-861	-888	-2 349	-3 339	-3 706	-3 944	-4 439	-5 245
Zambia (6)	209	309	50	186	448	376	799	1 394	1 368
Zimbabwe	-231	-761	-228	-317	-400	-510	-661	-707	-668
Middle Africa	*4 205*	*5 049*	*7 011*	*38 686*	*51 240*	*47 305*	*48 530*	*48 187*	*61 826*
Angola (7)	2 024	2 264	3 428	23 192	32 251	30 612	31 676	33 059	43 670
Cameroon*(8)	425	404	176	42	-149	-587	-863	-1 476	-2 113
Central African Republic*(8)	-6	5	31	-54	-89	-124	-153	-143	-130
Chad*(7)	-193	-232	-292	2 000	2 012	1 612	1 356	1 267	1 533
Congo*(8)	338	208	1 371	3 537	4 148	3 860	4 592	4 967	5 733
Dem. Rep. of the Congo*	475	580	152	-258	-129	-200	167	500	700
Equatorial Guinea (7)	-14	-42	600	6 464	8 315	7 553	6 669	5 233	6 600
Gabon*(9)	1 175	1 884	1 574	3 824	4 960	4 670	5 187	4 886	5 946
Sao Tome and Principe	-18	-22	-29	-59	-80	-90	-100	-106	-114
Northern Africa	*-3 972*	*-8 943*	*-1 883*	*33 801*	*39 941*	*21 054*	*9 273*	*-13 159*	*-11 945*
Algeria*	2 627	1 352	8 472	30 445	35 169	26 077	20 760	16 234	22 399
Egypt	-7 614	-8 170	-10 106	-12 662	-16 869	-20 639	-23 509	-26 348	-32 343
Libya	5 624	3 718	6 471	33 245	42 469	39 093	36 013	22 029	27 070
Morocco*	-2 467	-2 894	-3 769	-12 502	-16 642	-19 172	-19 486	-19 685	-21 196
Sudan (...2011) (10)	-498	-772	-213	-1 415	2	330	748	126	_
Sudan	_	_	_	_	_	_	_	_	_
Tunisia (11)	-1 644	-2 179	-2 739	-3 310	-4 188	-4 634	-5 253	-5 515	-6 444
Southern Africa	*3 537*	*-1 337*	*-10*	*-16 724*	*-20 831*	*-19 647*	*-19 092*	*-20 804*	*-29 571*
Botswana*	-112	417	575	1 272	764	-142	-832	-1 209	-1 469
Lesotho	-627	-864	-582	-845	-897	-1 000	-1 151	-1 289	-1 417
Namibia	-50	-188	-324	-448	-678	-1 210	-1 526	-1 777	-1 961
South Africa	4 431	-570	436	-16 628	-20 021	-17 300	-15 523	-16 423	-24 627
Swaziland	-105	-133	-115	-75	2	5	-60	-107	-97
Western Africa	*3 836*	*4 298*	*5 288*	*23 351*	*23 183*	*19 860*	*23 245*	*32 586*	*43 929*
Benin*	41	-162	-266	-641	-830	-946	-873	-801	-787
Burkina Faso	-369	-278	-419	-920	-1 098	-1 116	-919	-496	-495
Cape Verde (12)	-125	-223	-226	-558	-682	-733	-722	-750	-763
Côte d'Ivoire*	751	1 059	1 402	2 158	2 383	2 953	3 526	4 631	4 033
Gambia (13)	-152	-193	-159	-269	-288	-285	-265	-246	-260
Ghana	-334	-435	-1 502	-3 146	-3 964	-3 691	-3 389	-2 784	-3 715
Guinea*	-31	-82	88	32	13	-16	11	-206	-536
Guinea-Bissau	-62	-82	1	-63	-85	-88	-83	-60	-73
Liberia*	8	111	-164	-262	-393	-424	-487	-522	-590
Mali*	-162	-308	-260	-447	-713	-861	-1 129	-1 047	-1 069
Mauritania*	152	49	-79	-194	23	-88	-50	104	-28
Niger*	-91	-104	-125	-460	-571	-824	-1 104	-1 325	-1 392
Nigeria	4 977	5 546	7 994	31 231	33 434	30 311	32 974	40 367	54 422
Saint Helena	-12	-26	-31	-58	-53	-38	-22	-22	-19
Senegal (14)	-486	-366	-646	-2 398	-3 211	-3 417	-3 225	-2 895	-3 297
Sierra Leone*	-25	-97	-121	-181	-225	-269	-346	-695	-753
Togo*	-244	-111	-200	-472	-557	-608	-654	-668	-750

For sources and notes, see end of table.

Percentage of imports (1) Part dans les importations en pourcentage (1)									Régions, pays ou territoires
1989-91	1994-96	1999-01	2005-07	2006-08	2007-09	2008-10	2009-11	2010-12	
-3.26	-1.38	-2.96	-1.98	-1.77	-1.50	-1.29	-0.81	-0.65	MONDE
2.24	-4.33	5.76	12.40	11.87	9.84	8.01	7.30	7.07	ÉCONOMIES EN DÉVELOPPEMENT
-5.95	10.08	35.71	33.84	29.33	24.09	26.59	29.59	33.21	ÉCONOMIES EN TRANSITION
-4.75	-0.49	-7.39	-10.65	-10.43	-9.19	-8.46	-7.81	-8.08	ÉCONOMIES DÉVELOPPÉES
3.14	-6.02	2.31	20.02	18.52	9.63	6.58	2.89	5.43	Économies en développement : Afrique
-40.05	-38.42	-42.40	-46.71	-48.94	-51.39	-51.22	-48.91	-48.15	*Afrique orientale*
-63.42	-56.56	-64.17	-82.16	-84.59	-83.51	-83.03	-82.31	-81.97	Burundi*(2)
-59.86	-83.44	-72.92	-89.74	-92.59	-93.09	-93.47	-91.65	-91.72	Comores*
-89.25	-89.77	-84.73	-85.68	-86.44	-86.19	-82.69	-80.64	-80.90	Djibouti (3)
	-82.45	-94.54	-97.54	-97.69	-97.90	-98.18	-83.82	-68.44	Érythrée (4)
-62.06									Éthiopie (...1991)
	-65.75	-68.65	-78.64	-79.54	-79.19	-77.49	-73.16	-72.30	Éthiopie
-50.86	-30.39	-40.53	-49.23	-53.75	-55.30	-56.19	-58.19	-60.24	Kenya
-27.31	-18.64	-21.06	-49.44	-54.59	-61.83	-63.34	-56.65	-51.22	Madagascar*
-36.05	-22.64	-27.26	-45.97	-47.23	-46.11	-50.76	-44.49	-49.58	Malawi
-25.06	-24.56	-25.62	-36.81	-42.35	-46.45	-48.42	-48.89	-49.56	Maurice
-84.88	-77.38	-59.78	-21.29	-23.91	-32.55	-37.18	-40.19	-39.11	Mozambique
-67.65	-76.99	-73.54	-73.74	-75.79	-78.77	-79.49	-78.37	-76.18	Rwanda
-73.45	-71.71	-54.82	-52.53	-56.11	-56.23	-49.68	-41.41	-37.31	Seychelles
42.50	-40.87	-41.37	-61.34	-58.93	-51.78	-48.98	-45.01	-38.97	Somalie (5)
-14.69	-53.47	-68.95	-61.51	-62.00	-62.24	-63.43	-63.35	-62.65	Ouganda
-72.25	-56.09	-55.74	-54.01	-57.53	-57.00	-53.84	-52.73	-52.08	République-Unie de Tanzanie
22.28	43.72	7.02	2.88	12.88	9.51	16.21	24.42	21.87	Zambie (6)
-11.76	-24.17	-12.51	-13.40	-14.78	-17.69	-21.00	-19.25	-15.91	Zimbabwe
64.71	81.16	86.93	161.59	161.21	123.13	114.11	105.01	124.21	*Afrique centrale*
142.09	135.14	110.65	225.54	230.86	169.93	162.79	172.16	214.88	Angola (7)
33.43	34.69	13.15	2.99	-1.16	-12.34	-17.43	-26.02	-32.13	Cameroun*(8)
1.00	3.52	27.34	-25.88	-33.59	-44.71	-52.96	-49.20	-42.14	République centrafricaine*(8)
-45.99	-51.03	-55.08	158.76	120.13	84.04	64.75	52.07	57.78	Tchad*(7)
50.78	37.94	240.39	196.22	165.87	135.34	138.59	121.97	120.45	Congo*(8)
28.59	69.94	24.02	-8.66	-4.32	-5.58	3.28	9.17	13.69	Rép. dém. du Congo*
-22.67	-0.50	99.34	338.50	288.49	211.39	152.17	91.67	102.22	Guinée équatoriale (7)
139.04	217.03	169.90	217.59	227.23	193.29	192.87	157.28	174.62	Gabon*(9)
-77.52	-80.44	-91.65	-88.95	-90.40	-91.41	-91.03	-91.38	-91.21	Sao Tomé-et-Principe
-8.64	-20.28	-3.81	31.87	30.53	13.96	5.06	-7.42	-5.90	*Afrique septentrionale*
31.00	14.82	89.81	132.75	124.38	77.85	52.26	37.16	49.28	Algérie*
-63.12	-69.86	-68.51	-43.13	-44.23	-47.56	-48.18	-49.34	-52.30	Égypte
106.86	72.33	160.98	526.65	580.94	454.55	313.81	166.73	161.12	Libye
-38.43	-31.09	-34.48	-48.37	-50.30	-53.77	-53.00	-52.71	-51.01	Maroc*
-51.65	-57.79	-13.92	-19.12	-1.32	3.73	7.84	1.21		Soudan (...2011) (10)
									Soudan
-32.65	-29.44	-30.95	-21.01	-21.42	-22.18	-24.00	-25.30	-27.33	Tunisie (11)
15.34	-3.37	-0.05	-19.11	-20.79	-19.49	-18.40	-18.42	-22.05	*Afrique australe*
-5.78	23.98	28.90	38.00	23.00	-1.56	-16.31	-21.02	-20.58	Botswana*
-90.45	-84.01	-71.71	-54.45	-53.46	-55.65	-57.68	-58.42	-57.55	Lesotho
-3.97	-11.75	-20.64	-14.97	-17.62	-27.15	-30.73	-31.75	-31.87	Namibie
23.86	-1.23	1.53	-21.45	-22.57	-19.45	-17.13	-16.75	-21.10	Afrique du Sud
-16.01	-13.19	-10.67	-3.90	0.46	0.47	-2.88	-5.65	-4.91	Swaziland
26.57	23.39	24.13	43.55	34.85	26.38	28.16	35.87	43.54	*Afrique occidentale*
16.86	-23.56	-39.90	-43.96	-44.22	-44.42	-40.75	-38.06	-36.62	Bénin*
-75.87	-57.55	-64.73	-62.19	-63.12	-60.12	-46.70	-25.57	-18.51	Burkina Faso
-95.07	-96.22	-95.43	-96.54	-96.58	-96.20	-95.06	-93.94	-93.28	Cap-Vert (12)
35.72	42.48	53.28	35.53	35.72	41.42	47.25	65.53	53.39	Côte d'Ivoire*
-82.67	-88.72	-92.76	-96.20	-95.81	-90.04	-87.25	-79.48	-77.95	Gambie (13)
-29.06	-20.91	-46.69	-46.79	-47.16	-41.36	-34.41	-24.83	-24.94	Ghana
-4.23	-10.57	14.93	3.61	1.70	-1.31	0.66	-9.41	-23.57	Guinée*
-77.43	-65.64	2.46	-40.11	-45.47	-42.47	-39.64	-29.01	-31.71	Guinée-Bissau
-0.02	20.48	-34.88	-61.24	-65.43	-67.70	-70.64	-68.86	-63.49	Libéria*
-33.34	-43.33	-29.95	-24.09	-26.93	-31.54	-35.87	-33.29	-32.54	Mali*
67.66	11.84	-17.58	-12.53	3.57	-5.10	-3.23	3.57	0.98	Mauritanie*
-24.60	-27.22	-30.84	-45.63	-45.03	-47.72	-51.49	-53.93	-51.84	Niger*
88.70	81.13	85.86	118.61	95.12	77.10	76.65	87.23	107.27	Nigéria
-66.06	-83.55	-75.39	-71.43	-62.04	-48.65	-39.62	-39.07	-32.53	Sainte-Hélène
-40.35	-27.83	-39.58	-59.03	-62.99	-63.19	-59.58	-56.33	-57.48	Sénégal (14)
-14.34	-56.45	-89.19	-46.49	-48.36	-53.38	-56.99	-63.67	-54.94	Sierra Leone*
-48.31	-7.35	-35.02	-41.64	-43.56	-42.98	-42.46	-40.92	-42.86	Togo*

Pour les sources et les notes, se reporter à la fin du tableau.

Region, country or territory	Trade balance (1) - Balance commerciale (1) Millions of dollars - Millions de dollars								
	1989-91	1994-96	1999-01	2005-07	2006-08	2007-09	2008-10	2009-11	2010-12
Developing economies: America	14 110	-22 795	-27 104	43 507	21 094	4 805	-5 416	5 959	-2 444
Caribbean	*-4 815*	*-7 524*	*-13 766*	*-19 486*	*-23 843*	*-26 071*	*-27 364*	*-26 586*	*-28 092*
Anguilla	..	-55	-85	-188	-237	-215	-184	-143	-137
Antigua and Barbuda	-219	-306	-359	-547	-632	-610	-539	-451	-447
Aruba (15)	-415	-211	-204	67	-161	-324	-722	-774	-859
Bahamas (16)	-796	-1 047	-1 427	-1 983	-2 144	-2 074	-1 985	-1 948	-2 141
Barbados	-490	-506	-852	-1 218	-1 281	-1 242	-1 215	-1 180	-1 228
Bonaire, Sint Eustatius and Saba	–	–	–	–	–	–	–	–	–
British Virgin Islands (5)	-95	-120	-181	-257	-272	-272	-269	-266	-271
Cayman Islands (5)	-254	-356	-589	-1 066	-1 035	-981	-918	-860	-865
Cuba*	-491	-1 028	-3 071	-6 590	-8 473	-8 283	-8 175	-6 971	-7 377
Curaçao									
Dominica*	-60	-66	-88	-136	-164	-186	-195	-192	-183
Dominican Republic (17)	-805	-1 505	-3 383	-5 242	-7 082	-7 498	-8 265	-8 124	-8 746
Grenada	-83	-110	-175	-302	-313	-306	-293	-282	-298
Haiti	-184	-429	-716	-1 085	-1 369	-1 514	-1 983	-2 122	-2 391
Jamaica	-747	-1 328	-1 935	-3 850	-4 789	-4 805	-4 557	-4 154	-4 530
Montserrat*	-36	-27	-20	-28	-30	-29	-30	-29	-31
Netherlands Antilles*(18)	-349	-650	-525	-1 576	-1 793	-1 887	-1 888		
Saint Kitts and Nevis*	-81	-116	-149	-208	-240	-256	-257	-233	-208
Saint Lucia	-157	-206	-307	-479	-502	-454	-431	-447	-495
Saint Vincent and the Grenadines*	-60	-86	-137	-238	-278	-295	-301	-291	-302
Sint Maarten (Dutch part)									
Trinidad and Tobago*	509	609	580	5 884	7 488	5 654	5 244	4 035	4 617
Turks and Caicos Islands	..	..	-143	-444	-537	-495	-402	-312	-289
Central America	*-7 652*	*-10 161*	*-22 126*	*-36 378*	*-45 388*	*-44 243*	*-41 810*	*-36 335*	*-40 133*
Belize	-111	-97	-279	-396	-446	-455	-450	-424	-450
Costa Rica*	-374	-698	-593	-3 254	-4 277	-4 031	-4 200	-4 181	-5 353
El Salvador (19)	-757	-1 470	-1 918	-4 012	-4 647	-4 481	-4 184	-4 011	-4 501
Guatemala (20)	-560	-1 208	-2 556	-5 895	-6 459	-5 935	-5 501	-5 302	-6 200
Honduras (21)	-50	-169	-709	-2 209	-3 128	-3 301	-3 199	-2 845	-3 079
Mexico	-4 368	-3 990	-12 427	-15 325	-19 660	-19 089	-16 914	-11 734	-11 016
Nicaragua (22)	-363	-576	-1 221	-2 041	-2 402	-2 442	-2 420	-2 452	-2 812
Panama*(23)	-1 068	-1 954	-2 422	-3 246	-4 370	-4 509	-4 943	-5 386	-6 722
South America	*26 577*	*-5 110*	*8 788*	*99 370*	*90 326*	*75 119*	*63 758*	*68 880*	*65 781*
Argentina*	5 837	-1 578	1 737	11 710	12 008	13 505	13 692	12 843	11 354
Bolivia (Plurinational State of)	110	-333	-576	783	1 133	926	890	637	1 444
Brazil	10 688	-3 171	-2 458	38 958	30 513	22 962	15 087	16 263	12 894
Chile*	683	-887	907	16 538	14 268	11 729	8 734	10 235	5 618
Colombia	1 333	-3 409	626	-1 564	-2 240	-1 664	-984	613	1 015
Ecuador	602	403	651	285	336	-278	-1 454	-2 097	-2 138
Falkland Islands (Malvinas) (5)	-16	-4	41	79	86	92	88	52	47
Guyana*	-50	-48	-45	-306	-400	-432	-478	-521	-582
Paraguay	-290	-1 997	-1 249	-2 675	-3 522	-3 164	-3 326	-3 337	-4 138
Peru*	902	-1 788	-495	7 037	5 770	4 646	3 916	6 401	5 717
Suriname	-17	-75	-108	141	305	255	359	490	746
Uruguay	238	-853	-1 097	-795	-1 685	-1 913	-2 176	-2 071	-2 528
Venezuela (Bolivarian Rep. of)	6 559	8 630	10 853	29 178	33 755	28 455	29 409	29 373	36 332
Developing economies: Asia	2 449	-31 865	129 077	402 765	472 951	453 678	416 353	419 613	475 501
Eastern Asia	*7 026*	*-9 533*	*43 308*	*202 593*	*249 733*	*262 969*	*235 866*	*194 843*	*188 144*
China	3 421	11 392	25 289	181 286	246 661	252 718	225 107	177 364	188 904
China, Hong Kong SAR	-3 962	-18 995	-9 536	-13 958	-18 851	-22 095	-28 739	-39 592	-52 179
China, Macao SAR	46	-61	-150	-2 740	-3 354	-3 725	-4 144	-5 202	-6 593
China, Taiwan Province of	13 247	10 778	13 616	21 521	21 308	23 970	22 616	26 496	26 964
Korea, Dem. People's Rep. of	-1 031	-353	-846	-1 388	-1 435	-1 330	-1 198	-900	-867
Korea, Republic of (24)	-4 524	-12 340	15 020	17 969	5 819	13 942	22 784	37 474	33 419
Mongolia	-173	46	-85	-97	-416	-511	-561	-796	-1 505
Southern Asia	*-12 217*	*-6 240*	*-6 339*	*-52 738*	*-74 236*	*-90 822*	*-111 783*	*-122 442*	*-157 063*
Afghanistan	-514	-326	-1 171	-2 194	-2 325	-2 578	-3 393	-4 571	-5 303
Bangladesh	-2 005	-2 639	-2 755	-4 989	-6 288	-7 128	-7 956	-9 051	-9 807
Bhutan	-17	-21	-74	5	40	31	-89	-208	-357
India (25)	-4 336	-3 578	-9 162	-59 689	-87 339	-99 236	-114 127	-125 912	-160 317
Iran (Islamic Rep. of)*	-1 974	5 418	10 509	32 081	45 433	42 707	40 080	44 738	51 020
Maldives	-64	-184	-291	-718	-875	-906	-914	-935	-1 084
Nepal	-434	-885	-775	-1 776	-2 186	-2 822	-3 497	-4 231	-4 762
Pakistan	-2 044	-2 601	-1 524	-12 318	-16 551	-16 968	-17 516	-16 391	-18 205
Sri Lanka	-828	-1 425	-1 095	-3 140	-4 145	-3 922	-4 371	-5 882	-8 248

For sources and notes, see end of table.

Percentage of imports (1) Part dans les importations en pourcentage (1)									Régions, pays ou territoires
1989-91	1994-96	1999-01	2005-07	2006-08	2007-09	2008-10	2009-11	2010-12	
11.62	-9.47	-7.45	7.07	3.43	0.84	-0.47	0.68	-0.25	Économies en développement : Amérique
-26.27	-36.72	-44.20	-38.07	-39.24	-44.46	-47.79	-47.21	-45.29	*Caraïbes*
..	-97.39	-96.15	-93.08	-95.52	-92.80	-91.36	-89.21	-89.01	Anguilla
-88.95	-87.08	-89.14	-87.86	-90.39	-91.17	-90.85	-89.81	-89.21	Antigua-et-Barbuda
-61.31	-12.05	-10.13	1.47	-2.60	-9.32	-36.78	-37.73	-40.59	Aruba (15)
-59.56	-85.62	-74.60	-74.56	-72.51	-71.65	-71.66	-72.25	-71.91	Bahamas (16)
-70.68	-68.60	-76.27	-72.52	-71.52	-72.83	-73.72	-73.41	-71.53	Barbade
—	—	—	—	—	—	—	—	—	Bonaire, Saint-Eustache et Saba
-93.83	-86.13	-86.99	-87.61	-87.86	-87.75	-87.64	-87.55	-87.49	Îles Vierges britanniques (5)
-94.35	-94.58	-97.09	-96.79	-97.96	-97.98	-98.29	-97.95	-97.95	Îles Caïmanes (5)
3.11	37.70	65.60	-67.99	-68.97	-68.51	-66.46	-59.97	-56.17	Cuba*
—	—	—	—	—	—	—	—	—	Curaçao
-53.91	-57.43	-63.34	-77.02	-80.05	-83.38	-84.16	-85.12	-84.24	Dominique*
-25.98	-28.56	-38.50	-43.59	-50.28	-53.52	-56.54	-54.14	-51.96	République dominicaine (17)
-75.48	-83.07	-80.60	-91.31	-91.32	-90.70	-91.13	-90.99	-90.96	Grenade
-53.54	-78.96	-69.90	-68.40	-72.28	-73.71	-77.91	-76.35	-76.83	Haïti
-40.56	-49.40	-60.56	-66.84	-68.00	-70.83	-73.27	-74.46	-74.48	Jamaïque
-94.69	-90.00	-95.12	-93.90	-91.96	-89.86	-91.65	-92.78	-94.25	Montserrat*
-17.11	-29.56	-20.60	-70.28	-68.89	-69.01	-67.80			Antilles néerlandaises*(18)
-75.06	-84.59	-82.89	-85.04	-85.23	-86.29	-86.55	-85.73	-83.46	Saint-Kitts-et-Nevis*
-56.14	-66.72	-86.60	-85.00	-81.07	-75.71	-70.24	-70.89	-73.44	Sainte-Lucie
-44.22	-64.88	-74.83	-84.92	-85.79	-85.56	-86.34	-87.14	-88.06	Saint-Vincent-et-les Grenadines*
—	—	—	—	—	—	—	—	—	Saint-Martin (partie néerlandaise)
41.69	41.48	17.14	89.24	95.85	66.83	65.05	52.60	56.60	Trinité-et-Tobago*
..	..	-94.73	-96.27	-96.49	-95.83	-94.99	-94.28	-93.43	Îles Turques et Caïques
-14.03	-10.49	-11.49	-11.53	-12.72	-12.57	-11.65	-9.81	-9.39	*Amérique centrale*
-48.62	-37.72	-58.48	-61.49	-61.06	-62.29	-60.90	-57.93	-55.81	Belize
-19.90	-17.39	-9.05	-28.46	-31.69	-29.67	-30.49	-29.70	-33.68	Costa Rica*
-57.41	-48.61	-40.76	-51.68	-52.95	-51.48	-48.83	-46.83	-47.09	El Salvador (19)
-32.51	-39.48	-49.64	-49.12	-48.48	-44.48	-41.03	-37.89	-39.17	Guatemala (20)
-5.16	-9.35	-18.35	-28.51	-34.46	-36.72	-35.54	-31.66	-29.83	Honduras (21)
-9.12	-4.83	-7.44	-5.88	-6.66	-6.58	-5.74	-3.97	-3.19	Mexique
-53.79	-57.73	-67.29	-66.15	-65.76	-64.01	-60.51	-57.40	-55.46	Nicaragua (22)
-74.84	-76.14	-73.48	-28.51	-32.19	-31.30	-31.58	-30.12	-32.75	Panama*(23)
47.37	-3.59	5.91	36.97	27.35	19.91	15.28	15.18	12.00	*Amérique du Sud*
126.11	-7.21	8.91	33.90	27.64	30.05	28.66	25.89	17.42	Argentine*
18.94	-22.58	-32.56	25.81	29.85	21.06	17.36	10.86	19.25	Bolivie (État plurinational de)
50.06	-3.33	-4.47	41.11	26.39	16.61	9.47	9.31	5.81	Brésil
8.85	-4.81	5.33	40.99	33.22	25.48	17.42	19.26	8.90	Chili*
25.98	-26.06	5.80	-5.22	-6.92	-4.71	-2.47	0.92	1.62	Colombie
30.54	10.26	22.38	2.11	2.66	-1.74	-7.79	-10.43	-9.50	Équateur
-46.55	-10.04	90.80	119.89	131.00	145.96	135.96	74.85	41.28	Îles Falkland (Malvinas) (5)
-16.76	-9.11	-7.26	-33.23	-36.43	-36.57	-36.93	-36.00	-34.38	Guyana*
-15.40	-68.16	-59.10	-56.26	-54.94	-43.20	-37.61	-33.16	-36.49	Paraguay
39.58	-25.00	-6.98	44.16	32.37	21.70	15.20	21.53	16.09	Pérou*
-2.37	-15.82	-21.71	13.70	26.59	21.54	26.47	32.13	46.46	Suriname
19.01	-28.57	-33.28	-16.17	-23.73	-25.32	-26.08	-23.33	-24.32	Uruguay
81.69	84.82	67.13	92.93	79.49	60.68	66.27	67.55	75.04	Venezuela (Rép. bolivarienne du)
0.54	-2.85	10.14	12.92	13.12	11.94	10.07	9.23	8.77	Économies en développement : Asie
2.53	-1.72	6.66	11.94	12.96	13.21	10.95	8.47	6.51	*Asie orientale*
5.99	8.67	12.53	21.84	25.47	24.47	19.59	13.78	11.52	Chine
-4.45	-10.04	-4.74	-4.06	-5.09	-5.96	-7.16	-8.84	-10.33	Chine (RAS de Hong Kong)
3.81	-3.05	-4.66	-51.41	-58.37	-67.91	-76.78	-84.45	-87.40	Chine (RAS de Macao)
23.48	11.01	11.73	10.56	9.78	11.88	10.81	11.88	10.06	Province chinoise de Taiwan
-35.86	-26.53	-53.06	-48.25	-45.48	-40.95	-35.21	-25.86	-21.03	Corée, Rép. populaire dém. de
-5.76	-9.12	11.32	6.06	2.08	4.53	6.38	9.36	7.00	Corée, République de (24)
-19.05	15.78	-14.19	-5.67	-12.23	-17.10	-17.35	-16.43	-24.49	Mongolie
-21.89	-8.35	-6.99	-18.38	-19.68	-22.64	-24.75	-24.24	-25.98	*Asie méridionale*
-67.91	-64.91	-89.30	-83.68	-82.89	-84.13	-87.50	-91.50	-93.28	Afghanistan
-56.19	-43.15	-31.56	-30.83	-31.67	-33.18	-32.50	-31.48	-29.98	Bangladesh
-20.30	-19.02	-40.68	-2.05	7.66	5.97	-11.75	-22.36	-34.93	Bhoutan
-19.96	-10.43	-18.59	-32.18	-35.19	-36.58	-36.86	-35.35	-36.69	Inde (25)
-7.78	36.98	72.79	75.60	94.78	83.58	69.40	74.64	83.60	Iran (Rép. islamique d')*
-46.46	-69.26	-73.76	-77.73	-77.00	-79.25	-80.15	-80.23	-79.34	Maldives
-71.05	-69.72	-52.17	-66.92	-70.80	-75.76	-79.47	-82.88	-84.13	Népal
-26.98	-23.52	-14.57	-41.73	-46.83	-47.31	-46.68	-43.46	-43.35	Pakistan
-31.04	-27.99	-18.22	-30.85	-34.60	-32.61	-34.22	-37.58	-45.65	Sri Lanka

Pour les sources et les notes, se reporter à la fin du tableau.

Region, country or territory	Trade balance (1) - Balance commerciale (1) Millions of dollars - Millions de dollars								
	1989-91	1994-96	1999-01	2005-07	2006-08	2007-09	2008-10	2009-11	2010-12
South-Eastern Asia	**-14 067**	**-29 384**	**47 296**	**74 503**	**73 664**	**75 476**	**77 863**	**89 002**	**70 984**
Brunei Darussalam*	1 237	218	2 171	5 428	6 425	6 022	6 281	6 636	8 185
Cambodia (7)	-67	-338	-535	-1 088	-1 410	-1 595	-1 694	-1 861	-2 249
Indonesia (...2002)	4 384	6 579	19 853						
Indonesia	–	–	–	19 687	19 952	20 947	20 226	24 399	15 150
Lao People's Dem. Rep.*	-100	-303	-203	-217	-211	-288	-345	-302	-231
Malaysia (26)	154	-1 541	16 546	28 369	33 791	35 150	36 737	36 068	35 125
Myanmar	-51	-394	-807	2 313	2 567	2 663	2 955	2 145	1 273
Philippines	-4 117	-11 298	827	-7 477	-8 513	-8 771	-8 585	-9 934	-11 905
Singapore (27)	-6 830	-6 136	4 210	32 951	29 215	26 199	27 840	36 286	37 827
Thailand	-8 270	-13 385	6 056	2 536	4 468	10 389	9 217	7 629	-4 633
Timor-Leste (28)	–	–	–	-123	-174	-239	-275	-299	-326
Viet Nam	-406	-2 786	-821	-7 876	-12 446	-15 001	-14 494	-11 766	-7 232
Western Asia	**21 707**	**13 292**	**44 813**	**178 407**	**223 791**	**206 055**	**214 407**	**258 210**	**373 435**
Bahrain (7)	-286	229	1 166	1 560	2 056	2 085	2 274	3 802	5 160
Iraq*	2 040	-384	3 819	9 462	18 831	17 172	13 444	15 453	26 756
Jordan	-1 311	-2 121	-2 387	-6 832	-7 786	-8 292	-8 485	-9 107	-10 755
Kuwait*	1 526	5 358	8 387	36 390	47 573	46 021	48 012	52 727	72 244
Lebanon (29)	-2 328	-6 296	-5 778	-7 602	-9 270	-11 121	-12 709	-13 637	-14 952
Oman	1 941	1 946	4 589	9 645	11 265	10 988	13 642	16 472	21 080
Qatar*	1 507	729	6 723	17 301	25 203	27 028	38 017	53 019	78 246
Saudi Arabia*(30)	15 431	24 737	35 645	135 291	160 983	146 068	146 457	158 064	203 402
State of Palestine	..	-1 470	-2 120	-2 451	-2 677	-2 907	-3 159	-3 399	-3 737
Syrian Arab Republic*	1 127	-1 649	315	-1 944	-2 124	-3 464	-4 016	-5 384	-4 955
Turkey*	-6 988	-13 219	-16 811	-53 377	-62 256	-57 171	-60 128	-72 127	-87 224
United Arab Emirates	10 207	4 995	10 233	41 431	43 524	42 348	43 304	63 333	89 333
Yemen, Arab Republic	–	–							
Yemen, Democratic	–	–							
Yemen*	–	-51	1 032	-467	-1 531	-2 700	-2 248	-1 005	-1 163
Developing economies: Oceania	**-2 133**	**-1 141**	**-1 299**	**-3 458**	**-4 125**	**-4 559**	**-5 067**	**-5 231**	**-5 633**
American Samoa*(31)	-55	-182	-155	-162	-150	-147	-163	-267	-313
Cook Islands	-41	-43	-40	-91	-102	-92	-84	-84	-100
Fiji	-182	-261	-296	-1 021	-1 166	-1 066	-1 040	-963	-1 036
French Polynesia*	-768	-743	-762	-1 531	-1 687	-1 736	-1 705	-1 590	-1 589
Guam (5)	-321	-298	-346	-708	-729	-646	-749	-920	-1 038
Kiribati	-21	-27	-35	-62	-59	-60	-63	-71	-85
Marshall Islands	-47	-51	-50	-75	-78	-82	-89	-97	-104
Micronesia (Federated States of)	-76	-79	-84	-117	-122	-132	-140	-148	-157
Nauru (5)	35	12	5	-31	-17	-9	15	22	40
New Caledonia*	-315	-450	-448	-717	-1 135	-1 407	-1 778	-1 813	-1 927
Niue	-3	-3	-2	-5	-5	-6	-7	-7	-7
Northern Mariana Islands (5)	..	204	451	50	1	-26	-63	-71	-71
Palau (5)	..	-40	-92	-97	-104	-111	-116	-117	-120
Papua New Guinea	-121	1 030	794	1 729	1 948	1 708	1 726	1 708	1 709
Samoa (29)	-74	-85	-64	-177	-198	-190	-213	-235	-263
Solomon Islands*	-29	9	-17	-102	-109	-112	-129	-112	-78
Tokelau (5)	..	..	..	0	0	0	0	0	0
Tonga	-47	-61	-62	-117	-133	-143	-149	-155	-171
Tuvalu	-5	-6	-6	-14	-18	-19	-19	-18	-22
Vanuatu	-64	-66	-68	-153	-202	-225	-244	-237	-238
Wallis and Futuna Islands (5)	..	..	-35	-56	-63	-61	-61	-58	-63
Transition economies	**-8 958**	**10 294**	**37 277**	**111 303**	**128 463**	**115 597**	**129 631**	**150 269**	**190 905**
Albania	-181	-536	-908	-2 443	-3 089	-3 488	-3 406	-3 255	-3 073
Armenia*	–	-382	-562	-1 383	-2 230	-2 698	-2 896	-2 710	-2 786
Azerbaijan (32)	–	-162	450	8 756	15 327	17 607	19 109	19 547	22 092
Belarus	–	-868	-973	-2 588	-4 615	-6 164	-7 892	-7 073	-4 789
Bosnia and Herzegovina*(33)	–	-1 093	-1 981	-4 753	-5 586	-5 852	-5 469	-4 813	-4 827
Croatia*	–	-2 367	-3 811	-11 462	-13 739	-13 607	-11 867	-9 445	-8 675
Georgia (34)	–	-305	-424	-2 783	-3 844	-4 052	-3 918	-3 938	-4 638
Kazakhstan*(35)	–	928	2 727	13 356	20 952	21 023	25 645	31 399	42 386
Kyrgyzstan	–	-141	-63	-979	-1 575	-1 684	-1 682	-1 706	-2 411
Montenegro							-2 262	-1 861	-1 841
Republic of Moldova	–	-155	-250	-1 730	-2 432	-2 550	-2 539	-2 428	-2 780
Russian Federation (36)	–	18 980	45 290	129 517	149 977	140 749	147 775	153 920	181 328
Serbia and Montenegro*	–	-1 700	-2 240	-8 821		–	–		
Serbia	–	–	–	–	–	–	-9 334	-7 575	-7 561
SFR of Yugoslavia	-2 239								
Tajikistan (34)	–	-5	33	-577	-1 058	-1 470	-1 628	-1 657	-1 944
TFYR of Macedonia*	–	-464	-631	-1 477	-2 045	-2 380	-2 460	-2 345	-2 394

For sources and notes, see end of table.

Percentage of imports (1) Part dans les importations en pourcentage (1)									Régions, pays ou territoires
1989-91	1994-96	1999-01	2005-07	2006-08	2007-09	2008-10	2009-11	2010-12	
-8.51	*-8.56*	*13.81*	*10.69*	*9.56*	*9.60*	*9.13*	*9.77*	*6.69*	*Asie du Sud-Est*
120.77	11.18	186.27	313.23	307.27	253.42	247.62	228.16	250.96	Brunéi Darussalam*
-42.68	-34.00	-28.56	-22.91	-25.03	-26.84	-26.65	-25.67	-24.81	Cambodge (7)
22.09	17.68	52.21	_	_	_	_	_	_	Indonésie (...2002)
_	_	_	23.34	21.53	21.26	17.95	19.45	9.92	Indonésie
-55.47	-49.03	-38.82	-22.52	-17.48	-21.22	-21.79	-16.93	-10.29	Rép. dém. populaire lao*
1.94	-2.08	22.80	21.80	23.19	24.73	24.98	23.15	19.32	Malaisie (26)
-1.57	-30.37	-33.34	89.42	77.38	68.80	65.66	45.87	27.04	Myanmar
-33.21	-39.89	2.60	-13.98	-14.70	-15.99	-15.64	-17.43	-18.84	Philippines
-11.51	-5.17	3.55	14.13	11.12	9.76	9.58	11.65	10.91	Singapour (27)
-25.54	-20.04	10.78	1.51	3.29	7.71	6.29	5.65	-1.45	Thaïlande
			-93.21	-94.07	-95.90	-95.56	-96.00	-95.91	Timor-Leste (28)
-15.84	-32.80	-5.22	-15.27	-18.80	-21.08	-18.52	-14.15	-7.81	Viet Nam
25.78	*10.66*	*27.19*	*40.53*	*40.49*	*33.77*	*33.12*	*37.31*	*47.98*	*Asie occidentale*
-7.67	5.67	27.07	14.58	16.76	17.28	18.42	31.34	39.49	Bahreïn (7)
23.20	-15.79	37.33	44.35	72.67	62.19	38.09	32.86	51.71	Iraq*
-53.99	-55.91	-54.11	-57.37	-55.46	-55.56	-54.45	-55.92	-58.15	Jordanie
27.48	70.03	112.39	200.76	223.47	205.69	210.74	227.43	289.61	Koweït*
-81.44	-91.10	-87.61	-72.47	-71.69	-72.99	-73.65	-73.41	-73.31	Liban (29)
69.88	44.03	86.00	86.00	70.88	57.09	66.82	77.83	87.21	Oman
96.00	32.17	211.45	114.18	109.24	104.41	151.91	198.97	264.36	Qatar*
61.03	93.21	118.60	188.43	177.88	144.05	136.18	137.82	153.93	Arabie saoudite*(30)
..	-79.70	-85.51	-85.93	-84.91	-84.54	-85.14	-84.72	-82.97	État de Palestine
47.57	-31.42	7.42	-15.33	-13.68	-21.94	-23.91	-32.44	-37.61	République arabe syrienne*
-34.56	-36.14	-35.75	-37.57	-36.76	-33.02	-33.59	-36.71	-39.38	Turquie*
87.93	19.12	29.05	39.62	33.25	27.42	25.71	35.49	43.55	Émirats arabes unis
									Yémen, République arabe du
_	_	_	_	_	_	_	_	_	Yémen, Démocratique
_	-0.36	44.62	-4.05	-14.84	-28.64	-23.06	-11.15	-9.98	Yémen*
-41.35	*-18.20*	*-20.88*	*-30.74*	*-31.93*	*-35.00*	*-37.52*	*-37.18*	*-36.05*	*Économies en développement : Océanie*
-14.78	-39.14	-31.24	-27.72	-23.74	-22.87	-27.77	-42.37	-48.19	Samoa américaines*(31)
-90.21	-91.61	-86.37	-95.06	-95.97	-95.85	-95.34	-95.63	-96.08	Îles Cook
-26.68	-28.96	-33.82	-58.66	-59.63	-57.87	-56.34	-53.56	-50.03	Fidji
-87.59	-76.86	-77.16	-87.55	-88.74	-90.60	-91.16	-91.04	-91.21	Polynésie française*
-80.42	-77.92	-82.31	-90.72	-88.58	-88.17	-91.00	-95.07	-95.80	Guam (5)
-81.47	-81.73	-86.09	-90.10	-85.27	-85.47	-88.34	-91.98	-93.31	Kiribati
-90.19	-70.64	-83.14	-78.35	-80.61	-80.56	-78.69	-77.09	-75.36	Îles Marshall
-93.55	-82.34	-79.29	-85.91	-84.78	-84.24	-84.40	-85.08	-84.35	Micronésie (États fédérés de)
202.97	51.76	48.17	-83.12	-46.38	-22.77	51.85	88.89	136.11	Nauru (5)
-36.53	-48.26	-46.82	-33.22	-40.35	-48.77	-58.72	-57.14	-56.43	Nouvelle-Calédonie*
-99.17	-93.22	-86.94	-74.76	-75.34	-85.87	-99.69	-99.69	-99.71	Nioué
..	75.88	81.27	10.23	-4.79	-35.20	-69.84	-92.85	-95.13	Îles Mariannes du Nord (5)
..	-75.43	-88.55	-88.48	-89.96	-92.35	-94.02	-95.13	-94.76	Palaos (5)
-7.39	66.85	69.88	77.54	68.68	52.87	48.34	42.46	38.18	Papouasie-Nouvelle-Guinée
-88.35	-92.08	-54.71	-67.70	-71.54	-72.79	-77.46	-79.41	-78.72	Samoa (29)
-27.56	6.21	-19.41	-44.01	-40.22	-38.40	-38.64	-31.37	-18.65	Îles Salomon*
..	..	..	81.86	100.34	56.00	67.95	124.54	125.60	Tokélaou (5)
-80.72	-82.21	-87.10	-92.53	-93.44	-94.36	-94.61	-93.97	-93.17	Tonga
-97.67	-97.67	-99.31	-99.51	-99.42	-98.84	-98.41	-98.26	-98.58	Tuvalu
-75.95	-70.39	-73.87	-76.84	-79.25	-80.30	-81.84	-80.50	-80.77	Vanuatu
..	..	-99.88	-99.94	-99.94	-99.94	-99.94	-99.94	-99.94	Îles Wallis-et-Futuna (5)
-5.95	*10.08*	*35.71*	*33.84*	*29.33*	*24.09*	*26.59*	*29.59*	*33.21*	*Économies en transition*
-45.42	-74.63	-76.58	-74.35	-74.12	-74.83	-71.72	-68.27	-62.83	Albanie
_	-57.05	-66.12	-55.24	-65.30	-73.16	-75.65	-72.89	-68.86	Arménie*
_	-18.40	33.43	158.23	234.22	259.85	273.40	251.88	248.35	Azerbaïdjan (32)
_	-16.79	-12.27	-10.49	-14.80	-19.37	-23.41	-20.82	-12.64	Bélarus
_	-85.97	-67.76	-59.37	-56.95	-57.01	-53.89	-49.97	-47.83	Bosnie-Herzégovine*(33)
_	-33.09	-45.88	-52.21	-52.65	-52.28	-48.61	-44.30	-40.95	Croatie*
_	-62.31	-59.24	-72.06	-75.73	-75.82	-73.06	-70.63	-68.92	Géorgie (34)
_	22.67	56.50	55.94	65.06	61.89	77.56	93.75	112.13	Kazakhstan*(35)
_	-17.92	-10.37	-48.50	-53.64	-50.68	-48.27	-48.03	-54.62	Kirghizistan
						-82.24	-79.47	-78.33	Monténégro
_	-17.13	-32.03	-59.00	-64.03	-64.00	-62.80	-59.39	-58.61	République de Moldova
_	31.83	92.02	79.24	68.31	59.45	60.30	60.17	60.04	Fédération de Russie (36)
_	-47.27	-56.26	-54.69	_	_	_			Serbie-et-Monténégro*
				_	_	-48.12	-43.39	-40.82	Serbie
-12.91	_	_	_	_	_				RSF de Yougoslavie
	-0.86	4.95	-30.21	-38.65	-52.61	-57.55	-58.83	-59.96	Tadjikistan (34)
_	-28.74	-33.80	-36.20	-37.95	-41.42	-42.47	-40.55	-37.86	LERY de Macédoine*

Pour les sources et les notes, se reporter à la fin du tableau.

Region, country or territory	Trade balance (1) - Balance commerciale (1) Millions of dollars - Millions de dollars								
	1989-91	1994-96	1999-01	2005-07	2006-08	2007-09	2008-10	2009-11	2010-12
Turkmenistan (34)	–	523	293	3 969	5 418	3 286	1 782	1 467	4 267
Ukraine (34)	–	-2 000	281	-6 633	-12 191	-11 869	-11 240	-9 757	-13 225
USSR	-6 538								
Uzbekistan (34)	–	42	46	1 336	1 316	1 474	1 913	2 500	1 776
Developed economies: America	**-110 673**	**-166 818**	**-403 671**	**-834 094**	**-851 275**	**-751 409**	**-706 161**	**-690 201**	**-772 434**
Bermuda (7)	-494	-505	-671	-1 048	-1 114	-1 103	-1 048	-965	-916
Canada	2 935	20 383	27 558	32 583	32 381	18 051	2 813	-13 434	-15 538
Greenland	-14	-80	-93	-260	-332	-372	-406	-417	-416
Saint Pierre and Miquelon (5)	-55	-66	-97	-57	-90	-150	-191	-203	-191
United States (37)	-113 046	-186 550	-430 368	-865 313	-882 120	-767 834	-707 329	-675 182	-755 374
Developed economies: Asia	**59 832**	**87 050**	**81 166**	**75 319**	**54 604**	**42 364**	**37 646**	**20 050**	**-22 258**
Israel*	-4 909	-9 965	-6 685	-4 288	-4 937	-4 203	-3 486	-4 058	-7 694
Japan	64 741	97 015	87 851	79 606	59 541	46 567	41 132	24 107	-14 564
Developed economies: Europe	**-68 011**	**69 318**	**920**	**-72 803**	**-124 591**	**-105 648**	**-89 469**	**-45 713**	**-15 555**
Andorra*	..	-941	-1 005	-1 689	-1 747	-1 713	-1 604	-1 499	-1 518
Austria*	-8 021	-9 668	-4 606	-674	-961	-2 832	-5 176	-8 838	-10 806
Belgium*	-814	12 326	12 291	16 735	13 345	13 896	12 930	14 247	11 754
Bulgaria*	313	-357	-1 784	-8 691	-11 398	-11 070	-8 883	-5 492	-5 095
Cyprus*	-1 587	-2 368	-2 822	-5 889	-7 275	-7 603	-7 585	-6 868	-6 528
Czechoslovakia (38)	130								
Czech Republic*(39)	–	-3 454	-2 587	2 555	3 609	5 666	6 333	8 350	10 992
Denmark*(40)	2 909	5 576	5 550	7 245	6 585	7 852	10 600	13 480	14 404
Estonia*(34)	–	-734	-1 176	-3 649	-3 998	-3 109	-1 786	-924	-1 080
Faeroe Islands	71	59	-16	-184	-182	-142	-33	19	-41
Finland*	-99	9 048	10 789	7 628	6 942	4 987	2 451	-814	-2 545
France*	-20 607	5 068	-2 251	-52 666	-72 619	-82 632	-87 983	-95 650	-105 244
Germany, Federal Republic of	–								
Germany*	–	56 854	69 854	220 499	242 920	240 343	219 636	205 640	221 024
Gibraltar (41)	-281	-308	-344	-444	-508	-525	-505	-530	-576
Greece*	-11 062	-14 481	-20 604	-44 994	-54 674	-56 710	-52 419	-41 518	-34 420
Hungary*(42)	-240	-2 965	-3 381	-2 263	-1 203	1 549	4 039	7 475	8 596
Iceland	-105	17	-483	-2 176	-1 820	-775	105	548	494
Ireland*	3 267	11 584	27 693	38 141	38 361	44 233	50 400	56 193	56 604
Italy	-12 444	31 334	8 319	-16 372	-18 877	-13 049	-22 371	-27 824	-20 396
Latvia	–	-550	-1 356	-5 312	-6 133	-5 040	-3 422	-2 476	-2 807
Lithuania*(34)	–	-825	-1 771	-5 414	-6 651	-5 523	-3 986	-2 743	-2 985
Luxembourg*	-1 291	-2 094	-2 828	-3 980	-5 102	-5 210	-5 266	-5 596	-6 968
Malta	-776	-988	-845	-1 492	-1 671	-1 707	-1 638	-1 668	-1 910
Netherlands*	5 106	15 488	16 491	49 162	53 972	56 619	56 520	60 216	63 470
Norway	6 261	10 135	21 064	54 092	65 158	61 779	60 874	56 890	65 524
Poland*	453	-8 097	-16 664	-17 991	-26 706	-25 622	-23 209	-17 727	-17 609
Portugal*	-8 402	-9 818	-15 460	-25 334	-30 082	-31 453	-31 025	-26 195	-21 674
Romania	-659	-2 225	-2 936	-20 453	-27 682	-26 034	-20 268	-13 250	-12 784
Slovakia*	–	-802	-1 400	-2 662	-2 665	-1 479	-900	19	972
Slovenia*	–	-921	-1 276	-1 152	-1 758	-1 565	-1 377	-665	-500
Spain	-31 291	-13 931	-36 574	-115 708	-130 098	-113 731	-92 596	-69 511	-61 168
Sweden*	3 697	14 580	14 329	18 367	16 887	13 773	11 778	10 149	9 812
Switzerland*	-5 845	1 792	-1 179	7 237	11 513	15 060	17 870	21 008	24 697
United Kingdom*	-36 654	-29 017	-62 110	-155 276	-170 075	-173 880	-170 972	-170 157	-187 246
Developed economies: Oceania	**-2 871**	**-6 533**	**-7 625**	**-23 807**	**-21 518**	**-18 834**	**-5 604**	**9 081**	**11 271**
Australia	-3 278	-6 398	-7 079	-19 659	-17 603	-16 045	-4 387	8 847	11 140
New Zealand	408	-134	-546	-4 148	-3 914	-2 790	-1 217	234	131

For sources and notes, see next page.

1.3.1 Valeur de la balance commerciale et sa part dans les importations des pays et des régions géographiques

Percentage of imports (1) Part dans les importations en pourcentage (1)									Régions, pays ou territoires
1989-91	1994-96	1999-01	2005-07	2006-08	2007-09	2008-10	2009-11	2010-12	
–	37.51	13.54	131.37	146.55	77.88	33.62	19.54	50.59	Turkménistan (34)
–	-12.51	1.77	-12.92	-18.40	-17.65	-16.58	-15.05	-17.21	Ukraine (34)
-4.11									URSS
–	4.00	1.57	28.14	21.96	18.87	21.52	26.71	19.03	Ouzbékistan (34)
-17.60	**-18.06**	**-28.80**	**-37.17**	**-35.18**	**-32.26**	**-30.54**	**-29.39**	**-29.30**	**Économies développées : Amérique**
-90.34	-90.67	-93.58	-96.75	-97.71	-97.64	-97.92	-98.11	-98.56	Bermudes (7)
2.39	12.09	11.88	9.25	8.30	4.19	0.33	-3.47	-3.48	Canada
-3.36	-19.11	-24.92	-38.38	-42.86	-46.69	-50.00	-50.88	-48.53	Groenland
-65.76	-88.79	-94.00	-72.59	-75.94	-89.15	-95.82	-97.15	-96.92	Saint-Pierre-et-Miquelon (5)
-22.37	-24.57	-36.80	-45.89	-43.45	-39.35	-36.65	-34.65	-34.52	États-Unis (37)
24.01	**25.00**	**21.54**	**12.00**	**8.16**	**6.20**	**5.21**	**3.30**	**-1.67**	**Économies développées : Asie**
-29.00	-34.51	-18.98	-8.23	-8.25	-6.81	-5.54	-5.96	-10.47	Israël*
28.54	31.32	25.72	13.94	9.65	7.49	6.20	4.12	-0.90	Japon
-4.07	**3.19**	**0.06**	**-1.38**	**-2.13**	**-1.75**	**-1.48**	**-0.81**	**-0.28**	**Économies développées : Europe**
..	-95.19	-95.56	-92.33	-93.31	-94.80	-95.82	-95.87	-95.03	Andorre*
-17.26	-15.46	-6.35	-0.55	-0.54	-1.84	-3.31	-5.20	-6.03	Autriche*
-0.59	8.29	7.12	4.65	3.40	3.55	3.38	3.66	2.79	Belgique*
1.56	-7.23	-27.64	-36.27	-37.62	-36.09	-29.74	-21.08	-16.99	Bulgarie*
-63.79	-66.55	-74.30	-80.46	-83.08	-84.14	-84.08	-82.21	-79.62	Chypre*
1.33									Tchécoslovaquie (38)
–	-13.65	-7.97	2.54	2.96	4.85	5.29	6.54	7.79	République tchèque*(39)
8.93	13.24	12.20	8.71	6.80	8.40	12.03	15.37	15.96	Danemark*(40)
–	-28.16	-24.67	-27.45	-26.66	-20.94	-12.90	-7.33	-6.68	Estonie*(34)
22.41	20.73	-2.90	-21.17	-19.30	-14.36	-2.99	2.29	-2.62	Îles Féroé
-0.14	31.97	32.62	10.98	8.85	6.17	3.12	-0.60	-3.09	Finlande*
-9.13	1.70	-0.61	-9.29	-11.27	-12.96	-13.96	-15.00	-15.67	France*
–		–		–		–		–	Allemagne, Rép. fédérale d'
–	13.02	14.41	24.13	23.16	22.73	20.76	19.24	19.12	Allemagne*
-81.93	-72.17	-73.72	-64.09	-64.78	-64.91	-65.25	-67.19	-69.67	Gibraltar (41)
-57.37	-57.37	-64.39	-68.54	-69.62	-70.67	-69.33	-62.06	-53.16	Grèce*
-1.54	-18.92	-10.83	-3.15	-1.47	2.06	4.88	8.22	8.98	Hongrie*(42)
-6.11	1.89	-19.31	-36.89	-28.67	-9.90	5.59	13.50	11.35	Islande
16.76	37.29	55.95	51.21	47.81	59.87	75.96	88.98	89.60	Irlande*
-7.26	15.92	3.67	-3.71	-3.84	-2.56	-4.52	-5.50	-3.87	Italie
–	-28.92	-42.08	-44.37	-43.20	-34.81	-25.71	-19.79	-18.63	Lettonie
–	-22.04	-33.45	-26.95	-26.91	-21.28	-15.14	-11.06	-10.35	Lituanie*(34)
-17.35	-22.56	-24.48	-15.57	-17.56	-18.21	-19.05	-20.82	-25.38	Luxembourg*
-42.04	-36.23	-28.87	-35.09	-34.92	-35.28	-33.22	-31.88	-31.68	Malte
4.23	8.83	7.83	11.57	10.95	11.32	11.12	11.64	11.16	Pays-Bas*
24.30	31.19	62.43	82.33	83.41	76.45	76.18	71.63	76.66	Norvège
9.99	-26.45	-34.63	-13.40	-15.52	-14.15	-12.44	-9.79	-9.04	Pologne*
-35.36	-31.24	-38.86	-36.24	-36.85	-37.95	-38.08	-34.13	-27.77	Portugal*
-11.48	-21.94	-21.95	-36.88	-40.01	-36.27	-28.85	-21.03	-18.46	Roumanie
–	-7.20	-10.58	-6.13	-4.72	-2.15	-1.18	0.07	1.21	Slovaquie*
–	-10.23	-12.59	-4.58	-5.41	-4.57	-4.02	-2.13	-1.54	Slovénie*
-37.43	-13.01	-24.53	-34.40	-34.34	-30.17	-25.92	-21.09	-17.67	Espagne
7.26	23.09	21.01	14.43	11.62	9.36	8.11	7.05	6.05	Suède*
-9.13	2.43	-1.41	4.92	6.90	9.04	10.44	11.58	12.66	Suisse*
-17.45	-11.13	-18.30	-26.69	-27.44	-29.52	-29.56	-28.89	-28.75	Royaume-Uni*
-5.34	**-8.91**	**-9.02**	**-13.94**	**-11.12**	**-9.19**	**-2.75**	**2.87**	**4.34**	**Économies développées : Océanie**
-7.40	-10.74	-10.13	-13.72	-10.79	-9.24	-2.59	3.22	4.92	Australie
4.90	-0.81	-3.63	-15.02	-12.99	-8.76	-3.66	0.52	0.53	Nouvelle-Zélande

Pour les sources et les notes, se reporter à la page suivante.

Sources:

UNCTAD secretariat calculations, based on:

- UN DESA Statistics Division, *Yearbook of International Trade Statistics*
- UN DESA Statistics Division, *Monthly Bulletin of Statistics*
- UN DESA Statistics Division, UN *COMTRADE*
- IMF, *International Financial Statistics*
- IMF, *Direction of Trade Statistics*
- IMF, *Balance of Payments Statistics*
- WTO, *Statistics database*
- Eurostat, *Comext*
- World Bank, *World Development Indicators*
- OECD, *OECD.Stat Extracts*
- OPEC, *Annual Statistical Bulletin*
- Economist Intelligence Unit, *Country Data*
- Other international and national sources

Notes:

(*) Special Trade System.

(1) Average of three consecutive years.

(2) Excluding exports of gold.

(3) From 1996 onward, imports f.o.b.

(4) From 2011 onwards, commercial mining is included.

(5) Estimates based on UN *Comtrade* mirror structure.

(6) Prior to 2008, special trade.

(7) Imports f.o.b.

(8) Trade with other member countries of CEMAC is excluded. Imports f.o.b.

(9) Trade with other member countries of CEMAC is excluded.

(10) Prior to 1995, data refer to fiscal year ending June.

(11) Prior to 1974, special trade.

(12) Excluding re-exports (oil for bunkering).

(13) Prior to 2009, re-exports are excluded.

(14) Prior to 2005, special trade.

(15) Prior to 1986, included in Netherlands Antilles. Including exports and imports of crude oil and oil products. Prior to 2000, free zone trade is excluded. Imports f.o.b.

(16) From 1990 onwards, trade statistics exclude certain oil and chemical products. Imports f.o.b.

(17) Prior to 1993, excluding free trade processing zones. Imports f.o.b.

(18) Prior to 1986, including Aruba.

(19) Prior to 1992, excluding free trade processing zones.

(20) Prior to 2002, special trade.

(21) From 1990 onward, including goods for processing. Imports f.o.b.

(22) Excluding free trade processing zones.

(23) Prior to 2005, excluding customs free zones.

(24) Excluding imports of goods financed through foreign aid.

(25) Excluding military goods, fissionable materials, bunkers, ships and aircraft.

(26) Inter-trade between the States of Malaysia included. From 1965 onwards, excluding military imports and offshore installations of petroleum industry.

(27) Including trans-shipments to and from Peninsular Malaysia.

(28) Excluding exports of oil and gas.

(29) Prior to 2001, special trade.

(30) Excluding defense imports.

(31) Data refer to fiscal year ending September.

(32) Excluding military goods, precious metals and goods procured in foreign ports.

(33) Prior to 1998, data refer to the Federation of Bosnia and Herzegovina only. The other entity of Bosnia and Herzegovina, Republika Srpska, is not included.

(34) Prior to 1994, covers only trade with countries outside the CIS.

(35) Prior to 1994, covers only trade with countries outside the CIS. As of 2011, adjusted to include bilateral trade with Russian Federation.

(36) Prior to 1994, excluding trade with independent states which succeded from the former USSR.

(37) Prior to 1975, excludes non-monetary gold.

(38) From 1985 onwards, data are not comparable to those shown for prior periods due to revisions of the koruna-to-US dollar exchange rate.

(39) From 1995 onward, including goods for processing.

(40) Prior to 1988, excluding ships.

(41) Excluding petroleum products. Estimates based on UN *Comtrade* mirror structure.

(42) Prior to 1996, excluding customs free zones. .

Sources :

Calculs du secrétariat de la CNUCED, basés sur :

- ONU DAES Division de statistique, *Annuaire statistique du commerce international*
- ONU DAES Division de statistique, *Bulletin mensuel de statistique*
- ONU DAES Division de statistique, ONU *COMTRADE*
- FMI, *Statistiques financières internationales*
- FMI, *Direction of Trade Statistics*
- FMI, *Statistiques de la balance des paiements*
- OMC, *Base de données statistiques*
- Eurostat, *Comext*
- Banque mondiale, *Indicateurs du développement dans le monde*
- OCDE, *OECD.Stat Extracts*
- OPEP, *Bulletin statistique annuel*
- Economist Intelligence Unit, *Country Data*
- Autres sources internationales et nationales

Notes :

(*)   Système du commerce spécial.

(1)   Moyenne de trois années consécutives.

(2)   Non-compris les exportations d'or.

(3)   À partir de 1996, importations f.a.b.

(4)   À partir de 2011, l'exploitation minière commerciale est incluse.

(5)   Estimations basées sur la structure des données miroirs de UN *Comtrade*.

(6)   Avant 2008, commerce spécial.

(7)   Importations f.a.b.

(8)   Non-compris le commerce avec les autres pays membres de la CEMAC. Importations f.a.b.

(9)   Non-compris le commerce avec les autres pays membres de la CEMAC.

(10) Avant 1995, les données se rapportent à l'exercice budgétaire finissant juin.

(11) Avant 1974, commerce spécial.

(12) Non-compris les réexportations (huile pour mise en soute).

(13) Avant 2009, non-compris les réexportations.

(14) Avant 2005, commerce spécial.

(15) Avant 1986 compris dans Antilles néerlandaises. Les données comprennent les exportations et importations de pétrole brut et produits dérivés. Avant 2000, non-compris les zones
      franches douanières. Importations f.a.b.

(16) À partir de 1990, certains produits pétroliers et chimiques ne sont plus inclus dans les statistiques du commerce. Importations f.a.b.

(17) Avant 1993, non-compris les zones franches douanières. Importations f.a.b.

(18) Avant 1986, y compris Aruba.

(19) Avant 1992, non-compris les zones franches douanières.

(20) Avant 2002, commerce spécial.

(21) À partir de 1990, y compris les biens destinés à subir des transformations. Importations f.a.b.

(22) Non-compris les zones franches douanières.

(23) Avant 2005, non-compris les zones franches douanières.

(24) Non-compris les biens d'importation financés par l'aide à l'étranger.

(25) Non-compris les biens à usage militaire, le matériel fissile, le combustible de soute et l'avitaillement des navires et aéronefs.

(26) Y compris le commerce entre les États de la Malaisie. Non-compris les importations militaires et l'installation près des côtes de l'industrie pétrolière.

(27) Y compris les transbordements vers et en provenance de la Malaisie péninsulaire.

(28) Non-compris les exportations de pétrole et de gaz.

(29) Avant 2001, commerce spécial.

(30) Non-compris les importations de la défense.

(31) Les données se rapportent à l'exercice budgétaire finissant septembre.

(32) Non-compris les biens à usage militaire, les métaux précieux et les biens fournis dans les ports étrangers.

(33) Avant 1998, les données se réfèrent uniquement à la Fédération de la Bosnie-Herzégovine. L'autre entité de la Bosnie-Herzégovine, Republika Srpska, n'est pas incluse.

(34) Avant 1994, concerne seulement le commerce avec les pays extérieurs à la CEI.

(35) Avant 1994, concerne seulement le commerce avec les pays extérieurs à la CEI. A partir de 2011, y compris le commerce bilatéral avec la Fédération de Russie.

(36) Avant 1994, non-compris le commerce avec les républiques indépendantes de l'ancienne URSS.

(37) Avant 1975, non-compris l'or industriel.

(38) À partir de 1985, les chiffres ne sont pas comparables à ceux des années antérieures à cause des révisions du taux de change de la couronne par rapport au dollar des États-Unis.

(39) À partir de 1995, y compris les biens destinés à subir des transformations.

(40) Avant 1988, non-compris les navires.

(41) Non-compris les produits pétroliers. Estimations basées sur la structure des données miroirs de UN *Comtrade*.

(42) Avant 1996, non-compris les zones franches douanières.

1.3.2 Value of trade balance, and as percentage of imports of economic groupings

Economic grouping	Trade balance (1) - Balance commerciale (1) Millions of dollars - Millions de dollars								
	1989-91	1994-96	1999-01	2005-07	2006-08	2007-09	2008-10	2009-11	2010-12
DEVELOPING ECONOMIES	17 268	-62 796	103 772	504 144	559 980	495 482	438 426	436 744	496 460
Developing economies excluding China	13 847	-74 188	78 483	322 858	313 319	242 764	213 319	259 379	307 556
Developing economies excluding LDCs	25 219	-52 754	114 276	503 577	555 902	500 994	447 508	449 126	506 173
High-income developing economies	45 067	-14 180	83 387	364 490	382 266	356 216	360 992	407 172	491 235
Middle-income developing economies	-16 265	-32 290	37 028	214 184	286 777	275 692	233 493	186 936	181 957
Low-income developing economies	-11 534	-16 326	-16 642	-74 531	-109 063	-136 426	-156 060	-157 365	-176 732
Heavily indebted poor countries (IMF)	-4 294	-6 319	-10 579	-22 265	-27 791	-32 278	-33 412	-33 387	-40 951
Landlocked developing countries	-4 238	-7 312	-5 987	8 530	16 584	11 258	11 405	15 807	25 613
Small island developing States	-3 557	-3 956	-6 196	-6 602	-7 308	-9 568	-9 689	-10 348	-11 002
Least developed countries	*-7 951*	*-10 042*	*-10 505*	*566*	*4 078*	*-5 513*	*-9 082*	*-12 383*	*-9 713*
Africa and Haiti	-3 361	-4 841	-4 960	9 775	16 396	10 002	8 420	7 996	14 251
Asia	-4 349	-4 956	-5 289	-8 413	-11 345	-14 417	-16 267	-19 083	-22 599
Islands	-241	-245	-255	-795	-973	-1 098	-1 235	-1 296	-1 365
Major petroleum and gas exporters	*52 490*	*64 309*	*117 122*	*428 891*	*529 890*	*486 880*	*493 789*	*544 868*	*725 974*
Africa	15 252	12 881	26 365	118 113	143 323	126 093	121 423	111 689	147 561
America	6 559	8 630	10 853	29 178	33 755	28 455	29 409	29 373	36 332
Asia	30 679	42 798	79 904	281 600	352 813	332 331	342 957	403 807	542 081
Major exporters of manufactured goods	*-11 131*	*-34 217*	*58 773*	*255 349*	*302 752*	*321 184*	*298 649*	*269 991*	*254 411*
America	-4 368	-3 990	-12 427	-15 325	-19 660	-19 089	-16 914	-11 734	-11 016
Asia	-6 763	-30 227	71 200	270 673	322 412	340 273	315 563	281 724	265 427
Emerging economies	*7 518*	*-34 038*	*42 712*	*162 263*	*137 500*	*143 404*	*143 709*	*177 961*	*153 269*
America	13 741	-11 414	-12 736	58 918	42 899	33 754	24 514	34 009	24 567
Asia	-6 222	-22 624	55 448	103 345	94 601	109 650	119 195	143 953	128 702
Newly industrialized Asian economies	*-9 917*	*-46 338*	*66 591*	*101 598*	*87 190*	*99 730*	*102 097*	*118 825*	*79 768*
First tier	-2 069	-26 692	23 310	58 482	37 492	42 015	44 502	60 663	46 031
Second tier	-7 848	-19 646	43 281	43 116	49 698	57 715	57 595	58 162	33 738
Developing economies: Africa	2 843	-6 996	3 098	61 329	70 060	41 558	32 557	16 403	29 036
Northern Africa excluding Sudan	-3 475	-8 172	-1 670	35 216	39 939	20 724	8 525	-13 286	-10 514
Sub-Saharan Africa	6 318	1 176	4 768	26 113	30 121	20 834	24 032	29 688	39 550
Sub-Saharan Africa excluding South Africa	1 887	1 746	4 332	42 741	50 142	38 134	39 555	46 112	64 178
Developing economies: America	14 110	-22 795	-27 104	43 507	21 094	4 805	-5 416	5 959	-2 444
Central America and Greater Caribbean Islands excluding Puerto Rico	-9 880	-14 451	-31 231	-53 144	-67 102	-66 343	-64 791	-57 705	-63 177
Central America and Greater Caribbean Islands excluding Mexico and Puerto Rico	-5 513	-10 461	-18 804	-37 819	-47 442	-47 255	-47 877	-45 972	-52 161
South America and Central America	18 925	-15 270	-13 338	62 992	44 938	30 876	21 948	32 545	25 648
South America excluding Brazil	15 889	-1 939	11 245	60 412	59 813	52 157	48 672	52 617	52 887
Developing economies: Asia	2 449	-31 865	129 077	402 765	472 951	453 678	416 353	419 613	475 501
Eastern and South-Eastern Asia excluding China	-10 462	-50 308	65 315	95 810	76 735	85 726	88 622	106 481	70 224
Southern Asia excluding India	-7 880	-2 662	2 823	6 951	13 103	8 414	2 344	3 469	3 254

Source:

Data in this table are based on trade figures in table 1.1.1.

Notes:

(1) Average of three consecutive years.

Percentage of imports (1) Part dans les importations en pourcentage (1)									Groupements économiques
1989-91	1994-96	1999-01	2005-07	2006-08	2007-09	2008-10	2009-11	2010-12	
2.24	-4.33	5.76	12.40	11.87	9.84	8.01	7.30	7.07	**ÉCONOMIES EN DÉVELOPPEMENT**
2.02	-5.59	4.90	10.05	8.49	6.09	4.93	5.44	5.70	Économies en développement sans la Chine
3.34	-3.72	6.52	12.73	12.11	10.27	8.45	7.78	7.41	Économies en développement sans les PMA
9.23	-1.49	7.25	16.55	14.88	13.41	12.88	13.51	14.12	Économies en développement à revenu élevé
-7.66	-8.39	7.69	14.89	17.38	15.65	11.96	8.76	7.00	Économies en développement à revenu intermédiaire
-14.49	-15.16	-11.02	-16.91	-19.04	-22.10	-22.77	-20.95	-19.46	Économies en développement à revenu faible
-18.37	-21.62	-28.14	-25.35	-25.71	-27.79	-26.56	-24.73	-25.44	Pays pauvres très endettés (FMI)
-28.91	-21.55	-16.25	8.20	13.31	8.05	7.33	0.73	10.90	Pays en développement sans littoral
-31.74	-28.88	-36.74	-21.65	-20.25	-27.37	-28.20	-29.96	-28.49	Petits États insulaires en développement
-31.88	*-30.50*	*-23.92*	*0.09*	*3.09*	*-3.47*	*-5.83*	*-7.68*	*-4.72*	*Pays les moins avancés*
-19.78	-24.28	-20.06	13.93	19.19	10.87	7.76	6.36	11.63	Afrique et Haïti
-57.43	-39.58	-28.17	-22.65	-24.82	-29.04	-29.45	-29.68	-30.09	Asie
-63.96	-53.46	-59.03	-73.07	-74.38	-75.83	-77.40	-75.33	-71.30	Îles
52.45	*54.20*	*78.57*	*110.51*	*107.58*	*86.76*	*80.93*	*85.67*	*102.35*	*Principaux exportateurs de pétrole et de gaz*
68.74	54.92	101.34	177.39	167.50	124.14	103.68	91.93	111.08	Afrique
81.69	84.82	67.13	92.93	79.49	60.68	66.27	67.55	75.04	Amérique
44.18	50.81	74.88	97.54	96.98	80.84	76.57	85.68	102.73	Asie
-2.40	*-3.98*	*5.58*	*10.41*	*10.96*	*11.40*	*9.86*	*8.38*	*6.43*	*Principaux exportateurs d'articles manufacturés*
-9.12	-4.83	-7.44	-5.88	-6.66	-6.58	-5.74	-3.97	-3.19	Amérique
-1.64	-3.74	7.93	12.40	13.03	13.40	11.49	9.61	7.36	Asie
2.89	*-5.21*	*5.57*	*11.16*	*8.55*	*8.90*	*8.33*	*9.59*	*6.92*	*Économies émergentes*
18.11	-6.75	-4.75	13.23	8.87	6.61	4.55	5.73	3.36	Amérique
-2.10	-4.57	11.04	10.26	8.46	10.00	10.15	11.46	8.67	Asie
-2.37	*-6.16*	*8.65*	*6.85*	*5.42*	*6.24*	*5.97*	*6.56*	*3.73*	*Économies nouvellement industrialisées d'Asie*
-0.53	-4.92	4.17	5.48	3.29	3.69	3.62	4.59	2.95	Première génération
-7.58	-9.37	21.41	10.61	11.21	13.21	12.30	11.85	5.80	Deuxième génération
3.14	-6.02	2.31	20.02	18.52	9.63	6.58	2.89	5.43	Économies en développement : Afrique
-7.58	-19.10	-3.47	36.05	33.14	14.68	4.90	-7.87	-5.56	Afrique septentrionale sans le Soudan
10.98	1.53	5.71	12.56	11.61	7.25	7.64	8.48	11.04	Afrique subsaharienne
4.80	3.28	8.09	31.92	30.11	20.14	18.65	19.69	25.65	Afrique subsaharienne sans l'Afrique du Sud
11.62	-9.47	-7.45	7.07	3.43	0.84	-0.47	0.68	-0.25	Économies en développement : Amérique
-15.66	-13.44	-14.86	-15.43	-17.12	-17.18	-16.45	-14.26	-13.55	Amérique centrale et Grandes Antilles sans Porto Rico
-29.92	-38.77	-43.28	-45.61	-48.57	-47.96	-47.52	-44.59	-44.55	Amérique centrale et Grandes Antilles sans le Mexique et Porto Rico
18.33	-7.04	-4.04	10.98	7.05	4.47	3.03	4.00	2.63	Amérique du Sud et Amérique centrale
46.10	-2.83	12.54	34.70	28.06	22.02	19.13	19.14	16.17	Amérique du Sud sans le Brésil
0.54	-2.85	10.14	12.92	13.12	11.94	10.07	9.23	8.77	Économies en développement : Asie
-2.47	-6.53	8.23	6.19	4.60	5.11	4.91	5.55	3.11	Asie orientale et Asie du Sud-Est sans la Chine
-22.53	-6.62	6.47	6.13	10.89	6.51	1.55	1.63	1.71	Asie méridionale sans l'Inde

Source :

Les données dans ce tableau ont été calculées d'après les chiffres du tableau 1.1.1.

Notes :

(1)   Moyenne de trois années consécutives.

Trade group	Value of intra-trade (exports in millions of dollars) Valeur du commerce interne au groupement (exportations en millions de dollars)						Intra-trade of groups regional exports Commerce interne des exportations régionales		
	1995	2000	2005	2010	2011	2012	1995	2000	2005
AFRICA									
CEMAC	97	101	261	830	755	709	37.1	33.9	34.7
CEPGL	5	4	24	51	86	152	3.7	16.0	8.9
COMESA	1 363	1 404	3 399	8 876	9 332	9 297	43.9	44.7	52.8
EAC	539	489	1 133	2 222	2 595	3 086	61.2	59.7	55.3
ECCAS	135	157	350	1 394	1 062	990	32.8	46.0	25.5
ECOWAS	2 294	2 711	6 011	9 783	10 636	12 530	79.3	74.1	72.6
MRU	103	111	238	164	338	283	11.4	8.8	10.9
SADC	6 622	7 249	11 231	22 345	25 792	24 337	85.2	87.3	82.3
UMA	1 232	1 095	1 916	3 739	4 105	5 710	71.2	71.8	60.3
WAEMU	1 055	976	1 717	2 534	2 645	3 124	57.9	49.2	43.7
AMERICA									
ANCOM	1 804	2 039	4 574	7 942	9 336	9 948	14.5	11.2	12.5
CACM	1 470	2 413	3 727	5 490	6 391	6 260	22.6	20.1	22.1
CARICOM	842	1 249	1 949	2 439	3 219	3 146	22.8	21.5	16.7
FTAA	528 383	866 018	1 114 172	1 393 593	1 650 067	1 710 711	99.3	99.1	98.7
LAIA	36 983	45 834	78 146	140 321	172 287	172 532	26.1	17.8	20.4
MERCOSUR	17 677	21 042	26 970	57 087	70 130	66 614	34.7	28.0	20.9
NAFTA	392 902	681 263	824 515	955 315	1 101 207	1 150 305	87.2	90.8	90.4
OAS	529 606	867 927	1 118 147	1 400 479	1 658 407	1 720 011	99.4	99.3	99.0
OECS	31	28	34	56	54	60	19.9	20.3	26.3
ASIA									
APTA	21 988	37 785	128 116	278 555	325 535	326 030	12.8	15.8	22.2
ASEAN	80 081	98 189	165 406	262 987	310 488	325 513	41.9	39.1	39.4
ECO	4 908	4 693	14 565	32 945	42 740	48 430	24.5	16.2	20.4
GCC	7 041	8 340	19 453	34 523	47 015	51 191	9.6	6.6	6.9
SAARC	2 436	2 935	9 112	16 633	20 209	20 291	13.7	13.7	15.8
EUROPE									
EFTA	927	842	1 220	2 084	2 945	2 970	1.0	0.8	0.7
EU27	1 412 003	1 607 599	2 725 738	3 330 816	3 849 150	3 576 710	91.0	92.4	91.0
Euro area	883 190	956 886	1 619 956	1 945 931	2 215 974	2 038 696	70.3	69.8	68.8
OCEANIA									
MSG	..	19	44	76	89	106	0.0	1.7	2.3
INTERREGIONAL									
ACP	12 484	14 621	27 310	55 860	64 009	65 258	..	..	..
APEC	1 679 827	2 268 115	3 313 924	4 872 723	5 696 434	5 955 758	..	..	..
BSEC	24 741	24 832	66 417	101 456	129 021	126 235	..	..	..
CIS	29 333	29 341	61 230	97 592	138 038	127 552	..	..	..

Source:

UNCTAD secretariat calculations, based on UNCTAD, *UNCTADstat* Merchandise Trade Matrix

as percentage of of each group du groupement en pourcentage de chaque groupement			Intra-trade of groups as percentage of total exports of each group Commerce interne du groupement en pourcentage des exportations totales de chaque groupement						Groupements commerciaux
2010	2011	2012	1995	2000	2005	2010	2011	2012	
									AFRIQUE
47.9	46.3	46.0	1.7	1.2	1.1	2.3	1.7	1.6	CEMAC
3.3	5.1	30.9	0.3	0.4	0.9	0.9	1.2	2.2	CEPGL
60.1	58.8	57.6	5.6	4.7	5.2	7.5	9.5	6.9	COMESA
51.9	51.1	51.3	17.2	17.9	18.6	19.8	19.7	20.9	CAE
25.2	21.0	19.9	1.2	0.9	0.7	1.5	0.9	0.8	CEEAC
56.7	55.5	56.4	10.3	9.0	9.7	8.3	6.5	7.5	CEDEAO
4.9	9.8	6.4	1.9	2.4	2.9	1.2	2.3	1.8	UFM
80.2	83.5	83.0	15.0	14.3	12.0	13.1	12.5	11.7	SADC
58.6	60.7	62.2	3.9	2.3	1.9	2.6	3.0	3.3	UMA
36.8	37.0	38.2	16.1	15.2	14.2	12.2	11.1	13.5	UEMOA
									AMÉRIQUE
12.8	11.2	11.5	8.5	7.8	9.0	8.0	7.0	7.1	ANCOM
24.1	23.6	22.5	15.7	16.0	17.0	18.3	17.9	16.8	MCAC
18.6	19.2	19.9	14.5	15.4	13.4	13.8	14.0	14.5	CARICOM
99.1	99.1	98.7	52.8	61.3	60.5	54.8	54.6	55.0	ZLEA
27.2	27.5	26.9	17.7	13.9	14.6	16.9	16.7	16.5	ALADI
36.3	35.6	33.7	19.5	18.0	12.2	16.2	15.4	14.9	MERCOSUR
85.2	84.4	84.0	46.0	55.7	55.7	48.7	48.3	48.5	ALENA
99.4	99.4	99.1	52.9	61.3	60.7	55.0	54.7	55.2	OEA
27.3	27.4	27.1	9.8	9.1	10.0	12.6	13.1	13.5	OECO
									ASIE
24.5	23.1	21.4	7.0	7.9	11.0	12.1	11.7	11.1	ACAP
36.8	36.2	37.6	24.9	23.0	25.3	25.0	25.0	26.0	ANASE
21.0	20.8	22.3	8.1	5.7	7.4	9.6	9.6	11.1	ECO
6.6	6.4	6.2	6.8	4.8	4.9	5.4	5.1	5.0	CCG
12.3	11.8	11.9	5.1	4.6	6.8	6.1	5.5	5.8	SAARC
									EUROPE
0.9	1.1	1.1	0.7	0.6	0.5	0.6	0.7	0.8	AELE
89.6	88.8	87.9	65.9	67.5	67.6	64.8	63.9	61.8	UE27
67.6	66.5	65.5	51.7	51.6	51.5	48.7	47.6	45.7	Zone euro
									OCÉANIE
2.4	2.2	2.9	..	0.7	1.0	1.1	1.0	1.3	MSG
									INTERRÉGIONAUX
..	..	..	13.7	13.0	12.6	14.6	13.2	13.5	ACP
..	..	..	71.7	73.0	70.8	67.4	67.0	68.1	CEAP
..	..	..	17.8	14.2	15.9	14.6	14.4	13.8	CEMN
..	..	..	26.7	20.6	18.0	16.8	17.6	16.0	CEI

Source :

Calculs du secrétariat de la CNUCED, basés sur la matrice du commerce de marchandises de *UNCTADstat* de la CNUCED

2

INTERNATIONAL **MERCHANDISE** TRADE BY REGION

COMMERCE INTERNATIONAL DES **MARCHANDISES** PAR RÉGIONS

1

2

3

4

5

6

7

8

Destination / Origin / Origine	Year / Année	World (millions of dollars) (1) / Monde (millions de dollars) (1)	Developed economies / Économies développées Total	Europe Total	Europe EU UE	USA États-Unis	Japan Japon	Other Autres	Transition economies / Économies en transition	Developing economies / Économies en développement Total	Africa Afrique	America Amérique	Eastern, Southern and South-Eastern Asia / Asie orientale, méridionale et du Sud-Est	Western Asia / Asie occidentale	Oceania Océanie
Afghanistan	1995	(e)166	21.7	16.5	14.9	4.1	0.7	0.4	41.9	36.4	0.7	2.5	31.5	1.7	0.0
	2005	(e)384	39.4	14.1	13.9	23.1	1.0	1.2	3.4	57.2	2.0	1.2	48.0	5.9	0.0
	2012	(e)370	17.1	10.0	9.7	6.2	0.1	0.8	12.3	70.6	0.8	0.7	64.3	4.9	0.0
Albania - Albanie	1995	(e)202	90.0	84.8	84.3	3.4	0.9	0.8	6.1	3.9	0.3	0.3	0.3	2.9	..
	2005	(e)658	91.6	87.1	87.0	4.2	0.1	0.2	3.4	5.0	0.3	0.5	1.8	2.4	0.0
	2012	(e)1 968	78.1	76.7	76.0	1.0	0.1	0.3	6.1	15.7	0.8	0.4	9.3	5.3	0.0
Algeria - Algérie	1995	9 357	87.6	67.8	66.5	16.7	0.7	2.4	1.6	10.8	2.5	2.8	2.0	3.5	..
	2005	46 002	84.2	56.2	55.6	23.0	0.0	5.0	0.0	15.7	2.2	7.0	2.6	3.9	..
	2012	71 866	79.6	56.3	55.3	15.0	1.2	7.1	0.2	20.3	4.1	5.9	6.4	3.9	0.0
American Samoa - Samoa américaines	1995	272	..	..	..	..	..	..	..	..	..	..	..	..	..
	2005	(e)374	47.3	15.6	11.2	..	9.3	22.4	0.5	52.2	5.0	0.9	38.1	1.0	7.2
	2012	(e)420	19.4	2.1	2.1	..	0.1	17.2	5.6	75.0	4.1	2.2	67.6	0.2	0.8
Andorra - Andorre	1995	48	99.6	99.6	99.6	..	..	0.0	..	0.3	0.0	0.0	0.2	0.0	..
	2005	143	98.9	98.7	98.4	0.1	0.1	0.0	0.1	1.0	0.7	0.3	0.0	0.0	..
	2012	(e)110	69.6	68.2	64.1	0.3	..	1.1	0.6	29.8	2.0	7.2	20.6	0.0	0.0
Angola	1995	3 642	86.2	21.2	21.2	64.3	0.4	0.2	0.0	13.7	0.3	3.2	10.1	0.0	..
	2005	24 109	56.1	14.7	14.7	40.0	0.1	1.2	0.0	43.9	1.4	7.0	35.4	0.1	..
	2012	(e)74 000	29.6	12.5	12.4	13.9	0.5	2.7	0.0	70.4	4.0	0.1	66.4	0.0	0.0
Anguilla	1995	(e)1	4.3	2.9	2.9	0.8	0.5	0.1	44.0	51.7	0.2	43.9	7.6	0.0	..
	2005	(e)15	53.7	24.7	24.5	27.7	0.4	0.9	6.5	39.8	1.0	36.5	2.3	..	0.0
	2012	(e)21	63.7	15.4	7.1	40.9	0.1	7.2	15.3	21.1	0.5	11.3	8.6	0.7	0.0
Antigua and Barbuda - Antigua-et-Barbuda	1995	(e)53	42.9	27.4	24.1	5.9	0.3	9.3	0.0	57.1	0.6	52.1	4.1	0.3	..
	2005	(e)83	82.5	80.4	80.3	1.9	0.0	0.2	0.0	17.5	2.9	9.7	4.8	0.0	0.0
	2012	(e)60	3.3	2.6	2.6	0.5	0.0	0.1	0.0	96.7	86.5	6.2	1.1	2.9	0.0
Argentina - Argentine	1995	20 963	34.8	23.1	22.0	8.6	2.2	1.0	0.4	64.7	4.1	47.2	11.8	1.6	0.0
	2005	40 106	31.2	17.5	17.1	11.4	0.7	1.7	1.9	65.0	6.1	40.4	15.7	2.8	0.0
	2012	80 927	26.1	15.6	14.7	5.1	1.5	3.9	1.2	70.1	6.9	42.6	17.7	2.9	0.0
Armenia - Arménie	1995	(e)271	16.3	10.7	9.9	5.6	0.1	0.0	58.9	24.7	2.1	0.6	17.7	4.3	..
	2005	(e)937	72.0	52.2	50.3	7.2	0.1	12.4	19.0	9.0	0.1	3.3	4.1	1.4	0.0
	2012	(e)1 428	53.9	39.8	36.6	7.1	0.1	6.9	31.5	14.6	0.1	1.4	10.9	2.2	0.0
Aruba	1995	(e)1 347	73.3	4.7	4.7	66.5	..	2.0	0.0	26.7	0.9	25.6	0.1	0.1	..
	2005	(e)4 416	87.6	12.6	12.6	73.8	0.0	1.2	0.0	12.4	0.0	10.2	0.0	2.2	..
	2012	(e)1 850	60.0	5.3	5.3	54.7	0.0	0.0	0.0	40.0	2.5	22.8	14.3	0.3	..
Australia - Australie	1995	53 001	43.4	10.4	9.8	5.0	20.2	7.8	0.1	41.6	1.1	0.9	35.9	1.5	2.2
	2005	105 751	46.1	11.1	10.9	6.7	20.4	7.9	0.3	52.2	2.5	1.7	42.7	3.6	1.7
	2012	256 243	34.0	7.1	6.7	3.7	19.4	3.8	0.4	64.8	1.4	1.2	57.9	2.7	1.6
Austria - Autriche	1995	57 583	85.9	80.6	74.5	2.8	1.2	1.3	2.9	7.1	1.1	0.9	3.9	1.3	0.0
	2005	117 722	86.9	78.4	73.1	5.6	1.1	1.7	4.8	8.1	1.2	0.9	4.2	1.7	0.0
	2012	158 821	79.8	72.0	66.2	5.3	1.0	1.5	5.5	11.6	1.3	2.0	5.9	2.4	0.0
Azerbaijan - Azerbaïdjan	1995	(e)636	17.2	16.8	16.7	0.2	0.1	0.1	50.1	32.7	0.1	0.9	26.8	4.8	..
	2005	(e)7 649	63.1	59.8	59.5	1.0	0.0	2.2	22.3	14.7	0.5	0.0	7.1	7.0	0.0
	2012	(e)32 634	64.8	53.3	52.9	4.9	0.1	6.5	7.9	27.3	1.1	0.0	22.9	3.3	0.0
Bahamas	1995	(e)176	80.9	51.7	40.7	25.8	0.8	2.6	1.0	18.1	4.1	4.7	9.1	0.1	0.0
	2005	(e)549	87.4	57.3	55.1	27.9	0.0	2.1	0.1	12.4	0.2	8.0	4.0	0.2	0.0
	2012	(e)984	49.1	15.9	12.2	31.5	0.3	1.4	0.2	50.7	1.0	24.5	25.2	0.1	..
Bahrain - Bahreïn	1995	(e)4 113	30.0	11.4	10.2	6.1	12.2	0.4	0.0	69.1	0.9	0.1	47.8	20.3	0.0
	2005	(e)10 239	27.6	11.5	10.8	8.5	5.7	1.9	0.0	71.9	20.1	0.1	26.8	24.9	0.0
	2012	(e)19 766	24.1	12.6	11.8	5.6	4.5	1.4	0.1	75.7	13.8	0.6	29.2	32.1	0.0
Bangladesh	1995	(e)3 407	83.0	41.9	41.1	34.9	3.6	2.6	0.8	16.2	2.3	0.7	11.3	1.9	0.0
	2005	(e)9 332	88.6	54.5	53.6	28.4	1.3	4.4	0.3	11.1	0.8	0.5	7.7	2.0	0.0
	2012	(e)26 504	82.2	54.0	52.5	19.7	2.3	6.3	1.6	16.2	1.4	1.4	9.1	4.3	0.0
Barbados - Barbade	1995	238	44.0	20.6	20.4	17.2	0.6	5.6	0.1	41.6	0.4	40.5	0.7	0.0	..
	2005	361	32.1	22.3	22.1	8.2	0.0	1.6	0.0	48.8	0.1	48.1	0.5	0.1	0.0
	2012	566	31.3	9.5	8.7	17.8	0.0	3.9	0.2	68.5	0.2	64.1	3.9	0.2	0.0
Belarus - Bélarus	1995	(e)4 804	33.0	31.4	31.0	1.2	0.3	0.2	63.1	3.7	0.7	0.1	2.4	0.5	..
	2005	15 977	46.6	44.9	44.6	1.6	0.0	0.1	44.6	8.4	0.7	1.4	5.6	0.6	..
	2012	46 060	38.8	38.4	37.9	0.2	0.0	0.2	51.3	7.6	0.5	2.6	3.8	0.6	0.0

For sources and notes, see end of table.

Pour les sources et les notes, se reporter à la fin du tableau.

Destination / Origin / Origine	Year / Année	World (millions of dollars) (1) / Monde (millions de dollars) (1)	Developed economies / Économies développées — Total	Europe Total	Europe EU UE	USA États-Unis	Japan Japon	Other Autres	Transition economies / Économies en transition	Developing economies / Économies en développement — Total	Africa Afrique	America Amérique	Eastern, Southern and South-Eastern Asia / Asie orientale, méridionale et du Sud-Est	Western Asia / Asie occidentale	Oceania Océanie
													Percentage / En pourcentage		
Belgium - Belgique	1995	(e)177 831	86.4	77.3	74.6	4.7	1.7	2.7	1.1	12.1	2.1	1.5	6.7	1.8	0.0
	2005	334 106	88.0	78.2	76.7	6.4	1.0	2.3	1.2	10.2	1.8	1.1	5.2	2.1	0.0
	2012	446 854	81.1	72.3	70.0	5.9	1.1	1.8	2.2	15.4	3.3	1.9	7.3	2.9	0.0
Belize	1995	162	92.2	51.9	51.3	30.0	6.1	4.2	0.1	7.6	0.0	5.8	1.8	0.0	..
	2005	208	74.4	36.3	36.2	33.8	2.2	2.1	0.3	25.3	4.9	13.6	6.3	0.6	0.0
	2012	(e)390	76.4	36.3	36.1	35.2	4.1	0.9	1.1	22.5	1.0	15.7	5.0	0.7	0.0
Benin - Bénin	1995	420	35.9	30.8	30.2	4.9	0.2	0.0	0.7	61.1	20.0	20.0	21.1	0.1	..
	2005	(e)578	9.0	8.9	8.5	0.1	0.0	0.0	0.0	90.9	35.8	0.4	53.6	1.2	..
	2012	(e)1 400	6.5	6.0	6.0	0.3	0.1	0.0	0.0	93.5	39.1	0.2	40.2	14.0	..
Bermuda - Bermudes	1995	(e)56	75.0	60.1	59.8	12.0	1.1	1.8	0.2	24.8	0.4	23.5	1.0	0.1	..
	2005	(e)49	97.6	89.3	89.2	6.5	0.4	1.5	0.0	2.3	0.4	1.6	0.3	0.0	0.0
	2012	(e)12	66.5	3.8	3.7	29.0	0.0	33.7	0.2	33.3	7.5	1.2	24.5	0.2	..
Bhutan - Bhoutan	1995	(e)103	6.9	3.9	3.8	0.3	2.7	0.0	0.1	93.0	0.5	0.9	91.3	0.4	..
	2005	(e)258	1.1	0.7	0.6	0.3	0.1	0.0	..	98.9	0.1	2.0	96.8	0.0	..
	2012	(e)610	4.5	3.1	3.0	0.2	1.0	0.1	0.1	95.4	1.6	0.1	93.6	0.1	..
Bolivia (Plurinational State of) - Bolivie (État plurinational de)	1995	1 181	55.4	27.4	23.7	26.2	0.4	1.4	0.3	44.3	0.1	36.0	0.9	7.3	..
	2005	2 797	26.0	8.0	6.8	13.2	3.7	1.0	0.2	73.8	0.1	70.4	3.3	0.1	0.0
	2012	11 793	29.4	6.7	5.9	16.7	3.2	2.8	0.2	70.4	0.1	62.3	6.5	1.5	0.0
Bosnia and Herzegovina - Bosnie-Herzégovine	1995	(e)152	25.3	22.9	22.7	1.9	0.0	0.6	72.0	2.6	0.3	0.6	1.7	0.1	..
	2005	(e)2 388	63.8	60.6	60.1	2.7	0.1	0.4	30.9	5.3	0.7	0.1	3.7	0.7	0.0
	2012	(e)5 162	62.1	60.7	59.1	1.0	0.1	0.3	32.4	5.6	1.3	0.3	1.4	2.5	0.0
Botswana	1995	(e)2 142	89.0	86.9	78.0	1.6	0.0	0.5	0.0	11.0	10.8	0.1	0.1	0.0	0.0
	2005	4 431	85.9	81.8	74.0	3.6	0.4	0.1	0.0	14.1	12.0	0.0	2.0	0.0	0.0
	2012	5 971	82.5	77.1	70.8	3.1	0.3	2.0	0.0	17.5	13.5	0.0	3.8	0.1	0.0
Brazil - Brésil	1995	46 505	57.3	29.9	28.8	18.9	6.7	1.9	1.4	40.4	3.4	23.1	11.5	2.4	0.0
	2005	118 529	48.2	23.7	22.9	19.2	2.9	2.3	2.9	47.1	5.0	25.5	13.5	3.1	0.0
	2012	242 580	37.3	21.3	20.2	11.1	3.3	1.7	1.9	58.7	5.0	20.8	28.7	4.2	0.0
British Virgin Islands - Îles Vierges britanniques	1995	(e)19	66.9	55.7	49.4	11.1	0.0	0.1	0.1	30.1	1.1	29.0	0.0	..	..
	2005	(e)35	79.8	71.8	44.4	7.0	0.1	0.9	8.9	11.2	0.8	6.8	2.9	0.8	0.0
	2012	40	93.5	90.4	80.5	1.1	0.0	2.0	1.0	5.5	1.2	1.3	3.1	0.0	0.0
Brunei Darussalam - Brunéi Darussalam	1995	(e)2 379	58.2	1.2	1.2	2.5	53.1	1.4	..	41.8	0.0	0.0	41.7	0.1	..
	2005	(e)6 256	58.3	0.9	0.8	9.6	37.1	10.6	0.0	41.7	0.0	0.0	41.7	0.0	0.0
	2012	13 001	60.7	0.4	0.3	0.7	44.8	14.8	0.0	39.3	0.1	0.0	39.1	0.0	0.0
Bulgaria - Bulgarie	1995	(e)5 353	37.0	32.9	31.9	2.3	0.5	1.3	27.9	20.1	3.4	1.6	4.0	11.2	..
	2005	11 739	65.7	61.4	60.3	3.0	0.1	1.2	10.6	19.0	2.6	1.0	3.3	11.9	0.2
	2012	26 699	65.7	62.8	58.3	1.8	0.1	1.0	11.3	21.5	3.6	0.5	4.9	12.4	0.1
Burkina Faso	1995	(e)276	40.9	38.7	33.8	0.2	1.8	0.2	0.0	59.1	39.6	1.2	18.3	0.0	..
	2005	(e)468	28.5	26.4	16.9	0.4	1.6	0.1	0.3	71.3	30.3	0.2	40.7	0.1	0.0
	2012	(e)2 146	46.6	43.1	11.4	0.4	2.0	1.1	0.1	53.3	15.6	0.0	29.4	8.4	0.0
Burundi	1995	(e)106	92.8	86.8	80.7	5.9	0.0	0.1	0.1	7.1	6.0	0.1	1.0	0.1	..
	2005	(e)58	74.4	70.7	48.9	3.0	0.4	0.3	1.0	24.5	10.2	0.6	4.1	9.7	..
	2012	(e)134	46.5	43.2	34.4	2.3	0.5	0.5	1.2	52.4	20.4	0.3	17.8	13.8	0.1
Cambodia - Cambodge	1995	(e)855	18.8	15.1	14.6	1.5	2.0	0.3	1.5	79.7	3.2	0.1	76.3	0.1	0.0
	2005	(e)3 019	83.8	20.9	20.2	56.3	2.8	3.8	0.2	16.0	0.1	0.3	15.4	0.3	0.0
	2012	(e)7 838	73.7	29.9	28.7	31.5	4.5	7.8	1.3	25.1	0.3	1.1	22.8	0.8	0.0
Cameroon - Cameroun	1995	(e)1 539	81.2	77.2	77.0	2.3	1.3	0.4	0.0	18.8	8.7	0.9	8.6	0.6	0.0
	2005	(e)2 861	71.2	66.2	66.1	4.6	0.2	0.3	0.1	27.6	11.6	1.4	13.5	1.1	0.0
	2012	(e)4 500	52.8	46.9	46.8	5.6	0.1	0.2	0.3	47.0	15.3	2.7	28.1	0.9	0.0
Canada	1995	191 118	91.5	7.0	6.5	79.2	4.6	0.7	0.1	8.4	0.7	2.1	5.2	0.5	0.0
	2005	360 552	92.9	6.4	5.7	83.8	2.1	0.6	0.2	6.9	0.5	1.9	4.0	0.5	0.0
	2012	453 381	86.6	9.2	8.5	74.5	2.3	0.6	0.5	12.9	0.8	3.1	7.9	1.1	0.0
Cape Verde - Cap-Vert	1995	9	80.7	78.5	78.3	2.0	0.1	0.1	0.2	19.0	14.4	3.2	0.5	0.8	0.1
	2005	(e)18	71.6	64.5	64.4	7.0	0.1	0.0	0.0	28.4	23.6	0.9	0.4	3.5	..
	2012	56	90.4	84.7	84.6	4.3	0.2	1.2	0.0	9.6	2.0	2.2	5.4	0.0	0.0
Cayman Islands - Îles Caïmanes	1995	(e)19	62.4	39.9	39.9	13.7	0.6	8.2	0.1	37.5	1.1	36.2	0.1	0.1	..
	2005	(e)59	89.8	82.7	82.7	6.8	0.1	0.2	0.0	10.1	0.1	9.6	0.4	0.0	..
	2012	(e)20	89.1	84.7	84.3	3.7	0.0	0.7	0.0	10.9	0.1	3.3	6.5	1.0	0.0

For sources and notes, see end of table.

Pour les sources et les notes, se reporter à la fin du tableau.

Destination / Origin / Origine	Year / Année	World (millions of dollars) (1) / Monde (millions de dollars) (1)	Developed economies / Économies développées					Transition economies / Économies en transition	Developing economies / Économies en développement					
			Europe		USA États-Unis	Japan Japon	Other Autres		Total	Africa Afrique	America Amérique	Eastern, Southern and South-Eastern Asia / Asie orientale, méridionale et du Sud-Est	Western Asia / Asie occidentale	Oceania Océanie
			Total	Total	EU UE									
			Percentage / En pourcentage											
Central African Republic - République centrafricaine	1995	(e)171	88.4	87.6	87.2	0.2	0.2	0.4	0.0	11.5	9.8	0.1	1.3	0.4	..
	2005	(e)128	73.4	67.2	63.9	3.5	1.3	1.4	0.1	26.5	8.2	0.4	13.1	4.8	0.0
	2012	(e)210	53.2	46.8	46.6	3.2	2.6	0.7	0.1	46.7	16.2	0.8	24.3	5.4	0.0
Chad - Tchad	1995	(e)243	91.1	85.1	84.6	2.9	3.1	0.1	0.0	8.9	4.0	0.0	4.6	0.3	..
	2005	(e)3 081	86.8	12.8	12.8	74.1	0.0	0.0	0.1	13.1	0.5	0.0	12.5	0.0	0.0
	2012	(e)4 400	90.1	2.2	2.2	83.0	1.1	3.7	0.0	9.9	0.9	0.0	8.7	0.4	0.0
Chile - Chili	1995	15 901	60.6	28.2	27.4	13.4	17.9	1.1	0.7	37.5	0.8	19.4	16.4	0.8	0.1
	2005	41 973	54.6	23.6	23.4	16.0	11.9	3.0	0.4	44.2	0.3	18.2	24.4	1.2	0.0
	2012	78 277	43.1	16.8	15.3	12.3	10.7	3.4	0.6	55.7	0.4	17.4	36.7	1.1	0.0
China - Chine	1995	148 779	52.3	14.1	13.7	16.6	19.1	2.4	1.4	46.3	1.7	2.1	40.6	2.0	0.0
	2005	761 953	55.4	19.6	19.1	21.4	11.0	3.4	2.9	41.7	2.4	3.1	33.3	2.8	0.1
	2012	2 048 782	45.0	16.6	16.3	17.2	7.4	3.8	3.8	51.2	4.2	6.6	36.3	4.0	0.2
China, Hong Kong SAR - Chine (RAS de Hong Kong) (2)	1995	173 871	47.4	16.2	15.4	21.8	6.1	3.3	0.2	52.2	1.4	2.8	46.5	1.4	0.0
	2005	292 119	39.5	15.5	14.7	15.9	5.2	2.9	0.2	60.2	0.6	1.4	57.1	1.1	0.1
	2012	492 907	24.4	9.6	8.8	8.9	3.8	2.2	0.6	75.0	0.5	1.5	71.5	1.4	0.0
China, Macao SAR - Chine (RAS de Macao)	1995	2 025	78.8	31.9	31.4	43.5	1.4	2.0	0.0	21.2	0.2	0.5	20.4	0.1	0.1
	2005	2 474	70.7	18.9	18.5	49.4	1.0	1.5	0.0	29.2	0.3	2.7	26.3	0.1	0.0
	2012	1 021	12.9	5.6	5.3	4.7	1.3	1.3	0.1	86.9	35.1	1.2	50.5	0.1	0.0
China, Taiwan Province of - Province chinoise de Taiwan	1995	111 343	52.8	13.9	13.5	23.7	11.8	3.3	0.2	46.3	1.5	2.4	40.8	1.6	0.0
	2005	189 393	37.2	11.9	11.7	15.1	7.6	2.6	0.4	61.3	0.9	2.0	56.5	1.8	0.1
	2012	300 622	28.7	9.0	8.7	11.0	6.3	2.4	0.7	69.6	1.0	2.3	64.1	2.0	0.2
Colombia - Colombie	1995	10 201	67.1	25.9	25.1	35.6	3.6	2.1	0.1	32.3	0.3	29.4	2.3	0.2	0.0
	2005	21 190	59.9	14.1	13.4	41.8	1.6	2.4	0.5	37.9	0.2	34.3	2.6	0.7	0.0
	2012	60 274	55.5	16.3	15.1	36.9	0.6	1.7	0.4	43.7	0.8	30.9	10.5	1.4	0.0
Comoros - Comores	1995	11	95.6	69.6	69.5	20.2	1.9	3.9	0.4	4.1	2.0	0.9	1.2	0.0	..
	2005	(e)12	59.9	42.7	42.4	5.8	11.1	0.3	0.9	39.2	12.6	0.2	20.2	6.2	0.1
	2012	(e)19	41.4	37.8	37.8	3.3	0.1	0.3	0.5	58.1	2.1	0.5	18.9	36.6	0.1
Congo	1995	(e)1 090	69.5	47.2	46.5	20.5	1.0	0.8	..	30.5	2.3	0.0	28.0	0.1	..
	2005	(e)5 198	38.9	8.0	7.5	30.7	0.2	0.1	0.0	61.1	2.4	4.2	54.0	0.5	0.0
	2012	(e)10 699	48.4	26.7	26.5	13.1	0.0	8.6	0.0	51.6	1.7	0.0	49.5	0.3	0.0
Cook Islands - Îles Cook	1995	(e)5	88.2	21.6	21.5	16.5	18.6	31.4	0.9	11.0	0.6	3.8	6.6	..	..
	2005	(e)5	60.3	5.6	5.2	12.1	28.0	14.7	..	39.7	..	..	38.9	0.2	0.6
	2012	(e)3	90.7	46.3	46.3	3.1	40.0	1.4	0.1	9.2	1.6	0.0	4.0	3.5	0.0
Costa Rica	1995	(e)3 476	80.6	30.0	28.6	46.8	1.0	2.7	1.2	18.2	0.3	15.8	2.0	0.2	..
	2005	7 151	63.9	27.7	27.1	32.9	1.4	2.0	0.3	35.7	0.3	20.9	14.0	0.4	0.0
	2012	(e)11 248	56.7	23.2	22.8	30.9	0.7	1.9	0.6	42.7	0.2	18.2	24.1	0.2	0.0
Côte d'Ivoire	1995	3 737	69.0	63.5	63.4	4.4	0.5	0.6	2.2	28.2	22.7	0.6	4.1	0.7	0.0
	2005	7 248	57.6	42.9	42.3	14.1	0.1	0.5	1.6	40.5	29.8	5.2	5.0	0.6	0.0
	2012	(e)12 350	51.1	38.6	35.3	8.1	0.1	4.3	0.1	48.8	34.6	1.8	11.0	1.4	0.0
Croatia - Croatie	1995	4 633	80.0	77.5	76.1	1.9	0.0	0.5	13.8	6.2	3.3	1.0	1.3	0.6	0.0
	2005	8 773	69.3	64.5	63.4	3.5	0.6	0.8	21.8	8.9	4.3	0.3	0.5	3.7	0.0
	2012	12 369	64.0	59.7	58.2	2.9	0.5	0.8	24.8	10.4	3.7	2.1	1.4	3.0	0.2
Cuba	1995	(e)1 625	50.0	30.4	29.7	..	5.3	14.4	21.5	28.4	7.2	5.8	14.7	0.7	0.0
	2005	(e)2 319	66.6	43.3	42.1	0.0	1.3	21.9	3.6	29.8	1.7	16.2	11.5	0.3	0.0
	2012	(e)5 635	45.6	25.6	24.4	0.0	0.5	19.4	3.8	50.7	2.9	24.3	23.0	0.6	0.0
Cyprus - Chypre	1995	1 231	59.5	55.6	53.6	1.2	0.2	2.5	16.4	24.1	5.5	0.3	5.9	12.4	0.0
	2005	1 546	67.8	63.8	62.9	1.4	1.0	1.6	3.1	15.4	3.2	0.4	5.9	5.9	0.0
	2012	1 826	57.1	42.2	41.6	1.1	0.4	13.4	3.4	30.8	3.3	0.2	22.6	4.7	0.0
Czech Republic - République tchèque	1995	21 686	88.6	85.3	83.6	2.0	0.6	0.7	5.5	5.8	1.0	0.7	3.1	1.1	0.0
	2005	78 209	90.6	86.4	84.7	3.0	0.5	0.7	4.1	5.3	0.8	0.7	1.9	1.8	0.0
	2012	156 027	87.1	83.1	80.9	2.5	0.5	1.0	5.6	7.3	1.0	0.9	3.2	2.2	0.0
Dem. Rep. of the Congo - Rép. dém. du Congo	1995	1 563	88.3	62.8	61.4	18.0	5.3	2.2	0.0	11.5	7.7	0.1	3.6	0.1	..
	2005	2 403	77.2	59.3	59.3	17.6	0.2	0.0	0.1	22.8	10.1	0.0	12.5	0.0	0.0
	2012	(e)6 300	19.2	18.1	18.0	0.8	0.1	0.2	0.2	80.6	2.2	0.3	77.3	0.8	0.0
Denmark - Danemark	1995	48 789	77.5	68.9	60.8	3.5	3.4	1.7	1.8	10.0	1.7	1.7	4.9	1.6	0.0
	2005	82 415	81.7	71.9	64.8	5.5	2.0	2.3	1.9	8.5	0.8	1.1	5.0	1.5	0.1
	2012	105 584	82.8	71.4	63.1	6.8	2.0	2.6	2.7	14.1	1.5	2.5	7.7	2.3	0.0

For sources and notes, see end of table.   Pour les sources et les notes, se reporter à la fin du tableau.

60

Destination / Origin / Origine	Year / Année	World (millions of dollars) (1) / Monde (millions de dollars) (1)	Developed economies / Économies développées Total	Europe Total	Europe EU UE	USA États-Unis	Japan Japon	Other Autres	Transition economies / Économies en transition	Developing economies / Économies en développement Total	Africa Afrique	America Amérique	Eastern, Southern and South-Eastern Asia / Asie orientale, méridionale et du Sud-Est	Western Asia / Asie occidentale	Oceania Océanie
								Percentage / En pourcentage							
Djibouti	1995	(e)14	19.0	18.1	17.8	0.0	0.3	0.6	0.0	81.0	51.7	..	6.9	22.5	..
	2005	(e)40	8.4	7.1	6.9	1.0	0.2	0.2	0.0	91.6	67.0	0.6	6.0	18.0	..
	2012	(e)95	24.4	12.2	11.8	7.9	3.6	0.8	0.6	75.0	21.2	0.2	8.1	45.4	0.0
Dominica - Dominique	1995	45	54.3	46.2	46.2	8.1	0.0	0.0	..	45.2	..	45.2	..	..	..
	2005	42	32.5	27.8	27.8	4.5	0.0	0.3	..	60.8	0.0	60.7	0.0	..	..
	2012	37	15.2	10.9	10.9	4.2	..	0.0	..	80.4	0.0	79.6	0.7	0.0	..
Dominican Republic - République dominicaine	1995	(e)3 780	97.5	9.3	9.2	85.5	1.2	1.6	0.0	2.5	0.1	1.8	0.5	0.0	0.0
	2005	(e)6 183	90.8	9.7	9.4	78.8	0.8	1.5	0.1	9.2	0.1	6.4	2.6	0.1	0.0
	2012	(e)9 079	65.3	11.4	11.1	49.8	0.3	3.8	0.3	34.4	0.2	26.2	7.8	0.2	0.0
Ecuador - Équateur	1995	4 361	67.0	20.8	20.6	42.5	2.7	1.0	1.5	30.7	0.2	22.2	7.8	0.4	0.0
	2005	9 869	64.6	13.0	12.8	50.1	0.7	0.8	3.2	32.0	0.1	30.8	0.7	0.5	0.0
	2012	(e)23 869	55.7	12.3	11.8	37.5	4.6	1.3	6.1	38.2	2.0	28.0	7.4	0.8	0.0
Egypt - Égypte	1995	3 444	70.9	54.8	54.4	12.1	1.4	2.6	1.2	26.7	5.6	0.4	8.4	12.2	..
	2005	(e)12 912	50.4	37.1	36.8	11.6	0.9	0.8	1.0	34.2	7.5	0.9	9.6	16.2	0.0
	2012	29 417	41.0	28.4	27.8	7.8	3.4	1.4	1.5	53.7	13.7	1.2	15.7	23.0	0.0
El Salvador	1995	(e)1 652	66.6	25.8	25.4	37.8	1.2	1.8	0.1	33.3	0.0	32.6	0.6	0.0	..
	2005	3 436	63.3	6.2	6.1	55.5	0.5	1.0	0.7	36.0	0.1	34.7	1.1	0.1	0.0
	2012	5 339	54.8	5.0	4.9	47.3	0.7	1.8	0.0	45.1	0.1	42.3	2.6	0.0	0.0
Equatorial Guinea - Guinée équatoriale	1995	86	70.7	30.5	30.5	27.0	13.1	0.0	..	29.2	19.1	0.0	10.0	0.1	..
	2005	7 064	65.4	29.7	29.3	25.4	3.4	6.9	0.0	34.6	0.5	4.8	29.2	0.1	..
	2012	(e)15 500	77.8	44.8	43.5	11.3	18.8	2.9	0.0	22.2	0.6	1.2	20.3	0.0	..
Eritrea - Érythrée	1995	(e)86	30.5	24.7	24.5	1.9	3.9	0.0	0.0	69.5	20.9	0.1	..	48.4	..
	2005	(e)11	52.9	41.7	41.1	7.0	0.2	4.0	0.0	47.0	27.3	1.3	8.6	9.9	..
	2012	(e)457	95.5	1.4	1.4	0.0	0.0	94.0	0.0	4.5	0.7	0.1	3.3	0.5	..
Estonia - Estonie	1995	1 840	75.9	72.1	69.6	2.9	0.6	0.3	22.2	1.9	0.3	0.5	0.5	0.6	0.0
	2005	8 247	88.1	81.9	76.4	5.0	0.3	0.8	7.9	4.0	0.6	0.8	1.7	0.9	0.0
	2012	(e)16 124	74.7	68.6	64.4	4.3	1.1	0.7	13.4	9.6	1.8	1.2	4.5	2.1	0.0
Ethiopia - Éthiopie	1995	422	71.4	50.9	50.4	6.4	13.0	1.1	0.1	26.0	11.4	..	4.2	10.3	..
	2005	926	53.3	37.8	31.7	4.7	7.2	3.7	0.3	45.9	17.3	0.2	13.7	14.6	0.0
	2012	(e)2 728	47.0	38.1	32.6	4.0	1.4	3.5	0.4	52.6	22.8	0.1	15.6	14.0	..
Faeroe Islands - Îles Féroé	1995	(e)362	94.3	90.1	79.8	2.1	1.3	0.8	0.3	2.1	..	0.1	1.2	..	0.8
	2005	602	91.2	84.5	76.8	0.9	3.5	2.3	4.9	3.7	1.2	0.0	2.5	..	..
	2012	(e)948	73.4	63.5	58.8	8.9	..	0.9	8.2	18.4	13.6	0.2	4.6	0.0	0.0
Falkland Islands (Malvinas) - Îles Falkland (Malvinas)	1995	(e)30	98.9	94.3	92.4	1.7	3.0	0.0	..	1.1	0.8	0.0	0.3	..	..
	2005	(e)150	92.4	85.6	85.4	5.7	1.0	0.1	5.8	1.9	1.3	0.1	0.4	..	..
	2012	200	89.6	83.2	83.2	5.7	0.4	0.3	6.0	4.4	3.5	0.0	0.9	0.0	0.0
Fiji - Fidji	1995	(e)619	85.7	27.0	26.9	14.6	10.3	33.8	..	14.1	0.2	0.0	12.0	0.0	1.8
	2005	702	72.1	16.7	16.6	22.6	6.7	26.2	0.0	27.6	0.1	0.7	8.4	0.2	18.2
	2012	1 221	48.3	5.7	5.6	15.9	7.5	19.2	0.0	34.3	0.1	2.8	6.4	0.2	24.7
Finland - Finlande	1995	40 409	77.2	65.5	61.2	6.6	2.5	2.6	5.2	14.6	1.5	2.4	9.0	1.7	0.0
	2005	65 238	69.1	59.6	56.2	5.7	1.4	2.3	12.1	17.2	2.2	2.1	7.2	5.6	0.0
	2012	72 974	65.6	55.6	51.5	6.0	1.5	2.4	11.5	18.6	2.9	3.5	9.6	2.6	0.0
France (3)	1995	277 845	72.3	62.6	58.1	6.0	2.0	1.7	0.9	17.6	5.4	2.0	7.3	2.6	0.3
	2005	434 354	79.8	69.2	65.7	7.2	1.5	1.8	1.6	18.4	5.8	1.9	7.0	3.4	0.3
	2012	556 576	72.3	62.8	59.0	6.1	1.7	1.7	2.8	24.5	6.5	2.9	10.6	4.3	0.3
French Polynesia - Polynésie française	1995	(e)196	81.8	23.9	23.5	9.5	44.2	4.2	0.0	16.0	..	0.0	12.6	..	3.4
	2005	210	83.3	34.2	33.9	17.1	29.7	2.3	0.0	16.7	0.3	0.2	14.7	0.0	1.5
	2012	139	78.4	16.2	16.2	23.2	36.5	2.5	0.0	21.6	0.1	0.1	18.9	0.0	2.4
Gabon	1995	(e)2 718	79.8	12.2	11.0	64.1	2.1	1.5	0.0	14.6	2.2	5.0	6.7	0.7	..
	2005	5 068	77.6	14.7	12.5	60.8	0.2	2.0	1.3	21.1	4.7	4.0	12.1	0.4	0.0
	2012	(e)9 665	60.3	21.4	20.5	36.6	2.2	0.2	1.4	38.2	5.2	5.8	26.9	0.4	..
Gambia - Gambie	1995	(e)16	87.6	76.1	76.0	1.3	10.2	0.0	0.0	12.4	5.6	0.1	6.6	0.0	..
	2005	(e)8	30.3	25.1	25.0	1.1	2.0	2.0	0.3	69.4	17.2	0.6	50.5	1.1	0.0
	2012	(e)100	20.7	19.6	19.5	1.0	..	0.1	0.0	79.3	22.7	0.4	55.6	0.2	0.2
Georgia - Géorgie	1995	(e)158	19.7	19.0	15.2	0.7	0.0	0.1	64.7	14.6	0.0	..	1.6	13.0	..
	2005	865	32.9	25.4	25.0	3.1	0.2	4.2	47.1	19.8	1.6	0.9	2.7	14.6	0.0
	2012	2 377	31.1	15.4	14.9	9.5	0.2	6.0	52.4	16.5	1.7	2.2	4.3	8.3	0.0

For sources and notes, see end of table.

Pour les sources et les notes, se reporter à la fin du tableau.

Origin / Origine	Year Année	World (millions of dollars) (1) Monde (millions de dollars) (1)	Developed economies / Économies développées						Transition economies Économies en transition	Developing economies / Économies en développement					
			Total	Europe		USA États-Unis	Japan Japon	Other Autres		Total	Africa Afrique	America Amérique	Eastern, Southern and South-Eastern Asia / Asie orientale, méridionale et du Sud-Est	Western Asia / Asie occiden-tale	Oceania Océanie
				Total	EU UE										
Germany - Allemagne	1995	523 697	82.1	70.5	64.3	7.3	2.5	1.8	2.4	15.3	2.1	2.4	8.3	2.5	0.1
	2005	977 132	81.2	69.0	64.4	8.8	1.7	1.7	3.6	14.9	1.9	2.2	7.6	3.3	0.0
	2012	1 416 184	73.3	61.7	56.4	7.9	1.6	2.1	5.2	20.9	2.0	3.0	11.8	4.1	0.0
Ghana	1995	(e)1 754	84.3	68.1	59.1	11.0	4.4	0.8	1.2	14.6	6.5	0.3	6.4	1.3	0.0
	2005	(e)3 060	64.2	52.8	50.7	6.9	3.1	1.4	5.0	30.9	14.0	2.3	10.1	4.4	0.1
	2012	(e)13 000	54.5	49.2	47.2	3.3	1.6	0.5	3.2	42.3	14.9	1.5	19.5	6.3	0.0
Gibraltar	1995	117	77.1	74.0	33.2	2.9	0.0	0.3	0.2	15.2	6.2	3.9	4.8	0.3	..
	2005	(e)200	97.0	93.6	79.0	2.1	0.0	1.4	0.8	2.2	1.1	0.1	1.0	0.1	..
	2012	240	79.9	57.3	57.1	0.1	14.7	7.7	0.2	19.9	8.9	0.1	10.9	0.0	..
Greece - Grèce	1995	10 955	80.5	74.6	72.5	3.1	0.8	2.0	6.9	12.2	2.6	1.6	2.4	5.6	0.0
	2005	17 434	70.7	63.1	61.8	5.2	0.3	2.0	9.4	18.9	4.6	1.3	3.5	9.4	0.1
	2012	35 180	52.5	45.5	43.0	3.8	0.2	3.1	9.7	31.6	7.5	1.0	5.8	17.2	0.1
Greenland - Groenland	1995	364	99.0	93.7	93.3	0.6	4.6	0.0	..	0.2	..	..	0.2	..	..
	2005	402	99.1	97.2	95.6	1.2	0.6	0.0	..	0.9	..	..	0.9	..	..
	2012	(e)473	100.0	100.0	96.3	..	..	0.0	..	..	..	..	..	..	..
Grenada - Grenade	1995	22	68.6	42.2	40.4	24.9	..	1.5	0.1	31.3	0.2	31.0	0.1	0.1	..
	2005	28	51.4	34.2	33.9	15.1	0.2	2.0	0.5	48.0	0.2	46.1	1.6	0.2	..
	2012	(e)35	30.9	17.2	16.8	11.2	1.2	1.3	0.1	69.0	32.6	34.8	1.5	..	..
Guam	1995	85	..	..	..	..	..	..	..	..	..	..	..	..	..
	2005	(e)52	64.0	5.3	5.3	..	58.1	0.6	0.0	36.0	0.2	3.0	28.3	0.2	4.2
	2012	(e)46	59.3	3.5	2.3	..	55.1	0.7	0.0	40.7	0.1	0.1	40.4	..	0.0
Guatemala	1995	1 936	62.9	15.9	15.1	42.4	2.7	1.9	0.1	37.1	0.8	31.0	3.8	1.5	..
	2005	5 381	61.7	6.5	5.5	51.6	1.3	2.3	0.2	38.1	0.3	33.5	3.2	1.1	0.0
	2012	10 125	54.1	6.9	6.4	41.9	1.9	3.4	0.6	45.3	0.8	38.8	3.3	2.4	0.0
Guinea - Guinée	1995	(e)702	77.7	57.0	55.2	17.4	1.3	2.1	4.6	16.7	7.4	7.7	1.4	0.1	..
	2005	(e)796	52.9	43.7	43.5	7.1	0.1	2.0	28.7	18.4	3.4	0.0	14.9	0.1	0.0
	2012	(e)1 386	53.8	40.9	40.2	8.5	0.0	4.4	12.8	33.4	3.4	12.2	17.3	0.4	..
Guinea-Bissau - Guinée-Bissau	1995	(e)24	55.0	54.5	54.5	0.0	0.4	0.0	..	45.0	2.2	0.0	42.7	0.0	..
	2005	(e)89	1.8	1.6	1.6	0.2	0.1	0.0	0.0	98.1	1.5	0.1	96.6	0.0	..
	2012	(e)130	8.0	1.7	1.7	6.1	0.2	0.0	0.0	92.0	0.8	0.1	91.0	..	..
Guyana	1995	(e)455	80.8	33.2	33.0	26.1	1.6	19.9	0.0	17.7	0.5	15.5	1.3	0.4	0.0
	2005	539	72.3	32.8	32.6	18.7	0.6	20.2	0.1	27.6	1.1	20.5	5.8	0.2	0.0
	2012	(e)1 309	73.1	18.9	18.9	25.6	0.6	28.0	3.9	23.0	0.2	19.2	3.1	0.5	0.0
Haiti - Haïti	1995	(e)110	92.4	19.9	18.5	70.4	0.6	1.4	..	1.2	0.1	0.9	0.2	0.0	..
	2005	(e)473	90.1	4.0	3.7	81.6	0.2	4.3	0.0	9.9	0.7	7.8	1.3	0.0	..
	2012	(e)821	89.6	3.5	3.1	82.0	0.3	3.7	0.0	10.4	1.2	4.5	4.6	0.1	..
Honduras	1995	(e)1 769	88.3	21.3	20.8	60.4	5.2	1.4	0.2	11.5	0.0	9.5	1.9	0.0	..
	2005	(e)5 048	82.0	12.3	11.9	67.1	0.6	2.0	0.4	17.6	0.0	15.8	1.6	0.1	0.0
	2012	(e)7 931	76.2	15.1	14.7	58.6	0.6	2.0	0.1	23.6	0.4	20.7	2.5	0.1	0.0
Hungary - Hongrie	1995	12 452	83.9	78.8	77.2	3.6	0.7	0.7	11.2	4.9	0.9	0.6	1.6	1.8	0.0
	2005	62 272	86.1	80.9	79.3	3.7	0.8	0.7	6.0	7.3	1.2	0.6	2.0	3.5	0.0
	2012	103 006	81.9	77.4	76.1	2.8	0.7	1.0	8.5	9.6	1.4	1.1	3.9	3.1	0.0
Iceland - Islande	1995	1 803	95.9	69.0	63.0	12.4	11.3	3.2	0.6	3.5	0.6	0.5	2.3	0.1	..
	2005	3 091	93.2	79.6	74.6	8.9	3.2	1.4	1.5	5.4	1.8	1.7	1.7	0.2	..
	2012	5 063	88.9	81.1	73.2	4.5	2.0	1.2	4.6	6.5	2.8	0.7	2.8	0.3	0.0
India - Inde	1995	31 699	56.6	29.3	28.2	17.4	7.0	3.0	3.6	38.3	5.2	1.1	23.7	8.3	0.0
	2005	100 353	45.2	23.2	22.5	16.5	2.4	3.1	1.2	53.3	6.7	2.8	30.4	13.3	0.1
	2012	289 565	35.4	17.3	16.8	12.8	2.2	3.0	1.3	62.5	9.4	5.1	28.5	19.5	0.0
Indonesia (...2002) - Indonésie (...2002)	1995	45 443	59.6	15.5	15.3	13.9	27.0	3.1	0.3	39.8	1.3	1.6	33.9	3.0	0.1
Indonesia - Indonésie	2005	85 660	48.4	12.3	12.1	11.5	21.1	3.5	0.5	51.1	1.9	1.5	44.5	3.0	0.1
	2012	190 032	36.6	9.6	9.5	7.8	15.9	3.3	0.8	62.6	3.0	1.9	54.5	3.0	0.2
Iran (Islamic Rep. of) - Iran (Rép. islamique d')	1995	(e)18 360	61.8	41.5	40.8	1.2	18.1	0.9	3.6	34.6	8.1	1.5	17.6	7.4	0.0
	2005	(e)60 012	48.5	27.3	27.2	0.3	20.8	0.1	1.2	50.2	5.6	0.1	34.2	10.4	0.0
	2012	(e)102 853	17.8	9.3	9.3	0.0	8.4	0.1	1.6	80.5	2.1	0.2	62.5	15.6	0.0
Iraq	1995	(e)1 963	0.4	0.2	0.2	..	0.2	0.0	1.3	98.3	0.0	0.0	4.5	93.7	..
	2005	(e)23 697	80.4	23.1	23.1	49.9	2.3	5.0	0.0	19.6	0.3	2.9	12.0	4.5	0.0
	2012	(e)94 400	50.2	18.9	18.9	23.7	3.3	4.3	0.1	49.8	1.8	1.5	44.4	2.1	0.0

Percentage / En pourcentage

For sources and notes, see end of table.

Pour les sources et les notes, se reporter à la fin du tableau.

2.1 Country trade structure by partner
Exports by main region of destination

2.1 Structure du commerce des pays par partenaires
Exportations par principales régions de destination

Origin / Origine	Year / Année	World (millions of dollars) (1) / Monde (millions de dollars) (1)	Developed economies / Économies développées Total	Europe Total	Europe EU UE	USA États-Unis	Japan Japon	Other Autres	Transition economies / Économies en transition	Developing economies / Économies en développement Total	Africa Afrique	America Amérique	Eastern, Southern and South-Eastern Asia / Asie orientale, méridionale et du Sud-Est	Western Asia / Asie occidentale	Oceania Océanie
								Percentage / En pourcentage							
Ireland - Irlande	1995	43 789	89.3	76.3	73.3	8.3	3.0	1.7	0.9	7.1	1.6	1.0	3.3	1.2	0.0
	2005	110 003	90.8	67.8	63.4	18.7	2.6	1.7	0.4	8.3	0.9	1.2	5.1	1.1	0.0
	2012	118 296	89.2	64.8	59.0	19.7	2.3	2.3	0.9	9.4	1.4	1.4	4.5	2.1	0.0
Israel - Israël	1995	19 047	75.3	36.4	34.4	30.1	6.9	1.9	2.0	18.3	1.6	2.9	12.9	1.0	0.0
	2005	42 771	71.9	31.6	29.2	36.2	1.9	2.2	1.7	22.6	1.7	3.1	15.4	2.4	0.0
	2012	63 141	60.9	29.3	27.1	27.8	1.3	2.4	2.9	32.2	2.4	4.2	23.0	2.5	0.0
Italy - Italie	1995	230 441	78.7	66.4	62.1	7.3	2.3	2.7	2.5	18.6	3.5	3.5	7.7	3.9	0.0
	2005	372 957	76.9	65.2	60.7	8.0	1.5	2.3	4.3	17.5	3.8	2.7	6.4	4.6	0.0
	2012	500 743	70.7	60.1	53.5	6.8	1.4	2.3	5.1	23.2	4.9	3.9	7.8	6.6	0.1
Jamaica - Jamaïque	1995	1 424	86.5	36.6	29.1	36.9	1.9	11.0	2.6	10.8	3.5	6.7	0.6	0.0	0.0
	2005	1 514	77.5	30.9	24.0	25.6	1.0	20.0	1.4	21.0	0.0	11.7	7.6	1.8	0.0
	2012	1 712	78.5	22.3	20.6	48.1	0.6	7.5	5.6	14.7	0.7	8.9	1.1	4.0	0.0
Japan - Japon	1995	442 937	48.2	16.9	16.2	27.5	..	3.7	0.3	51.4	1.7	4.2	43.7	1.8	0.1
	2005	594 941	42.4	15.3	14.8	22.9	..	4.2	0.9	56.7	1.4	3.9	48.7	2.7	0.1
	2012	798 568	32.7	10.9	10.2	17.8	..	4.0	1.8	65.4	1.6	5.1	54.8	3.6	0.3
Jordan - Jordanie	1995	1 769	15.1	9.9	9.8	2.5	1.5	1.1	1.4	76.1	5.3	0.4	27.0	43.3	0.0
	2005	4 279	35.5	5.1	5.0	26.7	1.5	2.2	0.4	56.8	6.0	0.3	14.2	36.4	0.0
	2012	(e)7 843	21.3	4.8	4.3	13.6	1.0	1.9	0.6	69.4	7.6	0.3	21.8	39.7	0.0
Kazakhstan	1995	5 227	32.4	30.7	26.7	0.8	0.9	0.1	55.1	12.5	0.2	1.2	9.7	1.4	0.0
	2005	27 846	68.5	61.3	41.2	2.4	0.5	4.3	14.7	16.8	0.1	2.1	13.9	0.8	0.0
	2012	92 282	62.4	55.6	50.2	0.5	1.2	5.0	13.9	23.7	0.2	0.1	19.6	3.8	0.0
Kenya	1995	1 826	46.9	40.1	38.8	4.0	1.1	1.7	0.1	52.3	40.3	0.1	9.9	1.9	..
	2005	3 420	42.8	31.2	30.1	9.5	0.9	1.3	1.2	53.3	39.5	0.3	10.9	2.5	0.0
	2012	(e)6 127	35.4	26.8	25.2	6.7	0.8	1.1	3.3	61.3	46.6	0.2	11.0	3.6	0.0
Kiribati	1995	(e)7	37.8	2.2	2.2	13.2	21.2	1.3	..	62.2	0.1	0.2	54.7	0.1	7.1
	2005	(e)4	50.4	16.0	16.0	15.0	13.0	6.4	0.3	38.2	18.6	0.3	14.2	0.3	4.8
	2012	(e)6	21.9	0.8	0.8	1.2	19.4	0.5	0.0	78.0	0.1	6.3	68.1	3.2	0.3
Korea, Dem. People's Rep. of - Corée, Rép. populaire dém. de	1995	(e)959	45.7	10.9	10.8	..	34.6	0.2	0.1	53.9	2.5	26.5	20.7	4.1	..
	2005	(e)1 338	21.5	11.5	11.4	0.0	9.1	0.9	1.3	77.2	4.7	15.5	51.4	5.4	0.2
	2012	(e)3 750	2.7	2.4	2.4	..	..	0.3	1.0	96.3	2.3	3.1	89.9	1.1	0.0
Korea, Republic of - Corée, République de	1995	125 056	51.4	15.1	14.3	19.5	13.6	3.2	1.5	46.9	2.4	5.7	35.6	3.1	0.1
	2005	284 418	42.3	16.0	15.6	14.6	8.4	3.3	2.0	55.5	2.8	5.0	43.6	3.6	0.5
	2012	547 854	30.5	9.4	9.1	10.7	7.1	3.4	2.9	66.6	2.6	6.4	51.5	5.2	0.9
Kuwait - Koweït	1995	12 944	47.1	13.4	13.4	11.6	21.6	0.4	0.0	52.9	2.6	2.4	43.2	4.6	..
	2005	(e)44 902	42.0	10.0	9.9	11.7	19.4	0.8	0.0	58.0	2.8	0.2	51.7	3.4	..
	2012	(e)113 999	29.5	6.0	5.9	8.3	14.3	1.0	0.0	70.4	3.8	0.4	62.2	3.9	0.0
Kyrgyzstan - Kirghizistan	1995	(e)412	14.5	12.6	12.6	1.6	0.1	0.2	64.0	21.5	0.0	..	19.5	2.0	..
	2005	(e)672	9.8	5.9	3.9	0.7	0.1	3.1	48.1	42.1	0.1	0.1	15.9	26.1	..
	2012	(e)1 894	8.5	7.6	4.0	0.7	0.1	0.1	68.3	23.2	0.2	0.9	12.8	9.3	..
Lao People's Dem. Rep. - Rép. dém. populaire lao	1995	311	57.7	41.2	38.8	4.3	11.4	0.8	0.0	42.1	0.8	0.5	40.8	0.0	0.0
	2005	553	37.6	33.5	32.5	0.7	1.3	2.1	0.2	62.2	0.0	0.1	61.9	0.2	0.0
	2012	2 269	19.7	12.2	12.0	0.9	4.5	2.0	0.1	80.2	0.0	0.1	80.0	0.1	0.0
Latvia - Lettonie	1995	1 305	60.4	58.6	56.4	1.3	0.3	0.1	38.3	1.3	0.6	0.0	0.3	0.4	..
	2005	5 303	83.6	78.7	74.0	3.2	1.0	0.6	13.1	2.9	0.9	0.9	0.8	0.2	0.0
	2012	12 610	73.5	71.7	68.5	1.1	0.4	0.4	15.8	9.6	3.2	0.5	3.9	2.0	0.0
Lebanon - Liban	1995	(e)656	31.6	23.5	21.0	6.0	0.6	1.5	1.9	60.1	10.6	0.9	1.9	46.7	..
	2005	(e)2 337	24.8	20.5	12.4	3.0	0.2	1.1	0.9	73.4	14.1	0.4	6.0	52.8	0.1
	2012	(e)5 615	25.5	22.1	11.7	1.9	0.6	0.8	0.5	72.7	24.2	0.7	4.3	43.5	0.0
Lesotho	1995	(e)160	82.4	6.3	6.3	73.7	0.0	2.4	0.0	17.6	16.9	0.0	0.6	0.1	..
	2005	(e)651	90.9	5.9	5.9	83.4	0.1	1.5	..	9.1	8.7	0.0	0.2	0.2	..
	2012	(e)1 100	95.6	44.3	44.3	49.4	0.2	1.7	0.0	4.4	2.4	0.4	1.5	0.0	0.0
Liberia - Libéria	1995	(e)820	90.1	88.4	88.0	0.9	0.0	0.7	0.0	9.9	0.4	1.7	7.0	0.7	..
	2005	131	82.0	75.0	74.6	6.2	0.0	0.7	0.2	17.8	0.9	0.1	16.1	0.7	0.0
	2012	459	56.0	37.0	36.6	13.5	0.0	5.5	1.2	42.8	8.7	0.4	31.3	2.4	0.0
Libya - Libye	1995	(e)9 364	83.8	83.8	80.3	..	0.0	0.0	3.2	13.1	5.6	0.3	2.1	5.0	..
	2005	(e)31 358	86.5	80.7	77.3	5.3	0.0	0.4	0.6	12.9	2.3	0.2	3.0	7.5	..
	2012	(e)62 216	79.9	73.5	71.3	4.4	0.3	1.8	0.1	20.0	2.1	0.5	15.2	2.1	0.0

For sources and notes, see end of table.

Pour les sources et les notes, se reporter à la fin du tableau.

Origin / Origine	Year Année	World (millions of dollars) (1) Monde (millions de dollars) (1)	Developed economies Économies développées Total	Europe Total	EU UE	USA États-Unis	Japan Japon	Other Autres	Transition economies Économies en transition	Developing economies Économies en développement Total	Africa Afrique	America Amérique	Eastern, Southern and South-Eastern Asia Asie orientale, méridionale et du Sud-Est	Western Asia Asie occidentale	Oceania Océanie
Lithuania - Lituanie	1995	2 706	55.2	54.2	51.1	0.7	0.1	0.1	42.3	2.5	0.1	0.4	1.0	1.0	..
	2005	12 070	74.7	67.0	64.0	4.7	0.1	2.9	19.1	6.1	0.3	0.6	3.7	1.4	0.0
	2012	29 653	65.0	62.9	60.5	1.5	0.1	0.5	29.9	4.5	1.2	0.4	1.8	1.2	0.0
Luxembourg	1995	(e)7 244	84.3	69.0	65.4	5.6	0.5	9.3	0.7	14.6	2.8	5.6	4.0	2.1	0.1
	2005	(e)18 797	93.6	90.0	88.3	2.6	0.3	0.7	0.9	5.5	0.7	0.8	2.5	1.5	0.0
	2012	(e)19 447	89.1	84.3	81.5	2.8	0.4	1.5	2.0	8.9	1.3	1.1	3.9	2.6	0.0
Madagascar	1995	(e)507	86.1	71.3	70.1	8.1	5.5	1.2	0.1	12.4	7.0	0.1	4.8	0.4	0.0
	2005	836	84.7	53.6	53.0	27.6	2.4	1.1	0.1	15.1	3.5	0.2	8.7	2.7	0.0
	2012	(e)1 500	62.4	48.8	48.0	6.6	1.1	5.9	0.5	36.9	8.0	0.6	26.5	1.8	0.0
Malawi	1995	433	75.7	52.6	49.2	12.0	8.6	2.4	1.2	23.1	19.7	1.0	2.0	0.3	0.2
	2005	495	59.0	36.1	34.0	17.1	4.3	1.5	6.7	34.1	27.1	1.4	3.1	2.2	0.3
	2012	(e)1 184	47.5	30.4	29.4	6.0	2.0	9.1	7.1	45.3	31.3	0.9	11.3	1.8	0.1
Malaysia - Malaisie	1995	73 778	50.6	14.6	14.4	20.7	12.7	2.6	0.2	49.2	1.1	1.5	44.2	2.3	0.1
	2005	141 624	45.4	12.0	11.8	19.6	9.4	4.3	0.5	54.1	1.4	1.1	48.9	2.6	0.1
	2012	227 303	34.6	9.1	8.9	8.7	11.8	5.1	0.6	64.8	2.4	1.7	57.0	3.3	0.4
Maldives	1995	(e)85	63.6	38.7	38.4	19.1	5.7	0.1	0.0	36.2	0.1	0.0	35.7	0.3	..
	2005	154	42.4	23.9	23.9	3.0	15.3	0.2	0.1	57.5	2.9	0.0	47.9	6.7	..
	2012	(e)314	59.9	48.3	46.9	8.2	2.2	1.2	0.2	39.9	2.5	0.5	36.7	0.3	0.0
Mali	1995	(e)443	20.0	19.8	11.6	0.1	0.0	0.0	0.0	78.2	75.8	0.0	2.3	0.0	..
	2005	1 075	31.8	29.8	12.5	0.7	0.1	1.1	0.5	67.7	28.8	0.3	36.2	2.4	0.0
	2012	(e)2 164	12.9	12.0	5.3	0.4	0.2	0.3	0.8	86.4	43.0	0.1	40.5	2.9	0.0
Malta - Malte	1995	1 913	81.1	70.8	69.9	8.2	0.7	1.4	0.7	15.9	3.5	0.5	10.4	1.5	..
	2005	2 431	64.3	49.5	48.8	10.6	2.8	1.3	0.8	33.3	5.9	2.8	21.8	2.8	0.0
	2012	(e)4 250	40.3	31.1	29.8	3.7	1.7	3.9	1.6	41.3	10.4	1.5	24.7	4.6	0.0
Marshall Islands - Îles Marshall	1995	23	99.7	14.4	14.4	37.9	47.3	0.1	0.1	0.2	0.0	..	0.0	..	0.2
	2005	25	92.5	85.7	85.7	3.3	3.5	0.0	0.0	7.5	0.0	0.0	7.3	0.1	0.0
	2012	(e)35	27.5	24.2	24.2	2.3	0.9	0.1	0.1	72.4	2.5	1.3	68.0	0.6	0.0
Mauritania - Mauritanie	1995	(e)509	84.8	55.2	54.6	1.2	28.4	0.0	1.0	14.1	13.2	0.2	0.7	0.1	..
	2005	(e)556	73.6	60.7	59.7	0.1	12.5	0.4	5.6	20.8	19.3	0.0	1.1	0.3	0.0
	2012	(e)2 641	36.2	29.2	28.3	0.2	6.9	0.0	1.1	62.6	12.5	0.0	49.7	0.4	0.0
Mauritius - Maurice	1995	1 538	92.4	75.8	74.4	14.8	0.6	1.1	0.1	7.4	4.3	1.2	1.9	0.0	0.0
	2005	2 144	72.7	62.5	61.5	9.0	0.8	0.4	0.1	20.2	8.5	0.2	3.0	8.4	0.2
	2012	(e)2 673	61.4	50.9	49.7	8.5	1.3	0.7	0.3	22.5	16.9	0.4	4.3	0.9	0.0
Mexico - Mexique	1995	79 541	92.3	5.0	4.2	83.4	1.2	2.7	0.0	7.6	0.1	6.2	1.2	0.1	0.0
	2005	214 207	93.1	4.4	4.3	85.8	0.7	2.2	0.0	6.9	0.2	5.2	1.4	0.1	0.0
	2012	370 827	87.9	6.2	6.0	77.7	0.7	3.3	0.2	11.9	0.2	7.6	3.7	0.3	0.0
Micronesia (Federated States of) - Micronésie (États fédérés de)	1995	21	71.5	0.0	0.0	11.1	60.4	0.0	..	28.5	..	..	28.5	..	..
	2005	19	7.0	0.2	0.2	3.1	3.6	0.0	0.0	93.0	2.6	0.4	90.0	..	..
	2012	(e)35	19.7	0.7	0.7	1.4	17.5	0.0	0.0	80.3	..	2.1	78.2	0.0	0.0
Mongolia - Mongolie	1995	(e)473	14.4	13.6	13.6	0.2	0.5	0.1	63.2	21.6	..	0.0	21.6	..	..
	2005	1 064	38.9	9.8	9.4	15.0	0.6	13.5	5.0	56.2	0.0	0.5	55.5	0.2	0.0
	2012	(e)4 379	7.6	1.9	1.8	1.0	0.6	4.2	1.6	90.8	0.0	0.1	90.6	0.1	..
Montenegro - Monténégro	2012	469	30.0	29.1	28.3	0.3	0.5	0.1	58.5	5.1	0.6	0.0	1.1	3.3	..
Montserrat	1995	(e)3	86.4	71.0	70.9	15.2	..	0.1	0.0	13.6	10.9	2.7	0.0	0.0	..
	2005	(e)1	68.2	16.1	16.1	41.1	..	11.0	..	31.8	..	31.8	..	..	..
	2012	(e)2	90.2	15.3	14.8	65.7	..	9.1	0.8	9.0	2.7	2.8	3.5	0.0	0.0
Morocco - Maroc	1995	(e)6 881	81.1	70.3	69.3	3.5	6.1	1.2	0.5	18.0	6.4	1.8	7.3	2.5	0.0
	2005	11 185	79.0	73.2	72.0	3.0	1.1	1.7	1.4	18.8	3.5	3.6	9.1	2.7	0.0
	2012	21 417	63.4	57.0	55.1	4.4	0.9	1.1	2.3	33.1	8.8	7.5	13.6	3.3	0.0
Mozambique	1995	174	65.7	41.8	40.5	9.4	13.7	0.8	0.0	34.3	26.3	0.3	7.4	0.4	..
	2005	1 745	73.2	71.3	71.1	1.1	0.7	0.1	0.4	26.4	19.4	0.0	6.4	0.6	0.0
	2012	(e)4 100	39.5	37.3	35.5	1.1	0.8	0.3	2.0	58.5	34.1	0.8	20.2	3.4	0.0
Myanmar	1995	(e)860	19.9	5.2	4.9	6.5	7.0	1.2	0.0	79.0	1.3	0.1	77.2	0.5	..
	2005	(e)3 967	24.8	17.6	17.4	..	5.9	1.3	0.3	72.9	0.4	0.3	72.0	0.2	0.0
	2012	(e)8 900	9.0	4.4	4.3	..	4.1	0.5	0.1	90.1	0.3	0.2	89.2	0.4	..
Namibia - Namibie	1995	(e)1 409	71.5	63.6	62.4	4.3	0.9	2.7	0.1	28.2	25.7	0.8	1.4	0.2	0.1
	2005	(e)2 070	63.6	51.2	50.6	7.9	0.9	3.6	0.6	35.8	27.1	0.4	7.9	0.4	0.0
	2012	(e)4 034	54.6	43.8	41.5	5.2	0.3	5.3	0.1	45.3	36.3	0.3	8.4	0.3	0.0

For sources and notes, see end of table.

Pour les sources et les notes, se reporter à la fin du tableau.

Destination / Origin / Origine	Year / Année	World (millions of dollars) (1) / Monde (millions de dollars) (1)	Developed economies / Économies développées					Transition economies / Économies en transition	Developing economies / Économies en développement					
			Total	Europe Total	EU UE	USA États-Unis	Japan Japon	Other Autres		Total	Africa Afrique	America Amérique	Eastern, Southern and South-Eastern Asia / Asie orientale, méridionale et du Sud-Est	Western Asia / Asie occidentale	Oceania Océanie
													Percentage / En pourcentage		
Nauru	1995	(e)28	62.4	1.8	1.7	0.0	1.1	59.4	0.0	37.4	0.3	24.9	12.0	0.2	0.0
	2005	(e)3	56.6	24.7	24.7	3.5	5.1	23.3	2.0	41.5	4.6	1.9	31.8	2.9	0.2
	2012	90	28.7	1.9	1.9	0.5	3.4	22.9	0.0	71.2	0.1	0.0	70.6	0.4	0.1
Nepal - Népal	1995	(e)359	74.9	44.7	42.1	28.7	0.4	1.1	0.0	21.5	0.0	0.2	21.3	0.0	..
	2005	(e)888	28.4	12.9	12.3	13.4	0.9	1.2	0.0	71.6	0.1	0.1	70.7	0.7	..
	2012	(e)899	22.2	12.1	11.7	7.2	1.0	1.9	0.3	77.5	0.2	0.2	75.3	1.7	0.0
Netherlands - Pays-Bas	1995	(e)203 187	87.8	81.6	78.7	3.8	1.2	1.2	1.4	10.2	1.8	1.5	5.1	1.7	0.0
	2005	(e)406 372	87.9	81.4	78.8	4.6	0.7	1.2	1.7	9.8	1.8	1.3	4.6	2.1	0.0
	2012	(e)655 700	84.2	77.9	75.4	4.1	0.8	1.4	2.0	13.3	2.6	2.2	6.0	2.5	0.0
Netherlands Antilles - Antilles néerlandaises	1995	(e)1 522	61.8	31.5	28.5	24.9	1.0	4.3	0.0	38.2	0.9	34.5	2.7	0.1	..
	2005	(e)608	35.5	5.4	5.4	29.5	0.2	0.4	0.0	64.5	1.9	60.2	2.4	0.0	0.0
New Caledonia - Nouvelle-Calédonie	1995	(e)570	86.4	38.8	38.8	7.8	33.3	6.5	0.0	8.9	0.0	0.1	8.7	0.0	0.1
	2005	1 114	60.9	33.9	33.9	2.5	20.4	4.1	1.9	37.2	3.9	0.0	31.3	0.0	2.0
	2012	1 293	58.9	28.6	28.5	4.2	17.3	8.9	0.0	41.1	2.8	0.0	36.3	0.0	2.0
New Zealand - Nouvelle-Zélande	1995	13 745	63.0	14.7	14.3	10.0	16.2	22.1	0.9	32.8	1.2	3.1	23.2	2.3	3.0
	2005	21 729	63.6	15.6	15.1	14.2	10.6	23.1	0.7	34.0	2.1	3.5	22.3	2.7	3.5
	2012	37 092	48.7	9.8	9.5	9.2	7.0	22.8	0.9	48.8	4.0	3.0	34.9	3.9	3.0
Nicaragua	1995	509	78.0	31.4	29.6	43.3	1.9	1.4	0.0	22.0	0.2	19.9	1.9	0.0	..
	2005	866	66.4	8.8	8.6	53.9	0.8	2.9	1.3	32.3	0.1	30.1	1.9	0.1	0.0
	2012	2 690	68.8	7.6	7.2	51.5	0.6	9.2	0.5	30.7	0.2	25.7	4.7	0.1	0.0
Niger	1995	273	52.9	46.4	46.1	0.4	4.3	1.9	0.0	47.0	44.8	0.0	0.8	1.4	..
	2005	486	71.5	51.1	45.9	15.7	3.5	1.2	0.0	28.5	27.2	0.2	1.0	0.1	0.0
	2012	(e)1 500	50.6	39.7	36.9	8.5	2.0	0.4	0.0	49.3	32.7	1.1	14.8	0.7	0.0
Nigeria - Nigéria	1995	(e)12 342	77.1	34.7	33.3	38.0	1.0	3.4	0.1	22.8	7.3	5.2	10.3	0.1	0.0
	2005	(e)45 789	75.7	22.3	21.5	49.7	2.6	1.2	0.0	24.3	8.5	7.9	7.3	0.6	0.0
	2012	(e)127 287	61.8	33.8	33.3	20.4	3.3	4.3	0.1	38.0	9.4	9.3	17.9	0.3	1.1
Niue - Nioué	1995	0	66.5	8.5	8.5	10.2	..	47.8	17.8	15.7	5.8	2.1	7.8	..	..
	2005	0	46.1	22.3	22.3	8.4	..	15.3	2.9	51.1	25.9	0.4	24.6	0.1	0.1
	2012	(e)0	27.3	14.2	11.9	4.4	1.4	7.4	1.9	70.7	54.4	1.7	10.4	3.9	0.4
Northern Mariana Islands - Îles Mariannes du Nord	1995	(e)432	91.9	10.7	10.7	..	79.0	2.3	..	7.8	0.1	..	7.7	0.0	..
	2005	(e)691	41.9	24.6	24.5	..	16.7	0.6	0.0	58.1	0.6	24.7	32.6	0.2	..
	2012	(e)4	18.8	17.2	16.8	..	1.1	0.4	0.1	81.2	29.0	1.1	48.0	3.1	..
Norway - Norvège	1995	41 740	92.4	80.0	78.9	6.2	1.8	4.5	0.7	6.9	0.7	1.7	3.8	0.7	0.0
	2005	103 759	90.2	78.8	78.1	6.4	1.0	4.1	1.1	5.2	0.6	1.1	3.0	0.5	0.0
	2012	160 999	89.2	82.4	81.2	5.0	0.9	0.8	1.2	9.6	1.0	1.2	6.4	0.9	0.1
Oman	1995	5 917	37.5	1.7	1.7	4.3	30.6	0.9	0.2	62.4	1.8	0.0	49.8	10.7	..
	2005	18 692	21.3	2.9	2.9	2.8	15.2	0.4	0.1	78.5	1.6	0.0	67.3	9.6	0.0
	2012	52 138	18.5	1.4	1.4	2.9	12.4	1.8	0.1	81.3	2.2	0.1	63.9	15.1	0.0
Pakistan	1995	8 158	57.0	32.0	31.2	15.1	6.8	3.2	0.9	40.6	3.0	1.6	24.8	11.2	0.0
	2005	16 050	55.2	27.2	26.6	24.8	0.9	2.3	0.7	44.0	5.7	1.7	22.5	14.0	0.0
	2012	24 614	39.2	21.8	21.5	14.9	0.8	1.8	1.3	59.5	6.5	2.2	33.1	17.6	0.0
Palau - Palaos	1995	(e)14	54.0	0.9	0.9	15.1	38.0	0.0	0.0	45.9	0.1	1.2	44.6	..	..
	2005	13	95.1	1.5	1.5	2.4	91.2	0.0	0.0	4.9	0.0	0.2	4.4	0.3	0.0
	2012	(e)8	95.9	1.3	1.3	2.0	92.6	0.0	0.0	4.1	0.0	0.9	3.2	..	0.0
Panama	1995	577	42.8	26.8	24.2	12.9	2.4	0.7	0.3	56.6	0.2	32.7	22.1	1.6	..
	2005	(e)7 050	38.2	23.5	21.7	13.1	0.8	0.8	1.0	60.3	1.7	45.9	12.4	0.3	0.0
	2012	(e)16 220	27.6	7.0	6.0	15.5	3.2	1.8	0.3	72.1	0.4	62.6	8.8	0.3	0.0
Papua New Guinea - Papouasie-Nouvelle-Guinée	1995	(e)2 654	81.6	19.7	19.7	1.9	25.9	34.1	0.0	18.4	0.0	0.0	18.3	0.0	0.0
	2005	(e)3 492	76.2	14.9	14.8	2.0	13.1	46.2	0.1	23.5	0.5	0.0	22.4	0.0	0.6
	2012	(e)6 537	79.1	16.1	16.0	1.8	14.8	46.4	0.1	20.6	0.4	0.0	19.7	0.0	0.5
Paraguay	1995	919	27.5	20.1	19.7	4.6	1.7	1.1	0.0	72.4	0.5	64.3	7.6	0.1	..
	2005	1 655	17.9	12.5	12.0	3.1	1.0	1.3	4.8	77.3	2.4	66.3	5.7	2.7	0.0
	2012	7 271	21.9	17.4	16.8	2.9	0.5	1.1	12.4	65.7	2.7	55.0	5.3	2.8	0.0
Peru - Pérou	1995	5 440	63.5	34.8	31.0	17.2	8.4	3.1	0.4	35.2	0.7	17.5	16.8	0.2	0.0
	2005	17 114	62.6	22.0	17.3	30.7	3.5	6.4	0.2	36.8	0.4	20.7	15.4	0.3	0.0
	2012	(e)45 016	52.2	20.0	18.9	15.7	6.6	9.9	0.3	47.5	0.8	19.3	27.2	0.3	0.0

For sources and notes, see end of table.

Pour les sources et les notes, se reporter à la fin du tableau.

Destination / Origin	Year / Année	World (millions of dollars) (1) / Monde (millions de dollars) (1)	Developed economies / Économies développées						Transition economies / Économies en transition	Developing economies / Économies en développement					
			Total	Europe Total	EU UE	USA États-Unis	Japan Japon	Other Autres		Total	Africa Afrique	America Amérique	Eastern, Southern and South-Eastern Asia / Asie orientale, méridionale et du Sud-Est	Western Asia / Asie occidentale	Oceania Océanie
Philippines	1995	17 447	71.7	17.9	17.7	35.8	15.7	2.2	0.1	28.2	0.2	1.1	25.6	1.2	0.1
	2005	41 255	54.5	17.1	17.0	18.0	17.5	1.9	0.1	45.4	0.2	0.7	43.7	0.6	0.1
	2012	51 995	47.4	12.2	11.4	14.2	19.0	2.0	0.2	52.5	0.4	1.1	50.0	0.8	0.1
Poland - Pologne	1995	22 862	82.8	79.4	77.8	2.7	0.2	0.5	10.5	6.7	1.3	1.4	3.2	0.8	0.0
	2005	89 378	84.9	81.7	78.6	2.1	0.2	1.0	9.4	5.5	0.9	0.9	1.9	1.9	0.1
	2012	179 604	81.3	78.0	75.2	2.0	0.3	1.1	11.0	7.5	1.1	1.1	2.8	2.4	0.1
Portugal	1995	23 370	91.2	84.1	80.8	4.8	0.9	1.5	0.3	8.0	3.9	1.6	1.7	0.7	0.0
	2005	38 086	87.7	80.3	78.8	5.9	0.4	1.1	0.4	11.2	5.2	1.6	2.9	1.6	0.0
	2012	58 379	75.3	69.4	67.1	4.3	0.6	1.0	0.9	21.2	11.9	3.7	3.7	1.9	0.0
Qatar	1995	(e)3 557	63.1	1.3	1.3	2.6	55.5	3.6	0.0	36.9	1.5	0.0	27.7	7.7	0.0
	2005	(e)25 762	49.6	4.8	4.7	1.7	41.7	1.4	0.0	50.4	1.3	0.1	43.8	5.2	0.0
	2012	(e)132 968	41.1	10.8	10.5	0.8	28.5	1.0	0.1	58.9	0.7	1.0	55.4	1.8	0.0
Republic of Moldova - République de Moldova	1995	746	33.4	29.8	29.5	2.0	0.0	1.6	62.9	3.4	0.7	0.2	0.8	1.6	..
	2005	1 091	42.7	38.3	37.9	3.6	0.1	0.8	51.2	5.9	1.4	0.3	0.6	3.7	0.0
	2012	2 162	53.8	51.5	50.8	1.3	0.5	0.6	36.5	9.7	0.4	0.7	1.7	6.9	0.0
Romania - Roumanie	1995	7 910	65.3	60.5	59.3	2.5	0.4	1.8	6.8	27.5	7.2	2.2	9.2	8.9	0.0
	2005	27 730	77.1	71.8	70.5	4.1	0.3	0.9	6.2	16.6	2.2	0.6	3.2	10.7	0.0
	2012	57 904	75.0	71.8	70.2	1.9	0.5	0.8	8.9	16.0	4.0	1.1	3.2	7.6	0.1
Russian Federation - Fédération de Russie	1995	(e)78 217	51.0	43.4	38.8	4.3	2.8	0.5	18.0	15.2	0.7	3.3	9.1	2.2	0.0
	2005	241 452	67.1	62.2	57.3	2.6	1.5	0.7	14.1	18.7	1.1	2.0	10.3	5.3	0.0
	2012	524 565	52.2	46.8	45.1	2.3	2.9	0.3	11.1	18.9	1.4	1.0	12.9	3.6	0.0
Rwanda	1995	(e)52	72.6	69.2	68.8	2.9	0.2	0.2	0.0	27.4	21.9	0.0	5.4	0.1	..
	2005	(e)125	49.9	43.7	42.8	5.7	0.1	0.5	4.5	44.8	15.2	1.2	27.4	0.8	0.2
	2012	(e)591	16.1	9.6	9.4	5.7	0.4	0.5	0.9	83.0	55.3	0.1	27.1	0.5	0.0
Saint Helena - Sainte-Hélène	1995	(e)5	86.6	24.1	16.7	0.8	61.6	0.2	0.6	12.8	5.4	0.3	2.5	4.5	..
	2005	(e)20	61.3	16.4	16.4	23.4	20.7	0.8	0.4	38.3	24.0	9.8	4.2	0.2	0.1
	2012	(e)44	83.2	12.4	12.0	36.5	27.4	6.9	0.0	16.8	8.0	2.6	5.8	0.3	0.1
Saint Kitts and Nevis - Saint-Kitts-et-Nevis	1995	(e)19	91.2	34.5	34.3	51.9	0.1	4.7	0.2	8.6	0.0	8.4	0.1	0.0	..
	2005	(e)34	93.0	18.0	18.0	67.6	0.1	7.3	0.5	6.5	2.8	3.7	0.0	0.0	..
	2012	(e)45	77.3	7.3	6.5	61.3	..	8.8	2.0	20.7	0.2	9.6	8.7	2.3	..
Saint Lucia - Sainte-Lucie	1995	109	84.1	56.8	56.7	26.2	0.3	0.9	..	15.3	0.5	14.7	0.1	..	0.0
	2005	64	63.0	43.8	43.8	18.8	0.0	0.3	0.0	37.0	0.0	19.9	17.1	0.0	..
	2012	(e)160	54.3	30.4	30.3	23.7	0.0	0.2	0.0	45.6	0.0	32.6	12.9	0.1	..
Saint Pierre and Miquelon - Saint-Pierre-et-Miquelon	1995	(e)10	94.5	37.1	36.2	54.7	1.5	1.2	..	5.0	1.6	3.1	0.3	..	..
	2005	(e)12	59.4	51.2	47.4	8.0	..	0.2	0.1	40.5	4.5	0.1	35.9	0.0	..
	2012	(e)6	95.7	53.5	52.2	0.0	..	42.1	0.0	4.3	2.0	0.7	1.7	0.0	0.0
Saint Vincent and the Grenadines - Saint-Vincent-et-les Grenadines	1995	(e)43	61.2	43.0	43.0	7.9	6.9	3.4	..	38.8	0.3	30.5	7.9	..	..
	2005	40	83.5	77.7	77.5	5.7	0.0	0.1	0.7	15.8	0.4	14.5	0.3	0.7	..
	2012	43	15.8	12.7	11.1	2.8	0.0	0.3	0.4	83.8	2.7	63.3	4.6	13.2	0.0
Samoa	1995	(e)9	91.1	2.0	1.9	0.9	1.7	86.5	7.7	1.3	0.3	0.0	0.8	0.1	0.0
	2005	(e)87	77.9	1.4	1.4	7.0	0.9	68.6	0.1	22.0	1.1	1.5	0.5	0.1	18.8
	2012	(e)76	43.8	0.9	0.8	2.6	0.4	40.0	0.0	56.2	3.3	4.2	13.8	0.3	34.7
Sao Tome and Principe - Sao Tomé-et-Principe	1995	(e)5	67.6	63.0	57.7	2.0	2.5	0.1	1.0	14.4	3.7	1.5	8.6	0.5	..
	2005	(e)7	77.0	74.1	73.8	1.4	0.8	0.7	0.1	22.9	3.3	6.0	6.1	7.5	..
	2012	(e)11	57.8	54.3	54.1	3.0	..	0.5	0.1	42.1	7.0	30.6	3.4	1.1	..
Saudi Arabia - Arabie saoudite	1995	(e)49 030	56.1	19.8	19.5	16.8	17.3	2.2	0.0	43.9	2.8	2.3	29.7	9.2	0.0
	2005	(e)180 737	51.1	16.0	15.9	16.8	16.6	1.6	0.0	48.9	3.8	1.1	36.3	7.7	0.0
	2012	(e)388 329	35.7	9.7	9.7	12.6	12.3	1.0	0.1	64.2	4.2	1.0	53.0	6.0	0.0
Senegal - Sénégal	1995	(e)993	44.1	42.1	41.9	0.8	1.1	0.1	0.0	48.1	25.0	0.5	21.9	0.6	0.1
	2005	(e)1 471	30.9	29.4	29.1	0.6	0.9	0.1	0.0	58.3	39.2	0.3	18.2	0.5	0.2
	2012	(e)2 532	22.5	20.9	15.6	0.5	0.8	0.2	0.3	68.0	47.3	0.4	18.3	1.9	0.1
Serbia and Montenegro - Serbie-et-Monténégro	1995	(e)1 531	38.9	36.4	31.4	1.8	0.0	0.7	42.2	4.8	1.9	0.4	1.4	1.1	0.0
	2005	(d)5 065	54.0	52.3	51.5	1.2	0.0	0.6	30.5	3.4	1.0	0.1	0.5	1.7	0.0
Serbia - Serbie	2012	11 353	60.2	59.0	58.1	0.9	0.0	0.3	35.1	4.7	1.0	0.2	1.1	2.5	0.0
Seychelles	1995	53	58.1	50.2	50.1	3.9	3.3	0.7	..	41.8	2.6	0.0	21.5	17.7	..
	2005	340	79.6	69.9	69.8	1.1	7.7	0.9	0.8	19.6	6.2	0.1	3.3	9.9	0.0
	2012	(e)497	83.0	69.0	67.8	1.7	11.1	1.3	0.4	16.6	8.4	0.5	7.6	0.2	0.0

For sources and notes, see end of table.

Pour les sources et les notes, se reporter à la fin du tableau.

Destination / Origin / Origine	Year / Année	World (millions of dollars) (1) / Monde (millions de dollars) (1)	Developed economies / Économies développées — Total	Europe Total	EU UE	USA États-Unis	Japan Japon	Other Autres	Transition economies / Économies en transition	Developing economies / Économies en développement — Total	Africa Afrique	America Amérique	Eastern, Southern and South-Eastern Asia / Asie orientale, méridionale et du Sud-Est	Western Asia / Asie occidentale	Oceania Océanie
								Percentage / En pourcentage							
Sierra Leone	1995	(e)42	90.8	55.0	54.1	28.7	2.8	4.3	1.5	7.6	4.4	0.1	3.0	0.2	..
	2005	(e)159	88.4	79.5	79.5	7.3	0.4	1.3	1.5	10.1	3.2	0.8	4.0	2.1	0.0
	2012	(e)1 112	39.5	29.5	29.3	1.9	7.7	0.5	0.2	60.3	2.2	0.3	52.6	5.1	0.0
Singapore - Singapour (2)	1995	118 263	43.6	14.3	13.9	18.3	7.8	3.2	0.8	55.3	1.3	1.3	51.1	1.3	0.3
	2005	229 652	33.0	12.5	12.2	10.4	5.5	4.6	0.2	66.6	1.0	2.0	60.5	2.2	0.9
	2012	408 393	24.9	9.7	9.2	5.5	4.4	5.2	0.2	74.9	2.1	4.3	65.1	2.0	1.5
Sint Maarten (Dutch part) - Saint-Martin (partie néerlandaise)	2012	131	99.8	0.0	..	99.8		0.0	0.1	0.1	..	0.1	..	..	..
Slovakia - Slovaquie	1995	8 374	86.6	84.8	83.8	1.2	0.2	0.5	8.0	5.2	0.9	0.7	2.2	1.3	0.0
	2005	31 852	92.0	88.2	87.1	3.2	0.3	0.4	4.3	3.7	0.6	0.4	1.2	1.5	0.0
	2012	80 752	88.0	85.5	83.8	1.9	0.2	0.5	6.4	5.6	0.6	0.5	2.7	1.7	0.0
Slovenia - Slovénie	1995	8 316	77.7	73.6	72.5	3.1	0.3	0.7	19.0	3.3	0.7	0.5	1.3	0.8	0.0
	2005	17 896	73.8	71.1	69.5	2.0	0.1	0.5	22.0	4.1	0.9	0.4	1.3	1.5	0.0
	2012	(e)32 173	61.0	58.9	57.6	1.3	0.1	0.7	16.9	5.4	1.7	0.6	1.7	1.5	0.0
Solomon Islands - Îles Salomon	1995	(e)168	64.6	10.8	10.8	2.5	49.1	2.2	..	35.4	0.4	0.0	35.0	0.0	0.0
	2005	(e)103	19.4	9.4	9.4	1.0	7.1	1.8	0.0	80.6	0.3	0.0	78.2	0.0	2.1
	2012	(e)496	29.6	10.9	10.6	0.3	1.1	17.4	0.0	70.4	0.0	0.0	68.4	0.4	1.5
Somalia - Somalie	1995	(e)170	18.3	18.2	18.1	0.1	..	0.0	0.2	81.5	1.5	0.0	4.3	75.8	..
	2005	(e)250	1.2	0.8	0.8	0.2	0.2	0.0	0.1	98.7	2.7	0.1	13.1	82.9	0.0
	2012	510	3.7	3.3	3.3	0.2	0.0	0.1	0.1	96.2	0.8	2.8	16.4	76.1	0.0
South Africa - Afrique du Sud	1995	(e)27 853	60.2	37.7	36.4	11.4	7.2	3.9	0.3	37.7	19.7	1.9	14.1	1.9	0.0
	2005	46 991	61.0	37.1	35.0	9.9	9.6	4.5	0.4	38.0	18.2	1.4	15.3	3.1	0.0
	2012	86 712	36.5	21.7	20.1	7.5	5.4	1.9	0.5	62.6	17.8	1.9	39.9	3.0	0.1
Spain - Espagne	1995	89 616	83.8	76.5	74.0	4.2	1.4	1.6	0.6	15.6	3.8	5.6	4.2	1.9	0.0
	2005	192 798	80.8	74.6	71.1	4.1	0.7	1.3	1.1	15.8	4.3	5.2	3.2	3.0	0.1
	2012	285 936	72.1	65.0	61.1	4.1	0.9	2.1	1.9	22.2	6.8	6.3	4.8	4.2	0.0
Sri Lanka	1995	(e)3 798	75.5	30.0	29.0	36.3	6.3	2.9	1.8	15.5	2.0	1.4	9.3	2.7	0.0
	2005	6 160	69.3	31.8	31.0	32.2	2.3	3.1	3.3	25.4	1.4	1.7	16.1	6.3	0.0
	2012	9 370	64.2	35.3	34.1	22.6	2.3	4.0	4.3	31.3	2.4	2.6	18.3	7.9	0.1
State of Palestine - État de Palestine	1995	394	..	..	..	..	..	..	..	..	..	..	..	..	..
	2005	(e)335	92.8	4.1	4.0	1.1	0.0	87.5	0.0	7.2	0.9	0.4	0.7	5.2	..
	2012	(e)949	91.3	2.0	1.9	1.2	0.0	88.2	0.0	8.7	0.7	0.0	0.3	7.7	..
Sudan (...2011) - Soudan (...2011)	1995	(e)556	48.8	37.4	35.2	5.2	6.2	0.0	0.3	50.9	3.1	0.1	21.6	26.0	..
	2005	4 506	28.2	3.7	3.7	0.3	23.0	1.3	0.1	71.7	2.3	0.2	63.2	6.0	0.0
Sudan - Soudan	2012	3 384	11.1	3.4	3.3	0.1	5.3	2.4	0.1	88.8	4.9	0.2	26.6	57.1	0.0
Suriname	1995	483	85.5	59.7	34.2	20.0	5.5	0.3	0.8	13.7	0.4	12.5	0.9	0.0	..
	2005	997	81.0	48.0	25.6	14.3	1.0	17.8	0.0	18.9	1.3	11.0	1.5	5.1	0.0
	2012	(e)2 564	69.0	30.8	21.0	15.3	0.3	22.6	0.0	31.0	0.6	13.8	1.7	14.9	0.0
Swaziland	1995	(e)866	30.5	17.4	17.4	10.8	1.0	1.3	0.7	68.8	53.4	0.4	14.5	0.4	0.1
	2005	(e)1 770	48.6	13.6	13.5	14.3	0.6	20.2	0.3	51.1	27.9	0.4	20.4	2.4	0.0
	2012	(e)1 900	40.7	29.3	28.5	9.5	0.1	1.8	0.3	59.0	20.3	2.2	36.1	0.0	0.4
Sweden - Suède	1995	77 436	86.3	71.8	61.7	8.1	3.0	3.3	1.2	12.5	1.6	2.0	7.2	1.7	0.0
	2005	130 264	83.3	68.5	58.4	10.6	1.5	2.8	2.6	13.6	2.3	2.1	6.8	2.3	0.0
	2012	172 631	77.1	67.3	55.5	6.0	1.4	2.4	2.7	16.1	2.8	2.5	7.6	3.2	0.0
Switzerland - Suisse	1995	81 641	80.7	65.2	64.6	8.7	4.0	2.9	0.8	18.5	1.8	2.5	10.8	3.4	0.0
	2005	130 930	80.7	63.3	62.9	10.9	3.6	2.9	1.6	17.7	1.4	2.4	10.2	3.7	0.0
	2012	225 949	73.9	56.2	55.7	11.1	3.3	3.3	2.3	23.8	1.6	3.2	14.5	4.6	0.0
Syrian Arab Republic - République arabe syrienne	1995	(e)3 563	64.9	62.6	62.6	1.4	0.2	0.6	4.4	30.7	5.0	0.2	2.0	23.5	..
	2005	(e)8 708	46.8	42.5	42.4	3.9	0.2	0.2	1.8	51.2	5.2	0.8	0.9	44.4	0.0
	2012	(e)4 000	7.4	6.6	6.6	0.5	0.1	0.1	1.1	91.5	8.1	0.2	2.4	80.9	0.0
Tajikistan - Tadjikistan	1995	(e)749	62.2	49.5	47.0	8.5	4.1	0.0	28.3	9.5	3.2	0.1	4.5	1.7	..
	2005	(e)892	60.0	46.4	38.1	13.3	0.2	0.0	20.1	20.0	3.2	0.0	6.5	10.2	..
	2012	(e)1 333	15.5	12.2	9.2	2.4	0.9	0.0	13.6	70.9	2.5	0.0	37.9	30.5	0.0
TFYR of Macedonia - LERY de Macédoine	1995	1 204	71.0	67.8	64.7	3.0	0.1	0.1	14.7	6.7	1.0	0.0	2.2	3.5	0.0
	2005	2 041	60.2	57.4	57.0	2.2	0.4	0.2	31.6	8.2	0.2	4.3	1.3	2.4	0.0
	2012	4 002	65.4	63.6	62.8	1.4	0.0	0.3	25.9	8.7	0.1	0.2	6.4	2.0	0.0

For sources and notes, see end of table.

Destination / Origin / Origine	Year / Année	World (millions of dollars) (1) / Monde (millions de dollars) (1)	Developed economies / Économies développées Total	Europe Total	Europe EU UE	USA États-Unis	Japan Japon	Other Autres	Transition economies / Économies en transition	Developing economies / Économies en développement Total	Africa Afrique	America Amérique	Eastern, Southern and South-Eastern Asia / Asie orientale, méridionale et du Sud-Est	Western Asia / Asie occidentale	Oceania Océanie
Thailand - Thaïlande	1995	56 439	55.1	17.5	16.6	17.9	16.8	3.0	0.8	42.9	2.1	1.0	35.9	3.7	0.1
	2005	110 110	48.3	14.3	13.6	15.5	13.6	4.8	0.4	51.2	2.6	1.9	43.2	3.4	0.2
	2012	229 545	37.9	12.0	9.5	9.9	10.2	5.7	0.7	61.1	3.6	3.5	49.4	4.4	0.2
Timor-Leste	2005	(e)8	44.1	2.6	2.3	1.5	1.0	39.1	0.1	55.8	2.5	0.1	51.3	0.0	1.8
	2012	(e)12	15.8	1.0	1.0	0.0	14.2	0.5	0.0	84.2	0.1	0.0	84.2	0.0	..
Togo	1995	383	50.3	32.4	27.0	6.0	0.3	11.7	0.0	49.6	19.0	4.7	25.5	0.5	..
	2005	(e)660	19.4	16.7	16.4	1.1	0.0	1.6	0.1	80.1	60.2	1.7	17.7	0.5	0.0
	2012	900	21.2	18.1	17.5	3.1	0.0	0.0	0.5	78.2	45.4	0.4	21.1	11.3	0.0
Tokelau - Tokélaou	1995	(e)1	91.2	0.3	0.3	76.9	..	14.0	..	5.1	0.6	0.6	2.5	1.0	0.4
	2005	(e)0	50.7	11.7	11.7	38.0	1.0	0.0	0.0	49.2	8.1	3.4	37.6	0.1	0.0
	2012	(e)0	71.7	40.1	40.1	30.2	0.2	1.3	0.1	28.2	13.2	2.7	12.1	0.1	0.0
Tonga	1995	(e)15	95.0	4.1	4.1	32.6	49.3	9.0	0.1	4.9	..	0.1	4.5	0.2	..
	2005	(e)10	89.5	3.0	3.0	32.4	44.0	10.1	0.0	10.5	0.0	0.3	2.7	..	7.5
	2012	(e)16	55.8	2.8	2.7	16.6	10.6	25.8	0.0	44.2	0.9	0.3	25.1	0.0	17.9
Trinidad and Tobago - Trinité-et-Tobago	1995	2 467	60.1	16.6	16.5	41.7	0.4	1.4	0.2	38.8	0.7	37.6	0.6	0.0	0.0
	2005	9 611	73.1	5.6	5.6	65.7	0.0	1.8	0.0	26.8	0.1	26.5	0.3	0.0	0.0
	2012	(e)12 981	64.4	15.3	15.2	46.0	0.5	2.5	0.0	35.6	1.2	30.5	3.8	0.1	0.0
Tunisia - Tunisie	1995	5 475	82.3	80.6	79.6	1.3	0.3	0.1	0.0	14.6	8.4	0.8	3.5	1.8	0.0
	2005	10 494	81.9	80.6	80.1	0.9	0.2	0.1	0.2	14.3	9.0	0.7	2.5	2.1	0.0
	2012	(e)17 008	74.5	69.0	67.9	4.3	0.8	0.5	0.8	24.6	16.1	1.3	4.5	2.7	0.0
Turkey - Turquie	1995	21 599	68.4	58.8	57.4	7.0	0.8	1.8	10.3	19.3	4.9	0.7	6.2	7.5	0.0
	2005	73 476	68.4	58.5	57.3	6.7	0.3	2.9	8.1	19.4	4.9	0.9	3.8	9.5	0.2
	2012	152 537	47.7	41.3	39.5	3.7	0.2	2.5	11.8	39.0	8.8	1.9	10.9	17.3	0.1
Turkmenistan - Turkménistan	1995	(e)1 939	16.7	15.8	13.4	0.7	0.2	0.0	65.2	18.1	0.1	0.1	9.7	8.3	..
	2005	(e)4 944	25.0	21.3	21.3	2.8	0.0	0.9	63.0	12.1	0.0	0.1	6.2	5.7	0.0
	2012	(e)16 500	11.6	9.7	9.4	0.9	0.0	1.0	12.3	76.1	0.0	0.0	69.6	6.5	0.0
Turks and Caicos Islands - Iles Turques et Caïques	1995	(e)5	69.6	31.7	31.7	37.7	..	0.1	2.6	27.8	0.4	16.9	10.5	0.1	..
	2005	(e)15	99.3	..	..	69.1	..	30.1	..	0.7	..	0.7	..	..	..
	2012	(e)25	99.4	..	..	99.4	..	0.0	0.2	0.4	..	0.4	..	..	..
Tuvalu	1995	(e)0	30.1	28.4	28.4	..	0.4	1.3	8.9	61.0	40.5	0.9	19.3	0.2	0.1
	2005	(e)0	83.7	78.6	78.5	1.5	0.6	3.0	2.3	14.1	6.8	0.1	2.4	..	4.7
	2012	(e)0	57.4	1.5	1.5	0.1	54.2	1.6	0.5	42.1	1.4	0.1	23.0	16.4	1.3
Uganda - Ouganda	1995	(e)460	89.4	84.7	74.9	1.7	1.4	1.7	0.1	10.5	7.5	0.1	2.3	0.6	0.0
	2005	813	49.3	44.6	39.7	2.8	0.8	1.1	0.9	49.8	31.9	0.2	7.8	10.0	0.0
	2012	2 357	29.5	26.8	24.8	1.7	0.4	0.7	1.1	69.4	49.5	0.2	9.4	10.3	0.0
Ukraine	1995	(e)13 317	25.4	21.8	20.9	2.6	0.6	0.5	51.5	20.3	1.4	1.4	11.6	5.9	0.0
	2005	34 228	35.4	31.2	29.9	2.8	0.2	1.2	32.6	32.0	7.0	2.3	11.3	11.4	0.0
	2012	68 694	28.5	25.2	24.9	1.5	0.5	1.4	38.0	33.3	8.0	2.2	10.6	12.5	0.0
United Arab Emirates - Emirats arabes unis	1995	(e)27 753	55.2	4.4	4.4	2.2	46.4	2.2	0.5	44.3	2.1	0.1	32.4	9.7	0.0
	2005	(e)115 453	42.0	12.1	11.5	1.6	27.5	0.7	0.8	57.2	4.2	0.1	44.7	8.1	0.0
	2012	(e)324 424	22.8	4.3	3.8	0.9	16.2	1.5	0.6	76.6	4.2	0.3	62.4	9.7	0.0
United Kingdom - Royaume-Uni	1995	234 372	77.3	60.0	56.9	11.5	2.4	3.4	0.9	16.1	2.9	1.7	8.3	3.2	0.0
	2005	384 365	80.8	60.7	57.0	14.7	1.8	3.6	1.4	17.7	2.7	1.4	8.1	5.4	0.0
	2012	481 226	71.9	53.3	48.5	13.3	1.5	3.8	2.8	24.6	3.8	3.5	12.2	5.2	0.0
United Republic of Tanzania - République-Unie de Tanzanie	1995	(e)685	47.2	37.6	32.6	1.8	6.5	1.2	0.1	40.0	13.6	0.1	24.9	1.4	0.0
	2005	1 672	45.3	30.6	26.4	2.0	4.8	8.0	1.2	53.4	24.8	0.1	23.1	5.4	0.0
	2012	5 547	34.2	24.1	17.6	2.8	6.2	1.0	1.5	64.3	29.6	0.1	29.7	4.9	0.0
United States - États-Unis	1995	582 965	58.9	23.1	21.8	..	11.0	24.8	0.6	40.4	1.7	16.4	19.8	2.4	0.1
	2005	904 339	54.9	22.2	20.7	..	6.1	26.5	0.7	44.4	1.7	21.2	18.5	2.9	0.1
	2012	1 545 565	46.1	19.5	17.2	..	4.5	22.1	1.0	52.9	2.1	25.8	20.6	4.4	0.1
Uruguay	1995	2 106	32.1	21.9	21.2	6.0	0.9	3.2	0.3	66.8	0.7	53.4	11.6	1.1	..
	2005	3 405	46.5	19.1	17.6	23.2	0.9	3.4	1.3	49.1	3.9	34.7	9.4	1.0	0.1
	2012	8 743	19.9	13.2	11.3	3.8	0.1	2.8	4.8	58.8	3.9	39.1	13.0	2.7	0.1
Uzbekistan - Ouzbékistan	1995	3 430	60.0	52.8	52.4	1.1	5.7	0.3	19.1	20.9	0.0	2.4	14.9	3.5	..
	2005	4 749	25.7	18.5	18.3	2.6	3.3	1.3	42.6	31.7	0.1	0.1	24.4	7.1	0.0
	2012	10 836	11.2	8.0	7.9	0.6	2.5	0.1	42.3	46.6	0.3	0.1	27.4	18.8	0.0

For sources and notes, see end of table.

Pour les sources et les notes, se reporter à la fin du tableau.

Destination / Origin / Origine	Year / Année	World (millions of dollars) (1) / Monde (millions de dollars) (1)	Developed economies / Économies développées						Transition economies / Économies en transition	Developing economies / Économies en développement					
			Total	Europe		USA / États-Unis	Japan / Japon	Other / Autres		Total	Africa / Afrique	America / Amérique	Eastern, Southern and South-Eastern Asia / Asie orientale, méridionale et du Sud-Est	Western Asia / Asie occiden-tale	Oceania / Océanie
				Total	EU / UE										
													Percentage / En pourcentage		
Vanuatu	1995	(e)28	85.9	45.4	40.1	0.3	26.5	13.7	0.5	13.6	0.3	0.3	4.7	7.6	0.6
	2005	(e)38	24.2	13.9	13.9	1.0	6.1	3.2	0.0	75.8	0.2	0.1	64.9	8.4	2.2
	2012	(e)52	16.9	1.8	1.8	0.7	13.4	1.0	0.0	83.1	36.3	0.6	42.4	0.9	2.9
Venezuela (Bolivarian Rep. of) - Venezuela (Rép. bolivarienne du)	1995	19 093	67.8	10.2	10.1	53.5	2.0	2.0	0.2	32.0	0.2	31.0	0.7	0.1	..
	2005	55 413	71.7	8.8	8.6	60.0	0.5	2.4	0.1	28.2	0.3	22.9	4.8	0.2	0.0
	2012	(e)95 795	46.0	5.6	5.6	39.9	0.3	0.2	0.4	53.6	0.4	21.3	31.6	0.3	0.0
Viet Nam	1995	(e)5 449	44.7	19.9	16.1	3.1	18.2	3.5	1.6	48.0	0.4	0.8	45.3	1.3	0.0
	2005	32 447	58.9	17.5	17.1	18.3	13.4	9.7	1.0	39.6	2.0	1.8	34.6	1.1	0.1
	2012	(e)114 529	52.7	18.8	18.3	17.7	11.8	4.4	1.7	45.6	1.6	1.8	38.9	3.4	..
Wallis and Futuna Islands - Îles Wallis-et-Futuna	1995	(e)1	44.2	39.7	39.7	3.4	..	1.1	7.5	48.3	30.8	17.5	..	..	..
	2005	(e)0	41.3	40.4	40.4	0.8	..	0.1	0.1	58.6	52.3	0.1	5.4	..	0.7
	2012	(e)0	26.3	22.5	20.5	0.0	..	3.8	0.6	73.1	64.9	1.3	1.3	..	5.6
Western Sahara - Sahara occidental	1995	(e)8	30.0	6.4	6.4	..	23.6	0.0	3.2	66.8	6.5	59.1	1.2	..	..
Yemen - Yémen	1995	(e)1 917	18.4	2.5	2.5	1.6	14.3	0.0	0.0	81.5	8.6	8.0	61.0	3.9	..
	2005	(e)5 608	17.1	4.1	2.2	4.4	6.6	2.0	0.0	82.3	2.5	0.1	71.0	8.7	0.0
	2012	(e)8 600	7.2	1.4	1.4	1.0	3.9	0.8	0.0	92.8	2.3	0.6	76.2	13.6	0.0
Zambia - Zambie	1995	1 055	38.5	16.5	16.2	5.0	16.8	0.2	0.0	61.5	10.3	0.1	39.4	11.7	..
	2005	1 810	30.0	26.8	15.1	1.0	2.0	0.1	0.1	69.9	47.2	0.1	18.9	3.7	0.0
	2012	(e)8 600	11.2	9.2	9.2	1.0	0.8	0.1	0.2	88.7	26.5	0.1	57.5	4.6	..
Zimbabwe	1995	(e)2 121	60.8	44.2	42.5	5.4	9.1	2.2	0.6	38.6	29.6	0.8	7.7	0.5	0.0
	2005	(e)1 850	35.9	25.2	22.8	5.5	4.8	0.3	1.4	62.7	47.1	0.9	12.4	2.4	0.0
	2012	(e)3 884	22.5	19.0	18.7	1.9	1.3	0.3	1.7	75.8	46.8	0.4	26.2	2.4	0.0

Source:
UNCTAD secretariat calculations, based on UNCTAD, *UNCTADstat* Merchandise Trade Matrix

Source :
Calculs du secrétariat de la CNUCED, basés sur la matrice du commerce de marchandises d'*UNCTADstat* de la CNUCED

Notes:
(1) Includes unspecified destinations.
(2) Exports data include a considerable amount of re-exports.
(3) Estimates. France including French Guiana, Guadeloupe, Martinique, Monaco and Reunion (and excluding intra trade).

Notes :
(1) Y compris des destinations non-spécifiées.
(2) Les données des exportations comprennent une part importante de réexportations.
(3) Estimation. Les données sont dérivées des déclarations rapportées par la France métropolitaine et les départements d'outre-mer par agrégation diminuée des flux intra.

Origin / Origine / Destination	Year / Année	World (millions of dollars) (1) / Monde (millions de dollars) (1)	Developed economies / Économies développées — Total	Europe Total	Europe EU / UE	USA / États-Unis	Japan / Japon	Other / Autres	Transition economies / Économies en transition	Developing economies / Économies en développement — Total	Africa / Afrique	America / Amérique	Eastern, Southern and South-Eastern Asia / Asie orientale, méridionale et du Sud-Est	Western Asia / Asie occidentale	Oceania / Océanie
								Percentage / En pourcentage							
Afghanistan	1995	(e)387	43.4	17.1	17.0	1.1	23.3	1.9	13.1	43.5	0.0	0.1	42.4	1.0	..
	2005	(e)2 471	26.0	13.8	13.7	8.4	3.1	0.6	15.9	58.0	1.8	0.1	49.5	6.7	
	2012	(e)5 500	32.4	13.2	13.0	17.2	1.4	0.6	17.6	50.0	1.7	0.1	40.4	7.7	..
Albania - Albanie	1995	(e)714	74.9	72.2	68.9	2.6	0.1	0.1	7.7	10.5	1.5	0.9	1.1	7.0	..
	2005	2 614	73.1	71.3	70.3	1.1	0.2	0.4	9.9	16.8	0.7	1.5	6.5	8.0	0.0
	2012	4 880	69.2	66.2	64.8	1.5	0.2	1.4	13.1	17.6	0.6	1.5	9.4	6.1	0.0
Algeria - Algérie	1995	10 782	83.9	62.2	61.0	13.2	3.4	5.2	1.1	15.0	2.8	3.4	5.2	3.5	0.0
	2005	20 357	66.9	54.4	53.2	6.7	3.8	2.0	4.9	25.6	2.5	6.6	12.2	4.3	0.0
	2012	50 369	60.6	53.4	52.3	3.5	1.8	1.8	3.3	36.1	3.8	7.5	18.9	5.9	0.0
American Samoa - Samoa américaines	1995	416	..	..	..	..	..	..	..	..	..	..	..	..	..
	2005	(e)520	52.1	8.9	8.9	..	2.6	40.6	0.0	47.9	1.2	0.3	28.0	0.0	18.4
	2012	(e)690	16.1	2.4	2.1	..	1.8	11.9	0.0	83.9	0.7	0.4	65.8	0.1	16.8
Andorra - Andorre	1995	(e)1 025	97.0	92.3	91.1	2.8	1.8	0.1	0.1	2.9	0.2	0.2	2.5	0.1	..
	2005	(e)1 822	..	..	..	..	..	..	..	..	..	..	..	..	..
	2012	(e)1 704	97.6	97.4	96.9	0.2	0.0	0.0	0.0	2.4	0.0	0.0	2.3	0.0	..
Angola	1995	1 468	80.8	63.6	62.5	15.1	1.5	0.5	0.0	19.1	8.9	2.4	7.7	0.1	..
	2005	8 353	49.8	35.5	33.3	11.9	1.5	0.9	0.5	49.7	9.4	9.0	29.0	2.3	..
	2012	(e)24 000	51.1	41.6	40.0	7.4	1.3	0.8	0.2	48.7	8.5	7.2	31.3	1.7	..
Anguilla	1995	(e)53	6.3	1.6	1.6	4.3	0.1	0.2	0.3	93.4	0.0	93.4	0.0	0.0	..
	2005	(e)130	62.4	25.3	25.2	33.9	1.8	1.4	0.9	36.7	0.0	35.8	0.4	0.5	0.0
	2012	(e)149	86.5	23.1	22.2	59.9	2.1	1.5	4.1	9.4	0.4	4.7	2.9	1.4	..
Antigua and Barbuda - Antigua-et-Barbuda	1995	(e)346	77.7	36.7	35.9	34.2	4.8	2.0	0.1	18.5	0.5	14.4	3.5	0.0	..
	2005	525	58.6	28.4	27.7	26.7	1.5	1.9	0.0	41.4	0.7	15.3	23.4	2.0	0.0
	2012	(e)530	20.4	6.3	5.7	12.7	0.3	1.1	0.1	79.5	0.1	10.5	68.5	0.4	..
Argentina - Argentine	1995	20 122	58.8	32.0	30.5	20.9	3.5	2.4	0.5	39.2	1.3	29.3	8.5	0.1	..
	2005	28 689	38.6	19.9	19.1	15.8	1.9	1.0	0.7	59.5	0.6	47.3	11.4	0.2	0.0
	2012	68 507	35.0	19.0	17.9	12.4	2.2	1.4	1.8	61.9	0.7	38.8	21.1	1.3	0.0
Armenia - Arménie	1995	(e)674	37.2	20.2	18.5	16.5	0.1	0.3	44.1	18.7	0.3	0.6	11.7	6.1	..
	2005	(e)1 692	50.2	37.1	34.7	5.3	0.4	7.3	28.8	21.0	0.1	4.7	10.3	5.9	..
	2012	(e)4 267	37.1	30.6	28.6	3.0	1.5	2.0	34.4	28.4	0.5	2.9	18.6	6.3	0.0
Aruba	1995	(e)1 597	75.4	23.5	22.9	48.2	2.5	1.2	0.0	24.6	..	22.4	2.1	0.0	..
	2005	(e)4 288	47.1	12.8	12.2	33.0	0.8	0.6	0.9	52.0	0.1	50.2	1.7	0.0	0.0
	2012	(e)2 600	52.3	16.0	15.2	35.3	0.4	0.6	0.1	47.6	0.3	44.4	2.8	0.1	..
Australia - Australie	1995	57 423	69.9	26.5	25.0	21.3	15.2	6.9	0.1	27.9	0.6	1.2	22.0	2.1	1.9
	2005	118 922	54.7	24.4	23.2	13.9	11.0	5.4	0.1	45.1	1.3	1.4	39.2	1.8	1.5
	2012	250 465	43.2	18.9	17.6	11.7	7.9	4.7	0.4	53.3	2.9	2.0	44.6	2.2	1.6
Austria - Autriche	1995	66 406	89.5	82.2	78.2	4.2	2.5	0.6	1.2	7.1	1.3	0.7	4.2	0.9	0.0
	2005	119 950	85.7	79.9	76.0	3.3	2.0	0.6	4.4	9.8	1.1	1.0	6.5	1.3	0.0
	2012	169 663	79.2	74.3	68.8	3.1	1.3	0.5	3.5	12.2	1.7	0.8	8.1	1.6	0.0
Azerbaijan - Azerbaïdjan	1995	(e)668	25.2	20.2	20.0	3.6	1.1	0.3	35.8	38.6	0.0	..	20.6	18.0	..
	2005	4 211	37.1	31.2	29.9	3.4	1.7	0.8	34.4	28.4	1.3	0.4	18.5	8.3	0.0
	2012	9 642	40.4	29.2	27.7	7.4	2.5	1.2	26.3	33.3	0.4	2.7	13.2	17.1	0.0
Bahamas	1995	(e)1 243	94.3	2.7	2.3	90.4	0.3	1.0	..	5.3	0.0	4.6	0.7	0.0	..
	2005	(e)2 312	51.7	21.1	17.7	27.4	2.5	0.8	2.9	45.4	0.1	21.5	22.9	1.0	0.0
	2012	(e)3 386	46.4	8.7	6.5	32.2	4.3	1.1	0.6	53.0	0.2	9.9	42.8	0.1	..
Bahrain - Bahreïn	1995	(e)3 679	38.5	23.2	20.9	8.2	3.9	3.3	0.1	58.9	0.6	1.9	10.1	46.3	0.0
	2005	(e)9 339	39.0	24.6	22.8	5.4	6.8	2.3	0.3	60.6	1.1	2.4	14.5	42.7	0.0
	2012	(e)13 920	36.7	19.4	17.3	9.1	6.1	2.1	0.1	63.2	0.9	4.2	20.8	37.3	0.0
Bangladesh	1995	(e)6 694	27.9	12.1	11.3	5.9	7.2	2.8	0.9	70.7	0.5	2.1	65.9	2.2	0.1
	2005	12 631	20.6	10.8	9.8	2.7	4.6	2.4	3.8	75.6	1.7	2.7	58.4	12.7	0.1
	2012	(e)32 345	16.4	6.8	6.1	1.8	4.2	3.6	3.8	79.8	2.3	4.8	62.5	10.1	0.1
Barbados - Barbade	1995	766	72.6	22.7	21.5	37.5	6.1	6.2	0.1	27.2	0.1	23.5	3.6	0.0	..
	2005	1 672	60.0	15.3	14.0	34.1	5.6	5.0	0.5	39.5	0.2	33.9	5.2	0.1	0.0
	2012	1 768	44.1	10.0	9.3	27.7	1.7	4.7	0.7	55.2	0.2	46.1	8.6	0.3	0.0
Belarus - Bélarus	1995	(e)5 563	34.5	33.4	33.0	0.8	0.1	0.2	64.7	0.6	0.0	0.0	0.5	0.1	..
	2005	16 699	25.0	22.9	21.6	1.4	0.3	0.4	66.7	5.2	0.2	1.3	3.2	0.5	0.0
	2012	46 404	22.9	21.1	20.0	1.1	0.4	0.3	64.6	10.1	0.4	1.7	7.0	1.0	0.0

For sources and notes, see end of table.

Pour les sources et les notes, se reporter à la fin du tableau.

Origin / Origine — Destination	Year Année	World (millions of dollars) (1) — Monde (millions de dollars) (1)	Developed economies — Économies développées Total	Europe Total	Europe EU UE	USA États-Unis	Japan Japon	Other Autres	Transition economies — Économies en transition	Developing economies — Économies en développement Total	Africa Afrique	America Amérique	Eastern, Southern and South-Eastern Asia — Asie orientale, méridionale et du Sud-Est	Western Asia — Asie occidentale	Oceania Océanie
Belgium - Belgique	1995	(e)164 590	87.2	76.8	74.5	5.4	2.9	2.1	1.3	10.8	3.6	1.7	4.9	0.5	0.0
	2005	320 130	84.5	74.5	72.1	5.4	2.7	1.9	1.8	13.7	2.7	1.9	7.5	1.6	0.0
	2012	437 883	80.4	70.5	67.8	6.3	2.0	1.6	2.9	16.7	2.6	2.4	9.1	2.6	0.0
Belize	1995	259	65.5	13.8	13.4	44.6	5.0	2.2	0.0	34.5	0.1	30.7	3.7	0.0	..
	2005	(e)593	51.0	15.7	15.4	32.6	1.6	1.1	9.6	39.4	0.5	32.1	6.7	0.1	0.0
	2012	880	37.6	15.9	14.9	20.3	0.7	0.7	13.9	48.4	0.3	36.1	11.6	0.4	0.0
Benin - Bénin	1995	(e)719	54.6	45.1	44.4	5.1	3.9	0.5	0.0	41.2	16.9	1.3	21.2	1.7	0.2
	2005	(e)1 018	31.7	27.7	26.4	2.5	1.1	0.4	0.3	68.0	17.6	1.4	47.1	1.9	0.0
	2012	(e)2 200	33.9	25.7	25.0	7.2	0.5	0.5	0.5	65.6	8.8	2.0	52.6	2.2	0.0
Bermuda - Bermudes	1995	(e)550	75.2	19.0	16.5	45.0	7.1	4.1	8.2	16.7	0.0	10.9	5.7	0.0	0.0
	2005	(e)988	67.5	34.5	32.0	28.9	1.1	3.0	3.3	29.2	0.1	2.4	26.6	0.0	0.0
	2012	(e)867	31.7	8.0	6.3	20.9	0.1	2.6	4.4	63.9	1.0	0.9	61.9	0.0	0.0
Bhutan - Bhoutan	1995	(e)113	48.3	22.2	20.8	1.3	24.5	0.3	0.0	51.7	0.1	1.0	49.3	1.3	..
	2005	(e)387	16.4	9.2	7.8	1.2	6.0	0.1	0.8	82.8	0.3	0.1	81.0	1.3	..
	2012	(e)1 090	25.2	22.2	21.0	0.7	2.2	0.2	0.0	74.8	0.2	0.0	74.6	0.0	..
Bolivia (Plurinational State of) - Bolivie (État plurinational de)	1995	1 396	40.1	16.4	15.7	15.7	6.7	1.3	0.2	59.7	0.1	49.8	3.2	6.6	0.0
	2005	2 343	24.5	9.2	8.8	10.9	3.7	0.8	0.1	75.3	0.1	69.7	5.5	0.0	0.0
	2012	8 281	23.5	9.2	8.6	10.1	3.5	0.6	0.2	76.3	0.1	66.2	9.8	0.2	0.0
Bosnia and Herzegovina - Bosnie-Herzégovine	1995	(e)1 082	36.7	34.1	33.9	2.6	..	0.0	61.5	1.7	0.8	0.2	0.0	0.6	..
	2005	(e)7 054	60.5	59.9	59.1	0.4	0.1	0.1	35.5	4.0	0.2	0.5	1.1	2.3	0.0
	2012	(e)10 024	54.1	53.6	52.9	0.4	0.1	0.1	40.6	5.3	0.2	0.5	1.5	3.1	0.0
Botswana	1995	(e)1 911	23.5	18.0	17.7	3.0	0.3	2.2	0.0	76.2	72.7	0.4	3.1	0.0	0.0
	2005	3 162	15.5	10.5	10.3	3.2	0.6	1.2	0.0	84.5	78.7	0.3	5.4	0.2	..
	2012	8 025	34.7	28.2	27.3	2.1	1.2	3.2	0.0	65.3	57.4	0.0	7.6	0.3	0.0
Brazil - Brésil	1995	53 734	63.0	31.0	28.5	23.7	5.1	3.2	0.5	36.2	2.7	21.1	9.1	3.3	0.0
	2005	73 600	51.9	26.8	24.8	17.5	4.6	2.9	1.5	46.7	9.0	16.4	18.3	2.9	0.0
	2012	223 149	43.6	23.0	21.4	14.6	3.5	2.5	1.9	54.4	6.4	17.3	27.4	3.2	0.0
British Virgin Islands - Îles Vierges britanniques	1995	(e)131	84.2	68.9	55.6	14.0	1.0	0.3	0.0	15.7	0.1	15.3	0.4	..	..
	2005	(c)280	15.1	12.2	10.4	2.6	0.1	0.2	79.3	5.6	0.5	3.0	1.4	0.7	..
	2012	310	40.1	34.3	29.6	5.1	0.1	0.6	19.9	40.1	0.8	1.1	37.0	1.1	..
Brunei Darussalam - Brunéi Darussalam	1995	(e)2 078	40.4	16.0	15.4	10.0	11.2	3.3	0.0	56.7	0.0	0.1	55.5	1.1	0.0
	2005	(e)1 494	20.9	8.8	8.5	3.3	7.0	1.8	0.0	79.1	0.4	0.1	78.1	0.5	0.0
	2012	3 572	27.6	10.3	9.8	7.8	7.5	2.0	0.0	71.8	0.2	0.4	70.9	0.3	0.0
Bulgaria - Bulgarie	1995	(e)5 651	37.7	34.0	32.3	2.2	0.7	0.8	38.5	9.7	0.9	3.0	3.6	2.2	0.0
	2005	18 162	59.1	54.5	53.4	2.5	1.2	0.9	22.3	17.6	0.4	4.0	6.8	6.3	0.1
	2012	32 743	52.2	49.1	47.7	1.6	0.7	0.8	27.4	20.4	0.7	4.5	9.4	5.8	0.0
Burkina Faso	1995	484	60.2	49.9	49.3	4.3	5.3	0.6	0.1	39.7	31.3	1.8	6.5	0.1	0.0
	2005	1 161	43.0	36.4	36.2	3.2	1.6	1.7	2.4	54.6	41.2	1.8	8.9	2.7	0.0
	2012	(e)3 150	46.2	38.3	37.8	2.3	0.9	4.6	1.0	52.8	38.0	0.3	13.7	0.9	..
Burundi	1995	(e)234	67.7	57.0	56.0	3.4	6.7	0.6	0.0	32.2	15.9	0.3	11.8	4.2	..
	2005	258	48.2	38.3	36.0	2.8	5.8	1.3	0.6	51.1	33.2	0.3	11.4	6.3	0.0
	2012	(e)751	43.4	37.9	37.2	3.2	1.8	0.5	0.5	56.1	27.2	0.3	16.5	12.1	0.0
Cambodia - Cambodge	1995	(e)1 187	15.0	6.0	5.9	2.0	5.7	1.3	0.0	84.9	0.1	0.0	84.8	0.0	..
	2005	(e)3 927	10.7	5.6	5.4	1.7	2.5	0.9	0.1	89.1	0.1	0.2	88.7	0.1	0.0
	2012	(e)11 000	6.0	2.4	2.3	1.6	1.7	0.3	0.1	93.9	0.0	0.2	93.6	0.1	0.0
Cameroon - Cameroun	1995	1 079	74.2	63.6	62.8	4.5	4.6	1.6	0.2	25.6	16.9	1.6	6.7	0.4	0.0
	2005	2 735	50.7	43.3	42.8	4.8	1.4	1.2	0.9	48.3	26.0	4.5	16.0	1.7	0.1
	2012	(e)7 300	41.3	35.2	34.5	4.4	0.5	1.3	0.7	57.9	20.5	3.1	31.4	2.8	0.1
Canada	1995	164 371	84.7	11.7	10.3	66.8	5.4	0.8	0.3	13.3	0.8	4.2	8.0	0.3	0.0
	2005	314 444	76.4	14.2	12.1	56.5	3.9	1.8	0.6	23.0	1.8	7.0	13.2	1.0	0.0
	2012	462 369	67.9	12.5	10.9	50.6	3.3	1.5	1.3	30.8	2.9	9.2	16.8	1.9	0.0
Cape Verde - Cap-Vert	1995	(e)252	83.9	78.4	78.0	3.2	1.7	0.7	0.2	14.8	4.4	6.2	3.9	0.3	0.0
	2005	(e)438	74.3	70.0	69.8	2.5	1.5	0.3	0.1	25.6	4.5	13.0	2.6	5.5	..
	2012	(e)755	81.5	78.5	78.1	1.6	1.3	0.1	0.0	18.5	2.1	5.8	9.8	0.8	..
Cayman Islands - Îles Caïmanes	1995	(e)402	52.1	24.3	23.1	25.8	0.7	1.3	0.1	45.9	0.1	45.1	0.6	0.0	..
	2005	(e)1 214	83.8	49.7	44.7	31.3	0.8	2.1	0.0	16.2	0.0	11.6	4.6	0.0	..
	2012	(e)910	74.7	35.5	33.1	31.8	6.9	0.5	6.3	19.0	0.0	5.5	12.6	0.9	..

For sources and notes, see end of table.

Pour les sources et les notes, se reporter à la fin du tableau.

Origin / Origine	Year / Année	World (millions of dollars) (1) / Monde (millions de dollars) (1)	Developed economies / Économies développées						Transition economies / Économies en transition	Developing economies / Économies en développement					
			Total	Europe		USA États-Unis	Japan Japon	Other Autres		Total	Africa Afrique	America Amérique	Eastern, Southern and South-Eastern Asia / Asie orientale, méridionale et du Sud-Est	Western Asia / Asie occiden-tale	Oceania Océanie
Destination				Total	EU UE										
								Percentage / En pourcentage							
Central African Republic - République centrafricaine	1995	(e)174	82.7	55.5	55.2	3.2	23.9	0.2	0.1	17.2	14.5	0.5	1.8	0.4	..
	2005	185	59.8	48.9	48.4	8.5	2.0	0.3	0.0	40.1	26.6	1.6	8.6	3.3	..
	2012	(e)320	38.4	33.6	33.4	3.3	1.4	0.1	0.1	61.5	14.1	2.5	39.7	5.2	..
Chad - Tchad	1995	(e)488	69.6	59.8	59.5	6.6	2.6	0.7	0.5	29.9	21.2	0.2	7.8	0.6	..
	2005	(e)950	71.0	54.5	54.0	15.0	0.2	1.3	2.3	26.8	19.9	0.1	3.9	2.8	..
	2012	(e)2 800	65.3	51.3	50.8	12.7	0.3	1.0	2.4	32.4	21.1	0.7	9.4	1.2	..
Chile - Chili	1995	14 903	58.3	22.5	21.4	25.5	6.8	3.6	0.3	40.6	2.1	27.8	10.5	0.1	0.0
	2005	32 926	38.0	16.4	15.8	15.6	3.9	2.1	0.3	57.4	4.9	35.5	16.9	0.1	0.0
	2012	79 462	42.3	14.0	13.4	22.9	3.3	2.1	0.1	54.0	0.5	28.0	25.2	0.5	0.0
China - Chine	1995	132 083	55.8	17.3	16.5	12.2	22.0	4.3	3.7	38.7	1.1	2.2	33.9	1.4	0.1
	2005	659 953	38.5	12.0	11.2	7.4	15.2	4.0	3.2	58.3	3.2	4.0	47.4	3.6	0.1
	2012	1 818 199	36.6	13.1	11.7	7.4	9.8	6.4	4.0	59.0	6.2	6.9	39.2	6.6	0.1
China, Hong Kong SAR - Chine (RAS de Hong Kong) (2)	1995	196 072	37.1	12.2	10.8	7.9	14.6	2.3	0.3	62.7	0.8	0.6	60.6	0.6	0.0
	2005	300 160	26.7	8.9	7.6	5.2	11.0	1.6	0.2	73.2	0.4	0.7	71.4	0.7	0.0
	2012	553 486	26.4	10.5	7.3	6.0	7.7	2.2	0.3	73.3	1.2	1.0	69.9	1.1	0.0
China, Macao SAR - Chine (RAS de Macao)	1995	2 025	35.0	15.1	14.7	7.4	10.5	2.0	0.3	64.7	0.4	0.2	63.5	0.6	..
	2005	4 514	27.0	12.2	11.4	4.0	9.4	1.3	0.2	72.8	0.4	0.4	71.7	0.4	0.0
	2012	8 982	44.3	31.6	23.7	5.5	5.9	1.3	0.1	55.5	0.3	0.8	53.9	0.6	0.0
China, Taiwan Province of - Province chinoise de Taiwan	1995	103 506	70.1	16.3	14.8	20.1	29.2	4.5	1.8	27.7	1.8	2.3	20.3	3.3	0.0
	2005	181 592	51.5	10.7	9.7	11.6	25.3	4.0	1.3	45.6	2.0	1.9	32.8	8.8	0.1
	2012	270 863	40.2	9.2	8.3	8.8	17.6	4.6	1.7	56.3	3.5	2.6	35.0	15.1	0.1
Colombia - Colombie	1995	13 883	68.1	20.9	19.3	33.9	8.9	4.5	0.6	30.2	0.3	24.8	4.9	0.1	0.0
	2005	21 204	49.1	14.9	13.8	28.5	3.3	2.4	1.0	48.2	0.4	33.1	14.6	0.1	0.0
	2012	58 088	43.0	13.5	12.6	24.3	2.8	2.3	0.9	55.1	0.3	30.3	24.0	0.5	0.0
Comoros - Comores	1995	62	72.5	70.3	70.0	0.5	1.7	0.0	0.0	27.5	16.4	0.1	8.9	2.0	0.1
	2005	(e)99	36.7	35.7	35.6	0.2	0.3	0.5	0.4	62.8	24.2	2.2	17.8	18.6	0.0
	2012	(e)273	28.0	26.5	26.5	0.5	0.7	0.3	0.3	71.7	14.0	0.3	41.3	16.1	..
Congo	1995	(e)670	74.4	65.6	64.9	7.1	1.5	0.2	0.0	11.0	6.5	0.2	4.3	0.1	..
	2005	(e)1 166	55.8	47.6	47.0	6.8	0.5	0.9	0.3	43.9	14.1	5.1	22.9	1.8	..
	2012	(e)5 680	44.4	37.3	36.1	5.7	0.4	1.1	0.2	48.9	12.5	7.4	23.3	5.7	0.0
Cook Islands - Îles Cook	1995	(e)49	89.7	24.0	24.0	1.9	2.0	61.8	0.2	10.1	..	0.5	9.6	..	..
	2005	(e)81	92.4	5.8	5.8	1.5	2.7	82.5	0.0	7.6	0.0	0.0	5.9	0.0	1.6
	2012	(e)116	73.2	4.9	4.3	4.0	1.1	63.2	0.0	26.8	0.2	0.2	12.3	0.5	13.7
Costa Rica	1995	(e)4 090	67.3	13.8	13.0	48.6	3.4	1.5	0.3	32.4	0.1	27.0	5.3	0.0	0.0
	2005	9 173	64.5	13.4	12.7	42.8	5.8	2.5	0.6	34.9	0.0	26.2	8.6	0.1	0.0
	2012	(e)17 578	65.3	6.8	6.2	49.0	6.5	2.9	0.1	34.6	0.6	22.0	11.7	0.3	0.0
Côte d'Ivoire	1995	(e)2 946	52.4	43.4	42.5	4.0	4.2	0.8	1.6	29.9	17.8	2.3	9.2	0.6	0.0
	2005	5 865	46.4	42.6	41.4	2.0	1.4	0.4	1.4	51.9	30.3	3.4	16.8	1.4	0.0
	2012	(e)9 777	32.4	26.9	26.4	2.7	2.0	0.7	1.0	66.6	34.4	5.7	23.0	2.2	1.3
Croatia - Croatie	1995	7 509	86.3	82.0	79.1	2.7	1.1	0.5	3.6	10.1	3.5	1.9	3.6	1.0	0.0
	2005	18 560	73.6	69.7	67.9	2.2	1.5	0.3	13.9	12.5	1.0	1.6	7.9	2.0	0.0
	2012	20 834	68.6	65.0	62.5	2.2	0.9	0.4	16.2	15.2	0.9	2.0	10.7	1.7	0.0
Cuba	1995	(e)2 805	48.0	38.4	38.0	0.2	0.8	8.6	13.4	38.5	1.7	27.8	8.8	0.3	..
	2005	(e)8 084	41.2	25.9	25.6	5.8	2.9	6.7	2.6	56.0	2.8	38.5	14.5	0.1	0.1
	2012	(e)13 606	28.9	20.4	20.1	4.2	0.2	4.1	1.9	69.2	4.4	52.7	12.0	0.1	0.0
Cyprus - Chypre	1995	3 694	77.0	54.8	53.4	13.0	6.7	2.5	4.8	14.9	0.9	1.3	10.5	2.3	0.0
	2005	6 382	79.9	67.8	66.7	1.6	3.1	7.5	3.1	15.4	1.4	2.9	8.2	3.0	0.0
	2012	7 377	83.5	69.4	68.0	1.3	0.7	12.2	2.7	13.4	0.9	2.7	8.0	1.7	0.0
Czech Republic - République tchèque	1995	25 303	85.7	81.5	79.2	2.6	1.2	0.5	9.9	4.4	0.3	0.6	3.2	0.3	0.0
	2005	76 527	83.9	78.8	76.5	2.1	2.6	0.5	7.2	8.8	0.5	0.6	7.1	0.6	0.0
	2012	139 131	80.0	76.7	74.9	1.6	1.4	0.3	6.4	13.5	0.4	0.5	12.0	0.7	0.0
Dem. Rep. of the Congo - Rép. dém. du Congo	1995	871	50.1	40.3	39.4	6.4	0.9	2.4	0.0	49.8	27.8	0.8	21.1	0.1	..
	2005	2 690	47.4	41.0	40.1	4.2	1.1	1.2	0.2	52.4	44.1	1.9	5.9	0.5	..
	2012	(e)6 100	36.6	30.2	29.6	4.3	1.4	0.8	0.5	62.9	37.2	1.9	23.3	0.5	..
Denmark - Danemark	1995	43 142	84.7	76.1	68.8	4.5	2.6	1.4	1.1	8.2	0.5	1.5	5.9	0.4	0.0
	2005	74 265	82.9	77.8	71.6	2.7	1.0	1.4	2.2	14.6	0.5	1.6	10.1	2.2	0.1
	2012	91 907	83.0	78.7	70.7	2.6	0.5	1.3	1.2	15.7	1.1	2.0	10.8	1.8	0.0

For sources and notes, see end of table.

Pour les sources et les notes, se reporter à la fin du tableau.

Origin / Origine (Destination)	Year / Année	World (millions of dollars) (1) / Monde (millions de dollars) (1)	Developed economies / Économies développées Total	Europe Total	Europe EU UE	USA États-Unis	Japan Japon	Other Autres	Transition economies / Économies en transition	Developing economies / Économies en développement Total	Africa Afrique	America Amérique	Eastern, Southern and South-Eastern Asia / Asie orientale, méridionale et du Sud-Est	Western Asia / Asie occidentale	Oceania Océanie
Djibouti	1995	(e)177	44.7	35.5	34.9	2.6	5.5	1.1	0.0	55.3	11.9	1.7	36.1	5.6	..
	2005	(e)277	20.5	12.0	11.9	4.0	3.7	0.8	0.9	78.6	6.9	0.6	33.8	37.3	..
	2012	(e)580	15.3	8.9	8.8	4.3	1.7	0.5	4.0	80.6	8.6	2.1	60.5	9.4	..
Dominica - Dominique	1995	117	66.8	26.9	25.8	33.1	4.6	2.2	0.4	32.3	0.1	30.7	1.5	0.1	..
	2005	165	57.7	13.8	13.4	36.6	4.6	2.7	0.0	41.5	0.3	37.6	3.6	0.0	0.0
	2012	212	50.6	9.1	9.0	36.8	2.4	2.4	0.0	40.7	0.1	37.3	3.2	0.1	..
Dominican Republic - République dominicaine	1995	(e)5 170	77.4	9.4	9.0	63.8	2.7	1.4	0.0	22.6	0.0	18.2	4.3	0.1	..
	2005	(e)9 869	63.3	10.0	9.6	48.4	3.5	1.3	0.3	36.4	0.1	30.8	5.4	0.1	0.0
	2012	(e)18 491	55.9	10.7	10.3	43.9	0.3	1.0	0.2	43.9	0.2	31.8	11.4	0.4	0.1
Ecuador - Équateur	1995	4 195	58.5	16.8	15.8	30.7	8.6	2.3	0.0	39.3	0.8	32.6	5.6	0.3	0.0
	2005	9 609	36.0	11.6	11.0	19.2	3.6	1.6	1.0	62.7	1.1	46.8	14.0	0.7	0.0
	2012	(e)25 197	45.7	12.8	12.2	28.7	2.9	1.4	0.7	53.5	1.0	32.5	19.6	0.4	0.0
Egypt - Égypte	1995	11 739	68.7	44.3	42.3	18.6	4.0	1.8	4.0	23.2	1.9	3.7	13.5	4.1	0.0
	2005	(e)22 449	45.9	31.2	30.1	9.8	2.5	2.4	7.0	37.1	4.1	5.4	14.9	12.7	0.0
	2012	69 866	41.8	29.7	28.5	7.7	2.4	2.0	10.1	48.1	3.4	5.8	23.0	15.9	0.0
El Salvador	1995	(e)3 329	61.0	10.9	10.3	44.0	5.1	1.0	0.1	36.6	0.2	31.2	5.2	0.0	0.0
	2005	6 809	47.7	8.5	8.0	35.8	2.1	1.4	0.7	51.6	0.2	41.9	9.4	0.0	0.0
	2012	10 270	47.1	8.2	7.9	36.7	1.4	0.8	0.3	52.5	0.4	40.7	11.4	0.1	0.0
Equatorial Guinea - Guinée équatoriale	1995	121	63.2	55.5	54.0	6.7	0.4	0.6	..	35.2	29.4	1.5	4.3	0.0	..
	2005	1 310	80.9	53.7	52.5	25.2	0.6	1.4	0.3	18.8	12.7	1.0	3.3	1.7	..
	2012	(e)7 500	61.6	48.8	48.3	11.2	0.3	1.4	0.7	37.7	4.4	6.3	22.9	4.1	0.0
Eritrea - Érythrée	1995	(e)434	73.6	40.5	39.2	12.4	20.7	0.0	1.3	25.1	0.4	..	10.3	14.4	..
	2005	(e)482	61.4	49.3	48.6	11.0	0.4	0.8	7.0	31.5	5.5	3.9	6.5	15.6	..
	2012	(e)818	32.0	29.4	28.5	1.3	0.3	1.0	0.1	67.9	22.0	1.2	22.1	22.6	..
Estonia - Estonie	1995	2 546	78.4	73.1	71.7	3.9	1.1	0.3	18.5	3.1	0.1	1.0	1.8	0.2	0.0
	2005	11 018	73.6	69.0	67.6	1.6	2.7	0.3	17.8	8.6	0.4	0.6	7.0	0.6	0.0
	2012	19 597	73.4	71.0	68.9	1.1	1.1	0.3	15.7	10.9	0.8	0.5	8.8	0.8	0.0
Ethiopia - Éthiopie	1995	1 141	60.6	38.8	37.0	12.9	8.4	0.4	0.2	30.0	6.6	0.2	9.7	13.5	..
	2005	4 095	40.5	25.6	24.8	9.2	3.6	2.1	2.3	57.1	6.2	0.9	24.8	25.2	0.0
	2012	(e)12 656	39.0	18.8	18.4	16.6	1.7	1.9	3.3	57.7	5.9	0.7	32.7	18.5	..
Faeroe Islands - Îles Féroé	1995	(e)314	92.1	86.5	65.9	2.3	3.0	0.3	0.9	4.3	0.0	0.6	3.0	0.1	0.5
	2005	747	90.3	79.2	59.4	8.6	1.8	0.7	0.2	9.1	0.1	1.2	4.9	0.5	2.4
	2012	(e)1 149	98.3	97.6	59.8	0.1	..	0.6	0.2	1.5	0.0	0.9	0.5	0.0	..
Falkland Islands (Malvinas) - Îles Falkland (Malvinas)	1995	(e)44	98.1	97.2	97.1	0.7	0.1	0.1	0.1	1.6	0.4	..	1.2	..	..
	2005	(e)60	99.9	97.3	97.2	2.4	0.0	0.2	..	0.1	0.0	0.0	0.1	0.0	..
	2012	130	99.3	95.7	94.5	3.1	0.0	0.4	0.1	0.7	0.1	0.0	0.6	0.0	..
Fiji - Fidji	1995	(e)892	77.9	4.5	4.3	4.8	6.4	62.1	..	21.3	0.0	0.2	21.0	0.0	0.0
	2005	1 607	54.2	3.4	3.2	3.8	4.2	42.8	0.0	44.4	0.3	0.3	43.3	0.1	0.4
	2012	2 253	40.7	2.7	2.2	3.0	2.2	32.7	0.0	54.7	0.3	0.3	53.5	0.2	0.5
Finland - Finlande	1995	29 520	82.2	67.1	61.2	7.2	6.4	1.6	7.5	8.4	0.5	1.9	5.8	0.2	0.0
	2005	58 473	70.5	61.7	58.4	4.1	3.3	1.4	14.5	14.5	0.5	2.2	11.1	0.7	0.0
	2012	76 089	60.5	55.0	50.3	3.1	1.2	1.1	18.7	17.2	1.1	2.8	12.5	0.8	0.0
France (3)	1995	275 510	73.1	60.3	56.3	7.8	3.5	1.5	1.5	14.8	3.9	2.1	7.2	1.7	0.1
	2005	475 857	76.8	67.0	62.9	5.9	2.7	1.1	3.0	20.1	4.7	1.8	11.0	2.5	0.0
	2012	663 269	71.4	62.0	58.5	6.4	1.8	1.2	4.0	24.0	5.6	1.9	13.5	3.0	0.0
French Polynesia - Polynésie française	1995	(e)1 019	84.3	52.3	51.9	14.0	3.6	14.5	0.0	10.3	0.3	0.9	8.5	0.1	0.5
	2005	1 702	73.6	49.9	49.5	10.0	2.9	10.8	0.0	26.4	0.3	1.0	24.4	0.2	0.5
	2012	1 706	62.7	37.7	37.1	9.7	1.8	13.5	0.0	37.3	0.6	1.3	34.7	0.3	0.4
Gabon	1995	(e)884	78.6	61.2	60.7	10.4	6.0	1.0	0.1	12.2	5.7	1.3	4.8	0.4	0.0
	2005	1 451	76.9	66.7	65.4	6.6	2.9	0.6	0.1	23.0	11.2	2.8	7.4	1.7	0.0
	2012	(e)3 631	64.2	51.1	50.8	9.6	2.2	1.3	0.2	35.6	12.0	2.5	19.0	2.1	0.0
Gambia - Gambie	1995	(e)182	49.5	43.4	43.0	3.0	3.0	0.2	0.2	50.3	13.0	3.0	33.5	0.8	..
	2005	260	32.5	25.4	25.2	5.4	0.8	0.9	0.6	66.8	23.5	6.0	32.9	4.4	0.0
	2012	(e)380	23.1	19.1	18.7	3.1	0.6	0.3	0.2	76.7	17.6	10.4	42.3	6.4	..
Georgia - Géorgie	1995	(e)412	38.7	34.0	32.9	4.3	0.0	0.4	39.8	16.0	0.1	0.7	3.0	12.3	..
	2005	2 490	36.8	29.7	28.9	6.0	0.3	0.8	39.5	21.9	0.2	3.5	3.8	14.4	0.0
	2012	7 840	39.7	32.0	30.9	2.7	4.0	1.0	25.5	34.8	0.7	2.1	12.1	19.9	0.0

For sources and notes, see end of table.

Pour les sources et les notes, se reporter à la fin du tableau.

Origin / Origine / Destination	Year / Année	World (millions of dollars) (1) / Monde (millions de dollars) (1)	Developed economies / Économies développées — Total	Europe Total	Europe EU / UE	USA / États-Unis	Japan / Japon	Other / Autres	Transition economies / Économies en transition	Developing economies / Économies en développement — Total	Africa / Afrique	America / Amérique	Eastern, Southern and South-Eastern Asia / Asie orientale, méridionale et du Sud-Est	Western Asia / Asie occidentale	Oceania / Océanie
Germany - Allemagne	1995	464 145	82.3	68.7	62.8	6.8	5.3	1.4	2.6	15.0	2.1	2.3	9.0	1.6	0.1
	2005	779 819	76.3	65.3	59.1	6.7	3.5	0.9	4.5	19.0	2.2	2.2	12.8	1.8	0.1
	2012	1 173 288	72.2	63.0	55.8	5.7	2.5	1.0	5.9	21.8	2.6	2.7	14.7	1.8	0.0
Ghana	1995	(e)1 896	68.8	46.7	45.2	13.1	6.4	2.6	0.3	20.0	5.4	3.6	10.2	0.7	0.0
	2005	4 878	43.9	31.5	30.7	6.5	2.0	3.8	0.9	55.3	25.0	4.8	23.8	1.7	0.0
	2012	(e)18 000	37.4	25.5	25.0	7.8	1.2	2.8	1.2	61.3	16.4	2.5	40.1	2.5	0.0
Gibraltar	1995	411	94.7	86.8	84.3	2.9	4.9	0.1	0.8	4.3	1.1	0.1	2.4	0.7	..
	2005	(e)551	82.4	73.8	73.2	4.5	1.5	2.6	15.1	2.4	0.7	0.1	0.4	1.2	..
	2012	860	94.4	65.2	64.8	27.7	0.4	1.1	2.6	3.1	0.6	0.0	1.9	0.6	..
Greece - Grèce	1995	25 927	82.5	75.7	73.7	3.2	2.6	1.0	3.5	14.0	3.1	1.8	6.8	2.2	0.0
	2005	54 894	66.5	60.3	58.6	3.4	2.1	0.8	10.1	23.2	2.6	1.5	12.6	6.6	0.0
	2012	62 341	48.8	46.7	45.0	1.2	0.3	0.7	17.7	33.0	5.8	1.6	13.8	11.9	0.1
Greenland - Groenland	1995	421	98.4	93.2	85.2	1.8	2.1	1.3	0.1	1.6	0.1	0.2	1.3	0.0	0.0
	2005	(e)593	99.4	96.3	93.6	0.7	0.0	2.4	..	0.6	0.0	0.0	0.5	0.0	..
	2012	(e)901	99.4	96.0	92.0	2.0	0.0	1.4	0.1	0.6	0.0	0.0	0.5	0.0	0.0
Grenada - Grenade	1995	129	65.0	15.9	15.4	41.5	3.2	4.5	0.0	34.6	0.0	31.8	2.7	0.1	0.0
	2005	334	59.1	14.5	14.0	37.5	4.0	3.1	0.0	40.9	0.1	35.0	5.7	0.1	0.0
	2012	(e)335	51.0	12.0	11.4	32.0	3.7	3.4	0.0	49.0	0.1	43.2	5.6	0.2	0.0
Guam	1995	(e)442	..	..	..	..	..	..	..	..	..	..	..	..	..
	2005	(e)533	21.3	5.5	5.5	..	13.4	2.4	0.0	78.7	0.0	0.1	78.5	0.0	0.0
	2012	(e)1 200	19.3	5.8	4.9	..	11.6	1.9	6.6	74.1	0.0	0.1	73.8	0.1	0.0
Guatemala	1995	3 292	61.8	11.3	10.7	44.9	3.7	2.0	0.8	37.4	0.1	33.5	3.8	0.0	0.0
	2005	10 500	49.8	9.6	7.9	33.9	3.8	2.6	1.1	48.8	0.1	32.0	16.7	0.1	0.0
	2012	16 979	48.0	7.4	6.4	38.1	1.6	0.9	0.6	50.5	0.2	35.0	14.9	0.4	0.0
Guinea - Guinée	1995	819	62.7	48.3	47.5	8.0	6.0	0.5	1.0	36.3	14.4	5.2	16.0	0.7	0.0
	2005	(e)820	48.3	35.8	35.1	10.2	1.2	1.0	2.5	49.2	20.4	2.1	23.3	3.5	0.0
	2012	(e)2 300	54.0	44.8	44.5	4.7	1.4	3.2	1.6	44.4	11.7	2.9	25.7	4.1	0.0
Guinea-Bissau - Guinée-Bissau	1995	(e)133	56.4	48.5	48.0	0.7	7.1	0.1	0.2	43.4	7.3	0.7	35.4	0.0	..
	2005	(e)112	59.3	57.8	57.0	1.2	0.2	0.1	0.1	40.6	28.0	3.6	8.9	0.1	..
	2012	(e)227	53.5	46.8	46.0	6.6	0.1	0.0	0.1	46.4	25.5	6.8	13.5	0.7	..
Guyana	1995	(e)528	61.0	12.8	12.6	35.6	8.6	3.9	0.0	37.5	0.2	32.0	5.2	0.1	..
	2005	778	45.6	8.5	8.4	31.1	3.0	3.0	0.0	54.4	0.2	46.5	7.3	0.4	0.0
	2012	(e)1 885	36.7	8.1	8.0	22.3	3.4	3.0	0.3	63.0	0.8	42.0	19.2	1.0	..
Haiti - Haïti	1995	(e)654	81.0	12.2	11.6	61.7	4.3	2.8	0.0	17.1	0.1	12.5	4.5	0.0	..
	2005	(e)1 466	75.6	8.9	8.4	61.6	3.1	2.0	0.1	23.7	0.1	13.9	9.0	0.8	..
	2012	(e)3 196	75.6	8.7	8.3	61.7	3.2	2.0	0.1	23.8	0.1	13.9	9.0	0.8	..
Honduras	1995	1 728	69.7	12.4	11.5	53.0	3.6	0.8	0.1	30.1	0.1	23.9	6.0	0.0	0.0
	2005	(e)6 545	55.5	7.3	6.9	45.6	1.8	0.8	0.5	44.0	0.2	37.5	6.3	0.1	0.0
	2012	(e)11 179	51.4	5.3	5.1	44.3	1.3	0.5	0.6	48.0	0.2	38.7	8.9	0.2	0.0
Hungary - Hongrie	1995	15 186	78.4	72.5	69.8	3.1	2.2	0.6	14.8	6.7	1.0	1.5	3.9	0.3	0.0
	2005	65 920	76.4	71.0	69.9	1.7	3.4	0.3	9.7	13.8	0.1	0.4	12.6	0.7	0.0
	2012	94 266	75.4	70.9	70.2	2.0	1.3	1.1	11.8	12.9	0.1	0.8	11.3	0.6	0.0
Iceland - Islande	1995	1 751	91.2	73.9	62.3	8.4	4.4	4.5	2.4	6.3	0.2	0.7	5.3	0.1	0.0
	2005	4 979	87.7	71.1	62.1	9.3	5.3	2.0	0.6	11.7	0.4	1.8	8.5	1.0	0.0
	2012	4 772	76.1	62.7	44.8	10.2	1.5	1.6	0.9	23.0	0.9	9.8	11.3	1.1	0.0
India - Inde	1995	36 592	57.6	35.5	33.2	10.2	7.2	4.6	3.5	38.9	5.4	1.7	19.7	12.1	0.0
	2005	140 862	47.2	28.5	24.5	8.0	3.5	7.1	3.0	49.8	4.0	2.8	31.9	11.0	0.1
	2012	488 976	26.4	14.9	11.3	5.1	2.5	4.0	2.1	71.4	8.6	5.9	29.4	27.5	0.0
Indonesia (...2002) - Indonésie (...2002)	1995	(e)40 645	62.0	21.6	20.5	9.4	24.9	6.1	0.5	37.5	0.9	2.1	31.8	2.7	0.0
Indonesia - Indonésie	2005	(e)75 725	31.1	9.0	8.6	5.0	11.8	5.2	0.9	68.0	2.2	1.7	57.6	6.3	0.1
	2012	191 691	26.7	6.9	6.6	5.0	10.9	3.9	2.1	71.2	2.7	2.3	60.3	5.7	0.1
Iran (Islamic Rep. of) - Iran (Rép. islamique d')	1995	(e)13 882	51.3	36.6	32.8	0.3	6.2	8.2	8.2	30.3	1.0	9.2	12.9	7.2	..
	2005	38 675	47.6	43.3	40.8	0.2	3.2	1.0	8.0	43.6	0.6	2.8	20.7	19.6	..
	2012	(e)63 155	25.3	21.9	19.6	0.3	2.4	0.7	6.3	68.5	0.4	3.5	30.1	34.5	..
Iraq	1995	(e)2 891	22.0	21.4	14.5	0.0	0.0	0.5	0.1	77.9	0.6	0.0	11.5	65.7	..
	2005	(e)23 532	32.7	18.3	17.9	10.9	1.2	2.2	2.5	64.8	0.8	0.7	10.6	52.7	0.0
	2012	(e)57 000	23.3	15.6	14.7	5.4	1.0	1.4	4.3	72.3	1.6	1.1	24.2	45.4	0.0

For sources and notes, see end of table.

Pour les sources et les notes, se reporter à la fin du tableau.

Origin / Origine	Year / Année	World (millions of dollars) (1) / Monde (millions de dollars) (1)	Developed economies / Économies développées						Transition economies / Économies en transition	Developing economies / Économies en développement					
			Total	Europe		USA États-Unis	Japan Japon	Other Autres		Total	Africa Afrique	America Amérique	Eastern, Southern and South-Eastern Asia / Asie orientale, méridionale et du Sud-Est	Western Asia / Asie occiden-tale	Oceania Océanie
				Total	EU UE										
Destination								Percentage / En pourcentage							
Ireland - Irlande	1995	32 321	82.8	58.8	56.7	17.7	5.3	1.0	0.2	12.9	1.2	0.7	10.7	0.3	0.0
	2005	70 284	79.0	60.1	56.5	14.1	3.7	1.0	0.2	17.6	0.7	0.9	15.1	0.8	0.0
	2012	63 100	78.3	62.9	58.9	13.0	1.5	0.9	0.3	17.4	3.9	2.4	10.4	0.7	0.0
Israel - Israël	1995	28 344	82.0	59.1	52.9	18.6	3.3	1.1	1.0	9.9	1.4	0.9	6.7	0.9	0.0
	2005	45 032	61.9	44.7	39.1	13.5	2.7	1.0	3.0	20.8	0.7	2.2	15.1	2.9	0.0
	2012	73 112	56.1	40.2	34.4	12.9	2.4	0.7	1.5	22.9	0.5	1.3	18.0	3.2	0.0
Italy - Italie	1995	200 320	79.4	70.4	65.4	4.9	2.2	1.8	4.0	16.6	5.4	2.5	6.7	2.0	0.0
	2005	384 836	68.3	62.1	58.7	3.4	1.6	1.2	5.1	22.3	6.2	2.5	9.8	3.8	0.0
	2012	486 653	61.2	56.0	52.6	3.3	0.8	1.0	9.8	28.6	9.3	2.6	11.4	5.2	0.0
Jamaica - Jamaïque	1995	2 773	73.8	12.0	11.1	50.7	6.7	4.4	0.1	22.5	0.1	17.5	3.7	1.3	0.0
	2005	4 885	57.5	8.1	7.2	41.6	4.4	3.5	0.1	41.0	0.5	34.4	5.7	0.3	0.0
	2012	6 580	48.1	6.9	5.8	35.7	3.2	2.3	0.0	50.2	0.1	41.5	7.9	0.7	0.0
Japan - Japon	1995	336 094	47.6	16.3	14.7	22.6	..	8.7	1.5	50.9	1.4	3.4	37.5	8.3	0.4
	2005	515 866	32.5	12.6	11.4	12.7	..	7.1	1.3	66.2	1.9	2.8	46.4	14.9	0.2
	2012	885 843	27.7	10.6	9.4	8.8	..	8.3	2.5	69.8	2.4	3.8	45.2	18.2	0.2
Jordan - Jordanie	1995	3 696	49.6	35.0	33.4	9.3	3.5	1.7	2.8	45.0	2.8	2.9	14.9	24.4	..
	2005	10 455	36.9	26.0	24.6	5.6	2.8	2.5	4.2	58.9	4.6	1.8	20.1	32.3	0.0
	2012	(e)20 004	29.1	18.4	17.6	6.7	1.9	2.1	7.0	63.9	4.8	3.3	20.1	35.7	0.0
Kazakhstan	1995	3 805	20.1	17.6	16.6	1.7	0.3	0.5	70.3	9.7	0.0	0.5	5.6	3.5	0.0
	2005	17 333	33.8	25.8	24.9	4.8	2.2	1.1	44.6	21.6	0.2	1.0	17.3	3.0	0.0
	2012	44 538	24.8	19.9	19.3	2.8	1.5	0.6	44.0	31.2	0.3	0.7	27.6	2.6	0.0
Kenya	1995	2 818	56.2	41.2	40.0	3.9	9.4	1.6	0.3	43.5	9.8	1.8	21.2	10.7	..
	2005	5 846	38.2	21.5	20.6	10.4	4.4	1.8	1.3	60.6	13.0	1.7	23.4	22.4	0.0
	2012	(e)16 290	28.4	17.8	17.0	4.0	5.2	1.5	1.7	69.9	13.8	1.1	37.2	17.9	0.0
Kiribati	1995	(e)34	68.4	9.7	9.6	5.5	5.7	47.5	0.1	30.6	..	0.2	10.7	..	19.7
	2005	(e)74	61.9	1.4	1.0	3.1	16.7	40.7	..	38.1	0.0	0.5	11.6	..	26.0
	2012	(e)109	47.8	0.8	0.6	3.0	24.1	19.9	0.0	52.2	0.5	0.1	31.2	0.1	20.3
Korea, Dem. People's Rep. of - Corée, Rép. populaire dém. de	1995	(e)1 380	38.6	17.9	17.5	0.4	20.2	0.1	0.1	60.3	0.1	5.2	54.5	0.6	..
	2005	(e)2 718	12.4	8.9	8.7	0.2	2.6	0.7	9.6	78.0	1.3	7.4	59.8	9.5	0.0
	2012	(e)4 750	1.8	1.5	1.4	0.3	..	0.1	1.8	96.4	0.3	0.8	95.2	0.0	0.0
Korea, Republic of - Corée, République de	1995	135 113	68.0	15.0	13.7	22.5	24.1	6.4	1.7	29.6	1.7	2.9	17.3	7.4	0.2
	2005	261 236	46.8	11.2	10.5	11.8	18.5	5.3	1.7	51.4	1.3	2.6	31.0	16.4	0.1
	2012	519 576	37.8	11.2	9.7	8.4	12.4	5.9	2.5	59.7	1.5	3.7	31.9	22.5	0.1
Kuwait - Koweït	1995	7 790	68.3	40.2	38.9	16.1	9.4	2.7	0.3	31.3	1.4	1.6	15.3	13.0	..
	2005	(e)15 800	62.8	36.4	34.6	14.3	8.5	3.6	0.3	36.9	0.6	1.8	18.3	16.2	0.0
	2012	(e)25 880	46.2	23.2	21.1	11.8	8.2	3.0	0.4	53.4	1.4	2.0	29.2	20.8	0.0
Kyrgyzstan - Kirghizistan	1995	522	14.6	8.4	7.8	3.7	1.4	1.2	67.7	15.4	..	4.4	3.6	7.5	..
	2005	1 108	20.1	11.4	10.9	6.1	1.1	1.6	61.9	18.0	0.2	0.7	13.5	3.6	0.0
	2012	5 373	20.1	10.6	10.3	4.7	4.0	0.7	50.0	29.9	0.2	0.4	25.8	3.5	..
Lao People's Dem. Rep. - Rép. dém. populaire lao	1995	589	18.8	9.9	9.8	0.3	5.0	3.7	..	81.0	0.0	0.0	80.9	0.1	..
	2005	882	8.8	4.3	4.1	0.9	1.7	2.0	1.0	90.2	0.2	0.0	90.0	0.0	..
	2012	2 467	9.7	5.6	5.6	0.6	2.6	0.9	0.1	90.2	0.0	0.0	90.1	0.1	0.0
Latvia - Lettonie	1995	1 818	69.9	66.0	64.3	1.9	0.6	1.4	28.2	1.8	0.1	0.6	0.9	0.2	..
	2005	8 770	78.1	76.4	74.0	1.1	0.3	0.4	18.0	3.9	0.1	0.3	2.9	0.7	0.0
	2012	15 901	79.4	78.4	77.1	0.8	0.1	0.2	15.3	5.3	0.1	0.1	4.5	0.5	0.0
Lebanon - Liban	1995	(e)7 278	71.3	57.5	53.0	9.7	2.9	1.1	3.1	25.2	2.2	2.1	11.1	9.8	0.0
	2005	(e)9 327	59.7	50.2	46.3	5.9	2.7	0.8	6.8	33.5	4.5	2.5	13.5	12.9	0.0
	2012	(e)21 147	52.6	42.2	39.5	8.2	1.4	0.8	7.4	40.0	6.9	3.0	14.9	15.3	0.0
Lesotho	1995	(e)1 107	3.0	2.0	2.0	0.4	0.5	0.1	0.0	96.9	74.4	0.1	22.4	0.1	..
	2005	(e)1 390	9.5	7.3	7.3	1.6	0.4	0.2	0.0	90.5	7.4	0.6	82.2	0.3	..
	2012	(e)2 600	5.4	2.8	2.8	1.3	1.2	0.0	..	94.6	74.2	0.0	20.3	0.1	..
Liberia - Libéria	1995	(e)510	68.7	33.0	31.4	0.8	34.8	0.1	2.0	29.3	0.7	1.0	27.4	0.2	..
	2005	310	34.6	12.2	10.7	1.4	20.8	0.2	4.8	60.6	2.3	0.3	56.6	1.4	..
	2012	1 066	21.2	4.3	4.0	1.6	15.1	0.1	0.8	78.1	0.3	0.3	76.6	0.9	..
Libya - Libye	1995	(e)5 033	72.6	64.9	62.6	0.5	5.2	2.1	0.3	27.1	9.1	1.8	9.4	6.9	..
	2005	(e)6 082	62.9	58.6	56.7	1.0	2.2	1.1	3.3	33.8	7.9	3.2	13.1	9.5	..
	2012	(e)23 000	44.2	38.7	37.6	3.1	1.0	1.3	3.4	52.4	13.2	3.0	21.5	14.7	..

For sources and notes, see end of table.

Pour les sources et les notes, se reporter à la fin du tableau.

Origin / Origine — Destination	Year / Année	World (millions of dollars) (1) / Monde (millions de dollars) (1)	Developed economies / Économies développées — Total	Europe Total	Europe EU UE	USA États-Unis	Japan Japon	Other Autres	Transition economies / Économies en transition	Developing economies / Économies en développement — Total	Africa Afrique	America Amérique	Eastern, Southern and South-Eastern Asia / Asie orientale, méridionale et du Sud-Est	Western Asia / Asie occidentale	Oceania Océanie
Lithuania - Lituanie	1995	3 649	55.6	52.8	50.4	1.9	0.2	0.7	40.3	2.2	0.2	1.1	0.6	0.4	..
	2005	15 704	62.7	59.4	58.1	2.6	0.4	0.3	31.1	6.2	0.3	0.7	4.6	0.7	0.0
	2012	32 238	58.9	57.6	56.8	1.0	0.1	0.2	36.4	4.5	0.6	0.4	3.0	0.5	0.0
Luxembourg	1995	(e)8 983	95.9	72.1	66.9	19.8	3.7	0.2	0.3	3.8	0.5	2.0	1.2	0.1	0.0
	2005	(e)21 893	86.8	82.1	79.8	3.5	0.9	0.3	0.5	12.7	0.2	0.2	11.2	1.1	0.0
	2012	(e)27 555	89.8	80.4	78.9	7.7	1.0	0.7	0.3	9.3	0.1	1.1	7.7	0.3	0.0
Madagascar	1995	(e)628	61.5	52.8	51.7	2.9	5.3	0.5	0.2	35.9	10.9	0.7	22.0	2.2	0.0
	2005	1 686	33.4	28.3	27.8	2.4	2.1	0.6	0.1	66.5	14.7	1.9	33.3	16.7	0.0
	2012	(e)3 050	27.2	22.4	22.2	2.7	0.7	1.4	0.1	72.7	13.4	1.7	38.3	19.2	0.0
Malawi	1995	(e)500	35.8	27.1	26.5	3.3	4.1	1.3	0.0	64.2	52.8	0.5	10.3	0.5	0.0
	2005	(e)1 165	18.9	13.9	13.5	3.5	1.0	0.6	0.3	80.8	64.8	0.5	12.3	3.1	..
	2012	(e)2 724	21.6	14.4	13.4	4.1	2.4	0.6	0.2	78.3	46.3	0.6	26.9	4.4	0.0
Malaysia - Malaisie	1995	77 046	65.1	17.6	15.7	16.3	27.5	3.7	0.3	34.6	0.5	1.2	32.1	0.7	0.1
	2005	114 290	42.9	12.8	11.6	12.9	14.5	2.7	0.5	56.5	0.6	1.6	51.4	3.0	0.0
	2012	196 419	33.3	11.6	10.8	8.1	10.3	3.3	0.4	65.9	1.8	3.3	55.9	4.9	0.1
Maldives	1995	268	23.1	15.6	14.7	0.6	5.1	1.8	0.0	76.6	0.4	0.0	66.5	9.6	..
	2005	745	21.9	15.1	14.2	1.1	1.8	3.8	0.0	78.1	0.5	0.2	58.8	18.6	0.0
	2012	1 555	14.1	7.5	7.0	2.9	0.7	3.0	0.0	85.9	0.5	2.8	51.8	30.9	..
Mali	1995	(e)774	44.0	34.7	34.5	4.6	3.8	0.9	0.1	46.5	33.9	3.5	7.8	1.4	..
	2005	1 544	39.4	34.0	33.7	3.2	0.9	1.3	1.8	58.8	45.9	1.8	9.7	1.4	..
	2012	(e)2 941	35.7	30.6	30.3	2.5	0.6	2.0	1.6	62.7	42.6	1.1	17.7	1.3	0.0
Malta - Malte	1995	2 942	80.2	73.6	72.0	4.2	1.7	0.6	1.2	18.7	4.0	1.0	10.9	2.8	..
	2005	3 865	70.5	64.0	61.8	4.2	1.6	0.7	3.2	26.2	2.8	0.6	18.3	4.5	0.0
	2012	(e)6 598	50.7	44.8	43.4	2.2	2.4	1.3	11.9	37.3	1.2	0.8	30.0	5.3	0.0
Marshall Islands - Îles Marshall	1995	75	97.4	61.9	61.9	5.4	29.8	0.3	0.0	2.2	..	..	2.2	..	0.0
	2005	(e)94	31.6	20.7	19.4	3.2	7.5	0.3	0.6	67.8	0.0	0.0	63.4	4.3	0.0
	2012	(e)140	22.3	5.0	4.2	1.3	15.9	0.1	0.4	77.3	0.0	0.1	76.5	0.8	0.0
Mauritania - Mauritanie	1995	(e)455	70.4	58.4	58.0	6.9	4.6	0.5	0.3	26.8	10.9	0.5	14.8	0.5	..
	2005	(e)1 342	68.0	56.2	54.1	8.1	2.6	1.1	2.1	29.9	8.6	4.7	13.8	2.8	0.0
	2012	(e)3 151	56.2	45.7	45.3	7.8	1.3	1.3	1.0	42.8	9.2	6.5	20.8	6.3	0.0
Mauritius - Maurice	1995	2 000	48.6	36.5	34.0	2.6	4.7	4.8	0.1	50.9	15.1	2.0	29.7	4.2	0.0
	2005	3 160	41.9	32.0	30.7	2.2	3.6	4.1	0.1	58.0	12.0	1.8	30.8	13.4	0.1
	2012	5 772	32.5	23.3	22.4	2.1	2.6	4.5	0.2	67.3	10.5	2.6	51.3	2.8	0.0
Mexico - Mexique	1995	72 453	92.2	10.0	9.4	74.5	5.5	2.2	0.1	7.5	0.2	2.2	5.1	0.0	0.0
	2005	221 819	75.3	12.2	11.7	53.6	5.9	3.5	0.4	24.3	0.3	5.8	17.9	0.3	0.0
	2012	370 746	69.6	11.5	11.0	50.1	4.8	3.2	0.4	30.0	0.4	3.8	25.4	0.4	0.0
Micronesia (Federated States of) - Micronésie (États fédérés de)	1995	89	87.1	7.0	7.0	40.5	28.9	10.7	0.0	12.9	..	0.0	12.9	..	..
	2005	130	65.4	1.2	1.2	40.6	14.3	9.4	..	34.6	0.0	2.6	31.4	..	0.5
	2012	(e)210	63.8	0.7	0.7	38.6	16.8	7.7	..	36.2	0.0	0.2	35.8	..	0.2
Mongolia - Mongolie	1995	(e)415	26.9	12.7	11.4	2.3	11.7	0.2	37.5	24.4	0.0	0.0	24.4	0.0	..
	2005	1 183	23.6	10.3	10.2	3.4	6.4	3.5	41.0	35.4	0.0	0.6	34.5	0.2	..
	2012	(e)6 738	23.6	7.5	7.3	9.4	4.9	1.8	28.5	47.9	0.0	0.2	46.7	0.9	..
Montenegro - Monténégro	2012	2 336	41.5	39.8	38.4	0.8	0.9	0.2	45.5	12.7	0.2	1.5	9.4	1.6	0.0
Montserrat	1995	(e)30	77.8	63.2	63.1	12.9	1.5	0.3	..	22.2	0.1	21.5	0.5	0.0	..
	2005	(e)30	72.2	19.8	19.7	45.5	4.1	2.8	0.0	27.8	0.0	24.5	2.6	0.7	..
	2012	(e)37	89.8	14.6	14.3	69.6	2.4	3.2	..	10.2	0.5	7.8	1.9	..	..
Morocco - Maroc	1995	(e)10 023	60.7	52.0	50.8	5.6	1.2	1.9	3.8	20.7	5.0	3.6	6.0	6.1	..
	2005	20 803	61.0	54.6	53.2	3.3	1.7	1.3	8.0	30.8	5.3	4.2	11.3	9.9	0.0
	2012	44 790	57.5	48.4	47.4	6.4	1.5	1.2	8.5	34.0	5.1	4.5	11.1	13.4	0.0
Mozambique	1995	(e)727	34.2	23.9	23.2	5.6	2.8	1.8	0.0	65.8	52.7	1.7	9.1	2.2	..
	2005	(e)2 408	31.6	18.4	17.8	2.7	1.5	9.1	0.2	68.1	46.9	2.7	15.1	3.5	0.0
	2012	(e)6 177	26.0	13.6	13.3	5.4	1.9	5.1	0.6	73.4	33.4	3.4	33.3	3.2	0.0
Myanmar	1995	(e)1 348	14.4	6.7	6.5	0.7	6.3	0.7	0.5	84.3	0.0	0.0	84.2	0.1	..
	2005	(e)1 952	7.3	2.3	2.2	0.4	3.9	0.8	2.1	90.3	0.0	0.1	90.1	0.0	..
	2012	(e)9 201	8.0	1.0	0.8	0.5	4.9	1.6	0.8	90.9	0.0	0.2	90.6	0.2	..
Namibia - Namibie	1995	(e)1 616	28.6	15.8	14.5	10.9	0.5	1.4	0.6	70.8	64.1	2.0	4.1	0.6	0.0
	2005	2 525	20.4	13.5	12.8	5.3	0.3	1.4	0.1	79.4	70.7	1.1	6.5	1.2	0.0
	2012	(e)6 420	28.8	24.0	19.7	3.7	0.4	0.7	0.3	70.9	52.9	3.5	13.4	1.1	0.0

For sources and notes, see end of table.

Pour les sources et les notes, se reporter à la fin du tableau.

Origin / Origine (Destination)	Year / Année	World (millions of dollars) (1) / Monde (millions de dollars) (1)	Developed economies / Économies développées						Transition economies / Économies en transition	Developing economies / Économies en développement					
			Total	Europe Total	EU UE	USA États-Unis	Japan Japon	Other Autres		Total	Africa Afrique	America Amérique	Eastern, Southern and South-Eastern Asia / Asie orientale, méridionale et du Sud-Est	Western Asia / Asie occidentale	Oceania Océanie
			Percentage / En pourcentage												
Nauru	1995	(e)28	90.9	11.6	11.5	1.9	5.5	71.9	0.1	8.9	0.2	0.2	8.5	..	0.0
	2005	(e)25	48.2	5.6	5.5	6.2	0.6	35.8	..	51.8	1.3	..	49.9	..	0.6
	2012	40	63.3	0.6	0.6	4.6	1.0	57.1	0.0	36.7	0.1	..	19.3	..	17.3
Nepal - Népal	1995	(e)1 202	15.4	7.0	6.7	0.7	5.0	2.8	0.3	83.6	0.0	1.2	77.8	1.6	0.0
	2005	(e)2 243	9.7	4.5	4.3	1.2	1.8	2.2	1.0	89.3	0.1	1.3	84.9	3.0	..
	2012	(e)6 212	6.9	3.5	2.8	1.2	1.1	1.1	0.4	92.7	0.4	2.1	83.9	6.3	0.0
Netherlands - Pays-Bas	1995	(e)185 240	80.8	66.3	63.0	8.7	4.5	1.3	1.5	17.7	2.2	3.3	10.2	2.0	0.0
	2005	(e)363 822	66.4	54.6	51.2	7.3	3.1	1.3	6.1	27.5	2.8	3.8	17.3	3.5	0.0
	2012	(e)591 198	60.0	49.6	45.5	6.3	2.5	1.5	10.5	29.5	4.3	4.8	17.4	3.0	0.0
Netherlands Antilles - Antilles néerlandaises	1995	(e)1 841	62.9	32.9	26.8	25.8	2.9	1.4	0.0	37.1	2.5	29.0	5.6	0.0	..
	2005	(e)1 950	21.0	8.5	8.1	11.8	0.5	0.3	0.0	79.0	0.1	76.4	2.3	0.1	..
New Caledonia - Nouvelle-Calédonie	1995	(e)967	85.1	57.2	56.9	2.7	3.9	21.4	..	11.4	0.1	0.1	10.5	..	0.7
	2005	1 774	70.1	48.1	47.5	3.6	3.5	15.0	0.0	29.7	0.4	0.8	27.8	0.3	0.5
	2012	3 245	59.5	37.2	36.5	4.0	1.9	16.3	0.1	40.4	0.5	0.8	38.4	0.4	0.3
New Zealand - Nouvelle-Zélande	1995	13 958	79.0	22.9	21.7	18.7	13.9	23.5	0.0	20.5	0.6	1.1	15.8	2.2	0.8
	2005	26 232	63.6	19.6	18.7	11.0	10.9	22.1	0.1	35.9	1.7	1.1	28.4	4.3	0.4
	2012	38 079	49.2	16.2	15.5	9.3	6.5	17.2	0.6	50.1	1.0	1.5	39.9	7.5	0.3
Nicaragua	1995	1 009	48.1	11.0	10.3	30.2	5.0	1.9	0.7	51.1	0.1	47.1	3.9	0.0	0.0
	2005	2 536	34.2	7.4	6.8	20.7	4.6	1.4	1.7	64.0	0.0	53.4	10.4	0.1	0.0
	2012	5 917	28.0	6.1	5.8	18.0	2.9	0.9	1.4	70.5	0.0	55.5	14.8	0.3	0.0
Niger	1995	345	60.5	46.8	46.4	8.9	4.2	0.5	0.1	39.4	27.6	0.9	10.5	0.3	0.0
	2005	(e)943	50.3	37.2	35.6	10.2	1.2	1.7	0.3	49.4	27.3	2.0	17.1	2.9	..
	2012	(e)2 900	35.4	28.7	27.4	3.8	2.0	0.8	0.2	64.4	32.3	2.6	25.3	4.2	0.0
Nigeria - Nigéria	1995	(e)8 222	67.8	51.8	49.9	11.7	3.5	0.8	0.5	31.7	4.8	5.1	21.4	0.4	..
	2005	(e)20 754	54.2	33.5	31.5	16.9	3.0	0.8	1.9	38.6	6.2	4.5	24.3	3.5	0.1
	2012	(e)51 000	47.5	31.8	29.7	11.7	2.1	1.9	1.1	51.0	5.0	11.3	30.8	3.6	0.2
Niue - Nioué	1995	(e)4	98.8	2.7	2.7	81.3	1.6	13.2	0.0	1.2	..	0.0	1.1	..	..
	2005	(e)10	97.6	26.5	24.9	3.3	0.6	67.2	..	2.4	0.0	0.2	2.0	0.0	0.2
	2012	(e)7	88.3	1.0	1.0	5.8	0.5	81.0	0.0	11.7	1.6	1.3	7.4	..	1.3
Northern Mariana Islands - Îles Mariannes du Nord	1995	(e)240	63.1	4.1	4.1	..	57.4	1.6	0.0	36.9	0.1	0.1	36.6	0.1	..
	2005	(e)591	16.5	4.5	4.5	..	10.7	1.3	..	83.5	0.0	0.1	83.2	0.2	0.0
	2012	(e)67	28.7	6.8	6.7	..	17.0	4.9	..	71.3	0.6	0.0	70.7	..	..
Norway - Norvège	1995	32 706	87.9	74.8	73.1	6.7	3.8	2.6	2.0	10.2	0.9	2.5	6.4	0.3	0.0
	2005	55 488	82.0	70.8	69.5	5.1	3.2	2.9	2.8	15.2	1.3	2.7	10.3	0.9	0.0
	2012	87 321	76.9	65.9	64.2	5.4	2.3	3.2	2.7	20.4	1.7	3.0	14.7	1.0	0.0
Oman	1995	4 249	59.0	34.5	33.4	5.9	16.0	2.7	0.1	40.8	0.4	0.9	11.5	28.1	0.0
	2005	8 970	51.3	25.0	24.0	6.8	16.7	2.7	1.3	47.4	0.7	1.5	16.8	28.3	0.0
	2012	28 118	35.1	16.1	15.1	5.9	10.5	2.6	0.8	64.1	1.2	4.6	24.8	33.6	..
Pakistan	1995	11 704	50.7	27.9	24.7	9.3	10.7	2.7	1.4	47.5	2.3	1.7	25.1	18.4	0.0
	2005	25 097	35.0	19.6	17.6	6.1	6.5	2.8	2.8	61.4	3.3	1.7	28.2	28.1	0.0
	2012	43 813	21.0	10.9	10.2	3.4	4.3	2.4	1.1	77.5	3.1	0.8	34.5	39.1	0.0
Palau - Palaos	1995	(e)52	60.1	1.2	1.2	25.7	32.4	0.8	0.0	39.9	..	0.1	39.7	..	..
	2005	105	54.3	3.8	3.7	31.3	14.1	5.2	..	45.7	..	0.0	45.5	0.1	0.0
	2012	(e)140	41.4	0.5	0.5	23.3	14.4	3.2	..	58.6	..	0.0	58.5	0.0	0.0
Panama	1995	2 511	59.1	8.1	7.2	12.5	37.9	0.6	0.9	36.1	0.1	7.7	28.2	0.0	0.0
	2005	(e)9 600	46.9	8.4	7.6	11.8	26.2	0.5	1.1	46.9	1.7	15.9	29.1	0.3	0.0
	2012	(e)23 390	41.8	6.2	5.6	14.3	20.9	0.4	0.2	58.0	0.1	11.0	46.5	0.4	0.0
Papua New Guinea - Papouasie-Nouvelle-Guinée	1995	(e)1 452	70.8	5.4	5.3	4.4	10.3	50.6	0.0	28.6	0.0	1.0	27.5	0.0	..
	2005	(e)1 613	69.7	2.3	2.0	3.1	4.4	59.9	0.1	30.3	0.3	0.1	29.3	0.1	0.5
	2012	(e)4 608	64.4	4.1	3.9	5.3	4.5	50.6	0.1	35.4	0.3	0.1	34.5	0.1	0.4
Paraguay	1995	3 136	33.5	11.6	11.1	12.5	8.7	0.7	0.0	66.3	0.9	43.5	21.9	0.0	..
	2005	(e)3 715	17.8	9.7	5.8	4.9	2.7	0.6	0.0	69.5	0.3	47.0	22.1	0.0	..
	2012	11 555	18.3	7.1	6.6	8.1	2.7	0.4	1.6	80.2	0.2	46.2	33.5	0.3	0.0
Peru - Pérou	1995	7 584	54.6	19.3	18.3	25.2	7.0	3.1	0.2	44.5	0.2	34.7	9.4	0.3	0.0
	2005	12 502	36.8	12.9	12.0	17.8	3.6	2.6	1.1	62.1	3.4	42.1	16.1	0.4	0.0
	2012	(e)42 545	40.9	11.2	10.7	24.6	2.7	2.3	1.0	58.1	3.1	31.1	23.2	0.8	0.0

For sources and notes, see end of table.

Pour les sources et les notes, se reporter à la fin du tableau.

Origin / Origine Destination	Year Année	World (millions of dollars) (1) Monde (millions de dollars) (1)	Developed economies Économies développées						Transition economies Économies en transition	Developing economies Économies en développement					
			Total	Europe		USA États-Unis	Japan Japon	Other Autres		Total	Africa Afrique	America Amérique	Eastern, Southern and South-Eastern Asia Asie orientale, méridionale et du Sud-Est	Western Asia Asie occidentale	Oceania Océanie
				Total	EU UE										
								Percentage / En pourcentage							
Philippines	1995	28 487	57.5	11.5	10.9	18.9	22.1	5.0	1.7	40.8	0.6	1.7	30.6	7.4	0.4
	2005	49 487	47.1	8.5	7.9	18.9	17.1	2.6	0.9	52.0	0.2	1.4	44.4	5.7	0.3
	2012	65 350	33.9	8.0	7.5	11.6	10.7	3.6	1.6	64.5	0.2	1.1	53.0	9.8	0.3
Poland - Pologne	1995	29 019	80.6	74.3	71.2	3.9	1.6	0.7	9.5	9.9	1.6	1.4	6.5	0.3	0.0
	2005	101 539	73.8	68.9	66.2	2.4	2.0	0.5	11.8	14.2	0.7	1.8	10.1	1.5	0.0
	2012	191 430	63.3	58.7	56.3	2.6	1.5	0.6	16.9	19.3	0.9	1.7	15.2	1.4	0.1
Portugal	1995	33 565	85.5	79.7	76.8	3.0	2.2	0.5	0.7	13.8	4.7	2.9	5.0	1.1	0.0
	2005	61 167	82.1	78.6	76.7	1.9	1.2	0.4	2.2	15.6	6.6	3.1	3.8	2.1	0.0
	2012	72 293	73.4	70.6	68.9	1.7	0.6	0.5	3.4	23.1	10.1	4.1	6.3	2.6	0.0
Qatar	1995	3 398	72.6	50.8	47.6	9.4	10.7	1.7	0.2	26.0	0.5	1.2	10.8	13.4	0.0
	2005	10 061	61.9	38.1	36.3	10.9	11.0	1.8	0.4	37.7	0.7	1.9	18.6	16.5	..
	2012	(e)34 200	46.4	24.7	22.0	13.0	5.5	3.1	0.2	53.5	1.3	1.7	15.7	34.8	0.0
Republic of Moldova - République de Moldova	1995	841	34.5	32.7	31.9	1.1	0.1	0.6	64.3	1.2	0.0	0.1	0.3	0.8	..
	2005	2 292	48.7	46.3	45.6	1.6	0.5	0.4	42.9	8.4	0.2	0.9	3.7	3.5	0.0
	2012	5 213	55.8	53.7	52.9	1.0	0.2	0.9	32.0	12.2	0.2	0.8	5.6	5.6	0.0
Romania - Roumanie	1995	10 278	65.0	58.1	55.9	4.0	0.7	2.1	16.0	17.9	4.7	2.1	8.1	3.0	0.0
	2005	40 463	70.0	64.7	63.4	2.8	1.4	1.1	14.4	15.3	0.5	1.8	7.9	5.0	0.0
	2012	70 260	77.0	74.6	73.5	1.5	0.5	0.4	11.1	11.8	0.8	1.1	6.3	3.7	0.0
Russian Federation - Fédération de Russie	1995	(e)60 945	46.1	38.8	37.8	4.6	1.6	1.1	21.1	11.9	0.5	1.8	7.8	1.7	0.0
	2005	(e)125 434	61.8	52.9	51.2	3.6	4.3	1.0	15.8	22.4	0.7	3.7	16.0	2.0	0.0
	2012	(e)315 986	56.1	47.4	45.7	3.9	3.6	1.3	14.7	29.2	0.6	2.8	23.4	2.4	0.0
Rwanda	1995	(e)241	51.3	27.9	26.6	15.0	6.7	1.7	0.3	48.4	38.1	0.1	5.1	5.0	..
	2005	(e)412	38.9	26.8	26.5	2.9	3.6	5.7	1.5	59.6	42.8	2.5	7.9	6.3	0.1
	2012	(e)2 408	27.0	19.1	18.6	2.3	1.8	3.9	0.8	72.1	43.8	0.4	15.0	12.9	0.0
Saint Helena - Sainte-Hélène	1995	(e)23	83.0	80.7	78.8	1.5	0.5	0.2	0.1	16.7	15.0	0.4	1.3	0.0	..
	2005	(e)56	66.2	60.1	60.0	4.4	0.3	1.4	..	33.8	31.9	0.2	1.8	0.0	..
	2012	(e)51	43.0	36.2	35.6	6.5	0.0	0.4	..	57.0	56.4	..	0.5	..	0.1
Saint Kitts and Nevis - Saint-Kitts-et-Nevis	1995	132	76.7	13.8	13.3	55.1	5.3	2.5	0.0	22.8	0.0	21.0	1.7	0.0	0.0
	2005	210	73.8	9.6	9.3	57.9	3.8	2.4	0.1	26.2	0.1	24.3	1.8	0.0	0.0
	2012	(e)230	79.5	7.1	6.9	67.8	2.4	2.3	0.1	20.4	0.0	16.7	3.4	0.1	0.1
Saint Lucia - Sainte-Lucie	1995	306	70.6	30.8	30.6	32.0	3.8	4.0	0.0	29.4	0.0	26.0	3.3	0.1	0.0
	2005	486	59.6	28.3	27.7	26.2	3.0	2.1	0.0	40.3	0.1	37.8	2.4	0.1	0.0
	2012	(e)660	17.6	5.6	5.4	9.9	1.1	0.9	0.0	82.4	0.0	81.3	1.1	0.0	..
Saint Pierre and Miquelon - Saint-Pierre-et-Miquelon	1995	(e)74	98.4	54.4	54.0	0.9	0.0	43.1	..	1.2	0.4	0.5	0.3	..	..
	2005	(e)70	93.5	59.6	59.6	2.1	0.2	31.7	..	6.5	0.0	0.0	6.4	..	..
	2012	(e)190	99.9	63.2	63.2	0.3	..	36.4	..	0.1	0.0	0.0	0.0	..	..
Saint Vincent and the Grenadines - Saint-Vincent-et-les Grenadines	1995	134	67.3	36.7	36.2	25.6	3.1	1.9	0.0	32.5	1.8	22.9	7.8	0.0	..
	2005	240	55.5	35.6	35.3	14.4	3.2	2.3	2.6	41.9	5.2	22.8	12.8	1.2	0.0
	2012	(e)360	34.6	10.2	8.2	21.9	0.6	1.9	0.3	65.1	0.1	35.6	28.3	1.1	0.0
Samoa	1995	(e)95	89.4	1.8	1.8	6.4	23.0	58.2	..	10.6	0.0	1.5	9.1	..	0.0
	2005	(e)239	66.4	1.4	1.4	10.6	7.6	46.9	0.0	33.6	1.1	1.0	20.3	0.0	11.1
	2012	(e)346	39.8	1.6	1.6	7.1	3.7	27.4	0.4	59.9	0.2	0.6	43.8	0.1	15.3
Sao Tome and Principe - Sao Tomé-et-Principe	1995	(e)29	76.9	70.8	70.7	4.4	1.5	0.3	0.0	12.0	6.4	3.0	2.6	..	..
	2005	50	71.8	64.6	64.5	0.1	7.1	0.0	0.0	28.0	21.7	0.8	4.6	0.9	0.0
	2012	141	64.8	61.0	60.9	1.8	2.0	0.0	..	35.2	25.8	2.0	6.1	1.3	..
Saudi Arabia - Arabie saoudite	1995	28 085	71.6	39.0	34.0	21.5	8.9	2.2	0.9	25.4	2.9	2.3	14.7	5.5	0.0
	2005	59 510	62.0	34.0	31.7	14.8	9.0	4.2	1.7	35.4	3.1	3.7	20.9	7.8	0.0
	2012	(e)155 593	48.4	26.2	24.6	13.4	6.1	2.7	1.5	50.1	2.6	3.1	35.7	8.6	0.0
Senegal - Sénégal	1995	(e)1 412	51.0	41.5	41.0	5.0	3.2	1.3	1.2	28.5	10.0	5.4	12.7	0.4	..
	2005	3 498	53.4	46.8	46.3	4.3	1.3	1.1	1.8	44.7	21.2	6.0	14.8	2.7	0.0
	2012	6 434	50.4	45.0	44.1	2.2	1.2	2.1	3.4	46.2	18.5	4.9	19.2	3.6	0.0
Serbia and Montenegro - Serbie-et-Monténégro	1995	(e)2 666	53.3	48.2	45.3	2.9	1.4	0.8	18.3	12.7	2.3	5.4	3.8	1.2	0.0
	2005	(e)10 461	53.9	49.7	48.4	2.7	1.0	0.5	27.4	12.4	0.5	1.9	7.9	2.2	0.0
Serbia - Serbie	2012	19 013	62.4	59.4	58.2	1.7	1.0	0.3	23.0	14.7	0.5	1.0	10.6	2.5	0.0
Seychelles	1995	255	43.7	32.9	32.4	3.7	5.7	1.5	0.0	55.9	16.1	0.2	23.0	16.6	..
	2005	675	47.0	43.3	43.0	1.9	0.8	1.1	0.0	52.7	9.4	0.2	15.7	27.4	0.0
	2012	(e)752	36.9	31.7	31.3	1.4	2.1	1.7	0.0	63.1	10.9	0.3	20.1	31.8	0.0

For sources and notes, see end of table.

Pour les sources et les notes, se reporter à la fin du tableau.

Origin / Origine	Year / Année	World (millions of dollars) (1) / Monde (millions de dollars) (1)	Developed economies / Économies développées						Transition economies / Économies en transition	Developing economies / Économies en développement					
			Total	Europe		USA États-Unis	Japan Japon	Other Autres		Total	Africa Afrique	America Amérique	Eastern, Southern and South-Eastern Asia / Asie orientale, méridionale et du Sud-Est	Western Asia / Asie occiden-tale	Oceania Océanie
Destination				Total	EU UE										
			Percentage / En pourcentage												
Sierra Leone	1995	(e)134	58.8	48.8	46.7	8.6	1.0	0.4	0.8	31.5	11.9	1.2	17.7	0.7	..
	2005	(e)344	36.4	20.9	20.2	5.1	4.1	6.3	0.5	61.7	40.4	3.0	13.7	4.5	0.0
	2012	(e)1 569	35.4	19.7	19.0	5.1	4.2	6.4	0.5	62.7	41.3	3.1	13.7	4.5	0.0
Singapore - Singapour (2)	1995	124 503	59.7	15.0	13.0	15.1	21.1	2.2	0.3	40.0	0.5	0.9	38.5	6.0	0.0
	2005	200 050	36.6	13.0	11.6	11.7	9.6	2.2	0.5	62.8	0.6	1.0	52.2	9.0	0.0
	2012	379 723	32.5	14.1	12.6	10.2	6.2	2.0	1.4	66.1	0.5	2.9	49.6	13.1	0.0
Sint Maarten (Dutch part) - Saint-Martin (partie néerlandaise)	2012	768	99.8	0.0	..	99.8	..	0.0	0.0	0.2	0.0	0.1	0.0	..	..
Slovakia - Slovaquie	1995	8 162	79.7	74.9	72.9	2.6	1.6	0.6	14.1	5.7	0.6	1.1	3.6	0.4	0.0
	2005	34 226	67.4	63.9	62.9	1.4	1.9	0.2	13.1	10.4	0.2	0.7	8.9	0.6	0.0
	2012	77 695	53.5	50.7	50.1	0.9	1.7	0.2	11.5	20.5	0.4	0.4	19.0	0.7	0.0
Slovenia - Slovénie	1995	9 492	84.4	78.7	76.2	3.1	1.7	0.9	10.0	5.6	1.2	1.0	3.1	0.3	0.0
	2005	19 626	77.0	72.7	70.9	2.0	1.5	0.8	9.3	9.7	0.9	1.7	5.9	1.2	0.0
	2012	(e)32 009	62.6	59.3	57.8	2.0	0.7	0.6	8.9	13.4	1.0	1.3	9.3	1.8	0.0
Solomon Islands - Îles Salomon	1995	(e)154	71.6	3.3	3.3	2.2	11.7	54.4	0.0	28.4	0.2	0.0	28.1	0.0	0.0
	2005	(e)185	46.0	4.0	4.0	1.6	4.4	36.0	0.0	54.0	0.7	0.1	43.2	0.0	9.9
	2012	(e)495	40.9	2.1	2.0	1.5	4.3	33.1	..	59.1	0.7	0.1	50.5	0.0	7.8
Somalia - Somalie	1995	(e)268	22.7	15.5	15.4	5.8	0.6	0.8	0.0	73.9	24.2	11.5	23.7	14.5	..
	2005	(e)626	5.5	3.3	3.3	1.9	0.1	0.2	0.7	93.8	25.0	9.7	16.5	42.6	0.0
	2012	670	9.1	6.9	6.8	2.2	0.0	0.1	0.2	90.6	4.1	1.7	57.6	27.2	0.0
South Africa - Afrique du Sud	1995	(e)30 546	66.6	43.1	40.8	11.9	7.4	4.3	0.3	32.3	2.7	3.1	18.2	8.3	0.0
	2005	(e)62 304	51.0	34.9	33.7	7.0	6.0	3.1	0.3	36.4	4.1	3.5	22.0	6.8	0.1
	2012	(e)124 245	36.2	24.3	23.5	6.0	3.7	2.1	0.3	44.8	7.8	3.1	25.4	8.5	0.0
Spain - Espagne	1995	113 399	79.7	68.5	66.4	6.6	3.3	1.2	1.5	18.8	5.7	4.3	7.0	1.7	0.0
	2005	289 611	70.6	63.7	61.3	3.2	2.5	1.1	2.9	26.5	7.6	4.9	10.5	3.4	0.1
	2012	325 835	57.0	50.9	49.1	3.9	1.2	1.1	4.4	37.5	10.9	8.5	12.4	5.7	0.1
Sri Lanka	1995	(e)5 185	38.1	18.1	17.0	6.2	9.6	4.2	0.4	55.8	0.7	2.2	51.7	1.3	..
	2005	8 307	28.4	17.4	15.6	2.5	4.6	4.0	0.2	71.3	0.5	1.3	64.2	5.4	0.0
	2012	17 885	20.6	11.4	10.0	1.3	3.1	4.8	1.2	77.8	0.5	0.5	63.0	13.4	0.0
State of Palestine - Etat de Palestine	1995	1 658	..	..	..	..	..	..	..	..	..	..	..	..	..
	2005	(e)2 667	89.0	6.1	5.5	0.6	0.7	81.6	0.3	10.7	1.5	0.5	5.8	2.9	0.0
	2012	(e)4 790	85.1	8.1	7.1	0.3	0.1	76.5	0.1	14.7	1.5	0.8	5.7	6.8	0.0
Sudan (...2011) - Soudan (...2011)	1995	1 185	48.8	38.6	36.8	5.4	4.4	0.4	0.3	50.9	19.9	0.3	18.1	12.6	0.0
	2005	7 367	34.4	23.8	22.9	1.6	4.6	4.3	2.2	63.4	7.4	1.8	32.9	21.3	0.0
Sudan - Soudan	2012	(e)9 475	21.1	12.8	12.1	1.0	2.2	5.1	3.0	75.9	9.9	2.6	43.5	19.9	0.0
Suriname	1995	583	70.1	25.0	24.2	42.4	2.1	0.5	..	29.9	0.6	23.5	5.7	0.0	..
	2005	1 050	46.4	22.1	21.9	18.9	4.5	1.0	0.0	41.9	0.1	32.4	9.2	0.3	..
	2012	(e)1 782	51.7	21.3	21.2	26.3	2.9	1.2	0.0	48.2	0.0	37.8	10.2	0.2	0.0
Swaziland	1995	(e)1 008	10.0	5.3	5.0	2.9	1.5	0.3	0.0	90.0	79.0	0.3	10.5	0.1	0.1
	2005	(e)1 900	7.1	4.7	4.6	1.3	0.6	0.5	0.0	92.9	78.7	0.6	13.2	0.4	0.0
	2012	(e)1 990	35.2	12.9	11.7	18.3	2.7	1.3	0.1	64.8	13.5	0.5	50.6	0.1	0.0
Sweden - Suède	1995	61 647	91.7	82.0	72.2	5.7	3.0	1.0	0.8	7.5	0.5	1.3	5.1	0.5	0.0
	2005	111 351	87.0	80.7	71.4	3.4	2.1	0.9	3.2	9.7	0.5	1.3	6.8	1.1	0.0
	2012	162 686	82.7	77.8	67.7	3.2	1.1	0.6	5.5	11.6	1.1	1.3	8.2	1.0	0.0
Switzerland - Suisse	1995	80 152	91.7	81.2	80.8	6.4	3.2	0.9	0.6	7.6	1.3	1.1	4.5	0.7	0.0
	2005	126 574	88.8	80.4	80.2	5.6	1.9	0.9	0.9	10.3	2.3	1.0	5.7	1.2	0.0
	2012	197 787	83.6	74.8	74.6	5.7	2.3	0.8	1.0	15.4	2.0	1.7	10.4	1.3	0.0
Syrian Arab Republic - République arabe syrienne	1995	(e)4 709	43.9	32.3	31.7	6.8	4.4	0.4	9.1	34.4	2.9	3.4	17.4	10.6	0.0
	2005	(e)10 862	31.8	27.1	26.2	1.7	2.3	0.7	11.1	56.9	4.8	3.2	21.9	27.0	0.0
	2012	(e)7 300	26.7	22.5	21.3	2.3	1.3	0.6	10.3	63.0	6.0	4.2	25.4	27.4	..
Tajikistan - Tadjikistan	1995	(e)810	32.3	27.8	24.4	3.9	0.1	0.5	55.7	12.0	..	0.0	10.7	1.3	..
	2005	(e)1 330	15.3	13.4	12.9	1.5	0.3	0.2	63.8	20.8	0.6	2.1	13.5	4.7	..
	2012	(e)3 778	7.5	5.2	5.1	1.9	0.2	0.2	37.1	55.4	1.2	0.8	46.3	7.2	..
TFYR of Macedonia - LERY de Macédoine	1995	1 719	72.2	66.8	65.7	3.4	0.8	1.2	15.6	8.3	0.6	1.5	2.5	3.7	0.0
	2005	3 228	59.9	56.8	54.7	1.4	0.7	1.1	27.6	12.5	0.3	1.8	6.7	3.6	0.1
	2012	6 511	63.5	60.7	58.4	1.3	0.7	0.8	18.5	18.0	0.4	1.7	10.8	5.1	0.0

For sources and notes, see end of table.

Pour les sources et les notes, se reporter à la fin du tableau.

Origin / Origine Destination	Year Année	World (millions of dollars) (1) Monde (millions de dollars) (1)	Developed economies Économies développées Total	Europe Total	Europe EU UE	USA États-Unis	Japan Japon	Other Autres	Transition economies Économies en transition	Developing economies Économies en développement Total	Africa Afrique	America Amérique	Eastern, Southern and South-Eastern Asia Asie orientale, méridionale et du Sud-Est	Western Asia Asie occidentale	Oceania Océanie
			Percentage / En pourcentage												
Thailand - Thaïlande	1995	70 781	63.9	18.2	16.4	12.0	30.5	3.2	1.9	33.1	1.2	1.6	27.0	3.2	0.1
	2005	118 164	43.6	10.4	9.1	7.4	22.0	3.8	1.6	54.4	1.4	1.7	38.6	12.5	0.2
	2012	247 576	39.5	11.2	8.1	5.3	20.0	3.0	2.3	58.2	1.7	2.1	41.2	12.8	0.4
Timor-Leste	2005	(e)102	32.4	8.5	8.4	9.2	4.5	10.3	0.0	67.5	2.2	0.1	64.9	0.2	0.2
	2012	(e)354	7.5	0.6	0.6	0.2	1.7	5.0	0.0	92.5	0.3	0.5	91.7	0.0	..
Togo	1995	556	51.0	44.2	43.5	3.3	2.6	0.9	0.0	48.9	18.8	1.9	27.8	0.4	0.0
	2005	(e)1 060	39.3	36.3	35.7	1.3	0.9	0.8	0.9	58.4	13.8	2.1	39.3	3.2	0.0
	2012	1 665	40.7	35.0	34.8	3.8	0.7	1.1	1.0	58.4	7.2	2.7	45.1	3.4	0.0
Tokelau - Tokélaou	1995	(e)1	12.1	1.9	1.9	9.2	1.0	0.0	..	87.9	45.4	4.1	24.0	..	14.5
	2005	(e)0	96.4	44.8	44.8	51.6	0.0	0.0	..	3.6	0.6	0.1	2.4	..	0.5
	2012	(e)0	71.8	33.6	30.6	24.8	0.0	13.4	..	28.2	23.4	..	1.5	..	3.3
Tonga	1995	(e)77	96.8	8.9	8.8	13.1	5.1	69.6	..	3.2	0.0	0.7	2.4	0.0	..
	2005	(e)120	61.6	4.3	4.2	8.6	2.6	46.1	0.0	38.4	0.1	0.8	11.0	0.0	26.5
	2012	(e)199	46.3	1.5	1.3	11.3	3.3	30.3	0.0	53.7	0.2	0.6	23.7	0.2	29.0
Trinidad and Tobago - Trinité-et-Tobago	1995	1 724	80.6	20.8	19.6	50.6	3.2	6.0	0.1	18.8	0.4	12.6	5.7	0.1	0.0
	2005	5 694	48.4	12.4	11.9	29.2	3.9	2.9	0.4	51.2	12.9	31.6	6.5	0.1	0.0
	2012	(e)9 065	50.5	9.2	9.1	33.3	2.6	5.4	2.6	46.8	9.3	27.1	9.8	0.5	0.0
Tunisia - Tunisie	1995	7 903	82.7	74.8	73.2	5.1	1.8	1.1	3.0	13.7	6.8	1.4	2.7	2.8	0.0
	2005	13 174	75.2	70.8	69.7	2.5	1.6	0.3	4.7	19.3	6.4	2.4	6.3	4.1	0.0
	2012	(e)24 447	65.8	62.0	61.0	2.6	0.5	0.6	4.8	29.4	9.2	3.0	11.7	5.5	0.0
Turkey - Turquie	1995	35 707	69.6	53.0	50.5	10.4	3.9	2.2	9.5	20.1	3.9	2.0	9.1	5.1	0.0
	2005	116 774	57.6	49.0	45.2	4.6	2.7	1.3	15.0	26.6	5.2	1.7	17.0	2.7	0.0
	2012	236 544	48.2	39.2	37.0	6.0	1.5	1.5	15.3	30.7	2.5	2.2	23.0	3.0	0.0
Turkmenistan - Turkménistan	1995	(e)1 365	24.4	18.1	17.1	4.3	0.7	1.3	56.0	19.6	0.0	0.1	8.0	11.5	..
	2005	(e)2 947	30.2	18.3	18.0	9.7	1.1	1.2	36.6	33.2	0.0	0.2	11.3	21.7	..
	2012	(e)9 900	25.5	20.4	20.0	2.8	1.6	0.7	26.4	48.0	0.0	0.1	24.2	23.7	..
Turks and Caicos Islands - Iles Turques et Caïques	1995	(e)51	69.7	8.1	7.8	59.5	1.3	0.9	3.9	25.8	0.1	24.6	1.1	..	..
	2005	304	98.2	..	..	98.0	0.2	0.0	0.0	1.8	0.0	1.6	0.2	0.0	..
	2012	(e)309	84.1	2.5	1.4	80.6	0.3	0.6	0.1	15.8	..	15.5	0.3	0.0	..
Tuvalu	1995	(e)6	84.1	15.4	15.4	5.2	3.7	59.8	2.7	13.2	..	8.0	4.1	..	1.0
	2005	(e)13	49.1	18.8	18.7	0.1	15.0	15.2	0.2	50.7	0.3	0.0	22.2	..	28.2
	2012	(e)25	8.6	0.2	0.2	0.3	6.7	1.4	0.8	90.6	0.1	0.0	80.7	0.1	9.6
Uganda - Ouganda	1995	1 038	43.1	31.9	31.2	2.8	7.2	1.3	0.0	56.8	35.7	0.9	15.8	4.0	0.5
	2005	2 054	32.8	20.7	20.2	3.9	5.8	2.4	0.6	66.6	40.0	1.1	16.9	8.6	0.0
	2012	6 044	21.7	14.6	14.2	2.2	4.4	0.5	1.8	76.5	22.7	1.0	32.5	19.9	0.4
Ukraine	1995	(e)16 052	28.5	24.1	23.3	3.2	0.6	0.5	63.5	5.2	0.7	1.8	2.1	0.7	0.0
	2005	36 122	31.0	34.8	33.7	2.0	1.5	0.7	47.4	13.7	1.2	1.3	9.3	1.8	0.0
	2012	84 657	38.0	32.4	30.9	3.4	1.4	0.8	41.2	20.8	1.0	1.6	15.5	2.7	0.0
United Arab Emirates - Emirats arabes unis	1995	(e)23 778	53.4	34.5	32.8	8.2	8.9	1.7	0.5	46.1	0.8	0.8	35.5	8.9	..
	2005	(e)80 814	53.1	37.6	36.2	8.8	5.1	1.6	1.6	45.3	1.7	1.2	34.2	8.2	0.0
	2012	(e)251 921	39.0	22.4	20.7	10.5	4.2	1.9	0.7	60.3	2.8	1.6	45.8	10.1	0.0
United Kingdom - Royaume-Uni	1995	261 456	78.9	59.4	54.8	11.1	5.7	2.7	0.6	15.4	2.0	1.8	10.3	1.2	0.1
	2005	515 782	72.7	59.0	53.6	8.0	3.1	2.5	2.0	21.1	3.0	2.0	13.8	2.3	0.0
	2012	689 137	71.7	56.3	47.4	8.9	2.0	4.5	2.6	24.8	4.7	2.0	15.1	2.9	0.0
United Republic of Tanzania - République-Unie de Tanzanie	1995	1 653	45.0	33.3	32.2	3.9	6.9	1.0	0.1	54.9	22.1	0.7	20.1	11.9	0.0
	2005	3 247	30.4	21.1	20.5	3.1	3.9	2.4	1.6	68.0	24.1	1.4	24.2	18.3	0.0
	2012	11 716	24.9	17.2	12.6	2.3	3.4	2.0	1.0	74.1	15.5	1.5	40.8	16.3	0.0
United States - États-Unis	1995	770 821	56.8	19.6	18.1	..	16.5	20.7	0.7	42.5	2.1	14.0	24.6	1.8	0.0
	2005	1 732 321	46.3	19.7	18.5	..	8.2	18.5	1.2	52.5	3.9	17.5	28.0	3.1	0.0
	2012	2 333 805	40.1	18.1	16.7	..	6.4	15.6	1.5	58.4	2.9	19.6	31.4	4.4	0.0
Uruguay	1995	2 866	36.0	22.4	21.4	9.9	2.6	1.2	0.0	62.7	1.5	52.2	8.1	0.9	..
	2005	3 879	20.1	11.3	10.8	6.7	1.1	1.0	8.1	71.8	8.7	51.9	11.0	0.1	0.0
	2012	11 614	21.2	12.1	11.0	7.5	0.9	0.7	5.1	70.7	3.6	45.7	20.7	0.7	0.0
Uzbekistan - Ouzbékistan	1995	2 750	53.0	43.3	42.4	4.0	5.1	0.5	14.8	32.0	0.0	0.4	22.7	8.9	..
	2005	3 666	27.7	23.9	23.0	2.2	1.1	0.4	40.5	31.8	0.1	0.2	25.0	6.5	..
	2012	11 296	18.8	15.1	14.4	2.6	0.9	0.3	41.9	39.3	0.0	0.3	34.7	4.3	..

For sources and notes, see end of table.

Pour les sources et les notes, se reporter à la fin du tableau.

Origin / Origine — Destination	Year / Année	World (millions of dollars) (1) / Monde (millions de dollars) (1)	Developed economies / Économies développées — Total	Europe — Total	Europe — EU / UE	USA / États-Unis	Japan / Japon	Other / Autres	Transition economies / Économies en transition	Developing economies / Économies en développement — Total	Africa / Afrique	America / Amérique	Eastern, Southern and South-Eastern Asia / Asie orientale, méridionale et du Sud-Est	Western Asia / Asie occidentale	Oceania / Océanie
										Percentage / En pourcentage					
Vanuatu	1995	(e)95	80.7	9.5	7.0	0.9	45.0	25.3	0.3	18.1	1.4	0.3	16.3	0.0	0.1
	2005	(e)149	64.9	5.3	5.3	4.7	16.4	38.4	..	34.6	0.1	0.1	23.4	..	11.0
	2012	(e)274	37.1	7.9	7.8	1.4	6.2	21.6	0.0	62.9	0.5	0.1	52.7	0.2	9.4
Venezuela (Bolivarian Rep. of) - Venezuela (Rép. bolivarienne du)	1995	(e)12 649	71.6	20.7	19.7	41.3	4.4	5.3	0.1	28.3	0.3	24.0	0.0	0.2	0.0
	2005	21 848	53.2	16.1	15.2	31.0	3.5	2.7	0.2	46.6	0.2	37.6	8.6	0.3	0.0
	2012	(e)60 400	46.4	14.8	13.7	28.0	1.5	2.2	1.4	52.2	0.2	36.3	15.4	0.3	0.0
Viet Nam	1995	(e)8 155	29.1	11.7	10.4	2.2	13.0	2.2	1.7	63.7	0.1	0.1	62.2	1.3	0.0
	2005	36 761	25.2	9.5	7.1	2.4	11.1	2.2	2.8	71.9	0.6	1.4	68.2	1.7	0.1
	2012	(e)113 780	25.5	8.3	7.9	4.3	10.4	2.5	1.0	73.5	0.3	2.3	68.9	2.0	..
Wallis and Futuna Islands - Iles Wallis-et-Futuna	1995	(e)14	93.9	59.6	59.6	0.6	..	33.8	0.1	5.9	0.1	4.9	0.1	..	0.8
	2005	(e)51	66.2	35.4	35.3	1.2	2.8	26.8	0.0	33.8	0.7	1.1	6.5	0.0	25.4
	2012	(e)65	55.8	36.7	30.9	1.4	..	17.8	0.0	44.2	0.1	0.1	1.8	0.0	42.2
Western Sahara - Sahara occidental	1995	(e)14	11.7	..	..	2.0	0.2	9.4	0.3	88.0	47.1	..	40.2	0.7	..
Yemen - Yémen	1995	(e)1 582	40.5	27.1	26.8	8.6	3.5	1.3	0.4	59.1	4.3	2.8	20.0	31.9	..
	2005	(e)5 400	30.8	20.1	15.6	4.8	3.2	2.7	3.1	66.0	5.3	5.7	21.0	34.0	0.0
	2012	(e)12 000	19.4	10.6	10.3	3.7	2.4	2.7	2.3	78.3	4.1	5.0	35.4	33.8	0.0
Zambia - Zambie	1995	708	34.9	21.7	20.7	4.3	6.2	2.7	0.0	65.1	48.7	0.3	8.0	8.1	0.0
	2005	2 558	24.4	19.5	18.9	1.7	1.4	1.7	0.0	75.6	62.5	0.5	8.9	3.7	0.0
	2012	(e)8 200	14.1	8.8	8.6	2.2	2.2	0.9	0.1	85.8	61.6	0.3	15.2	8.7	..
Zimbabwe	1995	(e)2 659	37.7	24.7	23.0	5.2	6.5	1.3	0.1	62.1	53.7	1.5	6.4	0.5	0.0
	2005	(e)2 350	12.0	8.2	7.7	2.0	1.1	0.7	0.0	88.0	73.2	0.2	8.8	5.9	0.0
	2012	(e)4 400	11.1	8.6	8.3	1.2	0.7	0.6	0.1	88.8	67.7	0.8	15.9	4.4	..

Source:
UNCTAD secretariat calculations, based on UNCTAD, *UNCTADstat* Merchandise Trade Matrix

Source :
Calculs du secrétariat de la CNUCED, basés sur la matrice du commerce de marchandises d'*UNCTADstat* de la CNUCED

Notes:

(1) Includes unspecified destinations.

(2) Exports data include a considerable amount of re-exports.

(3) Estimates. France including French Guiana, Guadeloupe, Martinique, Monaco and Reunion (and excluding intra trade).

Notes :

(1) Y compris des destinations non-spécifiées.

(2) Les données des exportations comprennent une part importante de réexportations.

(3) Estimation. Les données sont dérivées des déclarations rapportées par la France métropolitaine et les départements d'outre-mer par agrégation diminuée des flux intra.

Destination / Product group	Year / Année	World (1) / Monde (1)	Developed economies - Économies développées							Transition economies / Économies en transition
			Total	Europe		Canada	USA / États-Unis	Japan / Japon	Other developed countries / Autres économies développées	
				Total	EU / UE					
Millions of dollars										
All products	1995	5 121 053	3 486 040	2 167 593	2 042 587	165 268	756 023	303 576	93 580	98 438
	2005	10 447 270	6 913 486	4 309 931	4 094 929	304 668	1 632 181	485 176	181 529	260 015
	2012	18 351 468	9 980 766	6 173 465	5 804 839	453 766	2 200 851	814 530	338 154	590 606
Share by destination (percentage)										
All products	1995	100.0	68.1	42.3	39.9	3.2	14.8	5.9	1.8	1.9
	2005	100.0	66.2	41.3	39.2	2.9	15.6	4.6	1.7	2.5
	2012	100.0	54.4	33.6	31.6	2.5	12.0	4.4	1.8	3.2
All food items	1995	100.0	67.8	47.4	45.8	2.1	7.5	9.6	1.1	4.4
(SITC 0 + 1 + 22 + 4) .	2005	100.0	68.6	48.4	46.9	2.6	9.9	6.4	1.4	4.4
	2012	100.0	56.1	39.4	38.1	2.5	7.8	4.9	1.5	4.9
Agricultural raw materials	1995	100.0	68.0	41.3	39.5	2.1	11.5	12.1	1.0	0.8
(SITC 2 - 22 - 27 - 28)	2005	100.0	61.8	39.5	38.1	2.3	12.9	6.2	0.9	1.8
	2012	100.0	47.3	31.5	30.5	1.6	8.9	4.5	0.8	2.4
Ores, metals, precious stones	1995	100.0	69.3	42.4	38.1	2.5	11.7	10.0	2.7	1.1
and non-monetary gold	2005	100.0	60.2	37.5	33.4	2.3	11.4	6.0	3.0	1.4
(SITC 27 + 28 + 68 + 667 + 971)	2012	100.0	47.1	31.4	25.5	2.2	7.3	4.4	1.8	1.2
Fuels (SITC 3)	1995	100.0	68.3	35.4	33.4	1.3	17.0	13.5	1.2	2.9
	2005	100.0	66.0	34.2	32.5	1.6	19.6	9.3	1.3	1.3
	2012	100.0	52.6	29.9	28.6	1.4	11.9	7.9	1.5	1.6
Manufactured goods	1995	100.0	67.8	41.8	39.3	3.7	15.9	4.4	1.9	1.5
(SITC 5 to 8 less 667 and 68)	2005	100.0	65.9	41.6	39.5	3.3	15.8	3.5	1.8	2.5
	2012	100.0	55.5	34.0	32.1	2.8	13.3	3.3	2.0	3.8
Share by major product group (percentage)										
All products	1995	100.0	100.0	100.0	100.0	100.0	100.0	100.0	100.0	100.0
	2005	100.0	100.0	100.0	100.0	100.0	100.0	100.0	100.0	100.0
	2012	100.0	100.0	100.0	100.0	100.0	100.0	100.0	100.0	100.0
All food items	1995	8.9	8.9	10.0	10.3	5.7	4.6	14.5	5.6	20.3
(SITC 0 + 1 + 22 + 4)	2005	6.5	6.8	7.7	7.8	5.7	4.2	9.0	5.1	11.6
	2012	7.5	7.8	8.8	9.1	7.6	4.9	8.3	6.3	11.5
Agricultural raw materials	1995	2.7	2.7	2.6	2.7	1.7	2.1	5.5	1.5	1.1
(SITC 2 - 22 - 27 - 28)	2005	1.6	1.5	1.5	1.5	1.3	1.3	2.1	0.8	1.1
	2012	1.5	1.3	1.4	1.5	1.0	1.1	1.5	0.7	1.1
Ores, metals, precious stones	1995	4.6	4.7	4.6	4.4	3.5	3.6	7.7	6.8	2.7
and non-monetary gold	2005	4.6	4.2	4.2	3.9	3.7	3.4	6.0	8.0	2.6
(SITC 27 + 28 + 68 + 667 + 971)	2012	6.4	5.6	6.0	5.2	5.8	3.9	6.3	6.4	2.3
Fuels (SITC 3)	1995	7.3	7.4	6.1	6.2	3.0	8.4	16.7	4.8	11.2
	2005	14.0	14.0	11.6	11.6	7.5	17.5	28.2	10.6	7.2
	2012	18.8	18.2	16.7	17.0	10.3	18.6	33.6	15.3	9.5
Manufactured goods	1995	72.7	72.4	71.8	71.6	83.2	78.4	54.0	77.4	56.3
(SITC 5 to 8 less 667 and 68)	2005	70.5	70.2	71.0	71.1	78.9	71.3	53.0	72.1	71.3
	2012	62.6	63.9	63.3	63.6	71.7	69.6	47.2	68.5	73.9

For sources and notes, see end of table 2.2.L.

| Developing economies - Économies en développement | | | | | | | | | | | |
Total	Africa Afrique	America Amérique	Asia Asie Total	Eastern, Southern and South-Eastern Asia Asie orientale, méridionale et du Sud-Est	China Chine	Western Asia Asie occidentale	Oceania Océanie	Major petroleum exporters and gas exporters Principaux exportateurs de pétrole et de gaz	Major manufactured goods exporters Principaux exportateurs d'articles manufacturés	Year Année	Destinations Groupes de produits
Millions de dollars											
1 452 438	119 410	245 531	1 082 759	957 087	147 414	125 672	4 738	115 472	856 695	1995	Total tous produits
3 223 918	250 609	495 813	2 465 836	2 122 848	594 585	342 988	11 660	313 109	1 910 934	2005	
7 591 837	585 450	1 131 649	5 843 984	5 065 541	1 621 435	778 443	30 754	774 857	4 251 496	2012	
Parts par destinations (en pourcentage)											
28.4	2.3	4.8	21.1	18.7	2.9	2.5	0.1	2.3	16.7	1995	Total tous produits
30.9	2.4	4.7	23.6	20.3	5.7	3.3	0.1	3.0	18.3	2005	
41.4	3.2	6.2	31.8	27.6	8.8	4.2	0.2	4.2	23.2	2012	
25.3	3.8	4.8	16.5	13.1	2.3	3.5	0.1	4.0	10.3	1995	Produits alimentaires
26.2	4.3	5.0	16.7	12.5	2.7	4.2	0.2	4.8	10.2	2005	(CTCI 0 + 1 + 22 + 4)
38.7	6.0	6.1	26.4	20.7	6.2	5.7	0.2	7.4	15.2	2012	
30.3	2.3	3.7	24.2	22.3	5.4	2.0	0.0	1.3	19.3	1995	Matières premières
35.8	2.2	3.9	29.6	26.9	13.5	2.6	0.1	1.5	23.4	2005	d'origine agricole
50.1	2.7	3.9	43.5	40.4	23.8	3.0	0.0	1.9	33.9	2012	(CTCI 2 - 22 - 27 - 28)
27.5	1.2	2.2	24.1	22.1	2.5	2.0	0.0	1.4	18.4	1995	Minerais, métaux, pierres
37.1	1.5	2.6	33.0	29.2	9.8	3.8	0.0	2.8	23.2	2005	précieuses et or (non monétaire)
51.0	1.8	2.3	46.9	41.5	20.1	5.4	0.0	4.1	33.5	2012	(CTCI 27 + 28 + 68 + 667 + 971)
25.9	2.0	4.8	19.1	16.8	1.5	2.2	0.1	0.5	13.6	1995	Combustibles (CTCI 3)
29.2	2.1	4.2	22.7	20.5	4.3	2.2	0.1	1.0	17.0	2005	
42.4	2.9	4.8	34.5	32.4	8.3	2.1	0.2	1.4	25.0	2012	
29.4	2.3	5.0	22.0	19.6	3.1	2.4	0.1	2.3	18.0	1995	Articles manufacturés
31.2	2.3	5.0	23.8	20.5	5.9	3.3	0.1	3.3	19.0	2005	(CTCI 5 à 8 moins 667 et 68)
40.5	3.1	6.9	30.3	25.8	7.9	4.6	0.2	4.7	22.6	2012	
Parts par principaux groupes de produits (en pourcentage)											
100.0	100.0	100.0	100.0	100.0	100.0	100.0	100.0	100.0	100.0	1995	Total tous produits
100.0	100.0	100.0	100.0	100.0	100.0	100.0	100.0	100.0	100.0	2005	
100.0	100.0	100.0	100.0	100.0	100.0	100.0	100.0	100.0	100.0	2012	
8.0	14.8	8.9	7.0	6.3	7.1	12.6	14.5	15.8	5.5	1995	Produits alimentaires
5.5	11.6	6.9	4.6	4.0	3.2	8.3	10.3	10.5	3.6	2005	(CTCI 0 + 1 + 22 + 4)
7.1	14.3	7.4	6.3	5.6	5.3	10.2	8.2	13.2	5.0	2012	
2.9	2.7	2.1	3.1	3.2	5.1	2.2	1.0	1.6	3.1	1995	Matières premières
1.8	1.5	1.3	2.0	2.1	3.7	1.3	1.0	0.8	2.0	2005	d'origine agricole
1.9	1.3	1.0	2.1	2.2	4.1	1.1	0.4	0.7	2.2	2012	(CTCI 2 - 22 - 27 - 28)
4.4	2.3	2.1	5.2	5.4	4.0	3.7	0.6	2.8	5.0	1995	Minerais, métaux, pierres
5.6	2.8	2.5	6.5	6.7	8.0	5.3	0.5	4.3	5.9	2005	précieuses et or (non monétaire)
7.9	3.6	2.4	9.4	9.6	14.6	8.1	0.5	6.2	9.3	2012	(CTCI 27 + 28 + 68 + 667 + 971)
6.7	6.2	7.3	6.6	6.6	3.9	6.7	8.5	1.5	6.0	1995	Combustibles (CTCI 3)
13.3	12.5	12.5	13.5	14.1	10.5	9.4	18.7	4.6	13.0	2005	
19.3	17.3	14.6	20.4	22.1	17.8	9.4	19.5	6.4	20.3	2012	
75.4	71.5	76.5	75.6	76.2	77.4	71.2	72.3	74.7	78.1	1995	Articles manufacturés
71.2	68.6	73.8	71.0	70.9	72.5	71.5	63.8	76.7	73.3	2005	(CTCI 5 à 8 moins 667 et 68)
61.3	61.2	70.3	59.6	58.4	55.9	67.3	60.4	70.2	61.0	2012	

Pour les sources et les notes, se reporter à la fin du tableau 2.2.L.

Product group	Year / Année	World (1) / Monde (1)	Developed economies - Économies développées							Transition economies / Économies en transition
			Total	Europe		Canada	USA / États-Unis	Japan / Japon	Other developed countries / Autres économies développées	
				Total	EU / UE					
Millions of dollars										
All products	1995	5 186 545	3 547 598	2 145 954	2 006 290	197 540	636 452	478 686	88 965	122 720
	2005	10 705 057	6 220 515	4 069 508	3 813 296	362 206	936 705	667 406	184 689	374 453
	2012	18 439 112	9 135 790	5 883 871	5 409 701	467 096	1 512 946	888 090	383 786	834 945
Share by origin (percentage)										
All products	1995	100.0	68.4	41.4	38.7	3.8	12.3	9.2	1.7	2.4
	2005	100.0	58.1	38.0	35.6	3.4	8.8	6.2	1.7	3.5
	2012	100.0	49.5	31.9	29.3	2.5	8.2	4.8	2.1	4.5
All food items	1995	100.0	64.8	42.9	41.2	3.5	13.8	0.5	4.0	1.9
(SITC 0 + 1 + 22 + 4)	2005	100.0	62.1	43.5	41.8	3.6	9.9	0.4	4.6	2.5
	2012	100.0	55.8	37.6	35.6	3.5	10.3	0.4	4.1	3.7
Agricultural raw materials	1995	100.0	65.9	29.7	28.6	12.4	16.7	1.7	5.4	5.3
(SITC 2 - 22 - 27 - 28)	2005	100.0	62.1	33.2	32.5	10.2	12.5	1.8	4.3	6.3
	2012	100.0	54.9	29.2	28.5	6.2	12.5	2.4	4.7	5.5
Ores, metals, precious stones	1995	100.0	60.4	34.8	29.1	6.4	8.5	2.4	8.4	7.5
and non-monetary gold	2005	100.0	52.6	29.8	25.0	4.7	5.6	2.5	10.0	7.7
(SITC 27 + 28 + 68 + 667 + 971)	2012	100.0	48.6	25.4	19.4	3.6	5.9	2.6	11.1	5.3
Fuels (SITC 3)	1995	100.0	30.1	19.2	13.8	4.3	3.2	0.5	2.8	8.8
	2005	100.0	28.7	18.9	14.2	4.9	2.2	0.3	2.3	12.4
	2012	100.0	25.9	15.5	12.7	3.5	4.0	0.4	2.6	14.1
Manufactured goods	1995	100.0	73.1	43.8	41.4	3.2	13.2	12.2	0.7	1.1
(SITC 5 to 8 less 667 and 68)	2005	100.0	63.3	41.5	39.7	2.7	10.0	8.4	0.7	1.4
	2012	100.0	54.9	36.2	34.2	1.8	9.2	7.0	0.7	1.6
Share by major product group (percentage)										
All products	1995	100.0	100.0	100.0	100.0	100.0	100.0	100.0	100.0	100.0
	2005	100.0	100.0	100.0	100.0	100.0	100.0	100.0	100.0	100.0
	2012	100.0	100.0	100.0	100.0	100.0	100.0	100.0	100.0	100.0
All food items	1995	9.0	8.6	9.4	9.6	8.4	10.2	0.5	21.2	7.4
(SITC 0 + 1 + 22 + 4)	2005	6.7	7.2	7.7	7.9	7.1	7.6	0.5	18.0	4.8
	2012	7.6	8.6	9.0	9.3	10.4	9.5	0.6	15.0	6.3
Agricultural raw materials	1995	2.9	2.8	2.1	2.1	9.3	3.9	0.5	9.1	6.4
(SITC 2 - 22 - 27 - 28)	2005	1.7	1.8	1.4	1.5	5.0	2.4	0.5	4.2	3.0
	2012	1.5	1.7	1.4	1.5	3.8	2.3	0.8	3.5	1.9
Ores, metals, precious stones	1995	5.0	4.4	4.2	3.7	8.3	3.4	1.3	24.2	15.6
and non-monetary gold	2005	4.9	4.4	3.8	3.4	6.7	3.1	1.9	28.2	10.7
(SITC 27 + 28 + 68 + 667 + 971)	2012	6.3	6.2	5.0	4.2	8.9	4.6	3.5	33.9	7.4
Fuels (SITC 3)	1995	7.3	3.2	3.4	2.6	8.3	1.9	0.4	12.1	27.2
	2005	13.4	6.6	6.7	5.4	19.3	3.5	0.6	18.3	47.6
	2012	18.5	9.7	9.0	8.0	25.2	8.9	1.6	22.8	57.5
Manufactured goods	1995	72.2	77.2	76.4	77.3	61.4	77.8	95.2	31.3	34.5
(SITC 5 to 8 less 667 and 68)	2005	70.8	77.2	77.2	78.9	57.3	81.2	95.1	28.8	28.2
	2012	63.3	70.1	71.7	73.9	46.1	71.1	92.3	20.8	22.0

For sources and notes, see end of table 2.2.L.

Developing economies - Économies en développement								Major petroleum exporters and gas exporters / Principaux exportateurs de pétrole et de gaz	Major manufactured goods exporters / Principaux exportateurs d'articles manufacturés	Year / Année	Origines / Groupes de produits
				Asia / Asie							
Total	Africa / Afrique	América / Amérique	Total	Eastern, Southern and South-Eastern Asia / Asie orientale, méridionale et du Sud-Est	China / Chine	Western Asia / Asie occidentale	Oceania / Océanie				
Millions de dollars											
1 428 732	115 624	245 775	1 062 603	927 068	233 463	135 535	4 729	176 738	852 752	1995	Total tous produits
4 031 392	318 539	625 587	3 080 195	2 604 081	1 073 485	476 114	7 071	615 926	2 397 172	2005	
8 341 762	677 759	1 213 851	6 436 759	5 205 846	2 387 460	1 230 913	13 393	1 525 511	4 662 286	2012	
Parts par origines (en pourcentage)											
27.5	2.2	4.7	20.5	17.9	4.5	2.6	0.1	3.4	16.4	1995	Total tous produits
37.7	3.0	5.8	28.8	24.3	10.0	4.4	0.1	5.8	22.4	2005	
45.2	3.7	6.6	34.9	28.2	12.9	6.7	0.1	8.3	25.3	2012	
31.9	3.8	12.6	15.3	13.6	2.7	1.7	0.3	0.8	10.3	1995	Produits alimentaires
35.2	3.9	15.1	16.0	13.6	3.7	2.3	0.2	1.0	9.9	2005	(CTCI 0 + 1 + 22 + 4)
40.3	3.7	16.8	19.6	16.8	3.7	2.8	0.2	1.4	11.0	2012	
28.0	4.0	6.4	17.1	16.5	2.3	0.6	0.5	0.6	12.4	1995	Matières premières
31.4	4.6	7.9	18.5	17.7	3.1	0.8	0.4	0.5	12.1	2005	d'origine agricole
39.5	4.2	8.6	26.3	25.5	3.8	0.7	0.4	0.6	14.5	2012	(CTCI 2 - 22 - 27 - 28)
29.4	6.2	9.9	12.8	11.0	1.9	1.7	0.6	1.7	7.4	1995	Minerais, métaux, pierres
39.2	7.4	12.2	19.2	16.0	3.4	3.3	0.4	3.3	9.2	2005	précieuses et or (non monétaire)
45.2	7.3	14.8	22.7	17.0	4.0	5.7	0.4	5.0	11.5	2012	(CTCI 27 + 28 + 68 + 667 + 971)
58.1	11.7	8.3	38.0	14.7	1.5	23.3	0.2	38.2	8.7	1995	Combustibles (CTCI 3)
56.7	12.3	8.8	35.4	13.3	1.3	22.1	0.1	36.5	8.8	2005	
57.7	11.4	7.7	38.6	13.4	0.7	25.2	0.0	37.8	8.5	2012	
24.5	0.7	3.1	20.7	19.8	5.5	0.9	0.0	0.5	19.2	1995	Articles manufacturés
35.0	0.8	4.0	30.2	28.7	13.2	1.6	0.0	0.8	27.7	2005	(CTCI 5 à 8 moins 667 et 68)
43.2	0.9	4.3	38.0	35.8	19.2	2.2	0.0	1.2	34.1	2012	
Parts par principaux groupes de produits (en pourcentage)											
100.0	100.0	100.0	100.0	100.0	100.0	100.0	100.0	100.0	100.0	1995	Total tous produits
100.0	100.0	100.0	100.0	100.0	100.0	100.0	100.0	100.0	100.0	2005	
100.0	100.0	100.0	100.0	100.0	100.0	100.0	100.0	100.0	100.0	2012	
10.5	15.3	24.1	6.8	6.9	5.5	6.0	25.9	2.1	5.7	1995	Produits alimentaires
6.3	8.8	17.4	3.7	3.8	2.5	3.5	22.7	1.2	3.0	2005	(CTCI 0 + 1 + 22 + 4)
6.8	7.6	19.5	4.3	4.5	2.2	3.2	22.1	1.3	3.3	2012	
2.9	5.2	3.9	2.4	2.6	1.5	0.7	15.3	0.5	2.2	1995	Matières premières
1.4	2.6	2.2	1.1	1.2	0.5	0.3	9.6	0.1	0.9	2005	d'origine agricole
1.3	1.8	2.0	1.2	1.4	0.4	0.2	9.0	0.1	0.9	2012	(CTCI 2 - 22 - 27 - 28)
5.3	13.7	10.4	3.1	3.1	2.1	3.3	30.0	2.5	2.2	1995	Minerais, métaux, pierres
5.1	12.1	10.2	3.3	3.2	1.7	3.6	26.4	2.8	2.0	2005	précieuses et or (non monétaire)
6.3	12.6	14.2	4.1	3.8	2.0	5.4	37.7	3.8	2.9	2012	(CTCI 27 + 28 + 68 + 667 + 971)
15.5	38.5	12.8	13.6	6.0	2.5	65.2	13.7	82.0	3.9	1995	Combustibles (CTCI 3)
20.2	55.7	20.3	16.6	7.4	1.7	66.9	15.5	85.3	5.3	2005	
23.6	57.5	21.5	20.4	8.7	0.9	69.7	12.3	84.4	6.2	2012	
64.3	24.1	46.9	73.0	80.1	87.7	24.0	14.4	11.4	84.5	1995	Articles manufacturés
65.9	19.8	47.9	74.4	83.5	93.0	24.8	23.6	9.7	87.6	2005	(CTCI 5 à 8 moins 667 et 68)
60.4	15.0	41.2	68.9	80.2	93.8	21.1	17.0	9.4	85.4	2012	

Pour les sources et les notes, se reporter à la fin du tableau 2.2.L.

2.2.B Export structure by partner and product group
Developing economies

Destination / Product group	Year Année	World (1) Monde (1)	Developed economies - Économies développées							Transition economies Économies en transition
			Total	Europe Total	Europe EU UE	Canada	USA États-Unis	Japan Japon	Other developed countries Autres économies développées	
Millions of dollars										
All products	1995	1 431 511	809 215	284 948	274 471	16 379	320 089	164 988	22 812	13 463
	2005	3 787 054	1 984 340	713 085	692 847	45 776	822 548	333 494	69 437	48 192
	2012	8 182 433	3 333 307	1 229 704	1 182 410	97 546	1 257 769	582 525	165 763	147 442
Share by destination (percentage)										
All products	1995	100.0	56.5	19.9	19.2	1.1	22.4	11.5	1.6	0.9
	2005	100.0	52.4	18.8	18.3	1.2	21.7	8.8	1.8	1.3
	2012	100.0	40.7	15.0	14.5	1.2	15.4	7.1	2.0	1.8
All food items	1995	100.0	56.7	27.7	26.8	0.9	12.9	14.1	1.2	2.8
(SITC 0 + 1 + 22 + 4)	2005	100.0	51.8	25.2	24.6	1.2	14.8	9.2	1.5	4.0
	2012	100.0	38.3	18.3	17.9	1.1	11.0	6.4	1.5	3.6
Agricultural raw materials	1995	100.0	51.3	23.7	23.1	0.6	11.9	14.1	0.9	0.3
(SITC 2 - 22 - 27 - 28)	2005	100.0	47.1	21.9	21.3	1.0	14.1	9.0	1.0	0.7
	2012	100.0	38.2	15.9	15.7	1.0	14.0	6.4	0.9	1.4
Ores, metals, precious stones	1995	100.0	59.4	28.1	25.6	1.2	12.3	16.1	1.7	0.8
and non-monetary gold	2005	100.0	48.3	23.8	20.8	2.1	11.1	9.0	2.4	0.6
(SITC 27 + 28 + 68 + 667 + 971)	2012	100.0	34.4	16.3	12.6	2.4	8.1	5.7	2.0	0.4
Fuels (SITC 3)	1995	100.0	62.4	20.0	19.7	0.8	19.3	20.7	1.6	0.3
	2005	100.0	56.8	17.3	17.0	1.0	22.0	14.7	1.8	0.1
	2012	100.0	41.9	14.0	13.8	1.0	13.1	11.7	2.1	0.1
Manufactured goods	1995	100.0	55.1	17.8	17.2	1.3	25.7	8.6	1.7	0.9
(SITC 5 to 8 less 667 and 68)	2005	100.0	51.6	18.4	17.9	1.2	23.4	6.7	1.8	1.5
	2012	100.0	41.6	14.9	14.5	1.1	17.8	5.6	2.1	2.5
Share by major product group (percentage)										
All products	1995	100.0	100.0	100.0	100.0	100.0	100.0	100.0	100.0	100.0
	2005	100.0	100.0	100.0	100.0	100.0	100.0	100.0	100.0	100.0
	2012	100.0	100.0	100.0	100.0	100.0	100.0	100.0	100.0	100.0
All food items	1995	9.9	9.9	13.8	13.8	7.9	5.7	12.1	7.2	30.0
(SITC 0 + 1 + 22 + 4)	2005	6.0	6.0	8.1	8.1	5.8	4.1	6.3	4.9	19.0
	2012	6.7	6.3	8.1	8.2	6.3	4.8	6.0	5.0	13.3
Agricultural raw materials	1995	2.7	2.5	3.3	3.3	1.5	1.5	3.4	1.6	0.7
(SITC 2 - 22 - 27 - 28)	2005	1.3	1.2	1.5	1.5	1.1	0.8	1.3	0.7	0.7
	2012	1.3	1.3	1.4	1.4	1.1	1.2	1.2	0.6	1.0
Ores, metals, precious stones	1995	5.4	5.6	7.6	7.2	5.5	2.9	7.5	5.7	4.7
and non-monetary gold	2005	5.0	4.6	6.3	5.7	8.6	2.6	5.1	6.5	2.5
(SITC 27 + 28 + 68 + 667 + 971)	2012	6.6	5.6	7.2	5.8	13.3	3.5	5.3	6.6	1.4
Fuels (SITC 3)	1995	15.1	16.7	15.3	15.6	10.1	13.0	27.2	15.3	4.1
	2005	22.5	24.4	20.7	21.0	18.6	22.8	37.6	22.4	1.3
	2012	24.8	25.4	23.1	23.7	21.1	21.0	40.8	25.1	1.3
Manufactured goods	1995	65.7	64.0	58.8	58.8	74.3	75.5	48.9	69.3	59.7
(SITC 5 to 8 less 667 and 68)	2005	64.3	63.3	62.8	63.1	65.0	69.3	49.2	64.4	76.2
	2012	59.6	60.8	59.2	59.9	57.4	69.1	46.5	62.0	82.8

For sources and notes, see end of table 2.2.L.

| Developing economies - Économies en développement | | | | | | | | | | Year | Destinations |
Total	Africa / Afrique	America / Amérique	Asia / Asie Total	Eastern, Southern and South-Eastern Asia / Asie orientale, méridionale et du Sud-Est	China / Chine	Western Asia / Asie occidentale	Oceania / Océanie	Major petroleum exporters and gas exporters / Principaux exportateurs de pétrole et de gaz	Major manufactured goods exporters / Principaux exportateurs d'articles manufacturés	Année	Groupes de produits
Millions de dollars											
601 512	38 103	73 341	489 254	446 480	83 170	42 775	814	38 503	374 647	1995	Total tous produits
1 740 065	109 734	184 313	1 440 701	1 302 455	367 705	138 246	5 317	137 564	1 082 718	2005	
4 679 454	317 571	495 355	3 848 091	3 456 694	998 600	391 397	18 437	438 230	2 647 219	2012	
Parts par destinations (en pourcentage)											
42.0	2.7	5.1	34.2	31.2	5.8	3.0	0.1	2.7	26.2	1995	Total tous produits
45.9	2.9	4.9	38.0	34.4	9.7	3.7	0.1	3.6	28.6	2005	
57.2	3.9	6.1	47.0	42.2	12.2	4.8	0.2	5.4	32.4	2012	
39.8	4.6	6.6	28.5	23.3	4.6	5.2	0.1	5.9	15.7	1995	Produits alimentaires
43.8	6.7	6.4	30.6	23.2	5.1	7.4	0.1	8.5	15.0	2005	(CTCI 0 + 1 + 22 + 4)
57.8	8.6	7.7	41.3	32.7	8.3	8.6	0.2	11.9	19.8	2012	
48.0	3.3	4.8	40.0	37.8	9.5	2.2	0.0	1.9	31.2	1995	Matières premières
51.9	2.7	4.4	44.8	42.1	19.8	2.7	0.0	1.9	33.3	2005	d'origine agricole
60.1	2.3	4.1	53.7	50.7	25.4	3.0	0.0	2.1	38.3	2012	(CTCI 2 - 22 - 27 - 28)
39.2	1.5	3.6	34.0	31.6	5.1	2.4	0.0	2.4	26.3	1995	Minerais, métaux, pierres
51.0	2.1	3.7	45.2	39.7	13.5	5.4	0.0	5.0	31.4	2005	précieuses et or (non monétaire)
65.1	2.2	2.7	60.2	53.1	26.0	7.1	0.0	7.4	40.9	2012	(CTCI 27 + 28 + 68 + 667 + 971)
36.2	2.6	5.3	28.3	25.2	2.4	3.0	0.1	0.3	19.8	1995	Combustibles (CTCI 3)
42.7	2.8	5.0	34.7	32.1	6.5	2.5	0.2	1.0	26.0	2005	
57.7	3.2	4.1	50.2	48.1	11.3	2.1	0.2	1.3	35.0	2012	
43.8	2.4	5.0	36.3	33.5	6.7	2.8	0.1	2.8	29.0	1995	Articles manufacturés
46.7	2.6	4.7	39.3	35.8	10.9	3.5	0.1	4.0	30.6	2005	(CTCI 5 à 8 moins 667 et 68)
55.9	3.8	7.0	44.9	39.7	11.1	5.1	0.2	6.2	31.7	2012	
Parts par principaux groupes de produits (en pourcentage)											
100.0	100.0	100.0	100.0	100.0	100.0	100.0	100.0	100.0	100.0	1995	Total tous produits
100.0	100.0	100.0	100.0	100.0	100.0	100.0	100.0	100.0	100.0	2005	
100.0	100.0	100.0	100.0	100.0	100.0	100.0	100.0	100.0	100.0	2012	
9.4	17.3	12.7	8.3	7.4	7.9	17.1	11.0	21.7	6.0	1995	Produits alimentaires
5.8	13.9	7.9	4.9	4.1	3.2	12.2	5.8	14.0	3.2	2005	(CTCI 0 + 1 + 22 + 4)
6.7	14.8	8.4	5.9	5.2	4.5	12.1	5.3	14.8	4.1	2012	
3.1	3.4	2.5	3.2	3.3	4.5	2.0	0.5	1.9	3.3	1995	Matières premières
1.5	1.2	1.2	1.5	1.6	2.7	1.0	0.2	0.7	1.5	2005	d'origine agricole
1.4	0.8	0.9	1.5	1.6	2.8	0.8	0.2	0.5	1.6	2012	(CTCI 2 - 22 - 27 - 28)
5.0	3.1	3.8	5.3	5.4	4.7	4.3	0.5	4.8	5.4	1995	Minerais, métaux, pierres
5.6	3.7	3.8	6.0	5.8	7.0	7.5	0.2	7.0	5.5	2005	précieuses et or (non monétaire)
7.6	3.8	2.9	8.5	8.3	14.1	9.9	0.4	9.2	8.4	2012	(CTCI 27 + 28 + 68 + 667 + 971)
13.0	14.8	15.6	12.5	12.3	6.4	15.3	15.2	1.5	11.5	1995	Combustibles (CTCI 3)
20.9	21.6	23.2	20.5	21.0	15.0	15.7	32.0	6.2	20.5	2005	
25.0	20.5	16.6	26.4	28.2	22.9	10.8	27.1	6.2	26.8	2012	
68.5	60.4	64.5	69.7	70.5	75.6	60.8	68.5	69.6	72.9	1995	Articles manufacturés
65.5	58.0	62.4	66.5	67.0	71.9	61.2	55.7	70.1	68.9	2005	(CTCI 5 à 8 moins 667 et 68)
58.2	58.6	68.8	56.8	56.0	54.4	64.0	53.0	69.0	58.4	2012	

Pour les sources et les notes, se reporter à la fin du tableau 2.2.L.

Product group	Year Année	World (1) Monde (1)	Developed economies - Économies développées							Transition economies Économies en transition
			Total	Europe Total	EU UE	Canada	USA États-Unis	Japan Japon	Other developed countries Autres économies développées	
Millions of dollars										
All products	1995	1 504 985	895 851	329 047	305 883	19 570	270 134	242 857	34 243	22 310
	2005	3 398 852	1 522 407	606 298	562 658	31 570	427 292	374 368	82 880	77 344
	2012	7 675 253	2 896 430	1 212 116	1 089 380	71 647	816 910	574 560	221 197	205 715
Share by origin (percentage)										
All products	1995	100.0	59.5	21.9	20.3	1.3	17.9	16.1	2.3	1.5
	2005	100.0	44.8	17.8	16.6	0.9	12.6	11.0	2.4	2.3
	2012	100.0	37.7	15.8	14.2	0.9	10.6	7.5	2.9	2.7
All food items	1995	100.0	54.7	20.2	19.4	3.7	22.9	1.5	6.4	0.8
(SITC 0 + 1 + 22 + 4)	2005	100.0	44.2	15.6	14.7	2.7	17.8	1.2	6.9	2.3
	2012	100.0	39.5	13.4	12.5	3.0	16.4	0.7	6.0	3.6
Agricultural raw materials	1995	100.0	53.6	12.0	11.6	4.6	24.9	4.3	7.8	4.7
(SITC 2 - 22 - 27 - 28)	2005	100.0	51.1	14.6	14.3	4.9	20.9	4.0	6.7	7.4
	2012	100.0	48.6	14.5	14.2	5.3	18.0	3.8	7.0	5.7
Ores, metals, precious stones	1995	100.0	56.2	23.0	17.4	2.8	11.9	6.9	11.5	4.0
and non-monetary gold	2005	100.0	45.4	18.8	13.5	1.6	6.7	5.3	13.0	5.0
(SITC 27 + 28 + 68 + 667 + 971)	2012	100.0	43.0	15.8	9.9	1.5	6.9	4.1	14.6	3.7
Fuels (SITC 3)	1995	100.0	16.4	4.4	4.3	0.7	5.8	1.6	4.0	1.9
	2005	100.0	12.5	3.4	3.0	0.3	4.3	0.7	3.8	4.7
	2012	100.0	15.4	5.1	4.8	0.4	5.9	0.8	3.1	6.4
Manufactured goods	1995	100.0	64.2	24.0	22.4	0.9	18.4	20.1	0.9	1.2
(SITC 5 to 8 less 667 and 68)	2005	100.0	50.1	20.4	19.3	0.7	13.9	14.3	0.8	1.4
	2012	100.0	43.3	19.3	18.1	0.7	11.6	11.0	0.7	1.0
Share by major product group (percentage)										
All products	1995	100.0	100.0	100.0	100.0	100.0	100.0	100.0	100.0	100.0
	2005	100.0	100.0	100.0	100.0	100.0	100.0	100.0	100.0	100.0
	2012	100.0	100.0	100.0	100.0	100.0	100.0	100.0	100.0	100.0
All food items	1995	8.1	7.4	7.5	7.7	23.0	10.3	0.8	22.7	4.4
(SITC 0 + 1 + 22 + 4)	2005	5.8	5.8	5.1	5.2	17.1	8.2	0.6	16.6	5.8
	2012	7.1	7.5	6.1	6.3	22.6	11.0	0.7	14.8	9.5
Agricultural raw materials	1995	3.0	2.7	1.6	1.7	10.4	4.1	0.8	10.2	9.4
(SITC 2 - 22 - 27 - 28)	2005	1.9	2.2	1.6	1.6	10.0	3.2	0.7	5.3	6.2
	2012	1.9	2.4	1.7	1.9	10.7	3.2	1.0	4.6	4.0
Ores, metals, precious stones	1995	4.9	4.6	5.2	4.2	10.6	3.3	2.1	25.0	13.4
and non-monetary gold	2005	6.3	6.4	6.6	5.1	11.0	3.3	3.0	33.5	13.9
(SITC 27 + 28 + 68 + 667 + 971)	2012	8.4	9.6	8.4	5.9	13.2	5.5	4.7	42.9	11.6
Fuels (SITC 3)	1995	6.7	1.9	1.4	1.4	3.6	2.2	0.7	11.7	8.5
	2005	12.3	3.4	2.3	2.2	4.2	4.2	0.7	19.3	25.3
	2012	18.4	7.5	6.0	6.1	8.0	10.1	2.0	20.0	43.7
Manufactured goods	1995	75.1	80.9	82.3	82.8	50.9	76.9	93.3	29.2	62.3
(SITC 5 to 8 less 667 and 68)	2005	72.2	80.8	82.5	84.0	57.3	79.9	94.0	22.8	43.0
	2012	61.8	70.9	75.6	78.6	44.0	67.4	90.9	14.1	23.4

For sources and notes, see end of table 2.2.L.

Developing economies - Économies en développement										Origines	
				Asia Asie				Major petroleum exporters and gas exporters	Major manufactured goods exporters	Year	
Total	Africa Afrique	America Amérique	Total	Eastern, Southern and South-Eastern Asia Asie orientale, méridionale et du Sud-Est	China Chine	Western Asia Asie occidentale	Oceania Océanie	Principaux exportateurs de pétrole et de gaz	Principaux exportateurs d'articles manufacturés	Année	Groupes de produits
Millions de dollars											
570 482	31 785	69 137	468 681	408 194	104 387	60 487	878	67 358	363 091	1995	Total tous produits
1 778 022	97 226	181 199	1 497 522	1 265 883	415 922	231 639	2 074	263 117	1 076 999	2005	
4 517 745	315 971	495 755	3 701 400	2 939 548	1 121 278	761 852	4 618	898 918	2 436 723	2012	
Parts par origines (en pourcentage)											
37.9	2.1	4.6	31.1	27.1	6.9	4.0	0.1	4.5	24.1	1995	Total tous produits
52.3	2.9	5.3	44.1	37.2	12.2	6.8	0.1	7.7	31.7	2005	
58.9	4.1	6.5	48.2	38.3	14.6	9.9	0.1	11.7	31.7	2012	
44.0	3.7	14.1	26.0	22.2	4.3	3.7	0.2	1.8	15.6	1995	Produits alimentaires
53.3	4.6	19.5	28.9	23.7	5.0	5.2	0.3	2.6	13.9	2005	(CTCI 0 + 1 + 22 + 4)
56.9	4.4	21.4	30.9	25.4	4.3	5.5	0.2	3.0	13.4	2012	
41.3	5.0	7.5	28.2	27.2	3.4	1.0	0.6	0.9	21.0	1995	Matières premières
41.4	5.8	7.0	27.7	26.6	2.7	1.2	0.9	0.9	17.5	2005	d'origine agricole
45.7	5.0	8.0	31.9	31.0	3.2	0.9	0.8	0.8	18.0	2012	(CTCI 2 - 22 - 27 - 28)
39.6	6.2	9.8	23.3	19.3	3.3	4.0	0.2	3.0	13.8	1995	Minerais, métaux, pierres
49.3	5.9	12.1	31.2	25.3	4.6	5.9	0.1	5.8	13.4	2005	précieuses et or (non monétaire)
53.2	7.8	13.7	31.5	23.1	5.3	8.4	0.1	7.7	14.1	2012	(CTCI 27 + 28 + 68 + 667 + 971)
81.0	8.6	7.8	64.6	27.4	2.6	37.2	0.1	48.9	16.7	1995	Combustibles (CTCI 3)
82.6	10.6	6.7	65.2	28.2	2.9	37.0	0.0	48.0	16.3	2005	
78.1	10.7	7.5	59.9	23.1	1.4	36.7	0.0	49.7	12.6	2012	
33.8	1.0	2.9	29.9	28.5	8.1	1.3	0.0	1.1	26.9	1995	Articles manufacturés
48.2	1.0	3.4	43.7	41.7	15.5	2.1	0.0	1.6	38.1	2005	(CTCI 5 à 8 moins 667 et 68)
55.5	1.1	3.6	50.7	47.4	21.8	3.3	0.0	2.5	43.2	2012	
Parts par principaux groupes de produits (en pourcentage)											
100.0	100.0	100.0	100.0	100.0	100.0	100.0	100.0	100.0	100.0	1995	Total tous produits
100.0	100.0	100.0	100.0	100.0	100.0	100.0	100.0	100.0	100.0	2005	
100.0	100.0	100.0	100.0	100.0	100.0	100.0	100.0	100.0	100.0	2012	
9.4	14.2	24.9	6.8	6.6	5.0	7.5	27.2	3.2	5.3	1995	Produits alimentaires
5.9	9.3	21.4	3.8	3.7	2.4	4.5	25.3	2.0	2.6	2005	(CTCI 0 + 1 + 22 + 4)
6.9	7.7	23.6	4.6	4.7	2.1	4.0	22.0	1.8	3.0	2012	
3.2	7.0	4.8	2.7	3.0	1.5	0.7	32.3	0.6	2.6	1995	Matières premières
1.5	3.8	2.5	1.2	1.4	0.4	0.3	26.8	0.2	1.0	2005	d'origine agricole
1.5	2.3	2.3	1.2	1.5	0.4	0.2	24.0	0.1	1.1	2012	(CTCI 2 - 22 - 27 - 28)
5.1	14.5	10.5	3.7	3.5	2.4	4.9	19.9	3.2	2.8	1995	Minerais, métaux, pierres
5.9	12.9	14.3	4.4	4.3	2.4	5.4	10.9	4.7	2.7	2005	précieuses et or (non monétaire)
7.6	16.0	17.9	5.5	5.1	3.1	7.2	14.9	5.5	3.7	2012	(CTCI 27 + 28 + 68 + 667 + 971)
14.4	27.3	11.5	14.0	6.8	2.6	62.3	8.2	73.6	4.7	1995	Combustibles (CTCI 3)
19.5	45.6	15.6	18.3	9.3	2.9	67.0	8.2	76.5	6.3	2005	
24.4	47.9	21.4	22.8	11.1	1.7	67.9	5.9	77.9	7.3	2012	
67.0	36.5	47.8	72.0	79.0	88.0	24.3	12.1	19.2	83.6	1995	Articles manufacturés
66.5	26.3	45.6	71.7	80.8	91.6	22.0	27.9	15.3	86.8	2005	(CTCI 5 à 8 moins 667 et 68)
58.2	16.7	34.2	65.0	76.5	92.2	20.7	30.2	13.4	84.1	2012	

Pour les sources et les notes, se reporter à la fin du tableau 2.2.L.

Destination / Product group	Year / Année	World (1) / Monde (1)	Developed economies - Économies développées							Transition economies / Économies en transition
			Total	Europe		Canada	USA / États-Unis	Japan / Japon	Other developed countries / Autres économies développées	
				Total	EU / UE					
Millions of dollars										
All products	1995	111 034	80 667	58 173	56 338	1 153	16 345	3 842	1 154	788
	2005	301 446	209 026	129 690	125 363	4 591	64 173	7 980	2 592	1 486
	2012	640 520	350 094	238 691	230 411	12 735	75 296	16 341	7 031	3 308
Share by destination (percentage)										
All products	1995	100.0	72.7	52.4	50.7	1.0	14.7	3.5	1.0	0.7
	2005	100.0	69.3	43.0	41.6	1.5	21.3	2.6	0.9	0.5
	2012	100.0	54.7	37.3	36.0	2.0	11.8	2.6	1.1	0.5
All food items	1995	100.0	72.8	60.9	59.4	0.8	3.9	6.4	0.8	1.6
(SITC 0 + 1 + 22 + 4)	2005	100.0	63.8	53.0	51.9	0.8	5.5	3.4	1.1	2.8
	2012	100.0	47.9	39.4	38.6	0.7	4.3	2.6	0.8	3.6
Agricultural raw materials	1995	100.0	58.4	48.6	47.6	0.2	3.2	5.8	0.6	0.1
(SITC 2 - 22 - 27 - 28)	2005	100.0	50.9	41.7	40.3	0.2	3.4	5.2	0.4	0.4
	2012	100.0	36.9	31.2	30.4	0.5	3.4	1.6	0.2	0.9
Ores, metals, precious stones	1995	100.0	77.6	54.5	50.3	0.9	11.7	9.5	1.1	0.3
and non-monetary gold	2005	100.0	69.1	49.2	43.3	1.2	9.7	8.0	1.1	1.3
(SITC 27 + 28 + 68 + 667 + 971)	2012	100.0	43.4	30.6	25.0	1.7	5.2	5.4	0.6	0.8
Fuels (SITC 3)	1995	100.0	79.7	51.0	49.4	1.5	25.9	0.7	0.6	0.8
	2005	100.0	73.9	40.4	39.4	2.0	29.9	1.4	0.2	0.0
	2012	100.0	61.0	39.3	38.5	2.6	15.3	2.4	1.3	0.1
Manufactured goods	1995	100.0	61.3	48.0	47.6	0.7	8.8	1.9	1.9	0.4
(SITC 5 to 8 less 667 and 68)	2005	100.0	61.0	45.4	44.9	0.7	8.9	3.2	2.8	0.6
	2012	100.0	47.8	36.6	36.1	0.6	8.3	1.3	1.0	0.7
Share by major product group (percentage)										
All products	1995	100.0	100.0	100.0	100.0	100.0	100.0	100.0	100.0	100.0
	2005	100.0	100.0	100.0	100.0	100.0	100.0	100.0	100.0	100.0
	2012	100.0	100.0	100.0	100.0	100.0	100.0	100.0	100.0	100.0
All food items	1995	14.9	15.0	17.4	17.5	10.8	3.9	27.7	12.0	33.1
(SITC 0 + 1 + 22 + 4)	2005	7.8	7.1	9.6	9.7	4.2	2.0	9.9	9.9	43.7
	2012	7.5	6.6	8.0	8.1	2.8	2.8	7.8	5.1	51.9
Agricultural raw materials	1995	5.2	4.2	4.8	4.9	0.9	1.1	8.7	3.1	0.9
(SITC 2 - 22 - 27 - 28)	2005	2.5	1.8	2.4	2.4	0.3	0.4	4.9	1.1	2.0
	2012	2.1	1.4	1.7	1.8	0.5	0.6	1.3	0.4	3.5
Ores, metals, precious stones	1995	15.5	16.5	16.1	15.3	13.9	12.3	42.3	16.5	7.6
and non-monetary gold	2005	10.6	10.5	12.1	11.0	8.1	4.8	31.9	13.4	28.5
(SITC 27 + 28 + 68 + 667 + 971)	2012	11.5	9.2	9.5	8.0	9.8	5.2	24.4	5.9	18.4
Fuels (SITC 3)	1995	37.9	41.6	36.9	36.9	56.0	66.8	7.2	21.9	41.8
	2005	60.5	64.5	56.7	57.3	79.1	85.1	32.0	16.8	5.4
	2012	62.5	69.8	65.9	66.9	83.0	81.4	59.6	75.7	7.8
Manufactured goods	1995	25.6	21.6	23.4	24.0	18.1	15.3	13.9	46.0	14.7
(SITC 5 to 8 less 667 and 68)	2005	17.8	15.6	18.7	19.2	8.2	7.4	21.2	58.6	20.4
	2012	13.9	12.2	13.7	14.0	4.0	9.8	6.9	12.7	18.1

For sources and notes, see end of table 2.2.L.

2.2.C Structure des exportations par partenaires et groupes de produits
Économies en développement : Afrique

Total	Africa / Afrique	America / Amérique	Asia / Asie — Total	Eastern, Southern and South-Eastern Asia / Asie orientale, méridionale et du Sud-Est	China / Chine	Western Asia / Asie occidentale	Oceania / Océanie	Major petroleum exporters and gas exporters / Principaux exportateurs de pétrole et de gaz	Major manufactured goods exporters / Principaux exportateurs d'articles manufacturés	Year / Année	Destinations / Groupes de produits
Millions de dollars											
28 428	13 735	2 196	12 483	9 770	1 372	2 713	15	2 877	6 238	1995	Total tous produits
87 886	28 775	11 124	47 962	37 801	19 923	10 161	26	6 655	29 993	2005	
284 793	71 519	22 008	189 840	168 733	93 241	21 107	1 427	20 233	120 736	2012	
Parts par destinations (en pourcentage)											
25.6	12.4	2.0	11.2	8.8	1.2	2.4	0.0	2.6	5.6	1995	Total tous produits
29.2	9.5	3.7	15.9	12.5	6.6	3.4	0.0	2.2	9.9	2005	
44.5	11.2	3.4	29.6	26.3	14.6	3.3	0.2	3.2	18.8	2012	
24.9	15.6	0.4	8.8	4.7	0.3	4.1	0.0	5.5	2.1	1995	Produits alimentaires
32.8	18.1	0.5	14.2	7.5	1.4	6.6	0.1	6.5	3.8	2005	(CTCI 0 + 1 + 22 + 4)
48.5	23.9	1.6	22.8	13.7	3.2	9.0	0.2	10.2	7.7	2012	
40.7	14.5	2.4	23.9	21.4	4.8	2.4	0.0	1.6	15.6	1995	Matières premières
48.7	9.9	0.6	38.2	35.1	17.4	3.1	0.0	1.3	25.3	2005	d'origine agricole
62.2	7.8	1.9	52.3	48.7	26.1	3.6	0.2	2.1	36.0	2012	(CTCI 2 - 22 - 27 - 28)
21.3	3.4	1.2	16.7	14.6	2.1	2.1	0.0	2.0	10.3	1995	Minerais, métaux, pierres
29.6	7.5	0.7	21.4	17.1	7.0	4.2	0.0	2.7	12.8	2005	précieuses et or (non monétaire)
55.7	7.8	0.7	47.2	40.0	24.5	7.2	0.0	5.2	32.5	2012	(CTCI 27 + 28 + 68 + 667 + 971)
17.4	6.0	3.0	8.4	6.3	0.6	2.1	0.0	0.3	4.0	1995	Combustibles (CTCI 3)
25.3	5.3	5.2	14.9	12.5	8.2	2.4	0.0	0.5	10.9	2005	
38.5	6.4	4.4	27.5	26.3	14.0	1.1	0.3	0.5	17.8	2012	
37.7	24.9	1.9	10.9	8.7	1.0	2.2	0.0	4.8	4.9	1995	Articles manufacturés
37.9	21.7	2.3	13.9	9.3	1.5	4.5	0.0	6.0	5.7	2005	(CTCI 5 à 8 moins 667 et 68)
51.5	31.1	3.2	17.0	10.1	2.8	6.9	0.2	10.2	6.0	2012	
Parts par principaux groupes de produits (en pourcentage)											
100.0	100.0	100.0	100.0	100.0	100.0	100.0	100.0	100.0	100.0	1995	Total tous produits
100.0	100.0	100.0	100.0	100.0	100.0	100.0	100.0	100.0	100.0	2005	
100.0	100.0	100.0	100.0	100.0	100.0	100.0	100.0	100.0	100.0	2012	
14.5	18.9	3.0	11.7	7.9	3.9	25.3	29.9	31.9	5.5	1995	Produits alimentaires
8.7	14.7	1.0	6.9	4.7	1.6	15.3	48.3	23.0	3.0	2005	(CTCI 0 + 1 + 22 + 4)
8.2	16.1	3.5	5.8	3.9	1.7	20.7	8.2	24.3	3.1	2012	
8.2	6.1	6.3	11.0	12.6	20.0	5.2	2.9	3.2	14.4	1995	Matières premières
4.2	2.6	0.4	6.0	7.0	6.5	2.3	6.4	1.4	6.3	2005	d'origine agricole
2.9	1.4	1.2	3.7	3.8	3.7	2.2	1.9	1.4	4.0	2012	(CTCI 2 - 22 - 27 - 28)
12.9	4.3	9.5	23.0	25.6	26.7	13.3	4.7	11.8	28.3	1995	Minerais, métaux, pierres
10.7	8.3	1.9	14.2	14.4	11.2	13.2	1.6	13.0	13.6	2005	précieuses et or (non monétaire)
14.5	8.0	2.4	18.4	17.5	19.4	25.2	2.1	18.8	19.9	2012	(CTCI 27 + 28 + 68 + 667 + 971)
25.8	18.5	56.9	28.3	27.1	19.0	32.4	16.9	5.0	27.0	1995	Combustibles (CTCI 3)
52.5	33.3	85.5	56.5	60.1	75.4	42.9	2.7	13.5	66.1	2005	
54.1	35.6	79.8	57.9	62.5	60.1	21.4	76.2	10.4	59.0	2012	
37.6	51.4	24.3	24.8	25.2	20.1	23.5	45.3	47.7	22.5	1995	Articles manufacturés
23.1	40.4	10.9	15.5	13.2	4.2	23.9	40.7	48.2	10.3	2005	(CTCI 5 à 8 moins 667 et 68)
16.1	38.8	13.0	8.0	5.3	2.6	29.3	11.5	44.8	4.4	2012	

Pour les sources et les notes, se reporter à la fin du tableau 2.2.L.

Product group	Year Année	World (1) Monde (1)	Developed economies - Économies développées							Transition economies Économies en transition
			Total	Europe Total	EU UE	Canada	USA États-Unis	Japan Japon	Other developed countries Autres économies développées	
Millions of dollars										
All products	1995	124 056	79 274	58 787	56 803	1 368	11 498	5 942	1 680	1 501
	2005	256 205	129 061	98 094	95 025	1 724	17 425	8 409	3 409	6 511
	2012	613 546	262 198	200 566	193 817	4 370	36 938	13 596	6 728	17 815
Share by origin (percentage)										
All products	1995	100.0	63.9	47.4	45.8	1.1	9.3	4.8	1.4	1.2
	2005	100.0	50.4	38.3	37.1	0.7	6.8	3.3	1.3	2.5
	2012	100.0	42.7	32.7	31.6	0.7	6.0	2.2	1.1	2.9
All food items	1995	100.0	60.7	39.2	37.9	3.8	15.5	0.2	2.0	0.6
(SITC 0 + 1 + 22 + 4)	2005	100.0	45.6	29.8	28.6	1.8	11.2	0.1	2.7	3.8
	2012	100.0	38.8	25.6	24.5	1.9	8.2	0.4	2.7	7.2
Agricultural raw materials	1995	100.0	62.0	47.6	47.0	1.9	9.3	0.9	2.4	6.4
(SITC 2 - 22 - 27 - 28)	2005	100.0	57.3	45.2	44.5	2.7	6.1	1.5	1.7	6.6
	2012	100.0	65.3	50.6	50.1	2.9	7.7	2.7	1.5	5.3
Ores, metals, precious stones	1995	100.0	67.6	46.1	41.5	3.4	3.2	1.2	13.8	3.0
and non-monetary gold	2005	100.0	38.4	24.2	22.7	1.0	3.4	0.3	9.4	4.8
(SITC 27 + 28 + 68 + 667 + 971)	2012	100.0	46.9	38.0	36.2	1.5	2.7	0.3	4.4	3.4
Fuels (SITC 3)	1995	100.0	18.7	13.8	13.7	0.2	3.1	0.0	1.5	1.3
	2005	100.0	18.0	15.6	14.9	0.2	1.4	0.1	0.7	4.4
	2012	100.0	30.6	26.5	25.5	0.1	3.5	0.1	0.3	5.3
Manufactured goods	1995	100.0	70.8	54.3	52.5	0.5	9.3	5.9	0.7	1.1
(SITC 5 to 8 less 667 and 68)	2005	100.0	59.3	46.2	44.8	0.5	7.6	4.2	0.8	1.9
	2012	100.0	48.1	37.2	36.0	0.6	6.6	3.1	0.7	1.3
Share by major product group (percentage)										
All products	1995	100.0	100.0	100.0	100.0	100.0	100.0	100.0	100.0	100.0
	2005	100.0	100.0	100.0	100.0	100.0	100.0	100.0	100.0	100.0
	2012	100.0	100.0	100.0	100.0	100.0	100.0	100.0	100.0	100.0
All food items	1995	15.2	14.5	12.6	12.6	52.5	25.5	0.6	22.8	7.6
(SITC 0 + 1 + 22 + 4)	2005	12.5	11.3	9.7	9.6	34.2	20.6	0.4	25.0	18.6
	2012	14.7	13.4	11.5	11.4	38.4	20.0	2.8	36.5	36.7
Agricultural raw materials	1995	2.5	2.5	2.5	2.6	4.4	2.5	0.5	4.5	13.3
(SITC 2 - 22 - 27 - 28)	2005	1.6	1.8	1.8	1.9	6.3	1.4	0.7	2.0	4.1
	2012	1.4	2.1	2.2	2.2	5.6	1.8	1.7	1.9	2.6
Ores, metals, precious stones	1995	2.6	2.8	2.6	2.4	8.1	0.9	0.6	26.9	6.5
and non-monetary gold	2005	2.8	2.2	1.8	1.7	4.2	1.4	0.2	20.0	5.4
(SITC 27 + 28 + 68 + 667 + 971)	2012	3.1	3.4	3.6	3.6	6.7	1.4	0.4	12.3	3.6
Fuels (SITC 3)	1995	8.4	2.5	2.4	2.5	1.4	2.8	0.0	9.4	9.3
	2005	11.7	4.2	4.8	4.7	3.7	2.3	0.5	6.4	20.5
	2012	15.9	11.4	12.9	12.9	2.0	9.4	0.8	4.5	28.9
Manufactured goods	1995	66.6	73.8	76.4	76.3	32.9	66.9	81.5	36.0	63.0
(SITC 5 to 8 less 667 and 68)	2005	64.8	76.3	78.3	78.4	50.7	72.2	82.0	37.3	49.7
	2012	59.6	67.2	67.9	68.0	46.5	65.5	82.2	39.0	27.5

For sources and notes, see end of table 2.2.L.

Developing economies - Économies en développement										Origines	
Total	Africa / Afrique	America / Amérique	Asia / Asie				Oceania / Océanie	Major petroleum exporters and gas exporters / Principaux exportateurs de pétrole et de gaz	Major manufactured goods exporters / Principaux exportateurs d'articles manufacturés	Year / Année	
			Total	Eastern, Southern and South-Eastern Asia / Asie orientale, méridionale et du Sud-Est	China / Chine	Western Asia / Asie occidentale					Groupes de produits
Millions de dollars											
39 627	14 216	3 416	21 980	16 050	3 231	5 930	15	7 988	11 384	1995	**Total tous produits**
108 849	32 596	9 711	66 456	47 268	18 169	19 188	86	22 930	35 245	2005	
309 738	75 960	27 481	206 000	152 421	77 715	53 579	297	54 845	115 720	2012	
Parts par origines (en pourcentage)											
31.9	11.5	2.8	17.7	12.9	2.6	4.8	0.0	6.4	9.2	1995	**Total tous produits**
42.5	12.7	3.8	25.9	18.4	7.1	7.5	0.0	8.9	13.8	2005	
50.5	12.4	4.5	33.6	24.8	12.7	8.7	0.0	8.9	18.9	2012	
37.7	13.9	9.7	14.2	11.7	1.8	2.5	0.0	0.9	6.9	1995	Produits alimentaires
49.8	15.5	15.9	18.3	15.3	2.1	2.9	0.1	1.5	9.0	2005	(CTCI 0 + 1 + 22 + 4)
53.9	13.7	19.3	21.0	17.8	2.8	3.2	0.0	1.7	9.7	2012	
31.0	15.8	3.4	11.8	8.7	0.5	3.1	0.0	1.0	6.3	1995	Matières premières
35.7	18.2	2.8	14.7	12.1	2.0	2.7	0.0	1.6	7.9	2005	d'origine agricole
29.3	10.1	2.6	16.5	14.4	3.9	2.1	0.0	1.3	9.7	2012	(CTCI 2 - 22 - 27 - 28)
28.6	14.3	3.9	10.3	4.1	1.3	6.2	0.1	4.5	3.1	1995	Minerais, métaux, pierres
52.5	33.2	6.8	12.6	6.4	2.4	6.2	0.0	5.2	4.7	2005	précieuses et or (non monétaire)
49.0	26.4	4.9	17.6	9.9	5.4	7.7	0.0	5.8	7.3	2012	(CTCI 27 + 28 + 68 + 667 + 971)
77.7	28.8	1.2	47.7	15.8	0.4	32.0	..	60.1	0.9	1995	Combustibles (CTCI 3)
77.4	32.1	1.6	43.7	11.7	0.4	32.0	0.0	55.8	1.0	2005	
64.1	25.5	0.9	37.7	10.4	0.2	27.2	0.0	41.0	3.4	2012	
26.8	9.1	1.4	16.3	14.1	3.4	2.2	0.0	1.7	11.6	1995	Articles manufacturés
37.8	8.8	1.9	27.1	22.4	10.2	4.8	0.0	3.1	18.5	2005	(CTCI 5 à 8 moins 667 et 68)
50.3	8.9	2.0	39.3	33.2	20.1	6.1	0.0	3.3	27.3	2012	
Parts par principaux groupes de produits (en pourcentage)											
100.0	100.0	100.0	100.0	100.0	100.0	100.0	100.0	100.0	100.0	1995	**Total tous produits**
100.0	100.0	100.0	100.0	100.0	100.0	100.0	100.0	100.0	100.0	2005	
100.0	100.0	100.0	100.0	100.0	100.0	100.0	100.0	100.0	100.0	2012	
18.0	18.5	53.6	12.2	13.8	10.3	7.8	13.1	2.2	11.5	1995	Produits alimentaires
14.7	15.3	52.5	8.8	10.4	3.7	4.9	26.0	2.0	8.2	2005	(CTCI 0 + 1 + 22 + 4)
15.7	16.3	63.4	9.2	10.5	3.3	5.5	3.0	2.9	7.6	2012	
2.5	3.5	3.2	1.7	1.7	0.5	1.6	0.4	0.4	1.7	1995	Matières premières
1.3	2.2	1.1	0.9	1.0	0.4	0.6	0.4	0.3	0.9	2005	d'origine agricole
0.8	1.2	0.8	0.7	0.8	0.4	0.3	0.5	0.2	0.7	2012	(CTCI 2 - 22 - 27 - 28)
2.4	3.3	3.8	1.5	0.8	1.3	3.4	12.8	1.8	0.9	1995	Minerais, métaux, pierres
3.5	7.4	5.0	1.4	1.0	1.0	2.3	0.5	1.7	1.0	2005	précieuses et or (non monétaire)
3.0	6.6	3.4	1.6	1.2	1.3	2.7	0.2	2.0	1.2	2012	(CTCI 27 + 28 + 68 + 667 + 971)
20.4	21.0	3.5	22.6	10.2	1.4	56.0	..	78.2	0.8	1995	Combustibles (CTCI 3)
21.3	29.5	4.9	19.7	7.4	0.7	50.0	2.0	73.0	0.9	2005	
20.2	32.8	3.3	17.9	6.7	0.3	49.7	8.2	73.1	2.9	2012	
55.8	52.9	33.4	61.2	72.4	86.1	30.9	73.4	17.3	84.0	1995	Articles manufacturés
57.7	44.6	32.3	67.8	78.6	93.3	41.4	71.1	22.6	87.2	2005	(CTCI 5 à 8 moins 667 et 68)
59.4	42.9	27.2	69.8	79.6	94.5	41.6	44.9	21.7	86.4	2012	

Pour les sources et les notes, se reporter à la fin du tableau 2.2.L.

2.2.D Export structure by partner and product group
Developing economies: America

| Product group | Year / Année | World (1) / Monde (1) | Developed economies - Économies développées | | | | | | | Transition economies / Économies en transition |
			Total	Europe Total	EU / UE	Canada	USA / États-Unis	Japan / Japon	Other developed countries / Autres économies développées	
Millions of dollars										
All products	1995	230 286	162 791	41 254	38 946	4 167	107 181	9 200	989	1 503
	2005	583 537	403 757	77 965	74 789	12 254	299 214	12 086	2 238	5 436
	2012	1 117 638	644 073	143 665	135 545	27 129	441 037	26 349	5 893	10 735
Share by destination (percentage)										
All products	1995	100.0	70.7	17.9	16.9	1.8	46.5	4.0	0.4	0.7
	2005	100.0	69.2	13.4	12.8	2.1	51.3	2.1	0.4	0.9
	2012	100.0	57.6	12.9	12.1	2.4	39.5	2.4	0.5	1.0
All food items	1995	100.0	65.2	34.3	33.3	1.1	23.6	5.4	0.7	2.5
(SITC 0 + 1 + 22 + 4)	2005	100.0	57.5	28.4	27.7	1.3	23.1	4.0	0.8	5.0
	2012	100.0	44.0	21.4	20.7	1.4	16.8	3.6	0.9	3.9
Agricultural raw materials	1995	100.0	66.3	30.6	29.1	0.4	25.0	10.0	0.2	0.1
(SITC 2 - 22 - 27 - 28)	2005	100.0	65.8	26.2	25.0	0.9	32.4	5.7	0.6	0.9
	2012	100.0	48.3	21.9	21.6	1.0	20.1	4.7	0.7	2.7
Ores, metals, precious stones	1995	100.0	73.5	33.8	30.1	2.8	20.5	16.1	0.3	0.4
and non-monetary gold	2005	100.0	60.9	26.1	22.9	5.1	19.3	10.3	0.2	0.3
(SITC 27 + 28 + 68 + 667 + 971)	2012	100.0	52.0	19.3	15.9	6.6	17.2	8.1	0.9	0.1
Fuels (SITC 3)	1995	100.0	72.9	8.8	8.7	1.6	60.7	1.6	0.3	0.0
	2005	100.0	73.0	7.6	7.6	1.6	63.6	0.0	0.2	0.0
	2012	100.0	59.1	10.6	10.6	1.1	46.7	0.6	0.2	0.2
Manufactured goods	1995	100.0	72.2	8.6	7.9	2.1	60.0	1.1	0.4	0.1
(SITC 5 to 8 less 667 and 68)	2005	100.0	73.7	7.9	7.8	1.9	62.9	0.5	0.4	0.1
	2012	100.0	65.8	7.8	7.6	2.1	54.8	0.7	0.4	0.3
Share by major product group (percentage)										
All products	1995	100.0	100.0	100.0	100.0	100.0	100.0	100.0	100.0	100.0
	2005	100.0	100.0	100.0	100.0	100.0	100.0	100.0	100.0	100.0
	2012	100.0	100.0	100.0	100.0	100.0	100.0	100.0	100.0	100.0
All food items	1995	22.3	20.6	42.7	44.0	13.4	11.3	30.2	38.9	87.1
(SITC 0 + 1 + 22 + 4)	2005	16.0	13.3	34.0	34.7	9.9	7.2	30.9	33.2	86.4
	2012	18.8	14.4	31.3	32.2	11.1	8.0	28.6	32.3	76.5
Agricultural raw materials	1995	3.7	3.5	6.3	6.4	0.8	2.0	9.3	1.7	0.3
(SITC 2 - 22 - 27 - 28)	2005	2.0	1.9	3.9	3.9	0.9	1.3	5.6	2.9	1.9
	2012	1.9	1.6	3.3	3.4	0.8	1.0	3.8	2.6	5.5
Ores, metals, precious stones	1995	10.1	10.5	19.1	18.0	15.8	4.5	40.9	6.7	6.7
and non-monetary gold	2005	10.2	9.0	19.9	18.2	24.8	3.8	50.7	4.2	3.6
(SITC 27 + 28 + 68 + 667 + 971)	2012	14.4	13.0	21.7	18.9	39.0	6.3	49.3	24.5	2.2
Fuels (SITC 3)	1995	14.3	14.7	7.0	7.4	12.3	18.6	5.9	9.2	0.6
	2005	21.1	22.2	12.0	12.5	16.1	26.1	0.0	13.6	1.1
	2012	21.8	22.3	17.9	19.0	9.6	25.7	5.4	8.7	4.0
Manufactured goods	1995	49.0	50.1	23.6	23.0	57.5	63.2	13.6	43.4	5.1
(SITC 5 to 8 less 667 and 68)	2005	49.9	53.1	29.7	30.3	45.2	61.2	12.7	45.9	7.0
	2012	41.9	47.8	25.5	26.2	36.6	58.1	12.6	31.7	11.7

For sources and notes, see end of table 2.2.L.

Total	Africa / Afrique	America / Amérique	Asia / Asie — Total	Eastern, Southern and South-Eastern Asia / Asie orientale, méridionale et du Sud-Est	China / Chine	Western Asia / Asie occidentale	Oceania / Océanie	Major petroleum exporters and gas exporters / Principaux exportateurs de pétrole et de gaz	Major manufactured goods exporters / Principaux exportateurs d'articles manufacturés	Year / Année	Destinations / Groupes de produits
Millions de dollars											
65 115	3 022	46 144	15 928	14 018	2 646	1 910	21	5 137	12 199	1995	Total tous produits
170 426	9 625	109 707	51 060	44 879	20 068	6 181	34	16 257	46 859	2005	
453 374	21 778	226 579	204 965	187 324	102 053	17 641	52	40 118	157 508	2012	
Parts par destinations (en pourcentage)											
28.3	1.3	20.0	6.9	6.1	1.1	0.8	0.0	2.2	5.3	1995	Total tous produits
29.2	1.6	18.8	8.8	7.7	3.4	1.1	0.0	2.8	8.0	2005	
40.6	1.9	20.3	18.3	16.8	9.1	1.6	0.0	3.6	14.1	2012	
31.8	3.3	17.1	11.3	9.4	2.8	1.9	0.0	4.4	6.2	1995	Produits alimentaires
37.1	5.4	14.1	17.6	14.0	6.3	3.6	0.0	6.2	11.3	2005	(CTCI 0 + 1 + 22 + 4)
51.4	7.0	17.5	26.8	22.4	11.1	4.5	0.0	9.7	17.7	2012	
33.3	1.0	14.6	17.6	15.9	3.4	1.7	0.0	2.6	13.6	1995	Matières premières
33.2	0.7	12.4	20.1	18.8	10.5	1.4	0.0	1.6	18.5	2005	d'origine agricole
47.8	1.3	10.7	35.7	33.7	18.5	2.0	0.0	1.9	29.2	2012	(CTCI 2 - 22 - 27 - 28)
25.6	1.2	10.7	13.7	12.8	2.0	1.0	0.0	1.6	12.2	1995	Minerais, métaux, pierres
38.7	1.1	10.9	26.7	25.3	14.3	1.4	0.0	1.6	24.8	2005	précieuses et or (non monétaire)
47.8	0.7	6.9	40.2	37.8	26.6	2.3	0.0	1.8	35.2	2012	(CTCI 27 + 28 + 68 + 667 + 971)
26.5	0.4	24.9	1.3	1.3	0.0	0.0	0.0	0.1	1.6	1995	Combustibles (CTCI 3)
26.5	0.6	22.7	3.2	3.1	0.9	0.2	0.0	0.3	3.0	2005	
40.5	0.3	19.0	21.3	20.8	9.2	0.4	0.0	0.4	13.0	2012	
27.6	0.8	22.4	4.4	3.9	0.4	0.5	0.0	2.0	4.0	1995	Articles manufacturés
26.1	1.1	20.7	4.2	3.7	1.1	0.5	0.0	3.0	5.4	2005	(CTCI 5 à 8 moins 667 et 68)
33.8	1.0	27.7	5.1	4.5	2.0	0.6	0.0	3.2	5.4	2012	
Parts par principaux groupes de produits (en pourcentage)											
100.0	100.0	100.0	100.0	100.0	100.0	100.0	100.0	100.0	100.0	1995	Total tous produits
100.0	100.0	100.0	100.0	100.0	100.0	100.0	100.0	100.0	100.0	2005	
100.0	100.0	100.0	100.0	100.0	100.0	100.0	100.0	100.0	100.0	2012	
25.0	55.9	19.1	36.5	34.5	54.9	50.9	38.7	43.8	26.1	1995	Produits alimentaires
20.4	52.1	12.0	32.3	29.2	29.5	55.0	61.7	35.7	22.5	2005	(CTCI 0 + 1 + 22 + 4)
23.9	67.9	16.3	27.6	25.1	22.9	53.3	43.3	51.1	23.6	2012	
4.4	2.8	2.7	9.4	9.7	11.0	7.6	0.4	4.3	9.5	1995	Matières premières
2.3	0.9	1.3	4.6	4.9	6.1	2.6	0.6	1.2	4.6	2005	d'origine agricole
2.3	1.3	1.0	3.8	3.9	3.9	2.4	2.2	1.0	4.0	2012	(CTCI 2 - 22 - 27 - 28)
9.2	9.0	5.4	20.1	21.3	17.8	11.7	0.1	7.2	23.3	1995	Minerais, métaux, pierres
13.5	6.8	5.9	31.1	33.5	42.3	13.6	0.2	6.0	31.5	2005	précieuses et or (non monétaire)
17.0	5.5	4.9	31.6	32.6	42.1	21.5	0.4	7.4	36.0	2012	(CTCI 27 + 28 + 68 + 667 + 971)
13.4	3.8	17.7	2.7	3.0	0.2	0.4	4.2	0.6	4.3	1995	Combustibles (CTCI 3)
19.1	7.1	25.4	7.8	8.4	5.6	3.1	1.5	2.3	7.9	2005	
21.7	3.3	20.3	25.2	27.0	21.9	5.9	2.3	2.5	20.0	2012	
47.8	28.4	54.8	31.3	31.5	16.0	29.4	56.4	44.0	36.7	1995	Articles manufacturés
44.5	33.0	55.0	24.2	24.0	16.5	25.4	35.6	54.6	33.4	2005	(CTCI 5 à 8 moins 667 et 68)
34.9	21.1	57.3	11.6	11.2	9.1	16.4	49.3	37.5	16.1	2012	

Pour les sources et les notes, se reporter à la fin du tableau 2.2.L.

Product group / Origin	Year / Année	World (1) / Monde (1)	Developed economies - Économies développées							Transition economies / Économies en transition
			Total	Europe		Canada	USA / États-Unis	Japan / Japon	Other developed countries / Autres économies développées	
				Total	EU / UE					
Millions of dollars										
All products	1995	244 698	174 475	48 786	45 707	5 373	104 978	13 720	1 618	1 076
	2005	523 914	308 930	80 067	75 323	10 359	188 296	26 021	4 187	4 086
	2012	1 113 096	575 821	160 241	150 988	19 394	346 174	42 431	7 579	11 107
Share by origin (percentage)										
All products	1995	100.0	71.3	19.9	18.7	2.2	42.9	5.6	0.7	0.4
	2005	100.0	59.0	15.3	14.4	2.0	35.9	5.0	0.8	0.8
	2012	100.0	51.7	14.4	13.6	1.7	31.1	3.8	0.7	1.0
All food items	1995	100.0	58.1	15.6	14.5	5.0	35.4	0.1	1.9	0.1
(SITC 0 + 1 + 22 + 4)	2005	100.0	57.9	9.4	8.8	5.0	41.3	0.0	2.2	0.1
	2012	100.0	49.8	8.4	7.9	4.5	35.3	0.0	1.5	0.2
Agricultural raw materials	1995	100.0	60.8	7.5	7.3	3.5	47.3	0.5	2.1	1.6
(SITC 2 - 22 - 27 - 28)	2005	100.0	63.3	8.4	8.3	2.8	50.4	0.6	1.0	0.5
	2012	100.0	55.6	8.9	8.7	2.0	43.1	0.9	0.8	2.0
Ores, metals, precious stones	1995	100.0	53.1	11.1	9.9	5.5	34.0	0.8	1.6	0.2
and non-monetary gold	2005	100.0	43.7	8.1	7.8	3.2	31.2	0.4	0.8	0.8
(SITC 27 + 28 + 68 + 667 + 971)	2012	100.0	44.3	8.4	7.7	4.0	29.9	0.4	1.6	2.3
Fuels (SITC 3)	1995	100.0	31.1	7.0	6.9	1.4	20.5	0.3	1.8	1.8
	2005	100.0	31.9	5.0	4.0	0.7	23.9	0.3	2.1	1.6
	2012	100.0	48.0	6.5	6.1	0.5	39.7	0.3	1.0	1.5
Manufactured goods	1995	100.0	76.6	22.5	21.1	1.7	45.4	6.6	0.4	0.4
(SITC 5 to 8 less 667 and 68)	2005	100.0	63.7	17.7	16.8	1.9	37.3	6.3	0.5	0.7
	2012	100.0	52.8	17.0	16.0	1.6	28.7	5.1	0.5	0.9
Share by major product group (percentage)										
All products	1995	100.0	100.0	100.0	100.0	100.0	100.0	100.0	100.0	100.0
	2005	100.0	100.0	100.0	100.0	100.0	100.0	100.0	100.0	100.0
	2012	100.0	100.0	100.0	100.0	100.0	100.0	100.0	100.0	100.0
All food items	1995	9.5	7.8	7.5	7.4	21.9	7.9	0.1	27.7	1.7
(SITC 0 + 1 + 22 + 4)	2005	7.0	6.9	4.3	4.3	17.6	8.1	0.1	19.4	0.5
	2012	7.8	7.5	4.6	4.5	20.2	8.9	0.1	17.2	1.7
Agricultural raw materials	1995	2.3	2.0	0.9	0.9	3.7	2.5	0.2	7.2	8.6
(SITC 2 - 22 - 27 - 28)	2005	1.3	1.4	0.7	0.8	1.9	1.9	0.1	1.7	0.8
	2012	1.1	1.1	0.7	0.7	1.2	1.5	0.2	1.3	2.2
Ores, metals, precious stones	1995	2.4	1.8	1.3	1.3	6.1	1.9	0.3	6.0	1.4
and non-monetary gold	2005	2.5	1.9	1.3	1.4	4.1	2.2	0.2	2.5	2.7
(SITC 27 + 28 + 68 + 667 + 971)	2012	2.3	1.9	1.3	1.3	5.1	2.2	0.3	5.1	5.1
Fuels (SITC 3)	1995	6.7	2.9	2.4	2.5	4.3	3.2	0.4	18.5	27.3
	2005	11.3	6.1	3.7	3.1	4.0	7.5	0.6	29.1	22.7
	2012	14.4	13.4	6.5	6.5	4.3	18.4	1.3	21.8	22.1
Manufactured goods	1995	76.1	81.7	85.9	85.9	59.8	80.6	89.3	40.6	61.0
(SITC 5 to 8 less 667 and 68)	2005	76.6	82.7	88.8	89.2	72.2	79.5	97.7	45.2	70.7
	2012	73.3	74.8	86.3	86.4	67.1	67.6	97.3	54.2	66.1

For sources and notes, see end of table 2.2.L.

Total	Africa / Afrique	America / Amérique	Asia / Asie Total	Eastern, Southern and South-Eastern Asia / Asie orientale, méridionale et du Sud-Est	China / Chine	Western Asia / Asie occidentale	Oceania / Océanie	Major petroleum and gas exporters / Principaux exportateurs de pétrole et de gaz	Major manufactured goods exporters / Principaux exportateurs d'articles manufacturés	Year / Année	Origines / Groupes de produits
Millions de dollars											
67 757	2 491	45 896	19 353	17 286	2 849	2 068	16	8 446	20 261	1995	**Total tous produits**
207 367	11 224	110 690	85 423	82 173	37 393	3 250	31	20 412	84 884	2005	
520 773	20 462	226 755	273 468	261 962	159 893	11 505	88	36 406	267 266	2012	
Parts par origines (en pourcentage)											
27.7	1.0	18.8	7.9	7.1	1.2	0.8	0.0	3.5	8.3	1995	**Total tous produits**
39.6	2.1	21.1	16.3	15.7	7.1	0.6	0.0	3.9	16.2	2005	
46.8	1.8	20.4	24.6	23.5	14.4	1.0	0.0	3.3	24.0	2012	
41.3	0.3	38.5	2.5	2.1	0.4	0.4	0.0	1.3	2.2	1995	Produits alimentaires
41.9	0.2	37.9	3.7	3.5	1.2	0.2	0.0	0.7	3.5	2005	(CTCI 0 + 1 + 22 + 4)
49.8	0.9	44.5	4.3	4.1	1.8	0.2	0.0	0.2	4.7	2012	
37.0	2.3	25.6	9.0	9.0	0.4	0.1	0.0	0.6	8.3	1995	Matières premières
36.2	0.6	24.0	11.4	11.2	1.4	0.2	0.1	0.5	8.9	2005	d'origine agricole
42.2	1.3	22.6	18.2	18.0	3.8	0.1	0.1	0.3	13.2	2012	(CTCI 2 - 22 - 27 - 28)
47.6	4.5	41.3	1.8	1.6	0.5	0.2	0.0	4.8	3.1	1995	Minerais, métaux, pierres
55.3	2.0	49.1	4.2	4.0	1.7	0.2	0.0	4.1	3.7	2005	précieuses et or (non monétaire)
53.4	2.4	39.6	11.4	9.9	7.5	1.4	0.0	2.8	12.1	2012	(CTCI 27 + 28 + 68 + 667 + 971)
67.0	8.9	44.4	13.7	3.1	0.9	10.6	..	35.3	4.4	1995	Combustibles (CTCI 3)
65.3	16.0	41.7	7.6	3.5	1.0	4.2	..	27.5	5.0	2005	
49.4	9.6	30.9	8.9	4.4	0.9	4.4	0.0	19.2	3.5	2012	
22.4	0.3	13.7	8.4	8.3	1.4	0.1	0.0	1.1	9.8	1995	Articles manufacturés
35.1	0.3	15.7	19.0	18.9	8.9	0.2	0.0	0.8	19.4	2005	(CTCI 5 à 8 moins 667 et 68)
46.0	0.4	15.3	30.2	29.8	18.7	0.5	0.0	0.6	30.6	2012	
Parts par principaux groupes de produits (en pourcentage)											
100.0	100.0	100.0	100.0	100.0	100.0	100.0	100.0	100.0	100.0	1995	**Total tous produits**
100.0	100.0	100.0	100.0	100.0	100.0	100.0	100.0	100.0	100.0	2005	
100.0	100.0	100.0	100.0	100.0	100.0	100.0	100.0	100.0	100.0	2012	
14.2	2.6	19.6	3.0	2.9	3.1	4.3	5.8	3.6	2.5	1995	Produits alimentaires
7.4	0.8	12.6	1.6	1.6	1.1	2.6	44.9	1.2	1.5	2005	(CTCI 0 + 1 + 22 + 4)
8.3	3.9	17.0	1.4	1.4	1.0	1.6	45.0	0.4	1.5	2012	
3.1	5.3	3.1	2.6	2.9	0.7	0.2	0.6	0.4	2.3	1995	Matières premières
1.2	0.4	1.5	0.9	1.0	0.3	0.5	12.2	0.2	0.7	2005	d'origine agricole
1.0	0.8	1.2	0.8	0.8	0.3	0.1	18.5	0.1	0.6	2012	(CTCI 2 - 22 - 27 - 28)
4.2	10.7	5.3	0.6	0.5	0.9	0.6	0.0	3.3	0.9	1995	Minerais, métaux, pierres
3.5	2.4	5.9	0.7	0.6	0.6	0.9	4.2	2.6	0.6	2005	précieuses et or (non monétaire)
2.6	3.0	4.4	1.0	1.0	1.2	3.1	0.1	1.9	1.1	2012	(CTCI 27 + 28 + 68 + 667 + 971)
16.3	58.8	15.9	11.7	2.9	5.3	84.8	..	68.8	3.6	1995	Combustibles (CTCI 3)
18.7	84.6	22.3	5.3	2.5	1.6	76.3	..	79.8	3.5	2005	
15.2	74.9	21.9	5.2	2.7	0.9	61.7	5.0	84.6	2.1	2012	
61.7	22.6	55.6	81.0	89.5	89.4	10.1	93.4	23.4	89.7	1995	Articles manufacturés
68.0	11.5	57.1	89.5	92.3	95.1	18.9	35.2	16.0	91.8	2005	(CTCI 5 à 8 moins 667 et 68)
72.0	17.1	55.1	90.2	92.7	95.5	33.2	31.0	13.0	93.5	2012	

Pour les sources et les notes, se reporter à la fin du tableau 2.2.L.

Product group	Year / Année	World (1) / Monde (1)	Developed economies - Économies développées							Transition economies / Économies en transition
			Total	Europe		Canada	USA / États-Unis	Japan / Japon	Other developed countries / Autres économies développées	
				Total	EU UE					
Millions of dollars										
All products	1995	1 085 043	561 785	184 479	178 148	11 031	196 334	150 449	19 493	11 170
	2005	2 895 127	1 366 885	504 073	491 357	28 908	458 853	312 423	62 628	41 244
	2012	6 413 798	2 332 150	845 756	814 869	57 672	741 029	538 445	149 247	133 368
Share by destination (percentage)										
All products	1995	100.0	51.8	17.0	16.4	1.0	18.1	13.9	1.8	1.0
	2005	100.0	47.2	17.4	17.0	1.0	15.8	10.8	2.2	1.4
	2012	100.0	36.4	13.2	12.7	0.9	11.6	8.4	2.3	2.1
All food items	1995	100.0	46.7	15.0	14.3	0.8	7.4	22.1	1.4	3.4
(SITC 0 + 1 + 22 + 4)	2005	100.0	44.1	16.3	16.0	1.1	9.8	14.8	2.0	3.4
	2012	100.0	32.2	12.3	12.1	1.0	7.8	9.1	2.1	3.4
Agricultural raw materials	1995	100.0	44.0	15.9	15.7	0.8	9.6	16.3	1.2	0.4
(SITC 2 - 22 - 27 - 28)	2005	100.0	39.3	15.6	15.5	1.3	9.9	11.3	1.2	0.8
	2012	100.0	35.7	11.5	11.4	1.1	14.3	7.7	1.1	1.1
Ores, metals, precious stones	1995	100.0	39.8	11.8	10.8	0.2	7.5	18.4	1.8	1.4
and non-monetary gold	2005	100.0	32.9	14.2	12.2	0.5	6.7	8.1	3.3	0.6
(SITC 27 + 28 + 68 + 667 + 971)	2012	100.0	22.2	11.3	7.9	0.4	4.0	4.3	2.3	0.4
Fuels (SITC 3)	1995	100.0	54.7	13.5	13.5	0.3	7.7	31.3	1.9	0.1
	2005	100.0	47.4	11.8	11.7	0.5	10.0	22.5	2.6	0.1
	2012	100.0	33.3	7.3	7.3	0.5	6.5	16.4	2.5	0.1
Manufactured goods	1995	100.0	52.4	18.0	17.4	1.2	21.5	9.9	1.8	1.0
(SITC 5 to 8 less 667 and 68)	2005	100.0	48.2	19.1	18.7	1.1	18.3	7.7	2.0	1.7
	2012	100.0	38.8	15.3	14.8	1.1	14.0	6.2	2.3	2.8
Share by major product group (percentage)										
All products	1995	100.0	100.0	100.0	100.0	100.0	100.0	100.0	100.0	100.0
	2005	100.0	100.0	100.0	100.0	100.0	100.0	100.0	100.0	100.0
	2012	100.0	100.0	100.0	100.0	100.0	100.0	100.0	100.0	100.0
All food items	1995	6.7	6.1	5.9	5.9	5.3	2.7	10.7	5.3	22.1
(SITC 0 + 1 + 22 + 4)	2005	3.8	3.6	3.6	3.6	4.2	2.4	5.2	3.5	9.2
	2012	4.4	3.9	4.1	4.2	4.8	3.0	4.8	4.0	7.2
Agricultural raw materials	1995	2.2	1.9	2.1	2.1	1.8	1.2	2.6	1.5	0.8
(SITC 2 - 22 - 27 - 28)	2005	1.0	0.9	0.9	0.9	1.3	0.6	1.1	0.6	0.5
	2012	1.1	1.1	1.0	1.0	1.4	1.4	1.1	0.6	0.6
Ores, metals, precious stones	1995	3.2	2.5	2.2	2.1	0.8	1.3	4.2	3.3	4.2
and non-monetary gold	2005	3.3	2.3	2.7	2.4	1.8	1.4	2.5	5.1	1.3
(SITC 27 + 28 + 68 + 667 + 971)	2012	4.7	2.9	4.1	3.0	1.9	1.6	2.4	4.6	1.0
Fuels (SITC 3)	1995	13.0	13.7	10.4	10.7	4.5	5.5	29.3	13.5	1.9
	2005	18.9	18.9	12.8	13.0	10.1	11.9	39.3	22.5	1.2
	2012	21.5	19.7	11.9	12.3	12.8	12.1	42.0	23.3	0.9
Manufactured goods	1995	73.6	74.4	78.0	77.9	86.7	87.3	52.3	75.5	70.2
(SITC 5 to 8 less 667 and 68)	2005	72.2	73.8	79.3	79.4	82.3	83.2	51.4	67.1	87.3
	2012	67.3	71.8	77.9	78.6	79.0	81.6	49.5	66.8	90.1

For sources and notes, see end of table 2.2.L.

	Developing economies - Économies en développement										Destinations
Total	Africa Afrique	America Amérique	Asia / Asie Total	Eastern, Southern and South-Eastern Asia Asie orientale, méridionale et du Sud-Est	China Chine	Western Asia Asie occidentale	Oceania Océanie	Major petroleum exporters and gas exporters Principaux exportateurs de pétrole et de gaz	Major manufactured goods exporters Principaux exportateurs d'articles manufacturés	Year Année	Groupes de produits
Millions de dollars											
507 185	21 343	24 993	460 091	421 942	79 065	38 149	759	30 489	355 571	1995	Total tous produits
1 479 517	71 249	63 298	1 339 936	1 218 042	327 285	121 894	5 034	114 647	1 004 404	2005	
3 938 056	224 172	246 717	3 450 615	3 097 973	802 343	352 642	16 552	377 875	2 366 838	2012	
Parts par destinations (en pourcentage)											
46.7	2.0	2.3	42.4	38.9	7.3	3.5	0.1	2.8	32.8	1995	Total tous produits
51.1	2.5	2.2	46.3	42.1	11.3	4.2	0.2	4.0	34.7	2005	
61.4	3.5	3.8	53.8	48.3	12.5	5.5	0.3	5.9	36.9	2012	
49.2	3.2	0.6	45.3	37.5	7.0	7.8	0.1	7.1	25.6	1995	Produits alimentaires
52.1	5.5	1.1	45.3	34.5	4.9	10.8	0.2	10.9	20.6	2005	(CTCI 0 + 1 + 22 + 4)
64.3	7.3	1.4	55.4	43.6	7.1	11.7	0.2	13.8	23.5	2012	
55.3	1.6	2.0	51.7	49.3	12.9	2.4	0.0	1.7	41.1	1995	Matières premières
59.6	1.7	2.3	55.6	52.3	23.6	3.2	0.0	2.1	40.6	2005	d'origine agricole
63.0	1.6	2.6	58.9	55.6	26.7	3.3	0.0	2.2	41.0	2012	(CTCI 2 - 22 - 27 - 28)
58.2	0.9	0.2	57.1	53.5	8.9	3.7	0.0	3.3	44.5	1995	Minerais, métaux, pierres
66.4	1.1	0.3	65.0	56.6	15.3	8.4	0.0	8.0	42.0	2005	précieuses et or (non monétaire)
77.3	1.7	0.9	74.6	64.9	26.3	9.7	0.0	11.0	46.3	2012	(CTCI 27 + 28 + 68 + 667 + 971)
44.2	2.1	1.4	40.6	36.6	3.5	4.0	0.1	0.3	28.8	1995	Combustibles (CTCI 3)
52.1	2.5	1.0	48.4	45.2	7.2	3.1	0.3	1.3	36.3	2005	
66.3	2.8	1.3	61.9	59.2	10.9	2.7	0.3	1.7	43.9	2012	
46.3	1.9	2.7	41.7	38.6	7.8	3.1	0.1	2.9	33.5	1995	Articles manufacturés
49.9	2.3	2.5	44.8	41.0	12.4	3.9	0.1	4.0	34.8	2005	(CTCI 5 à 8 moins 667 et 68)
58.3	3.6	4.8	49.7	44.1	12.3	5.6	0.2	6.4	35.1	2012	
Parts par principaux groupes de produits (en pourcentage)											
100.0	100.0	100.0	100.0	100.0	100.0	100.0	100.0	100.0	100.0	1995	Total tous produits
100.0	100.0	100.0	100.0	100.0	100.0	100.0	100.0	100.0	100.0	2005	
100.0	100.0	100.0	100.0	100.0	100.0	100.0	100.0	100.0	100.0	2012	
7.1	10.8	1.9	7.2	6.5	6.4	14.8	9.8	17.0	5.2	1995	Produits alimentaires
3.9	8.4	2.0	3.7	3.1	1.7	9.8	3.9	10.5	2.3	2005	(CTCI 0 + 1 + 22 + 4)
4.6	9.2	1.7	4.6	4.0	2.5	9.5	4.1	10.4	2.8	2012	
2.6	1.8	1.9	2.7	2.8	3.9	1.5	0.4	1.4	2.8	1995	Matières premières
1.2	0.7	1.1	1.2	1.3	2.1	0.8	0.1	0.5	1.2	2005	d'origine agricole
1.2	0.5	0.8	1.3	1.3	2.5	0.7	0.1	0.4	1.3	2012	(CTCI 2 - 22 - 27 - 28)
4.0	1.5	0.3	4.3	4.4	3.9	3.3	0.4	3.8	4.3	1995	Minerais, métaux, pierres
4.3	1.4	0.5	4.7	4.5	4.5	6.7	0.2	6.8	4.0	2005	précieuses et or (non monétaire)
6.0	2.3	1.2	6.6	6.4	10.0	8.4	0.2	8.9	6.0	2012	(CTCI 27 + 28 + 68 + 667 + 971)
12.3	13.9	8.1	12.4	12.2	6.3	14.8	15.5	1.3	11.4	1995	Combustibles (CTCI 3)
19.2	18.9	8.5	19.7	20.3	12.0	14.1	32.9	6.4	19.7	2005	
23.3	17.4	7.5	24.8	26.4	18.7	10.4	23.2	6.3	25.6	2012	
72.9	70.6	85.9	72.3	73.0	78.7	65.0	69.6	76.0	75.1	1995	Articles manufacturés
70.4	68.5	84.1	69.9	70.3	79.5	66.1	56.9	73.6	72.4	2005	(CTCI 5 à 8 moins 667 et 68)
64.0	68.5	84.5	62.2	61.5	66.2	68.4	57.0	73.7	64.0	2012	

Pour les sources et les notes, se reporter à la fin du tableau 2.2.L.

2.2.E Import structure by partner and product group
Developing economies: Asia

Product group	Year Année	World (1) Monde (1)	Developed economies - Économies développées							Transition economies Économies en transition
			Total	Europe Total	Europe EU UE	Canada	USA États-Unis	Japan Japon	Other developed countries Autres économies développées	
Millions of dollars										
All products	1995	1 130 030	637 904	220 156	202 067	12 816	153 303	222 620	29 009	19 732
	2005	2 609 117	1 078 676	426 162	390 363	19 456	221 088	339 427	72 543	66 744
	2012	5 932 676	2 050 201	849 042	742 377	47 787	433 006	517 852	202 514	176 703
Share by origin (percentage)										
All products	1995	100.0	56.5	19.5	17.9	1.1	13.6	19.7	2.6	1.7
	2005	100.0	41.3	16.3	15.0	0.7	8.5	13.0	2.8	2.6
	2012	100.0	34.6	14.3	12.5	0.8	7.3	8.7	3.4	3.0
All food items	1995	100.0	51.8	17.0	16.4	3.3	21.1	2.2	8.2	1.1
(SITC 0 + 1 + 22 + 4)	2005	100.0	39.5	13.8	12.9	2.3	12.7	1.8	8.9	2.6
	2012	100.0	37.0	11.6	10.7	2.9	14.0	0.9	7.6	3.5
Agricultural raw materials	1995	100.0	51.6	9.6	9.2	5.0	22.7	5.2	9.1	5.0
(SITC 2 - 22 - 27 - 28)	2005	100.0	49.0	13.2	12.8	5.3	18.2	4.6	7.8	8.4
	2012	100.0	46.7	12.5	12.3	5.8	16.3	4.2	7.9	6.1
Ores, metals, precious stones	1995	100.0	55.8	23.0	16.8	2.5	10.3	7.8	12.3	4.4
and non-monetary gold	2005	100.0	45.8	19.4	13.6	1.6	5.1	5.8	14.0	5.3
(SITC 27 + 28 + 68 + 667 + 971)	2012	100.0	42.8	15.4	9.1	1.4	6.1	4.4	15.5	3.8
Fuels (SITC 3)	1995	100.0	12.5	2.5	2.4	0.6	2.9	2.1	4.3	2.0
	2005	100.0	8.4	2.0	1.7	0.3	1.0	0.8	4.3	5.3
	2012	100.0	9.5	3.1	2.8	0.4	1.4	0.9	3.6	7.2
Manufactured goods	1995	100.0	60.8	21.3	19.8	0.7	13.4	24.4	0.9	1.4
(SITC 5 to 8 less 667 and 68)	2005	100.0	46.4	18.7	17.5	0.5	9.5	17.0	0.8	1.4
	2012	100.0	40.6	18.0	16.7	0.5	8.2	13.2	0.6	1.0
Share by major product group (percentage)										
All products	1995	100.0	100.0	100.0	100.0	100.0	100.0	100.0	100.0	100.0
	2005	100.0	100.0	100.0	100.0	100.0	100.0	100.0	100.0	100.0
	2012	100.0	100.0	100.0	100.0	100.0	100.0	100.0	100.0	100.0
All food items	1995	7.0	6.4	6.1	6.4	20.3	10.9	0.8	22.4	4.4
(SITC 0 + 1 + 22 + 4)	2005	4.9	4.7	4.1	4.2	15.3	7.4	0.7	15.7	4.9
	2012	6.2	6.6	5.0	5.3	22.2	11.9	0.7	13.8	7.3
Agricultural raw materials	1995	3.2	2.9	1.6	1.6	13.9	5.3	0.8	11.3	9.2
(SITC 2 - 22 - 27 - 28)	2005	2.1	2.4	1.7	1.8	14.7	4.4	0.7	5.7	6.7
	2012	2.1	2.8	1.8	2.0	15.0	4.6	1.0	4.8	4.3
Ores, metals, precious stones	1995	5.7	5.7	6.8	5.4	12.7	4.4	2.3	27.5	14.6
and non-monetary gold	2005	7.4	8.2	8.8	6.7	15.4	4.5	3.3	37.1	15.4
(SITC 27 + 28 + 68 + 667 + 971)	2012	10.2	12.6	10.9	7.4	17.1	8.5	5.2	46.2	12.8
Fuels (SITC 3)	1995	6.5	1.4	0.8	0.9	3.5	1.4	0.7	11.1	7.4
	2005	12.6	2.5	1.5	1.4	4.4	1.5	0.8	19.5	26.0
	2012	19.3	5.3	4.2	4.4	10.1	3.6	2.1	20.4	46.5
Manufactured goods	1995	75.9	81.7	83.1	84.0	49.0	75.1	93.9	26.4	62.3
(SITC 5 to 8 less 667 and 68)	2005	72.1	80.9	82.3	84.4	49.9	80.8	94.1	19.7	40.7
	2012	59.8	70.3	75.5	79.8	34.3	67.5	90.6	11.0	20.3

For sources and notes, see end of table 2.2.L.

	Developing economies - Économies en développement									Origines	
Total	Africa Afrique	America Amérique	Asia Asie Total	Eastern, Southern and South-Eastern Asia Asie orientale, méridionale et du Sud-Est	China Chine	Western Asia Asie occidentale	Oceania Océanie	Major petroleum exporters and gas exporters Principaux exportateurs de pétrole et de gaz	Major manufactured goods exporters Principaux exportateurs d'articles manufacturés	Year Année	Groupes de produits
Millions de dollars											
462 061	15 071	19 793	426 369	373 880	98 237	52 489	828	50 923	330 539	1995	**Total tous produits**
1 457 959	53 373	60 749	1 342 138	1 132 953	360 015	209 185	1 699	219 772	953 651	2005	
3 079 700	219 487	241 452	3 214 947	2 518 210	882 300	696 738	3 820	807 656	2 047 263	2012	
Parts par origines (en pourcentage)											
40.9	1.3	1.8	37.7	33.1	8.7	4.6	0.1	4.5	29.3	1995	**Total tous produits**
55.9	2.0	2.3	51.4	43.4	13.8	8.0	0.1	8.4	36.6	2005	
62.0	3.7	4.1	54.2	42.4	14.9	11.7	0.1	13.6	34.5	2012	
46.6	2.3	8.1	35.9	30.8	6.0	5.1	0.3	2.1	21.8	1995	Produits alimentaires
57.8	3.1	15.4	39.0	31.7	6.9	7.3	0.3	3.5	18.1	2005	(CTCI 0 + 1 + 22 + 4)
59.5	3.0	16.6	39.7	32.3	5.1	7.3	0.2	4.0	16.2	2012	
43.0	4.5	5.0	32.7	31.8	4.1	0.9	0.8	0.9	24.3	1995	Matières premières
42.6	5.5	5.1	30.9	29.7	3.0	1.2	1.0	0.9	19.3	2005	d'origine agricole
47.2	4.9	7.0	34.3	33.5	3.1	0.9	0.9	0.9	19.1	2012	(CTCI 2 - 22 - 27 - 28)
39.4	6.0	7.2	25.9	21.7	3.7	4.2	0.3	2.7	15.4	1995	Minerais, métaux, pierres
48.8	5.1	9.8	33.7	27.4	4.9	6.3	0.1	6.0	14.4	2005	précieuses et or (non monétaire)
53.3	7.5	12.9	32.8	24.0	5.2	8.8	0.1	8.0	14.4	2012	(CTCI 27 + 28 + 68 + 667 + 971)
85.0	5.7	0.7	78.5	34.4	3.4	44.1	0.1	50.7	21.6	1995	Combustibles (CTCI 3)
86.2	7.7	0.9	77.6	33.9	3.4	43.7	0.0	51.3	19.4	2005	
83.4	9.7	4.8	68.8	26.6	1.6	42.2	0.0	54.9	14.4	2012	
37.0	0.4	0.7	35.9	34.4	10.1	1.5	0.0	1.1	32.1	1995	Articles manufacturés
51.9	0.5	0.9	50.5	48.3	17.4	2.3	0.0	1.7	43.9	2005	(CTCI 5 à 8 moins 667 et 68)
58.2	0.5	1.0	56.7	53.0	22.7	3.7	0.0	2.9	47.8	2012	
Parts par principaux groupes de produits (en pourcentage)											
100.0	100.0	100.0	100.0	100.0	100.0	100.0	100.0	100.0	100.0	1995	**Total tous produits**
100.0	100.0	100.0	100.0	100.0	100.0	100.0	100.0	100.0	100.0	2005	
100.0	100.0	100.0	100.0	100.0	100.0	100.0	100.0	100.0	100.0	2012	
8.0	12.1	32.2	6.6	6.5	4.8	7.6	28.2	3.3	5.2	1995	Produits alimentaires
5.1	7.4	32.4	3.7	3.6	2.4	4.5	21.7	2.0	2.4	2005	(CTCI 0 + 1 + 22 + 4)
5.9	5.0	25.2	4.5	4.7	2.1	3.9	20.0	1.8	2.9	2012	
3.3	10.7	9.1	2.8	3.1	1.5	0.6	34.1	0.6	2.6	1995	Matières premières
1.6	5.6	4.5	1.2	1.4	0.4	0.3	32.2	0.2	1.1	2005	d'origine agricole
1.6	2.8	3.6	1.3	1.6	0.4	0.2	28.4	0.1	1.1	2012	(CTCI 2 - 22 - 27 - 28)
5.5	25.7	23.7	3.9	3.8	2.5	5.2	20.9	3.5	3.0	1995	Minerais, métaux, pierres
6.4	18.5	31.1	4.8	4.7	2.6	5.8	13.0	5.3	2.9	2005	précieuses et or (non monétaire)
8.7	20.5	32.4	6.2	5.8	3.6	7.6	17.7	5.9	4.2	2012	(CTCI 27 + 28 + 68 + 667 + 971)
13.6	28.1	2.6	13.6	6.8	2.5	62.2	8.4	73.6	4.8	1995	Combustibles (CTCI 3)
19.4	47.3	4.9	18.9	9.8	3.1	68.4	7.5	76.5	6.7	2005	
26.0	50.6	22.9	24.5	12.1	2.0	69.4	4.9	77.9	8.1	2012	
68.7	23.4	32.0	72.1	78.8	88.0	24.1	8.4	18.8	83.3	1995	Articles manufacturés
67.0	18.3	26.8	70.8	80.1	91.2	20.3	25.5	14.4	86.5	2005	(CTCI 5 à 8 moins 667 et 68)
56.2	7.6	15.4	62.6	74.7	91.4	18.8	28.7	12.9	82.9	2012	

Pour les sources et les notes, se reporter à la fin du tableau 2.2.L.

Product group / Destination	Year / Année	World (1) / Monde (1)	Developed economies - Économies développées Total	Europe Total	Europe EU / UE	Canada	USA / États-Unis	Japan / Japon	Other developed countries / Autres économies développées	Transition economies / Économies en transition
Millions of dollars										
All products	1995	949 867	489 249	155 886	150 094	10 540	183 710	121 511	17 602	8 583
	2005	2 380 903	1 110 932	400 595	390 159	25 559	400 962	226 471	57 344	34 059
	2012	5 108 231	1 892 011	686 953	661 668	49 167	646 703	372 667	136 522	112 453
Share by destination (percentage)										
All products	1995	100.0	51.5	16.4	15.8	1.1	19.3	12.8	1.9	0.9
	2005	100.0	46.7	16.8	16.4	1.1	16.8	9.5	2.4	1.4
	2012	100.0	37.0	13.4	13.0	1.0	12.7	7.3	2.7	2.2
All food items	1995	100.0	47.5	13.1	12.5	0.9	7.7	24.4	1.5	2.7
(SITC 0 + 1 + 22 + 4)	2005	100.0	45.5	13.9	13.7	1.2	11.0	17.2	2.1	3.0
	2012	100.0	34.4	12.0	11.8	1.1	8.7	10.5	2.2	3.0
Agricultural raw materials	1995	100.0	43.7	14.8	14.6	0.9	9.9	16.9	1.2	0.4
(SITC 2 - 22 - 27 - 28)	2005	100.0	39.4	14.9	14.8	1.4	10.2	11.7	1.2	0.7
	2012	100.0	36.0	11.3	11.2	1.1	14.6	7.9	1.1	1.0
Ores, metals, precious stones	1995	100.0	41.7	11.2	10.2	0.3	8.5	19.8	2.1	1.4
and non-monetary gold	2005	100.0	34.3	12.5	10.9	0.7	7.6	9.6	4.0	0.5
(SITC 27 + 28 + 68 + 667 + 971)	2012	100.0	24.7	10.5	7.2	0.4	5.0	5.7	3.1	0.4
Fuels (SITC 3)	1995	100.0	48.0	12.6	12.5	0.2	2.6	30.5	2.2	0.3
	2005	100.0	38.8	10.1	10.1	0.1	3.3	19.4	5.9	0.2
	2012	100.0	25.8	5.1	5.0	0.1	1.7	13.1	5.8	0.2
Manufactured goods	1995	100.0	52.6	17.2	16.5	1.2	22.1	10.2	1.9	0.8
(SITC 5 to 8 less 667 and 68)	2005	100.0	48.2	17.8	17.4	1.2	19.0	8.1	2.0	1.5
	2012	100.0	39.4	14.7	14.3	1.1	14.7	6.6	2.3	2.5
Share by major product group (percentage)										
All products	1995	100.0	100.0	100.0	100.0	100.0	100.0	100.0	100.0	100.0
	2005	100.0	100.0	100.0	100.0	100.0	100.0	100.0	100.0	100.0
	2012	100.0	100.0	100.0	100.0	100.0	100.0	100.0	100.0	100.0
All food items	1995	6.9	6.4	5.5	5.4	5.3	2.8	13.1	5.5	20.9
(SITC 0 + 1 + 22 + 4)	2005	3.9	3.8	3.3	3.3	4.5	2.6	7.1	3.4	8.3
	2012	4.8	4.5	4.3	4.4	5.3	3.3	6.9	3.9	6.7
Agricultural raw materials	1995	2.5	2.1	2.2	2.3	1.9	1.3	3.2	1.6	1.0
(SITC 2 - 22 - 27 - 28)	2005	1.2	1.0	1.1	1.1	1.5	0.7	1.5	0.6	0.6
	2012	1.4	1.4	1.2	1.2	1.6	1.6	1.5	0.6	0.6
Ores, metals, precious stones	1995	3.1	2.5	2.1	2.0	0.8	1.4	4.8	3.4	4.9
and non-monetary gold	2005	3.2	2.4	2.4	2.2	2.0	1.5	3.3	5.3	1.0
(SITC 27 + 28 + 68 + 667 + 971)	2012	4.2	2.8	3.3	2.3	1.6	1.7	3.3	4.8	0.7
Fuels (SITC 3)	1995	5.7	5.3	4.3	4.5	1.1	0.7	13.5	6.6	1.7
	2005	8.3	6.9	5.0	5.1	0.5	1.6	16.9	20.5	1.0
	2012	9.4	6.5	3.6	3.7	0.9	1.3	16.8	20.4	0.7
Manufactured goods	1995	80.5	82.2	84.3	84.3	89.9	91.9	64.3	81.8	70.5
(SITC 5 to 8 less 667 and 68)	2005	82.6	85.3	87.6	87.7	91.2	93.3	70.7	69.3	88.9
	2012	79.2	84.3	86.7	87.5	90.5	91.9	71.2	69.6	91.1

For sources and notes, see end of table 2.2.L.

	Developing economies - Économies en développement									Destinations	
				Asia / Asie				Major petroleum exporters and gas exporters / Principaux exportateurs de pétrole et de gaz	Major manufactured goods exporters / Principaux exportateurs d'articles manufacturés	Year / Année	
Total	Africa / Afrique	America / Amérique	Total	Eastern, Southern and South-Eastern Asia / Asie orientale, méridionale et du Sud-Est	China / Chine	Western Asia / Asie occidentale	Oceania / Océanie				Groupes de produits
Millions de dollars											
448 177	17 294	23 190	406 935	383 750	77 150	23 185	758	20 888	329 999	1995	**Total tous produits**
1 231 920	50 732	59 592	1 116 688	1 040 526	302 255	76 162	4 908	73 540	869 177	2005	
3 096 636	167 408	235 573	2 677 219	2 438 851	690 383	238 368	16 437	244 887	1 932 138	2012	
Parts par destinations (en pourcentage)											
47.2	1.8	2.4	42.8	40.4	8.1	2.4	0.1	2.2	34.7	1995	**Total tous produits**
51.7	2.1	2.5	46.9	43.7	12.7	3.2	0.2	3.1	36.5	2005	
60.6	3.3	4.6	52.4	47.7	13.5	4.7	0.3	4.8	37.8	2012	
49.0	2.9	0.6	45.4	40.9	7.7	4.6	0.1	4.1	28.2	1995	Produits alimentaires
51.2	5.2	1.3	44.5	38.6	5.7	5.9	0.2	6.2	23.9	2005	(CTCI 0 + 1 + 22 + 4)
62.5	7.1	1.6	53.5	47.1	8.2	6.4	0.3	7.6	26.7	2012	
55.5	1.2	2.0	52.3	50.4	13.2	1.9	0.0	1.5	42.3	1995	Matières premières
59.6	1.4	2.4	55.9	53.5	24.5	2.4	0.0	1.5	42.1	2005	d'origine agricole
62.9	1.4	2.6	58.9	56.1	27.3	2.8	0.0	1.6	41.9	2012	(CTCI 2 - 22 - 27 - 28)
56.5	0.4	0.2	55.8	54.8	10.2	1.0	0.0	1.0	48.1	1995	Minerais, métaux, pierres
65.1	0.6	0.3	64.2	57.9	18.4	6.2	0.0	6.2	49.0	2005	précieuses et or (non monétaire)
74.9	1.3	1.2	72.3	67.5	35.5	4.8	0.0	4.8	60.2	2012	(CTCI 27 + 28 + 68 + 667 + 971)
49.3	2.8	0.8	45.5	44.1	7.0	1.4	0.2	0.3	37.6	1995	Combustibles (CTCI 3)
60.0	2.2	1.3	55.7	53.0	9.4	2.7	0.8	1.4	38.7	2005	
73.1	2.5	2.4	67.4	63.3	11.8	4.1	0.8	3.3	45.7	2012	
46.4	1.7	2.8	41.8	39.4	8.1	2.4	0.1	2.3	34.5	1995	Articles manufacturés
50.2	2.0	2.7	45.4	42.4	13.0	3.0	0.1	3.0	36.4	2005	(CTCI 5 à 8 moins 667 et 68)
58.0	3.2	5.1	49.5	45.0	12.8	4.5	0.2	4.9	36.6	2012	
Parts par principaux groupes de produits (en pourcentage)											
100.0	100.0	100.0	100.0	100.0	100.0	100.0	100.0	100.0	100.0	1995	**Total tous produits**
100.0	100.0	100.0	100.0	100.0	100.0	100.0	100.0	100.0	100.0	2005	
100.0	100.0	100.0	100.0	100.0	100.0	100.0	100.0	100.0	100.0	2012	
7.2	10.8	1.8	7.3	7.0	6.6	12.9	9.8	12.8	5.6	1995	Produits alimentaires
3.9	9.7	2.0	3.7	3.5	1.8	7.3	4.0	7.9	2.6	2005	(CTCI 0 + 1 + 22 + 4)
5.0	10.4	1.7	4.9	4.7	2.9	6.6	4.1	7.7	3.4	2012	
2.9	1.7	2.1	3.0	3.1	4.0	1.9	0.4	1.6	3.0	1995	Matières premières
1.4	0.8	1.1	1.4	1.5	2.3	0.9	0.1	0.6	1.4	2005	d'origine agricole
1.5	0.6	0.8	1.6	1.6	2.8	0.8	0.1	0.5	1.6	2012	(CTCI 2 - 22 - 27 - 28)
3.7	0.8	0.3	4.0	4.2	3.9	1.3	0.4	1.3	4.3	1995	Minerais, métaux, pierres
4.1	0.9	0.4	4.4	4.3	4.7	6.3	0.2	6.5	4.3	2005	précieuses et or (non monétaire)
5.2	1.7	1.1	5.8	5.9	11.0	4.3	0.2	4.2	6.7	2012	(CTCI 27 + 28 + 68 + 667 + 971)
5.9	8.8	1.8	6.0	6.2	4.8	3.2	15.5	0.9	6.1	1995	Combustibles (CTCI 3)
9.6	8.4	4.2	9.8	10.1	6.2	7.1	33.7	3.7	8.8	2005	
11.3	7.1	5.0	12.1	12.5	8.2	8.2	23.2	6.5	11.3	2012	
79.1	76.3	91.9	78.5	78.4	79.9	79.9	69.6	82.6	79.9	1995	Articles manufacturés
80.1	77.8	88.1	79.9	80.2	84.9	76.3	55.9	79.9	82.5	2005	(CTCI 5 à 8 moins 667 et 68)
75.9	77.4	86.9	74.9	74.8	74.9	76.4	56.9	80.9	76.6	2012	

Pour les sources et les notes, se reporter à la fin du tableau 2.2.L.

2.2.F Import structure by partner and product group
Developing Asia: Eastern, Southern and South-Eastern Asia

Product group	Year Année	World (1) Monde (1)	Developed economies - Économies développées Total	Europe Total	EU UE	Canada	USA États-Unis	Japan Japon	Other developed countries Autres économies développées	Transition economies Économies en transition
Millions of dollars										
All products	1995	1 001 530	558 171	166 840	152 431	11 831	137 947	214 087	27 466	15 185
	2005	2 245 606	882 619	288 363	261 161	17 588	191 172	320 938	64 559	43 680
	2012	5 064 260	1 681 340	612 575	521 449	42 190	354 430	484 877	187 267	129 411
Share by origin (percentage)										
All products	1995	100.0	55.7	16.7	15.2	1.2	13.8	21.4	2.7	1.5
	2005	100.0	39.3	12.8	11.6	0.8	8.5	14.3	2.9	1.9
	2012	100.0	33.2	12.1	10.3	0.8	7.0	9.6	3.7	2.6
All food items	1995	100.0	53.3	13.6	13.1	4.1	23.3	2.8	9.5	0.7
(SITC 0 + 1 + 22 + 4)	2005	100.0	39.5	10.4	9.5	3.0	14.1	2.4	9.7	2.2
	2012	100.0	38.9	9.5	8.6	3.3	16.5	1.2	8.3	2.2
Agricultural raw materials	1995	100.0	51.4	7.3	7.0	5.2	23.9	5.7	9.3	4.0
(SITC 2 - 22 - 27 - 28)	2005	100.0	48.1	10.9	10.5	5.7	18.2	5.0	8.3	8.1
	2012	100.0	46.1	10.7	10.5	6.1	16.3	4.5	8.4	6.0
Ores, metals, precious stones	1995	100.0	54.9	20.1	15.0	2.5	10.5	8.5	13.3	4.4
and non-monetary gold	2005	100.0	46.2	16.8	12.4	1.7	5.3	6.6	15.8	4.1
(SITC 27 + 28 + 68 + 667 + 971)	2012	100.0	44.9	14.3	8.0	1.4	6.2	5.1	17.8	3.2
Fuels (SITC 3)	1995	100.0	12.3	1.7	1.6	0.7	2.9	2.3	4.7	0.9
	2005	100.0	7.5	1.0	0.8	0.3	1.0	0.9	4.4	3.6
	2012	100.0	8.1	2.0	1.7	0.4	1.2	1.0	3.6	7.0
Manufactured goods	1995	100.0	59.7	18.3	16.9	0.7	13.5	26.2	1.0	1.3
(SITC 5 to 8 less 667 and 68)	2005	100.0	43.8	14.6	13.5	0.5	9.5	18.5	0.7	1.2
	2012	100.0	39.0	15.4	14.1	0.5	7.9	14.6	0.6	0.8
Share by major product group (percentage)										
All products	1995	100.0	100.0	100.0	100.0	100.0	100.0	100.0	100.0	100.0
	2005	100.0	100.0	100.0	100.0	100.0	100.0	100.0	100.0	100.0
	2012	100.0	100.0	100.0	100.0	100.0	100.0	100.0	100.0	100.0
All food items	1995	6.1	5.9	5.0	5.3	21.2	10.4	0.8	21.2	2.9
(SITC 0 + 1 + 22 + 4)	2005	4.2	4.2	3.4	3.4	15.8	6.9	0.7	14.0	4.7
	2012	5.4	6.3	4.2	4.5	21.3	12.7	0.7	12.2	4.6
Agricultural raw materials	1995	3.3	3.0	1.4	1.5	14.3	5.7	0.9	11.2	8.6
(SITC 2 - 22 - 27 - 28)	2005	2.2	2.7	1.8	2.0	15.7	4.6	0.8	6.3	9.1
	2012	2.2	3.1	2.0	2.3	16.5	5.2	1.0	5.1	5.2
Ores, metals, precious stones	1995	5.9	5.8	7.1	5.8	12.6	4.5	2.3	28.5	17.0
and non-monetary gold	2005	7.4	8.7	9.7	7.9	16.1	4.6	3.4	40.8	15.7
(SITC 27 + 28 + 68 + 667 + 971)	2012	10.2	13.8	12.1	8.0	17.7	9.1	5.5	49.1	12.6
Fuels (SITC 3)	1995	6.6	1.5	0.7	0.7	3.7	1.4	0.7	11.3	4.0
	2005	13.2	2.5	1.0	0.9	4.3	1.5	0.8	20.1	24.3
	2012	21.4	5.2	3.5	3.5	11.0	3.7	2.2	20.6	58.5
Manufactured goods	1995	76.4	81.8	83.8	84.8	47.7	75.0	93.7	26.6	64.8
(SITC 5 to 8 less 667 and 68)	2005	72.4	80.7	82.2	84.1	47.7	81.1	93.8	17.2	45.5
	2012	58.9	69.2	75.0	80.5	32.0	66.5	90.0	9.5	18.6

For sources and notes, see end of table 2.2.L.

2.2.F Structure des importations par partenaires et groupes de produits
Économies en développement : Asie orientale, méridionale et du Sud-Est

| Developing economies - Économies en développement | | | | | | | | Major petroleum exporters and gas exporters / Principaux exportateurs de pétrole et de gaz | Major manufactured goods exporters / Principaux exportateurs d'articles manufacturés | Year Année | Origines |
Total	Africa / Afrique	America / Amérique	Asia / Asie Total	Eastern, Southern and South-Eastern Asia / Asie orientale, méridionale et du Sud-Est	China / Chine	Western Asia / Asie occidentale	Oceania / Océanie				Groupes de produits
Millions de dollars											
421 277	12 019	17 494	390 940	352 839	94 878	38 101	824	39 767	316 337	1995	Total tous produits
1 315 082	41 874	53 442	1 218 091	1 055 870	336 010	162 221	1 675	183 532	900 908	2005	
3 241 081	196 909	221 456	2 818 922	2 242 708	785 337	576 214	3 794	721 930	1 874 035	2012	
Parts par origines (en pourcentage)											
42.1	1.2	1.7	39.0	35.2	9.5	3.8	0.1	4.0	31.6	1995	Total tous produits
58.6	1.9	2.4	54.2	47.0	15.0	7.2	0.1	8.2	40.1	2005	
64.0	3.9	4.4	55.7	44.3	15.5	11.4	0.1	14.3	37.0	2012	
45.7	1.7	8.5	35.1	34.6	7.5	0.6	0.4	0.5	26.0	1995	Produits alimentaires
58.2	2.2	17.1	38.5	36.9	8.8	1.6	0.4	1.6	22.5	2005	(CTCI 0 + 1 + 22 + 4)
58.9	2.2	18.7	37.8	35.9	6.3	1.9	0.3	1.7	19.5	2012	
44.4	4.4	5.2	34.0	33.4	4.5	0.6	0.9	0.6	25.7	1995	Matières premières
43.8	5.6	5.2	31.9	31.2	3.0	0.7	1.1	0.7	20.3	2005	d'origine agricole
47.9	5.0	7.1	35.0	34.4	2.9	0.6	1.0	0.6	19.4	2012	(CTCI 2 - 22 - 27 - 28)
40.4	5.9	7.5	26.7	23.3	4.1	3.3	0.3	2.1	16.8	1995	Minerais, métaux, pierres
49.6	4.7	10.7	34.0	28.3	5.4	5.7	0.1	5.7	15.5	2005	précieuses et or (non monétaire)
51.9	7.4	14.2	30.1	23.8	5.8	6.3	0.1	6.2	15.8	2012	(CTCI 27 + 28 + 68 + 667 + 971)
86.3	4.8	0.7	80.6	37.1	3.7	43.5	0.1	49.0	24.0	1995	Combustibles (CTCI 3)
88.8	7.4	0.9	80.5	36.2	3.7	44.3	0.0	51.8	21.3	2005	
84.9	10.0	5.1	69.9	26.8	1.6	43.0	0.0	56.6	15.0	2012	
38.4	0.4	0.7	37.3	36.4	10.9	0.9	0.0	0.7	34.3	1995	Articles manufacturés
54.7	0.4	0.9	53.4	52.2	18.8	1.2	0.0	1.2	47.8	2005	(CTCI 5 à 8 moins 667 et 68)
60.0	0.3	1.1	58.5	56.2	24.0	2.4	0.0	2.3	51.6	2012	
Parts par principaux groupes de produits (en pourcentage)											
100.0	100.0	100.0	100.0	100.0	100.0	100.0	100.0	100.0	100.0	1995	Total tous produits
100.0	100.0	100.0	100.0	100.0	100.0	100.0	100.0	100.0	100.0	2005	
100.0	100.0	100.0	100.0	100.0	100.0	100.0	100.0	100.0	100.0	2012	
6.7	8.6	29.8	5.5	6.0	4.8	0.9	27.9	0.7	5.0	1995	Produits alimentaires
4.1	5.0	29.9	3.0	3.3	2.5	0.9	22.0	0.8	2.3	2005	(CTCI 0 + 1 + 22 + 4)
5.0	3.1	23.1	3.7	4.4	2.2	0.9	20.1	0.7	2.8	2012	
3.5	12.0	9.7	2.9	3.1	1.5	0.5	34.3	0.5	2.7	1995	Matières premières
1.6	6.5	4.7	1.3	1.4	0.4	0.2	32.7	0.2	1.1	2005	d'origine agricole
1.7	2.9	3.6	1.4	1.7	0.4	0.1	28.6	0.1	1.2	2012	(CTCI 2 - 22 - 27 - 28)
5.6	29.1	25.2	4.0	3.9	2.5	5.1	21.0	3.2	3.1	1995	Minerais, métaux, pierres
6.3	18.8	33.5	4.7	4.5	2.7	5.9	13.2	5.2	2.9	2005	précieuses et or (non monétaire)
8.3	19.5	33.3	5.5	5.5	3.8	5.6	17.9	4.5	4.4	2012	(CTCI 27 + 28 + 68 + 667 + 971)
13.6	26.4	2.8	13.7	7.0	2.6	75.6	8.4	81.6	5.0	1995	Combustibles (CTCI 3)
19.9	52.2	5.2	19.5	10.1	3.3	80.6	7.6	83.3	7.0	2005	
28.4	55.0	24.8	26.9	13.0	2.2	81.1	5.0	85.1	8.7	2012	
69.7	23.7	32.0	73.0	79.0	87.9	17.6	8.4	13.8	83.1	1995	Articles manufacturés
67.7	16.4	26.5	71.3	80.4	90.9	12.2	24.5	10.3	86.3	2005	(CTCI 5 à 8 moins 667 et 68)
55.2	4.9	15.0	61.9	74.7	90.9	12.2	28.3	9.6	82.1	2012	

Pour les sources et les notes, se reporter à la fin du tableau 2.2.L.

Product group	Year Année	World (1) Monde (1)	Developed economies - Économies développées							Transition economies Économies en transition
			Total	Europe		Canada	USA États-Unis	Japan Japon	Other developed countries Autres économies développées	
				Total	EU UE					
Millions of dollars										
All products	1995	135 176	72 536	28 593	28 054	491	12 624	28 938	1 891	2 587
	2005	514 225	255 954	103 478	101 199	3 350	57 891	85 952	5 284	7 184
	2012	1 305 568	440 138	158 803	153 201	8 505	94 327	165 778	12 725	20 914
Share by destination (percentage)										
All products	1995	100.0	53.7	21.2	20.8	0.4	9.3	21.4	1.4	1.9
	2005	100.0	49.8	20.1	19.7	0.7	11.3	16.7	1.0	1.4
	2012	100.0	33.7	12.2	11.7	0.7	7.2	12.7	1.0	1.6
All food items	1995	100.0	39.4	32.3	31.1	0.4	4.7	1.0	0.9	9.3
(SITC 0 + 1 + 22 + 4)	2005	100.0	36.0	30.1	29.1	0.4	3.0	1.0	1.5	5.9
	2012	100.0	18.0	13.8	13.4	0.5	1.8	0.5	1.5	5.5
Agricultural raw materials	1995	100.0	50.7	46.0	45.2	0.1	1.7	1.2	1.6	0.5
(SITC 2 - 22 - 27 - 28)	2005	100.0	35.6	32.2	31.8	0.1	1.3	1.0	1.0	1.7
	2012	100.0	24.3	21.5	21.2	0.1	1.2	0.5	1.0	5.2
Ores, metals, precious stones	1995	100.0	29.0	15.6	14.2	0.1	2.1	10.7	0.6	1.0
and non-monetary gold	2005	100.0	27.1	20.7	17.4	0.0	3.2	2.4	0.8	1.0
(SITC 27 + 28 + 68 + 667 + 971)	2012	100.0	16.3	13.3	9.7	0.4	1.4	0.9	0.4	0.5
Fuels (SITC 3)	1995	100.0	58.8	14.1	14.1	0.4	10.9	31.8	1.7	0.1
	2005	100.0	52.2	12.7	12.7	0.8	13.8	24.2	0.7	0.0
	2012	100.0	37.2	8.5	8.5	0.8	9.0	18.2	0.8	0.0
Manufactured goods	1995	100.0	47.4	37.5	36.5	0.3	7.3	1.5	0.9	5.3
(SITC 5 to 8 less 667 and 68)	2005	100.0	48.6	39.6	38.6	0.4	6.3	0.5	1.8	4.6
	2012	100.0	29.7	23.4	22.7	0.4	3.8	0.3	1.7	6.6
Share by major product group (percentage)										
All products	1995	100.0	100.0	100.0	100.0	100.0	100.0	100.0	100.0	100.0
	2005	100.0	100.0	100.0	100.0	100.0	100.0	100.0	100.0	100.0
	2012	100.0	100.0	100.0	100.0	100.0	100.0	100.0	100.0	100.0
All food items	1995	5.4	3.9	8.2	8.0	5.7	2.7	0.3	3.5	26.0
(SITC 0 + 1 + 22 + 4)	2005	3.2	2.3	4.7	4.7	1.8	0.9	0.2	4.8	13.4
	2012	3.0	1.6	3.4	3.4	2.1	0.7	0.1	4.6	10.3
Agricultural raw materials	1995	0.7	0.6	1.4	1.4	0.2	0.1	0.0	0.8	0.2
(SITC 2 - 22 - 27 - 28)	2005	0.2	0.2	0.4	0.4	0.0	0.0	0.0	0.2	0.3
	2012	0.2	0.1	0.3	0.3	0.0	0.0	0.0	0.2	0.5
Ores, metals, precious stones	1995	3.9	2.1	2.8	2.6	0.6	0.9	1.9	1.6	2.1
and non-monetary gold	2005	3.8	2.1	3.9	3.4	0.3	1.1	0.5	3.0	2.8
(SITC 27 + 28 + 68 + 667 + 971)	2012	6.9	3.3	7.5	5.7	3.7	1.3	0.5	2.6	2.3
Fuels (SITC 3)	1995	64.7	70.9	43.1	43.9	75.5	75.3	96.0	77.4	2.5
	2005	67.8	71.2	42.9	43.6	83.2	83.1	98.4	44.9	2.4
	2012	69.0	76.2	48.1	49.8	81.8	86.3	98.8	54.1	1.9
Manufactured goods	1995	24.8	21.9	44.0	43.6	18.0	19.3	1.7	16.4	69.1
(SITC 5 to 8 less 667 and 68)	2005	24.1	23.5	47.4	47.2	14.3	13.4	0.7	43.3	80.0
	2012	20.7	18.2	39.8	40.0	12.2	10.8	0.6	36.9	84.6

For sources and notes, see end of table 2.2.L.

| Developing economies - Économies en développement | | | | | | | | | | Year Année | Destinations |
Total	Africa Afrique	America Amérique	Asia Asie Total	Eastern, Southern and South-Eastern Asia Asie orientale, méridionale et du Sud-Est	China Chine	Western Asia Asie occidentale	Oceania Océanie	Major petroleum exporters and gas exporters Principaux exportateurs de pétrole et de gaz	Major manufactured goods exporters Principaux exportateurs d'articles manufacturés		Groupes de produits
Millions de dollars											
59 008	4 049	1 803	53 156	38 192	1 915	14 964	0	9 601	25 572	1995	**Total tous produits**
247 507	20 517	3 706	223 248	177 516	25 030	45 732	126	41 107	135 226	2005	
841 420	56 764	11 144	773 396	659 123	111 959	114 274	115	132 987	434 700	2012	
Parts par destinations (en pourcentage)											
43.7	3.0	1.3	39.3	28.3	1.4	11.1	0.0	7.1	18.9	1995	**Total tous produits**
48.1	4.0	0.7	43.4	34.5	4.9	8.9	0.0	8.0	26.3	2005	
64.4	4.3	0.9	59.2	50.5	8.6	8.8	0.0	10.2	33.3	2012	
50.7	6.0	0.6	44.1	7.3	0.1	36.8	0.0	34.6	2.2	1995	Produits alimentaires
57.0	6.6	0.5	49.9	11.0	0.2	38.8	0.0	37.7	1.6	2005	(CTCI 0 + 1 + 22 + 4)
75.7	8.2	0.5	67.0	21.7	0.5	45.3	0.0	52.6	3.0	2012	
48.1	10.3	0.2	37.5	22.7	3.0	14.8	0.0	9.3	7.9	1995	Matières premières
58.3	9.0	0.4	48.9	25.1	2.7	23.9	0.0	15.5	5.7	2005	d'origine agricole
68.4	7.4	1.0	59.9	40.2	5.4	19.7	0.0	24.9	8.3	2012	(CTCI 2 - 22 - 27 - 28)
68.3	3.5	0.2	64.6	45.9	1.6	18.7	0.0	16.6	24.1	1995	Minerais, métaux, pierres
71.4	2.9	0.2	68.3	51.3	3.1	17.0	0.0	15.0	14.8	2005	précieuses et or (non monétaire)
83.0	2.6	0.3	80.1	58.6	4.5	21.5	0.0	25.7	13.2	2012	(CTCI 27 + 28 + 68 + 667 + 971)
41.1	1.7	1.8	37.6	31.9	1.4	5.6	..	0.3	23.4	1995	Combustibles (CTCI 3)
47.7	2.6	0.8	44.2	40.9	5.9	3.4	0.0	1.3	34.9	2005	
62.7	3.0	0.8	58.9	57.0	10.4	1.9	0.0	0.9	42.9	2012	
45.7	5.6	0.4	39.7	20.9	1.7	18.7	0.0	17.6	10.7	1995	Articles manufacturés
44.3	7.5	0.6	36.1	17.9	3.0	18.2	0.1	20.7	8.0	2005	(CTCI 5 à 8 moins 667 et 68)
62.9	8.9	1.4	52.6	30.7	5.1	21.9	0.0	29.8	12.7	2012	
Parts par principaux groupes de produits (en pourcentage)											
100.0	100.0	100.0	100.0	100.0	100.0	100.0	100.0	100.0	100.0	1995	**Total tous produits**
100.0	100.0	100.0	100.0	100.0	100.0	100.0	100.0	100.0	100.0	2005	
100.0	100.0	100.0	100.0	100.0	100.0	100.0	100.0	100.0	100.0	2012	
6.2	10.7	2.5	6.0	1.4	0.3	17.8	6.5	26.1	0.6	1995	Produits alimentaires
3.8	5.3	2.4	3.6	1.0	0.1	13.9	1.3	15.0	0.2	2005	(CTCI 0 + 1 + 22 + 4)
3.5	5.6	1.7	3.4	1.3	0.2	15.5	3.5	15.4	0.3	2012	
0.7	2.3	0.1	0.6	0.5	1.4	0.9	7.5	0.9	0.3	1995	Matières premières
0.3	0.5	0.1	0.3	0.2	0.1	0.6	0.0	0.5	0.1	2005	d'origine agricole
0.2	0.3	0.2	0.2	0.1	0.1	0.3	0.0	0.4	0.0	2012	(CTCI 2 - 22 - 27 - 28)
6.0	4.6	0.4	6.3	6.3	4.4	6.5	19.7	9.0	4.9	1995	Minerais, métaux, pierres
5.7	2.7	0.8	6.0	5.7	2.5	7.3	0.1	7.1	2.1	2005	précieuses et or (non monétaire)
8.8	4.2	2.4	9.3	8.0	3.6	16.9	0.8	17.4	2.7	2012	(CTCI 27 + 28 + 68 + 667 + 971)
60.8	36.0	88.8	61.8	73.1	64.5	32.8	..	2.4	80.2	1995	Combustibles (CTCI 3)
67.2	44.8	76.1	69.1	80.3	82.0	25.7	0.1	11.2	90.1	2005	
67.1	47.6	61.5	68.7	78.0	83.5	15.1	18.5	6.1	89.0	2012	
26.0	46.4	8.2	25.0	18.4	29.4	42.0	66.3	61.6	14.0	1995	Articles manufacturés
22.2	45.5	19.6	20.0	12.5	14.8	49.2	97.3	62.3	7.3	2005	(CTCI 5 à 8 moins 667 et 68)
20.2	42.2	33.7	18.4	12.6	12.4	51.8	71.5	60.4	7.9	2012	

Pour les sources et les notes, se reporter à la fin du tableau 2.2.L.

Product group	Year Année	World (1) Monde (1)	Developed economies - Économies développées Total	Europe Total	Europe EU UE	Canada	USA États-Unis	Japan Japon	Other developed countries Autres économies développées	Transition economies Économies en transition
Millions of dollars										
All products	1995	128 501	79 733	53 316	49 637	985	15 356	8 533	1 543	4 547
	2005	363 511	196 056	137 799	129 202	1 868	29 916	18 489	7 984	23 064
	2012	868 417	368 861	236 467	220 928	5 597	78 576	32 975	15 247	47 292
Share by origin (percentage)										
All products	1995	100.0	62.0	41.5	38.6	0.8	11.9	6.6	1.2	3.5
	2005	100.0	53.9	37.9	35.5	0.5	8.2	5.1	2.2	6.3
	2012	100.0	42.5	27.2	25.4	0.6	9.0	3.8	1.8	5.4
All food items	1995	100.0	46.7	28.6	27.9	0.6	13.4	0.2	3.9	2.4
(SITC 0 + 1 + 22 + 4)	2005	100.0	39.6	23.0	22.1	0.5	9.1	0.1	6.8	3.6
	2012	100.0	31.6	17.7	16.8	1.7	6.7	0.1	5.4	7.4
Agricultural raw materials	1995	100.0	54.5	33.5	32.8	2.7	10.9	0.9	6.5	16.5
(SITC 2 - 22 - 27 - 28)	2005	100.0	58.5	36.0	35.6	2.0	17.6	0.6	2.4	10.9
	2012	100.0	54.0	32.8	32.5	1.8	15.9	0.8	2.7	7.6
Ores, metals, precious stones	1995	100.0	65.5	51.3	35.0	2.5	8.6	0.5	2.6	4.9
and non-monetary gold	2005	100.0	43.2	35.8	21.0	0.6	4.2	0.5	2.1	13.1
(SITC 27 + 28 + 68 + 667 + 971)	2012	100.0	30.5	22.0	15.7	0.8	5.5	0.2	2.0	7.4
Fuels (SITC 3)	1995	100.0	14.1	9.4	9.4	0.1	3.1	0.0	1.3	11.0
	2005	100.0	16.5	11.2	10.1	0.3	1.4	0.0	3.5	20.7
	2012	100.0	33.5	24.3	23.3	0.4	4.3	0.1	4.5	10.6
Manufactured goods	1995	100.0	70.1	47.0	44.2	0.7	12.8	9.2	0.4	2.7
(SITC 5 to 8 less 667 and 68)	2005	100.0	62.7	44.5	43.0	0.5	9.3	7.1	1.2	2.8
	2012	100.0	48.9	31.9	30.4	0.5	9.9	5.7	0.8	2.1
Share by major product group (percentage)										
All products	1995	100.0	100.0	100.0	100.0	100.0	100.0	100.0	100.0	100.0
	2005	100.0	100.0	100.0	100.0	100.0	100.0	100.0	100.0	100.0
	2012	100.0	100.0	100.0	100.0	100.0	100.0	100.0	100.0	100.0
All food items	1995	13.7	10.3	9.4	9.9	10.1	15.4	0.3	44.5	9.2
(SITC 0 + 1 + 22 + 4)	2005	9.5	6.9	5.7	5.9	10.0	10.5	0.2	29.2	5.3
	2012	10.8	8.1	7.0	7.1	28.3	8.0	0.3	33.5	14.6
Agricultural raw materials	1995	2.4	2.1	1.9	2.0	8.5	2.2	0.3	13.0	11.2
(SITC 2 - 22 - 27 - 28)	2005	1.4	1.5	1.3	1.4	5.3	2.9	0.2	1.5	2.3
	2012	1.1	1.4	1.4	1.4	3.1	2.0	0.3	1.7	1.6
Ores, metals, precious stones	1995	4.6	4.9	5.7	4.2	15.0	3.3	0.3	10.0	6.4
and non-monetary gold	2005	7.1	5.7	6.7	4.2	8.2	3.6	0.7	6.9	14.8
(SITC 27 + 28 + 68 + 667 + 971)	2012	9.9	7.1	8.0	6.1	12.6	6.0	0.6	11.2	13.6
Fuels (SITC 3)	1995	6.1	1.4	1.4	1.5	1.1	1.6	0.0	6.7	18.9
	2005	8.9	2.7	2.6	2.5	4.9	1.5	0.1	14.4	29.2
	2012	7.0	5.5	6.2	6.4	3.9	3.3	0.1	17.9	13.7
Manufactured goods	1995	71.3	80.5	80.7	81.5	65.0	76.6	98.5	23.0	54.2
(SITC 5 to 8 less 667 and 68)	2005	70.3	81.7	82.6	85.0	70.7	79.2	98.2	39.4	31.5
	2012	65.4	75.3	76.7	78.1	51.8	71.8	98.3	30.5	24.9

For sources and notes, see end of table 2.2.L.

			Developing economies - Économies en développement								Origines
			Asia Asie					Major petroleum exporters and gas exporters	Major manufactured goods exporters	Year	
Total	Africa Afrique	America Amérique	Total	Eastern, Southern and South-Eastern Asia Asie orientale, méridionale et du Sud-Est	China Chine	Western Asia Asie occidentale	Oceania Océanie	Principaux exportateurs de pétrole et de gaz	Principaux exportateurs d'articles manufacturés	Année	Groupes de produits
Millions de dollars											
40 784	3 052	2 299	35 429	21 041	3 359	14 387	4	11 157	14 202	1995	**Total tous produits**
142 877	11 499	7 307	124 047	77 083	24 006	46 964	24	36 240	52 743	2005	
438 625	22 578	19 996	396 025	275 501	96 963	120 524	26	85 727	173 227	2012	
Parts par origines (en pourcentage)											
31.7	2.4	1.8	27.6	16.4	2.6	11.2	0.0	8.7	11.1	1995	**Total tous produits**
39.3	3.2	2.0	34.1	21.2	6.6	12.9	0.0	10.0	14.5	2005	
50.5	2.6	2.3	45.6	31.7	11.2	13.9	0.0	9.9	19.9	2012	
49.7	4.4	6.5	38.7	17.8	1.0	20.9	0.0	7.9	7.1	1995	Produits alimentaires
56.8	5.5	10.8	40.5	17.5	1.5	23.0	0.0	8.7	6.0	2005	(CTCI 0 + 1 + 22 + 4)
61.0	5.3	10.5	45.2	22.1	1.7	23.2	0.0	10.4	6.5	2012	
28.0	5.1	3.5	19.4	15.0	0.5	4.4	0.0	3.9	9.8	1995	Matières premières
30.3	4.7	4.5	21.1	15.4	2.4	5.7	0.0	2.9	9.7	2005	d'origine agricole
38.3	4.8	6.5	27.0	23.0	5.2	4.0	0.0	3.5	14.6	2012	(CTCI 2 - 22 - 27 - 28)
29.7	6.4	4.8	18.5	5.4	0.4	13.1	0.0	8.5	1.5	1995	Minerais, métaux, pierres
43.4	7.7	4.0	31.7	21.7	1.2	10.0	0.0	7.6	7.7	2005	précieuses et or (non monétaire)
62.0	7.8	5.1	49.1	25.5	1.8	23.7	0.0	18.4	5.9	2012	(CTCI 27 + 28 + 68 + 667 + 971)
74.2	13.6	0.1	60.4	11.2	0.3	49.3	..	65.2	1.0	1995	Combustibles (CTCI 3)
62.5	10.5	0.8	51.2	13.1	0.9	38.1	..	46.9	1.7	2005	
55.8	4.8	0.5	50.5	23.2	1.3	27.3	0.0	24.2	3.6	2012	
25.7	0.7	0.8	24.2	17.7	3.4	6.5	0.0	4.4	13.6	1995	Articles manufacturés
34.0	1.1	0.8	32.1	23.2	8.9	8.8	0.0	5.0	18.5	2005	(CTCI 5 à 8 moins 667 et 68)
48.9	1.2	0.7	47.0	36.2	16.3	10.8	0.0	6.1	27.8	2012	
Parts par principaux groupes de produits (en pourcentage)											
100.0	100.0	100.0	100.0	100.0	100.0	100.0	100.0	100.0	100.0	1995	**Total tous produits**
100.0	100.0	100.0	100.0	100.0	100.0	100.0	100.0	100.0	100.0	2005	
100.0	100.0	100.0	100.0	100.0	100.0	100.0	100.0	100.0	100.0	2012	
21.4	25.5	49.9	19.2	14.9	5.4	25.5	88.1	12.5	8.8	1995	Produits alimentaires
13.7	16.4	50.6	11.2	7.8	2.1	16.8	2.6	8.2	3.9	2005	(CTCI 0 + 1 + 22 + 4)
13.1	22.0	49.5	10.7	7.5	1.7	18.1	9.9	11.4	3.5	2012	
2.1	5.2	4.7	1.7	2.2	0.5	1.0	0.0	1.1	2.1	1995	Matières premières
1.1	2.0	3.1	0.8	1.0	0.5	0.6	0.0	0.4	0.9	2005	d'origine agricole
0.9	2.1	3.2	0.7	0.8	0.5	0.3	3.4	0.4	0.8	2012	(CTCI 2 - 22 - 27 - 28)
4.3	12.5	12.4	3.1	1.5	0.7	5.4	1.3	4.5	0.6	1995	Minerais, métaux, pierres
7.9	17.4	14.1	6.6	7.3	1.3	5.5	0.4	5.4	3.8	2005	précieuses et or (non monétaire)
12.2	29.7	22.1	10.7	8.0	1.6	16.9	0.5	18.4	2.9	2012	(CTCI 27 + 28 + 68 + 667 + 971)
14.1	34.6	0.4	13.3	4.1	0.7	26.6	..	45.4	0.5	1995	Combustibles (CTCI 3)
14.2	29.7	3.3	13.4	5.5	1.3	26.3	..	42.0	1.0	2005	
7.7	12.8	1.7	7.8	5.1	0.8	13.8	0.0	17.2	1.3	2012	
57.8	22.2	32.5	62.5	76.9	92.5	41.4	10.5	36.4	87.6	1995	Articles manufacturés
60.9	25.1	28.4	66.1	77.0	94.4	48.1	96.9	35.3	89.7	2005	(CTCI 5 à 8 moins 667 et 68)
63.4	30.9	19.5	67.4	74.7	95.4	50.7	85.5	40.2	91.2	2012	

Pour les sources et les notes, se reporter à la fin du tableau 2.2.L.

2.2.H Export structure by partner and product group
Developing economies: Oceania

Destination Product group	Year Année	World (1) Monde (1)	Developed economies - Économies développées							Transition economies Économies en transition
			Total	Europe		Canada	USA États-Unis	Japan Japon	Other developed countries Autres économies développées	
				Total	EU UE					
Millions of dollars										
All products	1995	5 149	3 972	1 041	1 039	28	229	1 497	1 176	2
	2005	6 943	4 672	1 358	1 338	22	307	1 006	1 979	27
	2012	10 476	6 990	1 591	1 585	10	406	1 391	3 592	32
Share by destination (percentage)										
All products	1995	100.0	77.1	20.2	20.2	0.6	4.5	29.1	22.8	0.0
	2005	100.0	67.3	19.6	19.3	0.3	4.4	14.5	28.5	0.4
	2012	100.0	66.7	15.2	15.1	0.1	3.9	13.3	34.3	0.3
All food items	1995	100.0	82.1	53.4	53.4	2.3	5.3	12.8	8.4	0.1
(SITC 0 + 1 + 22 + 4)	2005	100.0	79.0	41.2	41.1	0.5	13.1	10.6	13.6	0.3
	2012	100.0	72.4	44.5	44.4	0.3	11.1	8.0	8.5	0.4
Agricultural raw materials	1995	100.0	61.7	1.4	1.4	0.0	0.3	58.3	1.7	..
(SITC 2 - 22 - 27 - 28)	2005	100.0	18.6	0.5	0.4	0.0	1.4	12.1	4.5	0.0
	2012	100.0	11.9	0.6	0.6	0.1	0.4	8.3	2.5	0.0
Ores, metals, precious stones	1995	100.0	87.2	15.9	15.8	0.0	2.4	39.6	29.4	0.0
and non-monetary gold	2005	100.0	83.8	15.5	15.4	0.0	1.5	24.4	42.4	1.1
(SITC 27 + 28 + 68 + 667 + 971)	2012	100.0	84.0	11.0	10.9	0.0	0.9	21.3	50.9	0.0
Fuels (SITC 3)	1995	100.0	89.3	0.0	0.0	..	3.4	1.9	84.0	..
	2005	100.0	77.2	0.0	0.0	0.0	2.5	5.2	69.5	0.0
	2012	100.0	60.8	0.0	0.0	0.0	2.3	6.5	52.0	0.0
Manufactured goods	1995	100.0	83.9	29.5	29.3	0.5	13.1	24.2	16.6	0.1
(SITC 5 to 8 less 667 and 68)	2005	100.0	50.0	26.5	25.6	0.8	3.1	11.4	8.3	0.1
	2012	100.0	45.5	14.4	14.3	0.3	6.5	9.3	15.1	1.8
Share by major product group (percentage)										
All products	1995	100.0	100.0	100.0	100.0	100.0	100.0	100.0	100.0	100.0
	2005	100.0	100.0	100.0	100.0	100.0	100.0	100.0	100.0	100.0
	2012	100.0	100.0	100.0	100.0	100.0	100.0	100.0	100.0	100.0
All food items	1995	20.2	21.5	53.3	53.5	84.3	24.0	8.9	7.4	50.1
(SITC 0 + 1 + 22 + 4)	2005	19.3	22.7	40.7	41.3	29.3	57.1	14.2	9.2	13.8
	2012	19.7	21.3	57.6	57.7	54.4	56.4	11.8	4.9	24.2
Agricultural raw materials	1995	12.8	10.2	0.9	0.9	0.2	0.8	25.6	0.9	..
(SITC 2 - 22 - 27 - 28)	2005	8.3	2.3	0.2	0.2	1.3	2.7	7.0	1.3	0.1
	2012	8.3	1.5	0.3	0.3	5.8	0.9	5.2	0.6	0.1
Ores, metals, precious stones	1995	27.1	30.7	21.3	21.3	0.4	14.6	36.9	34.9	0.2
and non-monetary gold	2005	27.7	34.5	22.0	22.2	2.7	9.1	46.7	41.2	77.9
(SITC 27 + 28 + 68 + 667 + 971)	2012	40.0	50.4	28.8	28.8	2.8	9.4	64.1	59.3	0.1
Fuels (SITC 3)	1995	12.3	14.2	0.0	0.0	..	9.4	0.8	45.2	..
	2005	14.8	17.0	0.0	0.0	0.0	8.4	5.3	36.1	0.0
	2012	17.1	15.6	0.0	0.0	0.1	10.0	8.3	25.9	0.0
Manufactured goods	1995	16.0	17.4	23.4	23.3	14.8	47.3	13.3	11.6	49.3
(SITC 5 to 8 less 667 and 68)	2005	27.2	20.2	36.9	36.1	66.3	18.8	21.3	7.9	8.1
	2012	13.1	9.0	12.4	12.4	35.5	22.0	9.2	5.8	75.7

For sources and notes, see end of table 2.2.L.

Total	Africa / Afrique	America / Amérique	Asia / Asie Total	Eastern, Southern and South-Eastern Asia / Asie orientale, méridionale et du Sud-Est	China / Chine	Western Asia / Asie occidentale	Oceania / Océanie	Major petroleum and gas exporters / Principaux exportateurs de pétrole et de gaz	Major manufactured goods exporters / Principaux exportateurs d'articles manufacturés	Year / Année	Destinations / Groupes de produits
Millions de dollars											
784	3	10	752	750	86	3	19	1	639	1995	Total tous produits
2 236	86	183	1 743	1 733	430	10	224	5	1 463	2005	
3 230	103	51	2 671	2 663	964	7	406	5	2 137	2012	
Parts par destinations (en pourcentage)											
15.2	0.1	0.2	14.6	14.6	1.7	0.1	0.4	0.0	12.4	1995	Total tous produits
32.2	1.2	2.6	25.1	25.0	6.2	0.1	3.2	0.1	21.1	2005	
30.8	1.0	0.5	25.5	25.4	9.2	0.1	3.9	0.1	20.4	2012	
17.5	0.1	0.1	17.1	16.9	1.2	0.2	0.3	0.0	14.7	1995	Produits alimentaires
20.2	0.5	0.3	13.5	13.4	0.3	0.0	6.0	0.0	10.8	2005	(CTCI 0 + 1 + 22 + 4)
26.5	0.3	0.7	17.4	17.2	1.0	0.2	8.2	0.1	15.0	2012	
38.0	0.0	0.0	37.8	37.8	4.3	0.0	0.2	..	33.7	1995	Matières premières
81.4	0.4	0.7	79.6	79.6	45.5	0.0	0.6	0.0	57.5	2005	d'origine agricole
88.1	0.5	1.6	85.6	85.5	69.9	0.0	0.5	0.2	77.4	2012	(CTCI 2 - 22 - 27 - 28)
12.7	0.0	0.0	12.7	12.7	..	0.0	0.0	..	8.6	1995	Minerais, métaux, pierres
15.1	0.5	0.0	14.4	14.4	2.6	0.0	0.1	0.0	7.1	2005	précieuses et or (non monétaire)
16.0	0.4	0.0	15.3	15.3	2.9	0.0	0.3	0.0	10.4	2012	(CTCI 27 + 28 + 68 + 667 + 971)
10.7	..	..	10.3	10.3	7.2	..	0.4	..	10.3	1995	Combustibles (CTCI 3)
22.6	0.2	0.0	18.2	18.2	3.4	..	4.2	0.1	12.9	2005	
27.5	0.1	0.9	22.1	22.1	5.4	0.0	4.5	0.0	17.9	2012	
12.5	0.2	1.0	9.9	9.8	0.0	0.1	1.3	0.0	9.5	1995	Articles manufacturés
49.9	3.4	9.2	33.4	32.8	4.2	0.5	3.9	0.2	37.6	2005	(CTCI 5 à 8 moins 667 et 68)
52.7	4.1	0.4	38.4	38.2	8.7	0.2	9.8	0.1	28.5	2012	
Parts par principaux groupes de produits (en pourcentage)											
100.0	100.0	100.0	100.0	100.0	100.0	100.0	100.0	100.0	100.0	1995	Total tous produits
100.0	100.0	100.0	100.0	100.0	100.0	100.0	100.0	100.0	100.0	2005	
100.0	100.0	100.0	100.0	100.0	100.0	100.0	100.0	100.0	100.0	2012	
23.2	22.7	9.2	23.6	23.4	14.2	84.4	14.3	53.0	23.9	1995	Produits alimentaires
12.1	8.0	2.2	10.4	10.4	0.8	1.3	35.8	6.3	9.9	2005	(CTCI 0 + 1 + 22 + 4)
16.9	6.6	28.7	13.4	13.3	2.0	44.7	41.4	28.7	14.5	2012	
31.9	0.3	0.6	33.0	33.2	32.7	0.0	5.8	..	34.7	1995	Matières premières
21.1	2.6	2.3	26.4	26.6	61.3	0.0	1.6	0.0	22.7	2005	d'origine agricole
23.7	3.8	26.9	27.9	27.9	63.1	0.4	1.2	27.5	31.5	2012	(CTCI 2 - 22 - 27 - 28)
22.7	0.2	0.1	23.6	23.7	..	0.3	1.4	..	18.8	1995	Minerais, métaux, pierres
13.0	11.7	0.3	15.9	16.0	11.6	0.6	1.1	0.2	9.3	2005	précieuses et or (non monétaire)
20.7	15.4	0.1	24.0	24.0	12.4	0.6	3.4	0.0	20.5	2012	(CTCI 27 + 28 + 68 + 667 + 971)
8.7	..	..	8.7	8.7	52.9	..	14.0	..	10.2	1995	Combustibles (CTCI 3)
10.4	2.2	0.0	10.8	10.8	8.0	..	19.3	16.9	9.1	2005	
15.2	1.0	31.9	14.8	14.8	10.1	0.0	19.6	0.0	15.0	2012	
13.1	75.9	90.0	10.9	10.8	0.1	15.3	55.2	47.0	12.2	1995	Articles manufacturés
42.1	75.3	94.8	36.2	35.8	18.3	97.7	32.6	75.9	48.6	2005	(CTCI 5 à 8 moins 667 et 68)
22.5	54.6	11.9	19.8	19.7	12.4	36.0	33.3	21.1	18.4	2012	

Pour les sources et les notes, se reporter à la fin du tableau 2.2.L.

Product group	Year / Année	World (1) / Monde (1)	Developed economies - Économies développées Total	Europe Total	Europe EU / UE	Canada	USA États-Unis	Japan Japon	Other developed countries / Autres économies développées	Transition economies / Économies en transition
Millions of dollars										
All products	1995	6 201	4 198	1 318	1 306	13	357	575	1 936	1
	2005	9 616	5 741	1 975	1 947	31	483	511	2 741	3
	2012	15 933	8 210	2 267	2 199	96	792	680	4 375	90
Share by origin (percentage)										
All products	1995	100.0	67.7	21.2	21.1	0.2	5.8	9.3	31.2	0.0
	2005	100.0	59.7	20.5	20.3	0.3	5.0	5.3	28.5	0.0
	2012	100.0	51.5	14.2	13.8	0.6	5.0	4.3	27.5	0.6
All food items	1995	100.0	86.5	23.3	23.2	0.2	10.7	3.8	48.5	0.0
(SITC 0 + 1 + 22 + 4)	2005	100.0	71.3	16.8	16.7	0.3	8.6	2.6	42.9	0.0
	2012	100.0	61.5	13.9	13.8	0.4	8.6	1.7	36.9	0.0
Agricultural raw materials	1995	100.0	90.5	6.5	6.5	0.0	28.1	2.4	53.5	0.3
(SITC 2 - 22 - 27 - 28)	2005	100.0	83.6	5.7	5.7	7.4	12.8	0.7	57.1	0.0
	2012	100.0	79.0	5.9	5.8	2.6	9.0	1.3	60.3	0.0
Ores, metals, precious stones	1995	100.0	81.0	27.7	27.7	0.0	3.6	0.9	48.7	0.0
and non-monetary gold	2005	100.0	74.4	31.4	31.1	1.0	2.3	1.9	37.9	0.0
(SITC 27 + 28 + 68 + 667 + 971)	2012	100.0	57.5	17.1	15.3	8.1	2.1	3.6	26.6	0.0
Fuels (SITC 3)	1995	100.0	68.0	0.6	0.6	0.0	1.6	0.0	65.8	0.0
	2005	100.0	20.3	0.3	0.3	0.0	0.3	0.0	19.8	0.0
	2012	100.0	22.6	0.5	0.3	0.0	0.4	0.8	20.8	2.0
Manufactured goods	1995	100.0	78.1	29.2	28.9	0.3	5.6	14.3	28.7	0.0
(SITC 5 to 8 less 667 and 68)	2005	100.0	69.2	29.4	29.0	0.3	5.3	8.1	26.1	0.0
	2012	100.0	62.4	22.0	21.3	0.8	5.6	7.3	26.6	0.1
Share by major product group (percentage)										
All products	1995	100.0	100.0	100.0	100.0	100.0	100.0	100.0	100.0	100.0
	2005	100.0	100.0	100.0	100.0	100.0	100.0	100.0	100.0	100.0
	2012	100.0	100.0	100.0	100.0	100.0	100.0	100.0	100.0	100.0
All food items	1995	14.1	18.1	15.5	15.6	11.4	26.4	5.8	22.0	8.6
(SITC 0 + 1 + 22 + 4)	2005	17.4	20.7	14.2	14.3	18.6	29.8	8.4	26.1	7.9
	2012	19.9	23.8	19.5	19.9	12.3	34.4	8.0	26.8	0.9
Agricultural raw materials	1995	0.9	1.2	0.3	0.3	0.1	4.3	0.2	1.5	18.1
(SITC 2 - 22 - 27 - 28)	2005	0.9	1.3	0.3	0.3	21.5	2.4	0.1	1.9	0.6
	2012	0.7	1.1	0.3	0.3	3.0	1.3	0.2	1.6	0.0
Ores, metals, precious stones	1995	0.6	0.7	0.8	0.8	0.0	0.4	0.1	0.9	0.9
and non-monetary gold	2005	0.8	1.0	1.2	1.2	2.5	0.4	0.3	1.1	0.0
(SITC 27 + 28 + 68 + 667 + 971)	2012	0.8	0.9	1.0	0.9	10.8	0.3	0.7	0.8	0.0
Fuels (SITC 3)	1995	8.5	8.5	0.2	0.2	0.2	2.4	0.0	17.9	8.4
	2005	20.8	7.1	0.3	0.3	0.1	1.1	0.1	14.4	28.8
	2012	26.9	11.8	1.0	0.6	0.0	2.2	5.3	20.4	94.5
Manufactured goods	1995	60.0	69.2	82.5	82.4	86.6	58.3	92.6	55.1	63.9
(SITC 5 to 8 less 667 and 68)	2005	58.3	67.6	83.5	83.4	56.1	61.6	88.9	53.4	62.4
	2012	49.2	59.5	75.9	76.0	68.3	55.6	84.1	47.7	4.6

For sources and notes, see end of table 2.2.L.

Total	Africa / Afrique	America / Amérique	Asia / Asie Total	Eastern, Southern and South-Eastern Asia / Asie orientale, méridionale et du Sud-Est	China / Chine	Western Asia / Asie occidentale	Oceania / Océanie	Major petroleum exporters and gas exporters / Principaux exportateurs de pétrole et de gaz	Major manufactured goods exporters / Principaux exportateurs d'articles manufacturés	Year / Année	Origines / Groupes de produits
Millions de dollars											
1 037	6	32	979	978	70	1	19	0	907	1995	**Total tous produits**
3 846	33	49	3 505	3 488	344	17	258	3	3 219	2005	
7 529	62	67	6 986	6 955	1 370	30	414	10	6 474	2012	
Parts par origines (en pourcentage)											
16.7	0.1	0.5	15.8	15.8	1.1	0.0	0.3	0.0	14.6	1995	**Total tous produits**
40.0	0.3	0.5	36.5	36.3	3.6	0.2	2.7	0.0	33.5	2005	
47.3	0.4	0.4	43.8	43.7	8.6	0.2	2.6	0.1	40.6	2012	
12.4	0.4	1.4	10.3	10.3	0.8	0.0	0.3	0.0	8.9	1995	Produits alimentaires
27.4	1.0	1.7	17.4	17.3	2.6	0.1	7.2	0.1	15.1	2005	(CTCI 0 + 1 + 22 + 4)
35.4	0.6	1.0	27.2	27.1	11.3	0.1	6.5	0.1	24.1	2012	
9.0	0.1	0.2	6.7	6.7	0.0	0.1	2.0	0.1	6.1	1995	Matières premières
16.3	1.4	0.4	8.7	8.7	1.1	0.0	5.8	0.0	6.3	2005	d'origine agricole
21.0	2.4	1.6	11.4	11.4	1.4	0.0	5.6	0.0	8.3	2012	(CTCI 2 - 22 - 27 - 28)
13.1	1.2	0.1	10.9	10.8	0.1	0.2	0.8	0.0	9.8	1995	Minerais, métaux, pierres
25.5	0.7	0.4	20.1	19.9	2.3	0.2	4.4	0.2	11.4	2005	précieuses et or (non monétaire)
42.5	0.4	0.1	35.4	35.4	6.1	0.0	6.6	1.3	25.3	2012	(CTCI 27 + 28 + 68 + 667 + 971)
31.5	0.2	0.1	30.7	30.7	0.0	..	0.5	..	30.0	1995	Combustibles (CTCI 3)
79.6	0.0	0.0	77.5	77.5	0.1	0.0	2.1	0.0	76.9	2005	
75.4	0.2	0.0	74.0	73.9	0.5	0.1	1.3	0.1	73.6	2012	
19.4	0.0	0.5	18.5	18.5	1.7	0.0	0.3	0.0	17.1	1995	Articles manufacturés
30.7	0.3	0.4	28.8	28.5	5.2	0.3	1.3	0.0	24.9	2005	(CTCI 5 à 8 moins 667 et 68)
37.5	0.4	0.4	35.0	34.8	12.4	0.3	1.7	0.0	30.9	2012	
Parts par principaux groupes de produits (en pourcentage)											
100.0	100.0	100.0	100.0	100.0	100.0	100.0	100.0	100.0	100.0	1995	**Total tous produits**
100.0	100.0	100.0	100.0	100.0	100.0	100.0	100.0	100.0	100.0	2005	
100.0	100.0	100.0	100.0	100.0	100.0	100.0	100.0	100.0	100.0	2012	
10.5	55.7	39.0	9.2	9.2	9.7	12.8	13.3	22.4	8.6	1995	Produits alimentaires
11.9	50.8	56.6	8.3	8.3	12.5	12.8	46.8	31.6	7.8	2005	(CTCI 0 + 1 + 22 + 4)
14.9	32.6	49.7	12.4	12.4	26.2	14.6	49.7	17.1	11.8	2012	
0.5	0.7	0.4	0.4	0.4	0.0	4.1	5.6	10.6	0.4	1995	Matières premières
0.4	3.7	0.8	0.2	0.2	0.3	0.0	2.0	0.2	0.2	2005	d'origine agricole
0.3	4.3	2.8	0.2	0.2	0.1	0.0	1.5	0.4	0.1	2012	(CTCI 2 - 22 - 27 - 28)
0.5	7.0	0.1	0.4	0.4	0.0	5.3	1.6	0.9	0.4	1995	Minerais, métaux, pierres
0.5	1.6	0.6	0.4	0.4	0.5	0.8	1.3	4.5	0.3	2005	précieuses et or (non monétaire)
0.7	0.9	0.1	0.6	0.7	0.6	0.0	2.0	16.8	0.5	2012	(CTCI 27 + 28 + 68 + 667 + 971)
16.0	20.6	2.1	16.5	16.5	0.1	..	13.4	..	17.4	1995	Combustibles (CTCI 3)
41.4	0.7	0.1	44.2	44.4	0.6	0.8	16.1	4.1	47.7	2005	
43.0	12.5	0.4	45.5	45.6	1.6	14.8	13.2	35.9	48.8	2012	
69.4	15.9	58.3	70.4	70.4	90.2	77.8	55.6	66.1	70.2	1995	Articles manufacturés
44.7	42.8	41.5	46.0	45.8	84.7	84.7	28.5	59.6	43.3	2005	(CTCI 5 à 8 moins 667 et 68)
39.1	47.9	46.6	39.3	39.2	70.6	68.4	32.8	28.2	37.4	2012	

Pour les sources et les notes, se reporter à la fin du tableau 2.2.L.

Product group	Year / Année	World (1) / Monde (1)	Developed economies - Économies développées							Transition economies / Économies en transition
			Total	Europe Total	Europe EU / UE	Canada	USA / États-Unis	Japan / Japon	Other developed countries / Autres économies développées	
Millions of dollars										
All products	1995	173 322	106 369	41 629	40 688	1 524	29 744	31 863	1 609	1 335
	2005	671 926	378 359	140 803	137 917	7 385	128 393	98 651	3 126	2 021
	2012	1 640 276	627 637	244 715	239 772	17 107	174 338	178 565	12 912	5 104
Share by destination (percentage)										
All products	1995	100.0	61.4	24.0	23.5	0.9	17.2	18.4	0.9	0.8
	2005	100.0	56.3	21.0	20.5	1.1	19.1	14.7	0.5	0.3
	2012	100.0	38.3	14.9	14.6	1.0	10.6	10.9	0.8	0.3
All food items	1995	100.0	27.5	22.2	21.8	0.5	3.0	1.7	0.2	8.6
(SITC 0 + 1 + 22 + 4)	2005	100.0	24.1	18.6	18.5	0.5	3.5	1.1	0.4	3.6
	2012	100.0	9.7	7.6	7.4	0.3	0.9	0.8	0.2	3.2
Agricultural raw materials	1995	100.0	54.4	50.2	48.7	0.2	3.3	0.5	0.0	0.7
(SITC 2 - 22 - 27 - 28)	2005	100.0	30.0	28.6	28.3	0.1	1.0	0.1	0.2	1.3
	2012	100.0	34.2	30.9	30.7	0.6	2.0	0.1	0.5	2.0
Ores, metals, precious stones	1995	100.0	46.4	20.7	19.9	0.4	10.5	14.7	0.1	1.2
and non-monetary gold	2005	100.0	29.4	20.8	18.0	0.8	4.9	2.8	0.1	0.5
(SITC 27 + 28 + 68 + 667 + 971)	2012	100.0	14.4	10.9	9.1	0.1	2.0	1.2	0.1	0.1
Fuels (SITC 3)	1995	100.0	66.9	24.6	24.1	1.0	18.8	21.5	1.0	0.3
	2005	100.0	60.9	21.0	20.7	1.2	21.3	17.0	0.4	0.0
	2012	100.0	43.5	16.1	15.9	1.2	12.4	13.0	0.8	0.1
Manufactured goods	1995	100.0	33.0	19.9	18.7	0.4	10.0	2.3	0.5	2.4
(SITC 5 to 8 less 667 and 68)	2005	100.0	30.6	21.9	21.0	0.5	6.6	0.8	0.9	2.2
	2012	100.0	12.7	8.5	8.0	0.2	2.5	0.5	0.9	1.9
Share by major product group (percentage)										
All products	1995	100.0	100.0	100.0	100.0	100.0	100.0	100.0	100.0	100.0
	2005	100.0	100.0	100.0	100.0	100.0	100.0	100.0	100.0	100.0
	2012	100.0	100.0	100.0	100.0	100.0	100.0	100.0	100.0	100.0
All food items	1995	2.3	1.0	2.1	2.1	1.2	0.4	0.2	0.6	25.9
(SITC 0 + 1 + 22 + 4)	2005	1.2	0.5	1.1	1.1	0.5	0.2	0.1	1.1	14.5
	2012	1.5	0.4	0.8	0.8	0.4	0.1	0.1	0.3	15.6
Agricultural raw materials	1995	0.5	0.4	1.0	1.0	0.1	0.1	0.0	0.0	0.5
(SITC 2 - 22 - 27 - 28)	2005	0.1	0.1	0.2	0.2	0.0	0.0	0.0	0.0	0.6
	2012	0.2	0.1	0.3	0.3	0.1	0.0	0.0	0.1	1.0
Ores, metals, precious stones	1995	2.5	1.9	2.1	2.1	1.2	1.5	2.0	0.1	3.7
and non-monetary gold	2005	2.7	1.4	2.7	2.4	2.0	0.7	0.5	0.4	4.3
(SITC 27 + 28 + 68 + 667 + 971)	2012	4.3	1.6	3.1	2.7	0.5	0.8	0.5	0.4	2.0
Fuels (SITC 3)	1995	82.3	89.7	84.2	84.6	92.2	90.2	96.2	92.4	28.5
	2005	85.2	92.1	85.2	85.7	93.1	95.0	98.7	73.8	6.2
	2012	82.7	94.1	89.3	90.1	96.9	96.1	98.9	85.1	16.6
Manufactured goods	1995	12.1	6.5	10.0	9.6	5.2	7.1	1.5	6.6	38.3
(SITC 5 to 8 less 667 and 68)	2005	10.1	5.5	10.6	10.3	4.3	3.5	0.5	18.8	72.4
	2012	10.7	3.6	6.1	5.9	2.1	2.5	0.5	12.6	64.6

For sources and notes, see end of table 2.2.L.

Developing economies - Économies en développement										Destinations	
			Asia Asie					Major petroleum exporters and gas exporters	Major manufactured goods exporters	Year	
Total	Africa Afrique	America Amérique	Total	Eastern, Southern and South-Eastern Asia Asie orientale, méridionale et du Sud-Est	China Chine	Western Asia Asie occidentale	Oceania Océanie	Principaux exportateurs de pétrole et de gaz	Principaux exportateurs d'articles manufacturés	Année	Groupes de produits
Millions de dollars											
65 612	5 649	8 725	51 237	38 525	1 886	12 712	0	6 445	26 049	1995	Total tous produits
291 510	23 124	24 200	244 181	204 381	39 735	39 801	4	26 636	160 567	2005	
1 007 343	59 859	45 011	901 099	808 705	188 176	92 394	1 374	84 933	543 540	2012	
Parts par destinations (en pourcentage)											
37.9	3.3	5.0	29.6	22.2	1.1	7.3	0.0	3.7	15.0	1995	Total tous produits
43.4	3.4	3.6	36.3	30.4	5.8	5.9	0.0	4.0	23.9	2005	
61.4	3.6	2.7	54.9	49.3	11.5	5.6	0.1	5.2	33.1	2012	
63.8	4.2	10.9	48.7	10.1	0.2	38.6	0.0	35.4	3.5	1995	Produits alimentaires
72.3	6.4	3.0	63.0	23.1	0.4	39.9	0.0	37.6	5.5	2005	(CTCI 0 + 1 + 22 + 4)
87.0	7.7	4.4	74.5	32.9	0.8	41.6	0.4	52.1	5.4	2012	
44.9	3.9	3.3	37.7	22.0	2.8	15.7	0.0	8.6	5.8	1995	Matières premières
68.7	10.9	3.4	54.4	34.9	3.1	19.5	0.0	16.4	7.1	2005	d'origine agricole
63.4	6.4	6.2	49.8	36.0	4.9	13.8	1.0	15.7	7.9	2012	(CTCI 2 - 22 - 27 - 28)
52.4	3.1	6.5	42.8	29.8	1.8	13.0	0.0	10.1	15.2	1995	Minerais, métaux, pierres
70.1	2.5	3.1	64.6	52.7	5.7	11.9	0.0	9.6	16.9	2005	précieuses et or (non monétaire)
85.5	1.9	1.2	82.4	64.7	7.0	17.7	0.0	13.9	17.5	2012	(CTCI 27 + 28 + 68 + 667 + 971)
32.8	2.7	4.3	25.8	21.6	0.8	4.2	..	0.3	15.4	1995	Combustibles (CTCI 3)
39.1	2.8	3.6	32.8	29.9	5.9	2.9	0.0	0.6	25.6	2005	
56.4	3.1	2.2	51.1	49.5	12.3	1.5	0.1	0.5	36.4	2012	
64.6	6.6	9.0	48.9	27.6	2.8	21.3	0.0	19.8	15.1	1995	Articles manufacturés
67.2	9.1	4.4	53.7	31.4	5.8	22.3	0.0	24.8	15.1	2005	(CTCI 5 à 8 moins 667 et 68)
85.4	8.1	7.7	69.6	46.7	9.5	22.9	0.1	31.2	20.8	2012	
Parts par principaux groupes de produits (en pourcentage)											
100.0	100.0	100.0	100.0	100.0	100.0	100.0	100.0	100.0	100.0	1995	Total tous produits
100.0	100.0	100.0	100.0	100.0	100.0	100.0	100.0	100.0	100.0	2005	
100.0	100.0	100.0	100.0	100.0	100.0	100.0	100.0	100.0	100.0	2012	
3.9	2.9	5.0	3.8	1.1	0.4	12.1	22.7	22.0	0.5	1995	Produits alimentaires
2.0	2.3	1.0	2.1	0.9	0.1	8.2	23.2	11.6	0.3	2005	(CTCI 0 + 1 + 22 + 4)
2.2	3.2	2.4	2.1	1.0	0.1	11.2	7.8	15.3	0.2	2012	
0.6	0.6	0.3	0.6	0.5	1.3	1.1	11.2	1.2	0.2	1995	Matières premières
0.2	0.4	0.1	0.2	0.2	0.1	0.4	0.1	0.6	0.0	2005	d'origine agricole
0.2	0.3	0.4	0.1	0.1	0.1	0.4	1.9	0.5	0.0	2012	(CTCI 2 - 22 - 27 - 28)
3.4	2.4	3.2	3.6	3.3	4.1	4.4	1.0	6.7	2.5	1995	Minerais, métaux, pierres
4.4	1.9	2.3	4.8	4.7	2.6	5.4	2.0	6.5	1.9	2005	précieuses et or (non monétaire)
5.9	2.3	1.8	6.4	5.6	2.6	13.4	1.0	11.4	2.2	2012	(CTCI 27 + 28 + 68 + 667 + 971)
71.2	69.2	69.7	71.7	79.8	63.5	47.2	..	5.6	84.6	1995	Combustibles (CTCI 3)
76.7	68.1	84.0	76.8	83.6	87.0	42.0	1.9	12.3	91.3	2005	
76.0	70.6	65.3	76.9	83.1	88.3	22.6	78.1	8.0	90.7	2012	
20.6	24.7	21.7	20.0	15.0	30.7	35.2	65.1	64.5	12.1	1995	Articles manufacturés
15.7	26.6	12.5	14.9	10.5	10.2	38.0	72.7	63.3	6.4	2005	(CTCI 5 à 8 moins 667 et 68)
14.9	23.7	30.0	13.6	10.2	8.9	43.6	11.2	64.7	6.7	2012	

Pour les sources et les notes, se reporter à la fin du tableau 2.2.L.

Product group	Year Année	World (1) Monde (1)	Developed economies - Économies développées							Transition economies Économies en transition
			Total	Europe Total	EU UE	Canada	USA États-Unis	Japan Japon	Other developed countries Autres économies développées	
Millions of dollars										
All products	1995	122 226	79 372	48 957	45 610	2 336	17 705	8 738	1 637	1 736
	2005	314 756	171 162	111 502	106 278	2 331	35 224	17 411	4 694	7 841
	2012	824 637	345 585	209 832	196 393	6 440	86 779	32 399	10 135	14 975
Share by origin (percentage)										
All products	1995	100.0	64.9	40.1	37.3	1.9	14.5	7.1	1.3	1.4
	2005	100.0	54.4	35.4	33.8	0.7	11.2	5.5	1.5	2.5
	2012	100.0	41.9	25.4	23.8	0.8	10.5	3.9	1.2	1.8
All food items	1995	100.0	51.3	28.6	27.8	5.4	11.6	0.1	5.6	1.0
(SITC 0 + 1 + 22 + 4)	2005	100.0	41.3	25.1	23.6	1.3	10.0	0.1	4.8	2.6
	2012	100.0	33.1	19.3	17.8	2.3	7.0	0.3	4.1	3.3
Agricultural raw materials	1995	100.0	57.7	30.3	30.0	4.5	18.6	2.9	1.5	3.4
(SITC 2 - 22 - 27 - 28)	2005	100.0	54.9	40.1	38.8	3.0	8.5	1.8	1.5	7.3
	2012	100.0	55.2	38.9	38.4	1.5	9.1	2.7	2.9	4.7
Ores, metals, precious stones	1995	100.0	56.1	42.9	22.0	2.4	8.8	0.7	1.3	2.0
and non-monetary gold	2005	100.0	34.2	26.0	20.9	0.9	4.9	0.8	1.6	4.5
(SITC 27 + 28 + 68 + 667 + 971)	2012	100.0	21.1	14.7	10.3	0.8	3.3	0.3	2.0	1.8
Fuels (SITC 3)	1995	100.0	60.1	42.8	42.7	0.7	13.3	0.2	3.2	6.3
	2005	100.0	24.8	20.7	20.4	0.0	3.2	0.2	0.7	8.8
	2012	100.0	37.9	32.0	31.2	0.0	5.6	0.1	0.2	5.4
Manufactured goods	1995	100.0	68.5	42.4	40.0	1.1	15.4	9.4	0.3	1.4
(SITC 5 to 8 less 667 and 68)	2005	100.0	58.9	38.1	36.5	0.7	12.4	7.1	0.8	1.9
	2012	100.0	45.2	27.3	25.8	0.5	11.5	5.4	0.5	1.2
Share by major product group (percentage)										
All products	1995	100.0	100.0	100.0	100.0	100.0	100.0	100.0	100.0	100.0
	2005	100.0	100.0	100.0	100.0	100.0	100.0	100.0	100.0	100.0
	2012	100.0	100.0	100.0	100.0	100.0	100.0	100.0	100.0	100.0
All food items	1995	17.5	13.8	12.5	13.1	49.0	14.1	0.3	73.1	11.8
(SITC 0 + 1 + 22 + 4)	2005	12.6	9.6	8.9	8.8	21.3	11.3	0.3	40.1	13.2
	2012	14.3	11.3	10.9	10.7	41.5	9.6	1.3	47.6	26.0
Agricultural raw materials	1995	1.7	1.5	1.3	1.3	3.9	2.1	0.7	1.8	4.0
(SITC 2 - 22 - 27 - 28)	2005	0.8	0.9	1.0	1.0	3.4	0.6	0.3	0.9	2.5
	2012	0.8	1.1	1.3	1.3	1.6	0.7	0.6	2.0	2.1
Ores, metals, precious stones	1995	3.7	3.2	4.0	2.2	4.7	2.3	0.4	3.7	5.4
and non-monetary gold	2005	5.0	3.1	3.7	3.1	6.2	2.2	0.7	5.4	9.1
(SITC 27 + 28 + 68 + 667 + 971)	2012	7.4	3.7	4.3	3.2	7.2	2.3	0.6	12.2	7.2
Fuels (SITC 3)	1995	1.4	1.3	1.5	1.7	0.5	1.3	0.0	3.5	6.4
	2005	3.6	1.6	2.1	2.2	0.1	1.0	0.1	1.6	12.7
	2012	5.3	4.8	6.7	7.0	0.2	2.9	0.1	0.7	16.0
Manufactured goods	1995	74.8	78.9	79.2	80.2	41.7	79.4	98.2	15.4	72.4
(SITC 5 to 8 less 667 and 68)	2005	76.0	82.4	81.7	82.2	68.2	83.9	97.3	38.6	58.1
	2012	71.1	76.7	76.2	77.1	49.4	77.7	97.0	30.1	47.9

For sources and notes, see end of table 2.2.L.

Total	Africa / Afrique	America / Amérique	Asia / Asie Total	Eastern, Southern and South-Eastern Asia / Asie orientale, méridionale et du Sud-Est	China / Chine	Western Asia / Asie occidentale	Oceania / Océanie	Major petroleum exporters and gas exporters / Principaux exportateurs de pétrole et de gaz	Major manufactured goods exporters / Principaux exportateurs d'articles manufacturés	Year / Année	Origines / Groupes de produits
Millions de dollars											
39 049	2 632	6 279	30 136	20 121	3 245	10 015	2	5 755	14 480	1995	Total tous produits
133 294	6 027	16 170	109 857	69 399	21 524	40 459	30	22 151	50 982	2005	
463 831	23 052	48 087	392 580	270 665	106 369	121 915	111	69 699	187 391	2012	
Parts par origines (en pourcentage)											
31.9	2.2	5.1	24.7	16.5	2.7	8.2	0.0	4.7	11.8	1995	Total tous produits
42.3	2.2	5.2	34.9	22.0	6.8	12.9	0.0	7.0	16.2	2005	
56.2	2.8	5.8	47.6	32.8	12.9	14.8	0.0	8.5	22.7	2012	
46.5	3.8	13.4	29.3	13.9	1.0	15.4	0.0	5.6	5.2	1995	Produits alimentaires
55.4	4.5	15.3	35.5	16.3	1.8	19.2	0.0	7.2	6.5	2005	(CTCI 0 + 1 + 22 + 4)
63.6	4.9	19.9	38.8	19.3	1.9	19.5	0.0	9.1	7.0	2012	
38.0	4.5	11.8	21.7	17.0	0.5	4.7	..	3.4	12.6	1995	Matières premières
37.3	3.7	7.5	26.1	18.5	2.1	7.5	0.0	4.7	12.4	2005	d'origine agricole
39.9	4.5	8.1	27.3	19.2	3.1	8.1	0.0	5.7	13.7	2012	(CTCI 2 - 22 - 27 - 28)
41.3	7.8	10.7	22.8	7.8	0.7	15.0	..	8.6	2.7	1995	Minerais, métaux, pierres
61.0	6.3	5.6	49.1	35.5	1.9	13.6	0.0	9.6	13.0	2005	précieuses et or (non monétaire)
77.2	8.1	6.0	63.1	35.6	3.0	27.5	0.0	19.7	8.7	2012	(CTCI 27 + 28 + 68 + 667 + 971)
32.5	7.2	2.5	22.8	9.9	0.7	12.9	..	19.7	2.4	1995	Combustibles (CTCI 3)
65.6	2.8	2.1	60.7	18.5	1.7	42.2	0.0	22.9	5.2	2005	
56.6	3.8	3.2	49.7	27.5	1.8	22.2	0.0	15.4	5.9	2012	
28.2	1.4	2.9	24.0	17.7	3.2	6.2	0.0	4.1	14.1	1995	Articles manufacturés
38.3	1.5	3.8	33.0	22.8	8.4	10.2	0.0	5.8	18.8	2005	(CTCI 5 à 8 moins 667 et 68)
53.5	1.8	3.2	48.5	36.3	17.3	12.2	0.0	6.8	29.0	2012	
Parts par principaux groupes de produits (en pourcentage)											
100.0	100.0	100.0	100.0	100.0	100.0	100.0	100.0	100.0	100.0	1995	Total tous produits
100.0	100.0	100.0	100.0	100.0	100.0	100.0	100.0	100.0	100.0	2005	
100.0	100.0	100.0	100.0	100.0	100.0	100.0	100.0	100.0	100.0	2012	
25.5	31.0	45.6	20.8	14.8	6.9	32.9	86.2	20.6	7.7	1995	Produits alimentaires
16.5	25.9	36.7	12.8	9.3	3.3	18.8	52.7	12.8	5.1	2005	(CTCI 0 + 1 + 22 + 4)
16.2	24.9	48.9	11.7	8.4	2.1	18.9	0.8	15.5	4.4	2012	
2.0	3.5	3.8	1.5	1.7	0.3	1.0	..	1.2	1.8	1995	Matières premières
0.7	1.4	1.2	0.6	0.7	0.3	0.5	0.5	0.6	0.6	2005	d'origine agricole
0.6	1.3	1.2	0.5	0.5	0.2	0.5	0.9	0.6	0.5	2012	(CTCI 2 - 22 - 27 - 28)
4.8	13.5	7.7	3.4	1.8	0.9	6.8	..	6.8	0.9	1995	Minerais, métaux, pierres
7.2	14.2	5.4	7.0	8.0	1.4	5.3	1.3	6.8	4.0	2005	précieuses et or (non monétaire)
10.1	21.4	7.5	9.8	8.0	1.7	13.7	0.1	17.2	2.8	2012	(CTCI 27 + 28 + 68 + 667 + 971)
1.5	4.8	0.7	1.3	0.9	0.4	2.3	..	6.1	0.3	1995	Combustibles (CTCI 3)
5.6	4.6	1.4	6.2	3.0	0.9	11.8	4.3	11.7	1.2	2005	
5.4	7.2	2.9	5.6	4.5	0.8	8.0	0.0	9.7	1.4	2012	
66.0	47.2	42.2	72.7	80.4	91.5	57.0	13.8	65.2	89.2	1995	Articles manufacturés
68.9	53.3	55.0	71.9	78.7	93.7	60.3	41.1	62.4	88.4	2005	(CTCI 5 à 8 moins 667 et 68)
67.7	45.0	39.4	72.5	78.6	95.2	58.9	98.2	57.0	90.7	2012	

Pour les sources et les notes, se reporter à la fin du tableau 2.2.L.

2.2.J Export structure by partner and product group
Developing economies: Major manufactured goods exporters

| Product group / Destination | Year / Année | World (1) / Monde (1) | Developed economies - Économies développées | | | | | | | Transition economies / Économies en transition |
			Total	Europe Total	Europe EU / UE	Canada	USA / États-Unis	Japan / Japon	Other developed countries / Autres économies développées	
Millions of dollars										
All products	1995	887 071	476 681	125 187	119 731	11 153	226 636	98 264	15 441	5 997
	2005	2 223 477	1 121 061	333 132	323 899	26 690	532 288	180 170	48 781	30 947
	2012	4 626 233	1 889 327	577 724	554 876	53 218	841 234	298 993	118 157	102 763
Share by destination (percentage)										
All products	1995	100.0	53.7	14.1	13.5	1.3	25.5	11.1	1.7	0.7
	2005	100.0	50.4	15.0	14.6	1.2	23.9	8.1	2.2	1.4
	2012	100.0	40.8	12.5	12.0	1.2	18.2	6.5	2.6	2.2
All food items	1995	100.0	51.9	8.9	8.3	0.9	15.9	24.6	1.6	1.5
(SITC 0 + 1 + 22 + 4)	2005	100.0	55.8	10.2	10.0	1.4	22.8	19.3	2.1	2.4
	2012	100.0	44.2	9.0	8.8	1.5	18.0	13.1	2.5	2.5
Agricultural raw materials	1995	100.0	44.7	13.2	12.8	0.7	10.4	19.2	1.2	0.2
(SITC 2 - 22 - 27 - 28)	2005	100.0	41.2	14.6	14.6	1.3	11.4	12.7	1.2	0.7
	2012	100.0	32.4	12.4	12.3	1.0	8.8	9.1	1.0	1.1
Ores, metals, precious stones	1995	100.0	38.7	9.1	7.8	0.4	13.0	14.3	1.9	0.4
and non-monetary gold	2005	100.0	37.8	13.1	10.9	0.8	11.2	8.6	4.1	0.6
(SITC 27 + 28 + 68 + 667 + 971)	2012	100.0	29.8	11.7	7.6	0.8	10.2	4.6	2.5	0.4
Fuels (SITC 3)	1995	100.0	46.9	3.8	3.7	0.2	22.0	19.0	1.9	0.3
	2005	100.0	45.0	4.5	4.5	0.6	23.7	10.3	5.9	0.2
	2012	100.0	36.0	4.8	4.8	0.4	15.1	9.0	6.7	0.2
Manufactured goods	1995	100.0	54.9	15.0	14.4	1.4	27.2	9.5	1.7	0.7
(SITC 5 to 8 less 667 and 68)	2005	100.0	51.1	15.9	15.5	1.2	24.6	7.5	1.9	1.5
	2012	100.0	41.8	13.2	12.9	1.2	19.0	6.1	2.3	2.5
Share by major product group (percentage)										
All products	1995	100.0	100.0	100.0	100.0	100.0	100.0	100.0	100.0	100.0
	2005	100.0	100.0	100.0	100.0	100.0	100.0	100.0	100.0	100.0
	2012	100.0	100.0	100.0	100.0	100.0	100.0	100.0	100.0	100.0
All food items	1995	6.0	5.7	3.7	3.7	4.2	3.7	13.2	5.4	13.6
(SITC 0 + 1 + 22 + 4)	2005	3.2	3.5	2.1	2.2	3.7	3.0	7.5	3.0	5.4
	2012	3.5	3.8	2.5	2.6	4.6	3.5	7.2	3.5	3.9
Agricultural raw materials	1995	2.1	1.7	1.9	2.0	1.1	0.8	3.6	1.5	0.5
(SITC 2 - 22 - 27 - 28)	2005	0.9	0.8	0.9	0.9	1.0	0.4	1.5	0.5	0.4
	2012	0.9	0.7	0.9	0.9	0.8	0.4	1.2	0.4	0.4
Ores, metals, precious stones	1995	2.4	1.7	1.5	1.4	0.7	1.2	3.1	2.7	1.3
and non-monetary gold	2005	2.2	1.7	1.9	1.7	1.4	1.0	2.4	4.1	0.9
(SITC 27 + 28 + 68 + 667 + 971)	2012	3.7	2.7	3.5	2.4	2.7	2.1	2.6	3.7	0.6
Fuels (SITC 3)	1995	3.6	3.2	1.0	1.0	0.7	3.1	6.2	3.8	1.4
	2005	5.7	5.1	1.7	1.7	2.9	5.6	7.3	15.3	0.9
	2012	6.5	5.7	2.5	2.6	2.4	5.4	9.0	16.9	0.6
Manufactured goods	1995	85.3	87.1	90.7	91.0	93.1	90.9	73.5	85.7	82.4
(SITC 5 to 8 less 667 and 68)	2005	87.3	88.5	92.5	92.8	90.8	89.6	80.7	76.1	92.3
	2012	84.4	86.4	89.5	90.5	88.8	88.1	79.6	74.9	94.4

For sources and notes, see end of table 2.2.L.

2.2.J Structure des exportations par partenaires et groupes de produits
Économies en développement : principaux exportateurs d'articles manufacturés

Total	Africa / Afrique	America / Amérique	Asia / Asie — Total	Eastern, Southern and South-Eastern Asia / Asie orientale, méridionale et du Sud-Est	China / Chine	Western Asia / Asie occidentale	Oceania / Océanie	Major petroleum exporters and gas exporters / Principaux exportateurs de pétrole et de gaz	Major manufactured goods exporters / Principaux exportateurs d'articles manufacturés	Year / Année	Destinations / Groupes de produits
Millions de dollars											
401 818	13 085	25 996	362 025	345 502	73 786	16 523	711	15 495	299 052	1995	Total tous produits
1 068 056	37 462	61 923	961 000	910 382	272 531	50 618	4 671	53 479	765 989	2005	
2 629 428	128 191	241 264	2 243 996	2 093 238	604 500	150 758	15 976	172 853	1 670 591	2012	
Parts par destinations (en pourcentage)											
45.3	1.5	2.9	40.8	38.9	8.3	1.9	0.1	1.7	33.7	1995	Total tous produits
48.0	1.7	2.9	43.2	40.9	12.3	2.3	0.2	2.4	34.5	2005	
56.8	2.8	5.2	48.5	45.2	13.1	3.3	0.3	3.7	36.1	2012	
46.2	2.1	0.9	43.0	40.6	8.6	2.4	0.1	1.9	29.0	1995	Produits alimentaires
41.6	3.8	1.9	35.7	33.0	5.2	2.7	0.2	3.2	22.8	2005	(CTCI 0 + 1 + 22 + 4)
53.3	5.5	2.6	44.8	41.8	7.3	2.9	0.3	4.3	25.4	2012	
54.8	1.2	2.4	51.2	49.5	14.7	1.7	0.0	1.4	41.6	1995	Matières premières
58.0	1.4	2.5	54.1	52.0	24.2	2.2	0.0	1.4	41.6	2005	d'origine agricole
66.5	1.6	3.4	61.5	58.4	24.9	3.2	0.0	2.0	42.7	2012	(CTCI 2 - 22 - 27 - 28)
60.3	0.5	0.7	59.1	58.7	12.5	0.4	0.0	0.5	51.7	1995	Minerais, métaux, pierres
61.6	0.7	0.9	59.9	55.4	16.5	4.5	0.0	4.7	46.0	2005	précieuses et or (non monétaire)
69.8	0.9	1.9	67.0	64.6	36.1	2.4	0.0	2.7	57.1	2012	(CTCI 27 + 28 + 68 + 667 + 971)
50.1	0.2	1.9	47.6	47.4	8.2	0.1	0.4	0.1	39.4	1995	Combustibles (CTCI 3)
53.2	0.2	3.0	48.7	48.2	5.6	0.5	1.3	0.5	30.7	2005	
62.5	1.3	2.7	57.4	56.5	7.8	0.9	1.3	0.9	36.4	2012	
44.3	1.5	3.1	39.6	37.6	8.0	1.9	0.1	1.9	33.1	1995	Articles manufacturés
47.4	1.7	2.9	42.7	40.3	12.8	2.3	0.1	2.4	34.8	2005	(CTCI 5 à 8 moins 667 et 68)
55.7	2.8	5.5	47.3	43.7	12.7	3.5	0.2	4.0	35.7	2012	
Parts par principaux groupes de produits (en pourcentage)											
100.0	100.0	100.0	100.0	100.0	100.0	100.0	100.0	100.0	100.0	1995	Total tous produits
100.0	100.0	100.0	100.0	100.0	100.0	100.0	100.0	100.0	100.0	2005	
100.0	100.0	100.0	100.0	100.0	100.0	100.0	100.0	100.0	100.0	2012	
6.1	8.6	1.9	6.3	6.2	6.2	7.7	9.4	6.6	5.1	1995	Produits alimentaires
2.7	7.1	2.0	2.6	2.6	1.3	3.8	3.1	4.2	2.1	2005	(CTCI 0 + 1 + 22 + 4)
3.3	7.0	1.8	3.3	3.3	2.0	3.2	3.6	4.1	2.5	2012	
2.5	1.7	1.7	2.6	2.6	3.6	1.9	0.3	1.6	2.5	1995	Matières premières
1.1	0.8	0.8	1.2	1.2	1.8	0.9	0.1	0.6	1.1	2005	d'origine agricole
1.0	0.5	0.6	1.1	1.1	1.7	0.9	0.1	0.5	1.0	2012	(CTCI 2 - 22 - 27 - 28)
3.2	0.8	0.6	3.5	3.6	3.6	0.5	0.4	0.7	3.7	1995	Minerais, métaux, pierres
2.8	0.9	0.7	3.1	3.0	3.0	4.4	0.2	4.3	3.0	2005	précieuses et or (non monétaire)
4.6	1.3	1.3	5.2	5.3	10.3	2.7	0.2	2.7	5.9	2012	(CTCI 27 + 28 + 68 + 667 + 971)
4.0	0.5	2.4	4.2	4.4	3.6	0.3	16.0	0.2	4.2	1995	Combustibles (CTCI 3)
6.3	0.8	5.8	6.4	6.7	2.6	1.3	35.4	1.2	5.1	2005	
7.1	2.9	3.3	7.7	8.1	3.9	1.7	23.9	1.5	6.5	2012	
83.4	86.3	91.7	82.7	82.4	82.2	89.1	69.4	90.4	83.8	1995	Articles manufacturés
86.1	87.3	87.0	86.1	86.0	91.0	88.8	54.9	88.7	88.3	2005	(CTCI 5 à 8 moins 667 et 68)
82.8	84.8	88.5	82.3	81.6	81.9	91.1	56.4	90.9	83.5	2012	

Pour les sources et les notes, se reporter à la fin du tableau 2.2.L.

Product group	Year / Année	World (1) Monde (1)	Developed economies - Économies développées			Canada	USA États-Unis	Japan Japon	Other developed countries Autres économies développées	Transition economies Économies en transition
			Total	Europe Total	EU / UE					
Millions of dollars										
All products	1995	911 557	539 863	136 610	124 433	11 106	176 513	193 664	21 970	11 550
	2005	2 057 264	890 856	234 359	214 957	20 700	282 012	302 726	51 058	32 487
	2012	4 356 588	1 662 350	526 094	455 419	45 399	488 020	443 253	159 584	105 398
Share by origin (percentage)										
All products	1995	100.0	59.2	15.0	13.7	1.2	19.4	21.2	2.4	1.3
	2005	100.0	43.3	11.4	10.4	1.0	13.7	14.7	2.5	1.6
	2012	100.0	38.2	12.1	10.5	1.0	11.2	10.2	3.7	2.4
All food items	1995	100.0	61.3	14.3	13.7	4.1	31.3	3.3	8.4	0.8
(SITC 0 + 1 + 22 + 4)	2005	100.0	51.9	9.9	9.3	3.7	26.4	2.7	9.1	1.9
	2012	100.0	48.9	9.9	9.1	4.0	26.0	1.5	7.6	1.5
Agricultural raw materials	1995	100.0	53.2	6.3	6.1	5.3	27.5	5.1	8.9	3.9
(SITC 2 - 22 - 27 - 28)	2005	100.0	52.4	9.8	9.6	6.0	23.2	5.1	8.2	8.1
	2012	100.0	50.3	10.5	10.3	6.9	19.5	4.5	8.9	5.8
Ores, metals, precious stones	1995	100.0	55.2	15.0	10.5	2.7	13.8	9.6	14.2	4.5
and non-monetary gold	2005	100.0	43.9	8.8	6.8	2.1	8.6	8.2	16.2	4.7
(SITC 27 + 28 + 68 + 667 + 971)	2012	100.0	44.8	10.1	5.9	1.8	7.4	5.9	19.6	3.5
Fuels (SITC 3)	1995	100.0	14.7	1.3	1.3	0.9	5.7	2.7	4.1	0.7
	2005	100.0	11.3	1.4	1.1	0.4	4.3	1.0	4.2	3.6
	2012	100.0	13.1	2.8	2.4	0.5	4.6	1.2	3.9	8.2
Manufactured goods	1995	100.0	62.6	16.4	15.1	0.8	19.2	25.4	0.8	1.0
(SITC 5 to 8 less 667 and 68)	2005	100.0	47.6	13.2	12.3	0.8	14.7	18.3	0.6	0.8
	2012	100.0	43.3	15.1	13.9	0.6	12.3	14.7	0.5	0.5
Share by major product group (percentage)										
All products	1995	100.0	100.0	100.0	100.0	100.0	100.0	100.0	100.0	100.0
	2005	100.0	100.0	100.0	100.0	100.0	100.0	100.0	100.0	100.0
	2012	100.0	100.0	100.0	100.0	100.0	100.0	100.0	100.0	100.0
All food items	1995	5.4	5.6	5.2	5.4	18.1	8.8	0.8	18.9	3.6
(SITC 0 + 1 + 22 + 4)	2005	3.8	4.5	3.3	3.4	14.0	7.3	0.7	14.0	4.7
	2012	4.9	6.3	4.0	4.3	18.7	11.4	0.7	10.1	3.1
Agricultural raw materials	1995	3.1	2.8	1.3	1.4	13.7	4.5	0.8	11.6	9.5
(SITC 2 - 22 - 27 - 28)	2005	2.0	2.4	1.7	1.9	12.1	3.4	0.7	6.7	10.4
	2012	2.2	2.9	1.9	2.2	14.5	3.8	1.0	5.3	5.3
Ores, metals, precious stones	1995	5.5	5.1	5.5	4.2	12.0	3.9	2.5	32.1	19.2
and non-monetary gold	2005	6.2	6.3	4.8	4.1	12.9	3.9	3.5	40.8	18.6
(SITC 27 + 28 + 68 + 667 + 971)	2012	9.7	11.4	8.1	5.5	16.3	6.4	5.6	51.8	13.8
Fuels (SITC 3)	1995	5.8	1.4	0.5	0.5	4.1	1.7	0.7	9.9	3.4
	2005	11.9	3.1	1.5	1.3	4.3	3.7	0.8	20.2	27.6
	2012	18.8	6.5	4.4	4.4	9.7	7.8	2.3	19.9	63.7
Manufactured goods	1995	78.7	83.2	86.0	87.1	50.6	77.9	94.3	27.0	60.9
(SITC 5 to 8 less 667 and 68)	2005	75.5	82.9	87.6	88.7	56.5	80.9	93.9	17.7	38.4
	2012	62.3	70.7	78.1	82.6	38.8	68.3	90.1	8.9	13.8

For sources and notes, see end of table 2.2.L.

2.2.J Structure des importations par partenaires et groupes de produits
Économies en développement : principaux exportateurs d'articles manufacturés

Developing economies - Économies en développement										Year	Origines
			Asia Asie					Major petroleum exporters and gas exporters	Major manufactured goods exporters		
Total	Africa Afrique	America Amérique	Total	Eastern, Southern and South-Eastern Asia Asie orientale, méridionale et du Sud-Est	China Chine	Western Asia Asie occidentale	Oceania Océanie	Principaux exportateurs de pétrole et de gaz	Principaux exportateurs d'articles manufacturés	Année	Groupes de produits
Millions de dollars											
355 471	9 110	15 310	330 359	303 475	88 607	26 884	692	28 091	274 096	1995	**Total tous produits**
1 129 979	33 397	57 624	1 037 692	915 800	311 240	121 824	1 265	142 765	787 008	2005	
2 576 645	147 739	194 171	2 231 436	1 853 538	679 453	377 898	3 298	475 180	1 561 328	2012	
Parts par origines (en pourcentage)											
39.0	1.0	1.7	36.2	33.3	9.7	2.9	0.1	3.1	30.1	1995	**Total tous produits**
54.9	1.6	2.8	50.4	44.5	15.1	5.9	0.1	6.9	38.3	2005	
59.1	3.4	4.5	51.2	42.5	15.6	8.7	0.1	10.9	35.8	2012	
37.9	1.3	6.9	29.4	29.1	7.9	0.3	0.4	0.3	22.7	1995	Produits alimentaires
46.2	1.3	16.8	27.6	27.3	8.5	0.3	0.4	0.5	18.8	2005	(CTCI 0 + 1 + 22 + 4)
49.6	1.7	20.0	27.5	27.2	5.7	0.3	0.3	0.3	15.8	2012	
42.8	4.2	5.2	32.5	32.3	4.6	0.2	0.9	0.2	24.6	1995	Matières premières
39.5	4.6	6.3	27.6	27.3	2.5	0.2	1.1	0.2	17.9	2005	d'origine agricole
43.9	4.3	7.8	30.7	30.6	2.0	0.2	1.0	0.2	16.9	2012	(CTCI 2 - 22 - 27 - 28)
40.0	6.2	8.4	25.2	23.1	4.4	2.1	0.2	1.4	16.4	1995	Minerais, métaux, pierres
51.3	4.5	13.8	33.0	31.1	6.3	1.9	0.0	2.3	15.9	2005	précieuses et or (non monétaire)
51.6	7.5	16.6	27.5	24.9	6.5	2.5	0.1	2.8	15.8	2012	(CTCI 27 + 28 + 68 + 667 + 971)
83.9	4.1	1.2	78.6	37.5	3.7	41.0	0.1	45.0	23.3	1995	Combustibles (CTCI 3)
85.0	8.1	1.3	75.5	30.9	2.8	44.6	0.0	52.7	15.6	2005	
78.7	8.9	4.2	65.6	25.1	1.1	40.5	0.0	52.1	12.4	2012	
36.0	0.3	0.8	34.9	34.4	11.0	0.5	0.0	0.5	32.6	1995	Articles manufacturés
51.4	0.3	1.3	49.8	49.2	18.5	0.6	0.0	0.6	45.3	2005	(CTCI 5 à 8 moins 667 et 68)
56.0	0.2	1.4	54.3	53.0	23.1	1.3	0.0	1.3	48.9	2012	
Parts par principaux groupes de produits (en pourcentage)											
100.0	100.0	100.0	100.0	100.0	100.0	100.0	100.0	100.0	100.0	1995	**Total tous produits**
100.0	100.0	100.0	100.0	100.0	100.0	100.0	100.0	100.0	100.0	2005	
100.0	100.0	100.0	100.0	100.0	100.0	100.0	100.0	100.0	100.0	2012	
5.3	7.0	22.1	4.4	4.7	4.4	0.6	28.2	0.5	4.1	1995	Produits alimentaires
3.2	3.1	22.8	2.1	2.3	2.1	0.2	25.2	0.3	1.9	2005	(CTCI 0 + 1 + 22 + 4)
4.1	2.5	22.0	2.6	3.1	1.8	0.2	21.7	0.2	2.2	2012	
3.4	13.2	9.8	2.8	3.0	1.5	0.3	36.4	0.2	2.6	1995	Matières premières
1.5	5.7	4.5	1.1	1.2	0.3	0.1	34.8	0.0	0.9	2005	d'origine agricole
1.6	2.8	3.8	1.3	1.6	0.3	0.0	30.3	0.0	1.0	2012	(CTCI 2 - 22 - 27 - 28)
5.6	33.9	27.3	3.8	3.8	2.5	3.8	16.4	2.5	3.0	1995	Minerais, métaux, pierres
5.8	17.2	30.7	4.1	4.4	2.6	2.0	3.7	2.1	2.6	2005	précieuses et or (non monétaire)
8.4	21.3	35.9	5.2	5.7	4.0	2.8	13.5	2.5	4.3	2012	(CTCI 27 + 28 + 68 + 667 + 971)
12.5	23.8	4.0	12.6	6.6	2.2	81.0	10.0	85.0	4.5	1995	Combustibles (CTCI 3)
18.5	59.8	5.5	17.9	8.3	2.2	89.8	7.2	90.6	4.9	2005	
25.1	49.5	17.6	24.1	11.1	1.4	87.9	5.6	89.9	6.5	2012	
72.6	22.1	36.3	75.8	81.3	89.0	14.3	8.9	11.8	85.2	1995	Articles manufacturés
70.7	12.7	35.5	74.5	83.4	92.4	7.9	29.0	7.0	89.3	2005	(CTCI 5 à 8 moins 667 et 68)
59.0	4.2	20.2	66.1	77.7	92.2	9.1	28.7	7.4	85.1	2012	

Pour les sources et les notes, se reporter à la fin du tableau 2.2.L.

Product group	Year / Année	World (1) / Monde (1)	Developed economies - Économies développées							Transition economies / Économies en transition
			Total	Europe Total	EU / UE	Canada	USA / États-Unis	Japan / Japon	Other developed countries / Autres économies développées	
Millions of dollars										
All products	1995	117 627	55 291	48 085	43 873	126	4 149	2 557	374	31 906
	2005	360 228	222 221	204 734	186 412	985	9 336	4 191	2 976	69 867
	2012	836 087	418 616	375 433	360 474	4 830	16 355	17 028	4 969	143 991
Share by destination (percentage)										
All products	1995	100.0	47.0	40.9	37.3	0.1	3.5	2.2	0.3	27.1
	2005	100.0	61.7	56.8	51.7	0.3	2.6	1.2	0.8	19.4
	2012	100.0	50.1	44.9	43.1	0.6	2.0	2.0	0.6	17.2
All food items	1995	100.0	31.9	26.7	25.8	0.1	1.8	2.3	1.0	59.3
(SITC 0 + 1 + 22 + 4)	2005	100.0	25.2	21.8	21.1	0.1	0.8	1.3	1.2	53.4
	2012	100.0	24.3	21.2	20.8	0.1	0.4	1.1	1.6	38.2
Agricultural raw materials	1995	100.0	64.7	55.5	53.5	0.0	0.9	8.1	0.1	7.2
(SITC 2 - 22 - 27 - 28)	2005	100.0	48.1	41.3	41.1	0.1	0.6	5.8	0.3	11.5
	2012	100.0	30.3	27.2	26.6	0.0	0.8	2.1	0.1	11.8
Ores, metals, precious stones	1995	100.0	80.7	58.9	51.2	0.0	10.4	11.4	0.1	10.7
and non-monetary gold	2005	100.0	69.1	56.8	45.7	0.2	5.5	5.3	1.4	11.4
(SITC 27 + 28 + 68 + 667 + 971)	2012	100.0	50.0	42.5	37.9	0.4	3.9	3.1	0.2	16.6
Fuels (SITC 3)	1995	100.0	62.2	60.2	54.2	0.0	0.8	0.6	0.5	22.7
	2005	100.0	66.5	63.6	57.6	0.3	1.2	0.7	0.7	8.1
	2012	100.0	62.1	56.5	54.4	0.8	1.6	2.6	0.6	8.4
Manufactured goods	1995	100.0	39.0	31.5	29.5	0.3	6.2	0.7	0.2	30.8
(SITC 5 to 8 less 667 and 68)	2005	100.0	38.1	32.4	31.6	0.4	4.3	0.4	0.5	31.0
	2012	100.0	35.2	30.5	29.6	0.4	2.9	1.0	0.5	38.7
Share by major product group (percentage)										
All products	1995	100.0	100.0	100.0	100.0	100.0	100.0	100.0	100.0	100.0
	2005	100.0	100.0	100.0	100.0	100.0	100.0	100.0	100.0	100.0
	2012	100.0	100.0	100.0	100.0	100.0	100.0	100.0	100.0	100.0
All food items	1995	5.6	3.8	3.7	3.9	4.7	2.9	6.0	17.5	12.3
(SITC 0 + 1 + 22 + 4)	2005	4.0	1.6	1.5	1.6	1.2	1.2	4.3	6.0	11.1
	2012	6.2	3.0	2.9	3.0	0.6	1.1	3.2	16.8	13.7
Agricultural raw materials	1995	5.5	7.5	7.4	7.9	0.6	1.5	20.5	2.4	1.5
(SITC 2 - 22 - 27 - 28)	2005	2.8	2.2	2.1	2.3	1.2	0.7	14.1	0.9	1.7
	2012	2.1	1.3	1.3	1.3	0.1	0.9	2.2	0.3	1.4
Ores, metals, precious stones	1995	10.1	17.3	14.5	13.8	2.3	29.6	52.7	2.7	4.0
and non-monetary gold	2005	7.7	8.7	7.7	6.8	5.1	16.3	35.1	13.3	4.6
(SITC 27 + 28 + 68 + 667 + 971)	2012	5.6	5.6	5.3	4.9	3.8	11.2	8.4	1.5	5.4
Fuels (SITC 3)	1995	32.8	43.4	48.3	47.6	13.3	7.7	9.5	51.8	27.5
	2005	52.9	57.0	59.2	58.9	55.6	23.8	31.3	45.2	22.1
	2012	59.7	74.0	75.1	75.2	81.8	47.4	74.9	62.9	29.2
Manufactured goods	1995	33.3	27.6	25.7	26.3	78.7	58.3	11.4	25.6	37.8
(SITC 5 to 8 less 667 and 68)	2005	26.5	16.3	15.1	16.1	36.5	44.3	9.8	14.9	42.3
	2012	21.9	15.4	14.9	15.1	13.6	32.2	11.0	17.6	49.3

For sources and notes, see end of table 2.2.L.

2.2.K Structure des exportations par partenaires et groupes de produits
Économies en transition

| Developing economies - Économies en développement | | | | | | | | | | | Destinations |
Total	Africa / Afrique	America / Amérique	Asia / Asie — Total	Eastern, Southern and South-Eastern Asia / Asie orientale, méridionale et du Sud-Est	China / Chine	Western Asia / Asie occidentale	Oceania / Océanie	Major petroleum exporters and gas exporters / Principaux exportateurs de pétrole et de gaz	Major manufactured goods exporters / Principaux exportateurs d'articles manufacturés	Year / Année	Groupes de produits
Millions de dollars											
17 441	1 019	2 958	13 463	10 428	4 790	3 035	1	1 174	8 207	1995	Total tous produits
67 433	5 638	6 686	55 092	35 894	17 510	10 100	17	8 304	24 592	2005	
178 997	14 340	8 400	156 127	118 757	66 787	37 370	130	13 692	93 257	2012	
Parts par destinations (en pourcentage)											
14.8	0.9	2.5	11.4	8.9	4.1	2.6	0.0	1.0	7.0	1995	Total tous produits
18.7	1.6	1.9	15.3	10.0	4.9	5.3	0.0	2.3	6.8	2005	
21.4	1.7	1.0	18.7	14.2	8.0	4.5	0.0	1.6	11.2	2012	
6.6	1.2	0.2	5.2	1.5	0.6	3.7	0.0	0.9	1.1	1995	Produits alimentaires
20.7	7.4	0.2	13.2	6.0	1.1	7.2	0.0	5.9	2.4	2005	(CTCI 0 + 1 + 22 + 4)
37.3	12.0	0.3	25.0	12.0	2.3	12.9	0.0	9.3	5.2	2012	
23.8	1.1	1.5	21.3	15.4	6.6	5.8	0.0	0.7	14.1	1995	Matières premières
40.4	2.4	0.1	37.8	33.3	25.1	4.5	..	2.1	27.7	2005	d'origine agricole
57.9	2.6	0.3	55.0	50.7	43.9	4.3	0.0	2.2	46.0	2012	(CTCI 2 - 22 - 27 - 28)
7.0	0.1	0.1	6.7	5.3	1.1	1.5	0.0	0.4	4.7	1995	Minerais, métaux, pierres
19.5	0.6	0.2	18.7	11.7	7.1	6.9	0.0	1.5	10.4	2005	précieuses et or (non monétaire)
33.4	1.1	0.9	31.4	18.3	14.6	13.0	0.0	0.4	17.3	2012	(CTCI 27 + 28 + 68 + 667 + 971)
9.7	0.1	5.5	4.2	2.2	0.1	1.9	0.0	0.6	1.3	1995	Combustibles (CTCI 3)
9.5	0.2	2.2	7.1	4.3	2.6	2.8	0.0	0.7	3.3	2005	
16.9	0.6	0.3	16.1	13.6	8.1	2.4	0.0	0.4	11.7	2012	
27.8	2.1	1.8	23.9	20.0	10.6	3.8	0.0	2.0	15.7	1995	Articles manufacturés
31.0	3.6	2.6	24.8	18.0	6.1	6.8	0.0	5.0	10.4	2005	(CTCI 5 à 8 moins 667 et 68)
26.0	2.4	3.4	20.2	13.9	5.6	6.3	0.0	3.4	8.4	2012	
Parts par principaux groupes de produits (en pourcentage)											
100.0	100.0	100.0	100.0	100.0	100.0	100.0	100.0	100.0	100.0	1995	Total tous produits
100.0	100.0	100.0	100.0	100.0	100.0	100.0	100.0	100.0	100.0	2005	
100.0	100.0	100.0	100.0	100.0	100.0	100.0	100.0	100.0	100.0	2012	
2.5	7.6	0.5	2.6	1.0	0.8	8.1	13.8	5.0	0.9	1995	Produits alimentaires
4.4	18.9	0.4	3.5	2.4	0.9	5.4	0.2	10.3	1.4	2005	(CTCI 0 + 1 + 22 + 4)
10.7	43.1	2.0	8.3	5.2	1.8	17.9	0.5	34.9	2.9	2012	
8.8	6.8	3.2	10.2	9.5	8.9	12.4	16.3	3.6	11.1	1995	Matières premières
6.1	4.4	0.2	7.0	9.5	14.7	2.4	..	2.6	11.5	2005	d'origine agricole
5.7	3.2	0.6	6.2	7.5	11.6	2.1	0.1	2.8	8.7	2012	(CTCI 2 - 22 - 27 - 28)
4.7	1.7	0.4	5.9	6.0	2.8	5.7	0.5	4.0	6.8	1995	Minerais, métaux, pierres
8.0	2.8	1.0	9.4	9.1	11.3	10.0	0.0	4.9	11.8	2005	précieuses et or (non monétaire)
8.8	3.5	5.3	9.5	7.3	10.3	16.4	0.0	1.4	8.7	2012	(CTCI 27 + 28 + 68 + 667 + 971)
21.5	2.4	71.7	11.9	8.3	0.8	24.6	9.9	19.8	6.2	1995	Combustibles (CTCI 3)
26.8	8.3	61.5	24.5	22.8	28.6	27.6	0.3	16.0	25.6	2005	
47.1	19.6	17.0	51.3	57.2	60.8	32.4	62.0	14.2	62.7	2012	
62.4	81.4	24.3	69.4	75.2	86.8	49.3	59.5	67.4	74.9	1995	Articles manufacturés
43.8	60.5	36.8	42.9	47.7	33.4	33.9	99.4	57.8	40.3	2005	(CTCI 5 à 8 moins 667 et 68)
26.7	30.1	74.9	23.7	21.5	15.3	31.0	37.0	45.9	16.5	2012	

Pour les sources et les notes, se reporter à la fin du tableau 2.2.L.

Product group	Year / Année	World (1) / Monde (1)	Developed economies - Économies développées							Transition economies / Économies en transition
			Total	Europe Total	EU / UE	Canada	USA / États-Unis	Japan / Japon	Other developed countries / Autres économies développées	
Millions of dollars										
All products	1995	108 097	48 462	41 939	40 659	283	4 207	1 424	609	34 307
	2005	257 241	135 778	118 689	115 056	924	7 933	6 951	1 282	72 898
	2012	612 493	288 716	247 950	239 092	2 565	19 858	14 849	3 494	164 609
Share by origin (percentage)										
All products	1995	100.0	44.8	38.8	37.6	0.3	3.9	1.3	0.6	31.7
	2005	100.0	52.8	46.1	44.7	0.4	3.1	2.7	0.5	28.3
	2012	100.0	47.1	40.5	39.0	0.4	3.2	2.4	0.6	26.9
All food items	1995	100.0	54.9	45.2	43.9	0.3	8.0	0.0	1.5	23.6
(SITC 0 + 1 + 22 + 4)	2005	100.0	42.2	36.5	33.5	0.5	4.3	0.1	0.8	26.0
	2012	100.0	42.5	36.0	32.8	1.3	3.7	0.0	1.5	26.7
Agricultural raw materials	1995	100.0	36.5	33.0	32.3	0.2	2.4	0.3	0.6	54.4
(SITC 2 - 22 - 27 - 28)	2005	100.0	44.9	40.8	40.5	0.3	3.3	0.3	0.1	42.1
	2012	100.0	45.2	39.5	39.1	0.2	3.6	1.0	0.8	29.8
Ores, metals, precious stones	1995	100.0	28.2	21.9	20.8	0.4	2.7	0.0	3.3	49.7
and non-monetary gold	2005	100.0	31.0	25.0	23.4	0.3	1.5	0.2	3.9	49.9
(SITC 27 + 28 + 68 + 667 + 971)	2012	100.0	26.9	23.4	21.1	0.0	0.8	0.1	2.5	56.7
Fuels (SITC 3)	1995	100.0	14.2	13.3	12.5	0.0	0.7	0.2	0.0	81.4
	2005	100.0	9.5	9.1	8.6	0.0	0.2	0.1	0.0	88.2
	2012	100.0	16.9	15.0	14.2	0.1	1.5	0.1	0.2	80.5
Manufactured goods	1995	100.0	63.2	55.5	53.8	0.4	4.4	2.6	0.4	22.6
(SITC 5 to 8 less 667 and 68)	2005	100.0	62.5	54.7	53.4	0.4	3.4	3.7	0.3	18.1
	2012	100.0	53.2	45.9	44.7	0.4	3.3	3.3	0.3	17.2
Share by major commodity group (percentage)										
All products	1995	100.0	100.0	100.0	100.0	100.0	100.0	100.0	100.0	100.0
	2005	100.0	100.0	100.0	100.0	100.0	100.0	100.0	100.0	100.0
	2012	100.0	100.0	100.0	100.0	100.0	100.0	100.0	100.0	100.0
All food items	1995	17.4	21.3	20.2	20.3	17.6	35.5	0.6	45.1	12.9
(SITC 0 + 1 + 22 + 4)	2005	12.2	9.7	9.6	9.1	15.3	17.0	0.4	20.3	11.1
	2012	11.5	10.4	10.2	9.7	34.4	13.1	0.2	29.8	11.4
Agricultural raw materials	1995	1.3	1.1	1.1	1.1	0.9	0.8	0.3	1.5	2.2
(SITC 2 - 22 - 27 - 28)	2005	1.2	1.0	1.0	1.1	1.1	1.3	0.1	0.3	1.8
	2012	1.1	1.1	1.1	1.1	0.6	1.2	0.5	1.6	1.2
Ores, metals, precious stones	1995	2.9	1.8	1.6	1.6	4.2	2.0	0.0	16.7	4.5
and non-monetary gold	2005	3.1	1.8	1.7	1.6	2.5	1.6	0.3	24.5	5.5
(SITC 27 + 28 + 68 + 667 + 971)	2012	2.6	1.5	1.5	1.4	0.2	0.7	0.1	11.6	5.5
Fuels (SITC 3)	1995	11.8	3.8	4.0	3.9	1.0	2.2	1.8	0.5	30.3
	2005	11.2	2.0	2.2	2.2	0.2	0.9	0.5	0.2	34.9
	2012	11.7	4.2	4.3	4.3	1.7	5.5	0.4	5.1	35.2
Manufactured goods	1995	49.2	69.4	70.3	70.4	75.4	55.8	95.3	34.1	35.0
(SITC 5 to 8 less 667 and 68)	2005	70.8	83.9	84.0	84.6	77.0	77.5	98.3	41.8	45.3
	2012	71.5	80.7	81.1	81.8	62.6	71.9	98.2	42.5	45.6

For sources and notes, see end of table 2.2.L.

			Developing economies - Économies en développement							Origines	
				Asia Asie						Year	
Total	Africa Afrique	America Amérique	Total	Eastern, Southern and South-Eastern Asia Asie orientale, méridionale et du Sud-Est	China Chine	Western Asia Asie occidentale	Oceania Océanie	Major petroleum exporters and gas exporters Principaux exportateurs de pétrole et de gaz	Major manufactured goods exporters Principaux exportateurs d'articles manufacturés	Année	Groupes de produits
Millions de dollars											
11 592	771	1 790	9 025	6 826	1 648	2 199	6	1 065	4 672	1995	Total tous produits
47 346	1 738	6 437	39 146	32 467	18 942	6 679	24	1 777	28 968	2005	
158 036	3 715	12 850	141 454	121 160	82 292	20 294	17	4 714	108 512	2012	
Parts par origines (en pourcentage)											
10.7	0.7	1.7	8.3	6.3	1.5	2.0	0.0	1.0	4.3	1995	Total tous produits
18.4	0.7	2.5	15.2	12.6	7.4	2.6	0.0	0.7	11.3	2005	
25.8	0.6	2.1	23.1	19.8	13.4	3.3	0.0	0.8	17.7	2012	
20.2	1.3	7.8	11.2	8.1	2.7	3.0	0.0	1.5	3.7	1995	Produits alimentaires
31.7	2.6	17.2	11.9	9.1	2.9	2.8	0.0	0.9	5.3	2005	(CTCI 0 + 1 + 22 + 4)
30.8	2.9	14.0	13.9	10.5	3.7	3.4	0.0	1.1	5.5	2012	
7.5	0.3	1.3	6.0	5.6	0.9	0.4	..	0.1	2.2	1995	Matières premières
12.9	1.1	3.8	8.1	7.3	1.1	0.7	0.0	0.3	5.1	2005	d'origine agricole
24.9	2.3	8.0	14.7	13.1	3.5	1.6	0.0	0.7	8.7	2012	(CTCI 2 - 22 - 27 - 28)
21.1	3.9	5.4	11.8	10.2	1.9	1.6	0.0	1.7	2.5	1995	Minerais, métaux, pierres
19.1	7.2	3.5	8.1	5.9	3.0	2.3	0.2	1.1	3.6	2005	précieuses et or (non monétaire)
16.4	3.6	2.0	10.8	7.6	4.6	3.2	0.0	0.7	5.3	2012	(CTCI 27 + 28 + 68 + 667 + 971)
4.0	2.1	0.1	1.8	1.3	0.2	0.4	..	2.6	0.7	1995	Combustibles (CTCI 3)
2.3	0.3	0.1	1.9	1.2	0.7	0.7	..	0.4	0.9	2005	
2.6	0.2	0.6	1.8	1.4	0.7	0.4	0.0	1.1	0.9	2012	
12.1	0.2	0.2	11.6	8.7	2.0	2.8	0.0	0.7	7.1	1995	Articles manufacturés
19.0	0.1	0.3	18.6	15.7	9.6	2.9	0.0	0.7	14.6	2005	(CTCI 5 à 8 moins 667 et 68)
29.6	0.2	0.4	29.1	25.2	17.8	3.8	0.0	0.7	23.4	2012	
Parts par principaux groupes de produits (en pourcentage)											
100.0	100.0	100.0	100.0	100.0	100.0	100.0	100.0	100.0	100.0	1995	Total tous produits
100.0	100.0	100.0	100.0	100.0	100.0	100.0	100.0	100.0	100.0	2005	
100.0	100.0	100.0	100.0	100.0	100.0	100.0	100.0	100.0	100.0	2012	
32.8	31.0	82.0	23.2	22.3	30.4	25.9	18.8	25.6	14.7	1995	Produits alimentaires
20.9	46.7	83.7	9.5	8.8	4.8	13.0	13.9	15.1	5.7	2005	(CTCI 0 + 1 + 22 + 4)
13.7	54.3	76.5	6.9	6.1	3.2	11.8	56.7	16.3	3.6	2012	
0.9	0.5	1.0	0.9	1.2	0.8	0.2	..	0.1	0.7	1995	Matières premières
0.8	1.9	1.8	0.6	0.7	0.2	0.3	0.4	0.5	0.5	2005	d'origine agricole
1.1	4.1	4.2	0.7	0.7	0.3	0.5	0.2	0.9	0.5	2012	(CTCI 2 - 22 - 27 - 28)
5.7	15.8	9.3	4.1	4.7	3.5	2.3	0.0	4.8	1.7	1995	Minerais, métaux, pierres
3.3	33.6	4.3	1.7	1.5	1.3	2.8	79.4	5.2	1.0	2005	précieuses et or (non monétaire)
1.7	15.6	2.5	1.2	1.0	0.9	2.5	0.5	2.2	0.8	2012	(CTCI 27 + 28 + 68 + 667 + 971)
4.4	34.7	1.0	2.5	2.5	1.9	2.5	..	30.9	2.0	1995	Combustibles (CTCI 3)
1.4	4.7	0.6	1.4	1.0	1.1	3.0	..	6.8	0.9	2005	
1.2	4.6	3.1	0.9	0.8	0.6	1.6	0.1	16.2	0.6	2012	
55.3	16.5	6.1	68.3	68.1	63.4	68.9	80.3	33.1	80.3	1995	Articles manufacturés
73.2	12.4	8.9	86.5	87.9	92.7	79.6	5.6	69.9	91.8	2005	(CTCI 5 à 8 moins 667 et 68)
82.1	21.1	13.4	90.0	91.1	94.9	83.0	42.6	63.8	94.3	2012	

Pour les sources et les notes, se reporter à la fin du tableau 2.2.L.

Destination / Product group	Year Année	World (1) Monde (1)	Developed economies - Économies développées							Transition economies Économies en transition
			Total	Europe Total	EU UE	Canada	USA États-Unis	Japan Japon	Other developed countries Autres économies développées	
Millions of dollars										
All products	1995	3 571 464	2 621 195	1 834 546	1 724 231	148 745	431 783	135 735	70 387	53 069
	2005	6 299 988	4 706 924	3 392 113	3 215 670	257 907	800 297	147 491	109 116	141 956
	2012	9 332 948	6 228 843	4 568 328	4 261 955	351 390	926 727	214 976	167 422	299 172
Share by destination (percentage)										
All products	1995	100.0	73.4	51.4	48.3	4.2	12.1	3.8	2.0	1.5
	2005	100.0	74.7	53.8	51.0	4.1	12.7	2.3	1.7	2.3
	2012	100.0	66.7	48.9	45.7	3.8	9.9	2.3	1.8	3.2
All food items	1995	100.0	73.6	56.9	55.0	2.6	5.2	7.7	1.1	3.9
(SITC 0 + 1 + 22 + 4)	2005	100.0	78.8	61.4	59.4	3.4	7.7	5.1	1.3	3.0
	2012	100.0	70.5	55.2	53.2	3.6	6.2	4.1	1.5	3.7
Agricultural raw materials	1995	100.0	75.3	47.8	45.5	2.9	12.1	11.5	1.1	0.5
(SITC 2 - 22 - 27 - 28)	2005	100.0	70.1	47.6	45.6	3.1	13.5	4.9	0.9	1.3
	2012	100.0	55.8	43.1	41.5	2.3	6.2	3.4	0.8	2.1
Ores, metals, precious stones	1995	100.0	73.6	48.5	43.5	3.4	11.5	6.8	3.5	0.5
and non-monetary gold	2005	100.0	67.8	45.3	41.1	2.7	12.2	3.9	3.6	0.9
(SITC 27 + 28 + 68 + 667 + 971)	2012	100.0	58.7	44.6	36.4	2.3	6.9	3.2	1.8	0.6
Fuels (SITC 3)	1995	100.0	80.8	55.0	51.4	2.7	18.0	4.4	0.7	1.4
	2005	100.0	84.5	55.2	52.7	3.3	23.1	2.3	0.6	0.6
	2012	100.0	70.8	50.3	46.9	2.4	14.8	2.5	0.8	1.3
Manufactured goods	1995	100.0	72.6	50.2	47.1	4.6	12.7	3.0	2.1	1.3
(SITC 5 to 8 less 667 and 68)	2005	100.0	73.7	53.5	50.6	4.4	12.2	1.9	1.8	2.5
	2012	100.0	66.7	48.6	45.6	4.2	10.2	1.7	2.0	3.8
Share by major product group (percentage)										
All products	1995	100.0	100.0	100.0	100.0	100.0	100.0	100.0	100.0	100.0
	2005	100.0	100.0	100.0	100.0	100.0	100.0	100.0	100.0	100.0
	2012	100.0	100.0	100.0	100.0	100.0	100.0	100.0	100.0	100.0
All food items	1995	8.7	8.7	9.6	9.9	5.4	3.8	17.5	4.9	22.7
(SITC 0 + 1 + 22 + 4)	2005	7.0	7.4	7.9	8.1	5.7	4.2	15.1	5.3	9.3
	2012	8.4	8.9	9.5	9.8	8.0	5.2	15.0	7.3	9.7
Agricultural raw materials	1995	2.6	2.6	2.4	2.4	1.8	2.6	7.7	1.4	0.9
(SITC 2 - 22 - 27 - 28)	2005	1.7	1.6	1.5	1.5	1.3	1.8	3.5	0.9	1.0
	2012	1.7	1.4	1.5	1.5	1.0	1.0	2.4	0.7	1.1
Ores, metals, precious stones	1995	4.1	4.1	3.8	3.7	3.3	3.9	7.2	7.2	1.5
and non-monetary gold	2005	4.2	3.8	3.5	3.4	2.8	4.0	7.1	8.8	1.7
(SITC 27 + 28 + 68 + 667 + 971)	2012	6.3	5.5	5.7	5.0	3.8	4.3	8.8	6.3	1.2
Fuels (SITC 3)	1995	3.4	3.7	3.6	3.6	2.2	5.0	3.9	1.1	3.2
	2005	6.7	7.5	6.8	6.9	5.3	12.1	6.7	2.1	1.9
	2012	9.9	10.5	10.2	10.2	6.3	14.8	10.9	4.2	4.0
Manufactured goods	1995	76.8	75.9	75.0	74.8	84.2	80.8	61.1	80.3	66.7
(SITC 5 to 8 less 667 and 68)	2005	76.6	75.6	76.1	76.0	81.6	73.8	62.8	78.5	83.9
	2012	68.9	68.8	68.4	68.7	76.5	71.0	51.8	76.5	81.3

For sources and notes, see end of table 2.2.L.

2.2.L Structure des exportations par partenaires et groupes de produits
Économies développées

Total	Africa / Afrique	America / Amérique	Asia / Asie — Total	Eastern, Southern and South-Eastern Asia / Asie orientale, méridionale et du Sud-Est	China / Chine	Western Asia / Asie occidentale	Oceania / Océanie	Major petroleum exporters and gas exporters / Principaux exportateurs de pétrole et de gaz	Major manufactured goods exporters / Principaux exportateurs d'articles manufacturés	Year / Année	Destinations / Groupes de produits
Millions de dollars											
833 374	80 267	169 214	579 971	500 109	59 455	79 861	3 923	75 794	473 775	1995	Total tous produits
1 416 419	135 237	304 814	970 043	784 499	209 302	105 543	6 326	167 241	803 624	2005	
2 733 386	253 539	627 894	1 839 766	1 490 090	556 047	349 676	12 187	322 935	1 511 019	2012	
Parts par destinations (en pourcentage)											
23.3	2.2	4.7	16.2	14.0	1.7	2.2	0.1	2.1	13.3	1995	Total tous produits
22.5	2.1	4.8	15.4	12.5	3.3	2.9	0.1	2.7	12.8	2005	
29.3	2.7	6.7	19.7	16.0	6.0	3.7	0.1	3.5	16.2	2012	
19.1	3.5	4.1	11.3	8.6	1.2	2.7	0.2	3.2	8.1	1995	Produits alimentaires
17.2	2.9	4.4	9.6	7.2	1.6	2.4	0.2	2.9	8.0	2005	(CTCI 0 + 1 + 22 + 4)
25.5	3.9	5.3	16.1	12.9	5.0	3.2	0.2	4.1	12.8	2012	
23.1	2.0	3.4	17.7	16.1	3.6	1.6	0.0	1.1	14.5	1995	Matières premières
27.8	2.0	4.1	21.6	19.2	9.5	2.4	0.1	1.2	18.3	2005	d'origine agricole
42.1	3.0	4.1	34.9	32.0	20.3	2.9	0.1	1.7	29.5	2012	(CTCI 2 - 22 - 27 - 28)
22.9	1.0	1.7	20.2	18.4	1.3	1.8	0.0	0.9	15.3	1995	Minerais, métaux, pierres
29.0	1.1	2.1	25.8	23.6	7.5	2.2	0.0	1.3	18.7	2005	précieuses et or (non monétaire)
39.2	1.4	2.1	35.7	32.6	15.1	3.1	0.0	1.4	28.1	2012	(CTCI 27 + 28 + 68 + 667 + 971)
12.6	1.4	3.7	7.3	6.4	0.4	1.0	0.2	0.8	6.2	1995	Combustibles (CTCI 3)
10.8	1.7	3.5	5.5	4.2	0.6	1.3	0.1	1.0	4.9	2005	
22.8	3.6	8.8	10.3	8.3	2.0	2.0	0.1	2.3	10.2	2012	
24.5	2.2	5.1	17.1	14.8	1.7	2.3	0.1	2.1	14.2	1995	Articles manufacturés
23.4	2.2	5.2	15.9	12.8	3.3	3.2	0.1	2.9	13.3	2005	(CTCI 5 à 8 moins 667 et 68)
29.3	2.6	7.0	19.6	15.5	5.5	4.1	0.1	3.7	16.1	2012	
Parts par principaux groupes de produits (en pourcentage)											
100.0	100.0	100.0	100.0	100.0	100.0	100.0	100.0	100.0	100.0	1995	Total tous produits
100.0	100.0	100.0	100.0	100.0	100.0	100.0	100.0	100.0	100.0	2005	
100.0	100.0	100.0	100.0	100.0	100.0	100.0	100.0	100.0	100.0	2012	
7.1	13.7	7.5	6.0	5.3	6.5	10.4	15.2	13.0	5.3	1995	Produits alimentaires
5.3	9.4	6.4	4.4	4.0	3.3	5.8	14.0	7.5	4.3	2005	(CTCI 0 + 1 + 22 + 4)
7.4	12.0	6.7	6.9	6.8	7.1	7.3	12.8	10.1	6.7	2012	
2.5	2.3	1.8	2.8	3.0	5.6	1.9	1.1	1.4	2.8	1995	Matières premières
2.1	1.6	1.4	2.3	2.6	4.7	1.4	1.6	0.8	2.4	2005	d'origine agricole
2.4	1.8	1.0	2.9	3.3	5.6	1.3	0.7	0.8	3.0	2012	(CTCI 2 - 22 - 27 - 28)
4.0	1.9	1.4	5.1	5.4	3.1	3.3	0.6	1.8	4.7	1995	Minerais, métaux, pierres
5.4	2.1	1.8	7.1	8.0	9.5	3.2	0.6	2.1	6.2	2005	précieuses et or (non monétaire)
8.4	3.2	1.9	11.4	12.8	15.9	5.2	0.8	2.5	10.9	2012	(CTCI 27 + 28 + 68 + 667 + 971)
1.8	2.1	2.6	1.5	1.5	0.7	1.4	7.1	1.2	1.6	1995	Combustibles (CTCI 3)
3.2	5.2	4.9	2.4	2.3	1.1	2.9	7.5	2.6	2.6	2005	
7.7	13.2	13.0	5.2	5.1	3.4	5.4	7.5	6.5	6.2	2012	
80.7	76.6	82.6	80.7	81.2	79.1	77.6	73.1	77.5	82.3	1995	Articles manufacturés
79.6	77.6	81.6	79.3	78.5	76.7	83.0	70.5	83.0	80.1	2005	(CTCI 5 à 8 moins 667 et 68)
68.9	66.2	71.4	68.4	66.8	63.4	74.8	72.0	72.7	68.4	2012	

Pour les sources et les notes, se reporter à la fin du tableau 2.2.L.

2.2.L Import structure by partner and product group
Developed economies

Product group	Year / Année	World (1) / Monde (1)	Developed economies - Économies développées								Transition economies / Économies en transition
			Total	Europe		Canada	USA / États-Unis	Japan / Japon	Other developed countries / Autres économies développées	
				Total	EU / UE					
Millions of dollars											
All products	1995	3 572 325	2 602 851	1 774 830	1 659 645	177 686	362 109	234 206	54 019	66 101
	2005	7 048 964	4 562 329	3 344 521	3 135 582	329 713	501 481	286 088	100 527	224 211
	2012	10 151 366	5 950 644	4 423 805	4 081 229	392 885	676 178	298 681	159 096	464 621
Share by origin (percentage)											
All products	1995	100.0	72.9	49.7	46.5	5.0	10.1	6.6	1.5	1.9
	2005	100.0	64.7	47.4	44.5	4.7	7.1	4.1	1.4	3.2
	2012	100.0	58.6	43.6	40.2	3.9	6.7	2.9	1.6	4.6
All food items	1995	100.0	69.2	51.3	49.1	3.7	10.8	0.2	3.3	1.1
(SITC 0 + 1 + 22 + 4)	2005	100.0	70.6	55.3	53.3	4.1	7.1	0.2	3.9	1.1
	2012	100.0	68.4	54.6	52.0	4.0	6.6	0.2	3.0	1.8
Agricultural raw materials	1995	100.0	71.7	37.4	36.0	16.0	13.3	0.5	4.5	4.9
(SITC 2 - 22 - 27 - 28)	2005	100.0	69.1	44.1	43.0	13.7	7.7	0.6	3.0	4.7
	2012	100.0	62.1	44.4	43.2	7.4	7.0	0.9	2.4	4.0
Ores, metals, precious stones	1995	100.0	62.8	39.8	34.0	8.0	7.2	0.6	7.2	8.2
and non-monetary gold	2005	100.0	58.2	37.8	33.2	6.9	5.0	0.5	8.0	8.4
(SITC 27 + 28 + 68 + 667 + 971)	2012	100.0	56.6	37.7	31.7	6.4	4.8	0.7	6.9	5.7
Fuels (SITC 3)	1995	100.0	36.2	25.2	17.5	5.9	2.3	0.1	2.5	8.0
	2005	100.0	36.1	25.8	19.1	6.9	1.5	0.1	1.8	13.4
	2012	100.0	33.9	23.1	18.5	5.8	2.7	0.1	2.2	17.3
Manufactured goods	1995	100.0	77.3	52.2	49.5	4.3	11.1	8.9	0.7	0.6
(SITC 5 to 8 less 667 and 68)	2005	100.0	69.9	51.5	49.3	3.8	8.4	5.6	0.7	0.8
	2012	100.0	63.5	47.8	45.4	2.8	7.9	4.4	0.7	0.9
Share by major product group (percentage)											
All products	1995	100.0	100.0	100.0	100.0	100.0	100.0	100.0	100.0	100.0
	2005	100.0	100.0	100.0	100.0	100.0	100.0	100.0	100.0	100.0
	2012	100.0	100.0	100.0	100.0	100.0	100.0	100.0	100.0	100.0
All food items	1995	9.2	8.7	9.5	9.7	6.8	9.8	0.3	19.9	5.5
(SITC 0 + 1 + 22 + 4)	2005	6.9	7.6	8.1	8.3	6.1	6.9	0.3	19.1	2.5
	2012	7.7	9.0	9.7	10.0	8.0	7.7	0.4	14.9	3.0
Agricultural raw materials	1995	2.9	2.8	2.2	2.2	9.2	3.8	0.2	8.5	7.6
(SITC 2 - 22 - 27 - 28)	2005	1.5	1.7	1.4	1.5	4.5	1.7	0.2	3.3	2.3
	2012	1.3	1.4	1.4	1.4	2.5	1.4	0.4	2.0	1.2
Ores, metals, precious stones	1995	5.0	4.3	4.0	3.7	8.1	3.6	0.5	23.8	22.2
and non-monetary gold	2005	4.3	3.8	3.4	3.2	6.3	3.0	0.6	23.9	11.3
(SITC 27 + 28 + 68 + 667 + 971)	2012	5.0	4.8	4.3	3.9	8.2	3.6	1.3	21.9	6.2
Fuels (SITC 3)	1995	7.4	3.7	3.8	2.8	8.9	1.7	0.1	12.5	32.0
	2005	14.1	7.8	7.6	6.0	20.8	2.9	0.5	17.7	59.5
	2012	19.0	11.0	10.0	8.7	28.5	7.6	0.8	27.0	71.6
Manufactured goods	1995	71.8	76.1	75.4	76.4	62.5	78.7	97.3	32.6	25.0
(SITC 5 to 8 less 667 and 68)	2005	70.1	75.7	76.1	77.7	57.2	82.4	96.4	33.5	17.5
	2012	63.9	69.3	70.1	72.1	46.4	75.5	94.8	29.7	13.1

Source:
UNCTAD secretariat calculations, based on UNCTAD, *UNCTADstat* Merchandise Trade Matrix

Notes:
- It is recognized that the structure of trade and partner distribution for certain countries and years might vary. In this regard, reader should know the coverage and limitations of the main data used in this table. For further information, please visit http://comtrade.un.org/db/help/uReadMeFirst.aspx.
(1) Includes special category exports, ship stores and bunkers and other exports of minor importance whose destination could not be determined.

2.2.L Structure des importations par partenaires et groupes de produits
Économies développées

			Developing economies - Économies en développement								Origines
				Asia / Asie				Major petroleum exporters and gas exporters	Major manufactured goods exporters	Year	
Total	Africa / Afrique	America / Amérique	Total	Eastern, Southern and South-Eastern Asia / Asie orientale, méridionale et du Sud-Est	China / Chine	Western Asia / Asie occidentale	Oceania / Océanie	Principaux exportateurs de pétrole et de gaz	Principaux exportateurs d'articles manufacturés	Année	Groupes de produits
Millions de dollars											
845 956	83 067	174 837	584 207	511 358	127 428	72 849	3 845	108 316	484 317	1995	Total tous produits
2 206 025	219 574	437 951	1 543 527	1 305 731	638 021	237 796	4 973	351 032	1 291 205	2005	
3 665 980	358 072	705 247	2 593 904	2 145 138	1 183 889	448 766	8 757	621 880	2 117 051	2012	
Parts par origines (en pourcentage)											
23.7	2.3	4.9	16.4	14.3	3.6	2.0	0.1	3.0	13.6	1995	Total tous produits
31.3	3.1	6.2	21.9	18.5	9.1	3.4	0.1	5.0	18.3	2005	
36.1	3.5	6.9	25.6	21.1	11.7	4.4	0.1	6.1	20.9	2012	
28.1	3.9	12.3	11.6	10.7	2.2	0.9	0.3	0.4	8.7	1995	Produits alimentaires
28.1	3.7	13.2	11.0	9.8	3.2	1.1	0.2	0.4	8.6	2005	(CTCI 0 + 1 + 22 + 4)
29.5	3.2	13.9	12.2	11.3	3.3	0.9	0.2	0.3	9.8	2012	
22.5	3.6	6.0	12.4	11.9	1.9	0.5	0.4	0.5	8.9	1995	Matières premières
26.0	4.0	8.5	13.3	12.8	3.4	0.5	0.1	0.3	9.1	2005	d'origine agricole
33.6	3.5	9.2	20.8	20.3	4.4	0.5	0.1	0.4	11.0	2012	(CTCI 2 - 22 - 27 - 28)
25.4	6.2	10.1	8.4	7.6	1.3	0.8	0.7	1.2	4.8	1995	Minerais, métaux, pierres
32.6	8.4	12.5	11.1	9.6	2.6	1.5	0.5	1.5	6.3	2005	précieuses et or (non monétaire)
36.0	6.8	16.6	11.7	9.4	2.3	2.3	0.9	1.7	8.5	2012	(CTCI 27 + 28 + 68 + 667 + 971)
52.0	13.4	8.0	29.5	10.4	1.2	19.1	0.2	35.8	5.9	1995	Combustibles (CTCI 3)
47.3	13.4	10.0	23.8	7.4	0.6	16.4	0.1	32.7	5.8	2005	
44.8	12.4	8.0	24.3	6.7	0.1	17.7	0.1	30.5	5.9	2012	
20.7	0.6	3.2	16.8	16.2	4.4	0.6	0.0	0.3	16.1	1995	Articles manufacturés
29.1	0.8	4.4	24.0	22.7	12.1	1.3	0.0	0.4	23.0	2005	(CTCI 5 à 8 moins 667 et 68)
35.2	0.7	5.1	29.4	28.0	17.4	1.3	0.0	0.3	28.2	2012	
Parts par principaux groupes de produits (en pourcentage)											
100.0	100.0	100.0	100.0	100.0	100.0	100.0	100.0	100.0	100.0	1995	Total tous produits
100.0	100.0	100.0	100.0	100.0	100.0	100.0	100.0	100.0	100.0	2005	
100.0	100.0	100.0	100.0	100.0	100.0	100.0	100.0	100.0	100.0	2012	
10.9	15.6	23.2	6.5	6.8	5.6	4.1	25.6	1.1	5.9	1995	Produits alimentaires
6.2	8.2	14.8	3.5	3.7	2.4	2.4	21.7	0.6	3.3	2005	(CTCI 0 + 1 + 22 + 4)
6.3	7.1	15.5	3.7	4.1	2.2	1.5	22.0	0.3	3.6	2012	
2.7	4.5	3.5	2.2	2.4	1.5	0.7	11.4	0.4	1.9	1995	Matières premières
1.3	2.0	2.1	0.9	1.1	0.6	0.2	2.5	0.1	0.8	2005	d'origine agricole
1.2	1.3	1.8	1.1	1.3	0.5	0.2	1.0	0.1	0.7	2012	(CTCI 2 - 22 - 27 - 28)
5.4	13.4	10.4	2.6	2.7	1.9	2.0	32.4	2.0	1.8	1995	Minerais, métaux, pierres
4.4	11.5	8.6	2.2	2.2	1.2	1.9	32.7	1.3	1.5	2005	précieuses et or (non monétaire)
4.9	9.6	11.8	2.3	2.2	1.0	2.6	49.8	1.4	2.0	2012	(CTCI 27 + 28 + 68 + 667 + 971)
16.3	42.8	13.4	13.4	5.4	2.5	69.5	15.0	87.8	3.2	1995	Combustibles (CTCI 3)
21.3	60.6	22.6	15.3	5.6	0.9	68.5	18.6	92.3	4.4	2005	
23.5	66.5	21.9	18.1	6.0	0.2	75.8	15.8	94.4	5.3	2012	
62.7	19.4	46.9	73.8	81.2	87.7	22.4	14.8	6.4	85.3	1995	Articles manufacturés
65.2	17.0	49.4	76.7	86.0	94.0	26.1	21.9	5.2	88.2	2005	(CTCI 5 à 8 moins 667 et 68)
62.3	13.4	46.6	73.4	84.8	95.3	19.0	9.9	3.2	86.5	2012	

Source :

Calculs du secrétariat de la CNUCED, basés sur la matrice du commerce de marchandises de *UNCTADstat* de la CNUCED

Notes :

- Il est reconnu que la structure du commerce et la distribution au niveau partenaire pour certains pays et sur certaines années peuvent varier. À cet égard, le lecteur devrait connaître la couverture ainsi que les limites des données principales utilisées dans ce tableau. Pour de plus amples renseignements, veuillez visiter http://comtrade.un.org/db/help/uReadMeFirst.aspx.

(1) Y compris les exportations de catégorie spéciale, approvisionnements des navires et combustibles de soute et autres exportations de moindre importance dont la destination n'a pas pu être déterminée.

3

INTERNATIONAL
MERCHANDISE
TRADE BY PRODUCT

COMMERCE
INTERNATIONAL DES
MARCHANDISES
PAR PRODUITS

1

2

3

4

5

6

7

8

Country or territory / Pays ou territoires	Year / Année	Total value (millions of dollars) (1) / Valeur totale (millions de dollars) (1)	By main SITC Revision 3 product group (percentage) / Par principaux groupes de produits de la CTCI Révision 3 (en pourcentage)					Of which: / dont :		
			All food items / Produits alimentaires	Agricultural raw materials / Matières premières agricoles	Fuels / Combustibles	Ores, metals, precious stones and non-monetary gold / Minerais, métaux, pierres précieuses et or (non monétaire)	Manufactured goods / Articles manufacturés	Chemical products / Produits chimiques	Machinery and transport equipment / Machines et matériel de transport	Other manufactured goods / Articles manufacturés divers
			0 + 1 + 22 + 4	2 - (22 + 27 + 28)	3	27 + 28 + 68 + 667 + 971	5 + 6 +7 + 8 - (667 + 68)	5	7	6 + 8 - (667 + 68)
Afghanistan	1995	(e)166	53.3	26.0	0.1	2.6	16.7	3.1	2.5	11.0
	2005	(e)384	36.3	18.6	10.0	7.3	14.0	2.2	6.0	5.8
	2012	(e)370	23.6	16.2	8.8	7.9	11.6	0.4	4.2	7.0
Albania - Albanie	1995	(e)202	11.2	12.4	2.7	12.3	60.0	1.7	3.4	54.9
	2005	(e)658	5.4	4.7	6.0	8.9	74.0	0.7	5.1	68.2
	2012	(e)1 968	4.4	2.7	25.2	13.4	54.0	1.4	3.9	48.7
Algeria - Algérie	1995	9 357	1.2	0.1	95.2	0.5	3.0	1.2	0.4	1.4
	2005	46 002	0.2	0.0	98.4	0.5	1.0	0.7	0.1	0.2
	2012	71 866	0.4	0.0	98.4	0.2	0.9	0.7	0.0	0.2
American Samoa - Samoa américaines	1995	272	..	..	..	..	..	..	..	..
	2005	(e)374	24.5	23.1	0.3	8.3	39.3	4.0	26.2	9.1
	2012	(e)420	16.6	1.9	37.2	3.0	41.0	5.8	32.0	3.2
Andorra - Andorre	1995	48	6.5	1.6	0.2	2.3	89.3	3.6	33.8	52.0
	2005	143	28.9	0.5	0.0	2.2	67.4	3.6	39.7	24.1
	2012	(e)110	12.7	0.2	0.0	0.9	59.4	1.4	32.5	25.6
Angola	1995	3 642	1.0	0.0	93.9	4.5	0.5	0.0	0.2	0.3
	2005	24 109	0.2	0.0	96.3	3.2	0.2	0.0	0.2	0.0
	2012	(e)74 000	0.0	0.0	98.3	1.4	0.2	0.0	0.1	0.1
Anguilla	1995	(e)1	13.1	2.1	3.0	1.8	79.2	15.2	30.1	33.9
	2005	(e)15	25.6	0.1	5.7	0.1	59.5	25.5	15.5	18.6
	2012	(e)21	21.2	1.1	0.2	1.6	70.2	2.1	40.1	28.1
Antigua and Barbuda - Antigua-et-Barbuda	1995	(e)53	18.8	4.2	47.5	4.4	23.2	6.3	11.0	5.8
	2005	(e)83	4.1	0.1	9.5	0.1	85.0	1.5	81.0	2.5
	2012	(e)60	46.3	0.3	5.9	0.6	46.6	4.3	30.7	11.6
Argentina - Argentine	1995	20 963	49.8	4.3	10.3	1.6	33.9	6.4	10.9	16.6
	2005	40 106	46.5	1.4	16.4	3.6	30.6	8.5	10.7	11.4
	2012	80 927	52.4	0.9	6.1	6.8	31.2	8.8	16.0	6.5
Armenia - Arménie	1995	(e)271	12.8	4.9	5.5	22.6	53.0	3.3	27.0	22.7
	2005	(e)937	12.4	0.8	2.5	39.6	43.7	0.4	3.2	40.1
	2012	(e)1 428	24.1	0.0	5.5	45.8	24.4	1.6	5.2	17.6
Aruba	1995	(e)1 347	2.9	0.1	93.6	0.4	2.0	0.9	0.5	0.5
	2005	(e)4 416	2.5	0.0	92.7	0.8	1.5	0.1	1.0	0.4
	2012	(e)1 850	10.6	0.1	80.0	1.4	3.0	0.6	1.2	1.1
Australia - Australie	1995	53 001	19.6	8.1	16.7	26.4	26.5	4.1	12.8	9.6
	2005	105 751	16.1	3.9	25.6	27.4	20.2	4.6	9.5	6.0
	2012	256 243	12.0	3.0	28.4	40.5	12.2	3.4	5.4	3.4
Austria - Autriche	1995	57 583	3.8	2.9	1.0	3.1	81.6	7.2	36.0	38.3
	2005	117 722	6.2	1.8	4.6	2.9	80.6	8.7	41.1	30.8
	2012	158 821	7.1	1.5	3.7	4.5	79.3	11.8	38.0	29.5
Azerbaijan - Azerbaïdjan	1995	(e)636	10.1	13.0	46.1	3.9	26.9	5.2	12.6	9.0
	2005	(e)7 649	6.2	1.3	77.0	3.7	11.8	2.3	7.1	2.4
	2012	(e)32 634	2.8	0.1	93.9	0.9	2.3	0.9	0.3	1.0
Bahamas	1995	(e)176	20.3	0.8	10.6	6.8	60.1	17.0	36.2	7.0
	2005	(e)549	11.2	0.1	23.4	3.1	58.5	9.3	44.4	4.9
	2012	(e)984	5.1	0.2	65.2	2.8	26.7	9.3	11.5	5.8
Bahrain - Bahreïn	1995	(e)4 113	3.0	0.4	18.4	45.0	32.6	10.7	4.8	17.1
	2005	(e)10 239	1.4	0.1	42.7	32.6	21.7	6.0	4.2	11.5
	2012	(e)19 766	3.6	0.3	42.5	27.8	25.5	5.4	6.7	13.4
Bangladesh	1995	(e)3 407	9.2	2.6	0.3	0.0	86.9	3.1	1.1	82.7
	2005	(e)9 332	5.8	1.4	0.4	0.2	92.0	1.9	1.3	88.8
	2012	(e)26 504	5.0	1.7	0.8	0.4	91.7	1.9	1.4	88.4

For sources and notes, see end of table.

Pour les sources et les notes, se reporter à la fin du tableau.

3.1 Country trade structure
by product group
Exports

3.1 Structure du commerce des pays
par groupes de produits
Exportations

Country or territory Pays ou territoires	Year Année	Total value (millions of dollars) (1) Valeur totale (millions de dollars) (1)	By main SITC Revision 3 product group (percentage) Par principaux groupes de produits de la CTCI Révision 3 (en pourcentage)					Of which: / dont :		
			All food items Produits alimentaires	Agricultural raw materials Matières premières agricoles	Fuels Combustibles	Ores, metals, precious stones and non-monetary gold Minerais, métaux, pierres précieuses et or (non monétaire)	Manufactured goods Articles manufacturés	Chemical products Produits chimiques	Machinery and transport equipment Machines et matériel de transport	Other manufactured goods Articles manufacturés divers
			0 + 1 + 22 + 4	2 - (22 + 27 + 28)	3	27 + 28 + 68 + 667 + 971	5 + 6 +7 + 8 - (667 + 68)	5	7	6 + 8 - (667 + 68)
Barbados - Barbade	1995	238	27.3	1.0	14.3	2.2	54.0	12.0	18.0	22.3
	2005	361	20.9	0.2	40.3	0.5	36.8	12.6	10.2	14.1
	2012	566	24.1	0.3	11.8	2.6	59.8	26.4	6.7	26.8
Belarus - Bélarus	1995	(e)4 804	1.8	5.0	4.5	3.9	33.1	10.7	9.0	13.3
	2005	15 977	8.3	2.5	34.8	0.5	51.9	11.1	18.7	22.2
	2012	46 060	9.8	1.3	35.6	0.6	48.7	18.0	15.3	15.4
Belgium - Belgique	1995	(e)177 831	7.6	0.8	1.8	8.7	53.4	12.7	22.3	18.4
	2005	334 106	8.1	1.2	6.9	7.6	73.9	27.6	25.2	21.1
	2012	446 854	9.2	1.4	11.5	8.2	67.8	28.6	20.6	18.6
Belize	1995	162	78.6	1.5	2.8	0.3	15.5	1.6	3.9	10.0
	2005	208	73.2	1.0	4.5	0.3	20.2	2.3	9.5	8.4
	2012	(e)390	64.4	2.7	20.4	1.0	10.7	2.7	2.9	5.2
Benin - Bénin	1995	420	17.6	71.6	4.7	1.7	5.5	0.6	0.4	4.4
	2005	(e)578	20.7	47.2	17.4	5.8	8.6	0.8	2.2	5.6
	2012	(e)1 400	28.8	22.1	16.0	22.0	11.0	1.8	3.4	5.8
Bermuda - Bermudes	1995	(e)56	7.3	12.9	2.1	0.2	68.3	18.5	45.6	4.2
	2005	(e)49	2.0	0.1	0.7	0.4	90.3	2.6	81.3	6.4
	2012	(e)12	5.9	0.1	21.3	2.2	44.1	33.3	9.3	1.5
Bhutan - Bhoutan	1995	(e)103	20.0	8.5	0.3	1.7	69.2	22.5	7.0	39.8
	2005	(e)258	9.2	0.3	28.9	10.1	51.3	8.1	3.5	39.7
	2012	(e)610	8.9	0.8	20.1	13.7	56.5	10.4	1.2	44.9
Bolivia (Plurinational State of) - Bolivie (État plurinational de)	1995	1 181	19.6	13.3	10.8	40.3	15.7	1.3	2.2	12.2
	2005	2 797	18.3	2.0	52.9	15.1	11.4	1.3	1.6	8.5
	2012	11 793	12.4	0.8	50.5	31.1	5.1	2.7	0.2	2.1
Bosnia and Herzegovina - Bosnie-Herzégovine	1995	(e)152	16.6	20.4	3.8	6.6	51.8	2.6	14.5	34.6
	2005	(e)2 388	5.1	8.4	8.9	23.0	53.6	3.2	16.6	33.9
	2012	(e)5 162	7.6	6.8	9.1	14.1	61.8	6.0	15.0	40.8
Botswana	1995	(a)2 142	3.5	0.3	0.1	80.7	8.7	1.1	3.9	3.6
	2005	4 431	2.2	0.1	0.1	91.0	6.5	0.6	2.6	3.3
	2012	5 971	1.3	0.2	0.7	91.6	6.1	1.1	3.1	1.9
Brazil - Brésil	1995	46 505	28.5	5.2	0.9	11.3	52.8	6.6	19.0	27.2
	2005	118 529	25.7	3.9	6.0	10.5	52.1	6.2	25.8	20.2
	2012	242 580	31.8	3.8	10.9	17.3	33.8	6.2	15.8	11.9
British Virgin Islands - Îles Vierges britanniques	1995	(e)19	4.1	0.5	3.2	28.4	57.8	19.4	30.8	7.6
	2005	(e)35	4.5	0.1	5.1	32.4	52.9	3.4	36.0	13.5
	2012	40	1.8	0.1	0.3	8.0	89.1	1.1	80.9	7.1
Brunei Darussalam - Brunéi Darussalam	1995	(e)2 379	0.1	0.0	91.1	0.0	8.2	0.1	4.5	3.6
	2005	(e)6 256	0.1	0.1	92.4	0.5	7.0	0.0	1.2	5.8
	2012	13 001	0.0	0.0	96.2	0.3	3.3	1.9	0.7	0.7
Bulgaria - Bulgarie	1995	(e)5 353	18.1	3.0	6.5	9.7	60.1	18.3	12.4	29.4
	2005	11 739	10.5	1.8	10.4	14.2	59.3	7.6	14.2	37.5
	2012	26 699	15.3	1.3	16.2	17.3	47.5	8.2	16.4	23.0
Burkina Faso	1995	(e)276	18.6	60.0	0.7	11.7	8.8	0.4	2.6	5.8
	2005	(e)468	13.6	76.7	0.1	2.0	7.3	0.8	2.2	4.4
	2012	(e)2 146	14.6	32.6	0.0	46.8	5.9	1.2	2.1	2.6
Burundi	1995	(e)106	57.5	3.8	0.0	36.5	2.1	0.2	0.4	1.5
	2005	(e)58	65.8	2.1	0.0	27.2	4.7	0.2	3.0	1.5
	2012	(e)134	58.5	1.8	0.1	18.7	20.4	8.7	6.6	5.1
Cambodia - Cambodge	1995	(e)855	4.0	74.4	0.0	0.3	20.8	0.3	0.7	19.7
	2005	(e)3 019	2.4	3.7	0.0	1.2	92.4	0.1	0.6	91.7
	2012	(e)7 838	4.9	5.0	0.0	4.8	85.2	0.4	4.4	80.4

For sources and notes, see end of table.

Pour les sources et les notes, se reporter à la fin du tableau.

Country or territory / Pays ou territoires	Year / Année	Total value (millions of dollars) (1) / Valeur totale (millions de dollars) (1)	By main SITC Revision 3 product group (percentage) / Par principaux groupes de produits de la CTCI Révision 3 (en pourcentage)					Of which: / dont :		
			All food items / Produits alimentaires	Agricultural raw materials / Matières premières agricoles	Fuels / Combustibles	Ores, metals, precious stones and non-monetary gold / Minerais, métaux, pierres précieuses et or (non monétaire)	Manufactured goods / Articles manufacturés	Chemical products / Produits chimiques	Machinery and transport equipment / Machines et matériel de transport	Other manufactured goods / Articles manufacturés divers
			0 + 1 + 22 + 4	2 - (22 + 27 + 28)	3	27 + 28 + 68 + 667 + 971	5 + 6 +7 + 8 - (667 + 68)	5	7	6 + 8 - (667 + 68)
Cameroon - Cameroun	1995	(e)1 539	26.2	31.1	29.0	7.0	6.6	0.6	0.9	5.1
	2005	(e)2 861	18.9	18.0	49.5	4.8	6.0	0.9	1.2	4.0
	2012	(e)4 500	19.5	17.8	48.3	2.4	11.8	1.7	3.6	6.5
Canada	1995	191 118	7.6	9.2	9.1	7.8	62.0	5.9	38.5	17.6
	2005	360 552	6.7	4.7	20.2	7.0	56.9	7.2	32.8	16.8
	2012	453 381	10.2	3.6	25.6	11.4	46.2	8.1	26.3	11.7
Cape Verde - Cap-Vert	1995	9	14.0	0.5	9.1	6.0	68.6	1.8	15.7	51.0
	2005	(e)18	23.1	0.1	32.4	0.3	43.2	0.4	23.4	19.4
	2012	56	64.4	0.1	10.9	3.5	20.8	0.1	7.3	13.4
Cayman Islands - Îles Caïmanes	1995	(e)19	20.7	2.1	0.0	18.8	55.3	16.0	33.7	5.6
	2005	(e)59	0.5	0.1	8.7	0.1	84.5	0.4	82.6	1.4
	2012	(e)20	0.2	0.0	2.9	1.4	92.7	0.0	91.6	1.0
Central African Republic - République centrafricaine	1995	(e)171	14.3	17.7	0.1	57.0	8.2	0.5	5.3	2.5
	2005	(e)128	1.7	45.8	1.4	44.8	6.1	1.1	2.2	2.9
	2012	(e)210	3.6	42.3	0.1	44.8	9.2	0.9	6.3	2.0
Chad - Tchad	1995	(e)243	1.4	90.3	0.0	0.0	6.0	0.1	5.1	0.8
	2005	(e)3 081	0.1	6.3	90.9	0.1	2.2	0.1	1.8	0.3
	2012	(e)4 400	0.6	3.8	94.7	0.1	0.8	0.2	0.2	0.4
Chile - Chili	1995	15 901	23.7	13.6	0.2	49.5	11.7	3.5	1.8	6.5
	2005	41 973	19.3	6.3	2.7	57.1	14.6	5.0	2.7	6.9
	2012	78 277	18.5	5.7	0.9	61.6	13.3	4.9	3.0	5.5
China - Chine	1995	148 779	8.3	1.8	3.6	2.4	83.6	6.1	21.1	56.4
	2005	761 953	3.2	0.5	2.3	2.0	91.7	4.7	46.2	40.8
	2012	2 048 782	2.7	0.5	1.5	1.4	93.8	5.5	47.1	41.1
China, Hong Kong SAR - Chine (RAS de Hong Kong)	1995	173 871	3.0	1.3	1.0	2.6	91.6	6.2	32.4	53.1
	2005	292 119	0.9	0.6	0.3	4.1	94.0	4.8	52.3	36.9
	2012	492 907	1.5	0.4	0.2	14.9	82.8	4.0	55.5	23.4
China, Macao SAR - Chine (RAS de Macao)	1995	2 025	2.1	1.7	0.0	0.1	95.9	1.2	4.2	90.6
	2005	2 474	1.2	0.3	0.1	2.0	96.2	2.3	8.0	85.9
	2012	1 021	2.6	0.5	0.1	9.4	76.5	14.5	31.4	30.6
China, Taiwan Province of - Province chinoise de Taiwan	1995	111 343	3.4	1.6	0.7	1.5	92.7	6.8	48.1	37.8
	2005	189 393	1.2	1.2	4.7	1.8	90.7	10.5	49.8	30.4
	2012	300 622	1.3	1.1	7.2	2.9	87.1	12.6	47.9	26.6
Colombia - Colombie	1995	10 201	30.8	5.4	27.2	6.8	29.8	7.9	2.6	19.3
	2005	21 190	17.2	4.5	39.2	4.6	34.4	8.4	6.0	20.0
	2012	60 274	8.7	2.3	65.7	6.9	16.3	5.7	2.5	8.2
Comoros - Comores	1995	11	60.4	0.4	..	0.0	38.6	35.0	1.8	1.8
	2005	(e)12	71.2	1.0	..	1.2	26.4	11.0	12.1	3.3
	2012	(e)19	43.0	0.4	0.0	1.8	54.8	13.8	38.3	2.6
Congo	1995	(e)1 090	1.7	11.9	79.8	1.8	4.5	0.3	0.4	3.9
	2005	(e)5 198	0.8	5.4	87.2	5.6	0.9	0.3	0.2	0.4
	2012	(e)10 699	0.4	3.2	87.2	4.9	4.3	0.8	2.1	1.3
Cook Islands - Îles Cook	1995	(e)5	32.7	5.0	0.5	33.8	24.7	5.4	4.6	14.7
	2005	(e)5	76.8	1.3	..	11.8	8.6	0.6	2.4	5.6
	2012	(e)3	43.9	0.1	0.0	5.1	49.8	0.1	49.2	0.5
Costa Rica	1995	(e)3 476	56.2	4.6	0.4	1.2	35.3	5.0	4.7	25.6
	2005	7 151	26.4	2.3	0.2	1.1	69.2	5.0	43.7	20.4
	2012	(e)11 248	25.1	1.5	0.5	1.1	71.9	2.9	57.1	11.8
Côte d'Ivoire	1995	3 737	58.7	16.0	9.8	0.8	14.2	4.2	1.4	8.6
	2005	7 248	38.2	8.2	27.7	0.5	24.9	3.6	9.8	11.4
	2012	(e)12 350	38.5	11.3	32.7	5.0	12.5	3.3	4.4	4.7

For sources and notes, see end of table.

Pour les sources et les notes, se reporter à la fin du tableau.

Country or territory / Pays ou territoires	Year / Année	Total value (millions of dollars) (1) / Valeur totale (millions de dollars) (1)	By main SITC Revision 3 product group (percentage) / Par principaux groupes de produits de la CTCI Révision 3 (en pourcentage)					Of which: / dont :		
			All food items / Produits alimentaires	Agricultural raw materials / Matières premières agricoles	Fuels / Combustibles	Ores, metals, precious stones and non-monetary gold / Minerais, métaux, pierres précieuses et or (non monétaire)	Manu-factured goods / Articles manu-facturés	Chemical products / Produits chimiques	Machinery and transport equipment / Machines et matériel de transport	Other manu-factured goods / Articles manu-facturés divers
			0 + 1 + 22 + 4	2 - (22 + 27 + 28)	3	27 + 28 + 68 + 667 + 971	5 + 6 +7 + 8 - (667 + 68)	5	7	6 + 8 - (667 + 68)
Croatia - Croatie	1995	4 633	10.8	4.6	8.4	2.3	73.8	17.0	16.8	39.5
	2005	8 773	10.5	3.4	13.9	3.8	68.5	9.9	28.9	29.6
	2012	12 369	12.7	4.1	13.7	7.1	62.5	10.9	26.8	24.8
Cuba	1995	(e)1 625	76.2	0.3	0.3	15.9	7.1	3.8	1.3	2.0
	2005	(e)2 319	27.7	0.6	2.2	33.1	14.3	4.3	3.5	6.5
	2012	(e)5 635	32.3	1.3	10.4	22.8	23.9	10.1	6.5	7.3
Cyprus - Chypre	1995	1 231	45.4	0.7	1.9	2.0	49.2	5.0	20.0	24.2
	2005	1 546	14.7	1.1	12.4	4.5	65.6	13.7	35.9	16.0
	2012	1 826	11.6	0.8	38.5	6.7	35.0	14.0	13.7	7.3
Czech Republic - République tchèque	1995	21 686	6.1	3.9	4.7	3.0	80.8	9.4	28.0	43.4
	2005	78 209	4.1	1.5	3.2	1.7	87.0	6.2	50.3	30.4
	2012	156 027	4.7	1.5	3.9	2.4	85.5	5.9	53.8	25.8
Dem. Rep. of the Congo - Rép. dém. du Congo	1995	1 563	6.7	6.3	10.3	75.5	2.8	0.3	0.9	1.5
	2005	2 403	2.8	6.5	16.3	70.1	3.3	0.7	1.0	1.6
	2012	(e)6 300	0.9	3.2	15.2	77.3	1.0	0.5	0.3	0.3
Denmark - Danemark	1995	48 789	24.0	2.9	2.6	1.2	59.8	9.7	25.1	25.0
	2005	82 415	17.6	2.5	9.4	1.3	65.3	13.2	28.1	24.1
	2012	105 584	17.9	3.1	9.6	1.7	59.5	11.3	24.6	23.6
Djibouti	1995	(e)14	18.7	5.0	10.2	11.6	53.2	7.9	19.0	26.3
	2005	(e)40	21.7	3.5	2.5	13.0	58.1	10.5	34.6	12.9
	2012	(e)95	40.5	3.3	4.2	16.6	21.3	3.8	9.9	7.6
Dominica - Dominique	1995	45	50.3	0.3	0.0	1.3	48.1	42.7	2.7	2.7
	2005	42	33.8	0.1	0.0	6.5	59.6	53.7	4.2	1.7
	2012	37	11.3	0.0	0.0	9.7	79.0	50.9	11.6	16.5
Dominican Republic - République dominicaine	1995	(e)3 780	15.8	0.4	0.0	2.2	79.4	0.9	6.1	72.4
	2005	(e)6 183	14.4	0.4	0.0	2.7	80.7	2.8	14.3	63.6
	2012	(e)9 079	23.1	0.8	3.0	8.0	63.6	5.4	10.2	48.0
Ecuador - Équateur	1995	4 361	51.8	3.0	35.1	2.5	7.6	1.2	2.0	4.4
	2005	9 869	28.2	4.4	59.5	0.6	7.3	1.2	2.2	3.9
	2012	(e)23 869	32.8	6.6	52.1	1.7	6.8	1.3	2.3	3.3
Egypt - Égypte	1995	3 444	9.5	4.4	46.0	4.7	34.7	5.0	2.5	27.2
	2005	(e)12 912	9.4	2.0	43.9	4.3	31.1	5.6	3.2	22.3
	2012	29 417	12.5	2.0	37.0	9.0	39.1	13.4	4.6	21.1
El Salvador	1995	(e)1 652	44.2	1.1	0.2	1.9	52.3	9.0	3.9	39.4
	2005	3 436	18.8	0.4	1.5	1.5	76.8	7.0	5.4	64.4
	2012	5 339	23.0	1.0	2.5	2.8	69.9	6.9	5.4	57.6
Equatorial Guinea - Guinée équatoriale	1995	86	21.4	44.3	28.1	0.0	5.8	0.0	0.4	5.4
	2005	7 064	0.0	1.4	94.0	0.0	4.2	3.7	0.1	0.4
	2012	(e)15 500	0.0	0.9	95.0	0.1	3.8	2.4	1.3	0.1
Eritrea - Érythrée	1995	(e)86	59.1	8.5	..	0.0	30.9	1.4	15.3	14.2
	2005	(e)11	24.6	14.1	0.0	2.5	55.6	5.3	12.2	38.1
	2012	(e)457	1.2	0.1	..	96.7	2.0	0.1	0.3	1.5
Estonia - Estonie	1995	1 840	13.9	9.9	10.8	5.2	59.9	8.1	17.8	34.1
	2005	8 247	7.1	6.3	14.0	2.7	65.7	5.0	32.2	28.5
	2012	(e)16 124	9.3	4.6	13.0	4.1	63.8	6.5	32.3	25.0
Ethiopia - Éthiopie	1995	422	72.5	13.4	2.9	0.1	11.2	0.3	0.0	10.8
	2005	926	73.5	15.3	..	5.8	5.1	0.0	0.0	5.0
	2012	(e)2 728	74.0	8.8	0.0	6.9	10.3	0.3	3.5	6.4
Faeroe Islands - Îles Féroé	1995	(e)362	91.1	2.2	..	..	6.7	0.1	4.8	1.8
	2005	602	91.6	1.5	..	0.0	6.9	0.1	5.4	1.4
	2012	(e)948	84.5	2.1	5.6	0.2	7.0	0.1	5.9	1.0

For sources and notes, see end of table.

Pour les sources et les notes, se reporter à la fin du tableau.

Country or territory / Pays ou territoires	Year / Année	Total value (millions of dollars) (1) / Valeur totale (millions de dollars) (1)	By main SITC Revision 3 product group (percentage) / Par principaux groupes de produits de la CTCI Révision 3 (en pourcentage)					Of which: / dont :		
			All food items / Produits alimentaires	Agricultural raw materials / Matières premières agricoles	Fuels / Combustibles	Ores, metals, precious stones and non-monetary gold / Minerais, métaux, pierres précieuses et or (non monétaire)	Manu-factured goods / Articles manu-facturés	Chemical products / Produits chimiques	Machinery and transport equipment / Machines et matériel de transport	Other manu-factured goods / Articles manu-facturés divers
			0 + 1 + 22 + 4	2 - (22 + 27 + 28)	3	27 + 28 + 68 + 667 + 971	5 + 6 +7 + 8 - (667 + 68)	5	7	6 + 8 - (667 + 68)
Falkland Islands (Malvinas) - Îles Falkland (Malvinas)	1995	(e)30	68.0	16.3	..	..	16.0	1.0	12.6	2.4
	2005	(e)150	95.0	2.4	..	0.5	0.8	0.1	0.5	0.3
	2012	200	91.4	5.4	0.0	0.0	0.6	0.1	0.5	0.0
Fiji - Fidji	1995	(e)619	51.5	7.0	0.4	7.6	33.1	0.3	1.0	31.8
	2005	702	52.6	5.0	9.8	6.6	23.8	1.8	2.5	19.5
	2012	1 221	41.9	4.2	24.7	9.3	19.1	2.9	5.2	11.1
Finland - Finlande	1995	40 409	2.4	8.4	1.9	3.1	83.3	6.0	35.4	42.0
	2005	65 238	1.9	5.2	4.4	3.6	84.3	7.6	44.1	32.6
	2012	72 974	2.9	6.1	10.9	6.3	71.6	11.0	29.2	31.3
France	1995	277 845	14.3	1.5	2.4	2.7	76.6	12.9	39.4	24.3
	2005	434 354	10.7	0.9	4.1	2.3	80.1	15.9	41.6	22.5
	2012	556 576	12.6	1.0	4.5	3.0	76.5	17.5	38.3	20.6
French Polynesia - Polynésie française	1995	(e)196	2.7	1.0	0.0	61.8	28.6	0.8	20.8	7.1
	2005	210	15.2	1.1	0.0	55.2	27.0	2.8	17.3	7.0
	2012	139	19.0	1.5	0.0	62.4	13.1	1.4	8.2	3.5
Gabon	1995	(e)2 718	0.2	13.1	82.7	2.0	1.9	0.4	0.4	1.1
	2005	5 068	0.9	10.8	78.8	5.6	3.8	0.0	0.9	2.9
	2012	(e)9 665	0.5	9.9	78.7	6.3	4.6	0.2	2.4	2.0
Gambia - Gambie	1995	(e)16	28.4	0.8	0.5	61.5	8.5	2.1	1.7	4.8
	2005	(e)8	66.0	2.1	0.9	3.4	26.8	1.3	18.3	7.2
	2012	(e)100	51.1	12.5	0.8	20.1	15.5	1.0	3.4	11.1
Georgia - Géorgie	1995	(e)158	29.3	3.3	18.8	8.0	40.6	11.1	5.7	23.8
	2005	865	34.9	2.1	3.2	21.1	38.5	6.8	16.9	14.8
	2012	2 377	21.3	0.6	2.1	10.9	63.6	11.3	31.1	21.2
Germany - Allemagne	1995	523 697	5.1	1.1	1.0	2.8	83.4	13.2	46.1	24.2
	2005	977 132	4.5	0.8	2.2	2.7	86.0	13.9	50.2	21.8
	2012	1 416 184	5.4	0.8	2.7	3.7	82.0	14.4	46.9	20.6
Ghana	1995	(e)1 754	41.9	13.2	4.3	34.8	7.1	0.6	0.8	5.7
	2005	(e)3 060	54.9	8.3	8.1	13.9	13.2	0.7	2.3	10.2
	2012	(e)13 000	41.1	3.0	33.4	14.9	7.3	1.1	2.1	4.0
Gibraltar	1995	117	15.0	0.4	0.7	17.1	64.5	3.9	22.0	38.6
	2005	(e)200	0.3	0.4	12.3	5.4	78.0	1.1	62.4	14.5
	2012	240	0.1	0.0	74.2	0.5	24.7	0.1	23.0	1.5
Greece - Grèce	1995	10 955	29.5	4.4	6.5	7.9	49.2	4.9	8.0	36.3
	2005	17 434	22.0	2.4	9.4	8.3	55.3	14.6	12.7	28.0
	2012	35 180	17.1	2.3	38.9	7.7	32.0	9.0	8.4	14.6
Greenland - Groenland	1995	364	95.1	0.6	0.8	0.0	1.5	0.0	0.3	1.2
	2005	402	87.4	0.0	0.0	6.4	2.6	0.0	0.5	2.1
	2012	(e)473	96.7	0.0	0.0	0.7	2.6	0.0	1.7	0.9
Grenada - Grenade	1995	22	70.2	0.2	1.5	0.4	26.7	2.3	8.0	16.4
	2005	28	64.1	0.2	0.1	0.2	33.9	3.7	16.9	13.3
	2012	(e)35	36.2	0.2	0.1	11.2	52.3	11.4	22.2	18.7
Guam	1995	85	..	..	..	..	..	..	..	..
	2005	(e)52	12.9	2.0	8.1	9.4	19.8	3.5	9.3	7.1
	2012	(e)46	5.5	0.2	0.1	24.0	21.2	1.0	9.5	10.7
Guatemala	1995	1 936	57.3	3.7	1.7	0.4	36.1	8.8	1.8	25.5
	2005	5 381	36.4	3.4	5.6	0.9	53.3	9.2	2.0	42.0
	2012	10 125	47.2	4.4	4.1	6.7	37.1	10.6	2.1	24.4
Guinea - Guinée	1995	(e)702	11.8	2.8	1.0	77.6	6.8	5.7	0.9	0.1
	2005	(e)796	8.4	1.9	6.3	81.6	1.6	0.1	0.5	1.1
	2012	(e)1 386	7.1	2.8	27.2	59.7	2.9	1.1	0.9	0.9

For sources and notes, see end of table.

Pour les sources et les notes, se reporter à la fin du tableau.

Country or territory Pays ou territoires	Year Année	Total value (millions of dollars) (1) Valeur totale (millions de dollars) (1)	By main SITC Revision 3 product group (percentage) Par principaux groupes de produits de la CTCI Révision 3 (en pourcentage)					Of which: / dont :		
			All food items Produits alimentaires	Agricultural raw materials Matières premières agricoles	Fuels Combustibles	Ores, metals, precious stones and non-monetary gold Minerais, métaux, pierres précieuses et or (non monétaire)	Manufactured goods Articles manufacturés	Chemical products Produits chimiques	Machinery and transport equipment Machines et matériel de transport	Other manufactured goods Articles manufacturés divers
			0 + 1 + 22 + 4	2 - (22 + 27 + 28)	3	27 + 28 + 68 + 667 + 971	5 + 6 +7 + 8 - (667 + 68)	5	7	6 + 8 - (667 + 68)
Guinea-Bissau - Guinée-Bissau	1995	(e)24	84.6	5.5	7.5	..	2.6	0.5	0.7	1.4
	2005	(e)89	96.3	1.3	0.3	0.8	1.2	0.0	0.2	0.9
	2012	(e)130	90.9	1.1	6.2	0.5	1.3	0.1	0.4	0.8
Guyana	1995	(e)455	44.9	2.2	0.0	42.1	10.8	0.7	1.1	9.0
	2005	539	45.3	6.6	0.0	38.1	9.0	1.6	1.9	5.6
	2012	(e)1 309	31.8	5.1	0.1	56.5	6.5	1.2	2.5	2.8
Haiti - Haïti	1995	(e)110	25.4	0.8	0.3	0.3	69.4	7.2	2.8	59.4
	2005	(e)473	6.5	0.6	0.0	0.6	83.5	1.1	2.6	79.9
	2012	(e)821	7.3	1.0	0.0	1.7	85.0	1.8	3.3	79.8
Honduras	1995	(e)1 769	52.5	2.3	0.1	0.9	43.7	3.0	1.5	39.2
	2005	(e)5 048	32.4	2.2	0.3	4.0	59.8	2.5	6.7	50.6
	2012	(e)7 931	37.0	1.6	2.1	7.7	51.5	2.9	7.3	41.3
Hungary - Hongrie	1995	12 452	19.3	2.3	3.0	5.0	69.9	11.6	28.8	29.5
	2005	62 272	6.6	0.7	2.8	1.9	85.0	7.8	60.1	17.1
	2012	103 006	9.3	0.8	3.7	2.1	80.2	9.9	51.9	18.4
Iceland - Islande	1995	1 803	75.5	0.5	0.0	12.0	11.6	0.7	5.1	5.8
	2005	3 091	58.5	0.8	1.4	19.0	19.3	3.5	9.3	6.5
	2012	5 063	44.6	0.8	2.0	37.7	14.3	3.3	4.7	6.2
India - Inde	1995	31 699	18.7	1.3	1.7	18.6	58.2	8.1	7.5	42.5
	2005	100 353	9.0	1.3	10.5	19.8	58.4	11.4	10.5	36.4
	2012	289 565	10.5	4.1	18.8	11.3	54.4	11.9	13.7	28.7
Indonesia (...2002) - Indonésie (...2002)	1995	45 443	11.4	6.7	25.3	6.1	50.5	3.4	8.4	38.7
Indonesia - Indonésie	2005	85 660	11.7	5.1	27.7	8.7	46.9	5.2	15.9	25.8
	2012	190 032	17.7	6.0	33.3	7.3	35.6	5.6	12.0	18.0
Iran (Islamic Rep. of) - Iran (Rép. islamique d')	1995	(e)18 360	5.8	1.8	77.3	1.6	13.1	2.3	0.7	10.0
	2005	(e)60 012	2.7	0.4	85.3	2.2	8.1	2.8	1.3	4.0
	2012	(e)102 853	2.5	0.3	74.6	3.8	11.0	7.4	1.2	2.4
Iraq	1995	(e)1 963	0.1	0.2	95.3	0.0	4.1	0.4	3.4	0.3
	2005	(e)23 697	0.4	0.2	97.1	0.2	0.8	0.7	0.0	0.0
	2012	(e)94 400	0.1	0.1	98.9	0.3	0.6	0.5	0.1	0.0
Ireland - Irlande	1995	43 789	19.4	1.1	0.4	1.2	71.0	18.4	34.5	18.0
	2005	110 003	8.4	0.4	0.7	0.9	85.7	45.6	26.5	13.6
	2012	118 296	10.1	0.6	2.0	1.3	84.6	59.6	11.3	13.6
Israel - Israël	1995	19 047	5.4	1.8	0.0	31.6	58.9	14.7	26.8	17.3
	2005	42 771	2.5	0.7	0.1	38.6	45.2	14.8	18.2	12.2
	2012	63 141	3.2	0.6	1.7	29.4	64.9	26.8	24.6	13.6
Italy - Italie	1995	230 441	6.6	0.7	1.2	1.5	89.2	8.0	37.7	43.6
	2005	372 957	6.5	0.6	3.4	1.7	85.0	10.6	36.8	37.6
	2012	500 743	7.7	0.7	6.0	4.3	79.7	11.5	34.1	34.1
Jamaica - Jamaïque	1995	1 424	21.7	0.3	0.5	49.4	28.1	2.7	3.1	22.4
	2005	1 514	17.2	0.1	7.4	68.5	6.8	3.7	1.1	2.0
	2012	1 712	22.0	0.1	22.7	39.1	15.8	12.4	1.3	2.0
Japan - Japon	1995	442 937	0.5	0.6	0.6	1.2	95.1	6.8	70.3	18.0
	2005	594 941	0.5	0.5	0.7	2.1	91.8	8.8	64.1	18.9
	2012	798 568	0.6	0.8	1.7	3.7	88.8	9.9	59.6	19.3
Jordan - Jordanie	1995	1 769	25.0	1.5	0.2	18.5	54.1	32.6	9.5	12.0
	2005	4 279	13.8	0.3	0.6	10.9	73.5	24.1	11.8	37.7
	2012	(e)7 843	14.2	0.4	1.2	14.5	69.6	32.4	10.7	26.6
Kazakhstan	1995	5 227	9.9	2.8	25.0	24.1	38.1	10.3	6.0	21.9
	2005	27 846	2.4	0.7	70.1	14.7	12.0	1.9	1.2	8.9
	2012	92 282	3.3	0.1	69.9	14.2	12.5	3.8	1.4	7.3

For sources and notes, see end of table.

Pour les sources et les notes, se reporter à la fin du tableau.

Country or territory / Pays ou territoires	Year / Année	Total value (millions of dollars) (1) / Valeur totale (millions de dollars) (1)	By main SITC Revision 3 product group (percentage) / Par principaux groupes de produits de la CTCI Révision 3 (en pourcentage)					Of which: / dont :		
			All food items / Produits alimentaires	Agricultural raw materials / Matières premières agricoles	Fuels / Combustibles	Ores, metals, precious stones and non-monetary gold / Minerais, métaux, pierres précieuses et or (non monétaire)	Manufactured goods / Articles manufacturés	Chemical products / Produits chimiques	Machinery and transport equipment / Machines et matériel de transport	Other manufactured goods / Articles manufacturés divers
			0 + 1 + 22 + 4	2 - (22 + 27 + 28)	3	27 + 28 + 68 + 667 + 971	5 + 6 +7 + 8 - (667 + 68)	5	7	6 + 8 - (667 + 68)
Kenya	1995	1 826	54.7	8.3	5.0	2.7	28.9	6.6	3.2	19.1
	2005	3 420	37.9	12.5	15.5	2.8	31.0	7.0	3.1	20.9
	2012	(e)6 127	42.5	12.9	4.9	4.0	35.7	9.0	5.3	21.3
Kiribati	1995	(e)7	85.3	2.0	..	0.6	5.8	0.1	0.4	5.3
	2005	(e)4	76.5	-0.1	0.0	0.7	20.1	1.9	1.9	16.3
	2012	(e)6	90.5	0.3	0.1	0.1	7.8	0.1	5.6	2.1
Korea, Dem. People's Rep. of - Corée, Rép. populaire dém. de	1995	(e)959	15.5	2.7	2.0	9.5	69.3	5.4	27.6	36.2
	2005	(e)1 338	11.1	2.3	10.1	13.5	61.2	7.7	28.7	24.7
	2012	(e)3 750	4.5	1.3	42.8	16.8	34.6	3.7	7.0	24.0
Korea, Republic of - Corée, République de	1995	125 056	2.3	1.3	2.0	3.0	91.5	7.2	52.5	31.8
	2005	284 418	1.1	0.8	5.5	1.8	90.8	9.8	61.0	20.1
	2012	547 854	1.2	1.1	10.5	2.7	84.5	11.2	52.5	20.8
Kuwait - Koweït	1995	12 944	0.5	0.1	89.8	1.1	8.2	3.2	2.6	2.5
	2005	(e)44 902	0.3	0.1	90.5	0.8	8.3	6.5	0.6	1.3
	2012	(e)113 999	0.2	0.2	91.7	0.8	7.1	5.0	1.3	0.8
Kyrgyzstan - Kirghizistan	1995	(e)412	21.4	15.0	13.1	13.6	36.2	7.0	9.7	19.5
	2005	(e)672	12.3	9.3	10.1	34.3	32.4	1.1	8.9	22.4
	2012	(e)1 894	14.8	3.9	13.6	17.6	47.8	3.2	21.9	22.7
Lao People's Dem. Rep. - Rép. dém. populaire lao	1995	311	11.1	42.3	0.3	5.3	40.7	1.6	0.3	38.8
	2005	553	6.6	28.1	11.0	16.8	35.5	0.3	1.5	33.7
	2012	2 269	8.3	13.9	18.7	42.4	16.3	3.1	1.3	11.9
Latvia - Lettonie	1995	1 305	14.4	23.0	1.7	1.0	58.1	6.9	16.3	34.9
	2005	5 303	11.3	17.1	8.9	3.5	55.4	6.0	12.4	37.0
	2012	12 610	18.6	9.4	7.9	3.7	52.6	6.8	17.5	28.3
Lebanon - Liban	1995	(e)656	19.5	1.5	0.1	10.6	68.3	12.5	14.4	41.4
	2005	(e)2 337	15.7	2.5	0.6	16.7	63.5	10.5	17.4	35.6
	2012	(e)5 615	16.2	1.1	2.2	32.0	48.1	11.2	13.2	23.7
Lesotho	1995	(a)160	3.7	0.9	0.0	3.7	91.6	0.3	3.9	87.4
	2005	(e)651	2.6	0.5	0.0	6.8	90.0	0.1	1.4	88.5
	2012	(e)1 100	0.1	0.5	0.0	45.7	51.7	0.0	1.4	50.3
Liberia - Libéria	1995	(e)820	0.1	1.9	2.1	81.2	14.7	0.4	13.9	0.3
	2005	131	0.4	11.0	0.8	2.7	85.0	0.1	84.6	0.3
	2012	459	2.9	31.4	17.8	24.0	23.8	0.1	23.3	0.3
Libya - Libye	1995	(e)9 364	0.2	0.2	92.0	0.0	7.4	4.1	0.1	3.2
	2005	(e)31 358	0.1	0.0	95.4	0.6	3.9	2.7	0.1	1.2
	2012	(e)62 216	0.0	0.0	97.1	0.8	2.0	1.3	0.1	0.6
Lithuania - Lituanie	1995	2 706	18.1	7.8	11.4	5.0	57.7	14.3	15.7	27.7
	2005	12 070	12.4	3.3	26.6	1.5	55.5	8.4	21.5	25.5
	2012	29 653	17.6	2.2	24.5	1.5	52.3	13.0	17.4	22.0
Luxembourg	1995	(e)7 244	4.9	0.9	0.8	5.5	57.7	6.2	15.9	35.6
	2005	(e)18 797	6.0	0.6	0.9	5.5	84.4	8.6	29.1	46.7
	2012	(e)19 447	7.7	2.5	1.4	6.4	78.5	9.0	20.8	48.7
Madagascar	1995	(e)507	63.7	4.8	2.6	5.5	22.3	1.7	0.6	20.0
	2005	836	32.2	4.9	2.7	4.8	51.5	1.4	2.7	47.4
	2012	(e)1 500	39.7	2.7	2.6	18.6	36.0	1.9	1.3	32.7
Malawi	1995	433	86.2	2.3	0.1	0.1	11.1	0.3	1.7	9.1
	2005	495	79.8	4.0	0.1	0.3	15.3	0.6	2.4	12.3
	2012	(e)1 184	75.0	4.1	0.2	7.2	13.6	5.6	2.7	5.3
Malaysia - Malaisie	1995	73 778	9.5	6.2	7.0	1.5	74.5	3.0	55.1	16.4
	2005	141 624	6.9	2.5	13.4	1.3	74.5	5.8	54.0	14.7
	2012	227 303	12.5	2.4	20.3	2.6	61.6	6.6	38.0	17.0

For sources and notes, see end of table.

Pour les sources et les notes, se reporter à la fin du tableau.

Country or territory / Pays ou territoires	Year / Année	Total value (millions of dollars) (1) / Valeur totale (millions de dollars) (1)	By main SITC Revision 3 product group (percentage) / Par principaux groupes de produits de la CTCI Révision 3 (en pourcentage)					Of which: / dont :		
			All food items / Produits alimentaires	Agricultural raw materials / Matières premières agricoles	Fuels / Combustibles	Ores, metals, precious stones and non-monetary gold / Minerais, métaux, pierres précieuses et or (non monétaire)	Manufactured goods / Articles manufacturés	Chemical products / Produits chimiques	Machinery and transport equipment / Machines et matériel de transport	Other manufactured goods / Articles manufacturés divers
			0 + 1 + 22 + 4	2 - (22 + 27 + 28)	3	27 + 28 + 68 + 667 + 971	5 + 6 +7 + 8 - (667 + 68)	5	7	6 + 8 - (667 + 68)
Maldives	1995	(e)85	68.7	0.6	..	0.2	30.0	0.3	0.5	29.2
	2005	154	77.8	0.1	6.6	0.9	14.4	1.9	3.8	8.7
	2012	(e)314	72.1	0.1	0.0	2.5	5.2	0.1	3.9	1.2
Mali	1995	(e)443	18.2	58.1	1.0	17.1	5.3	0.3	1.1	3.9
	2005	1 075	5.5	48.3	0.6	37.3	8.0	0.7	4.2	3.1
	2012	(e)2 164	7.7	35.6	3.0	41.3	12.3	6.0	3.5	2.8
Malta - Malte	1995	1 913	2.2	0.1	4.8	0.8	91.0	2.0	62.0	26.9
	2005	2 431	5.1	0.1	3.5	0.3	89.1	6.1	62.5	20.4
	2012	(e)4 250	3.5	0.2	40.2	0.9	54.3	8.2	33.2	12.9
Marshall Islands - Îles Marshall	1995	23	58.6	0.5	..	0.4	17.3	0.0	15.6	1.6
	2005	25	10.9	0.0	0.0	0.0	88.1	0.0	88.0	0.1
	2012	(e)35	15.3	0.0	2.7	0.1	81.7	0.0	81.4	0.3
Mauritania - Mauritanie	1995	(e)509	59.4	0.5	0.3	38.4	1.3	0.0	0.7	0.5
	2005	(e)556	44.0	0.2	0.0	50.0	1.4	0.1	0.8	0.6
	2012	(e)2 641	26.7	0.2	7.7	64.5	1.0	0.2	0.5	0.4
Mauritius - Maurice	1995	1 538	28.9	0.7	0.0	2.0	68.4	0.8	2.3	65.3
	2005	2 144	26.9	0.3	0.1	2.8	63.0	1.4	15.1	46.6
	2012	(e)2 673	30.5	0.6	0.1	3.7	49.6	2.9	3.1	43.7
Mexico - Mexique	1995	79 541	7.7	1.3	10.3	3.1	77.5	5.0	52.3	20.2
	2005	214 207	5.4	0.5	14.9	2.0	77.0	3.7	53.2	20.1
	2012	370 827	5.8	0.4	14.1	5.9	72.7	4.2	54.4	14.2
Micronesia (Federated States of) - Micronésie (États fédérés de)	1995	21	86.3	0.3	..	0.0	8.8	..	0.0	8.8
	2005	19	94.3	0.9	..	1.5	2.9	0.0	0.3	2.6
	2012	(e)35	96.7	0.2	0.1	0.8	1.0	0.0	0.1	0.9
Mongolia - Mongolie	1995	(e)473	2.2	27.7	0.0	59.9	10.2	0.6	1.7	7.8
	2005	1 064	1.4	8.2	3.9	70.2	16.3	0.1	0.8	15.4
	2012	(e)4 379	1.7	8.7	11.9	74.1	3.6	0.1	0.5	3.0
Montenegro - Monténégro	2012	469	15.5	6.5	13.8	44.6	19.6	3.3	7.1	9.2
Montserrat	1995	(e)3	74.0	0.0	..	0.2	22.6	1.3	17.8	3.5
	2005	(e)1	0.2	1.1	13.6	6.4	69.4	7.1	44.4	17.9
	2012	(e)2	13.2	1.1	0.0	10.2	66.3	0.2	44.8	21.3
Morocco - Maroc	1995	(e)6 881	27.1	2.9	1.8	9.6	58.4	16.5	7.0	34.9
	2005	11 185	20.8	1.7	5.9	8.2	62.5	11.2	17.8	33.6
	2012	21 417	17.5	1.1	6.4	11.7	62.8	19.1	20.4	23.3
Mozambique	1995	174	64.1	14.2	2.2	5.7	13.2	1.1	3.9	8.1
	2005	1 745	11.5	3.4	14.6	67.3	3.2	0.3	1.7	1.2
	2012	(e)4 100	13.9	3.6	38.7	35.1	6.8	1.6	2.4	2.9
Myanmar	1995	(e)860	41.9	38.5	0.2	7.4	11.9	1.0	0.9	10.0
	2005	(e)3 967	20.7	19.0	33.3	4.2	22.8	0.2	0.7	21.9
	2012	(e)8 900	19.3	13.7	39.3	18.2	9.4	0.3	0.5	8.7
Namibia - Namibie	1995	(a)1 409	39.4	1.0	1.5	38.3	15.6	3.8	3.7	8.1
	2005	(e)2 070	29.8	0.6	1.2	43.0	25.2	10.4	4.6	10.1
	2012	(e)4 034	23.9	0.7	1.3	53.3	20.6	6.0	9.5	5.1
Nauru	1995	(e)28	1.0	0.5	..	70.0	27.9	0.7	25.3	1.9
	2005	(e)3	7.5	1.0	0.6	25.2	62.8	7.4	38.8	16.7
	2012	90	0.3	0.1	0.1	96.0	3.5	0.4	1.0	2.1
Nepal - Népal	1995	(e)359	7.8	1.1	..	0.1	83.7	1.2	0.1	82.4
	2005	(e)888	23.1	1.1	0.0	7.4	68.3	7.8	0.5	60.0
	2012	(e)899	22.5	3.2	0.0	4.3	70.1	5.4	1.4	63.3
Netherlands - Pays-Bas	1995	(e)203 187	20.5	4.1	8.1	3.2	61.4	17.4	24.3	19.7
	2005	(e)406 372	13.1	3.0	12.0	2.7	60.0	15.7	28.3	16.0
	2012	(e)655 700	14.4	2.8	19.1	3.0	53.7	16.5	22.9	14.3

For sources and notes, see end of table.

Pour les sources et les notes, se reporter à la fin du tableau.

Country or territory / Pays ou territoires	Year / Année	Total value (millions of dollars) (1) / Valeur totale (millions de dollars) (1)	By main SITC Revision 3 product group (percentage) / Par principaux groupes de produits de la CTCI Révision 3 (en pourcentage)					Of which: / dont :		
			All food items / Produits alimentaires	Agricultural raw materials / Matières premières agricoles	Fuels / Combustibles	Ores, metals, precious stones and non-monetary gold / Minerais, métaux, pierres précieuses et or (non monétaire)	Manu-factured goods / Articles manu-facturés	Chemical products / Produits chimiques	Machinery and transport equipment / Machines et matériel de transport	Other manu-factured goods / Articles manu-facturés divers
			0 + 1 + 22 + 4	2 - (22 + 27 + 28)	3	27 + 28 + 68 + 667 + 971	5 + 6 +7 + 8 - (667 + 68)	5	7	6 + 8 - (667 + 68)
Netherlands Antilles - Antilles néerlandaises	1995	(e)1 522	12.1	0.1	65.9	3.0	14.2	2.0	6.5	5.7
	2005	(e)608	1.9	0.1	75.9	1.0	15.4	3.7	6.3	5.4
New Caledonia - Nouvelle-Calédonie	1995	(e)570	2.7	0.4	..	41.0	55.5	0.1	0.6	54.7
	2005	1 114	2.9	0.1	1.0	28.8	66.6	0.2	1.7	64.6
	2012	1 293	1.9	0.2	0.0	37.2	58.8	5.1	1.7	52.0
New Zealand - Nouvelle-Zélande	1995	13 745	42.4	18.0	1.6	6.3	30.5	7.6	8.6	14.3
	2005	21 729	49.6	10.3	2.5	5.0	31.2	5.8	11.5	13.9
	2012	37 092	54.0	10.7	4.7	4.7	22.3	5.0	7.5	9.8
Nicaragua	1995	509	68.8	2.8	0.6	2.7	24.8	1.6	5.7	17.6
	2005	866	51.4	1.6	0.9	4.0	41.4	2.6	8.9	30.0
	2012	2 690	50.9	2.5	1.5	12.3	32.2	0.9	7.9	23.3
Niger	1995	273	15.9	4.6	4.6	20.9	53.8	40.7	5.9	7.3
	2005	486	20.7	3.8	15.0	20.2	38.0	29.7	4.9	3.4
	2012	(e)1 500	14.9	5.0	31.8	17.5	28.1	24.0	1.5	2.5
Nigeria - Nigéria	1995	(e)12 342	3.0	2.3	91.7	0.3	2.5	0.5	0.3	1.7
	2005	(e)45 789	1.4	0.3	96.3	0.2	1.2	0.1	0.5	0.6
	2012	(e)127 287	1.6	0.9	94.8	0.6	2.1	0.3	0.9	0.8
Niue - Nioué	1995	0	62.1	0.4	2.5	0.2	38.5	5.0	13.3	20.2
	2005	0	6.2	1.4	0.1	25.9	66.4	5.9	28.9	31.7
	2012	(e)0	44.4	0.0	0.5	0.3	53.4	6.5	35.6	11.3
Northern Mariana Islands - Îles Mariannes du Nord	1995	(e)432	2.8	0.1	0.0	3.2	44.7	0.5	21.8	22.5
	2005	(e)691	0.8	2.1	0.0	4.5	88.7	1.2	13.1	74.5
	2012	(e)4	0.2	0.0	0.0	24.1	74.3	14.8	24.8	34.7
Norway - Norvège	1995	41 740	8.3	1.5	47.3	8.8	26.8	3.1	13.3	10.4
	2005	103 759	5.2	0.5	67.7	6.0	17.1	2.7	8.2	6.2
	2012	160 999	6.0	0.5	69.8	5.4	15.2	2.2	7.9	5.1
Oman	1995	5 917	4.1	0.0	81.2	2.0	12.3	0.6	7.7	4.1
	2005	18 692	2.8	0.0	84.9	1.0	7.0	2.0	2.0	3.0
	2012	52 138	3.7	0.0	74.7	4.7	16.8	8.8	3.4	4.6
Pakistan	1995	8 158	11.8	3.8	1.0	0.2	83.0	0.7	0.5	81.8
	2005	16 050	12.0	1.5	4.2	0.4	81.8	3.0	1.8	76.9
	2012	24 614	17.0	3.2	1.3	2.0	75.2	3.8	1.5	69.9
Palau - Palaos	1995	(e)14	75.2	1.8	0.0	0.1	22.5	0.1	3.9	18.6
	2005	13	92.5	1.2	..	0.9	3.8	0.0	2.1	1.7
	2012	(e)8	93.1	0.1	0.0	4.0	2.2	0.4	1.1	0.7
Panama	1995	577	32.6	0.4	2.8	1.8	61.7	5.1	40.3	16.3
	2005	(e)7 050	25.8	0.4	6.5	2.5	63.0	5.6	35.8	21.5
	2012	(e)16 220	9.3	0.4	9.7	3.1	77.6	25.0	22.6	30.0
Papua New Guinea - Papouasie-Nouvelle-Guinée	1995	(e)2 654	20.4	18.9	23.7	36.1	0.8	0.1	0.6	0.1
	2005	(e)3 492	19.6	10.2	26.9	39.2	2.6	0.2*	1.3	1.1
	2012	(e)6 537	18.4	7.6	20.3	50.7	1.5	0.1	0.8	0.6
Paraguay	1995	919	48.0	31.7	4.0	0.3	15.6	2.2	0.9	12.5
	2005	1 655	70.0	8.7	8.6	1.2	11.4	2.3	0.7	8.3
	2012	7 271	59.7	2.9	23.2	1.9	11.6	3.2	1.0	7.4
Peru - Pérou	1995	5 440	28.8	2.5	4.9	50.2	13.6	2.2	0.6	10.8
	2005	17 114	17.0	1.5	9.3	57.9	14.3	2.4	0.8	11.0
	2012	(e)45 016	18.6	1.1	12.9	55.1	12.3	3.5	1.0	7.8
Philippines	1995	17 447	12.8	1.2	1.5	5.4	40.8	2.0	22.2	16.7
	2005	41 255	6.1	0.5	1.9	2.4	89.0	1.3	74.4	13.3
	2012	51 995	8.9	0.8	2.4	6.0	81.8	3.7	59.6	18.4
Poland - Pologne	1995	22 862	10.4	2.8	8.2	7.3	71.1	7.7	21.1	42.4
	2005	89 378	9.4	1.2	5.1	4.0	78.1	6.7	38.6	32.9
	2012	179 604	12.0	1.3	5.0	5.2	76.5	9.1	37.8	29.6

For sources and notes, see end of table.

Pour les sources et les notes, se reporter à la fin du tableau.

Country or territory / Pays ou territoires	Year / Année	Total value (millions of dollars) (1) / Valeur totale (millions de dollars) (1)	All food items / Produits alimentaires	Agricultural raw materials / Matières premières agricoles	Fuels / Combustibles	Ores, metals, precious stones and non-monetary gold / Minerais, métaux, pierres précieuses et or (non monétaire)	Manufactured goods / Articles manufacturés	Chemical products / Produits chimiques	Machinery and transport equipment / Machines et matériel de transport	Other manufactured goods / Articles manufacturés divers
			0 + 1 + 22 + 4	2 - (22 + 27 + 28)	3	27 + 28 + 68 + 667 + 971	5 + 6 +7 + 8 - (667 + 68)	5	7	6 + 8 - (667 + 68)
Portugal	1995	23 370	7.4	4.8	3.2	2.1	81.1	4.9	26.1	50.8
	2005	38 086	8.4	2.7	3.9	2.7	78.9	7.0	33.0	38.9
	2012	58 379	11.2	2.7	8.2	4.5	72.5	8.7	26.6	37.1
Qatar	1995	(e)3 557	0.3	0.1	81.4	0.8	17.1	9.2	1.3	6.6
	2005	(e)25 762	0.1	0.0	84.7	0.3	10.1	8.3	0.7	1.2
	2012	(e)132 968	0.0	0.0	91.5	1.3	6.8	5.6	0.5	0.7
Republic of Moldova - République de Moldova	1995	746	67.0	1.5	0.6	3.0	27.8	1.6	7.7	18.5
	2005	1 091	46.5	2.6	0.1	2.1	48.5	1.7	5.2	41.6
	2012	2 162	37.2	0.7	2.1	3.1	56.9	4.2	15.5	37.2
Romania - Roumanie	1995	7 910	6.6	3.3	7.9	3.5	78.3	10.7	13.1	54.4
	2005	27 730	3.0	2.3	10.7	4.2	79.2	5.7	25.4	48.1
	2012	57 904	8.5	2.3	5.5	3.8	77.1	6.4	39.8	30.8
Russian Federation - Fédération de Russie	1995	(e)78 217	1.8	3.3	43.1	9.9	26.1	5.9	7.0	13.1
	2005	241 452	1.6	2.8	61.8	7.2	18.2	4.2	4.1	9.9
	2012	524 565	3.2	1.8	70.3	3.9	14.2	4.7	2.7	6.8
Rwanda	1995	(e)52	72.7	9.7	0.1	8.3	7.8	1.2	2.5	4.1
	2005	(e)125	44.7	1.0	1.5	39.9	9.7	1.9	4.9	2.9
	2012	(e)591	52.8	3.3	5.9	29.3	8.6	0.6	3.3	4.7
Saint Helena - Sainte-Hélène	1995	(e)5	70.6	0.0	0.0	7.4	25.7	5.0	12.4	8.3
	2005	(e)20	40.0	0.7	0.0	0.1	56.9	6.4	28.8	21.7
	2012	(e)44	62.1	0.0	..	0.2	37.4	10.1	19.4	8.0
Saint Kitts and Nevis - Saint-Kitts-et-Nevis	1995	(e)19	40.0	0.2	0.1	0.1	56.7	0.4	50.1	6.2
	2005	(e)34	10.3	1.9	0.0	0.4	81.8	0.1	76.9	4.8
	2012	(e)45	5.7	-0.2	0.0	1.0	85.3	0.6	70.1	14.6
Saint Lucia - Sainte-Lucie	1995	109	58.3	0.5	0.0	0.1	37.1	1.0	10.3	25.8
	2005	64	24.0	0.1	52.8	0.7	19.8	1.0	10.2	8.6
	2012	(e)160	31.5	0.1	31.0	2.3	35.1	3.1	13.5	18.5
Saint Pierre and Miquelon - Saint-Pierre-et-Miquelon	1995	(e)10	82.5	1.9	..	0.1	14.2	0.9	4.8	8.5
	2005	(e)12	51.6	5.7	2.8	0.4	39.5	0.6	1.4	37.4
	2012	(e)6	56.6	0.0	..	4.7	34.4	1.4	1.6	31.3
Saint Vincent and the Grenadines - Saint-Vincent-et-les Grenadines	1995	(e)43	67.0	0.2	0.0	0.2	32.2	0.7	21.4	10.1
	2005	40	20.4	0.2	0.0	0.1	79.2	4.7	70.8	3.6
	2012	43	49.5	0.1	1.0	4.1	44.9	1.0	30.0	13.9
Samoa	1995	(e)9	12.7	1.1	..	2.0	83.7	0.1	75.7	7.9
	2005	(e)87	25.9	0.4	1.2	0.2	28.9	0.3	26.8	1.8
	2012	(e)76	38.2	2.2	0.0	1.7	43.4	1.7	30.8	11.0
Sao Tome and Principe - Sao Tomé-et-Principe	1995	(e)5	58.6	2.2	..	0.1	38.1	5.0	18.4	14.8
	2005	(e)7	67.1	0.8	..	0.4	29.7	0.4	19.2	10.1
	2012	(e)11	51.3	0.4	0.3	2.7	45.1	1.0	8.3	35.8
Saudi Arabia - Arabie saoudite	1995	(e)49 030	1.1	0.2	83.8	1.0	13.7	9.0	1.8	3.0
	2005	(e)180 737	0.6	0.1	88.4	0.5	10.3	7.7	1.1	1.6
	2012	(e)388 329	1.3	0.0	84.9	0.7	13.0	10.3	0.7	2.0
Senegal - Sénégal	1995	(e)993	39.8	6.7	13.1	11.1	28.9	22.2	1.8	4.9
	2005	(e)1 471	32.5	2.5	19.0	4.3	41.5	23.1	8.3	10.1
	2012	(e)2 532	29.7	1.5	20.6	12.2	35.6	16.9	5.2	13.4
Serbia and Montenegro - Serbie-et-Monténégro	1995	(e)1 531	28.2	4.0	2.1	14.8	49.0	9.0	12.1	27.9
	2005	(e)5 065	17.5	2.6	3.2	8.2	56.8	9.8	8.7	38.3
Serbia - Serbie	2012	11 353	23.4	1.7	3.5	9.0	61.6	8.1	22.4	31.0
Seychelles	1995	53	68.4	0.2	19.2	0.2	10.6	1.3	5.5	3.7
	2005	340	68.9	0.0	10.2	0.3	20.3	2.7	10.9	6.7
	2012	(e)497	86.3	0.2	3.0	0.8	9.7	0.4	3.4	5.9

For sources and notes, see end of table.

Pour les sources et les notes, se reporter à la fin du tableau.

Country or territory / Pays ou territoires	Year / Année	Total value (millions of dollars) (1) / Valeur totale (millions de dollars) (1)	By main SITC Revision 3 product group (percentage) / Par principaux groupes de produits de la CTCI Révision 3 (en pourcentage)					Of which: / dont :		
			All food items / Produits alimentaires	Agricultural raw materials / Matières premières agricoles	Fuels / Combustibles	Ores, metals, precious stones and non-monetary gold / Minerais, métaux, pierres précieuses et or (non monétaire)	Manufactured goods / Articles manufacturés	Chemical products / Produits chimiques	Machinery and transport equipment / Machines et matériel de transport	Other manufactured goods / Articles manufacturés divers
			0 + 1 + 22 + 4	2 - (22 + 27 + 28)	3	27 + 28 + 68 + 667 + 971	5 + 6 +7 + 8 - (667 + 68)	5	7	6 + 8 - (667 + 68)
Sierra Leone	1995	(e)42	52.8	1.0	0.6	30.1	14.6	1.2	3.9	9.6
	2005	(e)159	10.7	0.8	0.7	58.2	29.1	4.0	13.1	12.0
	2012	(e)1 112	30.0	-4.1	0.0	53.2	19.8	0.3	7.4	12.1
Singapore - Singapour	1995	118 263	3.9	1.1	6.8	2.3	83.6	6.0	65.6	12.0
	2005	229 652	1.7	0.3	12.2	2.1	79.9	11.4	58.7	9.8
	2012	408 393	2.2	0.3	18.5	1.8	69.1	13.2	45.3	10.5
Sint Maarten (Dutch part) - Saint-Martin (partie néerlandaise)	2012	131	0.2	0.0	0.3	8.7	1.5	0.0	0.9	0.6
Slovakia - Slovaquie	1995	8 374	6.2	3.6	4.2	3.6	82.3	12.6	19.0	50.8
	2005	31 852	4.6	1.8	5.9	2.6	83.3	5.5	44.2	33.6
	2012	80 752	5.9	1.1	5.9	3.3	83.8	4.3	54.8	24.8
Slovenia - Slovénie	1995	8 316	3.9	1.8	1.2	3.4	89.5	10.5	31.4	47.6
	2005	17 896	2.8	1.2	2.1	4.8	89.0	12.9	39.2	36.8
	2012	(e)32 173	3.2	1.7	5.4	4.0	69.0	14.8	29.8	24.3
Solomon Islands - Îles Salomon	1995	(e)168	36.7	61.9	..	0.1	1.2	0.0	0.5	0.8
	2005	(e)103	24.5	73.1	0.1	0.4	1.8	0.2	0.9	0.7
	2012	(e)496	20.2	62.2	0.1	15.8	1.5	0.1	0.8	0.6
Somalia - Somalie	1995	(e)170	90.1	6.8	0.0	0.2	2.6	0.5	0.8	1.3
	2005	(e)250	68.6	11.1	0.7	5.4	2.9	0.7	1.1	1.1
	2012	510	74.3	14.3	0.0	0.2	11.1	2.0	3.5	5.6
South Africa - Afrique du Sud	1995	(a)27 853	10.0	3.2	10.9	29.8	43.5	7.2	17.3	19.1
	2005	46 991	8.9	2.5	10.0	32.1	45.2	7.5	17.9	19.8
	2012	86 712	7.0	1.7	9.0	32.8	33.0	6.1	15.4	11.4
Spain - Espagne	1995	89 616	15.4	1.6	1.7	2.6	77.9	8.5	42.4	27.1
	2005	192 798	14.1	1.2	4.3	2.5	76.3	12.0	40.2	24.2
	2012	285 936	15.3	1.2	7.4	5.0	66.6	13.3	30.8	22.5
Sri Lanka	1995	(e)3 798	18.7	4.3	0.4	6.9	69.0	0.9	3.6	64.5
	2005	6 160	22.2	2.1	0.0	8.6	65.2	1.3	4.5	59.4
	2012	9 370	25.9	3.3	0.4	5.1	65.2	1.5	6.1	57.6
State of Palestine - État de Palestine	1995	394	..	..	..	..	..	..	..	..
	2005	(e)335	19.3	2.6	3.6	3.8	70.6	8.5	5.4	56.7
	2012	(e)949	22.9	1.4	0.1	15.4	59.8	4.5	3.0	52.3
Sudan (...2011) - Soudan (...2011)	1995	(e)556	47.7	41.6	0.2	3.1	7.2	0.2	0.9	6.2
	2005	4 506	5.3	4.1	85.6	3.0	1.8	0.2	1.3	0.3
Sudan - Soudan	2012	3 384	11.1	2.6	30.4	49.5	6.4	2.5	0.8	3.1
Suriname	1995	483	18.6	0.7	1.9	73.9	3.8	0.4	1.1	2.2
	2005	997	13.4	0.4	4.0	62.6	5.2	1.4	2.8	1.1
	2012	(e)2 564	11.5	1.3	9.5	71.8	5.9	0.9	2.6	2.5
Swaziland	1995	(a)866	34.6	9.8	0.4	1.3	53.8	22.5	9.1	22.2
	2005	(e)1 770	26.3	7.6	2.3	3.3	60.4	27.1	11.6	21.6
	2012	(e)1 900	26.1	16.5	0.4	8.1	43.0	14.1	10.4	18.5
Sweden - Suède	1995	77 436	2.2	6.5	1.9	3.2	78.6	6.6	42.1	29.9
	2005	130 264	3.5	4.0	5.0	3.3	78.4	10.6	41.8	26.1
	2012	172 631	4.9	3.6	9.3	5.9	71.6	10.6	36.3	24.7
Switzerland - Suisse	1995	81 641	3.0	0.7	0.1	5.3	90.9	26.0	31.4	33.5
	2005	130 930	2.6	0.4	2.1	4.3	90.6	34.7	25.5	30.4
	2012	225 949	3.7	0.3	3.2	5.8	85.3	37.0	19.0	29.2
Syrian Arab Republic - République arabe syrienne	1995	(e)3 563	12.8	9.0	63.4	1.0	13.7	0.6	1.1	12.0
	2005	(e)8 708	21.6	2.8	49.4	1.6	24.0	8.6	3.3	12.2
	2012	(e)4 000	40.5	1.0	17.3	3.3	37.8	8.6	4.9	24.3
Tajikistan - Tadjikistan	1995	(e)749	12.4	34.1	0.9	37.3	15.2	1.9	3.1	10.2
	2005	(e)892	4.5	10.8	7.6	57.9	17.6	2.3	3.7	11.6
	2012	(e)1 333	4.2	16.6	1.5	58.7	12.5	2.6	1.5	8.4

For sources and notes, see end of table.

Pour les sources et les notes, se reporter à la fin du tableau.

Country or territory / Pays ou territoires	Year / Année	Total value (millions of dollars) (1) / Valeur totale (millions de dollars) (1)	By main SITC Revision 3 product group (percentage) / Par principaux groupes de produits de la CTCI Révision 3 (en pourcentage)					Of which: / dont :		
			All food items / Produits alimentaires	Agricultural raw materials / Matières premières agricoles	Fuels Combustibles	Ores, metals, precious stones and non-monetary gold / Minerais, métaux, pierres précieuses et or (non monétaire)	Manu-factured goods / Articles manu-facturés	Chemical products / Produits chimiques	Machinery and transport equipment / Machines et matériel de transport	Other manu-factured goods / Articles manu-facturés divers
			0 + 1 + 22 + 4	2 - (22 + 27 + 28)	3	27 + 28 + 68 + 667 + 971	5 + 6 +7 + 8 - (667 + 68)	5	7	6 + 8 - (667 + 68)
TFYR of Macedonia - LERY de Macédoine	1995	1 204	18.3	5.2	0.4	17.9	58.2	6.5	12.9	39.7
	2005	2 041	16.4	0.8	8.0	3.0	71.6	4.4	5.4	61.8
	2012	4 002	14.9	0.6	6.4	6.3	71.8	17.0	9.9	44.9
Thailand - Thaïlande	1995	56 439	19.3	5.4	0.7	2.9	70.9	4.4	33.7	32.9
	2005	110 110	11.6	4.5	4.3	2.4	75.7	8.1	44.7	22.9
	2012	229 545	13.4	4.9	6.5	5.2	70.0	10.1	40.5	19.4
Timor-Leste	2005	(e)8	7.6	0.6	83.7	0.5	7.2	0.2	3.6	3.5
	2012	(e)12	1.6	0.2	97.4	0.1	0.5	0.1	0.3	0.2
Togo	1995	383	16.8	30.1	6.5	35.1	11.4	0.9	3.7	6.8
	2005	(e)660	27.7	11.7	11.2	12.1	37.2	3.9	4.7	28.5
	2012	900	15.5	7.9	9.9	28.7	37.8	6.2	7.6	24.0
Tokelau - Tokélaou	1995	(e)1	11.9	0.1	..	0.9	84.6	0.1	57.3	27.2
	2005	(e)0	1.6	30.9	0.3	3.0	46.3	2.9	9.8	33.6
	2012	(e)0	5.5	0.1	0.0	1.4	86.8	8.0	33.4	45.4
Tonga	1995	(e)15	84.1	0.5	..	0.5	2.9	0.2	1.1	1.6
	2005	(e)10	54.1	14.2	0.0	2.0	7.5	1.1	2.9	3.4
	2012	(e)16	58.1	7.9	0.1	7.4	24.0	2.6	11.9	9.5
Trinidad and Tobago - Trinité-et-Tobago	1995	2 467	10.3	0.2	43.0	1.5	44.6	26.5	2.4	15.7
	2005	9 611	2.7	0.0	66.7	0.7	28.9	21.7	1.2	5.9
	2012	(e)12 981	2.4	0.0	63.9	2.2	31.5	23.3	1.2	7.0
Tunisia - Tunisie	1995	5 475	9.8	0.6	8.5	1.8	79.3	11.9	9.4	57.9
	2005	10 494	10.4	0.6	12.9	1.2	74.9	9.4	19.2	46.3
	2012	(e)17 008	11.0	0.6	15.3	1.9	71.2	10.3	26.4	34.4
Turkey - Turquie	1995	21 599	19.6	1.5	1.3	3.3	74.3	4.1	11.1	59.1
	2005	73 476	10.5	0.5	3.6	2.7	81.4	3.8	29.3	48.3
	2012	152 537	9.9	0.4	4.9	12.7	70.8	5.2	24.5	41.1
Turkmenistan - Turkménistan	1995	(e)1 939	1.1	20.3	70.3	1.3	6.8	0.5	0.4	5.9
	2005	(e)4 944	0.2	2.5	89.1	0.3	7.6	1.2	1.0	5.4
	2012	(e)16 500	0.1	20.4	61.5	0.4	17.5	8.1	0.6	8.7
Turks and Caicos Islands - Îles Turques et Caïques	1995	(e)5	72.9	0.2	17.6	0.1	7.2	3.7	0.8	2.8
	2005	(e)15	52.3	29.8	0.0	0.1	15.2	0.1	7.9	7.2
	2012	(e)25	17.1	2.3	0.0	7.9	45.9	0.1	7.6	38.3
Tuvalu	1995	(e)0	1.0	1.2	..	1.3	96.4	14.5	31.0	50.9
	2005	(e)0	1.8	0.2	0.5	0.6	95.2	2.5	42.5	50.1
	2012	(e)0	66.2	0.0	0.0	0.0	32.1	4.5	25.1	2.5
Uganda - Ouganda	1995	(e)460	88.7	4.3	0.0	4.5	2.4	0.5	0.8	1.1
	2005	813	60.4	12.7	1.9	9.4	14.8	2.2	4.8	7.7
	2012	2 357	51.9	8.9	0.9	1.6	33.1	3.4	13.9	15.8
Ukraine	1995	(e)13 317	19.0	1.0	4.3	8.2	66.4	12.8	14.1	39.4
	2005	34 228	12.4	1.5	9.8	7.2	68.4	9.1	13.1	46.3
	2012	68 694	25.9	1.0	5.3	7.7	59.5	7.3	18.8	33.4
United Arab Emirates - Émirats arabes unis	1995	(e)27 753	3.3	0.3	72.4	5.1	18.0	2.9	6.3	8.8
	2005	(e)115 453	2.9	0.2	61.7	10.1	24.4	3.1	13.1	8.2
	2012	(e)324 424	3.6	0.2	58.1	16.4	21.5	3.3	8.8	9.4
United Kingdom - Royaume-Uni	1995	234 372	7.6	0.7	6.2	4.8	80.0	12.4	43.8	23.8
	2005	384 365	5.2	0.6	9.5	5.3	74.6	14.9	39.6	20.1
	2012	481 226	6.1	0.7	13.7	6.5	64.2	16.2	30.3	17.7
United Republic of Tanzania - République-Unie de Tanzanie	1995	(e)685	65.2	23.1	0.3	3.9	7.1	0.7	1.3	5.0
	2005	1 672	38.8	10.3	4.0	36.4	10.3	1.5	2.3	6.5
	2012	5 547	36.1	7.9	1.4	36.2	17.4	3.4	4.8	9.3
United States - États-Unis	1995	582 965	10.1	3.7	1.8	3.8	77.5	10.6	48.3	18.7
	2005	904 339	6.8	2.3	2.9	4.3	80.4	13.3	48.0	19.1
	2012	1 545 565	8.9	2.2	8.9	6.8	64.4	13.4	34.4	16.6

For sources and notes, see end of table.　　　　Pour les sources et les notes, se reporter à la fin du tableau.

Country or territory / Pays ou territoires	Year / Année	Total value (millions of dollars) (1) / Valeur totale (millions de dollars) (1)	By main SITC Revision 3 product group (percentage) / Par principaux groupes de produits de la CTCI Révision 3 (en pourcentage)					Of which: / dont :		
			All food items / Produits alimentaires	Agricultural raw materials / Matières premières agricoles	Fuels / Combustibles	Ores, metals, precious stones and non-monetary gold / Minerais, métaux, pierres précieuses et or (non monétaire)	Manufactured goods / Articles manufacturés	Chemical products / Produits chimiques	Machinery and transport equipment / Machines et matériel de transport	Other manufactured goods / Articles manufacturés divers
			0 + 1 + 22 + 4	2 - (22 + 27 + 28)	3	27 + 28 + 68 + 667 + 971	5 + 6 +7 + 8 - (667 + 68)	5	7	6 + 8 - (667 + 68)
Uruguay	1995	2 106	44.2	14.9	1.0	0.9	38.7	5.6	6.0	27.1
	2005	3 405	54.5	9.2	4.8	1.9	29.6	5.8	2.9	20.9
	2012	8 743	65.4	8.4	1.1	1.8	22.6	6.7	3.0	12.9
Uzbekistan - Ouzbékistan	1995	3 430	1.3	62.3	15.0	14.1	7.2	3.0	0.8	3.4
	2005	4 749	11.5	25.8	16.2	16.6	28.3	8.8	10.7	8.8
	2012	10 836	12.7	18.8	8.0	21.2	39.2	14.1	6.1	19.1
Vanuatu	1995	(e)28	82.7	4.8	..	0.0	12.3	0.0	6.1	6.1
	2005	(e)38	64.5	11.3	0.5	0.0	23.0	0.3	22.2	0.4
	2012	(e)52	54.9	1.4	0.8	0.3	6.1	0.3	5.2	0.6
Venezuela (Bolivarian Rep. of) - Venezuela (Rép. bolivarienne du)	1995	19 093	3.1	0.2	72.4	8.1	16.0	5.0	3.1	7.9
	2005	55 413	0.9	0.1	83.5	4.2	11.1	3.1	1.5	6.6
	2012	(e)95 795	1.1	0.1	82.1	2.3	14.4	2.4	7.4	4.6
Viet Nam	1995	(e)5 449	30.2	3.1	18.0	0.8	43.7	1.1	7.0	35.6
	2005	32 447	20.2	3.1	25.8	0.7	49.8	1.6	9.6	38.5
	2012	(e)114 529	18.6	3.8	14.4	1.0	62.1	2.8	17.3	41.9
Wallis and Futuna Islands - Îles Wallis-et-Futuna	1995	(e)1	16.4	..	..	..	83.6	7.9	49.0	26.7
	2005	(e)0	5.2	11.4	0.0	0.8	81.4	8.4	32.6	40.5
	2012	(e)0	4.5	4.5	..	0.7	81.5	8.0	27.2	46.3
Western Sahara - Sahara occidental	1995	(e)8	58.9	23.6	2.3	..	15.0	6.4	5.1	3.6
Yemen - Yémen	1995	(e)1 917	3.2	0.6	92.9	1.0	2.2	0.5	0.9	0.8
	2005	(e)5 608	5.8	0.3	90.3	1.9	1.6	0.4	0.8	0.4
	2012	(e)8 600	6.6	0.3	87.4	3.2	2.4	0.9	0.7	0.8
Zambia - Zambie	1995	1 055	3.6	0.8	2.3	87.4	5.8	0.3	1.5	4.0
	2005	1 810	12.3	6.3	0.6	68.8	10.9	0.7	1.6	8.6
	2012	(e)8 600	8.7	1.9	0.7	75.7	13.1	2.9	3.9	6.3
Zimbabwe	1995	(e)2 121	42.0	8.8	2.3	14.9	31.7	2.0	2.5	27.1
	2005	(e)1 850	25.3	10.0	0.9	36.6	26.8	2.0	2.3	22.4
	2012	(e)3 884	34.0	12.4	9.3	24.0	22.6	1.4	2.8	18.4

Source:
UNCTAD secretariat calculations, based on UNCTAD, *UNCTADstat* Merchandise Trade Matrix

Source :
Calculs du secrétariat de la CNUCED, basés sur la matrice du commerce de marchandises d'*UNCTADstat* de la CNUCED

Notes:
(a) More than 30% of total trade under SITC Rev.3, code 931: "Special transactions & commodities not classified".
(1) Includes unallocated product groups, SITC Rev.3, 911 and 931.

Notes :
(a) Plus de 30% du commerce sous la position 931 de la CTCI rév. 3 : "Transactions et articles spéciaux non classés".
(1) Y compris les groupes de produits non-distribués, CTCI Rév.3, 911 et 931.

Country or territory / Pays ou territoires	Year / Année	Total value (millions of dollars) (1) / Valeur totale (millions de dollars) (1)	All food items / Produits alimentaires	Agricultural raw materials / Matières premières agricoles	Fuels / Combustibles	Ores, metals, precious stones and non-monetary gold / Minerais, métaux, pierres précieuses et or (non monétaire)	Manufactured goods / Articles manufacturés	Of which: / dont :		
								Chemical products / Produits chimiques	Machinery and transport equipment / Machines et matériel de transport	Other manufactured goods / Articles manufacturés divers
			0 + 1 + 22 + 4	2 - (22 + 27 + 28)	3	27 + 28 + 68 + 667 + 971	5 + 6 +7 + 8 - (667 + 68)	5	7	6 + 8 - (667 + 68)
Afghanistan	1995	(e)387	23.7	0.8	7.0	0.5	67.4	9.7	10.0	37.8
	2005	(e)2 471	22.0	1.3	18.1	0.4	56.1	6.2	22.0	27.9
	2012	(e)5 500	21.1	1.0	13.8	0.2	54.4	3.8	27.1	23.5
Albania - Albanie	1995	(e)714	55.8	1.5	4.2	1.7	99.6	9.6	37.1	52.9
	2005	2 614	17.7	1.1	7.9	2.4	70.4	8.6	22.7	39.0
	2012	4 880	17.3	1.0	18.0	2.6	60.8	11.2	17.7	32.0
Algeria - Algérie	1995	10 782	29.5	3.2	1.1	1.6	64.7	11.3	30.5	22.9
	2005	20 357	19.3	1.7	1.0	1.5	76.5	12.0	43.0	21.5
	2012	50 369	19.8	1.5	9.7	1.6	67.4	11.7	35.0	20.7
American Samoa - Samoa américaines	1995	416	..	..	..	..	..	..	..	..
	2005	(e)520	51.2	2.7	7.0	1.3	33.5	2.2	14.7	16.6
	2012	(e)690	34.9	0.4	44.5	0.6	19.1	1.3	4.5	13.3
Andorra - Andorre	1995	(e)1 025	28.4	0.8	4.3	1.2	65.2	9.5	20.4	35.2
	2005	(e)1 822	..	..	..	..	..	..	..	..
	2012	(e)1 704	23.1	0.4	12.2	0.9	63.2	11.8	18.5	32.9
Angola	1995	1 468	26.2	0.9	0.6	0.4	70.5	6.1	42.4	22.0
	2005	8 353	16.1	0.7	0.7	0.4	80.6	4.9	53.5	22.2
	2012	(e)24 000	19.4	0.8	5.4	0.8	72.9	7.3	36.5	29.2
Anguilla	1995	(e)53	24.8	0.2	67.1	0.1	7.1	0.8	2.8	3.5
	2005	(e)130	20.0	2.0	19.9	1.8	54.1	4.4	28.7	21.0
	2012	(e)149	15.5	2.2	1.2	3.2	75.8	6.0	32.2	37.6
Antigua and Barbuda - Antigua-et-Barbuda	1995	(e)346	14.9	1.7	4.9	0.4	70.5	7.3	47.2	16.0
	2005	525	9.5	1.0	17.1	0.3	60.4	3.1	46.1	11.2
	2012	(e)530	9.9	0.9	31.1	0.4	57.7	2.7	46.3	8.6
Argentina - Argentine	1995	20 122	5.5	2.0	4.2	2.7	85.5	17.8	44.5	23.1
	2005	28 689	2.8	1.5	5.0	3.5	86.4	19.8	46.6	19.9
	2012	68 507	2.5	1.1	13.0	2.8	79.6	17.6	44.9	17.0
Armenia - Arménie	1995	(e)674	32.7	0.2	31.8	1.2	31.4	8.8	10.7	12.0
	2005	(e)1 692	16.7	0.8	13.5	19.4	48.5	7.8	21.0	19.7
	2012	(e)4 267	20.8	1.3	16.5	6.5	54.4	10.2	22.4	21.9
Aruba	1995	(e)1 597	27.9	2.0	14.0	3.0	50.0	6.9	19.6	23.5
	2005	(e)4 288	6.2	0.4	49.0	2.2	29.0	2.8	10.6	15.6
	2012	(e)2 600	17.2	0.3	47.1	1.0	32.4	4.9	11.1	16.3
Australia - Australie	1995	57 423	5.0	1.7	5.0	2.5	85.7	11.0	47.0	27.7
	2005	118 922	4.6	0.9	11.1	3.2	79.9	11.4	44.3	24.2
	2012	250 465	5.0	0.6	16.9	4.1	71.0	10.0	39.6	21.5
Austria - Autriche	1995	66 406	5.7	3.2	4.4	4.3	81.6	10.7	36.8	34.1
	2005	119 950	6.1	2.2	12.2	3.8	74.9	10.7	36.8	27.4
	2012	169 663	7.3	2.2	13.1	6.7	70.4	12.3	31.9	26.2
Azerbaijan - Azerbaïdjan	1995	(e)668	37.2	0.9	6.5	1.0	53.9	10.2	14.1	29.6
	2005	4 211	10.5	1.0	11.9	2.2	74.2	5.5	43.5	25.2
	2012	9 642	14.6	2.0	0.9	1.9	80.2	10.0	42.0	28.3
Bahamas	1995	(e)1 243	18.8	1.9	12.6	0.5	64.5	8.1	25.8	30.6
	2005	(e)2 312	4.6	0.7	32.1	0.2	57.5	3.1	45.0	9.4
	2012	(e)3 386	4.9	0.4	47.5	0.2	46.9	7.4	31.2	8.2
Bahrain - Bahreïn	1995	(e)3 679	10.9	0.5	36.7	4.8	45.1	5.5	17.0	22.6
	2005	(e)9 339	6.7	0.3	32.1	4.9	53.6	4.4	29.3	20.0
	2012	(e)13 920	15.5	0.8	2.4	7.5	71.7	9.4	34.8	27.5
Bangladesh	1995	(e)6 694	16.6	3.4	5.7	2.1	70.9	9.3	18.3	43.3
	2005	12 631	13.1	5.3	12.8	2.7	65.5	11.4	24.5	29.5
	2012	(e)32 345	21.8	5.5	9.6	2.9	60.2	14.3	18.5	27.4

For sources and notes, see end of table.

Pour les sources et les notes, se reporter à la fin du tableau.

145

3.1 Country trade structure
by product group
Imports

3.1 Structure du commerce des pays
par groupes de produits
Importations

Country or territory / Pays ou territoires	Year / Année	Total value (millions of dollars) (1) / Valeur totale (millions de dollars) (1)	By main SITC Revision 3 product group (percentage) / Par principaux groupes de produits de la CTCI Révision 3 (en pourcentage)					Of which: / dont :		
			All food items / Produits alimentaires	Agricultural raw materials / Matières premières agricoles	Fuels / Combustibles	Ores, metals, precious stones and non-monetary gold / Minerais, métaux, pierres précieuses et or (non monétaire)	Manufactured goods / Articles manufacturés	Chemical products / Produits chimiques	Machinery and transport equipment / Machines et matériel de transport	Other manufactured goods / Articles manufacturés divers
			0 + 1 + 22 + 4	2 - (22 + 27 + 28)	3	27 + 28 + 68 + 667 + 971	5 + 6 +7 + 8 - (667 + 68)	5	7	6 + 8 - (667 + 68)
Barbados - Barbade	1995	766	18.5	2.3	8.4	1.3	67.4	11.3	26.8	29.3
	2005	1 672	14.4	1.9	21.7	1.2	59.0	8.2	26.4	24.4
	2012	1 768	17.7	1.2	35.7	0.9	42.3	7.8	14.7	19.7
Belarus - Bélarus	1995	(e)5 563	11.8	0.5	1.1	1.1	32.7	6.0	13.6	13.1
	2005	16 699	9.4	1.7	33.0	3.2	46.3	9.5	18.2	18.6
	2012	46 404	7.6	1.5	38.5	3.3	46.4	9.4	20.5	16.4
Belgium - Belgique	1995	(e)164 590	7.0	1.6	5.2	9.9	48.4	10.6	20.1	17.7
	2005	320 130	7.6	1.2	12.4	8.4	69.7	25.0	25.7	19.0
	2012	437 883	8.7	1.3	17.5	8.9	62.5	23.2	22.2	17.0
Belize	1995	259	16.3	0.7	14.5	0.5	65.6	9.2	28.0	28.4
	2005	(e)593	12.3	0.9	25.6	1.9	56.9	10.8	24.1	22.0
	2012	880	11.4	0.5	26.7	1.6	44.1	6.8	24.2	13.1
Benin - Bénin	1995	(e)719	27.3	2.7	9.4	1.0	59.4	13.7	18.0	27.7
	2005	(e)1 018	21.4	2.3	12.3	0.7	63.0	7.4	17.8	37.7
	2012	(e)2 200	22.9	1.9	15.9	0.5	58.9	5.2	15.3	38.4
Bermuda - Bermudes	1995	(e)550	18.0	0.9	14.0	0.3	60.7	6.3	35.2	19.3
	2005	(e)988	9.1	0.4	5.5	0.3	80.8	3.2	64.0	13.5
	2012	(e)867	4.7	0.1	6.1	0.1	72.4	1.7	59.5	11.2
Bhutan - Bhoutan	1995	(e)113	16.1	1.0	1.7	1.7	60.7	5.3	40.3	15.1
	2005	(e)387	13.6	0.6	11.4	5.0	68.4	6.7	33.7	27.9
	2012	(e)1 090	11.2	2.3	14.8	14.5	57.0	4.0	32.3	20.8
Bolivia (Plurinational State of) - Bolivie (État plurinational de)	1995	1 396	14.3	1.5	3.7	2.7	77.3	13.7	35.9	27.7
	2005	2 343	9.5	1.3	8.7	1.0	79.1	17.5	31.9	29.7
	2012	8 281	7.5	0.5	14.0	0.9	76.4	13.4	37.6	25.4
Bosnia and Herzegovina - Bosnie-Herzégovine	1995	(e)1 082	37.8	0.9	10.7	1.0	46.4	9.0	12.6	24.8
	2005	(e)7 054	17.6	1.3	12.6	2.1	64.0	11.0	22.7	30.3
	2012	(e)10 024	19.1	1.8	17.7	3.4	57.7	13.7	17.7	26.3
Botswana	1995	(a)1 911	13.5	0.9	5.6	4.1	72.2	6.6	35.8	29.8
	2005	3 162	12.7	0.8	12.1	5.3	65.3	8.8	31.0	25.5
	2012	8 025	7.1	1.4	12.5	38.4	39.2	4.9	20.9	13.4
Brazil - Brésil	1995	53 734	10.7	2.7	12.1	3.4	71.1	15.2	39.2	16.7
	2005	73 600	4.4	1.5	18.3	3.9	71.9	19.9	37.9	14.2
	2012	223 149	4.8	1.1	18.0	3.0	73.1	18.9	38.4	15.8
British Virgin Islands - Îles Vierges britanniques	1995	(e)131	11.4	0.7	2.2	0.2	83.7	1.6	75.6	6.5
	2005	(e)280	0.9	0.2	72.7	2.5	23.3	0.4	13.4	9.5
	2012	310	2.0	0.1	10.5	9.0	77.7	2.0	70.7	5.0
Brunei Darussalam - Brunéi Darussalam	1995	(e)2 078	13.6	0.6	0.2	3.3	81.8	6.4	39.0	36.5
	2005	(e)1 494	20.1	0.3	1.2	1.6	76.7	9.3	29.3	38.0
	2012	3 572	14.0	0.2	9.6	1.7	72.5	6.8	29.1	36.7
Bulgaria - Bulgarie	1995	(e)5 651	7.6	2.6	33.7	4.4	47.9	11.1	16.0	20.8
	2005	18 162	4.7	1.4	5.4	6.5	65.5	9.5	30.1	25.9
	2012	32 743	8.9	1.0	24.9	9.3	53.1	11.2	22.8	19.1
Burkina Faso	1995	484	17.7	1.7	11.0	1.1	68.0	17.1	24.2	26.7
	2005	1 161	18.6	0.7	13.0	0.6	66.1	18.4	23.4	24.4
	2012	(e)3 150	16.0	0.9	18.0	0.9	64.2	16.3	23.4	24.4
Burundi	1995	(e)234	19.0	4.2	6.2	1.1	68.4	14.1	30.8	23.5
	2005	258	9.9	1.6	9.8	2.4	75.2	14.4	29.8	31.1
	2012	(e)751	32.2	1.0	16.8	1.4	47.7	10.7	16.1	20.8
Cambodia - Cambodge	1995	(e)1 187	23.8	1.6	9.0	7.8	56.3	5.9	34.2	16.2
	2005	(e)3 927	10.1	1.4	10.9	0.9	75.6	6.9	16.3	52.4
	2012	(e)11 000	12.9	0.9	19.3	2.2	64.6	6.6	19.9	38.1

For sources and notes, see end of table.

Pour les sources et les notes, se reporter à la fin du tableau.

Country or territory / Pays ou territoires	Year / Année	Total value (millions of dollars) (1) / Valeur totale (millions de dollars) (1)	All food items / Produits alimentaires	Agricultural raw materials / Matières premières agricoles	Fuels / Combustibles	Ores, metals, precious stones and non-monetary gold / Minerais, métaux, pierres précieuses et or (non monétaire)	Manufactured goods / Articles manufacturés	Of which: / dont : Chemical products / Produits chimiques	Machinery and transport equipment / Machines et matériel de transport	Other manufactured goods / Articles manufacturés divers
			0 + 1 + 22 + 4	2 - (22 + 27 + 28)	3	27 + 28 + 68 + 667 + 971	5 + 6 +7 + 8 - (667 + 68)	5	7	6 + 8 - (667 + 68)
Cameroon - Cameroun	1995	1 079	18.5	3.0	2.0	3.4	72.8	17.2	30.8	24.0
	2005	2 735	18.2	2.2	22.2	3.5	53.2	11.1	22.6	19.4
	2012	(e)7 300	19.5	2.3	15.7	1.9	60.7	12.0	25.3	23.4
Canada	1995	164 371	5.7	1.7	3.6	3.7	82.7	8.1	51.6	23.1
	2005	314 444	5.6	1.2	9.2	3.6	78.9	10.1	45.5	23.2
	2012	462 369	7.2	1.0	11.1	5.4	73.7	10.1	41.1	22.4
Cape Verde - Cap-Vert	1995	(e)252	32.0	2.1	14.5	0.4	49.9	5.8	19.6	24.6
	2005	(e)438	26.9	1.5	11.3	5.4	52.7	6.5	20.4	25.8
	2012	(e)755	26.6	0.8	21.1	0.8	49.3	5.8	18.5	25.0
Cayman Islands - Îles Caïmanes	1995	(e)402	10.6	0.7	1.2	2.4	78.7	20.4	30.9	27.3
	2005	(e)1 214	9.8	0.5	5.0	0.4	74.4	1.4	61.8	11.2
	2012	(e)910	5.5	0.3	10.7	0.7	69.3	1.6	58.6	9.1
Central African Republic - République centrafricaine	1995	(e)174	14.2	1.3	0.9	2.0	81.0	12.0	50.3	18.6
	2005	185	19.5	3.6	15.9	1.5	58.4	10.0	28.8	19.5
	2012	(e)320	16.2	1.1	50.5	0.9	31.3	6.9	11.8	12.5
Chad - Tchad	1995	(e)488	17.5	0.5	14.0	0.5	66.8	9.3	31.2	26.3
	2005	(e)950	12.4	1.2	6.9	1.0	78.0	11.1	42.8	24.1
	2012	(e)2 800	16.8	0.8	8.3	1.0	72.7	11.2	38.8	22.7
Chile - Chili	1995	14 903	6.7	1.7	9.0	2.2	79.2	12.2	42.3	24.7
	2005	32 926	5.8	1.0	21.6	3.2	68.4	10.6	37.2	20.6
	2012	79 462	7.4	0.6	22.6	1.8	67.6	10.1	36.6	20.8
China - Chine	1995	132 083	7.0	5.2	3.9	4.6	78.1	12.9	39.8	25.4
	2005	659 953	3.3	3.6	9.7	8.8	74.4	11.8	44.0	18.6
	2012	1 818 199	5.0	3.6	17.2	12.5	57.9	9.8	35.9	12.1
China, Hong Kong SAR - Chine (RAS de Hong Kong)	1995	196 072	5.4	1.6	1.9	5.6	85.1	7.4	36.5	41.3
	2005	300 160	2.9	0.8	2.7	4.9	88.7	6.2	52.1	30.3
	2012	553 486	4.0	0.5	3.3	13.8	78.3	4.2	52.8	21.3
China, Macao SAR - Chine (RAS de Macao)	1995	2 025	14.0	2.7	5.1	0.8	77.3	4.5	18.9	53.9
	2005	4 514	10.9	0.3	8.4	0.7	79.6	4.2	22.3	53.2
	2012	8 982	13.8	0.2	10.6	0.4	72.4	5.6	24.1	42.6
China, Taiwan Province of - Province chinoise de Taiwan	1995	103 506	5.4	4.2	6.9	7.4	74.2	13.3	40.2	20.7
	2005	181 592	3.6	1.6	15.5	6.3	72.1	12.6	41.0	18.4
	2012	270 863	4.2	1.4	25.9	7.8	60.0	13.2	32.3	14.4
Colombia - Colombie	1995	13 883	9.4	2.5	2.8	2.5	78.0	18.1	37.3	22.6
	2005	21 204	8.7	1.6	2.6	2.6	83.7	20.8	40.4	22.5
	2012	58 088	10.1	0.9	9.7	1.6	76.7	16.9	37.6	22.1
Comoros - Comores	1995	62	25.1	1.5	5.0	0.5	67.4	7.4	32.5	27.5
	2005	(e)99	33.6	1.2	9.3	0.4	53.6	3.8	23.2	26.6
	2012	(e)273	41.7	0.9	3.3	0.4	53.5	3.6	23.1	26.8
Congo	1995	(e)670	11.9	0.4	15.5	0.6	70.6	8.9	26.7	35.1
	2005	(e)1 166	21.2	2.2	2.6	1.3	71.6	12.7	29.9	29.1
	2012	(e)5 680	15.4	1.4	2.7	0.7	78.8	7.8	47.4	23.5
Cook Islands - Îles Cook	1995	(e)49	22.7	1.7	11.5	1.2	62.5	5.8	31.0	25.6
	2005	(e)81	28.0	2.6	6.1	0.7	57.4	7.4	20.9	29.1
	2012	(e)116	24.7	2.1	17.5	0.9	46.9	5.1	20.1	21.7
Costa Rica	1995	(e)4 090	9.2	1.3	7.0	2.0	79.1	17.1	26.8	35.2
	2005	9 173	7.0	1.1	9.5	1.9	78.7	14.5	39.1	25.1
	2012	(e)17 578	9.3	1.2	14.7	2.1	72.7	13.2	36.5	23.0
Côte d'Ivoire	1995	(e)2 946	17.5	0.8	16.1	1.3	47.5	10.9	20.5	16.1
	2005	5 865	14.6	0.5	28.0	1.0	54.8	9.4	24.2	21.2
	2012	(e)9 777	20.4	0.8	26.0	1.1	50.4	12.7	23.4	14.4

For sources and notes, see end of table.

Pour les sources et les notes, se reporter à la fin du tableau.

Country or territory / Pays ou territoires	Year / Année	Total value (millions of dollars) (1) / Valeur totale (millions de dollars) (1)	By main SITC Revision 3 product group (percentage) / Par principaux groupes de produits de la CTCI Révision 3 (en pourcentage)					Of which: / dont :		
			All food items / Produits alimentaires	Agricultural raw materials / Matières premières agricoles	Fuels / Combustibles	Ores, metals, precious stones and non-monetary gold / Minerais, métaux, pierres précieuses et or (non monétaire)	Manufactured goods / Articles manufacturés	Chemical products / Produits chimiques	Machinery and transport equipment / Machines et matériel de transport	Other manu-factured goods / Articles manu-facturés divers
			0 + 1 + 22 + 4	2 - (22 + 27 + 28)	3	27 + 28 + 68 + 667 + 971	5 + 6 +7 + 8 - (667 + 68)	5	7	6 + 8 - (667 + 68)
Croatia - Croatie	1995	7 509	11.8	1.8	11.6	2.5	66.6	10.8	26.7	29.0
	2005	18 560	8.3	1.3	15.1	2.3	72.9	11.1	32.9	28.9
	2012	20 834	11.8	1.0	23.2	2.6	61.5	13.5	22.3	25.6
Cuba	1995	(e)2 805	20.9	1.7	21.4	1.6	53.5	12.3	20.4	20.9
	2005	(e)8 084	19.2	0.7	26.3	1.5	51.0	7.5	24.6	18.9
	2012	(e)13 606	14.7	0.9	25.0	2.2	55.6	11.4	18.0	26.2
Cyprus - Chypre	1995	3 694	20.4	1.3	7.7	2.3	68.3	8.8	27.6	31.9
	2005	6 382	12.4	1.1	16.1	1.3	67.5	8.9	30.9	27.7
	2012	7 377	17.5	0.7	30.2	0.8	50.3	10.8	16.3	23.2
Czech Republic - République tchèque	1995	25 303	6.6	2.5	8.6	4.3	76.4	11.6	35.1	29.7
	2005	76 527	5.2	1.5	6.8	3.4	78.3	10.6	40.2	27.5
	2012	139 131	6.4	1.4	9.4	4.0	77.1	11.2	40.6	25.2
Dem. Rep. of the Congo - Rép. dém. du Congo	1995	871	21.8	3.2	10.2	1.2	62.3	9.5	20.9	31.9
	2005	2 690	23.2	2.9	13.4	0.8	58.7	11.0	26.6	21.1
	2012	(e)6 100	19.9	1.9	4.1	1.3	71.3	11.2	35.0	25.1
Denmark - Danemark	1995	43 142	12.0	3.0	3.3	2.1	72.7	11.2	32.0	29.5
	2005	74 265	11.3	2.2	6.7	1.8	76.4	10.9	36.3	29.2
	2012	91 907	13.5	2.4	9.8	1.7	69.9	11.2	29.9	28.8
Djibouti	1995	(e)177	28.7	11.3	2.1	0.3	56.8	5.3	15.2	36.3
	2005	(e)277	12.7	3.7	30.6	0.6	51.2	6.8	15.8	28.6
	2012	(e)580	25.5	1.2	1.6	1.1	69.4	13.7	20.5	35.2
Dominica - Dominique	1995	117	26.2	2.0	5.6	0.4	65.7	14.3	24.0	27.5
	2005	165	19.4	1.3	13.3	0.5	65.5	11.4	25.4	28.8
	2012	212	24.9	2.0	22.1	0.6	50.3	8.0	17.0	25.2
Dominican Republic - République dominicaine	1995	(e)5 170	12.4	1.6	11.6	0.7	71.6	7.7	20.5	43.3
	2005	(e)9 869	11.6	1.3	13.2	1.5	70.6	9.5	24.4	36.7
	2012	(e)18 491	14.0	1.0	27.2	1.3	55.4	9.7	20.0	25.7
Ecuador - Équateur	1995	4 195	7.6	2.8	5.9	1.9	81.8	17.6	40.1	24.1
	2005	9 609	8.0	1.3	12.0	1.2	77.4	16.8	36.8	23.9
	2012	(e)25 197	7.7	1.0	22.4	1.2	67.7	15.9	31.2	20.6
Egypt - Égypte	1995	11 739	23.3	5.8	1.1	2.3	66.7	10.9	32.0	23.8
	2005	(e)22 449	15.8	3.2	11.6	3.9	53.5	10.7	23.7	19.2
	2012	69 866	21.9	2.8	18.0	4.8	51.9	11.7	20.0	20.3
El Salvador	1995	(e)3 329	14.3	2.4	7.8	1.4	73.0	15.1	27.4	30.5
	2005	6 809	14.3	1.4	13.3	1.4	66.6	13.9	18.0	34.7
	2012	10 270	16.2	2.0	16.3	1.0	61.6	15.4	17.0	29.1
Equatorial Guinea - Guinée équatoriale	1995	121	25.7	2.6	3.2	0.6	69.0	9.7	27.9	31.4
	2005	1 310	10.2	0.8	9.5	0.5	77.1	2.8	56.4	17.9
	2012	(e)7 500	15.0	0.6	2.9	0.6	79.1	5.6	39.8	33.7
Eritrea - Érythrée	1995	(e)434	12.0	1.5	5.2	0.4	79.2	4.3	46.1	28.8
	2005	(e)482	33.2	0.7	2.3	1.2	59.4	6.5	33.3	19.6
	2012	(e)818	25.1	0.6	3.1	0.9	69.3	13.5	32.8	23.1
Estonia - Estonie	1995	2 546	14.2	2.6	11.5	2.4	68.5	8.9	29.1	30.5
	2005	11 018	8.0	3.5	12.8	1.5	69.0	9.0	35.2	24.9
	2012	19 597	9.2	1.9	20.7	1.4	61.1	10.1	31.0	20.0
Ethiopia - Éthiopie	1995	1 141	13.8	1.9	11.1	0.8	72.4	14.1	35.5	22.7
	2005	4 095	10.6	0.9	15.1	1.2	72.1	12.3	34.7	25.1
	2012	(e)12 656	15.5	0.7	15.3	0.6	67.9	11.7	33.1	23.1
Faeroe Islands - Îles Féroé	1995	(e)314	22.3	3.5	11.7	1.2	57.9	7.3	27.5	23.0
	2005	747	13.2	2.3	16.2	1.1	65.6	6.4	36.8	22.3
	2012	(e)1 149	18.6	2.4	26.1	1.1	51.8	8.0	20.1	23.7

For sources and notes, see end of table.

Pour les sources et les notes, se reporter à la fin du tableau.

Country or territory / Pays ou territoires	Year / Année	Total value (millions of dollars) (1) / Valeur totale (millions de dollars) (1)	By main SITC Revision 3 product group (percentage) / Par principaux groupes de produits de la CTCI Révision 3 (en pourcentage)					Of which: / dont :		
			All food items / Produits alimentaires	Agricultural raw materials / Matières premières agricoles	Fuels / Combustibles	Ores, metals, precious stones and non-monetary gold / Minerais, métaux, pierres précieuses et or (non monétaire)	Manufactured goods / Articles manufacturés	Chemical products / Produits chimiques	Machinery and transport equipment / Machines et matériel de transport	Other manufactured goods / Articles manufacturés divers
			0 + 1 + 22 + 4	2 - (22 + 27 + 28)	3	27 + 28 + 68 + 667 + 971	5 + 6 +7 + 8 - (667 + 68)	5	7	6 + 8 - (667 + 68)
Falkland Islands (Malvinas) - Îles Falkland (Malvinas)	1995	(e)44	18.1	1.4	4.4	0.1	74.1	2.0	57.9	14.1
	2005	(e)60	1.5	0.1	1.6	0.1	12.1	0.2	5.4	6.5
	2012	130	7.9	0.3	22.3	1.1	63.9	6.0	25.3	32.6
Fiji - Fidji	1995	(e)892	14.1	0.6	13.3	0.9	68.8	6.9	23.6	38.3
	2005	1 607	14.7	0.4	28.8	0.9	54.9	7.7	21.7	25.5
	2012	2 253	21.1	0.3	30.1	1.1	46.5	7.9	18.9	19.7
Finland - Finlande	1995	29 520	6.0	3.6	8.8	5.7	74.3	12.2	38.7	23.3
	2005	58 473	5.2	2.9	13.7	6.5	70.0	11.3	39.2	19.5
	2012	76 089	7.4	2.3	22.0	7.3	57.9	11.7	27.1	19.1
France	1995	275 510	10.7	2.5	6.9	3.9	76.0	12.5	35.4	28.1
	2005	475 857	7.8	1.5	13.4	2.8	74.6	13.3	35.7	25.5
	2012	663 269	8.4	1.2	17.3	2.9	70.0	14.1	32.5	23.5
French Polynesia - Polynésie française	1995	(e)1 019	21.6	1.5	5.5	0.9	70.5	8.5	34.7	27.4
	2005	1 702	19.0	1.3	9.6	0.9	69.2	8.4	35.8	25.0
	2012	1 706	25.3	1.0	17.3	0.7	55.6	9.9	23.4	22.3
Gabon	1995	(e)884	19.1	0.7	3.4	1.1	75.6	10.7	39.3	25.7
	2005	1 451	16.9	0.7	4.1	1.3	76.2	9.1	41.9	25.2
	2012	(e)3 631	16.5	0.8	4.2	1.4	76.1	8.9	40.1	27.1
Gambia - Gambie	1995	(e)182	30.4	1.2	8.8	0.3	57.6	5.5	16.4	35.7
	2005	260	30.8	1.1	13.1	3.4	51.1	5.5	15.3	30.3
	2012	(e)380	34.8	1.1	8.7	0.8	54.6	6.9	12.6	35.1
Georgia - Géorgie	1995	(e)412	36.1	0.2	38.8	0.5	24.4	4.8	9.7	9.9
	2005	2 490	17.4	0.4	19.9	0.6	60.0	9.6	29.4	21.1
	2012	7 840	16.0	0.8	17.1	1.8	63.9	9.5	30.3	24.2
Germany - Allemagne	1995	464 145	9.8	2.6	6.2	4.4	69.9	9.1	31.8	28.9
	2005	779 819	7.0	1.5	11.5	4.1	71.6	11.7	37.4	22.4
	2012	1 173 288	7.4	1.5	14.8	5.3	65.2	12.3	31.9	21.0
Ghana	1995	(e)1 896	7.9	1.0	5.8	2.6	74.9	9.3	43.7	21.9
	2005	4 878	15.6	1.7	16.4	1.9	63.1	10.2	28.0	24.9
	2012	(e)18 000	13.0	1.1	12.5	1.0	71.7	10.9	32.8	28.0
Gibraltar	1995	411	12.0	0.6	51.9	1.3	33.2	2.8	15.8	14.6
	2005	(e)551	3.7	0.1	67.2	1.2	24.7	1.3	18.1	5.3
	2012	860	1.0	0.0	85.5	0.0	5.7	1.5	3.6	0.6
Greece - Grèce	1995	25 927	16.0	2.5	7.2	3.2	70.6	13.2	27.4	30.0
	2005	54 894	11.2	1.2	17.9	3.1	66.4	14.4	28.9	23.1
	2012	62 341	12.3	1.1	37.7	3.2	45.8	13.3	17.3	15.2
Greenland - Groenland	1995	421	13.7	1.3	6.4	0.4	66.2	5.3	28.3	32.6
	2005	(e)593	17.7	1.2	21.3	0.4	58.0	4.8	28.6	24.6
	2012	(e)901	22.4	0.7	22.9	0.8	53.2	6.6	22.5	24.1
Grenada - Grenade	1995	129	27.5	2.5	7.8	0.4	61.8	8.8	21.3	31.7
	2005	334	16.4	6.2	7.2	0.6	69.6	8.2	23.5	38.0
	2012	(e)335	23.4	2.0	17.8	0.8	56.1	8.4	19.3	28.4
Guam	1995	(e)442	..	..	..	..	..	..	..	..
	2005	(e)533	9.4	0.1	58.0	0.0	31.5	2.0	11.6	17.9
	2012	(e)1 200	7.7	0.1	56.8	0.3	33.8	2.6	8.6	22.6
Guatemala	1995	3 292	11.9	1.5	12.4	1.2	73.0	17.2	31.5	24.3
	2005	10 500	10.9	1.2	15.5	1.3	71.1	15.8	23.1	32.3
	2012	16 979	13.3	1.4	19.7	1.1	64.3	17.1	22.5	24.8
Guinea - Guinée	1995	819	29.6	1.1	14.4	0.6	53.1	7.5	21.2	24.4
	2005	(e)820	20.2	0.8	12.1	0.5	55.5	9.0	21.0	25.4
	2012	(e)2 300	19.0	1.1	21.3	0.5	58.2	9.6	26.0	22.6

For sources and notes, see end of table.

Pour les sources et les notes, se reporter à la fin du tableau.

Country or territory / Pays ou territoires	Year / Année	Total value (millions of dollars) (1) / Valeur totale (millions de dollars) (1)	By main SITC Revision 3 product group (percentage) / Par principaux groupes de produits de la CTCI Révision 3 (en pourcentage)					Of which: / dont :		
			All food items / Produits alimentaires	Agricultural raw materials / Matières premières agricoles	Fuels / Combustibles	Ores, metals, precious stones and non-monetary gold / Minerais, métaux, pierres précieuses et or (non monétaire)	Manufactured goods / Articles manufacturés	Chemical products / Produits chimiques	Machinery and transport equipment / Machines et matériel de transport	Other manufactured goods / Articles manufacturés divers
			0 + 1 + 22 + 4	2 - (22 + 27 + 28)	3	27 + 28 + 68 + 667 + 971	5 + 6 +7 + 8 - (667 + 68)	5	7	6 + 8 - (667 + 68)
Guinea-Bissau - Guinée-Bissau	1995	(e)133	18.8	0.4	5.4	0.3	74.0	5.7	23.1	45.1
	2005	(e)112	30.6	0.5	36.0	0.1	30.8	5.3	13.1	12.3
	2012	(e)227	33.1	0.5	19.0	3.9	42.6	5.3	16.0	21.3
Guyana	1995	(e)528	14.1	0.4	5.6	0.5	68.7	11.1	34.8	22.8
	2005	778	15.1	0.5	29.4	0.7	53.4	10.6	22.0	20.8
	2012	(e)1 885	13.4	0.6	22.5	1.0	62.5	10.3	26.1	26.1
Haiti - Haïti	1995	(e)654	38.5	1.8	3.8	0.6	48.1	5.6	21.7	20.8
	2005	(e)1 466	40.1	1.6	5.7	0.5	52.1	5.9	15.4	30.8
	2012	(e)3 196	46.1	1.5	6.0	0.4	45.9	5.7	12.3	27.9
Honduras	1995	1 728	11.5	1.1	6.0	1.2	77.9	14.2	26.1	37.6
	2005	(e)6 545	12.5	0.8	13.9	0.7	68.8	12.6	18.8	37.3
	2012	(e)11 179	15.7	1.2	16.9	0.7	65.5	14.4	16.8	34.3
Hungary - Hongrie	1995	15 186	5.7	3.0	11.9	4.3	75.2	14.5	30.1	30.6
	2005	65 920	4.1	1.1	10.1	1.9	77.5	9.1	48.9	19.5
	2012	94 266	5.0	1.3	12.7	2.8	68.9	10.9	41.6	16.5
Iceland - Islande	1995	1 751	11.8	1.6	7.2	4.6	74.6	9.3	32.4	32.9
	2005	4 979	7.8	1.3	9.4	4.1	77.3	7.8	41.9	27.6
	2012	4 772	10.3	1.0	15.0	13.1	60.4	8.9	32.4	19.1
India - Inde	1995	36 592	4.6	4.1	14.2	16.7	56.0	15.8	26.4	13.8
	2005	140 862	4.4	2.4	12.5	25.0	53.8	12.0	27.2	14.5
	2012	488 976	3.9	1.6	39.0	17.7	35.9	9.4	16.9	9.6
Indonesia (...2002) - Indonésie (...2002)	1995	(e)40 645	8.5	5.3	6.4	3.6	75.3	14.0	42.0	19.3
Indonesia - Indonésie	2005	(e)75 725	6.6	3.0	23.6	3.1	62.3	12.5	33.2	16.6
	2012	191 691	8.0	2.5	21.9	3.0	63.0	11.8	33.2	18.0
Iran (Islamic Rep. of) - Iran (Rép. islamique d')	1995	(e)13 882	20.9	2.4	1.8	5.1	69.8	13.3	35.6	20.9
	2005	38 675	8.1	1.8	8.2	2.4	72.9	9.6	39.4	24.0
	2012	(e)63 155	15.5	1.8	4.3	3.0	75.5	10.7	34.2	30.6
Iraq	1995	(e)2 891	63.9	0.2	0.1	0.1	34.8	30.6	1.4	2.8
	2005	(e)23 532	22.9	0.3	9.1	0.6	63.0	9.8	32.9	20.3
	2012	(e)57 000	25.4	0.3	5.7	0.7	66.1	6.8	31.4	28.0
Ireland - Irlande	1995	32 321	8.5	1.2	3.3	2.2	75.7	12.8	42.3	20.7
	2005	70 284	7.9	1.0	6.9	1.4	76.8	12.9	43.9	20.1
	2012	63 100	13.6	0.7	14.3	1.6	65.1	20.8	25.5	18.9
Israel - Israël	1995	28 344	6.6	1.6	5.9	19.3	65.1	9.3	34.0	21.9
	2005	45 032	5.5	1.0	15.0	23.6	54.5	10.2	27.6	16.7
	2012	73 112	7.1	1.0	22.0	12.7	56.6	11.3	28.8	16.4
Italy - Italie	1995	200 320	11.5	5.6	7.3	6.3	66.7	13.1	29.8	23.8
	2005	384 836	8.6	2.6	11.9	5.2	65.7	12.9	30.0	22.7
	2012	486 653	9.5	2.2	22.4	6.5	58.4	14.7	22.3	21.4
Jamaica - Jamaïque	1995	2 773	14.3	1.6	12.7	0.9	67.6	9.9	27.5	30.3
	2005	4 885	14.7	1.4	28.3	0.8	53.3	11.8	19.1	22.4
	2012	6 580	16.6	0.6	36.3	0.4	44.4	14.0	13.9	16.5
Japan - Japon	1995	336 094	16.1	6.2	16.0	8.5	52.0	7.1	22.6	22.3
	2005	515 866	10.4	2.4	25.8	6.6	53.3	7.3	25.7	20.3
	2012	885 843	8.9	1.7	34.1	6.9	47.0	8.3	21.5	17.2
Jordan - Jordanie	1995	3 696	20.6	2.1	12.9	3.4	60.5	12.3	24.5	23.7
	2005	10 455	13.6	1.2	23.1	2.5	57.7	8.8	25.1	23.7
	2012	(e)20 004	17.9	1.2	26.7	2.4	51.8	10.4	18.7	22.7
Kazakhstan	1995	3 805	10.0	2.1	23.5	4.2	59.5	9.9	26.4	23.2
	2005	17 333	6.6	0.9	11.0	1.6	79.2	8.6	37.9	32.7
	2012	44 538	8.3	0.6	10.1	1.9	78.3	9.7	36.5	32.2

For sources and notes, see end of table.

Pour les sources et les notes, se reporter à la fin du tableau.

Country or territory / Pays ou territoires	Year / Année	Total value (millions of dollars) (1) / Valeur totale (millions de dollars) (1)	By main SITC Revision 3 product group (percentage) / Par principaux groupes de produits de la CTCI Révision 3 (en pourcentage)						Of which: / dont :		
			All food items / Produits alimentaires	Agricultural raw materials / Matières premières agricoles	Fuels / Combustibles	Ores, metals, precious stones and non-monetary gold / Minerais, métaux, pierres précieuses et or (non monétaire)	Manufactured goods / Articles manufacturés		Chemical products / Produits chimiques	Machinery and transport equipment / Machines et matériel de transport	Other manufactured goods / Articles manufacturés divers
			0 + 1 + 22 + 4	2 - (22 + 27 + 28)	3	27 + 28 + 68 + 667 + 971	5 + 6 +7 + 8 - (667 + 68)		5	7	6 + 8 - (667 + 68)
Kenya	1995	2 818	11.1	2.5	11.7	1.8	72.4		14.7	34.3	23.3
	2005	5 846	8.6	1.9	20.2	1.8	66.0		13.8	30.5	21.8
	2012	(e)16 290	12.9	1.5	24.9	1.4	59.3		12.7	25.9	20.7
Kiribati	1995	(e)34	32.9	1.8	10.2	0.4	51.1		8.9	16.4	25.8
	2005	(e)74	31.2	1.2	14.1	0.9	43.7		4.4	21.8	17.5
	2012	(e)109	22.4	1.0	10.2	0.9	58.2		3.8	31.2	23.2
Korea, Dem. People's Rep. of - Corée, Rép. populaire dém. de	1995	(e)1 380	14.0	5.4	18.6	3.6	53.9		8.7	18.4	26.7
	2005	(e)2 718	18.5	2.2	28.6	4.2	44.4		6.9	16.7	20.8
	2012	(e)4 750	15.1	2.5	20.4	2.2	59.3		9.1	22.1	28.1
Korea, Republic of - Corée, République de	1995	135 113	5.4	5.5	14.1	8.4	66.6		9.7	36.6	20.3
	2005	261 236	4.4	2.0	25.8	7.1	60.6		9.4	31.6	19.7
	2012	519 576	4.8	1.6	35.8	8.2	49.6		9.1	24.6	15.9
Kuwait - Koweït	1995	7 790	15.5	1.1	0.5	2.0	80.8		7.3	41.2	32.3
	2005	(e)15 800	23.0	0.7	1.5	2.8	72.0		7.2	34.3	30.6
	2012	(e)25 880	17.2	0.7	0.7	3.5	77.9		8.7	35.6	33.7
Kyrgyzstan - Kirghizistan	1995	522	18.3	2.7	35.9	2.6	40.5		6.3	18.4	15.9
	2005	1 108	15.0	1.7	28.9	2.2	52.0		14.2	18.0	19.8
	2012	5 373	14.5	1.5	21.7	1.3	60.5		10.1	25.2	25.2
Lao People's Dem. Rep. - Rép. dém. populaire lao	1995	589	17.6	0.2	7.7	3.8	69.1		6.7	35.1	27.3
	2005	882	14.1	0.6	18.3	2.2	62.3		7.5	30.0	24.8
	2012	2 467	12.1	0.4	17.7	1.3	68.1		5.7	42.7	19.8
Latvia - Lettonie	1995	1 818	10.5	1.7	21.2	1.1	65.6		12.7	25.4	27.5
	2005	8 770	10.8	2.7	15.1	1.5	66.5		10.2	28.7	27.6
	2012	15 901	13.2	1.4	17.2	3.7	53.8		9.8	23.1	20.8
Lebanon - Liban	1995	(e)7 278	20.1	1.9	7.5	6.0	64.2		8.5	25.0	30.7
	2005	(e)9 327	14.8	1.3	21.5	5.7	56.2		11.4	21.0	23.8
	2012	(e)21 147	14.9	1.2	23.1	8.4	52.4		10.2	18.3	23.9
Lesotho	1995	(a)1 107	19.0	0.8	11.5	1.6	60.3		7.2	13.3	39.8
	2005	(e)1 390	5.7	1.1	0.7	1.3	88.1		4.7	14.5	68.9
	2012	(e)2 600	25.0	2.1	11.0	0.8	61.0		7.8	18.1	35.2
Liberia - Libéria	1995	(e)510	1.5	0.1	0.7	0.1	93.1		0.5	92.0	0.6
	2005	310	2.8	0.2	2.5	0.1	80.1		0.6	77.1	2.4
	2012	1 066	2.0	0.1	4.5	0.1	65.7		0.6	61.7	3.4
Libya - Libye	1995	(e)5 033	21.5	0.9	4.4	2.0	69.6		8.8	31.1	29.6
	2005	(e)6 082	15.1	0.7	10.4	3.1	66.5		6.0	35.1	25.3
	2012	(e)23 000	17.2	0.7	10.2	2.0	69.4		7.5	32.2	29.6
Lithuania - Lituanie	1995	3 649	13.1	3.9	19.4	3.9	57.8		12.5	21.7	23.6
	2005	15 704	8.0	2.3	24.2	1.5	62.5		11.0	29.7	21.8
	2012	32 238	12.3	1.7	33.8	1.7	47.6		12.5	19.3	15.7
Luxembourg	1995	(e)8 983	8.7	0.9	2.0	5.8	54.2		7.1	28.9	18.3
	2005	(e)21 893	8.9	0.9	9.7	6.1	71.3		8.8	38.1	24.4
	2012	(e)27 555	9.4	2.4	14.0	7.9	61.1		8.8	31.2	21.0
Madagascar	1995	(e)628	14.0	2.0	11.7	0.6	70.4		11.5	26.9	32.0
	2005	1 686	14.6	0.5	16.0	0.4	66.8		7.6	24.7	34.5
	2012	(e)3 050	17.7	2.1	16.8	0.8	61.9		12.0	18.8	31.1
Malawi	1995	(e)500	17.8	0.8	8.4	0.6	71.3		16.6	30.4	24.3
	2005	(e)1 165	19.4	1.0	8.7	0.9	69.2		21.5	21.9	25.7
	2012	(e)2 724	13.7	0.9	6.9	1.6	76.1		23.4	24.0	28.6
Malaysia - Malaisie	1995	77 046	4.8	1.2	2.3	5.9	83.4		7.1	60.0	16.3
	2005	114 290	5.1	1.2	8.1	4.8	79.0		7.8	57.5	13.7
	2012	196 419	8.4	2.5	14.2	6.6	67.8		9.0	44.0	14.8
Maldives	1995	268	24.0	2.1	11.4	1.9	60.7		5.9	26.5	28.4
	2005	745	15.6	3.6	15.5	2.3	63.0		5.3	30.8	26.9
	2012	1 555	21.2	2.0	31.3	2.1	43.3		5.7	17.1	20.5

For sources and notes, see end of table.

Pour les sources et les notes, se reporter à la fin du tableau.

Country or territory Pays ou territoires	Year Année	Total value (millions of dollars) (1) Valeur totale (millions de dollars) (1)	By main SITC Revision 3 product group (percentage) Par principaux groupes de produits de la CTCI Révision 3 (en pourcentage)						Of which: / dont :		
			All food items Produits alimentaires	Agricultural raw materials Matières premières agricoles	Fuels Combustibles	Ores, metals, precious stones and non-monetary gold Minerais, métaux, pierres précieuses et or (non monétaire)	Manufactured goods Articles manufacturés	Chemical products Produits chimiques	Machinery and transport equipment Machines et matériel de transport	Other manufactured goods Articles manufacturés divers
			0 + 1 + 22 + 4	2 - (22 + 27 + 28)	3	27 + 28 + 68 + 667 + 971	5 + 6 +7 + 8 - (667 + 68)	5	7	6 + 8 - (667 + 68)
Mali	1995	(e)774	19.9	0.8	15.6	1.1	62.5	14.9	21.6	26.0
	2005	1 544	16.7	0.5	16.5	0.7	64.7	16.8	23.1	24.9
	2012	(e)2 941	15.7	0.7	18.3	0.6	64.2	15.8	25.1	23.2
Malta - Malte	1995	2 942	8.1	0.7	10.8	1.6	77.5	7.1	49.7	20.8
	2005	3 865	8.9	0.6	14.1	1.1	71.3	7.5	46.2	17.5
	2012	(e)6 598	6.1	0.2	38.3	0.6	50.0	5.0	34.0	11.0
Marshall Islands - Îles Marshall	1995	75	2.1	0.2	0.6	0.5	94.6	0.4	92.5	1.7
	2005	(e)94	0.9	0.1	0.4	0.0	89.0	0.3	88.2	0.6
	2012	(e)140	0.2	0.0	3.2	0.0	74.3	0.1	73.1	1.0
Mauritania - Mauritanie	1995	(e)455	26.0	0.9	12.6	0.4	59.0	7.3	27.3	24.3
	2005	(e)1 342	25.1	0.6	6.2	0.4	66.2	6.6	34.9	24.7
	2012	(e)3 151	23.7	0.4	18.9	0.5	55.3	6.1	26.2	23.0
Mauritius - Maurice	1995	2 000	16.6	3.1	6.9	3.1	70.3	7.7	19.2	43.4
	2005	3 160	16.7	1.9	16.4	3.0	62.0	7.9	28.1	26.0
	2012	5 772	21.5	2.0	20.9	3.2	52.5	7.8	20.5	24.2
Mexico - Mexique	1995	72 453	6.3	2.3	2.1	2.3	80.1	9.8	43.2	27.1
	2005	221 819	6.0	1.4	5.5	2.6	83.4	11.0	48.1	24.2
	2012	370 746	6.2	1.1	9.0	2.7	78.2	11.3	46.4	20.5
Micronesia (Federated States of) - Micronésie (États fédérés de)	1995	89	37.2	2.1	1.0	0.9	52.5	2.7	28.2	21.7
	2005	130	33.8	3.1	1.2	0.5	51.5	3.7	18.8	29.0
	2012	(e)210	31.7	1.0	5.6	0.8	47.8	2.9	20.8	24.0
Mongolia - Mongolie	1995	(e)415	14.3	0.7	19.3	0.7	65.1	5.0	39.7	20.3
	2005	1 183	13.0	0.4	26.6	0.5	59.5	5.0	31.2	23.2
	2012	(e)6 738	12.9	0.5	21.2	0.5	64.9	6.4	29.2	29.3
Montenegro - Monténégro	2012	2 336	24.1	0.8	18.4	3.3	53.5	9.3	18.3	25.9
Montserrat	1995	(e)30	16.1	0.7	4.2	0.1	74.6	3.4	58.6	12.6
	2005	(e)30	16.8	2.2	18.9	2.5	56.7	5.5	27.7	23.5
	2012	(e)37	20.4	1.5	22.9	1.0	46.8	5.8	20.5	20.5
Morocco - Maroc	1995	(e)10 023	16.6	5.4	11.7	3.4	48.0	10.2	19.8	18.1
	2005	20 803	10.6	2.8	21.4	3.4	61.8	9.3	26.6	26.0
	2012	44 790	12.5	1.9	27.6	4.2	53.8	9.5	24.3	20.1
Mozambique	1995	(e)727	25.7	1.4	5.8	0.7	65.2	9.7	31.5	24.0
	2005	(e)2 408	15.9	0.9	13.8	0.4	50.9	7.9	23.0	19.9
	2012	(e)6 177	14.4	1.2	18.7	1.9	59.4	9.9	27.8	21.7
Myanmar	1995	(e)1 348	21.7	0.7	4.0	1.8	71.0	9.5	32.8	28.7
	2005	(e)1 952	10.8	0.6	19.3	1.0	68.3	11.6	27.6	29.1
	2012	(e)9 201	10.9	0.7	24.3	1.0	63.2	10.5	24.0	28.7
Namibia - Namibie	1995	(a)1 616	14.7	0.8	5.5	2.7	73.8	8.6	39.8	25.4
	2005	2 525	16.0	0.7	2.2	4.0	75.2	10.2	35.7	29.2
	2012	(e)6 420	11.5	0.8	10.0	14.1	62.1	8.7	30.9	22.5
Nauru	1995	(e)28	24.2	2.3	11.4	0.6	55.7	5.7	28.1	21.9
	2005	(e)25	10.0	1.0	46.8	0.6	21.8	1.2	12.6	8.1
	2012	40	12.9	0.6	16.4	0.1	49.5	11.1	19.5	18.8
Nepal - Népal	1995	(e)1 292	9.8	2.3	9.5	22.3	37.1	8.6	15.0	13.4
	2005	(e)2 243	15.3	3.8	24.7	4.2	51.8	10.1	12.6	29.2
	2012	(e)6 212	13.7	1.7	22.1	8.6	53.9	10.9	19.3	23.7
Netherlands - Pays-Bas	1995	(e)185 240	14.0	2.3	7.2	4.1	70.9	12.1	33.2	25.5
	2005	(e)363 822	8.8	1.5	17.4	3.8	62.5	11.0	32.3	19.2
	2012	(e)591 198	10.2	1.5	28.3	3.9	52.9	11.1	25.1	16.6
Netherlands Antilles - Antilles néerlandaises	1995	(e)1 841	13.6	0.7	32.2	0.6	50.2	3.8	23.0	23.4
	2005	(e)1 950	3.9	0.2	76.4	1.8	16.7	2.6	5.8	8.4

For sources and notes, see end of table.

Pour les sources et les notes, se reporter à la fin du tableau.

Country or territory / Pays ou territoires	Year / Année	Total value (millions of dollars) (1) / Valeur totale (millions de dollars) (1)	All food items / Produits alimentaires	Agricultural raw materials / Matières premières agricoles	Fuels / Combustibles	Ores, metals, precious stones and non-monetary gold / Minerais, métaux, pierres précieuses et or (non monétaire)	Manufactured goods / Articles manufacturés	Chemical products / Produits chimiques	Machinery and transport equipment / Machines et matériel de transport	Other manufactured goods / Articles manufacturés divers
			0 + 1 + 22 + 4	2 - (22 + 27 + 28)	3	27 + 28 + 68 + 667 + 971	5 + 6 +7 + 8 - (667 + 68)	5	7	6 + 8 - (667 + 68)
New Caledonia - Nouvelle-Calédonie	1995	(e)967	15.4	1.0	11.2	0.8	69.9	9.0	33.7	27.2
	2005	1 774	13.2	0.8	15.8	1.0	68.9	9.2	35.0	24.7
	2012	3 245	13.1	0.9	23.0	1.1	56.0	8.2	27.6	20.3
New Zealand - Nouvelle-Zélande	1995	13 958	7.4	1.2	5.3	3.7	82.4	13.1	42.2	27.1
	2005	26 232	7.7	0.8	12.1	2.5	76.7	11.3	40.7	24.7
	2012	38 079	10.6	0.6	17.7	2.4	68.0	11.1	33.7	23.2
Nicaragua	1995	1 009	17.9	0.9	17.9	0.6	62.6	17.5	23.1	22.0
	2005	2 536	13.2	0.5	18.2	0.4	64.9	17.5	23.0	24.4
	2012	5 917	15.4	0.7	23.9	0.4	59.4	15.9	22.5	21.0
Niger	1995	345	28.2	2.5	8.1	2.6	57.8	10.2	23.5	24.2
	2005	(e)943	26.3	4.2	9.4	1.4	57.9	7.8	25.0	25.0
	2012	(e)2 900	28.2	4.5	12.4	1.4	53.1	12.4	22.2	18.6
Nigeria - Nigéria	1995	(e)8 222	11.6	0.9	5.2	1.0	79.5	17.6	34.9	27.1
	2005	(e)20 754	18.5	0.7	4.1	1.9	74.8	12.6	39.3	22.9
	2012	(e)51 000	19.6	1.8	13.2	1.4	64.1	10.4	34.9	18.8
Niue - Nioué	1995	(e)4	4.0	0.3	0.1	0.1	91.4	3.4	22.8	65.2
	2005	(e)10	13.1	2.1	12.7	5.6	66.3	4.6	29.5	32.2
	2012	(e)7	26.7	3.4	14.9	0.4	53.7	6.0	22.6	25.1
Northern Mariana Islands - Îles Mariannes du Nord	1995	(e)240	9.3	0.2	14.4	0.1	73.9	2.4	24.0	47.5
	2005	(e)591	3.4	0.2	27.1	0.0	68.7	0.7	4.0	64.0
	2012	(e)67	15.2	0.1	14.3	0.1	69.7	0.7	11.4	57.6
Norway - Norvège	1995	32 706	6.8	2.7	2.9	6.8	79.9	9.6	37.7	32.7
	2005	55 488	6.8	1.9	4.2	7.8	78.9	9.4	39.5	30.1
	2012	87 321	9.0	1.3	6.2	6.7	75.4	9.0	38.2	28.2
Oman	1995	4 249	18.4	0.7	1.3	4.7	71.9	6.3	42.3	23.3
	2005	8 970	11.4	0.6	3.1	4.2	77.4	7.6	48.9	20.9
	2012	28 118	10.7	0.5	11.3	7.3	69.2	9.0	36.7	23.5
Pakistan	1995	11 704	17.5	5.5	16.1	4.0	56.7	17.0	28.9	10.8
	2005	25 097	10.4	4.2	21.1	5.1	59.0	16.3	29.4	13.3
	2012	43 813	11.1	3.8	36.4	3.1	45.4	15.0	18.5	11.8
Palau - Palaos	1995	(e)52	26.3	3.2	4.2	0.3	59.7	3.8	26.9	29.1
	2005	105	25.8	2.1	2.1	2.4	58.9	5.2	25.9	27.8
	2012	(e)140	39.5	1.0	20.1	0.2	33.5	1.9	18.5	13.0
Panama	1995	2 511	3.2	0.2	4.4	0.7	89.6	5.5	62.0	22.1
	2005	(e)9 600	4.3	0.2	13.9	0.5	74.1	6.6	48.8	18.7
	2012	(e)23 390	3.7	0.2	13.5	0.4	82.3	20.8	42.2	19.2
Papua New Guinea - Papouasie-Nouvelle-Guinée	1995	(e)1 452	14.3	0.8	10.8	0.6	69.8	6.4	39.4	24.0
	2005	(e)1 613	16.7	0.7	26.0	0.8	55.8	7.4	27.4	21.1
	2012	(e)4 608	22.3	0.7	25.7	0.7	50.6	8.5	22.4	19.7
Paraguay	1995	3 136	18.5	0.2	6.5	0.7	74.0	9.0	42.3	22.7
	2005	(e)3 715	7.6	0.7	14.5	0.9	64.4	14.8	29.0	20.6
	2012	11 555	7.9	0.7	15.9	0.7	74.5	15.1	37.1	22.3
Peru - Pérou	1995	7 584	13.5	1.9	8.8	0.8	75.0	13.2	39.2	22.6
	2005	12 502	11.4	1.8	19.8	1.0	66.0	16.1	28.3	21.6
	2012	(e)42 545	11.4	1.6	16.0	1.2	69.8	15.5	32.5	21.8
Philippines	1995	28 487	8.3	2.2	9.2	3.2	57.8	9.2	32.5	16.2
	2005	49 487	6.9	0.9	13.2	2.6	76.4	7.3	57.8	11.3
	2012	65 350	10.4	0.6	21.6	3.6	63.7	10.3	42.2	11.3
Poland - Pologne	1995	29 019	9.6	3.2	9.1	3.3	74.4	14.9	29.9	29.5
	2005	101 539	6.1	1.8	11.4	2.9	75.5	14.0	35.1	26.4
	2012	191 430	8.3	1.9	13.7	3.5	69.7	13.8	32.0	23.9

For sources and notes, see end of table.

Pour les sources et les notes, se reporter à la fin du tableau.

Country or territory / Pays ou territoires	Year / Année	Total value (millions of dollars) (1) / Valeur totale (millions de dollars) (1)	By main SITC Revision 3 product group (percentage) / Par principaux groupes de produits de la CTCI Révision 3 (en pourcentage)					Of which: / dont :		
			All food items / Produits alimentaires	Agricultural raw materials / Matières premières agricoles	Fuels / Combustibles	Ores, metals, precious stones and non-monetary gold / Minerais, métaux, pierres précieuses et or (non monétaire)	Manufactured goods / Articles manufacturés	Chemical products / Produits chimiques	Machinery and transport equipment / Machines et matériel de transport	Other manufactured goods / Articles manufacturés divers
			0 + 1 + 22 + 4	2 - (22 + 27 + 28)	3	27 + 28 + 68 + 667 + 971	5 + 6 +7 + 8 - (667 + 68)	5	7	6 + 8 - (667 + 68)
Portugal	1995	33 565	13.4	3.4	7.2	2.6	72.5	10.0	34.4	28.1
	2005	61 167	11.1	1.5	13.4	3.5	68.7	10.5	33.3	24.9
	2012	72 293	15.4	1.7	19.0	2.8	60.3	14.2	22.9	23.2
Qatar	1995	3 398	9.6	0.6	0.4	2.8	86.0	5.3	47.4	33.3
	2005	10 061	6.0	0.6	0.4	2.9	88.3	5.8	51.8	30.7
	2012	(e)34 200	7.8	0.4	1.5	27.3	56.8	4.6	29.8	22.4
Republic of Moldova - République de Moldova	1995	841	10.6	2.3	43.4	1.6	41.6	8.5	14.6	18.5
	2005	2 292	12.4	3.4	17.3	7.7	56.6	11.4	18.1	27.2
	2012	5 213	15.6	1.5	15.5	1.0	61.8	13.3	21.8	26.7
Romania - Roumanie	1995	10 278	8.5	2.3	21.4	3.6	63.3	10.6	24.8	28.0
	2005	40 463	6.0	1.0	13.9	2.7	76.0	10.2	33.2	32.6
	2012	70 260	8.1	1.7	12.1	2.7	72.6	13.5	32.8	26.4
Russian Federation - Fédération de Russie	1995	(e)60 945	19.9	0.9	2.3	2.8	48.8	6.7	21.9	20.2
	2005	(e)125 434	15.4	1.0	1.4	2.7	78.0	11.4	40.0	26.6
	2012	(e)315 986	12.8	1.0	1.6	2.2	80.9	11.6	44.0	25.3
Rwanda	1995	(e)241	27.3	2.7	10.0	2.0	56.5	7.5	30.1	18.8
	2005	(e)412	14.7	2.1	12.5	2.2	67.1	15.2	28.6	23.3
	2012	(e)2 408	18.4	2.8	5.8	1.1	70.3	14.2	28.3	27.8
Saint Helena - Sainte-Hélène	1995	(e)23	21.5	1.5	16.8	2.4	61.9	7.0	32.9	22.1
	2005	(e)56	11.2	1.8	15.9	13.2	57.2	3.2	38.6	15.3
	2012	(e)51	10.7	0.4	8.0	1.3	73.3	5.6	46.4	21.2
Saint Kitts and Nevis - Saint-Kitts-et-Nevis	1995	132	21.1	2.5	4.3	0.9	71.2	8.3	27.8	35.1
	2005	210	18.5	1.5	8.8	0.8	70.4	6.9	31.2	32.3
	2012	(e)230	22.0	2.0	4.0	1.0	70.9	7.6	24.5	38.9
Saint Lucia - Sainte-Lucie	1995	306	20.4	1.8	23.6	0.7	51.4	7.7	17.4	26.3
	2005	486	15.1	1.3	41.0	1.0	39.7	4.8	15.3	19.5
	2012	(e)660	5.7	0.5	78.5	0.2	15.1	2.1	5.3	7.8
Saint Pierre and Miquelon - Saint-Pierre-et-Miquelon	1995	(e)74	14.5	1.4	7.8	0.8	69.8	8.4	31.5	29.9
	2005	(e)70	22.6	1.6	2.6	0.3	68.6	8.4	32.3	27.9
	2012	(e)190	25.3	1.5	0.8	0.7	65.2	9.2	27.8	28.3
Saint Vincent and the Grenadines - Saint-Vincent-et-les Grenadines	1995	134	18.2	1.6	8.7	0.3	65.0	7.7	34.7	22.5
	2005	240	10.4	1.1	17.3	0.5	60.3	4.1	41.6	14.7
	2012	(e)360	17.5	1.0	23.2	0.4	34.1	5.1	12.8	16.2
Samoa	1995	(e)95	15.7	0.9	7.4	0.3	74.4	5.1	47.2	22.1
	2005	(e)239	20.7	2.2	14.1	0.7	47.1	5.2	16.4	25.5
	2012	(e)346	23.9	2.3	20.8	1.6	48.6	6.3	17.3	25.0
Sao Tome and Principe - Sao Tomé-et-Principe	1995	(e)29	25.3	0.4	1.9	0.5	71.5	6.6	39.0	25.9
	2005	50	38.5	0.9	20.2	0.2	40.2	4.5	21.3	14.4
	2012	141	30.4	0.8	25.7	0.9	42.2	5.6	19.9	16.7
Saudi Arabia - Arabie saoudite	1995	28 085	16.1	1.2	0.2	7.0	75.0	9.6	35.6	29.7
	2005	59 510	14.6	0.7	0.2	5.4	79.0	9.7	45.2	24.0
	2012	(e)155 593	16.0	0.7	0.3	4.7	78.3	10.6	41.3	26.4
Senegal - Sénégal	1995	(e)1 412	28.2	1.9	8.7	1.4	46.5	12.1	15.7	18.8
	2005	3 498	26.6	1.8	22.4	2.0	46.6	9.1	21.0	16.5
	2012	6 434	21.5	1.4	35.0	2.2	39.3	8.2	16.5	14.7
Serbia and Montenegro - Serbie-et-Monténégro	1995	(e)2 666	14.2	4.1	13.9	7.1	59.8	14.3	19.4	26.1
	2005	(e)10 461	7.1	1.5	19.4	6.2	65.5	14.0	25.7	25.8
Serbia - Serbie	2012	19 013	7.4	1.8	17.6	4.3	61.5	16.3	23.2	22.0
Seychelles	1995	255	21.2	1.4	17.4	0.7	59.1	6.5	27.0	25.5
	2005	675	21.5	1.0	23.5	0.4	48.2	4.3	24.6	19.3
	2012	(e)752	21.9	1.9	25.2	0.7	50.2	4.3	24.7	21.2

For sources and notes, see end of table.

Pour les sources et les notes, se reporter à la fin du tableau.

Country or territory / Pays ou territoires	Year / Année	Total value (millions of dollars) (1) / Valeur totale (millions de dollars) (1)	By main SITC Revision 3 product group (percentage) / Par principaux groupes de produits de la CTCI Révision 3 (en pourcentage)					Of which: / dont :		
			All food items / Produits alimentaires	Agricultural raw materials / Matières premières agricoles	Fuels / Combustibles	Ores, metals, precious stones and non-monetary gold / Minerais, métaux, pierres précieuses et or (non monétaire)	Manufactured goods / Articles manufacturés	Chemical products / Produits chimiques	Machinery and transport equipment / Machines et matériel de transport	Other manufactured goods / Articles manufacturés divers
			0 + 1 + 22 + 4	2 - (22 + 27 + 28)	3	27 + 28 + 68 + 667 + 971	5 + 6 +7 + 8 - (667 + 68)	5	7	6 + 8 - (667 + 68)
Sierra Leone	1995	(e)134	31.1	3.0	10.0	0.9	53.4	7.5	26.9	19.0
	2005	(e)344	21.0	7.0	38.6	1.6	31.8	4.9	13.1	13.8
	2012	(e)1 569	23.4	7.3	40.1	1.4	27.8	4.8	11.0	12.0
Singapore - Singapour	1995	124 503	4.6	0.9	8.1	2.9	82.6	6.5	57.9	18.3
	2005	200 050	2.8	0.4	17.7	3.1	75.1	6.2	55.8	13.1
	2012	379 723	3.3	0.4	32.6	2.4	59.5	6.8	40.8	12.0
Sint Maarten (Dutch part) - Saint-Martin (partie néerlandaise)	2012	768	8.6	0.6	2.1	14.2	69.4	3.2	13.3	53.0
Slovakia - Slovaquie	1995	8 162	8.9	2.8	12.7	6.0	69.6	14.5	30.2	24.9
	2005	34 226	6.1	1.3	13.2	3.4	75.3	9.8	37.8	27.7
	2012	77 695	6.8	1.4	13.1	4.2	74.4	8.4	41.1	24.9
Slovenia - Slovénie	1995	9 492	7.8	4.6	6.6	4.4	73.8	12.1	33.8	28.0
	2005	19 626	6.1	2.6	10.6	5.8	74.8	12.8	32.6	29.3
	2012	(e)32 009	7.1	2.7	14.9	5.7	57.8	12.7	24.0	21.1
Solomon Islands - Îles Salomon	1995	(e)154	12.4	0.6	15.4	0.6	67.6	4.1	34.2	29.2
	2005	(e)185	16.3	0.5	23.8	0.8	48.9	5.3	24.4	19.3
	2012	(e)495	18.1	0.6	28.1	0.5	43.2	5.7	21.4	16.2
Somalia - Somalie	1995	(e)268	65.5	2.7	1.3	0.1	31.1	8.3	7.3	15.5
	2005	(e)626	48.4	13.0	0.8	0.1	36.0	6.9	6.6	22.5
	2012	670	60.1	0.5	0.4	0.2	38.4	4.7	8.3	25.4
South Africa - Afrique du Sud	1995	(a)30 546	4.6	1.4	14.2	4.2	66.9	11.7	37.4	17.8
	2005	(e)62 304	3.9	1.0	12.6	3.8	59.4	8.9	34.8	15.7
	2012	(e)124 245	5.3	0.7	18.4	2.3	50.1	8.4	28.1	13.6
Spain - Espagne	1995	113 399	13.6	3.0	8.3	4.3	70.8	12.1	35.6	23.1
	2005	289 611	9.2	1.4	14.0	3.5	71.4	11.6	37.9	22.0
	2012	325 835	11.1	1.3	24.4	4.4	58.4	14.1	24.1	20.2
Sri Lanka	1995	(e)5 185	14.8	1.6	2.2	5.2	73.1	9.2	24.9	38.9
	2005	8 307	12.4	1.2	13.4	7.1	65.8	10.0	20.2	35.6
	2012	17 885	11.4	1.3	21.4	4.5	60.7	10.1	22.4	28.2
State of Palestine - État de Palestine	1995	1 658	..	..	..	..	..	..	..	..
	2005	(e)2 667	23.3	1.2	31.1	2.7	41.6	8.0	13.7	19.9
	2012	(e)4 790	21.7	0.4	38.8	2.1	36.9	7.7	11.9	17.3
Sudan (...2011) - Soudan (...2011)	1995	1 185	20.0	1.9	10.4	0.5	66.9	10.7	24.1	32.1
	2005	7 367	11.9	0.6	4.6	0.9	79.4	8.5	43.5	27.4
Sudan - Soudan	2012	(e)9 475	18.3	0.6	8.4	2.8	67.2	13.6	25.9	27.7
Suriname	1995	583	14.0	0.1	11.8	1.2	73.0	16.0	35.7	21.3
	2005	1 050	9.5	0.0	17.2	0.3	41.0	3.9	23.1	13.9
	2012	(e)1 782	14.2	0.1	21.8	1.3	62.7	15.3	25.7	21.7
Swaziland	1995	(a)1 008	17.5	2.4	10.4	2.7	66.0	12.0	24.4	29.6
	2005	(e)1 900	16.0	1.1	11.0	1.0	69.8	19.9	19.3	30.7
	2012	(e)1 990	13.4	1.1	2.9	7.3	73.3	23.5	14.7	35.1
Sweden - Suède	1995	61 647	6.7	2.2	5.8	3.8	80.0	10.7	41.8	27.5
	2005	111 351	7.4	1.6	11.7	3.3	73.3	10.3	38.6	24.3
	2012	162 686	9.2	1.4	16.1	3.3	66.8	10.9	34.2	21.7
Switzerland - Suisse	1995	80 152	6.4	2.0	2.9	5.6	83.1	14.6	33.4	35.0
	2005	126 574	5.4	1.1	7.2	5.8	80.5	21.7	28.5	30.3
	2012	197 787	5.7	0.9	9.5	5.5	78.3	22.2	25.7	30.3
Syrian Arab Republic - République arabe syrienne	1995	(e)4 709	16.7	3.3	1.1	1.3	75.6	10.2	31.6	33.9
	2005	(e)10 862	14.1	2.6	11.0	2.3	67.8	17.3	26.5	24.0
	2012	(e)7 300	19.4	1.9	14.6	3.0	61.0	18.1	21.0	22.0
Tajikistan - Tadjikistan	1995	(e)810	25.4	0.9	14.5	12.1	46.4	7.3	26.5	12.6
	2005	(e)1 330	12.5	1.8	24.2	12.9	43.7	13.6	14.4	15.6
	2012	(e)3 778	14.5	1.1	18.1	7.3	56.5	9.7	14.6	32.2

For sources and notes, see end of table.　　　　Pour les sources et les notes, se reporter à la fin du tableau.

Country or territory / Pays ou territoires	Year / Année	Total value (millions of dollars) (1) / Valeur totale (millions de dollars) (1)	All food items / Produits alimentaires	Agricultural raw materials / Matières premières agricoles	Fuels Combustibles	Ores, metals, precious stones and non-monetary gold / Minerais, métaux, pierres précieuses et or (non monétaire)	Manufactured goods / Articles manufacturés	Of which: / dont : Chemical products / Produits chimiques	Machinery and transport equipment / Machines et matériel de transport	Other manufactured goods / Articles manufacturés divers
			0 + 1 + 22 + 4	2 - (22 + 27 + 28)	3	27 + 28 + 68 + 667 + 971	5 + 6 +7 + 8 - (667 + 68)	5	7	6 + 8 - (667 + 68)
TFYR of Macedonia - LERY de Macédoine	1995	1 719	17.4	3.3	11.6	3.0	54.2	11.9	19.5	22.8
	2005	3 228	12.7	1.3	19.2	3.2	63.6	10.3	17.4	35.8
	2012	6 511	13.0	0.9	21.3	10.8	53.8	11.3	15.8	26.7
Thailand - Thaïlande	1995	70 781	3.8	4.1	6.7	5.4	78.7	10.5	47.5	20.7
	2005	118 164	4.0	2.0	17.7	6.8	68.2	10.2	38.0	20.0
	2012	247 576	5.1	1.7	19.3	8.6	65.3	9.7	36.7	19.0
Timor-Leste	2005	(e)102	21.7	3.7	21.0	1.5	44.6	5.2	18.0	21.3
	2012	(e)354	28.3	6.1	16.7	1.0	46.1	3.8	20.9	21.3
Togo	1995	556	19.8	2.6	16.5	0.9	59.7	8.0	16.1	35.7
	2005	(e)1 060	16.7	4.1	22.4	1.0	55.4	8.5	15.0	31.9
	2012	1 665	9.9	0.9	37.8	0.3	50.8	4.9	9.9	36.0
Tokelau - Tokélaou	1995	(e)1	4.7	3.4	..	47.5	43.4	3.0	15.3	25.1
	2005	(e)0	0.9	25.8	0.3	0.6	69.2	18.2	32.3	18.8
	2012	(e)0	5.4	0.3	22.7	9.6	60.5	7.8	39.3	13.3
Tonga	1995	(e)77	33.3	3.8	4.3	0.7	53.8	6.6	25.4	21.8
	2005	(e)120	22.5	1.6	18.7	0.4	34.0	3.2	12.6	18.2
	2012	(e)199	30.5	1.5	19.5	1.0	45.0	5.0	18.5	21.5
Trinidad and Tobago - Trinité-et-Tobago	1995	1 724	15.1	0.3	0.5	4.6	59.4	6.5	32.7	20.2
	2005	5 694	9.0	0.6	34.8	4.3	51.2	7.3	26.4	17.4
	2012	(e)9 065	13.3	0.7	27.0	5.4	53.5	8.9	25.6	19.0
Tunisia - Tunisie	1995	7 903	12.5	4.2	7.2	3.3	72.8	9.1	25.9	37.8
	2005	13 174	8.5	2.6	13.7	3.2	72.0	10.5	28.8	32.7
	2012	(e)24 447	10.6	1.8	14.5	3.5	69.6	10.5	31.5	27.6
Turkey - Turquie	1995	35 707	7.0	5.6	12.9	5.9	68.6	15.0	32.2	21.5
	2005	116 774	2.8	2.7	13.5	9.2	66.4	13.8	32.4	20.2
	2012	236 544	4.4	2.5	8.7	11.2	55.9	12.4	26.0	17.5
Turkmenistan - Turkménistan	1995	(e)1 365	29.5	0.5	1.9	1.5	65.0	9.6	27.8	27.7
	2005	(e)2 947	7.1	0.6	0.8	0.6	89.4	7.9	55.4	26.1
	2012	(e)9 900	7.2	1.0	1.2	1.0	86.1	8.6	44.5	32.9
Turks and Caicos Islands - Îles Turques et Caïques	1995	(e)51	11.7	1.7	0.9	0.3	59.7	20.8	16.9	22.0
	2005	304	9.6	2.9	7.9	1.1	59.7	3.5	27.1	29.1
	2012	(e)309	14.8	1.4	28.6	0.5	36.7	3.6	13.6	19.5
Tuvalu	1995	(e)6	31.7	3.1	1.4	..	60.2	2.2	38.4	19.6
	2005	(e)13	19.1	1.3	7.3	0.2	58.7	1.7	46.9	10.1
	2012	(e)25	7.1	0.4	4.3	0.2	67.2	1.2	50.4	15.7
Uganda - Ouganda	1995	1 038	15.3	2.5	4.2	2.2	75.4	11.7	30.7	33.0
	2005	2 054	13.2	1.2	17.2	1.2	66.5	14.6	25.4	26.4
	2012	6 044	9.1	1.4	20.6	1.3	65.0	15.0	29.8	20.3
Ukraine	1995	(e)16 052	7.9	2.4	47.8	3.1	37.9	6.7	17.0	14.2
	2005	36 122	7.2	1.3	29.5	4.3	57.0	11.8	26.4	18.7
	2012	84 657	8.5	1.0	30.9	3.0	56.1	13.2	25.2	17.7
United Arab Emirates - Émirats arabes unis	1995	(e)23 778	10.3	0.9	1.7	2.6	83.1	6.6	36.3	40.2
	2005	(e)80 814	5.9	0.5	4.1	11.2	76.3	5.2	43.5	27.6
	2012	(e)251 921	7.6	0.5	6.3	14.3	69.3	5.7	32.6	31.1
United Kingdom - Royaume-Uni	1995	261 456	10.1	2.4	3.5	5.2	78.1	10.3	41.3	26.6
	2005	515 782	8.5	1.3	8.3	4.1	70.4	10.4	35.8	24.3
	2012	689 137	8.7	1.0	13.8	6.0	59.4	10.9	27.6	20.9
United Republic of Tanzania - République-Unie de Tanzanie	1995	1 653	14.4	1.7	5.0	3.0	75.0	13.7	34.7	26.6
	2005	3 247	10.7	1.3	13.8	2.3	70.3	15.2	29.8	25.4
	2012	11 716	10.0	1.1	21.9	1.4	64.2	11.9	30.1	22.2
United States - États-Unis	1995	770 821	4.8	2.1	8.2	3.8	78.1	5.5	46.4	26.2
	2005	1 732 321	4.2	1.3	17.2	3.4	70.6	7.6	38.3	24.7
	2012	2 333 805	5.0	1.1	18.6	3.9	68.6	8.6	38.0	22.0

For sources and notes, see end of table.

Pour les sources et les notes, se reporter à la fin du tableau.

Country or territory / Pays ou territoires	Year / Année	Total value (millions of dollars) (1) / Valeur totale (millions de dollars) (1)	All food items / Produits alimentaires	Agricultural raw materials / Matières premières agricoles	Fuels / Combustibles	Ores, metals, precious stones and non-monetary gold / Minerais, métaux, pierres précieuses et or (non monétaire)	Manufactured goods / Articles manufacturés	Chemical products / Produits chimiques	Machinery and transport equipment / Machines et matériel de transport	Other manufactured goods / Articles manufacturés divers
			0 + 1 + 22 + 4	2 - (22 + 27 + 28)	3	27 + 28 + 68 + 667 + 971	5 + 6 +7 + 8 - (667 + 68)	5	7	6 + 8 - (667 + 68)
Uruguay	1995	2 866	10.4	4.0	10.1	1.2	74.3	15.3	34.5	24.5
	2005	3 879	8.1	3.1	24.3	1.6	62.9	19.4	23.2	20.3
	2012	11 614	9.4	1.9	26.7	1.0	61.0	16.6	26.1	18.3
Uzbekistan - Ouzbékistan	1995	2 750	19.6	0.4	2.3	2.8	73.4	8.9	41.7	22.7
	2005	3 666	7.7	3.2	2.8	2.9	80.9	11.1	43.5	26.3
	2012	11 296	10.4	3.6	6.4	3.5	73.4	11.6	37.9	24.0
Vanuatu	1995	(e)95	8.6	0.3	2.3	0.3	80.6	2.9	59.8	17.9
	2005	(e)149	18.9	0.7	17.9	1.0	61.6	6.8	33.8	21.0
	2012	(e)274	14.0	0.8	17.4	0.3	67.5	5.7	47.4	14.5
Venezuela (Bolivarian Rep. of) - Venezuela (Rép. bolivarienne du)	1995	(e)12 649	13.8	4.3	1.3	3.5	75.5	15.2	38.7	21.6
	2005	21 848	10.5	1.1	1.2	1.6	85.0	13.7	48.5	22.7
	2012	(e)60 400	18.1	1.1	4.1	1.4	75.4	17.8	35.7	21.9
Viet Nam	1995	(e)8 155	4.9	2.4	10.3	2.4	75.9	16.7	28.3	30.9
	2005	36 761	6.3	3.7	14.6	5.4	69.7	14.4	25.1	30.2
	2012	(e)113 780	8.1	3.0	13.4	4.5	71.0	14.9	28.9	27.1
Wallis and Futuna Islands - Îles Wallis-et-Futuna	1995	(e)14	32.7	1.2	4.5	0.2	60.8	8.3	38.3	14.2
	2005	(e)51	27.1	0.8	11.2	1.2	55.6	11.1	22.3	22.2
	2012	(e)65	29.6	0.9	10.3	0.9	55.3	12.8	16.6	25.8
Western Sahara - Sahara occidental	1995	(e)14	19.5	21.0	9.3	1.5	48.6	8.1	5.8	34.8
Yemen - Yémen	1995	(e)1 582	32.2	1.8	9.9	1.0	54.4	7.3	21.0	26.1
	2005	(e)5 400	25.0	0.7	19.9	1.1	49.8	8.5	19.9	21.3
	2012	(e)12 000	29.4	0.7	25.6	0.8	43.4	7.2	14.4	21.7
Zambia - Zambie	1995	708	10.8	1.9	8.6	2.7	75.4	12.7	39.8	22.9
	2005	2 558	7.4	1.1	10.3	3.0	76.6	19.0	31.7	25.9
	2012	(e)8 200	4.8	0.7	9.4	17.3	67.8	18.2	31.5	18.1
Zimbabwe	1995	(e)2 659	8.1	2.4	6.7	4.9	76.9	17.5	38.8	20.6
	2005	(e)2 350	13.6	1.6	12.6	25.6	45.8	10.6	20.2	15.0
	2012	(e)4 400	22.2	0.6	10.0	3.2	63.7	16.1	28.8	18.7

Source:
UNCTAD secretariat calculations, based on UNCTAD, *UNCTADstat* Merchandise Trade Matrix

Source :
Calculs du secrétariat de la CNUCED, basés sur la matrice du commerce de marchandises d'*UNCTADstat* de la CNUCED

Notes:
(a) More than 30% of total trade under SITC Rev.3, code 931: "Special transactions & commodities not classified".
(1) Includes unallocated product groups, SITC Rev.3, 911 and 931.

Notes :
(a) Plus de 30% du commerce sous la position 931 de la CTCI rév. 3 : "Transactions et articles spéciaux non classés".
(1) Y compris les groupes de produits non-distribués, CTCI Rév.3, 911 et 931.

Products ranked by average 2011-2012 values SITC Revision 3 (3-digit level) / Produits classés d'après la moyenne des valeurs de 2011-2012 CTCI révision 3 (positions à 3 chiffres)	2005 Value (millions of dollars) / Valeur (millions de dollars)	2005 % of the country grouping exports / En % des exportations du groupe de pays	2005 % of world product exports / En % des exportations mondiales des produits	2012 Value (millions of dollars) / Valeur (millions de dollars)	2012 % of the country grouping exports / En % des exportations du groupe de pays	2012 % of world product exports / En % des exportations mondiales des produits	Growth rates (%) 2005-2012 Value / Valeur	Difference from world / Différence par rapport au monde
All commodity groups	10 447 270	100.00	100.00	18 351 468	100.00	100.00	6.35	–
333 Crude petroleum & bituminous oil	796 723	7.63	100.00	1 770 439	9.65	100.00	8.58	–
334 Heavy petroleum & bituminous oil	377 933	3.62	100.00	1 018 259	5.55	100.00	12.58	–
781 Passenger cars and race cars	487 521	4.67	100.00	646 149	3.52	100.00	1.70	–
776 Valves tubes; diodes, transistors	367 379	3.52	100.00	555 287	3.03	100.00	5.00	–
764 Telecom equipment part nes	360 145	3.45	100.00	521 442	2.84	100.00	3.54	–
784 Motor vehicle parts and accessories	234 800	2.25	100.00	360 448	1.96	100.00	4.82	–
752 Computer equipment nes	275 924	2.64	100.00	358 975	1.96	100.00	2.92	–
343 Natural gas, liquefied or not	151 721	1.45	100.00	361 508	1.97	100.00	10.48	–
542 Medicines including veterinary	207 800	1.99	100.00	334 151	1.82	100.00	5.40	–
971 Gold non-monetary excluding ores	38 254	0.37	100.00	274 698	1.50	100.00	29.02	–
772 Electrical circuit equipment	142 267	1.36	100.00	237 345	1.29	100.00	5.78	–
778 Electrical machinery apparatus nes	148 363	1.42	100.00	225 844	1.23	100.00	4.90	–
759 Office equipment part & accessories	201 037	1.92	100.00	186 879	1.02	100.00	-2.72	–
728 Special industrial machine part nes	98 502	0.94	100.00	174 474	0.95	100.00	6.90	–
874 Measure analyze control device nes	111 473	1.07	100.00	185 142	1.01	100.00	6.10	–
793 Ships boats floating structures	71 259	0.68	100.00	157 997	0.86	100.00	11.38	–
541 Pharmaceuticals excluding medicines	66 898	0.64	100.00	168 463	0.92	100.00	13.87	–
713 Internal combustion engine part nes	113 367	1.09	100.00	159 303	0.87	100.00	3.35	–
792 Aircraft, spacecraft & equipment	128 436	1.23	100.00	169 645	0.92	100.00	-2.07	–
667 Pearls, precious semiprecious stone	94 656	0.91	100.00	143 644	0.78	100.00	8.65	–
821 Furniture part; bedding furnishing	97 385	0.93	100.00	156 813	0.85	100.00	4.89	–
699 Base metal manufactures nes	90 760	0.87	100.00	145 143	0.79	100.00	3.62	–
682 Copper	64 284	0.62	100.00	138 272	0.75	100.00	3.79	–
845 Articles of apparel nes	95 979	0.92	100.00	138 072	0.75	100.00	3.26	–
893 Articles of plastic nes	86 159	0.82	100.00	142 130	0.77	100.00	5.85	–
281 Iron ore and concentrates	28 967	0.28	100.00	122 285	0.67	100.00	27.81	–
782 Goods and service vehicles	90 481	0.87	100.00	136 207	0.74	100.00	2.06	–
321 Coal excluding non-agglomomerated	46 280	0.44	100.00	127 026	0.69	100.00	18.74	–
598 Miscellaneous chemical products nes	64 362	0.62	100.00	122 037	0.67	100.00	8.02	–
897 Jewellery nes (667)	40 985	0.39	100.00	137 881	0.75	100.00	17.78	–
743 Gas pump, compressor, fan, filter	69 566	0.67	100.00	123 361	0.67	100.00	6.66	–
723 Civil engineering plant & equipment	69 427	0.66	100.00	124 005	0.68	100.00	4.11	–
641 Paper and paperboard	96 888	0.93	100.00	114 543	0.62	100.00	1.37	–
684 Aluminium	79 133	0.76	100.00	112 100	0.61	100.00	0.58	–
851 Footwear	66 671	0.64	100.00	117 449	0.64	100.00	7.73	–
575 Other plastics, in primary forms	66 862	0.64	100.00	110 978	0.60	100.00	5.94	–
773 Electrical distribute equipment nes	61 377	0.59	100.00	112 287	0.61	100.00	5.27	–
741 Heating and cooling equipment parts nes	68 910	0.66	100.00	111 790	0.61	100.00	3.79	–
515 Organo-inorganic compound acid salt	79 978	0.77	100.00	111 877	0.61	100.00	3.79	–
871 Optical instruments apparatus nes	44 800	0.43	100.00	109 161	0.59	100.00	10.59	–
582 Plastic sheet film foil & strips	57 973	0.55	100.00	97 255	0.53	100.00	6.27	–
511 Hydrocarbons nes; derivatives	50 723	0.49	100.00	97 917	0.53	100.00	7.91	–
679 Iron steel pipe tube fittings etc	54 442	0.52	100.00	97 695	0.53	100.00	3.07	–
716 Rotating electric plant parts nes	51 629	0.49	100.00	97 219	0.53	100.00	6.71	–
775 Household equipment nes	64 073	0.61	100.00	95 437	0.52	100.00	4.17	–
894 Baby carriages, toys, games, sporting goods	64 736	0.62	100.00	92 505	0.50	100.00	2.97	–
625 Rubber for wheels, incl inner tube	43 822	0.42	100.00	92 564	0.50	100.00	10.31	–
771 Electric power machine part excluding 716	45 865	0.44	100.00	92 592	0.50	100.00	8.05	–
676 Iron steel bar rod section piling	52 927	0.51	100.00	89 487	0.49	100.00	1.98	–
761 Television video receive project	57 558	0.55	100.00	87 983	0.48	100.00	1.89	–
714 Non-electric engines excluding 712, 713, and 718	69 025	0.66	100.00	93 670	0.51	100.00	1.35	–
872 Medical instruments appliances nes	52 831	0.51	100.00	91 359	0.50	100.00	8.02	–
673 Flat iron non-alloy steel products	66 920	0.64	100.00	80 645	0.44	100.00	0.20	–
057 Fruit nut (exc oil), fresh or dried	48 457	0.46	100.00	88 995	0.48	100.00	9.00	–
842 Female clothing, woven	65 542	0.63	100.00	80 584	0.44	100.00	1.77	–
744 Mechanical handling equipment nes	52 441	0.50	100.00	83 182	0.45	100.00	2.10	–
899 Manufactured articles nes	44 410	0.43	100.00	83 152	0.45	100.00	8.74	–
747 Pipe, boiler, tank & vat appliances	41 059	0.39	100.00	80 544	0.44	100.00	6.50	–
571 Primary form ethylene polymers	42 002	0.40	100.00	76 693	0.42	100.00	7.77	–
553 Perfume toilet cosmetics, excluding soap	43 885	0.42	100.00	77 704	0.42	100.00	7.27	–

For sources and notes, see end of table.

Pour les sources et les notes, se reporter à la fin du tableau.

Products ranked by average 2011-2012 values SITC Revision 3 (3-digit level) / Produits classés d'après la moyenne des valeurs de 2011-2012 CTCI révision 3 (positions à 3 chiffres)	2005			2012			Growth rates (%) Taux d'accroissement (%) 2005-2012	
	Value (millions of dollars) / Valeur (millions de dollars)	% of the country grouping exports / En % des exportations du groupe de pays	% of world product exports / En % des exportations mondiales des produits	Value (millions of dollars) / Valeur (millions de dollars)	% of the country grouping exports / En % des exportations du groupe de pays	% of world product exports / En % des exportations mondiales des produits	Value / Valeur	Difference from world / Différence par rapport au monde
112 Alcoholic beverages	46 384	0.44	100.00	77 944	0.42	100.00	5.94	–
562 Manufactured fertilizer excluding crude	24 770	0.24	100.00	74 420	0.41	100.00	16.59	–
081 Animal feed excluding unmilled cereal	30 757	0.29	100.00	76 854	0.42	100.01	13.41	–
012 Meat nes, fresh chilled frozen	40 049	0.38	100.00	72 667	0.40	100.00	9.51	–
841 Male clothing, woven	53 455	0.51	100.00	70 553	0.38	100.00	3.10	–
222 Oil seed etc for soft oil	21 492	0.21	100.00	75 023	0.41	100.00	19.87	–
675 Flat rolled products of alloy steel	44 209	0.42	100.00	65 512	0.36	100.00	1.19	–
681 Silver, platinum, platinum metals	21 003	0.20	100.00	61 595	0.34	100.00	9.43	–
533 Pigment, paint, varnish & related	39 346	0.38	100.00	62 590	0.34	100.00	5.84	–
512 Alcohols, phenols; derivatives	32 240	0.31	100.00	60 705	0.33	100.00	8.71	–
098 Edible products & preparations nes	33 160	0.32	100.00	63 283	0.34	100.00	9.05	–
742 Liquid pump; liquid elevator parts	33 739	0.32	100.00	61 705	0.34	100.00	7.14	–
522 Inorganic chemical elem oxide salt	29 034	0.28	100.00	58 973	0.32	100.00	9.24	–
763 Sound TV recorder or reproducer	62 265	0.60	100.00	59 867	0.33	100.00	-1.02	–
034 Fish, fresh live chilled frozen	34 603	0.33	100.00	60 361	0.33	100.00	8.43	–
054 Vegetable & vegetable products nes	33 772	0.32	100.00	58 553	0.32	100.00	7.42	–
642 Cut paper and paperboard articles	36 707	0.35	100.00	60 146	0.33	100.00	6.22	–
674 Flat plated iron non-alloy steel	34 969	0.33	100.00	56 446	0.31	100.00	4.56	–
342 Liquefied propane and butane	29 017	0.28	100.00	58 654	0.32	100.00	8.96	–
898 Music instrument device recording	51 236	0.49	100.00	56 474	0.31	100.00	0.07	–
651 Textile yarn	40 853	0.39	100.00	55 523	0.30	100.00	4.15	–
745 Non-electrical machinery tool nes	39 689	0.38	100.00	56 982	0.31	100.00	2.91	–
574 Polyacetals and polyesters, etc	36 494	0.35	100.00	55 123	0.30	100.00	4.97	–
884 Optical goods fibres nes	30 639	0.29	100.00	57 501	0.31	100.00	8.36	–
844 Female clothing, knitted crocheted	26 080	0.25	100.00	58 555	0.32	100.00	9.03	–
691 Iron steel aluminium structures nes	27 222	0.26	100.00	56 791	0.31	100.00	5.59	–
748 Mechanical transmission equipment	29 602	0.28	100.00	55 220	0.30	100.00	7.46	–
831 Case bag: storage travel shopping	23 724	0.23	100.00	56 058	0.31	100.00	12.38	–
283 Copper ores and concentrates	19 520	0.19	100.00	54 463	0.30	100.00	9.15	–
282 Ferrous iron & steel, waste & scrap	25 001	0.24	100.00	50 238	0.27	100.00	6.28	–
514 Nitrogen function compounds	34 137	0.33	100.00	53 197	0.29	100.00	6.33	–
658 Made-up textile articles nes	31 704	0.30	100.00	51 602	0.28	100.00	6.99	–
751 Office machines	15 302	0.15	100.00	51 266	0.28	100.00	12.77	–
513 Carboxylic acid and compounds	33 219	0.32	100.00	48 487	0.26	100.00	4.81	–
335 Residual petroleum products nes	18 566	0.18	100.00	50 273	0.27	100.00	12.96	–
885 Watches and clocks	25 297	0.24	100.00	52 251	0.28	100.00	10.58	–
892 Printed matter	39 247	0.38	100.00	47 143	0.26	100.00	1.81	–
695 Tools for use in hand or in machine	30 620	0.29	100.00	49 617	0.27	100.00	5.20	–
422 Fixed veg fat and oil, excluding "soft"	13 659	0.13	100.00	47 070	0.26	100.00	18.50	–
041 Wheat meslin, incl spelt, unmilled	17 920	0.17	100.00	49 119	0.27	100.00	11.92	–
251 Pulp and waste paper	26 328	0.25	100.00	44 947	0.24	100.00	6.85	–
657 Special yarn and textile fabric etc	30 224	0.29	100.00	46 475	0.25	100.00	6.03	–
288 Non ferrous base metal waste nes	17 441	0.17	100.00	45 976	0.25	100.00	6.58	–
785 Motorcycles, mopeds and cycles	32 495	0.31	100.00	47 915	0.26	100.00	3.76	–
783 Road motor vehicles nes	30 526	0.29	100.00	46 828	0.26	100.00	2.49	–
048 Cereal & preparation flour starch	25 370	0.24	100.00	46 791	0.25	100.00	7.86	–
061 Sugar, mollasses and honey	17 823	0.17	100.00	44 361	0.24	100.00	13.95	–
653 Man-made woven fabrics	32 055	0.31	100.00	43 246	0.24	100.00	4.08	–
292 Crude vegetable materials nes	24 371	0.23	100.00	45 553	0.25	100.00	8.86	–
672 Ingots, Iron steel primary products	28 980	0.28	100.00	41 488	0.23	100.00	2.38	–
774 Electrodiagnostic equipment	26 136	0.25	100.00	42 895	0.23	100.00	5.90	–
022 Milk products, excluding butter & cheese	22 897	0.22	100.00	41 470	0.23	100.00	7.69	–
671 Pig & sponge iron, ferro alloys etc	26 415	0.25	100.00	40 042	0.22	100.00	4.91	–
516 Other organic chemicals	25 574	0.24	100.00	42 111	0.23	100.00	6.75	–
071 Coffee and coffee substitutes	15 712	0.15	100.00	38 457	0.21	100.00	13.54	–
554 Soaps cleansers polishes	22 723	0.22	100.00	40 445	0.22	100.00	7.43	–
731 Machine tools for material removal	27 272	0.26	100.00	41 526	0.23	100.00	2.82	–
421 Fixed veg fat and oil, "soft"	16 861	0.16	100.00	40 368	0.22	100.00	10.52	–
011 Beef, fresh chilled frozen	21 762	0.21	100.00	39 683	0.22	100.00	8.31	–
351 Electric current	24 884	0.24	100.00	38 344	0.21	100.00	4.28	–

For sources and notes, see end of table.

Pour les sources et les notes, se reporter à la fin du tableau.

Products ranked by average 2011-2012 values SITC Revision 3 (3-digit level) / Produits classés d'après la moyenne des valeurs de 2011-2012 CTCI révision 3 (positions à 3 chiffres)	2005			2012			Growth rates (%) Taux d'accroissement (%) 2005-2012	
	Value (millions of dollars) / Valeur (millions de dollars)	% of the country grouping exports / En % des exportations du groupe de pays	% of world product exports / En % des exportations mondiales des produits	Value (millions of dollars) / Valeur (millions de dollars)	% of the country grouping exports / En % des exportations du groupe de pays	% of world product exports / En % des exportations mondiales des produits	Value / Valeur	Difference from world / Différence par rapport au monde
664 Glass	25 531	0.24	100.00	38 547	0.21	100.00	4.52	_
721 Agricultural machine nes excluding tractor	20 712	0.20	100.00	38 880	0.21	100.00	7.38	_
813 Lighting fixtures and fittings nes	19 131	0.18	100.00	41 650	0.23	100.00	9.80	_
694 Nails screws nuts bolts rivets	21 481	0.21	100.00	37 463	0.20	100.00	6.23	_
248 Wood simply worked, railway sleeper	35 506	0.34	100.00	36 651	0.20	100.00	-1.65	_
663 Mineral manufactures nes	21 488	0.21	100.00	35 220	0.19	100.00	4.79	_
044 Maize unmilled, excluding sweet corn	11 392	0.11	100.00	35 789	0.20	100.00	14.59	_
786 Trailer caravan transport container	23 283	0.22	100.00	33 197	0.18	100.00	1.20	_
634 Veneer, plywood & other wood nes	29 905	0.29	100.00	34 457	0.19	100.00	-0.35	_
746 Ball or roller bearings	19 702	0.19	100.00	32 731	0.18	100.00	6.60	_
231 Natural rubber, latex, gum, etc	9 841	0.09	100.00	27 439	0.15	100.00	14.64	_
652 Woven cotton fabrics	29 003	0.28	100.00	31 877	0.17	100.00	1.46	_
287 Base metal ores & concentrates nes	18 792	0.18	100.00	31 116	0.17	100.00	3.58	_
036 Crustacean mollusc aquat invertebra	20 087	0.19	100.00	32 052	0.17	100.00	7.50	_
791 Railway vehicles and equipment	16 386	0.16	100.00	33 398	0.18	100.00	8.60	_
122 Manufactured tabacco	19 245	0.18	100.00	30 878	0.17	100.00	7.36	_
749 Non-electric machinery part nes	21 824	0.21	100.00	31 130	0.17	100.00	3.44	_
655 Knitted or crocheted fabrics nes	19 847	0.19	100.00	30 377	0.17	100.00	5.56	_
843 Male clothing, knitted crocheted	15 130	0.14	100.00	31 209	0.17	100.00	7.64	_
724 Textile leather machinery parts nes	25 515	0.24	100.00	28 561	0.16	100.00	0.58	_
629 Articles of rubber nes	18 285	0.18	100.00	30 078	0.16	100.00	5.88	_
848 Headgear, non-textile clothing	21 131	0.20	100.00	30 393	0.17	100.00	6.87	_
024 Cheese and curd	17 433	0.17	100.00	29 513	0.16	100.00	6.87	_
697 Base metal household equipment nes	18 638	0.18	100.00	30 531	0.17	100.00	5.51	_
661 Lime cement construction material	19 262	0.18	100.00	30 319	0.17	100.00	3.39	_
591 Household and garden chemicals	16 281	0.16	100.00	30 088	0.16	100.00	9.60	_
846 Clothing accessory excluding 831, 848, and 851	17 673	0.17	100.00	28 741	0.16	100.00	7.47	_
056 Vegetables roots tubers nes	16 177	0.15	100.00	27 998	0.15	100.00	7.07	_
232 Synthetic & reclaimed rubber; waste	11 977	0.11	100.00	27 095	0.15	100.00	12.25	_
665 Glassware	17 510	0.17	100.00	27 747	0.15	100.00	4.85	_
037 Fish shellfish, prepared preserved	14 883	0.14	100.00	27 385	0.15	100.00	6.94	_
662 Clay and refractory materials	17 076	0.16	100.00	27 256	0.15	100.00	4.01	_
621 Rubber material e.g. paste tube rod	13 046	0.12	100.00	26 089	0.14	100.00	8.70	_
263 Cotton	11 039	0.11	100.00	25 523	0.14	100.00	15.36	_
635 Wood manufactures nes	21 082	0.20	100.00	25 788	0.14	100.00	0.16	_
592 Starches, glutenes, glues, etc	14 185	0.14	100.00	25 912	0.14	100.00	8.38	_
572 Primary form styrene polymers	19 331	0.19	100.00	24 830	0.14	100.00	2.02	_
551 Essential oils, perfumes & flavours	15 682	0.15	100.00	25 216	0.14	100.00	6.74	_
718 Power generating machinery part nes	11 449	0.11	100.00	24 966	0.14	100.00	10.27	_
042 Rice	10 155	0.10	100.00	24 772	0.13	100.00	13.96	_
073 Chocolate & cocoa preparations nes	12 757	0.12	100.00	24 172	0.13	100.00	8.39	_
611 Leather	20 764	0.20	100.00	23 508	0.13	100.00	-0.18	_
722 Tractors	14 272	0.14	100.00	24 313	0.13	100.00	4.83	_
597 Additive e.g. lubricate, antifreeze	11 413	0.11	100.00	23 592	0.13	100.00	9.57	_
896 Work of art & collections; antiques	14 912	0.14	100.00	23 790	0.13	100.00	2.59	_
737 Metalwork machinery nes excluding tools	16 053	0.15	100.00	21 664	0.12	100.00	1.07	_
001 Live animal excluding fish & crustacean	13 775	0.13	100.00	22 092	0.12	100.00	6.64	_
523 Inorganic acid metal salt peroxy	12 319	0.12	100.00	21 909	0.12	100.00	6.23	_
683 Nickel	13 665	0.13	100.00	19 787	0.11	100.00	-3.67	_
581 Plastic tube pipe hose & fittings	11 902	0.11	100.00	21 727	0.12	100.00	6.24	_
072 Cocoa	9 427	0.09	100.00	18 726	0.10	100.00	13.14	_
692 Metal storage transport container	11 437	0.11	100.00	20 039	0.11	100.00	4.66	_
573 Vinyl chloride etc polymers	12 492	0.12	100.00	19 375	0.11	100.00	5.49	_
017 Meat offal preserved nes	10 822	0.10	100.00	20 166	0.11	100.00	8.20	_
111 Non alcoholic beverage nes	11 164	0.11	100.00	19 967	0.11	100.00	6.05	_
058 Fruit preserve preparation excluding juice	10 105	0.10	100.00	19 584	0.11	100.00	8.04	_
289 Prec metal ore concentrate excluding gold	4 050	0.04	100.00	17 937	0.10	100.00	17.58	_
525 Radio active & associated materials	7 744	0.07	100.00	16 135	0.09	100.00	7.43	_
882 Photo cinematographic supply excluding 883	19 717	0.19	100.00	17 543	0.10	100.00	-1.85	_
278 Other crude minerals	10 775	0.10	100.00	17 355	0.09	100.00	6.12	_

For sources and notes, see end of table.

Pour les sources et les notes, se reporter à la fin du tableau.

Products ranked by average 2011-2012 values SITC Revision 3 (3-digit level) Produits classés d'après la moyenne des valeurs de 2011-2012 CTCI révision 3 (positions à 3 chiffres)	2005			2012			Growth rates (%) Taux d'accroissement (%) 2005-2012	
	Value (millions of dollars) Valeur (millions de dollars)	% of the country grouping exports En % des exportations du groupe de pays	% of world product exports En % des exportations mondiales des produits	Value (millions of dollars) Valeur (millions de dollars)	% of the country grouping exports En % des exportations du groupe de pays	% of world product exports En % des exportations mondiales des produits	Value Valeur	Difference from world Différence par rapport au monde
059 Fruit & vegetable juice unfermented	9 147	0.09	100.00	17 078	0.09	100.00	5.38	–
735 Machine part accessory for 731 and 733	11 817	0.11	100.00	16 600	0.09	100.00	3.12	–
762 Radio broadcast receivers	18 772	0.18	100.00	16 685	0.09	100.00	-3.05	–
895 Office and stationery supplies nes	10 619	0.10	100.00	16 452	0.09	100.00	5.31	–
693 Wire products and fencing grills	9 134	0.09	100.00	15 682	0.09	100.00	4.39	–
726 Printing bookbinding machines parts	18 633	0.18	100.00	14 905	0.08	100.00	-5.71	–
659 Floor coverings etc	11 806	0.11	100.00	15 382	0.08	100.00	2.41	–
247 Wood in rough or roughly squared	11 064	0.11	100.00	14 606	0.08	100.00	2.10	–
285 Aluminium ore concentrate alumina	10 612	0.10	100.00	14 816	0.08	100.00	1.16	–
727 Food processing machine excluding domestic	9 357	0.09	100.00	15 246	0.08	100.00	4.67	–
812 Sanitary plumb heat fixtures nes	11 455	0.11	100.00	14 877	0.08	100.00	0.23	–
431 Processed animal & veg fats & oils	5 741	0.05	100.00	14 458	0.08	100.00	13.16	–
344 Petroleum and hydrocarbon gas nes	10 235	0.10	100.00	15 530	0.08	100.00	-0.08	–
524 Other inorganic chemicals	6 665	0.06	100.00	12 521	0.07	100.00	7.13	–
733 Metal work tool no material removal	9 059	0.09	100.00	13 650	0.07	100.00	2.41	–
686 Zinc	6 952	0.07	100.00	12 386	0.07	100.00	-4.06	–
678 Wire of iron or steel	7 191	0.07	100.00	12 100	0.07	100.00	5.57	–
531 Synthetic organic colour agents	10 413	0.10	100.00	12 248	0.07	100.00	1.32	–
873 Meters and counters nes	6 722	0.06	100.00	12 513	0.07	100.00	8.71	–
121 Unmanufactured tabacco and refuse	7 100	0.07	100.00	12 585	0.07	100.00	7.63	–
273 Stone, sand and gravel	6 260	0.06	100.00	13 343	0.07	100.00	7.35	–
891 Arms and ammunition	7 459	0.07	100.00	12 036	0.07	100.00	5.25	–
696 Cutlery	7 231	0.07	100.00	11 516	0.06	100.00	6.38	–
725 Paper & pulp mill, cut manufacture	9 405	0.09	100.00	11 198	0.06	100.00	0.45	–
654 Other woven textile fabrics nes	11 115	0.11	100.00	10 677	0.06	100.00	-1.78	–
062 Sugar confectionery	6 637	0.06	100.00	10 960	0.06	100.00	6.55	–
284 Nickel ores, concentrates, etc	5 449	0.05	100.00	10 151	0.06	100.00	2.75	–
689 Misc non-ferrous base metals	7 451	0.07	100.00	9 686	0.05	100.00	0.43	–
656 Tulle lace embroidery trim etc	8 188	0.08	100.00	9 664	0.05	100.00	0.67	–
711 Steam generating boilers & parts	3 911	0.04	100.00	9 337	0.05	100.00	12.98	–
666 Pottery	6 357	0.06	100.00	9 857	0.05	100.00	6.90	–
291 Crude animal materials nes	5 160	0.05	100.00	9 461	0.05	100.00	9.32	–
811 Prefabricated buildings	5 531	0.05	100.00	9 062	0.05	100.00	3.18	–
325 Coke, semi coke, retort carbon	6 211	0.06	100.00	7 765	0.04	100.00	3.66	–
266 Synthetic fibres for spinning	5 973	0.06	100.00	8 088	0.04	100.00	5.75	–
075 Spices	2 992	0.03	100.00	8 599	0.05	100.00	16.26	–
712 Steam vapour turbines & parts nes	4 233	0.04	100.00	8 001	0.04	100.00	11.80	–
074 Tea and maté	4 155	0.04	100.00	8 479	0.05	100.00	10.41	–
211 Raw hides & skins, excluding furskins	5 799	0.06	100.00	8 176	0.04	100.00	5.29	–
023 Butter fats oils derived from milk	4 349	0.04	100.00	7 138	0.04	100.00	9.76	–
043 Barley grain unmilled	3 632	0.03	100.00	7 956	0.04	100.00	9.61	–
687 Tin	3 211	0.03	100.00	7 146	0.04	100.00	11.63	–
268 Wool & animal hair, incl wool tops	4 909	0.05	100.00	6 939	0.04	100.00	5.66	–
579 Plastic waste, parings and scrap	3 701	0.04	100.00	7 280	0.04	100.00	7.91	–
881 Photographic device nes	17 211	0.16	100.00	7 060	0.04	100.00	-12.32	–
091 Margarine and shortening	2 779	0.03	100.00	6 457	0.04	100.00	11.33	–
685 Lead	2 871	0.03	100.00	6 205	0.03	100.00	5.96	–
411 Animals oils and fats	2 526	0.02	100.00	6 424	0.04	100.00	13.22	–
246 Wood chips, particles and waste	2 951	0.03	100.00	6 040	0.03	100.00	10.51	–
035 Fish, dried salted smoked	3 808	0.04	100.00	5 903	0.03	100.00	5.59	–
046 Wheat meal & flour, meslin flour	2 545	0.02	100.00	5 756	0.03	100.00	11.62	–
025 Eggs, yolks and albumin	2 408	0.02	100.00	5 939	0.03	100.00	13.00	–
274 Sulphur and unroasted iron pyrites	1 627	0.02	100.00	5 534	0.03	100.00	17.35	–
583 Plastic rod stick & profile shapes	3 676	0.04	100.00	5 123	0.03	100.00	2.66	–
212 Raw furskins and furskin pieces	2 349	0.02	100.00	5 815	0.03	100.00	12.43	–
267 Man made fibre for spinning; waste	3 195	0.03	100.00	5 096	0.03	100.00	5.03	–
272 Crude fertilizer, excluding manufactured	1 817	0.02	100.00	5 189	0.03	100.00	16.62	–
269 Worn clothing, textile article; rag	2 141	0.02	100.00	5 072	0.03	100.00	12.33	–
016 Meat offal preserved	2 673	0.03	100.00	4 671	0.03	100.00	6.12	–
677 Iron steel rail railway materials	2 307	0.02	100.00	4 499	0.02	100.00	8.01	–

For sources and notes, see end of table.

Pour les sources et les notes, se reporter à la fin du tableau.

Products ranked by average 2011-2012 values SITC Revision 3 (3-digit level) Produits classés d'après la moyenne des valeurs de 2011-2012 CTCI révision 3 (positions à 3 chiffres)	2005			2012			Growth rates (%) Taux d'accroissement (%) 2005-2012	
	Value (millions of dollars) Valeur (millions de dollars)	% of the country grouping exports En % des exportations du groupe de pays	% of world product exports En % des exportations mondiales des produits	Value (millions of dollars) Valeur (millions de dollars)	% of the country grouping exports En % des exportations du groupe de pays	% of world product exports En % des exportations mondiales des produits	Value Valeur	Difference from world Différence par rapport au monde
322 Briquettes, lignite and peat	990	0.01	100.00	3 838	0.02	100.00	23.81	_
612 Leather manufactures nes	3 088	0.03	100.00	3 733	0.02	100.00	0.90	_
593 Explosives and pyrotechnic products	1 914	0.02	100.00	3 648	0.02	100.00	8.08	_
045 Grain, excluding wheat rice barley maize	1 613	0.02	100.00	3 446	0.02	100.00	7.64	_
223 Oil seed for non soft oil	1 461	0.01	100.00	3 990	0.02	100.00	12.86	_
532 Dyeing and tanning extracts	1 418	0.01	100.00	2 225	0.01	100.00	7.90	_
613 Furskin tanned dressed etc	1 727	0.02	100.00	2 246	0.01	100.00	2.88	_
633 Cork manufactures	1 525	0.01	100.00	1 494	0.01	100.00	-2.03	_
277 Natural abrasives nes	1 137	0.01	100.00	1 367	0.01	100.00	4.51	_
047 Other cereal meals and flours	651	0.01	100.00	1 292	0.01	100.00	8.86	_
245 Fuel wood excluding waste; wood charcoal	555	0.01	100.00	1 287	0.01	100.00	11.77	_
265 Veg textile fibre, excluding cotton jute	699	0.01	100.00	970	0.01	100.00	5.89	_
286 Uranium & thorium ore concentrates	516	0.00	100.00	716	0.00	100.00	-1.85	_
261 Silk	360	0.00	100.00	591	0.00	100.00	8.60	_
961 Coins, nongold and non currency	195	0.00	100.00	338	0.00	100.00	7.53	_
883 Cinematographic film, developed	674	0.01	100.00	166	0.00	100.00	-18.37	_
264 Jute & bast fibre nes, raw & retted	120	0.00	100.00	316	0.00	100.00	16.04	_
244 Natural cork, raw and wastes	238	0.00	100.00	193	0.00	100.00	-5.39	_
345 Coal, water, producer gas etc	17	0.00	100.00	11	0.00	100.00	-1.60	_

Source:
UNCTAD secretariat calculations, based on UNCTAD, *UNCTADstat* Merchandise Trade Matrix

Source :
Calculs du secrétariat de la CNUCED, basés sur la matrice du commerce de marchandises d'*UNCTADstat* de la CNUCED

3.2.B Export structure by product
Developing economies

3.2.B Structure des exportations par produits
Économies en développement

Products ranked by average 2011-2012 values SITC Revision 3 (3-digit level) / Produits classés d'après la moyenne des valeurs de 2011-2012 CTCI révision 3 (positions à 3 chiffres)	2005			2012			Growth rates (%) Taux d'accroissement (%) 2005-2012	
	Value (millions of dollars) Valeur (millions de dollars)	% of the country grouping exports En % des exportations du groupe de pays	% of world product exports En % des exportations mondiales des produits	Value (millions of dollars) Valeur (millions de dollars)	% of the country grouping exports En % des exportations du groupe de pays	% of world product exports En % des exportations mondiales des produits	Value Valeur	Difference from world Différence par rapport au monde
All commodity groups	3 787 054	100.00	36.25	8 182 433	100.00	44.59	9.69	3.35
333 Crude petroleum & bituminous oil	577 959	15.26	72.54	1 299 580	15.88	73.40	8.55	-0.02
334 Heavy petroleum & bituminous oil	174 243	4.60	46.10	432 613	5.29	42.49	11.88	-0.70
776 Valves tubes; diodes, transistors	214 573	5.67	58.41	409 958	5.01	73.83	8.05	3.04
764 Telecom equipment part nes	181 721	4.80	50.46	360 290	4.40	69.10	8.50	4.96
752 Computer equipment nes	154 005	4.07	55.81	257 492	3.15	71.73	6.38	3.46
343 Natural gas, liquefied or not	49 325	1.30	32.51	170 733	2.09	47.23	16.61	6.13
971 Gold non-monetary excluding ores	19 181	0.51	50.14	152 486	1.86	55.51	30.72	1.71
759 Office equipment part & accessories	113 688	3.00	56.55	114 475	1.40	61.26	-1.60	1.12
793 Ships boats floating structures	31 105	0.82	43.65	104 698	1.28	66.27	19.67	8.29
781 Passenger cars and race cars	62 125	1.64	12.74	115 920	1.42	17.94	6.76	5.06
778 Electrical machinery apparatus nes	60 739	1.60	40.94	114 129	1.39	50.53	7.93	3.02
772 Electrical circuit equipment	54 626	1.44	38.40	108 495	1.33	45.71	8.58	2.79
845 Articles of apparel nes	64 387	1.70	67.09	97 988	1.20	70.97	3.51	0.25
784 Motor vehicle parts and accessories	42 456	1.12	18.08	99 563	1.22	27.62	11.15	6.32
871 Optical instruments apparatus nes	33 928	0.90	75.73	89 230	1.09	81.74	10.45	-0.14
897 Jewellery nes (667)	19 737	0.52	48.16	94 467	1.15	68.51	25.86	8.08
667 Pearls, precious semiprecious stone	36 976	0.98	39.06	73 811	0.90	51.38	15.49	6.84
821 Furniture part; bedding furnishing	34 291	0.91	35.21	81 369	0.99	51.89	11.14	6.26
682 Copper	30 499	0.81	47.44	68 843	0.84	49.79	4.79	1.00
851 Footwear	37 606	0.99	56.40	74 926	0.92	63.79	9.84	2.12
281 Iron ore and concentrates	14 849	0.39	51.26	50 364	0.62	41.19	24.29	-3.52
894 Baby carriages, toys, games, sporting goods	38 311	1.01	59.18	58 615	0.72	63.36	3.86	0.90
893 Articles of plastic nes	27 967	0.74	32.46	60 761	0.74	42.75	10.46	4.61
761 Television video receive project	33 407	0.88	58.04	53 920	0.66	61.28	3.42	1.54
842 Female clothing, woven	42 654	1.13	65.08	53 398	0.65	66.26	2.39	0.62
775 Household equipment nes	27 738	0.73	43.29	55 077	0.67	57.71	8.54	4.37
773 Electrical distribute equipment nes	24 548	0.65	40.00	54 958	0.67	48.94	8.44	3.17
699 Base metal manufactures nes	25 842	0.68	28.47	54 013	0.66	37.21	7.87	4.25
771 Electric power machine part excluding 716	23 417	0.62	51.06	51 091	0.62	55.18	8.73	0.68
841 Male clothing, woven	34 764	0.92	65.04	48 872	0.60	69.27	4.28	1.17
782 Goods and service vehicles	20 128	0.53	22.25	51 291	0.63	37.66	10.29	8.23
321 Coal excluding non-agglomomerated	15 761	0.42	34.06	44 377	0.54	34.94	18.85	0.11
422 Fixed veg fat and oil, excluding "soft"	11 732	0.31	85.90	42 422	0.52	90.12	19.40	0.90
844 Female clothing, knitted crocheted	18 925	0.50	72.57	47 007	0.57	80.28	9.91	0.89
057 Fruit nut (exc oil), fresh or dried	21 809	0.58	45.01	45 189	0.55	50.78	11.58	2.58
741 Heating and cooling equipment parts nes	19 616	0.52	28.47	44 335	0.54	39.66	9.19	5.40
728 Special industrial machine part nes	15 710	0.41	15.95	43 605	0.53	24.99	14.88	7.97
511 Hydrocarbons nes; derivatives	16 108	0.43	31.76	42 013	0.51	42.91	13.09	5.18
874 Measure analyze control device nes	16 596	0.44	14.89	43 912	0.54	23.72	13.12	7.01
342 Liquefied propane and butane	19 597	0.52	67.54	38 701	0.47	65.98	8.46	-0.50
283 Copper ores and concentrates	15 646	0.41	80.16	39 835	0.49	73.14	7.48	-1.67
658 Made-up textile articles nes	22 224	0.59	70.10	39 866	0.49	77.26	8.76	1.78
684 Aluminium	21 012	0.55	26.55	36 847	0.45	32.87	4.34	3.77
625 Rubber for wheels, incl inner tube	13 529	0.36	30.87	39 152	0.48	42.30	15.20	4.89
575 Other plastics, in primary forms	14 118	0.37	21.12	38 459	0.47	34.65	15.85	9.91
679 Iron steel pipe tube fittings etc	14 849	0.39	27.27	39 870	0.49	40.81	7.79	4.72
571 Primary form ethylene polymers	16 315	0.43	38.84	37 812	0.46	49.30	14.75	6.99
723 Civil engineering plant & equipment	13 596	0.36	19.58	39 084	0.48	31.52	11.92	7.81
651 Textile yarn	22 610	0.60	55.34	37 043	0.45	66.72	7.50	3.35
713 Internal combustion engine part nes	16 206	0.43	14.30	36 129	0.44	22.68	10.96	7.61
831 Case bag: storage travel shopping	14 311	0.38	60.32	36 555	0.45	65.21	14.36	1.98
763 Sound TV recorder or reproducer	37 079	0.98	59.55	35 397	0.43	59.13	-0.54	0.48
743 Gas pump, compressor, fan, filter	15 650	0.41	22.50	35 743	0.44	28.97	11.03	4.37
512 Alcohols, phenols; derivatives	15 079	0.40	46.77	33 903	0.41	55.85	11.10	2.39
716 Rotating electric plant parts nes	16 386	0.43	31.74	35 252	0.43	36.26	9.54	2.83
751 Office machines	7 261	0.19	47.45	33 787	0.41	65.91	19.11	6.34
653 Man-made woven fabrics	19 577	0.52	61.07	32 336	0.40	74.77	7.51	3.42
081 Animal feed excluding unmilled cereal	12 150	0.32	39.50	34 242	0.42	44.56	15.67	2.26
231 Natural rubber, latex, gum, etc	9 590	0.25	97.46	25 876	0.32	94.30	14.04	-0.61
061 Sugar, molasses and honey	9 736	0.26	54.63	30 268	0.37	68.23	17.98	4.03

For sources and notes, see end of table.

Pour les sources et les notes, se reporter à la fin du tableau.

Products ranked by average 2011-2012 values SITC Revision 3 (3-digit level) / Produits classés d'après la moyenne des valeurs de 2011-2012 CTCI révision 3 (positions à 3 chiffres)	2005			2012			Growth rates (%) Taux d'accroissement (%) 2005-2012	
	Value (millions of dollars) / Valeur (millions de dollars)	% of the country grouping exports / En % des exportations du groupe de pays	% of world product exports / En % des exportations mondiales des produits	Value (millions of dollars) / Valeur (millions de dollars)	% of the country grouping exports / En % des exportations du groupe de pays	% of world product exports / En % des exportations mondiales des produits	Value / Valeur	Difference from world / Différence par rapport au monde
676 Iron steel bar rod section piling	14 770	0.39	27.91	32 413	0.40	36.22	3.30	1.31
598 Miscellaneous chemical products nes	9 987	0.26	15.52	29 405	0.36	24.10	14.76	6.74
582 Plastic sheet film foil & strips	12 176	0.32	21.00	30 728	0.38	31.59	13.77	7.50
222 Oil seed etc for soft oil	10 376	0.27	48.28	29 354	0.36	39.13	18.81	-1.05
899 Manufactured articles nes	13 512	0.36	30.43	30 211	0.37	36.33	11.37	2.63
681 Silver, platinum, platinum metals	8 871	0.23	42.24	26 194	0.32	42.53	10.76	1.33
522 Inorganic chemical elem oxide salt	11 047	0.29	38.05	27 780	0.34	47.11	13.69	4.45
898 Music instrument device recording	15 935	0.42	31.10	28 057	0.34	49.68	6.32	6.25
542 Medicines including veterinary	9 852	0.26	4.74	29 711	0.36	8.89	13.24	7.84
673 Flat iron non-alloy steel products	19 424	0.51	29.03	25 071	0.31	31.09	-0.50	-0.70
034 Fish, fresh live chilled frozen	13 841	0.37	40.00	27 502	0.34	45.56	10.29	1.86
562 Manufactured fertilizer excluding crude	7 006	0.19	28.29	26 241	0.32	35.26	19.92	3.33
513 Carboxylic acid and compounds	12 564	0.33	37.82	24 572	0.30	50.68	10.31	5.51
884 Optical goods fibres nes	9 664	0.26	31.54	27 385	0.33	47.63	14.26	5.91
785 Motorcycles, mopeds and cycles	12 543	0.33	38.60	26 965	0.33	56.28	10.30	6.54
843 Male clothing, knitted crocheted	12 001	0.32	79.32	26 394	0.32	84.57	8.08	0.44
674 Flat plated iron non-alloy steel	10 161	0.27	29.06	24 872	0.30	44.06	10.30	5.74
071 Coffee and coffee substitutes	10 103	0.27	64.30	23 128	0.28	60.14	12.74	-0.80
652 Woven cotton fabrics	17 700	0.47	61.03	24 313	0.30	76.27	4.87	3.41
574 Polyacetals and polyesters, etc	13 477	0.36	36.93	24 362	0.30	44.20	8.34	3.37
054 Vegetable & vegetable products nes	11 451	0.30	33.91	23 494	0.29	40.12	11.01	3.59
515 Organo-inorganic compound acid salt	9 678	0.26	12.10	24 286	0.30	21.71	14.44	10.66
691 Iron steel aluminium structures nes	7 384	0.19	27.12	25 640	0.31	45.15	11.72	6.13
655 Knitted or crocheted fabrics nes	12 796	0.34	64.47	23 717	0.29	78.07	8.33	2.77
792 Aircraft, spacecraft & equipment	10 416	0.28	8.11	23 371	0.29	13.78	7.02	9.09
641 Paper and paperboard	11 964	0.32	12.35	21 679	0.26	18.93	8.18	6.82
747 Pipe, boiler, tank & vat appliances	8 605	0.23	20.96	23 572	0.29	29.27	10.44	3.93
813 Lighting fixtures and fittings nes	8 691	0.23	45.43	26 326	0.32	63.21	15.78	5.98
675 Flat rolled products of alloy steel	10 170	0.27	23.00	20 353	0.25	31.07	6.74	5.55
671 Pig & sponge iron, ferro alloys etc	13 825	0.37	52.34	19 739	0.24	49.30	3.81	-1.09
036 Crustacean mollusc aquat invertebra	12 472	0.33	62.09	21 529	0.26	67.17	9.08	1.58
848 Headgear, non-textile clothing	15 001	0.40	70.99	21 517	0.26	70.80	8.37	1.51
657 Special yarn and textile fabric etc	9 715	0.26	32.14	20 141	0.25	43.34	12.18	6.14
541 Pharmaceuticals excluding medicines	6 726	0.18	10.05	20 973	0.26	12.45	17.34	3.46
042 Rice	7 774	0.21	76.55	20 404	0.25	82.37	15.24	1.28
642 Cut paper and paperboard articles	8 317	0.22	22.66	20 495	0.25	34.07	13.00	6.78
872 Medical instruments appliances nes	9 649	0.25	18.26	20 400	0.25	22.33	10.96	2.94
744 Mechanical handling equipment nes	7 296	0.19	13.91	20 279	0.25	24.38	10.77	8.66
846 Clothing accessory excluding 831, 848, and 851	9 683	0.26	54.79	19 029	0.23	66.21	10.58	3.11
335 Residual petroleum products nes	6 655	0.18	35.84	19 978	0.24	39.74	14.83	1.87
287 Base metal ores & concentrates nes	10 384	0.27	55.26	18 191	0.22	58.46	5.52	1.93
037 Fish shellfish, prepared preserved	9 263	0.24	62.24	19 544	0.24	71.37	8.65	1.71
514 Nitrogen function compounds	8 174	0.22	23.94	19 264	0.24	36.21	11.10	4.77
553 Perfume toilet cosmetics, excluding soap	6 940	0.18	15.81	19 097	0.23	24.58	14.64	7.37
697 Base metal household equipment nes	9 455	0.25	50.73	19 118	0.23	62.62	9.31	3.84
885 Watches and clocks	9 932	0.26	39.26	18 349	0.22	35.12	9.51	-1.07
661 Lime cement construction material	9 710	0.26	50.41	17 465	0.21	57.60	5.44	2.05
695 Tools for use in hand or in machine	8 298	0.22	27.10	17 397	0.21	35.06	9.43	4.23
098 Edible products & preparations nes	6 766	0.18	20.40	17 189	0.21	27.16	14.65	5.59
292 Crude vegetable materials nes	5 907	0.16	24.24	18 200	0.22	39.95	17.69	8.83
786 Trailer caravan transport container	8 709	0.23	37.40	14 334	0.18	43.18	6.26	5.06
012 Meat nes, fresh chilled frozen	7 371	0.19	18.41	15 443	0.19	21.25	12.85	3.34
516 Other organic chemicals	8 332	0.22	32.58	15 713	0.19	37.31	11.46	4.71
892 Printed matter	7 301	0.19	18.60	13 274	0.16	28.16	9.32	7.51
634 Veneer, plywood & other wood nes	9 617	0.25	32.16	15 359	0.19	44.58	3.59	3.94
572 Primary form styrene polymers	10 419	0.28	53.90	14 367	0.18	57.86	4.13	2.12
694 Nails screws nuts bolts rivets	7 218	0.19	33.60	14 096	0.17	37.63	8.15	1.92
112 Alcoholic beverages	6 678	0.18	14.40	14 734	0.18	18.90	10.76	4.82
664 Glass	6 484	0.17	25.39	14 483	0.18	37.57	11.51	6.99
072 Cocoa	6 012	0.16	63.77	12 498	0.15	66.74	13.61	0.47

For sources and notes, see end of table.

Pour les sources et les notes, se reporter à la fin du tableau.

3

Products ranked by average 2011-2012 values SITC Revision 3 (3-digit level) / Produits classés d'après la moyenne des valeurs de 2011-2012 CTCI révision 3 (positions à 3 chiffres)	2005			2012			Growth rates (%) Taux d'accroissement (%) 2005-2012	
	Value (millions of dollars) / Valeur (millions de dollars)	% of the country grouping exports / En % des exportations du groupe de pays	% of world product exports / En % des exportations mondiales des produits	Value (millions of dollars) / Valeur (millions de dollars)	% of the country grouping exports / En % des exportations du groupe de pays	% of world product exports / En % des exportations mondiales des produits	Value / Valeur	Difference from world / Différence par rapport au monde
783 Road motor vehicles nes	4 895	0.13	16.04	14 127	0.17	30.17	15.53	13.04
714 Non-electric engines excluding 712, 713, and 718	5 484	0.14	7.94	14 189	0.17	15.15	13.42	12.07
421 Fixed veg fat and oil, "soft"	6 582	0.17	39.04	12 666	0.15	31.38	6.89	-3.63
611 Leather	11 314	0.30	54.49	13 073	0.16	55.61	0.39	0.58
742 Liquid pump; liquid elevator parts	4 474	0.12	13.26	13 469	0.16	21.83	14.32	7.17
665 Glassware	4 954	0.13	28.29	13 830	0.17	49.84	14.35	9.51
533 Pigment, paint, varnish & related	6 448	0.17	16.39	12 719	0.16	20.32	10.31	4.47
745 Non-electrical machinery tool nes	5 942	0.16	14.97	13 120	0.16	23.02	9.33	6.43
672 Ingots, Iron steel primary products	9 473	0.25	32.69	12 550	0.15	30.25	2.45	0.07
044 Maize unmilled, excluding sweet corn	3 183	0.08	27.94	13 936	0.17	38.94	22.55	7.96
748 Mechanical transmission equipment	4 217	0.11	14.25	12 713	0.16	23.02	16.20	8.75
724 Textile leather machinery parts nes	7 144	0.19	28.00	12 163	0.15	42.59	7.26	6.68
011 Beef, fresh chilled frozen	5 697	0.15	26.18	12 714	0.16	32.04	10.22	1.91
251 Pulp and waste paper	5 360	0.14	20.36	11 297	0.14	25.13	10.06	3.20
662 Clay and refractory materials	4 531	0.12	26.53	12 854	0.16	47.16	13.59	9.58
554 Soaps cleansers polishes	4 329	0.11	19.05	11 959	0.15	29.57	14.02	6.58
263 Cotton	3 913	0.10	35.44	11 475	0.14	44.96	18.04	2.68
749 Non-electric machinery part nes	5 569	0.15	25.52	11 271	0.14	36.21	9.84	6.40
762 Radio broadcast receivers	12 281	0.32	65.42	10 852	0.13	65.04	-3.32	-0.26
288 Non ferrous base metal waste nes	3 643	0.10	20.89	10 334	0.13	22.48	6.83	0.25
056 Vegetables roots tubers nes	4 732	0.12	29.25	9 408	0.11	33.60	9.87	2.80
048 Cereal & preparation flour starch	3 671	0.10	14.47	10 138	0.12	21.67	15.55	7.68
635 Wood manufactures nes	6 903	0.18	32.74	9 976	0.12	38.69	3.10	2.94
523 Inorganic acid metal salt peroxy	4 293	0.11	34.85	9 583	0.12	43.74	9.85	3.62
746 Ball or roller bearings	4 234	0.11	21.49	9 107	0.11	27.82	11.31	4.71
621 Rubber material e.g. paste tube rod	2 154	0.06	16.51	9 805	0.12	37.58	21.53	12.83
058 Fruit preserve preparation excluding juice	4 465	0.12	44.18	9 505	0.12	48.53	10.24	2.19
731 Machine tools for material removal	4 715	0.12	17.29	9 429	0.12	22.71	6.24	3.43
232 Synthetic & reclaimed rubber; waste	3 090	0.08	25.80	8 198	0.10	30.26	17.12	4.86
663 Mineral manufactures nes	3 586	0.09	16.69	9 196	0.11	26.11	12.17	7.39
122 Manufactured tabacco	4 158	0.11	21.61	9 040	0.11	29.28	11.34	3.99
591 Household and garden chemicals	3 891	0.10	23.90	9 262	0.11	30.78	14.81	5.21
431 Processed animal & veg fats & oils	3 004	0.08	52.33	8 301	0.10	57.42	14.13	0.97
629 Articles of rubber nes	3 794	0.10	20.75	8 629	0.11	28.69	10.70	4.82
121 Unmanufactured tabacco and refuse	4 290	0.11	60.42	8 754	0.11	69.55	9.49	1.86
248 Wood simply worked, railway sleeper	7 274	0.19	20.49	7 966	0.10	21.73	-1.51	0.14
592 Starches, glutenes, glues, etc	2 848	0.08	20.08	8 173	0.10	31.54	15.45	7.07
059 Fruit & vegetable juice unfermented	3 403	0.09	37.20	7 693	0.09	45.05	8.00	2.62
659 Floor coverings etc	4 359	0.12	36.92	7 750	0.09	50.38	8.51	6.10
278 Other crude minerals	3 587	0.09	33.29	7 794	0.10	44.91	11.13	5.00
344 Petroleum and hydrocarbon gas nes	3 269	0.09	31.94	8 490	0.10	54.67	6.51	6.58
693 Wire products and fencing grills	3 269	0.09	35.79	7 137	0.09	45.51	8.11	3.71
791 Railway vehicles and equipment	1 591	0.04	9.71	8 034	0.10	24.06	22.29	13.69
075 Spices	2 198	0.06	73.46	7 003	0.09	81.44	18.24	1.98
289 Prec metal ore concentrate excluding gold	1 307	0.03	32.26	6 940	0.08	38.69	21.36	3.78
017 Meat offal preserved nes	3 518	0.09	32.51	7 056	0.09	34.99	9.18	0.98
692 Metal storage transport container	2 652	0.07	23.19	7 023	0.09	35.04	10.00	5.34
666 Pottery	3 379	0.09	53.14	7 127	0.09	72.30	12.85	5.94
656 Tulle lace embroidery trim etc	4 604	0.12	56.23	6 603	0.08	68.32	2.88	2.21
687 Tin	2 743	0.07	85.42	6 069	0.07	84.93	12.14	0.51
696 Cutlery	3 533	0.09	48.85	6 552	0.08	56.90	9.01	2.63
074 Tea and maté	3 079	0.08	74.10	6 422	0.08	75.75	11.49	1.08
282 Ferrous iron & steel, waste & scrap	2 726	0.07	10.90	5 860	0.07	11.67	6.12	-0.16
273 Stone, sand and gravel	2 196	0.06	35.08	7 885	0.10	59.09	13.50	6.14
774 Electrodiagnostic equipment	2 262	0.06	8.65	6 606	0.08	15.40	13.94	8.04
284 Nickel ores, concentrates, etc	2 733	0.07	50.15	5 822	0.07	57.35	6.71	3.96
351 Electric current	2 670	0.07	10.73	6 004	0.07	15.66	16.99	12.70
531 Synthetic organic colour agents	3 506	0.09	33.67	6 137	0.08	50.11	6.49	5.17
895 Office and stationery supplies nes	3 854	0.10	36.30	6 094	0.07	37.04	5.97	0.65
022 Milk products, excluding butter & cheese	2 714	0.07	11.85	5 983	0.07	14.43	10.46	2.77

For sources and notes, see end of table.

Pour les sources et les notes, se reporter à la fin du tableau.

Products ranked by average 2011-2012 values SITC Revision 3 (3-digit level) Produits classés d'après la moyenne des valeurs de 2011-2012 CTCI révision 3 (positions à 3 chiffres)	2005			2012			Growth rates (%) Taux d'accroissement (%) 2005-2012	
	Value (millions of dollars) Valeur (millions de dollars)	% of the country grouping exports En % des exportations du groupe de pays	% of world product exports En % des exportations mondiales des produits	Value (millions of dollars) Valeur (millions de dollars)	% of the country grouping exports En % des exportations du groupe de pays	% of world product exports En % des exportations mondiales des produits	Value Valeur	Difference from world Différence par rapport au monde
285 Aluminium ore concentrate alumina	3 543	0.09	33.39	5 709	0.07	38.53	3.70	2.54
573 Vinyl chloride etc polymers	3 138	0.08	25.12	5 660	0.07	29.21	7.54	2.05
737 Metalwork machinery nes excluding tools	3 087	0.08	19.23	5 859	0.07	27.04	6.18	5.11
041 Wheat meslin, incl spelt, unmilled	1 907	0.05	10.64	6 271	0.08	12.77	13.39	1.47
711 Steam generating boilers & parts	914	0.02	23.38	5 348	0.07	57.27	25.52	12.54
678 Wire of iron or steel	2 238	0.06	31.12	5 171	0.06	42.74	10.51	4.94
581 Plastic tube pipe hose & fittings	2 012	0.05	16.91	5 787	0.07	26.64	14.09	7.85
266 Synthetic fibres for spinning	3 377	0.09	56.55	5 026	0.06	62.14	8.28	2.53
551 Essential oils, perfumes & flavours	2 136	0.06	13.62	5 487	0.07	21.76	15.63	8.90
721 Agricultural machine nes excluding tractor	1 753	0.05	8.47	5 271	0.06	13.56	16.59	9.20
247 Wood in rough or roughly squared	2 959	0.08	26.75	5 145	0.06	35.22	6.18	4.08
111 Non alcoholic beverage nes	2 330	0.06	20.87	5 015	0.06	25.12	11.62	5.56
654 Other woven textile fabrics nes	4 158	0.11	37.41	4 684	0.06	43.87	1.65	3.43
001 Live animal excluding fish & crustacean	2 910	0.08	21.12	4 724	0.06	21.38	10.70	4.06
873 Meters and counters nes	1 664	0.04	24.76	4 898	0.06	39.14	17.34	8.63
689 Misc non-ferrous base metals	2 657	0.07	35.65	4 164	0.05	42.99	2.94	2.51
686 Zinc	2 280	0.06	32.80	3 805	0.05	30.72	-5.09	-1.03
062 Sugar confectionery	2 235	0.06	33.67	4 420	0.05	40.33	8.59	2.03
291 Crude animal materials nes	1 981	0.05	38.40	4 076	0.05	43.08	12.10	2.78
881 Photographic device nes	4 525	0.12	26.29	4 255	0.05	60.27	-1.80	10.52
718 Power generating machinery part nes	917	0.02	8.01	4 089	0.05	16.38	21.42	11.16
272 Crude fertilizer, excluding manufactured	1 324	0.03	72.87	3 884	0.05	74.85	16.80	0.17
812 Sanitary plumb heat fixtures nes	2 347	0.06	20.49	3 775	0.05	25.37	3.37	3.14
597 Additive e.g. lubricate, antifreeze	1 491	0.04	13.07	3 564	0.04	15.11	13.58	4.01
524 Other inorganic chemicals	2 254	0.06	33.82	3 277	0.04	26.17	7.81	0.68
722 Tractors	1 596	0.04	11.18	3 658	0.04	15.05	11.44	6.61
735 Machine part accessory for 731 733	1 750	0.05	14.81	3 132	0.04	18.87	6.98	3.86
733 Metal work tool no material removal	1 875	0.05	20.70	3 404	0.04	24.94	6.37	3.95
073 Chocolate & cocoa preparations nes	1 362	0.04	10.67	3 205	0.04	13.26	13.53	5.14
882 Photo cinematographic supply excluding 883	3 592	0.09	18.22	3 169	0.04	18.06	-0.46	1.39
811 Prefabricated buildings	868	0.02	15.70	3 236	0.04	35.71	10.33	7.15
046 Wheat meal & flour, meslin flour	1 060	0.03	41.65	2 861	0.03	49.70	17.29	5.67
683 Nickel	1 318	0.03	9.65	2 539	0.03	12.83	2.96	6.63
525 Radio active & associated materials	711	0.02	9.19	1 870	0.02	11.59	21.84	14.41
274 Sulphur and unroasted iron pyrites	758	0.02	46.60	2 819	0.03	50.94	18.46	1.12
268 Wool & animal hair, incl wool tops	1 442	0.04	29.37	2 498	0.03	36.00	9.04	3.38
579 Plastic waste, parings and scrap	1 576	0.04	42.57	2 642	0.03	36.29	5.88	-2.03
727 Food processing machine excluding domestic	885	0.02	9.46	2 799	0.03	18.36	14.19	9.51
325 Coke, semi coke, retort carbon	2 675	0.07	43.07	2 010	0.02	25.88	-6.41	-10.07
712 Steam vapour turbines & parts nes	453	0.01	10.70	2 337	0.03	29.21	27.36	15.55
091 Margarine and shortening	826	0.02	29.73	2 168	0.03	33.58	13.51	2.18
726 Printing bookbinding machines parts	1 632	0.04	8.76	2 245	0.03	15.06	2.67	8.39
246 Wood chips, particles and waste	1 010	0.03	34.24	2 151	0.03	35.60	15.23	4.71
267 Man made fibre for spinning; waste	618	0.02	19.34	2 055	0.03	40.33	16.59	11.56
024 Cheese and curd	668	0.02	3.83	2 059	0.03	6.98	18.69	11.82
322 Briquettes, lignite and peat	22	0.00	2.20	2 044	0.02	53.26	101.67	77.86
685 Lead	1 009	0.03	35.15	1 802	0.02	29.04	1.77	-4.20
896 Work of art & collections; antiques	1 218	0.03	8.17	2 018	0.02	8.48	1.19	-1.40
725 Paper & pulp mill, cut manufacture	969	0.03	10.30	1 991	0.02	17.78	9.70	9.25
035 Fish, dried salted smoked	989	0.03	25.98	1 754	0.02	29.71	9.26	3.67
612 Leather manufactures nes	1 503	0.04	48.68	1 718	0.02	46.02	-0.92	-1.82
269 Worn clothing, textile article; rag	558	0.01	26.05	1 641	0.02	32.36	14.69	2.36
891 Arms and ammunition	981	0.03	13.15	1 624	0.02	13.50	6.93	1.68
593 Explosives and pyrotechnic products	673	0.02	35.16	1 398	0.02	38.32	8.39	0.31
025 Eggs, yolks and albumin	393	0.01	16.34	1 371	0.02	23.08	21.85	8.86
411 Animals oils and fats	373	0.01	14.78	1 418	0.02	22.07	17.66	4.44
613 Furskin tanned dressed etc	926	0.02	53.61	1 274	0.02	56.76	5.21	2.33
583 Plastic rod stick & profile shapes	315	0.01	8.57	941	0.01	18.37	12.21	9.54
045 Grain, excluding wheat rice barley maize	187	0.00	11.58	1 093	0.01	31.71	27.49	19.86
277 Natural abrasives nes	687	0.02	60.39	916	0.01	66.96	6.11	1.60

For sources and notes, see end of table.

Pour les sources et les notes, se reporter à la fin du tableau.

Products ranked by average 2011-2012 values SITC Revision 3 (3-digit level) / Produits classés d'après la moyenne des valeurs de 2011-2012 CTCI révision 3 (positions à 3 chiffres)	2005 Value (millions of dollars) Valeur (millions de dollars)	2005 % of the country grouping exports En % des exportations du groupe de pays	2005 % of world product exports En % des exportations mondiales des produits	2012 Value (millions of dollars) Valeur (millions de dollars)	2012 % of the country grouping exports En % des exportations du groupe de pays	2012 % of world product exports En % des exportations mondiales des produits	Growth rates (%) Taux d'accroissement (%) 2005-2012 Value Valeur	Growth rates (%) Taux d'accroissement (%) 2005-2012 Difference from world Différence par rapport au monde
211 Raw hides & skins, excluding furskins	996	0.03	17.17	933	0.01	11.41	-0.75	-6.03
212 Raw furskins and furskin pieces	518	0.01	22.05	932	0.01	16.02	8.77	-3.67
043 Barley grain unmilled	92	0.00	2.53	996	0.01	12.52	28.79	19.18
532 Dyeing and tanning extracts	541	0.01	38.12	821	0.01	36.91	7.01	-0.88
286 Uranium & thorium ore concentrates	71	0.00	13.81	712	0.01	99.48	22.24	24.09
223 Oil seed for non soft oil	416	0.01	28.47	799	0.01	20.02	9.47	-3.39
016 Meat offal preserved	50	0.00	1.86	733	0.01	15.68	34.73	28.61
677 Iron steel rail railway materials	139	0.00	6.03	735	0.01	16.34	17.92	9.90
023 Butter fats oils derived from milk	177	0.00	4.08	516	0.01	7.23	20.62	10.87
047 Other cereal meals and flours	279	0.01	42.94	522	0.01	40.40	11.81	2.95
245 Fuel wood excluding waste; wood charcoal	209	0.01	37.54	553	0.01	42.93	13.06	1.29
265 Veg textile fibre, excluding cotton jute	186	0.00	26.59	480	0.01	49.49	16.49	10.60
261 Silk	299	0.01	83.05	426	0.01	72.04	5.70	-2.89
264 Jute & bast fibre nes, raw & retted	112	0.00	93.50	307	0.00	97.00	16.27	0.22
883 Cinematographic film, developed	64	0.00	9.46	72	0.00	43.39	7.08	25.45
633 Cork manufactures	109	0.00	7.16	83	0.00	5.55	-6.47	-4.43
961 Coins, nongold and non currency	7	0.00	3.67	22	0.00	6.64	6.40	-1.13
244 Natural cork, raw and wastes	18	0.00	7.36	17	0.00	8.65	-1.07	4.32
345 Coal, water, producer gas etc	15	0.00	83.52	9	0.00	85.79	2.64	4.24

Source:
UNCTAD secretariat calculations, based on UNCTAD, *UNCTADstat* Merchandise Trade Matrix

Source :
Calculs du secrétariat de la CNUCED, basés sur la matrice du commerce de marchandises d'*UNCTADstat* de la CNUCED

3

Products ranked by average 2011-2012 values SITC Revision 3 (3-digit level) / Produits classés d'après la moyenne des valeurs de 2011-2012 CTCI révision 3 (positions à 3 chiffres)	2005 Value (millions of dollars) / Valeur (millions de dollars)	2005 % of the country grouping exports / En % des exportations du groupe de pays	2005 % of world product exports / En % des exportations mondiales des produits	2012 Value (millions of dollars) / Valeur (millions de dollars)	2012 % of the country grouping exports / En % des exportations du groupe de pays	2012 % of world product exports / En % des exportations mondiales des produits	Growth rates (%) 2005-2012 Value / Valeur	Growth rates (%) 2005-2012 Difference from world / Différence par rapport au monde
All commodity groups	**6 299 988**	**100.00**	**60.30**	**9 332 948**	**100.00**	**50.86**	**3.72**	**-2.62**
781 Passenger cars and race cars	424 276	6.73	87.03	528 648	5.66	81.82	0.79	-0.92
334 Heavy petroleum & bituminous oil	158 739	2.52	42.00	457 669	4.90	44.95	13.31	0.73
542 Medicines including veterinary	197 359	3.13	94.98	302 497	3.24	90.53	4.78	-0.62
784 Motor vehicle parts and accessories	191 327	3.04	81.49	259 944	2.79	72.12	3.02	-1.81
333 Crude petroleum & bituminous oil	116 462	1.85	14.62	202 963	2.17	11.46	5.72	-2.85
764 Telecom equipment part nes	177 755	2.82	49.36	159 480	1.71	30.58	-3.62	-7.17
776 Valves tubes; diodes, transistors	152 573	2.42	41.53	144 942	1.55	26.10	-1.17	-6.18
541 Pharmaceuticals excluding medicines	59 973	0.95	89.65	147 142	1.58	87.34	13.43	-0.44
874 Measure analyze control device nes	94 108	1.49	84.42	139 651	1.50	75.43	4.44	-1.67
728 Special industrial machine part nes	82 313	1.31	83.57	130 027	1.39	74.53	5.03	-1.87
792 Aircraft, spacecraft & equipment	116 974	1.86	91.08	144 944	1.55	85.44	-3.23	-1.17
772 Electrical circuit equipment	86 988	1.38	61.14	127 394	1.36	53.67	3.75	-2.03
713 Internal combustion engine part nes	96 563	1.53	85.18	122 244	1.31	76.74	1.70	-1.65
971 Gold non-monetary excluding ores	18 353	0.29	47.98	120 381	1.29	43.82	27.44	-1.57
778 Electrical machinery apparatus nes	86 809	1.38	58.51	110 080	1.18	48.74	2.28	-2.62
343 Natural gas, liquefied or not	67 029	1.06	44.18	110 682	1.19	30.62	6.01	-4.46
752 Computer equipment nes	121 739	1.93	44.12	100 864	1.08	28.10	-3.40	-6.32
598 Miscellaneous chemical products nes	54 022	0.86	83.94	91 607	0.98	75.06	6.27	-1.75
641 Paper and paperboard	83 044	1.32	85.71	89 847	0.96	78.44	-0.02	-1.38
699 Base metal manufactures nes	63 715	1.01	70.20	88 760	0.95	61.15	1.59	-2.03
743 Gas pump, compressor, fan, filter	53 396	0.85	76.76	86 418	0.93	70.05	5.12	-1.54
515 Organo-inorganic compound acid salt	69 685	1.11	87.13	86 754	0.93	77.54	1.74	-2.04
723 Civil engineering plant & equipment	55 183	0.88	79.48	83 959	0.90	67.71	1.53	-2.57
782 Goods and service vehicles	68 870	1.09	76.12	82 725	0.89	60.73	-1.27	-3.33
893 Articles of plastic nes	57 695	0.92	66.96	79 840	0.86	56.17	3.17	-2.68
759 Office equipment part & accessories	87 281	1.39	43.42	72 225	0.77	38.65	-4.34	-1.62
821 Furniture part; bedding furnishing	61 986	0.98	63.65	73 235	0.78	46.70	0.21	-4.68
714 Non-electric engines excluding 712, 713, and 718	62 520	0.99	90.58	76 730	0.82	81.92	-0.42	-1.76
575 Other plastics, in primary forms	52 398	0.83	78.37	71 402	0.77	64.34	2.27	-3.67
667 Pearls, precious semiprecious stone	55 727	0.88	58.87	69 731	0.75	48.54	3.57	-5.08
321 Coal excluding non-agglomomerated	26 058	0.41	56.30	68 049	0.73	53.57	18.60	-0.14
281 Iron ore and concentrates	11 603	0.18	40.06	66 253	0.71	54.18	32.48	4.67
684 Aluminium	51 303	0.81	64.83	65 497	0.70	58.43	-0.97	-1.54
872 Medical instruments appliances nes	43 058	0.68	81.50	70 710	0.76	77.40	7.28	-0.74
741 Heating and cooling equipment parts nes	48 827	0.78	70.86	66 438	0.71	59.43	1.02	-2.77
582 Plastic sheet film foil & strips	45 558	0.72	78.59	65 689	0.70	67.54	3.68	-2.59
744 Mechanical handling equipment nes	44 698	0.71	85.23	62 198	0.67	74.77	0.07	-2.03
112 Alcoholic beverages	38 533	0.61	83.07	61 572	0.66	79.00	5.04	-0.91
716 Rotating electric plant parts nes	34 826	0.55	67.46	60 839	0.65	62.58	5.26	-1.45
682 Copper	28 934	0.46	45.01	57 661	0.62	41.70	2.35	-1.44
553 Perfume toilet cosmetics, excluding soap	36 684	0.58	83.59	57 702	0.62	74.26	5.39	-1.89
012 Meat nes, fresh chilled frozen	32 557	0.52	81.29	56 390	0.60	77.60	8.51	-1.00
773 Electrical distribute equipment nes	36 077	0.57	58.78	54 613	0.59	48.64	2.40	-2.87
747 Pipe, boiler, tank & vat appliances	32 143	0.51	78.28	56 279	0.60	69.87	5.13	-1.37
793 Ships boats floating structures	37 976	0.60	53.29	51 095	0.55	32.34	1.76	-9.61
679 Iron steel pipe tube fittings etc	36 695	0.58	67.40	53 363	0.57	54.62	0.65	-2.42
511 Hydrocarbons nes; derivatives	33 402	0.53	65.85	53 656	0.57	54.80	4.83	-3.09
676 Iron steel bar rod section piling	33 307	0.53	62.93	49 579	0.53	55.40	1.38	-0.61
899 Manufactured articles nes	30 801	0.49	69.35	52 753	0.57	63.44	7.43	-1.31
625 Rubber for wheels, incl inner tube	29 354	0.47	66.98	51 126	0.55	55.23	7.54	-2.77
673 Flat iron non-alloy steel products	37 602	0.60	56.19	46 597	0.50	57.78	0.87	0.67
533 Pigment, paint, varnish & related	32 475	0.52	82.54	46 241	0.50	73.88	3.98	-1.86
742 Liquid pump; liquid elevator parts	28 914	0.46	85.70	47 456	0.51	76.91	5.65	-1.49
675 Flat rolled products of alloy steel	32 724	0.52	74.02	43 699	0.47	66.70	-0.48	-1.67
282 Ferrous iron & steel, waste & scrap	19 214	0.30	76.85	41 920	0.45	83.44	7.18	0.91
098 Edible products & preparations nes	25 885	0.41	78.06	44 899	0.48	70.95	7.33	-1.72
745 Non-electrical machinery tool nes	33 615	0.53	84.69	43 640	0.47	76.59	1.41	-1.50
897 Jewellery nes (667)	21 039	0.33	51.33	43 305	0.46	31.41	8.23	-9.55
748 Mechanical transmission equipment	25 143	0.40	84.94	42 052	0.45	76.15	5.57	-1.88
851 Footwear	28 189	0.45	42.28	40 867	0.44	34.80	4.57	-3.16

For sources and notes, see end of table.

Pour les sources et les notes, se reporter à la fin du tableau.

Products ranked by average 2011-2012 values SITC Revision 3 (3-digit level) / Produits classés d'après la moyenne des valeurs de 2011-2012 CTCI révision 3 (positions à 3 chiffres)	2005			2012			Growth rates (%) Taux d'accroissement (%) 2005-2012	
	Value (millions of dollars) Valeur (millions de dollars)	% of the country grouping exports En % des exportations du groupe de pays	% of world product exports En % des exportations mondiales des produits	Value (millions of dollars) Valeur (millions de dollars)	% of the country grouping exports En % des exportations du groupe de pays	% of world product exports En % des exportations mondiales des produits	Value Valeur	Difference from world Différence par rapport au monde
771 Electric power machine part excluding 716	21 968	0.35	47.90	40 167	0.43	43.38	7.32	-0.73
057 Fruit nut (exc oil), fresh or dried	25 795	0.41	63.23	41 700	0.45	46.06	6.43	-2.57
845 Articles of apparel nes	30 859	0.49	32.15	38 657	0.41	28.00	2.50	-0.76
775 Household equipment nes	35 720	0.57	55.75	39 063	0.42	40.93	-0.49	-4.66
642 Cut paper and paperboard articles	28 098	0.45	76.55	38 742	0.42	64.41	3.51	-2.70
571 Primary form ethylene polymers	24 891	0.40	59.26	37 902	0.41	49.42	3.06	-4.70
081 Animal feed excluding unmilled cereal	18 285	0.29	59.45	40 518	0.43	52.72	11.39	-2.02
222 Oil seed etc for soft oil	10 858	0.17	50.52	43 484	0.47	57.96	20.36	0.49
681 Silver, platinum, platinum metals	11 900	0.19	56.66	34 392	0.37	55.84	10.17	0.74
288 Non ferrous base metal waste nes	13 579	0.22	77.86	34 919	0.37	75.95	6.49	-0.09
774 Electrodiagnostic equipment	23 832	0.38	91.18	36 184	0.39	84.36	4.81	-1.09
894 Baby carriages, toys, games, sporting goods	26 263	0.42	40.57	33 536	0.36	36.25	1.52	-1.45
041 Wheat meslin, incl spelt, unmilled	13 968	0.22	77.95	34 116	0.37	69.46	11.34	-0.58
761 Television video receive project	24 031	0.38	41.75	32 912	0.35	37.41	-0.70	-2.59
048 Cereal & preparation flour starch	21 326	0.34	84.06	35 555	0.38	75.99	6.11	-1.75
022 Milk products, excluding butter & cheese	19 549	0.31	85.38	34 021	0.36	82.04	7.22	-0.47
251 Pulp and waste paper	20 177	0.32	76.64	32 342	0.35	71.95	5.90	-0.96
054 Vegetable & vegetable products nes	21 851	0.35	64.70	33 834	0.36	57.78	5.06	-2.35
514 Nitrogen function compounds	25 786	0.41	75.54	33 544	0.36	63.06	4.21	-2.12
892 Printed matter	31 410	0.50	80.03	32 728	0.35	69.42	-0.77	-2.58
885 Watches and clocks	15 345	0.24	60.66	33 877	0.36	64.83	11.20	0.61
783 Road motor vehicles nes	25 174	0.40	82.47	31 986	0.34	68.31	-0.99	-3.48
721 Agricultural machine nes excluding tractor	18 606	0.30	89.83	32 810	0.35	84.39	6.23	-1.15
695 Tools for use in hand or in machine	22 084	0.35	72.12	31 730	0.34	63.95	3.31	-1.89
674 Flat plated iron non-alloy steel	23 786	0.38	68.02	30 334	0.33	53.74	1.25	-3.31
562 Manufactured fertilizer excluding crude	11 501	0.18	46.43	31 068	0.33	41.75	15.57	-1.02
574 Polyacetals and polyesters, etc	22 904	0.36	62.76	30 340	0.33	55.04	2.61	-2.36
034 Fish, fresh live chilled frozen	20 248	0.32	58.51	30 494	0.33	50.52	6.03	-2.40
351 Electric current	21 015	0.33	84.45	29 883	0.32	77.94	2.29	-2.00
731 Machine tools for material removal	22 429	0.36	82.24	31 903	0.34	76.83	1.96	-0.86
691 Iron steel aluminium structures nes	19 225	0.31	70.62	30 091	0.32	52.99	2.10	-3.49
335 Residual petroleum products nes	11 411	0.18	61.46	28 621	0.31	56.93	12.19	-0.77
884 Optical goods fibres nes	20 929	0.33	68.31	30 014	0.32	52.20	4.43	-3.93
898 Music instrument device recording	35 192	0.56	68.69	28 230	0.30	49.99	-4.32	-4.39
554 Soaps cleansers polishes	18 028	0.29	79.34	27 728	0.30	68.56	5.39	-2.04
522 Inorganic chemical elem oxide salt	15 966	0.25	54.99	26 594	0.28	45.10	5.40	-3.84
292 Crude vegetable materials nes	18 378	0.29	75.41	26 887	0.29	59.02	4.91	-3.95
512 Alcohols, phenols; derivatives	16 359	0.26	50.74	25 720	0.28	42.37	6.54	-2.17
842 Female clothing, woven	21 852	0.35	33.34	26 147	0.28	32.45	0.75	-1.01
011 Beef, fresh chilled frozen	15 786	0.25	72.54	26 339	0.28	66.37	7.32	-0.99
024 Cheese and curd	16 250	0.26	93.21	26 369	0.28	89.35	5.96	-0.91
657 Special yarn and textile fabric etc	20 252	0.32	67.01	25 491	0.27	54.85	2.18	-3.85
516 Other organic chemicals	16 879	0.27	66.00	25 976	0.28	61.68	4.65	-2.10
663 Mineral manufactures nes	17 599	0.28	81.90	25 236	0.27	71.65	2.77	-2.02
763 Sound TV recorder or reproducer	25 169	0.40	40.42	24 362	0.26	40.69	-1.70	-0.68
664 Glass	18 811	0.30	73.68	23 649	0.25	61.35	1.57	-2.95
248 Wood simply worked, railway sleeper	25 478	0.40	71.76	24 300	0.26	66.30	-2.44	-0.79
513 Carboxylic acid and compounds	20 205	0.32	60.83	23 474	0.25	48.41	0.55	-4.26
746 Ball or roller bearings	15 165	0.24	76.97	23 030	0.25	70.36	5.06	-1.54
694 Nails screws nuts bolts rivets	14 083	0.22	65.56	23 003	0.25	61.40	5.17	-1.06
629 Articles of rubber nes	14 362	0.23	78.55	21 201	0.23	70.49	4.34	-1.54
122 Manufactured tabacco	14 559	0.23	75.65	20 627	0.22	66.80	5.82	-1.53
785 Motorcycles, mopeds and cycles	19 906	0.32	61.26	20 915	0.22	43.65	-1.86	-5.62
841 Male clothing, woven	17 860	0.28	33.41	20 705	0.22	29.35	0.76	-2.34
421 Fixed veg fat and oil, "soft"	9 381	0.15	55.64	21 019	0.23	52.07	10.30	-0.22
591 Household and garden chemicals	12 347	0.20	75.84	20 675	0.22	68.72	7.76	-1.84
871 Optical instruments apparatus nes	10 747	0.17	23.99	19 602	0.21	17.96	11.22	0.63
896 Work of art & collections; antiques	13 672	0.22	91.68	21 745	0.23	91.41	2.74	0.15
551 Essential oils, perfumes & flavours	13 526	0.21	86.25	19 690	0.21	78.09	4.97	-1.77
749 Non-electric machinery part nes	16 160	0.26	74.04	19 662	0.21	63.16	0.61	-2.83

For sources and notes, see end of table.

Pour les sources et les notes, se reporter à la fin du tableau.

Products ranked by average 2011-2012 values SITC Revision 3 (3-digit level) / Produits classés d'après la moyenne des valeurs de 2011-2012 CTCI révision 3 (positions à 3 chiffres)	2005			2012			Growth rates (%) Taux d'accroissement (%) 2005-2012	
	Value (millions of dollars) Valeur (millions de dollars)	% of the country grouping exports En % des exportations du groupe de pays	% of world product exports En % des exportations mondiales des produits	Value (millions of dollars) Valeur (millions de dollars)	% of the country grouping exports En % des exportations du groupe de pays	% of world product exports En % des exportations mondiales des produits	Value Valeur	Difference from world Différence par rapport au monde
073 Chocolate & cocoa preparations nes	10 825	0.17	84.85	19 545	0.21	80.86	7.48	-0.91
718 Power generating machinery part nes	9 580	0.15	83.67	19 298	0.21	77.30	8.96	-1.31
597 Additive e.g. lubricate, antifreeze	9 845	0.16	86.26	18 796	0.20	79.67	8.28	-1.29
791 Railway vehicles and equipment	13 291	0.21	81.11	19 439	0.21	58.20	3.93	-4.67
831 Case bag: storage travel shopping	9 377	0.15	39.52	19 420	0.21	34.64	9.14	-3.24
722 Tractors	12 122	0.19	84.93	19 505	0.21	80.22	3.90	-0.93
786 Trailer caravan transport container	14 375	0.23	61.74	18 595	0.20	56.02	-2.05	-3.25
044 Maize unmilled, excluding sweet corn	7 796	0.12	68.43	16 746	0.18	46.79	7.72	-6.88
751 Office machines	8 023	0.13	52.43	17 423	0.19	33.99	4.96	-7.81
056 Vegetables roots tubers nes	11 263	0.18	69.62	18 219	0.20	65.07	5.74	-1.33
651 Textile yarn	17 585	0.28	43.05	16 837	0.18	30.32	-1.77	-5.91
724 Textile leather machinery parts nes	18 323	0.29	71.81	16 338	0.18	57.20	-2.90	-3.49
634 Veneer, plywood & other wood nes	19 302	0.31	64.54	17 158	0.18	49.79	-3.57	-3.21
592 Starches, glutenes, glues, etc	11 114	0.18	78.35	17 531	0.19	67.65	5.99	-2.39
001 Live animal excluding fish & crustacean	10 844	0.17	78.72	17 104	0.18	77.42	5.46	-1.18
621 Rubber material e.g. paste tube rod	10 799	0.17	82.78	16 089	0.17	61.67	4.10	-4.60
342 Liquefied propane and butane	8 606	0.14	29.66	17 022	0.18	29.02	8.64	-0.32
232 Synthetic & reclaimed rubber; waste	7 875	0.13	65.75	16 180	0.17	59.71	9.73	-2.52
737 Metalwork machinery nes excluding tools	12 754	0.20	79.44	15 547	0.17	71.77	-0.41	-1.48
581 Plastic tube pipe hose & fittings	9 723	0.15	81.69	15 567	0.17	71.65	4.19	-2.05
635 Wood manufactures nes	13 839	0.22	65.64	15 065	0.16	58.42	-1.59	-1.75
672 Ingots, Iron steel primary products	11 031	0.18	38.07	14 139	0.15	34.08	0.85	-1.53
071 Coffee and coffee substitutes	5 572	0.09	35.46	15 112	0.16	39.30	14.81	1.27
813 Lighting fixtures and fittings nes	10 353	0.16	54.12	15 135	0.16	36.34	3.43	-6.37
882 Photo cinematographic supply excluding 883	16 107	0.26	81.69	14 362	0.15	81.86	-2.13	-0.28
683 Nickel	8 750	0.14	64.03	13 366	0.14	67.55	-2.76	0.92
111 Non alcoholic beverage nes	8 621	0.14	77.22	14 423	0.15	72.23	4.46	-1.59
662 Clay and refractory materials	12 188	0.19	71.38	13 631	0.15	50.01	-1.35	-5.36
573 Vinyl chloride etc polymers	9 197	0.15	73.62	13 464	0.14	69.49	4.61	-0.89
665 Glassware	12 327	0.20	70.40	13 329	0.14	48.04	-0.99	-5.84
283 Copper ores and concentrates	3 673	0.06	18.82	13 427	0.14	24.65	13.94	4.80
735 Machine part accessory for 731 733	9 958	0.16	84.27	13 350	0.14	80.42	2.31	-0.81
726 Printing bookbinding machines parts	16 980	0.27	91.13	12 624	0.14	84.70	-6.84	-1.13
692 Metal storage transport container	8 625	0.14	75.41	12 658	0.14	63.17	2.38	-2.29
727 Food processing machine excluding domestic	8 418	0.13	89.97	12 346	0.13	80.98	3.16	-1.51
287 Base metal ores & concentrates nes	7 962	0.13	42.37	11 763	0.13	37.80	0.46	-3.12
017 Meat offal preserved nes	7 081	0.11	65.43	12 414	0.13	61.56	7.37	-0.83
061 Sugar, mollasses and honey	7 344	0.12	41.21	12 776	0.14	28.80	6.67	-7.27
525 Radio active & associated materials	6 481	0.10	83.69	10 378	0.11	64.32	2.19	-5.24
658 Made-up textile articles nes	9 219	0.15	29.08	11 317	0.12	21.93	2.06	-4.93
289 Prec metal ore concentrate excluding gold	2 630	0.04	64.95	10 649	0.11	59.37	15.52	-2.06
661 Lime cement construction material	8 892	0.14	46.17	11 702	0.13	38.60	1.08	-2.31
523 Inorganic acid metal salt peroxy	7 641	0.12	62.03	11 330	0.12	51.71	3.49	-2.74
844 Female clothing, knitted crocheted	6 931	0.11	26.58	10 890	0.12	18.60	5.64	-3.39
812 Sanitary plumb heat fixtures nes	8 979	0.14	78.39	10 782	0.12	72.47	-0.85	-1.07
653 Man-made woven fabrics	12 404	0.20	38.69	10 761	0.12	24.88	-3.20	-7.28
697 Base metal household equipment nes	8 903	0.14	47.77	10 851	0.12	35.54	0.56	-4.95
263 Cotton	5 453	0.09	49.40	10 057	0.11	39.40	12.21	-3.15
572 Primary form styrene polymers	8 793	0.14	45.49	10 327	0.11	41.59	-0.49	-2.51
036 Crustacean mollusc aquat invertebra	7 551	0.12	37.59	10 152	0.11	31.67	4.11	-3.39
611 Leather	8 791	0.14	42.34	9 911	0.11	42.16	0.00	0.18
895 Office and stationery supplies nes	6 752	0.11	63.59	10 335	0.11	62.82	4.95	-0.37
733 Metal work tool no material removal	7 101	0.11	78.39	10 154	0.11	74.39	1.35	-1.07
891 Arms and ammunition	6 383	0.10	85.58	10 249	0.11	85.15	5.03	-0.22
671 Pig & sponge iron, ferro alloys etc	7 176	0.11	27.17	9 198	0.10	22.97	3.34	-1.56
846 Clothing accessory excluding 831, 848, and 851	7 819	0.12	44.24	9 065	0.10	31.54	2.19	-5.28
725 Paper & pulp mill, cut manufacture	8 390	0.13	89.21	9 183	0.10	82.01	-0.84	-1.29
058 Fruit preserve preparation excluding juice	5 350	0.08	52.94	9 464	0.10	48.32	6.13	-1.91
059 Fruit & vegetable juice unfermented	5 556	0.09	60.74	9 006	0.10	52.74	3.57	-1.81
848 Headgear, non-textile clothing	6 033	0.10	28.55	8 716	0.09	28.68	3.75	-3.12

For sources and notes, see end of table.

Pour les sources et les notes, se reporter à la fin du tableau.

Products ranked by average 2011-2012 values SITC Revision 3 (3-digit level) / Produits classés d'après la moyenne des valeurs de 2011-2012 CTCI révision 3 (positions à 3 chiffres)	2005			2012			Growth rates (%) Taux d'accroissement (%) 2005-2012	
	Value (millions of dollars) Valeur (millions de dollars)	% of the country grouping exports En % des exportations du groupe de pays	% of world product exports En % des exportations mondiales des produits	Value (millions of dollars) Valeur (millions de dollars)	% of the country grouping exports En % des exportations du groupe de pays	% of world product exports En % des exportations mondiales des produits	Value Valeur	Difference from world Différence par rapport au monde
278 Other crude minerals	6 666	0.11	61.87	8 354	0.09	48.14	2.24	-3.88
524 Other inorganic chemicals	4 041	0.06	60.63	7 945	0.09	63.45	0.05	-1.00
693 Wire products and fencing grills	5 600	0.09	61.32	8 183	0.09	52.18	2.12	-2.27
285 Aluminium ore concentrate alumina	6 110	0.10	57.58	8 105	0.09	54.71	0.24	-0.92
247 Wood in rough or roughly squared	4 988	0.08	45.08	7 564	0.08	51.79	6.30	4.20
652 Woven cotton fabrics	11 011	0.17	37.96	7 187	0.08	22.54	-6.37	-7.83
659 Floor coverings etc	7 352	0.12	62.28	7 389	0.08	48.03	-2.24	-4.64
686 Zinc	4 235	0.07	60.92	7 151	0.08	57.74	-4.13	-0.07
873 Meters and counters nes	5 006	0.08	74.48	7 513	0.08	60.04	4.94	-3.78
037 Fish shellfish, prepared preserved	5 419	0.09	36.41	7 507	0.08	27.41	3.40	-3.54
211 Raw hides & skins, excluding furskins	4 587	0.07	79.10	6 917	0.07	84.60	6.06	0.77
023 Butter fats oils derived from milk	4 022	0.06	92.47	6 281	0.07	87.98	8.89	-0.86
072 Cocoa	3 401	0.05	36.07	6 190	0.07	33.06	12.19	-0.95
678 Wire of iron or steel	4 593	0.07	63.87	6 475	0.07	53.51	3.21	-2.36
655 Knitted or crocheted fabrics nes	6 992	0.11	35.23	6 506	0.07	21.42	-1.81	-7.37
531 Synthetic organic colour agents	6 897	0.11	66.23	6 092	0.07	49.74	-2.42	-3.74
062 Sugar confectionery	4 247	0.07	63.99	6 113	0.07	55.77	4.77	-1.79
431 Processed animal & veg fats & oils	2 666	0.04	46.43	5 989	0.06	41.42	11.75	-1.41
654 Other woven textile fabrics nes	6 746	0.11	60.69	5 812	0.06	54.43	-4.07	-2.29
712 Steam vapour turbines & parts nes	3 633	0.06	85.82	5 533	0.06	69.15	8.16	-3.65
762 Radio broadcast receivers	6 483	0.10	34.54	5 821	0.06	34.89	-2.58	0.47
811 Prefabricated buildings	4 581	0.07	82.82	5 603	0.06	61.82	0.30	-2.85
344 Petroleum and hydrocarbon gas nes	6 752	0.11	65.97	5 952	0.06	38.32	-7.53	-7.45
043 Barley grain unmilled	2 867	0.05	78.94	5 279	0.06	66.35	8.23	-1.37
411 Animals oils and fats	2 146	0.03	84.96	4 985	0.05	77.60	12.21	-1.02
291 Crude animal materials nes	3 128	0.05	60.62	5 282	0.06	55.83	7.43	-1.88
273 Stone, sand and gravel	3 867	0.06	61.77	4 875	0.05	36.54	1.47	-5.89
696 Cutlery	3 648	0.06	50.45	4 893	0.05	42.49	3.58	-2.81
325 Coke, semi coke, retort carbon	2 742	0.04	44.15	4 479	0.05	57.68	8.41	4.75
422 Fixed veg fat and oil, excluding "soft"	1 907	0.03	13.96	4 575	0.05	9.72	12.20	-6.30
689 Misc non-ferrous base metals	4 237	0.07	56.86	4 677	0.05	48.29	-1.54	-1.97
284 Nickel ores, concentrates, etc	2 714	0.04	49.81	4 327	0.05	42.62	-1.27	-4.02
843 Male clothing, knitted crocheted	3 062	0.05	20.24	4 601	0.05	14.74	5.12	-2.52
579 Plastic waste, parings and scrap	2 115	0.03	57.14	4 590	0.05	63.05	9.09	1.17
268 Wool & animal hair, incl wool tops	3 416	0.05	69.59	4 316	0.05	62.20	3.99	-1.66
212 Raw furskins and furskin pieces	1 741	0.03	74.09	4 684	0.05	80.55	13.55	1.12
583 Plastic rod stick & profile shapes	3 335	0.05	90.74	4 040	0.04	78.85	0.80	-1.86
042 Rice	2 362	0.04	23.26	4 159	0.04	16.79	8.34	-5.62
035 Fish, dried salted smoked	2 781	0.04	73.04	4 062	0.04	68.81	4.27	-1.32
025 Eggs, yolks and albumin	1 978	0.03	82.18	4 387	0.05	73.87	10.65	-2.35
685 Lead	1 745	0.03	60.79	3 826	0.04	61.66	7.28	1.31
091 Margarine and shortening	1 854	0.03	66.74	3 941	0.04	61.04	9.94	-1.39
016 Meat offal preserved	2 617	0.04	97.87	3 899	0.04	83.47	3.97	-2.15
711 Steam generating boilers & parts	2 858	0.05	73.08	3 672	0.04	39.33	3.18	-9.80
246 Wood chips, particles and waste	1 874	0.03	63.53	3 483	0.04	57.67	7.08	-3.43
121 Unmanufactured tabacco and refuse	2 639	0.04	37.17	3 536	0.04	28.09	3.81	-3.82
677 Iron steel rail railway materials	1 976	0.03	85.67	3 355	0.04	74.56	6.48	-1.53
269 Worn clothing, textile article; rag	1 568	0.02	73.24	3 419	0.04	67.41	11.41	-0.92
656 Tulle lace embroidery trim etc	3 568	0.06	43.57	2 989	0.03	30.92	-3.40	-4.08
881 Photographic device nes	12 676	0.20	73.65	2 799	0.03	39.64	-19.21	-6.89
266 Synthetic fibres for spinning	2 431	0.04	40.70	2 842	0.03	35.14	2.04	-3.71
267 Man made fibre for spinning; waste	2 537	0.04	79.42	3 014	0.03	59.14	0.15	-4.88
666 Pottery	2 934	0.05	46.15	2 687	0.03	27.26	-2.29	-9.19
045 Grain, excluding wheat rice barley maize	1 405	0.02	87.11	2 222	0.02	64.48	2.86	-4.78
223 Oil seed for non soft oil	1 021	0.02	69.88	2 744	0.03	68.78	11.58	-1.28
046 Wheat meal & flour, meslin flour	1 279	0.02	50.24	2 096	0.02	36.41	5.27	-6.35
593 Explosives and pyrotechnic products	1 190	0.02	62.18	2 083	0.02	57.09	7.86	-0.22
074 Tea and maté	1 012	0.02	24.35	1 916	0.02	22.60	7.57	-2.84
231 Natural rubber, latex, gum, etc	244	0.00	2.48	1 561	0.02	5.69	29.84	15.20
612 Leather manufactures nes	1 517	0.02	49.13	1 855	0.02	49.68	2.11	1.21

For sources and notes, see end of table.

Pour les sources et les notes, se reporter à la fin du tableau.

Products ranked by average 2011-2012 values SITC Revision 3 (3-digit level) Produits classés d'après la moyenne des valeurs de 2011-2012 CTCI révision 3 (positions à 3 chiffres)	2005			2012			Growth rates (%) Taux d'accroissement (%) 2005-2012	
	Value (millions of dollars) Valeur (millions de dollars)	% of the country grouping exports En % des exportations du groupe de pays	% of world product exports En % des exportations mondiales des produits	Value (millions of dollars) Valeur (millions de dollars)	% of the country grouping exports En % des exportations du groupe de pays	% of world product exports En % des exportations mondiales des produits	Value Valeur	Difference from world Différence par rapport au monde
274 Sulphur and unroasted iron pyrites	756	0.01	46.45	1 683	0.02	30.41	10.74	-6.61
322 Briquettes, lignite and peat	911	0.01	92.08	1 548	0.02	40.32	7.34	-16.47
075 Spices	776	0.01	25.92	1 544	0.02	17.96	9.29	-6.97
633 Cork manufactures	1 414	0.02	92.75	1 408	0.02	94.28	-1.73	0.30
532 Dyeing and tanning extracts	875	0.01	61.70	1 399	0.01	62.88	8.44	0.54
687 Tin	453	0.01	14.10	1 066	0.01	14.91	9.39	-2.24
613 Furskin tanned dressed etc	780	0.01	45.20	876	0.01	39.01	-0.65	-3.53
272 Crude fertilizer, excluding manufactured	309	0.00	17.02	879	0.01	16.94	18.61	1.98
047 Other cereal meals and flours	353	0.01	54.17	716	0.01	55.42	7.21	-1.65
245 Fuel wood excluding waste; wood charcoal	286	0.00	51.49	528	0.01	41.04	9.77	-2.00
277 Natural abrasives nes	430	0.01	37.81	451	0.00	32.99	1.47	-3.04
265 Veg textile fibre, excluding cotton jute	496	0.01	70.92	472	0.01	48.64	-0.24	-6.13
961 Coins, nongold and non currency	188	0.00	96.16	315	0.00	93.34	6.05	-1.48
883 Cinematographic film, developed	608	0.01	90.18	92	0.00	55.34	-23.51	-5.13
244 Natural cork, raw and wastes	221	0.00	92.63	176	0.00	91.34	-5.72	-0.32
261 Silk	45	0.00	12.40	49	0.00	8.29	-3.05	-11.65
264 Jute & bast fibre nes, raw & retted	8	0.00	6.49	9	0.00	2.93	7.90	-8.14
286 Uranium & thorium ore concentrates	437	0.01	84.83	4	0.00	0.49	-71.57	-69.72
345 Coal, water, producer gas etc	3	0.00	16.48	2	0.00	14.21	-13.79	-12.19

Source:
UNCTAD secretariat calculations, based on UNCTAD, *UNCTADstat* Merchandise Trade Matrix

Source :
Calculs du secrétariat de la CNUCED, basés sur la matrice du commerce de marchandises d'*UNCTADstat* de la CNUCED

Leading products exported based on average 2011-2012 values SITC Revision 3 (3-digit level) / Principaux produits exportés d'après la moyenne des valeurs de 2011-2012 CTCI révision 3 (positions à 3 chiffres)	Value (f.o.b., thousands of dollars) Valeur (f.a.b., milliers de dollars)	2011-2012 As percentage En pourcentage of country total du total du pays	of ** (1) des ** (1)	of world du monde
Afghanistan (**=Developing) (2)				
All commodity groups	372 925	100.0	0.00	0.00
057 Fruit nut (exc oil), fresh or dried	69 079	18.5	0.16	0.08
292 Crude vegetable materials nes	29 320	7.9	0.19	0.07
282 Ferrous iron & steel, waste & scrap	26 605	7.1	0.42	0.05
075 Spices	23 221	6.2	0.33	0.27
263 Cotton	21 001	5.8	0.20	0.08
321 Coal excluding non-agglomomerated	20 722	5.6	0.05	0.02
659 Floor coverings etc	16 338	4.4	0.22	0.11
054 Vegetable & vegetable products nes	13 965	3.7	0.06	0.02
661 Lime cement construction material	9 163	2.5	0.05	0.03
222 Oil seed etc for soft oil	8 254	2.2	0.03	0.01
Remainder	134 577	36.1		
Albania - Albanie (**=Transition) (2)				
All commodity groups	1 958 063	100.0	0.24	0.01
333 Crude petroleum & bituminous oil	388 955	19.9	0.15	0.02
851 Footwear	310 143	15.8	18.13	0.27
841 Male clothing, woven	116 751	6.0	11.45	0.16
845 Articles of apparel nes	88 774	4.5	6.79	0.06
287 Base metal ores & concentrates nes	88 071	4.5	5.87	0.27
672 Ingots, Iron steel primary products	85 740	4.4	0.56	0.20
699 Base metal manufactures nes	53 653	2.7	2.37	0.04
283 Copper ores and concentrates	48 893	2.5	3.88	0.09
288 Non ferrous base metal waste nes	46 924	2.4	6.26	0.10
671 Pig & sponge iron, ferro alloys etc	42 356	2.2	0.39	0.10
Remainder	687 803	35.1		
Algeria - Algérie (**=Developing)				
All commodity groups	72 651 028	100.0	0.91	0.40
333 Crude petroleum & bituminous oil	33 953 461	46.7	2.71	1.98
343 Natural gas, liquefied or not	20 996 296	28.9	13.16	6.05
334 Heavy petroleum & bituminous oil	10 496 114	14.4	2.48	1.06
342 Liquefied propane and butane	5 143 769	7.1	13.01	8.71
335 Residual petroleum products nes	872 226	1.2	4.67	1.72
522 Inorganic chemical elem oxide salt	429 451	0.6	1.49	0.70
061 Sugar, mollasses and honey	239 868	0.3	0.75	0.53
272 Crude fertilizer, excl. manufactured	140 572	0.2	3.69	2.79
512 Alcohols, phenols; derivatives	37 878	0.1	0.11	0.06
111 Non alcoholic beverage nes	29 073	0.0	0.59	0.15
Remainder	312 320	0.5		
American Samoa - Samoa américaines (**=Developing) (2)				
All commodity groups	350 000	100.0	0.00	0.00
333 Crude petroleum & bituminous oil	76 724	21.9	0.01	0.00
712 Steam vapour turbines & parts nes	41 754	11.9	1.71	0.49
542 Medicines including veterinary	33 192	9.5	0.12	0.01
081 Animal feed excluding unmilled cereal	32 456	9.3	0.10	0.04
897 Jewellery nes (667)	20 446	5.8	0.03	0.02
034 Fish, fresh live chilled frozen	19 842	5.7	0.07	0.03
776 Valves tubes; diodes, transistors	16 012	4.6	0.00	0.00
282 Ferrous iron & steel, waste & scrap	8 785	2.5	0.14	0.02
411 Animals oils and fats	8 639	2.5	0.71	0.13
743 Gas pump, compressor, fan, filter	8 540	2.4	0.02	0.01
Remainder	83 610	23.9		
Andorra - Andorre (**=Developed) (2)				
All commodity groups	93 684	100.0	0.00	0.00
781 Passenger cars and race cars	33 813	36.1	0.01	0.01
778 Electrical machinery apparatus nes	10 023	10.7	0.01	0.00
061 Sugar, mollasses and honey	6 736	7.2	0.06	0.01
896 Work of art & collections; antiques	3 808	4.1	0.02	0.02
898 Music instrument device recording	3 111	3.3	0.01	0.00
844 Female clothing, knitted crocheted	2 850	3.0	0.03	0.01
764 Telecom equipment part nes	2 083	2.2	0.00	0.00
611 Leather	1 070	1.1	0.01	0.00
744 Mechanical handling equipment nes	1 041	1.1	0.00	0.00
759 Office equipment part & accessories	1 014	1.1	0.00	0.00
Remainder	28 135	30.1		

Leading products exported based on average 2011-2012 values SITC Revision 3 (3-digit level) / Principaux produits exportés d'après la moyenne des valeurs de 2011-2012 CTCI révision 3 (positions à 3 chiffres)	Value (f.o.b., thousands of dollars) Valeur (f.a.b., milliers de dollars)	2011-2012 As percentage En pourcentage of country total du total du pays	of ** (1) des ** (1)	of world du monde
Angola (**=Developing)				
All commodity groups	70 655 150	100.0	0.88	0.39
333 Crude petroleum & bituminous oil	68 546 991	97.0	5.47	3.99
334 Heavy petroleum & bituminous oil	703 620	1.0	0.17	0.07
667 Pearls, precious semiprecious stone	687 089	1.0	0.87	0.45
342 Liquefied propane and butane	373 212	0.5	0.94	0.63
282 Ferrous iron & steel, waste & scrap	87 388	0.1	1.06	0.13
273 Stone, sand and gravel	38 196	0.1	0.62	0.32
691 Iron steel aluminium structures nes	30 860	0.0	0.13	0.06
288 Non ferrous base metal waste nes	24 789	0.0	0.24	0.05
344 Petroleum and hydrocarbon gas nes	20 030	0.0	0.27	0.14
747 Pipe, boiler, tank & vat appliances	15 349	0.0	0.07	0.02
Remainder	147 626	0.3		
Anguilla (**=Developing) (2)				
All commodity groups	18 787	100.0	0.00	0.00
112 Alcoholic beverages	2 554	13.6	0.02	0.00
723 Civil engineering plant & equipment	1 663	8.8	0.00	0.00
896 Work of art & collections; antiques	1 342	7.1	0.07	0.01
782 Goods and service vehicles	1 172	6.2	0.00	0.00
781 Passenger cars and race cars	880	4.7	0.00	0.00
744 Mechanical handling equipment nes	851	4.5	0.00	0.00
898 Music instrument device recording	738	3.9	0.00	0.00
691 Iron steel aluminium structures nes	721	3.8	0.00	0.00
793 Ships boats floating structures	434	2.3	0.00	0.00
743 Gas pump, compressor, fan, filter	410	2.2	0.00	0.00
Remainder	8 022	42.9		
Antigua and Barbuda - Antigua-et-Barbuda (**=Developing) (2)				
All commodity groups	58 076	100.0	0.00	0.00
098 Edible products & preparations nes	32 862	56.6	0.20	0.05
334 Heavy petroleum & bituminous oil	2 612	4.5	0.00	0.00
793 Ships boats floating structures	1 811	3.1	0.00	0.00
781 Passenger cars and race cars	1 795	3.1	0.00	0.00
782 Goods and service vehicles	1 349	2.3	0.00	0.00
072 Cocoa	961	1.7	0.01	0.00
778 Electrical machinery apparatus nes	835	1.4	0.00	0.00
783 Road motor vehicles nes	825	1.4	0.01	0.00
727 Food processing machine excl. domesti	680	1.2	0.03	0.00
634 Veneer, plywood & other wood nes	663	1.1	0.00	0.00
Remainder	13 683	23.6		
Argentina - Argentine (**=Developing)				
All commodity groups	82 489 130	100.0	1.03	0.45
081 Animal feed excluding unmilled cereal	11 227 334	13.6	34.89	15.39
421 Fixed veg fat and oil, "soft"	6 023 180	7.3	45.33	15.09
222 Oil seed etc for soft oil	4 816 628	5.8	16.21	6.83
044 Maize unmilled, excluding sweet corn	4 680 149	5.7	37.52	13.33
781 Passenger cars and race cars	4 335 347	5.3	3.82	0.67
782 Goods and service vehicles	3 674 355	4.5	7.96	2.78
041 Wheat meslin, incl spelt, unmilled	2 730 303	3.3	47.31	5.62
333 Crude petroleum & bituminous oil	2 395 194	2.9	0.19	0.14
971 Gold non-monetary excluding ores	2 287 442	2.8	1.72	0.91
598 Miscellaneous chemical products nes	2 191 469	2.7	7.31	1.74
Remainder	38 127 729	46.1		
Armenia - Arménie (**=Transition) (2)				
All commodity groups	1 374 266	100.0	0.17	0.01
283 Copper ores and concentrates	184 318	13.4	14.61	0.34
112 Alcoholic beverages	157 631	11.5	10.57	0.21
671 Pig & sponge iron, ferro alloys etc	120 274	8.8	1.10	0.29
682 Copper	110 045	8.0	0.98	0.08
667 Pearls, precious semiprecious stone	101 985	7.4	5.27	0.07
684 Aluminium	92 036	6.7	0.92	0.08
351 Electric current	80 915	5.9	3.24	0.21
971 Gold non-monetary excluding ores	80 022	5.8	4.41	0.03
792 Aircraft, spacecraft & equipment	34 452	2.5	3.67	0.02
122 Manufactured tabacco	26 294	1.9	2.52	0.08
Remainder	386 294	28.1		

For sources and notes, see end of table.

Pour les sources et les notes, se reporter à la fin du tableau.

173

Leading products exported based on average 2011-2012 values SITC Revision 3 (3-digit level) / Principaux produits exportés d'après la moyenne des valeurs de 2011-2012 CTCI révision 3 (positions à 3 chiffres)	Value (f.o.b., thousands of dollars) Valeur (f.a.b., milliers de dollars)	2011-2012 As percentage / En pourcentage of country total / du total du pays	of ** (1) / des ** (1)	of world / du monde
Aruba (**=Developing) (2)				
All commodity groups	3 514 721	100.0	0.04	0.02
334 Heavy petroleum & bituminous oil	2 947 317	83.9	0.70	0.30
112 Alcoholic beverages	103 444	2.9	0.74	0.14
335 Residual petroleum products nes	72 301	2.1	0.39	0.14
122 Manufactured tabacco	62 720	1.8	0.74	0.20
044 Maize unmilled, excluding sweet corn	57 374	1.6	0.46	0.16
333 Crude petroleum & bituminous oil	43 129	1.2	0.00	0.00
081 Animal feed excluding unmilled cereal	32 311	0.9	0.10	0.04
041 Wheat meslin, incl spelt, unmilled	17 872	0.5	0.31	0.04
061 Sugar, mollasses and honey	11 086	0.3	0.03	0.02
971 Gold non-monetary excluding ores	7 920	0.2	0.01	0.00
Remainder	159 247	4.6		
Australia - Australie (**=Developed)				
All commodity groups	262 833 149	100.0	2.78	1.44
281 Iron ore and concentrates	61 471 888	23.4	86.55	44.92
321 Coal excluding non-agglomomerated	45 466 681	17.3	62.62	34.40
971 Gold non-monetary excluding ores	15 826 142	6.0	13.55	6.29
343 Natural gas, liquefied or not	12 750 280	4.9	11.79	3.67
333 Crude petroleum & bituminous oil	11 573 861	4.4	5.82	0.67
041 Wheat meslin, incl spelt, unmilled	6 518 235	2.5	18.27	13.42
283 Copper ores and concentrates	5 542 231	2.1	40.32	10.19
285 Aluminium ore concentrate alumina	5 540 010	2.1	66.67	36.52
011 Beef, fresh chilled frozen	4 881 226	1.9	18.16	12.28
287 Base metal ores & concentrates nes	4 498 244	1.7	36.27	13.81
Remainder	88 764 351	33.7		
Austria - Autriche (**=Developed) (2)				
All commodity groups	164 166 193	100.0	1.74	0.90
713 Internal combustion engine part nes	6 427 766	3.9	5.10	3.95
542 Medicines including veterinary	5 802 930	3.5	1.89	1.72
781 Passenger cars and race cars	5 110 900	3.1	0.97	0.79
784 Motor vehicle parts and accessories	4 973 478	3.0	1.90	1.39
699 Base metal manufactures nes	4 349 787	2.6	4.80	3.01
728 Special industrial machine part nes	4 341 635	2.6	3.10	2.37
641 Paper and paperboard	3 688 700	2.2	3.91	3.08
541 Pharmaceuticals excluding medicines	3 354 245	2.0	2.35	2.05
772 Electrical circuit equipment	2 807 132	1.7	2.17	1.20
778 Electrical machinery apparatus nes	2 556 822	1.6	2.28	1.14
Remainder	120 752 798	73.8		
Azerbaijan - Azerbaïdjan (**=Transition) (2)				
All commodity groups	33 564 469	100.0	4.05	0.18
333 Crude petroleum & bituminous oil	29 696 496	88.5	11.25	1.73
334 Heavy petroleum & bituminous oil	1 271 888	3.8	1.04	0.13
343 Natural gas, liquefied or not	627 550	1.9	0.79	0.18
061 Sugar, mollasses and honey	230 167	0.7	18.52	0.51
057 Fruit nut (exc oil), fresh or dried	191 770	0.6	9.46	0.22
344 Petroleum and hydrocarbon gas nes	92 029	0.3	9.08	0.65
897 Jewellery nes (667)	82 541	0.2	57.34	0.07
571 Primary form ethylene polymers	81 022	0.2	7.69	0.10
672 Ingots, Iron steel primary products	74 687	0.2	0.49	0.17
421 Fixed veg fat and oil, "soft"	73 780	0.2	1.31	0.18
Remainder	1 142 539	3.4		
Bahamas (**=Developing) (2)				
All commodity groups	908 750	100.0	0.01	0.00
334 Heavy petroleum & bituminous oil	546 346	60.1	0.13	0.06
793 Ships boats floating structures	68 041	7.5	0.06	0.04
572 Primary form styrene polymers	49 621	5.5	0.34	0.19
335 Residual petroleum products nes	48 238	5.3	0.26	0.09
896 Work of art & collections; antiques	40 458	4.5	2.09	0.18
036 Crustacean mollusc aquat invertebra	30 852	3.4	0.15	0.10
515 Organo-inorganic compound acid salt	20 487	2.3	0.09	0.02
553 Perfume toilet cosmetics, excl. soap	12 004	1.3	0.07	0.02
112 Alcoholic beverages	8 473	0.9	0.06	0.01
273 Stone, sand and gravel	7 722	0.8	0.12	0.07
Remainder	76 508	8.4		

Leading products exported based on average 2011-2012 values SITC Revision 3 (3-digit level) / Principaux produits exportés d'après la moyenne des valeurs de 2011-2012 CTCI révision 3 (positions à 3 chiffres)	Value (f.o.b., thousands of dollars) Valeur (f.a.b., milliers de dollars)	2011-2012 As percentage / En pourcentage of country total / du total du pays	of ** (1) / des ** (1)	of world / du monde
Bahrain - Bahrein (**=Developing) (2)				
All commodity groups	19 706 900	100.0	0.25	0.11
334 Heavy petroleum & bituminous oil	6 273 091	31.8	1.48	0.64
684 Aluminium	3 512 274	17.8	9.15	2.95
281 Iron ore and concentrates	2 370 211	12.0	4.08	1.73
344 Petroleum and hydrocarbon gas nes	456 370	2.3	6.12	3.23
562 Manufactured fertilizer excl. crude	435 693	2.2	1.65	0.58
693 Wire products and fencing grills	425 941	2.2	6.06	2.69
781 Passenger cars and race cars	405 388	2.1	0.36	0.06
671 Pig & sponge iron, ferro alloys etc	352 042	1.8	1.63	0.84
335 Residual petroleum products nes	335 934	1.7	1.80	0.66
897 Jewellery nes (667)	251 424	1.3	0.31	0.20
Remainder	4 888 532	24.8		
Bangladesh (**=Developing) (2)				
All commodity groups	26 148 336	100.0	0.33	0.14
845 Articles of apparel nes	7 970 342	30.5	8.07	5.67
841 Male clothing, woven	5 767 594	22.1	11.79	8.10
842 Female clothing, woven	2 683 500	10.3	4.98	3.27
844 Female clothing, knitted crocheted	1 476 004	5.6	3.34	2.64
843 Male clothing, knitted crocheted	1 474 480	5.6	5.75	4.83
658 Made-up textile articles nes	1 030 991	3.9	2.62	2.00
036 Crustacean mollusc aquat invertebra	775 955	3.0	3.67	2.43
651 Textile yarn	613 483	2.3	1.63	1.07
611 Leather	412 084	1.6	3.17	1.73
562 Manufactured fertilizer excl. crude	390 305	1.5	1.48	0.52
Remainder	3 553 598	13.6		
Barbados - Barbade (**=Developing) (2)				
All commodity groups	537 443	100.0	0.01	0.00
334 Heavy petroleum & bituminous oil	79 128	14.7	0.02	0.01
542 Medicines including veterinary	60 655	11.3	0.21	0.02
112 Alcoholic beverages	37 730	7.0	0.27	0.05
333 Crude petroleum & bituminous oil	33 279	6.2	0.00	0.00
793 Ships boats floating structures	17 765	3.3	0.02	0.01
892 Printed matter	15 429	2.9	0.10	0.03
091 Margarine and shortening	14 039	2.6	0.61	0.21
899 Manufactured articles nes	12 340	2.3	0.04	0.02
661 Lime cement construction material	11 204	2.1	0.07	0.04
022 Milk products, excl. butter & cheese	10 679	2.0	0.18	0.03
Remainder	245 195	45.6		
Belarus - Bélarus (**=Transition)				
All commodity groups	43 739 304	100.0	5.27	0.24
334 Heavy petroleum & bituminous oil	13 618 946	31.1	11.16	1.38
562 Manufactured fertilizer excl. crude	3 394 621	7.8	19.99	4.50
533 Pigment, paint, varnish & related	2 241 440	5.1	74.94	3.52
782 Goods and service vehicles	1 609 241	3.7	68.51	1.22
333 Crude petroleum & bituminous oil	1 303 842	3.0	0.49	0.08
722 Tractors	1 030 591	2.4	90.83	4.39
022 Milk products, excl. butter & cheese	847 841	1.9	63.40	2.00
597 Additive e.g. lubricate, antifreeze	726 071	1.7	86.03	3.11
625 Rubber for wheels, incl inner tube	675 922	1.5	31.68	0.73
676 Iron steel bar rod section piling	618 964	1.4	8.25	0.67
Remainder	17 671 825	40.4		
Belgium - Belgique (**=Developed)				
All commodity groups	462 389 828	100.0	4.90	2.53
334 Heavy petroleum & bituminous oil	36 519 901	7.9	8.29	3.70
542 Medicines including veterinary	33 000 051	7.1	10.76	9.80
781 Passenger cars and race cars	27 959 127	6.0	5.30	4.35
667 Pearls, precious semiprecious stone	19 159 409	4.1	26.15	12.43
541 Pharmaceuticals excluding medicines	15 465 643	3.3	10.84	9.47
515 Organo-inorganic compound acid salt	12 418 343	2.7	14.29	11.11
575 Other plastics, in primary forms	10 676 529	2.3	14.40	9.41
343 Natural gas, liquefied or not	7 946 191	1.7	7.35	2.29
784 Motor vehicle parts and accessories	7 385 083	1.6	2.82	2.06
571 Primary form ethylene polymers	6 567 296	1.4	16.81	8.42
Remainder	285 292 255	61.9		

For sources and notes, see end of table.

Pour les sources et les notes, se reporter à la fin du tableau.

3.2.D Export structure by product
Individual countries and territories

3.2.D Structure des exportations par produits
Pays et territoires individuels

Leading products exported based on average 2011-2012 values SITC Revision 3 (3-digit level) / Principaux produits exportés d'après la moyenne des valeurs de 2011-2012 CTCI révision 3 (positions à 3 chiffres)	2011-2012 Value (f.o.b., thousands of dollars) / Valeur (f.a.b., milliers de dollars)	As percentage / En pourcentage: of country total / du total du pays	of ** (1) / des ** (1)	of world / du monde
Belize (=Developing) (2)**				
All commodity groups	393 092	100.0	0.00	0.00
333 Crude petroleum & bituminous oil	84 837	21.6	0.01	0.00
057 Fruit nut (exc oil), fresh or dried	54 202	13.8	0.12	0.06
061 Sugar, mollasses and honey	46 064	11.7	0.14	0.10
059 Fruit & vegetable juice unfermented	43 142	11.0	0.57	0.25
036 Crustacean mollusc aquat invertebra	18 933	4.8	0.09	0.00
041 Wheat meslin, incl spelt, unmilled	17 359	4.4	0.30	0.04
034 Fish, fresh live chilled frozen	15 086	3.8	0.06	0.03
793 Ships boats floating structures	7 687	2.0	0.01	0.00
781 Passenger cars and race cars	5 963	1.5	0.01	0.00
001 Live animal excl. fish & crustacean	5 737	1.5	0.12	0.03
Remainder	94 082	23.9		
Benin - Bénin (=Developing) (2)**				
All commodity groups	1 405 000	100.0	0.02	0.01
263 Cotton	289 751	20.6	2.63	1.11
334 Heavy petroleum & bituminous oil	191 718	13.6	0.05	0.02
971 Gold non-monetary excluding ores	181 518	12.9	0.14	0.07
057 Fruit nut (exc oil), fresh or dried	155 448	11.1	0.35	0.18
012 Meat nes, fresh chilled frozen	79 380	5.6	0.51	0.11
288 Non ferrous base metal waste nes	78 400	5.6	0.77	0.17
676 Iron steel bar rod section piling	37 767	2.7	0.12	0.04
042 Rice	37 369	2.7	0.18	0.15
282 Ferrous iron & steel, waste & scrap	32 122	2.3	0.51	0.06
247 Wood in rough or roughly squared	28 055	2.0	0.55	0.18
Remainder	293 472	20.9		
Bermuda - Bermudes (=Developed) (2)**				
All commodity groups	12 727	100.0	0.00	0.00
793 Ships boats floating structures	4 203	33.0	0.01	0.00
542 Medicines including veterinary	2 728	21.4	0.00	0.00
342 Liquefied propane and butane	1 725	13.6	0.01	0.00
034 Fish, fresh live chilled frozen	191	1.5	0.00	0.00
971 Gold non-monetary excluding ores	164	1.3	0.00	0.00
041 Wheat meslin, incl spelt, unmilled	145	1.1	0.00	0.00
112 Alcoholic beverages	122	1.0	0.00	0.00
044 Maize unmilled, excluding sweet corn	64	0.5	0.00	0.00
896 Work of art & collections; antiques	61	0.5	0.00	0.00
081 Animal feed excluding unmilled cereal	49	0.4	0.00	0.00
Remainder	3 275	25.7		
Bhutan - Bhoutan (=Developing) (2)**				
All commodity groups	642 322	100.0	0.01	0.00
671 Pig & sponge iron, ferro alloys etc	182 685	28.4	0.85	0.43
351 Electric current	88 902	13.8	1.48	0.23
682 Copper	57 387	8.9	0.08	0.04
524 Other inorganic chemicals	44 363	6.9	1.28	0.33
676 Iron steel bar rod section piling	34 734	5.4	0.11	0.04
689 Misc non-ferrous base metals	23 463	3.7	0.53	0.23
273 Stone, sand and gravel	22 443	3.5	0.36	0.19
057 Fruit nut (exc oil), fresh or dried	22 047	3.4	0.05	0.03
278 Other crude minerals	19 980	3.1	0.27	0.11
661 Lime cement construction material	18 198	2.8	0.11	0.06
Remainder	128 120	20.1		
Bolivia (Plurinational State of) - Bolivie (État plurinational de) (=Developing)**				
All commodity groups	10 453 015	100.0	0.13	0.06
343 Natural gas, liquefied or not	4 752 320	45.5	2.98	1.37
287 Base metal ores & concentrates nes	1 116 432	10.7	5.98	3.43
289 Prec metal ore concentrate excl. gold	833 970	8.0	11.99	4.39
971 Gold non-monetary excluding ores	713 142	6.8	0.54	0.28
081 Animal feed excluding unmilled cereal	402 298	3.8	1.25	0.55
687 Tin	392 567	3.8	6.09	5.14
333 Crude petroleum & bituminous oil	381 846	3.7	0.03	0.02
421 Fixed veg fat and oil, "soft"	287 264	2.7	2.16	0.72
057 Fruit nut (exc oil), fresh or dried	181 712	1.7	0.41	0.21
681 Silver, platinum, platinum metals	169 345	1.6	0.59	0.25
Remainder	1 222 119	11.7		

Leading products exported based on average 2011-2012 values SITC Revision 3 (3-digit level) / Principaux produits exportés d'après la moyenne des valeurs de 2011-2012 CTCI révision 3 (positions à 3 chiffres)	2011-2012 Value (f.o.b., thousands of dollars) / Valeur (f.a.b., milliers de dollars)	As percentage / En pourcentage: of country total / du total du pays	of ** (1) / des ** (1)	of world / du monde
Bonaire, Sint Eustatius and Saba - Bonaire, Saint-Eustache et Saba (=Developing)**				
All commodity groups	5 172	100.0	0.00	0.00
773 Electrical distribute equipment nes	2 202	42.6	0.00	0.00
723 Civil engineering plant & equipment	1 078	20.8	0.00	0.00
772 Electrical circuit equipment	1 001	19.4	0.00	0.00
278 Other crude minerals	331	6.4	0.00	0.00
740 Ball or roller bearings	185	3.6	0.00	0.00
743 Gas pump, compressor, fan, filter	173	3.3	0.00	0.00
676 Iron steel bar rod section piling	77	1.5	0.00	0.00
749 Non-electric machinery part nes	66	1.3	0.00	0.00
778 Electrical machinery apparatus nes	36	0.7	0.00	0.00
621 Rubber material e.g. paste tube rod	15	0.3	0.00	0.00
Remainder	8	0.1		
Bosnia and Herzegovina - Bosnie-Herzégovine (=Transition) (2)**				
All commodity groups	5 505 924	100.0	0.66	0.03
684 Aluminium	404 538	7.3	4.02	0.34
851 Footwear	404 304	7.3	23.63	0.35
821 Furniture part; bedding furnishing	321 862	5.8	15.14	0.21
676 Iron steel bar rod section piling	217 767	4.0	2.90	0.24
334 Heavy petroleum & bituminous oil	205 196	3.7	0.17	0.02
248 Wood simply worked, railway sleeper	165 286	3.0	3.74	0.45
743 Gas pump, compressor, fan, filter	135 130	2.5	12.42	0.11
325 Coke, semi coke, retort carbon	122 636	2.2	8.90	1.38
282 Ferrous iron & steel, waste & scrap	119 071	2.2	4.48	0.22
351 Electric current	111 942	2.0	4.49	0.28
Remainder	3 298 192	60.0		
Botswana (=Developing)**				
All commodity groups	5 926 582	100.0	0.07	0.03
667 Pearls, precious semiprecious stone	4 712 525	79.5	5.97	3.06
284 Nickel ores, concentrates, etc	397 594	6.7	6.62	3.70
283 Copper ores and concentrates	100 816	1.7	0.26	0.19
277 Natural abrasives nes	78 705	1.3	8.49	5.39
971 Gold non-monetary excluding ores	52 855	0.9	0.04	0.02
781 Passenger cars and race cars	36 762	0.6	0.03	0.01
842 Female clothing, woven	33 862	0.6	0.06	0.04
011 Beef, fresh chilled frozen	32 585	0.5	0.27	0.08
841 Male clothing, woven	27 077	0.5	0.06	0.04
782 Goods and service vehicles	26 411	0.4	0.06	0.02
Remainder	427 390	7.3		
Brazil - Brésil (=Developing)**				
All commodity groups	249 309 239	100.0	3.11	1.36
281 Iron ore and concentrates	36 403 272	14.6	62.66	26.60
333 Crude petroleum & bituminous oil	20 954 608	8.4	1.67	1.22
222 Oil seed etc for soft oil	16 891 844	6.8	56.85	23.97
061 Sugar, mollasses and honey	13 872 770	5.6	43.61	30.66
012 Meat nes, fresh chilled frozen	8 785 829	3.5	56.91	12.13
071 Coffee and coffee substitutes	7 597 912	3.0	30.30	18.71
081 Animal feed excluding unmilled cereal	6 445 229	2.6	20.03	8.84
784 Motor vehicle parts and accessories	4 934 457	2.0	5.17	1.38
251 Pulp and waste paper	4 853 777	1.9	41.32	10.19
334 Heavy petroleum & bituminous oil	4 839 612	1.9	1.14	0.49
Remainder	123 729 929	49.7		
British Virgin Islands - Îles Vierges britanniques (=Developing)**				
All commodity groups	39 250	100.0	0.00	0.00
793 Ships boats floating structures	18 528	47.2	0.02	0.01
667 Pearls, precious semiprecious stone	6 952	17.7	0.01	0.00
896 Work of art & collections; antiques	2 503	6.4	0.13	0.01
334 Heavy petroleum & bituminous oil	2 359	6.0	0.00	0.00
897 Jewellery nes (667)	1 381	3.5	0.00	0.00
792 Aircraft, spacecraft & equipment	905	2.3	0.00	0.00
516 Other organic chemicals	696	1.8	0.00	0.00
562 Manufactured fertilizer excl. crude	476	1.2	0.00	0.00
772 Electrical circuit equipment	444	1.1	0.00	0.00
043 Barley grain unmilled	323	0.8	0.04	0.00
Remainder	4 683	12.0		

For sources and notes, see end of table.

Pour les sources et les notes, se reporter à la fin du tableau.

3

Leading products exported based on average 2011-2012 values SITC Revision 3 (3-digit level) Principaux produits exportés d'après la moyenne des valeurs de 2011-2012 CTCI révision 3 (positions à 3 chiffres)	2011-2012			
	Value (f.o.b., thousands of dollars) Valeur (f.a.b., milliers de dollars)	As percentage En pourcentage		
		of country total du total du pays	of ** (1) des ** (1)	of world du monde
Brunei Darussalam - Brunéi Darussalam (**=Developing) (2)				
All commodity groups	12 729 597	100.0	0.16	0.07
333 Crude petroleum & bituminous oil	6 667 486	52.4	0.53	0.39
343 Natural gas, liquefied or not	5 556 394	43.6	3.48	1.60
512 Alcohols, phenols; derivatives	121 065	1.0	0.35	0.19
845 Articles of apparel nes	28 152	0.2	0.03	0.02
334 Heavy petroleum & bituminous oil	27 530	0.2	0.01	0.00
897 Jewellery nes (667)	18 991	0.1	0.02	0.02
792 Aircraft, spacecraft & equipment	18 472	0.1	0.08	0.01
728 Special industrial machine part nes	13 782	0.1	0.03	0.01
282 Ferrous iron & steel, waste & scrap	11 984	0.1	0.19	0.02
667 Pearls, precious semiprecious stone	11 485	0.1	0.01	0.01
Remainder	254 256	2.1		
Bulgaria - Bulgarie (**=Developed)				
All commodity groups	27 432 000	100.0	0.29	0.15
334 Heavy petroleum & bituminous oil	3 390 257	12.4	0.77	0.34
682 Copper	2 937 926	10.7	4.92	2.04
222 Oil seed etc for soft oil	812 311	3.0	2.10	1.15
041 Wheat meslin, incl spelt, unmilled	647 036	2.4	1.81	1.33
542 Medicines including veterinary	645 333	2.4	0.21	0.19
351 Electric current	551 502	2.0	1.79	1.40
772 Electrical circuit equipment	506 853	1.8	0.39	0.22
289 Prec metal ore concentrate excl. gold	496 979	1.8	4.25	2.62
842 Female clothing, woven	472 361	1.7	1.75	0.58
676 Iron steel bar rod section piling	454 724	1.7	0.86	0.50
Remainder	16 516 718	60.1		
Burkina Faso (**=Developing) (2)				
All commodity groups	2 229 377	100.0	0.03	0.01
971 Gold non-monetary excluding ores	1 046 747	47.0	0.79	0.42
263 Cotton	725 431	32.5	6.59	2.77
222 Oil seed etc for soft oil	109 224	4.9	0.37	0.15
057 Fruit nut (exc oil), fresh or dried	76 293	3.4	0.17	0.09
223 Oil seed for non soft oil	37 535	1.7	4.80	1.13
001 Live animal excl. fish & crustacean	29 415	1.3	0.63	0.13
054 Vegetable & vegetable products nes	20 008	0.9	0.08	0.03
287 Base metal ores & concentrates nes	19 793	0.9	0.11	0.06
744 Mechanical handling equipment nes	9 002	0.4	0.05	0.01
676 Iron steel bar rod section piling	8 496	0.4	0.03	0.01
Remainder	147 433	6.6		
Burundi (**=Developing) (2)				
All commodity groups	128 500	100.0	0.00	0.00
071 Coffee and coffee substitutes	58 782	45.7	0.23	0.14
074 Tea and maté	16 102	12.5	0.25	0.19
971 Gold non-monetary excluding ores	15 524	12.1	0.01	0.01
287 Base metal ores & concentrates nes	9 711	7.6	0.05	0.03
554 Soaps cleansers polishes	5 617	4.4	0.05	0.01
211 Raw hides & skins, excluding furskins	1 829	1.4	0.20	0.02
782 Goods and service vehicles	1 646	1.3	0.00	0.00
665 Glassware	1 392	1.1	0.01	0.01
723 Civil engineering plant & equipment	981	0.8	0.00	0.00
282 Ferrous iron & steel, waste & scrap	974	0.8	0.02	0.00
Remainder	15 942	12.3		
Cambodia - Cambodge (**=Developing) (2)				
All commodity groups	7 271 119	100.0	0.09	0.04
845 Articles of apparel nes	2 114 888	29.1	2.14	1.51
844 Female clothing, knitted crocheted	1 210 601	16.6	2.74	2.16
851 Footwear	598 014	8.2	0.83	0.52
843 Male clothing, knitted crocheted	566 500	7.8	2.21	1.86
842 Female clothing, woven	528 531	7.3	0.98	0.64
841 Male clothing, woven	515 192	7.1	1.05	0.72
231 Natural rubber, latex, gum, etc	276 592	3.8	0.86	0.82
892 Printed matter	188 161	2.6	1.25	0.38
785 Motorcycles, mopeds and cycles	170 244	2.3	0.66	0.36
971 Gold non-monetary excluding ores	149 947	2.1	0.11	0.06
Remainder	952 449	13.1		

Leading products exported based on average 2011-2012 values SITC Revision 3 (3-digit level) Principaux produits exportés d'après la moyenne des valeurs de 2011-2012 CTCI révision 3 (positions à 3 chiffres)	2011-2012			
	Value (f.o.b., thousands of dollars) Valeur (f.a.b., milliers de dollars)	As percentage En pourcentage		
		of country total du total du pays	of ** (1) des ** (1)	of world du monde
Cameroon - Cameroun (**=Developing) (2)				
All commodity groups	4 508 425	100.0	0.06	0.02
333 Crude petroleum & bituminous oil	1 709 773	37.9	0.14	0.10
072 Cocoa	526 925	11.7	3.85	2.55
248 Wood simply worked, railway sleeper	353 578	7.8	4.40	0.95
334 Heavy petroleum & bituminous oil	304 110	6.7	0.07	0.03
247 Wood in rough or roughly squared	211 167	4.7	4.15	1.38
057 Fruit nut (exc oil), fresh or dried	199 889	4.4	0.46	0.23
231 Natural rubber, latex, gum, etc	145 469	3.2	0.45	0.43
263 Cotton	126 963	2.8	1.15	0.48
684 Aluminium	87 965	2.0	0.23	0.07
071 Coffee and coffee substitutes	85 463	1.9	0.34	0.21
Remainder	757 123	16.9		
Canada (**=Developed)				
All commodity groups	451 905 451	100.0	4.79	2.47
333 Crude petroleum & bituminous oil	71 955 805	15.9	36.21	4.19
781 Passenger cars and race cars	43 354 018	9.6	8.22	6.74
334 Heavy petroleum & bituminous oil	18 720 911	4.1	4.25	1.90
971 Gold non-monetary excluding ores	17 013 445	3.8	14.57	6.77
343 Natural gas, liquefied or not	11 109 767	2.5	10.27	3.20
784 Motor vehicle parts and accessories	10 071 314	2.2	3.85	2.81
792 Aircraft, spacecraft & equipment	10 021 852	2.2	7.31	6.22
684 Aluminium	7 735 397	1.7	10.93	6.49
562 Manufactured fertilizer excl. crude	7 685 800	1.7	23.95	10.18
641 Paper and paperboard	7 227 346	1.6	7.67	6.04
Remainder	247 009 796	54.7		
Cape Verde - Cap-Vert (**=Developing) (2)				
All commodity groups	62 333	100.0	0.00	0.00
037 Fish shellfish, prepared preserved	22 415	36.0	0.12	0.08
034 Fish, fresh live chilled frozen	18 266	29.3	0.07	0.03
851 Footwear	3 992	6.4	0.01	0.00
333 Crude petroleum & bituminous oil	3 017	4.8	0.00	0.00
282 Ferrous iron & steel, waste & scrap	1 529	2.5	0.02	0.00
845 Articles of apparel nes	1 350	2.2	0.00	0.00
841 Male clothing, woven	1 343	2.2	0.00	0.00
764 Telecom équipment part nes	1 029	1.7	0.00	0.00
843 Male clothing, knitted crocheted	971	1.6	0.00	0.00
036 Crustacean mollusc aquat invertebra	806	1.3	0.00	0.00
Remainder	7 615	12.0		
Cayman Islands - Îles Caïmanes (**=Developing) (2)				
All commodity groups	20 700	100.0	0.00	0.00
793 Ships boats floating structures	18 345	88.6	0.02	0.01
714 Non-electric engines excl. 712 713 718	505	2.4	0.00	0.00
334 Heavy petroleum & bituminous oil	286	1.4	0.00	0.00
792 Aircraft, spacecraft & equipment	272	1.3	0.00	0.00
897 Jewellery nes (667)	206	1.0	0.00	0.00
896 Work of art & collections; antiques	110	0.5	0.01	0.00
971 Gold non-monetary excluding ores	83	0.4	0.00	0.00
282 Ferrous iron & steel, waste & scrap	80	0.4	0.00	0.00
781 Passenger cars and race cars	49	0.2	0.00	0.00
713 Internal combustion engine part nes	39	0.2	0.00	0.00
Remainder	725	3.6		
Central African Republic - République centrafricaine (**=Developing) (2)				
All commodity groups	200 000	100.0	0.00	0.00
667 Pearls, precious semiprecious stone	50 377	25.2	0.06	0.03
247 Wood in rough or roughly squared	45 096	22.5	0.89	0.29
277 Natural abrasives nes	38 240	19.1	4.13	2.62
248 Wood simply worked, railway sleeper	20 555	10.3	0.26	0.06
263 Cotton	19 086	9.5	0.17	0.07
971 Gold non-monetary excluding ores	2 715	1.4	0.00	0.00
071 Coffee and coffee substitutes	2 573	1.3	0.01	0.01
684 Aluminium	2 298	1.1	0.01	0.00
741 Heating, cooling equipment parts nes	2 295	1.1	0.01	0.00
781 Passenger cars and race cars	1 470	0.7	0.00	0.00
Remainder	15 295	7.8		

For sources and notes, see end of table.

Pour les sources et les notes, se reporter à la fin du tableau.

Leading products exported based on average 2011-2012 values SITC Revision 3 (3-digit level) / Principaux produits exportés d'après la moyenne des valeurs de 2011-2012 CTCI révision 3 (positions à 3 chiffres)	Value (f.o.b., thousands of dollars) Valeur (f.a.b., milliers de dollars)	2011-2012 As percentage En pourcentage		
		of country total du total du pays	of ** (1) des ** (1)	of world du monde
Chad - Tchad (**=Developing) (2)				
All commodity groups	4 500 000	100.0	0.06	0.02
333 Crude petroleum & bituminous oil	3 916 919	87.0	0.31	0.23
334 Heavy petroleum & bituminous oil	352 136	7.8	0.08	0.04
263 Cotton	113 314	2.5	1.03	0.43
292 Crude vegetable materials nes	37 713	0.8	0.24	0.09
792 Aircraft, spacecraft & equipment	26 208	0.6	0.11	0.02
222 Oil seed etc for soft oil	9 327	0.2	0.03	0.01
811 Prefabricated buildings	3 805	0.1	0.13	0.04
523 Inorganic acid metal salt peroxy	2 534	0.1	0.03	0.01
657 Special yarn and textile fabric etc	2 124	0.0	0.01	0.00
662 Clay and refractory materials	1 908	0.0	0.02	0.01
Remainder	34 012	0.9		
Chile - Chili (**=Developing)				
All commodity groups	79 844 057	100.0	1.00	0.44
682 Copper	27 946 458	35.0	38.17	19.39
283 Copper ores and concentrates	15 362 901	19.2	39.01	28.25
057 Fruit nut (exc oil), fresh or dried	4 620 387	5.8	10.54	5.32
034 Fish, fresh live chilled frozen	3 160 208	4.0	11.82	5.26
251 Pulp and waste paper	2 696 307	3.4	22.96	5.66
112 Alcoholic beverages	1 785 545	2.2	12.79	2.34
971 Gold non-monetary excluding ores	1 541 645	1.9	1.16	0.61
281 Iron ore and concentrates	1 481 017	1.9	2.55	1.08
287 Base metal ores & concentrates nes	1 406 220	1.8	7.53	4.32
522 Inorganic chemical elem oxide salt	1 015 028	1.3	3.53	1.66
Remainder	18 828 341	23.5		
China - Chine (**=Developing)				
All commodity groups	1 973 585 334	100.0	24.60	10.79
764 Telecom equipment part nes	172 526 680	8.7	49.36	33.35
752 Computer equipment nes	164 745 172	8.3	66.23	46.74
776 Valves tubes; diodes, transistors	75 950 418	3.8	18.85	13.66
821 Furniture part; bedding furnishing	50 478 561	2.6	68.01	33.37
778 Electrical machinery apparatus nes	46 690 275	2.4	41.95	20.74
845 Articles of apparel nes	45 441 359	2.3	46.00	32.35
851 Footwear	44 266 800	2.2	61.68	38.32
793 Ships boats floating structures	41 222 499	2.1	36.03	24.02
759 Office equipment part & accessories	38 552 144	2.0	33.50	20.17
894 Baby carriage, toy, game, sport goods	37 285 107	1.9	64.62	39.65
Remainder	1 256 426 319	63.7		
China, Hong Kong SAR - Chine (RAS de Hong Kong) (**=Developing)				
All commodity groups	474 240 426	100.0	5.91	2.59
764 Telecom equipment part nes	68 850 520	14.5	19.70	13.31
776 Valves tubes; diodes, transistors	68 844 314	14.5	17.09	12.38
971 Gold non-monetary excluding ores	38 239 296	8.1	28.79	15.21
759 Office equipment part & accessories	31 998 181	6.7	27.80	16.74
772 Electrical circuit equipment	20 369 163	4.3	19.61	8.68
752 Computer equipment nes	18 306 107	3.9	7.36	5.19
667 Pearls, precious semiprecious stone	15 548 149	3.3	19.71	10.09
894 Baby carriage, toy, game, sport goods	11 708 473	2.5	20.29	12.45
778 Electrical machinery apparatus nes	11 449 397	2.4	10.29	5.09
771 Electric power machine part excl. 716	10 125 339	2.1	20.40	10.94
Remainder	178 801 487	37.7		
China, Macao SAR - Chine (RAS de Macao) (**=Developing)				
All commodity groups	944 806	100.0	0.01	0.01
713 Internal combustion engine part nes	79 479	8.4	0.22	0.05
897 Jewellery nes (667)	72 640	7.7	0.09	0.06
845 Articles of apparel nes	50 349	5.3	0.05	0.04
885 Watches and clocks	48 800	5.2	0.28	0.10
288 Non ferrous base metal waste nes	42 968	4.5	0.42	0.09
764 Telecom equipment part nes	42 344	4.5	0.01	0.01
842 Female clothing, woven	34 849	3.7	0.06	0.04
682 Copper	32 098	3.4	0.04	0.02
553 Perfume toilet cosmetics, excl. soap	28 679	3.0	0.16	0.04
579 Plastic waste, parings and scrap	24 868	2.6	0.94	0.34
Remainder	487 732	51.7		
China, Taiwan Province of - Province chinoise de Taiwan (**=Developing)				
All commodity groups	303 809 826	100.0	3.79	1.66
776 Valves tubes; diodes, transistors	65 891 438	21.7	16.36	11.85
334 Heavy petroleum & bituminous oil	18 961 347	6.2	4.47	1.92
871 Optical instruments apparatus nes	17 027 199	5.6	19.92	16.06
764 Telecom equipment part nes	15 130 557	5.0	4.33	2.92
772 Electrical circuit equipment	9 103 283	3.0	8.76	3.88
778 Electrical machinery apparatus nes	7 558 384	2.5	6.79	3.36
898 Music instrument device recording	6 080 097	2.0	21.17	10.38
759 Office equipment part & accessories	5 831 474	1.9	5.07	3.05
728 Special industrial machine part nes	4 752 320	1.6	11.16	2.59
785 Motorcycles, mopeds and cycles	4 589 932	1.5	17.70	9.68
Remainder	148 883 795	49.0		
Colombia - Colombie (**=Developing)				
All commodity groups	58 613 567	100.0	0.73	0.32
333 Crude petroleum & bituminous oil	24 788 479	42.3	1.98	1.44
321 Coal excluding non-agglomerated	7 577 629	12.9	16.75	5.73
334 Heavy petroleum & bituminous oil	4 610 893	7.9	1.09	0.47
971 Gold non-monetary excluding ores	3 095 944	5.3	2.33	1.23
071 Coffee and coffee substitutes	2 576 479	4.4	10.27	6.35
292 Crude vegetable materials nes	1 286 318	2.2	8.22	2.97
057 Fruit nut (exc oil), fresh or dried	875 280	1.5	2.00	1.01
671 Pig & sponge iron, ferro alloys etc	854 541	1.5	3.96	2.03
061 Sugar, mollasses and honey	546 632	0.9	1.72	1.21
325 Coke, semi coke, retort carbon	523 388	0.9	20.37	5.90
Remainder	11 877 984	20.2		
Comoros - Comores (**=Developing) (2)				
All commodity groups	22 007	100.0	0.00	0.00
075 Spices	9 223	41.9	0.13	0.11
793 Ships boats floating structures	8 094	36.8	0.01	0.00
551 Essential oils, perfumes & flavours	3 082	14.0	0.06	0.01
971 Gold non-monetary excluding ores	373	1.7	0.00	0.00
651 Textile yarn	87	0.4	0.00	0.00
774 Electrodiagnostic equipment	77	0.3	0.00	0.00
231 Natural rubber, latex, gum, etc	67	0.3	0.00	0.00
661 Lime cement construction material	61	0.3	0.00	0.00
842 Female clothing, woven	59	0.3	0.00	0.00
843 Male clothing, knitted crocheted	57	0.3	0.00	0.00
Remainder	827	3.7		
Congo (**=Developing) (2)				
All commodity groups	11 149 664	100.0	0.14	0.06
333 Crude petroleum & bituminous oil	9 040 551	81.1	0.72	0.53
793 Ships boats floating structures	453 930	4.1	0.40	0.26
334 Heavy petroleum & bituminous oil	317 680	2.8	0.07	0.03
682 Copper	257 064	2.3	0.35	0.18
247 Wood in rough or roughly squared	251 065	2.3	4.93	1.64
342 Liquefied propane and butane	111 824	1.0	0.28	0.19
287 Base metal ores & concentrates nes	93 444	0.8	0.50	0.29
283 Copper ores and concentrates	82 260	0.7	0.21	0.15
573 Vinyl chloride etc polymers	75 439	0.7	1.30	0.38
679 Iron steel pipe tube fittings etc	74 803	0.7	0.20	0.08
Remainder	391 604	3.5		
Cook Islands - Îles Cook (**=Developing) (2)				
All commodity groups	3 090	100.0	0.00	0.00
793 Ships boats floating structures	1 327	43.0	0.00	0.00
034 Fish, fresh live chilled frozen	1 309	42.4	0.00	0.00
667 Pearls, precious semiprecious stone	132	4.3	0.00	0.00
059 Fruit & vegetable juice unfermented	71	2.3	0.00	0.00
282 Ferrous iron & steel, waste & scrap	23	0.8	0.00	0.00
511 Hydrocarbons nes; derivatives	21	0.7	0.00	0.00
112 Alcoholic beverages	19	0.6	0.00	0.00
896 Work of art & collections; antiques	14	0.5	0.00	0.00
961 Coins, nongold and non currency	10	0.3	0.04	0.00
057 Fruit nut (exc oil), fresh or dried	9	0.3	0.00	0.00
Remainder	155	4.8		

For sources and notes, see end of table.

Pour les sources et les notes, se reporter à la fin du tableau.

Leading products exported based on average 2011-2012 values SITC Revision 3 (3-digit level) / Principaux produits exportés d'après la moyenne des valeurs de 2011-2012 CTCI révision 3 (positions à 3 chiffres)	Value (f.o.b., thousands of dollars) Valeur (f.a.b., milliers de dollars)	of country total du total du pays	of ** (1) des ** (1)	of world du monde
Costa Rica (=Developing) (2)**				
All commodity groups	10 735 035	100.0	0.13	0.06
776 Valves tubes; diodes, transistors	4 156 517	38.7	1.03	0.75
057 Fruit nut (exc oil), fresh or dried	1 550 006	14.4	3.54	1.79
759 Office equipment part & accessories	1 478 597	13.8	1.28	0.77
872 Medical instruments appliances nes	433 480	4.0	2.22	0.48
071 Coffee and coffee substitutes	196 279	1.8	0.78	0.48
772 Electrical circuit equipment	154 304	1.4	0.15	0.07
098 Edible products & preparations nes	153 618	1.4	0.92	0.25
422 Fixed veg fat and oil, excl. "soft"	145 566	1.4	0.33	0.30
899 Manufactured articles nes	142 019	1.3	0.49	0.17
542 Medicines including veterinary	114 310	1.1	0.41	0.03
Remainder	2 210 339	20.7		
Côte d'Ivoire (=Developing)**				
All commodity groups	12 445 968	100.0	0.16	0.07
072 Cocoa	3 630 030	29.2	26.54	17.55
333 Crude petroleum & bituminous oil	1 660 467	13.3	0.13	0.10
334 Heavy petroleum & bituminous oil	1 483 993	11.9	0.35	0.15
231 Natural rubber, latex, gum, etc	1 003 537	8.1	3.13	2.97
971 Gold non-monetary excluding ores	573 139	4.6	0.43	0.23
057 Fruit nut (exc oil), fresh or dried	491 349	3.9	1.12	0.57
422 Fixed veg fat and oil, excl. "soft"	268 993	2.2	0.61	0.55
263 Cotton	233 561	1.9	2.12	0.89
335 Residual petroleum products nes	214 404	1.7	1.15	0.42
071 Coffee and coffee substitutes	183 456	1.5	0.73	0.45
Remainder	2 703 039	21.7		
Croatia - Croatie (=Transition)**				
All commodity groups	12 866 503	100.0	1.55	0.07
334 Heavy petroleum & bituminous oil	1 307 331	10.2	1.07	0.13
793 Ships boats floating structures	1 147 297	8.9	48.29	0.67
542 Medicines including veterinary	487 636	3.8	27.93	0.14
562 Manufactured fertilizer excl. crude	371 462	2.9	2.19	0.49
771 Electric power machine part excl. 716	367 919	2.9	28.22	0.40
821 Furniture part; bedding furnishing	336 498	2.6	15.83	0.22
248 Wood simply worked, railway sleeper	297 005	2.3	6.72	0.80
684 Aluminium	249 193	1.9	2.48	0.21
845 Articles of apparel nes	210 897	1.6	16.13	0.15
282 Ferrous iron & steel, waste & scrap	209 124	1.6	7.87	0.39
Remainder	7 882 141	61.3		
Cuba (=Developing) (2)**				
All commodity groups	5 855 242	100.0	0.07	0.03
284 Nickel ores, concentrates, etc	1 182 458	20.2	19.69	11.02
061 Sugar, mollasses and honey	907 617	15.5	2.85	2.01
122 Manufactured tabacco	460 256	7.9	5.41	1.48
334 Heavy petroleum & bituminous oil	417 823	7.1	0.10	0.04
542 Medicines including veterinary	323 490	5.5	1.15	0.10
288 Non ferrous base metal waste nes	166 128	2.8	1.62	0.35
672 Ingots, Iron steel primary products	154 003	2.6	1.22	0.36
036 Crustacean mollusc aquat invertebra	146 514	2.5	0.69	0.46
541 Pharmaceuticals excluding medicines	116 370	2.0	0.57	0.07
778 Electrical machinery apparatus nes	101 134	1.7	0.09	0.04
Remainder	1 879 449	32.2		
Cyprus - Chypre (=Developed)**				
All commodity groups	1 890 394	100.0	0.02	0.01
334 Heavy petroleum & bituminous oil	572 041	30.3	0.13	0.06
542 Medicines including veterinary	130 591	6.9	0.04	0.04
793 Ships boats floating structures	89 096	4.7	0.16	0.05
515 Organo-inorganic compound acid salt	55 653	2.9	0.06	0.05
776 Valves tubes; diodes, transistors	47 502	2.5	0.03	0.01
764 Telecom equipment part nes	38 846	2.1	0.02	0.01
024 Cheese and curd	34 961	1.8	0.13	0.12
054 Vegetable & vegetable products nes	34 854	1.8	0.10	0.06
282 Ferrous iron & steel, waste & scrap	31 053	1.6	0.07	0.06
541 Pharmaceuticals excluding medicines	27 015	1.4	0.02	0.02
Remainder	828 782	44.0		

Leading products exported based on average 2011-2012 values SITC Revision 3 (3-digit level) / Principaux produits exportés d'après la moyenne des valeurs de 2011-2012 CTCI révision 3 (positions à 3 chiffres)	Value (f.o.b., thousands of dollars) Valeur (f.a.b., milliers de dollars)	of country total du total du pays	of ** (1) des ** (1)	of world du monde
Czech Republic - République tchèque (=Developed)**				
All commodity groups	159 209 184	100.0	1.69	0.87
781 Passenger cars and race cars	15 502 886	9.7	2.94	2.41
784 Motor vehicle parts and accessories	11 000 780	6.9	4.20	3.07
752 Computer equipment nes	9 384 976	5.9	9.09	2.66
764 Telecom equipment part nes	5 087 684	3.2	3.06	0.98
772 Electrical circuit equipment	4 462 189	2.8	3.45	1.90
699 Base metal manufactures nes	4 173 597	2.6	4.60	2.89
778 Electrical machinery apparatus nes	3 828 937	2.4	3.41	1.70
741 Heating, cooling equipment parts nes	2 943 526	1.8	4.32	2.63
773 Electrical distribute equipment nes	2 696 224	1.7	4.80	2.40
761 Television video receive project	2 602 969	1.6	7.30	2.84
Remainder	97 525 416	61.4		
Dem. Rep. of the Congo - Rép. dém. du Congo (=Developing) (2)**				
All commodity groups	6 450 000	100.0	0.08	0.04
682 Copper	2 806 008	43.5	3.83	1.95
333 Crude petroleum & bituminous oil	998 255	15.5	0.08	0.06
287 Base metal ores & concentrates nes	691 156	10.7	3.70	2.12
689 Misc non-ferrous base metals	587 245	9.1	13.35	5.82
283 Copper ores and concentrates	489 972	7.6	1.24	0.90
667 Pearls, precious semiprecious stone	250 292	3.9	0.32	0.16
247 Wood in rough or roughly squared	116 947	1.8	2.30	0.76
522 Inorganic chemical elem oxide salt	106 683	1.7	0.37	0.17
248 Wood simply worked, railway sleeper	50 638	0.8	0.63	0.14
334 Heavy petroleum & bituminous oil	33 782	0.5	0.01	0.00
Remainder	319 022	4.9		
Denmark - Danemark (=Developed)**				
All commodity groups	109 183 863	100.0	1.16	0.60
333 Crude petroleum & bituminous oil	5 299 630	4.9	2.92	0.54
334 Heavy petroleum & bituminous oil	4 548 679	4.2	1.11	0.52
012 Meat nes, fresh chilled frozen	4 033 923	3.7	7.32	5.71
542 Medicines including veterinary	3 091 568	2.8	1.05	0.96
541 Pharmaceuticals excluding medicines	2 825 845	2.6	2.09	1.82
716 Rotating electric plant parts nes	2 410 269	2.2	4.11	2.61
821 Furniture part; bedding furnishing	2 214 412	2.0	3.18	1.55
874 Measure analyze control device nes	1 884 423	1.7	1.37	1.05
098 Edible products & preparations nes	1 761 416	1.6	4.12	2.94
212 Raw furskins and furskin pieces	1 746 234	1.6	41.64	33.74
Remainder	79 367 464	72.7		
Djibouti (=Developing) (2)**				
All commodity groups	93 851	100.0	0.00	0.00
001 Live animal excl. fish & crustacean	21 679	23.1	0.47	0.10
971 Gold non-monetary excluding ores	10 586	11.3	0.01	0.00
334 Heavy petroleum & bituminous oil	10 298	11.0	0.00	0.00
071 Coffee and coffee substitutes	3 731	4.0	0.01	0.01
054 Vegetable & vegetable products nes	1 548	1.6	0.01	0.00
674 Flat plated iron non-alloy steel	1 270	1.4	0.00	0.00
723 Civil engineering plant & equipment	1 268	1.4	0.00	0.00
041 Wheat meslin, incl spelt, unmilled	1 136	1.2	0.02	0.00
335 Residual petroleum products nes	1 083	1.2	0.01	0.00
792 Aircraft, spacecraft & equipment	1 078	1.1	0.00	0.00
Remainder	40 174	42.7		
Dominica - Dominique (=Developing) (2)**				
All commodity groups	33 446	100.0	0.00	0.00
554 Soaps cleansers polishes	13 447	40.2	0.12	0.03
057 Fruit nut (exc oil), fresh or dried	3 996	11.9	0.01	0.00
892 Printed matter	3 113	9.3	0.02	0.01
273 Stone, sand and gravel	2 806	8.4	0.05	0.02
533 Pigment, paint, varnish & related	1 866	5.6	0.01	0.00
054 Vegetable & vegetable products nes	1 660	5.0	0.01	0.00
764 Telecom equipment part nes	1 091	3.3	0.00	0.00
763 Sound TV recorder or reproducer	565	1.7	0.00	0.00
716 Rotating electric plant parts nes	389	1.2	0.00	0.00
551 Essential oils, perfumes & flavours	386	1.2	0.01	0.00
Remainder	4 127	12.2		

For sources and notes, see end of table.

Pour les sources et les notes, se reporter à la fin du tableau.

Leading products exported based on average 2011-2012 values SITC Revision 3 (3-digit level) / Principaux produits exportés d'après la moyenne des valeurs de 2011-2012 CTCI révision 3 (positions à 3 chiffres)	Value (f.o.b., thousands of dollars) / Valeur (f.a.b., milliers de dollars)	2011-2012 As percentage En pourcentage		
		of country total / du total du pays	of ** (1) / des ** (1)	of world / du monde

Dominican Republic - République dominicaine (**=Developing) (2)

All commodity groups	8 845 650	100.0	0.11	0.05
872 Medical instruments appliances nes	852 836	9.6	4.37	0.95
845 Articles of apparel nes	467 885	5.3	0.47	0.33
772 Electrical circuit equipment	450 812	5.1	0.43	0.19
122 Manufactured tabacco	445 639	5.0	5.24	1.43
057 Fruit nut (exc oil), fresh or dried	422 556	4.8	0.90	0.49
652 Woven cotton fabrics	415 544	4.7	1.67	1.26
851 Footwear	333 792	3.8	0.47	0.29
893 Articles of plastic nes	330 652	3.7	0.60	0.24
971 Gold non-monetary excluding ores	267 866	3.0	0.20	0.11
897 Jewellery nes (667)	255 421	2.9	0.32	0.21
Remainder	4 602 647	52.1		

Ecuador - Équateur (**=Developing)

All commodity groups	23 105 554	100.0	0.29	0.13
333 Crude petroleum & bituminous oil	11 790 919	51.0	0.94	0.69
057 Fruit nut (exc oil), fresh or dried	2 699 555	11.7	6.16	3.11
036 Crustacean mollusc aquat invertebra	1 163 098	5.0	5.50	3.65
037 Fish shellfish, prepared preserved	905 250	3.9	4.88	3.42
292 Crude vegetable materials nes	888 188	3.8	5.68	2.05
334 Heavy petroleum & bituminous oil	782 986	3.4	0.18	0.08
072 Cocoa	521 960	2.3	3.82	2.52
422 Fixed veg fat and oil, excl. "soft"	357 875	1.5	0.81	0.73
034 Fish, fresh live chilled frozen	325 461	1.4	1.22	0.54
071 Coffee and coffee substitutes	245 720	1.1	0.98	0.61
Remainder	3 424 542	14.9		

Egypt - Égypte (**=Developing)

All commodity groups	30 499 722	100.0	0.38	0.17
333 Crude petroleum & bituminous oil	4 940 151	16.2	0.39	0.29
334 Heavy petroleum & bituminous oil	2 947 207	9.7	0.70	0.30
343 Natural gas, liquefied or not	2 411 039	7.9	1.51	0.69
562 Manufactured fertilizer excl. crude	1 328 766	4.4	5.03	1.76
971 Gold non-monetary excluding ores	1 122 888	3.7	0.85	0.45
057 Fruit nut (exc oil), fresh or dried	916 929	3.0	2.09	1.06
054 Vegetable & vegetable products nes	791 041	2.6	3.30	1.32
773 Electrical distribute equipment nes	753 922	2.5	1.41	0.67
682 Copper	521 857	1.7	0.71	0.36
522 Inorganic chemical elem oxide salt	517 858	1.7	1.80	0.85
Remainder	14 248 064	46.6		

El Salvador (**=Developing) (2)

All commodity groups	5 323 634	100.0	0.07	0.03
845 Articles of apparel nes	1 065 486	20.0	1.08	0.76
071 Coffee and coffee substitutes	417 579	7.8	1.67	1.03
843 Male clothing, knitted crocheted	276 907	5.2	1.08	0.91
846 Clothing accessory excl. 831 848 851	239 535	4.5	1.28	0.83
061 Sugar, mollasses and honey	214 283	4.0	0.67	0.47
778 Electrical machinery apparatus nes	210 867	4.0	0.19	0.09
893 Articles of plastic nes	199 075	3.7	0.36	0.14
642 Cut paper and paperboard articles	181 343	3.4	0.93	0.30
844 Female clothing, knitted crocheted	156 850	2.9	0.35	0.28
048 Cereal & preparation flour starch	133 553	2.5	1.38	0.29
Remainder	2 228 156	42.0		

Equatorial Guinea - Guinée équatoriale (**=Developing) (2)

All commodity groups	14 500 000	100.0	0.18	0.08
333 Crude petroleum & bituminous oil	10 685 199	73.7	0.85	0.62
343 Natural gas, liquefied or not	2 822 415	19.5	1.77	0.81
512 Alcohols, phenols; derivatives	360 316	2.5	1.05	0.58
342 Liquefied propane and butane	253 913	1.8	0.64	0.43
247 Wood in rough or roughly squared	135 508	0.9	2.66	0.89
792 Aircraft, spacecraft & equipment	95 812	0.7	0.42	0.06
334 Heavy petroleum & bituminous oil	49 933	0.3	0.01	0.01
971 Gold non-monetary excluding ores	22 504	0.2	0.02	0.01
634 Veneer, plywood & other wood nes	13 144	0.1	0.09	0.04
511 Hydrocarbons nes; derivatives	3 795	0.0	0.01	0.00
Remainder	57 461	0.3		

Eritrea - Érythrée (**=Developing) (2)

All commodity groups	422 209	100.0	0.01	0.00
971 Gold non-monetary excluding ores	388 365	92.0	0.29	0.15
681 Silver, platinum, platinum metals	12 568	3.0	0.04	0.02
281 Iron ore and concentrates	5 272	1.2	0.01	0.00
611 Leather	2 047	0.5	0.02	0.01
041 Male clothing, woven	1 136	0.3	0.00	0.00
651 Textile yarn	1 316	0.3	0.00	0.00
667 Pearls, precious semiprecious stone	1 238	0.3	0.00	0.00
075 Spices	927	0.2	0.01	0.01
282 Ferrous iron & steel, waste & scrap	810	0.2	0.01	0.00
071 Coffee and coffee substitutes	799	0.2	0.00	0.00
Remainder	7 431	1.8		

Estonia - Estonie (**=Developed)

All commodity groups	17 128 126	100.0	0.18	0.09
764 Telecom equipment part nes	2 315 288	13.5	1.39	0.45
334 Heavy petroleum & bituminous oil	1 705 872	10.0	0.39	0.17
821 Furniture part; bedding furnishing	568 871	3.3	0.76	0.38
773 Electrical distribute equipment nes	353 570	2.1	0.63	0.32
635 Wood manufactures nes	352 938	2.1	2.26	1.36
772 Electrical circuit equipment	346 841	2.0	0.27	0.15
248 Wood simply worked, railway sleeper	328 149	1.9	1.33	0.89
282 Ferrous iron & steel, waste & scrap	313 729	1.8	0.70	0.58
781 Passenger cars and race cars	307 403	1.8	0.06	0.05
351 Electric current	279 075	1.6	0.90	0.71
Remainder	10 256 390	59.9		

Ethiopia - Éthiopie (**=Developing)

All commodity groups	2 671 601	100.0	0.03	0.01
071 Coffee and coffee substitutes	811 023	30.4	3.23	2.00
054 Vegetable & vegetable products nes	429 818	16.1	1.79	0.72
222 Oil seed etc for soft oil	381 416	14.3	1.28	0.54
292 Crude vegetable materials nes	211 188	7.9	1.35	0.49
001 Live animal excl. fish & crustacean	174 359	6.5	3.75	0.80
971 Gold non-monetary excluding ores	142 167	5.3	0.11	0.06
611 Leather	103 999	3.9	0.80	0.44
012 Meat nes, fresh chilled frozen	64 072	2.4	0.42	0.09
075 Spices	39 694	1.5	0.57	0.46
223 Oil seed for non soft oil	27 936	1.0	3.57	0.84
Remainder	285 929	10.7		

Faeroe Islands - Îles Féroé (**=Developed) (2)

All commodity groups	977 912	100.0	0.01	0.01
034 Fish, fresh live chilled frozen	674 321	69.0	2.18	1.12
035 Fish, dried salted smoked	88 913	9.1	2.13	1.50
334 Heavy petroleum & bituminous oil	43 025	4.4	0.01	0.00
793 Ships boats floating structures	39 166	4.0	0.07	0.02
081 Animal feed excluding unmilled cereal	38 088	3.9	0.10	0.05
036 Crustacean mollusc aquat invertebra	31 492	3.2	0.30	0.10
291 Crude animal materials nes	17 449	1.8	0.34	0.19
792 Aircraft, spacecraft & equipment	4 984	0.5	0.00	0.00
037 Fish shellfish, prepared preserved	4 781	0.5	0.06	0.02
251 Pulp and waste paper	4 262	0.4	0.01	0.01
Remainder	31 431	3.2		

Falkland Islands (Malvinas) - Îles Falkland (Malvinas) (**=Developing) (2)

All commodity groups	190 000	100.0	0.00	0.00
036 Crustacean mollusc aquat invertebra	137 674	72.5	0.65	0.43
034 Fish, fresh live chilled frozen	33 828	17.8	0.13	0.06
268 Wool & animal hair, incl wool tops	9 704	5.1	0.35	0.13
012 Meat nes, fresh chilled frozen	2 575	1.4	0.02	0.00
723 Civil engineering plant & equipment	323	0.2	0.00	0.00
874 Measure analyze control device nes	155	0.1	0.00	0.00
037 Fish shellfish, prepared preserved	145	0.1	0.00	0.00
792 Aircraft, spacecraft & equipment	104	0.1	0.00	0.00
897 Jewellery nes (667)	82	0.0	0.00	0.00
342 Liquefied propane and butane	59	0.0	0.00	0.00
Remainder	5 351	2.7		

For sources and notes, see end of table.

Pour les sources et les notes, se reporter à la fin du tableau.

Left side

Leading products exported based on average 2011-2012 values SITC Revision 3 (3-digit level) Principaux produits exportés d'après la moyenne des valeurs de 2011-2012 CTCI révision 3 (positions à 3 chiffres)	2011-2012			
	Value (f.o.b., thousands of dollars) Valeur (f.a.b., milliers de dollars)	As percentage En pourcentage		
		of country total du total du pays	of ** (1) des ** (1)	of world du monde
Fiji - Fidji (**=Developing) (2)				
All commodity groups	1 145 037	100.0	0.01	0.01
334 Heavy petroleum & bituminous oil	287 108	25.1	0.07	0.03
034 Fish, fresh live chilled frozen	124 280	10.9	0.46	0.21
111 Non alcoholic beverage nes	93 373	8.2	1.88	0.47
061 Sugar, mollasses and honey	76 656	6.7	0.24	0.17
971 Gold non-monetary excluding ores	75 849	6.6	0.06	0.03
048 Cereal & preparation flour starch	52 976	4.6	0.55	0.12
037 Fish shellfish, prepared preserved	26 621	2.3	0.14	0.10
841 Male clothing, woven	25 009	2.2	0.05	0.04
046 Wheat meal & flour, meslin flour	21 330	1.9	0.73	0.36
248 Wood simply worked, railway sleeper	20 398	1.8	0.25	0.06
Remainder	341 437	29.7		
Finland - Finlande (**=Developed)				
All commodity groups	75 884 354	100.0	0.80	0.41
641 Paper and paperboard	9 657 215	12.7	10.25	8.07
334 Heavy petroleum & bituminous oil	7 428 229	9.8	1.69	0.75
675 Flat rolled products of alloy steel	3 437 225	4.5	7.24	4.88
764 Telecom equipment part nes	2 467 912	3.3	1.48	0.48
251 Pulp and waste paper	1 844 196	2.4	5.35	3.87
728 Special industrial machine part nes	1 753 268	2.3	1.25	0.96
716 Rotating electric plant parts nes	1 689 050	2.2	2.80	1.77
248 Wood simply worked, railway sleeper	1 667 698	2.2	6.77	4.50
723 Civil engineering plant & equipment	1 641 734	2.2	1.93	1.33
771 Electric power machine part excl. 716	1 394 006	1.8	3.35	1.51
Remainder	42 903 821	56.6		
France (**=Developed)				
All commodity groups	569 058 777	100.0	6.03	3.11
792 Aircraft, spacecraft & equipment	52 135 464	9.2	38.01	32.36
542 Medicines including veterinary	27 273 640	4.8	8.89	8.10
781 Passenger cars and race cars	21 670 038	3.8	4.11	3.37
784 Motor vehicle parts and accessories	18 564 532	3.3	7.09	5.18
334 Heavy petroleum & bituminous oil	16 454 437	2.9	3.74	1.67
112 Alcoholic beverages	15 141 721	2.7	24.82	19.80
553 Perfume toilet cosmetics, excl. soap	13 799 755	2.4	23.71	17.84
714 Non-electric engines excl. 712 713 718	10 845 689	1.9	14.62	12.02
776 Valves tubes; diodes, transistors	10 178 591	1.8	6.66	1.83
772 Electrical circuit equipment	9 471 410	1.7	7.32	4.04
Remainder	373 523 500	65.5		
French Polynesia - Polynésie française (**=Developing)				
All commodity groups	144 425	100.0	0.00	0.00
667 Pearls, precious semiprecious stone	86 084	59.6	0.11	0.06
792 Aircraft, spacecraft & equipment	8 285	5.7	0.04	0.01
034 Fish, fresh live chilled frozen	8 244	5.7	0.03	0.01
422 Fixed veg fat and oil, excl. "soft"	5 879	4.1	0.01	0.01
058 Fruit preserve preparation excl. juice	4 709	3.3	0.05	0.02
971 Gold non-monetary excluding ores	2 358	1.6	0.00	0.00
897 Jewellery nes (667)	2 316	1.6	0.00	0.00
714 Non-electric engines excl. 712 713 718	1 987	1.4	0.01	0.00
075 Spices	1 937	1.3	0.03	0.02
713 Internal combustion engine part nes	1 762	1.2	0.00	0.00
Remainder	20 864	14.5		
Gabon (**=Developing) (2)				
All commodity groups	9 715 199	100.0	0.12	0.05
333 Crude petroleum & bituminous oil	7 412 686	76.3	0.59	0.43
247 Wood in rough or roughly squared	752 057	7.7	14.78	4.92
287 Base metal ores & concentrates nes	594 208	6.1	3.18	1.82
334 Heavy petroleum & bituminous oil	220 184	2.3	0.05	0.02
634 Veneer, plywood & other wood nes	163 584	1.7	1.09	0.47
793 Ships boats floating structures	135 077	1.4	0.12	0.08
248 Wood simply worked, railway sleeper	115 565	1.2	1.44	0.31
231 Natural rubber, latex, gum, etc	82 091	0.8	0.26	0.24
792 Aircraft, spacecraft & equipment	21 522	0.2	0.09	0.01
122 Manufactured tabacco	20 939	0.2	0.25	0.07
Remainder	197 286	2.1		

Right side

Leading products exported based on average 2011-2012 values SITC Revision 3 (3-digit level) Principaux produits exportés d'après la moyenne des valeurs de 2011-2012 CTCI révision 3 (positions à 3 chiffres)	2011-2012			
	Value (f.o.b., thousands of dollars) Valeur (f.a.b., milliers de dollars)	As percentage En pourcentage		
		of country total du total du pays	of ** (1) des ** (1)	of world du monde
Gambia - Gambie (**=Developing)				
All commodity groups	97 366	100.0	0.00	0.00
057 Fruit nut (exc oil), fresh or dried	20 541	21.1	0.05	0.02
247 Wood in rough or roughly squared	12 239	12.6	0.24	0.08
287 Base metal ores & concentrates nes	11 149	11.5	0.06	0.03
653 Man-made woven fabrics	7 410	7.6	0.02	0.02
421 Fixed veg fat and oil, "soft"	6 586	6.8	0.05	0.02
282 Ferrous iron & steel, waste & scrap	4 787	4.9	0.08	0.01
072 Cocoa	3 865	4.0	0.03	0.02
034 Fish, fresh live chilled frozen	3 645	3.7	0.01	0.01
222 Oil seed etc for soft oil	3 280	3.4	0.01	0.00
036 Crustacean mollusc aquat invertebra	1 604	1.6	0.01	0.01
Remainder	22 260	22.8		
Georgia - Géorgie (**=Transition) (2)				
All commodity groups	2 283 288	100.0	0.28	0.01
781 Passenger cars and race cars	518 796	22.7	24.61	0.08
671 Pig & sponge iron, ferro alloys etc	259 558	11.4	2.37	0.62
562 Manufactured fertilizer excl. crude	140 671	6.2	0.83	0.19
112 Alcoholic beverages	137 718	6.0	9.24	0.18
057 Fruit nut (exc oil), fresh or dried	117 197	5.1	5.78	0.13
971 Gold non-monetary excluding ores	98 936	4.3	5.45	0.04
282 Ferrous iron & steel, waste & scrap	80 365	3.5	3.03	0.15
111 Non alcoholic beverage nes	71 443	3.1	14.59	0.36
283 Copper ores and concentrates	69 335	3.0	5.50	0.13
288 Non ferrous base metal waste nes	61 622	2.7	8.22	0.13
Remainder	727 647	32.0		
Germany - Allemagne (**=Developed)				
All commodity groups	1 449 193 237	100.0	15.35	7.92
781 Passenger cars and race cars	150 295 752	10.4	28.50	23.38
784 Motor vehicle parts and accessories	54 078 997	3.7	20.65	15.09
542 Medicines including veterinary	46 034 063	3.2	15.01	13.67
792 Aircraft, spacecraft & equipment	40 141 760	2.8	29.27	24.91
772 Electrical circuit equipment	31 492 940	2.2	24.33	13.42
874 Measure analyze control device nes	30 953 948	2.1	22.08	16.97
728 Special industrial machine part nes	26 989 017	1.9	19.28	14.72
713 Internal combustion engine part nes	26 259 643	1.8	20.84	16.14
541 Pharmaceuticals excluding medicines	23 144 861	1.6	16.22	14.18
743 Gas pump, compressor, fan, filter	20 563 505	1.4	23.52	16.61
Remainder	999 238 751	68.9		
Ghana (**=Developing) (2)				
All commodity groups	12 892 710	100.0	0.16	0.07
072 Cocoa	3 871 301	30.0	28.30	18.71
333 Crude petroleum & bituminous oil	3 825 028	29.7	0.31	0.22
971 Gold non-monetary excluding ores	1 068 871	8.3	0.80	0.43
057 Fruit nut (exc oil), fresh or dried	742 671	5.8	1.69	0.86
287 Base metal ores & concentrates nes	387 191	3.0	2.07	1.19
342 Liquefied propane and butane	324 986	2.5	0.82	0.55
334 Heavy petroleum & bituminous oil	231 696	1.8	0.05	0.02
037 Fish shellfish, prepared preserved	153 602	1.2	0.83	0.58
248 Wood simply worked, railway sleeper	122 224	0.9	1.52	0.33
684 Aluminium	117 290	0.9	0.31	0.10
Remainder	2 047 850	15.9		
Gibraltar (**=Developed)				
All commodity groups	243 210	100.0	0.00	0.00
334 Heavy petroleum & bituminous oil	155 767	64.0	0.04	0.02
793 Ships boats floating structures	50 233	20.7	0.09	0.03
781 Passenger cars and race cars	10 094	4.2	0.00	0.00
723 Civil engineering plant & equipment	6 956	2.9	0.01	0.01
716 Rotating electric plant parts nes	3 664	1.5	0.01	0.00
714 Non-electric engines excl. 712 713 718	2 522	1.0	0.00	0.00
792 Aircraft, spacecraft & equipment	1 639	0.7	0.00	0.00
335 Residual petroleum products nes	811	0.3	0.00	0.00
885 Watches and clocks	791	0.3	0.00	0.00
342 Liquefied propane and butane	721	0.3	0.00	0.00
Remainder	10 012	4.1		

For sources and notes, see end of table.

Pour les sources et les notes, se reporter à la fin du tableau.

Left table

Leading products exported based on average 2011-2012 values SITC Revision 3 (3-digit level) / Principaux produits exportés d'après la moyenne des valeurs de 2011-2012 CTCI révision 3 (positions à 3 chiffres)	Value (f.o.b., thousands of dollars) Valeur (f.a.b., milliers de dollars)	2011-2012 As percentage En pourcentage of country total du total du pays	of ** (1) des ** (1)	of world du monde
Greece - Grèce (**=Developed)				
All commodity groups	33 445 390	100.0	0.35	0.18
334 Heavy petroleum & bituminous oil	11 003 021	32.9	2.50	1.12
684 Aluminium	1 436 918	4.3	2.03	1.21
542 Medicines including veterinary	1 187 154	3.5	0.39	0.35
057 Fruit nut (exc oil), fresh or dried	902 367	2.7	2.20	1.04
034 Fish, fresh live chilled frozen	688 052	2.1	2.22	1.15
676 Iron steel bar rod section piling	663 432	2.0	1.26	0.72
682 Copper	612 356	1.8	1.02	0.42
056 Vegetables roots tubers nes	568 960	1.7	3.09	2.00
058 Fruit preserve preparation excl. juice	514 757	1.5	5.54	2.68
263 Cotton	459 134	1.4	4.15	1.75
Remainder	15 409 239	46.1		
Greenland - Groenland (**=Developed) (2)				
All commodity groups	473 412	100.0	0.01	0.00
037 Fish shellfish, prepared preserved	149 950	31.7	1.98	0.57
036 Crustacean mollusc aquat invertebra	139 447	29.5	1.34	0.44
034 Fish, fresh live chilled frozen	134 643	28.4	0.43	0.22
035 Fish, dried salted smoked	10 814	2.3	0.26	0.18
971 Gold non-monetary excluding ores	2 852	0.6	0.00	0.00
792 Aircraft, spacecraft & equipment	2 778	0.6	0.00	0.00
896 Work of art & collections; antiques	1 724	0.4	0.01	0.01
613 Furskin tanned dressed etc	1 652	0.3	0.19	0.08
273 Stone, sand and gravel	928	0.2	0.02	0.01
282 Ferrous iron & steel, waste & scrap	755	0.2	0.00	0.00
Remainder	27 869	5.8		
Grenada - Grenade (**=Developing) (2)				
All commodity groups	32 061	100.0	0.00	0.00
046 Wheat meal & flour, meslin flour	4 123	12.9	0.14	0.07
793 Ships boats floating structures	3 023	9.4	0.00	0.00
581 Plastic tube pipe hose & fittings	2 778	8.7	0.05	0.01
075 Spices	2 748	8.6	0.04	0.03
684 Aluminium	2 657	8.3	0.01	0.00
034 Fish, fresh live chilled frozen	2 010	6.3	0.01	0.00
892 Printed matter	1 726	5.4	0.01	0.00
642 Cut paper and paperboard articles	1 326	4.1	0.01	0.00
081 Animal feed excluding unmilled cereal	1 254	3.9	0.00	0.00
748 Mechanical transmission equipment	1 068	3.3	0.01	0.00
Remainder	9 348	29.1		
Guam (**=Developing) (2)				
All commodity groups	44 762	100.0	0.00	0.00
282 Ferrous iron & steel, waste & scrap	9 946	22.2	0.16	0.02
288 Non ferrous base metal waste nes	2 420	5.4	0.02	0.01
034 Fish, fresh live chilled frozen	1 692	3.8	0.01	0.00
885 Watches and clocks	1 527	3.4	0.01	0.00
723 Civil engineering plant & equipment	1 372	3.1	0.00	0.00
831 Case bag: storage travel shopping	1 162	2.6	0.00	0.00
897 Jewellery nes (667)	1 155	2.6	0.00	0.00
776 Valves tubes; diodes, transistors	512	1.1	0.00	0.00
781 Passenger cars and race cars	499	1.1	0.00	0.00
612 Leather manufactures nes	390	0.9	0.02	0.01
Remainder	24 087	53.8		
Guatemala (**=Developing)				
All commodity groups	10 142 798	100.0	0.13	0.06
071 Coffee and coffee substitutes	1 120 072	11.0	4.47	2.76
057 Fruit nut (exc oil), fresh or dried	953 628	9.4	2.18	1.10
061 Sugar, mollasses and honey	847 668	8.4	2.66	1.87
845 Articles of apparel nes	471 508	4.6	0.48	0.34
289 Prec metal ore concentrate excl. gold	353 674	3.5	5.09	1.86
231 Natural rubber, latex, gum, etc	330 272	3.3	1.03	0.98
075 Spices	306 046	3.0	4.38	3.58
333 Crude petroleum & bituminous oil	303 832	3.0	0.02	0.02
844 Female clothing, knitted crocheted	300 057	3.0	0.68	0.54
422 Fixed veg fat and oil, excl. "soft"	268 409	2.6	0.61	0.55
Remainder	4 887 632	48.2		

Right table

Leading products exported based on average 2011-2012 values SITC Revision 3 (3-digit level) / Principaux produits exportés d'après la moyenne des valeurs de 2011-2012 CTCI révision 3 (positions à 3 chiffres)	Value (f.o.b., thousands of dollars) Valeur (f.a.b., milliers de dollars)	2011-2012 As percentage En pourcentage of country total du total du pays	of ** (1) des ** (1)	of world du monde
Guinea - Guinée (**=Developing) (2)				
All commodity groups	1 456 491	100.0	0.02	0.01
285 Aluminium ore concentrate alumina	641 386	44.0	10.98	4.23
343 Natural gas, liquefied or not	327 558	22.5	0.21	0.09
333 Crude petroleum & bituminous oil	158 672	10.9	0.01	0.01
971 Gold non-monetary excluding ores	68 804	4.7	0.05	0.03
071 Coffee and coffee substitutes	33 055	2.3	0.13	0.08
231 Natural rubber, latex, gum, etc	26 973	1.9	0.08	0.08
072 Cocoa	25 420	1.7	0.19	0.12
283 Copper ores and concentrates	22 444	1.5	0.06	0.04
667 Pearls, precious semiprecious stone	19 728	1.4	0.03	0.01
034 Fish, fresh live chilled frozen	15 541	1.1	0.06	0.03
Remainder	116 910	8.0		
Guinea-Bissau - Guinée-Bissau (**=Developing) (2)				
All commodity groups	180 000	100.0	0.00	0.00
057 Fruit nut (exc oil), fresh or dried	161 808	89.9	0.37	0.19
333 Crude petroleum & bituminous oil	10 786	6.0	0.00	0.00
247 Wood in rough or roughly squared	1 003	0.6	0.02	0.01
282 Ferrous iron & steel, waste & scrap	890	0.5	0.01	0.00
672 Ingots, Iron steel primary products	826	0.5	0.01	0.00
263 Cotton	620	0.3	0.01	0.00
035 Fish, dried salted smoked	412	0.2	0.02	0.01
036 Crustacean mollusc aquat invertebra	289	0.2	0.00	0.00
725 Paper & pulp mill, cut manufacture	281	0.2	0.01	0.00
034 Fish, fresh live chilled frozen	271	0.2	0.00	0.00
Remainder	2 814	1.4		
Guyana (**=Developing)				
All commodity groups	1 178 747	100.0	0.01	0.01
971 Gold non-monetary excluding ores	508 946	43.2	0.38	0.20
285 Aluminium ore concentrate alumina	144 069	12.2	2.47	0.95
061 Sugar, mollasses and honey	131 515	11.2	0.41	0.29
042 Rice	117 063	9.9	0.58	0.48
248 Wood simply worked, railway sleeper	48 096	4.1	0.60	0.13
036 Crustacean mollusc aquat invertebra	33 520	2.8	0.16	0.11
786 Trailer caravan transport container	26 968	2.3	0.17	0.08
112 Alcoholic beverages	24 829	2.1	0.18	0.03
034 Fish, fresh live chilled frozen	24 682	2.1	0.09	0.04
247 Wood in rough or roughly squared	11 687	1.0	0.23	0.08
Remainder	107 372	9.1		
Haiti - Haïti (**=Developing) (2)				
All commodity groups	796 518	100.0	0.01	0.00
845 Articles of apparel nes	365 155	45.8	0.37	0.26
844 Female clothing, knitted crocheted	68 908	8.7	0.16	0.12
843 Male clothing, knitted crocheted	51 503	6.5	0.20	0.17
841 Male clothing, woven	41 758	5.2	0.09	0.06
057 Fruit nut (exc oil), fresh or dried	22 151	2.8	0.05	0.03
773 Electrical distribute equipment nes	15 929	2.0	0.03	0.01
658 Made-up textile articles nes	14 435	1.8	0.04	0.03
551 Essential oils, perfumes & flavours	12 835	1.6	0.25	0.05
846 Clothing accessory excl. 831 848 851	12 684	1.6	0.07	0.04
071 Coffee and coffee substitutes	12 047	1.5	0.05	0.03
Remainder	179 113	22.5		
Honduras (**=Developing) (2)				
All commodity groups	7 865 450	100.0	0.10	0.04
845 Articles of apparel nes	1 481 248	18.8	1.50	1.05
071 Coffee and coffee substitutes	996 400	12.7	3.97	2.45
057 Fruit nut (exc oil), fresh or dried	578 107	7.3	1.32	0.67
773 Electrical distribute equipment nes	426 777	5.4	0.80	0.38
843 Male clothing, knitted crocheted	375 894	4.8	1.47	1.23
971 Gold non-monetary excluding ores	320 053	4.1	0.24	0.13
422 Fixed veg fat and oil, excl. "soft"	292 626	3.7	0.66	0.59
841 Male clothing, woven	251 670	3.2	0.51	0.35
036 Crustacean mollusc aquat invertebra	250 132	3.2	1.18	0.78
844 Female clothing, knitted crocheted	247 896	3.2	0.56	0.44
Remainder	2 644 647	33.6		

For sources and notes, see end of table.

Pour les sources et les notes, se reporter à la fin du tableau.

Leading products exported based on average 2011-2012 values SITC Revision 3 (3-digit level) / Principaux produits exportés d'après la moyenne des valeurs de 2011-2012 CTCI révision 3 (positions à 3 chiffres)	Value (f.o.b., thousands of dollars) Valeur (f.a.b., milliers de dollars)	2011-2012 As percentage En pourcentage — of country total / du total du pays	of ** (1) / des ** (1)	of world / du monde
Hungary - Hongrie (=Developed)**				
All commodity groups	107 111 424	100.0	1.13	0.59
764 Telecom equipment part nes	10 799 452	10.1	6.50	2.09
713 Internal combustion engine part nes	6 820 401	6.4	5.41	4.19
781 Passenger cars and race cars	4 866 148	4.5	0.92	0.76
761 Television video receive project	4 334 583	4.0	12.16	4.73
784 Motor vehicle parts and accessories	4 178 684	3.9	1.60	1.17
542 Medicines including veterinary	3 488 670	3.3	1.14	1.04
772 Electrical circuit equipment	3 384 955	3.2	2.62	1.44
752 Computer equipment nes	3 158 459	2.9	3.06	0.90
874 Measure analyze control device nes	2 539 756	2.4	1.81	1.39
778 Electrical machinery apparatus nes	2 511 356	2.3	2.24	1.12
Remainder	61 028 960	57.0		
Iceland - Islande (=Developed)**				
All commodity groups	5 206 116	100.0	0.06	0.03
684 Aluminium	1 996 489	38.3	2.82	1.67
034 Fish, fresh live chilled frozen	1 420 516	27.3	4.58	2.37
035 Fish, dried salted smoked	356 812	6.9	8.56	6.01
671 Pig & sponge iron, ferro alloys etc	190 117	3.7	1.98	0.45
081 Animal feed excluding unmilled cereal	166 162	3.2	0.43	0.23
542 Medicines including veterinary	121 969	2.3	0.04	0.04
037 Fish shellfish, prepared preserved	121 390	2.3	1.60	0.46
411 Animals oils and fats	110 623	2.1	2.13	1.72
334 Heavy petroleum & bituminous oil	102 629	2.0	0.02	0.01
899 Manufactured articles nes	61 365	1.2	0.12	0.08
Remainder	558 044	10.7		
India - Inde (=Developing)**				
All commodity groups	295 524 010	100.0	3.68	1.62
334 Heavy petroleum & bituminous oil	53 687 473	18.2	12.67	5.44
667 Pearls, precious semiprecious stone	27 670 114	9.4	35.07	17.96
897 Jewellery nes (667)	18 060 135	6.1	22.28	14.53
542 Medicines including veterinary	8 331 384	2.8	29.52	2.47
793 Ships boats floating structures	5 586 444	1.9	4.88	3.26
651 Textile yarn	5 207 965	1.8	13.88	9.11
042 Rice	5 100 641	1.7	25.22	20.73
292 Crude vegetable materials nes	4 756 404	1.6	30.40	10.97
764 Telecom equipment part nes	4 415 482	1.5	1.26	0.85
842 Female clothing, woven	4 048 195	1.4	7.51	4.94
Remainder	158 659 773	53.6		
Indonesia - Indonésie (=Developing)**				
All commodity groups	196 764 229	100.0	2.45	1.08
321 Coal excluding non-agglomomerated	24 899 682	12.7	55.03	18.84
343 Natural gas, liquefied or not	21 548 960	11.0	13.50	6.21
422 Fixed veg fat and oil, excl. "soft"	20 196 544	10.3	45.64	41.06
333 Crude petroleum & bituminous oil	13 061 044	6.6	1.04	0.76
231 Natural rubber, latex, gum, etc	9 815 385	5.0	30.65	29.01
283 Copper ores and concentrates	3 647 517	1.9	9.26	6.71
641 Paper and paperboard	3 569 105	1.8	15.90	2.98
851 Footwear	3 413 267	1.7	4.76	2.95
682 Copper	2 781 760	1.4	3.80	1.93
284 Nickel ores, concentrates, etc	2 554 450	1.3	42.53	23.80
Remainder	91 276 515	46.3		
Iran (Islamic Rep. of) - Iran (Rép. islamique d') (=Developing) (2)**				
All commodity groups	116 698 424	100.0	1.45	0.64
333 Crude petroleum & bituminous oil	79 818 474	68.4	6.37	4.65
334 Heavy petroleum & bituminous oil	2 751 469	2.4	0.65	0.28
342 Liquefied propane and butane	2 491 558	2.1	6.30	4.22
571 Primary form ethylene polymers	1 990 286	1.7	5.25	2.55
511 Hydrocarbons nes; derivatives	1 886 198	1.6	4.53	1.92
512 Alcohols, phenols; derivatives	1 783 214	1.5	5.21	2.85
281 Iron ore and concentrates	1 769 068	1.5	3.04	1.29
057 Fruit nut (exc oil), fresh or dried	1 418 792	1.2	3.24	1.63
344 Petroleum and hydrocarbon gas nes	937 466	0.8	12.57	6.63
562 Manufactured fertilizer excl. crude	852 258	0.7	3.23	1.13
Remainder	20 999 641	18.1		
Iraq (=Developing) (2)**				
All commodity groups	88 850 000	100.0	1.11	0.49
333 Crude petroleum & bituminous oil	87 208 866	98.2	6.95	5.08
334 Heavy petroleum & bituminous oil	605 367	0.7	0.14	0.06
525 Radio active & associated materials	140 039	0.2	5.09	0.77
971 Gold non-monetary excluding ores	138 918	0.2	0.10	0.06
057 Fruit nut (exc oil), fresh or dried	92 917	0.1	0.21	0.11
274 Sulphur and unroasted iron pyrites	70 253	0.1	2.56	1.27
511 Hydrocarbons nes; derivatives	69 479	0.1	0.17	0.07
598 Miscellaneous chemical products nes	67 694	0.1	0.23	0.05
522 Inorganic chemical elem oxide salt	56 804	0.1	0.20	0.09
728 Special industrial machine part nes	40 237	0.0	0.09	0.02
Remainder	359 426	0.2		
Ireland - Irlande (=Developed)**				
All commodity groups	122 649 785	100.0	1.30	0.67
515 Organo-inorganic compound acid salt	24 490 826	20.0	28.18	21.91
542 Medicines including veterinary	22 416 883	18.3	7.31	6.66
541 Pharmaceuticals excluding medicines	11 480 842	9.4	8.05	7.03
551 Essential oils, perfumes & flavours	7 279 149	5.9	36.79	29.09
899 Manufactured articles nes	4 649 180	3.8	8.83	5.70
872 Medical instruments appliances nes	3 747 372	3.1	5.36	4.18
598 Miscellaneous chemical products nes	3 565 777	2.9	3.75	2.83
752 Computer equipment nes	2 965 097	2.4	2.87	0.84
011 Beef, fresh chilled frozen	2 062 138	1.7	7.67	5.19
098 Edible products & preparations nes	1 947 081	1.6	4.36	3.12
Remainder	38 045 440	30.9		
Israel - Israël (=Developed)**				
All commodity groups	65 468 480	100.0	0.69	0.36
667 Pearls, precious semiprecious stone	19 124 812	29.2	26.10	12.41
542 Medicines including veterinary	6 624 767	10.1	2.16	1.97
598 Miscellaneous chemical products nes	2 885 848	4.4	3.03	2.29
764 Telecom equipment part nes	2 583 972	3.9	1.55	0.50
776 Valves tubes; diodes, transistors	2 433 916	3.7	1.59	0.44
562 Manufactured fertilizer excl. crude	1 952 446	3.0	6.09	2.59
792 Aircraft, spacecraft & equipment	1 773 168	2.7	1.29	1.10
874 Measure analyze control device nes	1 754 764	2.7	1.25	0.96
772 Electrical circuit equipment	1 135 435	1.7	0.88	0.48
778 Electrical machinery apparatus nes	1 015 215	1.6	0.90	0.45
Remainder	24 184 137	37.0		
Italy - Italie (=Developed)**				
All commodity groups	511 999 497	100.0	5.42	2.80
334 Heavy petroleum & bituminous oil	24 539 347	4.8	5.57	2.49
542 Medicines including veterinary	17 371 787	3.4	5.66	5.16
784 Motor vehicle parts and accessories	14 857 877	2.9	5.67	4.15
728 Special industrial machine part nes	13 011 141	2.5	9.30	7.10
851 Footwear	11 127 731	2.2	26.48	9.63
821 Furniture part; bedding furnishing	11 120 664	2.2	14.84	7.35
699 Base metal manufactures nes	10 254 804	2.0	11.31	7.09
971 Gold non-monetary excluding ores	9 449 985	1.8	8.09	3.76
741 Heating, cooling equipment parts nes	9 298 870	1.8	13.66	8.31
781 Passenger cars and race cars	9 197 867	1.8	1.74	1.43
Remainder	381 769 424	74.6		
Jamaica - Jamaïque (=Developing) (2)**				
All commodity groups	1 667 325	100.0	0.02	0.01
285 Aluminium ore concentrate alumina	681 239	40.9	11.67	4.49
334 Heavy petroleum & bituminous oil	356 773	21.4	0.08	0.04
112 Alcoholic beverages	97 959	5.9	0.70	0.13
512 Alcohols, phenols; derivatives	94 054	5.6	0.27	0.15
061 Sugar, mollasses and honey	78 649	4.7	0.25	0.17
098 Edible products & preparations nes	30 163	1.8	0.18	0.05
054 Vegetable & vegetable products nes	26 314	1.6	0.11	0.04
351 Electric current	22 401	1.3	0.37	0.06
971 Gold non-monetary excluding ores	20 261	1.2	0.02	0.01
071 Coffee and coffee substitutes	19 200	1.2	0.08	0.05
Remainder	240 312	14.4		

For sources and notes, see end of table.

Pour les sources et les notes, se reporter à la fin du tableau.

Leading products exported based on average 2011-2012 values SITC Revision 3 (3-digit level) / Principaux produits exportés d'après la moyenne des valeurs de 2011-2012 CTCI révision 3 (positions à 3 chiffres)	Value (f.o.b., thousands of dollars) Valeur (f.a.b., milliers de dollars)	2011-2012 As percentage En pourcentage of country total du total du pays	of ** (1) des ** (1)	of world du monde
Japan - Japon (**=Developed)				
All commodity groups	810 875 673	100.0	8.59	4.43
781 Passenger cars and race cars	92 399 048	11.4	17.52	14.37
776 Valves tubes; diodes, transistors	43 304 787	5.3	28.35	7.79
784 Motor vehicle parts and accessories	40 080 957	4.9	15.31	11.18
728 Special industrial machine part nes	32 863 991	4.1	23.48	17.92
793 Ships boats floating structures	24 142 094	3.0	44.04	14.07
778 Electrical machinery apparatus nes	22 935 471	2.8	20.43	10.19
772 Electrical circuit equipment	20 765 458	2.6	16.04	8.85
713 Internal combustion engine part nes	20 345 886	2.5	16.14	12.51
874 Measure analyze control device nes	19 310 492	2.4	13.78	10.59
723 Civil engineering plant & equipment	14 787 604	1.8	17.43	11.98
Remainder	479 939 885	59.2		
Jordan - Jordanie (**=Developing)				
All commodity groups	7 903 307	100.0	0.10	0.04
562 Manufactured fertilizer excl. crude	1 099 851	13.9	4.16	1.46
272 Crude fertilizer, excl. manufactured	739 310	9.4	19.42	14.66
845 Articles of apparel nes	636 271	8.1	0.64	0.45
542 Medicines including veterinary	590 160	7.5	2.09	0.18
054 Vegetable & vegetable products nes	401 912	5.1	1.68	0.67
522 Inorganic chemical elem oxide salt	275 633	3.5	0.96	0.45
971 Gold non-monetary excluding ores	262 516	3.3	0.20	0.10
773 Electrical distribute equipment nes	179 689	2.3	0.34	0.16
523 Inorganic acid metal salt peroxy	178 584	2.3	1.88	0.82
842 Female clothing, woven	134 688	1.7	0.25	0.16
Remainder	3 404 693	42.9		
Kazakhstan (**=Transition) (2)				
All commodity groups	90 194 727	100.0	10.88	0.49
333 Crude petroleum & bituminous oil	55 808 391	61.9	21.14	3.25
671 Pig & sponge iron, ferro alloys etc	3 631 962	4.0	33.17	8.62
682 Copper	3 456 157	3.8	30.91	2.40
334 Heavy petroleum & bituminous oil	2 830 073	3.1	2.32	0.29
281 Iron ore and concentrates	2 580 863	2.9	33.39	1.89
525 Radio active & associated materials	2 466 459	2.7	65.96	13.50
343 Natural gas, liquefied or not	2 305 621	2.6	2.90	0.66
321 Coal excluding non-agglomerated	1 408 340	1.6	9.85	1.07
342 Liquefied propane and butane	1 232 006	1.4	43.08	2.09
041 Wheat meslin, incl spelt, unmilled	1 104 273	1.2	15.53	2.27
Remainder	13 370 582	14.8		
Kenya (**=Developing) (2)				
All commodity groups	5 941 301	100.0	0.07	0.03
074 Tea and maté	1 084 074	18.2	17.07	12.94
292 Crude vegetable materials nes	715 519	12.0	4.57	1.65
071 Coffee and coffee substitutes	308 769	5.2	1.23	0.76
054 Vegetable & vegetable products nes	272 453	4.6	1.14	0.46
334 Heavy petroleum & bituminous oil	256 210	4.3	0.06	0.03
523 Inorganic acid metal salt peroxy	134 385	2.3	1.41	0.62
661 Lime cement construction material	100 834	1.7	0.59	0.34
554 Soaps cleansers polishes	100 651	1.7	0.88	0.25
122 Manufactured tabacco	97 295	1.6	1.14	0.31
893 Articles of plastic nes	93 577	1.6	0.17	0.07
Remainder	2 777 534	46.8		
Kiribati (**=Developing) (2)				
All commodity groups	7 207	100.0	0.00	0.00
034 Fish, fresh live chilled frozen	5 914	82.1	0.02	0.01
422 Fixed veg fat and oil, excl. "soft"	417	5.8	0.00	0.00
793 Ships boats floating structures	203	2.8	0.00	0.00
072 Cocoa	133	1.8	0.00	0.00
036 Crustacean mollusc aquat invertebra	77	1.1	0.00	0.00
872 Medical instruments appliances nes	70	1.0	0.00	0.00
786 Trailer caravan transport container	55	0.8	0.00	0.00
081 Animal feed excluding unmilled cereal	51	0.7	0.00	0.00
728 Special industrial machine part nes	30	0.4	0.00	0.00
748 Mechanical transmission equipment	19	0.3	0.00	0.00
Remainder	238	3.2		

Leading products exported based on average 2011-2012 values SITC Revision 3 (3-digit level) / Principaux produits exportés d'après la moyenne des valeurs de 2011-2012 CTCI révision 3 (positions à 3 chiffres)	Value (f.o.b., thousands of dollars) Valeur (f.a.b., milliers de dollars)	2011-2012 As percentage En pourcentage of country total du total du pays	of ** (1) des ** (1)	of world du monde
Korea, Dem. People's Rep. of - Corée, Rép. populaire dém. de (**=Developing) (2)				
All commodity groups	3 727 500	100.0	0.05	0.02
321 Coal excluding non-agglomerated	1 412 609	37.9	3.12	1.07
281 Iron ore and concentrates	334 543	9.0	0.58	0.24
841 Male clothing, woven	239 405	6.4	0.49	0.34
842 Female clothing, woven	178 941	4.8	0.33	0.22
671 Pig & sponge iron, ferro alloys etc	139 463	3.7	0.65	0.33
845 Articles of apparel nes	106 985	2.9	0.11	0.08
036 Crustacean mollusc aquat invertebra	103 688	2.8	0.49	0.33
278 Other crude minerals	64 514	1.7	0.86	0.37
686 Zinc	62 539	1.7	1.45	0.48
334 Heavy petroleum & bituminous oil	58 661	1.6	0.01	0.01
Remainder	1 026 152	27.5		
Korea, Republic of - Corée, République de (**=Developing)				
All commodity groups	551 531 673	100.0	6.87	3.01
334 Heavy petroleum & bituminous oil	52 548 697	9.5	12.40	5.33
776 Valves tubes; diodes, transistors	46 046 717	8.3	11.43	8.28
793 Ships boats floating structures	45 980 767	8.3	40.19	26.79
781 Passenger cars and race cars	41 648 700	7.6	36.70	6.48
764 Telecom equipment part nes	32 341 083	5.9	9.25	6.25
871 Optical instruments apparatus nes	27 635 581	5.0	32.34	26.07
784 Motor vehicle parts and accessories	22 193 590	4.0	23.23	6.19
778 Electrical machinery apparatus nes	15 036 736	2.7	13.51	6.68
511 Hydrocarbons nes; derivatives	12 138 936	2.2	29.16	12.39
673 Flat iron non-alloy steel products	10 602 384	1.9	39.04	12.12
Remainder	245 358 482	44.6		
Kuwait - Koweït (**=Developing) (2)				
All commodity groups	106 124 202	100.0	1.32	0.58
333 Crude petroleum & bituminous oil	78 879 591	74.3	6.29	4.59
334 Heavy petroleum & bituminous oil	15 460 676	14.6	3.65	1.57
571 Primary form ethylene polymers	2 681 996	2.5	7.08	3.44
342 Liquefied propane and butane	2 619 516	2.5	6.63	4.44
512 Alcohols, phenols; derivatives	1 090 644	1.0	3.19	1.74
562 Manufactured fertilizer excl. crude	628 593	0.6	2.38	0.83
274 Sulphur and unroasted iron pyrites	417 195	0.4	15.18	7.52
781 Passenger cars and race cars	400 097	0.4	0.35	0.06
575 Other plastics, in primary forms	310 973	0.3	0.81	0.27
335 Residual petroleum products nes	208 445	0.2	1.12	0.41
Remainder	3 426 476	3.2		
Kyrgyzstan - Kirghizistan (**=Transition) (2)				
All commodity groups	1 936 366	100.0	0.23	0.01
971 Gold non-monetary excluding ores	174 147	9.0	9.60	0.07
334 Heavy petroleum & bituminous oil	169 219	8.7	0.14	0.02
782 Goods and service vehicles	141 496	7.3	6.02	0.11
054 Vegetable & vegetable products nes	116 448	6.0	8.88	0.19
842 Female clothing, woven	115 954	6.0	10.75	0.14
351 Electric current	109 902	5.7	4.41	0.28
057 Fruit nut (exc oil), fresh or dried	64 900	3.4	3.20	0.07
289 Prec metal ore concentrate excl. gold	54 665	2.8	16.67	0.29
263 Cotton	47 180	2.4	1.14	0.18
288 Non ferrous base metal waste nes	44 254	2.3	5.90	0.09
Remainder	898 201	46.4		
Lao People's Dem. Rep. - Rép. dém. populaire lao (**=Developing) (2)				
All commodity groups	2 242 610	100.0	0.03	0.01
682 Copper	505 840	22.6	0.69	0.35
283 Copper ores and concentrates	398 970	17.8	1.01	0.73
351 Electric current	376 130	16.8	6.27	0.96
248 Wood simply worked, railway sleeper	188 409	8.4	2.34	0.51
247 Wood in rough or roughly squared	161 138	7.2	3.17	1.05
841 Male clothing, woven	92 353	4.1	0.19	0.13
071 Coffee and coffee substitutes	68 165	3.0	0.27	0.17
845 Articles of apparel nes	44 630	2.0	0.05	0.03
522 Inorganic chemical elem oxide salt	42 113	1.9	0.15	0.07
231 Natural rubber, latex, gum, etc	36 320	1.6	0.11	0.11
Remainder	328 542	14.6		

For sources and notes, see end of table.

Pour les sources et les notes, se reporter à la fin du tableau.

Latvia - Lettonie (**=Developed)

Leading products exported based on average 2011-2012 values SITC Revision 3 (3-digit level) / Principaux produits exportés d'après la moyenne des valeurs de 2011-2012 CTCI révision 3 (positions à 3 chiffres)	Value (f.o.b., thousands of dollars) / Valeur (f.a.b., milliers de dollars)	of country total / du total du pays	of ** (1) / des ** (1)	of world / du monde
All commodity groups	12 299 162	100.0	0.13	0.07
334 Heavy petroleum & bituminous oil	625 950	5.1	0.14	0.06
248 Wood simply worked, railway sleeper	602 097	4.9	2.45	1.62
676 Iron steel bar rod section piling	525 706	4.3	1.00	0.57
112 Alcoholic beverages	478 082	3.9	0.78	0.63
634 Veneer, plywood & other wood nes	385 779	3.1	2.17	1.12
542 Medicines including veterinary	323 825	2.6	0.11	0.10
781 Passenger cars and race cars	322 616	2.6	0.06	0.05
041 Wheat meslin, incl spelt, unmilled	283 222	2.3	0.79	0.58
247 Wood in rough or roughly squared	275 786	2.2	3.44	1.80
635 Wood manufactures nes	264 629	2.2	1.69	1.02
Remainder	8 211 470	66.8		

Lithuania - Lituanie (**=Developed)

Leading products	Value	of country total	of ** (1)	of world
All commodity groups	28 860 655	100.0	0.31	0.16
334 Heavy petroleum & bituminous oil	6 713 974	23.3	1.52	0.68
562 Manufactured fertilizer excl. crude	1 310 793	4.5	4.09	1.74
821 Furniture part; bedding furnishing	1 302 179	4.5	1.74	0.86
781 Passenger cars and race cars	874 691	3.0	0.17	0.14
574 Polyacetals and polyesters, etc	731 392	2.5	2.34	1.29
057 Fruit nut (exc oil), fresh or dried	481 601	1.7	1.18	0.55
893 Articles of plastic nes	450 698	1.6	0.55	0.33
054 Vegetable & vegetable products nes	425 859	1.5	1.23	0.71
041 Wheat meslin, incl spelt, unmilled	409 646	1.4	1.15	0.84
542 Medicines including veterinary	348 028	1.2	0.11	0.10
Remainder	15 811 794	54.8		

Lebanon - Liban (**=Developing) (2)

Leading products	Value	of country total	of ** (1)	of world
All commodity groups	5 639 500	100.0	0.07	0.03
971 Gold non-monetary excluding ores	868 190	15.4	0.65	0.35
667 Pearls, precious semiprecious stone	382 368	6.8	0.48	0.25
897 Jewellery nes (667)	270 318	4.8	0.33	0.22
282 Ferrous iron & steel, waste & scrap	264 975	4.7	4.18	0.49
716 Rotating electric plant parts nes	256 689	4.6	0.75	0.27
288 Non ferrous base metal waste nes	199 638	3.5	1.95	0.42
562 Manufactured fertilizer excl. crude	145 064	2.6	0.55	0.19
057 Fruit nut (exc oil), fresh or dried	128 280	2.3	0.29	0.15
892 Printed matter	127 796	2.3	0.85	0.26
642 Cut paper and paperboard articles	127 283	2.3	0.65	0.21
Remainder	2 868 899	50.7		

Luxembourg (**=Developed) (2)

Leading products	Value	of country total	of ** (1)	of world
All commodity groups	20 656 202	100.0	0.22	0.11
676 Iron steel bar rod section piling	2 726 300	13.2	5.18	2.97
625 Rubber for wheels, incl inner tube	980 895	4.7	1.87	1.06
674 Flat plated iron non-alloy steel	865 007	4.2	2.69	1.46
893 Articles of plastic nes	811 133	3.9	1.00	0.59
764 Telecom equipment part nes	708 717	3.4	0.43	0.14
684 Aluminium	653 650	3.2	0.92	0.55
657 Special yarn and textile fabric etc	607 018	2.9	2.30	1.28
582 Plastic sheet film foil & strips	576 461	2.8	0.85	0.59
641 Paper and paperboard	510 553	2.5	0.54	0.43
781 Passenger cars and race cars	440 054	2.1	0.08	0.07
Remainder	11 776 414	57.1		

Lesotho (**=Developing) (2)

Leading products	Value	of country total	of ** (1)	of world
All commodity groups	1 136 083	100.0	0.01	0.01
667 Pearls, precious semiprecious stone	398 016	35.0	0.50	0.26
845 Articles of apparel nes	188 558	16.6	0.19	0.13
841 Male clothing, woven	148 668	13.1	0.30	0.21
843 Male clothing, knitted crocheted	91 209	8.0	0.36	0.30
842 Female clothing, woven	88 064	7.8	0.16	0.11
844 Female clothing, knitted crocheted	77 103	6.8	0.17	0.14
652 Woven cotton fabrics	28 594	2.5	0.11	0.09
268 Wool & animal hair, incl wool tops	13 364	1.2	0.49	0.18
761 Television video receive project	13 238	1.2	0.02	0.01
772 Electrical circuit equipment	11 908	1.0	0.01	0.01
Remainder	77 361	6.8		

Madagascar (**=Developing) (2)

Leading products	Value	of country total	of ** (1)	of world
All commodity groups	1 485 762	100.0	0.02	0.01
075 Spices	338 546	22.8	4.85	3.96
845 Articles of apparel nes	193 044	13.0	0.20	0.14
287 Base metal ores & concentrates nes	124 810	8.4	0.67	0.38
036 Crustacean mollusc aquat invertebra	101 601	6.8	0.48	0.32
841 Male clothing, woven	70 007	4.7	0.14	0.10
842 Female clothing, woven	57 924	3.9	0.11	0.07
334 Heavy petroleum & bituminous oil	48 428	3.3	0.01	0.00
037 Fish shellfish, prepared preserved	42 556	2.9	0.23	0.16
551 Essential oils, perfumes & flavours	32 114	2.2	0.62	0.13
846 Clothing accessory excl. 831 848 851	31 847	2.1	0.17	0.11
Remainder	444 885	29.9		

Liberia - Libéria (**=Developing)

Leading products	Value	of country total	of ** (1)	of world
All commodity groups	413 200	100.0	0.01	0.00
231 Natural rubber, latex, gum, etc	132 671	32.1	0.41	0.39
793 Ships boats floating structures	81 664	19.8	0.07	0.05
281 Iron ore and concentrates	52 386	12.7	0.09	0.04
334 Heavy petroleum & bituminous oil	38 844	9.4	0.01	0.00
333 Crude petroleum & bituminous oil	31 243	7.6	0.00	0.00
247 Wood in rough or roughly squared	16 919	4.1	0.33	0.11
072 Cocoa	11 634	2.8	0.09	0.06
246 Wood chips, particles and waste	5 339	1.3	0.25	0.09
667 Pearls, precious semiprecious stone	4 005	1.0	0.01	0.00
282 Ferrous iron & steel, waste & scrap	3 705	0.9	0.06	0.01
Remainder	34 790	8.3		

Malawi (**=Developing) (2)

Leading products	Value	of country total	of ** (1)	of world
All commodity groups	1 304 801	100.0	0.02	0.01
121 Unmanufactured tabacco and refuse	605 322	46.4	7.22	4.95
061 Sugar, mollasses and honey	117 224	9.0	0.37	0.26
286 Uranium & thorium ore concentrates	97 077	7.4	12.37	12.34
074 Tea and maté	80 856	6.2	1.27	0.97
525 Radio active & associated materials	62 469	4.8	2.27	0.34
044 Maize unmilled, excluding sweet corn	43 370	3.3	0.35	0.12
263 Cotton	42 703	3.3	0.39	0.16
054 Vegetable & vegetable products nes	31 337	2.4	0.13	0.05
222 Oil seed etc for soft oil	20 762	1.6	0.07	0.03
057 Fruit nut (exc oil), fresh or dried	14 679	1.1	0.03	0.02
Remainder	189 002	14.5		

Libya - Libye (**=Developing) (2)

Leading products	Value	of country total	of ** (1)	of world
All commodity groups	40 606 242	100.0	0.51	0.22
333 Crude petroleum & bituminous oil	33 390 914	82.2	2.66	1.95
334 Heavy petroleum & bituminous oil	2 380 999	5.9	0.56	0.24
343 Natural gas, liquefied or not	1 921 459	4.7	1.20	0.55
344 Petroleum and hydrocarbon gas nes	960 199	2.4	12.87	6.79
971 Gold non-monetary excluding ores	338 679	0.8	0.25	0.13
342 Liquefied propane and butane	335 253	0.8	0.85	0.57
511 Hydrocarbons nes; derivatives	177 437	0.4	0.43	0.18
562 Manufactured fertilizer excl. crude	163 292	0.4	0.62	0.22
512 Alcohols, phenols; derivatives	103 023	0.3	0.30	0.16
522 Inorganic chemical elem oxide salt	100 927	0.2	0.35	0.16
Remainder	734 060	1.9		

Malaysia - Malaisie (**=Developing)

Leading products	Value	of country total	of ** (1)	of world
All commodity groups	227 147 705	100.0	2.83	1.24
776 Valves tubes; diodes, transistors	34 053 317	15.0	8.45	6.12
422 Fixed veg fat and oil, excl. "soft"	17 710 996	7.8	40.02	36.01
343 Natural gas, liquefied or not	17 151 735	7.6	10.75	4.94
334 Heavy petroleum & bituminous oil	13 108 356	5.8	3.09	1.33
333 Crude petroleum & bituminous oil	10 600 180	4.7	0.85	0.62
752 Computer equipment nes	9 978 225	4.4	4.01	2.83
759 Office equipment part & accessories	6 473 472	2.8	5.63	3.39
764 Telecom equipment part nes	5 834 531	2.6	1.67	1.13
772 Electrical circuit equipment	5 483 567	2.4	5.28	2.34
874 Measure analyze control device nes	4 733 999	2.1	11.62	2.60
Remainder	102 019 327	44.8		

For sources and notes, see end of table.

Pour les sources et les notes, se reporter à la fin du tableau.

184

Leading products exported based on average 2011-2012 values SITC Revision 3 (3-digit level) / Principaux produits exportés d'après la moyenne des valeurs de 2011-2012 CTCI révision 3 (positions à 3 chiffres)	2011-2012			
	Value (f.o.b., thousands of dollars) / Valeur (f.a.b., milliers de dollars)	As percentage En pourcentage		
		of country total du total du pays	of ** (1) des ** (1)	of world du monde

Maldives (**=Developing) (2)

All commodity groups	330 409	100.0	0.00	0.00
034 Fish, fresh live chilled frozen	217 454	65.8	0.81	0.36
035 Fish, dried salted smoked	17 067	5.2	1.01	0.29
037 Fish shellfish, prepared preserved	16 516	5.0	0.09	0.06
344 Petroleum and hydrocarbon gas nes	5 350	1.6	0.07	0.04
036 Crustacean mollusc aquat invertebra	5 139	1.6	0.02	0.02
764 Telecom equipment part nes	4 980	1.5	0.00	0.00
342 Liquefied propane and butane	4 443	1.3	0.01	0.01
282 Ferrous iron & steel, waste & scrap	4 081	1.2	0.06	0.01
743 Gas pump, compressor, fan, filter	3 289	1.0	0.01	0.00
776 Valves tubes; diodes, transistors	2 506	0.8	0.00	0.00
Remainder	49 584	15.0		

Mali (**=Developing) (2)

All commodity groups	2 269 266	100.0	0.03	0.01
971 Gold non-monetary excluding ores	980 961	43.2	0.74	0.39
263 Cotton	682 314	30.1	6.20	2.60
562 Manufactured fertilizer excl. crude	127 683	5.6	0.48	0.17
334 Heavy petroleum & bituminous oil	109 440	4.8	0.03	0.01
001 Live animal excl. fish & crustacean	66 896	2.9	1.44	0.31
222 Oil seed etc for soft oil	55 280	2.4	0.19	0.08
611 Leather	29 993	1.3	0.23	0.13
281 Iron ore and concentrates	29 612	1.3	0.05	0.02
723 Civil engineering plant & equipment	24 805	1.1	0.07	0.02
057 Fruit nut (exc oil), fresh or dried	18 706	0.8	0.04	0.02
Remainder	143 576	6.5		

Malta - Malte (**=Developed) (2)

All commodity groups	4 317 904	100.0	0.05	0.02
334 Heavy petroleum & bituminous oil	1 680 904	38.9	0.38	0.17
776 Valves tubes; diodes, transistors	1 021 720	23.7	0.67	0.18
542 Medicines including veterinary	253 574	5.9	0.08	0.08
793 Ships boats floating structures	126 103	2.9	0.23	0.07
772 Electrical circuit equipment	106 886	2.5	0.08	0.05
894 Baby carriage, toy, game, sport goods	105 629	2.4	0.29	0.11
792 Aircraft, spacecraft & equipment	81 113	1.9	0.06	0.05
892 Printed matter	73 513	1.7	0.22	0.15
034 Fish, fresh live chilled frozen	66 188	1.5	0.21	0.11
893 Articles of plastic nes	51 546	1.2	0.06	0.04
Remainder	750 728	17.4		

Marshall Islands - Îles Marshall (**=Developing) (2)

All commodity groups	35 000	100.0	0.00	0.00
793 Ships boats floating structures	26 015	74.3	0.02	0.02
034 Fish, fresh live chilled frozen	7 388	21.1	0.03	0.01
334 Heavy petroleum & bituminous oil	599	1.7	0.00	0.00
037 Fish shellfish, prepared preserved	395	1.1	0.00	0.00
035 Fish, dried salted smoked	77	0.2	0.00	0.00
714 Non-electric engines excl. 712 713 718	43	0.1	0.00	0.00
897 Jewellery nes (667)	26	0.1	0.00	0.00
081 Animal feed excluding unmilled cereal	24	0.1	0.00	0.00
288 Non ferrous base metal waste nes	24	0.1	0.00	0.00
671 Pig & sponge iron, ferro alloys etc	23	0.1	0.00	0.00
Remainder	386	1.1		

Mauritania - Mauritanie (**=Developing) (2)

All commodity groups	2 708 360	100.0	0.03	0.01
281 Iron ore and concentrates	1 279 832	47.3	2.20	0.94
034 Fish, fresh live chilled frozen	377 936	14.0	1.41	0.63
283 Copper ores and concentrates	336 957	12.4	0.86	0.62
036 Crustacean mollusc aquat invertebra	244 037	9.0	1.15	0.77
333 Crude petroleum & bituminous oil	172 379	6.4	0.01	0.01
081 Animal feed excluding unmilled cereal	35 249	1.3	0.11	0.05
971 Gold non-monetary excluding ores	21 755	0.8	0.02	0.01
288 Non ferrous base metal waste nes	6 572	0.2	0.06	0.01
282 Ferrous iron & steel, waste & scrap	6 176	0.2	0.10	0.01
037 Fish shellfish, prepared preserved	5 351	0.2	0.03	0.02
Remainder	222 116	8.2		

Mauritius - Maurice (**=Developing) (2)

All commodity groups	2 618 921	100.0	0.03	0.01
845 Articles of apparel nes	400 446	15.3	0.41	0.29
037 Fish shellfish, prepared preserved	311 079	11.9	1.68	1.18
061 Sugar, mollasses and honey	288 157	11.0	0.91	0.64
841 Male clothing, woven	254 224	9.7	0.52	0.36
844 Female clothing, knitted crocheted	93 251	3.6	0.21	0.17
667 Pearls, precious semiprecious stone	65 374	2.5	0.08	0.04
034 Fish, fresh live chilled frozen	64 828	2.5	0.24	0.11
897 Jewellery nes (667)	62 058	2.4	0.08	0.05
843 Male clothing, knitted crocheted	47 878	1.8	0.19	0.16
842 Female clothing, woven	47 258	1.8	0.09	0.06
Remainder	984 368	37.5		

Mexico - Mexique (**=Developing)

All commodity groups	360 197 940	100.0	4.49	1.97
333 Crude petroleum & bituminous oil	48 161 179	13.4	3.84	2.81
781 Passenger cars and race cars	28 006 715	7.8	24.68	4.36
764 Telecom equipment part nes	19 523 441	5.4	5.59	3.77
784 Motor vehicle parts and accessories	18 032 957	5.0	18.88	5.03
761 Television video receive project	18 009 055	5.0	32.74	19.66
752 Computer equipment nes	17 739 770	4.9	7.13	5.03
782 Goods and service vehicles	13 676 047	3.8	29.61	10.34
773 Electrical distribute equipment nes	8 501 979	2.4	15.92	7.58
971 Gold non-monetary excluding ores	8 005 951	2.2	6.03	3.18
713 Internal combustion engine part nes	7 927 127	2.2	22.09	4.87
Remainder	172 613 719	47.9		

Micronesia (Federated States of) - Micronésie (États fédérés de) (**=Developing) (2)

All commodity groups	31 500	100.0	0.00	0.00
034 Fish, fresh live chilled frozen	29 222	92.8	0.11	0.05
036 Crustacean mollusc aquat invertebra	546	1.7	0.00	0.00
689 Misc non-ferrous base metals	193	0.6	0.00	0.00
288 Non ferrous base metal waste nes	180	0.6	0.00	0.00
625 Rubber for wheels, incl inner tube	114	0.4	0.00	0.00
899 Manufactured articles nes	106	0.3	0.00	0.00
282 Ferrous iron & steel, waste & scrap	103	0.3	0.00	0.00
851 Footwear	100	0.3	0.00	0.00
291 Crude animal materials nes	58	0.2	0.00	0.00
657 Special yarn and textile fabric etc	53	0.2	0.00	0.00
Remainder	825	2.6		

Mongolia - Mongolie (**=Developing) (2)

All commodity groups	4 595 089	100.0	0.06	0.03
283 Copper ores and concentrates	2 344 872	51.0	5.95	4.31
287 Base metal ores & concentrates nes	465 890	10.1	2.50	1.43
971 Gold non-monetary excluding ores	427 377	9.3	0.32	0.17
321 Coal excluding non-agglomerated	384 852	8.4	0.85	0.29
268 Wool & animal hair, incl wool tops	372 448	8.1	13.58	4.98
333 Crude petroleum & bituminous oil	135 776	3.0	0.01	0.01
281 Iron ore and concentrates	75 845	1.7	0.13	0.06
611 Leather	52 477	1.1	0.40	0.22
278 Other crude minerals	45 241	1.0	0.60	0.26
682 Copper	38 767	0.8	0.05	0.03
Remainder	251 544	5.5		

Montenegro - Monténégro (**=Transition)

All commodity groups	548 160	100.0	0.07	0.00
684 Aluminium	209 256	38.2	2.08	0.18
351 Electric current	58 692	10.7	2.35	0.15
112 Alcoholic beverages	29 934	5.5	2.01	0.04
282 Ferrous iron & steel, waste & scrap	20 481	3.7	0.77	0.04
676 Iron steel bar rod section piling	19 350	3.5	0.26	0.02
248 Wood simply worked, railway sleeper	17 113	3.1	0.39	0.05
288 Non ferrous base metal waste nes	15 484	2.8	2.06	0.03
334 Heavy petroleum & bituminous oil	13 928	2.5	0.01	0.00
748 Mechanical transmission equipment	12 305	2.2	2.83	0.02
542 Medicines including veterinary	11 397	2.1	0.65	0.00
Remainder	140 220	25.7		

For sources and notes, see end of table.   Pour les sources et les notes, se reporter à la fin du tableau.

185

Leading products exported based on average 2011-2012 values SITC Revision 3 (3-digit level) Principaux produits exportés d'après la moyenne des valeurs de 2011-2012 CTCI révision 3 (positions à 3 chiffres)	2011-2012			
	Value (f.o.b., thousands of dollars) Valeur (f.a.b., milliers de dollars)	As percentage / En pourcentage		
		of country total du total du pays	of ** (1) des ** (1)	of world du monde

Montserrat (**=Developing) (2)

Product	Value	% country	% **	% world
All commodity groups	2 367	100.0	0.00	0.00
723 Civil engineering plant & equipment	250	10.6	0.00	0.00
872 Medical instruments appliances nes	120	5.1	0.00	0.00
782 Goods and service vehicles	101	4.3	0.00	0.00
034 Fish, fresh live chilled frozen	88	3.7	0.00	0.00
873 Meters and counters nes	62	2.6	0.00	0.00
971 Gold non-monetary excluding ores	59	2.5	0.00	0.00
874 Measure analyze control device nes	54	2.3	0.00	0.00
776 Valves tubes; diodes, transistors	41	1.7	0.00	0.00
273 Stone, sand and gravel	31	1.3	0.00	0.00
764 Telecom equipment part nes	29	1.2	0.00	0.00
Remainder	1 532	64.7		

Morocco - Maroc (**=Developing) (2)

Product	Value	% country	% **	% world
All commodity groups	21 533 559	100.0	0.27	0.12
562 Manufactured fertilizer excl. crude	2 208 415	10.3	8.36	2.93
773 Electrical distribute equipment nes	1 932 640	9.0	3.62	1.72
522 Inorganic chemical elem oxide salt	1 849 501	8.6	6.43	3.02
842 Female clothing, woven	1 477 286	6.9	2.74	1.80
272 Crude fertilizer, excl. manufactured	1 462 070	6.8	38.41	29.00
334 Heavy petroleum & bituminous oil	919 065	4.3	0.22	0.09
054 Vegetable & vegetable products nes	835 778	3.9	3.49	1.40
845 Articles of apparel nes	828 404	3.8	0.84	0.59
776 Valves tubes; diodes, transistors	745 308	3.5	0.19	0.13
841 Male clothing, woven	623 580	2.9	1.27	0.88
Remainder	8 651 512	40.0		

Mozambique (**=Developing) (2)

Product	Value	% country	% **	% world
All commodity groups	3 852 059	100.0	0.05	0.02
684 Aluminium	1 289 333	33.5	3.36	1.08
334 Heavy petroleum & bituminous oil	376 021	9.8	0.09	0.04
351 Electric current	292 516	7.6	4.87	0.74
343 Natural gas, liquefied or not	257 073	6.7	0.16	0.07
287 Base metal ores & concentrates nes	189 560	4.9	1.02	0.58
121 Unmanufactured tabacco and refuse	169 154	4.4	2.02	1.38
321 Coal excluding non-agglomomerated	163 893	4.3	0.36	0.12
325 Coke, semi coke, retort carbon	150 454	3.9	5.86	1.70
061 Sugar, mollasses and honey	119 315	3.1	0.38	0.26
057 Fruit nut (exc oil), fresh or dried	95 789	2.5	0.22	0.11
Remainder	748 951	19.3		

Myanmar (**=Developing) (2)

Product	Value	% country	% **	% world
All commodity groups	9 069 220	100.0	0.11	0.05
343 Natural gas, liquefied or not	3 374 747	37.2	2.11	0.97
667 Pearls, precious semiprecious stone	1 387 670	15.3	1.76	0.90
054 Vegetable & vegetable products nes	910 200	10.0	3.80	1.52
247 Wood in rough or roughly squared	897 199	9.9	17.63	5.87
036 Crustacean mollusc aquat invertebra	245 192	2.7	1.16	0.77
845 Articles of apparel nes	198 513	2.2	0.20	0.14
841 Male clothing, woven	196 837	2.2	0.40	0.28
248 Wood simply worked, railway sleeper	186 114	2.1	2.32	0.50
231 Natural rubber, latex, gum, etc	169 341	1.9	0.53	0.50
682 Copper	145 467	1.6	0.20	0.10
Remainder	1 357 940	14.9		

Namibia - Namibie (**=Developing) (2)

Product	Value	% country	% **	% world
All commodity groups	4 220 568	100.0	0.05	0.02
667 Pearls, precious semiprecious stone	955 836	22.6	1.21	0.62
034 Fish, fresh live chilled frozen	536 861	12.7	2.01	0.89
286 Uranium & thorium ore concentrates	386 850	9.2	49.28	49.16
682 Copper	331 753	7.9	0.45	0.23
686 Zinc	276 663	6.6	6.43	2.10
525 Radio active & associated materials	246 229	5.8	8.96	1.35
112 Alcoholic beverages	109 985	2.6	0.79	0.14
892 Printed matter	96 117	2.3	0.64	0.19
011 Beef, fresh chilled frozen	84 614	2.0	0.69	0.21
283 Copper ores and concentrates	66 628	1.6	0.17	0.12
Remainder	1 129 032	26.7		

Nauru (**=Developing)

Product	Value	% country	% **	% world
All commodity groups	80 000	100.0	0.00	0.00
272 Crude fertilizer, excl. manufactured	74 788	93.5	1.96	1.48
034 Fish, fresh live chilled frozen	381	0.5	0.00	0.00
683 Nickel	369	0.5	0.01	0.00
022 Milk products, excl. butter & cheese	346	0.4	0.01	0.00
772 Electrical circuit equipment	340	0.4	0.01	0.00
282 Ferrous iron & steel, waste & scrap	326	0.4	0.01	0.00
776 Valves tubes; diodes, transistors	251	0.3	0.00	0.00
813 Lighting fixtures and fittings nes	228	0.3	0.00	0.00
874 Measure analyze control device nes	207	0.3	0.00	0.00
288 Non ferrous base metal waste nes	186	0.2	0.00	0.00
Remainder	2 578	3.2		

Nepal - Népal (**=Developing) (2)

Product	Value	% country	% **	% world
All commodity groups	903 418	100.0	0.01	0.00
674 Flat plated iron non-alloy steel	83 372	9.2	0.33	0.14
651 Textile yarn	78 284	8.7	0.21	0.14
659 Floor coverings etc	76 523	8.5	1.01	0.50
653 Man-made woven fabrics	54 141	6.0	0.17	0.12
658 Made-up textile articles nes	39 884	4.4	0.10	0.08
075 Spices	37 832	4.2	0.54	0.44
054 Vegetable & vegetable products nes	33 061	3.7	0.14	0.06
059 Fruit & vegetable juice unfermented	27 983	3.1	0.37	0.16
846 Clothing accessory excl. 831 848 851	26 331	2.9	0.14	0.09
292 Crude vegetable materials nes	25 231	2.8	0.16	0.06
Remainder	420 776	46.5		

Netherlands - Pays-Bas (**=Developed) (2)

Product	Value	% country	% **	% world
All commodity groups	661 400 785	100.0	7.00	3.62
334 Heavy petroleum & bituminous oil	84 970 969	12.8	19.29	8.62
752 Computer equipment nes	19 225 256	2.9	18.62	5.45
764 Telecom equipment part nes	17 892 059	2.7	10.76	3.46
333 Crude petroleum & bituminous oil	16 898 950	2.6	8.50	0.98
542 Medicines including veterinary	15 491 366	2.3	5.05	4.60
759 Office equipment part & accessories	14 814 906	2.2	19.51	7.75
292 Crude vegetable materials nes	14 026 361	2.1	51.38	32.35
511 Hydrocarbons nes; derivatives	12 728 305	1.9	23.50	12.99
728 Special industrial machine part nes	12 010 819	1.8	8.58	6.55
343 Natural gas, liquefied or not	9 948 634	1.5	9.20	2.87
Remainder	443 393 160	67.2		

New Caledonia - Nouvelle-Calédonie (**=Developing) (2)

Product	Value	% country	% **	% world
All commodity groups	1 475 235	100.0	0.02	0.01
671 Pig & sponge iron, ferro alloys etc	757 584	51.4	3.51	1.80
284 Nickel ores, concentrates, etc	494 433	33.5	8.23	4.61
522 Inorganic chemical elem oxide salt	68 649	4.7	0.24	0.11
281 Iron ore and concentrates	49 585	3.4	0.09	0.04
036 Crustacean mollusc aquat invertebra	12 209	0.8	0.06	0.04
792 Aircraft, spacecraft & equipment	5 899	0.4	0.03	0.00
034 Fish, fresh live chilled frozen	5 658	0.4	0.02	0.01
874 Measure analyze control device nes	3 894	0.3	0.01	0.00
551 Essential oils, perfumes & flavours	2 954	0.2	0.06	0.01
282 Ferrous iron & steel, waste & scrap	2 879	0.2	0.05	0.01
Remainder	71 491	4.7		

New Zealand - Nouvelle-Zélande (**=Developed)

Product	Value	% country	% **	% world
All commodity groups	37 362 367	100.0	0.40	0.20
022 Milk products, excl. butter & cheese	6 428 668	17.2	18.28	15.16
012 Meat nes, fresh chilled frozen	2 608 863	7.0	4.64	3.60
023 Butter fats oils derived from milk	1 786 774	4.8	25.60	22.71
011 Beef, fresh chilled frozen	1 648 910	4.4	6.13	4.15
333 Crude petroleum & bituminous oil	1 577 772	4.2	0.79	0.09
247 Wood in rough or roughly squared	1 287 769	3.4	16.04	8.42
057 Fruit nut (exc oil), fresh or dried	1 247 597	3.3	3.04	1.44
024 Cheese and curd	1 124 428	3.0	4.20	3.77
098 Edible products & preparations nes	1 048 655	2.8	2.35	1.68
112 Alcoholic beverages	1 031 690	2.8	1.69	1.35
Remainder	17 571 241	47.1		

For sources and notes, see end of table.

Pour les sources et les notes, se reporter à la fin du tableau.

186

Leading products exported based on average 2011-2012 values SITC Revision 3 (3-digit level) / Principaux produits exportés d'après la moyenne des valeurs de 2011-2012 CTCI révision 3 (positions à 3 chiffres)	2011-2012			
	Value (f.o.b., thousands of dollars) Valeur (f.a.b., milliers de dollars)	of country total du total du pays	of ** (1) des ** (1)	of world du monde
Nicaragua (=Developing)**				
All commodity groups	2 485 456	100.0	0.03	0.01
071 Coffee and coffee substitutes	332 680	13.4	1.33	0.82
845 Articles of apparel nes	329 245	13.2	0.33	0.23
971 Gold non-monetary excluding ores	264 974	10.7	0.20	0.11
011 Beef, fresh chilled frozen	261 031	10.5	2.13	0.66
773 Electrical distribute equipment nes	171 490	6.9	0.32	0.15
061 Sugar, mollasses and honey	126 820	5.1	0.40	0.28
841 Male clothing, woven	118 069	4.8	0.24	0.17
036 Crustacean mollusc aquat invertebra	99 611	4.0	0.47	0.31
222 Oil seed etc for soft oil	66 941	2.7	0.23	0.09
024 Cheese and curd	52 403	2.1	2.64	0.18
Remainder	662 192	26.6		
Niger (=Developing) (2)**				
All commodity groups	1 375 000	100.0	0.02	0.01
525 Radio active & associated materials	323 384	23.5	11.77	1.77
334 Heavy petroleum & bituminous oil	304 257	22.1	0.07	0.03
286 Uranium & thorium ore concentrates	294 971	21.5	37.57	37.48
001 Live animal excl. fish & crustacean	123 365	9.0	2.66	0.56
054 Vegetable & vegetable products nes	55 981	4.1	0.23	0.09
269 Worn clothing, textile article; rag	52 503	3.8	3.46	1.08
343 Natural gas, liquefied or not	41 576	3.0	0.03	0.01
652 Woven cotton fabrics	15 338	1.1	0.06	0.05
042 Rice	13 682	1.0	0.07	0.06
061 Sugar, mollasses and honey	12 600	0.9	0.04	0.03
Remainder	137 343	10.0		
Nigeria - Nigéria (=Developing) (2)**				
All commodity groups	126 464 007	100.0	1.58	0.69
333 Crude petroleum & bituminous oil	98 908 522	78.2	7.89	5.76
343 Natural gas, liquefied or not	10 558 570	8.3	6.62	3.04
334 Heavy petroleum & bituminous oil	7 819 800	6.2	1.85	0.79
342 Liquefied propane and butane	1 566 312	1.2	3.96	2.65
231 Natural rubber, latex, gum, etc	1 408 492	1.1	4.40	4.16
072 Cocoa	954 384	0.8	6.98	4.61
793 Ships boats floating structures	870 700	0.7	0.76	0.51
611 Leather	424 909	0.3	3.27	1.79
344 Petroleum and hydrocarbon gas nes	399 693	0.3	5.36	2.83
222 Oil seed etc for soft oil	339 565	0.3	1.14	0.48
Remainder	3 213 060	2.6		
Niue - Nioué (=Developing) (2)**				
All commodity groups	20	100.0	0.00	0.00
272 Crude fertilizer, excl. manufactured	4	18.7	0.00	0.00
046 Wheat meal & flour, meslin flour	4	18.6	0.00	0.00
728 Special industrial machine part nes	2	11.2	0.00	0.00
745 Non-electrical machinery tool nes	1	4.2	0.00	0.00
059 Fruit & vegetable juice unfermented	1	3.7	0.00	0.00
764 Telecom equipment part nes	1	3.0	0.00	0.00
775 Household equipment nes	1	2.9	0.00	0.00
751 Office machines	0	2.4	0.00	0.00
773 Electrical distribute equipment nes	0	2.1	0.00	0.00
575 Other plastics, in primary forms	0	1.3	0.00	0.00
Remainder	6	31.9		
Northern Mariana Islands - Îles Mariannes du Nord (=Developing) (2)**				
All commodity groups	3 000	100.0	0.00	0.00
282 Ferrous iron & steel, waste & scrap	434	14.5	0.01	0.00
533 Pigment, paint, varnish & related	327	10.9	0.00	0.00
895 Office and stationery supplies nes	271	9.0	0.00	0.00
885 Watches and clocks	269	9.0	0.00	0.00
751 Office machines	256	8.5	0.00	0.00
831 Case bag: storage travel shopping	253	8.4	0.00	0.00
288 Non ferrous base metal waste nes	199	6.6	0.00	0.00
761 Television video receive project	177	5.9	0.00	0.00
541 Pharmaceuticals excluding medicines	85	2.8	0.00	0.00
695 Tools for use in hand or in machine	62	2.1	0.00	0.00
Remainder	667	22.3		

Leading products exported based on average 2011-2012 values SITC Revision 3 (3-digit level) / Principaux produits exportés d'après la moyenne des valeurs de 2011-2012 CTCI révision 3 (positions à 3 chiffres)	2011-2012			
	Value (f.o.b., thousands of dollars) Valeur (f.a.b., milliers de dollars)	of country total du total du pays	of ** (1) des ** (1)	of world du monde
Norway - Norvège (=Developed)**				
All commodity groups	160 180 019	100.0	1.70	0.88
333 Crude petroleum & bituminous oil	56 722 634	35.4	28.55	3.30
343 Natural gas, liquefied or not	39 277 482	24.5	36.33	11.32
334 Heavy petroleum & bituminous oil	8 994 685	5.6	2.04	0.91
034 Fish, fresh live chilled frozen	7 763 595	4.8	25.06	12.93
684 Aluminium	4 534 461	2.8	6.40	3.80
342 Liquefied propane and butane	3 659 212	2.3	21.97	6.20
683 Nickel	1 903 420	1.2	13.03	8.79
874 Measure analyze control device nes	1 662 825	1.0	1.19	0.91
793 Ships boats floating structures	1 406 516	0.9	2.57	0.82
598 Miscellaneous chemical products nes	1 288 685	0.8	1.35	1.02
Remainder	32 966 504	20.7		
Oman (=Developing) (2)**				
All commodity groups	49 615 049	100.0	0.62	0.27
333 Crude petroleum & bituminous oil	28 510 665	57.5	2.27	1.66
343 Natural gas, liquefied or not	5 188 510	10.5	3.25	1.49
334 Heavy petroleum & bituminous oil	2 738 679	5.5	0.65	0.28
511 Hydrocarbons nes; derivatives	1 195 962	2.4	2.87	1.22
562 Manufactured fertilizer excl. crude	985 107	2.0	3.73	1.30
684 Aluminium	897 754	1.8	2.34	0.75
512 Alcohols, phenols; derivatives	680 035	1.4	1.99	1.09
281 Iron ore and concentrates	495 639	1.0	0.85	0.36
671 Pig & sponge iron, ferro alloys etc	483 546	1.0	2.24	1.15
773 Electrical distribute equipment nes	402 292	0.8	0.75	0.36
Remainder	8 036 860	16.1		
Pakistan (=Developing)**				
All commodity groups	24 978 722	100.0	0.31	0.14
658 Made-up textile articles nes	3 395 734	13.6	8.62	6.59
652 Woven cotton fabrics	2 631 540	10.5	10.58	7.97
651 Textile yarn	2 127 222	8.5	5.67	3.72
042 Rice	1 972 095	7.9	9.75	8.01
897 Jewellery nes (667)	1 047 119	4.2	1.29	0.84
841 Male clothing, woven	1 015 574	4.1	2.08	1.43
843 Male clothing, knitted crocheted	975 891	3.9	3.81	3.20
334 Heavy petroleum & bituminous oil	819 222	3.3	0.19	0.08
842 Female clothing, woven	623 114	2.5	1.16	0.76
845 Articles of apparel nes	552 624	2.2	0.56	0.39
Remainder	9 818 587	39.3		
Palau - Palaos (=Developing)**				
All commodity groups	7 000	100.0	0.00	0.00
034 Fish, fresh live chilled frozen	6 434	91.9	0.02	0.01
282 Ferrous iron & steel, waste & scrap	122	1.7	0.00	0.00
288 Non ferrous base metal waste nes	69	1.0	0.00	0.00
971 Gold non-monetary excluding ores	58	0.8	0.00	0.00
112 Alcoholic beverages	56	0.8	0.00	0.00
036 Crustacean mollusc aquat invertebra	24	0.3	0.00	0.00
784 Motor vehicle parts and accessories	17	0.2	0.00	0.00
743 Gas pump, compressor, fan, filter	14	0.2	0.00	0.00
713 Internal combustion engine part nes	12	0.2	0.00	0.00
048 Cereal & preparation flour starch	12	0.2	0.00	0.00
Remainder	182	2.7		
Panama (=Developing)**				
All commodity groups	15 387 408	100.0	0.19	0.08
541 Pharmaceuticals excluding medicines	2 156 194	14.0	10.64	1.32
793 Ships boats floating structures	1 180 394	7.7	1.03	0.69
542 Medicines including veterinary	1 118 419	7.3	3.96	0.33
851 Footwear	863 448	5.6	1.20	0.75
333 Crude petroleum & bituminous oil	554 598	3.6	0.04	0.03
334 Heavy petroleum & bituminous oil	509 324	3.3	0.12	0.05
842 Female clothing, woven	461 904	3.0	0.86	0.56
057 Fruit nut (exc oil), fresh or dried	422 491	2.7	0.96	0.49
553 Perfume toilet cosmetics, excl. soap	408 278	2.7	2.23	0.53
845 Articles of apparel nes	403 375	2.6	0.41	0.29
Remainder	7 308 983	47.5		

For sources and notes, see end of table.

Pour les sources et les notes, se reporter à la fin du tableau.

Leading products exported based on average 2011-2012 values SITC Revision 3 (3-digit level) / Principaux produits exportés d'après la moyenne des valeurs de 2011-2012 CTCI révision 3 (positions à 3 chiffres)	2011-2012			
	Value (f.o.b., thousands of dollars) / Valeur (f.a.b., milliers de dollars)	As percentage / En pourcentage		
		of country total / du total du pays	of ** (1) / des ** (1)	of world / du monde
Papua New Guinea - Papouasie-Nouvelle-Guinée (**=Developing) (2)				
All commodity groups	6 953 086	100.0	0.09	0.04
971 Gold non-monetary excluding ores	1 704 524	24.5	1.28	0.68
283 Copper ores and concentrates	1 383 341	19.9	3.51	2.54
333 Crude petroleum & bituminous oil	1 222 042	17.6	0.10	0.07
422 Fixed veg fat and oil, excl. "soft"	535 848	7.7	1.21	1.09
247 Wood in rough or roughly squared	414 468	6.0	8.14	2.71
289 Prec metal ore concentrate excl. gold	388 356	5.6	5.59	2.05
071 Coffee and coffee substitutes	227 539	3.3	0.91	0.56
681 Silver, platinum, platinum metals	185 450	2.7	0.64	0.28
334 Heavy petroleum & bituminous oil	135 448	1.9	0.03	0.01
072 Cocoa	116 769	1.7	0.85	0.56
Remainder	639 301	9.1		
Paraguay (**=Developing)				
All commodity groups	7 517 415	100.0	0.09	0.04
222 Oil seed etc for soft oil	2 105 794	28.0	7.09	2.99
351 Electric current	1 618 235	21.5	26.95	4.11
011 Beef, fresh chilled frozen	779 612	10.4	6.36	1.96
081 Animal feed excluding unmilled cereal	459 026	6.1	1.43	0.63
044 Maize unmilled, excluding sweet corn	425 055	5.7	3.41	1.21
421 Fixed veg fat and oil, "soft"	273 676	3.6	2.06	0.69
041 Wheat meslin, incl spelt, unmilled	204 023	2.7	3.54	0.42
611 Leather	161 529	2.1	1.24	0.68
061 Sugar, mollasses and honey	118 121	1.6	0.37	0.26
122 Manufactured tabacco	77 636	1.0	0.91	0.25
Remainder	1 294 708	17.3		
Peru - Pérou (**=Developing)				
All commodity groups	45 325 863	100.0	0.56	0.25
283 Copper ores and concentrates	8 404 327	18.5	21.34	15.45
971 Gold non-monetary excluding ores	7 523 574	16.6	5.66	2.99
287 Base metal ores & concentrates nes	3 674 259	8.1	19.68	11.28
682 Copper	3 582 412	7.9	4.89	2.49
334 Heavy petroleum & bituminous oil	3 006 300	6.6	0.71	0.30
081 Animal feed excluding unmilled cereal	2 340 302	5.2	7.27	3.21
343 Natural gas, liquefied or not	1 480 713	3.3	0.93	0.43
071 Coffee and coffee substitutes	1 335 899	2.9	5.33	3.29
281 Iron ore and concentrates	936 038	2.1	1.61	0.68
845 Articles of apparel nes	758 590	1.7	0.77	0.54
Remainder	12 283 449	27.1		
Philippines (**=Developing)				
All commodity groups	50 018 676	100.0	0.62	0.27
776 Valves tubes; diodes, transistors	10 163 981	20.3	2.52	1.83
752 Computer equipment nes	3 464 733	6.9	1.39	0.98
635 Wood manufactures nes	1 921 381	3.8	20.12	7.41
784 Motor vehicle parts and accessories	1 730 016	3.5	1.81	0.48
771 Electric power machine part excl. 716	1 548 239	3.1	3.12	1.67
759 Office equipment part & accessories	1 532 794	3.1	1.33	0.80
773 Electrical distribute equipment nes	1 353 254	2.7	2.53	1.21
778 Electrical machinery apparatus nes	1 249 574	2.5	1.12	0.56
422 Fixed veg fat and oil, excl. "soft"	1 244 120	2.5	2.81	2.53
682 Copper	1 005 660	2.0	1.37	0.70
Remainder	24 804 924	49.6		
Poland - Pologne (**=Developed)				
All commodity groups	183 854 345	100.0	1.95	1.00
784 Motor vehicle parts and accessories	9 061 449	4.9	3.46	2.53
821 Furniture part; bedding furnishing	8 919 795	4.9	11.90	5.90
781 Passenger cars and race cars	8 151 060	4.4	1.55	1.27
761 Television video receive project	5 497 980	3.0	15.42	6.00
713 Internal combustion engine part nes	4 777 446	2.6	3.79	2.94
793 Ships boats floating structures	4 515 593	2.5	8.24	2.63
682 Copper	4 327 853	2.4	7.24	3.00
775 Household equipment nes	4 147 903	2.3	10.34	4.36
334 Heavy petroleum & bituminous oil	3 999 834	2.2	0.91	0.41
893 Articles of plastic nes	3 611 130	2.0	4.43	2.62
Remainder	126 844 302	68.8		

Leading products exported based on average 2011-2012 values SITC Revision 3 (3-digit level) / Principaux produits exportés d'après la moyenne des valeurs de 2011-2012 CTCI révision 3 (positions à 3 chiffres)	2011-2012			
	Value (f.o.b., thousands of dollars) / Valeur (f.a.b., milliers de dollars)	As percentage / En pourcentage		
		of country total / du total du pays	of ** (1) / des ** (1)	of world / du monde
Portugal (**=Developed)				
All commodity groups	58 655 590	100.0	0.62	0.32
334 Heavy petroleum & bituminous oil	3 849 543	6.6	0.87	0.39
781 Passenger cars and race cars	2 875 726	4.9	0.55	0.45
784 Motor vehicle parts and accessories	2 400 705	4.1	0.92	0.67
851 Footwear	2 207 355	3.8	5.25	1.91
641 Paper and paperboard	1 781 422	3.0	1.89	1.49
845 Articles of apparel nes	1 613 772	2.8	4.00	1.15
821 Furniture part; bedding furnishing	1 399 164	2.4	1.87	0.92
112 Alcoholic beverages	1 229 185	2.1	2.01	1.61
625 Rubber for wheels, incl inner tube	1 032 066	1.8	1.97	1.11
676 Iron steel bar rod section piling	1 021 007	1.7	1.94	1.11
Remainder	39 245 645	66.8		
Qatar (**=Developing) (2)				
All commodity groups	123 633 097	100.0	1.54	0.68
343 Natural gas, liquefied or not	46 522 158	37.6	29.15	13.40
333 Crude petroleum & bituminous oil	44 824 387	36.3	3.57	2.61
334 Heavy petroleum & bituminous oil	8 868 351	7.2	2.09	0.90
342 Liquefied propane and butane	8 441 256	6.8	21.35	14.29
571 Primary form ethylene polymers	2 200 665	1.8	5.81	2.82
562 Manufactured fertilizer excl. crude	1 355 660	1.1	5.13	1.80
511 Hydrocarbons nes; derivatives	978 088	0.8	2.35	1.00
684 Aluminium	922 624	0.7	2.40	0.77
344 Petroleum and hydrocarbon gas nes	777 918	0.6	10.43	5.50
512 Alcohols, phenols; derivatives	537 075	0.4	1.57	0.86
Remainder	8 204 915	6.7		
Republic of Moldova - République de Moldova (**=Transition)				
All commodity groups	2 189 347	100.0	0.26	0.01
057 Fruit nut (exc oil), fresh or dried	177 895	8.1	8.77	0.20
112 Alcoholic beverages	165 088	7.5	11.07	0.22
222 Oil seed etc for soft oil	163 123	7.5	8.07	0.23
773 Electrical distribute equipment nes	156 163	7.1	5.97	0.14
842 Female clothing, woven	98 327	4.5	9.12	0.12
676 Iron steel bar rod section piling	90 357	4.1	1.20	0.10
421 Fixed veg fat and oil, "soft"	81 070	3.7	1.44	0.20
851 Footwear	80 940	3.7	4.73	0.07
821 Furniture part; bedding furnishing	67 270	3.1	3.16	0.04
841 Male clothing, woven	62 827	2.9	6.16	0.09
Remainder	1 046 287	47.8		
Romania - Roumanie (**=Developed)				
All commodity groups	60 298 166	100.0	0.64	0.33
784 Motor vehicle parts and accessories	3 540 236	5.9	1.35	0.99
773 Electrical distribute equipment nes	3 323 705	5.5	5.92	2.96
781 Passenger cars and race cars	3 270 683	5.4	0.62	0.51
334 Heavy petroleum & bituminous oil	2 670 363	4.4	0.61	0.27
764 Telecom equipment part nes	2 244 238	3.7	1.35	0.43
821 Furniture part; bedding furnishing	1 807 127	3.0	2.41	1.19
851 Footwear	1 694 200	2.8	4.03	1.47
772 Electrical circuit equipment	1 627 277	2.7	1.26	0.69
625 Rubber for wheels, incl inner tube	1 358 579	2.3	2.59	1.46
842 Female clothing, woven	1 239 967	2.1	4.60	1.51
Remainder	37 521 791	62.2		
Russian Federation - Fédération de Russie (**=Transition) (2)				
All commodity groups	520 778 804	100.0	62.79	2.85
333 Crude petroleum & bituminous oil	176 307 934	33.9	66.78	10.27
334 Heavy petroleum & bituminous oil	97 546 957	18.7	79.90	9.89
343 Natural gas, liquefied or not	67 465 652	13.0	84.99	19.44
321 Coal excluding non-agglomerated	12 193 502	2.3	85.27	9.23
562 Manufactured fertilizer excl. crude	10 623 334	2.0	62.56	14.07
672 Ingots, Iron steel primary products	8 075 454	1.6	52.83	18.65
684 Aluminium	7 403 787	1.4	73.66	6.21
682 Copper	5 300 993	1.0	47.41	3.68
671 Pig & sponge iron, ferro alloys etc	4 547 802	0.9	41.54	10.80
673 Flat iron non-alloy steel products	4 479 246	0.9	43.23	5.12
Remainder	126 834 143	24.3		

For sources and notes, see end of table.   Pour les sources et les notes, se reporter à la fin du tableau.

188

Leading products exported based on average 2011-2012 values SITC Revision 3 (3-digit level) / Principaux produits exportés d'après la moyenne des valeurs de 2011-2012 CTCI révision 3 (positions à 3 chiffres)	Value (f.o.b., thousands of dollars) Valeur (f.a.b., milliers de dollars)	of country total / du total du pays	of ** (1) / des ** (1)	of world / du monde
Rwanda (**=Developing) (2)				
All commodity groups	504 071	100.0	0.01	0.00
287 Base metal ores & concentrates nes	159 793	31.7	0.86	0.49
074 Tea and maté	122 920	24.4	1.94	1.47
071 Coffee and coffee substitutes	83 739	16.6	0.33	0.21
334 Heavy petroleum & bituminous oil	21 039	4.2	0.00	0.00
046 Wheat meal & flour, meslin flour	10 130	2.0	0.34	0.17
851 Footwear	10 071	2.0	0.01	0.01
211 Raw hides & skins, excluding furskins	7 983	1.6	0.87	0.10
781 Passenger cars and race cars	6 465	1.3	0.01	0.00
292 Crude vegetable materials nes	5 834	1.2	0.04	0.01
001 Live animal excl. fish & crustacean	5 607	1.1	0.12	0.03
Remainder	70 490	13.9		
Saint Helena - Sainte-Hélène (**=Developing) (2)				
All commodity groups	40 586	100.0	0.00	0.00
034 Fish, fresh live chilled frozen	13 746	33.9	0.05	0.02
036 Crustacean mollusc aquat invertebra	11 480	28.3	0.05	0.04
764 Telecom equipment part nes	3 015	7.4	0.00	0.00
752 Computer equipment nes	1 794	4.4	0.00	0.00
776 Valves tubes; diodes, transistors	1 580	3.9	0.00	0.00
562 Manufactured fertilizer excl. crude	1 351	3.3	0.01	0.00
582 Plastic sheet film foil & strips	1 228	3.0	0.00	0.00
874 Measure analyze control device nes	462	1.1	0.00	0.00
899 Manufactured articles nes	448	1.1	0.00	0.00
728 Special industrial machine part nes	363	0.9	0.00	0.00
Remainder	5 119	12.7		
Saint Kitts and Nevis - Saint-Kitts-et-Nevis (**=Developing) (2)				
All commodity groups	44 943	100.0	0.00	0.00
772 Electrical circuit equipment	12 582	28.0	0.01	0.01
764 Telecom equipment part nes	8 316	18.5	0.00	0.00
716 Rotating electric plant parts nes	3 338	7.4	0.01	0.00
793 Ships boats floating structures	2 610	5.8	0.00	0.00
892 Printed matter	1 918	4.3	0.01	0.00
771 Electric power machine part excl. 716	1 849	4.1	0.00	0.00
842 Female clothing, woven	1 683	3.7	0.00	0.00
112 Alcoholic beverages	1 020	2.3	0.01	0.00
111 Non alcoholic beverage nes	747	1.7	0.02	0.00
778 Electrical machinery apparatus nes	661	1.5	0.00	0.00
Remainder	10 219	22.7		
Saint Lucia - Sainte-Lucie (**=Developing) (2)				
All commodity groups	160 721	100.0	0.00	0.00
334 Heavy petroleum & bituminous oil	46 523	28.9	0.01	0.00
057 Fruit nut (exc oil), fresh or dried	32 089	20.0	0.07	0.04
112 Alcoholic beverages	12 055	7.5	0.09	0.02
642 Cut paper and paperboard articles	4 962	3.1	0.03	0.01
764 Telecom equipment part nes	4 691	2.9	0.00	0.00
885 Watches and clocks	3 365	2.1	0.02	0.01
897 Jewellery nes (667)	3 129	1.9	0.00	0.00
874 Measure analyze control device nes	3 077	1.9	0.01	0.00
111 Non alcoholic beverage nes	2 548	1.6	0.05	0.01
321 Coal excluding non-agglomomerated	2 330	1.4	0.01	0.00
Remainder	45 952	28.7		
Saint Pierre and Miquelon - Saint-Pierre-et-Miquelon (**=Developed) (2)				
All commodity groups	6 275	100.0	0.00	0.00
792 Aircraft, spacecraft & equipment	1 618	25.8	0.00	0.00
036 Crustacean mollusc aquat invertebra	1 234	19.7	0.01	0.00
034 Fish, fresh live chilled frozen	682	10.9	0.00	0.00
035 Fish, dried salted smoked	626	10.0	0.02	0.01
842 Female clothing, woven	520	8.3	0.00	0.00
845 Articles of apparel nes	437	7.0	0.00	0.00
844 Female clothing, knitted crocheted	212	3.4	0.00	0.00
682 Copper	88	1.4	0.00	0.00
831 Case bag: storage travel shopping	75	1.2	0.00	0.00
851 Footwear	71	1.1	0.00	0.00
Remainder	712	11.2		

Leading products exported based on average 2011-2012 values SITC Revision 3 (3-digit level) / Principaux produits exportés d'après la moyenne des valeurs de 2011-2012 CTCI révision 3 (positions à 3 chiffres)	Value (f.o.b., thousands of dollars) Valeur (f.a.b., milliers de dollars)	of country total / du total du pays	of ** (1) / des ** (1)	of world / du monde
Saint Vincent and the Grenadines-Saint-Vincent-et-les Grenadines(**=Developing)(2)				
All commodity groups	40 737	100.0	0.00	0.00
793 Ships boats floating structures	11 058	27.1	0.01	0.01
046 Wheat meal & flour, meslin flour	6 613	16.2	0.23	0.11
054 Vegetable & vegetable products nes	3 260	8.0	0.01	0.01
792 Aircraft, spacecraft & equipment	2 244	5.5	0.01	0.00
042 Rice	1 904	4.7	0.01	0.01
081 Animal feed excluding unmilled cereal	1 893	4.6	0.01	0.00
111 Non alcoholic beverage nes	1 149	2.8	0.02	0.01
112 Alcoholic beverages	1 075	2.6	0.01	0.00
057 Fruit nut (exc oil), fresh or dried	1 068	2.6	0.00	0.00
674 Flat plated iron non-alloy steel	973	2.4	0.00	0.00
Remainder	9 500	23.5		
Samoa (**=Developing) (2)				
All commodity groups	71 183	100.0	0.00	0.00
773 Electrical distribute equipment nes	19 821	27.8	0.04	0.02
112 Alcoholic beverages	11 102	15.6	0.08	0.01
034 Fish, fresh live chilled frozen	5 866	8.2	0.02	0.01
772 Electrical circuit equipment	2 734	3.8	0.00	0.00
422 Fixed veg fat and oil, excl. "soft"	2 138	3.0	0.00	0.00
054 Vegetable & vegetable products nes	1 968	2.8	0.01	0.00
884 Optical goods fibres nes	1 907	2.7	0.01	0.00
782 Goods and service vehicles	1 276	1.8	0.00	0.00
111 Non alcoholic beverage nes	1 210	1.7	0.02	0.01
851 Footwear	1 145	1.6	0.00	0.00
Remainder	22 016	31.0		
Sao Tome and Principe - Sao Tomé-et-Príncipe (**=Developing) (2)				
All commodity groups	11 021	100.0	0.00	0.00
072 Cocoa	4 594	41.7	0.03	0.02
885 Watches and clocks	2 547	23.1	0.01	0.01
897 Jewellery nes (667)	1 500	13.6	0.00	0.00
784 Motor vehicle parts and accessories	147	1.3	0.00	0.00
073 Chocolate & cocoa preparations nes	125	1.1	0.00	0.00
971 Gold non-monetary excluding ores	123	1.1	0.00	0.00
282 Ferrous iron & steel, waste & scrap	117	1.1	0.00	0.00
057 Fruit nut (exc oil), fresh or dried	108	1.0	0.00	0.00
334 Heavy petroleum & bituminous oil	106	1.0	0.00	0.00
781 Passenger cars and race cars	102	0.9	0.00	0.00
Remainder	1 552	14.1		
Saudi Arabia - Arabie saoudite (**=Developing) (2)				
All commodity groups	376 513 540	100.0	4.69	2.06
333 Crude petroleum & bituminous oil	288 573 005	76.6	23.01	16.81
334 Heavy petroleum & bituminous oil	20 633 049	5.5	4.87	2.09
571 Primary form ethylene polymers	10 194 851	2.7	26.90	13.07
512 Alcohols, phenols; derivatives	9 260 193	2.5	27.05	14.81
342 Liquefied propane and butane	6 308 128	1.7	15.96	10.68
575 Other plastics, in primary forms	6 118 317	1.6	16.02	5.39
511 Hydrocarbons nes; derivatives	4 152 035	1.1	9.97	4.24
516 Other organic chemicals	2 432 279	0.6	15.96	5.82
562 Manufactured fertilizer excl. crude	2 082 926	0.6	7.88	2.76
522 Inorganic chemical elem oxide salt	1 185 542	0.3	4.12	1.94
Remainder	25 573 215	6.8		
Senegal - Sénégal (**=Developing) (2)				
All commodity groups	2 536 685	100.0	0.03	0.01
334 Heavy petroleum & bituminous oil	504 089	19.9	0.12	0.05
522 Inorganic chemical elem oxide salt	303 195	12.0	1.05	0.50
034 Fish, fresh live chilled frozen	224 038	8.8	0.84	0.37
661 Lime cement construction material	172 804	6.8	1.01	0.58
971 Gold non-monetary excluding ores	142 439	5.6	0.11	0.06
036 Crustacean mollusc aquat invertebra	128 212	5.1	0.61	0.40
421 Fixed veg fat and oil, "soft"	76 653	3.0	0.58	0.19
098 Edible products & preparations nes	72 521	2.9	0.43	0.12
122 Manufactured tabacco	64 387	2.5	0.76	0.21
676 Iron steel bar rod section piling	57 244	2.3	0.18	0.06
Remainder	791 103	31.1		

For sources and notes, see end of table.

Pour les sources et les notes, se reporter à la fin du tableau.

Leading products exported based on average 2011-2012 values SITC Revision 3 (3-digit level) / Principaux produits exportés d'après la moyenne des valeurs de 2011-2012 CTCI révision 3 (positions à 3 chiffres)	2011-2012			
	Value (f.o.b., thousands of dollars) / Valeur (f.a.b., milliers de dollars)	As percentage / En pourcentage		
		of country total / du total du pays	of ** (1) / des ** (1)	of world / du monde
Serbia - Serbie (=Transition)**				
All commodity groups	11 566 292	100.0	1.39	0.06
044 Maize unmilled, excluding sweet corn	513 527	4.4	13.14	1.46
682 Copper	509 815	4.4	4.56	0.35
673 Flat iron non-alloy steel products	394 075	3.4	3.80	0.45
773 Electrical distribute equipment nes	370 467	3.2	14.15	0.33
625 Rubber for wheels, incl inner tube	320 099	2.8	15.00	0.34
058 Fruit preserve preparation excl. juice	301 354	2.6	47.83	1.57
851 Footwear	256 541	2.2	15.00	0.22
893 Articles of plastic nes	237 507	2.1	17.36	0.17
684 Aluminium	236 011	2.0	2.35	0.20
846 Clothing accessory excl. 831 848 851	224 760	1.9	36.09	0.78
Remainder	8 202 136	71.0		
Seychelles (=Developing) (2)**				
All commodity groups	489 851	100.0	0.01	0.00
037 Fish shellfish, prepared preserved	244 536	49.9	1.32	0.93
034 Fish, fresh live chilled frozen	97 761	20.0	0.37	0.16
035 Fish, dried salted smoked	56 789	11.6	3.37	0.96
872 Medical instruments appliances nes	15 405	3.1	0.08	0.02
334 Heavy petroleum & bituminous oil	14 031	2.9	0.00	0.00
036 Crustacean mollusc aquat invertebra	7 034	1.4	0.03	0.02
411 Animals oils and fats	5 902	1.2	0.49	0.09
899 Manufactured articles nes	5 257	1.1	0.02	0.01
081 Animal feed excluding unmilled cereal	4 297	0.9	0.01	0.01
282 Ferrous iron & steel, waste & scrap	2 913	0.6	0.05	0.01
Remainder	35 926	7.3		
Sierra Leone (=Developing) (2)**				
All commodity groups	730 954	100.0	0.01	0.00
281 Iron ore and concentrates	123 469	16.9	0.21	0.09
667 Pearls, precious semiprecious stone	113 854	15.6	0.14	0.07
001 Live animal excl. fish & crustacean	103 053	14.1	2.22	0.47
287 Base metal ores & concentrates nes	73 011	10.0	0.39	0.22
697 Base metal household equipment nes	48 636	6.7	0.27	0.16
072 Cocoa	45 441	6.2	0.33	0.22
285 Aluminium ore concentrate alumina	41 430	5.7	0.71	0.27
793 Ships boats floating structures	36 990	5.1	0.03	0.02
034 Fish, fresh live chilled frozen	22 538	3.1	0.08	0.04
282 Ferrous iron & steel, waste & scrap	7 675	1.0	0.12	0.01
Remainder	114 857	15.6		
Singapore - Singapour (=Developing)**				
All commodity groups	408 948 325	100.0	5.10	2.24
776 Valves tubes; diodes, transistors	82 701 502	20.2	20.53	14.87
334 Heavy petroleum & bituminous oil	76 225 229	18.6	17.99	7.73
759 Office equipment part & accessories	16 132 170	3.9	14.02	8.44
764 Telecom equipment part nes	10 781 535	2.6	3.08	2.08
752 Computer equipment nes	9 162 749	2.2	3.68	2.60
728 Special industrial machine part nes	7 546 883	1.8	17.72	4.12
772 Electrical circuit equipment	6 841 720	1.7	6.59	2.92
515 Organo-inorganic compound acid salt	6 827 318	1.7	28.61	6.11
778 Electrical machinery apparatus nes	6 706 232	1.6	6.03	2.98
874 Measure analyze control device nes	6 541 729	1.6	16.06	3.59
Remainder	179 481 258	44.1		
Sint Maarten (Dutch part) - Saint-Martin (partie néerlandaise) (=Developing)**				
All commodity groups	128 816	100.0	0.00	0.00
971 Gold non-monetary excluding ores	10 590	8.2	0.01	0.00
288 Non ferrous base metal waste nes	3 031	2.4	0.03	0.01
897 Jewellery nes (667)	3 011	2.3	0.00	0.00
764 Telecom equipment part nes	1 710	1.3	0.00	0.00
112 Alcoholic beverages	680	0.5	0.00	0.00
763 Sound TV recorder or reproducer	464	0.4	0.00	0.00
335 Residual petroleum products nes	351	0.3	0.00	0.00
122 Manufactured tabacco	313	0.2	0.00	0.00
289 Prec metal ore concentrate excl. gold	297	0.2	0.00	0.00
781 Passenger cars and race cars	242	0.2	0.00	0.00
Remainder	108 127	84.0		

Leading products exported based on average 2011-2012 values SITC Revision 3 (3-digit level) / Principaux produits exportés d'après la moyenne des valeurs de 2011-2012 CTCI révision 3 (positions à 3 chiffres)	2011-2012			
	Value (f.o.b., thousands of dollars) / Valeur (f.a.b., milliers de dollars)	As percentage / En pourcentage		
		of country total / du total du pays	of ** (1) / des ** (1)	of world / du monde
Slovakia - Slovaquie (=Developed)**				
All commodity groups	79 619 620	100.0	0.84	0.44
781 Passenger cars and race cars	12 506 848	15.7	2.37	1.95
761 Television video receive project	6 974 830	8.8	19.56	7.61
784 Motor vehicle parts and accessories	4 797 884	6.0	1.83	1.34
334 Heavy petroleum & bituminous oil	3 825 695	4.8	0.87	0.39
764 Telecom equipment part nes	3 595 866	4.5	2.16	0.70
673 Flat iron non-alloy steel products	1 713 561	2.2	3.43	1.96
773 Electrical distribute equipment nes	1 552 930	2.0	2.76	1.38
699 Base metal manufactures nes	1 519 103	1.9	1.68	1.05
625 Rubber for wheels, incl inner tube	1 407 512	1.8	2.69	1.52
851 Footwear	1 208 157	1.5	2.87	1.05
Remainder	40 517 234	50.8		
Slovenia - Slovénie (=Developed) (2)**				
All commodity groups	33 464 033	100.0	0.35	0.18
542 Medicines including veterinary	2 415 632	7.2	0.79	0.72
781 Passenger cars and race cars	2 280 664	6.8	0.43	0.35
775 Household equipment nes	1 130 385	3.4	2.82	1.19
778 Electrical machinery apparatus nes	1 030 373	3.1	0.92	0.46
334 Heavy petroleum & bituminous oil	848 967	2.5	0.19	0.09
351 Electric current	841 994	2.5	2.73	2.14
684 Aluminium	737 939	2.2	1.04	0.62
821 Furniture part; bedding furnishing	724 149	2.2	0.97	0.48
784 Motor vehicle parts and accessories	709 803	2.1	0.27	0.20
716 Rotating electric plant parts nes	595 113	1.8	0.99	0.62
Remainder	22 149 014	66.2		
Solomon Islands - Îles Salomon (=Developing) (2)**				
All commodity groups	456 598	100.0	0.01	0.00
247 Wood in rough or roughly squared	277 436	60.8	5.45	1.81
971 Gold non-monetary excluding ores	57 890	12.7	0.04	0.02
422 Fixed veg fat and oil, excl. "soft"	29 483	6.5	0.07	0.06
034 Fish, fresh live chilled frozen	21 029	4.6	0.08	0.04
037 Fish shellfish, prepared preserved	20 134	4.4	0.11	0.08
072 Cocoa	9 136	2.0	0.07	0.04
223 Oil seed for non soft oil	7 748	1.7	0.99	0.23
248 Wood simply worked, railway sleeper	6 526	1.4	0.08	0.02
001 Live animal excl. fish & crustacean	3 086	0.7	0.07	0.01
282 Ferrous iron & steel, waste & scrap	2 078	0.5	0.03	0.00
Remainder	22 052	4.7		
Somalia - Somalie (=Developing) (2)**				
All commodity groups	515 000	100.0	0.01	0.00
001 Live animal excl. fish & crustacean	371 075	72.1	7.99	1.70
245 Fuel wood excl. waste; wood charcoal	33 948	6.6	6.60	2.64
211 Raw hides & skins, excluding furskins	22 882	4.4	2.49	0.28
611 Leather	17 223	3.3	0.13	0.07
222 Oil seed etc for soft oil	17 103	3.3	0.06	0.02
043 Barley grain unmilled	12 490	2.4	1.47	0.16
781 Passenger cars and race cars	8 401	1.6	0.01	0.00
292 Crude vegetable materials nes	5 662	1.1	0.04	0.01
574 Polyacetals and polyesters, etc	4 209	0.8	0.02	0.01
742 Liquid pump; liquid elevator parts	4 137	0.8	0.03	0.01
Remainder	17 870	3.6		
South Africa - Afrique du Sud (=Developing) (2)**				
All commodity groups	89 843 792	100.0	1.12	0.49
681 Silver, platinum, platinum metals	8 618 277	9.6	29.94	12.80
281 Iron ore and concentrates	6 810 981	7.6	11.72	4.98
971 Gold non-monetary excluding ores	5 755 219	6.4	4.33	2.29
321 Coal excluding non-agglomomerated	5 421 252	6.0	11.98	4.10
671 Pig & sponge iron, ferro alloys etc	3 889 227	4.3	18.01	9.23
781 Passenger cars and race cars	3 509 005	3.9	3.09	0.55
287 Base metal ores & concentrates nes	3 392 328	3.8	18.17	10.42
667 Pearls, precious semiprecious stone	2 478 551	2.8	3.14	1.61
057 Fruit nut (exc oil), fresh or dried	2 323 604	2.6	5.30	2.68
743 Gas pump, compressor, fan, filter	2 071 706	2.3	5.88	1.67
Remainder	45 573 642	50.7		

For sources and notes, see end of table.

Pour les sources et les notes, se reporter à la fin du tableau.

Leading products exported based on average 2011-2012 values SITC Revision 3 (3-digit level) / Principaux produits exportés d'après la moyenne des valeurs de 2011-2012 CTCI révision 3 (positions à 3 chiffres)	Value (f.o.b., thousands of dollars) Valeur (f.a.b., milliers de dollars)	As percentage / En pourcentage		
		of country total / du total du pays	of ** (1) / des ** (1)	of world / du monde
Spain - Espagne (**=Developed) (2)				
All commodity groups	292 053 705	100.0	3.09	1.60
781 Passenger cars and race cars	27 797 854	9.5	5.27	4.32
334 Heavy petroleum & bituminous oil	16 375 475	5.6	3.72	1.66
784 Motor vehicle parts and accessories	11 073 605	3.8	4.23	3.09
542 Medicines including veterinary	9 569 138	3.3	3.12	2.84
057 Fruit nut (exc oil), fresh or dried	7 752 195	2.7	18.92	8.93
782 Goods and service vehicles	5 645 878	1.9	6.75	4.27
054 Vegetable & vegetable products nes	5 515 319	1.9	15.99	9.23
676 Iron steel bar rod section piling	5 482 659	1.9	10.42	5.97
792 Aircraft, spacecraft & equipment	4 505 426	1.5	3.28	2.80
112 Alcoholic beverages	4 101 292	1.4	6.72	5.36
Remainder	194 234 864	66.5		
Sri Lanka (**=Developing)				
All commodity groups	9 690 533	100.0	0.12	0.05
074 Tea and maté	1 452 061	15.0	22.87	17.34
845 Articles of apparel nes	1 157 444	11.9	1.17	0.82
844 Female clothing, knitted crocheted	826 218	8.5	1.87	1.48
842 Female clothing, woven	783 998	8.1	1.45	0.96
841 Male clothing, woven	588 899	6.1	1.20	0.83
625 Rubber for wheels, incl inner tube	556 328	5.7	1.45	0.60
667 Pearls, precious semiprecious stone	425 994	4.4	0.54	0.28
843 Male clothing, knitted crocheted	272 138	2.8	1.06	0.89
846 Clothing accessory excl. 831 848 851	253 779	2.6	1.35	0.88
075 Spices	228 915	2.4	3.28	2.68
Remainder	3 144 759	32.5		
State of Palestine - État de Palestine (**=Developing)				
All commodity groups	834 300	100.0	0.01	0.00
661 Lime cement construction material	139 574	16.7	0.82	0.47
821 Furniture part; bedding furnishing	72 767	8.7	0.10	0.05
282 Ferrous iron & steel, waste & scrap	72 610	8.7	1.15	0.13
851 Footwear	42 293	5.1	0.06	0.04
893 Articles of plastic nes	36 275	4.3	0.07	0.03
288 Non ferrous base metal waste nes	28 750	3.4	0.28	0.06
122 Manufactured tabacco	25 800	3.1	0.30	0.08
022 Milk products, excl. butter & cheese	23 087	2.8	0.39	0.05
421 Fixed veg fat and oil, "soft"	19 100	2.3	0.14	0.05
635 Wood manufactures nes	16 077	1.9	0.17	0.06
Remainder	357 967	43.0		
Sudan - Soudan (**=Developing)				
All commodity groups	3 383 882	100.0	0.02	0.01
971 Gold non-monetary excluding ores	1 648 086	48.7	0.62	0.33
333 Crude petroleum & bituminous oil	947 976	28.0	0.04	0.03
222 Oil seed etc for soft oil	153 574	4.5	0.26	0.11
001 Live animal excl. fish & crustacean	98 954	2.9	1.07	0.23
335 Residual petroleum products nes	78 916	2.3	0.21	0.08
611 Leather	75 312	2.2	0.29	0.16
511 Hydrocarbons nes; derivatives	69 040	2.0	0.08	0.04
292 Crude vegetable materials nes	60 036	1.8	0.19	0.07
061 Sugar, mollasses and honey	31 558	0.9	0.05	0.03
081 Animal feed excluding unmilled cereal	23 112	0.7	0.04	0.02
Remainder	98 659	6.0		
Suriname (**=Developing) (2)				
All commodity groups	2 515 225	100.0	0.03	0.01
971 Gold non-monetary excluding ores	788 306	31.3	0.59	0.31
285 Aluminium ore concentrate alumina	552 565	22.0	9.46	3.64
334 Heavy petroleum & bituminous oil	234 687	9.3	0.06	0.02
034 Fish, fresh live chilled frozen	66 561	2.6	0.25	0.11
057 Fruit nut (exc oil), fresh or dried	50 661	2.0	0.12	0.06
042 Rice	38 330	1.5	0.19	0.16
036 Crustacean mollusc aquat invertebra	26 864	1.1	0.13	0.08
723 Civil engineering plant & equipment	21 909	0.9	0.06	0.02
247 Wood in rough or roughly squared	17 906	0.7	0.35	0.12
111 Non alcoholic beverage nes	17 779	0.7	0.36	0.09
Remainder	699 657	27.9		
Swaziland (**=Developing) (2)				
All commodity groups	1 905 000	100.0	0.02	0.01
061 Sugar, mollasses and honey	299 610	15.7	0.94	0.66
251 Pulp and waste paper	157 713	8.3	1.34	0.33
551 Essential oils, perfumes & flavours	155 708	8.2	3.00	0.62
971 Gold non-monetary excluding ores	99 200	5.2	0.07	0.04
057 Fruit nut (exc oil), fresh or dried	90 724	4.8	0.21	0.10
845 Articles of apparel nes	53 496	2.8	0.05	0.04
512 Alcohols, phenols; derivatives	49 060	2.6	0.14	0.08
671 Pig & sponge iron, ferro alloys etc	41 465	2.2	0.19	0.10
098 Edible products & preparations nes	40 351	2.1	0.24	0.06
058 Fruit preserve preparation excl. juice	40 261	2.1	0.43	0.21
Remainder	877 412	46.0		
Sweden - Suède (**=Developed)				
All commodity groups	179 905 034	100.0	1.91	0.98
334 Heavy petroleum & bituminous oil	12 431 589	6.9	2.82	1.26
641 Paper and paperboard	10 273 135	5.7	10.90	8.59
764 Telecom equipment part nes	9 488 371	5.3	5.71	1.83
784 Motor vehicle parts and accessories	6 978 302	3.9	2.67	1.95
542 Medicines including veterinary	6 765 643	3.8	2.21	2.01
781 Passenger cars and race cars	6 182 782	3.4	1.17	0.96
713 Internal combustion engine part nes	3 572 162	2.0	2.83	2.20
675 Flat rolled products of alloy steel	3 559 239	2.0	7.50	5.05
281 Iron ore and concentrates	3 446 274	1.9	4.85	2.52
248 Wood simply worked, railway sleeper	3 376 509	1.9	13.71	9.11
Remainder	113 831 028	63.2		
Switzerland - Suisse (**=Developed)				
All commodity groups	230 384 012	100.0	2.44	1.26
542 Medicines including veterinary	31 816 726	13.8	10.37	9.45
541 Pharmaceuticals excluding medicines	26 987 054	11.7	18.91	16.53
885 Watches and clocks	22 314 130	9.7	67.87	44.54
897 Jewellery nes (667)	8 941 374	3.9	20.74	7.19
515 Organo-inorganic compound acid salt	8 127 831	3.5	9.35	7.27
899 Manufactured articles nes	6 441 677	2.8	12.24	7.89
351 Electric current	6 420 990	2.8	20.80	16.31
874 Measure analyze control device nes	5 073 453	2.2	3.62	2.78
728 Special industrial machine part nes	4 809 734	2.1	3.44	2.62
681 Silver, platinum, platinum metals	4 725 171	2.1	12.53	7.02
Remainder	104 725 872	45.4		
Syrian Arab Republic - République arabe syrienne (**=Developing) (2)				
All commodity groups	7 000 000	100.0	0.09	0.04
333 Crude petroleum & bituminous oil	1 387 487	19.8	0.11	0.08
334 Heavy petroleum & bituminous oil	709 350	10.1	0.17	0.07
111 Non alcoholic beverage nes	429 254	6.1	8.64	2.17
054 Vegetable & vegetable products nes	383 543	5.5	1.60	0.64
057 Fruit nut (exc oil), fresh or dried	298 913	4.3	0.68	0.34
001 Live animal excl. fish & crustacean	170 115	2.4	3.66	0.78
554 Soaps cleansers polishes	162 835	2.3	1.42	0.40
773 Electrical distribute equipment nes	142 866	2.0	0.27	0.13
272 Crude fertilizer, excl. manufactured	138 522	2.0	3.64	2.75
025 Eggs, yolks and albumin	129 284	1.8	9.90	2.32
Remainder	3 047 831	43.7		
Tajikistan - Tadjikistan (**=Transition) (2)				
All commodity groups	1 283 244	100.0	0.15	0.01
684 Aluminium	618 149	48.2	6.15	0.52
263 Cotton	211 013	16.4	5.10	0.81
652 Woven cotton fabrics	49 059	3.8	13.24	0.15
287 Base metal ores & concentrates nes	46 604	3.6	3.11	0.14
057 Fruit nut (exc oil), fresh or dried	28 025	2.2	1.38	0.03
351 Electric current	20 090	1.6	0.81	0.05
841 Male clothing, woven	17 903	1.4	1.76	0.03
651 Textile yarn	15 992	1.2	1.04	0.03
288 Non ferrous base metal waste nes	12 365	1.0	1.65	0.03
283 Copper ores and concentrates	11 932	0.9	0.95	0.02
Remainder	252 112	19.7		

For sources and notes, see end of table.

Pour les sources et les notes, se reporter à la fin du tableau.

Leading products exported based on average 2011-2012 values — SITC Revision 3 (3-digit level)
Principaux produits exportés d'après la moyenne des valeurs de 2011-2012 — CTCI révision 3 (positions à 3 chiffres)

Columns: Value (f.o.b., thousands of dollars) / Valeur (f.a.b., milliers de dollars) — As percentage (En pourcentage): of country total (du total du pays) · of ** (1) (des ** (1)) · of world (du monde) — period 2011-2012

TFYR of Macedonia - l'ERY de Macédoine (**=Transition) (2)

Product	Value	of country total	of ** (1)	of world
All commodity groups	4 228 616	100.0	0.51	0.02
598 Miscellaneous chemical products nes	524 262	12.4	50.85	0.42
671 Pig & sponge iron, ferro alloys etc	488 789	11.6	4.46	1.16
842 Female clothing, woven	257 749	6.1	23.90	0.31
334 Heavy petroleum & bituminous oil	250 405	5.9	0.21	0.03
841 Male clothing, woven	213 109	5.0	20.91	0.30
673 Flat iron non-alloy steel products	190 681	4.5	1.84	0.22
743 Gas pump, compressor, fan, filter	141 275	3.3	12.99	0.11
121 Unmanufactured tabacco and refuse	119 708	2.8	42.94	0.98
679 Iron steel pipe tube fittings etc	111 144	2.6	2.63	0.11
287 Base metal ores & concentrates nes	98 316	2.3	6.55	0.30
Remainder	1 833 178	43.5		

Thailand - Thaïlande (**=Developing)

Product	Value	of country total	of ** (1)	of world
All commodity groups	229 184 243	100.0	2.86	1.25
752 Computer equipment nes	12 521 554	5.5	5.03	3.55
231 Natural rubber, latex, gum, etc	10 961 073	4.8	34.23	32.39
334 Heavy petroleum & bituminous oil	10 740 850	4.7	2.53	1.09
776 Valves tubes; diodes, transistors	8 442 704	3.7	2.10	1.52
782 Goods and service vehicles	7 961 847	3.5	17.24	6.02
971 Gold non-monetary excluding ores	6 307 838	2.8	4.75	2.51
781 Passenger cars and race cars	5 972 513	2.6	5.26	0.93
042 Rice	5 569 871	2.4	27.54	22.63
784 Motor vehicle parts and accessories	5 251 021	2.3	5.50	1.46
037 Fish shellfish, prepared preserved	5 123 251	2.2	27.61	19.38
Remainder	150 331 721	65.5		

Timor-Leste (**=Developing) (2)

Product	Value	of country total	of ** (1)	of world
All commodity groups	12 000	100.0	0.00	0.00
333 Crude petroleum & bituminous oil	7 059	58.8	0.00	0.00
342 Liquefied propane and butane	2 220	18.5	0.01	0.00
071 Coffee and coffee substitutes	939	7.8	0.00	0.00
723 Civil engineering plant & equipment	436	3.6	0.00	0.00
772 Electrical circuit equipment	67	0.6	0.00	0.00
782 Goods and service vehicles	36	0.3	0.00	0.00
247 Wood in rough or roughly squared	34	0.3	0.00	0.00
764 Telecom equipment part nes	31	0.3	0.00	0.00
598 Miscellaneous chemical products nes	31	0.3	0.00	0.00
579 Plastic waste, parings and scrap	29	0.2	0.00	0.00
Remainder	1 118	9.3		

Togo (**=Developing) (2)

Product	Value	of country total	of ** (1)	of world
All commodity groups	1 000 203	100.0	0.01	0.01
661 Lime cement construction material	116 944	11.7	0.68	0.40
272 Crude fertilizer, excl. manufactured	115 990	11.6	3.05	2.30
072 Cocoa	115 787	11.6	0.85	0.56
263 Cotton	90 811	9.1	0.83	0.35
971 Gold non-monetary excluding ores	89 264	8.9	0.07	0.04
071 Coffee and coffee substitutes	40 975	4.1	0.16	0.10
334 Heavy petroleum & bituminous oil	40 809	4.1	0.01	0.00
893 Articles of plastic nes	30 061	3.0	0.05	0.02
553 Perfume toilet cosmetics, excl. soap	24 473	2.4	0.13	0.03
562 Manufactured fertilizer excl. crude	23 816	2.4	0.09	0.03
Remainder	311 273	31.1		

Tokelau - Tokélaou (**=Developing) (2)

Product	Value	of country total	of ** (1)	of world
All commodity groups	111	100.0	0.00	0.00
676 Iron steel bar rod section piling	35	31.5	0.00	0.00
821 Furniture part; bedding furnishing	8	7.2	0.00	0.00
781 Passenger cars and race cars	5	4.2	0.00	0.00
542 Medicines including veterinary	3	3.1	0.00	0.00
741 Heating, cooling equipment parts nes	3	3.1	0.00	0.00
742 Liquid pump; liquid elevator parts	2	1.9	0.00	0.00
896 Work of art & collections; antiques	2	1.8	0.00	0.00
694 Nails screws nuts bolts rivets	2	1.7	0.00	0.00
845 Articles of apparel nes	2	1.6	0.00	0.00
642 Cut paper and paperboard articles	2	1.5	0.00	0.00
Remainder	47	42.4		

Tonga (**=Developing) (2)

Product	Value	of country total	of ** (1)	of world
All commodity groups	14 988	100.0	0.00	0.00
054 Vegetable & vegetable products nes	3 762	25.1	0.02	0.01
034 Fish, fresh live chilled frozen	1 934	12.9	0.01	0.00
292 Crude vegetable materials nes	1 777	11.9	0.01	0.00
036 Crustacean mollusc aquat invertebra	754	5.0	0.00	0.00
057 Fruit nut (exc oil), fresh or dried	529	3.5	0.00	0.00
892 Printed matter	509	3.4	0.00	0.00
247 Wood in rough or roughly squared	449	3.0	0.01	0.00
282 Ferrous iron & steel, waste & scrap	413	2.8	0.01	0.00
744 Mechanical handling equipment nes	366	2.4	0.00	0.00
288 Non ferrous base metal waste nes	297	2.0	0.00	0.00
Remainder	4 198	28.0		

Trinidad and Tobago - Trinité-et-Tobago (**=Developing) (2)

Product	Value	of country total	of ** (1)	of world
All commodity groups	13 962 651	100.0	0.17	0.08
343 Natural gas, liquefied or not	3 819 746	27.4	2.39	1.10
334 Heavy petroleum & bituminous oil	2 957 681	21.2	0.70	0.30
522 Inorganic chemical elem oxide salt	2 062 286	14.8	7.17	3.37
333 Crude petroleum & bituminous oil	1 580 077	11.3	0.13	0.09
512 Alcohols, phenols; derivatives	887 167	6.4	2.59	1.42
671 Pig & sponge iron, ferro alloys etc	516 343	3.7	2.39	1.23
281 Iron ore and concentrates	312 410	2.2	0.54	0.23
342 Liquefied propane and butane	253 207	1.8	0.64	0.43
562 Manufactured fertilizer excl. crude	227 398	1.6	0.86	0.30
676 Iron steel bar rod section piling	222 387	1.6	0.70	0.24
Remainder	1 123 949	8.0		

Tunisia - Tunisie (**=Developing) (2)

Product	Value	of country total	of ** (1)	of world
All commodity groups	17 427 247	100.0	0.22	0.10
333 Crude petroleum & bituminous oil	2 262 843	13.0	0.18	0.13
845 Articles of apparel nes	1 603 574	9.2	1.62	1.14
773 Electrical distribute equipment nes	1 516 239	8.7	2.84	1.35
841 Male clothing, woven	850 649	4.9	1.74	1.19
772 Electrical circuit equipment	755 330	4.3	0.73	0.32
421 Fixed veg fat and oil, "soft"	654 011	3.8	4.92	1.64
562 Manufactured fertilizer excl. crude	589 580	3.4	2.23	0.78
851 Footwear	521 952	3.0	0.73	0.45
842 Female clothing, woven	487 763	2.8	0.90	0.60
761 Television video receive project	459 057	2.6	0.83	0.50
Remainder	7 726 249	44.3		

Turkey - Turquie (**=Developing)

Product	Value	of country total	of ** (1)	of world
All commodity groups	143 725 952	100.0	1.79	0.79
971 Gold non-monetary excluding ores	7 409 782	5.2	5.58	2.95
676 Iron steel bar rod section piling	7 314 373	5.1	23.09	7.97
334 Heavy petroleum & bituminous oil	6 299 632	4.4	1.49	0.64
781 Passenger cars and race cars	6 277 351	4.4	5.53	0.98
845 Articles of apparel nes	4 940 874	3.4	5.00	3.52
782 Goods and service vehicles	3 822 309	2.7	8.28	2.89
057 Fruit nut (exc oil), fresh or dried	3 799 799	2.6	8.67	4.38
775 Household equipment nes	3 567 665	2.5	6.63	3.75
784 Motor vehicle parts and accessories	3 483 527	2.4	3.65	0.97
842 Female clothing, woven	2 933 751	2.0	5.44	3.58
Remainder	93 876 889	65.3		

Turkmenistan - Turkménistan (**=Transition) (2)

Product	Value	of country total	of ** (1)	of world
All commodity groups	14 750 000	100.0	1.78	0.08
343 Natural gas, liquefied or not	7 736 283	52.4	9.75	2.23
263 Cotton	1 984 608	13.5	47.99	7.57
334 Heavy petroleum & bituminous oil	1 593 693	10.8	1.31	0.16
522 Inorganic chemical elem oxide salt	486 653	3.3	10.82	0.79
333 Crude petroleum & bituminous oil	475 847	3.2	0.18	0.03
657 Special yarn and textile fabric etc	367 039	2.5	47.54	0.77
575 Other plastics, in primary forms	357 937	2.4	32.94	0.32
651 Textile yarn	307 605	2.1	19.99	0.54
292 Crude vegetable materials nes	198 252	1.3	48.43	0.46
845 Articles of apparel nes	119 578	0.8	9.14	0.09
Remainder	1 122 505	7.7		

For sources and notes, see end of table.

Pour les sources et les notes, se reporter à la fin du tableau.

Leading products exported based on average 2011-2012 values SITC Revision 3 (3-digit level) Principaux produits exportés d'après la moyenne des valeurs de 2011-2012 CTCI révision 3 (positions à 3 chiffres)	2011-2012 Value (f.o.b., thousands of dollars) Valeur (f.a.b., milliers de dollars)	As percentage / En pourcentage of country total du total du pays	of ** (1) des ** (1)	of world du monde
Turks and Caicos Islands - Îles Turques et Caïques (=Developing) (2)**				
All commodity groups	22 500	100.0	0.00	0.00
892 Printed matter	9 086	40.4	0.06	0.02
036 Crustacean mollusc aquat invertebra	3 581	15.9	0.02	0.01
282 Ferrous iron & steel, waste & scrap	708	3.1	0.01	0.00
288 Non ferrous base metal waste nes	587	2.6	0.01	0.00
723 Civil engineering plant & equipment	473	2.1	0.00	0.00
971 Gold non-monetary excluding ores	421	1.9	0.00	0.00
716 Rotating electric plant parts nes	392	1.7	0.00	0.00
289 Prec metal ore concentrate excl. gold	307	1.4	0.00	0.00
782 Goods and service vehicles	289	1.3	0.00	0.00
793 Ships boats floating structures	263	1.2	0.00	0.00
Remainder	6 393	28.4		
Tuvalu (=Developing) (2)**				
All commodity groups	297	100.0	0.00	0.00
034 Fish, fresh live chilled frozen	201	67.7	0.00	0.00
793 Ships boats floating structures	37	12.4	0.00	0.00
421 Fixed veg fat and oil, "soft"	9	2.9	0.00	0.00
282 Ferrous iron & steel, waste & scrap	4	1.4	0.00	0.00
692 Metal storage transport container	4	1.3	0.00	0.00
516 Other organic chemicals	4	1.3	0.00	0.00
655 Knitted or crocheted fabrics nes	3	1.1	0.00	0.00
571 Primary form ethylene polymers	2	0.7	0.00	0.00
743 Gas pump, compressor, fan, filter	2	0.5	0.00	0.00
742 Liquid pump; liquid elevator parts	1	0.5	0.00	0.00
Remainder	30	10.2		
Uganda - Ouganda (=Developing) (2)**				
All commodity groups	2 258 285	100.0	0.03	0.01
071 Coffee and coffee substitutes	430 805	19.1	1.72	1.06
764 Telecom equipment part nes	177 942	7.9	0.05	0.03
034 Fish, fresh live chilled frozen	112 102	5.0	0.42	0.19
074 Tea and maté	100 306	4.4	1.58	1.20
263 Cotton	99 744	4.4	0.91	0.38
661 Lime cement construction material	98 835	4.4	0.58	0.33
121 Unmanufactured tabacco and refuse	85 535	3.8	1.02	0.70
292 Crude vegetable materials nes	70 953	3.1	0.45	0.16
061 Sugar, mollasses and honey	54 481	2.4	0.17	0.12
072 Cocoa	52 943	2.3	0.39	0.26
Remainder	974 639	43.2		
Ukraine (=Transition)**				
All commodity groups	68 543 765	100.0	8.26	0.37
672 Ingots, Iron steel primary products	6 038 655	8.8	39.51	13.95
673 Flat iron non-alloy steel products	4 225 280	6.2	40.78	4.83
676 Iron steel bar rod section piling	4 039 545	5.9	53.87	4.40
791 Railway vehicles and equipment	3 950 593	5.8	75.16	12.62
421 Fixed veg fat and oil, "soft"	3 615 189	5.3	64.05	9.06
281 Iron ore and concentrates	3 458 992	5.0	44.75	2.53
044 Maize unmilled, excluding sweet corn	2 937 858	4.3	75.17	8.37
334 Heavy petroleum & bituminous oil	2 362 831	3.4	1.94	0.24
679 Iron steel pipe tube fittings etc	1 979 822	2.9	46.94	2.04
671 Pig & sponge iron, ferro alloys etc	1 797 719	2.6	16.42	4.27
Remainder	34 137 281	49.8		
United Arab Emirates - Émirats arabes unis (=Developing) (2)**				
All commodity groups	302 177 626	100.0	3.77	1.65
333 Crude petroleum & bituminous oil	133 493 660	44.2	10.65	7.78
334 Heavy petroleum & bituminous oil	26 432 655	8.7	6.24	2.68
971 Gold non-monetary excluding ores	21 687 567	7.2	16.33	8.63
667 Pearls, precious semiprecious stone	16 115 278	5.3	20.43	10.46
342 Liquefied propane and butane	6 977 823	2.3	17.65	11.82
343 Natural gas, liquefied or not	5 858 865	1.9	3.67	1.69
897 Jewellery nes (667)	4 595 289	1.5	5.67	3.70
684 Aluminium	4 055 298	1.3	10.56	3.40
781 Passenger cars and race cars	3 890 002	1.3	3.43	0.61
764 Telecom equipment part nes	3 336 077	1.1	0.95	0.64
Remainder	75 735 112	25.2		

Leading products exported based on average 2011-2012 values SITC Revision 3 (3-digit level) Principaux produits exportés d'après la moyenne des valeurs de 2011-2012 CTCI révision 3 (positions à 3 chiffres)	2011-2012 Value (f.o.b., thousands of dollars) Valeur (f.a.b., milliers de dollars)	As percentage / En pourcentage of country total du total du pays	of ** (1) des ** (1)	of world du monde
United Kingdom - Royaume-Uni (=Developed)**				
All commodity groups	477 491 434	100.0	5.06	2.61
781 Passenger cars and race cars	33 161 022	6.9	6.29	5.16
333 Crude petroleum & bituminous oil	29 036 465	6.1	14.61	1.69
334 Heavy petroleum & bituminous oil	28 321 920	5.9	6.43	2.87
542 Medicines including veterinary	26 109 121	5.5	8.51	7.75
714 Non-electric engines excl 712 713 718	19 510 563	4.1	26.30	21.63
112 Alcoholic beverages	10 202 009	2.1	16.72	13.34
541 Pharmaceuticals excluding medicines	10 127 165	2.1	7.10	6.20
874 Measure analyze control device nes	9 655 292	2.0	6.89	5.29
667 Pearls, precious semiprecious stone	9 137 952	1.9	12.47	5.93
764 Telecom equipment part nes	8 725 579	1.8	5.25	1.69
Remainder	293 504 346	61.6		
United Republic of Tanzania - République-Unie de Tanzanie (=Developing)**				
All commodity groups	5 141 094	100.0	0.06	0.03
971 Gold non-monetary excluding ores	830 511	16.2	0.63	0.33
289 Prec metal ore concentrate excl. gold	551 111	10.7	7.93	2.90
121 Unmanufactured tabacco and refuse	328 179	6.4	3.91	2.68
071 Coffee and coffee substitutes	240 402	4.7	0.96	0.59
287 Base metal ores & concentrates nes	234 531	4.6	1.26	0.72
057 Fruit nut (exc oil), fresh or dried	227 078	4.4	0.52	0.26
034 Fish, fresh live chilled frozen	186 046	3.6	0.70	0.31
263 Cotton	168 701	3.3	1.53	0.64
222 Oil seed etc for soft oil	156 852	3.1	0.53	0.22
054 Vegetable & vegetable products nes	145 018	2.8	0.60	0.24
Remainder	2 072 665	40.2		
United States - États-Unis (=Developed)**				
All commodity groups	1 512 647 677	100.0	16.02	8.27
334 Heavy petroleum & bituminous oil	96 865 484	6.4	21.99	9.82
781 Passenger cars and race cars	51 446 625	3.4	9.76	8.00
776 Valves tubes; diodes, transistors	42 947 628	2.8	28.12	7.72
784 Motor vehicle parts and accessories	40 374 371	2.7	15.42	11.26
764 Telecom equipment part nes	39 099 906	2.6	23.52	7.56
971 Gold non-monetary excluding ores	34 728 543	2.3	29.74	13.81
874 Measure analyze control device nes	32 891 136	2.2	23.46	18.04
752 Computer equipment nes	28 766 768	1.9	27.87	8.16
542 Medicines including veterinary	25 699 225	1.7	8.38	7.63
723 Civil engineering plant & equipment	22 410 682	1.5	26.41	18.15
Remainder	1 097 417 309	72.5		
Uruguay (=Developing) (2)**				
All commodity groups	8 327 433	100.0	0.10	0.05
011 Beef, fresh chilled frozen	1 347 576	16.2	11.00	3.39
222 Oil seed etc for soft oil	1 101 398	13.2	3.71	1.56
042 Rice	516 188	6.2	2.55	2.10
022 Milk products, excl. butter & cheese	392 026	4.7	6.63	0.92
041 Wheat meslin, incl spelt, unmilled	349 555	4.2	6.06	0.72
247 Wood in rough or roughly squared	263 001	3.2	5.17	1.72
268 Wool & animal hair, incl wool tops	251 904	3.0	9.19	3.37
024 Cheese and curd	250 019	3.0	12.60	0.84
611 Leather	234 975	2.8	1.81	0.99
048 Cereal & preparation flour starch	225 588	2.7	2.33	0.49
Remainder	3 395 203	40.8		
Uzbekistan - Ouzbékistan (=Transition)**				
All commodity groups	12 044 945	100.0	1.45	0.07
263 Cotton	1 798 537	14.9	43.49	6.86
682 Copper	1 510 302	12.5	13.51	1.05
343 Natural gas, liquefied or not	1 123 777	9.3	1.42	0.32
057 Fruit nut (exc oil), fresh or dried	939 475	7.8	46.33	1.08
525 Radio active & associated materials	788 711	6.5	21.09	4.32
781 Passenger cars and race cars	766 374	6.4	36.36	0.12
651 Textile yarn	747 641	6.2	48.59	1.31
334 Heavy petroleum & bituminous oil	698 144	5.8	0.57	0.07
562 Manufactured fertilizer excl. crude	478 107	4.0	2.82	0.63
054 Vegetable & vegetable products nes	359 298	3.0	27.41	0.60
Remainder	2 834 579	23.6		

For sources and notes, see end of table.

Pour les sources et les notes, se reporter à la fin du tableau.

Leading products exported based on average 2011-2012 values SITC Revision 3 (3-digit level) / Principaux produits exportés d'après la moyenne des valeurs de 2011-2012 CTCI révision 3 (positions à 3 chiffres)	Value (f.o.b., thousands of dollars) Valeur (f.a.b., milliers de dollars)	of country total du total du pays	of ** (1) des ** (1)	of world du monde
Vanuatu (**=Developing) (2)				
All commodity groups	57 601	100.0	0.00	0.00
034 Fish, fresh live chilled frozen	33 463	58.1	0.13	0.06
793 Ships boats floating structures	8 041	14.0	0.01	0.00
422 Fixed veg fat and oil, excl. "soft"	1 146	2.0	0.00	0.00
292 Crude vegetable materials nes	727	1.3	0.00	0.00
223 Oil seed for non soft oil	622	1.1	0.08	0.02
011 Beef, fresh chilled frozen	447	0.8	0.00	0.00
344 Petroleum and hydrocarbon gas nes	446	0.8	0.01	0.00
072 Cocoa	444	0.8	0.00	0.00
778 Electrical machinery apparatus nes	339	0.6	0.00	0.00
054 Vegetable & vegetable products nes	332	0.6	0.00	0.00
Remainder	11 594	19.9		
Venezuela (Bolivarian Rep.of)-Venezuela (Rép. bolivarienne du) (**=Developing) (2)				
All commodity groups	93 566 827	100.0	1.17	0.51
333 Crude petroleum & bituminous oil	62 618 900	66.9	4.99	3.65
334 Heavy petroleum & bituminous oil	16 367 003	17.5	3.86	1.66
793 Ships boats floating structures	3 243 021	3.5	2.83	1.89
674 Flat plated iron non-alloy steel	1 126 524	1.2	4.40	1.91
281 Iron ore and concentrates	1 021 389	1.1	1.76	0.75
676 Iron steel bar rod section piling	912 281	1.0	2.88	0.99
671 Pig & sponge iron, ferro alloys etc	847 576	0.9	3.93	2.01
684 Aluminium	758 614	0.8	1.98	0.64
335 Residual petroleum products nes	540 618	0.6	2.90	1.06
591 Household and garden chemicals	530 678	0.6	6.25	1.82
Remainder	5 600 223	5.9		
Viet Nam (**=Developing) (2)				
All commodity groups	105 717 422	100.0	1.32	0.58
333 Crude petroleum & bituminous oil	9 293 036	8.8	0.74	0.54
851 Footwear	7 572 992	7.2	10.55	6.56
764 Telecom equipment part nes	6 685 883	6.3	1.91	1.29
845 Articles of apparel nes	4 208 942	4.0	4.26	3.00
821 Furniture part; bedding furnishing	3 740 553	3.5	5.04	2.47
042 Rice	3 610 288	3.4	17.85	14.67
841 Male clothing, woven	3 590 683	3.4	7.34	5.04
842 Female clothing, woven	3 246 086	3.1	6.02	3.96
231 Natural rubber, latex, gum, etc	3 018 789	2.9	9.43	8.92
034 Fish, fresh live chilled frozen	2 976 691	2.8	11.14	4.96
Remainder	57 773 479	54.6		
Wallis and Futuna Islands - Îles Wallis-et-Futuna (**=Developing) (2)				
All commodity groups	36	100.0	0.00	0.00
676 Iron steel bar rod section piling	14	39.9	0.00	0.00
772 Electrical circuit equipment	5	14.2	0.00	0.00
598 Miscellaneous chemical products nes	2	5.0	0.00	0.00
292 Crude vegetable materials nes	1	2.8	0.00	0.00
592 Starches, glutenes, glues, etc	1	2.7	0.00	0.00
036 Crustacean mollusc aquat invertebra	1	2.5	0.00	0.00
764 Telecom equipment part nes	1	2.3	0.00	0.00
745 Non-electrical machinery tool nes	1	2.3	0.00	0.00
752 Computer equipment nes	1	2.0	0.00	0.00
759 Office equipment part & accessories	0	1.3	0.00	0.00
Remainder	9	25.0		

Leading products exported based on average 2011-2012 values SITC Revision 3 (3-digit level) / Principaux produits exportés d'après la moyenne des valeurs de 2011-2012 CTCI révision 3 (positions à 3 chiffres)	Value (f.o.b., thousands of dollars) Valeur (f.a.b., milliers de dollars)	of country total du total du pays	of ** (1) des ** (1)	of world du monde
Yemen - Yémen (**=Developing) (2)				
All commodity groups	9 700 000	100.0	0.12	0.05
333 Crude petroleum & bituminous oil	5 487 764	56.6	0.44	0.32
343 Natural gas, liquefied or not	2 219 514	22.9	1.39	0.64
334 Heavy petroleum & bituminous oil	737 982	7.6	0.17	0.07
971 Gold non-monetary excluding ores	185 258	1.9	0.14	0.07
034 Fish, fresh live chilled frozen	140 835	1.5	0.53	0.23
057 Fruit nut (exc oil), fresh or dried	114 805	1.2	0.26	0.13
335 Residual petroleum products nes	97 350	1.0	0.52	0.19
036 Crustacean mollusc aquat invertebra	38 488	0.4	0.18	0.12
122 Manufactured tabacco	36 561	0.4	0.43	0.12
579 Plastic waste, parings and scrap	34 950	0.4	1.32	0.47
Remainder	606 493	6.1		
Zambia - Zambie (**=Developing) (2)				
All commodity groups	8 800 473	100.0	0.11	0.05
682 Copper	5 934 237	67.4	8.10	4.12
699 Base metal manufactures nes	221 039	2.5	0.43	0.15
121 Unmanufactured tabacco and refuse	216 919	2.5	2.59	1.77
689 Misc non-ferrous base metals	215 081	2.4	4.89	2.13
061 Sugar, mollasses and honey	188 107	2.1	0.59	0.42
283 Copper ores and concentrates	145 191	1.6	0.37	0.27
772 Electrical circuit equipment	140 639	1.6	0.14	0.06
044 Maize unmilled, excluding sweet corn	138 895	1.6	1.11	0.40
263 Cotton	122 452	1.4	1.11	0.47
288 Non ferrous base metal waste nes	109 549	1.2	1.07	0.23
Remainder	1 368 364	15.7		
Zimbabwe (**=Developing) (2)				
All commodity groups	3 698 063	100.0	0.05	0.02
121 Unmanufactured tabacco and refuse	745 562	20.2	8.89	6.09
671 Pig & sponge iron, ferro alloys etc	294 670	8.0	1.36	0.70
263 Cotton	280 981	7.6	2.55	1.07
325 Coke, semi coke, retort carbon	273 582	7.4	10.65	3.08
284 Nickel ores, concentrates, etc	227 814	6.2	3.79	2.12
061 Sugar, mollasses and honey	215 398	5.8	0.68	0.48
971 Gold non-monetary excluding ores	214 844	5.8	0.16	0.09
667 Pearls, precious semiprecious stone	105 632	2.9	0.13	0.07
661 Lime cement construction material	86 316	2.3	0.50	0.29
892 Printed matter	77 973	2.1	0.52	0.16
Remainder	1 175 291	31.7		

Source:

UNCTAD secretariat calculations, based on UNCTAD, *UNCTADstat* Merchandise Trade Matrix

Notes:

(1) The symbol ** indicates the grouping to which the country belongs and to which the percentage share shown applies. The percentage is the share of exports of each commodity shown by the country in the relevant grouping total exports for that commodity (i.e. "developing", which refers to developing economies; "transition", which refers to transition economies and "developed", which refers to developed economies).

(2) Data are estimated at least for one of the reference years.

Source :

Calculs du secrétariat de la CNUCED, basés sur la matrice du commerce de marchandises d'*UNCTADstat* de la CNUCED

Notes :

(1) Le symbole ** indique le groupement auquel le pays appartient et par rapport auquel est calculé le pourcentage. Ce pourcentage est la part que représentent les exportations du produit par le pays par rapport aux exportations du même produit par le groupement auquel le pays appartient («developing» se réfère aux économies en développement, «transition» aux économies en transition et «developed» aux économies développées).

(2) Données estimées pour au moins une des années de référence.

3.2.E Export structure by product
Major exporters for leading products
among developing economies

3.2.E Structure des exportations par produits
Principaux exportateurs de produits majeurs
parmi les économies en développement

3

Leading exporting developing economies (1) based on average 2011-12 exports (2) SITC Revision 3 (3-digit level) / Principales économies en dévelopement exportatrices (1) d'après la moyenne des exportations de 2011-12 (2) CTCI révision 3 (positions à 3 chiffres)	2011-2012			
	Value (f.o.b., thousands of dollars) Valeur (f.a.b., milliers de dollars)	As percentage / En pourcentage		
		of country total / du total du pays	of developing economies / des économies en déve-loppement	of world / du monde
012 - Meat nes, fresh chilled frozen				
World	72 428 565	0.40	_	100.00
Developed economies	56 283 160	0.60	_	77.71
Transition economies	707 590	0.10	_	0.98
Developing economies	15 437 814	0.20	100.00	21.31
Brazil	8 785 829	3.50	56.91	12.13
China, Hong Kong SAR	1 453 054	0.30	9.41	2.01
China	925 009	0.00	5.99	1.28
Chile	793 516	1.00	5.14	1.10
Argentina	772 477	0.90	5.00	1.07
Turkey	462 989	0.30	3.00	0.64
Mexico	458 626	0.10	2.97	0.63
Uruguay	181 709	2.20	1.18	0.25
Thailand	170 612	0.10	1.11	0.24
Saudi Arabia	147 676	0.00	0.96	0.20
057 - Fruit nut (exc oil), fresh or dried				
World	86 828 465	0.50	_	100.00
Developed economies	40 977 832	0.40	_	47.19
Transition economies	2 027 627	0.20	_	2.34
Developing economies	43 823 006	0.50	100.00	50.47
Chile	4 620 387	5.80	10.54	5.32
Turkey	3 799 799	2.60	8.67	4.38
China	3 121 690	0.20	7.12	3.60
Mexico	2 708 113	0.80	6.18	3.12
Ecuador	2 699 555	11.70	6.16	3.11
South Africa	2 323 604	2.60	5.30	2.68
Viet Nam	1 913 286	1.80	4.37	2.20
China, Hong Kong SAR	1 749 750	0.40	3.99	2.02
Costa Rica	1 550 006	14.40	3.54	1.79
Iran (Islamic Rep. of)	1 418 792	1.20	3.24	1.63
081 - Animal feed excluding unmilled cereal				
World	72 939 856	0.40	_	100.00
Developed economies	39 032 295	0.40	_	53.51
Transition economies	1 723 748	0.20	_	2.36
Developing economies	32 183 813	0.40	100.00	44.12
Argentina	11 227 334	13.60	34.89	15.39
Brazil	6 445 229	2.60	20.03	8.84
India	2 696 572	0.90	8.38	3.70
China	2 523 478	0.10	7.84	3.46
Peru	2 340 302	5.20	7.27	3.21
Thailand	1 196 678	0.50	3.72	1.64
Indonesia	564 709	0.30	1.75	0.77
United Arab Emirates	519 438	0.20	1.61	0.71
Chile	513 839	0.60	1.60	0.70
Malaysia	476 242	0.20	1.48	0.65
112 - Alcoholic beverages				
World	76 456 281	0.40	_	100.00
Developed economies	61 009 674	0.60	_	79.80
Transition economies	1 490 869	0.20	_	1.95
Developing economies	13 955 738	0.20	100.00	18.25
Mexico	3 072 686	0.90	22.02	4.02
Singapore	2 374 449	0.60	17.01	3.11
Chile	1 785 545	2.20	12.79	2.34
Argentina	943 296	1.10	6.76	1.23
South Africa	842 870	0.90	6.04	1.10
China, Hong Kong SAR	800 174	0.20	5.73	1.05
China	608 811	0.00	4.36	0.80
Malaysia	398 388	0.20	2.85	0.52
Korea, Republic of	397 661	0.10	2.85	0.52
Venezuela (Bolivarian Rep. of)	372 989	0.40	2.67	0.49

Leading exporting developing economies (1) based on average 2011-12 exports (2) SITC Revision 3 (3-digit level) / Principales économies en dévelopement exportatrices (1) d'après la moyenne des exportations de 2011-12 (2) CTCI révision 3 (positions à 3 chiffres)	2011-2012			
	Value (f.o.b., thousands of dollars) Valeur (f.a.b., milliers de dollars)	As percentage / En pourcentage		
		of country total / du total du pays	of developing economies / des économies en déve-loppement	of world / du monde
222 - Oil seed etc for soft oil				
World	70 480 995	0.40	_	100.00
Developed economies	38 748 126	0.40	_	54.98
Transition economies	2 020 835	0.20	_	2.87
Developing economies	29 712 034	0.40	100.00	42.16
Brazil	16 891 844	6.80	56.85	23.97
Argentina	4 816 628	5.80	16.21	6.83
Paraguay	2 105 794	28.00	7.09	2.99
India	1 513 684	0.50	5.09	2.15
Uruguay	1 101 398	13.20	3.71	1.56
China	819 985	0.00	2.76	1.16
Ethiopia	381 416	14.30	1.28	0.54
Nigeria	339 565	0.30	1.14	0.48
United Arab Emirates	286 225	0.10	0.96	0.41
United Republic of Tanzania	156 852	3.10	0.53	0.22
281 - Iron ore and concentrates				
World	136 859 480	0.70	_	100.00
Developed economies	71 028 624	0.80	_	51.90
Transition economies	7 729 874	0.90	_	5.65
Developing economies	58 100 982	0.70	100.00	42.45
Brazil	36 403 272	14.60	62.66	26.60
South Africa	6 810 981	7.60	11.72	4.98
India	3 292 308	1.10	5.67	2.41
Bahrain	2 370 211	12.00	4.08	1.73
Iran (Islamic Rep. of)	1 769 068	1.50	3.04	1.29
Chile	1 481 017	1.90	2.55	1.08
Mauritania	1 279 832	47.30	2.20	0.94
Venezuela (Bolivarian Rep. of)	1 021 389	1.10	1.76	0.75
Peru	936 038	2.10	1.61	0.68
Oman	495 639	1.00	0.85	0.36
321 - Coal excluding non-agglomerated				
World	132 157 659	0.70	_	100.00
Developed economies	72 610 018	0.80	_	54.94
Transition economies	14 300 344	1.70	_	10.82
Developing economies	45 247 298	0.60	100.00	34.24
Indonesia	24 899 682	12.70	55.03	18.84
Colombia	7 577 629	12.90	16.75	5.73
South Africa	5 421 252	6.00	11.98	4.10
China	2 109 509	0.10	4.66	1.60
Viet Nam	2 016 307	1.90	4.46	1.53
Korea, Dem. People's Rep. of	1 412 609	37.90	3.12	1.07
Venezuela (Bolivarian Rep. of)	513 314	0.50	1.13	0.39
Mongolia	384 852	8.40	0.85	0.29
India	191 227	0.10	0.42	0.14
Mozambique	163 893	4.30	0.36	0.12
333 - Crude petroleum & bituminous oil				
World	1 716 651 623	9.40	_	100.00
Developed economies	198 696 418	2.10	_	11.57
Transition economies	264 017 412	31.80	_	15.38
Developing economies	1 253 937 793	15.60	100.00	73.05
Saudi Arabia	288 573 005	76.60	23.01	16.81
United Arab Emirates	133 493 660	44.20	10.65	7.78
Nigeria	98 908 522	78.20	7.89	5.76
Iraq	87 208 866	98.20	6.95	5.08
Iran (Islamic Rep. of)	79 818 474	68.40	6.37	4.65
Kuwait	78 879 591	74.30	6.29	4.59
Angola	68 546 991	97.00	5.47	3.99
Venezuela (Bolivarian Rep. of)	62 618 900	66.90	4.99	3.65
Mexico	48 161 179	13.40	3.84	2.81
Qatar	44 824 387	36.30	3.57	2.61

For sources and notes, see end of table.

Pour les sources et les notes, se reporter à la fin du tableau.

3.2.E Export structure by product
Major exporters for leading products among developing economies

3.2.E Structure des exportations par produits
Principaux exportateurs de produits majeurs parmi les économies en développement

Left table

Leading exporting developing economies (1) based on average 2011-12 exports (2) SITC Revision 3 (3-digit level) / Principales économies en dévelopement exportatrices (1) d'après la moyenne des exportations de 2011-12 (2) CTCI révision 3 (positions à 3 chiffres)	Value (f.o.b., thousands of dollars) / Valeur (f.a.b., milliers de dollars)	2011-2012 As percentage / En pourcentage		
		of country total / du total du pays	of developing economies / des économies en déve-loppement	of world / du monde
334 - Heavy petroleum & bituminous oil				
World	986 216 183	5.40	_	100.00
Developed economies	440 405 491	4.70	_	44.66
Transition economies	122 087 521	14.70	_	12.38
Developing economies	423 723 171	5.30	100.00	42.96
Singapore	76 225 229	18.60	17.99	7.73
India	53 687 473	18.20	12.67	5.44
Korea, Republic of	52 548 697	9.50	12.40	5.33
United Arab Emirates	26 432 655	8.70	6.24	2.68
China	21 041 189	1.10	4.97	2.13
Saudi Arabia	20 633 049	5.50	4.87	2.09
China, Taiwan Province of	18 961 347	6.20	4.47	1.92
Venezuela (Bolivarian Rep. of)	16 367 003	17.50	3.86	1.66
Kuwait	15 460 676	14.60	3.65	1.57
Malaysia	13 108 356	5.80	3.09	1.33
343 - Natural gas, liquefied or not				
World	347 082 847	1.90	_	100.00
Developed economies	108 125 895	1.10	_	31.15
Transition economies	79 383 578	9.60	_	22.87
Developing economies	159 573 374	2.00	100.00	45.98
Qatar	46 522 158	37.60	29.15	13.40
Indonesia	21 548 960	11.00	13.50	6.21
Algeria	20 996 296	28.90	13.16	6.05
Malaysia	17 151 735	7.60	10.75	4.94
Nigeria	10 558 570	8.30	6.62	3.04
United Arab Emirates	5 858 865	1.90	3.67	1.69
Brunei Darussalam	5 556 394	43.60	3.48	1.60
Oman	5 188 510	10.50	3.25	1.49
Bolivia (Plurinational State of)	4 752 320	45.50	2.98	1.37
Trinidad and Tobago	3 819 746	27.40	2.39	1.10
511 - Hydrocarbons nes; derivatives				
World	97 995 081	0.50	_	100.00
Developed economies	54 159 754	0.60	_	55.27
Transition economies	2 203 564	0.30	_	2.25
Developing economies	41 631 762	0.50	100.00	42.48
Korea, Republic of	12 138 936	2.20	29.16	12.39
Saudi Arabia	4 152 035	1.10	9.97	4.24
China	3 694 821	0.20	8.88	3.77
China, Taiwan Province of	3 160 897	1.00	7.59	3.23
Singapore	3 106 673	0.80	7.46	3.17
India	2 890 076	1.00	6.94	2.95
Thailand	2 405 782	1.00	5.78	2.46
Iran (Islamic Rep. of)	1 886 198	1.60	4.53	1.92
Brazil	1 200 349	0.50	2.88	1.22
Oman	1 195 962	2.40	2.87	1.22
512 - Alcohols, phenols; derivatives				
World	62 505 690	0.30	_	100.00
Developed economies	27 199 135	0.30	_	43.51
Transition economies	1 067 726	0.10	_	1.71
Developing economies	34 238 830	0.40	100.00	54.78
Saudi Arabia	9 260 193	2.50	27.05	14.81
China, Taiwan Province of	2 940 555	1.00	8.59	4.70
Singapore	2 738 498	0.70	8.00	4.38
Brazil	2 095 339	0.80	6.12	3.35
Malaysia	2 029 984	0.90	5.93	3.25
Iran (Islamic Rep. of)	1 783 214	1.50	5.21	2.85
China	1 551 954	0.10	4.53	2.48
Korea, Republic of	1 537 844	0.30	4.49	2.46
India	1 269 566	0.40	3.71	2.03
Indonesia	1 141 583	0.60	3.33	1.83

Right table

Leading exporting developing economies (1) based on average 2011-12 exports (2) SITC Revision 3 (3-digit level) / Principales économies en dévelopement exportatrices (1) d'après la moyenne des exportations de 2011-12 (2) CTCI révision 3 (positions à 3 chiffres)	Value (f.o.b., thousands of dollars) / Valeur (f.a.b., milliers de dollars)	2011-2012 As percentage / En pourcentage		
		of country total / du total du pays	of developing economies / des économies en déve-loppement	of world / du monde
515 - Organo-inorganic compound acid salt				
World	111 781 981	0.60	_	100.00
Developed economies	86 921 641	0.90	_	77.76
Transition economies	1 001 104	0.10	_	0.90
Developing economies	23 859 236	0.30	100.00	21.34
China	12 479 959	0.60	52.31	11.16
Singapore	6 827 318	1.70	28.61	6.11
India	1 377 831	0.50	5.77	1.23
Korea, Republic of	642 294	0.10	2.69	0.57
China, Hong Kong SAR	451 927	0.10	1.89	0.40
Mexico	442 547	0.10	1.85	0.40
China, Taiwan Province of	273 813	0.10	1.15	0.24
Brazil	210 641	0.10	0.88	0.19
Saudi Arabia	182 433	0.00	0.76	0.16
Indonesia	165 612	0.10	0.69	0.15
533 - Pigment, paint, varnish & related				
World	63 626 945	0.30	_	100.00
Developed economies	47 916 143	0.50	_	75.31
Transition economies	2 990 809	0.40	_	4.70
Developing economies	12 719 994	0.20	100.00	19.99
China	2 803 601	0.10	22.04	4.41
Korea, Republic of	1 524 996	0.30	11.99	2.40
China, Taiwan Province of	1 331 009	0.40	10.46	2.09
Singapore	1 008 621	0.20	7.93	1.59
China, Hong Kong SAR	862 280	0.20	6.78	1.36
Malaysia	592 199	0.30	4.66	0.93
Turkey	541 466	0.40	4.26	0.85
Mexico	491 753	0.10	3.87	0.77
Saudi Arabia	481 387	0.10	3.78	0.76
India	462 140	0.20	3.63	0.73
541 - Pharmaceuticals excluding medicines				
World	163 229 226	0.90	_	100.00
Developed economies	142 677 484	1.50	_	87.41
Transition economies	282 643	0.00	_	0.17
Developing economies	20 269 098	0.30	100.00	12.42
China	9 254 217	0.50	45.66	5.67
Singapore	3 179 531	0.80	15.69	1.95
Panama	2 156 194	14.00	10.64	1.32
India	1 849 778	0.60	9.13	1.13
Korea, Republic of	771 316	0.10	3.81	0.47
Mexico	505 863	0.10	2.50	0.31
Brazil	496 282	0.20	2.45	0.30
Argentina	238 062	0.30	1.17	0.15
China, Hong Kong SAR	210 222	0.00	1.04	0.13
Thailand	180 939	0.10	0.89	0.11
542 - Medicines including veterinary				
World	336 742 393	1.80	_	100.00
Developed economies	306 776 446	3.20	_	91.10
Transition economies	1 745 974	0.20	_	0.52
Developing economies	28 219 973	0.40	100.00	8.38
India	8 331 384	2.80	29.52	2.47
Singapore	4 892 434	1.20	17.34	1.45
China	2 610 757	0.10	9.25	0.78
China, Hong Kong SAR	1 521 596	0.30	5.39	0.45
Mexico	1 493 080	0.40	5.29	0.44
Panama	1 118 419	7.30	3.96	0.33
Brazil	1 088 059	0.40	3.86	0.32
Argentina	696 692	0.80	2.47	0.21
Korea, Republic of	638 913	0.10	2.26	0.19
Jordan	590 160	7.50	2.09	0.18

For sources and notes, see end of table.

Pour les sources et les notes, se reporter à la fin du tableau.

3.2.E Export structure by product
Major exporters for leading products among developing economies

3.2.E Structure des exportations par produits
Principaux exportateurs de produits majeurs parmi les économies en développement

Leading exporting developing economies (1) based on average 2011-12 exports (2) SITC Revision 3 (3-digit level) / Principales économies en dévelopement exportatrices (1) d'après la moyenne des exportations de 2011-12 (2) CTCI révision 3 (positions à 3 chiffres)	2011-2012			
	Value (f.o.b., thousands of dollars) / Valeur (f.a.b., milliers de dollars)	As percentage / En pourcentage		
		of country total / du total du pays	of developing economies / des économies en déve-loppement	of world / du monde
553 - Perfume toilet cosmetics, excl. soap				
World	77 345 564	0.40	_	100.00
Developed economies	58 210 366	0.60	_	75.26
Transition economies	788 242	0.10	_	1.02
Developing economies	18 346 955	0.20	100.00	23.72
Singapore	2 743 425	0.70	14.95	3.55
China	2 652 187	0.10	14.46	3.43
Mexico	1 909 390	0.50	10.41	2.47
Thailand	1 827 085	0.80	9.96	2.36
China, Hong Kong SAR	1 320 066	0.30	7.20	1.71
Korea, Republic of	930 824	0.20	5.07	1.20
United Arab Emirates	799 722	0.30	4.36	1.03
Argentina	543 956	0.70	2.96	0.70
Turkey	534 014	0.40	2.91	0.69
India	526 130	0.20	2.87	0.68
562 - Manufactured fertilizer excl. crude				
World	75 490 004	0.40	_	100.00
Developed economies	32 084 932	0.30	_	42.50
Transition economies	16 981 727	2.00	_	22.50
Developing economies	26 423 345	0.30	100.00	35.00
China	7 535 766	0.40	28.52	9.98
Morocco	2 208 415	10.30	8.36	2.93
Saudi Arabia	2 082 926	0.60	7.88	2.76
Qatar	1 355 660	1.10	5.13	1.80
Egypt	1 328 766	4.40	5.03	1.76
Jordan	1 099 851	13.90	4.16	1.46
Oman	985 107	2.00	3.73	1.30
Iran (Islamic Rep. of)	852 258	0.70	3.23	1.13
Chile	761 581	1.00	2.88	1.01
South Africa	631 901	0.70	2.39	0.84
571 - Primary form ethylene polymers				
World	78 023 592	0.40	_	100.00
Developed economies	39 071 965	0.40	_	50.08
Transition economies	1 052 939	0.10	_	1.35
Developing economies	37 898 688	0.50	100.00	48.57
Saudi Arabia	10 194 851	2.70	26.90	13.07
Singapore	4 174 000	1.00	11.01	5.35
Korea, Republic of	3 727 256	0.70	9.83	4.78
Thailand	3 355 959	1.50	8.86	4.30
Kuwait	2 681 996	2.50	7.08	3.44
United Arab Emirates	2 216 595	0.70	5.85	2.84
Qatar	2 200 665	1.80	5.81	2.82
Iran (Islamic Rep. of)	1 990 286	1.70	5.25	2.55
Brazil	1 422 536	0.60	3.75	1.82
China, Taiwan Province of	1 184 014	0.40	3.12	1.52
575 - Other plastics, in primary forms				
World	113 413 058	0.60	_	100.00
Developed economies	74 144 470	0.80	_	65.38
Transition economies	1 086 535	0.10	_	0.96
Developing economies	38 182 053	0.50	100.00	33.67
Korea, Republic of	6 893 630	1.20	18.05	6.08
Saudi Arabia	6 118 317	1.60	16.02	5.39
Singapore	4 604 092	1.10	12.06	4.06
China	4 349 547	0.20	11.39	3.84
China, Taiwan Province of	3 915 996	1.30	10.26	3.45
China, Hong Kong SAR	2 349 985	0.50	6.15	2.07
Thailand	2 001 510	0.90	5.24	1.76
India	1 473 794	0.50	3.86	1.30
Brazil	1 027 358	0.40	2.69	0.91
United Arab Emirates	912 455	0.30	2.39	0.80

Leading exporting developing economies (1) based on average 2011-12 exports (2) SITC Revision 3 (3-digit level) / Principales économies en dévelopement exportatrices (1) d'après la moyenne des exportations de 2011-12 (2) CTCI révision 3 (positions à 3 chiffres)	2011-2012			
	Value (f.o.b., thousands of dollars) / Valeur (f.a.b., milliers de dollars)	As percentage / En pourcentage		
		of country total / du total du pays	of developing economies / des économies en déve-loppement	of world / du monde
582 - Plastic sheet film foil & strips				
World	98 464 299	0.50	_	100.00
Developed economies	67 764 017	0.70	_	68.82
Transition economies	725 090	0.10	_	0.74
Developing economies	29 975 192	0.40	100.00	30.44
China	7 418 941	0.40	24.75	7.53
Korea, Republic of	4 713 603	0.90	15.73	4.79
China, Taiwan Province of	3 685 083	1.20	12.29	3.74
China, Hong Kong SAR	2 457 563	0.50	8.20	2.50
Malaysia	1 194 610	0.50	3.99	1.21
Turkey	1 141 707	0.80	3.81	1.16
Thailand	1 094 397	0.50	3.65	1.11
Mexico	1 067 987	0.30	3.56	1.08
Singapore	1 059 197	0.30	3.53	1.08
India	1 054 722	0.40	3.52	1.07
598 - Miscellaneous chemical products nes				
World	126 171 241	0.70	_	100.00
Developed economies	95 159 900	1.00	_	75.42
Transition economies	1 030 935	0.10	_	0.82
Developing economies	29 980 407	0.40	100.00	23.76
China	8 537 279	0.40	28.48	6.77
China, Taiwan Province of	3 150 422	1.00	10.51	2.50
Korea, Republic of	3 123 813	0.60	10.42	2.48
Singapore	2 614 858	0.60	8.72	2.07
Argentina	2 191 469	2.70	7.31	1.74
Indonesia	1 835 136	0.90	6.12	1.45
China, Hong Kong SAR	1 610 731	0.30	5.37	1.28
Malaysia	1 382 949	0.60	4.61	1.10
India	783 869	0.30	2.61	0.62
Mexico	629 023	0.20	2.10	0.50
625 - Rubber for wheels, incl inner tube				
World	92 832 808	0.50	_	100.00
Developed economies	52 420 665	0.60	_	56.47
Transition economies	2 133 698	0.30	_	2.30
Developing economies	38 278 445	0.50	100.00	41.23
China	16 154 586	0.80	42.20	17.40
Korea, Republic of	4 615 348	0.80	12.06	4.97
Thailand	3 639 668	1.60	9.51	3.92
Indonesia	1 827 674	0.90	4.77	1.97
India	1 745 180	0.60	4.56	1.88
Brazil	1 633 739	0.70	4.27	1.76
Turkey	1 311 690	0.90	3.43	1.41
United Arab Emirates	1 260 724	0.40	3.29	1.36
China, Taiwan Province of	1 183 806	0.40	3.09	1.28
Mexico	909 241	0.30	2.38	0.98
641 - Paper and paperboard				
World	119 662 629	0.70	_	100.00
Developed economies	94 238 065	1.00	_	78.75
Transition economies	2 983 762	0.40	_	2.49
Developing economies	22 440 801	0.30	100.00	18.75
China	5 426 326	0.30	24.18	4.53
Indonesia	3 569 105	1.80	15.90	2.98
Korea, Republic of	2 623 844	0.50	11.69	2.19
Brazil	1 845 182	0.70	8.22	1.54
Thailand	1 623 043	0.70	7.23	1.36
Singapore	1 182 481	0.30	5.27	0.99
China, Taiwan Province of	937 887	0.30	4.18	0.78
Chile	573 822	0.70	2.56	0.48
India	531 425	0.20	2.37	0.44
Turkey	408 103	0.30	1.82	0.34

For sources and notes, see end of table.

Pour les sources et les notes, se reporter à la fin du tableau.

3.2.E Export structure by product
Major exporters for leading products among developing economies

3.2.E Structure des exportations par produits
Principaux exportateurs de produits majeurs parmi les économies en développement

Leading exporting developing economies (1) based on average 2011-12 exports (2) SITC Revision 3 (3-digit level) / Principales économies en dévelopement exportatrices (1) d'après la moyenne des exportations de 2011-12 (2) CTCI révision 3 (positions à 3 chiffres)	Value (f.o.b., thousands of dollars) Valeur (f.a.b., milliers de dollars)	2011-2012		
		of country total du total du pays	of developing economies des économies en déve-loppement	of world du monde
667 - Pearls, precious semiprecious stone				
World	154 096 843	0.80	_	100.00
Developed economies	73 262 777	0.80	_	47.54
Transition economies	1 936 088	0.20	_	1.26
Developing economies	78 897 979	1.00	100.00	51.20
India	27 670 114	9.40	35.07	17.96
United Arab Emirates	16 115 278	5.30	20.43	10.46
China, Hong Kong SAR	15 548 149	3.30	19.71	10.09
Botswana	4 712 525	79.50	5.97	3.06
China	3 478 571	0.20	4.41	2.26
South Africa	2 478 551	2.80	3.14	1.61
Thailand	2 214 141	1.00	2.81	1.44
Myanmar	1 387 670	15.30	1.76	0.90
Namibia	955 836	22.60	1.21	0.62
Angola	687 089	1.00	0.87	0.45
673 - Flat iron non-alloy steel products				
World	87 478 281	0.50	_	100.00
Developed economies	49 961 139	0.50	_	57.11
Transition economies	10 360 740	1.20	_	11.84
Developing economies	27 156 402	0.30	100.00	31.04
Korea, Republic of	10 602 384	1.90	39.04	12.12
China, Taiwan Province of	3 453 611	1.10	12.72	3.95
China	3 275 843	0.20	12.06	3.74
India	1 398 301	0.50	5.15	1.60
Turkey	1 106 573	0.80	4.07	1.26
United Arab Emirates	1 056 990	0.30	3.89	1.21
Brazil	1 023 662	0.40	3.77	1.17
Singapore	668 086	0.20	2.46	0.76
South Africa	629 279	0.70	2.32	0.72
Viet Nam	590 798	0.60	2.18	0.68
675 - Flat rolled products of alloy steel				
World	70 478 120	0.40	_	100.00
Developed economies	47 448 098	0.50	_	67.32
Transition economies	1 381 946	0.20	_	1.96
Developing economies	21 648 076	0.30	100.00	30.72
China	10 385 262	0.50	47.97	14.74
Korea, Republic of	3 858 242	0.70	17.82	5.47
China, Taiwan Province of	3 067 780	1.00	14.17	4.35
India	673 126	0.20	3.11	0.96
South Africa	630 575	0.70	2.91	0.89
China, Hong Kong SAR	547 961	0.10	2.53	0.78
Brazil	471 479	0.20	2.18	0.67
Mexico	327 979	0.10	1.52	0.47
Malaysia	288 852	0.10	1.33	0.41
Singapore	285 591	0.10	1.32	0.41
676 - Iron steel bar rod section piling				
World	91 815 798	0.50	_	100.00
Developed economies	52 633 721	0.60	_	57.33
Transition economies	7 499 249	0.90	_	8.17
Developing economies	31 682 828	0.40	100.00	34.51
China	9 315 862	0.50	29.40	10.15
Turkey	7 314 373	5.10	23.09	7.97
Korea, Republic of	2 878 094	0.50	9.08	3.13
United Arab Emirates	1 526 339	0.50	4.82	1.66
China, Taiwan Province of	1 496 443	0.50	4.72	1.63
India	1 140 810	0.40	3.60	1.24
Mexico	925 171	0.30	2.92	1.01
Venezuela (Bolivarian Rep. of)	912 281	1.00	2.88	0.99
Brazil	887 053	0.40	2.80	0.97
Thailand	579 815	0.30	1.83	0.63

Leading exporting developing economies (1) based on average 2011-12 exports (2) SITC Revision 3 (3-digit level) / Principales économies en dévelopement exportatrices (1) d'après la moyenne des exportations de 2011-12 (2) CTCI révision 3 (positions à 3 chiffres)	Value (f.o.b., thousands of dollars) Valeur (f.a.b., milliers de dollars)	2011-2012		
		of country total du total du pays	of developing economies des économies en déve-loppement	of world du monde
679 - Iron steel pipe tube fittings etc				
World	96 974 425	0.50	_	100.00
Developed economies	54 628 453	0.60	_	56.33
Transition economies	4 218 207	0.50	_	4.35
Developing economies	38 127 765	0.50	100.00	39.32
China	15 484 343	0.80	40.61	15.97
Korea, Republic of	4 851 274	0.90	12.72	5.00
India	2 822 964	1.00	7.40	2.91
Turkey	1 822 608	1.30	4.78	1.88
Mexico	1 740 904	0.50	4.57	1.80
Singapore	1 604 513	0.40	4.21	1.65
China, Taiwan Province of	1 292 010	0.40	3.39	1.33
Malaysia	1 198 335	0.50	3.14	1.24
Argentina	1 158 718	1.40	3.04	1.19
United Arab Emirates	1 041 415	0.30	2.73	1.07
681 - Silver, platinum, platinum metals				
World	67 329 780	0.40	_	100.00
Developed economies	37 713 490	0.40	_	56.01
Transition economies	833 874	0.10	_	1.24
Developing economies	28 782 416	0.40	100.00	42.75
South Africa	8 618 277	9.60	29.94	12.80
China, Hong Kong SAR	4 687 402	1.00	16.29	6.96
Mexico	4 400 071	1.20	15.29	6.54
Korea, Republic of	2 543 197	0.50	8.84	3.78
United Arab Emirates	2 363 786	0.80	8.21	3.51
China, Taiwan Province of	2 015 627	0.70	7.00	2.99
China	1 235 172	0.10	4.29	1.83
Chile	581 142	0.70	2.02	0.86
Argentina	360 569	0.40	1.25	0.54
Peru	320 412	0.70	1.11	0.48
682 - Copper				
World	144 153 332	0.80	_	100.00
Developed economies	59 748 901	0.60	_	41.45
Transition economies	11 182 040	1.30	_	7.76
Developing economies	73 222 391	0.90	100.00	50.79
Chile	27 946 458	35.00	38.17	19.39
China	6 261 808	0.30	8.55	4.34
Zambia	5 934 237	67.40	8.10	4.12
Korea, Republic of	4 263 470	0.80	5.82	2.96
Peru	3 582 412	7.90	4.89	2.49
China, Taiwan Province of	3 172 046	1.00	4.33	2.20
Dem. Rep. of the Congo	2 806 008	43.50	3.83	1.95
Indonesia	2 781 760	1.40	3.80	1.93
India	2 509 702	0.80	3.43	1.74
China, Hong Kong SAR	1 932 100	0.40	2.64	1.34
684 - Aluminium				
World	119 241 274	0.70	_	100.00
Developed economies	70 804 214	0.70	_	59.38
Transition economies	10 051 314	1.20	_	8.43
Developing economies	38 385 746	0.50	100.00	32.19
China	11 708 051	0.60	30.50	9.82
United Arab Emirates	4 055 298	1.30	10.56	3.40
Bahrain	3 512 274	17.80	9.15	2.95
Korea, Republic of	1 943 363	0.40	5.06	1.63
South Africa	1 574 288	1.80	4.10	1.32
Turkey	1 539 390	1.10	4.01	1.29
Brazil	1 455 515	0.60	3.79	1.22
Malaysia	1 316 590	0.60	3.43	1.10
Mozambique	1 289 333	33.50	3.36	1.08
India	936 588	0.30	2.44	0.79

For sources and notes, see end of table.

Pour les sources et les notes, se reporter à la fin du tableau.

3.2.E Export structure by product
Major exporters for leading products
among developing economies

3.2.E Structure des exportations par produits
Principaux exportateurs de produits majeurs
parmi les économies en développement

3

Leading exporting developing economies (1) based on average 2011-12 exports (2) SITC Revision 3 (3-digit level) / Principales économies en dévelopement exportatrices (1) d'après la moyenne des exportations de 2011-12 (2) CTCI révision 3 (positions à 3 chiffres)	2011-2012		
	Value (f.o.b., thousands of dollars) Valeur (f.a.b., milliers de dollars)	As percentage En pourcentage	
		of country total du total du pays	of developing economies des économies en déve-loppement	of world du monde

699 - Base metal manufactures nes

	Value	of country total	of developing economies	of world
World	144 629 408	0.80	_	100.00
Developed economies	90 643 783	1.00	_	62.67
Transition economies	2 261 624	0.30	_	1.56
Developing economies	51 724 001	0.60	100.00	35.76
China	22 867 828	1.20	44.21	15.81
China, Taiwan Province of	4 124 627	1.40	7.97	2.85
Mexico	3 759 403	1.00	7.27	2.60
Korea, Republic of	3 416 794	0.60	6.61	2.36
India	3 038 508	1.00	5.87	2.10
Thailand	2 369 476	1.00	4.58	1.64
China, Hong Kong SAR	1 963 533	0.40	3.80	1.36
Turkey	1 851 519	1.30	3.58	1.28
Brazil	1 643 916	0.70	3.18	1.14
Malaysia	1 210 415	0.50	2.34	0.84

713 - Internal combustion engine part nes

	Value	of country total	of developing economies	of world
World	162 681 095	0.90	_	100.00
Developed economies	126 022 425	1.30	_	77.47
Transition economies	774 233	0.10	_	0.48
Developing economies	35 884 437	0.40	100.00	22.06
Mexico	7 927 127	2.20	22.09	4.87
China	7 063 603	0.40	19.68	4.34
Korea, Republic of	5 473 768	1.00	15.25	3.36
Brazil	3 096 549	1.20	8.63	1.90
Thailand	3 073 510	1.30	8.57	1.89
Singapore	2 447 379	0.60	6.82	1.50
Turkey	1 705 604	1.20	4.75	1.05
India	1 414 656	0.50	3.94	0.87
United Arab Emirates	637 984	0.20	1.78	0.39
China, Hong Kong SAR	494 405	0.10	1.38	0.30

714 - Non-electric engines excl. 712, 713, and 718

	Value	of country total	of developing economies	of world
World	90 193 189	0.50	_	100.00
Developed economies	74 187 482	0.80	_	82.25
Transition economies	2 447 721	0.30	_	2.71
Developing economies	13 557 986	0.20	100.00	15.03
China, Hong Kong SAR	2 877 704	0.60	21.23	3.19
Singapore	2 445 630	0.60	18.04	2.71
China	1 969 419	0.10	14.53	2.18
Mexico	1 913 401	0.50	14.11	2.12
United Arab Emirates	1 423 047	0.50	10.50	1.58
Korea, Republic of	491 545	0.10	3.63	0.54
Thailand	343 216	0.10	2.53	0.38
Brazil	338 088	0.10	2.49	0.37
Iran (Islamic Rep. of)	321 064	0.30	2.37	0.36
Turkey	244 113	0.20	1.80	0.27

716 - Rotating electric plant parts nes

	Value	of country total	of developing economies	of world
World	95 500 554	0.50	_	100.00
Developed economies	60 408 214	0.60	_	63.25
Transition economies	1 027 225	0.10	_	1.08
Developing economies	34 065 115	0.40	100.00	35.67
China	16 381 809	0.80	48.09	17.15
Mexico	3 123 550	0.90	9.17	3.27
China, Hong Kong SAR	2 632 216	0.60	7.73	2.76
Korea, Republic of	1 876 057	0.30	5.51	1.96
Brazil	1 477 548	0.60	4.34	1.55
Singapore	1 357 852	0.30	3.99	1.42
Thailand	1 242 911	0.50	3.65	1.30
Viet Nam	1 119 492	1.10	3.29	1.17
China, Taiwan Province of	1 005 854	0.30	2.95	1.05
India	842 114	0.30	2.47	0.88

723 - Civil engineering plant & equipment

	Value	of country total	of developing economies	of world
World	123 475 364	0.70	_	100.00
Developed economies	84 856 322	0.90	_	68.72
Transition economies	894 757	0.10	_	0.72
Developing economies	37 724 285	0.50	100.00	30.55
China	12 551 761	0.60	33.27	10.17
Korea, Republic of	7 445 949	1.40	19.74	6.03
Singapore	5 640 229	1.40	14.95	4.57
Brazil	2 403 676	1.00	6.37	1.95
United Arab Emirates	1 651 864	0.50	4.38	1.34
Mexico	1 440 577	0.40	3.82	1.17
Thailand	981 970	0.40	2.60	0.80
India	833 781	0.30	2.21	0.68
Turkey	698 271	0.50	1.85	0.57
Indonesia	667 206	0.30	1.77	0.54

728 - Special industrial machine part nes

	Value	of country total	of developing economies	of world
World	183 375 302	1.00	_	100.00
Developed economies	139 958 781	1.50	_	76.32
Transition economies	825 912	0.10	_	0.45
Developing economies	42 590 609	0.50	100.00	23.23
China	10 645 858	0.50	25.00	5.81
Korea, Republic of	8 095 185	1.50	19.01	4.41
Singapore	7 546 883	1.80	17.72	4.12
China, Taiwan Province of	4 752 320	1.60	11.16	2.59
China, Hong Kong SAR	2 952 889	0.60	6.93	1.61
Malaysia	1 450 305	0.60	3.41	0.79
Mexico	1 038 985	0.30	2.44	0.57
Brazil	978 463	0.40	2.30	0.53
India	956 748	0.30	2.25	0.52
Turkey	815 719	0.60	1.92	0.44

741 - Heating and cooling equipment parts nes

	Value	of country total	of developing economies	of world
World	111 841 256	0.60	_	100.00
Developed economies	68 071 601	0.70	_	60.86
Transition economies	885 480	0.10	_	0.79
Developing economies	42 884 175	0.50	100.00	38.34
China	19 693 428	1.00	45.92	17.61
Thailand	4 580 704	2.00	10.68	4.10
Korea, Republic of	4 448 565	0.80	10.37	3.98
Mexico	3 819 341	1.10	8.91	3.41
Malaysia	1 723 767	0.80	4.02	1.54
Singapore	1 307 666	0.30	3.05	1.17
Turkey	1 017 671	0.70	2.37	0.91
China, Hong Kong SAR	1 014 379	0.20	2.37	0.91
United Arab Emirates	940 754	0.30	2.19	0.84
China, Taiwan Province of	912 745	0.30	2.13	0.82

743 - Gas pump, compressor, fan, filter

	Value	of country total	of developing economies	of world
World	123 774 273	0.70	_	100.00
Developed economies	87 434 687	0.90	_	70.64
Transition economies	1 087 824	0.10	_	0.88
Developing economies	35 251 762	0.40	100.00	28.48
China	13 703 470	0.70	38.87	11.07
Mexico	3 665 088	1.00	10.40	2.96
Korea, Republic of	3 218 441	0.60	9.13	2.60
Thailand	2 225 409	1.00	6.31	1.80
South Africa	2 071 706	2.30	5.88	1.67
Singapore	1 648 634	0.40	4.68	1.33
Brazil	1 456 676	0.60	4.13	1.18
China, Taiwan Province of	1 240 298	0.40	3.52	1.00
China, Hong Kong SAR	1 237 827	0.30	3.51	1.00
India	1 067 741	0.40	3.03	0.86

For sources and notes, see end of table.

Pour les sources et les notes, se reporter à la fin du tableau.

3.2.E Export structure by product
Major exporters for leading products among developing economies

3.2.E Structure des exportations par produits
Principaux exportateurs de produits majeurs parmi les économies en développement

Leading exporting developing economies (1) based on average 2011-12 exports (2) SITC Revision 3 (3-digit level) / Principales économies en dévelopement exportatrices (1) d'après la moyenne des exportations de 2011-12 (2) CTCI révision 3 (positions à 3 chiffres)	2011-2012 Value (f.o.b., thousands of dollars) / Valeur (f.a.b., milliers de dollars)	As percentage / En pourcentage: of country total / du total du pays	of developing economies / des économies en développement	of world / du monde
744 - Mechanical handling equipment nes				
World	81 842 170	0.40	_	100.00
Developed economies	61 725 784	0.70	_	75.42
Transition economies	675 718	0.10	_	0.83
Developing economies	19 440 668	0.20	100.00	23.75
China	10 969 563	0.60	56.43	13.40
Korea, Republic of	2 126 794	0.40	10.94	2.60
Singapore	1 289 629	0.30	6.63	1.58
China, Taiwan Province of	726 490	0.20	3.74	0.89
Mexico	629 446	0.20	3.24	0.77
Thailand	565 741	0.20	2.91	0.69
United Arab Emirates	464 866	0.20	2.39	0.57
Turkey	349 056	0.20	1.80	0.43
Malaysia	328 204	0.10	1.69	0.40
China, Hong Kong SAR	265 833	0.10	1.37	0.32
747 - Pipe, boiler, tank & vat appliances				
World	78 955 256	0.40	_	100.00
Developed economies	55 979 792	0.60	_	70.90
Transition economies	602 796	0.10	_	0.76
Developing economies	22 372 668	0.30	100.00	28.34
China	12 487 668	0.60	55.82	15.82
Mexico	1 865 808	0.50	8.34	2.36
Korea, Republic of	1 796 234	0.30	8.03	2.28
China, Taiwan Province of	1 138 326	0.40	5.09	1.44
India	903 066	0.30	4.04	1.14
Singapore	866 628	0.20	3.87	1.10
Thailand	608 099	0.30	2.72	0.77
Brazil	576 590	0.20	2.58	0.73
Turkey	423 334	0.30	1.89	0.54
China, Hong Kong SAR	332 589	0.10	1.49	0.42
752 - Computer equipment nes				
World	352 479 646	1.90	_	100.00
Developed economies	103 225 712	1.10	_	29.29
Transition economies	501 156	0.10	_	0.14
Developing economies	248 752 778	3.10	100.00	70.57
China	164 745 172	8.30	66.23	46.74
China, Hong Kong SAR	18 306 107	3.90	7.36	5.19
Mexico	17 739 770	4.90	7.13	5.03
Thailand	12 521 554	5.50	5.03	3.55
Malaysia	9 978 225	4.40	4.01	2.83
Singapore	9 162 749	2.20	3.68	2.60
Korea, Republic of	5 168 156	0.90	2.08	1.47
China, Taiwan Province of	4 173 795	1.40	1.68	1.18
Philippines	3 464 733	6.90	1.39	0.98
United Arab Emirates	1 234 240	0.40	0.50	0.35
759 - Office equipment part & accessories				
World	191 177 632	1.00	_	100.00
Developed economies	75 927 110	0.80	_	39.72
Transition economies	167 293	0.00	_	0.09
Developing economies	115 083 228	1.40	100.00	60.20
China	38 552 144	2.00	33.50	20.17
China, Hong Kong SAR	31 998 181	6.70	27.80	16.74
Singapore	16 132 170	3.90	14.02	8.44
Malaysia	6 473 472	2.80	5.63	3.39
China, Taiwan Province of	5 831 474	1.90	5.07	3.05
Korea, Republic of	4 899 149	0.90	4.26	2.56
Thailand	3 981 232	1.70	3.46	2.08
Philippines	1 532 794	3.10	1.33	0.80
Costa Rica	1 478 597	13.80	1.28	0.77
Mexico	1 420 510	0.40	1.23	0.74

Leading exporting developing economies (1) based on average 2011-12 exports (2) SITC Revision 3 (3-digit level) / Principales économies en dévelopement exportatrices (1) d'après la moyenne des exportations de 2011-12 (2) CTCI révision 3 (positions à 3 chiffres)	2011-2012 Value (f.o.b., thousands of dollars) / Valeur (f.a.b., milliers de dollars)	As percentage / En pourcentage: of country total / du total du pays	of developing economies / des économies en développement	of world / du monde
761 - Television video receive project				
World	91 616 356	0.50	_	100.00
Developed economies	35 658 107	0.40	_	38.92
Transition economies	947 341	0.10	_	1.03
Developing economies	55 010 907	0.70	100.00	60.04
China	22 003 639	1.10	40.00	24.02
Mexico	18 009 055	5.00	32.74	19.66
Malaysia	4 142 353	1.80	7.53	4.52
Turkey	2 016 603	1.40	3.67	2.20
Korea, Republic of	1 893 298	0.30	3.44	2.07
Thailand	1 674 313	0.70	3.04	1.83
Indonesia	1 216 097	0.60	2.21	1.33
China, Taiwan Province of	1 092 815	0.40	1.99	1.19
China, Hong Kong SAR	790 609	0.20	1.44	0.86
Singapore	487 526	0.10	0.89	0.53
764 - Telecom equipment part nes				
World	517 324 722	2.80	_	100.00
Developed economies	166 268 979	1.80	_	32.14
Transition economies	1 498 698	0.20	_	0.29
Developing economies	349 557 045	4.40	100.00	67.57
China	172 526 680	8.70	49.36	33.35
China, Hong Kong SAR	68 850 520	14.50	19.70	13.31
Korea, Republic of	32 341 083	5.90	9.25	6.25
Mexico	19 523 441	5.40	5.59	3.77
China, Taiwan Province of	15 130 557	5.00	4.33	2.92
Singapore	10 781 535	2.60	3.08	2.08
Viet Nam	6 685 883	6.30	1.91	1.29
Malaysia	5 834 531	2.60	1.67	1.13
India	4 415 482	1.50	1.26	0.85
Thailand	4 356 349	1.90	1.25	0.84
771 - Electric power machine part excl. 716				
World	92 593 752	0.50	_	100.00
Developed economies	41 658 069	0.40	_	44.99
Transition economies	1 303 624	0.20	_	1.41
Developing economies	49 632 058	0.60	100.00	53.60
China	23 007 074	1.20	46.36	24.85
China, Hong Kong SAR	10 125 339	2.10	20.40	10.94
Korea, Republic of	2 752 247	0.50	5.55	2.97
Mexico	2 547 540	0.70	5.13	2.75
China, Taiwan Province of	1 651 189	0.50	3.33	1.78
Philippines	1 548 239	3.10	3.12	1.67
Singapore	1 486 744	0.40	3.00	1.61
Thailand	1 433 416	0.60	2.89	1.55
India	1 021 155	0.30	2.06	1.10
Turkey	742 408	0.50	1.50	0.80
772 - Electrical circuit equipment				
World	234 681 346	1.30	_	100.00
Developed economies	129 441 579	1.40	_	55.16
Transition economies	1 350 884	0.20	_	0.58
Developing economies	103 888 882	1.30	100.00	44.27
China	33 221 266	1.70	31.98	14.16
China, Hong Kong SAR	20 369 163	4.30	19.61	8.68
Korea, Republic of	9 482 545	1.70	9.13	4.04
China, Taiwan Province of	9 103 283	3.00	8.76	3.88
Mexico	7 250 283	2.00	6.98	3.09
Singapore	6 841 720	1.70	6.59	2.92
Malaysia	5 483 567	2.40	5.28	2.34
Thailand	3 032 761	1.30	2.92	1.29
India	1 498 367	0.50	1.44	0.64
Turkey	1 165 389	0.80	1.12	0.50

For sources and notes, see end of table.

Pour les sources et les notes, se reporter à la fin du tableau.

3.2.E Export structure by product
Major exporters for leading products
among developing economies

3.2.E Structure des exportations par produits
Principaux exportateurs de produits majeurs
parmi les économies en développement

3

Leading exporting developing economies (1) based on average 2011-12 exports (2) SITC Revision 3 (3-digit level) Principales économies en développement exportatrices (1) d'après la moyenne des exportations de 2011-12 (2) CTCI révision 3 (positions à 3 chiffres)	2011-2012		
	Value (f.o.b., thousands of dollars) Valeur (f.a.b., milliers de dollars)	As percentage En pourcentage		
		of country total du total du pays	of developing economies des économies en déve-loppement	of world du monde

773 - Electrical distribution equipment nes				
World	112 199 989	0.60	_	100.00
Developed economies	56 174 801	0.60	_	50.07
Transition economies	2 617 512	0.30	_	2.33
Developing economies	53 407 677	0.70	100.00	47.60
China	17 382 729	0.90	32.55	15.49
Mexico	8 501 979	2.40	15.92	7.58
Korea, Republic of	3 771 893	0.70	7.06	3.36
China, Hong Kong SAR	3 531 084	0.70	6.61	3.15
Turkey	2 395 232	1.70	4.48	2.13
Morocco	1 932 640	9.00	3.62	1.72
Viet Nam	1 734 755	1.60	3.25	1.55
Tunisia	1 516 239	8.70	2.84	1.35
Philippines	1 353 254	2.70	2.53	1.21
Thailand	1 185 350	0.50	2.22	1.06

775 - Household equipment nes				
World	95 177 612	0.50	_	100.00
Developed economies	40 127 598	0.40	_	42.16
Transition economies	1 222 206	0.10	_	1.28
Developing economies	53 827 808	0.70	100.00	56.56
China	31 086 335	1.60	57.75	32.66
Mexico	4 607 249	1.30	8.56	4.84
Korea, Republic of	3 569 330	0.60	6.63	3.75
Turkey	3 567 665	2.50	6.63	3.75
Thailand	3 216 449	1.40	5.98	3.38
China, Hong Kong SAR	2 377 099	0.50	4.42	2.50
Malaysia	1 314 939	0.60	2.44	1.38
Singapore	885 396	0.20	1.64	0.93
United Arab Emirates	720 551	0.20	1.34	0.76
Indonesia	590 157	0.30	1.10	0.62

776 - Valves tubes; diodes, transistors				
World	555 996 807	3.00	_	100.00
Developed economies	152 727 387	1.60	_	27.47
Transition economies	400 177	0.00	_	0.07
Developing economies	402 869 243	5.00	100.00	72.46
Singapore	82 701 502	20.20	20.53	14.87
China	75 950 418	3.80	18.85	13.66
China, Hong Kong SAR	68 844 314	14.50	17.09	12.38
China, Taiwan Province of	65 891 438	21.70	16.36	11.85
Korea, Republic of	46 046 717	8.30	11.43	8.28
Malaysia	34 053 317	15.00	8.45	6.12
Philippines	10 163 981	20.30	2.52	1.83
Thailand	8 442 704	3.70	2.10	1.52
Costa Rica	4 156 517	38.70	1.03	0.75
Mexico	2 728 447	0.80	0.68	0.49

778 - Electrical machinery apparatus nes				
World	225 086 329	1.20	_	100.00
Developed economies	112 271 646	1.20	_	49.88
Transition economies	1 518 225	0.20	_	0.67
Developing economies	111 296 459	1.40	100.00	49.45
China	46 690 275	2.40	41.95	20.74
Korea, Republic of	15 036 736	2.70	13.51	6.68
China, Hong Kong SAR	11 449 397	2.40	10.29	5.09
China, Taiwan Province of	7 558 384	2.50	6.79	3.36
Mexico	7 550 553	2.10	6.78	3.35
Singapore	6 706 232	1.60	6.03	2.98
Thailand	3 756 944	1.60	3.38	1.67
Malaysia	2 887 994	1.30	2.59	1.28
Indonesia	1 862 377	0.90	1.67	0.83
Philippines	1 249 574	2.50	1.12	0.56

Leading exporting developing economies (1) based on average 2011-12 exports (2) SITC Revision 3 (3-digit level) Principales économies en développement exportatrices (1) d'après la moyenne des exportations de 2011-12 (2) CTCI révision 3 (positions à 3 chiffres)	2011-2012		
	Value (f.o.b., thousands of dollars) Valeur (f.a.b., milliers de dollars)	As percentage En pourcentage		
		of country total du total du pays	of developing economies des économies en déve-loppement	of world du monde

781 - Passenger cars and race cars				
World	642 904 162	3.50	_	100.00
Developed economies	527 296 741	5.60	_	82.02
Transition economies	2 107 866	0.30	_	0.33
Developing economies	113 499 556	1.40	100.00	17.65
Korea, Republic of	41 648 700	7.00	36.70	6.48
Mexico	28 006 715	7.80	24.68	4.36
Turkey	6 277 351	4.40	5.53	0.98
Thailand	5 972 513	2.60	5.26	0.93
Argentina	4 335 347	5.30	3.82	0.67
China	4 253 719	0.20	3.75	0.66
Brazil	4 050 484	1.60	3.57	0.63
India	3 931 571	1.30	3.46	0.61
United Arab Emirates	3 890 002	1.30	3.43	0.61
South Africa	3 509 005	3.90	3.09	0.55

782 - Goods and service vehicles				
World	132 235 005	0.70	_	100.00
Developed economies	83 702 472	0.90	_	63.30
Transition economies	2 348 923	0.30	_	1.78
Developing economies	46 183 609	0.60	100.00	34.93
Mexico	13 676 047	3.80	29.61	10.34
Thailand	7 961 847	3.50	17.24	6.02
China	5 753 234	0.30	12.46	4.35
Turkey	3 822 309	2.70	8.28	2.89
Argentina	3 674 355	4.50	7.96	2.78
Korea, Republic of	2 665 676	0.50	5.77	2.02
Brazil	2 157 739	0.90	4.67	1.63
South Africa	1 963 251	2.20	4.25	1.48
India	1 120 008	0.40	2.43	0.85
United Arab Emirates	929 659	0.30	2.01	0.70

784 - Motor vehicle parts and accessories				
World	358 447 779	2.00	_	100.00
Developed economies	261 824 487	2.80	_	73.04
Transition economies	1 088 513	0.10	_	0.30
Developing economies	95 534 780	1.20	100.00	26.65
Korea, Republic of	22 193 590	4.00	23.23	6.19
China	21 682 861	1.10	22.70	6.05
Mexico	18 032 957	5.00	18.88	5.03
Thailand	5 251 021	2.30	5.50	1.46
Brazil	4 934 457	2.00	5.17	1.38
China, Taiwan Province of	3 534 145	1.20	3.70	0.99
Turkey	3 483 527	2.40	3.65	0.97
India	3 401 434	1.20	3.56	0.95
Singapore	2 786 852	0.70	2.92	0.78
United Arab Emirates	1 740 348	0.60	1.82	0.49

792 - Aircraft, spacecraft & equipment				
World	161 123 983	0.90	_	100.00
Developed economies	137 155 767	1.50	_	85.12
Transition economies	937 632	0.10	_	0.58
Developing economies	23 030 584	0.30	100.00	14.29
Singapore	5 639 980	1.40	24.49	3.50
Brazil	4 778 648	1.90	20.75	2.97
India	2 038 936	0.70	8.85	1.27
China	1 588 247	0.10	6.90	0.99
Thailand	1 262 875	0.60	5.48	0.78
Korea, Republic of	1 031 992	0.20	4.48	0.64
Argentina	870 432	1.10	3.78	0.54
Malaysia	861 995	0.40	3.74	0.53
United Arab Emirates	845 172	0.30	3.67	0.52
Mexico	556 248	0.20	2.42	0.35

For sources and notes, see end of table.

Pour les sources et les notes, se reporter à la fin du tableau.

3.2.E Export structure by product
Major exporters for leading products
among developing economies

3.2.E Structure des exportations par produits
Principaux exportateurs de produits majeurs
parmi les économies en développement

Leading exporting developing economies (1) based on average 2011-12 exports (2) SITC Revision 3 (3-digit level) Principales économies en dévelopement exportatrices (1) d'après la moyenne des exportations de 2011-12 (2) CTCI révision 3 (positions à 3 chiffres)	2011-2012			
	Value (f.o.b., thousands of dollars) Valeur (f.a.b., milliers de dollars)	As percentage En pourcentage		
		of country total du total du pays	of developing economies des économies en déve-loppement	of world du monde
793 - Ships boats floating structures				
World	171 614 251	0.90	_	100.00
Developed economies	54 817 246	0.60	_	31.94
Transition economies	2 375 768	0.30	_	1.38
Developing economies	114 421 237	1.40	100.00	66.67
Korea, Republic of	45 980 767	8.30	40.19	26.79
China	41 222 499	2.10	36.03	24.02
India	5 586 444	1.90	4.88	3.26
Singapore	4 481 616	1.10	3.92	2.61
Venezuela (Bolivarian Rep. of)	3 243 021	3.50	2.83	1.89
Thailand	1 577 441	0.70	1.38	0.92
Brazil	1 350 799	0.50	1.18	0.79
Panama	1 180 394	7.70	1.03	0.69
Turkey	1 041 318	0.70	0.91	0.61
Indonesia	1 008 023	0.50	0.88	0.59
821 - Furniture part; bedding furnishing				
World	151 289 473	0.80	_	100.00
Developed economies	74 941 877	0.80	_	49.54
Transition economies	2 126 297	0.30	_	1.41
Developing economies	74 221 299	0.90	100.00	49.06
China	50 478 561	2.60	68.01	33.37
Mexico	5 315 161	1.50	7.16	3.51
Viet Nam	3 740 553	3.50	5.04	2.47
Malaysia	2 625 041	1.20	3.54	1.74
Indonesia	1 770 178	0.90	2.38	1.17
Turkey	1 749 193	1.20	2.36	1.16
China, Taiwan Province of	1 382 362	0.50	1.86	0.91
Thailand	1 151 539	0.50	1.55	0.76
Korea, Republic of	985 992	0.20	1.33	0.65
India	775 452	0.30	1.04	0.51
841 - Male clothing, woven				
World	71 238 016	0.40	_	100.00
Developed economies	21 299 104	0.20	_	29.90
Transition economies	1 019 304	0.10	_	1.43
Developing economies	48 919 609	0.60	100.00	68.67
China	20 535 957	1.00	41.98	28.83
Bangladesh	5 767 594	22.10	11.79	8.10
Viet Nam	3 590 683	3.40	7.34	5.04
China, Hong Kong SAR	2 967 140	0.60	6.07	4.17
Turkey	2 093 076	1.50	4.28	2.94
India	2 001 417	0.70	4.09	2.81
Mexico	1 932 092	0.50	3.95	2.71
Indonesia	1 688 730	0.90	3.45	2.37
Pakistan	1 015 574	4.10	2.08	1.43
Tunisia	850 649	4.90	1.74	1.19
842 - Female clothing, woven				
World	81 945 271	0.40	_	100.00
Developed economies	26 942 963	0.30	_	32.88
Transition economies	1 078 509	0.10	_	1.32
Developing economies	53 923 799	0.70	100.00	65.80
China	26 144 660	1.30	48.48	31.91
China, Hong Kong SAR	4 937 946	1.00	9.16	6.03
India	4 048 195	1.40	7.51	4.94
Viet Nam	3 246 086	3.10	6.02	3.96
Turkey	2 933 751	2.00	5.44	3.58
Bangladesh	2 683 500	10.30	4.98	3.27
Indonesia	1 607 198	0.80	2.98	1.96
Morocco	1 477 286	6.90	2.74	1.80
Sri Lanka	783 998	8.10	1.45	0.96
Pakistan	623 114	2.50	1.16	0.76

Leading exporting developing economies (1) based on average 2011-12 exports (2) SITC Revision 3 (3-digit level) Principales économies en dévelopement exportatrices (1) d'après la moyenne des exportations de 2011-12 (2) CTCI révision 3 (positions à 3 chiffres)	2011-2012			
	Value (f.o.b., thousands of dollars) Valeur (f.a.b., milliers de dollars)	As percentage En pourcentage		
		of country total du total du pays	of developing economies des économies en déve-loppement	of world du monde
845 - Articles of apparel nes				
World	140 462 440	0.80	_	100.00
Developed economies	40 368 376	0.40	_	28.74
Transition economies	1 307 608	0.20	_	0.93
Developing economies	98 786 456	1.20	100.00	70.33
China	45 441 359	2.30	46.00	32.35
China, Hong Kong SAR	10 092 699	2.10	10.22	7.19
Bangladesh	7 970 342	30.50	8.07	5.67
Turkey	4 940 874	3.40	5.00	3.52
Viet Nam	4 208 942	4.00	4.26	3.00
India	3 872 170	1.30	3.92	2.76
Indonesia	2 360 844	1.20	2.39	1.68
Cambodia	2 114 888	29.10	2.14	1.51
Tunisia	1 603 574	9.20	1.62	1.14
Honduras	1 481 248	18.80	1.50	1.05
851 - Footwear				
World	115 508 218	0.60	_	100.00
Developed economies	42 028 353	0.40	_	36.39
Transition economies	1 710 816	0.20	_	1.48
Developing economies	71 769 050	0.90	100.00	62.13
China	44 266 800	2.20	61.68	38.32
Viet Nam	7 572 992	7.20	10.55	6.56
China, Hong Kong SAR	5 416 666	1.10	7.55	4.69
Indonesia	3 413 267	1.70	4.76	2.95
India	2 024 413	0.70	2.82	1.75
Brazil	1 392 527	0.60	1.94	1.21
Panama	863 448	5.60	1.20	0.75
Thailand	832 359	0.40	1.16	0.72
Cambodia	598 014	8.20	0.83	0.52
Mexico	527 949	0.10	0.74	0.46
871 - Optical instruments apparatus nes				
World	106 025 076	0.60	_	100.00
Developed economies	20 266 153	0.20	_	19.11
Transition economies	299 291	0.00	_	0.28
Developing economies	85 459 631	1.10	100.00	80.60
China	35 706 395	1.80	41.78	33.68
Korea, Republic of	27 635 581	5.00	32.34	26.07
China, Taiwan Province of	17 027 199	5.60	19.92	16.06
China, Hong Kong SAR	3 711 507	0.80	4.34	3.50
Singapore	480 916	0.10	0.56	0.45
Thailand	329 242	0.10	0.39	0.31
Mexico	219 089	0.10	0.26	0.21
Malaysia	112 327	0.00	0.13	0.11
United Arab Emirates	45 265	0.00	0.05	0.04
Viet Nam	44 680	0.00	0.05	0.04
872 - Medical instruments appliances nes				
World	89 673 640	0.50	_	100.00
Developed economies	69 928 417	0.70	_	77.98
Transition economies	235 600	0.00	_	0.26
Developing economies	19 509 623	0.20	100.00	21.76
China	5 164 199	0.30	26.47	5.76
Mexico	4 863 506	1.40	24.93	5.42
Singapore	2 666 396	0.70	13.67	2.97
China, Hong Kong SAR	933 711	0.20	4.79	1.04
Dominican Republic	852 836	9.60	4.37	0.95
Malaysia	726 760	0.30	3.73	0.81
Korea, Republic of	684 704	0.10	3.51	0.76
Thailand	477 511	0.20	2.45	0.53
China, Taiwan Province of	475 104	0.20	2.44	0.53
Costa Rica	433 480	4.00	2.22	0.48

For sources and notes, see end of table.

Pour les sources et les notes, se reporter à la fin du tableau.

3.2.E Export structure by product
Major exporters for leading products among developing economies

3.2.E Structure des exportations par produits
Principaux exportateurs de produits majeurs parmi les économies en développement

Leading exporting developing economies (1) based on average 2011-12 exports (2) SITC Revision 3 (3-digit level) / Principales économies en dévelopement exportatrices (1) d'après la moyenne des exportations de 2011-12 (2) CTCI révision 3 (positions à 3 chiffres)	2011-2012			
	Value (f.o.b., thousands of dollars) / Valeur (f.a.b., milliers de dollars)	As percentage / En pourcentage		
		of country total / du total du pays	of developing economies / des économies en développement	of world / du monde
874 - Measure analyze control device nes				
World	182 363 086	1.00	_	100.00
Developed economies	140 172 044	1.50	_	76.86
Transition economies	1 448 329	0.20	_	0.79
Developing economies	40 742 713	0.50	100.00	22.34
China	11 080 000	0.60	27.20	6.08
Singapore	6 541 729	1.60	16.06	3.59
China, Hong Kong SAR	5 124 360	1.10	12.58	2.81
Malaysia	4 733 999	2.10	11.62	2.60
Mexico	3 632 064	1.00	8.91	1.99
Korea, Republic of	3 167 405	0.60	7.77	1.74
China, Taiwan Province of	2 035 318	0.70	5.00	1.12
Thailand	936 283	0.40	2.30	0.51
India	737 175	0.20	1.81	0.40
United Arab Emirates	409 802	0.10	1.01	0.22
893 - Articles of plastic nes				
World	137 861 883	0.80	_	100.00
Developed economies	81 435 800	0.90	_	59.07
Transition economies	1 367 855	0.20	_	0.99
Developing economies	55 058 228	0.70	100.00	39.94
China	27 530 619	1.40	50.00	19.97
China, Taiwan Province of	3 185 704	1.00	5.79	2.31
China, Hong Kong SAR	2 949 640	0.60	5.36	2.14
Mexico	2 823 786	0.80	5.13	2.05
Korea, Republic of	2 542 659	0.50	4.62	1.84
Thailand	2 148 765	0.90	3.90	1.56
Malaysia	1 936 943	0.90	3.52	1.40
Turkey	1 593 603	1.10	2.89	1.16
Singapore	1 350 324	0.30	2.45	0.98
Viet Nam	1 215 507	1.10	2.21	0.88
894 - Baby carriages, toys, games, sporting goods				
World	94 027 266	0.50	_	100.00
Developed economies	35 981 041	0.40	_	38.27
Transition economies	347 127	0.00	_	0.37
Developing economies	57 699 098	0.70	100.00	61.36
China	37 285 107	1.90	64.62	39.65
China, Hong Kong SAR	11 708 473	2.50	20.29	12.45
China, Taiwan Province of	2 129 332	0.70	3.69	2.26
Mexico	1 262 159	0.40	2.19	1.34
Thailand	834 886	0.40	1.45	0.89
Singapore	782 926	0.20	1.36	0.83
Indonesia	524 045	0.30	0.91	0.56
Viet Nam	476 403	0.50	0.83	0.51
Korea, Republic of	439 124	0.10	0.76	0.47
Pakistan	341 573	1.40	0.59	0.36

Leading exporting developing economies (1) based on average 2011-12 exports (2) SITC Revision 3 (3-digit level) / Principales économies en dévelopement exportatrices (1) d'après la moyenne des exportations de 2011-12 (2) CTCI révision 3 (positions à 3 chiffres)	2011-2012			
	Value (f.o.b., thousands of dollars) / Valeur (f.a.b., milliers de dollars)	As percentage / En pourcentage		
		of country total / du total du pays	of developing economies / des économies en développement	of world / du monde
897 - Jewellery nes (667)				
World	124 308 840	0.70	_	100.00
Developed economies	43 112 730	0.50	_	34.68
Transition economies	143 950	0.00	_	0.12
Developing economies	81 052 159	1.00	100.00	65.20
China	31 565 109	1.00	38.94	25.39
India	18 060 135	6.10	22.28	14.53
China, Hong Kong SAR	7 672 659	1.60	9.47	6.17
United Arab Emirates	4 595 289	1.50	5.67	3.70
Thailand	4 131 663	1.80	5.10	3.32
Singapore	3 021 325	0.70	3.73	2.43
Turkey	2 334 241	1.60	2.88	1.88
Malaysia	2 324 005	1.00	2.87	1.87
Viet Nam	1 747 221	1.70	2.16	1.41
Pakistan	1 047 119	4.20	1.29	0.84
899 - Manufactured articles nes				
World	81 610 684	0.40	_	100.00
Developed economies	52 629 564	0.60	_	64.49
Transition economies	171 999	0.00	_	0.21
Developing economies	28 809 122	0.40	100.00	35.30
China	18 918 989	1.00	65.67	23.18
China, Hong Kong SAR	2 267 934	0.50	7.87	2.78
Mexico	1 060 404	0.30	3.68	1.30
Singapore	987 698	0.20	3.43	1.21
Korea, Republic of	710 630	0.10	2.47	0.87
Viet Nam	658 712	0.60	2.29	0.81
China, Taiwan Province of	615 890	0.20	2.14	0.75
Indonesia	597 496	0.30	2.07	0.73
India	588 628	0.20	2.04	0.72
Thailand	342 328	0.10	1.19	0.42
971 - Gold non-monetary excluding ores				
World	251 422 403	1.40	_	100.00
Developed economies	116 767 675	1.20	_	46.44
Transition economies	1 813 832	0.20	_	0.72
Developing economies	132 840 896	1.70	100.00	52.84
China, Hong Kong SAR	38 239 296	8.10	28.79	15.21
United Arab Emirates	21 687 567	7.20	16.33	8.63
Mexico	8 005 951	2.20	6.03	3.18
Peru	7 523 574	16.60	5.66	2.99
Turkey	7 409 782	5.20	5.58	2.95
Thailand	6 307 838	2.80	4.75	2.51
South Africa	5 755 219	6.40	4.33	2.29
Korea, Republic of	3 116 956	0.60	2.35	1.24
Colombia	3 095 944	5.30	2.33	1.23
Brazil	2 508 090	1.00	1.89	1.00

Source:

UNCTAD secretariat calculations, based on UNCTAD, *UNCTADstat* Merchandise Trade Matrix

Notes:

(1) In addition, are presented for each product group the world total exports and the exports from developed, transition and developing economies.

(2) Commodity groups are selected on the basis of ranking by value.

Source :

Calculs du secrétariat de la CNUCED, basés sur la matrice du commerce de marchandises de *UNCTADstat* de la CNUCED

Notes :

(1) Les exportations mondiales totales et les exportations des économies développées, en transition et en développement sont également présentées pour chaque groupe de produits.

(2) Les groupes de produits sont sélectionnés d'après le classement par valeur.

SITC group Revision 3 (3-digit level) ranked according to the concentration index in 2012 Groupes de la CTCI Révision 3 (positions à 3 chiffres) classés d'après l'indice de concentration en 2012	Concentration index (1) Indice de concentration (1)			Structural change index (2) Indice de changement structurel (2) 1995=0	
	2005	2010	2012	2005	2012
264 Jute, other textile bast fibres n.e.s., raw, processed, not spun; waste of	0.825	0.771	0.747	0.086	0.135
261 Silk	0.738	0.650	0.659	0.291	0.319
633 Cork manufactures	0.601	0.613	0.641	0.076	0.078
666 Pottery	0.355	0.494	0.575	0.276	0.479
244 Cork, natural, raw and waste (including natural cork in blocks or sheets)	0.582	0.564	0.556	0.116	0.034
286 Uranium or thorium ores and concentrates	0.810	0.567	0.547	0.228	0.241
422 Fixed vegetable fats and oils, crude, refined or fractionated, other than "soft"	0.460	0.522	0.520	0.181	0.204
844 Women's textiles, knitted (articles as code 841, plus dresses skirts)	0.233	0.413	0.491	0.322	0.559
281 Iron ore and concentrates	0.356	0.461	0.490	0.164	0.248
813 Lighting fixtures and fittings, n.e.s.	0.277	0.389	0.484	0.260	0.462
322 Briquettes, lignites and peat	0.293	0.255	0.465	0.262	0.356
831 Cases bags(storage hand executive equipment instrument gun travel shopping back)	0.364	0.449	0.456	0.221	0.334
752 Automatic data-processing transcibing machines; magnetic optical readers, n.e.s.	0.284	0.447	0.456	0.436	0.627
885 Watches & clocks	0.432	0.443	0.453	0.168	0.222
843 Men's textile, knitted (coat suit trouser short shirt underwear nightwear)	0.242	0.414	0.449	0.334	0.523
658 Made-up articles, wholly or chiefly of textile materials, n.e.s.	0.314	0.417	0.438	0.254	0.357
871 Optical instruments and apparatus, n.e.s.	0.379	0.429	0.435	0.551	0.624
345 Coal gas, water gas, producer gas, similar gas (exclude other gas hydrocarbons)	0.680	0.326	0.424	0.822	0.452
697 Household equipment of base metal, n.e.s.	0.270	0.364	0.420	0.291	0.452
896 Works of art, collectors' pieces and antiques	0.440	0.441	0.419	0.162	0.144
846 Clothing accessories of textiles, knitted or crocheted or not (exluding babies)	0.260	0.370	0.407	0.261	0.442
231 Natural rubber, balata, gutta-percha, guayule, chicle, natural gums	0.444	0.417	0.406	0.157	0.206
894 Baby carriages, toys, games and sporting goods	0.344	0.364	0.405	0.241	0.353
652 Cotton fabrics, woven (not including narrow or special fabrics)	0.260	0.380	0.396	0.180	0.366
891 Arms and ammunition	0.402	0.405	0.393	0.254	0.318
222 Oil-seed, oleaginous fruit for soft fixed vegetable oils (exclude flours, meals)	0.379	0.388	0.384	0.302	0.294
851 Footwear	0.297	0.360	0.384	0.274	0.412
792 Aircraft, associated equipment; spacecraft, satellites, launch vehicles; parts	0.423	0.384	0.381	0.156	0.471
751 Office machines	0.318	0.360	0.379	0.375	0.461
653 Fabrics, woven, of man-made textiles (excluding narrow or special fabrics)	0.252	0.332	0.376	0.292	0.449
655 Knitted, crocheted fabric (include tubular knit, pile, openwork fabric), n.e.s.	0.260	0.341	0.372	0.250	0.422
321 Coal, whether or not pulverized, excluding agglomerated	0.355	0.394	0.372	0.213	0.238
268 Wool and other animal hair (including wool tops)	0.347	0.353	0.368	0.164	0.250
848 Apparel articles accessories other than textile fabrics; headgear (all material)	0.374	0.347	0.365	0.217	0.258
786 Trailers semi-trailers vehicles not mechanically-propelled; transport containers	0.339	0.373	0.361	0.244	0.311
285 Aluminium ores and concentrates (including alumina)	0.308	0.334	0.356	0.164	0.220
764 Telecommunications equipment and parts, n.e.s.; accessories within division 76	0.212	0.308	0.355	0.295	0.507
212 Furskins, raw, other than hides and skins of group 211	0.339	0.366	0.351	0.219	0.238
763 Sound or television image recorder reproducer; prepared unrecorded media	0.369	0.349	0.349	0.407	0.440
696 Cutlery	0.300	0.319	0.348	0.324	0.500
223 Oil-seed, oleaginous fruit to extract other vegetable oil; flour, meal of n.e.s.	0.281	0.240	0.342	0.416	0.533
821 Furniture and parts; bedding, mattresses, mattress supports, cushions	0.203	0.294	0.342	0.250	0.444
793 Ships, boats (including hovercraft) and floating structures	0.269	0.354	0.333	0.306	0.439
662 Clay construction materials and refractory construction materials	0.298	0.301	0.332	0.222	0.419
583 Plastic monofilament, cross-section > 1 mm, rods, sticks, profile shapes	0.357	0.362	0.331	0.174	0.266
284 Nickel ores, concentrates; mattes, oxide sinters, intermediate product of	0.296	0.331	0.328	0.192	0.164
731 Machine tools working by removing metal or other material	0.320	0.308	0.327	0.093	0.163
775 Household-type electrical and non-electrical equipment, n.e.s.	0.236	0.299	0.327	0.274	0.477
042 Rice	0.306	0.315	0.316	0.183	0.252
044 Maize (not including sweet corn), unmilled	0.443	0.424	0.313	0.288	0.516
897 Jewellery, articles of goldsmiths' silversmiths' B2 semiprecious, n.e.s.	0.206	0.200	0.313	0.233	0.436
656 Tulles, lace, embroidery, ribbons, trimmings and other smallwares	0.211	0.284	0.312	0.215	0.369
882 Photographic and cinematographic supplies	0.282	0.310	0.311	0.142	0.223
283 Copper ores and concentrates; copper mattes; cement copper	0.389	0.311	0.310	0.255	0.287
845 Articles of apparel, textile fabrics, knitted or crocheted or not, n.e.s.	0.243	0.306	0.307	0.253	0.393
711 Steam vapour superheated water boiler, auxiliary plant for use with; parts of	0.188	0.317	0.305	0.266	0.529
292 Crude vegetable materials, n.e.s.	0.360	0.308	0.305	0.091	0.230
842 Women's textiles not knitted (articles as code 841, plus dresses skirts)	0.242	0.310	0.305	0.230	0.329
654 Other textile fabrics, woven n.e.s.	0.272	0.289	0.305	0.187	0.283
551 Essential oils, perfume and flavour materials	0.367	0.312	0.302	0.325	0.332
774 Electrodiagnostic apparatus, medical surgical dental veterinary radiological	0.326	0.313	0.299	0.111	0.172
687 Tin	0.303	0.313	0.298	0.272	0.290
761 Television receiver, video monitor projector, w wo radio video-record reproduce	0.222	0.285	0.297	0.362	0.569
613 Furskin, tanned, dressed, unassembled, assembled (without other materials)	0.310	0.296	0.297	0.411	0.455

For sources and notes, see end of table 3.3 Imports.

Pour les sources et les notes, se reporter à la fin du tableau 3.3 Importations.

SITC group Revision 3 (3-digit level) ranked according to the concentration index in 2012 Groupes de la CTCI Révision 3 (positions à 3 chiffres) classés d'après l'indice de concentration en 2012	Concentration index (1) Indice de concentration (1)			Structural change index (2) Indice de changement structurel (2) 1995=0	
	2005	2010	2012	2005	2012
431 Animal, vegetable fats, oils, processed; waxes; inedible preparations of, n.e.s.	0.280	0.333	0.296	0.208	0.241
785 Motor cycles, mopeds, cycles, motorized and non-motorized; invalid carriages	0.291	0.290	0.295	0.254	0.402
265 Vegetable textile fibre (exclu cotton, jute), raw, processed, not spun; waste of	0.369	0.329	0.294	0.191	0.294
762 Radio-broadcast receivers, with without sound-recording reproducing or clock	0.247	0.262	0.293	0.322	0.460
593 Explosives and pyrotechnic products	0.309	0.289	0.293	0.234	0.269
726 Printing and bookbinding machinery, and parts thereof	0.354	0.303	0.285	0.131	0.183
272 Fertilizers, crude (excluding those of division 56)	0.300	0.276	0.285	0.193	0.257
263 Cotton	0.348	0.351	0.284	0.226	0.380
759 Parts, accessories for machines of groups 751, 752	0.230	0.254	0.281	0.318	0.407
037 Fish, crustaceans, molluscs, aquatic invertebrates (prepared preserved) n.e.s.	0.236	0.254	0.280	0.244	0.326
072 Cocoa	0.286	0.283	0.277	0.108	0.177
841 Men's textile, not knitted (coat suit trouser short shirt underwear nightwear)	0.216	0.281	0.274	0.223	0.322
597 Prepared additives: mineral oil; transmission; anti-freeze, de-ice; lubricating	0.286	0.274	0.270	0.119	0.180
267 Other man-made fibres suitable for spinning; waste of man-made fibres	0.371	0.269	0.270	0.174	0.368
061 Sugar, molasses and honey	0.209	0.316	0.269	0.313	0.416
023 Butter and other fats and oils derived from milk	0.227	0.255	0.268	0.187	0.248
781 Vehicles to transport less than 10 persons, including station-wagons race cars	0.274	0.272	0.268	0.122	0.196
899 Miscellaneous manufactured articles, n.e.s.	0.222	0.244	0.268	0.231	0.292
667 Pearls and precious or semiprecious stones, unworked or worked	0.267	0.267	0.266	0.205	0.346
665 Glassware	0.179	0.219	0.266	0.208	0.386
211 Hides and skins (except furskins), raw	0.268	0.294	0.266	0.194	0.188
771 Electric power machinery parts (excluding rotating electric plant, group 716)	0.225	0.253	0.265	0.212	0.297
712 Steam turbines and other vapour turbines, and parts thereof, n.e.s.	0.311	0.272	0.264	0.266	0.326
515 Organo-inorganic and heterocyclic compounds, nucleic acids-salts, sulphonamides	0.280	0.269	0.263	0.283	0.312
776 Thermionic cold cathode photo-cathode valves tubes; diodes, transistors	0.236	0.256	0.262	0.249	0.382
895 Office and stationery supplies, n.e.s.	0.205	0.238	0.262	0.213	0.341
525 Radio-actives and associated materials	0.316	0.280	0.261	0.250	0.399
745 Non-electrical machinery, tools and mechanical apparatus, parts thereof, n.e.s.	0.281	0.265	0.261	0.106	0.191
748 Transmission shaft camshaft crankshaft; bearing housing; gearbox speed changer	0.282	0.266	0.261	0.144	0.219
025 Eggs, birds', yolks, fresh, dried, preserved, sweetened or not; albumin	0.283	0.281	0.260	0.200	0.279
714 Engines, motors, non-electric (exclude group 712, 713 and 718); parts of, n.e.s.	0.354	0.253	0.260	0.126	0.277
045 Cereals, unmilled (excluding wheat, rice, barley, maize)	0.364	0.331	0.259	0.176	0.437
016 Meat, edible meat offal (salted dried); flours, meals	0.304	0.259	0.256	0.195	0.343
724 Textile and leather machinery, and parts thereof, n.e.s.	0.252	0.246	0.254	0.174	0.317
883 Cinematographic film, exposed developed, whether or not incorporating soundtrack	0.492	0.454	0.253	0.543	0.499
872 Instruments and appliances, n.e.s., (medical, surgical, dental or veterinary)	0.244	0.254	0.253	0.172	0.195
722 Tractors (excluding headings 714.14 & 744.15)	0.262	0.245	0.252	0.159	0.245
961 Coin (other than gold coin), not being legal tender	0.315	0.360	0.249	0.350	0.608
884 Optical goods, n.e.s.	0.279	0.245	0.248	0.168	0.277
733 Machine tool to work metal sintered metal carbide cermet, not removing material	0.249	0.232	0.247	0.157	0.190
251 Pulp and waste paper	0.263	0.247	0.247	0.139	0.201
121 Tobacco, unmanufactured; tobacco refuse	0.243	0.238	0.245	0.262	0.343
531 Synthetic organic colouring matter and colour lakes, preparations based thereon	0.232	0.234	0.244	0.216	0.372
874 Measuring, checking, analysing and controlling instruments and apparatus, n.e.s.	0.274	0.250	0.244	0.122	0.209
043 Barley, unmilled	0.263	0.241	0.242	0.313	0.452
541 Medicinal and pharmaceutical products, excluding medicines of group 542	0.247	0.257	0.241	0.144	0.222
721 Agricultural machinery (excluding tractors), and parts thereof	0.246	0.228	0.240	0.118	0.178
041 Wheat (including spelt) and meslin, unmilled	0.287	0.261	0.239	0.201	0.321
747 Appliances for pipes boiler shells tanks vats; pressure and temperature valves	0.224	0.233	0.238	0.165	0.264
737 Metalworking machinery (other than machine tools), and parts thereof, n.e.s.	0.222	0.236	0.238	0.146	0.224
694 Nails, screws, nuts, bolts, rivets, of iron, steel, copper or aluminium	0.224	0.233	0.237	0.134	0.192
273 Stone, sand and gravel	0.137	0.138	0.237	0.219	0.450
735 Parts, n.e.s. and accessories for machines of groups 731, 733; tool holder	0.244	0.227	0.236	0.136	0.196
728 Other machinery or specialized industrial equipment; parts thereof, n.e.s.	0.262	0.259	0.235	0.089	0.202
659 Floor coverings, etc.	0.232	0.227	0.233	0.169	0.328
657 Special yarns, special textile fabrics and related products	0.181	0.219	0.233	0.173	0.317
778 Electrical machinery and apparatus, n.e.s.	0.200	0.225	0.233	0.208	0.284
266 Synthetic fibres suitable for spinning	0.218	0.223	0.233	0.199	0.307
742 Liquid pump, with without a fitted measuring device; liquid elevator; parts for	0.256	0.232	0.233	0.153	0.251
683 Nickel	0.281	0.271	0.233	0.128	0.182
725 Paper mill pulp mill paper-cutting other paper manufacture machines; parts of	0.252	0.247	0.232	0.140	0.219
325 Coke, semi-coke of coal, lignite, peat, agglomerated or not; retort carbon	0.373	0.263	0.232	0.283	0.507
112 Alcoholic beverages	0.249	0.233	0.232	0.141	0.176
291 Crude animal materials, nes	0.222	0.219	0.232	0.157	0.187

For sources and notes, see end of table 3.3 Imports.

Pour les sources et les notes, se reporter à la fin du tableau 3.3 Importations.

SITC group Revision 3 (3-digit level) ranked according to the concentration index in 2012 / Groupes de la CTCI Révision 3 (positions à 3 chiffres) classés d'après l'indice de concentration en 2012	Concentration index (1) / Indice de concentration (1)			Structural change index (2) / Indice de changement structurel (2) 1995=0	
	2005	2010	2012	2005	2012
748 Ball or roller bearings	0.224	0.236	0.231	0.143	0.217
893 Articles, n.e.s., of plastics	0.188	0.197	0.231	0.176	0.282
074 Tea and maté	0.241	0.240	0.228	0.201	0.233
122 Tobacco, manufactured (whether or not containing tobacco substitutes)	0.271	0.242	0.228	0.400	0.470
727 Food-processing machines (excluding domestic); parts thereof	0.250	0.235	0.228	0.109	0.176
523 Metallic salts and peroxysalts, of inorganic acids	0.213	0.217	0.227	0.208	0.297
723 Civil engineering and contractors' plant and equipment; parts thereof	0.242	0.229	0.227	0.123	0.253
691 Structures and parts of structures, n.e.s., of iron, steel or aluminium	0.179	0.215	0.226	0.248	0.361
232 Synthetic rubber; reclaimed rubber; waste, parings, scrap of unhardened rubber	0.223	0.223	0.225	0.189	0.276
672 Ingots, other primary forms of iron or steel; semi-finished products of	0.209	0.231	0.224	0.212	0.340
695 Tools for use in the hand or in machine	0.211	0.216	0.224	0.137	0.220
024 Cheese and curd	0.240	0.227	0.223	0.169	0.234
572 Polymers of styrene, in primary forms	0.216	0.240	0.222	0.178	0.278
573 Polymers of vinyl chloride or of other halogenated olefins, in primary forms	0.186	0.227	0.222	0.168	0.281
783 Road motor vehicles, n.e.s.	0.246	0.215	0.222	0.235	0.368
612 Manufactures of leather or of composition leather, n.e.s.; saddlery and harness	0.220	0.217	0.221	0.361	0.400
791 Railway vehicles (including hovertrains) and associated equipment	0.232	0.230	0.221	0.255	0.375
343 Natural gas, whether or not liquefied	0.256	0.218	0.220	0.276	0.378
056 Vegetables, roots and tubers (prepared preserved) n.e.s.	0.203	0.222	0.220	0.167	0.198
743 Pump (non liquid), air gas compressor, fan ventilation filter; centrifuge; parts	0.220	0.215	0.220	0.148	0.236
744 Mechanical handling equipment, and parts thereof, n.e.s.	0.212	0.219	0.219	0.141	0.217
677 Rails or railway track construction material, of iron or steel	0.197	0.210	0.219	0.244	0.292
282 Ferrous waste and scrap; remelting scrap ingots of iron or steel	0.201	0.217	0.219	0.229	0.199
898 Musical instrument, parts accessory; tape, sound recording (excluding 763 & 883)	0.207	0.211	0.218	0.245	0.398
716 Rotating electric plant, and parts thereof, n.e.s.	0.189	0.212	0.218	0.189	0.279
516 Other organic chemicals	0.199	0.211	0.216	0.189	0.246
713 Internal combustion piston engines, and parts thereof, n.e.s.	0.239	0.222	0.215	0.194	0.235
971 Gold, non-monetary (excluding gold ores and concentrates)	0.200	0.167	0.215	0.349	0.472
651 Textile yarn	0.169	0.202	0.214	0.159	0.340
514 Nitrogen-function compounds	0.190	0.204	0.214	0.255	0.339
741 Heating and cooling equipment, and parts thereof, n.e.s.	0.193	0.208	0.214	0.218	0.325
579 Waste, parings and scrap, of plastics	0.255	0.246	0.214	0.253	0.345
081 Feeding stuff for animals (excluding unmilled cereals)	0.213	0.219	0.214	0.147	0.215
075 Spices	0.162	0.199	0.213	0.206	0.291
772 Electrical apparatus to switch protect circuits or make circuit connections	0.201	0.211	0.213	0.185	0.287
881 Photographic apparatus and equipment, n.e.s.	0.338	0.203	0.212	0.229	0.451
873 Meters and counters, n.e.s.	0.220	0.202	0.212	0.267	0.402
012 Other meat and edible meat offal (fresh chilled frozen)	0.207	0.207	0.211	0.275	0.338
749 Non-electric parts and accessories of machinery, n.e.s.	0.203	0.206	0.211	0.142	0.258
664 Glass	0.182	0.209	0.210	0.164	0.278
718 Power-generating machinery, and parts thereof, n.e.s.	0.222	0.215	0.210	0.195	0.249
782 Motor vehicles for the transport of goods and special-purpose motor vehicles	0.219	0.211	0.210	0.196	0.353
784 Parts and accessories of the motor vehicles of groups 722, 781, 782 and 783	0.215	0.207	0.210	0.209	0.323
689 Miscellaneous non-ferrous base metals employed in metallurgy, and cermets	0.259	0.229	0.209	0.308	0.281
675 Flat-rolled products of alloy steel	0.190	0.200	0.209	0.228	0.309
674 Flat-rolled products of iron or non-alloy steel, clad, plated or coated	0.180	0.195	0.208	0.223	0.368
553 Perfumery, cosmetic or toilet preparations (excluding soaps)	0.254	0.218	0.207	0.149	0.230
598 Miscellaneous chemical products, n.e.s.	0.233	0.211	0.207	0.119	0.192
513 Carboxylic acid, anhydrides, halides, peroxides, peroxyacids; halogenate derivatives	0.188	0.198	0.205	0.290	0.401
611 Leather	0.222	0.208	0.205	0.192	0.195
663 Mineral manufactures, n.e.s.	0.200	0.208	0.205	0.136	0.244
634 Veneers, plywood, particle board, and other wood, worked, n.e.s.	0.185	0.183	0.203	0.235	0.323
699 Manufactures of base metal, n.e.s.	0.196	0.197	0.203	0.154	0.261
542 Medicines (including veterinary medicines)	0.229	0.216	0.203	0.183	0.183
022 Milk, cream and milk products (excluding butter, cheese)	0.209	0.202	0.203	0.201	0.309
511 Hydrocarbons, n.e.s., halogenated, sulphonated, nitrated, nitrosated derivatives	0.204	0.196	0.202	0.165	0.278
277 Natural abrasives, n.e.s. (including industrial diamonds)	0.168	0.175	0.201	0.404	0.456
011 Meat of bovine animals (fresh chilled frozen)	0.216	0.191	0.200	0.297	0.303
524 Other inorganic chemicals; organic and inorganic compounds of precious metals	0.253	0.219	0.200	0.211	0.251
581 Tubes, pipes and hoses, and fittings therefor, of plastics	0.205	0.205	0.199	0.197	0.286
812 Sanitary, plumbing and heating fixtures and fittings, n.e.s.	0.212	0.208	0.199	0.206	0.321
342 Liquefied propane and butane	0.217	0.192	0.198	0.192	0.340
625 Rubber tyres, interchangeable tyre treads, tyre flaps, inner tubes for wheels	0.172	0.187	0.197	0.184	0.331
073 Chocolate and other food preparations containing cocoa, n.e.s.	0.199	0.197	0.197	0.199	0.220

For sources and notes, see end of table 3.3 Imports.

Pour les sources et les notes, se reporter à la fin du tableau 3.3 Importations.

SITC group Revision 3 (3-digit level) ranked according to the concentration index in 2012 Groupes de la CTCI Révision 3 (positions à 3 chiffres) classés d'après l'indice de concentration en 2012	Concentration index (1) Indice de concentration (1)			Structural change index (2) Indice de changement structurel (2) 1995=0	
	2005	2010	2012	2005	2012
591 Insecticide, rodenticide, fungicide, herbicide, plant-growth reg, disinfectant	0.210	0.194	0.197	0.203	0.275
679 Tubes, pipes and hollow profiles, and tube or pipe fittings, of iron or steel	0.175	0.184	0.196	0.162	0.286
892 Printed matter	0.214	0.190	0.195	0.129	0.240
248 Wood, simply worked, and railway sleepers of wood	0.251	0.188	0.195	0.211	0.292
287 Ores and concentrates of base metals, n.e.s.	0.211	0.192	0.194	0.282	0.231
661 Lime, cement, fabricated construction material (excluding glass, clay material)	0.175	0.191	0.193	0.287	0.383
533 Pigments, paints, varnishes and related materials	0.208	0.204	0.193	0.102	0.191
635 Wood manufactures, n.e.s.	0.185	0.188	0.193	0.232	0.315
017 Meat, edible meat offal (prepared preserved) n.e.s.	0.188	0.194	0.192	0.265	0.330
621 Materials of rubber (e.g., pastes, plates, sheets, rods, thread, tubes, of rubber)	0.218	0.192	0.192	0.131	0.342
811 Prefabricated buildings	0.145	0.187	0.192	0.253	0.394
288 Non-ferrous base metal waste and scrap, n.e.s.	0.185	0.195	0.191	0.201	0.218
091 Margarine and shortening	0.171	0.179	0.190	0.252	0.296
673 Flat-rolled products of iron or non-alloy steel, not clad, plated or coated	0.157	0.185	0.190	0.170	0.207
592 Starches, inulin and wheat gluten; albuminoidal substances; glues	0.196	0.193	0.189	0.132	0.214
693 Wire products (excluding insulated electrical wiring) and fencing grills	0.167	0.186	0.189	0.205	0.317
582 Plates, sheets, film, foil and strip, of plastics	0.201	0.199	0.189	0.125	0.246
421 Fixed vegetable fats and oils, "soft", crude, refined or fractionated	0.225	0.207	0.189	0.210	0.313
682 Copper	0.191	0.201	0.188	0.183	0.253
054 Vegetables and veg products (fresh chilled frozen preserved dried edible) n.e.s.	0.210	0.196	0.188	0.145	0.193
575 Other plastics, in primary forms	0.230	0.195	0.188	0.144	0.268
333 Petroleum oils and oils obtained from bituminous minerals, crude	0.180	0.172	0.188	0.136	0.206
629 Articles of rubber, n.e.s.	0.192	0.188	0.186	0.159	0.250
289 Ores and concentrates of precious metals; waste of (excluding gold)	0.258	0.401	0.186	0.324	0.444
071 Coffee and coffee substitutes	0.207	0.207	0.186	0.227	0.284
269 Worn clothing and other worn textile articles; rags	0.201	0.201	0.186	0.286	0.354
411 Animals oils and fats	0.207	0.230	0.185	0.232	0.292
059 Fruit and vegetable juice (unfermented, no added spirit, sweetened or not)	0.187	0.188	0.185	0.214	0.248
035 Fish (dried, salted, in brine, smoked); flours, meals, pellets for human consump	0.203	0.201	0.184	0.242	0.357
641 Paper and paperboard	0.202	0.188	0.183	0.119	0.213
773 Equipment for distributing electricity, n.e.s.	0.169	0.171	0.183	0.224	0.343
678 Wire of iron or steel	0.147	0.175	0.183	0.186	0.305
001 Live animals other than animals of division 03	0.198	0.185	0.183	0.156	0.248
642 Paper and paperboard, cut to size or shape, and articles of paper or paperboard	0.182	0.176	0.183	0.175	0.287
681 Silver, platinum, other metals of the platinum group	0.268	0.231	0.182	0.200	0.334
562 Fertilizers (excluding group 272)	0.184	0.180	0.181	0.215	0.306
274 Sulphur and unroasted iron pyrites	0.251	0.190	0.180	0.270	0.410
574 Polyacetal, polyether, epoxide resin; polycarbonate, alkyd resin, polyester	0.188	0.179	0.180	0.181	0.261
351 Electric current	0.201	0.161	0.178	0.364	0.411
047 Other cereal meals and flours	0.188	0.183	0.178	0.260	0.309
571 Polymers of ethylene, in primary forms	0.180	0.180	0.175	0.222	0.340
512 Alcohol, phenol, phenol-alcohol;halogenate, sulphonate, nitrate, nitrosate deriv	0.165	0.169	0.174	0.230	0.350
685 Lead	0.212	0.162	0.172	0.211	0.297
246 Wood in chips or particles and wood waste	0.222	0.172	0.172	0.337	0.459
058 Fruit, preserved, and fruit preparations (excluding fruit juices)	0.158	0.166	0.171	0.192	0.264
335 Residual petroleum products, n.e.s., related mater.	0.162	0.190	0.170	0.220	0.262
046 Meal and flour of wheat and flour of meslin	0.182	0.179	0.169	0.412	0.480
671 Pig-iron, spiegeleisen, sponge iron, iron steel granules, powders, ferro-alloys	0.182	0.166	0.169	0.235	0.311
247 Wood in the rough or roughly squared	0.264	0.188	0.168	0.320	0.330
034 Fish, fresh (live dead chilled frozen)	0.151	0.171	0.166	0.182	0.281
554 Soaps, cleansing and polishing preparations	0.182	0.167	0.166	0.123	0.208
048 Cereal preparations and preparations of flour or starch of fruits or vegetables	0.190	0.173	0.165	0.151	0.203
111 Non-alcoholic beverages, n.e.s.	0.198	0.177	0.164	0.268	0.315
036 Crustaceans, mollusks and aquatic invertebrates	0.134	0.148	0.162	0.230	0.259
278 Other crude minerals	0.164	0.167	0.161	0.166	0.257
686 Zinc	0.156	0.155	0.161	0.234	0.304
532 Dyeing and tanning extracts, and synthetic tanning materials	0.173	0.171	0.161	0.207	0.268
522 Inorganic chemical elements, oxides and halogen salts	0.174	0.180	0.160	0.150	0.245
057 Fruits and nuts (excluding oil nuts), fresh or dried	0.166	0.159	0.160	0.157	0.210
676 Iron and steel bars, rods, angles, shapes and sections (including sheet piling)	0.143	0.145	0.159	0.183	0.294
334 Petroleum oil, oil from bituminous (excl crude); preparations, n.e.s., > 70% oil	0.129	0.153	0.159	0.185	0.264
098 Edible products and preparations, n.e.s.	0.170	0.156	0.158	0.209	0.245
692 Metal containers for storage or transport	0.158	0.157	0.157	0.180	0.277
684 Aluminium	0.143	0.138	0.143	0.138	0.243
344 Petroleum gases and other gaseous hydrocarbons, n.e.s.	0.377	0.159	0.139	0.452	0.592
062 Sugar confectionery	0.139	0.132	0.134	0.206	0.262
245 Fuel wood (excluding wood waste) and wood charcoal	0.097	0.116	0.106	0.307	0.358

For sources and notes, see end of table 3.3 Imports.

Pour les sources et les notes, se reporter à la fin du tableau 3.3 Importations.

SITC group Revision 3 (3-digit level) ranked according to the concentration index in 2012 Groupes de la CTCI Révision 3 (positions à 3 chiffres) classés d'après l'indice de concentration en 2012	Concentration index (1) Indice de concentration (1)			Structural change index (2) Indice de changement structurel (2) 1995=0	
	2005	2010	2012	2005	2012
286 Uranium or thorium ores and concentrates	0.884	0.915	0.968	0.275	0.496
579 Waste, parings and scrap, of plastics	0.498	0.606	0.637	0.361	0.605
871 Optical instruments and apparatus, n.e.s.	0.596	0.618	0.615	0.641	0.693
322 Briquettes, lignites and peat	0.212	0.420	0.599	0.261	0.691
961 Coin (other than gold coin), not being legal tender	0.173	0.436	0.599	0.450	0.380
281 Iron ore and concentrates	0.428	0.584	0.589	0.376	0.519
263 Cotton	0.292	0.346	0.501	0.357	0.524
244 Cork, natural, raw and waste (including natural cork in blocks or sheets)	0.511	0.432	0.461	0.268	0.254
284 Nickel ores, concentrates; mattes, oxide sinters, intermediate product of	0.294	0.356	0.460	0.239	0.485
222 Oil-seed, oleaginous fruit for soft fixed vegetable oils (exclude flours, meals)	0.306	0.426	0.452	0.384	0.557
265 Vegetable textile fibre (exclu cotton, jute), raw, processed, not spun; waste of	0.356	0.462	0.451	0.459	0.535
896 Works of art, collectors' pieces and antiques	0.438	0.425	0.447	0.121	0.194
613 Furskin, tanned, dressed, unassembled, assembled (without other materials)	0.375	0.488	0.428	0.403	0.463
247 Wood in the rough or roughly squared	0.262	0.391	0.418	0.396	0.586
261 Silk	0.430	0.396	0.410	0.406	0.455
345 Coal gas, water gas, producer gas, similar gas (exclude other gas hydrocarbons)	0.434	0.356	0.405	0.808	0.767
268 Wool and other animal hair (including wool tops)	0.296	0.384	0.402	0.276	0.415
212 Furskins, raw, other than hides and skins of group 211	0.376	0.380	0.381	0.296	0.318
211 Hides and skins (except furskins), raw	0.276	0.334	0.376	0.308	0.400
274 Sulphur and unroasted iron pyrites	0.342	0.369	0.374	0.426	0.440
283 Copper ores and concentrates; copper mattes; cement copper	0.330	0.359	0.371	0.359	0.465
273 Stone, sand and gravel	0.153	0.205	0.348	0.252	0.588
246 Wood in chips or particles and wood waste	0.526	0.374	0.347	0.241	0.507
776 Thermionic cold cathode photo-cathode valves tubes; diodes, transistors	0.250	0.301	0.344	0.314	0.424
264 Jute, other textile bast fibres n.e.s., raw, processed, not spun; waste of	0.346	0.334	0.337	0.332	0.379
288 Non-ferrous base metal waste and scrap, n.e.s.	0.255	0.346	0.336	0.266	0.395
251 Pulp and waste paper	0.228	0.282	0.329	0.238	0.390
287 Ores and concentrates of base metals, n.e.s.	0.218	0.363	0.319	0.239	0.392
891 Arms and ammunition	0.244	0.333	0.308	0.312	0.354
043 Barley, unmilled	0.262	0.326	0.306	0.248	0.294
971 Gold, non-monetary (excluding gold ores and concentrates)	0.243	0.254	0.290	0.524	0.517
016 Meat, edible meat offal (salted dried); flours, meals	0.380	0.326	0.289	0.201	0.309
667 Pearls and precious or semiprecious stones, unworked or worked	0.293	0.313	0.287	0.205	0.332
761 Television receiver, video monitor projector, w wo radio video-record reproduce	0.339	0.285	0.287	0.314	0.299
525 Radio-actives and associated materials	0.318	0.293	0.275	0.230	0.235
762 Radio-broadcast receivers, with without sound-recording reproducing or clock	0.276	0.253	0.272	0.168	0.236
289 Ores and concentrates of precious metals; waste of (excluding gold)	0.366	0.307	0.271	0.272	0.372
681 Silver, platinum, other metals of the platinum group	0.268	0.252	0.270	0.225	0.293
731 Machine tools working by removing metal or other material	0.199	0.270	0.269	0.203	0.323
682 Copper	0.184	0.251	0.267	0.217	0.365
321 Coal, whether or not pulverized, excluding agglomerated	0.233	0.249	0.264	0.161	0.307
231 Natural rubber, balata, gutta-percha, guayule, chicle, natural gums	0.243	0.257	0.263	0.193	0.340
894 Baby carriages, toys, games and sporting goods	0.316	0.280	0.261	0.097	0.129
036 Crustaceans, mollusks and aquatic invertebrates	0.299	0.265	0.253	0.233	0.250
897 Jewellery, articles of goldsmiths' silversmiths' B2 semiprecious, n.e.s.	0.268	0.245	0.252	0.156	0.396
658 Made-up articles, wholly or chiefly of textile materials, n.e.s.	0.299	0.263	0.250	0.193	0.212
821 Furniture and parts; bedding, mattresses, mattress supports, cushions	0.304	0.252	0.249	0.209	0.209
511 Hydrocarbons, n.e.s., halogenated, sulphonated, nitrated, nitrosated derivatives	0.191	0.220	0.248	0.203	0.289
272 Fertilizers, crude (excluding those of division 56)	0.178	0.166	0.243	0.235	0.389
512 Alcohol, phenol, phenol-alcohol;halogenate, sulphonate, nitrate, nitrosate deriv	0.208	0.251	0.242	0.261	0.316
752 Automatic data-processing transcibing machines; magnetic optical readers, n.e.s.	0.231	0.236	0.240	0.144	0.252
633 Cork manufactures	0.252	0.246	0.238	0.159	0.253
285 Aluminium ores and concentrates (including alumina)	0.239	0.208	0.236	0.247	0.354
848 Apparel articles accessories other than textile fabrics; headgear (all material)	0.274	0.239	0.235	0.166	0.204
845 Articles of apparel, textile fabrics, knitted or crocheted or not, n.e.s.	0.270	0.241	0.234	0.163	0.187
843 Men's textile, knitted (coat suit trouser short shirt underwear nightwear)	0.317	0.257	0.233	0.177	0.218
689 Miscellaneous non-ferrous base metals employed in metallurgy, and cermets	0.250	0.227	0.232	0.136	0.202
572 Polymers of styrene, in primary forms	0.249	0.262	0.230	0.200	0.280
343 Natural gas, whether or not liquefied	0.260	0.209	0.230	0.333	0.341
885 Watches & clocks	0.232	0.224	0.229	0.121	0.144
844 Women's textiles, knitted (articles as code 841, plus dresses skirts)	0.285	0.236	0.229	0.152	0.224
515 Organo-inorganic and heterocyclic compounds, nucleic acids-salts, sulphonamides	0.266	0.241	0.226	0.203	0.227
342 Liquefied propane and butane	0.266	0.211	0.225	0.264	0.296
884 Optical goods, n.e.s.	0.215	0.222	0.225	0.290	0.347

For sources and notes, see end of table.

Pour les sources et les notes, se reporter à la fin du tableau.

SITC group Revision 3 (3-digit level) ranked according to the concentration index in 2012 Groupes de la CTCI Révision 3 (positions à 3 chiffres) classés d'après l'indice de concentration en 2012	Concentration index (1) Indice de concentration (1)			Structural change index (2) Indice de changement structurel (2) 1995=0	
	2005	2010	2012	2005	2012
683 Nickel	0.202	0.243	0.225	0.185	0.335
781 Vehicles to transport less than 10 persons, including station-wagons race cars	0.259	0.209	0.224	0.165	0.257
333 Petroleum oils and oils obtained from bituminous minerals, crude	0.241	0.233	0.222	0.121	0.233
611 Leather	0.227	0.222	0.222	0.204	0.223
841 Men's textile, not knitted (coat suit trouser short shirt underwear nightwear)	0.277	0.230	0.220	0.140	0.183
759 Parts, accessories for machines of groups 751, 752	0.204	0.217	0.219	0.238	0.364
017 Meat, edible meat offal (prepared preserved) n.e.s.	0.230	0.212	0.219	0.197	0.245
763 Sound or television image recorder reproducer; prepared unrecorded media	0.262	0.205	0.218	0.133	0.291
792 Aircraft, associated equipment; spacecraft, satellites, launch vehicles; parts	0.214	0.226	0.217	0.312	0.355
774 Electrodiagnostic apparatus, medical surgical dental veterinary radiological	0.244	0.210	0.215	0.172	0.176
714 Engines, motors, non-electric (exclude group 712, 713 and 718); parts of, n.e.s.	0.225	0.202	0.213	0.149	0.241
831 Cases bags(storage hand executive equipment instrument gun travel shopping back)	0.267	0.220	0.212	0.171	0.243
842 Women's textiles not knitted (articles as code 841, plus dresses skirts)	0.282	0.225	0.212	0.172	0.236
112 Alcoholic beverages	0.257	0.222	0.211	0.172	0.206
851 Footwear	0.253	0.216	0.209	0.142	0.206
267 Other man-made fibres suitable for spinning; waste of man-made fibres	0.165	0.189	0.208	0.235	0.349
422 Fixed vegetable fats and oils, crude, refined or fractionated, other than "soft"	0.175	0.189	0.208	0.206	0.300
621 Materials of rubber (e.g., pastes, plates, sheets, rods, thread, tubes, of rubber)	0.155	0.200	0.207	0.175	0.327
282 Ferrous waste and scrap; remelting scrap ingots of iron or steel	0.178	0.187	0.206	0.256	0.312
697 Household equipment of base metal, n.e.s.	0.268	0.215	0.206	0.178	0.187
037 Fish, crustaceans, molluscs, aquatic invertebrates (prepared preserved) n.e.s.	0.247	0.214	0.206	0.168	0.227
813 Lighting fixtures and fittings, n.e.s.	0.274	0.199	0.205	0.185	0.177
718 Power-generating machinery, and parts thereof, n.e.s.	0.188	0.186	0.205	0.232	0.315
071 Coffee and coffee substitutes	0.213	0.203	0.205	0.118	0.135
687 Tin	0.207	0.193	0.204	0.336	0.369
292 Crude vegetable materials, n.e.s.	0.193	0.173	0.201	0.125	0.227
277 Natural abrasives, n.e.s. (including industrial diamonds)	0.177	0.192	0.200	0.276	0.432
045 Cereals, unmilled (excluding wheat, rice, barley, maize)	0.271	0.228	0.200	0.254	0.344
072 Cocoa	0.226	0.211	0.199	0.139	0.195
764 Telecommunications equipment and parts, n.e.s.; accessories within division 76	0.182	0.190	0.198	0.158	0.212
058 Fruit, preserved, and fruit preparations (excluding fruit juices)	0.217	0.193	0.195	0.154	0.240
635 Wood manufactures, n.e.s.	0.273	0.194	0.194	0.217	0.187
899 Miscellaneous manufactured articles, n.e.s.	0.201	0.197	0.194	0.164	0.177
671 Pig-iron, spiegeleisen, sponge iron, iron steel granules, powders, ferro-alloys	0.192	0.195	0.194	0.165	0.224
025 Eggs, birds', yolks, fresh, dried, preserved, sweetened or not; albumin	0.217	0.219	0.193	0.181	0.310
751 Office machines	0.249	0.210	0.192	0.117	0.211
344 Petroleum gases and other gaseous hydrocarbons, n.e.s.	0.233	0.201	0.192	0.501	0.555
784 Parts and accessories of the motor vehicles of groups 722, 781, 782 and 783	0.212	0.178	0.189	0.150	0.262
873 Meters and counters, n.e.s.	0.201	0.178	0.187	0.164	0.184
872 Instruments and appliances, n.e.s., (medical, surgical, dental or veterinary)	0.208	0.186	0.187	0.181	0.177
248 Wood, simply worked, and railway sleepers of wood	0.285	0.170	0.187	0.217	0.336
846 Clothing accessories of textiles, knitted or crocheted or not (exluding babies)	0.194	0.183	0.186	0.204	0.242
325 Coke, semi-coke of coal, lignite, peat, agglomerated or not; retort carbon	0.193	0.166	0.186	0.287	0.389
771 Electric power machinery parts (excluding rotating electric plant, group 716)	0.194	0.185	0.184	0.163	0.231
772 Electrical apparatus to switch protect circuits or make circuit connections	0.171	0.184	0.184	0.215	0.298
541 Medicinal and pharmaceutical products, excluding medicines of group 542	0.196	0.183	0.183	0.159	0.187
713 Internal combustion piston engines, and parts thereof, n.e.s.	0.210	0.174	0.183	0.184	0.274
666 Pottery	0.251	0.198	0.183	0.154	0.255
335 Residual petroleum products, n.e.s., related mater.	0.165	0.175	0.183	0.255	0.358
874 Measuring, checking, analysing and controlling instruments and apparatus, n.e.s.	0.171	0.175	0.182	0.122	0.203
612 Manufactures of leather or of composition leather, n.e.s.; saddlery and harness	0.217	0.189	0.182	0.278	0.294
733 Machine tool to work metal sintered metal carbide cermet, not removing material	0.188	0.177	0.182	0.229	0.311
035 Fish (dried, salted, in brine, smoked); flours, meals, pellets for human consump	0.197	0.184	0.180	0.152	0.252
686 Zinc	0.179	0.174	0.179	0.239	0.278
059 Fruit and vegetable juice (unfermented, no added spirit, sweetened or not)	0.190	0.178	0.177	0.149	0.179
724 Textile and leather machinery, and parts thereof, n.e.s.	0.174	0.188	0.176	0.192	0.201
034 Fish, fresh (live dead chilled frozen)	0.211	0.175	0.176	0.190	0.255
232 Synthetic rubber; reclaimed rubber; waste, parings, scrap of unhardened rubber	0.165	0.190	0.175	0.167	0.306
735 Parts, n.e.s. and accessories for machines of groups 731, 733; tool holder	0.168	0.167	0.175	0.164	0.224
122 Tobacco, manufactured (whether or not containing tobacco substitutes)	0.185	0.165	0.174	0.283	0.301
775 Household-type electrical and non-electrical equipment, n.e.s.	0.188	0.175	0.174	0.182	0.218
514 Nitrogen-function compounds	0.158	0.168	0.174	0.174	0.207
748 Transmission shaft camshaft crankshaft; bearing housing; gearbox speed changer	0.178	0.169	0.174	0.164	0.226
895 Office and stationery supplies, n.e.s.	0.177	0.160	0.173	0.149	0.224

For sources and notes, see end of table.

Pour les sources et les notes, se reporter à la fin du tableau.

SITC group Revision 3 (3-digit level) ranked according to the concentration index in 2012 / Groupes de la CTCI Révision 3 (positions à 3 chiffres) classés d'après l'indice de concentration en 2012	Concentration index (1) Indice de concentration (1)			Structural change index (2) Indice de changement structurel (2) 1995=0	
	2005	2010	2012	2005	2012
882 Photographic and cinematographic supplies	0.147	0.157	0.172	0.211	0.333
524 Other inorganic chemicals; organic and inorganic compounds of precious metals	0.169	0.168	0.172	0.147	0.225
513 Carboxylic acid, anhydrides, halides, peroxides, peroxyacids; halogenate derivatives	0.216	0.189	0.171	0.248	0.277
659 Floor coverings, etc.	0.221	0.173	0.170	0.242	0.277
778 Electrical machinery and apparatus, n.e.s.	0.170	0.173	0.169	0.167	0.217
728 Other machinery or specialized industrial equipment; parts thereof, n.e.s.	0.159	0.199	0.168	0.152	0.156
291 Crude animal materials, nes	0.185	0.165	0.166	0.209	0.220
024 Cheese and curd	0.192	0.170	0.166	0.186	0.244
898 Musical instrument, parts accessory; tape, sound recording (excluding 763 & 883)	0.171	0.151	0.165	0.159	0.264
747 Appliances for pipes boiler shells tanks vats; pressure and temperature valves	0.173	0.156	0.164	0.162	0.213
625 Rubber tyres, interchangeable tyre treads, tyre flaps, inner tubes for wheels	0.186	0.163	0.163	0.154	0.229
542 Medicines (including veterinary medicines)	0.202	0.179	0.163	0.233	0.203
001 Live animals other than animals of division 03	0.200	0.166	0.163	0.221	0.290
571 Polymers of ethylene, in primary forms	0.160	0.167	0.162	0.202	0.278
696 Cutlery	0.193	0.166	0.162	0.181	0.243
746 Ball or roller bearings	0.160	0.164	0.162	0.147	0.218
593 Explosives and pyrotechnic products	0.221	0.187	0.162	0.263	0.302
812 Sanitary, plumbing and heating fixtures and fittings, n.e.s.	0.182	0.168	0.160	0.238	0.239
694 Nails, screws, nuts, bolts, rivets, of iron, steel, copper or aluminium	0.194	0.155	0.160	0.149	0.242
562 Fertilizers (excluding group 272)	0.148	0.159	0.159	0.210	0.294
773 Equipment for distributing electricity, n.e.s.	0.186	0.154	0.158	0.146	0.212
685 Lead	0.159	0.156	0.157	0.246	0.302
786 Trailers semi-trailers vehicles not mechanically-propelled; transport containers	0.163	0.150	0.157	0.190	0.259
075 Spices	0.166	0.149	0.157	0.140	0.241
742 Liquid pump, with without a fitted measuring device; liquid elevator; parts for	0.151	0.143	0.157	0.164	0.240
722 Tractors (excluding headings 714.14 & 744.15)	0.213	0.153	0.157	0.181	0.264
881 Photographic apparatus and equipment, n.e.s.	0.226	0.155	0.155	0.246	0.282
056 Vegetables, roots and tubers (prepared preserved) n.e.s.	0.184	0.158	0.155	0.153	0.202
893 Articles, n.e.s., of plastics	0.175	0.155	0.154	0.141	0.175
712 Steam turbines and other vapour turbines, and parts thereof, n.e.s.	0.161	0.146	0.154	0.392	0.473
351 Electric current	0.180	0.147	0.154	0.334	0.347
629 Articles of rubber, n.e.s.	0.173	0.151	0.154	0.137	0.198
054 Vegetables and veg products (fresh chilled frozen preserved dried edible) n.e.s.	0.188	0.155	0.153	0.175	0.272
575 Other plastics, in primary forms	0.148	0.159	0.152	0.165	0.264
266 Synthetic fibres suitable for spinning	0.187	0.150	0.152	0.166	0.266
551 Essential oils, perfume and flavour materials	0.184	0.159	0.151	0.221	0.231
664 Glass	0.148	0.137	0.151	0.168	0.254
011 Meat of bovine animals (fresh chilled frozen)	0.204	0.154	0.150	0.245	0.283
057 Fruits and nuts (excluding oil nuts), fresh or dried	0.177	0.158	0.150	0.162	0.244
651 Textile yarn	0.149	0.147	0.150	0.200	0.351
695 Tools for use in the hand or in machine	0.162	0.147	0.149	0.140	0.201
684 Aluminium	0.178	0.151	0.149	0.155	0.200
044 Maize (not including sweet corn), unmilled	0.193	0.163	0.149	0.193	0.268
725 Paper mill pulp mill paper-cutting other paper manufacture machines; parts of	0.139	0.161	0.148	0.198	0.228
522 Inorganic chemical elements, oxides and halogen salts	0.176	0.160	0.148	0.140	0.201
516 Other organic chemicals	0.163	0.155	0.148	0.148	0.245
574 Polyacetal, polyether, epoxide resin; polycarbonate, alkyd resin, polyester	0.144	0.165	0.147	0.233	0.310
023 Butter and other fats and oils derived from milk	0.185	0.154	0.147	0.232	0.300
223 Oil-seed, oleaginous fruit to extract other vegetable oil; flour, meal of n.e.s.	0.192	0.168	0.147	0.384	0.430
883 Cinematographic film, exposed developed, whether or not incorporating soundtrack	0.512	0.453	0.147	0.367	0.479
592 Starches, inulin and wheat gluten; albuminoidal substances; glues	0.143	0.141	0.146	0.141	0.231
245 Fuel wood (excluding wood waste) and wood charcoal	0.174	0.151	0.145	0.219	0.333
782 Motor vehicles for the transport of goods and special-purpose motor vehicles	0.195	0.141	0.144	0.183	0.310
062 Sugar confectionery	0.184	0.150	0.144	0.196	0.226
737 Metalworking machinery (other than machine tools), and parts thereof, n.e.s.	0.180	0.153	0.143	0.194	0.248
699 Manufactures of base metal, n.e.s.	0.169	0.137	0.141	0.124	0.179
598 Miscellaneous chemical products, n.e.s.	0.147	0.145	0.141	0.144	0.185
672 Ingots, other primary forms of iron or steel; semi-finished products of	0.165	0.150	0.141	0.255	0.345
743 Pump (non liquid), air gas compressor, fan ventilation filter; centrifuge; parts	0.159	0.138	0.141	0.143	0.192
663 Mineral manufactures, n.e.s.	0.164	0.139	0.140	0.159	0.201
111 Non-alcoholic beverages, n.e.s.	0.166	0.142	0.140	0.267	0.289
785 Motor cycles, mopeds, cycles, motorized and non-motorized; invalid carriages	0.203	0.141	0.140	0.232	0.206
679 Tubes, pipes and hollow profiles, and tube or pipe fittings, of iron or steel	0.130	0.120	0.140	0.189	0.297
582 Plates, sheets, film, foil and strip, of plastics	0.136	0.142	0.139	0.167	0.264

For sources and notes, see end of table.

Pour les sources et les notes, se reporter à la fin du tableau.

SITC group Revision 3 (3-digit level) ranked according to the concentration index in 2012 Groupes de la CTCI Révision 3 (positions à 3 chiffres) classés d'après l'indice de concentration en 2012	Concentration index (1) Indice de concentration (1)			Structural change index (2) Indice de changement structurel (2) 1995=0	
	2005	2010	2012	2005	2012
749 Non-electric parts and accessories of machinery, n.e.s.	0.146	0.138	0.139	0.164	0.225
721 Agricultural machinery (excluding tractors), and parts thereof	0.150	0.136	0.138	0.153	0.206
745 Non-electrical machinery, tools and mechanical apparatus, parts thereof, n.e.s.	0.153	0.139	0.138	0.140	0.179
655 Knitted, crocheted fabric (include tubular knit, pile, openwork fabric), n.e.s.	0.161	0.143	0.137	0.307	0.418
634 Veneers, plywood, particle board, and other wood, worked, n.e.s.	0.243	0.136	0.136	0.287	0.294
073 Chocolate and other food preparations containing cocoa, n.e.s.	0.155	0.138	0.136	0.196	0.214
121 Tobacco, unmanufactured; tobacco refuse	0.148	0.126	0.136	0.263	0.358
012 Other meat and edible meat offal (fresh chilled frozen)	0.181	0.144	0.135	0.238	0.340
675 Flat-rolled products of alloy steel	0.190	0.140	0.135	0.239	0.245
783 Road motor vehicles, n.e.s.	0.135	0.118	0.135	0.287	0.340
716 Rotating electric plant, and parts thereof, n.e.s.	0.165	0.133	0.134	0.172	0.214
532 Dyeing and tanning extracts, and synthetic tanning materials	0.138	0.138	0.133	0.202	0.249
791 Railway vehicles (including hovertrains) and associated equipment	0.139	0.143	0.131	0.315	0.391
421 Fixed vegetable fats and oils, "soft", crude, refined or fractionated	0.147	0.130	0.131	0.241	0.247
278 Other crude minerals	0.142	0.136	0.131	0.141	0.238
431 Animal, vegetable fats, oils, processed; waxes; inedible preparations of, n.e.s.	0.123	0.111	0.131	0.257	0.299
892 Printed matter	0.156	0.135	0.131	0.133	0.160
726 Printing and bookbinding machinery, and parts thereof	0.149	0.130	0.130	0.165	0.275
654 Other textile fabrics, woven n.e.s.	0.140	0.138	0.129	0.241	0.275
411 Animals oils and fats	0.129	0.137	0.129	0.277	0.339
048 Cereal preparations and preparations of flour or starch of fruits or vegetables	0.152	0.134	0.127	0.213	0.242
334 Petroleum oil, oil from bituminous (excl crude); preparations, n.e.s., > 70% oil	0.168	0.133	0.127	0.227	0.249
711 Steam vapour superheated water boiler, auxiliary plant for use with; parts of	0.124	0.160	0.127	0.306	0.404
665 Glassware	0.153	0.131	0.127	0.180	0.256
744 Mechanical handling equipment, and parts thereof, n.e.s.	0.157	0.114	0.126	0.172	0.199
573 Polymers of vinyl chloride or of other halogenated olefins, in primary forms	0.151	0.137	0.126	0.265	0.345
597 Prepared additives: mineral oil; transmission; anti-freeze, de-ice; lubricating	0.113	0.123	0.124	0.165	0.223
723 Civil engineering and contractors' plant and equipment; parts thereof	0.148	0.113	0.123	0.192	0.265
642 Paper and paperboard, cut to size or shape, and articles of paper or paperboard	0.148	0.129	0.123	0.133	0.185
074 Tea and maté	0.130	0.123	0.121	0.205	0.234
657 Special yarns, special textile fabrics and related products	0.133	0.123	0.121	0.157	0.234
741 Heating and cooling equipment, and parts thereof, n.e.s.	0.127	0.115	0.121	0.184	0.241
641 Paper and paperboard	0.164	0.128	0.121	0.126	0.217
678 Wire of iron or steel	0.151	0.125	0.119	0.157	0.256
531 Synthetic organic colouring matter and colour lakes, preparations based thereon	0.127	0.124	0.119	0.151	0.244
677 Rails or railway track construction material, of iron or steel	0.140	0.126	0.119	0.313	0.381
793 Ships, boats (including hovercraft) and floating structures	0.122	0.163	0.119	0.423	0.382
693 Wire products (excluding insulated electrical wiring) and fencing grills	0.149	0.112	0.116	0.172	0.213
553 Perfumery, cosmetic or toilet preparations (excluding soaps)	0.133	0.115	0.116	0.139	0.191
656 Tulles, lace, embroidery, ribbons, trimmings and other smallwares	0.124	0.115	0.115	0.235	0.319
652 Cotton fabrics, woven (not including narrow or special fabrics)	0.128	0.116	0.114	0.241	0.358
583 Plastic monofilament, cross-section > 1 mm, rods, sticks, profile shapes	0.145	0.122	0.113	0.301	0.324
042 Rice	0.088	0.103	0.112	0.289	0.304
673 Flat-rolled products of iron or non-alloy steel, not clad, plated or coated	0.137	0.123	0.111	0.247	0.282
653 Fabrics, woven, of man-made textiles (excluding narrow or special fabrics)	0.116	0.111	0.111	0.249	0.369
047 Other cereal meals and flours	0.117	0.107	0.110	0.377	0.413
674 Flat-rolled products of iron or non-alloy steel, clad, plated or coated	0.142	0.113	0.108	0.209	0.286
811 Prefabricated buildings	0.124	0.101	0.107	0.447	0.434
091 Margarine and shortening	0.115	0.101	0.106	0.348	0.418
691 Structures and parts of structures, n.e.s., of iron, steel or aluminium	0.125	0.101	0.105	0.262	0.327
081 Feeding stuff for animals (excluding unmilled cereals)	0.122	0.110	0.104	0.144	0.244
046 Meal and flour of wheat and flour of meslin	0.149	0.113	0.103	0.418	0.452
591 Insecticide, rodenticide, fungicide, herbicide, plant-growth reg, disinfectant	0.115	0.100	0.103	0.162	0.231
581 Tubes, pipes and hoses, and fittings therefor, of plastics	0.123	0.102	0.102	0.172	0.226
022 Milk, cream and milk products (excluding butter, cheese)	0.121	0.103	0.100	0.243	0.313
533 Pigments, paints, varnishes and related materials	0.110	0.102	0.099	0.136	0.178
661 Lime, cement, fabricated construction material (excluding glass, clay material)	0.229	0.101	0.098	0.336	0.340
692 Metal containers for storage or transport	0.115	0.095	0.098	0.169	0.226
727 Food-processing machines (excluding domestic); parts thereof	0.103	0.086	0.095	0.198	0.219
676 Iron and steel bars, rods, angles, shapes and sections (including sheet piling)	0.122	0.098	0.094	0.205	0.311
523 Metallic salts and peroxysalts, of inorganic acids	0.107	0.099	0.092	0.121	0.203
098 Edible products and preparations, n.e.s.	0.110	0.096	0.092	0.159	0.227
554 Soaps, cleansing and polishing preparations	0.115	0.096	0.092	0.133	0.191
061 Sugar, molasses and honey	0.107	0.086	0.090	0.227	0.248
041 Wheat (including spelt) and meslin, unmilled	0.102	0.091	0.089	0.276	0.306
662 Clay construction materials and refractory construction materials	0.145	0.089	0.084	0.251	0.343
269 Worn clothing and other worn textile articles; rags	0.075	0.068	0.069	0.356	0.418

For sources and notes, see next page

Pour les sources et les notes, se reporter à la page suivante.

3

Source:

UNCTAD secretariat calculations, based on UNCTAD, *UNCTADstat* Merchandise Trade Matrix

Source :

Calculs du secrétariat de la CNUCED, basés sur la matrice du commerce de marchandises de *UNCTADstat* de la CNUCED

Notes:

(1)   Concentration index:

The Herfindahl-Hirschmann index is a measure of the degree of market concentration. It has been normalized to obtain values ranking from 0 to 1 (maximum concentration), according to the following formula:

$$H_i = \frac{\sqrt{\sum_{j=1}^{n}(\frac{x_{ij}}{X_i})^2} - \sqrt{\frac{1}{n}}}{1 - \sqrt{\frac{1}{n}}}$$

where

H_i = Value of concentration index for product i

x_{ij} = Value of exports or imports for country j and product i

$$X_i = \sum_{j=1}^{n} x_{ij}$$

and

n = maximum number of individual economies

An index value that is close to 1 indicates a very concentrated market. On the contrary, values closer to 0 reflect a more equal distribution of market shares among exporters or importers.

(2)   Structural change index:

This index, ranging from 0 to 1 reveals the structural change in trade for a particular product as compared to the reference year (1995 = 0).

An index value close to 1 indicates a significant change in the composition of exporters (importers). On the contrary, values closer to 0 would demonstrate a higher degree of "traditionality" in the markets over the period concerned.

The value is calculated as follows:

$$I_i = \frac{\sum_{j=1}^{} \left| S_{ij}^{1} - S_{ij}^{0} \right|}{2}$$

where

I_i = Value of structure index for product *i*

S^0_{ij} = Share of trade of product *i* for country *j* in 1995

S^1_{ij} = Share of trade of product *i* for the country *j* in the concerned year

Notes :

(1)   Indice de concentration :

L'indice Herfindahl-Hirschmann mesure le degré de concentration des marchés. Il a été normalisé afin d'obtenir des valeurs comprises entre 0 et 1 (concentration maximale), d'après la formule suivante :

$$H_i = \frac{\sqrt{\sum_{j=1}^{n}(\frac{x_{ij}}{X_i})^2} - \sqrt{\frac{1}{n}}}{1 - \sqrt{\frac{1}{n}}}$$

où

H_i = Valeur de l'indice de concentration pour le produit i

x_{ij} = Valeur des exportations ou des importations du pays j pour le produit i

$$X_i = \sum_{j=1}^{n} x_{ij}$$

et

n = nombre maximum d'économies individuelles

Un indice proche de 1 indique une concentration très forte du marché pour ce produit en particulier. En revanche, une valeur proche de 0 démontre une répartition plus homogène du commerce entre les exportateurs ou les importateurs.

(2)   Indice de changement structurel :

Cet indice, dont la valeur est comprise entre 0 et 1, représente les changements de structure du commerce par rapport à une année de référence (1995 = 0).

Une valeur proche de 1 indique un important changement structurel du commerce de ce produit, c'est à dire, une grande variation des parts de marché au sein des exportateurs ou importateurs, par rapport à l'année de référence. Plus la valeur de l'indice est proche de 0, plus la structure du commerce de ce produit est stable.

Il est calculé comme suit :

$$I_i = \frac{\sum_{j=1}^{} \left| S_{ij}^{1} - S_{ij}^{0} \right|}{2}$$

où

I_i = Valeur de l'indice de changement structurel, pour le produit *i*

S^0_{ij} = Part du commerce du produit *i* pour le pays *j* par rapport au commerce total de ce produit pour l'année 1995

S^1_{ij} = Part du commerce du produit *i* pour le pays *j*, par rapport au commerce total de ce produit pour l'année concernée

4

INTERNATIONAL **MERCHANDISE** TRADE INDICATORS

INDICATEURS DU COMMERCE INTERNATIONAL DES **MARCHANDISES**

4.1.1 Export and import concentration and diversification indices of countries and geographical regions

Region, country or territory	Exports - Exportations					
	2005			2012		
	Number of products exported	Diversification index	Concentration index	Number of products exported	Diversification index	Concentration index
	Nombre de produits exportés (1)	Indice de diversification (2)	Indice de concentration (3)	Nombre de produits exportés (1)	Indice de diversification (2)	Indice de concentration (3)
WORLD	260	0.000	0.077	260	0.000	0.089
DEVELOPING ECONOMIES	260	0.247	0.140	260	0.199	0.141
TRANSITION ECONOMIES	257	0.578	0.293	257	0.544	0.332
DEVELOPED ECONOMIES	260	0.159	0.066	260	0.189	0.066
Developing economies: Africa	260	0.600	0.433	260	0.551	0.452
Eastern Africa	255	0.676	0.115	256	0.658	0.135
Burundi	18	0.790	0.608	52	0.746	0.437
Comoros	12	0.679	0.543	6	0.768	0.542
Djibouti	54	0.650	0.152	85	0.616	0.239
Eritrea	52	0.634	0.155	31	0.785	0.883
Ethiopia	52	0.643	0.379	149	0.772	0.338
Kenya	227	0.709	0.209	237	0.645	0.192
Madagascar	123	0.732	0.228	147	0.756	0.235
Malawi	74	0.825	0.565	152	0.790	0.465
Mauritius	166	0.703	0.280	180	0.697	0.241
Mozambique	101	0.813	0.633	129	0.760	0.293
Rwanda	36	0.757	0.450	96	0.812	0.380
Seychelles	44	0.830	0.460	74	0.831	0.517
Somalia	41	0.777	0.567	51	0.748	0.659
Uganda	141	0.750	0.259	192	0.721	0.173
United Republic of Tanzania	174	0.760	0.235	218	0.758	0.185
Zambia	126	0.875	0.519	201	0.824	0.617
Zimbabwe	176	0.753	0.203	202	0.788	0.217
Middle Africa	209	0.832	0.817	234	0.808	0.835
Angola	73	0.835	0.944	82	0.824	0.967
Cameroon	149	0.761	0.422	196	0.689	0.404
Central African Republic	31	0.798	0.440	56	0.770	0.350
Chad	55	0.774	0.720	75	0.763	0.814
Congo	91	0.825	0.787	131	0.804	0.814
Dem. Rep. of the Congo	94	0.780	0.415	92	0.793	0.526
Equatorial Guinea	31	0.788	0.921	34	0.730	0.740
Gabon	85	0.857	0.769	139	0.817	0.754
Sao Tome and Principe	20	0.677	0.614	25	0.649	0.470
Northern Africa	253	0.687	0.474	255	0.624	0.447
Algeria	108	0.810	0.588	98	0.724	0.540
Egypt	239	0.606	0.237	242	0.539	0.178
Libya	119	0.816	0.833	140	0.784	0.821
Morocco	220	0.670	0.157	229	0.653	0.160
Sudan (...2011)	75	0.806	0.608	–	–	–
Sudan	–	–	–	84	0.793	0.534
Tunisia	200	0.599	0.180	226	0.530	0.157
Southern Africa	257	0.560	0.141	255	0.590	0.169
Botswana	142	0.916	0.776	149	0.900	0.788
Lesotho	43	0.853	0.414	29	0.868	0.486
Namibia	191	0.803	0.310	199	0.771	0.272
South Africa	257	0.557	0.131	253	0.590	0.182
Swaziland	180	0.763	0.230	190	0.713	0.194
Western Africa	245	0.755	0.643	251	0.701	0.612
Benin	90	0.779	0.436	131	0.761	0.263
Burkina Faso	96	0.814	0.746	143	0.818	0.534
Cape Verde	21	0.699	0.376	23	0.664	0.397
Côte d'Ivoire	161	0.731	0.319	189	0.674	0.309
Gambia	36	0.691	0.339	57	0.746	0.252
Ghana	179	0.812	0.396	214	0.751	0.408
Guinea	51	0.844	0.642	110	0.782	0.504
Guinea-Bissau	11	0.722	0.926	13	0.753	0.892
Liberia	8	0.853	0.839	35	0.747	0.375
Mali	123	0.813	0.576	119	0.842	0.501
Mauritania	36	0.857	0.542	88	0.835	0.506
Niger	101	0.786	0.335	96	0.807	0.359
Nigeria	199	0.851	0.880	235	0.783	0.775

For sources and notes, see end of table.

214

Imports - Importations						Régions, pays ou territoires
2005			2012			
Number of products imported	Diversification index	Concentration index	Number of products imported	Diversification index	Concentration index	
Nombre de produits importés	Indice de diversification	Indice de concentration	Nombre de produits importés	Indice de diversification	Indice de concentration	
(1)	(2)	(3)	(1)	(2)	(3)	
260	0.000	0.075	260	0.000	0.088	MONDE
260	0.191	0.091	260	0.141	0.097	ÉCONOMIES EN DÉVELOPPEMENT
258	0.249	0.056	259	0.269	0.056	ÉCONOMIES EN TRANSITION
260	0.091	0.080	260	0.102	0.093	ÉCONOMIES DÉVELOPPÉES
259	0.276	0.074	259	0.286	0.085	Économies en développement : Afrique
255	0.389	0.097	259	0.395	0.111	Afrique orientale
159	0.492	0.103	176	0.536	0.182	Burundi
108	0.551	0.121	154	0.576	0.147	Comores
173	0.559	0.268	205	0.564	0.099	Djibouti
216	0.521	0.099	204	0.530	0.073	Érythrée
212	0.481	0.139	230	0.472	0.138	Éthiopie
243	0.413	0.132	249	0.387	0.150	Kenya
209	0.525	0.139	217	0.493	0.124	Madagascar
202	0.545	0.125	224	0.506	0.089	Malawi
218	0.450	0.140	227	0.434	0.150	Maurice
222	0.516	0.167	230	0.464	0.104	Mozambique
181	0.419	0.111	219	0.453	0.073	Rwanda
174	0.604	0.253	195	0.567	0.243	Seychelles
137	0.697	0.165	148	0.644	0.252	Somalie
217	0.481	0.145	230	0.448	0.169	Ouganda
230	0.438	0.113	239	0.469	0.177	République-Unie de Tanzanie
229	0.441	0.085	241	0.463	0.115	Zambie
233	0.548	0.135	240	0.458	0.080	Zimbabwe
246	0.452	0.096	252	0.451	0.058	Afrique centrale
222	0.565	0.182	231	0.472	0.063	Angola
218	0.459	0.172	232	0.415	0.104	Cameroun
133	0.494	0.142	149	0.610	0.476	République centrafricaine
201	0.526	0.100	223	0.487	0.105	Tchad
217	0.474	0.061	239	0.528	0.160	Congo
223	0.482	0.114	222	0.477	0.062	Rép. dém. du Congo
176	0.620	0.213	205	0.552	0.079	Guinée équatoriale
206	0.447	0.070	227	0.475	0.078	Gabon
60	0.581	0.203	116	0.517	0.222	Sao Tomé-et-Principe
258	0.307	0.061	257	0.344	0.083	Afrique septentrionale
236	0.455	0.086	234	0.465	0.111	Algérie
249	0.388	0.109	253	0.392	0.094	Égypte
239	0.461	0.097	250	0.445	0.089	Libye
249	0.355	0.109	249	0.344	0.116	Maroc
229	0.454	0.080	–	–	–	Soudan (…2011)
–	–	–	229	0.453	0.084	Soudan
242	0.396	0.087	249	0.365	0.075	Tunisie
258	0.271	0.165	258	0.289	0.200	Afrique australe
234	0.417	0.093	234	0.556	0.352	Botswana
186	0.782	0.310	230	0.530	0.081	Lesotho
233	0.387	0.066	238	0.431	0.108	Namibie
252	0.291	0.190	256	0.312	0.232	Afrique du Sud
233	0.464	0.093	214	0.570	0.117	Swaziland
255	0.401	0.076	258	0.389	0.102	Afrique occidentale
192	0.551	0.142	204	0.589	0.192	Bénin
188	0.524	0.120	218	0.502	0.148	Burkina Faso
185	0.466	0.098	191	0.497	0.166	Cap-Vert
211	0.527	0.254	224	0.475	0.219	Côte d'Ivoire
156	0.587	0.135	174	0.587	0.138	Gambie
226	0.413	0.125	237	0.390	0.082	Ghana
192	0.555	0.137	219	0.516	0.183	Guinée
93	0.622	0.327	145	0.570	0.170	Guinée-Bissau
69	0.854	0.746	115	0.775	0.624	Libéria
205	0.545	0.138	208	0.528	0.161	Mali
211	0.490	0.092	226	0.550	0.152	Mauritanie
202	0.513	0.096	205	0.574	0.118	Niger
247	0.480	0.077	252	0.432	0.107	Nigéria

Pour les sources et les notes, se reporter à la fin du tableau.

Region, country or territory	Exports - Exportations					
	2005			2012		
	Number of products exported	Diversification index	Concentration index	Number of products exported	Diversification index	Concentration index
	Nombre de produits exportés (1)	Indice de diversification (2)	Indice de concentration (3)	Nombre de produits exportés (1)	Indice de diversification (2)	Indice de concentration (3)
Saint Helena	35	0.555	0.270	28	0.550	0.395
Senegal	182	0.679	0.208	201	0.706	0.227
Sierra Leone	110	0.677	0.498	114	0.808	0.308
Togo	143	0.718	0.211	123	0.717	0.199
Developing economies: America	**257**	**0.327**	**0.122**	**257**	**0.329**	**0.135**
Caribbean	*235*	*0.643*	*0.267*	*251*	*0.571*	*0.185*
Anguilla	40	0.538	0.235	44	0.527	0.187
Antigua and Barbuda	29	0.773	0.776	69	0.601	0.376
Aruba	103	0.835	0.910	102	0.822	0.781
Bahamas	48	0.795	0.464	103	0.822	0.584
Barbados	111	0.638	0.348	136	0.598	0.175
Bonaire, Sint Eustatius and Saba	–	–	–	2	0.509	0.987
British Virgin Islands	21	0.712	0.331	15	0.771	0.752
Cayman Islands	9	0.781	0.811	9	0.748	0.838
Cuba	132	0.783	0.369	193	0.709	0.250
Dominica	20	0.729	0.356	23	0.716	0.435
Dominican Republic	194	0.723	0.175	235	0.669	0.124
Grenada	26	0.701	0.322	30	0.679	0.189
Haiti	58	0.771	0.552	73	0.743	0.493
Jamaica	111	0.786	0.657	124	0.792	0.412
Montserrat	27	0.481	0.250	27	0.508	0.213
Netherlands Antilles	101	0.797	0.715	–	–	–
Saint Kitts and Nevis	18	0.690	0.375	31	0.656	0.342
Saint Lucia	37	0.666	0.520	94	0.618	0.324
Saint Vincent and the Grenadines	18	0.828	0.674	37	0.703	0.278
Sint Maarten (Dutch part)	–	–	–	10	(a)0.610	(a)0.877
Trinidad and Tobago	184	0.770	0.370	199	0.726	0.369
Turks and Caicos Islands	18	0.701	0.407	24	0.623	0.474
Central America	*252*	*0.356*	*0.126*	*256*	*0.354*	*0.126*
Belize	60	0.785	0.302	77	0.744	0.295
Costa Rica	207	0.661	0.268	214	0.746	0.394
El Salvador	187	0.729	0.260	205	0.644	0.198
Guatemala	217	0.682	0.157	224	0.681	0.146
Honduras	187	0.792	0.288	222	0.775	0.215
Mexico	252	0.387	0.144	251	0.400	0.146
Nicaragua	119	0.774	0.187	154	0.806	0.217
Panama	218	0.609	0.222	239	0.568	0.154
South America	*255*	*0.487*	*0.153*	*255*	*0.484*	*0.176*
Argentina	243	0.556	0.136	243	0.606	0.155
Bolivia (Plurinational State of)	153	0.766	0.393	146	0.815	0.453
Brazil	250	0.476	0.087	251	0.514	0.146
Chile	229	0.744	0.322	228	0.718	0.364
Colombia	231	0.582	0.210	230	0.643	0.435
Ecuador	170	0.746	0.535	210	0.720	0.485
Falkland Islands (Malvinas)	10	0.698	0.807	8	0.654	0.717
Guyana	80	0.813	0.287	121	0.862	0.441
Paraguay	128	0.812	0.354	160	0.774	0.320
Peru	215	0.787	0.243	237	0.712	0.236
Suriname	87	0.781	0.441	136	0.760	0.503
Uruguay	181	0.669	0.209	193	0.704	0.206
Venezuela (Bolivarian Rep. of)	233	0.776	0.649	225	0.736	0.636
Developing economies: Asia	**259**	**0.282**	**0.129**	**260**	**0.232**	**0.125**
Eastern Asia	*258*	*0.396*	*0.107*	*258*	*0.398*	*0.104*
China	256	0.460	0.110	256	0.469	0.101
China, Hong Kong SAR	242	0.512	0.150	243	0.545	0.206
China, Macao SAR	155	0.753	0.332	128	0.575	0.186
China, Taiwan Province of	240	0.455	0.156	245	0.478	0.205
Korea, Dem. People's Rep. of	185	0.472	0.102	182	0.713	0.395
Korea, Republic of	242	0.441	0.161	248	0.462	0.147
Mongolia	84	0.861	0.395	124	0.834	0.515
Southern Asia	*258*	*0.540*	*0.232*	*260*	*0.442*	*0.173*
Afghanistan	134	0.710	0.258	72	0.766	0.270
Bangladesh	165	0.828	0.381	221	0.800	0.359

For sources and notes, see end of table.

| Imports - Importations | | | | | | Régions, pays ou territoires |
| 2005 | | | 2012 | | | |
Number of products imported / Nombre de produits importés (1)	Diversification index / Indice de diversification (2)	Concentration index / Indice de concentration (3)	Number of products imported / Nombre de produits importés (1)	Diversification index / Indice de diversification (2)	Concentration index / Indice de concentration (3)	
66	0.615	0.296	66	0.555	0.171	Sainte-Hélène
226	0.418	0.131	229	0.446	0.211	Sénégal
183	0.616	0.352	214	0.628	0.368	Sierra Leone
188	0.611	0.201	195	0.634	0.307	Togo
259	**0.196**	**0.063**	**259**	**0.220**	**0.076**	**Économies en développement : Amérique**
255	*0.367*	*0.158*	*256*	*0.347*	*0.149*	*Caraïbes*
130	0.534	0.136	152	0.508	0.083	Anguilla
164	0.636	0.363	150	0.708	0.466	Antigua-et-Barbuda
208	0.606	0.424	210	0.577	0.423	Aruba
205	0.628	0.408	210	0.682	0.485	Bahamas
215	0.437	0.151	209	0.467	0.313	Barbade
–	–	–	11	0.474	0.734	Bonaire, Saint-Eustache et Saba
60	0.788	0.495	88	0.727	0.627	Îles Vierges britanniques
145	0.655	0.452	150	0.649	0.500	Îles Caïmanes
235	0.432	0.145	246	0.419	0.145	Cuba
145	0.414	0.100	144	0.473	0.170	Dominique
245	0.381	0.077	251	0.365	0.136	République dominicaine
156	0.459	0.080	169	0.502	0.133	Grenade
207	0.587	0.134	224	0.600	0.153	Haïti
217	0.428	0.203	221	0.426	0.218	Jamaïque
75	0.472	0.136	75	0.430	0.192	Montserrat
191	0.700	0.674	–	–	–	Antilles néerlandaises
144	0.412	0.084	161	0.485	0.070	Saint-Kitts-et-Nevis
173	0.503	0.264	156	0.644	0.680	Sainte-Lucie
142	0.576	0.295	155	0.606	0.287	Saint-Vincent-et-les Grenadines
–	–	–	147	0.595	0.394	Saint-Martin (partie néerlandaise)
226	0.446	0.275	237	0.407	0.214	Trinité-et-Tobago
163	0.519	0.174	156	0.563	0.292	Îles Turques et Caïques
257	*0.256*	*0.072*	*258*	*0.271*	*0.089*	*Amérique centrale*
199	0.493	0.183	190	0.549	0.260	Belize
240	0.347	0.146	246	0.338	0.131	Costa Rica
238	0.404	0.080	238	0.399	0.091	El Salvador
235	0.430	0.112	240	0.433	0.139	Guatemala
234	0.486	0.117	241	0.486	0.133	Honduras
254	0.243	0.079	254	0.304	0.094	Mexique
208	0.387	0.105	220	0.425	0.150	Nicaragua
232	0.546	0.343	243	0.556	0.293	Panama
258	*0.209*	*0.068*	*259*	*0.228*	*0.075*	*Amérique du Sud*
244	0.325	0.071	248	0.338	0.101	Argentine
221	0.426	0.081	234	0.430	0.114	Bolivie (État plurinational de)
250	0.293	0.100	254	0.258	0.087	Brésil
250	0.294	0.107	250	0.284	0.111	Chili
240	0.341	0.072	246	0.338	0.089	Colombie
232	0.389	0.080	241	0.389	0.111	Équateur
14	(a)0.747	(a)0.835	102	0.498	0.212	Îles Falkland (Malvinas)
183	0.548	0.245	201	0.464	0.190	Guyana
208	0.454	0.150	224	0.457	0.141	Paraguay
242	0.341	0.114	248	0.304	0.088	Pérou
159	(a)0.502	(a)0.320	201	0.426	0.186	Suriname
233	0.356	0.156	240	0.320	0.141	Uruguay
241	0.343	0.072	252	0.381	0.050	Venezuela (Rép. bolivarienne du)
260	**0.232**	**0.108**	**260**	**0.180**	**0.113**	**Économies en développement : Asie**
259	*0.308*	*0.129*	*259*	*0.284*	*0.138*	*Asie orientale*
258	0.386	0.140	258	0.345	0.150	Chine
249	0.442	0.153	252	0.502	0.192	Chine (RAS de Hong Kong)
203	0.501	0.121	189	0.472	0.160	Chine (RAS de Macao)
256	0.376	0.156	255	0.344	0.160	Province chinoise de Taiwan
230	0.449	0.157	226	0.389	0.122	Corée, Rép. populaire dém. de
256	0.353	0.155	257	0.326	0.189	Corée, République de
188	0.502	0.226	229	0.479	0.184	Mongolie
258	*0.352*	*0.081*	*259*	*0.373*	*0.217*	*Asie méridionale*
229	0.497	0.148	215	0.518	0.139	Afghanistan
242	0.532	0.112	250	0.547	0.098	Bangladesh

Pour les sources et les notes, se reporter à la fin du tableau.

Region, country or territory	Exports - Exportations					
	2005			2012		
	Number of products exported	Diversification index	Concentration index	Number of products exported	Diversification index	Concentration index
	Nombre de produits exportés	Indice de diversification	Indice de concentration	Nombre de produits exportés	Indice de diversification	Indice de concentration
	(1)	(2)	(3)	(1)	(2)	(3)
Bhutan	55	0.761	0.278	87	0.796	0.344
India	252	0.542	0.133	255	0.502	0.173
Iran (Islamic Rep. of)	238	0.778	0.795	255	0.726	0.676
Maldives	35	0.760	0.545	38	0.768	0.629
Nepal	100	0.520	0.136	132	0.702	0.142
Pakistan	207	0.769	0.226	216	0.722	0.183
Sri Lanka	169	0.747	0.211	199	0.771	0.203
South-Eastern Asia	**257**	**0.345**	**0.152**	**258**	**0.312**	**0.116**
Brunei Darussalam	108	0.832	0.641	119	0.845	0.657
Cambodia	98	0.829	0.354	138	0.789	0.314
Indonesia	247	0.493	0.130	243	0.555	0.170
Lao People's Dem. Rep.	76	0.767	0.266	108	0.766	0.304
Malaysia	252	0.467	0.186	254	0.455	0.164
Myanmar	149	0.827	0.337	170	0.817	0.397
Philippines	227	0.620	0.356	236	0.566	0.223
Singapore	246	0.489	0.246	249	0.496	0.246
Thailand	245	0.389	0.086	251	0.399	0.082
Timor-Leste	11	0.790	0.825	3	0.829	0.920
Viet Nam	229	0.638	0.226	248	0.520	0.123
Western Asia	**258**	**0.591**	**0.518**	**259**	**0.563**	**0.520**
Bahrain	214	0.754	0.422	234	0.698	0.353
Iraq	86	0.825	0.952	133	0.880	0.981
Jordan	220	0.594	0.135	234	0.623	0.164
Kuwait	224	0.813	0.632	233	0.777	0.743
Lebanon	215	0.625	0.102	227	0.643	0.159
Oman	197	0.768	0.717	223	0.665	0.541
Qatar	175	0.790	0.571	233	0.768	0.523
Saudi Arabia	248	0.809	0.745	254	0.747	0.756
State of Palestine	127	0.591	0.167	136	0.680	0.182
Syrian Arab Republic	214	0.671	0.367	222	0.619	0.136
Turkey	246	0.529	0.091	250	0.441	0.092
United Arab Emirates	256	0.594	0.458	259	0.553	0.429
Yemen	135	0.815	0.817	192	0.737	0.590
Developing economies: Oceania	**225**	**0.691**	**0.181**	**234**	**0.700**	**0.229**
American Samoa	116	0.633	0.245	76	0.675	0.389
Cook Islands	17	0.654	0.543	12	0.728	0.580
Fiji	143	0.762	0.232	159	0.727	0.261
French Polynesia	46	0.766	0.536	35	0.731	0.569
Guam	29	(a)0.649	(a)0.461	19	(a)0.692	(a)0.494
Kiribati	24	0.665	0.312	7	0.746	0.845
Marshall Islands	5	0.763	0.866	4	0.727	0.803
Micronesia (Federated States of)	7	0.745	0.928	5	0.695	0.951
Nauru	43	0.561	0.231	12	0.747	0.944
New Caledonia	85	0.873	0.656	101	0.844	0.582
Niue	30	0.515	0.267	38	0.534	0.326
Northern Mariana Islands	70	0.584	0.328	26	0.562	0.212
Palau	8	0.644	0.898	8	0.717	0.907
Papua New Guinea	120	0.818	0.327	136	0.793	0.336
Samoa	26	(a)0.755	(a)0.472	47	0.718	0.273
Solomon Islands	16	0.824	0.694	49	0.824	0.597
Tokelau	40	0.585	0.307	59	0.450	0.142
Tonga	20	0.674	0.404	31	0.722	0.287
Tuvalu	37	0.588	0.254	8	0.726	0.683
Vanuatu	16	0.781	0.563	16	0.811	0.794
Wallis and Futuna Islands	26	0.546	0.289	26	0.470	0.349
Transition economies	**257**	**0.578**	**0.293**	**257**	**0.544**	**0.332**
Albania	142	0.717	0.265	179	0.689	0.258
Armenia	131	0.778	0.350	153	0.787	0.198
Azerbaijan	172	0.763	0.579	162	0.769	0.865
Belarus	214	0.569	0.276	224	0.586	0.293
Bosnia and Herzegovina	202	0.663	0.136	225	0.604	0.103
Croatia	232	0.458	0.110	234	0.454	0.104
Georgia	122	0.747	0.198	184	0.702	0.251
Kazakhstan	195	0.757	0.605	230	0.733	0.592

For sources and notes, see end of table.

Imports - Importations						Régions, pays ou territoires
2005			2012			
Number of products imported	Diversification index	Concentration index	Number of products imported	Diversification index	Concentration index	
Nombre de produits importés	Indice de diversification	Indice de concentration	Nombre de produits importés	Indice de diversification	Indice de concentration	
(1)	(2)	(3)	(1)	(2)	(3)	
189	0.468	0.090	203	0.529	0.121	Bhoutan
257	0.412	0.115	256	0.458	0.291	Inde
251	0.425	0.084	253	0.414	0.052	Iran (Rép. islamique d')
170	0.500	0.123	188	0.499	0.243	Maldives
220	0.561	0.195	232	0.488	0.151	Népal
243	0.439	0.128	246	0.442	0.224	Pakistan
234	0.445	0.094	240	0.404	0.115	Sri Lanka
258	**0.287**	**0.162**	**259**	**0.242**	**0.136**	**Asie du Sud-Est**
210	0.469	0.078	211	0.454	0.111	Brunéi Darussalam
209	0.551	0.159	226	0.554	0.174	Cambodge
255	0.347	0.136	256	0.343	0.124	Indonésie
185	0.464	0.142	212	0.463	0.151	Rép. dém. populaire lao
255	0.373	0.221	257	0.313	0.140	Malaisie
220	0.472	0.119	242	0.517	0.174	Myanmar
250	0.469	0.319	249	0.336	0.182	Philippines
250	0.380	0.217	252	0.362	0.238	Singapour
254	0.322	0.135	256	0.287	0.127	Thaïlande
120	0.516	0.197	169	0.558	0.151	Timor-Leste
249	0.455	0.114	256	0.375	0.090	Viet Nam
259	**0.243**	**0.063**	**259**	**0.293**	**0.071**	**Asie occidentale**
241	0.419	0.269	247	0.462	0.079	Bahreïn
236	0.503	0.077	248	0.474	0.065	Iraq
232	0.347	0.143	244	0.329	0.138	Jordanie
198	0.416	0.058	253	0.420	0.091	Koweït
245	0.420	0.169	250	0.447	0.188	Liban
244	0.416	0.138	249	0.437	0.119	Oman
250	0.482	0.105	244	0.560	0.186	Qatar
249	0.338	0.093	245	0.304	0.071	Arabie saoudite
205	0.517	0.185	209	0.577	0.213	État de Palestine
240	0.447	0.095	244	0.466	0.101	République arabe syrienne
251	0.286	0.083	252	0.322	0.153	Turquie
257	0.371	0.117	259	0.355	0.103	Émirats arabes unis
229	0.515	0.168	236	0.550	0.221	Yémen
247	**0.428**	**0.162**	**250**	**0.443**	**0.211**	**Économies en développement : Océanie**
136	0.562	0.244	122	0.689	0.465	Samoa américaines
125	0.483	0.068	135	0.524	0.143	Îles Cook
207	0.478	0.244	211	0.495	0.256	Fidji
201	0.426	0.103	199	0.401	0.138	Polynésie française
127	0.665	0.558	140	0.642	0.536	Guam
103	0.550	0.151	125	0.567	0.171	Kiribati
7	0.844	0.842	8	0.829	0.742	Îles Marshall
102	0.507	0.100	125	0.520	0.144	Micronésie (États fédérés de)
32	0.592	0.466	60	0.491	0.227	Nauru
208	0.418	0.129	213	0.423	0.175	Nouvelle-Calédonie
63	0.483	0.110	70	0.482	0.126	Nioué
112	0.712	0.390	59	0.580	0.255	Îles Mariannes du Nord
108	0.504	0.102	101	0.522	0.225	Palaos
216	0.500	0.195	232	0.507	0.203	Papouasie-Nouvelle-Guinée
159	0.575	0.164	169	0.540	0.172	Samoa
154	0.530	0.215	186	0.550	0.254	Îles Salomon
36	0.593	0.268	35	0.576	0.238	Tokélaou
112	0.613	0.229	154	0.525	0.156	Tonga
39	0.625	0.396	33	0.652	0.431	Tuvalu
150	0.512	0.169	157	0.592	0.320	Vanuatu
93	0.472	0.107	109	0.485	0.088	Îles Wallis-et-Futuna
258	**0.249**	**0.056**	**259**	**0.269**	**0.056**	**Économies en transition**
230	0.452	0.062	233	0.468	0.102	Albanie
221	0.454	0.142	231	0.414	0.111	Arménie
216	0.484	0.126	227	0.517	0.079	Azerbaïdjan
241	0.414	0.225	245	0.335	0.186	Bélarus
243	0.400	0.077	247	0.379	0.072	Bosnie-Herzégovine
249	0.245	0.075	249	0.274	0.088	Croatie
215	0.449	0.127	235	0.440	0.117	Géorgie
248	0.365	0.065	251	0.361	0.065	Kazakhstan

Pour les sources et les notes, se reporter à la fin du tableau.

Region, country or territory	Exports - Exportations					
	2005			2012		
	Number of products exported	Diversification index	Concentration index	Number of products exported	Diversification index	Concentration index
	Nombre de produits exportés	Indice de diversification	Indice de concentration	Nombre de produits exportés	Indice de diversification	Indice de concentration
	(1)	(2)	(3)	(1)	(2)	(3)
Kyrgyzstan	147	0.717	0.240	182	0.569	0.149
Montenegro	–	–	–	110	0.600	0.330
Republic of Moldova	163	0.719	0.252	183	0.633	0.137
Russian Federation	248	0.662	0.352	235	0.576	0.386
Serbia and Montenegro	235	0.580	0.105	–	–	–
Serbia	–	–	–	245	0.515	0.067
Tajikistan	82	0.828	0.546	122	0.853	0.534
TFYR of Macedonia	185	0.646	0.174	206	0.618	0.164
Turkmenistan	99	0.767	0.661	119	0.803	0.569
Ukraine	246	0.609	0.144	249	0.595	0.121
Uzbekistan	146	0.731	0.282	178	0.746	0.229
Developed economies: America	**259**	**0.226**	**0.072**	**260**	**0.227**	**0.086**
Bermuda	20	0.773	0.522	11	0.735	0.435
Canada	256	0.366	0.126	257	0.346	0.165
Greenland	24	0.771	0.445	24	0.810	0.510
Saint Pierre and Miquelon	14	0.628	0.434	24	0.587	0.294
United States	257	0.268	0.074	259	0.259	0.090
Developed economies: Asia	**250**	**0.401**	**0.127**	**251**	**0.437**	**0.115**
Israel	214	0.616	0.365	229	0.588	0.266
Japan	247	0.418	0.135	245	0.415	0.123
Developed economies: Europe	**259**	**0.178**	**0.065**	**260**	**0.218**	**0.066**
Andorra	71	0.631	0.258	47	0.646	0.261
Austria	251	0.327	0.072	250	0.340	0.060
Belgium	256	0.356	0.106	258	0.378	0.098
Bulgaria	233	0.496	0.120	244	0.441	0.140
Cyprus	207	0.442	0.152	209	0.548	0.344
Czech Republic	251	0.394	0.095	256	0.421	0.106
Denmark	246	0.399	0.084	247	0.421	0.084
Estonia	241	0.488	0.157	243	0.465	0.136
Faeroe Islands	14	0.533	0.577	44	0.736	0.661
Finland	236	0.520	0.194	244	0.495	0.139
France	258	0.298	0.082	257	0.341	0.091
Germany	258	0.293	0.096	258	0.342	0.094
Gibraltar	40	0.690	0.553	33	0.716	0.727
Greece	234	0.488	0.100	245	0.539	0.337
Hungary	248	0.404	0.149	252	0.427	0.103
Iceland	120	0.777	0.385	129	0.769	0.434
Ireland	246	0.656	0.224	240	0.682	0.252
Italy	258	0.368	0.055	259	0.371	0.057
Latvia	218	0.526	0.124	234	0.456	0.096
Lithuania	236	0.531	0.213	243	0.483	0.200
Luxembourg	243	0.524	0.125	242	0.498	0.123
Malta	166	0.619	0.407	175	0.680	0.432
Netherlands	257	0.342	0.101	259	0.349	0.120
Norway	232	0.648	0.453	235	0.606	0.406
Poland	254	0.438	0.081	253	0.402	0.065
Portugal	250	0.374	0.081	254	0.423	0.078
Romania	235	0.505	0.124	242	0.416	0.091
Slovakia	239	0.397	0.119	247	0.464	0.165
Slovenia	236	0.497	0.119	238	0.489	0.162
Spain	256	0.350	0.110	256	0.348	0.091
Sweden	251	0.382	0.117	252	0.367	0.095
Switzerland	244	0.539	0.136	246	0.603	0.179
United Kingdom	257	0.258	0.098	258	0.320	0.118
Developed economies: Oceania	**256**	**0.575**	**0.139**	**253**	**0.630**	**0.220**
Australia	255	0.590	0.167	253	0.649	0.256
New Zealand	236	0.638	0.130	236	0.657	0.172

For sources and notes, see next page.

Imports - Importations						Régions, pays ou territoires
2005			2012			
Number of products imported / Nombre de produits importés (1)	Diversification index / Indice de diversification (2)	Concentration index / Indice de concentration (3)	Number of products imported / Nombre de produits importés (1)	Diversification index / Indice de diversification (2)	Concentration index / Indice de concentration (3)	
206	0.532	0.201	225	0.486	0.165	Kirghizistan
			221	0.432	0.099	Monténégro
230	0.460	0.103	238	0.441	0.102	République de Moldova
256	0.336	0.062	259	0.349	0.064	Fédération de Russie
248	0.315	0.084	–	–	–	Serbie-et-Monténégro
–	–	–	249	0.317	0.081	Serbie
204	0.575	0.154	229	0.551	0.083	Tadjikistan
234	0.391	0.103	240	0.434	0.102	L'ERY de Macédoine
230	0.494	0.124	238	0.461	0.092	Turkménistan
249	0.336	0.135	251	0.390	0.154	Ukraine
220	0.409	0.092	232	0.460	0.086	Ouzbékistan
260	**0.166**	**0.105**	**260**	**0.189**	**0.118**	**Économies développées : Amérique**
170	0.595	0.330	151	0.744	0.479	Bermudes
258	0.213	0.082	258	0.235	0.077	Canada
171	0.462	0.176	183	0.452	0.192	Groenland
95	0.391	0.072	137	0.478	0.078	Saint-Pierre-et-Miquelon
259	0.188	0.112	259	0.205	0.130	États-Unis
257	**0.268**	**0.126**	**257**	**0.276**	**0.156**	**Économies développées : Asie**
248	0.298	0.198	248	0.261	0.149	Israël
257	0.283	0.131	257	0.297	0.162	Japon
260	**0.104**	**0.069**	**260**	**0.117**	**0.079**	**Économies développées : Europe**
..	..	..	193	0.532	0.115	Andorre
258	0.227	0.062	258	0.246	0.060	Autriche
258	0.282	0.103	258	0.267	0.095	Belgique
245	0.337	0.143	250	0.281	0.127	Bulgarie
226	0.371	0.152	227	0.467	0.256	Chypre
256	0.248	0.064	259	0.293	0.065	République tchèque
254	0.253	0.058	257	0.288	0.056	Danemark
246	0.328	0.110	249	0.350	0.162	Estonie
184	0.480	0.191	198	0.539	0.229	Îles Féroé
254	0.196	0.085	253	0.191	0.104	Finlande
259	0.160	0.073	258	0.198	0.082	France
258	0.144	0.072	258	0.175	0.077	Allemagne
108	0.725	0.585	61	0.850	0.836	Gibraltar
254	0.283	0.116	253	0.372	0.241	Grèce
254	0.275	0.101	252	0.313	0.112	Hongrie
229	0.401	0.102	230	0.449	0.159	Islande
256	0.300	0.113	252	0.352	0.093	Irlande
257	0.211	0.096	257	0.233	0.104	Italie
243	0.344	0.098	249	0.379	0.121	Lettonie
251	0.332	0.179	252	0.352	0.202	Lituanie
248	0.370	0.114	244	0.383	0.120	Luxembourg
227	0.432	0.202	228	0.591	0.395	Malte
258	0.220	0.105	259	0.237	0.145	Pays-Bas
252	0.300	0.059	252	0.338	0.061	Norvège
257	0.239	0.061	254	0.199	0.083	Pologne
253	0.171	0.076	256	0.249	0.097	Portugal
247	0.288	0.074	247	0.257	0.062	Roumanie
251	0.279	0.075	253	0.320	0.100	Slovaquie
249	0.309	0.066	250	0.291	0.125	Slovénie
258	0.179	0.091	257	0.230	0.125	Espagne
253	0.174	0.076	255	0.183	0.094	Suède
252	0.287	0.076	254	0.354	0.090	Suisse
256	0.214	0.088	257	0.239	0.112	Royaume-Uni
257	**0.230**	**0.092**	**257**	**0.235**	**0.108**	**Économies développées : Océanie**
253	0.231	0.092	256	0.245	0.108	Australie
249	0.268	0.095	249	0.275	0.114	Nouvelle-Zélande

Pour les sources et les notes, se reporter à la page suivante.

4.1.1 Export and import concentration and diversification indices of countries and geographical regions

Source:

UNCTAD secretariat calculations, based on UNCTAD, *UNCTADstat* Merchandise Trade Matrix

Notes:

(a)　More than 30% of total trade under SITC Rev.3, code 931: "Special transactions & commodities not classified"

(1)　Number of products exported (or imported) at the three-digit SITC, Rev. 3 level; this figure includes only those products that are greater than $100,000 or more than 0.3 per cent of the country's total exports (or imports).

　　　Data for the country groupings are calculated as weighted averages of individual countries data, including those that are estimated and not shown separately.

(2)　The diversification index signals whether the structure of exports or imports by product of a given country or group of countries differ from the structure of product of the world. This index that ranges from 0 to 1 reveals the extent of the differences between the structure of trade of the country or country group and the world average. The index value closer to 1 indicates a bigger difference from the world average.

　　　Diversification index is computed by measuring absolute deviation of the country share from world structure, as follows:

$$S_j = \frac{\sum_i \left| h_{ij} - h_i \right|}{2}$$

where

　　　hij = share of product i in total exports or imports of country or country group j

　　　hi = share of product i in total world exports or imports.

　　　This index is a modified Finger-Kreinin measure of similarity in trade. For more information, please consult the article of Finger, J. M. and M. E. Kreinin (1979), "A measure of 'export similarity' and its possible uses" in the Economic Journal, 89: 905-12.

(3)　Concentration index, also named Herfindahl-Hirschmann index, is a measure of the degree of market concentration. It has been normalized to obtain values ranking from 0 to 1 (maximum concentration), according to the following formula:

$$H_j = \frac{\sqrt{\sum_{i=1}^{n} \left(\frac{x_{ij}}{X_j} \right)^2} - \sqrt{1/n}}{1 - \sqrt{1/n}}$$

where

　　　Hj　= country or country group index

　　　Xij = value of exports for country j and product i

$$X_j = \sum_{i=1}^{n} x_{ij}$$

and

　　　n = number of products (SITC Revision 3 at 3-digit group level)

Source :

Calculs du secrétariat de la CNUCED, basés sur la matrice du commerce de marchandises de *UNCTADstat* de la CNUCED

Notes :

(a) Plus de 30% du commerce sous la position 931 de la CTCI rév. 3 : "Transactions et articles spéciaux non classés"

(1) Nombre de produits au niveau de groupes de la CTCI (rév. 3, position à 3 chiffres) exportés (ou importés) par chaque pays ; cependant, seuls les produits ayant une valeur supérieure à 100.000 dollars ou comptant pour plus de 0,3 % des exportations (ou des importations) totales du pays sont inclus.

Les indices de concentration et de diversification calculés au niveau des groupes de pays et du monde sont les moyennes arithmétiques des indices respectifs des pays, pondérées par la valeur de leurs exportations.

(2) L'indice de Diversification indique si la structure par produits des exportations d'un pays ou groupe de pays diverge peu ou beaucoup de la structure par produits des exportations totales dans le monde. Cet indice dont la valeur est comprise entre de 0 à 1, révèle l'ampleur des différences entre la structure des échanges d'un pays ou du groupe de pays et la moyenne mondiale. Plus l'indice est proche de 1, plus la divergence est forte.

L'indice de diversification mesure la déviation absolue de la structure du pays par rapport à la structure mondiale comme ci-dessous :

$$S_j = \frac{\sum_i \left| h_{ij} - h_i \right|}{2}$$

où

h_{ij} = part du produit i dans le total des exportations (ou importations) du pays j

h_i = part du produit i dans le total des exportations (ou importations) mondiales.

Cet indice est une variante de l'indicateur de Finger-Kreinin sur la similarité de la structure du commerce. Pour plus d'information, veuillez consulter l'article de Finger, J. M. et M. E. Kreinin (1979), "A measure of 'export similarity' and its possible uses", dans l'*Economic Journal*, 89: 905-12.

(3) L'indice de concentration, aussi appelé indice de Herfindahl-Hirschmann, mesure le degré de concentration des marchés. Il a été normalisé afin d'obtenir des valeurs comprises entre 0 et 1 (concentration maximale), d'après la formule suivante :

$$H_j = \frac{\sqrt{\sum_{i=1}^{n} \left(\frac{x_{ij}}{X_j} \right)^2} - \sqrt{1/n}}{1 - \sqrt{1/n}}$$

où

H_j = Indice du pays ou groupe de pays

X_{ij} = valeur des exportations du pays j pour le produit i

$$X_j = \sum_{i=1}^{n} x_{ij}$$

et

n = nombre de produits (de la CTCI Révision 3, position à 3 chiffres)

Region, country or territory	Exports - Exportations					
	2005			2012		
	Number of products exported Nombre de produits exportés (1)	Diversification index Indice de diversification (2)	Concentration index Indice de concentration (3)	Number of products exported Nombre de produits exportés (1)	Diversification index Indice de diversification (2)	Concentration index Indice de concentration (3)
DEVELOPING ECONOMIES	260	0.247	0.140	260	0.199	0.141
Developing economies excluding China	260	0.259	0.172	260	0.231	0.190
Developing economies excluding LDCs	259	0.244	0.135	260	0.194	0.136
High-income developing economies	259	0.254	0.160	260	0.237	0.181
Middle-income developing economies	259	0.322	0.106	260	0.306	0.090
Low-income developing economies	260	0.539	0.258	260	0.450	0.250
Heavily indebted poor countries (IMF)	255	0.644	0.211	259	0.588	0.195
Landlocked developing countries	259	0.624	0.305	259	0.612	0.369
Small island developing States	235	0.666	0.208	247	0.603	0.203
Least developed countries	*257*	*0.688*	*0.457*	*258*	*0.659*	*0.432*
Africa and Haiti	253	0.730	0.581	257	0.689	0.574
Asia	247	0.720	0.265	249	0.694	0.230
Islands	67	0.817	0.333	105	0.832	0.453
Major petroleum and gas exporters	*258*	*0.735*	*0.683*	*260*	*0.667*	*0.649*
Africa	219	0.836	0.771	243	0.790	0.758
America	233	0.776	0.649	225	0.736	0.636
Asia	258	0.714	0.662	260	0.649	0.621
Major exporters of manufactured goods	*259*	*0.335*	*0.109*	*259*	*0.322*	*0.099*
America	252	0.387	0.144	251	0.400	0.146
Asia	259	0.361	0.116	259	0.345	0.104
Emerging economies	*259*	*0.268*	*0.108*	*259*	*0.252*	*0.100*
America	256	0.317	0.085	256	0.364	0.096
Asia	257	0.366	0.151	258	0.344	0.143
Newly industrialized Asian economies	*258*	*0.346*	*0.137*	*259*	*0.323*	*0.129*
First tier	256	0.390	0.151	259	0.389	0.158
Second tier	257	0.373	0.127	257	0.368	0.095
Developing economies: Africa	260	0.600	0.433	260	0.551	0.452
Northern Africa excluding Sudan	253	0.687	0.470	254	0.633	0.451
Sub-Saharan Africa	260	0.605	0.422	259	0.579	0.460
Sub-Saharan Africa excluding South Africa	259	0.699	0.576	258	0.671	0.584
Developing economies: America	257	0.327	0.122	257	0.329	0.135
Central America and Greater Caribbean Islands excluding Puerto Rico	253	0.350	0.120	256	0.344	0.120
Central America and Greater Caribbean Islands excluding Mexico and Puerto Rico	246	0.575	0.118	254	0.543	0.098
South America and Central America	257	0.327	0.125	257	0.336	0.138
South America excluding Brazil	255	0.595	0.239	255	0.534	0.238
Developing economies: Asia	259	0.282	0.129	260	0.232	0.125
Eastern and South-Eastern Asia excluding China	258	0.336	0.132	259	0.305	0.121
Southern Asia excluding India	255	0.697	0.497	257	0.645	0.406

For sources and notes, see end of table 4.1.1.

| Imports - Importations | | | | | | Régions, pays ou territoires |
| 2005 | | | 2012 | | | |
Number of products imported Nombre de produits importés (1)	Diversification index Indice de diversification (2)	Concentration index Indice de concentration (3)	Number of products imported Nombre de produits importés (1)	Diversification index Indice de diversification (2)	Concentration index Indice de concentration (3)	
260	**0.191**	**0.091**	**260**	**0.141**	**0.097**	**ÉCONOMIES EN DÉVELOPPEMENT**
260	0.167	0.084	260	0.142	0.090	Économies en développement sans la Chine
260	0.192	0.093	260	0.140	0.099	Économies en développement sans les PMA
260	0.165	0.097	260	0.148	0.093	Économies en développement à revenu élevé
260	0.269	0.105	260	0.215	0.109	Économies en développement à revenu intermédiaire
259	0.330	0.067	259	0.292	0.144	Économies en développement à revenu faible
257	0.374	0.080	259	0.387	0.092	Pays pauvres très endettés (FMI)
259	0.338	0.065	260	0.339	0.070	Pays en développement sans littoral
253	0.368	0.152	254	0.368	0.176	Petits États insulaires en développement
258	*0.426*	*0.085*	*259*	*0.412*	*0.093*	*Pays les moins avancés*
256	0.419	0.077	259	0.413	0.088	Afrique et Haïti
257	0.471	0.115	258	0.473	0.112	Asie
212	0.516	0.148	224	0.517	0.164	Îles
259	*0.310*	*0.062*	*259*	*0.314*	*0.056*	*Principaux exportateurs de pétrole et de gaz*
254	0.410	0.067	258	0.394	0.086	Afrique
241	0.343	0.072	252	0.381	0.050	Amérique
259	0.320	0.068	259	0.335	0.062	Asie
260	*0.264*	*0.128*	*259*	*0.226*	*0.129*	*Principaux exportateurs d'articles manufacturés*
254	0.243	0.079	254	0.304	0.094	Amérique
260	0.290	0.140	259	0.249	0.138	Asie
259	*0.218*	*0.122*	*259*	*0.174*	*0.119*	*Économies émergentes*
258	0.219	0.068	257	0.226	0.079	Amérique
259	0.289	0.158	258	0.247	0.156	Asie
259	*0.260*	*0.145*	*259*	*0.220*	*0.135*	*Économies nouvellement industrialisées d'Asie*
259	0.278	0.143	259	0.274	0.150	Première génération
258	0.294	0.153	258	0.238	0.106	Deuxième génération
259	0.276	0.074	259	0.286	0.085	Économies en développement : Afrique
257	0.303	0.062	257	0.346	0.085	Afrique septentrionale sans le Soudan
259	0.290	0.086	259	0.302	0.097	Afrique subsaharienne
259	0.374	0.066	259	0.371	0.083	Afrique subsaharienne sans l'Afrique du Sud
259	0.196	0.063	259	0.220	0.076	Économies en développement : Amérique
257	0.245	0.069	259	0.262	0.087	Amérique centrale et Grandes Antilles sans Porto Rico
257	0.334	0.092	259	0.347	0.113	Amérique centrale et Grandes Antilles sans le Mexique et Porto Rico
258	0.206	0.062	259	0.224	0.075	Amérique du Sud et Amérique centrale
258	0.230	0.063	259	0.253	0.073	Amérique du Sud sans le Brésil
260	0.232	0.108	260	0.180	0.113	Économies en développement : Asie
259	0.254	0.139	260	0.212	0.129	Asie orientale et Asie du Sud-Est sans la Chine
257	0.370	0.078	259	0.376	0.087	Asie méridionale sans l'Inde

Pour les sources et les notes, se reporter à la fin du tableau 4.1.1.

4.2.1 Volume indices of exports and imports
of countries and geographical regions
2000 = 100

Region, country or territory	Exports (1) - Exportations (1)							
	2005	2006	2007	2008	2009	2010	2011	2012
WORLD	127	138	147	149	129	147	155	158
DEVELOPING ECONOMIES	157	173	190	196	177	205	217	225
TRANSITION ECONOMIES	141	148	163	163	139	155	162	163
DEVELOPED ECONOMIES	114	123	128	130	110	124	130	131
Developing economies: Africa	126	127	136	131	119	129	119	125
Eastern Africa	138	141	151	155	150	167	172	190
Burundi	84	76	70	57	69	86	80	99
Comoros	135	99	113	45	101	122	124	117
Djibouti	103	128	125	125	170	175	168	170
Eritrea (2)	29	30	28	22	22	21	540	606
Ethiopia	137	150	164	174	184	233	233	256
Kenya	162	156	175	184	166	180	172	186
Madagascar	110	121	142	136	113	105	128	121
Malawi	135	162	193	174	207	175	205	197
Mauritius	153	168	151	151	138	160	163	169
Mozambique	365	397	387	373	382	441	464	582
Rwanda	119	129	144	140	135	153	219	237
Seychelles	163	178	170	177	164	150	155	151
Somalia	106	109	121	124	125	126	131	133
Uganda	166	177	229	254	238	221	243	296
United Republic of Tanzania	177	164	175	208	201	230	215	261
Zambia	127	163	187	202	213	260	275	283
Zimbabwe	74	66	65	57	59	74	70	84
Middle Africa	158	165	189	199	192	195	192	199
Angola	163	179	226	240	238	231	225	241
Cameroon	94	101	109	107	85	77	75	76
Central African Republic	71	83	86	69	59	62	75	87
Chad	903	823	814	685	706	691	667	560
Congo	104	111	93	102	108	130	122	116
Dem. Rep. of the Congo	211	199	210	231	253	300	309	305
Equatorial Guinea	344	336	381	401	369	335	338	369
Gabon	108	98	102	112	92	120	128	127
Sao Tome and Principe	154	172	136	168	122	157	157	182
Northern Africa	123	127	136	130	115	123	93	110
Algeria	110	106	109	100	89	98	95	92
Egypt	155	171	184	189	199	204	190	183
Libya	132	141	150	144	133	141	39	123
Morocco	122	132	143	121	91	108	105	102
Sudan (...2011)	148	146	208	202	201	221	139	–
Tunisia	156	167	199	208	170	181	172	163
Southern Africa	127	121	131	122	100	115	114	109
Botswana	151	137	139	146	110	135	154	156
Lesotho	298	318	346	386	316	366	438	402
Namibia	131	129	127	135	148	173	167	157
South Africa	124	118	130	120	98	112	111	105
Swaziland	153	138	142	109	99	102	95	98
Western Africa	121	120	121	115	114	129	132	131
Benin	123	139	180	183	194	162	139	152
Burkina Faso	213	248	231	217	300	392	441	492
Cape Verde	133	143	129	189	205	245	322	240
Côte d'Ivoire	116	115	104	98	117	100	94	101
Gambia	45	59	59	51	276	132	327	353
Ghana	109	133	130	121	133	162	227	226
Guinea	95	86	94	95	103	120	97	102
Guinea-Bissau	136	96	138	132	127	126	203	114
Liberia	41	43	49	46	28	31	41	56
Mali	163	193	173	192	159	140	128	120
Mauritania	123	230	231	204	191	209	239	243
Niger	107	97	92	127	157	173	151	177
Nigeria	129	124	128	120	120	143	145	141
Saint Helena	244	248	289	384	359	341	363	442
Senegal	132	122	117	121	133	125	114	111
Sierra Leone	1 114	1 502	1 500	1 124	1 295	1 736	1 654	3 220
Togo	257	229	213	169	208	182	187	189

For sources and notes, see end of table.

Imports (1) - Importations (1)								Régions, pays ou territoires
2005	2006	2007	2008	2009	2010	2011	2012	
129	**139**	**148**	**151**	**131**	**149**	**156**	**159**	**MONDE**
155	170	189	202	181	215	231	242	ÉCONOMIES EN DÉVELOPPEMENT
203	244	310	359	258	298	345	359	ÉCONOMIES EN TRANSITION
117	125	129	128	109	121	125	124	ÉCONOMIES DÉVELOPPÉES
156	**173**	**196**	**219**	**205**	**223**	**229**	**247**	**Économies en développement : Afrique**
148	*164*	*181*	*204*	*202*	*215*	*227*	*253*	*Afrique orientale*
149	226	154	174	184	222	285	299	Burundi
187	209	232	246	300	311	326	355	Comores
95	106	135	139	122	94	111	130	Djibouti
87	80	71	69	72	78	88	95	Érythrée (2)
258	309	318	386	407	428	379	516	Éthiopie
140	159	183	193	199	217	224	249	Kenya
126	125	170	213	196	145	139	148	Madagascar
182	180	185	247	245	252	248	243	Malawi
146	160	160	158	152	161	165	166	Maurice
166	185	181	194	204	234	278	304	Mozambique
164	201	257	347	415	431	469	539	Rwanda
144	148	157	172	141	104	103	108	Seychelles
155	178	182	150	128	134	152	165	Somalie
105	122	154	176	183	189	199	211	Ouganda
166	200	231	287	259	292	344	368	République-Unie de Tanzanie
230	261	315	349	300	368	432	488	Zambie
89	77	76	76	84	102	104	106	Zimbabwe
214	*237*	*308*	*379*	*419*	*376*	*400*	*441*	*Afrique centrale*
252	254	368	515	586	415	447	532	Angola
142	149	202	208	181	192	213	233	Cameroun
123	134	152	157	152	151	123	126	République centrafricaine
247	335	406	406	429	494	489	475	Tchad
237	351	405	442	427	555	656	648	Congo
319	323	345	387	379	414	448	499	Rép. dém. du Congo
216	318	404	523	846	843	763	761	Guinée équatoriale
133	151	174	187	192	218	244	256	Gabon
129	171	174	213	219	223	232	249	Sao Tomé-et-Principe
147	*158*	*184*	*213*	*212*	*223*	*207*	*236*	*Afrique septentrionale*
188	187	215	279	294	295	304	305	Algérie
122	138	170	191	196	212	203	246	Égypte
130	121	123	149	223	291	115	331	Libye
140	155	183	207	180	178	189	192	Maroc
366	419	429	421	456	449	376	—	Soudan (…2011)
126	133	156	176	149	162	151	156	Tunisie
156	*180*	*190*	*190*	*162*	*189*	*212*	*215*	*Afrique australe*
126	115	142	165	161	181	207	229	Botswana
156	162	179	165	184	208	190	201	Lesotho
147	157	181	201	245	251	254	271	Namibie
159	187	197	196	160	190	216	217	Afrique du Sud
145	139	123	90	108	110	95	96	Swaziland
167	*184*	*214*	*249*	*206*	*241*	*261*	*266*	*Afrique occidentale*
135	157	240	221	223	195	173	180	Bénin
169	191	194	196	206	212	217	286	Burkina Faso
155	178	224	219	210	204	223	180	Cap-Vert
181	164	174	163	167	172	125	181	Côte d'Ivoire
110	104	117	98	99	84	86	99	Gambie
145	170	188	206	177	226	292	329	Ghana
105	115	135	129	111	137	172	189	Guinée
148	160	192	179	187	171	194	187	Guinée-Bissau
54	75	72	91	56	66	94	89	Libéria
155	172	188	246	204	260	218	191	Mali
269	204	223	257	223	262	282	325	Mauritanie
191	183	204	258	368	399	381	414	Niger
197	235	283	358	264	329	369	338	Nigéria
113	146	184	82	76	87	68	62	Sainte-Hélène
168	164	196	209	176	163	168	185	Sénégal
155	157	162	153	184	240	433	439	Sierra Leone
57	54	58	60	64	62	60	63	Togo

Pour les sources et les notes, se reporter à la fin du tableau.

4

4.2.1 Volume indices of exports and imports of countries and geographical regions
2000 = 100

Region, country or territory	Exports (1) - Exportations (1)							
	2005	2006	2007	2008	2009	2010	2011	2012
Developing economies: America	127	134	138	136	126	136	143	146
Caribbean	96	104	99	92	69	76	84	86
Anguilla	319	211	154	179	372	206	248	324
Antigua and Barbuda	176	144	103	92	71	63	70	83
Aruba	52	51	42	30	42	38	43	48
Bahamas	81	95	102	99	91	77	72	84
Barbados	90	116	112	88	73	78	73	88
British Virgin Islands	119	115	114	101	97	92	84	81
Cayman Islands	360	129	131	62	73	46	75	77
Cuba	91	96	102	102	83	107	120	129
Curaçao	–	–	–	–	–	–	(a)14	..
Dominica	63	58	49	46	38	41	30	35
Dominican Republic	100	103	103	92	80	94	111	119
Grenada	61	51	61	48	50	39	39	47
Haiti	135	143	143	127	138	140	182	187
Jamaica	93	94	105	100	69	58	61	63
Montserrat	114	101	196	276	232	80	117	..
Netherlands Antilles	18	18	16	20	20	17	–	–
Saint Kitts and Nevis	105	120	100	145	108	92	125	123
Saint Lucia	101	130	129	186	216	258	166	194
Saint Vincent and the Grenadines	85	74	84	72	63	49	41	45
Trinidad and Tobago	136	159	140	134	92	100	86	82
Turks and Caicos Islands	179	213	188	268	234	172	151	154
Central America	117	130	133	134	124	142	146	153
Belize	84	97	93	92	82	87	89	96
Costa Rica	127	148	167	167	164	180	192	211
El Salvador	112	118	121	135	117	132	143	145
Guatemala	185	198	214	218	210	227	249	252
Honduras	166	167	174	173	145	162	167	185
Mexico	112	124	126	127	117	135	138	144
Nicaragua	137	160	179	200	196	238	258	306
Panama (3)	790	883	932	988	1 101	1 096	1 356	1 453
South America	143	146	151	149	140	146	154	155
Argentina	136	144	155	156	149	173	181	175
Bolivia (Plurinational State of)	174	179	183	249	204	216	236	293
Brazil	179	185	195	190	170	186	191	189
Chile	141	145	156	149	151	149	155	162
Colombia	131	139	148	154	168	168	197	204
Ecuador	173	186	190	202	193	203	214	225
Falkland Islands (Malvinas)	209	175	210	204	185	202	175	202
Guyana	88	77	89	82	78	77	82	100
Paraguay	182	189	270	363	468	573	610	556
Peru	173	174	178	188	187	190	199	203
Suriname	200	183	200	223	196	229	233	242
Uruguay	140	154	159	159	173	192	197	211
Venezuela (Bolivarian Rep. of)	96	92	86	85	77	70	75	77
Developing economies: Asia	168	190	212	221	199	236	254	264
Eastern Asia	203	240	277	299	266	330	365	384
China	300	376	459	507	436	563	636	682
China, Hong Kong SAR	150	164	174	177	156	181	191	200
China, Macao SAR	95	96	93	70	33	28	26	30
China, Taiwan Province of	140	156	167	170	152	192	200	200
Korea, Dem. People's Rep. of	167	169	185	185	189	222	239	242
Korea, Republic of	178	202	224	244	251	288	316	321
Mongolia	119	118	131	138	124	144	199	195
Southern Asia	146	167	176	189	177	195	212	190
Afghanistan	194	185	203	187	144	122	100	98
Bangladesh	144	183	190	222	213	258	295	301
Bhutan	152	219	350	200	229	265	235	229
India	180	210	224	262	244	278	318	310
Iran (Islamic Rep. of)	108	123	129	122	125	129	125	91
Maldives	127	155	173	211	109	113	174	155
Nepal	93	82	79	77	71	68	60	65
Pakistan	172	177	180	182	161	160	179	140
Sri Lanka	113	117	128	127	107	119	126	115
South-Eastern Asia	142	156	167	169	152	180	188	192
Brunei Darussalam	88	86	81	75	79	86	91	92
Cambodia	214	253	273	296	258	295	367	429

For sources and notes, see end of table.

Imports (1) - Importations (1)								Régions, pays ou territoires
2005	2006	2007	2008	2009	2010	2011	2012	
121	**137**	**153**	**166**	**136**	**167**	**185**	**189**	**Économies en développement : Amérique**
104	*115*	*119*	*122*	*101*	*102*	*108*	*108*	*Caraïbes*
111	180	187	187	119	106	93	92	Anguilla
107	122	130	108	76	64	51	54	Antigua-et-Barbuda
107	103	102	93	94	83	91	94	Aruba
92	97	96	83	74	66	63	71	Bahamas
111	109	104	98	82	77	72	70	Barbade
74	67	65	57	50	47	46	47	Îles Vierges britanniques
184	149	129	102	79	66	68	67	Îles Caïmanes
142	178	167	195	139	150	153	157	Cuba
–	–	–	–	–	–	(a)32	..	Curaçao
90	86	93	105	107	96	82	75	Dominique
93	109	116	123	110	127	126	126	République dominicaine
117	102	116	103	88	91	82	83	Grenade
118	124	122	116	126	181	141	133	Haïti
107	118	133	134	94	87	90	90	Jamaïque
108	103	94	105	103	..	..	..	Montserrat
40	39	41	40	42	38	–	–	Antilles néerlandaises
90	102	104	114	110	96	80	74	Saint-Kitts-et-Nevis
103	114	108	87	96	100	80	79	Sainte-Lucie
130	136	149	144	136	126	106	111	Saint-Vincent-et-les Grenadines
124	128	139	143	120	99	122	119	Trinité-et-Tobago
172	269	293	268	186	140	119	118	Îles Turques et Caïques
120	*132*	*139*	*144*	*115*	*140*	*152*	*158*	*Amérique centrale*
86	90	86	90	84	83	78	103	Belize
143	164	180	202	164	192	214	232	Costa Rica
126	138	150	156	125	134	146	150	El Salvador
173	184	194	184	164	180	191	194	Guatemala
157	161	183	187	152	167	180	180	Honduras
114	126	131	136	107	132	143	149	Mexique
121	130	148	156	144	159	175	196	Nicaragua
256	274	321	346	326	375	446	479	Panama (3)
127	*148*	*179*	*205*	*172*	*218*	*246*	*249*	*Amérique du Sud*
108	126	153	178	138	190	225	201	Argentine
110	122	135	187	176	195	255	262	Bolivie (État plurinational de)
109	126	154	182	150	207	225	220	Brésil
162	181	213	249	202	264	304	309	Chili
165	194	229	253	226	261	319	337	Colombie
239	258	276	332	305	382	410	422	Équateur
94	91	111	75	80	137	201	146	Îles Falkland (Malvinas)
100	105	114	121	124	136	146	154	Guyana
150	184	216	303	259	357	400	373	Paraguay
141	161	195	235	185	232	266	294	Pérou
155	140	134	147	175	163	159	159	Suriname
96	109	116	151	142	163	180	193	Uruguay
132	179	236	229	209	188	210	259	Venezuela (Rép. bolivarienne du)
164	**180**	**199**	**211**	**192**	**229**	**246**	**257**	**Économies en développement : Asie**
170	*187*	*206*	*208*	*197*	*242*	*260*	*271*	*Asie orientale*
251	284	324	332	329	412	454	481	Chine
143	157	169	172	154	181	194	205	Chine (RAS de Hong Kong)
154	172	189	168	144	165	209	241	Chine (RAS de Macao)
115	119	119	115	97	124	121	118	Province chinoise de Taiwan
119	114	110	103	101	104	113	130	Corée, Rép. populaire dém. de
139	153	166	167	164	192	200	202	Corée, République de
145	169	222	321	215	307	526	539	Mongolie
199	*230*	*253*	*305*	*289*	*329*	*349*	*356*	*Asie méridionale*
173	171	170	153	195	276	292	283	Afghanistan
125	136	141	145	144	163	176	174	Bangladesh
184	182	204	178	193	291	317	312	Bhoutan
224	280	322	416	413	470	512	542	Inde
225	217	220	241	223	276	234	217	Iran (Rép. islamique d')
157	183	201	220	172	178	206	218	Maldives
106	104	118	112	151	162	154	175	Népal
170	181	179	182	124	123	135	113	Pakistan
113	121	122	127	103	124	157	150	Sri Lanka
141	*150*	*160*	*172*	*145*	*177*	*189*	*200*	*Asie du Sud-Est*
118	128	146	160	159	151	159	187	Brunéi Darussalam
173	200	214	224	218	223	256	311	Cambodge

Pour les sources et les notes, se reporter à la fin du tableau.

Region, country or territory	Exports (1) - Exportations (1)							
	2005	2006	2007	2008	2009	2010	2011	2012
Indonesia	96	99	101	95	95	109	112	110
Lao People's Dem. Rep.	141	169	170	184	208	276	302	363
Malaysia	134	148	154	150	132	157	160	161
Myanmar	170	174	232	197	220	281	253	246
Philippines	132	145	151	143	116	149	129	140
Singapore	174	192	208	218	196	236	247	248
Thailand	143	159	178	187	159	185	202	207
Viet Nam	181	206	238	256	249	293	344	410
Western Asia	**131**	**136**	**146**	**150**	**143**	**151**	**161**	**172**
Bahrain	109	107	111	113	103	107	117	127
Iraq	67	69	88	96	103	101	117	130
Jordan	173	191	177	160	142	179	181	165
Kuwait	125	132	135	140	131	136	150	174
Lebanon	270	295	340	369	358	400	395	394
Oman	88	83	89	88	115	113	108	112
Qatar	122	132	153	172	185	256	303	326
Saudi Arabia	127	126	127	126	115	122	133	139
State of Palestine	72	76	96	94	92	96	113	154
Syrian Arab Republic	122	137	131	134	116	118	74	30
Turkey	199	223	248	265	244	260	275	324
United Arab Emirates	149	159	180	189	181	183	188	196
Yemen	76	75	65	58	69	77	75	56
Developing economies: Oceania	**89**	**79**	**80**	**70**	**57**	**58**	**55**	**55**
American Samoa	89	62	60	70	60	35	30	32
Cook Islands	51	32	..	..	..	..	..	..
Fiji	100	84	89	95	64	76	67	71
French Polynesia	94	99	79	75	59	59	59	48
Guam	54	50	82	83	40	33	28	30
Kiribati	120	162	211	267	114	65	123	140
Marshall Islands	304	196	181	155	150	211	217	201
Micronesia (Federated States of)	81	68	93	98	91	85	82	100
Nauru	9	11	30	47	25	49	46	59
New Caledonia	114	109	134	77	60	71	70	66
Niue	60	339	842	5	6	6	5	5
Northern Mariana Islands	66	47	28	9	1	0	0	0
Palau	99	88	81	61	37	35	30	34
Papua New Guinea	93	87	85	87	77	77	72	70
Samoa	115	79	114	79	54	65	54	76
Solomon Islands	115	124	146	170	158	191	310	361
Tokelau	..	..	..	..	..	..	..	..
Tonga	93	86	78	74	64	62	97	108
Vanuatu	135	155	173	156	157	123	148	119
Wallis and Futuna Islands	77	71	66	51	58	55	41	42
Transition economies	**141**	**148**	**163**	**163**	**139**	**155**	**162**	**163**
Albania	222	255	326	357	308	397	442	450
Armenia	270	226	245	193	144	177	200	227
Azerbaijan	253	361	538	571	600	595	572	522
Belarus	153	175	194	206	167	176	240	266
Bosnia and Herzegovina	180	226	264	285	245	274	291	266
Croatia	170	185	206	203	161	169	171	159
Georgia	198	183	219	214	172	231	269	300
Kazakhstan	175	191	214	239	202	224	251	267
Kyrgyzstan	95	113	156	190	177	165	157	154
Republic of Moldova	260	254	285	288	311	355	461	520
Russian Federation	133	136	144	140	124	140	141	140
Serbia and Montenegro	228	287	356					
Serbia	−	−	−	356	291	318	337	333
Tajikistan	85	103	105	89	74	67	60	76
TFYR of Macedonia	125	138	181	181	125	146	171	156
Turkmenistan	115	127	156	137	82	97	145	171
Ukraine	159	167	188	204	134	159	178	187
Uzbekistan	123	120	160	156	204	181	164	143
Developed economies: America	**105**	**113**	**119**	**122**	**104**	**118**	**126**	**131**
Bermuda	96	47	44	30	50	24	20	18
Canada	100	101	101	98	80	88	92	95
Greenland	161	147	159	160	122	119	124	122
Saint Pierre and Miquelon	231	541	396	194	100	73	67	68
United States	108	119	126	134	115	133	142	148

For sources and notes, see end of table.

Imports (1) - Importations (1)								Régions, pays ou territoires
2005	2006	2007	2008	2009	2010	2011	2012	
133	131	139	162	133	178	199	216	Indonésie
131	147	138	160	184	243	245	276	Rép. dém. populaire lao
134	147	157	147	124	156	159	169	Malaisie
63	78	91	101	114	115	180	222	Myanmar
139	130	134	121	102	122	115	118	Philippines
134	149	158	175	151	177	184	190	Singapour
164	168	174	·197	151	191	217	232	Thaïlande
184	207	265	295	281	317	350	378	Viet Nam
173	*187*	*218*	*251*	*216*	*234*	*253*	*267*	***Asie occidentale***
153	155	156	185	129	145	135	159	Bahreïn
177	149	140	195	242	265	260	304	Iraq
154	155	162	167	157	140	135	150	Jordanie
191	200	231	248	203	223	231	231	Koweït
118	110	129	153	166	170	163	173	Liban
145	167	226	302	246	260	277	336	Oman
266	418	558	623	565	511	592	710	Qatar
169	187	224	254	219	234	263	288	Arabie saoudite
77	72	77	69	85	87	83	97	État de Palestine
223	218	258	275	255	270	221	103	République arabe syrienne
156	171	190	188	163	198	222	223	Turquie
214	235	292	400	309	322	358	382	Émirats arabes unis
175	180	227	237	239	219	195	234	Yémen
125	**137**	**140**	**136**	**126**	**137**	**137**	**139**	**Économies en développement : Océanie**
90	93	102	83	76	64	66	65	Samoa américaines
139	164	162	..	..	..	..	..	Îles Cook
148	153	140	149	110	124	135	141	Fidji
150	138	144	152	131	122	112	106	Polynésie française
83	151	88	70	115	113	105	112	Guam
148	118	119	103	102	102	113	123	Kiribati
208	184	180	140	130	151	154	143	Îles Marshall
107	108	105	101	117	111	103	119	Micronésie (États fédérés de)
66	77	134	173	84	50	63	73	Nauru
159	181	224	230	199	242	237	207	Nouvelle-Calédonie
423	147	254	253	185	181	189	175	Nioué
77	60	34	15	8	9	8	8	Îles Mariannes du Nord
72	76	67	63	71	63	56	65	Palaos
112	135	161	151	155	178	183	207	Papouasie-Nouvelle-Guinée
209	227	201	190	170	210	202	203	Samoa
150	163	203	178	177	249	242	258	Îles Salomon
57	9	8	7	7	6	6	6	Tokélaou
134	120	134	137	131	130	134	146	Tonga
145	200	194	215	211	187	179	168	Vanuatu
124	134	123	110	117	108	95	96	Îles Wallis-et-Futuna
203	**244**	**310**	**359**	**258**	**298**	**345**	**359**	**Économies en transition**
196	216	275	303	286	262	279	258	Albanie
166	187	259	306	250	269	261	266	Arménie
293	327	348	398	352	355	489	500	Azerbaïdjan
135	162	192	213	187	212	230	229	Bélarus
182	177	215	237	187	183	192	176	Bosnie-Herzégovine
193	209	236	241	183	162	160	147	Croatie
272	373	493	519	412	451	543	604	Géorgie
280	360	466	478	376	398	432	521	Kazakhstan
144	231	306	392	308	301	343	432	Kirghizistan
318	391	488	525	485	565	665	773	République de Moldova
223	281	364	444	300	375	454	471	Fédération de Russie
242	286	390	—	—	—	—	—	Serbie-et-Monténégro
—	—	—	374	274	266	276	270	Serbie
141	161	213	234	207	193	203	243	Tadjikistan
117	127	164	180	141	139	148	143	LERY de Macédoine
144	120	158	221	273	221	265	346	Turkménistan
188	212	268	311	191	243	282	284	Ukraine
114	130	175	232	236	218	226	250	Ouzbékistan
124	**130**	**132**	**128**	**108**	**123**	**128**	**132**	**Économies développées : Amérique**
131	136	131	107	94	79	69	65	Bermudes
116	120	125	128	109	123	131	133	Canada
132	140	148	155	141	141	138	127	Groenland
86	86	104	182	246	207	193	184	Saint-Pierre-et-Miquelon
125	132	133	129	107	123	128	132	États-Unis

Pour les sources et les notes, se reporter à la fin du tableau.

4

4.2.1 Volume indices of exports and imports of countries and geographical regions
2000 = 100

Region, country or territory	Exports (1) - Exportations (1)							
	2005	2006	2007	2008	2009	2010	2011	2012
Developed economies: Asia	**128**	**142**	**156**	**158**	**120**	**152**	**152**	**150**
Israel	119	125	136	133	112	132	143	128
Japan	129	144	157	161	121	154	153	152
Developed economies: Europe	**117**	**126**	**131**	**131**	**112**	**125**	**131**	**131**
Andorra	290	268	227	160	102	86	119	175
Austria	133	138	147	148	121	138	147	146
Belgium	123	129	136	133	119	128	133	132
Bulgaria	163	184	194	206	174	209	249	246
Cyprus	105	90	84	83	81	87	100	102
Czech Republic	174	203	234	249	210	246	270	272
Denmark	117	122	127	129	114	118	122	119
Estonia	144	174	169	170	140	175	221	226
Faeroe Islands	112	101	126	121	110	110	116	106
Finland	105	117	118	118	87	93	94	92
France	99	101	101	100	85	93	96	96
Germany	125	137	146	146	120	136	145	145
Gibraltar	164	176	202	164	197	159	128	120
Greece	103	114	117	114	105	105	135	154
Hungary	169	201	232	243	200	236	254	251
Iceland	139	137	169	170	171	168	176	175
Ireland	110	106	108	103	104	103	103	99
Italy	104	110	115	112	91	100	104	104
Latvia	186	209	232	254	227	271	330	370
Lithuania	232	255	266	312	266	314	357	387
Luxembourg	179	214	193	212	202	184	184	174
Malta	83	88	85	85	69	83	85	87
Netherlands	131	141	148	154	137	152	153	158
Norway	107	105	107	107	104	101	96	97
Poland	187	221	246	266	240	276	295	304
Portugal	114	123	134	133	113	124	135	139
Romania	168	183	206	224	206	244	271	263
Slovakia	171	219	277	310	270	320	358	392
Slovenia	149	174	200	206	173	193	206	203
Spain	114	120	126	126	112	125	136	136
Sweden	111	119	122	122	98	113	121	117
Switzerland	145	157	172	188	168	186	205	200
United Kingdom	94	103	91	87	75	84	90	85
Developed economies: Oceania	**107**	**110**	**113**	**119**	**111**	**126**	**126**	**127**
Australia	109	111	114	120	114	129	129	131
New Zealand	102	109	112	121	102	125	122	119

Sources:

UNCTAD secretariat calculations, based on:

- ECLAC, *CEPALSTAT* External trade deflator

- EUROSTAT, online database, Trade unit value indices by reporting country

- IMF, *International Financial Statistics*

- U.S. Bureau of Labor Statistics, External trade price indices

- Unit value indices of Japan Customs and Price indices of Bank of Japan

- UNCTAD, *UNCTADstat Commodity Price Statistics*

- UNCTAD, *UNCTADstat Merchandise Trade Matrix*

- UNCTAD secretariat estimates

Notes:

(a)　Data refer to Netherlands Antilles.

(1)　Volume indices or quantum: The ratio of the export or import value index to the corresponding unit value index.

(2)　From 2011 onwards, exports include commercial mining.

(3)　From 2005 onwards, including customs free zones.

Imports (1) - Importations (1)								Régions, pays ou territoires
2005	2006	2007	2008	2009	2010	2011	2012	
116	121	123	122	107	118	123	128	Économies développées : Asie
104	105	113	114	98	113	122	125	Israël
118	123	124	123	108	119	124	128	Japon
115	123	129	128	110	120	123	120	Économies développées : Europe
..	..	..	..	..	..	..	..	Andorre
119	122	129	129	110	123	130	127	Autriche
123	129	137	134	119	126	131	128	Belgique
181	217	245	266	203	209	229	241	Bulgarie
114	118	130	142	121	129	114	99	Chypre
165	190	215	225	187	221	236	225	République tchèque
117	126	137	137	113	116	117	119	Danemark
139	173	177	157	118	137	171	176	Estonie
117	118	141	122	104	96	104	119	Îles Féroé
118	129	135	136	105	112	119	112	Finlande
100	102	105	105	91	97	100	97	France
110	121	126	127	110	125	132	127	Allemagne
71	75	87	65	86	71	62	59	Gibraltar
107	114	127	129	113	99	81	83	Grèce
151	171	189	196	157	177	189	186	Hongrie
155	180	176	137	94	97	106	106	Islande
103	104	108	99	83	79	78	75	Irlande
110	116	120	114	95	107	107	97	Italie
190	234	272	247	176	207	253	269	Lettonie
209	232	254	268	196	229	261	265	Lituanie
138	158	150	162	148	139	143	139	Luxembourg
88	101	101	102	96	111	120	123	Malte
121	129	136	141	124	136	139	142	Pays-Bas
122	135	148	155	133	144	151	150	Norvège
142	167	193	212	177	202	211	204	Pologne
105	108	118	121	105	109	105	96	Portugal
208	248	309	325	239	268	290	279	Roumanie
176	217	262	283	243	280	311	322	Slovaquie
134	153	176	184	149	165	173	164	Slovénie
122	130	136	128	104	111	111	101	Espagne
109	116	127	126	102	120	126	121	Suède
117	127	134	134	123	133	134	137	Suisse
107	117	110	102	92	99	99	101	Royaume-Uni
147	158	173	193	167	184	198	207	Économies développées : Océanie
150	163	181	200	178	195	208	219	Australie
135	141	142	167	123	141	154	154	Nouvelle-Zélande

Sources :

Calculs du secrétariat de la CNUCED, basés sur :

- CEPALC, *CEPALSTAT* Déflateur du commerce extérieur

- EUROSTAT, base de données en ligne, Indices de valeur unitaire par pays déclarant

- FMI, *Statistiques financières internationales*

- Bureau des statistiques du travail des États-Unis (BLS), Indices de prix du commerce extérieur

- Indices des valeurs unitaires des douanes japonaises et Indices de prix de la Banque du Japon

- CNUCED, *UNCTADstat Statistiques de prix des produits de base*

- CNUCED, *UNCTADstat Matrice du commerce de marchandises*

- Estimations du secrétariat de la CNUCED

Notes :

(a) Les données se réfèrent aux Antilles néerlandaises.

(1) Indices du volume ou quantum : représentent le rapport de l'indice de la valeur des exportations ou des importations à l'indice de la valeur unitaire correspondant.

(2) À partir de 2011, les exportations comprennent l'exploitation minière commerciale.

(3) À partir de 2005, y compris les zones franches douanières.

4.2.1 Unit value indices of exports and imports of countries and geographical regions
2000 = 100

Region, country or territory	Exports (1) - Exportations (1)							
	2005	2006	2007	2008	2009	2010	2011	2012
WORLD	**128**	**137**	**148**	**168**	**151**	**161**	**183**	**180**
DEVELOPING ECONOMIES	118	128	135	157	138	153	176	177
TRANSITION ECONOMIES	167	199	220	294	222	260	332	334
DEVELOPED ECONOMIES	131	137	150	165	152	157	174	169
Developing economies: Africa	**167**	**198**	**217**	**290**	**224**	**267**	**341**	**341**
Eastern Africa	*122*	*148*	*160*	*179*	*167*	*196*	*231*	*219*
Burundi	137	154	167	201	195	236	308	263
Comoros	66	74	90	106	109	124	150	157
Djibouti	122	136	148	174	144	154	175	177
Eritrea (2)	105	112	129	141	135	157	200	209
Ethiopia	135	143	161	189	181	206	254	241
Kenya	121	129	134	156	155	166	193	190
Madagascar	94	99	106	117	113	123	151	151
Malawi	99	109	118	133	151	161	183	174
Mauritius	90	89	95	102	90	91	101	101
Mozambique	134	165	171	195	154	187	213	193
Rwanda	198	216	232	361	326	367	400	374
Seychelles	107	110	109	125	124	138	160	169
Somalia	122	138	150	175	175	184	206	210
Uganda	122	135	145	169	164	182	220	201
United Republic of Tanzania	129	160	174	204	202	240	300	288
Zambia	160	259	277	282	227	310	367	339
Zimbabwe	130	157	191	199	198	226	259	234
Middle Africa	*183*	*218*	*240*	*327*	*218*	*275*	*366*	*372*
Angola	187	224	248	336	217	276	376	382
Cameroon	166	193	211	268	227	275	336	322
Central African Republic	113	117	128	135	126	140	157	150
Chad	186	223	246	333	217	277	377	381
Congo	184	221	244	328	228	287	377	381
Dem. Rep. of the Congo	141	168	183	236	171	219	265	256
Equatorial Guinea	187	223	244	346	225	272	364	383
Gabon	181	214	237	330	223	279	361	363
Sao Tome and Principe	147	150	167	211	221	231	231	202
Northern Africa	*173*	*204*	*221*	*308*	*225*	*262*	*336*	*344*
Algeria	190	235	251	359	229	265	350	364
Egypt	158	185	198	263	219	246	305	304
Libya	187	224	247	338	218	271	366	376
Morocco	128	135	149	233	215	230	286	291
Sudan (...2011)	180	215	237	320	227	286	385	_
Tunisia	115	120	130	159	145	155	177	178
Southern Africa	*136*	*160*	*175*	*214*	*201*	*229*	*278*	*262*
Botswana	109	124	139	127	117	130	143	143
Lesotho	99	99	101	104	105	109	121	124
Namibia	119	155	174	176	161	176	200	197
South Africa	139	164	180	225	210	242	296	277
Swaziland	126	142	145	170	183	193	220	212
Western Africa	*182*	*216*	*239*	*323*	*241*	*296*	*386*	*385*
Benin	120	135	149	178	161	202	259	236
Burkina Faso	105	114	129	153	144	194	255	228
Cape Verde	120	131	136	154	156	165	193	201
Côte d'Ivoire	171	190	214	273	249	296	343	314
Gambia	119	129	141	178	159	176	193	189
Ghana	154	168	193	260	263	294	336	317
Guinea	135	179	191	211	153	184	222	207
Guinea-Bissau	105	124	125	156	153	162	182	183
Liberia	98	112	125	160	162	221	272	247
Mali	124	147	165	200	204	262	342	329
Mauritania	143	168	177	247	201	280	327	290
Niger	161	185	254	254	226	235	292	300
Nigeria	187	226	248	342	225	280	376	384
Saint Helena	92	95	95	100	95	101	113	111
Senegal	130	142	155	195	165	187	242	245
Sierra Leone	109	118	125	147	137	151	162	155
Togo	71	75	87	138	119	136	161	146

For sources and notes, see end of table.

234

	Imports (1) - Importations (1)							Régions, pays ou territoires
2005	2006	2007	2008	2009	2010	2011	2012	
126	**134**	**145**	**164**	**146**	**156**	**177**	**175**	**MONDE**
116	123	131	149	134	146	166	165	ÉCONOMIES EN DÉVELOPPEMENT
122	130	138	155	145	152	169	169	ÉCONOMIES EN TRANSITION
131	139	151	171	151	159	180	177	ÉCONOMIES DÉVELOPPÉES
127	**135**	**147**	**169**	**154**	**165**	**189**	**188**	**Économies en développement : Afrique**
126	*135*	*147*	*172*	*153*	*166*	*193*	*191*	*Afrique orientale*
122	129	140	157	148	155	178	176	Burundi
122	128	138	169	162	173	197	195	Comores
141	153	169	200	179	193	222	215	Djibouti
120	131	153	184	174	188	215	213	Érythrée (2)
126	134	145	170	149	160	186	184	Éthiopie
135	147	158	186	165	180	213	211	Kenya
124	132	142	162	149	159	191	188	Madagascar
120	126	140	168	155	162	184	182	Malawi
98	103	110	134	111	124	141	142	Maurice
126	134	146	178	160	170	196	193	Mozambique
123	128	141	159	148	156	178	174	Rwanda
137	150	160	185	165	182	213	217	Seychelles
118	130	142	173	171	183	211	195	Somalie
127	137	147	168	151	161	184	183	Ouganda
130	139	152	176	156	169	199	198	République-Unie de Tanzanie
125	133	143	163	144	163	187	185	Zambie
142	161	181	209	185	199	226	223	Zimbabwe
117	*123*	*134*	*149*	*138*	*147*	*166*	*166*	*Afrique centrale*
109	114	122	134	127	132	149	148	Angola
130	142	155	185	165	180	206	205	Cameroun
121	129	140	164	152	170	216	218	République centrafricaine
121	127	140	156	147	153	174	173	Tchad
118	123	134	148	146	155	170	173	Congo
124	131	144	163	151	159	180	179	Rép. dém. du Congo
120	126	136	149	122	134	156	157	Guinée équatoriale
116	120	131	144	137	144	160	160	Gabon
129	139	153	180	158	169	190	189	Sao Tomé-et-Principe
124	*131*	*146*	*166*	*153*	*163*	*188*	*185*	*Afrique septentrionale*
118	125	140	154	146	149	170	167	Algérie
127	135	150	174	158	171	199	195	Égypte
125	133	146	164	155	163	187	186	Libye
129	134	152	177	158	172	203	200	Maroc
119	124	132	143	137	144	158	_	Soudan (…2011)
122	132	143	163	149	161	185	183	Tunisie
130	*139*	*149*	*171*	*153*	*165*	*188*	*187*	*Afrique australe*
120	128	138	152	141	150	169	168	Botswana
112	115	120	135	124	137	162	160	Lesotho
113	118	125	139	131	143	162	161	Namibie
132	142	151	175	156	167	190	190	Afrique du Sud
124	131	143	169	157	169	196	193	Swaziland
128	*137*	*150*	*174*	*158*	*168*	*193*	*192*	*Afrique occidentale*
123	128	138	169	151	171	207	200	Bénin
122	129	141	168	149	158	181	180	Burkina Faso
123	132	146	164	147	158	185	185	Cap-Vert
131	143	155	195	168	184	217	218	Côte d'Ivoire
126	134	146	176	164	181	213	205	Gambie
124	133	144	167	153	162	184	184	Ghana
127	135	147	174	156	168	200	199	Guinée
140	152	167	212	182	192	225	225	Guinée-Bissau
85	93	104	133	146	162	167	178	Libéria
124	131	144	169	151	164	193	191	Mali
117	126	141	166	148	163	192	190	Mauritanie
125	131	142	167	151	157	179	177	Niger
121	129	141	160	148	154	174	173	Nigéria
128	141	149	169	158	182	215	214	Sainte-Hélène
134	144	160	201	172	189	226	224	Sénégal
149	166	184	233	189	215	264	267	Sierra Leone
330	355	383	450	416	462	535	507	Togo

Pour les sources et les notes, se reporter à la fin du tableau.

4.2.1 Unit value indices of exports and imports of countries and geographical regions
2000 = 100

Region, country or territory	Exports (1) - Exportations (1)							
	2005	2006	2007	2008	2009	2010	2011	2012
Developing economies: America	125	142	155	182	153	179	213	212
Caribbean	141	165	180	231	191	214	261	261
Anguilla	117	144	148	159	153	152	164	162
Antigua and Barbuda	91	99	111	137	138	141	154	151
Aruba	113	124	134	191	185	188	197	194
Bahamas	117	127	137	168	136.	159	202	208
Barbados	146	162	172	203	190	203	238	237
British Virgin Islands	109	116	123	142	140	152	170	..
Cayman Islands	92	100	111	133	145	160	161	174
Cuba	152	196	233	232	223	273	306	277
Curaçao	—	—	—	—	—	—	(a)307	..
Dominica	124	133	140	162	165	169	186	184
Dominican Republic	107	111	121	128	119	125	135	134
Grenada	94	103	115	131	121	134	155	154
Haiti	110	112	115	119	131	130	133	138
Jamaica	127	160	166	187	147	175	206	196
Montserrat	113	116	124	132	121	123	135	..
Netherlands Antilles	170	196	213	276	197	235	—	—
Saint Kitts and Nevis	100	102	106	108	107	107	110	113
Saint Lucia	148	168	177	205	178	193	227	228
Saint Vincent and the Grenadines	100	109	121	154	167	181	199	207
Trinidad and Tobago	171	208	223	325	231	257	353	373
Turks and Caicos Islands	93	94	98	104	100	105	120	118
Central America	113	119	127	135	117	131	150	152
Belize	114	130	132	152	142	161	194	192
Costa Rica	95	95	96	98	92	90	93	92
El Salvador	104	107	113	117	112	116	126	125
Guatemala	107	112	119	131	127	137	154	148
Honduras	91	95	99	107	100	113	140	130
Mexico	115	121	129	138	118	133	152	155
Nicaragua	98	102	106	115	111	121	137	136
Panama (3)	104	106	110	116	113	117	125	126
South America	133	159	177	218	179	217	264	259
Argentina	113	122	137	171	142	149	176	176
Bolivia (Plurinational State of)	130	176	199	213	196	237	287	303
Brazil	120	135	150	189	164	197	243	233
Chile	152	210	227	225	191	248	274	253
Colombia	124	135	155	188	150	182	223	228
Ecuador	119	139	153	189	146	175	212	216
Falkland Islands (Malvinas)	83	85	88	96	87	97	118	114
Guyana	125	152	151	193	196	228	272	269
Paraguay	107	109	120	141	125	131	146	150
Peru	143	195	223	235	205	267	331	320
Suriname	126	162	172	197	180	223	267	266
Uruguay	106	113	124	163	136	153	175	181
Venezuela (Bolivarian Rep. of)	174	214	244	334	223	281	367	375
Developing economies: Asia	112	119	125	142	127	139	157	158
Eastern Asia	97	99	102	107	101	106	113	114
China	102	104	107	113	111	112	120	121
China, Hong Kong SAR	96	97	99	103	104	109	118	122
China, Macao SAR	103	105	108	112	115	121	132	133
China, Taiwan Province of	94	95	97	99	89	95	102	99
Korea, Dem. People's Rep. of	113	122	128	157	149	162	195	196
Korea, Republic of	93	93	96	101	84	94	102	99
Mongolia	166	245	269	343	286	376	451	419
Southern Asia	139	152	170	202	173	209	251	254
Afghanistan	144	160	179	211	204	231	274	259
Bangladesh	101	101	103	109	111	116	130	131
Bhutan	165	184	187	253	210	235	279	250
India	130	137	158	175	159	192	225	223
Iran (Islamic Rep. of)	182	217	239	325	219	273	362	365
Maldives	117	134	122	144	143	160	184	187
Nepal	116	128	138	151	144	157	189	183
Pakistan	103	106	110	123	120	148	157	195
Sri Lanka	104	109	112	123	126	133	149	152
South-Eastern Asia	107	115	120	137	125	136	153	152
Brunei Darussalam	182	227	243	353	234	265	352	377
Cambodia	104	105	108	115	117	125	136	138

For sources and notes, see end of table.

236

			Imports (1) - Importations (1)					Régions, pays ou territoires
2005	2006	2007	2008	2009	2010	2011	2012	
114	120	128	144	132	139	153	155	Économies en développement : Amérique
124	132	144	172	150	166	196	197	Caraïbes
124	132	140	154	150	158	174	172	Anguilla
116	125	138	169	172	191	225	235	Antigua-et-Barbuda
115	121	131	145	140	146	158	159	Aruba
121	135	148	186	165	190	226	235	Bahamas
125	134	145	169	153	175	218	220	Barbade
159	182	201	243	245	272	293	..	Îles Vierges britanniques
99	107	120	159	170	189	201	209	Îles Caïmanes
117	119	135	163	143	158	191	191	Cuba
–	–	–	–	–	–	(a)307	..	Curaçao
124	130	142	158	142	153	179	179	Dominique
112	117	123	137	118	128	146	146	République dominicaine
118	122	132	148	134	145	168	169	Grenade
119	126	133	192	163	167	206	203	Haïti
134	145	157	191	163	181	224	226	Jamaïque
128	136	145	168	133	..	..	..	Montserrat
169	197	216	268	216	250	–	–	Antilles néerlandaises
120	125	134	145	138	144	158	158	Saint-Kitts-et-Nevis
133	146	160	212	152	187	246	249	Sainte-Lucie
113	122	134	159	151	165	191	193	Saint-Vincent-et-les Grenadines
139	153	167	202	175	198	237	238	Trinité-et-Tobago
119	124	133	148	136	145	171	172	Îles Turques et Caïques
111	116	123	132	125	131	142	143	Amérique centrale
131	140	151	177	151	161	204	204	Belize
107	110	113	119	109	111	119	119	Costa Rica
108	112	119	127	118	127	138	139	El Salvador
117	125	136	153	136	149	168	169	Guatemala
104	114	122	140	122	134	153	154	Honduras
111	116	123	131	126	131	141	142	Mexique
120	129	135	153	135	145	165	165	Nicaragua
111	117	122	135	126	132	145	146	Panama (3)
115	122	130	152	135	142	159	161	Amérique du Sud
105	108	116	128	112	118	131	135	Argentine
117	126	140	148	141	151	164	169	Bolivie (État plurinational de)
121	130	140	171	152	158	180	181	Brésil
109	115	120	137	115	122	133	139	Chili
111	117	125	136	126	135	149	151	Colombie
116	126	135	153	133	145	159	161	Équateur
108	115	122	136	117	124	151	151	Îles Falkland (Malvinas)
137	147	162	190	163	179	212	210	Guyana
110	114	120	132	119	125	136	136	Paraguay
119	128	142	172	159	175	193	195	Pérou
129	138	148	169	151	163	195	197	Suriname
117	128	139	174	141	153	172	173	Uruguay
113	116	121	134	123	130	142	143	Venezuela (Rép. bolivarienne du)
115	122	129	147	132	145	166	165	Économies en développement : Asie
112	118	125	143	127	140	159	157	Asie orientale
117	124	131	152	136	151	171	168	Chine
98	100	103	107	107	114	123	127	Chine (RAS de Hong Kong)
111	116	122	134	125	130	144	144	Chine (RAS de Macao)
113	121	131	149	128	143	166	162	Province chinoise de Taiwan
135	149	165	206	181	201	236	228	Corée, Rép. populaire dém. de
117	126	134	162	123	138	164	160	Corée, République de
133	143	155	183	161	174	204	203	Mongolie
126	129	144	161	139	163	194	195	Asie méridionale
121	129	141	167	145	159	186	186	Afghanistan
125	133	149	186	170	192	232	221	Bangladesh
120	132	147	174	157	168	190	186	Bhoutan
124	124	138	150	121	145	176	175	Inde
128	135	147	171	163	170	190	188	Iran (Rép. islamique d')
122	130	140	162	144	158	183	183	Maldives
137	152	169	205	184	201	238	236	Népal
138	151	167	214	236	283	299	361	Pakistan
124	135	147	175	156	173	206	202	Sri Lanka
112	121	127	143	132	142	160	160	Asie du Sud-Est
114	118	130	145	139	147	167	166	Brunéi Darussalam
117	123	131	150	138	158	188	183	Cambodge

Pour les sources et les notes, se reporter à la fin du tableau.

Region, country or territory	Exports (1) - Exportations (1)							
	2005	2006	2007	2008	2009	2010	2011	2012
Indonesia	139	160	178	224	193	222	273	261
Lao People's Dem. Rep.	119	158	164	180	154	191	222	200
Malaysia	107	111	117	135	121	129	145	144
Myanmar	139	163	169	217	187	190	225	236
Philippines	83	87	88	91	88	91	99	98
Singapore	96	103	104	113	100	108	120	120
Thailand	113	118	125	138	139	151	160	161
Viet Nam	124	134	141	169	158	171	195	193
Western Asia	*168*	*195*	*214*	*281*	*206*	*245*	*315*	*318*
Bahrain	151	184	198	248	185	226	271	261
Iraq	188	226	250	340	218	278	380	387
Jordan	131	143	170	261	237	207	233	252
Kuwait	185	218	240	321	211	264	354	358
Lebanon	121	133	147	169	164	176	201	199
Oman	188	231	244	378	212	287	385	410
Qatar	182	223	236	338	224	252	325	340
Saudi Arabia	183	216	237	320	215	265	353	357
State of Palestine	117	121	134	148	140	149	167	163
Syrian Arab Republic	154	172	190	247	201	234	292	290
Turkey	133	138	155	180	151	158	176	170
United Arab Emirates	158	183	199	254	205	241	304	307
Yemen	181	217	239	321	222	267	354	370
Developing economies: Oceania	**145**	**190**	**218**	**263**	**239**	**301**	**374**	**356**
American Samoa	121	204	217	236	227	251	267	272
Cook Islands	113	121	..	..	..	..	..	..
Fiji	120	142	144	166	169	189	228	227
French Polynesia	104	108	113	118	114	117	129	130
Guam	130	144	151	171	175	189	208	206
Kiribati	100	108	129	156	153	167	195	199
Marshall Islands	91	100	111	143	152	168	177	191
Micronesia (Federated States of)	105	120	107	129	126	136	159	162
Nauru	117	124	170	806	346	355	521	522
New Caledonia	158	204	259	279	275	349	394	333
Niue	114	117	116	125	121	123	152	151
Northern Mariana Islands	103	107	114	130	130	148	159	162
Palau	117	134	118	144	139	150	175	178
Papua New Guinea	171	233	265	317	276	360	466	447
Samoa	117	126	131	140	131	141	156	153
Solomon Islands	131	142	164	179	151	170	194	189
Tokelau	109	113	120	136	134	136	188	188
Tonga	122	127	123	143	139	153	169	169
Vanuatu	107	121	111	140	139	153	175	178
Wallis and Futuna Islands	123	127	137	175	156	164	222	216
Transition economies	**167**	**199**	**220**	**294**	**222**	**260**	**332**	**334**
Albania	113	119	126	145	135	149	169	167
Armenia	123	148	160	186	168	200	227	214
Azerbaijan	173	207	227	307	202	255	345	351
Belarus	142	154	171	215	175	196	236	236
Bosnia and Herzegovina	125	137	147	165	151	164	188	181
Croatia	116	126	135	157	147	158	176	175
Georgia	135	158	175	216	205	225	252	246
Kazakhstan	181	227	254	337	242	303	396	393
Kyrgyzstan	138	154	166	191	186	208	246	241
Republic of Moldova	89	88	100	117	87	92	102	88
Russian Federation	175	213	235	321	233	272	354	360
Serbia and Montenegro	129	146	157	–	–	–	–	–
Serbia	–	–	–	179	166	179	203	198
Tajikistan	136	173	178	201	173	226	269	228
TFYR of Macedonia	124	131	142	167	164	174	197	193
Turkmenistan	171	225	228	347	243	266	358	374
Ukraine	148	158	180	225	204	223	264	252
Uzbekistan	137	167	178	235	187	229	287	278
Developed economies: America	**113**	**118**	**125**	**135**	**125**	**133**	**145**	**144**
Bermuda	100	112	122	158	113	125	128	120
Canada	130	140	150	169	142	160	177	173
Greenland	91	99	99	112	108	117	140	144
Saint Pierre and Miquelon	104	111	106	124	119	137	150	147
United States	107	111	116	123	117	123	133	134

For sources and notes, see end of table.

Imports (1) - Importations (1)								Régions, pays ou territoires
2005	2006	2007	2008	2009	2010	2011	2012	
130	142	153	181	161	175	203	202	Indonésie
126	135	144	164	148	158	183	183	Rép. dém. populaire lao
105	109	115	130	122	129	144	142	Malaisie
129	138	153	180	160	175	211	209	Myanmar
96	112	117	135	122	130	150	150	Philippines
111	119	123	135	121	130	148	148	Singapour
116	124	130	147	143	154	170	173	Thaïlande
128	139	151	175	159	171	195	192	Viet Nam
125	*134*	*145*	*165*	*152*	*162*	*184*	*183*	*Asie occidentale*
132	146	159	175	168	183	204	202	Bahreïn
121	127	139	154	144	151	171	170	Iraq
148	162	184	221	197	243	305	300	Jordanie
115	121	129	140	137	142	157	157	Koweït
131	141	153	176	160	174	204	204	Liban
121	129	138	149	142	149	168	168	Oman
116	121	129	138	136	140	155	156	Qatar
116	123	133	150	144	151	165	166	Arabie saoudite
145	161	172	216	179	192	226	221	État de Palestine
128	138	149	173	159	171	201	198	République arabe syrienne
138	150	164	197	159	172	199	195	Turquie
113	121	130	143	139	146	164	165	Émirats arabes unis
132	145	162	191	166	182	221	221	Yémen
126	**135**	**145**	**172**	**155**	**167**	**196**	**198**	**Économies en développement : Océanie**
114	123	126	162	157	170	209	211	Samoa américaines
115	120	130	..	..	..	..	..	Îles Cook
131	142	155	183	157	175	209	210	Fidji
118	124	133	147	135	146	165	165	Polynésie française
153	173	185	222	175	200	248	254	Guam
126	136	149	182	166	182	205	206	Kiribati
82	90	101	131	148	164	166	179	Îles Marshall
114	118	127	144	137	144	163	165	Micronésie (États fédérés de)
146	160	165	200	138	155	184	185	Nauru
121	127	136	153	140	148	169	170	Nouvelle-Calédonie
124	129	139	159	141	145	194	194	Nioué
126	135	144	172	147	163	184	191	Îles Mariannes du Nord
116	120	130	149	144	149	168	169	Palaos
135	145	159	202	179	193	228	231	Papouasie-Nouvelle-Guinée
127	135	146	169	150	164	190	189	Samoa
134	145	158	191	165	177	209	210	Îles Salomon
103	106	116	142	140	144	151	149	Tokélaou
130	139	153	176	159	175	207	207	Tonga
118	125	136	167	160	175	196	202	Vanuatu
111	116	127	142	133	143	164	163	Îles Wallis-et-Futuna
122	**130**	**138**	**155**	**145**	**152**	**169**	**169**	**Économies en transition**
123	130	140	159	146	154	177	174	Albanie
123	133	143	164	150	158	180	182	Arménie
127	138	148	162	158	162	177	176	Azerbaïdjan
143	160	173	214	176	190	231	234	Bélarus
125	134	145	165	151	162	186	183	Bosnie-Herzégovine
122	131	139	161	147	157	180	179	Croatie
129	139	149	171	154	164	183	183	Géorgie
123	130	140	157	150	155	170	170	Kazakhstan
137	150	163	186	177	192	222	223	Kirghizistan
93	89	97	120	87	88	100	87	République de Moldova
114	118	125	133	130	134	145	144	Fédération de Russie
130	141	150	—	—	—	—	—	Serbie-et-Monténégro
—	—	—	175	158	170	194	190	Serbie
140	158	171	207	183	203	234	230	Tadjikistan
131	142	154	183	172	189	226	218	LERY de Macédoine
115	120	129	142	140	142	157	157	Turkménistan
137	152	162	197	171	180	210	213	Ukraine
120	125	134	149	142	148	163	161	Ouzbékistan
111	**116**	**121**	**134**	**120**	**128**	**141**	**142**	**Économies développées : Amérique**
104	112	124	151	158	174	184	193	Bermudes
114	122	127	133	124	133	145	146	Canada
123	129	140	158	145	157	182	183	Groenland
116	118	126	132	132	138	148	148	Saint-Pierre-et-Miquelon
110	115	120	134	119	127	141	141	États-Unis

Pour les sources et les notes, se reporter à la fin du tableau.

4

4.2.1 Unit value indices of exports and imports of countries and geographical regions
2000 = 100

Region, country or territory	Exports (1) - Exportations (1)							
	2005	2006	2007	2008	2009	2010	2011	2012
Developed economies: Asia	**97**	**95**	**97**	**104**	**102**	**107**	**115**	**113**
Israel	114	119	126	147	136	141	151	157
Japan	96	94	95	101	100	104	112	110
Developed economies: Europe	**141**	**149**	**167**	**185**	**168**	**170**	**190**	**182**
Andorra	108	125	124	133	137	139	143	139
Austria	140	146	165	182	168	163	179	168
Belgium	144	151	169	188	166	169	190	180
Bulgaria	148	168	197	224	193	203	234	223
Cyprus	146	156	175	206	164	169	192	180
Czech Republic	154	161	180	203	185	186	207	198
Denmark	142	148	159	178	160	161	179	173
Estonia	140	145	170	191	168	173	197	186
Faeroe Islands	113	135	125	148	146	161	184	188
Finland	135	144	166	177	156	163	183	172
France	143	150	170	188	174	172	190	182
Germany	141	147	165	180	170	168	184	176
Gibraltar	96	108	118	136	106	128	151	157
Greece	143	155	173	197	166	176	200	190
Hungary	132	133	146	159	147	144	157	147
Iceland	117	132	149	166	125	144	160	152
Ireland	130	133	146	157	144	147	158	152
Italy	150	158	180	202	187	186	208	200
Latvia	149	158	191	214	182	188	213	203
Lithuania	143	156	182	213	174	186	222	216
Luxembourg	125	128	139	145	126	128	142	133
Malta	118	129	147	168	170	177	211	186
Netherlands	134	141	160	178	156	162	187	178
Norway	161	193	212	266	188	216	276	273
Poland	151	158	180	202	179	183	201	190
Portugal	137	145	162	177	161	162	181	173
Romania	159	170	188	212	189	195	223	211
Slovakia	158	161	178	194	176	171	189	175
Slovenia	147	153	172	189	173	173	192	181
Spain	146	154	175	194	176	176	196	188
Sweden	136	143	159	173	154	161	179	170
Switzerland	113	117	124	132	128	131	143	140
United Kingdom	144	154	170	186	166	174	196	194
Developed economies: Oceania	**153**	**171**	**192**	**235**	**208**	**248**	**313**	**297**
Australia	153	174	195	244	212	259	328	308
New Zealand	153	148	174	182	177	181	222	226

Sources:

UNCTAD secretariat calculations, based on:

- ECLAC, *CEPALSTAT* External trade deflator

- EUROSTAT, online database, Trade unit value indices by reporting country

- IMF, *International Financial Statistics*

- U.S. Bureau of Labor Statistics, External trade price indices

- Unit value indices of Japan Customs and Price indices of Bank of Japan

- UNCTAD, *UNCTADstat Commodity Price Statistics*

- UNCTAD, *UNCTADstat Merchandise Trade Matrix*

- UNCTAD secretariat estimates

Notes:

(a)   Data refer to Netherlands Antilles.

(1)   To improve data coverage, especially for the latest periods, the following procedure was used in the calculation of unit value indices:

- A set of average prices indices at SITC (Revision 3, 3-digit) group level was constructed using UNCTAD, *Commodity Price Statistics*, international and national sources and UNCTAD secretariat estimates.

- At the country level, unit value indices were calculated using previous year's trade values at the SITC 3-digit level, available in table 3.2 as weights.

In some instances these indices may differ from the estimates published in official sources, since the main aim is to provide tentative estimates for most countries on a comparable basis.

(2)   From 2011 onwards, exports include commercial mining.

(3)   From 2005 onwards, including customs free zones.

4.2.1 Indices de la valeur unitaire des exportations et importations des pays et des régions géographiques
2000 = 100

Imports (1) - Importations (1)								Régions, pays ou territoires
2005	2006	2007	2008	2009	2010	2011	2012	
116	**125**	**133**	**163**	**135**	**154**	**181**	**180**	**Économies développées : Asie**
120	127	138	158	134	144	165	161	Israël
115	125	132	164	135	154	182	182	Japon
144	**153**	**171**	**193**	**171**	**176**	**201**	**194**	**Économies développées : Europe**
..	..	..	..	..	..	..	..	Andorre
148	156	175	199	179	180	203	194	Autriche
146	153	170	196	168	176	201	191	Belgique
153	164	187	212	177	187	217	208	Bulgarie
144	152	172	194	169	173	198	191	Chypre
145	154	172	197	175	180	201	196	République tchèque
143	149	158	176	161	161	180	173	Danemark
145	154	175	202	171	177	205	198	Estonie
119	126	135	151	141	153	178	181	Îles Féroé
145	156	176	197	169	179	207	198	Finlande
149	157	178	202	182	185	212	205	France
142	152	169	188	170	170	192	185	Allemagne
161	186	204	263	180	219	292	301	Gibraltar
152	166	185	215	184	194	224	218	Grèce
137	143	157	173	154	155	169	159	Hongrie
124	131	148	175	148	156	177	174	Islande
131	138	152	167	148	149	168	164	Irlande
147	160	179	207	182	190	220	211	Italie
143	154	176	204	174	176	201	197	Lettonie
143	160	184	222	179	196	234	231	Lituanie
141	149	164	177	152	160	182	176	Luxembourg
123	125	138	152	136	134	153	147	Malte
138	149	167	190	164	174	198	192	Pays-Bas
132	139	158	170	151	156	175	169	Norvège
146	155	176	201	172	180	203	196	Pologne
146	155	174	196	171	174	198	189	Portugal
148	157	173	197	173	176	201	191	Roumanie
155	162	182	205	180	182	201	190	Slovaquie
150	155	177	198	175	180	203	192	Slovénie
152	163	184	211	182	189	219	212	Espagne
142	152	166	185	161	170	193	184	Suède
132	135	145	166	153	161	188	175	Suisse
139	148	164	179	162	172	196	195	Royaume-Uni
120	**122**	**132**	**141**	**133**	**147**	**166**	**169**	**Économies développées : Océanie**
117	120	128	140	130	145	163	166	Australie
136	132	153	145	146	152	169	175	Nouvelle-Zélande

Sources :

Calculs du secrétariat de la CNUCED, basés sur :

- CEPALC, *CEPALSTAT* Déflateur du commerce extérieur

- EUROSTAT, base de données en ligne, Indices de valeur unitaire par pays déclarant

- FMI, *Statistiques financières internationales*

- Bureau des statistiques du travail des États-Unis (BLS), Indices de prix du commerce extérieur

- Indices des valeurs unitaires des douanes japonaises et Indices de prix de la Banque du Japon

- CNUCED, *UNCTADstat Statistiques de prix des produits de base*

- CNUCED, *UNCTADstat Matrice du commerce de marchandises*

- Estimations du secrétariat de la CNUCED

Notes :

(a)   Les données se réfèrent aux Antilles néerlandaises.

(1)   Afin d'améliorer la couverture des données et spécialement pour les années récentes, la méthode suivante a été utilisée pour le calcul des valeurs unitaires :

- Un ensemble d'indices de prix moyens au niveau des groupes de la CTCI (révision 3, position à 3 chiffres) a été construit en utilisant des données de CNUCED, *Statistiques des produits de base*, des sources internationales et nationales ainsi que des estimations du secrétariat de la CNUCED.

- Au niveau des pays individuels, les indices de la valeur unitaire ont été calculés en utilisant comme pondération les valeurs des exportations et des importations de l'année précédente, disponibles dans la table 3.2.

Dans certains cas ces indices peuvent différer des estimations publiées dans les sources officielles, le but principal étant de fournir des estimations approximatives et comparables pour la plupart des pays.

(2)   À partir de 2011, les exportations comprennent l'exploitation minière commerciale.

(3)   À partir de 2005, y compris les zones franches douanières.

Terms of trade indices and purchasing power indices of exports of countries and geographical regions
2000 = 100

Region, country or territory	Terms of trade (1) - Termes de l'échange (1)							
	2005	2006	2007	2008	2009	2010	2011	2012
WORLD	**102**	**102**	**102**	**103**	**103**	**103**	**104**	**103**
DEVELOPING ECONOMIES	102	104	104	106	103	105	106	107
TRANSITION ECONOMIES	136	154	160	190	153	171	197	198
DEVELOPED ECONOMIES	100	99	99	97	100	98	96	95
Developing economies: Africa	**132**	**147**	**147**	**171**	**145**	**162**	**181**	**182**
Eastern Africa	*97*	*109*	*109*	*104*	*109*	*118*	*120*	*115*
Burundi	112	120	119	128	132	153	172	149
Comoros	54	58	65	63	67	71	76	80
Djibouti	87	89	87	87	80	80	79	82
Eritrea (3)	87	85	85	76	78	84	93	99
Ethiopia	108	107	111	111	121	129	136	131
Kenya	90	88	85	84	94	92	90	90
Madagascar	76	75	75	72	76	78	79	80
Malawi	83	87	85	80	98	99	100	96
Mauritius	92	87	86	76	81	73	71	71
Mozambique	107	123	118	110	97	110	109	100
Rwanda	161	168	165	227	220	236	225	215
Seychelles	78	74	68	68	75	75	75	78
Somalia	104	106	105	101	102	101	98	108
Uganda	96	98	98	101	109	113	120	110
United Republic of Tanzania	99	115	114	116	130	142	151	145
Zambia	128	195	193	173	158	191	196	184
Zimbabwe	92	97	106	95	107	113	114	105
Middle Africa	*156*	*177*	*180*	*219*	*158*	*188*	*221*	*225*
Angola	172	198	203	251	170	209	253	258
Cameroon	128	136	136	145	138	153	163	157
Central African Republic	93	91	91	83	83	82	73	69
Chad	154	175	176	214	148	181	216	221
Congo	155	179	182	221	156	185	221	221
Dem. Rep. of the Congo	114	128	127	145	114	138	147	143
Equatorial Guinea	156	177	180	233	184	203	233	245
Gabon	156	178	182	229	163	194	226	226
Sao Tome and Principe	114	107	110	117	140	137	122	107
Northern Africa	*139*	*155*	*152*	*185*	*147*	*161*	*179*	*186*
Algeria	161	188	179	233	157	177	206	217
Egypt	124	137	132	151	139	144	153	156
Libya	150	168	169	205	141	166	196	201
Morocco	99	100	98	132	136	133	141	145
Sudan (...2011)	152	173	180	223	166	199	243	_
Tunisia	94	91	91	97	97	97	96	97
Southern Africa	*104*	*115*	*118*	*125*	*131*	*139*	*148*	*140*
Botswana	91	96	101	83	83	87	85	85
Lesotho	89	86	84	77	85	79	75	78
Namibia	105	131	139	127	122	123	123	123
South Africa	105	116	119	129	135	145	156	145
Swaziland	101	108	101	100	116	114	112	110
Western Africa	*143*	*158*	*160*	*185*	*153*	*176*	*200*	*201*
Benin	98	105	107	106	107	118	125	118
Burkina Faso	86	88	92	91	96	122	141	127
Cape Verde	97	99	93	94	106	104	104	109
Côte d'Ivoire	131	133	138	140	149	161	158	144
Gambia	95	97	97	101	97	98	91	92
Ghana	124	126	134	156	172	181	183	172
Guinea	106	132	130	122	98	109	111	104
Guinea-Bissau	75	82	75	74	84	84	81	82
Liberia	114	120	120	120	111	136	163	139
Mali	100	112	115	119	135	160	177	172
Mauritania	123	134	126	149	136	172	170	153
Niger	129	142	178	152	149	150	163	169
Nigeria	155	175	176	214	153	182	216	222
Saint Helena	72	67	64	59	60	55	53	52
Senegal	96	99	97	97	96	99	107	109
Sierra Leone	73	71	68	63	72	70	61	58
Togo	21	21	23	31	29	29	30	29

For sources and notes, see end of table.

Purchasing power of exports (2) - Pouvoir d'achat des exportations (2)								Régions, pays ou territoires
2005	2006	2007	2008	2009	2010	2011	2012	
129	141	150	153	133	152	161	163	**MONDE**
160	181	197	206	182	215	231	240	ÉCONOMIES EN DÉVELOPPEMENT
192	228	260	309	214	266	318	323	ÉCONOMIES EN TRANSITION
114	121	127	126	110	122	126	125	ÉCONOMIES DÉVELOPPÉES
166	186	201	225	173	210	214	228	Économies en développement : Afrique
134	154	164	161	164	198	207	219	*Afrique orientale*
95	90	84	73	91	131	138	147	Burundi
72	57	74	28	68	87	94	94	Comores
89	114	108	109	136	140	132	140	Djibouti
26	25	23	16	17	17	503	597	Érythrée (3)
148	161	182	194	223	301	318	335	Éthiopie
146	137	148	155	156	166	156	167	Kenya
84	91	106	98	86	82	101	97	Madagascar
112	140	164	138	202	173	204	189	Malawi
141	146	131	115	112	117	117	120	Maurice
390	489	455	409	370	485	505	583	Mozambique
191	217	237	318	298	360	493	509	Rwanda
127	131	116	120	123	113	117	118	Seychelles
110	116	127	126	127	127	128	144	Somalie
159	174	225	256	258	250	291	326	Ouganda
176	188	200	242	261	326	324	378	République-Unie de Tanzanie
162	318	361	349	336	496	539	519	Zambie
68	64	69	55	64	83	81	89	Zimbabwe
247	291	340	436	302	365	424	447	*Afrique centrale*
280	354	459	602	405	483	569	621	Angola
120	137	149	155	117	118	122	119	Cameroun
66	76	79	57	49	51	55	60	République centrafricaine
1 390	1 439	1 432	1 465	1 041	1 249	1 444	1 235	Tchad
161	198	169	225	168	241	271	256	Congo
241	256	267	335	288	413	455	436	Rép. dém. du Congo
536	593	686	934	680	679	788	902	Guinée équatoriale
168	175	186	256	150	233	289	288	Gabon
176	184	149	197	171	215	191	194	Sao Tomé-et-Principe
172	197	207	240	169	199	166	204	*Afrique septentrionale*
176	198	195	233	141	173	197	201	Algérie
193	234	243	286	278	293	291	286	Égypte
197	237	252	297	188	235	76	249	Libye
121	132	141	160	124	143	147	148	Maroc
224	253	373	451	334	438	339	_	Soudan (...2011)
147	151	181	203	165	175	165	158	Tunisie
132	139	154	152	131	160	169	152	*Afrique australe*
137	132	141	122	92	117	130	133	Botswana
264	274	290	296	267	291	327	312	Lesotho
138	169	177	171	182	213	206	193	Namibie
130	137	154	154	132	162	172	153	Afrique du Sud
156	149	144	110	116	116	107	108	Swaziland
173	189	194	212	175	226	264	262	*Afrique occidentale*
120	147	193	194	207	191	174	179	Bénin
183	218	211	197	290	479	621	624	Burkina Faso
130	142	120	178	218	255	337	261	Cap-Vert
152	153	144	137	174	162	149	146	Côte d'Ivoire
42	57	57	52	269	129	297	325	Gambie
135	167	174	189	229	294	416	390	Ghana
100	115	123	116	101	131	108	105	Guinée
103	78	103	97	107	106	165	93	Guinée-Bissau
47	51	58	55	31	42	67	78	Libéria
163	217	198	228	215	224	227	206	Mali
151	307	290	303	260	360	406	372	Mauritanie
138	137	165	193	234	259	246	299	Niger
199	216	225	257	183	260	314	314	Nigéria
175	167	184	227	217	189	192	231	Sainte-Hélène
128	120	114	118	127	124	122	122	Sénégal
815	1 069	1 024	710	937	1 220	1 016	1 870	Sierra Leone
55	49	49	52	60	53	56	54	Togo

Pour les sources et les notes, se reporter à la fin du tableau.

4

4.2.1 Terms of trade indices and purchasing power indices of exports of countries and geographical regions
2000 = 100

Region, country or territory	Terms of trade (1) - Termes de l'échange (1)							
	2005	2006	2007	2008	2009	2010	2011	2012
Developing economies: America	110	118	121	126	116	129	139	136
Caribbean	114	125	125	134	128	129	133	132
Anguilla	94	109	106	103	102	96	94	95
Antigua and Barbuda	78	79	80	81	80	73	68	64
Aruba	98	103	102	131	132	129	125	122
Bahamas	97	94	92	90	82	84	89	89
Barbados	117	120	119	120	124	116	109	108
British Virgin Islands	68	64	61	58	57	56	58	65
Cayman Islands	92	94	92	84	86	85	80	83
Cuba	130	164	173	143	156	173	160	145
Curaçao	–	–	–	–	–	–	(a)100	..
Dominica	101	102	99	103	117	110	104	103
Dominican Republic	96	95	98	94	101	98	92	91
Grenada	80	84	87	89	91	92	92	91
Haiti	92	89	86	62	80	78	65	68
Jamaica	95	110	105	98	90	97	92	87
Montserrat	88	86	85	78	91	..	..	..
Netherlands Antilles	101	99	99	103	91	94	–	–
Saint Kitts and Nevis	84	82	79	74	78	75	70	71
Saint Lucia	112	115	110	97	117	103	92	91
Saint Vincent and the Grenadines	88	89	90	97	111	110	104	107
Trinidad and Tobago	123	136	134	161	132	130	149	157
Turks and Caicos Islands	78	75	74	70	74	72	70	68
Central America	102	102	103	103	94	100	106	106
Belize	87	93	87	86	94	100	95	94
Costa Rica	88	86	85	82	84	81	78	78
El Salvador	97	95	95	92	95	91	91	90
Guatemala	91	90	88	86	93	92	92	88
Honduras	87	83	82	77	82	84	91	84
Mexico	104	104	105	106	94	101	108	109
Nicaragua	81	79	79	75	82	83	83	82
Panama (4)	94	91	90	86	90	88	86	86
South America	116	131	136	144	133	152	166	161
Argentina	107	113	118	133	127	127	135	130
Bolivia (Plurinational State of)	112	140	142	144	139	158	175	179
Brazil	99	104	107	110	108	125	135	129
Chile	140	183	189	165	167	204	205	182
Colombia	111	115	124	138	119	134	150	151
Ecuador	102	110	113	124	110	121	133	135
Falkland Islands (Malvinas)	76	74	72	70	74	78	78	76
Guyana	91	103	94	102	120	128	128	128
Paraguay	97	96	100	107	105	105	107	111
Peru	119	152	158	137	129	152	172	164
Suriname	97	118	116	117	119	137	137	135
Uruguay	91	89	89	94	97	100	102	104
Venezuela (Bolivarian Rep. of)	154	184	202	249	182	216	260	262
Developing economies: Asia	98	98	97	96	96	95	95	96
Eastern Asia	87	83	82	75	80	76	71	72
China	87	84	81	75	81	75	70	72
China, Hong Kong SAR	98	97	97	96	98	96	96	96
China, Macao SAR	92	91	89	84	92	93	92	93
China, Taiwan Province of	83	78	74	67	69	66	61	61
Korea, Dem. People's Rep. of	84	82	78	76	82	81	82	86
Korea, Republic of	79	74	72	62	68	68	62	62
Mongolia	125	171	173	187	177	216	221	206
Southern Asia	110	118	118	125	124	128	129	130
Afghanistan	119	125	126	126	141	146	147	139
Bangladesh	81	76	69	58	65	61	56	59
Bhutan	137	140	127	145	134	140	147	134
India	105	111	114	117	132	133	128	127
Iran (Islamic Rep. of)	142	161	163	190	134	160	191	194
Maldives	96	103	87	89	99	101	100	102
Nepal	85	84	82	74	78	78	80	78
Pakistan	75	70	66	58	51	52	52	54
Sri Lanka	83	81	76	70	81	77	73	75
South-Eastern Asia	96	95	95	95	95	96	95	95
Brunei Darussalam	160	192	187	243	168	181	210	226

For sources and notes, see end of table.

Purchasing power of exports (2) - Pouvoir d'achat des exportations (2)								Régions, pays ou territoires
2005	2006	2007	2008	2009	2010	2011	2012	
140	159	167	172	146	176	198	199	**Économies en développement : Amérique**
109	*131*	*124*	*124*	*88*	*98*	*111*	*114*	*Caraïbes*
299	230	162	185	381	199	233	306	Anguilla
138	114	83	74	57	46	48	53	Antigua-et-Barbuda
51	52	43	40	56	49	54	58	Aruba
78	89	94	89	75	64	64	74	Bahamas
106	140	133	106	91	90	80	95	Barbade
81	73	70	59	56	51	49	53	Îles Vierges britanniques
331	121	121	52	63	39	60	64	Îles Caïmanes
118	158	176	145	129	186	192	187	Cuba
–	–	–	–	–	–	(a)14	..	Curaçao
63	60	48	47	44	46	31	37	Dominique
96	98	101	86	81	92	103	108	République dominicaine
49	43	53	43	46	36	36	43	Grenade
125	127	123	79	111	109	117	127	Haïti
88	104	111	98	62	57	56	55	Jamaïque
101	86	166	216	211	..	..	..	Montserrat
18	18	16	20	19	16	–	–	Antilles néerlandaises
88	98	79	108	84	68	87	87	Saint-Kitts-et-Nevis
113	149	142	180	254	267	153	177	Sainte-Lucie
75	66	76	70	69	54	43	49	Saint-Vincent-et-les Grenadines
168	216	188	216	122	130	128	129	Trinité-et-Tobago
140	160	138	189	172	125	106	105	Îles Turques et Caïques
120	*133*	*137*	*137*	*116*	*142*	*155*	*162*	*Amérique centrale*
73	90	81	79	77	87	85	90	Belize
112	127	142	136	138	146	150	164	Costa Rica
108	112	115	124	111	121	131	131	El Salvador
169	177	188	186	195	210	229	221	Guatemala
145	139	142	133	119	137	152	156	Honduras
116	129	133	134	110	137	150	157	Mexique
112	127	141	150	161	198	214	252	Nicaragua
739	802	839	849	991	967	1 172	1 253	Panama (4)
166	*190*	*206*	*214*	*186*	*223*	*256*	*249*	*Amérique du Sud*
145	164	182	208	189	219	244	228	Argentine
195	250	259	358	284	340	413	525	Bolivie (État plurinational de)
177	193	208	210	183	232	258	244	Brésil
197	266	295	246	252	304	318	296	Chili
146	160	184	212	199	226	296	308	Colombie
177	205	215	250	212	245	284	303	Équateur
160	130	150	144	137	158	137	152	Îles Falkland (Malvinas)
80	80	84	84	93	98	105	128	Guyana
177	180	271	390	491	601	656	615	Paraguay
207	264	280	257	241	289	342	332	Pérou
195	215	231	261	234	315	319	326	Suriname
127	136	141	149	168	192	200	220	Uruguay
148	169	173	212	140	151	195	203	Venezuela (Rép. bolivarienne du)
165	186	205	213	192	225	241	252	**Économies en développement : Asie**
177	*200*	*226*	*224*	*213*	*250*	*261*	*277*	*Asie orientale*
262	314	374	379	355	420	447	490	Chine
147	159	168	171	152	174	183	192	Chine (RAS de Hong Kong)
88	87	82	59	30	26	24	28	Chine (RAS de Macao)
117	122	125	114	105	126	123	123	Province chinoise de Taiwan
140	139	145	141	155	179	197	207	Corée, Rép. populaire dém. de
141	149	161	151	171	196	197	199	Corée, République de
149	201	227	259	220	311	441	402	Mongolie
161	*196*	*209*	*236*	*220*	*250*	*274*	*247*	*Asie méridionale*
231	231	256	235	202	178	147	137	Afghanistan
117	139	131	130	139	157	165	178	Bangladesh
209	306	446	290	307	372	345	307	Bhoutan
190	232	256	307	322	369	406	395	Inde
153	199	210	231	168	207	239	177	Iran (Rép. islamique d')
121	159	149	188	108	115	174	158	Maldives
78	69	64	57	56	53	48	51	Népal
129	124	118	105	82	84	94	75	Pakistan
94	94	97	89	87	91	92	86	Sri Lanka
136	*148*	*158*	*160*	*144*	*172*	*179*	*182*	*Asie du Sud-Est*
141	165	152	182	133	156	191	208	Brunéi Darussalam

Pour les sources et les notes, se reporter à la fin du tableau.

Region, country or territory	Terms of trade (1) - Termes de l'échange (1)							
	2005	2006	2007	2008	2009	2010	2011	2012
Cambodia	88	85	82	76	85	80	72	75
Indonesia	107	113	116	124	120	127	134	129
Lao People's Dem. Rep.	94	117	114	109	104	121	121	109
Malaysia	102	102	102	104	99	100	101	101
Myanmar	108	118	110	121	117	109	107	113
Philippines	86	77	75	67	72	70	66	66
Singapore	87	86	84	83	83	83	81	81
Thailand	97	96	96	94	97	98	94	93
Viet Nam	97	96	93	97	99	100	100	101
Western Asia	*135*	*145*	*147*	*170*	*136*	*151*	*171*	*174*
Bahrain	114	126	124	142	110	124	133	129
Iraq	156	178	179	221	151	185	222	227
Jordan	88	88	92	118	120	85	77	84
Kuwait	161	181	185	230	154	186	226	228
Lebanon	93	95	96	96	102	101	98	98
Oman	156	180	177	253	149	192	230	244
Qatar	156	184	183	246	165	180	209	218
Saudi Arabia	157	175	178	214	149	175	214	216
State of Palestine	81	75	78	68	78	78	74	73
Syrian Arab Republic	120	124	128	143	127	137	146	147
Turkey	97	92	95	91	95	92	89	87
United Arab Emirates	140	151	153	178	148	165	186	186
Yemen	137	150	148	168	134	147	160	168
Developing economies: Oceania	**116**	**141**	**150**	**152**	**154**	**180**	**191**	**180**
American Samoa	106	165	172	146	145	148	128	129
Cook Islands	99	101	..	..	..	..	..	..
Fiji	91	100	93	91	107	108	109	108
French Polynesia	88	87	84	80	84	80	79	79
Guam	85	83	81	77	100	95	84	81
Kiribati	79	79	86	86	92	92	95	97
Marshall Islands	111	111	109	109	103	103	107	106
Micronesia (Federated States of)	92	102	84	90	92	94	98	98
Nauru	80	78	104	402	251	229	283	283
New Caledonia	131	161	191	183	197	235	233	196
Niue	92	91	83	78	86	85	78	78
Northern Mariana Islands	82	79	79	75	89	91	86	85
Palau	101	112	91	97	97	101	104	105
Papua New Guinea	127	160	166	157	154	186	204	193
Samoa	92	94	90	83	87	86	82	81
Solomon Islands	98	98	104	94	92	96	93	90
Tokelau	105	107	103	96	96	95	124	126
Tonga	94	91	81	81	87	87	82	82
Vanuatu	91	97	81	83	87	87	89	88
Wallis and Futuna Islands	111	109	108	124	117	115	135	133
Transition economies	**136**	**154**	**160**	**190**	**153**	**171**	**197**	**198**
Albania	92	92	90	91	93	96	95	96
Armenia	100	112	112	113	112	127	126	118
Azerbaijan	136	150	153	189	128	157	195	200
Belarus	99	97	99	101	99	103	102	101
Bosnia and Herzegovina	100	103	101	100	100	101	101	99
Croatia	95	97	97	97	100	101	98	98
Georgia	105	114	117	126	133	137	138	134
Kazakhstan	147	174	182	215	161	196	233	231
Kyrgyzstan	101	103	102	103	105	109	111	108
Republic of Moldova	96	99	102	98	100	105	101	101
Russian Federation	153	180	189	241	179	203	244	249
Serbia and Montenegro	100	103	105					
Serbia	–	–	–	102	105	105	105	104
Tajikistan	97	109	104	97	94	111	115	99
TFYR of Macedonia	94	93	92	91	95	92	87	89
Turkmenistan	149	188	178	245	174	187	229	238
Ukraine	107	104	111	114	119	124	126	118
Uzbekistan	115	134	133	158	132	155	176	172
Developed economies: America	**102**	**102**	**103**	**100**	**104**	**104**	**102**	**102**
Bermuda	96	99	98	104	72	72	70	62
Canada	114	114	118	127	115	120	122	119
Greenland	75	76	71	70	74	75	77	79
Saint Pierre and Miquelon	90	94	84	93	90	99	101	99
United States	97	96	97	92	99	97	95	95

For sources and notes, see end of table.

Purchasing power of exports (2) - Pouvoir d'achat des exportations (2)								Régions, pays ou territoires
2005	2006	2007	2008	2009	2010	2011	2012	
190	216	224	225	218	235	266	323	Cambodge
102	112	118	118	113	138	151	142	Indonésie
133	198	193	202	215	334	367	398	Rép. dém. populaire lao
137	150	157	156	132	157	161	163	Malaisie
182	206	255	238	257	306	270	277	Myanmar
113	112	114	96	83	105	85	92	Philippines
151	165	176	181	162	196	201	200	Singapour
138	152	171	176	155	182	190	193	Thaïlande
176	198	222	248	248	292	344	412	Viet Nam
177	**198**	**215**	**256**	**195**	**229**	**276**	**300**	**Asie occidentale**
125	135	138	160	114	132	155	164	Bahreïn
105	123	158	213	155	186	259	296	Iraq
153	169	164	109	171	153	138	138	Jordanie
200	239	250	322	203	253	339	397	Koweït
250	280	327	354	365	403	389	386	Liban
137	148	158	223	172	216	248	273	Oman
191	243	281	422	305	462	635	711	Qatar
200	221	226	270	172	214	285	301	Arabie saoudite
58	57	74	64	72	75	84	113	État de Palestine
147	171	168	192	148	162	108	44	République arabe syrienne
192	206	235	241	232	238	244	282	Turquie
208	241	276	336	268	302	349	365	Émirats arabes unis
104	113	96	97	93	113	120	94	Yémen
103	**111**	**120**	**106**	**88**	**104**	**105**	**98**	**Économies en développement : Océanie**
95	103	103	101	87	51	39	41	Samoa américaines
50	32	44	..	..	..	..	..	Îles Cook
91	83	83	86	68	82	73	77	Fidji
83	86	67	60	50	48	46	38	Polynésie française
46	41	67	64	40	31	24	25	Guam
95	129	183	230	105	60	117	135	Kiribati
337	217	198	169	154	216	231	214	Îles Marshall
75	69	79	88	84	80	80	98	Micronésie (États fédérés de)
7	9	31	189	62	111	131	168	Nauru
149	176	256	141	117	166	162	128	Nouvelle-Calédonie
56	309	702	4	5	5	4	4	Nioué
54	37	22	7	1	0	0	0	Îles Mariannes du Nord
101	98	74	58	36	35	31	36	Palaos
117	138	142	137	118	144	146	136	Papouasie-Nouvelle-Guinée
106	74	103	66	47	56	44	62	Samoa
112	122	151	159	145	183	288	324	Îles Salomon
..	..	..	..	..	..	..	..	Tokélaou
88	78	63	60	56	54	79	88	Tonga
123	150	141	130	136	107	132	105	Vanuatu
86	78	71	64	68	63	55	55	Îles Wallis-et-Futuna
192	**228**	**260**	**309**	**214**	**266**	**318**	**323**	**Économies en transition**
205	235	295	326	286	383	420	433	Albanie
269	252	274	219	161	224	252	267	Arménie
346	542	822	1 079	766	937	1 114	1 044	Azerbaïdjan
152	169	192	208	165	181	245	268	Bélarus
180	233	267	284	245	278	295	263	Bosnie-Herzégovine
162	179	201	197	161	170	168	156	Croatie
208	208	256	270	228	316	370	402	Géorgie
257	333	388	514	327	439	584	617	Kazakhstan
96	117	158	195	185	180	174	166	Kirghizistan
249	251	292	281	313	372	467	528	République de Moldova
203	244	271	337	223	284	344	349	Fédération de Russie
227	296	373						Serbie-et-Monténégro
—	—	—	363	307	335	353	347	Serbie
83	113	109	87	70	75	68	75	Tadjikistan
118	128	167	165	119	134	149	139	LERY de Macédoine
172	239	277	336	143	183	331	407	Turkménistan
171	173	209	233	160	197	224	221	Ukraine
141	160	212	246	269	280	288	246	Ouzbékistan
108	**115**	**122**	**123**	**108**	**123**	**129**	**133**	**Économies développées : Amérique**
92	47	43	31	36	17	14	11	Bermudes
115	115	119	124	92	105	113	113	Canada
120	112	113	113	91	89	95	96	Groenland
207	508	334	181	91	72	68	68	Saint-Pierre-et-Miquelon
105	114	122	123	114	129	135	140	États-Unis

Pour les sources et les notes, se reporter à la fin du tableau.

4.2.1 Terms of trade indices and purchasing power indices of exports of countries and geographical regions
2000 = 100

Region, country or territory	Terms of trade (1) - Termes de l'échange (1)							
	2005	2006	2007	2008	2009	2010	2011	2012
Developed economies: Asia	**84**	**76**	**73**	**64**	**76**	**69**	**63**	**62**
Israel	95	94	91	93	102	98	91	98
Japan	83	75	72	62	74	68	62	60
Developed economies: Europe	**98**	**98**	**98**	**96**	**98**	**96**	**95**	**94**
Austria	95	94	94	92	94	91	88	87
Belgium	99	98	99	96	99	96	95	94
Bulgaria	97	103	105	106	109	109	108	107
Cyprus	102	103	102	106	97	98	97	94
Czech Republic	106	104	105	103	106	103	103	101
Denmark	100	99	101	101	100	100	100	100
Estonia	96	94	97	95	99	98	96	94
Faeroe Islands	95	107	92	98	104	105	103	104
Finland	93	92	94	90	92	91	88	87
France	96	96	96	93	96	93	90	89
Germany	99	97	97	96	100	98	96	95
Gibraltar	60	58	58	52	59	58	52	52
Greece	94	93	93	92	90	91	89	87
Hungary	97	93	93	92	95	93	93	93
Iceland	94	101	101	95	84	92	91	87
Ireland	99	97	96	95	97	98	94	93
Italy	102	99	101	98	102	98	95	95
Latvia	104	103	109	105	104	107	106	103
Lithuania	100	98	99	96	97	95	95	93
Luxembourg	89	86	85	82	83	80	78	76
Malta	96	103	106	110	124	132	138	126
Netherlands	97	95	96	94	95	93	94	93
Norway	122	139	134	157	124	139	158	162
Poland	103	102	102	100	104	102	99	97
Portugal	94	93	93	90	94	93	92	91
Romania	107	109	109	108	109	110	111	111
Slovakia	102	99	98	95	98	94	94	92
Slovenia	98	98	97	95	99	96	95	94
Spain	96	95	95	92	97	93	90	89
Sweden	96	95	96	94	95	95	93	92
Switzerland	85	87	86	80	83	81	76	80
United Kingdom	104	104	104	104	103	102	100	99
Developed economies: Oceania	**128**	**140**	**146**	**166**	**156**	**169**	**189**	**176**
Australia	131	146	152	175	163	179	200	185
New Zealand	113	112	114	126	121	119	132	129

Sources:

UNCTAD secretariat calculations, based on:

- ECLAC, *CEPALSTAT* External trade deflator

- EUROSTAT, online database, Trade unit value indices by reporting country

- IMF, *International Financial Statistics*

- U.S. Bureau of Labor Statistics, External trade price indices

- Unit value indices of Japan Customs and Price indices of Bank of Japan

- UNCTAD, *UNCTADstat Commodity Price Statistics*

- UNCTAD, *UNCTADstat Merchandise Trade Matrix*

- UNCTAD secretariat estimates

Notes:

(a)   Data refer to Netherlands Antilles.

(1)   The "net barter" terms of trade, defined as the ratio of the export unit value index to the import unit value index.

(2)   The purchasing power index of exports is the value index of exports deflated by the import unit value index.

(3)   From 2011 onwards, exports include commercial mining.

(4)   From 2005 onwards, including customs free zones.

Purchasing power of exports (2) - Pouvoir d'achat des exportations (2)								Régions, pays ou territoires
2005	2006	2007	2008	2009	2010	2011	2012	
108	**109**	**113**	**101**	**91**	**106**	**96**	**94**	**Économies développées : Asie**
114	117	125	124	114	129	131	125	Israël
108	108	113	100	90	104	94	92	Japon
116	**123**	**128**	**126**	**111**	**120**	**124**	**123**	**Économies développées : Europe**
126	130	138	135	113	126	129	127	Autriche
122	127	135	128	117	124	126	124	Belgique
158	189	204	218	190	228	268	265	Bulgarie
107	92	85	88	78	85	97	96	Chypre
185	212	245	256	221	255	278	275	République tchèque
117	121	128	130	114	118	121	119	Danemark
138	164	164	161	138	171	213	212	Estonie
106	109	116	119	114	116	119	110	Îles Féroé
98	107	111	106	81	85	83	80	Finlande
95	96	96	93	81	86	86	85	France
124	133	142	140	120	134	139	138	Allemagne
98	102	117	85	115	93	66	63	Gibraltar
97	106	109	105	95	96	121	134	Grèce
163	187	216	223	191	219	236	232	Hongrie
131	138	170	162	144	155	159	153	Islande
108	102	103	98	101	101	97	92	Irlande
106	108	116	109	93	98	99	99	Italie
193	214	253	266	236	289	349	381	Lettonie
233	250	263	300	259	299	338	361	Lituanie
159	184	164	174	168	148	144	132	Luxembourg
79	91	91	93	85	109	117	109	Malte
126	134	142	145	130	142	145	147	Pays-Bas
130	147	144	168	129	140	152	157	Norvège
193	225	251	267	249	280	292	295	Pologne
108	115	124	120	106	115	124	127	Portugal
180	199	224	242	225	270	301	291	Roumanie
174	218	272	293	264	301	335	361	Slovaquie
147	171	194	196	171	185	196	191	Slovénie
110	114	120	116	109	117	122	120	Espagne
106	112	117	114	93	107	112	108	Suède
124	136	147	150	140	151	155	161	Suisse
97	106	94	90	77	85	90	84	Royaume-Uni
137	**154**	**164**	**198**	**173**	**214**	**239**	**224**	**Économies développées : Océanie**
142	161	173	210	186	230	259	242	Australie
115	122	127	152	123	148	161	154	Nouvelle-Zélande

Sources :

Calculs du secrétariat de la CNUCED, basés sur :

- CEPALC, *CEPALSTAT* Déflateur du commerce extérieur

- EUROSTAT, base de données en ligne, Indices de valeur unitaire par pays déclarant

- FMI, *Statistiques financières internationales*

- Bureau des statistiques du travail des États-Unis (BLS), Indices de prix du commerce extérieur

- Indices des valeurs unitaires des douanes japonaises et Indices de prix de la Banque du Japon

- CNUCED, *UNCTADstat Statistiques de prix des produits de base*

- CNUCED, *UNCTADstat Matrice du commerce de marchandises*

- Estimations du secrétariat de la CNUCED

Notes :

(a)   Les données se réfèrent aux Antilles néerlandaises.

(1)   Le terme de l'échange, appelé aussi "troc net", est le rapport de l'indice de la valeur unitaire des exportations à l'indice de la valeur unitaire des importations exprimé en pourcentage.

(2)   Le pouvoir d'achat des exportations est l'indice de la valeur des exportations corrigé par l'indice de la valeur unitaire des importations.

(3)   À partir de 2011, les exportations comprennent l'exploitation minière commerciale.

(4)   À partir de 2005, y compris les zones franches douanières.

Economic grouping	Exports (1) - Exportations (1)							
	2005	2006	2007	2008	2009	2010	2011	2012
DEVELOPING ECONOMIES	**157**	**173**	**190**	**196**	**177**	**205**	**217**	**225**
Developing economies excluding China	137	147	157	158	145	163	169	174
Developing economies excluding LDCs	157	174	191	196	177	205	218	226
High-income developing economies	141	151	161	162	148	167	174	180
Middle-income developing economies	199	233	271	285	250	304	330	342
Low-income developing economies	141	151	164	174	166	185	203	206
Heavily indebted poor countries (IMF)	135	139	145	146	145	153	152	159
Landlocked developing countries	151	164	192	201	182	195	209	215
Small island developing States	116	126	118	113	84	87	80	79
Least developed countries	*150*	*161*	*184*	*188*	*182*	*192*	*190*	*198*
Africa and Haiti	169	177	209	216	209	212	204	221
Asia	129	145	153	153	154	183	194	191
Islands	121	114	138	133	118	131	182	207
Major petroleum and gas exporters	*120*	*123*	*130*	*131*	*126*	*132*	*135*	*141*
Africa	126	127	137	132	126	137	116	132
America	96	92	86	85	77	70	75	77
Asia	122	127	135	138	134	141	150	154
Major exporters of manufactured goods	*178*	*207*	*233*	*247*	*220*	*269*	*292*	*305*
America	112	124	126	127	117	135	138	144
Asia	189	220	251	267	237	292	319	333
Emerging economies	*147*	*162*	*173*	*177*	*164*	*191*	*201*	*203*
America	130	138	144	141	131	146	150	152
Asia	156	175	190	197	183	217	231	233
Newly industrialized Asian economies	*149*	*165*	*177*	*182*	*166*	*197*	*207*	*210*
First tier	159	177	191	200	186	220	234	238
Second tier	126	137	145	143	127	150	154	155
Developing economies: Africa	**126**	**127**	**136**	**131**	**119**	**129**	**119**	**125**
Northern Africa excluding Sudan	123	126	134	127	112	120	91	111
Sub-Saharan Africa	128	128	138	135	124	136	135	135
Sub-Saharan Africa excluding South Africa	135	136	147	145	140	152	151	154
Developing economies: America	**127**	**134**	**138**	**136**	**126**	**136**	**143**	**146**
Central America and Greater Caribbean Islands excluding Puerto Rico	116	128	131	132	122	139	144	151
Central America and Greater Caribbean Islands excluding Mexico and Puerto Rico	146	157	167	167	157	171	191	204
South America and Central America	129	135	140	138	129	140	146	149
South America excluding Brazil	126	127	131	130	126	128	136	139
Developing economies: Asia	**168**	**190**	**212**	**221**	**199**	**236**	**254**	**264**
Eastern and South-Eastern Asia excluding China	149	165	177	182	167	197	208	213
Southern Asia excluding India	119	133	139	134	129	135	136	106

For sources and notes, see end of table 4.2.1 (Volume indices of exports and imports).

4.2.2 Indices du volume des exportations et importations des groupements économiques
2000 = 100

			Imports (1) - Importations (1)					Groupements économiques
2005	2006	2007	2008	2009	2010	2011	2012	
155	**170**	**189**	**202**	**181**	**215**	**231**	**242**	**ÉCONOMIES EN DÉVELOPPEMENT**
142	155	171	185	162	189	201	210	Économies en développement sans la Chine
155	170	188	202	180	215	231	241	Économies en développement sans les PMA
134	148	162	171	147	174	186	192	Économies en développement à revenu élevé
195	212	237	252	235	287	311	328	Économies en développement à revenu intermédiaire
183	209	237	281	269	300	323	341	Économies en développement à revenu faible
163	177	197	213	205	225	236	256	Pays pauvres très endettés (FMI)
168	192	229	260	241	261	285	316	Pays en développement sans littoral
119	127	135	133	113	108	114	116	Petits États insulaires en développement
160	*174*	*198*	*219*	*228*	*232*	*242*	*263*	*Pays les moins avancés*
184	200	232	269	279	273	278	306	Afrique et Haïti
130	141	153	157	165	180	195	211	Asie
166	187	193	192	191	213	212	219	Îles
187	*204*	*244*	*298*	*263*	*277*	*291*	*318*	*Principaux exportateurs de pétrole et de gaz*
190	202	243	314	304	321	313	347	Afrique
132	179	236	229	209	188	210	259	Amérique
195	209	246	305	261	280	297	320	Asie
154	*170*	*184*	*189*	*171*	*210*	*224*	*234*	*Principaux exportateurs d'articles manufacturés*
114	126	131	136	107	132	143	149	Amérique
162	178	194	198	183	224	239	250	Asie
127	*139*	*149*	*156*	*133*	*164*	*174*	*177*	*Économies émergentes*
116	130	144	158	126	163	179	181	Amérique
134	144	152	156	136	166	172	176	Asie
136	*145*	*154*	*158*	*138*	*167*	*175*	*181*	*Économies nouvellement industrialisées d'Asie*
134	145	154	158	141	168	174	178	Première génération
143	147	154	161	131	166	179	190	Deuxième génération
156	173	196	219	205	223	229	247	Économies en développement : Afrique
140	149	176	206	204	216	202	234	Afrique septentrionale sans le Soudan
165	186	208	227	207	227	245	255	Afrique subsaharienne
171	188	217	248	237	252	266	282	Afrique subsaharienne sans l'Afrique du Sud
121	137	153	166	136	167	185	189	Économies en développement : Amérique
119	132	138	143	115	138	149	155	Amérique centrale et Grandes Antilles sans Porto Rico
138	154	166	175	147	164	175	181	Amérique centrale et Grandes Antilles sans le Mexique et Porto Rico
123	139	156	170	139	173	192	197	Amérique du Sud et Amérique centrale
138	163	195	222	188	225	260	269	Amérique du Sud sans le Brésil
164	180	199	211	192	229	246	257	Économies en développement : Asie
137	146	156	161	141	170	179	186	Asie orientale et Asie du Sud-Est sans la Chine
168	172	174	182	158	181	181	167	Asie méridionale sans l'Inde

Pour les sources et les notes, se reporter à la fin du tableau 4.2.1 (Indices du volume des exportations et importations).

4

Economic grouping	Exports (1) - Exportations (1)							
	2005	2006	2007	2008	2009	2010	2011	2012
DEVELOPING ECONOMIES	118	128	135	157	138	153	176	177
Developing economies excluding China	123	135	144	171	145	165	195	195
Developing economies excluding LDCs	118	127	134	155	137	151	174	174
High-income developing economies	118	128	136	158	134	151	177	176
Middle-income developing economies	114	121	127	144	134	142	159	159
Low-income developing economies	144	161	178	216	184	220	267	268
Heavily indebted poor countries (IMF)	146	173	190	234	202	245	301	289
Landlocked developing countries	155	192	210	271	212	258	328	325
Small island developing States	148	179	192	257	206	238	308	312
Least developed countries	*152*	*178*	*193*	*247*	*194*	*234*	*296*	*296*
Africa and Haiti	164	197	217	285	209	262	341	340
Asia	125	136	142	165	153	166	193	196
Islands	116	126	137	154	140	155	177	174
Major petroleum and gas exporters	*179*	*214*	*234*	*318*	*219*	*268*	*353*	*360*
Africa	189	229	250	347	225	276	370	380
America	174	214	244	334	223	281	367	375
Asia	177	209	228	307	216	263	346	351
Major exporters of manufactured goods	*100*	*103*	*106*	*113*	*106*	*112*	*121*	*122*
America	115	121	129	138	118	133	152	155
Asia	99	101	104	111	104	110	118	118
Emerging economies	*105*	*111*	*117*	*128*	*112*	*125*	*140*	*138*
America	121	136	148	169	145	169	199	197
Asia	98	101	105	112	100	109	119	117
Newly industrialized Asian economies	*99*	*103*	*107*	*115*	*105*	*114*	*125*	*125*
First tier	95	97	100	104	95	102	111	111
Second tier	112	119	127	147	136	149	168	166
Developing economies: Africa	167	198	217	290	224	267	341	341
Northern Africa excluding Sudan	172	203	220	307	225	261	333	341
Sub-Saharan Africa	164	194	214	279	221	268	342	337
Sub-Saharan Africa excluding South Africa	169	201	222	292	219	269	348	347
Developing economies: America	125	142	155	182	153	179	213	212
Central America and Greater Caribbean Islands excluding Puerto Rico	114	120	128	136	119	132	151	153
Central America and Greater Caribbean Islands excluding Mexico and Puerto Rico	105	111	118	125	119	126	139	136
South America and Central America	125	141	154	180	151	177	211	210
South America excluding Brazil	142	175	196	236	189	229	276	274
Developing economies: Asia	112	119	125	142	127	139	157	158
Eastern and South-Eastern Asia excluding China	100	104	108	117	107	116	128	127
Southern Asia excluding India	149	170	183	235	185	223	279	291

For sources and notes, see end of table 4.2.1 (Unit value indices).

4.2.2 Indices de la valeur unitaire des exportations et importations des groupements économiques
2000 = 100

			Imports (1) - Importations (1)					Groupements économiques
2005	2006	2007	2008	2009	2010	2011	2012	
116	123	131	149	134	146	166	165	**ÉCONOMIES EN DÉVELOPPEMENT**
115	122	130	148	133	145	164	165	Économies en développement sans la Chine
115	122	130	148	133	145	165	165	Économies en développement sans les PMA
113	119	126	143	129	138	156	156	Économies en développement à revenu élevé
118	126	134	154	140	154	174	172	Économies en développement à revenu intermédiaire
126	132	145	165	144	164	194	194	Économies en développement à revenu faible
124	133	144	169	152	164	189	188	Pays pauvres très endettés (FMI)
123	131	141	161	149	157	178	176	Pays en développement sans littoral
127	137	149	180	157	175	209	211	Petits États insulaires en développement
125	*133*	*145*	*170*	*154*	*168*	*196*	*193*	*Pays les moins avancés*
124	132	143	165	150	161	186	184	Afrique et Haïti
126	135	149	180	162	181	217	212	Asie
126	134	146	176	161	174	200	201	Îles
118	*124*	*134*	*149*	*142*	*149*	*166*	*166*	*Principaux exportateurs de pétrole et de gaz*
119	126	138	154	145	150	170	169	Afrique
113	116	121	134	123	130	142	143	Amérique
118	125	134	149	144	151	168	168	Asie
112	*118*	*124*	*141*	*127*	*139*	*156*	*156*	*Principaux exportateurs d'articles manufacturés*
111	116	123	131	126	131	141	142	Amérique
112	118	124	141	127	139	158	157	Asie
113	*121*	*128*	*146*	*128*	*139*	*157*	*157*	*Économies émergentes*
113	119	127	143	131	138	151	154	Amérique
113	121	128	147	127	139	159	158	Asie
109	*116*	*122*	*138*	*124*	*135*	*153*	*153*	*Économies nouvellement industrialisées d'Asie*
109	115	121	136	120	131	149	149	Première génération
111	120	126	145	135	145	164	164	Deuxième génération
127	135	147	169	154	165	189	188	Économies en développement : Afrique
124	132	147	168	154	164	190	187	Afrique septentrionale sans le Soudan
128	137	148	170	154	165	188	188	Afrique subsaharienne
124	132	143	165	150	161	184	183	Afrique subsaharienne sans l'Afrique du Sud
114	120	128	144	132	139	153	155	Économies en développement : Amérique
112	117	124	134	127	133	145	146	Amérique centrale et Grandes Antilles sans Porto Rico
114	120	127	144	129	138	157	157	Amérique centrale et Grandes Antilles sans le Mexique et Porto Rico
113	119	127	142	130	137	151	153	Amérique du Sud et Amérique centrale
112	117	125	141	125	134	147	150	Amérique du Sud sans le Brésil
115	122	129	147	132	145	166	165	Économies en développement : Asie
110	117	123	139	125	136	155	155	Asie orientale et Asie du Sud-Est sans la Chine
129	139	152	185	181	200	226	235	Asie méridionale sans l'Inde

Pour les sources et les notes, se reporter à la fin du tableau 4.2.1 (Indices de la valeur unitaire).

4

4.2.2 Terms of trade indices and purchasing power indices
of exports of economic groupings
2000 = 100

Economic grouping	Terms of trade (1) - Termes de l'échange (1)							
	2005	2006	2007	2008	2009	2010	2011	2012
DEVELOPING ECONOMIES	**102**	**104**	**104**	**106**	**103**	**105**	**106**	**107**
Developing economies excluding China	106	110	110	116	109	114	119	118
Developing economies excluding LDCs	102	104	103	105	103	104	106	106
High-income developing economies	105	107	107	111	104	109	113	113
Middle-income developing economies	97	96	95	93	96	93	91	92
Low-income developing economies	114	122	122	131	128	134	138	138
Heavily indebted poor countries (IMF)	117	130	131	139	133	150	159	154
Landlocked developing countries	126	146	149	168	142	164	184	184
Small island developing States	117	130	129	143	131	136	147	148
Least developed countries	*122*	*134*	*133*	*145*	*126*	*140*	*151*	*153*
Africa and Haiti	132	150	152	173	139	163	184	185
Asia	99	101	95	92	94	92	89	93
Islands	92	94	94	88	87	89	89	86
Major petroleum and gas exporters	*153*	*172*	*175*	*213*	*154*	*180*	*213*	*217*
Africa	159	182	181	225	155	183	218	225
America	154	184	202	249	182	216	260	262
Asia	150	167	170	206	150	175	206	209
Major exporters of manufactured goods	*90*	*87*	*86*	*81*	*84*	*81*	*78*	*78*
America	104	104	105	106	94	101	108	109
Asia	88	85	84	78	82	79	75	76
Emerging economies	*92*	*92*	*91*	*88*	*87*	*90*	*89*	*88*
America	107	115	117	118	110	123	132	128
Asia	87	84	82	76	79	78	74	74
Newly industrialized Asian economies	*91*	*88*	*87*	*83*	*85*	*85*	*82*	*81*
First tier	87	84	83	77	79	78	75	74
Second tier	100	100	101	101	101	103	103	101
Developing economies: Africa	**132**	**147**	**147**	**171**	**145**	**162**	**181**	**182**
Northern Africa excluding Sudan	138	154	150	183	146	159	175	182
Sub-Saharan Africa	128	142	145	164	144	163	182	180
Sub-Saharan Africa excluding South Africa	137	152	155	177	146	167	189	190
Developing economies: America	**110**	**118**	**121**	**126**	**116**	**129**	**139**	**136**
Central America and Greater Caribbean Islands excluding Puerto Rico	102	102	103	102	94	99	104	104
Central America and Greater Caribbean Islands excluding Mexico and Puerto Rico	93	93	93	86	92	91	89	87
South America and Central America	110	119	122	127	116	130	140	137
South America excluding Brazil	127	149	157	168	151	171	188	183
Developing economies: Asia	**98**	**98**	**97**	**96**	**96**	**95**	**95**	**96**
Eastern and South-Eastern Asia excluding China	91	89	88	84	86	85	83	82
Southern Asia excluding India	115	122	120	127	102	112	123	124

For sources and notes, see end of table 4.2.1 (Terms of trade and purchasing power indices).

4.2.2 Indices des termes de l'échange et du pouvoir d'achat des exportations des groupements économiques
2000 = 100

Purchasing power of exports (2) - Pouvoir d'achat des exportations (2)								Groupements économiques
2005	2006	2007	2008	2009	2010	2011	2012	
160	181	197	206	182	215	231	240	**ÉCONOMIES EN DÉVELOPPEMENT**
146	162	173	182	158	186	201	205	Économies en développement sans la Chine
160	180	197	205	181	214	230	239	Économies en développement sans les PMA
147	162	172	180	154	183	197	204	Économies en développement à revenu élevé
192	225	257	265	238	282	301	316	Économies en développement à revenu intermédiaire
160	185	201	228	212	249	280	285	Économies en développement à revenu faible
158	180	190	203	192	229	243	244	Pays pauvres très endettés (FMI)
191	240	286	338	259	320	385	396	Pays en développement sans littoral
135	164	152	161	110	118	118	118	Petits États insulaires en développement
183	*216*	*245*	*273*	*229*	*268*	*286*	*303*	*Pays les moins avancés*
222	266	318	373	291	345	375	408	Afrique et Haïti
128	146	145	141	145	168	173	177	Asie
111	107	130	117	102	117	162	179	Îles
183	*211*	*228*	*279*	*193*	*238*	*286*	*305*	*Principaux exportateurs de pétrole et de gaz*
201	231	248	297	195	251	252	297	Afrique
148	169	173	212	140	151	195	203	Amérique
183	212	230	284	201	246	310	323	Asie
160	*180*	*199*	*199*	*184*	*218*	*227*	*239*	*Principaux exportateurs d'articles manufacturés*
116	129	133	134	110	137	150	157	Amérique
167	188	210	209	195	230	240	252	Asie
136	*149*	*159*	*155*	*144*	*172*	*179*	*179*	*Économies émergentes*
139	158	168	168	145	179	197	195	Amérique
136	146	155	151	144	170	172	172	Asie
135	*146*	*155*	*151*	*141*	*166*	*170*	*171*	*Économies nouvellement industrialisées d'Asie*
139	149	158	154	147	172	175	177	Première génération
126	137	146	145	128	153	158	157	Deuxième génération
166	186	201	225	173	210	214	228	**Économies en développement : Afrique**
170	194	202	233	164	191	160	202	Afrique septentrionale sans le Soudan
165	182	201	221	179	221	245	243	Afrique subsaharienne
184	207	227	257	204	254	285	291	Afrique subsaharienne sans l'Afrique du Sud
140	159	167	172	146	176	198	199	**Économies en développement : Amérique**
118	131	135	134	114	139	150	158	Amérique centrale et Grandes Antilles sans Porto Rico
136	146	154	144	144	156	170	177	Amérique centrale et Grandes Antilles sans le Mexique et Porto Rico
142	161	170	176	150	181	204	205	Amérique du Sud et Amérique centrale
160	190	205	219	190	219	256	255	Amérique du Sud sans le Brésil
165	186	205	213	192	225	241	252	**Économies en développement : Asie**
136	146	156	153	143	168	173	176	Asie orientale et Asie du Sud-Est sans la Chine
137	163	167	170	132	151	168	132	Asie méridionale sans l'Inde

Pour les sources et les notes, se reporter à la fin du tableau 4.2.1 (Indices des termes de l'échange et du pouvoir d'achat).

Market / Marchés	Year / Année	MFN rate - Simple average (2) / Droit NPF - Moyenne simple (2)						MFN rate - Weighted average (3) / Droit NPF - Moyenne pondérée (3)					
		Total of non-agricultural and non-fuel products / Total des produits non-agricoles et non-pétroliers	Ores and metals / Minérais et métaux	Manufactured products / Produits manufacturés	Chemical products / Produits chimiques	Machinery and transport equipment / Machines et matériel de transport	Other manufactured products / Produits manufacturés divers	Total of non-agricultural and non-fuel products / Total des produits non-agricoles et non-pétroliers	Ores and metals / Minérais et métaux	Manufactured products / Produits manufacturés	Chemical products / Produits chimiques	Machinery and transport equipment / Machines et matériel de transport	Other manufactured products / Produits manufacturés divers
SITC Rev.3 (1) / CTCI Rév.3 (1)		5+6+7+8 +27+28-667	27+28+68	(5+6+7+8) -(667+68)	5	7	(6+8) -(667+68)	5+6+7+8 +27+28-667	27+28+68	(5+6+7+8) -(667+68)	5	7	(6+8) -(667+68)
Afghanistan	2007	6.1	5.7	6.1	5.1	5.0	6.9	6.2	6.1	6.2	4.5	6.7	6.2
	2008	6.1	5.4	6.1	5.0	4.8	7.0	6.3	4.8	6.3	4.9	6.9	5.4
	2012	6.3	5.8	6.3	4.8	5.0	7.3	6.4	8.1	6.4	4.9	6.9	6.1
Albania - Albanie	2005	6.5	3.0	6.6	2.8	2.6	9.4	7.4	0.9	7.6	3.2	4.2	10.7
	2007	5.7	2.8	5.8	2.3	2.5	8.2	6.0	1.4	6.2	2.5	3.6	8.5
	2008	5.4	3.0	5.5	2.2	1.6	8.2	5.1	1.1	5.3	2.6	1.5	8.4
	2009	5.4	1.0	5.6	2.4	1.6	8.2	4.8	0.6	5.0	2.7	1.4	8.0
	2011	5.3	1.1	5.4	2.2	1.6	8.1	4.6	1.2	4.9	2.7	1.5	7.6
	2012	3.6	1.0	3.7	2.1	1.6	5.2	2.9	0.9	3.1	2.5	1.4	4.2
Algeria - Algérie	2005	18.2	11.9	18.6	14.2	12.1	23.2	11.9	9.3	12.0	8.8	10.5	16.7
	2007	17.9	11.9	18.2	14.2	11.4	22.9	12.1	9.4	12.1	8.2	11.3	15.2
	2008	17.9	12.0	18.2	14.2	11.3	23.0	11.7	9.7	11.7	8.3	11.1	14.2
	2009	17.9	12.2	18.2	14.2	11.3	22.9	12.0	9.8	12.0	8.3	11.2	14.8
Angola	2005	6.7	7.9	6.7	5.2	3.1	8.8	5.0	6.5	5.0	7.9	2.8	9.9
	2008	6.5	7.3	6.5	5.1	2.8	8.6	6.2	8.1	6.2	8.8	3.3	10.9
	2009	6.5	7.3	6.5	5.1	2.8	8.6	5.9	8.0	5.9	8.7	3.2	10.9
Antigua and Barbuda - Antigua-et-Barbuda	2000	12.1	5.4	12.4	8.5	9.7	14.4	15.3	10.0	15.4	16.7	13.6	17.0
	2005	10.4	5.0	10.6	7.5	8.9	12.0	13.8	6.3	13.9	12.7	14.4	13.6
	2007	10.3	5.0	10.5	6.7	8.9	12.0	13.4	6.4	13.5	9.3	14.4	13.5
	2008	10.2	5.2	10.3	6.5	8.7	12.0	14.1	6.0	14.2	11.7	13.3	15.5
	2009	10.3	5.2	10.4	7.2	8.7	12.0	14.4	5.9	14.5	14.2	13.3	15.5
Argentina - Argentine	2000	15.8	9.7	16.2	11.6	14.8	18.6	15.1	8.2	15.3	12.6	15.1	18.0
	2005	11.8	6.5	12.1	8.1	8.6	15.2	12.5	4.0	12.8	8.7	14.3	13.6
	2007	11.7	6.5	12.0	8.1	8.5	15.1	12.8	4.7	13.1	8.3	14.7	13.8
	2008	10.3	6.5	10.5	8.1	7.8	13.4	11.1	4.6	11.4	8.1	12.2	12.9
	2009	10.5	6.5	10.8	8.1	8.4	13.7	13.1	3.7	13.5	7.8	16.1	13.4
	2010	13.4	6.5	13.8	8.1	8.5	18.4	13.5	4.4	13.8	8.7	15.2	15.8
	2011	10.5	6.5	10.8	8.1	8.4	13.7	13.9	4.0	14.3	8.2	17.0	13.7
	2012	10.5	6.5	10.7	8.2	8.4	13.6	13.8	4.4	14.2	8.3	17.0	13.4
Armenia - Arménie	2008	2.5	0.7	2.6	0.1	1.8	3.8	2.9	0.1	3.0	0.2	3.2	3.9
	2012	3.3	1.2	3.3	0.2	3.1	4.6	3.2	0.1	3.4	0.1	3.4	4.9
Australia - Australie	2000	5.2	1.2	5.5	2.0	3.9	7.5	4.7	2.4	4.7	1.8	4.2	7.1
	2005	4.1	1.1	4.2	1.6	3.0	5.8	3.8	2.6	3.8	1.6	3.4	5.6
	2007	4.1	1.2	4.3	1.6	3.2	5.8	4.2	2.2	4.2	1.6	4.0	5.7
	2008	4.1	1.2	4.3	1.6	3.2	5.8	4.2	2.2	4.2	1.6	4.0	5.7
	2009	4.1	1.2	4.3	1.6	3.2	5.8	4.1	2.0	4.1	1.5	4.0	5.6
	2010	3.2	1.2	3.3	1.6	2.9	4.2	3.4	2.0	3.4	1.5	3.4	4.3
	2011	3.2	1.2	3.3	1.6	2.9	4.2	3.3	1.2	3.4	1.4	3.4	4.4
Azerbaijan - Azerbaïdjan	2005	9.2	4.9	9.4	5.2	6.2	12.1	5.8	2.1	6.0	5.7	2.9	10.8
	2007	8.6	5.0	8.7	5.2	5.0	12.0	5.5	2.4	5.6	4.8	3.4	10.0
	2008	8.6	5.0	8.7	5.2	5.0	12.0	5.5	2.4	5.6	4.8	3.4	10.0
	2009	8.5	4.4	8.7	5.1	4.8	12.1	5.3	4.0	5.4	5.3	.3.2	10.0
	2011	8.5	4.8	8.7	5.0	4.7	12.0	5.2	4.1	5.2	5.3	2.8	10.0
	2012	8.6	4.9	8.7	5.1	4.8	12.0	5.8	4.0	5.8	5.1	3.4	9.9
Bahamas	2010	37.8	41.7	37.6	40.2	38.0	36.6	32.5	29.3	32.6	31.5	32.0	33.5
	2011	37.7	40.7	37.6	40.2	37.9	36.5	31.5	30.9	31.5	26.7	33.0	32.7
Bahrain - Bahreïn	2005	4.9	5.0	4.9	4.8	4.9	5.0	4.9	5.0	4.9	4.3	5.0	5.0
	2007	4.8	5.0	4.8	4.6	4.6	4.9	4.8	5.0	4.7	4.1	4.8	5.0
	2008	4.8	4.8	4.8	4.6	4.5	4.9	4.6	5.0	4.6	3.5	4.5	4.9
	2009	4.8	4.8	4.8	4.6	4.5	4.9	4.5	5.0	4.5	3.6	4.2	4.9
	2011	4.8	5.2	4.8	4.7	4.5	5.0	4.8	5.2	4.7	3.8	4.6	5.1
	2012	4.8	5.2	4.8	4.7	4.5	5.0	4.8	5.2	4.7	3.8	4.6	5.1

For sources and notes, see end of table.

Pour les sources et les notes, se reporter à la fin du tableau.

Market / Marchés	Year / Année	MFN rate - Simple average (2) / Droit NPF - Moyenne simple (2)						MFN rate - Weighted average (3) / Droit NPF - Moyenne pondérée (3)					
		Total of non-agricultural and non-fuel products / Total des produits non-agricoles et non-pétroliers	of which: / dont :					Total of non-agricultural and non-fuel products / Total des produits non-agricoles et non-pétroliers	of which: / dont :				
			Ores and metals / Minérais et métaux	Manu-factured products / Produits manu-facturés	Of which: / dont :				Ores and metals / Minérais et métaux	Manu-factured products / Produits manu-facturés	Of which: / dont :		
					Chemical products / Produits chimiques	Machinery and transport equipment / Machines et matériel de transport	Other manu-factured products / Produits manu-facturés divers				Chemical products / Produits chimiques	Machinery and transport equipment / Machines et matériel de transport	Other manu-factured products / Produits manu-facturés divers
SITC Rev.3 (1) / CTCI Rév.3 (1)		5+6+7+8 +27+28-667	27+28+68	(5+6+7+8) -(667+68)	5	7	(6+8) -(667+68)	5+6+7+8 +27+28-667	27+28+68	(5+6+7+8) -(667+68)	5	7	(6+8) -(667+68)
Bangladesh	2000	21.9	14.9	22.2	17.0	13.6	28.1	18.5	11.7	18.7	11.7	10.8	25.9
	2005	15.2	10.5	15.5	11.5	10.7	19.1	25.5	9.5	26.0	8.7	14.7	43.0
	2007	14.4	9.7	14.7	10.2	9.8	18.5	12.9	8.7	13.0	6.8	9.4	19.1
	2008	14.3	10.4	14.5	11.1	8.6	18.3	13.9	8.6	14.0	8.0	8.9	20.1
Barbados - Barbade	2000	17.9	18.7	17.9	12.2	16.9	19.1	21.5	18.2	21.5	14.4	26.1	21.1
	2007	11.6	5.4	11.8	6.7	8.2	15.2	13.8	5.4	14.0	12.0	12.0	16.9
Belarus - Bélarus	2000	10.1	8.1	10.2	6.7	10.0	11.9	9.2	7.6	9.3	8.2	8.9	10.2
	2008	8.9	7.7	8.9	6.7	6.4	11.3	7.8	6.8	7.9	8.6	6.1	9.6
	2009	8.8	7.5	8.9	6.7	6.3	11.3	7.6	5.4	7.7	8.7	5.4	10.2
	2010	7.8	7.0	7.8	6.3	4.7	10.2	6.6	3.8	6.9	8.1	4.2	9.1
	2011	7.7	6.6	7.8	6.2	4.7	10.1	6.4	3.3	6.6	8.0	4.0	8.9
	2012	7.8	6.9	7.9	6.3	4.8	10.2	6.6	5.4	6.6	8.1	4.5	9.1
Belize	2007	10.1	4.9	10.2	6.7	8.1	12.3	11.5	8.8	11.5	9.5	10.6	13.1
	2008	10.1	4.9	10.2	6.7	8.1	12.3	11.5	8.8	11.5	9.5	10.6	13.1
	2009	10.0	4.8	10.1	7.0	7.7	12.3	9.3	4.3	9.4	8.0	6.8	13.6
	2010	10.3	4.8	10.4	7.1	7.7	12.7	10.0	4.3	10.1	8.1	6.9	14.6
	2011	9.8	4.9	10.0	6.6	7.5	12.2	12.9	11.0	12.9	9.4	9.9	15.1
	2012	9.9	4.7	10.0	6.7	7.5	12.3	10.6	7.2	10.6	7.8	10.0	12.3
Benin - Bénin	2005	13.2	8.9	13.3	7.9	9.5	16.9	12.7	6.9	12.8	4.6	11.6	15.6
	2007	13.0	9.1	13.1	8.0	9.1	16.7	12.7	7.0	12.9	4.4	11.9	15.6
	2008	13.0	8.6	13.1	8.0	8.7	16.5	17.6	10.7	17.6	6.8	16.3	19.1
	2009	13.0	8.4	13.1	8.0	8.7	16.5	17.6	10.2	17.6	6.9	16.3	19.0
	2010	12.7	8.4	12.8	7.6	8.6	16.3	17.1	9.1	17.2	6.5	15.4	19.2
	2011	12.8	8.5	12.9	7.6	8.6	16.3	17.2	9.1	17.2	7.8	16.1	19.1
	2012	12.5	8.4	12.6	7.1	8.8	16.3	16.8	9.7	16.9	5.5	16.6	18.5
Bermuda - Bermudes	2005	19.5	19.8	19.5	17.8	24.2	17.6	28.2	21.9	28.2	13.8	31.0	14.8
	2007	19.7	20.4	19.7	18.3	24.6	17.7	30.8	21.7	30.8	13.8	31.9	16.3
	2008	19.7	20.9	19.7	17.9	24.9	17.7	31.0	22.2	31.4	13.6	33.4	15.8
	2009	19.6	20.9	19.6	17.9	24.6	17.7	28.8	22.2	28.9	13.6	30.3	15.9
	2010	19.6	20.2	19.6	18.2	24.2	17.8	27.7	21.0	27.7	13.8	29.9	16.8
	2011	19.3	19.5	19.3	18.9	23.8	17.4	18.6	17.1	18.6	13.5	29.2	14.1
	2012	19.2	19.4	19.2	19.1	23.6	17.4	16.5	17.7	16.4	13.6	27.7	12.3
Bhutan - Bhoutan	2005	18.0	25.8	17.7	19.6	11.3	21.4	14.7	26.0	14.5	27.0	9.1	21.4
	2007	16.6	22.5	16.4	15.6	11.0	21.4	16.2	26.2	16.0	6.4	16.0	18.1
Bolivia (Plurinational State of) - Bolivie (État plurinational de)	2000	9.2	9.9	9.1	9.9	6.9	9.9	8.2	10.0	8.2	9.7	6.4	9.7
	2005	8.2	8.5	8.1	7.7	5.7	9.4	8.4	9.5	8.4	9.5	6.6	9.5
	2007	8.0	8.5	8.0	7.5	5.5	9.3	8.1	9.4	8.1	9.3	6.5	9.5
	2008	8.0	8.5	8.0	7.5	5.5	9.3	8.0	9.4	7.9	9.2	6.3	9.5
	2009	9.8	6.9	10.0	7.0	5.4	13.2	8.0	8.1	8.0	8.2	6.0	10.6
	2010	11.1	6.9	11.3	7.0	5.4	15.6	8.3	8.1	8.3	8.2	6.0	11.4
	2011	11.1	6.8	11.3	7.0	5.3	15.5	8.2	8.4	8.2	8.0	5.9	11.9
	2012	11.1	6.8	11.3	7.0	5.3	15.5	8.2	8.4	8.2	8.0	5.9	11.9
Bosnia and Herzegovina - Bosnie-Herzégovine	2007	6.8	2.3	7.0	3.1	6.4	8.6	7.3	3.7	7.6	6.0	7.5	8.2
	2008	6.5	2.3	6.7	3.1	5.9	8.4	7.2	3.5	7.5	5.9	7.6	8.0
	2009	6.5	2.3	6.7	3.1	5.9	8.3	7.3	4.6	7.5	5.9	7.4	8.2
	2010	6.5	2.2	6.7	3.0	5.9	8.4	7.3	4.3	7.4	5.9	7.4	8.2
	2011	6.5	2.3	6.7	3.1	5.9	8.3	7.1	4.5	7.2	5.7	7.3	7.9
	2012	6.5	2.3	6.7	3.1	5.9	8.4	7.1	4.7	7.3	5.6	7.5	8.0

For sources and notes, see end of table.

Pour les sources et les notes, se reporter à la fin du tableau.

Market / Marchés	Year / Année	MFN rate - Simple average (2) / Droit NPF - Moyenne simple (2)						MFN rate - Weighted average (3) / Droit NPF - Moyenne pondérée (3)					
		Total of non-agricultural and non-fuel products / Total des produits non-agricoles et non-pétroliers	Ores and metals / Minérais et métaux	Manu-factured products / Produits manu-facturés	Chemical products / Produits chimiques	Machinery and transport equipment / Machines et matériel de transport	Other manu-factured products / Produits manu-facturés divers	Total of non-agricultural and non-fuel products / Total des produits non-agricoles et non-pétroliers	Ores and metals / Minérais et métaux	Manu-factured products / Produits manu-facturés	Chemical products / Produits chimiques	Machinery and transport equipment / Machines et matériel de transport	Other manu-factured products / Produits manu-facturés divers
SITC Rev.3 (1) / CTCI Rév.3 (1)		5+6+7+8 +27+28-667	27+28+68	(5+6+7+8) -(667+68)	5	7	(6+8) -(667+68)	5+6+7+8 +27+28-667	27+28+68	(5+6+7+8) -(667+68)	5	7	(6+8) -(667+68)
Botswana	2005	11.5	2.5	11.7	5.2	4.0	16.8	12.0	0.1	13.6	1.0	10.7	22.7
	2007	10.7	2.0	10.9	6.3	4.1	15.6	13.1	0.7	13.2	1.2	5.2	26.4
	2008	10.8	2.3	11.0	6.0	3.8	15.9	14.3	0.4	14.4	1.4	5.0	26.5
	2009	10.6	2.0	10.9	6.0	3.8	15.6	13.9	0.4	13.9	1.5	7.1	23.1
	2010	10.5	1.1	10.7	4.9	3.6	15.6	8.0	0.2	8.0	0.9	2.5	17.2
	2011	10.0	1.1	10.2	4.1	3.7	14.8	4.7	0.2	4.8	1.3	4.9	5.0
	2012	9.9	1.6	10.1	5.1	3.8	14.2	10.7	1.6	10.7	2.6	7.7	18.5
Brazil - Brésil	2000	16.4	9.3	16.8	11.6	17.6	18.6	14.7	8.2	15.0	11.1	16.1	16.5
	2005	13.1	6.1	13.5	8.3	13.9	15.5	10.5	4.7	10.8	7.4	11.5	13.5
	2007	13.0	6.0	13.4	8.2	13.7	15.4	11.0	4.8	11.5	6.8	13.6	13.2
	2008	14.2	6.0	14.7	8.2	13.7	17.7	11.1	4.2	11.5	6.1	13.9	13.8
	2009	14.8	6.1	15.3	8.1	13.8	18.7	12.2	5.0	12.5	6.9	14.5	14.7
	2010	14.9	6.1	15.4	8.1	13.7	19.0	12.3	5.0	12.6	6.9	14.5	15.1
	2011	14.9	6.1	15.4	8.1	13.8	18.9	13.0	5.2	13.4	6.9	15.8	15.8
	2012	14.9	6.1	15.4	8.1	13.8	19.0	12.9	5.2	13.2	6.8	15.2	16.4
Brunei Darussalam - Brunéi Darussalam	2000	3.7	0.0	3.9	0.5	10.0	2.0	10.5	0.0	10.6	1.0	18.9	0.9
	2005	3.7	0.1	3.8	0.5	9.7	2.1	6.5	0.0	6.6	0.9	11.4	2.5
	2007	3.8	0.1	3.9	0.5	10.0	2.1	6.3	0.0	6.3	1.1	10.0	2.7
	2008	3.5	0.0	3.6	0.5	9.1	2.0	4.2	0.0	4.3	1.1	5.8	2.7
	2010	3.5	0.1	3.6	0.5	9.4	1.9	4.9	0.0	5.0	1.2	7.2	2.9
Bulgaria - Bulgarie (4)	2000	11.6	4.0	12.0	8.1	7.9	15.2	10.2	1.8	11.0	9.0	7.2	15.5
	2005	9.3	3.3	9.6	7.5	5.9	11.9	8.2	1.5	8.9	7.2	6.8	12.0
Burkina Faso	2005	12.7	8.6	12.9	7.4	9.3	16.3	12.6	8.4	12.6	5.9	13.8	14.8
	2007	12.6	8.9	12.7	7.5	8.7	16.2	12.6	8.5	12.7	5.1	14.0	14.6
	2008	12.4	8.6	12.5	7.9	8.7	16.2	9.9	8.2	9.9	6.0	9.0	16.1
	2009	12.3	8.7	12.4	7.8	8.7	16.2	9.7	8.3	9.8	5.8	8.8	16.0
	2010	12.5	8.8	12.7	7.6	8.6	16.2	10.5	7.2	10.5	5.0	10.2	14.0
	2011	12.5	8.6	12.6	7.4	8.4	16.3	10.4	7.8	10.4	4.5	10.3	13.8
	2012	12.4	8.6	12.5	7.2	8.6	16.2	10.0	7.7	10.0	4.6	10.5	13.6
Burundi	2005	18.6	11.1	18.7	16.0	15.5	21.5	17.9	14.9	18.0	15.8	16.5	21.2
	2007	14.8	6.0	15.0	11.9	10.3	18.1	14.0	9.2	14.1	14.2	15.0	13.0
	2008	14.7	5.8	14.8	11.9	10.3	17.8	13.6	8.5	13.6	14.5	13.0	13.7
	2009	12.8	10.7	12.9	6.8	7.3	17.7	16.4	16.6	16.4	6.3	8.1	24.1
	2010	12.5	12.0	12.5	6.3	7.3	17.7	14.6	19.3	14.5	5.6	7.5	22.9
	2011	13.0	9.4	13.1	6.4	6.8	17.8	12.1	16.9	12.1	4.6	8.4	18.6
	2012	12.4	9.8	12.5	7.1	7.1	17.7	9.9	13.9	9.8	3.8	5.9	18.4
Cambodia - Cambodge	2005	14.5	9.3	14.6	9.8	17.4	14.8	10.9	9.9	10.9	6.0	16.4	10.2
	2007	14.3	9.3	14.5	9.8	17.3	14.5	10.9	9.9	10.9	6.0	16.4	10.2
	2008	14.5	8.9	14.6	10.1	17.2	14.8	11.2	11.3	11.2	5.9	16.7	9.1
Cameroon - Cameroun	2005	18.0	10.9	18.3	11.3	14.4	22.5	14.8	10.7	15.1	7.8	16.5	17.7
	2007	17.4	11.0	17.7	11.2	13.9	22.0	14.3	10.4	14.6	8.9	16.7	16.1
	2009	17.7	10.7	18.0	11.6	13.9	22.1	15.8	13.9	15.9	8.5	16.0	18.9
	2011	17.8	10.7	18.1	11.3	14.4	22.3	14.2	10.5	14.3	8.1	15.5	16.5
	2012	17.7	10.8	18.0	11.2	14.3	22.3	14.1	11.5	14.3	8.3	14.6	17.2
Canada	2000	4.7	0.7	5.0	2.9	2.1	7.0	3.1	0.6	3.2	3.3	2.5	4.7
	2005	4.2	0.7	4.4	2.6	2.2	6.0	3.1	0.6	3.2	2.6	2.8	4.2
	2007	3.9	0.7	4.1	2.6	2.2	5.5	3.3	0.6	3.4	2.6	3.0	4.4
	2008	3.9	0.7	4.1	2.6	2.3	5.5	3.3	0.6	3.4	2.6	3.0	4.4
	2009	3.8	0.7	4.0	2.6	1.7	5.5	3.1	0.7	3.2	2.3	2.6	4.7
	2010	2.8	0.0	2.9	0.8	1.3	4.5	2.7	0.0	2.8	1.3	2.4	4.1
	2012	2.6	0.0	2.7	0.7	1.2	4.2	2.6	0.0	2.7	1.2	2.3	4.0

For sources and notes, see end of table.

Pour les sources et les notes, se reporter à la fin du tableau.

Market / Marchés	Year / Année	MFN rate - Simple average (2) / Droit NPF - Moyenne simple (2)						MFN rate - Weighted average (3) / Droit NPF - Moyenne pondérée (3)					
		Total of non-agricultural and non-fuel products / Total des produits non-agricoles et non-pétroliers	Ores and metals / Minérais et métaux	Manufactured products / Produits manufacturés	Chemical products / Produits chimiques	Machinery and transport equipment / Machines et matériel de transport	Other manufactured products / Produits manufacturés divers	Total of non-agricultural and non-fuel products / Total des produits non-agricoles et non-pétroliers	Ores and metals / Minérais et métaux	Manufactured products / Produits manufacturés	Chemical products / Produits chimiques	Machinery and transport equipment / Machines et matériel de transport	Other manufactured products / Produits manufacturés divers
SITC Rev.3 (1) / CTCI Rév.3 (1)		5+6+7+8 +27+28-667	27+28+68	(5+6+7+8) -(667+68)	5	7	(6+8) -(667+68)	5+6+7+8 +27+28-667	27+28+68	(5+6+7+8) -(667+68)	5	7	(6+8) -(667+68)
Cape Verde - Cap-Vert	2005	12.6	1.4	12.9	5.1	9.1	16.6	13.4	1.5	13.5	11.4	12.9	14.6
	2007	11.5	1.2	11.8	4.9	7.9	15.7	9.5	0.1	10.8	11.8	8.4	12.9
	2008	12.0	1.4	12.4	4.9	7.9	16.4	11.6	1.7	11.8	9.6	12.4	11.9
	2009	12.1	1.7	12.4	4.8	7.7	16.5	11.4	2.1	11.6	8.9	10.5	13.4
	2010	11.6	1.7	11.9	4.8	6.7	16.2	10.8	2.1	11.0	8.6	9.8	12.8
	2011	11.5	1.2	11.8	4.9	6.6	16.0	9.6	2.1	9.7	9.1	8.1	11.6
Central African Republic - République centrafricaine	2005	18.8	13.3	18.9	13.3	15.7	22.1	15.4	22.2	15.2	7.5	15.7	18.9
	2007	17.8	12.7	18.0	12.1	15.0	21.5	13.4	13.3	13.4	7.0	14.2	17.8
Chad - Tchad	2005	17.9	13.6	18.0	13.0	14.9	21.7	11.4	14.5	11.3	9.1	10.6	16.0
	2007	17.5	12.7	17.6	12.9	14.4	21.3	12.6	8.9	12.7	8.1	12.2	17.7
	2009	17.4	11.3	17.5	12.5	14.3	21.3	13.8	6.8	13.9	9.2	13.2	17.8
	2011	17.7	11.0	17.8	12.5	14.1	21.5	14.3	8.8	14.3	9.5	13.0	18.3
Chile - Chili	2000	9.0	9.0	9.0	9.0	9.0	9.0	9.0	9.0	9.0	9.0	9.0	9.0
	2005	6.0	6.0	6.0	6.0	6.0	6.0	6.0	6.0	6.0	6.0	6.0	6.0
	2007	6.0	6.0	6.0	6.0	6.0	6.0	6.0	6.0	6.0	6.0	5.9	6.0
	2008	6.0	6.0	6.0	6.0	6.0	6.0	6.0	6.0	6.0	6.0	5.9	6.0
	2009	6.0	6.0	6.0	6.0	5.9	6.0	6.0	6.0	6.0	6.0	5.9	6.0
	2010	6.0	6.0	6.0	6.0	5.9	6.0	6.0	6.0	6.0	6.0	6.0	6.0
China - Chine	2000	15.9	5.3	16.5	11.2	16.2	18.7	13.0	5.2	13.7	13.0	12.6	16.1
	2005	9.2	3.7	9.6	6.9	9.2	10.8	5.0	1.8	5.4	7.3	4.0	7.3
	2007	9.2	3.7	9.6	6.9	8.9	10.9	5.6	1.5	6.4	6.4	5.5	7.9
	2008	8.9	3.4	9.3	6.6	8.4	10.8	5.1	0.7	6.1	5.9	5.1	7.7
	2009	8.9	3.3	9.3	6.6	8.4	10.7	5.1	0.5	6.3	6.0	5.6	7.6
	2010	9.0	3.3	9.3	6.5	8.6	10.7	5.3	0.4	6.6	5.8	6.2	7.9
	2011	9.0	3.3	9.3	6.5	8.6	10.7	5.3	0.4	6.8	5.6	6.7	7.9
China, Taiwan Province of - Province chinoise de Taiwan	2000	6.1	1.6	6.4	3.9	6.0	7.5	2.9	1.4	3.0	3.4	2.5	4.1
	2005	4.5	0.9	4.7	2.8	4.5	5.5	2.3	0.6	2.4	1.9	2.7	2.2
	2007	4.3	0.9	4.5	2.8	4.1	5.4	1.8	0.5	1.9	1.9	1.7	2.3
	2008	4.3	0.9	4.5	2.8	4.0	5.4	1.7	0.4	1.9	1.8	1.8	2.2
	2009	4.3	0.8	4.6	2.8	4.1	5.5	2.4	0.6	2.7	1.8	3.4	2.6
	2010	4.3	0.9	4.6	2.8	4.1	5.4	2.6	0.5	2.9	2.0	3.8	2.7
	2012	4.3	0.9	4.5	2.8	4.0	5.5	2.7	0.5	2.9	2.0	3.9	2.7
Colombia - Colombie	2000	11.9	6.7	12.2	8.1	10.0	14.8	10.5	6.6	10.6	8.0	10.7	13.0
	2005	11.9	6.5	12.2	8.1	9.8	14.9	10.7	6.4	10.9	8.2	10.9	13.2
	2007	11.9	6.5	12.2	8.1	9.8	14.8	11.8	6.1	12.1	8.5	13.0	13.1
	2008	11.8	6.6	12.1	8.1	9.7	14.8	12.1	6.1	12.4	8.5	14.0	13.1
	2009	11.8	6.5	12.2	8.0	9.8	14.8	10.6	6.8	10.7	7.7	10.7	13.3
	2010	11.9	6.5	12.2	8.0	9.9	14.8	10.5	6.8	10.6	7.5	10.7	13.3
	2011	7.3	4.8	7.4	5.6	6.4	8.6	8.8	4.9	8.9	5.5	10.9	8.0
	2012	5.2	1.5	5.5	2.6	3.6	7.3	7.4	3.3	7.5	3.5	9.5	7.4
Comoros - Comores	2008	11.5	14.5	11.5	11.3	13.3	10.5	11.2	13.0	11.2	7.9	12.4	10.4
	2010	11.4	13.8	11.3	11.6	13.2	10.2	12.2	11.7	12.2	5.8	13.1	11.6
	2011	11.2	14.5	11.1	10.6	13.0	10.3	8.8	13.5	8.7	9.1	12.9	6.3
	2012	8.2	9.3	8.2	9.8	6.9	8.6	5.9	10.0	5.9	5.8	7.1	5.1
Congo	2005	18.4	11.5	18.6	11.7	14.5	22.7	15.9	17.0	15.9	9.4	14.3	20.6
	2007	18.0	11.8	18.2	11.7	14.0	22.3	14.1	14.9	14.1	10.8	12.6	18.3
Cook Islands - Îles Cook	2010	0.5	0.0	0.5	0.0	2.1	0.0	1.7	0.0	1.7	0.0	4.0	0.0
	2012	0.3	0.0	0.3	0.0	1.1	0.0	0.6	0.0	0.6	0.0	1.5	0.0
Costa Rica	2000	4.8	1.6	5.0	1.4	2.2	7.5	3.8	1.6	3.9	3.1	1.9	6.9
	2005	5.1	1.3	5.3	1.4	2.3	8.0	3.6	1.3	3.7	3.0	1.9	6.8
	2007	4.9	1.3	5.1	1.5	2.1	7.8	4.0	0.9	4.1	2.8	3.1	6.0
	2008	5.6	2.3	5.7	2.4	2.8	8.3	4.4	1.9	4.4	3.3	2.7	6.8
	2009	4.6	1.3	4.7	1.4	1.8	7.3	3.5	0.9	3.5	2.3	2.0	5.7
	2010	4.6	1.3	4.7	1.4	1.8	7.3	3.5	1.1	3.5	2.5	1.9	5.8

For sources and notes, see end of table.

Pour les sources et les notes, se reporter à la fin du tableau.

Market / Marchés	Year / Année	MFN rate - Simple average (2) / Droit NPF - Moyenne simple (2)						MFN rate - Weighted average (3) / Droit NPF - Moyenne pondérée (3)					
		Total of non-agricultural and non-fuel products / Total des produits non-agricoles et non-pétroliers	Ores and metals / Minérais et métaux	Manufactured products / Produits manufacturés	Chemical products / Produits chimiques	Machinery and transport equipment / Machines et matériel de transport	Other manufactured products / Produits manufacturés divers	Total of non-agricultural and non-fuel products / Total des produits non-agricoles et non-pétroliers	Ores and metals / Minérais et métaux	Manufactured products / Produits manufacturés	Chemical products / Produits chimiques	Machinery and transport equipment / Machines et matériel de transport	Other manufactured products / Produits manufacturés divers
SITC Rev.3 (1) / CTCI Rév.3 (1)		5+6+7+8 +27+28-667	27+28+68	(5+6+7+8) -(667+68)	5	7	(6+8) -(667+68)	5+6+7+8 +27+28-667	27+28+68	(5+6+7+8) -(667+68)	5	7	(6+8) -(667+68)
Côte d'Ivoire	2005	12.3	8.2	12.4	6.8	8.9	16.1	10.4	7.0	10.4	5.1	8.2	15.3
	2007	12.1	8.2	12.2	6.9	8.4	16.0	10.6	7.1	10.7	5.3	10.3	14.6
	2008	12.0	8.1	12.2	6.9	8.3	15.9	9.7	6.8	9.8	5.1	10.9	12.6
	2009	12.0	8.1	12.2	6.9	8.3	15.9	9.7	6.8	9.8	5.1	10.9	12.6
	2010	12.0	8.1	12.2	6.9	8.3	16.0	9.4	7.2	9.5	5.0	10.0	12.6
	2011	11.9	7.9	12.1	6.8	8.3	15.8	9.2	6.5	9.3	4.6	10.2	12.9
	2012	11.9	7.9	12.1	6.8	8.3	15.8	9.2	6.5	9.3	4.6	10.2	12.9
Croatia - Croatie	2005	4.0	1.8	4.2	1.3	3.1	5.6	3.8	2.0	3.9	2.3	3.6	4.9
	2007	4.2	1.6	4.3	1.4	3.6	5.7	4.2	1.8	4.3	2.3	4.1	5.2
	2008	4.1	1.6	4.3	1.4	3.6	5.7	4.2	1.8	4.3	2.3	4.1	5.2
	2009	4.1	1.6	4.3	1.4	3.5	5.7	4.2	2.1	4.3	2.3	4.1	5.4
	2010	4.1	1.6	4.3	1.3	3.5	5.7	4.2	2.1	4.3	2.2	4.1	5.4
	2011	4.1	1.6	4.3	1.3	3.6	5.7	4.0	1.7	4.1	2.0	4.2	5.2
	2012	4.2	1.7	4.3	1.4	3.6	5.7	4.0	1.7	4.1	2.1	4.1	5.3
Cuba	2000	11.4	5.7	11.6	9.3	10.0	13.3	10.5	3.7	10.6	8.0	10.0	12.3
	2005	11.5	5.6	11.7	9.3	10.1	13.5	9.8	3.9	9.9	8.1	9.3	11.4
	2007	11.5	5.6	11.7	9.2	10.1	13.5	10.0	3.9	10.1	8.6	9.4	11.6
	2008	11.4	5.9	11.7	9.1	10.1	13.4	9.8	2.6	10.0	8.1	9.4	11.7
	2009	11.3	5.3	11.6	9.3	9.8	13.3	10.0	6.3	10.0	9.4	9.1	11.7
	2010	11.4	5.7	11.6	9.4	9.9	13.3	10.3	6.0	10.4	9.9	9.5	11.6
	2011	11.3	5.1	11.6	9.3	9.8	13.3	10.2	4.5	10.3	9.6	9.7	11.3
	2012	11.3	5.8	11.6	9.5	9.9	13.2	10.1	4.6	10.2	9.1	9.4	11.3
Cyprus - Chypre (5)	2000	4.6	2.2	4.7	5.0	2.4	5.6	5.0	4.1	5.0	3.3	5.4	5.2
Czech Republic - République tchèque (5)	2000	4.6	1.3	4.8	4.2	4.0	5.4	4.4	1.6	4.5	3.7	4.0	5.5
Dem. Rep. of the Congo - Rép. dém. du Congo	2007	12.4	9.7	12.5	8.9	8.6	15.6	11.3	9.6	11.3	14.0	7.7	15.2
	2008	12.0	8.9	12.2	8.8	8.3	15.3	10.8	6.0	11.1	13.1	7.6	15.2
	2009	12.0	8.9	12.2	8.8	8.3	15.3	10.8	6.0	11.1	13.0	7.6	15.1
Djibouti	2005	28.7	29.2	28.7	30.4	28.8	28.2	27.7	31.2	27.7	25.8	28.5	27.6
	2009	21.6	22.7	21.5	23.6	20.5	21.4	18.6	21.1	18.6	16.0	18.1	19.9
	2011	22.1	20.6	22.2	22.9	21.7	22.3	19.9	16.1	20.0	20.8	19.4	20.6
	2012	22.1	20.6	22.2	22.9	21.7	22.3	19.9	16.1	20.0	20.8	19.4	20.6
Dominica - Dominique	2000	14.1	12.8	14.1	10.6	16.1	14.6	15.0	14.4	15.0	10.3	21.8	12.5
	2007	10.2	4.4	10.4	9.3	7.7	11.8	11.7	4.6	11.7	10.7	10.7	13.0
	2011	10.0	4.4	10.1	9.6	7.0	11.7	12.6	6.6	12.6	15.5	10.4	13.5
Dominican Republic - République dominicaine	2000	18.2	10.2	18.5	10.4	13.4	24.1	17.5	13.6	17.6	9.8	17.8	21.3
	2005	8.1	4.7	8.3	4.9	5.5	10.7	9.1	5.1	9.2	6.2	8.1	10.7
	2007	6.5	2.7	6.6	2.5	3.2	9.8	7.7	3.1	7.8	3.7	8.3	8.7
	2008	8.1	5.2	8.2	4.9	5.1	10.9	8.7	5.5	8.7	5.3	9.0	9.8
	2010	6.3	2.1	6.5	2.4	3.2	9.4	7.5	6.1	7.5	3.8	7.2	9.2
Ecuador - Équateur	2005	11.5	6.0	11.7	7.2	8.3	15.0	10.3	6.6	10.4	7.1	10.5	12.5
	2007	11.5	6.0	11.8	7.2	8.4	15.0	10.2	6.6	10.2	7.3	10.1	12.5
	2008	10.8	4.4	11.1	4.7	6.2	15.9	8.5	6.1	8.5	5.0	8.5	10.9
	2009	10.1	1.1	10.6	3.1	4.8	16.1	7.3	2.7	7.3	4.6	6.8	10.2
	2010	10.1	1.1	10.6	3.1	4.8	16.1	7.2	2.7	7.3	4.6	6.8	10.2
	2011	8.7	0.9	9.0	3.1	5.1	13.1	7.0	2.3	7.1	4.3	7.4	8.8
	2012	8.7	0.9	9.1	3.1	5.1	13.1	7.3	2.3	7.4	4.3	8.2	8.8
Egypt - Égypte	2005	13.1	5.6	13.5	6.8	8.0	18.5	11.6	2.3	12.1	16.5	10.0	13.0
	2008	10.2	5.1	10.4	6.1	7.0	13.6	9.1	1.8	10.3	10.7	11.5	8.8
	2009	10.0	4.9	10.3	5.9	6.7	13.6	8.9	1.8	10.0	10.1	11.2	8.8

For sources and notes, see end of table.

Pour les sources et les notes, se reporter à la fin du tableau.

Market / Marchés	Year / Année	MFN rate - Simple average (2) / Droit NPF - Moyenne simple (2)						MFN rate - Weighted average (3) / Droit NPF - Moyenne pondérée (3)					
		Total of non-agricultural and non-fuel products / Total des produits non-agricoles et non-pétroliers	of which: / dont :					Total of non-agricultural and non-fuel products / Total des produits non-agricoles et non-pétroliers	of which: / dont :				
			Ores and metals / Minérais et métaux	Manu-factured products / Produits manu-facturés	Of which: / dont :				Ores and metals / Minérais et métaux	Manu-factured products / Produits manu-facturés	Of which: / dont :		
					Chemical products / Produits chimiques	Machinery and transport equipment / Machines et matériel de transport	Other manu-factured products / Produits manu-facturés divers				Chemical products / Produits chimiques	Machinery and transport equipment / Machines et matériel de transport	Other manu-factured products / Produits manu-facturés divers
SITC Rev 3 (1) / CTCI Rév.3 (1)		5+6+7+8 +27+28-667	27+28+68	(5+6+7+8) -(667+68)	5	7	(6+8) -(667+68)	5+6+7+8 +27+28-667	27+28+68	(5+6+7+8) -(667+68)	5	7	(6+8) -(667+68)
El Salvador	2000	6.7	1.2	7.0	1.6	2.4	11.2	5.4	1.6	5.5	4.6	3.5	8.4
	2005	5.3	1.3	5.5	1.7	2.3	8.3	6.0	1.3	6.1	6.0	4.6	7.5
	2007	5.2	1.3	5.3	1.7	2.1	8.1	6.8	1.2	6.9	8.4	4.8	7.4
	2008	5.2	1.3	5.3	1.7	2.1	8.1	6.7	1.2	6.8	8.4	4.8	7.2
	2009	5.1	1.4	5.3	1.6	2.0	8.0	6.6	1.8	6.7	5.9	4.0	8.4
	2010	5.1	1.4	5.3	1.7	2.0	8.0	6.6	1.8	6.7	5.9	4.0	8.4
	2012	5.0	1.4	5.2	1.7	1.9	8.0	6.5	1.4	6.6	6.0	4.4	7.8
Equatorial Guinea - Guinée équatoriale	2005	18.5	12.1	18.7	13.0	14.6	22.4	14.3	9.9	14.3	16.4	12.9	18.3
	2007	18.0	11.0	18.2	12.6	14.3	21.9	14.3	11.5	14.3	14.2	12.1	18.7
Estonia - Estonie (5)	2000	0.1	0.0	0.1	0.3	0.0	0.0	0.0	0.0	0.0	0.1	0.0	0.0
Ethiopia - Éthiopie	2008	16.9	8.3	17.3	10.7	11.3	22.7	12.7	6.9	12.8	6.5	12.1	17.2
	2009	16.9	8.3	17.3	10.7	11.3	22.7	12.7	6.9	12.8	6.5	12.1	17.2
	2010	16.9	8.3	17.3	10.6	11.3	22.7	13.1	6.7	13.2	6.5	12.1	18.3
	2011	16.9	8.3	17.2	10.5	11.2	22.7	12.9	6.9	13.0	6.5	11.3	18.6
	2012	16.8	8.3	17.2	10.5	11.1	22.6	12.8	6.9	12.9	6.5	11.1	18.5
EU27 - UE27 (6)	2000	4.2	1.6	4.4	4.2	2.3	5.4	3.3	1.8	3.4	2.9	2.3	5.4
	2005	3.9	1.6	4.1	4.6	2.3	4.7	3.3	1.7	3.4	3.2	2.4	5.0
	2007	3.7	1.6	3.9	3.7	2.2	4.6	3.3	1.7	3.5	2.2	2.8	4.7
	2008	3.7	1.6	3.9	3.7	2.2	4.6	3.2	1.3	3.4	2.2	2.7	4.7
	2009	3.7	1.6	3.8	3.7	2.2	4.6	3.2	1.3	3.4	2.1	2.7	4.7
	2010	3.9	1.6	4.0	4.6	2.2	4.6	3.2	1.3	3.4	2.9	2.2	5.0
	2011	3.9	1.6	4.0	4.6	2.2	4.6	3.3	1.3	3.5	3.0	2.3	5.0
	2012	3.9	1.6	4.0	4.6	2.2	4.6	3.3	1.3	3.5	2.9	2.3	5.1
Fiji - Fidji	2007	8.2	3.6	8.4	5.1	5.9	10.6	9.1	3.0	9.2	6.2	7.7	11.8
	2008	9.6	5.5	9.8	6.6	7.9	11.7	10.4	5.0	10.5	7.0	9.4	12.9
	2009	10.8	5.3	10.9	7.2	8.7	12.9	12.8	5.0	12.9	7.1	13.9	14.6
	2010	10.5	5.2	10.7	6.9	8.4	12.9	12.0	5.0	12.2	8.2	11.1	14.6
	2011	10.2	5.0	10.4	6.9	8.1	12.6	11.7	5.0	11.8	7.4	11.1	14.1
French Polynesia - Polynésie française	2008	11.7	10.0	11.7	10.9	10.1	12.6	11.3	11.1	11.3	13.5	10.6	11.4
	2009	11.7	9.9	11.8	11.1	10.3	12.6	11.7	10.9	11.7	13.8	11.2	11.3
	2011	11.7	9.7	11.8	11.1	10.4	12.6	11.8	10.8	11.8	13.8	11.3	11.3
	2012	10.0	8.8	10.0	9.3	8.4	11.0	10.3	9.2	10.4	12.9	9.6	9.9
Gabon	2000	18.2	11.1	18.4	11.4	14.6	22.3	13.3	17.7	13.3	8.7	12.1	18.1
	2005	18.3	11.5	18.5	11.6	14.8	22.5	15.5	16.4	15.5	9.7	15.2	18.2
	2007	17.8	11.0	18.1	11.6	14.2	22.1	14.9	14.8	14.9	11.4	14.4	16.9
	2008	17.9	11.1	18.2	11.8	14.0	22.1	14.2	14.4	14.2	9.8	13.5	17.3
	2009	17.9	11.1	18.1	11.8	14.0	22.0	14.3	14.2	14.3	9.8	13.6	17.4
Gambia - Gambie	2007	19.3	19.0	19.3	18.5	19.1	19.5	17.0	17.7	17.0	12.1	18.1	16.7
	2008	19.3	18.9	19.3	18.6	19.3	19.6	17.4	16.4	17.4	11.7	18.8	17.0
	2009	19.3	18.8	19.3	18.7	19.2	19.6	16.9	15.2	17.0	14.5	18.2	16.6
	2011	14.3	8.5	14.5	12.1	10.8	17.1	12.9	13.4	12.9	7.0	15.1	12.7
	2012	14.3	8.5	14.5	12.1	10.8	17.1	12.9	13.4	12.9	7.0	15.1	12.7
Georgia - Géorgie	2007	0.3	3.2	0.2	0.1	0.0	0.3	0.3	3.3	0.2	0.0	0.0	0.6
	2008	0.3	3.2	0.2	0.1	0.0	0.3	0.3	3.3	0.2	0.0	0.0	0.6
	2009	0.3	3.5	0.2	0.1	0.0	0.3	0.3	1.7	0.3	0.0	0.0	0.7
	2010	0.3	3.5	0.2	0.1	0.0	0.3	0.3	1.7	0.3	0.0	0.0	0.7
	2011	0.8	3.6	0.7	0.7	0.1	1.0	1.2	2.4	1.1	1.7	0.0	1.9
	2012	0.8	3.4	0.7	0.7	0.1	1.0	1.2	3.7	1.1	1.7	0.0	2.3
Ghana	2000	13.8	11.2	13.9	12.1	5.4	18.6	8.9	10.2	8.9	11.4	5.2	13.3
	2007	12.4	11.0	12.4	11.2	5.9	15.9	8.9	10.2	8.8	10.2	6.4	13.1
	2008	12.3	11.0	12.4	11.2	5.8	15.9	8.8	10.2	8.8	10.2	6.4	13.1
	2009	12.4	11.4	12.4	11.2	5.8	15.9	8.5	10.8	8.5	9.2	5.5	13.0

For sources and notes, see end of table.

Pour les sources et les notes, se reporter à la fin du tableau.

4

Market / Marchés	Year / Année	MFN rate - Simple average (2) / Droit NPF - Moyenne simple (2)						MFN rate - Weighted average (3) / Droit NPF - Moyenne pondérée (3)					
		Total of non-agricultural and non-fuel products / Total des produits non-agricoles et non-pétroliers	Ores and metals / Minérais et métaux	Manu-factured products / Produits manu-facturés	Chemical products / Produits chimiques	Machinery and transport equipment / Machines et matériel de transport	Other manu-factured products / Produits manu-facturés divers	Total of non-agricultural and non-fuel products / Total des produits non-agricoles et non-pétroliers	Ores and metals / Minérais et métaux	Manu-factured products / Produits manu-facturés	Chemical products / Produits chimiques	Machinery and transport equipment / Machines et matériel de transport	Other manu-factured products / Produits manu-facturés divers
SITC Rev.3 (1) / CTCI Rév.3 (1)		5+6+7+8 +27+28-667	27+28+68	(5+6+7+8) -(667+68)	5	7	(6+8) -(667+68)	5+6+7+8 +27+28-667	27+28+68	(5+6+7+8) -(667+68)	5	7	(6+8) -(667+68)
Grenada - Grenade	2007	10.2	5.7	10.3	7.7	8.4	11.9	11.1	7.0	11.1	12.8	10.3	11.2
	2008	10.2	5.8	10.4	7.6	8.5	12.0	10.5	8.1	10.5	13.0	11.0	9.7
	2010	10.7	6.3	10.8	9.1	9.1	12.0	11.3	6.9	11.4	12.1	10.8	11.7
	2011	10.6	6.3	10.7	8.9	9.1	11.9	12.0	6.0	12.1	12.2	12.3	11.9
	2012	10.8	6.2	10.9	10.0	9.4	11.9	13.3	7.4	13.3	10.2	12.9	14.3
Guatemala	2000	6.7	1.4	7.0	1.5	2.6	11.0	5.1	2.0	5.2	3.5	4.7	7.0
	2005	5.2	1.4	5.3	1.6	2.5	8.0	5.9	1.7	6.0	3.2	5.5	7.7
	2007	5.0	1.3	5.2	1.5	2.3	7.8	5.6	1.7	5.7	3.0	5.3	7.3
	2008	5.0	1.3	5.2	1.5	2.3	7.8	5.6	1.7	5.7	3.0	5.3	7.3
	2009	5.0	1.2	5.2	1.6	2.3	7.8	5.4	1.9	5.4	3.1	5.4	6.9
	2010	5.0	1.3	5.2	1.6	2.3	7.8	5.4	2.1	5.5	3.4	5.2	7.1
	2011	5.0	1.3	5.2	1.6	2.3	7.8	5.2	2.2	5.3	3.4	4.9	6.9
	2012	4.9	1.2	5.1	1.6	2.2	7.7	5.3	1.9	5.4	3.5	4.9	7.1
Guinea - Guinée	2005	12.7	9.8	12.8	7.8	9.2	16.2	11.2	8.8	11.2	4.3	11.8	15.0
	2008	12.6	9.6	12.6	7.5	9.2	16.0	11.2	8.0	11.2	4.1	11.8	15.1
	2009	12.6	10.2	12.7	7.3	8.9	16.0	10.2	9.9	10.2	5.2	8.9	14.7
	2010	12.6	10.2	12.7	7.3	8.9	16.0	10.2	9.9	10.2	5.2	8.9	14.7
	2012	12.7	10.2	12.7	7.7	8.9	16.0	10.2	9.9	10.2	5.3	8.9	14.7
Guinea-Bissau - Guinée-Bissau	2005	13.7	11.0	13.7	9.6	10.0	16.9	13.5	13.4	13.5	10.9	10.2	17.0
	2007	13.5	10.1	13.6	10.3	9.4	16.9	12.4	7.6	12.4	9.7	9.8	16.5
	2008	13.5	10.7	13.5	9.8	9.4	16.5	13.8	10.8	13.8	11.2	10.3	16.9
	2009	13.4	10.7	13.5	9.8	9.4	16.5	13.8	10.8	13.8	11.5	10.4	16.8
	2010	13.5	10.0	13.6	9.7	9.3	16.6	12.3	11.1	12.3	11.4	8.5	16.2
	2011	13.5	10.7	13.6	9.3	9.5	16.6	13.6	10.6	13.6	11.0	10.0	16.3
	2012	13.3	10.3	13.4	9.2	9.2	16.5	13.1	6.0	13.2	10.3	8.7	17.3
Guyana	2000	17.7	14.1	17.7	13.6	16.9	18.7	16.1	16.2	16.1	12.2	20.3	14.9
	2008	9.6	5.8	9.7	7.1	6.7	11.9	9.1	8.1	9.1	10.2	7.8	10.0
	2010	9.5	5.6	9.6	7.3	6.5	11.9	9.5	6.4	9.5	11.1	7.5	11.1
	2011	9.5	5.6	9.7	7.1	6.5	12.1	8.7	6.8	8.7	10.6	6.8	10.6
	2012	9.5	5.6	9.7	7.1	6.5	12.1	8.7	6.8	8.7	10.6	6.8	10.6
Haiti - Haïti	2007	2.4	0.8	2.4	2.2	0.9	3.3	1.9	0.5	2.0	3.5	1.6	2.0
	2008	2.3	0.8	2.4	2.0	0.9	3.3	5.5	0.0	5.6	3.5	2.4	7.6
	2009	2.4	0.8	2.4	2.1	0.9	3.3	5.8	0.0	5.9	3.6	2.7	7.8
	2011	5.4	3.0	5.4	5.0	3.7	6.4	7.8	1.7	7.9	6.1	5.9	9.1
	2012	2.4	0.2	2.5	2.3	1.0	3.3	3.0	0.1	3.0	3.6	2.6	3.2
Honduras	2000	7.2	2.1	7.4	2.5	3.6	10.8	6.0	3.8	6.0	2.5	8.0	8.7
	2005	5.3	1.4	5.4	1.6	2.5	8.1	5.3	2.6	5.3	2.7	5.0	7.5
	2007	5.1	1.5	5.2	1.6	2.2	7.9	5.6	2.6	5.7	2.6	5.8	7.7
	2008	5.1	1.5	5.2	1.6	2.2	7.9	5.6	2.6	5.7	2.6	5.8	7.7
	2009	5.1	1.5	5.2	1.6	2.1	7.9	5.4	2.6	5.5	2.6	5.3	7.7
Iceland - Islande	2007	2.7	0.0	2.8	0.9	1.2	4.2	2.3	0.0	2.5	3.0	0.5	5.4
	2008	2.7	0.0	2.8	0.9	1.2	4.2	2.3	0.0	2.5	3.0	0.5	5.4
	2009	2.8	0.0	2.9	1.0	1.3	4.2	2.2	0.0	2.6	2.7	0.5	5.4
	2010	2.7	0.0	2.9	0.9	1.2	4.2	2.1	0.0	2.7	2.7	0.6	5.3
	2011	2.7	0.0	2.9	0.9	1.2	4.2	2.0	0.0	2.5	2.6	0.5	5.4
	2012	2.7	0.0	2.8	0.9	1.2	4.1	1.9	0.0	2.3	2.7	0.4	5.3
India - Inde	2005	15.3	14.0	15.4	15.9	15.1	15.3	12.0	13.6	11.8	14.5	9.4	14.9
	2007	13.1	11.8	13.2	13.4	13.3	13.0	11.1	9.6	11.4	11.9	9.7	14.1
	2008	8.6	5.2	8.9	8.5	9.0	9.0	6.9	4.7	7.1	7.0	6.8	7.9
	2009	9.0	5.3	9.3	8.8	9.6	9.3	7.6	6.2	7.8	7.5	7.8	8.1

For sources and notes, see end of table.

Pour les sources et les notes, se reporter à la fin du tableau.

4.3 Average applied import MFN tariff rates on non-agricultural and non-fuel products

4.3 Droits de douane moyens NPF appliqués à l'importation des produits non-agricoles et non-pétroliers

Market / Marchés	Year / Année	MFN rate - Simple average (2) / Droit NPF - Moyenne simple (2)						MFN rate - Weighted average (3) / Droit NPF - Moyenne pondérée (3)					
		Total of non-agricultural and non-fuel products / Total des produits non-agricoles et non-pétroliers	Ores and metals / Minérais et métaux	Manufactured products / Produits manufacturés	Chemical products / Produits chimiques	Machinery and transport equipment / Machines et matériel de transport	Other manufactured products / Produits manufacturés divers	Total of non-agricultural and non-fuel products / Total des produits non-agricoles et non-pétroliers	Ores and metals / Minérais et métaux	Manufactured products / Produits manufacturés	Chemical products / Produits chimiques	Machinery and transport equipment / Machines et matériel de transport	Other manufactured products / Produits manufacturés divers
SITC Rev.3 (1) / CTCI Rév.3 (1)		5+6+7+8 +27+28-667	27+28+68	(5+6+7+8) -(667+68)	5	7	(6+8) -(667+68)	5+6+7+8 +27-28-667	27+28+68	(5+6+7+8) -(667+68)	5	7	(6+8) -(667+68)
Indonesia (…2002) - Indonésie (…2002)	2000	8.7	4.8	8.9	6.1	5.4	11.6	6.5	2.9	6.7	5.6	6.1	8.9
Indonesia - Indonésie	2005	7.0	4.3	7.2	5.2	4.8	8.9	6.4	3.4	6.5	5.8	5.5	9.1
	2007	6.9	4.3	7.1	5.1	4.5	9.0	6.3	3.5	6.5	5.9	5.5	8.5
	2009	6.8	4.2	7.0	4.9	4.3	8.9	6.3	3.2	6.4	5.5	5.7	8.4
	2010	7.2	4.2	7.4	5.5	6.1	8.7	6.7	3.0	6.8	7.1	6.0	8.1
	2011	7.2	4.3	7.4	5.5	6.1	8.7	6.5	2.9	6.7	6.2	6.4	7.6
Iran (Islamic Rep. of) - Iran (Rép. islamique d')	2000	41.8	16.8	43.1	17.0	42.0	60.1	28.1	13.3	28.6	12.7	34.8	28.9
	2007	24.0	9.0	24.7	11.2	16.7	35.1	18.3	8.5	18.5	14.0	20.9	17.2
	2008	27.0	8.1	28.0	11.2	16.0	39.8	21.0	9.4	21.2	13.2	20.5	25.1
	2011	27.2	8.0	28.2	11.1	17.1	39.9	23.0	8.2	23.4	12.9	23.7	27.2
Israel - Israël	2005	4.6	0.7	4.8	1.8	3.6	6.5	3.7	0.5	3.8	3.0	2.6	6.4
	2007	4.5	0.7	4.7	1.7	3.8	6.3	3.9	0.7	4.1	2.9	3.1	6.2
	2008	4.5	0.7	4.7	1.7	3.8	6.2	3.9	0.7	4.0	2.8	3.1	6.0
	2009	4.5	0.7	4.7	1.8	3.8	6.2	4.3	0.8	4.4	3.4	3.3	6.7
Jamaica - Jamaïque	2000	6.1	1.4	6.3	2.5	4.2	8.6	9.9	1.1	10.0	6.9	10.4	10.9
	2007	6.1	1.6	6.3	2.8	3.9	8.6	9.3	2.4	9.4	9.4	9.9	9.0
	2010	6.1	1.7	6.2	2.8	3.9	8.6	9.9	3.5	9.9	9.1	9.9	10.5
	2011	6.1	1.5	6.3	2.8	3.9	8.7	10.4	3.2	10.4	9.9	10.8	10.6
Japan - Japon	2000	2.8	1.2	2.9	2.8	0.1	4.2	2.0	0.1	2.2	1.8	0.1	5.1
	2005	2.5	1.2	2.6	2.7	0.1	3.6	1.7	0.2	1.8	1.7	0.1	4.1
	2007	2.5	1.3	2.6	2.8	0.1	3.6	1.9	0.6	2.1	1.8	0.1	4.2
	2008	2.5	1.2	2.6	2.7	0.1	3.6	1.7	0.1	2.0	1.7	0.1	3.9
	2009	2.5	1.2	2.6	2.8	0.1	3.6	1.7	0.1	2.0	1.7	0.1	3.9
	2010	2.5	1.2	2.6	2.8	0.1	3.5	2.0	0.1	2.2	1.6	0.1	4.3
	2011	2.5	1.2	2.6	2.7	0.0	3.5	1.7	0.1	2.0	1.5	0.0	4.0
Jordan - Jordanie	2000	22.5	17.9	22.7	18.2	15.4	27.6	19.8	14.3	19.9	14.1	18.7	24.9
	2005	13.3	9.1	13.5	3.0	11.5	18.2	12.1	6.6	12.3	4.3	12.4	15.2
	2007	10.5	7.4	10.6	1.5	8.8	14.7	8.7	6.0	8.9	2.7	9.9	10.5
	2008	10.0	6.9	10.1	1.3	8.8	14.1	8.0	5.5	8.1	1.5	9.1	10.2
	2009	9.3	6.2	9.4	1.2	8.0	13.2	7.4	5.4	7.5	1.6	7.6	10.4
Kazakhstan	2008	4.6	4.2	4.6	4.6	0.8	6.7	4.0	4.8	4.0	3.8	0.7	7.9
	2010	7.3	5.9	7.4	5.4	4.3	10.1	7.1	3.8	7.2	5.5	3.9	11.7
	2011	7.4	6.5	7.4	5.4	4.4	10.1	7.2	5.2	7.3	5.5	4.0	11.9
	2012	7.4	6.8	7.5	5.5	4.7	10.0	7.1	4.8	7.2	7.3	4.9	10.8
Kenya	2000	17.6	11.8	17.9	11.6	13.6	23.8	12.9	7.7	13.0	7.2	12.3	19.7
	2005	11.9	7.2	12.1	3.4	6.4	18.1	6.9	3.4	7.0	3.4	4.7	13.4
	2007	11.7	7.0	11.9	3.4	6.3	17.8	7.1	3.8	7.3	2.8	5.5	13.0
	2008	11.4	7.0	11.6	3.6	5.8	17.6	7.2	4.8	7.2	2.5	5.8	12.7
	2009	11.4	7.0	11.6	3.6	5.8	17.5	7.2	4.8	7.2	2.5	5.8	12.7
	2010	11.5	6.8	11.7	3.6	5.7	17.6	7.2	5.0	7.3	2.8	5.8	13.0
	2011	11.4	7.1	11.6	3.6	5.7	17.5	7.1	4.9	7.2	3.0	5.5	12.8
	2012	11.7	7.0	11.9	4.0	5.7	17.7	10.4	6.0	10.4	3.8	6.7	16.7
Korea, Republic of - Corée, République de	2007	7.3	3.7	7.5	9.7	6.1	7.3	4.6	1.5	5.2	6.8	4.9	4.7
	2009	7.2	3.7	7.5	9.6	6.2	7.2	4.3	1.5	4.9	6.6	4.9	4.0
	2010	7.3	3.7	7.5	9.6	6.1	7.2	4.8	1.5	5.3	6.9	4.9	4.8
Kuwait - Koweït	2005	4.9	4.8	4.9	4.7	4.9	5.0	4.8	5.0	4.8	3.2	4.8	5.0
	2007	4.8	4.8	4.8	4.6	4.6	4.9	4.4	5.0	4.4	3.4	4.3	4.9
	2008	4.8	4.8	4.8	4.5	4.6	4.9	4.7	5.0	4.6	3.1	4.7	4.9
	2009	4.8	4.8	4.8	4.5	4.6	4.9	4.7	5.0	4.6	3.2	4.7	4.9
	2012	4.7	4.8	4.7	4.4	4.4	4.9	4.6	5.0	4.6	2.8	4.7	4.8

For sources and notes, see end of table.

Pour les sources et les notes, se reporter à la fin du tableau.

Market / Marchés	Year / Année	MFN rate - Simple average (2) / Droit NPF - Moyenne simple (2)						MFN rate - Weighted average (3) / Droit NPF - Moyenne pondérée (3)					
		Total of non-agricultural and non-fuel products / Total des produits non-agricoles et non-pétroliers	of which: / dont :					Total of non-agricultural and non-fuel products / Total des produits non-agricoles et non-pétroliers	of which: / dont :				
			Ores and metals / Minérais et métaux	Manu-factured products / Produits manu-facturés	Of which: / dont :				Ores and metals / Minérais et métaux	Manu-factured products / Produits manu-facturés	Of which: / dont :		
					Chemical products / Produits chimiques	Machinery and transport equipment / Machines et matériel de transport	Other manu-factured products / Produits manu-facturés divers				Chemical products / Produits chimiques	Machinery and transport equipment / Machines et matériel de transport	Other manu-factured products / Produits manu-facturés divers
SITC Rev.3 (1) / CTCI Rév.3 (1)		5+6+7+8 +27+28-667	27+28+68	(5+6+7+8) -(667+68)	5	7	(6+8) -(667+68)	5+6+7+8 +27+28-667	27+28+68	(5+6+7+8) -(667+68)	5	7	(6+8) -(667+68)
Kyrgyzstan - Kirghizistan	2007	3.9	2.5	4.0	1.9	3.2	5.0	2.1	2.3	2.1	0.8	2.1	2.7
	2008	4.2	1.5	4.3	1.8	3.0	5.5	9.4	0.2	9.5	0.6	4.5	10.0
	2009	4.2	1.5	4.3	1.8	3.0	5.5	9.4	0.2	9.4	0.5	5.0	10.0
	2010	4.1	2.1	4.2	2.2	2.9	5.4	4.1	2.3	4.1	0.4	4.6	5.5
	2011	4.1	2.0	4.2	2.2	2.9	5.4	4.3	2.5	4.4	0.3	5.4	5.4
	2012	4.1	2.0	4.2	2.2	2.9	5.4	4.3	2.5	4.4	0.3	5.4	5.4
Lao People's Dem. Rep. - Rép. dém. populaire lao	2000	8.3	5.3	8.4	8.3	7.5	9.0	12.6	5.0	12.7	9.7	16.6	8.4
	2005	8.4	5.1	8.5	8.0	7.7	9.1	12.3	5.0	12.4	11.7	15.4	8.6
	2007	8.4	5.5	8.5	8.1	7.8	9.0	13.3	5.0	13.4	12.5	16.8	8.3
	2008	8.3	5.4	8.4	7.9	7.6	8.9	12.7	6.5	12.7	12.5	16.2	8.0
Lebanon - Liban	2000	14.6	7.6	14.9	7.9	12.0	18.6	16.1	6.4	16.6	10.7	15.7	19.6
	2005	4.5	2.6	4.6	2.7	3.8	5.5	6.1	1.5	6.3	5.5	4.9	7.9
	2007	4.2	2.8	4.3	2.9	3.8	5.0	5.8	1.6	6.0	5.6	4.9	7.4
Lesotho	2005	10.4	3.5	10.6	4.8	4.1	14.7	17.3	2.4	17.4	2.4	8.0	20.2
	2007	9.6	2.5	9.7	5.8	4.2	13.9	14.3	0.4	14.3	3.8	4.6	19.9
	2008	10.0	0.4	10.1	5.3	4.0	14.3	17.3	0.0	17.4	1.0	5.8	20.0
	2009	9.9	0.4	10.1	5.5	4.0	14.2	13.7	0.0	13.8	0.9	4.1	20.0
	2010	9.6	2.2	9.7	4.1	4.1	13.7	12.0	4.3	12.0	0.8	5.8	19.0
	2011	9.8	3.9	9.9	3.8	3.8	14.4	11.2	0.9	11.2	1.8	3.9	14.9
	2012	9.7	2.5	9.7	4.1	4.0	14.1	13.6	0.1	13.6	1.3	7.7	18.1
Madagascar	2005	11.1	10.1	11.2	9.8	6.8	13.6	6.1	8.4	6.1	7.9	4.9	6.5
	2007	12.4	8.2	12.6	7.3	10.9	15.1	11.9	8.4	11.9	6.9	10.9	13.6
	2008	12.5	8.2	12.7	7.3	10.9	15.3	11.9	8.4	11.9	6.9	10.8	13.6
	2010	11.6	8.4	11.7	7.3	8.2	14.7	9.8	7.3	9.9	6.6	7.1	11.9
	2011	11.5	8.4	11.6	7.3	7.9	14.6	8.9	9.3	8.9	6.6	6.8	11.5
	2012	11.5	8.7	11.6	7.6	7.9	14.5	11.5	9.1	11.5	7.1	8.8	13.9
Malawi	2008	13.2	7.4	13.4	7.1	8.9	17.5	7.7	3.2	7.8	2.3	7.1	15.0
	2009	13.1	7.4	13.3	7.1	8.6	17.5	7.6	3.2	7.7	2.3	6.9	15.0
	2010	12.6	10.2	12.6	4.0	7.9	17.9	8.7	6.1	8.7	2.1	9.3	14.4
	2011	12.8	10.4	12.9	3.9	8.1	18.5	8.2	2.9	8.5	4.0	4.3	14.6
	2012	12.4	9.9	12.5	4.0	7.9	17.9	8.0	2.9	8.2	2.4	6.8	15.1
Malaysia - Malaisie	2005	8.4	2.6	8.8	3.0	5.5	12.5	4.8	4.0	4.9	5.1	2.8	13.3
	2007	8.2	2.5	8.6	2.9	5.2	12.4	4.7	3.9	4.7	4.8	2.2	14.0
	2008	8.0	2.7	8.3	2.8	4.7	12.1	5.5	3.9	5.6	4.1	3.2	13.4
	2009	8.0	2.7	8.3	2.8	4.7	12.1	5.5	3.9	5.6	4.1	3.2	13.4
Maldives	2000	22.1	23.9	22.0	15.6	24.4	22.4	21.4	19.2	21.5	19.5	23.8	20.0
	2005	21.7	23.6	21.6	14.8	24.3	22.3	21.9	20.1	22.0	20.3	23.7	20.3
	2008	22.2	23.6	22.1	15.0	26.0	22.4	22.6	19.9	22.8	20.9	25.3	20.7
	2009	22.2	23.6	22.1	15.0	26.0	22.4	22.6	19.9	22.8	20.9	25.3	20.7
Mali	2005	12.5	9.0	12.6	7.6	9.0	16.1	10.6	8.1	10.6	5.2	9.7	15.4
	2007	12.4	8.8	12.5	7.6	8.5	16.1	11.3	8.4	11.3	4.6	10.9	16.2
	2008	12.4	8.6	12.5	7.4	8.5	16.1	10.8	8.1	10.8	5.1	9.3	15.4
	2009	12.4	8.6	12.5	7.4	8.5	16.1	10.8	8.1	10.8	5.1	9.3	15.4
	2010	12.4	8.6	12.5	7.4	8.5	16.1	10.8	8.1	10.8	5.1	9.3	15.4
	2011	12.3	7.9	12.4	7.3	8.5	16.0	10.4	7.8	10.5	3.5	9.8	15.6
	2012	12.3	7.9	12.4	7.3	8.5	16.0	10.4	7.8	10.5	3.5	9.8	15.6
Malta - Malte (5)	2000	8.0	7.7	8.0	7.1	7.2	8.7	10.3	4.5	10.3	4.3	11.7	8.1
Mauritania - Mauritanie	2007	12.7	9.0	12.8	8.3	9.8	15.8	11.0	8.2	11.0	6.9	9.5	14.0

For sources and notes, see end of table.

Pour les sources et les notes, se reporter à la fin du tableau.

Market / Marchés	Year / Année	MFN rate - Simple average (2) / Droit NPF - Moyenne simple (2)						MFN rate - Weighted average (3) / Droit NPF - Moyenne pondérée (3)					
		Total of non-agricultural and non-fuel products / Total des produits non-agricoles et non-pétroliers	Ores and metals / Minérais et métaux	Manu-factured products / Produits manu-facturés	of which: / dont :			Total of non-agricultural and non-fuel products / Total des produits non-agricoles et non-pétroliers	Ores and metals / Minérais et métaux	Manu-factured products / Produits manu-facturés	of which: / dont :		
					Chemical products / Produits chimiques	Machinery and transport equipment / Machines et matériel de transport	Other manu-factured products / Produits manu-facturés divers				Chemical products / Produits chimiques	Machinery and transport equipment / Machines et matériel de transport	Other manu-factured products / Produits manu-facturés divers
SITC Rev.3 (1) / CTCI Rév.3 (1)		5+6+7+8 +27+28-667	27+28+68	(5+6+7+8) -(667+68)	5	7	(6+8) -(667+68)	5+6+7+8 +27+28-667	27+28+68	(5+6+7+8) -(667+68)	5	7	(6+8) -(667+68)
Mauritius - Maurice	2005	6.1	1.5	6.3	4.2	5.9	7.3	4.9	1.7	4.9	6.0	3.6	6.1
	2007	2.7	0.3	2.8	1.7	2.8	3.2	2.7	0.3	2.8	3.4	1.9	3.2
	2008	2.7	0.4	2.8	1.8	2.3	3.3	3.0	0.3	3.0	3.9	1.9	3.5
	2009	1.4	0.1	1.4	0.9	0.8	1.9	1.8	0.5	1.8	2.4	0.5	2.6
	2010	1.4	0.1	1.4	0.9	0.8	1.9	1.8	0.4	1.8	2.5	0.4	2.7
	2011	1.3	0.1	1.4	0.9	0.8	1.9	2.0	0.2	2.0	2.7	0.6	2.7
	2012	1.1	0.1	1.1	0.5	0.7	1.5	1.4	0.2	1.5	1.2	0.7	2.1
Mexico - Mexique	2000	17.1	12.4	17.4	12.4	14.1	20.7	14.6	11.9	14.7	11.8	13.2	18.4
	2005	13.6	9.4	13.8	9.3	10.4	17.0	11.8	9.4	11.9	9.0	11.1	14.7
	2008	11.2	6.5	11.5	6.9	8.8	14.5	10.0	5.6	10.2	6.4	10.8	11.0
	2009	10.0	4.8	10.4	5.3	7.3	13.7	8.4	4.5	8.6	5.2	9.0	9.5
	2010	7.3	0.7	7.7	2.5	4.0	11.2	4.8	1.3	5.0	3.0	4.5	6.9
Mongolia - Mongolie	2005	4.2	5.0	4.2	5.0	2.1	5.0	3.8	5.0	3.7	5.0	2.6	5.0
	2007	4.9	5.0	4.9	5.0	4.8	5.0	4.9	5.0	4.9	5.0	4.8	5.0
	2008	4.9	5.0	4.9	5.0	4.8	5.0	4.9	5.0	4.9	5.0	4.8	5.0
	2009	4.9	5.0	4.9	5.0	4.8	5.0	4.9	5.0	4.9	5.0	4.8	5.0
	2011	4.9	5.0	4.9	5.0	4.8	5.0	4.9	5.0	4.9	5.0	4.8	5.0
Montenegro - Monténégro	2008	4.6	3.4	4.6	2.7	2.5	6.1	5.0	2.5	5.2	4.8	2.9	7.2
	2009	4.6	3.4	4.6	2.7	2.6	6.1	5.0	2.5	5.2	4.8	2.9	7.2
	2010	4.5	3.7	4.6	2.6	2.6	6.0	5.1	2.0	5.3	4.6	2.9	7.2
	2011	4.5	3.6	4.6	2.6	2.6	6.0	5.5	1.7	5.8	4.7	3.6	7.6
	2012	4.5	3.6	4.6	2.6	2.6	6.0	5.4	2.1	5.6	4.7	3.5	7.3
Montserrat	2012	10.4	4.8	10.6	8.7	8.5	11.9	10.6	5.6	10.7	12.3	12.1	8.9
Morocco - Maroc	2000	28.2	24.1	28.4	26.7	13.2	35.7	25.9	12.8	26.4	26.1	15.5	36.2
	2005	23.7	13.6	24.2	17.6	11.1	32.2	21.2	7.5	21.8	19.4	14.3	30.2
	2007	20.2	13.3	20.6	15.5	9.0	27.4	17.9	7.9	18.5	17.0	13.4	24.9
	2008	18.0	12.7	18.3	14.5	8.3	24.0	16.3	7.7	16.8	15.5	12.4	22.4
	2009	15.0	10.4	15.3	11.3	8.1	19.9	12.9	3.1	13.9	10.7	11.9	17.6
	2012	9.1	4.9	9.3	5.9	5.3	12.4	8.1	2.7	8.4	5.6	7.1	11.4
Mozambique	2005	11.9	4.9	12.2	5.5	8.3	16.2	8.8	6.2	8.8	5.7	8.1	11.1
	2007	10.1	4.7	10.4	5.1	7.6	13.4	7.9	7.0	7.9	4.7	7.6	9.6
	2009	9.7	4.7	9.9	5.0	6.8	13.1	7.6	2.7	7.9	5.6	6.9	10.2
	2010	9.6	4.7	9.9	5.0	6.9	13.0	7.9	3.5	8.0	5.5	6.2	11.4
Myanmar	2005	4.9	3.1	5.0	2.2	3.0	6.9	4.1	2.8	4.1	2.6	3.0	5.6
	2007	4.9	2.9	4.9	2.1	3.0	6.8	4.1	2.6	4.1	2.6	3.2	5.4
	2008	5.0	3.1	5.1	2.2	2.8	7.1	3.9	2.9	3.9	2.7	3.2	5.2
Namibia - Namibie	2005	8.6	1.6	9.0	3.1	3.1	13.4	11.0	1.9	11.1	6.0	10.6	13.7
	2007	8.4	1.7	8.8	3.2	3.1	13.1	10.5	1.5	10.6	6.1	9.3	13.5
	2008	8.4	1.7	8.8	3.1	3.1	13.1	10.3	1.5	10.4	6.1	9.1	13.3
	2009	8.3	1.7	8.6	3.1	3.1	12.9	10.1	1.8	10.2	5.8	9.5	13.0
	2010	8.2	1.1	8.6	2.4	2.9	13.2	10.2	1.2	10.3	5.5	9.2	13.6
	2011	8.1	1.1	8.5	2.4	2.9	13.1	10.0	0.4	10.5	5.2	9.9	13.6
	2012	8.7	1.5	8.9	3.7	3.5	13.1	7.5	0.1	9.7	6.0	5.6	16.9
Nepal - Népal	2000	13.7	8.0	13.9	12.6	12.3	15.2	19.5	5.4	20.4	12.1	33.2	12.5
	2005	14.1	10.0	14.3	13.0	11.4	16.0	16.4	7.2	17.0	14.8	19.6	16.4
	2007	12.5	9.2	12.7	11.9	10.4	14.0	15.6	7.0	16.2	13.0	18.8	16.0
	2009	12.8	9.8	12.9	12.6	10.2	14.2	16.5	6.0	16.9	13.1	18.9	16.3
	2010	12.3	9.2	12.4	11.6	9.7	14.0	14.4	6.9	14.9	12.5	18.9	11.7
	2011	12.2	9.1	12.4	11.5	9.8	13.9	14.3	6.9	14.8	12.0	18.9	11.6
	2012	12.2	9.1	12.4	11.5	9.1	14.1	13.1	7.0	13.6	13.1	16.1	12.1

For sources and notes, see end of table.

Pour les sources et les notes, se reporter à la fin du tableau.

Market / Marchés	Year / Année	MFN rate - Simple average (2) / Droit NPF - Moyenne simple (2)						MFN rate - Weighted average (3) / Droit NPF - Moyenne pondérée (3)					
		Total of non-agricultural and non-fuel products / Total des produits non-agricoles et non-pétroliers	Ores and metals / Minérais et métaux	Manu-factured products / Produits manu-facturés	Chemical products / Produits chimiques	Machinery and transport equipment / Machines et matériel de transport	Other manu-factured products / Produits manu-facturés divers	Total of non-agricultural and non-fuel products / Total des produits non-agricoles et non-pétroliers	Ores and metals / Minérais et métaux	Manu-factured products / Produits manu-facturés	Chemical products / Produits chimiques	Machinery and transport equipment / Machines et matériel de transport	Other manu-factured products / Produits manu-facturés divers
SITC Rev.3 (1) / CTCI Rév.3 (1)		5+6+7+8 +27+28-667	27+28+68	(5+6+7+8) -(667+68)	5	7	(6+8) -(667+68)	5+6+7+8 +27+28-667	27+28+68	(5+6+7+8) -(667+68)	5	7	(6+8) -(667+68)
New Zealand - Nouvelle-Zélande	2000	3.0	0.8	3.1	0.7	3.2	4.1	3.6	1.3	3.7	1.4	3.8	4.6
	2005	3.6	1.0	3.8	0.9	3.9	4.8	4.3	2.2	4.4	1.8	4.6	5.3
	2007	3.5	1.1	3.6	1.0	4.0	4.5	4.5	2.0	4.6	2.0	5.0	5.3
	2008	2.6	0.8	2.7	0.8	2.9	3.3	3.3	1.5	3.4	1.6	3.7	3.8
	2009	2.4	0.8	2.5	0.7	2.9	3.0	2.8	1.5	2.9	1.6	2.8	3.5
	2010	2.4	0.8	2.5	0.7	2.9	3.0	2.8	1.6	2.9	1.6	2.8	3.5
Nicaragua	2000	3.5	1.3	3.6	1.3	1.7	5.2	3.9	2.3	3.9	3.0	3.5	4.9
	2005	5.4	1.6	5.5	1.8	2.4	8.1	5.4	4.7	5.4	3.6	4.2	7.9
	2007	5.1	1.7	5.2	1.8	2.1	7.9	5.6	3.8	5.6	3.7	4.2	7.9
	2009	5.1	1.7	5.2	1.8	2.1	7.8	5.3	3.8	5.3	3.8	4.3	7.1
	2010	5.1	1.5	5.2	1.8	2.1	7.8	5.0	4.7	5.0	3.6	3.9	7.1
Niger	2005	12.8	8.1	13.0	7.3	9.5	16.3	11.8	5.6	12.0	5.6	11.0	15.6
	2007	12.7	7.8	12.8	7.4	9.0	16.2	11.8	5.6	12.0	5.5	11.2	15.4
	2008	12.8	8.5	12.9	7.6	8.8	16.2	9.6	5.4	9.7	3.1	9.3	15.7
	2009	12.8	8.5	12.9	7.6	8.8	16.2	9.6	5.4	9.7	3.1	9.3	15.7
	2010	12.8	8.5	12.9	7.6	8.8	16.2	9.6	5.4	9.7	3.1	9.3	15.7
	2011	12.6	9.1	12.7	7.7	8.7	16.1	10.5	5.3	10.6	3.4	9.8	16.1
	2012	12.6	9.1	12.7	7.7	8.7	16.1	10.5	5.3	10.6	3.4	9.8	16.1
Nigeria - Nigéria	2000	24.6	17.0	24.9	18.3	16.7	31.9	18.2	15.4	18.2	17.0	17.6	20.5
	2005	11.6	7.5	11.8	7.3	6.0	16.3	9.8	10.1	9.8	10.2	6.6	14.8
	2008	10.8	7.4	11.0	7.2	5.6	16.0	8.7	10.1	8.7	7.7	5.3	15.4
	2009	10.7	6.6	10.9	7.2	5.2	15.0	10.0	11.9	10.0	8.6	8.1	14.7
	2010	10.7	6.8	10.9	7.1	7.4	14.8	10.8	9.6	10.8	8.1	10.0	14.2
Norway - Norvège	2000	2.5	0.3	2.6	1.6	0.3	4.0	1.6	0.3	1.7	3.3	0.2	3.9
	2007	0.7	0.0	0.8	0.4	0.0	1.2	0.4	0.0	0.5	0.5	0.0	1.1
	2008	0.7	0.0	0.8	0.4	0.0	1.2	0.4	0.0	0.5	0.4	0.0	1.1
	2009	0.6	0.0	0.7	0.4	0.0	1.0	0.5	0.0	0.5	0.4	0.0	1.2
	2010	0.7	0.0	0.7	0.7	0.0	1.0	0.5	0.0	0.5	0.7	0.0	1.2
	2011	0.7	0.0	0.7	0.7	0.0	1.0	0.5	0.0	0.5	0.6	0.0	1.2
	2012	0.7	0.0	0.7	0.7	0.0	1.1	0.3	0.0	0.3	0.4	0.0	0.8
Oman	2005	4.9	4.9	4.9	4.8	4.9	5.0	4.7	5.0	4.7	3.8	4.8	5.0
	2007	4.8	4.8	4.8	4.5	4.6	5.0	4.8	5.0	4.8	4.2	4.7	4.9
	2008	4.8	4.8	4.8	4.5	4.6	5.0	4.8	5.0	4.8	4.2	4.7	4.9
	2009	4.8	4.8	4.8	4.5	4.6	5.0	4.8	5.0	4.8	4.2	4.7	4.9
	2012	4.7	4.9	4.7	4.5	4.4	4.9	4.7	5.0	4.6	4.1	4.7	4.8
Pakistan	2005	14.5	8.9	14.8	9.9	13.7	17.4	14.4	9.4	14.7	8.5	18.0	14.9
	2007	14.3	8.4	14.6	9.5	12.9	17.5	13.1	8.1	13.4	8.2	15.5	15.3
	2008	13.8	7.3	14.1	9.2	12.4	16.9	12.0	5.5	12.5	6.8	16.1	14.0
	2009	14.0	7.2	14.4	9.6	12.9	17.1	11.8	5.2	12.3	6.9	15.3	14.6
Palau - Palaos	2005	3.2	2.9	3.2	3.9	3.1	3.0	3.2	3.0	3.2	2.6	3.5	3.0
	2010	3.2	2.8	3.2	4.8	3.0	3.0	3.1	2.9	3.1	4.1	3.0	3.0
	2011	3.2	2.8	3.3	5.0	3.0	3.0	3.1	3.0	3.1	5.8	2.8	3.0
	2012	3.2	2.8	3.2	5.1	3.0	3.0	3.2	3.0	3.2	5.6	3.0	3.0
Panama	2000	7.2	7.4	7.2	4.2	6.8	8.4	7.7	6.9	7.7	5.0	7.8	8.6
	2005	6.4	7.0	6.4	2.1	6.6	7.8	6.7	4.3	6.7	2.8	7.5	7.7
	2007	6.4	6.6	6.4	1.9	6.6	7.9	6.7	4.6	6.8	2.6	7.6	7.5
	2008	6.3	6.8	6.3	1.9	6.5	7.7	7.0	4.9	7.1	2.7	8.1	7.5
	2009	6.2	6.8	6.2	1.8	6.4	7.7	7.2	5.3	7.3	2.6	8.2	8.2
Papua New Guinea - Papouasie-Nouvelle-Guinée	2005	4.5	0.0	4.6	1.5	0.2	7.9	1.7	0.0	1.8	2.7	0.1	3.7
	2007	3.3	0.1	3.4	1.1	0.2	5.9	1.1	1.3	1.1	1.3	0.0	2.6
	2008	3.4	0.1	3.5	1.4	0.3	5.7	2.2	1.2	2.2	2.1	0.1	5.9
	2010	3.2	0.1	3.4	0.9	0.2	5.7	2.8	0.6	2.8	1.9	0.1	8.1

For sources and notes, see end of table.

Pour les sources et les notes, se reporter à la fin du tableau.

Market / Marchés	Year / Année	MFN rate - Simple average (2) / Droit NPF - Moyenne simple (2)						MFN rate - Weighted average (3) / Droit NPF - Moyenne pondérée (3)					
		Total of non-agricultural and non-fuel products / Total des produits non-agricoles et non-pétroliers	Ores and metals / Minérais et métaux	Manufactured products / Produits manufacturés	of which: Chemical products / Produits chimiques	of which: Machinery and transport equipment / Machines et matériel de transport	of which: Other manufactured products / Produits manufacturés divers	Total of non-agricultural and non-fuel products / Total des produits non-agricoles et non-pétroliers	Ores and metals / Minérais et métaux	Manufactured products / Produits manufacturés	of which: Chemical products / Produits chimiques	of which: Machinery and transport equipment / Machines et matériel de transport	of which: Other manufactured products / Produits manufacturés divers
SITC Rev 3 (1) / CTCI Rév.3 (1)		5+6+7+8 +27+28-667	27+28+68	(5+6+7+8) -(667+68)	5	7	(6+8) -(667+68)	5+6+7+8 +27+28-667	27+28+68	(5+6+7+8) -(667+68)	5	7	(6+8) -(667+68)
Paraguay	2000	13.9	9.6	14.0	11.2	9.1	17.3	11.7	8.8	11.7	11.2	10.0	14.1
	2005	11.4	7.1	11.5	8.2	6.3	15.2	10.1	6.2	10.1	7.4	9.0	13.6
	2007	11.0	6.4	11.1	7.9	5.7	14.9	6.9	6.8	6.9	5.8	5.2	12.2
	2008	11.0	6.5	11.2	8.1	5.6	15.0	7.1	7.0	7.1	5.4	5.6	11.9
	2009	11.0	6.6	11.1	8.1	5.6	14.9	8.0	6.9	8.0	5.9	6.7	11.0
	2010	11.0	6.6	11.1	8.1	5.2	15.0	8.2	7.0	8.2	6.1	6.8	11.3
	2011	11.0	6.8	11.2	8.1	5.2	15.1	8.8	8.3	8.8	6.2	7.4	12.3
	2012	11.0	6.8	11.2	8.1	5.2	15.1	9.0	8.1	9.0	6.5	7.7	12.3
Peru - Pérou	2000	13.2	12.0	13.3	12.0	12.3	14.2	12.3	12.0	12.4	12.0	12.2	12.8
	2005	9.6	8.5	9.7	6.7	6.1	12.4	8.2	9.4	8.1	6.9	7.3	10.2
	2007	9.6	8.3	9.7	6.6	6.1	12.5	7.6	8.4	7.6	6.6	6.5	10.0
	2008	5.4	3.9	5.5	2.9	1.5	8.3	3.0	5.6	2.9	3.1	1.8	4.5
	2009	5.5	4.0	5.5	2.9	1.5	8.4	3.0	5.6	2.9	3.1	1.9	4.5
	2010	5.4	3.3	5.5	2.8	1.5	8.3	3.3	3.0	3.4	3.6	2.0	5.0
	2011	3.8	1.2	3.9	1.8	1.0	6.0	2.3	1.5	2.3	2.1	1.3	3.7
Philippines	2000	7.2	3.4	7.4	3.9	5.1	9.8	3.5	3.4	3.5	5.2	2.1	7.7
	2005	5.8	2.5	6.0	3.4	3.5	8.1	3.3	2.5	3.3	5.5	2.0	6.2
	2007	5.8	2.5	6.0	3.4	3.6	8.0	3.8	2.7	3.8	4.7	2.9	6.2
	2008	5.8	2.5	6.0	3.6	3.6	8.0	4.9	2.6	5.0	4.8	4.1	6.5
	2009	5.8	2.5	6.0	3.6	3.6	8.0	5.6	2.9	5.8	5.0	5.0	7.2
	2010	5.8	2.5	6.0	3.6	3.6	8.0	5.6	2.9	5.8	5.0	5.0	7.2
Poland - Pologne (5)	2000	10.5	6.0	10.8	9.0	9.2	12.1	10.0	5.6	10.1	7.8	10.7	10.7
Qatar	2005	4.9	4.9	4.9	4.8	4.9	5.0	4.9	5.0	4.9	4.2	5.0	5.0
	2007	4.8	4.9	4.8	4.6	4.6	4.9	4.7	5.0	4.7	4.1	4.6	4.9
	2008	4.8	4.9	4.8	4.5	4.5	4.9	4.4	5.0	4.4	3.8	4.1	4.9
	2009	4.8	4.9	4.8	4.5	4.5	4.9	4.4	5.0	4.3	3.9	4.0	4.9
	2012	4.7	4.8	4.7	4.4	4.3	4.9	4.2	5.0	4.2	3.4	4.0	4.8
Republic of Moldova - République de Moldova	2000	4.5	1.9	4.6	3.5	1.7	6.1	2.8	1.8	2.8	1.5	1.2	4.1
	2008	4.0	1.1	4.1	2.7	1.7	5.5	2.9	0.1	3.1	2.5	1.8	4.4
	2010	3.9	1.0	4.0	2.8	1.7	5.5	3.2	0.6	3.2	2.1	2.0	4.7
	2012	4.0	0.9	4.1	2.8	1.7	5.5	3.4	1.1	3.5	2.3	2.3	4.9
Romania - Roumanie (4)	2005	15.5	6.7	16.0	13.9	12.8	18.2	13.9	4.3	14.3	10.1	13.9	15.9
Russian Federation - Fédération de Russie	2005	9.5	7.6	9.6	6.6	8.4	11.6	8.4	5.6	8.5	8.9	7.6	10.5
	2007	8.6	7.7	8.7	6.6	6.0	11.1	6.8	3.6	6.9	8.8	5.4	9.5
	2008	8.5	7.3	8.6	6.6	5.7	11.0	6.5	3.8	6.6	8.8	5.2	9.2
	2009	8.5	7.2	8.6	6.5	5.7	11.0	6.7	3.8	6.8	8.8	5.5	9.2
	2010	7.8	6.5	7.8	6.2	4.8	10.1	5.8	3.5	5.9	8.5	3.5	9.2
	2011	7.7	6.5	7.8	6.2	4.8	10.1	5.8	4.4	5.8	8.4	3.8	9.0
	2012	7.6	6.9	7.7	6.3	4.4	10.0	6.2	4.2	6.3	8.2	3.8	9.0
Rwanda	2005	21.6	13.4	21.8	16.4	19.2	24.8	16.2	15.2	16.2	9.8	15.5	22.3
	2008	21.2	11.4	21.6	16.0	19.1	24.5	17.1	6.8	17.5	10.5	19.5	18.6
	2009	12.4	8.2	12.6	5.2	6.2	17.7	12.9	11.9	12.9	6.1	8.1	20.6
	2010	12.5	7.6	12.7	5.0	6.1	17.8	11.2	11.1	11.3	6.7	7.2	18.7
	2011	12.5	8.0	12.7	5.1	6.0	18.0	11.1	11.0	11.1	6.7	8.5	15.5
	2012	12.6	9.2	12.7	6.3	6.6	17.7	11.5	19.3	11.5	9.3	5.0	21.8
Saint Kitts and Nevis - Saint-Kitts-et-Nevis	2000	11.1	3.8	11.3	7.1	9.6	13.1	13.3	4.4	13.4	13.5	12.5	14.1
	2007	11.1	4.1	11.4	7.4	8.9	13.5	13.7	7.6	13.8	13.1	12.2	15.3
	2008	11.0	3.9	11.3	7.3	9.1	13.3	13.6	5.3	13.7	14.2	11.9	15.4
	2009	11.0	3.9	11.3	7.3	9.1	13.3	13.6	5.3	13.7	14.2	11.9	15.4
	2010	11.2	4.8	11.4	9.6	8.9	13.1	12.9	5.9	13.0	14.9	10.0	16.0
	2011	11.9	4.8	12.1	9.6	9.4	13.8	13.4	1.7	13.7	13.8	9.6	18.5
Saint Lucia - Sainte-Lucie	2000	17.6	13.3	17.6	12.8	18.8	18.1	17.7	13.1	17.7	14.3	24.3	15.6
	2005	9.6	2.7	9.8	7.3	6.3	11.9	13.5	2.8	13.6	13.2	12.8	14.3
	2007	9.5	2.2	9.7	7.2	6.4	11.8	14.0	3.7	14.1	13.8	14.2	14.1

For sources and notes, see end of table.

Pour les sources et les notes, se reporter à la fin du tableau.

Market / Marchés	Year / Année	MFN rate - Simple average (2) / Droit NPF - Moyenne simple (2)						MFN rate - Weighted average (3) / Droit NPF - Moyenne pondérée (3)					
		Total of non-agricultural and non-fuel products / Total des produits non-agricoles et non-pétroliers	Ores and metals / Minérais et métaux	Manufactured products / Produits manufacturés	Chemical products / Produits chimiques	Machinery and transport equipment / Machines et matériel de transport	Other manufactured products / Produits manufacturés divers	Total of non-agricultural and non-fuel products / Total des produits non-agricoles et non-pétroliers	Ores and metals / Minérais et métaux	Manufactured products / Produits manufacturés	Chemical products / Produits chimiques	Machinery and transport equipment / Machines et matériel de transport	Other manufactured products / Produits manufacturés divers
SITC Rev.3 (1) / CTCI Rév.3 (1)		5+6+7+8 +27+28-667	27+28+68	(5+6+7+8) -(667+68)	5	7	(6+8) -(667+68)	5+6+7+8 +27+28-667	27+28+68	(5+6+7+8) -(667+68)	5	7	(6+8) -(667+68)
Saint Vincent and the Grenadines - Saint-Vincent-et-les Grenadines	2000	17.2	12.3	17.2	13.2	17.4	17.8	16.5	14.5	16.6	12.8	22.3	15.5
	2007	10.1	5.0	10.3	7.6	8.3	11.8	10.8	5.8	10.8	11.8	9.9	11.2
Saudi Arabia - Arabie saoudite	2000	12.1	12.2	12.0	11.8	11.8	12.3	11.3	13.1	11.2	8.5	11.4	12.0
	2005	4.9	4.8	4.9	4.8	4.9	5.0	4.7	5.0	4.7	3.4	4.8	5.0
	2007	4.8	4.8	4.7	4.4	4.6	5.0	4.5	5.0	4.4	3.1	4.4	4.9
	2008	4.7	4.8	4.7	4.5	4.6	4.9	4.5	5.0	4.4	3.1	4.4	4.9
	2009	4.7	4.8	4.7	4.4	4.6	4.9	4.5	5.0	4.4	3.1	4.4	4.9
	2012	4.7	4.8	4.7	4.4	4.4	4.9	4.4	5.0	4.4	2.9	4.4	4.9
Senegal - Sénégal	2005	12.5	8.7	12.7	7.0	8.9	16.2	10.2	6.0	10.4	5.8	10.1	13.6
	2007	12.3	8.1	12.4	7.0	8.3	16.0	10.7	6.9	10.8	5.9	10.5	13.6
	2008	12.2	8.0	12.4	7.1	8.3	16.0	10.4	5.9	10.6	6.3	9.9	13.7
	2009	12.2	8.0	12.4	7.1	8.3	16.0	10.4	5.9	10.6	6.3	9.9	13.7
	2010	12.3	8.3	12.4	7.1	8.4	16.1	10.4	7.8	10.4	6.2	9.7	13.8
	2011	12.1	8.3	12.3	7.0	8.3	16.0	10.0	7.6	10.0	5.9	9.4	13.5
	2012	12.1	7.7	12.3	6.9	8.3	16.0	9.4	5.7	9.7	5.3	9.3	13.4
Serbia and Montenegro - Serbie-et-Monténégro	2005	6.6	3.6	6.8	3.1	5.2	8.8	6.4	2.3	6.8	4.2	7.2	7.9
Seychelles	2000	25.3	21.2	25.4	32.1	21.4	25.7	18.5	21.3	18.5	23.1	17.3	20.9
	2005	7.5	2.1	7.7	1.4	8.1	9.1	11.3	1.4	11.3	3.8	17.2	5.6
	2007	4.6	0.0	4.8	1.6	3.6	6.2	6.4	0.0	6.4	1.9	10.2	2.4
Sierra Leone	2010	12.0	5.7	12.1	8.2	9.1	15.0	9.3	5.6	9.3	7.6	8.5	12.0
	2011	12.0	5.5	12.1	8.2	9.0	15.1	9.1	5.1	9.2	8.2	7.3	14.1
	2012	12.0	5.5	12.1	8.2	9.0	15.1	9.1	5.1	9.2	8.2	7.3	14.1
Solomon Islands - Îles Salomon	2007	9.1	8.2	9.1	8.4	9.1	9.3	7.6	7.8	7.6	8.5	7.0	8.5
	2008	9.1	8.5	9.1	8.5	9.1	9.3	8.6	8.0	8.6	8.7	8.5	8.8
	2010	9.2	8.5	9.2	8.9	9.2	9.3	8.8	7.3	8.8	8.0	8.7	9.0
	2011	9.2	8.5	9.2	8.9	9.2	9.3	9.1	6.7	9.1	8.5	9.0	9.3
South Africa - Afrique du Sud	2005	8.2	1.3	8.6	2.6	3.0	13.4	7.2	0.6	7.4	3.1	7.0	10.9
	2007	8.0	1.3	8.4	2.6	3.0	13.0	7.4	0.6	7.8	3.3	7.6	10.8
	2008	8.0	1.3	8.4	2.6	3.0	13.0	7.2	0.6	7.6	3.3	7.4	10.3
	2009	7.9	1.3	8.4	2.6	3.0	13.0	6.4	0.7	6.8	3.0	6.1	10.5
	2010	7.8	0.9	8.3	2.0	2.8	13.1	7.1	0.4	7.3	2.4	6.4	11.8
	2011	7.8	0.9	8.3	2.0	2.8	13.1	7.3	0.4	7.6	2.4	7.3	11.6
	2012	7.8	0.9	8.3	2.0	2.8	13.1	7.2	0.4	7.5	2.3	7.0	11.9
Sri Lanka	2000	8.0	5.5	8.2	6.4	6.2	9.7	5.7	5.3	5.7	5.4	6.9	5.1
	2005	9.7	5.8	9.9	5.3	8.0	12.4	6.8	4.4	7.0	5.0	9.8	5.9
	2007	9.3	5.6	9.5	5.2	7.2	12.2	6.7	3.9	6.9	4.3	10.8	5.6
	2009	9.0	5.5	9.2	5.1	7.1	11.8	6.3	4.1	6.4	4.0	10.0	5.5
	2010	8.0	4.6	8.2	3.3	4.7	11.7	6.6	2.2	6.7	2.9	10.3	5.7
	2011	7.5	4.1	7.7	3.1	4.5	11.0	6.6	2.0	6.7	2.7	10.7	4.7
	2012	7.5	4.5	7.7	3.4	4.5	10.7	6.2	2.8	6.3	3.8	7.4	6.1
Sudan (...2011) - Soudan (...2011)	2008	18.8	16.0	18.9	7.4	10.9	27.1	14.0	12.6	14.0	10.3	11.0	24.4
	2009	19.1	15.2	19.2	7.8	10.9	27.5	10.6	12.7	10.6	10.9	5.8	30.7
	2010	18.0	14.5	18.1	8.4	10.6	25.7	19.1	13.1	19.2	10.7	15.0	26.9
	2011	18.0	14.5	18.1	8.4	10.6	25.7	19.1	13.1	19.2	10.7	15.0	26.9
Sudan - Soudan	2012	19.4	14.2	19.5	8.8	11.0	27.5	22.0	11.4	22.0	11.1	13.2	29.7
Suriname	2000	10.6	11.5	10.6	9.5	7.1	12.1	11.7	14.1	11.6	9.7	10.9	12.9
	2007	9.9	6.2	10.0	7.8	7.9	11.8	11.7	9.7	11.7	9.6	11.0	12.8
	2010	9.5	5.9	9.7	7.7	7.5	11.3	10.3	9.9	10.3	8.3	10.7	11.2

For sources and notes, see end of table.

Pour les sources et les notes, se reporter à la fin du tableau.

Market / Marchés	Year / Année	MFN rate - Simple average (2) / Droit NPF - Moyenne simple (2)						MFN rate - Weighted average (3) / Droit NPF - Moyenne pondérée (3)					
		Total of non-agricultural and non-fuel products / Total des produits non-agricoles et non-pétroliers	Ores and metals / Minérais et métaux	Manu-factured products / Produits manu-facturés	Chemical products / Produits chimiques	Machinery and transport equipment / Machines et matériel de transport	Other manu-factured products / Produits manu-facturés divers	Total of non-agricultural and non-fuel products / Total des produits non-agricoles et non-pétroliers	Ores and metals / Minérais et métaux	Manu-factured products / Produits manu-facturés	Chemical products / Produits chimiques	Machinery and transport equipment / Machines et matériel de transport	Other manu-factured products / Produits manu-facturés divers
SITC Rev.3 (1) / CTCI Rév.3 (1)		5+6+7+8 +27+28-667	27+28+68	(5+6+7+8) -(667+68)	5	7	(6+8) -(667+68)	5+6+7+8 +27+28-667	27+28+68	(5+6+7+8) -(667+68)	5	7	(6+8) -(667+68)
Swaziland	2005	11.2	2.9	11.3	4.7	4.2	16.2	10.1	1.9	10.1	2.1	5.2	16.3
	2007	10.6	2.1	10.7	5.4	3.8	15.4	9.4	1.0	10.0	3.8	4.2	15.6
	2008	11.1	2.0	11.2	5.6	4.4	16.0	6.8	0.3	7.4	2.8	2.8	16.5
	2009	10.7	1.8	10.8	5.4	4.4	15.4	6.1	0.1	7.6	2.6	2.9	15.3
	2010	11.0	1.3	11.2	3.6	3.8	16.3	14.6	0.0	16.3	0.6	4.7	26.2
	2011	11.0	1.3	11.2	3.2	3.8	16.2	4.8	0.1	5.1	0.7	1.3	15.9
	2012	10.1	2.4	10.3	3.8	4.5	14.6	7.8	8.4	7.8	2.5	6.3	11.1
Syrian Arab Republic - République arabe syrienne	2009	13.5	2.3	13.9	4.8	7.2	20.1	12.7	1.3	13.1	6.3	16.1	12.2
	2010	10.0	1.7	10.3	4.5	7.5	15.0	6.8	1.4	7.3	3.4	16.6	4.8
Tajikistan - Tadjikistan	2010	7.2	7.9	7.2	6.2	5.0	8.6	8.9	4.2	9.0	6.0	5.0	10.5
	2012	7.1	7.6	7.1	5.9	5.0	8.6	8.1	7.1	8.1	5.5	5.0	9.6
TFYR of Macedonia - LERY de Macédoine	2005	8.4	3.4	8.6	3.6	6.3	11.3	7.0	1.9	7.3	5.7	5.9	8.4
	2007	7.4	2.6	7.6	3.2	6.5	9.7	5.6	0.7	6.2	4.4	6.4	6.5
	2008	7.4	2.6	7.6	3.1	6.5	9.7	5.6	0.7	6.1	4.2	6.4	6.5
	2009	7.1	2.5	7.3	2.8	5.6	9.6	6.3	2.5	6.4	3.8	6.0	7.5
	2010	6.6	2.5	6.8	2.8	5.6	8.7	5.9	2.5	6.0	3.6	5.5	7.2
	2011	6.6	2.7	6.7	2.7	5.7	8.6	5.3	3.9	5.7	3.7	5.6	6.6
	2012	6.5	2.3	6.7	2.6	5.7	8.7	5.0	0.3	6.0	3.5	6.1	7.0
Thailand - Thaïlande	2000	15.7	6.7	16.2	11.3	12.2	19.8	10.2	5.4	10.4	10.6	8.8	14.0
	2005	10.4	2.5	10.9	4.7	8.1	14.4	6.5	2.0	6.8	7.0	6.1	7.9
	2007	8.3	1.2	8.8	2.9	7.2	12.3	5.1	1.2	5.5	3.6	5.8	6.2
	2008	8.3	1.2	8.8	3.0	7.2	12.3	5.5	1.1	5.9	3.8	6.4	6.4
	2009	8.4	1.2	8.9	3.0	7.2	12.3	5.9	1.2	6.2	4.1	6.3	7.3
Togo	2005	13.5	9.1	13.6	8.4	9.9	16.8	10.8	5.6	11.0	4.3	10.7	13.1
	2007	13.3	8.9	13.4	8.5	9.3	16.7	10.8	5.6	11.0	4.1	10.8	13.0
	2008	13.0	9.2	13.1	7.9	8.7	16.6	16.2	8.9	16.2	8.5	13.6	18.6
	2009	13.0	8.7	13.1	7.8	8.7	16.6	16.1	7.9	16.1	8.3	13.6	18.6
	2010	12.7	8.9	12.8	7.4	8.7	16.4	15.1	7.2	15.1	6.7	11.9	18.4
	2011	12.9	9.9	12.9	8.3	8.9	16.4	11.8	6.1	11.9	5.7	11.6	13.9
	2012	12.9	9.9	12.9	8.3	8.9	16.4	11.8	6.1	11.9	5.7	11.6	13.9
Tonga	2009	10.8	14.0	10.7	12.2	4.8	13.2	9.0	10.8	9.0	9.7	3.2	13.2
	2010	10.9	13.5	10.8	12.0	4.8	13.3	9.0	12.4	9.0	10.8	4.0	12.5
	2011	10.9	14.4	10.8	12.0	4.5	13.5	8.0	11.5	7.9	8.8	2.4	12.0
	2012	11.3	13.6	11.2	11.1	6.1	13.6	8.6	11.4	8.5	8.7	4.2	11.2
Trinidad and Tobago - Trinité-et-Tobago	2007	5.9	1.4	6.1	2.5	3.9	8.5	5.0	0.4	5.8	6.4	5.5	6.0
	2008	5.9	1.4	6.1	2.5	3.9	8.5	5.0	0.4	5.8	6.4	5.5	6.0
Tunisia - Tunisie	2005	21.4	15.0	21.7	14.3	14.2	27.7	20.2	9.3	20.7	13.1	16.8	26.5
	2008	18.7	7.8	19.3	12.0	11.7	25.2	16.9	3.6	18.2	11.4	15.1	23.5
Turkey - Turquie	2005	4.2	1.9	4.3	4.7	2.2	5.1	4.0	1.5	4.2	4.1	3.9	4.8
	2007	4.3	2.7	4.3	4.9	2.3	5.0	3.7	1.5	4.0	4.6	3.1	4.6
	2008	4.2	1.9	4.3	4.7	2.3	5.0	3.9	1.3	4.2	4.3	3.6	4.9
	2009	4.2	1.9	4.4	4.7	2.3	5.1	3.9	1.2	4.3	4.0	3.3	5.8
	2010	4.2	1.8	4.4	4.8	2.3	5.1	3.9	1.1	4.3	4.2	3.6	5.3
	2011	4.2	1.8	4.3	4.8	2.3	4.9	3.9	1.1	4.3	4.5	3.7	5.0
Tuvalu	2010	7.5	0.0	7.6	4.5	5.9	9.1	0.4	0.0	0.4	1.2	0.3	2.6
Uganda - Ouganda	2000	8.6	7.9	8.6	7.3	4.1	11.2	7.0	7.2	7.0	4.9	6.3	8.6
	2005	12.3	7.7	12.5	4.1	6.6	18.1	11.5	12.5	11.5	6.1	8.1	17.7
	2007	12.2	8.0	12.3	3.9	6.6	18.1	10.2	11.7	10.2	3.9	6.8	17.8
	2008	11.7	6.9	11.9	4.0	5.8	17.7	10.6	12.7	10.5	3.8	7.6	17.0
	2009	11.7	6.9	11.9	4.0	5.8	17.7	10.6	12.7	10.5	3.8	7.6	17.0
	2010	11.7	6.9	11.9	4.0	5.8	17.7	10.6	12.7	10.6	3.8	7.6	17.1
	2011	11.6	6.8	11.8	3.9	5.7	17.6	10.2	12.5	10.2	4.5	7.2	16.4
	2012	11.6	7.3	11.8	3.9	5.7	17.5	9.4	13.4	9.3	4.9	6.2	16.7

For sources and notes, see end of table. | Pour les sources et les notes, se reporter à la fin du tableau.

Market / Marchés	Year / Année	MFN rate - Simple average (2) / Droit NPF - Moyenne simple (2)						MFN rate - Weighted average (3) / Droit NPF - Moyenne pondérée (3)					
		Total of non-agricultural and non-fuel products / Total des produits non-agricoles et non-pétroliers	Ores and metals / Minérais et métaux	Manufactured products / Produits manufacturés	Chemical products / Produits chimiques	Machinery and transport equipment / Machines et matériel de transport	Other manufactured products / Produits manufacturés divers	Total of non-agricultural and non-fuel products / Total des produits non-agricoles et non-pétroliers	Ores and metals / Minérais et métaux	Manufactured products / Produits manufacturés	Chemical products / Produits chimiques	Machinery and transport equipment / Machines et matériel de transport	Other manufactured products / Produits manufacturés divers
SITC Rev.3 (1) / CTCI Rév.3 (1)		5+6+7+8 +27+28-667	27+28+68	(5+6+7+8) -(667+68)	5	7	(6+8) -(667+68)	5+6+7+8 +27+28-667	27+28+68	(5+6+7+8) -(667+68)	5	7	(6+8) -(667+68)
Ukraine	2008	4.7	2.6	4.8	3.2	4.2	5.6	6.4	1.9	6.7	2.5	9.7	4.5
	2009	4.0	1.9	4.1	3.3	3.1	4.9	3.6	1.3	3.8	2.5	4.6	3.3
	2010	4.0	1.9	4.1	3.3	3.0	4.9	2.9	1.1	3.1	2.3	3.2	3.6
	2011	4.0	1.6	4.1	3.2	2.9	5.0	3.2	0.9	3.3	2.3	4.0	3.3
	2012	4.0	1.7	4.1	3.2	2.9	5.0	3.3	1.0	3.4	2.2	3.7	4.0
United Arab Emirates - Émirats arabes unis	2005	4.9	4.8	4.9	4.8	4.9	5.0	4.6	4.8	4.6	4.3	4.5	5.0
	2007	4.8	4.8	4.8	4.5	4.6	4.9	4.6	3.1	4.7	4.3	4.4	4.9
	2008	4.8	4.8	4.8	4.5	4.5	4.9	4.5	2.4	4.7	4.3	4.5	5.0
	2009	4.8	4.8	4.8	4.5	4.5	4.9	4.5	2.4	4.7	4.3	4.5	5.0
	2012	4.7	4.8	4.7	4.5	4.4	4.9	4.1	4.7	4.1	3.8	3.5	4.9
United Republic of Tanzania - République-Unie de Tanzanie	2000	16.5	11.9	16.7	8.7	13.4	21.2	13.0	10.4	13.0	8.9	11.0	18.4
	2005	11.8	7.5	12.0	3.7	6.4	17.9	8.6	8.5	8.6	4.3	7.8	13.0
	2007	11.9	7.8	12.0	3.7	6.4	17.9	7.9	4.1	8.0	2.3	8.0	12.1
	2008	11.9	7.1	12.0	4.4	5.9	17.6	11.6	10.5	11.6	4.6	8.1	18.1
	2009	11.8	7.1	12.0	4.3	5.9	17.6	11.5	10.4	11.5	4.4	8.1	18.1
	2010	11.5	7.2	11.7	3.9	5.6	17.6	8.7	7.4	8.7	3.1	7.3	14.3
	2011	11.5	6.9	11.7	4.0	5.6	17.5	7.7	5.8	7.7	3.8	6.2	13.1
	2012	11.7	7.6	11.9	4.4	5.7	17.5	11.5	12.2	11.5	4.9	7.3	18.2
United States - États-Unis	2000	3.9	1.3	4.0	3.4	1.7	5.3	3.0	1.1	3.0	3.1	1.8	5.2
	2005	3.5	1.3	3.6	3.1	1.6	4.7	2.8	1.4	2.8	2.3	1.9	4.4
	2007	3.5	1.3	3.7	3.0	1.7	4.8	2.9	1.3	3.0	2.0	2.1	4.5
	2008	3.5	1.4	3.7	3.0	1.7	4.8	2.7	1.3	2.8	2.0	1.9	4.3
	2009	3.5	1.4	3.7	3.1	1.7	4.8	2.8	1.3	2.9	1.9	1.7	4.7
	2010	3.5	1.4	3.7	3.1	1.7	4.8	2.8	1.3	2.9	1.9	1.7	4.7
	2011	3.3	1.2	3.4	2.7	1.4	4.6	2.3	1.3	2.4	1.5	1.1	4.5
	2012	3.3	1.3	3.4	2.6	1.4	4.7	2.3	1.3	2.3	1.5	1.1	4.5
Uruguay	2000	14.9	10.5	15.1	11.4	10.9	18.4	14.4	9.6	14.5	12.6	12.8	17.6
	2005	11.8	7.0	12.0	8.4	7.1	15.3	10.5	4.5	10.6	9.2	8.7	14.2
	2007	11.4	6.3	11.6	7.9	6.8	15.0	9.6	2.8	9.8	7.2	8.7	13.9
	2008	11.4	6.3	11.6	7.9	6.6	15.2	10.0	2.8	10.2	6.7	9.5	14.4
	2009	11.4	6.3	11.6	7.8	6.6	15.1	10.2	3.5	10.3	7.4	8.8	14.9
	2010	11.4	6.3	11.6	7.8	6.6	15.1	10.5	3.5	10.6	7.4	9.4	14.9
	2011	11.4	6.3	11.6	7.8	6.6	15.1	10.5	3.9	10.6	7.4	9.4	14.8
	2012	11.3	6.3	11.5	7.8	6.5	15.1	10.9	3.8	11.1	7.1	10.6	15.1
Uzbekistan - Ouzbékistan	2007	14.7	15.0	14.7	9.3	10.8	19.0	10.4	7.8	10.5	10.3	9.6	12.2
	2008	14.9	15.7	14.9	9.7	10.2	19.3	10.4	10.7	10.4	10.0	10.0	11.0
	2009	14.6	15.6	14.5	9.4	9.1	19.3	10.1	10.7	10.0	9.9	9.4	11.2
	2012	14.5	15.0	14.5	9.0	9.1	19.5	9.5	7.8	9.6	9.2	8.3	11.2
Vanuatu	2007	15.3	10.1	15.5	12.4	15.1	16.2	9.9	7.0	10.0	9.4	7.4	15.2
	2008	14.8	11.5	14.9	11.4	13.8	16.3	14.3	9.5	14.4	14.5	12.7	16.0
	2009	14.8	11.5	14.9	11.4	13.8	16.3	14.3	9.5	14.4	14.5	12.7	16.0
	2012	9.4	3.8	9.6	8.4	7.4	10.9	2.7	4.3	2.7	6.2	1.0	11.1
Venezuela (Bolivarian Rep. of) - Venezuela (Rép. bolivarienne du)	2000	12.1	6.8	12.4	8.4	10.3	14.9	13.3	8.5	13.4	9.5	14.0	14.4
	2005	12.1	7.0	12.4	8.4	10.4	14.9	13.5	8.7	13.5	10.1	14.4	13.7
	2007	12.9	7.0	13.2	8.4	10.5	16.3	14.1	8.9	14.2	9.8	14.3	16.6
	2008	13.1	7.0	13.4	8.3	10.6	16.6	15.5	9.0	15.7	10.1	16.4	16.8
	2009	13.0	7.0	13.4	8.4	10.5	16.5	13.5	8.3	13.7	10.0	12.2	17.6
	2010	13.0	7.0	13.4	8.3	10.5	16.6	12.1	7.8	12.2	9.6	10.4	16.5
	2011	13.0	7.1	13.3	8.4	10.5	16.5	10.6	8.3	10.7	8.7	9.6	14.6
	2012	13.0	7.1	13.3	8.4	10.5	16.5	10.6	8.3	10.7	8.7	9.6	14.6
Viet Nam	2005	15.8	1.9	16.6	4.3	10.1	24.2	13.9	1.1	14.3	4.4	13.2	19.8
	2007	15.3	2.0	16.1	4.1	10.1	23.6	13.0	1.1	13.5	3.9	12.5	19.0
	2008	9.4	1.9	9.9	3.7	7.3	13.5	6.8	0.9	7.2	3.0	7.4	8.9
	2010	8.7	1.9	9.1	3.3	6.7	12.5	6.8	1.0	7.1	2.8	7.9	8.7

For sources and notes, see end of table.   Pour les sources et les notes, se reporter à la fin du tableau.

Market / Marchés	Year / Année	MFN rate - Simple average (2) / Droit NPF - Moyenne simple (2)						MFN rate - Weighted average (3) / Droit NPF - Moyenne pondérée (3)					
		Total of non-agricultural and non-fuel products / Total des produits non-agricoles et non-pétroliers	Ores and metals / Minérais et métaux	Manufactured products / Produits manufacturés	of which: / dont : Chemical products / Produits chimiques	Machinery and transport equipment / Machines et matériel de transport	Other manufactured products / Produits manufacturés divers	Total of non-agricultural and non-fuel products / Total des produits non-agricoles et non-pétroliers	Ores and metals / Minérais et métaux	Manufactured products / Produits manufacturés	of which: / dont : Chemical products / Produits chimiques	Machinery and transport equipment / Machines et matériel de transport	Other manufactured products / Produits manufacturés divers
SITC Rev.3 (1) / CTCI Rév.3 (1)		5+6+7+8 +27+28-667	27+28+68	(5+6+7+8) -(667+68)	5	7	(6+8) -(667+68)	5+6+7+8 +27+28-667	27+28+68	(5+6+7+8) -(667+68)	5	7	(6+8) -(667+68)
Yemen - Yémen	2000	12.5	11.3	12.6	9.8	11.1	14.3	12.5	10.5	12.5	8.5	13.2	13.2
	2009	6.2	6.8	6.1	5.9	5.0	6.8	5.3	5.6	5.3	5.2	4.5	6.5
	2011	6.2	6.9	6.2	5.9	5.0	6.9	5.1	5.7	5.0	5.2	4.5	5.4
	2012	6.2	6.3	6.2	5.8	5.0	6.9	6.1	6.1	6.1	5.9	4.6	7.0
Zambia - Zambie	2005	13.6	9.5	13.7	7.3	10.6	17.5	9.9	3.6	10.1	3.9	11.2	12.8
	2008	12.8	9.6	12.9	6.9	9.7	16.9	7.9	0.8	9.2	3.7	9.3	13.7
	2009	12.8	9.4	12.9	7.1	9.5	16.6	8.1	3.8	9.0	4.0	8.9	14.2
	2011	12.3	9.1	12.5	5.6	9.3	16.6	7.3	3.2	8.7	3.2	8.4	15.2
	2012	12.5	9.8	12.6	5.6	9.5	16.9	10.7	2.0	11.0	7.1	9.2	16.1
Zimbabwe	2007	13.1	7.7	13.4	7.9	9.3	18.1	9.7	5.1	14.7	7.5	16.7	16.4

Source:
UNCTAD/WITS, *TRAINS*

Notes:

(1) Product categories are defined in terms of SITC Revision 3, and all corresponding Harmonized System (HS) 6-digit codes have been aggregated for each category.

(2) Simple average for each product group calculated from simple average at HS 6-digit level.

(3) Weighted average for each product group calculated from simple average at HS 6-digit level. Country's own imports at HS 6-digit level for corresponding years are used as weights. Where imports are not reported, mirror imports have been compiled using exports of partner countries.

(4) From 2008 onwards, member of the European Union.

(5) From 2004 onwards, member of the European Union.

(6) For the Union, data refer to the composition of the group during that year.

Source :
CNUCED/WITS, *TRAINS*

Notes :

(1) Les catégories de produits sont définies sur la base de la CTCI, révision 3, et pour chaque catégorie, les codes à 6 chiffres du Système harmonisé (SH) correspondants ont été agrégés.

(2) Moyenne arithmétique, pour chaque catégorie de produits, calculée à partir des moyennes arithmétiques au niveau du code à 6 chiffres du SH.

(3) Moyenne arithmétique pondérée, pour chaque catégorie de produits, calculée à partir des moyennes simples au niveau du code à 6 chiffres du SH. Pour chaque année, les coefficients de pondération sont les importations de chaque marché au niveau du code à 6 chiffres du SH. Lorsque les importations n'étaient pas disponibles, elles ont été évaluées par les données miroir basées sur les exportations des pays partenaires.

(4) À partir de 2008, membre de l'Union européenne.

(5) À partir de 2004, membre de l'Union européenne.

(6) Pour une année donnée, les tarifs de l'Union se réfèrent à la composition du groupe durant cette année.

4

Region, country or territory	Exports - Exportations Millions of dollars							
	1980	1990	2000	2005	2009	2010	2011	2012
WORLD	**395 700**	**831 300**	**1 521 300**	**2 569 400**	**3 547 200**	**3 887 300**	**4 333 600**	**4 425 800**
DEVELOPING ECONOMIES	73 400	150 400	352 000	629 400	922 700	1 110 600	1 251 100	1 345 900
TRANSITION ECONOMIES	9 800	16 700	24 300	57 500	95 000	103 000	122 000	129 400
DEVELOPED ECONOMIES	312 500	664 300	1 145 100	1 882 500	2 529 500	2 673 700	2 960 500	2 950 500
Developing economies: Africa	**13 400**	**21 700**	**33 300**	**59 700**	**81 600**	**90 500**	**92 400**	**97 400**
Eastern Africa	*1 800*	*3 100*	*5 300*	*8 800*	*13 400*	*15 800*	*18 600*	*20 600*
Burundi	-	17	4	35	50	79	112	-
Comoros	2	17	-	43	59	65	74	68
Djibouti	-	-	162	248	322	336	327	-
Eritrea	_	_	61	-	-	-	-	-
Ethiopia (...1991)	125	305	_	_	_	_	_	
Ethiopia	_	_	506	1 012	1 895	2 244	2 834	(e)2 776
Kenya	577	1 138	993	1 880	2 883	3 760	4 100	(e)5 090
Madagascar	79	153	364	498	892	1 039	1 103	(e)1 348
Malawi	32	37	34	67	79	81	82	-
Mauritius	140	484	1 070	1 618	2 239	2 695	3 283	3 408
Mozambique	118	103	325	342	612	599	716	(e)813
Rwanda	34	42	59	129	341	310	431	(e)424
Seychelles	91	172	287	369	600	592	614	(e)569
Somalia	66	-	-	-	-	..	..	..
Uganda	10	-	213	525	990	1 241	1 721	1 994
United Republic of Tanzania	165	131	627	1 269	1 855	2 046	2 363	(e)2 697
Zambia	151	107	115	273	241	311	375	-
Zimbabwe	169	264	427	362	262	307	362	-
Middle Africa	*1 100*	*1 200*	*1 400*	*2 000*	*3 500*	*3 500*	*3 900*	*-*
Angola	-	109	267	177	623	857	732	-
Cameroon	401	382	682	970	1 249	1 159	(e)1 168	-
Central African Republic	54	69	31	44	65	(e)69	(e)74	-
Chad	0	41	51	108	457	(e)390	-	-
Congo	111	99	137	220	378	399	473	-
Dem. Rep. of the Congo	103	230	62	308	541	389	739	(e)719
Equatorial Guinea	-	5	9	36	50	52	57	-
Gabon	325	242	178	146	-	-	-	-
Sao Tome and Principe	3	4	14	9	10	13	18	18
Northern Africa	*5 200*	*10 500*	*16 700*	*29 900*	*43 100*	*46 400*	*42 500*	*44 600*
Algeria	476	497	910	2 507	2 983	3 566	3 738	(e)3 540
Egypt	2 393	5 971	9 803	14 643	21 520	23 807	19 140	(e)21 767
Libya	164	117	172	534	385	410	30	-
Morocco	783	2 009	3 034	8 098	12 336	12 545	13 963	(e)13 516
Sudan (...2011)	292	173	(b)27	114	392	254	838	_
Tunisia	1 067	1 688	2 767	4 021	5 499	5 805	4 779	(e)5 237
Southern Africa	*2 700*	*3 900*	*5 800*	*12 900*	*13 200*	*15 500*	*16 600*	*16 500*
Botswana	101	210	325	834	(b)238	283	517	266
Lesotho	32	41	24	36	44	41	47	-
Namibia	-	132	174	413	653	897	944	(e)829
South Africa	2 463	3 407	5 046	11 300	12 020	14 004	14 824	15 148
Swaziland	36	108	273	283	200	257	(e)242	-
Western Africa	*2 600*	*3 000*	*4 000*	*(b)6 100*	*8 400*	*9 200*	*10 800*	*11 600*
Benin	62	126	136	194	221	376	(e)360	(e)400
Burkina Faso	49	69	31	68	153	304	(e)395	-
Cape Verde	10	35	108	269	480	501	577	597
Côte d'Ivoire	564	590	482	832	1 020	1 046	(e)927	(e)994
Gambia	19	59	-	82	104	131	153	-
Ghana	107	86	504	1 106	1 770	1 477	1 871	(e)2 971
Guinea	-	157	68	83	72	62	77	(e)170
Guinea-Bissau	-	7	(e)5	5	33	44	(e)18	-
Liberia	13	-	-	213	274	158	604	-
Mali	58	85	99	274	354	384	(e)408	-
Mauritania	56	27	47	80	159	119	210	161
Niger	41	44	38	88	100	119	(e)137	-
Nigeria	1 127	965	1 833	(b)1 793	2 218	3 092	3 387	(e)2 930
Senegal	337	515	387	777	1 022	1 052	(e)1 134	(e)1 053
Sierra Leone	49	61	42	78	104	60	160	-
Togo	74	149	62	177	294	320	(e)407	-

For sources and notes, see end of table.

1980	1990	2000	2005	2009	2010	2011	2012	Régions, pays ou territoires
			Imports - Importations Millions de dollars					
447 800	875 200	1 520 000	2 475 300	3 418 600	3 742 600	4 169 300	4 274 000	**MONDE**
139 600	193 800	416 500	700 900	1 092 400	1 306 000	1 497 400	1 594 400	ÉCONOMIES EN DÉVELOPPEMENT
12 400	30 600	28 400	68 500	107 900	123 600	144 400	166 900	ÉCONOMIES EN TRANSITION
295 800	650 900	1 075 100	1 705 900	2 218 300	2 313 000	2 527 600	2 512 800	ÉCONOMIES DÉVELOPPÉES
29 400	30 300	41 700	77 500	136 000	152 100	168 100	169 300	**Économies en développement : Afrique**
3 400	*4 200*	*6 100*	*8 900*	*14 100*	*16 200*	*19 500*	*21 200*	*Afrique orientale*
-	129	43	134	177	168	213	-	Burundi
12	44	-	46	84	94	107	105	Comores
-	-	71	84	128	110	164	-	Djibouti
		-	28	-	-	-	-	Érythrée
208	359							Éthiopie (…1991)
-	-	490	1 194	2 227	2 546	3 322	(e)3 869	Éthiopie
502	700	719	1 137	1 812	2 016	2 141	(e)2 505	Kenya
311	242	522	615	1 262	1 135	1 179	(e)1 184	Madagascar
179	268	167	159	239	212	224	-	Malawi
174	421	763	1 198	1 607	1 979	2 492	2 439	Maurice
124	206	446	649	1 069	1 318	1 510	(e)2 363	Mozambique
133	129	200	304	519	557	618	(e)512	Rwanda
40	80	190	235	383	427	423	(e)371	Seychelles
133	-	-	-	-	-	-	-	Somalie
123	195	459	609	1 394	1 803	2 430	2 419	Ouganda
295	288	682	1 207	1 709	1 852	2 165	(e)2 313	République-Unie de Tanzanie
651	386	335	471	705	940	1 193	-	Zambie
394	495	842	636	612	836	1 096	-	Zimbabwe
3 600	*5 800*	*6 400*	*14 500*	*31 400*	*34 400*	*41 400*	*-*	*Afrique centrale*
-	1 807	2 699	6 791	19 169	18 754	23 670	-	Angola
717	1 045	1 017	1 455	1 780	1 746	(e)1 756	-	Cameroun
142	169	114	105	156	(e)183	(e)186	-	République centrafricaine
24	228	241	1 567	1 881	(e)2 176	-	-	Tchad
480	769	738	1 417	3 213	4 854	5 462	-	Congo
834	758	215	1 167	1 783	2 663	2 889	(e)3 071	Rép. dém. du Congo
-	36	552	921	2 092	2 003	2 489	-	Guinée équatoriale
789	1 007	858	1 042	-	-	-	-	Gabon
6	9	13	11	19	24	31	25	Sao Tomé-et-Principe
9 700	*9 000*	*14 500*	*25 500*	*42 500*	*45 900*	*45 000*	*45 800*	*Afrique septentrionale*
2 697	1 321	2 360	4 783	11 679	11 906	12 529	(e)11 507	Algérie
2 343	3 788	7 513	10 508	13 935	14 718	14 070	(e)16 361	Égypte
2 303	1 385	895	2 349	5 063	6 127	4 435	-	Libye
1 436	1 445	1 892	3 845	6 899	7 436	8 574	(e)8 136	Maroc
353	228	(b)648	1 844	1 907	2 321	2 153	-	Soudan (…2011)
600	846	1 218	2 191	2 974	3 345	3 286	(e)3 288	Tunisie
3 800	*4 700*	*7 200*	*14 100*	*17 000*	*21 000*	*22 500*	*20 400*	*Afrique australe*
216	376	547	864	633	679	791	648	Botswana
50	81	249	369	372	476	542	-	Lesotho
-	354	320	369	575	701	724	(e)648	Namibie
3 295	3 738	5 823	12 125	14 808	18 456	19 664	17 671	Afrique du Sud
80	179	310	403	562	670	(e)796	-	Swaziland
8 900	*6 600*	*7 300*	*(b)14 500*	*31 100*	*34 700*	*39 700*	*38 200*	*Afrique occidentale*
109	131	192	279	496	515	(e)575	(e)643	Bénin
209	216	140	360	559	832	(e)1 081	-	Burkina Faso
7	28	100	209	318	302	319	294	Cap-Vert
1 531	1 626	1 227	2 124	2 608	2 825	(e)2 709	(e)2 902	Côte d'Ivoire
43	53	-	47	83	73	68	-	Gambie
270	301	584	1 273	2 943	3 003	3 667	(e)3 570	Ghana
-	367	285	278	331	396	572	(e)977	Guinée
-	20	(e)29	42	87	103	(e)85	-	Guinée-Bissau
73	-	-	855	1 145	1 079	1 243	-	Libéria
212	374	335	588	826	1 017	(e)1 070	-	Mali
128	137	149	379	638	670	761	1 024	Mauritanie
279	227	132	279	735	843	(e)940	-	Niger
5 285	1 976	3 300	(b)6 624	18 697	21 411	24 573	(e)22 332	Nigéria
340	676	405	806	1 151	1 122	(e)1 240	(e)1 156	Sénégal
85	74	113	91	138	160	255	-	Sierra Leone
167	244	118	251	375	398	(e)502	-	Togo

Pour les sources et les notes, se reporter à la fin du tableau.

5

Region, country or territory	Exports - Exportations Millions of dollars							
	1980	1990	2000	2005	2009	2010	2011	2012
Developing economies: America	**19 000**	**31 600**	**61 800**	**88 100**	**117 700**	**132 100**	**154 200**	**160 400**
Caribbean	*3 900*	*7 500*	*15 500*	*23 100*	*26 000*	*28 300*	*(b)34 800*	*35 200*
Anguilla	-	41	65	99	108	111	119	(e)115
Antigua and Barbuda	45	312	415	463	511	479	493	(e)508
Aruba	-	411	1 012	1 308	1 523	1 546	1 677	(e)1 756
Bahamas	746	1 500	1 973	2 511	2 351	2 494	2 606	2 741
Barbados	345	654	1 020	1 454	1 503	1 638	(e)1 763	(e)1 801
Cuba	-	525	2 642	7 075	8 444	10 212	10 986	(e)10 220
Curaçao	–	–	–	–	–	–	1 227	(e)1 420
Dominica	6	33	90	86	120	131	133	(e)132
Dominican Republic	309	1 097	3 228	3 935	4 836	5 154	5 341	(e)5 554
Grenada	21	64	153	116	139	138	148	(e)143
Haiti	90	52	172	141	379	239	249	(e)278
Jamaica (1)	401	1 027	2 026	2 330	2 651	2 634	2 620	2 674
Montserrat	-	18	16	15	12	11	10	(e)10
Netherlands Antilles	878	1 161	1 571	1 875	2 035	(e)1 987		
Saint Kitts and Nevis	8	54	99	163	132	160	173	(e)176
Saint Lucia	41	151	324	436	353	390	380	(e)397
Saint Vincent and the Grenadines	18	45	128	158	139	139	143	(e)147
Sint Maarten (Dutch part)	–	–	–	–	–	–	902	(e)1 040
Trinidad and Tobago	411	329	554	897	765	874	(e,b)5 812	-
Central America	*6 200*	*10 800*	*19 800*	*25 100*	*28 500*	*30 900*	*33 000*	*36 500*
Belize (1)	-	115	153	302	344	354	340	413
Costa Rica	194	609	1 936	2 622	3 593	4 320	4 990	(e)5 579
El Salvador	139	329	698	(b)946	863	976	1 073	(e)1 320
Guatemala	211	356	777	1 308	1 925	2 291	2 359	(e)2 450
Honduras	82	137	507	700	946	976	1 023	(e)1 073
Mexico	4 591	8 094	13 480	15 666	14 730	15 168	15 298	16 018
Nicaragua (1)	44	60	221	309	563	578	663	712
Panama, excl. Canal Zone	902	–	–	–	–	–	–	–
Panama	–	1 092	1 994	3 231	5 525	6 220	7 261	8 918
South America	*8 900*	*13 300*	*26 500*	*39 900*	*63 200*	*72 900*	*86 400*	*88 700*
Argentina	1 876	2 446	4 936	6 634	10 967	13 648	15 606	15 239
Bolivia (Plurinational State of)	88	146	224	489	515	550	801	(e)860
Brazil	1 737	3 762	9 498	16 048	27 728	31 821	38 209	39 864
Chile (1)	1 263	1 848	4 083	7 134	8 493	10 836	13 133	12 626
Colombia	1 342	1 600	2 049	2 668	4 202	4 446	4 856	5 240
Ecuador	367	538	849	1 012	1 337	1 472	1 587	(e)1 808
Guyana	20	-	169	148	170	248	-	-
Paraguay	164	418	595	656	1 432	1 473	1 917	-
Peru	715	798	1 555	2 289	3 636	3 693	4 364	(e)5 120
Suriname	176	37	91	204	287	241	201	(e)175
Uruguay	468	466	1 276	1 311	2 245	2 576	3 395	(e)3 197
Venezuela (Bolivarian Rep. of)	693	1 183	1 182	1 342	2 227	1 858	1 993	2 205
Developing economies: Asia	**40 700**	**96 300**	**256 100**	**478 600**	**720 400**	**884 900**	**1 000 900**	**1 084 200**
Eastern Asia	*15 200*	*42 900*	*125 800*	*222 700*	*338 500*	*423 000*	*476 100*	*521 000*
China	-	5 855	30 431	74 404	(e)129 476	(e)162 165	(e)176 422	(e)191 430
China, Hong Kong SAR (1)	(e)5 876	(e)18 294	(e)40 433	(e)63 700	84 484	104 048	118 123	(e)123 461
China, Macao SAR (1)	379	1 473	3 280	8 567	18 791	28 693	39 778	(e)45 469
China, Taiwan Province of	1 944	7 008	20 010	25 827	31 774	40 357	45 920	49 064
Korea, Republic of	4 915	10 240	31 540	49 745	73 580	87 282	95 257	110 854
Mongolia	-	48	78	414	415	486	622	(e)755
Southern Asia	*5 000*	*7 700*	*22 500*	*(b)64 800*	*111 300*	*149 500*	*163 500*	*169 400*
Afghanistan	36	-	-	-	1 896	3 156	-	-
Bangladesh (1)	211	392	815	1 249	1 975	2 412	2 423	(e)2 021
Bhutan	-	28	20	42	57	69	82	(e)102
India (1)	2 971	4 625	16 685	(b)52 527	92 627	124 046	137 678	(e)141 207
Iran (Islamic Rep. of)	731	436	1 797	4 999	6 777	8 282	8 817	-
Maldives	52	101	348	323	1 436	1 810	1 981	(e)1 991
Nepal	155	204	506	380	705	672	863	(e)925
Pakistan	652	1 429	1 380	3 678	3 983	6 593	5 041	6 559
Sri Lanka	231	440	939	1 540	1 892	2 474	3 084	(e)3 788
South-Eastern Asia	*9 700*	*29 500*	*68 900*	*119 100*	*(b)167 400*	*202 400*	*237 500*	*255 500*
Brunei Darussalam	-	-	198	616	915	(e)1 054	(e)915	-
Cambodia	-	-	428	1 118	1 525	1 669	2 213	(e)2 545
Indonesia (...2002)	-	2 488	5 214	–	–	–	–	–
Indonesia	–	–	–	12 927	13 156	16 766	20 690	23 143

For sources and notes, see end of table.

Imports - Importations Millions de dollars								Régions, pays ou territoires
1980	1990	2000	2005	2009	2010	2011	2012	
29 900	37 900	74 100	95 300	142 200	171 800	208 400	220 000	Économies en développement : Amérique
2 800	(b)4 800	7 700	9 500	10 900	12 000	(b)17 600	18 300	Caraïbes
-	15	41	56	62	57	56	(e)52	Anguilla
17	105	156	227	228	226	217	(e)219	Antigua-et-Barbuda
-	135	644	712	686	672	857	(e)832	Aruba
226	573	1 026	1 286	1 196	1 181	1 292	1 538	Bahamas
129	250	485	656	711	733	(e)570	(e)392	Barbade
-	(b)1 313	778	1 015	1 673	1 923	2 213	(e)2 278	Cuba
						794	(e)876	Curaçao
6	30	53	50	66	67	68	(e)68	Dominique
399	440	1 073	1 478	1 849	2 185	2 232	(e)2 279	République dominicaine
11	33	89	96	98	94	96	(e)94	Grenade
162	72	282	544	772	1 277	1 140	(e)1 090	Haïti
370	697	1 423	1 722	1 881	1 824	1 946	2 035	Jamaïque (1)
-	12	23	26	18	17	16	(e)17	Montserrat
529	518	668	734	930	(e)917	_		Antilles néerlandaises
6	35	76	95	96	99	97	(e)95	Saint-Kitts-et-Nevis
22	81	133	177	190	203	207	(e)200	Sainte-Lucie
11	32	56	79	94	91	92	(e)97	Saint-Vincent-et-les Grenadines
						237	(e)259	Saint-Martin (partie néerlandaise)
645	479	388	541	383	387	(e,b)5 504	-	Trinité-et-Tobago
8 500	12 700	22 200	28 200	31 500	35 200	40 600	41 400	Amérique centrale
-	60	123	159	162	162	171	188	Belize (1)
286	550	1 273	1 506	1 405	1 783	1 780	(e)2 035	Costa Rica
273	315	933	(b)1 075	953	1 070	1 106	(e)1 184	El Salvador
487	384	825	1 450	2 084	2 381	2 504	(e)2 564	Guatemala
174	220	694	929	964	1 169	1 461	(e)1 492	Honduras
6 514	10 323	16 891	20 823	23 078	25 198	29 391	29 194	Mexique
104	112	351	448	664	720	838	919	Nicaragua (1)
588								Panama, sans la zone du canal
_	689	1 141	1 811	2 199	2 730	3 383	3 860	Panama
18 600	20 400	44 200	57 600	99 800	124 600	150 100	160 300	Amérique du Sud
3 788	3 120	9 219	7 626	12 252	14 808	17 844	18 699	Argentine
259	311	468	683	1 015	1 152	1 661	(e)1 885	Bolivie (État plurinational de)
4 871	7 523	16 660	24 356	46 974	62 592	76 161	80 939	Brésil
1 583	2 076	4 802	7 756	10 503	12 972	15 711	15 061	Chili (1)
1 170	1 750	3 307	4 770	7 023	8 070	9 503	10 577	Colombie
704	804	1 269	2 142	2 618	3 010	3 166	(e)3 251	Équateur
107	-	193	201	272	344	-	-	Guyana
165	434	420	343	538	755	903	-	Paraguay
880	1 164	2 290	3 123	4 812	6 038	6 497	(e)7 385	Pérou
364	171	216	352	285	259	563	(e)594	Suriname
476	393	882	939	1 315	1 553	2 014	(e)2 297	Uruguay
4 253	2 534	4 435	5 339	12 176	13 055	15 690	18 164	Venezuela (Rép. bolivarienne du)
79 700	124 800	299 400	(b)524 500	809 600	976 300	1 114 600	1 198 000	Économies en développement : Asie
12 600	42 700	121 900	213 000	318 000	386 500	449 700	502 600	Asie orientale
-	4 352	36 031	83 966	(e)158 856	(e)193 321	(e)238 068	(e)281 204	Chine
(e)4 029	(e)12 937	(e)24 699	(e)33 977	43 833	51 317	56 417	(e)57 384	Chine (RAS de Hong Kong) (1)
22	247	828	2 384	4 783	7 298	10 302	(e)10 941	Chine (RAS de Macao) (1)
2 554	14 658	26 647	32 480	29 783	37 864	42 026	42 855	Province chinoise de Taiwan
3 738	10 341	33 577	59 696	80 221	95 908	101 107	108 178	Corée, République de
-	155	163	476	558	780	1 782	(e)2 029	Mongolie
10 200	13 800	28 200	(b)70 800	112 800	157 800	164 300	169 400	Asie méridionale
144	-	-	-	820	1 293	-		Afghanistan
481	700	1 620	2 207	3 409	4 392	5 274	(e)5 202	Bangladesh (1)
-	28	46	128	75	90	117	(e)142	Bhoutan
2 981	6 090	19 188	(b)47 287	80 350	117 086	124 592	(e)128 178	Inde (1)
5 223	3 962	3 127	10 840	17 847	23 394	19 504	-	Iran (Rép. islamique d')
43	38	110	213	400	451	540	(e)582	Maldives
88	167	200	435	842	871	782	(e)898	Népal
877	2 073	2 252	7 508	6 551	7 105	7 969	8 163	Pakistan
351	639	1 621	2 089	2 522	3 113	4 012	(e)4 458	Sri Lanka
14 100	28 800	87 900	138 600	(b)190 500	227 100	266 000	279 800	Asie du Sud-Est
-	-	768	1 110	1 434	(e)1 612	(e)1 382		Brunéi Darussalam
-	-	328	642	909	972	1 323	(e)1 546	Cambodge
-	6 056	15 637						Indonésie (…2002)
_	_	_	22 049	22 896	26 089	31 323	33 912	Indonésie

Pour les sources et les notes, se reporter à la fin du tableau.

Region, country or territory	Exports - Exportations Millions of dollars							
	1980	1990	2000	2005	2009	2010	2011	2012
Lao People's Dem. Rep.	-	24	176	204	397	511	550	-
Malaysia (1)	1 135	3 859	13 941	19 576	28 769	31 727	35 859	37 616
Myanmar	53	93	471	257	313	363	612	-
Philippines (1)	1 447	3 244	3 377	4 525	11 014	14 095	17 723	18 490
Singapore (2)	4 856	12 811	(e)28 547	(e)55 702	(b)75 336	94 345	108 656	112 243
Thailand (1)	1 490	6 419	13 868	19 892	30 157	34 326	41 573	49 517
Timor-Leste	–	–	–	-	52	70	65	-
Vlet Nam	-	(e)182	2 702	4 265	5 766	7 460	8 691	9 600
Western Asia	..	..	**38 900**	**(b)72 100**	**103 100**	**109 900**	**123 700**	**138 300**
Bahrain	333	359	933	3 048	3 653	4 047	3 040	(e)2 819
Iraq	-	-	-	355	2 199	2 835	2 828	-
Jordan	1 003	1 447	1 640	2 334	4 554	5 600	5 138	(e)5 684
Kuwait (1)	1 225	1 279	1 823	4 775	11 571	9 324	10 193	(e)10 346
Lebanon	-	-	-	10 858	16 889	16 020	19 736	
Oman	9	-	452	(b)939	1 620	1 899	2 148	(e)2 519
Qatar	-	-	363	3 221	2 002	3 011	7 394	9 922
Saudi Arabia (1)	5 191	3 027	4 779	(b)11 410	9 749	10 689	11 489	11 050
State of Palestine	-	-	473	282	579	831	(e)955	(e)903
Syrian Arab Republic	365	874	1 699	2 910	4 798	7 333	-	-
Turkey	711	8 016	20 429	26 770	34 111	35 004	38 982	(e)42 788
United Arab Emirates	789	764	2 170	4 784	10 157	11 736	12 798	15 069
Yemen, Arab Republic	164	–	–	–	–	–	–	–
Yemen, Democratic	87							
Yemen	–	106	211	372	1 237	1 612	1 248	(e)1 159
Developing economies: Oceania	**300**	**800**	**1 000**	**3 000**	**2 900**	**3 200**	**-**	**-**
Fiji (1)	201	417	432	851	706	859	-	-
French Polynesia	-	-	-	1 081	1 019	900	963	-
Kiribati	4	8	6	11	5	-	-	-
Micronesia (Federated States of)	–	-	18	19	-	-	-	-
New Caledonia	-	-	-	380	499	489	520	-
Papua New Guinea	43	206	243	305	185	310	(e)424	(e)513
Samoa (1)	8	36	(e)59	113	148	159	171	-
Solomon Islands	12	25	52	41	70	107	138	(e)145
Tonga	9	26	14	35	35	(e)41	(e)50	(e)64
Tuvalu	-	-	1	2	2	3	3	-
Vanuatu	-	60	130	139	248	277	286	(e)319
Transition economies	**9 800**	**16 700**	**24 300**	**57 500**	**95 000**	**103 000**	**122 000**	**129 400**
Albania	11	32	448	1 165	2 484	2 308	2 437	2 118
Armenia (1)	–	–	137	411	590	762	824	823
Azerbaijan	–	–	260	683	1 779	2 114	2 732	4 281
Belarus (1)	–	–	1 000	2 073	3 501	4 534	5 289	5 913
Bosnia and Herzegovina (1)	–	–	450	989	1 336	1 201	1 220	1 096
Croatia	–	–	4 071	9 967	11 725	11 579	12 644	(e)11 956
Georgia (1)	–	–	360	715	1 314	1 599	2 008	2 541
Kazakhstan	–	–	1 053	2 228	4 236	4 253	4 509	(e)4 952
Kyrgyzstan	–	–	62	259	860	693	1 117	(e)1 220
Montenegro	–	–	–	–	945	989	1 175	(e)1 172
Republic of Moldova	–	–	165	399	673	700	881	936
Russian Federation (1)	–	–	(e)9 758	24 970	42 411	45 080	55 227	59 174
Serbia and Montenegro	–	–	624	1 909				
Serbia	–	–	–	–	4 156	4 231	5 104	4 822
Tajikistan	–	–	-	146	180	334	564	(e)817
TFYR of Macedonia	–	–	317	519	858	902	1 120	(e)1 068
Ukraine (1)	–	–	(e)3 896	9 354	13 494	16 538	18 806	19 384
Uzbekistan	–	–	447	660	1 036	1 328	1 773	(e)2 152
Developed economies: America	**55 000**	**167 000**	**329 400**	**432 500**	**578 600**	**630 400**	**689 000**	**720 900**
Bermuda (1)	-	-	-	-	1 327	1 400	1 428	(e)1 381
Canada (1)	7 445	19 210	40 230	55 829	65 186	73 577	79 802	79 181
United States	47 550	147 832	289 141	376 674	512 117	555 466	607 743	(e)640 321
Developed economies: Asia	**23 000**	**46 000**	**84 900**	**127 200**	**149 900**	**165 600**	**172 300**	**175 200**
Israel	2 722	4 569	15 701	16 873	21 647	24 348	26 839	29 673
Japan	20 240	41 384	69 245	110 302	128 242	141 284	145 507	(e)145 503
Developed economies: Europe	**229 600**	**438 600**	**706 500**	**1 283 100**	**1 751 900**	**1 821 500**	**2 037 300**	**1 991 600**
Austria	9 423	23 279	22 996	42 446	54 497	54 484	61 113	(e)61 453
Belgium	(a)12 925	(a)28 417	(a)49 747	56 166	86 376	91 665	95 481	(e)96 720
Bulgaria	1 211	837	2 175	4 428	6 836	6 634	7 437	(e)7 275
Cyprus	482	2 004	4 068	6 511	8 028	8 012	(e)8 705	(e)7 927

For sources and notes, see end of table.

278

Imports - Importations Millions de dollars								Régions, pays ou territoires
1980	1990	2000	2005	2009	2010	2011	2012	
-	26	43	39	136	263	331	-	Rép. dém. populaire lao
2 957	5 485	16 747	21 956	27 472	32 245	38 005	42 182	Malaisie (1)
74	72	324	497	617	789	1 090	-	Myanmar
1 439	1 761	5 247	5 865	8 900	11 360	12 367	14 390	Philippines (1)
2 912	8 642	(e)30 112	(e)55 259	(b)82 646	97 738	114 733	117 949	Singapour (2)
1 644	6 309	15 460	26 762	36 515	45 029	52 136	52 739	Thaïlande (1)
_	_	-	-	828	1 031	1 484	-	Timor-Leste
-	(e)126	3 252	4 450	8 187	9 921	11 859	12 520	Viet Nam
..	..	**61 300**	**(b)102 000**	**188 200**	**204 900**	**234 600**	**246 100**	*Asie occidentale*
474	474	757	1 416	1 741	1 905	1 778	(e)1 495	Bahreïn
-	-	-	6 095	8 570	9 869	11 082	-	Iraq
1 094	1 268	1 722	2 542	3 818	4 419	4 475	(e)4 538	Jordanie
3 067	3 359	4 921	8 715	13 636	14 877	17 660	(e)19 140	Koweït (1)
-	-	-	7 895	14 051	13 442	12 956	-	Liban
518	719	1 759	3 145	5 482	6 291	7 066	(e)7 961	Oman
-	-	1 640	4 144	5 918	8 780	16 867	23 906	Qatar
30 231	22 384	25 228	(b)33 120	74 991	76 772	78 017	73 407	Arabie saoudite (1)
-	-	548	504	931	1 143	(e)1 058	(e)1 151	État de Palestine
521	892	1 667	2 359	2 719	3 473	-	-	République arabe syrienne
569	3 071	9 061	11 505	16 795	19 511	20 986	(e)20 651	Turquie
2 279	3 075	8 574	19 367	37 433	42 100	56 518	63 922	Émirats arabes unis
375	_	_	_	_	_	_	_	Yémen, République arabe du
130	_	_	_	_	_	_	_	Yémen, Démocratique
_	683	809	1 241	2 133	2 349	2 273	(e)2 499	Yémen
500	**800**	**1 400**	**3 700**	**4 600**	**5 900**	**6 200**	**-**	*Économies en développement : Océanie*
124	257	329	506	448	509	-	-	Fidji (1)
-	-	-	737	710	597	556	-	Polynésie française
9	19	23	44	50	-	-	-	Kiribati
_	-	57	60	-	-	-	-	Micronésie (États fédérés de)
-	-	-	841	1 102	1 395	1 435	-	Nouvelle-Calédonie
302	403	772	1 278	1 840	2 757	(e)2 978	(e)3 653	Papouasie-Nouvelle-Guinée
15	25	(e)29	56	83	83	76	-	Samoa (1)
28	79	73	58	105	187	194	(e)205	Îles Salomon
6	23	18	41	49	(e)47	(e)60	(e)68	Tonga
-	-	11	12	20	24	33	-	Tuvalu
-	24	70	74	109	121	145	(e)145	Vanuatu
12 400	**30 600**	**28 400**	**68 500**	**107 900**	**123 600**	**144 400**	**166 900**	*Économies en transition*
18	29	429	1 383	2 233	2 008	2 248	1 872	Albanie
_	_	193	531	858	1 004	1 136	1 155	Arménie (1)
_	_	485	2 653	3 389	3 846	5 729	7 203	Azerbaïdjan
_	_	536	1 093	2 109	2 880	3 172	3 637	Bélarus (1)
_	_	263	436	660	534	567	509	Bosnie-Herzégovine (1)
_	_	1 822	3 401	3 853	3 523	3 627	(e)3 718	Croatie
_	_	295	631	974	1 085	1 261	1 440	Géorgie (1)
_	_	1 850	7 496	10 040	11 332	10 921	(e)12 692	Kazakhstan
_	_	148	290	869	924	1 138	(e)1 534	Kirghizistan
_	_	_	_	460	446	440	(e)494	Monténégro
_	_	202	420	713	764	884	957	République de Moldova
_	_	(e)16 847	38 745	62 018	73 411	89 414	106 280	Fédération de Russie (1)
_	_	293	1 478	_	_	_	_	Serbie-et-Monténégro
_	_	_	_	3 856	4 034	4 507	4 128	Serbie
_	_	-	252	291	528	671	(e)1 009	Tadjikistan
_	_	268	555	835	853	984	(e)1 038	LERY de Macédoine
_	_	3 004	7 548	11 505	12 660	13 331	14 141	Ukraine (1)
_	_	_	-	415	486	557	(e)659	Ouzbékistan
51 600	**146 000**	**264 200**	**370 300**	**468 300**	**502 400**	**535 800**	**549 000**	*Économies développées : Amérique*
-	-	-	-	982	1 010	962	(e)949	Bermudes (1)
10 666	28 303	44 118	65 749	81 822	96 353	105 653	106 384	Canada (1)
40 970	117 657	220 108	304 566	385 514	405 079	429 211	(e)441 704	États-Unis
34 700	**89 200**	**127 200**	**148 100**	**165 200**	**175 200**	**187 000**	**197 100**	*Économies développées : Asie*
2 310	4 921	12 047	13 826	16 550	17 830	19 408	20 513	Israël
32 360	84 281	115 106	134 271	148 689	157 395	167 580	(e)176 630	Japon
201 100	**398 600**	**660 300**	**1 148 700**	**1 534 800**	**1 575 000**	**1 733 500**	**1 691 500**	*Économies développées : Europe*
6 204	14 197	16 483	30 791	36 883	37 034	42 138	(e)42 601	Autriche
(a)12 827	(a)26 581	(a)41 847	51 190	77 779	82 630	91 303	(e)92 440	Belgique
549	600	1 670	3 411	5 028	4 162	4 219	(e)4 188	Bulgarie
268	674	1 585	2 708	3 357	3 267	(e)3 720	(e)3 554	Chypre

Pour les sources et les notes, se reporter à la fin du tableau.

5

Region, country or territory	Exports - Exportations Millions of dollars							
	1980	1990	2000	2005	2009	2010	2011	2012
Czech Republic	–	–	6 827	11 856	19 295	20 910	23 078	(e)22 008
Denmark	4 785	12 830	23 960	43 436	56 089	62 052	66 654	(e)65 150
Estonia	–	–	1 502	3 248	4 448	4 561	5 421	(e)5 451
Faeroe Islands	-	-	54	133	170	191	(e)207	-
Finland	2 733	4 649	7 684	16 995	27 738	27 003	30 121	(e)29 725
France	43 506	(e)67 782	80 603	122 331	(b)190 705	192 159	224 461	(e)211 515
Germany, Federal Republic of	32 817	–	–	–	–	–	–	–
Germany	–	62 447	83 136	163 814	237 728	243 502	264 729	(e)261 763
Greece	3 947	6 560	19 337	34 273	37 484	37 717	39 771	(e)33 951
Hungary	-	2 884	6 086	12 867	18 399	19 404	21 635	(e)20 090
Iceland	280	560	1 043	2 034	2 349	2 490	2 969	(e)3 058
Ireland	1 381	3 445	16 885	59 965	93 912	98 419	113 224	(e)115 970
Italy	19 192	49 666	56 447	89 410	94 185	97 963	106 645	(e)104 289
Latvia	–	–	1 172	2 169	3 831	3 680	4 481	(e)4 530
Lithuania	–	–	1 059	3 115	3 655	4 090	5 202	(e)5 894
Luxembourg	-	-	-	40 477	57 792	63 767	71 182	(e)70 205
Malta	481	752	1 095	2 011	3 957	4 497	4 984	(e)4 885
Netherlands	17 150	29 302	52 395	92 023	113 808	118 005	138 257	(e)133 615
Norway	8 615	12 765	17 718	29 318	38 446	39 721	42 445	(e)43 871
Poland	2 018	3 200	10 425	16 292	28 679	32 746	37 542	(e)37 814
Portugal	2 006	5 096	9 057	15 206	22 669	23 281	26 633	(e)24 549
Romania	1 063	610	1 746	5 089	9 817	8 785	10 095	(e)9 828
Slovakia	–	–	2 301	4 408	6 032	5 823	6 602	(e)7 157
Slovenia	–	–	1 893	3 995	6 039	6 114	6 727	(e)6 547
Spain	11 593	27 937	52 582	94 820	123 296	124 324	142 100	(e)136 649
Sweden	7 489	13 726	21 624	43 043	58 043	63 729	74 550	(e)76 415
Switzerland	6 888	20 110	30 693	49 821	76 247	83 498	96 419	(e)92 681
United Kingdom	36 452	56 422	120 150	207 672	258 104	267 350	293 789	(e)283 608
Developed economies: Oceania	**4 900**	**12 700**	**24 300**	**39 700**	**49 100**	**56 100**	**61 900**	**62 800**
Australia (1)	3 862	10 204	19 894	31 047	40 969	47 119	51 791	(e)52 811
New Zealand	1 009	2 494	(e)4 380	(e)8 682	(e)8 130	(e)9 025	(e)10 124	(e)10 035

Sources:

UNCTAD and WTO and ITC secretariats' calculations, based on:

- IMF, *Balance of Payments Statistics*
- Eurostat, online database
- UN/DESA/Statistics Division, *UN Service Trade Statistical Database*
- OECD, *OECD.Stat*
- Other international and national sources

Notes:

- The statistics presented correspond to the concepts and definitions from the IMF *Balance of Payments Manual* (*BPM5, 1993*).

  Total services cover the following main categories: transport, travel, communications, construction, insurance, financial services, computer and information services, royalties and license fees, other business services, personal, cultural and recreational services, and government services.

(a) Refers to Belgium-Luxembourg Economic Union.
(1) From 2009 onwards, data adjusted according to BPM5 methodology.
(2) From 2009 onwards, data adjusted according to BPM5 methodology. Data do not include merchanting.

Imports - Importations Millions de dollars								Régions, pays ou territoires
1980	1990	2000	2005	2009	2010	2011	2012	
–	–	5 414	10 274	15 416	16 966	19 331	(e)18 988	République tchèque
3 596	10 218	21 083	37 047	52 210	53 349	59 044	(e)57 834	Danemark
–	–	938	2 204	2 516	2 785	3 698	(e)3 883	Estonie
-	-	97	230	343	366	(e)394	-	Îles Féroé
2 555	7 627	9 405	17 749	27 198	26 622	29 686	(e)30 289	Finlande
32 148	(e)51 947	60 802	107 026	(b)165 257	171 149	190 783	(e)172 555	France
45 143								Allemagne, Rép. fédérale d'
–	85 125	138 138	212 672	260 843	267 670	296 278	(e)294 505	Allemagne
1 428	3 000	11 292	14 748	19 923	20 170	19 433	(e)15 551	Grèce
–	2 400	4 950	11 354	15 674	15 514	17 182	(e)15 674	Hongrie
263	556	1 164	2 550	2 036	2 206	2 610	(e)2 780	Islande
1 593	5 178	28 922	71 533	103 499	107 213	115 740	(e)112 166	Irlande
16 249	46 795	55 395	00 076	105 903	110 171	116 353	(e)106 782	Italie
–	–	697	1 562	2 269	2 198	2 632	(e)2 594	Lettonie
–	–	679	2 060	3 046	3 013	3 816	(e)4 282	Lituanie
-	-	-	24 243	33 340	36 776	41 417	(e)40 503	Luxembourg
243	514	758	1 205	2 570	2 854	3 070	(e)2 963	Malte
18 148	29 708	53 260	84 482	108 348	106 244	121 637	(e)119 957	Pays-Bas
6 996	12 358	14 991	29 568	36 724	42 911	46 057	(e)49 018	Norvège
2 023	2 847	9 011	15 562	23 935	29 651	31 967	(e)31 680	Pologne
1 525	4 005	7 023	10 341	14 354	14 392	15 867	(e)13 319	Portugal
1 045	787	1 992	5 518	10 223	8 241	9 610	(e)9 120	Roumanie
–	–	1 861	4 087	7 458	6 809	7 118	(e)6 772	Slovaquie
–	–	1 442	2 851	4 420	4 411	4 722	(e)4 359	Slovénie
5 732	16 055	33 207	67 164	88 522	87 884	94 501	(e)89 508	Espagne
7 018	17 058	23 977	35 349	45 273	47 136	54 919	(e)55 059	Suède
4 885	8 651	12 801	22 862	34 043	36 461	45 103	(e)46 819	Suisse
27 933	48 737	99 383	162 950	170 202	171 160	180 701	(e)179 871	Royaume-Uni
8 400	**17 100**	**23 400**	**38 700**	**49 900**	**60 400**	**71 200**	**75 100**	**Économies développées : Océanie**
6 568	13 772	18 934	30 505	41 982	51 053	60 287	(e)63 940	Australie (1)
1 843	3 324	(e)4 498	(e)8 243	(e)7 952	(e)9 324	(e)10 931	(e)11 110	Nouvelle-Zélande

Sources :

Calculs des secrétariats de la CNUCED et de l'OMC et du CCI, sur la base de :

- FMI, *Statistiques de la balance des paiements*

- Eurostat, base de données en ligne

- ONU/DAES/Division des statistiques, *ONU Service Trade Statistical Database*

- OCDE, *OECD.Stat*

- Autres sources internationales et nationales

Notes :

- Les statistiques présentées correspondent aux concepts et définitions du *Manuel de la balance des paiements* du FMI (*MBP5, 1993*).

  Les services totaux comprennent les catégories suivantes : transports, voyages, communications, bâtiment et travaux publics (BTP), assurances, services financiers, informatique et information, redevances et droits de licence, autres services aux entreprises, services personnels, culturels et relatifs aux loisirs, et les services fournis ou reçus par les administrations publiques.

(a)   Se réfère à l'Union économique belgo-luxembourgeoise.

(1)   À partir de 2009, les données ont été ajustées conformément à la méthodologie MBP5.

(2)   À partir de 2009, les données ont été ajustées conformément à la méthodologie MBP5. Les données ne couvrent pas le négoce international.

5

5.1.2 Value of exports and imports of services of economic groupings

Economic grouping	Exports - Exportations Millions of dollars							
	1980	1990	2000	2005	2009	2010	2011	2012
DEVELOPING ECONOMIES	**73 400**	**150 400**	**352 000**	**629 400**	**922 700**	**1 110 600**	**1 251 100**	**1 345 900**
Developing economies excluding China	71 300	144 500	321 600	555 000	793 200	948 400	1 074 600	1 154 500
Developing economies excluding LDCs	70 200	146 200	344 900	617 700	901 200	1 085 600	1 221 300	1 315 100
High-income developing economies	45 400	96 500	225 600	369 400	(b)505 800	595 400	686 800	740 800
Middle-income developing economies	17 600	39 800	93 600	180 500	281 700	339 000	368 800	400 900
Low-income developing economies	10 400	14 100	32 900	(b)79 500	135 100	176 200	195 500	204 300
Heavily indebted poor countries (IMF)	3 600	4 500	6 700	12 000	20 400	22 200	27 200	-
Landlocked developing countries	1 800	3 200	7 500	12 500	24 500	28 300	34 700	-
Small island developing States	2 700	5 800	9 600	12 800	15 000	16 600	(b)23 000	23 900
Least developed countries	*3 200*	*4 200*	*7 100*	*11 700*	*21 500*	*25 000*	*29 700*	*(u)30 900*
Africa and Haiti	2 400	3 100	4 200	7 600	12 800	13 800	17 400	18 200
Asia	700	900	2 600	3 700	8 100	10 500	11 500	-
Islands	100	100	300	400	600	700	800	-
Major petroleum and gas exporters	*11 400*	*8 700*	*15 900*	*(b)36 800*	*52 500*	*57 600*	*65 500*	*70 400*
Africa	1 900	1 700	3 200	(b)5 000	6 200	7 900	7 900	7 400
America	700	1 200	1 200	1 300	2 200	1 900	2 000	2 200
Asia	8 800	5 900	11 500	(b)30 500	44 100	47 800	55 700	60 800
Major exporters of manufactured goods	*26 900*	*72 600*	*192 200*	*324 500*	*(b)468 300*	*569 400*	*637 100*	*690 200*
America	4 600	8 100	13 500	15 700	14 700	15 200	15 300	16 000
Asia	22 300	64 500	178 800	308 800	(b)453 600	554 300	621 800	674 200
Emerging economies	*24 500*	*57 300*	*141 500*	*218 500*	*(b)305 200*	*363 200*	*413 900*	*448 200*
America	10 200	16 900	33 600	47 800	65 600	75 200	86 600	88 900
Asia	14 300	40 300	107 900	170 700	(b)239 600	288 000	327 300	359 300
Newly industrialized Asian economies	*22 100*	*64 400*	*156 900*	*251 900*	*(b)348 300*	*422 900*	*483 800*	*524 400*
First tier	17 600	48 400	120 500	195 000	(b)265 200	326 000	368 000	395 600
Second tier	4 500	16 000	36 400	56 900	83 100	96 900	115 800	128 800
Developing economies: Africa	**13 400**	**21 700**	**33 300**	**59 700**	**81 600**	**90 500**	**92 400**	**97 400**
Northern Africa excluding Sudan	4 900	10 300	16 700	29 800	42 700	46 100	41 600	44 100
Sub-Saharan Africa	8 600	11 400	16 600	29 900	38 900	44 300	50 800	53 300
Sub-Saharan Africa excluding South Africa	6 100	8 000	11 500	(b)18 600	26 900	30 300	35 900	38 200
Developing economies: America	**19 000**	**31 600**	**61 800**	**88 100**	**117 700**	**132 100**	**154 200**	**160 400**
Central America and Greater Caribbean Islands excluding Puerto Rico	7 400	13 500	27 800	38 600	44 800	49 100	52 200	55 200
Central America and Greater Caribbean Islands excluding Mexico and Puerto Rico	2 800	5 400	14 400	22 900	30 100	34 000	36 900	39 200
South America and Central America	15 100	24 100	46 300	65 000	91 700	103 700	119 400	125 100
South America excluding Brazil	7 200	9 600	17 000	23 900	35 500	41 000	48 200	48 800
Developing economies: Asia	**40 700**	**96 300**	**256 100**	**478 600**	**720 400**	**884 900**	**1 000 900**	**1 084 200**
Eastern and South-Eastern Asia excluding China	22 800	66 600	164 300	267 300	(b)376 400	463 300	537 200	585 100
Southern Asia excluding India	2 100	3 000	5 800	12 300	18 700	25 500	25 800	-

Sources:

UNCTAD and WTO and ITC secretariats' calculations, based on:

- IMF, *Balance of Payments Statistics*
- Eurostat, online database
- UN/DESA/Statistics Division, *UN Service Trade Statistical Database*
- OECD, *OECD.Stat*
- Other international and national sources

Imports - Importations Millions de dollars								Groupements économiques
1980	1990	2000	2005	2009	2010	2011	2012	
139 600	**193 800**	**416 500**	**700 900**	**1 092 400**	**1 306 000**	**1 497 400**	**1 594 400**	**ÉCONOMIES EN DÉVELOPPEMENT**
137 300	189 400	380 500	617 000	933 600	1 112 700	1 259 300	1 313 200	Économies en développement sans la Chine
131 900	183 300	402 100	672 200	1 037 900	1 245 500	1 425 500	1 517 600	Économies en développement sans les PMA
85 100	123 200	256 800	391 400	582 600	680 700	782 700	817 400	Économies en développement à revenu élevé
31 600	44 500	113 400	208 500	342 300	406 600	474 100	529 700	Économies en développement à revenu intermédiaire
22 800	26 000	46 300	(b)101 000	167 600	218 700	240 600	247 300	Économies en développement à revenu faible
9 400	11 100	12 500	23 700	36 900	43 800	49 800	-	Pays pauvres très endettés (FMI)
4 500	0 500	10 900	23 600	35 800	42 100	49 700	-	Pays en développement sans littoral
2 200	3 800	6 500	9 000	11 300	13 100	(b)19 700	21 000	Petits États insulaires en développement
7 700	*10 500*	*14 400*	*28 700*	*54 500*	*60 600*	*71 900*	*76 800*	*Pays les moins avancés*
6 200	8 500	10 700	23 200	44 300	47 900	57 100	61 200	Afrique et Haïti
1 400	1 800	3 400	5 300	8 900	11 000	12 700	13 400	Asie
100	200	300	300	1 300	1 600	2 100	-	Îles
60 000	*46 000*	*60 800*	*(b)111 300*	*230 700*	*253 300*	*287 600*	*301 900*	*Principaux exportateurs de pétrole et de gaz*
10 800	6 500	9 300	(b)20 500	54 600	58 200	65 200	63 800	Afrique
4 300	2 500	4 400	5 300	12 200	13 100	15 700	18 200	Amérique
44 900	37 000	47 100	(b)85 400	163 900	182 100	206 700	219 900	Asie
26 600	*73 000*	*200 200*	*334 900*	*(b)482 400*	*578 600*	*671 900*	*731 700*	*Principaux exportateurs d'articles manufacturés*
6 500	10 300	16 900	20 800	23 100	25 200	29 400	29 200	Amérique
20 100	62 700	183 300	314 100	(b)459 300	553 400	642 500	702 500	Asie
31 400	*69 600*	*172 400*	*259 800*	*(b)354 300*	*430 400*	*493 600*	*515 200*	*Économies émergentes*
17 600	24 200	49 900	63 700	97 600	121 600	145 600	151 300	Amérique
13 800	45 400	122 500	196 200	(b)256 600	308 800	348 000	363 900	Asie
24 100	*66 200*	*168 100*	*258 000*	*(b)332 300*	*397 600*	*448 100*	*469 600*	*Économies nouvellement industrialisées d'Asie*
13 200	46 600	115 000	181 400	(b)236 500	282 800	314 300	326 400	Première génération
10 900	19 600	53 100	76 600	95 800	114 700	133 800	143 200	Deuxième génération
29 400	**30 300**	**41 700**	**77 500**	**136 000**	**152 100**	**168 100**	**169 300**	Économies en développement : Afrique
9 400	8 800	13 900	23 700	40 600	43 500	42 900	43 800	Afrique septentrionale sans le Soudan
20 000	21 500	27 800	53 800	95 500	108 600	125 200	125 400	Afrique subsaharienne
16 700	17 800	22 000	(b)41 700	80 700	90 200	105 600	107 800	Afrique subsaharienne sans l'Afrique du Sud
29 900	**37 900**	**74 100**	**95 300**	**142 200**	**171 800**	**208 400**	**220 000**	Économies en développement : Amérique
9 600	15 200	26 100	33 000	37 700	42 400	48 200	49 100	Amérique centrale et Grandes Antilles sans Porto Rico
3 100	(b)4 900	9 200	12 100	14 600	17 200	18 800	19 900	Amérique centrale et Grandes Antilles sans le Mexique et Porto Rico
27 100	33 000	66 400	85 800	131 300	159 800	190 800	201 700	Amérique du Sud et Amérique centrale
13 700	12 900	27 500	33 300	52 800	62 000	74 000	79 300	Amérique du Sud sans le Brésil
79 700	**124 800**	**299 400**	**(b)524 500**	**809 600**	**976 300**	**1 114 600**	**1 198 000**	Économies en développement : Asie
24 500	67 200	173 800	267 600	(b)349 700	420 200	477 700	501 200	Asie orientale et Asie du Sud-Est sans la Chine
7 200	7 700	9 000	23 500	32 500	40 700	39 700	-	Asie méridionale sans l'Inde

Sources :

Calculs des secrétariats de la CNUCED et de l'OMC et du CCI, sur la base de :

- FMI, *Statistiques de la balance des paiements*

- Eurostat, base de données en ligne

- ONU/DAES/Division des statistiques, *ONU Service Trade Statistical Database*

- OCDE, *OECD.Stat*

- Autres sources internationales et nationales

5

Trade group	Exports - Exportations Millions of dollars							
	1980	1990	2000	2005	2009	2010	2011	2012
AFRICA								
CEMAC	900	800	1 100	1 500	2 400	2 200	2 400	-
CEPGL	100	300	100	500	900	800	1 300	1 300
COMESA	4 500	9 500	14 700	23 100	34 000	38 300	36 500	40 300
EAC	800	1 400	1 900	3 800	6 100	7 400	8 700	10 300
ECCAS	1 200	1 200	1 500	2 200	3 900	3 900	4 400	-
ECOWAS	2 600	3 000	3 900	(b)6 000	8 200	9 100	10 600	11 500
MRU	700	900	700	1 200	1 500	1 300	1 800	-
SADC	3 900	5 700	9 400	18 100	21 100	24 400	26 900	27 800
UMA	2 500	4 300	6 900	15 200	21 400	22 400	22 700	22 500
WAEMU	1 200	1 600	1 200	2 400	3 200	3 600	3 800	-
AMERICA								
ANCOM	2 500	3 100	4 700	6 500	9 700	10 200	11 600	13 000
CACM	700	1 500	4 100	(b)5 900	7 900	9 100	10 100	11 100
CARICOM	2 400	4 500	7 400	9 400	9 900	10 200	(b)15 400	16 100
FTAA	72 500	196 500	385 800	510 200	682 900	747 300	826 800	865 300
LAIA	14 600	22 900	44 400	65 600	91 500	104 000	119 400	123 300
MERCOSUR	5 000	8 400	17 700	26 500	45 100	51 900	61 900	63 400
NAFTA	59 600	175 100	342 900	448 200	592 000	644 200	702 800	735 500
OAS	72 900	197 000	388 500	517 300	691 400	757 500	837 800	875 600
OECS	100	700	1 300	1 500	1 500	1 600	1 600	1 600
ASIA								
APTA	10 400	21 600	80 600	(b)179 700	299 900	378 900	415 400	449 900
ASEAN	9 700	29 500	68 900	119 100	(b)167 300	202 300	237 500	255 400
ECO	2 600	10 700	26 600	40 300	58 200	65 600	71 600	80 500
GCC	..	..	10 500	(b)28 200	38 800	40 700	47 100	51 700
SAARC	4 300	7 200	20 700	(b)59 800	104 600	141 200	154 700	160 400
EUROPE								
EFTA	15 800	33 400	49 500	81 200	117 000	125 700	141 800	139 600
EU27	213 800	405 100	657 000	1 198 100	1 631 400	1 690 700	1 890 600	1 845 000
Euro area	157 700	311 500	461 700	848 100	b)1 168 700	1 201 300	1 346 200	1 312 400
OCEANIA								
MSG	300	700	900	1 300	1 200	1 600	-	-
INTERREGIONAL								
ACP	11 900	18 300	30 800	51 800	63 500	71 700	84 600	87 500
APEC	114 500	309 600	642 300	964 100	1 308 500	1 495 200	1 653 200	1 747 700
BSEC	11 700	25 400	58 700	108 300	154 500	160 800	183 400	187 100
CIS	–	–	18 000	41 900	72 100	80 200	96 300	104 600

Sources:

UNCTAD and WTO and ITC secretariats' calculations, based on:

- IMF, *Balance of Payments Statistics*
- Eurostat, online database
- UN/DESA/Statistics Division, *UN Service Trade Statistical Database*
- OECD, *OECD.Stat*
- Other international and national sources

Imports - Importations Millions de dollars								Groupements commerciaux
1980	1990	2000	2005	2009	2010	2011	2012	
								AFRIQUE
2 200	3 300	3 500	6 500	10 400	12 900	14 800	-	CEMAC
1 100	1 000	500	1 600	2 500	3 400	3 700	3 800	CEPGL
8 800	9 900	14 400	23 100	34 400	39 400	40 000	43 100	COMESA
1 100	1 400	2 100	3 400	5 600	6 400	7 600	8 000	CAE
3 800	6 100	6 700	14 900	32 100	35 100	42 200	-	CEEAC
8 800	6 400	7 100	(b)14 100	30 500	34 100	38 900	37 200	CEDEAO
1 800	2 200	1 800	3 300	4 200	4 500	4 800	-	UFM
7 400	9 700	14 100	27 300	45 500	51 100	59 400	60 100	SADC
7 200	5 100	6 500	13 500	27 300	29 500	29 600	28 500	UMA
2 900	3 500	2 600	4 700	6 800	7 700	8 200	-	UEMOA
								AMÉRIQUE
3 000	4 000	7 300	10 700	15 500	18 300	20 800	23 100	ANCOM
1 300	1 600	4 100	(b)5 400	6 100	7 100	7 700	8 200	MCAC
2 100	2 700	4 700	6 200	6 500	7 000	(b)12 400	13 000	CARICOM
80 700	181 800	336 200	463 100	606 200	669 600	739 100	763 800	ZLEA
25 500	32 400	62 600	80 700	126 200	153 900	184 100	194 500	ALADI
13 800	14 300	32 100	39 300	74 300	93 900	114 300	122 900	MERCOSUR
58 100	156 300	281 100	391 100	490 400	526 600	564 300	577 300	ALENA
81 000	183 100	336 900	464 100	607 900	671 500	741 300	766 100	OEA
100	300	600	800	900	900	800	800	OECO
								ASIE
9 800	22 100	92 100	(b)195 300	325 500	414 100	473 400	527 600	ACAP
14 100	28 800	87 900	138 600	(b)189 700	226 000	264 500	278 300	ANASE
7 500	10 500	18 700	41 800	59 800	71 700	72 700	-	ECO
..	..	42 900	(b)69 900	139 200	150 700	177 900	189 800	CCG
5 000	9 800	25 100	(b)60 000	95 000	134 400	144 800	149 200	SAARC
								EUROPE
12 100	21 600	29 000	55 000	72 800	81 600	93 800	98 600	AELE
188 900	377 000	631 200	1 080 200	1 405 400	1 439 500	1 580 900	1 531 000	UE27
144 100	291 500	462 400	795 100	b)1 062 200	1 088 100	1 197 500	1 151 700	Zone euro
								OCÉANIE
500	800	1 200	1 900	2 500	3 600	3 900	4 600	MSG
								INTERRÉGIONAUX
23 300	26 800	36 000	64 600	109 000	124 600	147 800	149 500	ACP
133 800	344 700	652 500	962 600	1 269 000	1 442 000	1 617 100	1 726 100	CEAP
10 200	21 800	45 500	87 100	137 100	150 400	172 200	186 300	CEMN
_	_	25 000	60 200	95 000	111 100	130 700	153 700	CEI

Sources :

Calculs des secrétariats de la CNUCED et de l'OMC et du CCI, sur la base de :

- FMI, *Statistiques de la balance des paiements*

- Eurostat, base de données en ligne

- ONU/DAES/Division des statistiques, *ONU Service Trade Statistical Database*

- OCDE, *OECD.Stat*

- Autres sources internationales et nationales

5

Country or territory Pays ou territoires	Exports (1) - Exportations (1)							
	Millions of dollars / Millions de dollars				As % of total services En % du total des services			
	2000	2010	2011	2012	2000	2010	2011	2012
SELECTED COUNTRY GROUPINGS **SÉLECTION DE GROUPEMENTS DE PAYS**								
World - Monde	346 400	806 700	879 300	891 900	22.8	20.8	20.3	20.2
Developing economies - Économies en développement	84 000	264 200	285 700	301 800	23.9	23.8	22.8	22.4
Transition economies - Économies en transition	9 500	35 200	40 700	42 500	39.3	34.2	33.4	32.8
Developed economies - Économies développées	252 800	507 300	552 900	547 700	22.1	19.0	18.7	18.6
Developing economies: Africa - Économies en développement : Afrique	7 900	23 000	24 400	26 500	23.8	25.4	26.4	27.2
Developing economies: America - Économies en développement : Amérique	11 100	26 000	29 900	29 400	18.0	19.7	19.4	18.3
Developing economies: Asia - Économies en développement : Asie	64 800	214 500	230 600	245 000	25.3	24.2	23.0	22.6
Developing economies: Oceania - Économies en développement : Océanie	200	700	-	-	18.6	22.2	-	-
Developed economies: America - Économies développées : Amérique	53 100	83 000	92 800	96 100	16.1	13.2	13.5	13.3
Developed economies: Asia - Économies développées : Asie	28 100	43 100	42 700	44 600	33.1	26.0	24.8	25.5
Developed economies: Europe - Économies développées : Europe	166 200	374 400	410 000	399 700	23.5	20.6	20.1	20.1
Developed economies: Oceania - Économies développées : Océanie	5 500	6 700	7 400	7 400	22.8	12.0	12.0	11.7
Least developed countries - Pays les moins avancés	1 200	4 200	5 400	5 900	16.6	16.8	18.2	(u)19.1
Developing economies excluding LDCs - Économies en développement sans les PMA	82 800	260 000	280 300	295 900	24.0	23.9	23.0	22.5
Developing economies excluding China - Économies en développement sans la Chine	80 300	230 000	250 200	262 900	25.0	24.2	23.3	22.8
25 LEADING EXPORTERS: DEVELOPING AND TRANSITION ECONOMIES **25 PRINCIPAUX EXPORTATEURS : ÉCONOMIES EN DÉVELOPPEMENT ET EN TRANSITION**								
Singapore - Singapour (11)	(e)11 729	38 726	41 273	42 483	(e)41.1	41.0	38.0	37.8
Korea, Republic of - Corée, République de	13 687	38 982	36 938	40 701	43.4	44.7	38.8	36.7
China - Chine	3 671	34 211	35 570	38 912	12.1	(e)21.1	(e)20.2	(e)20.3
China, Hong Kong SAR - Chine (RAS de Hong Kong) (12)	(e)12 773	29 562	31 804	(e)31 928	(e)31.6	28.4	26.9	(e)25.9
India - Inde (13)	1 979	13 241	17 477	(e)17 093	11.9	10.7	12.7	(e)12.1
Russian Federation - Fédération de Russie (14)	3 555	14 785	17 226	19 017	(e)36.4	32.8	31.2	32.1
Turkey - Turquie	2 955	9 586	10 690	(e)13 237	14.5	27.4	27.4	(e)30.9
China, Taiwan Province of - Province chinoise de Taiwan	4 121	9 765	9 696	9 986	20.6	24.2	21.1	20.4
Ukraine (12)	2 920	7 763	9 004	8 483	(e)75.0	46.9	47.9	43.8
Egypt - Égypte	2 645	7 916	8 199	(e)8 867	27.0	33.3	42.8	(e)40.7
Chile - Chili (15)	2 188	6 394	7 652	6 727	53.6	59.0	58.3	53.3
Thailand - Thaïlande (16)	3 250	5 916	5 830	5 978	23.4	17.2	14.0	12.1
Brazil - Brésil	1 409	4 931	5 819	5 422	14.8	15.5	15.2	13.6
Kuwait - Koweït (17)	1 383	4 413	5 498	(e)5 715	75.9	47.3	53.9	(e)55.2
Malaysia - Malaisie (12)	2 802	4 873	5 060	4 424	20.1	15.4	14.1	11.8
Panama	1 153	3 372	3 935	4 685	57.8	54.2	54.2	52.5
Qatar	206	1 752	3 929	4 671	56.6	58.2	53.1	47.1
Iran (Islamic Rep. of) - Iran (Rép. islamique d')	561	3 651	-	-	31.2	44.1	-	-
Belarus - Bélarus (12)	584	2 993	3 490	3 560	58.3	66.0	66.0	60.2
Indonesia - Indonésie	_	2 665	3 456	3 821	_	15.9	16.7	16.5
United Arab Emirates - Émirats arabes unis	781	2 451	2 859	3 899	36.0	20.9	22.3	25.9
Morocco - Maroc	485	2 152	2 724	(e)2 779	16.0	17.2	19.5	(e)20.6
Turkmenistan - Turkménistan	-	-	-	-	-	-	-	-
Viet Nam	-	2 306	2 227	2 070	-	30.9	25.6	21.6
Kazakhstan	461	2 276	2 221	(e)2 551	43.8	53.5	49.3	(e)51.5
15 LEADING EXPORTERS: DEVELOPED ECONOMIES **15 PRINCIPAUX EXPORTATEURS : ÉCONOMIES DÉVELOPPÉES**								
United States - États-Unis	45 515	71 564	79 458	(e)82 827	15.7	12.9	13.1	(e)12.9
Germany - Allemagne	19 802	57 088	59 817	(e)56 488	23.8	23.4	22.6	(e)21.6
France	18 498	42 017	45 363	(e)44 353	22.9	21.9	20.2	(e)21.0
Denmark - Danemark	14 265	38 016	40 177	(e)40 181	59.5	61.3	60.3	(e)61.7
Japan - Japon	25 606	38 902	38 319	(e)40 101	37.0	27.5	26.3	(e)27.6
United Kingdom - Royaume-Uni	19 087	31 943	37 043	(e)37 217	15.9	11.9	12.6	(e)13.1
Netherlands - Pays-Bas	19 775	25 573	29 882	(e)29 892	37.7	21.7	21.6	(e)22.4
Belgium - Belgique (18)	(a)10 672	26 220	26 228	(e)25 982	(a)21.5	28.6	27.5	(e)26.9
Spain - Espagne	8 449	21 143	23 838	(e)23 234	16.1	17.0	16.8	(e)17.0
Greece - Grèce	7 969	20 421	19 596	(e)17 081	41.2	54.1	49.3	(e)50.3
Norway - Norvège	9 606	15 686	17 433	(e)17 988	54.2	39.5	41.1	(e)41.0
Italy - Italie	9 231	14 645	15 296	(e)14 191	16.4	14.9	14.3	(e)13.6
Austria - Autriche	4 210	12 900	14 513	(e)13 833	18.3	23.7	23.7	(e)22.5
Canada (19)	7 539	11 417	13 266	13 192	18.7	15.5	16.6	16.7
Sweden - Suède	4 965	10 239	11 269	(e)11 189	23.0	16.1	15.1	(e)14.6

For sources and notes, see end of table.   Pour les sources et les notes, se reporter à la fin du tableau.

Country or territory / Pays ou territoires	Imports (1) - Importations (1)							
	Millions of dollars / Millions de dollars				As % of total services / En % du total des services			
	2000	2010	2011	2012	2000	2010	2011	2012
SELECTED COUNTRY GROUPINGS / **SÉLECTION DE GROUPEMENTS DE PAYS**								
World - Monde	419 200	980 600	1 117 700	1 143 100	27.6	26.2	26.8	26.7
Developing economies - Économies en développement	138 600	450 300	537 000	564 100	33.3	34.5	35.9	35.4
Transition economies - Économies en transition	4 900	25 500	30 000	32 000	17.2	20.6	20.8	19.2
Developed economies - Économies développées	275 700	504 800	550 700	547 100	25.6	21.8	21.8	21.8
Developing economies: Africa - Économies en développement : Afrique	14 700	55 700	60 000	62 300	35.3	36.6	35.7	36.8
Developing economies: America - Économies en développement : Amérique	26 300	54 900	64 100	66 400	35.6	32.0	30.8	30.2
Developing economies: Asia - Économies en développement : Asie	97 100	338 000	411 000	433 300	32.4	34.6	36.9	36.2
Developing economies: Oceania - Économies en développement : Océanie	500	1 700	1 900	-	33.0	29.1	30.9	-
Developed economies: America - Économies développées : Amérique	69 700	90 200	109 100	113 200	26.4	19.7	20.4	20.6
Developed economies: Asia - Économies développées : Asie	37 500	52 300	56 000	61 700	29.5	29.8	29.9	31.3
Developed economies: Europe - Économies développées : Europe	160 700	337 200	367 100	351 800	24.3	21.4	21.2	20.8
Developed economies: Oceania - Économies développées : Océanie	7 700	16 200	18 600	20 300	32.9	26.8	26.1	27.1
Least developed countries - Pays les moins avancés	6 100	23 500	27 500	29 100	42.4	38.9	38.3	37.9
Developing economies excluding LDCs - Économies en développement sans les PMA	132 500	426 700	509 500	535 000	33.0	34.3	35.7	35.3
Developing economies excluding China - Économies en développement sans la Chine	128 200	387 000	456 500	478 200	33.7	34.8	36.3	36.4
25 LEADING IMPORTERS: DEVELOPING AND TRANSITION ECONOMIES / **25 PRINCIPAUX IMPORTATEURS : ÉCONOMIES EN DÉVELOPPEMENT ET EN TRANSITION**								
China - Chine	10 396	63 257	80 445	85 862	28.9	(e)32.7	(e)33.8	(e)30.5
India - Inde (13)	8 703	46 237	56 641	(e)58 877	45.4	39.5	45.5	(e)45.9
United Arab Emirates - Émirats arabes unis	4 557	25 780	41 948	47 703	53.2	61.2	74.2	74.6
Singapore - Singapour (11)	(e)12 617	29 752	34 392	35 319	(e)41.9	30.4	30.0	29.9
Korea, Republic of - Corée, République de	11 048	29 675	29 537	30 146	32.9	30.9	29.2	27.9
Thailand - Thaïlande (16)	6 760	22 431	26 719	28 514	43.7	49.8	51.2	54.1
China, Hong Kong SAR - Chine (RAS de Hong Kong) (12)	(e)6 242	14 579	16 624	(e)16 437	(e)25.3	28.4	29.5	(e)28.6
Russian Federation - Fédération de Russie (14)	2 330	11 866	15 398	16 422	(e)13.8	16.2	17.2	15.5
Saudi Arabia - Arabie saoudite (20)	2 244	12 724	15 348	17 869	8.9	16.6	19.7	24.3
Brazil - Brésil	4 305	11 339	14 153	14 191	25.8	18.1	18.6	17.5
Malaysia - Malaisie (12)	5 890	11 824	13 250	13 493	35.2	36.7	34.9	32.0
Indonesia - Indonésie	_	8 673	12 149	12 936	_	33.2	38.8	38.1
Mexico - Mexique	6 186	10 774	12 120	11 785	36.6	42.8	41.2	40.4
China, Taiwan Province of - Province chinoise de Taiwan	6 247	9 895	10 268	10 482	23.4	26.1	24.4	24.5
Qatar	293	5 758	9 845	9 888	17.9	65.6	58.4	41.4
Turkey - Turquie	2 463	8 104	8 460	(e)8 562	27.2	41.5	40.3	(e)41.5
South Africa - Afrique du Sud	2 441	7 088	8 262	7 991	41.9	38.4	42.0	45.2
Viet Nam	-	6 596	8 226	8 715	-	66.5	69.4	69.6
Nigeria - Nigéria	624	8 524	8 056	(e)8 099	18.9	39.8	32.8	(e)36.3
Chile - Chili (15)	2 191	6 573	7 721	7 191	45.6	50.7	49.1	47.7
Egypt - Égypte	2 212	6 575	6 474	(e)7 482	29.4	44.7	46.0	(e)45.7
Kuwait - Koweït (17)	1 536	5 400	6 166	(e)6 489	31.2	36.3	34.9	(e)33.9
Iraq	-	4 918	5 359	-	-	49.8	48.4	-
Venezuela (Bolivarian Rep. of) - Venezuela (Rép. bolivarienne du)	1 808	4 037	5 058	6 439	40.8	30.9	32.2	35.4
Argentina - Argentine	2 413	3 700	4 535	4 650	26.2	25.0	25.4	24.9
15 LEADING IMPORTERS: DEVELOPED ECONOMIES / **15 PRINCIPAUX IMPORTATEURS : ÉCONOMIES DÉVELOPPÉES**								
United States - États-Unis	60 325	78 147	85 453	(e)89 830	27.4	19.3	19.9	(e)20.3
Germany - Allemagne	26 270	65 464	69 956	(e)67 880	19.0	24.5	23.6	(e)23.0
France	17 908	46 208	52 774	(e)48 414	29.5	27.0	27.7	(e)28.1
Japan - Japon	33 331	46 447	49 447	(e)55 264	29.0	29.5	29.5	(e)31.3
United Kingdom - Royaume-Uni	24 166	28 779	31 966	(e)31 930	24.3	16.8	17.7	(e)17.8
Denmark - Danemark	11 115	27 422	30 830	(e)30 719	52.7	51.4	52.2	(e)53.1
Italy - Italie	13 067	25 921	27 027	(e)24 273	23.6	23.5	23.2	(e)22.7
Spain - Espagne	10 134	21 824	23 795	(e)22 414	30.5	24.8	25.2	(e)25.0
Canada (19)	9 373	20 766	23 369	23 167	21.2	21.6	22.1	21.8
Belgium - Belgique (18)	(a)8 402	20 850	21 840	(e)21 539	(a)20.1	25.2	23.9	(e)23.3
Netherlands - Pays-Bas	14 656	18 831	21 536	(e)21 422	27.5	17.7	17.7	(e)17.9
Australia - Australie (21)	6 292	13 411	15 552	(e)17 245	33.2	26.3	25.8	(e)27.0
Austria - Autriche	3 753	12 153	14 591	(e)14 086	22.8	32.8	34.6	(e)33.1
Greece - Grèce	4 108	10 801	10 056	(e)8 135	36.4	53.6	51.7	(e)52.3
Norway - Norvège	5 138	11 679	8 461	(e)9 013	34.3	27.2	18.4	(e)18.4

For sources and notes, see end of table.

Pour les sources et les notes, se reporter à la fin du tableau.

Country or territory / Pays ou territoires	Exports (2) - Exportations (2)							
	Millions of dollars / Millions de dollars				As % of total services / En % du total des services			
	2000	2010	2011	2012	2000	2010	2011	2012
SELECTED COUNTRY GROUPINGS **SÉLECTION DE GROUPEMENTS DE PAYS**								
World - Monde	476 200	949 500	1 066 900	1 110 700	31.3	24.4	24.6	25.1
Developing economies - Économies en développement	130 300	362 100	410 200	444 400	37.0	32.6	32.8	33.0
Transition economies - Économies en transition	8 400	29 500	35 900	37 700	34.8	28.6	29.4	29.1
Developed economies - Économies développées	337 400	557 900	620 800	628 600	29.5	20.9	21.0	21.3
Developing economies: Africa - Économies en développement : Afrique	14 500	42 100	40 300	42 700	43.5	46.5	43.6	43.9
Developing economies: America - Économies en développement : Amérique	31 600	54 600	58 100	61 200	51.2	41.4	37.7	38.2
Developing economies: Asia - Économies en développement : Asie	83 900	263 900	310 200	338 700	32.8	29.8	31.0	31.2
Developing economies: Oceania - Économies en développement : Océanie	300	1 500	-	-	33.4	47.2	-	-
Developed economies: America - Économies développées : Amérique	111 500	150 400	166 500	180 600	33.9	23.9	24.2	25.1
Developed economies: Asia - Économies développées : Asie	7 500	17 900	15 800	19 700	8.8	10.8	9.2	11.2
Developed economies: Europe - Économies développées : Europe	206 900	355 500	401 400	391 300	29.3	19.5	19.7	19.6
Developed economies: Oceania - Économies développées : Océanie	11 500	34 000	37 000	37 100	47.5	60.6	59.8	59.0
Least developed countries - Pays les moins avancés	2 500	9 800	11 400	12 200	35.9	39.0	38.3	(u)39.4
Developing economies excluding LDCs - Économies en développement sans les PMA	127 800	352 300	398 900	432 300	37.0	32.5	32.7	32.9
Developing economies excluding China - Économies en développement sans la Chine	114 100	316 300	361 800	394 400	35.5	33.3	33.7	34.2
25 LEADING EXPORTERS: DEVELOPING AND TRANSITION ECONOMIES **25 PRINCIPAUX EXPORTATEURS : ÉCONOMIES EN DÉVELOPPEMENT ET EN TRANSITION**								
China - Chine	16 231	45 814	48 464	50 028	53.3	(e)28.3	(e)27.5	(e)26.1
China, Macao SAR - Chine (RAS de Macao) (22)	3 011	27 802	38 453	(e)43 882	91.8	96.9	96.7	(e)96.5
China, Hong Kong SAR - Chine (RAS de Hong Kong) (12)	(e)5 907	22 200	27 665	(e)32 090	(e)14.6	21.3	23.4	(e)26.0
Thailand - Thaïlande (16)	7 483	20 116	27 186	33 632	54.0	58.6	65.4	67.9
Turkey - Turquie	7 636	20 807	23 020	(e)23 819	37.4	59.4	59.1	(e)55.7
Malaysia - Malaisie (12)	5 011	18 115	19 656	20 250	35.9	57.1	54.8	53.8
Singapore - Singapour (11)	(e)5 142	14 178	18 082	19 261	(e)18.0	15.0	16.6	17.2
India - Inde (13)	3 460	14 160	17 518	(e)17 781	20.7	11.4	12.7	(e)12.6
Korea, Republic of - Corée, République de	6 834	10 359	12 525	14 231	21.7	11.9	13.1	12.8
Mexico - Mexique	8 294	11 992	11 869	12 720	61.5	79.1	77.6	79.4
Russian Federation - Fédération de Russie (14)	3 429	8 830	11 328	11 187	(e)35.1	19.6	20.5	18.9
China, Taiwan Province of - Province chinoise de Taiwan	3 738	8 721	11 065	11 707	18.7	21.6	24.1	23.9
South Africa - Afrique du Sud	2 677	9 085	9 515	9 996	53.0	64.9	64.2	66.0
United Arab Emirates - Émirats arabes unis	1 062	8 577	9 204	10 380	48.9	73.1	71.9	68.9
Croatia - Croatie	2 758	8 219	9 183	(e)8 775	67.7	71.0	72.6	(e)73.4
Egypt - Égypte	4 345	12 528	8 707	(e)9 940	44.3	52.6	45.5	(e)45.7
Saudi Arabia - Arabie saoudite (20)	-	6 712	8 459	7 432	-	62.8	73.6	67.3
Indonesia - Indonésie	_	6 958	7 997	8 342	_	41.5	38.6	36.0
Morocco - Maroc	2 039	6 702	7 321	(e)6 721	67.2	53.4	52.4	(e)49.7
Lebanon - Liban	-	8 064	6 871	-	-	50.3	34.8	-
Brazil - Brésil	1 810	5 919	6 555	6 645	19.1	18.6	17.2	16.7
Syrian Arab Republic - République arabe syrienne	1 082	6 190	-	-	63.7	84.4	-	-
Viet Nam	-	4 450	5 710	6 830	-	59.7	65.7	71.1
Argentina - Argentine	2 904	4 942	5 354	4 895	58.8	36.2	34.3	32.1
Dominican Republic - République dominicaine	2 860	4 209	4 353	(e)4 550	88.6	81.7	81.5	(e)81.9
15 LEADING EXPORTERS: DEVELOPED ECONOMIES **15 PRINCIPAUX EXPORTATEURS : ÉCONOMIES DÉVELOPPÉES**								
United States - États-Unis	100 716	134 167	149 256	(e)162 793	34.8	24.2	24.6	(e)25.4
Spain - Espagne	29 893	52 475	59 812	(e)55 944	56.8	42.2	42.1	(e)40.9
France	30 681	46 871	54 438	(e)53 724	38.1	24.4	24.3	(e)25.4
Italy - Italie	27 552	38 749	42 942	(e)41 220	48.8	39.6	40.3	(e)39.5
Germany - Allemagne	18 648	34 642	38 789	(e)38 107	22.4	14.2	14.7	(e)14.6
United Kingdom - Royaume-Uni	21 857	32 401	35 069	(e)36 614	18.2	12.1	11.9	(e)12.9
Australia - Australie (21)	9 289	29 141	31 486	(e)31 618	46.7	61.8	60.8	(e)59.9
Austria - Autriche	9 760	18 578	19 833	(e)18 904	42.4	34.1	32.5	(e)30.8
Switzerland - Suisse	6 646	14 910	17 540	(e)16 477	21.7	17.9	18.2	(e)17.8
Canada (19)	10 778	15 759	16 800	17 364	26.8	21.4	21.1	21.9
Greece - Grèce	9 276	12 729	14 603	(e)12 886	48.0	33.7	36.7	(e)38.0
Netherlands - Pays-Bas	7 198	12 870	14 329	(e)13 894	13.7	10.9	10.4	(e)10.4
Sweden - Suède	4 068	11 040	13 762	(e)15 496	18.8	17.3	18.5	(e)20.3
Belgium - Belgique (18)	(a)7 435	10 357	11 651	(e)11 400	(a)14.9	11.3	12.2	(e)11.8
Portugal	5 270	10 067	11 323	(e)11 062	58.2	43.2	42.5	(e)45.1

For sources and notes, see end of table.   Pour les sources et les notes, se reporter à la fin du tableau.

Country or territory / Pays ou territoires	Imports (2) - Importations (2)							
	Millions of dollars / Millions de dollars				As % of total services / En % du total des services			
	2000	2010	2011	2012	2000	2010	2011	2012
SELECTED COUNTRY GROUPINGS / SÉLECTION DE GROUPEMENTS DE PAYS								
World - Monde	441 200	859 500	945 300	994 600	29.0	23.0	22.7	23.3
Developing economies - Économies en développement	103 800	297 700	331 500	373 900	24.9	22.8	22.1	23.5
Transition economies - Économies en transition	11 600	38 700	47 700	59 300	41.0	31.3	33.0	35.5
Developed economies - Économies développées	325 700	523 100	566 100	561 300	30.3	22.6	22.4	22.3
Developing economies: Africa - Économies en développement : Afrique	8 300	25 600	27 200	26 100	19.9	16.8	16.2	15.4
Developing economies: America - Économies en développement : Amérique	20 700	40 800	48 600	51 900	27.9	23.7	23.3	23.6
Developing economies: Asia - Économies en développement : Asie	74 700	230 700	255 000	295 100	24.9	23.6	22.9	24.6
Developing economies: Oceania - Économies en développement : Océanie	200	700	800	-	12.3	11.4	12.3	-
Developed economies: America - Économies développées : Amérique	80 300	112 400	119 800	127 400	30.4	22.4	22.4	23.2
Developed economies: Asia - Économies développées : Asie	34 700	31 300	30 700	31 300	27.3	17.9	10.4	16.9
Developed economies: Europe - Économies développées : Europe	202 900	354 200	385 500	371 500	30.7	22.5	22.2	22.0
Developed economies: Oceania - Économies développées : Océanie	7 800	25 300	30 000	31 200	33.4	41.9	42.2	41.6
Least developed countries - Pays les moins avancés	2 300	6 600	7 200	7 600	15.9	10.8	10.0	9.8
Developing economies excluding LDCs - Économies en développement sans les PMA	101 500	291 200	324 400	366 400	25.2	23.4	22.8	24.1
Developing economies excluding China - Économies en développement sans la Chine	90 700	242 900	259 000	271 900	23.8	21.8	20.6	20.7
25 LEADING IMPORTERS: DEVELOPING AND TRANSITION ECONOMIES / 25 PRINCIPAUX IMPORTATEURS : ÉCONOMIES EN DÉVELOPPEMENT ET EN TRANSITION								
China - Chine	13 114	54 880	72 585	102 000	36.4	(e)28.4	(e)30.5	(e)36.3
Russian Federation - Fédération de Russie (14)	8 848	26 693	32 902	42 798	(e)52.5	36.4	36.8	40.3
Singapore - Singapour (11)	(e)4 938	18 700	21 437	22 412	(e)16.4	19.1	18.7	19.0
Brazil - Brésil	3 894	16 422	21 264	22 233	23.4	26.2	27.9	27.5
Korea, Republic of - Corée, République de	7 132	18 780	19 934	20 101	21.2	19.6	19.7	18.6
China, Hong Kong SAR - Chine (RAS de Hong Kong) (12)	(e)12 502	17 503	19 172	(e)20 246	(e)50.6	34.1	34.0	(e)35.3
Saudi Arabia - Arabie saoudite (20)	-	21 135	17 271	17 023	-	27.5	22.1	23.2
India - Inde (13)	2 690	10 549	13 722	(e)12 356	14.0	9.0	11.0	(e)9.6
Iran (Islamic Rep. of) - Iran (Rép. islamique d')	668	14 186	-	-	21.4	60.6	-	-
Malaysia - Malaisie (12)	2 075	8 299	10 192	11 543	12.4	25.7	26.8	27.4
China, Taiwan Province of - Province chinoise de Taiwan	8 107	9 357	10 112	10 630	30.4	24.7	24.1	24.8
Kuwait - Koweït (17)	2 495	6 429	8 129	(e)8 747	50.7	43.2	46.0	(e)45.7
United Arab Emirates - Émirats arabes unis	3 017	11 818	8 005	8 741	35.2	28.1	14.2	13.7
Mexico - Mexique	5 499	7 255	7 832	8 387	32.6	28.8	26.6	28.7
Nigeria - Nigéria	591	5 587	6 599	(e)6 193	17.9	26.1	26.9	(e)27.7
Indonesia - Indonésie	_	6 395	6 255	6 771	_	24.5	20.0	20.0
Thailand - Thaïlande (16)	2 772	5 623	5 716	6 131	17.9	12.5	11.0	11.6
Argentina - Argentine	4 425	4 878	5 542	5 879	48.0	32.9	31.1	31.4
Philippines (12)	1 642	3 416	5 368	6 247	31.3	30.1	43.4	43.4
South Africa - Afrique du Sud	2 085	5 595	5 283	4 069	35.8	30.3	26.9	23.0
Turkey - Turquie	1 713	4 826	4 976	(e)4 173	18.9	24.7	23.7	(e)20.2
Ukraine (12)	470	3 742	4 461	5 104	15.6	29.6	33.5	36.1
Lebanon - Liban	-	4 926	4 215	-	-	36.6	32.5	-
Libya - Libye	397	2 047	2 269	-	44.4	33.4	51.2	-
Colombia - Colombie	1 060	1 826	2 243	2 608	32.0	22.6	23.6	24.7
15 LEADING IMPORTERS: DEVELOPED ECONOMIES / 15 PRINCIPAUX IMPORTATEURS : ÉCONOMIES DÉVELOPPÉES								
United States - États-Unis	67 860	82 507	86 184	(e)91 825	30.8	20.4	20.1	(e)20.8
Germany - Allemagne	52 909	78 054	85 752	(e)83 861	38.3	29.2	28.9	(e)28.5
United Kingdom - Royaume-Uni	38 408	50 002	50 998	(e)52 732	38.6	29.2	28.2	(e)29.3
France	17 714	39 002	44 045	(e)37 180	29.1	22.8	23.1	(e)21.5
Canada (19)	12 438	29 573	33 323	35 223	28.2	30.7	31.5	33.1
Italy - Italie	15 672	27 039	28 613	(e)26 177	28.3	24.5	24.6	(e)24.5
Japan - Japon	31 890	27 867	27 210	(e)27 831	27.7	17.7	16.2	(e)15.8
Australia - Australie (21)	6 387	22 240	26 597	(e)27 495	33.7	43.6	44.1	(e)43.0
Belgium - Belgique (18)	(a)10 181	18 890	22 232	(e)21 908	(a)24.3	22.9	24.4	(e)23.7
Netherlands - Pays-Bas	12 199	19 611	20 501	(e)20 186	22.9	18.5	16.9	(e)16.8
Spain - Espagne	5 946	16 771	17 268	(e)15 402	17.9	19.1	18.3	(e)17.2
Norway - Norvège	4 601	14 024	16 075	(e)16 876	30.7	32.7	34.9	(e)34.4
Sweden - Suède	8 036	13 250	15 786	(e)16 116	33.5	28.1	28.7	(e)29.3
Switzerland - Suisse	5 428	11 164	13 956	(e)14 196	42.4	30.6	30.9	(e)30.3
Austria - Autriche	6 235	10 222	10 469	(e)10 131	37.8	27.6	24.8	(e)23.8

For sources and notes, see end of table.

Pour les sources et les notes, se reporter à la fin du tableau.

5

Country or territory Pays ou territoires	Exports (3) - Exportations (3)							
	Millions of dollars / Millions de dollars				As % of total services En % du total des services			
	2000	2010	2011	2012	2000	2010	2011	2012
SELECTED COUNTRY GROUPINGS **SÉLECTION DE GROUPEMENTS DE PAYS**								
World - Monde	34 300	95 800	106 200	111 500	2.3	2.5	2.5	2.5
Developing economies - Économies en développement	10 300	25 000	26 600	27 500	2.9	2.3	2.1	2.0
Transition economies - Économies en transition	900	3 500	3 900	4 000	3.9	3.4	3.2	3.1
Developed economies - Économies développées	23 100	67 200	75 700	80 000	2.0	2.5	2.6	2.7
Developing economies: Africa - Économies en développement : Afrique	1 600	4 000	4 200	4 400	4.7	4.4	4.5	4.5
Developing economies: America - Économies en développement : Amérique	3 200	4 100	3 900	4 300	5.2	3.1	2.5	2.7
Developing economies: Asia - Économies en développement : Asie	5 500	16 900	18 500	18 800	2.2	1.9	1.9	1.7
Developing economies: Oceania - Économies en développement : Océanie	-	100	0	-	-	1.6	-	-
Developed economies: America - Économies développées : Amérique	5 500	14 100	16 100	17 200	1.7	2.2	2.3	2.4
Developed economies: Asia - Économies développées : Asie	1 000	1 000	1 100	1 200	1.2	0.6	0.6	0.7
Developed economies: Europe - Économies développées : Europe	15 500	50 900	57 200	60 200	2.2	2.8	2.8	3.0
Developed economies: Oceania - Économies développées : Océanie	1 100	1 200	1 400	1 400	4.5	2.1	2.2	2.3
Least developed countries - Pays les moins avancés	300	1 800	2 100	2 100	4.6	7.2	7.1	(u)6.9
Developing economies excluding LDCs - Économies en développement sans les PMA	10 000	23 200	24 500	25 400	2.9	2.1	2.0	1.9
Developing economies excluding China - Économies en développement sans la Chine	9 000	23 800	24 900	25 700	2.8	2.5	2.3	2.2
25 LEADING EXPORTERS: DEVELOPING AND TRANSITION ECONOMIES **25 PRINCIPAUX EXPORTATEURS : ÉCONOMIES EN DÉVELOPPEMENT ET EN TRANSITION**								
Kuwait - Koweït (17)	-	3 558	3 601	(e)3 447	-	38.2	35.3	(e)33.3
Singapore - Singapour (11)	(e)433	-	-	-	(e)1.5	-	-	-
China - Chine	1 345	1 220	1 726	1 793	4.4	(e)0.8	(e)1.0	(e)0.9
India - Inde (13)	599	1 548	1 672	(e)1 647	3.6	1.2	1.2	(e)1.2
China, Hong Kong SAR - Chine (RAS de Hong Kong) (12)	(e)362	1 241	1 568	-	(e)0.9	1.2	1.3	-
Russian Federation - Fédération de Russie (14)	385	1 351	1 473	1 550	(e)3.9	3.0	2.7	2.6
Indonesia - Indonésie	_	1 126	1 450	1 090	_	6.7	7.0	4.7
Korea, Republic of - Corée, République de	387	834	828	860	1.2	1.0	0.9	0.8
Morocco - Maroc	114	713	772	(e)676	3.7	5.7	5.5	(e)5.0
Egypt - Égypte	306	844	730	-	3.1	3.5	3.8	-
Malaysia - Malaisie (12)	181	685	653	828	1.3	2.2	1.8	2.2
Bahrain - Bahreïn	-	799	627	-	-	19.8	20.6	-
Ukraine (12)	89	518	577	550	(e)2.3	3.1	3.1	2.8
Turkey - Turquie	0	538	526	(e)453	0.0	1.5	1.3	(e)1.1
Thailand - Thaïlande (16)	132	456	512	466	1.0	1.3	1.2	0.9
China, Taiwan Province of - Province chinoise de Taiwan	294	392	439	499	1.5	1.0	1.0	1.0
Lebanon - Liban	-	387	424	-	-	2.4	2.1	-
Cuba	-	-	-	-	-	-	-	-
Bangladesh (23)	22	278	399	-	2.6	11.5	16.5	-
Philippines (12)	182	305	395	486	5.4	2.2	2.2	2.6
Kenya	22	360	390	-	2.2	9.6	9.5	-
Serbia - Serbie	_	259	374	351	_	6.1	7.3	7.3
Tunisia - Tunisie	12	302	345	-	0.4	5.2	7.2	-
Guatemala	0	316	343	(e)372	0.0	13.8	14.6	(e)15.2
Brazil - Brésil	36	435	320	381	0.4	1.4	0.8	1.0
15 LEADING EXPORTERS: DEVELOPED ECONOMIES **15 PRINCIPAUX EXPORTATEURS : ÉCONOMIES DÉVELOPPÉES**								
United States - États-Unis	4 128	11 335	12 886	(e)14 047	1.4	2.0	2.1	(e)2.2
United Kingdom - Royaume-Uni	2 820	8 128	10 358	(e)11 695	2.3	3.0	3.5	(e)4.1
Italy - Italie	1 282	6 756	6 699	(e)5 643	2.3	6.9	6.3	(e)5.4
France	1 330	5 624	6 378	(e)5 936	1.7	2.9	2.8	(e)2.8
Netherlands - Pays-Bas	1 424	4 931	5 934	(e)5 288	2.7	4.2	4.3	(e)4.0
Germany - Allemagne	1 455	5 386	5 675	(e)11 807	1.7	2.2	2.1	(e)4.5
Belgium - Belgique (18)	(a)1 884	4 126	4 526	(e)4 170	(a)3.8	4.5	4.7	(e)4.3
Canada (19)	1 379	2 716	3 156	-	3.4	3.7	4.0	-
Luxembourg	..	2 633	2 571	(e)2 532	..	4.1	3.6	(e)3.6
Spain - Espagne	673	2 119	2 298	(e)2 116	1.3	1.7	1.6	(e)1.5
Sweden - Suède	647	1 832	2 174	(e)1 776	3.0	2.9	2.9	(e)2.3
Switzerland - Suisse	879	1 433	1 448	(e)882	2.9	1.7	1.5	(e)1.0
Austria - Autriche	(e)482	1 393	1 407	(e)1 388	(e)2.1	2.6	2.3	(e)2.3
Norway - Norvège	291	739	1 278	(e)957	1.6	1.9	3.0	(e)2.2
Australia - Australie (21)	889	1 042	1 167	(e)1 257	4.5	2.2	2.3	(e)2.4

For sources and notes, see end of table.   Pour les sources et les notes, se reporter à la fin du tableau.

290

Country or territory / Pays ou territoires	Imports (3) - Importations (3)							
	Millions of dollars / Millions de dollars				As % of total services / En % du total des services			
	2000	2010	2011	2012	2000	2010	2011	2012
SELECTED COUNTRY GROUPINGS / SÉLECTION DE GROUPEMENTS DE PAYS								
World - Monde	..	..	..	..	..	..	..	..
Developing economies - Économies en développement	..	..	..	..	..	..	..	..
Transition economies - Économies en transition	..	..	..	..	..	..	..	..
Developed economies - Économies développées	..	..	..	..	..	..	..	..
Developing economies: Africa - Économies en développement : Afrique	..	..	..	..	..	..	..	..
Developing economies: America - Économies en développement : Amérique	..	..	..	..	..	..	..	..
Developing economies: Asia - Économies en développement : Asie	..	..	..	..	..	..	..	..
Developing economies: Oceania - Économies en développement : Océanie	..	..	..	..	..	..	..	..
Developed economies: America - Économies développées : Amérique	..	..	..	..	..	..	..	..
Developed economies: Asia - Économies développées : Asie	..	..	..	..	..	..	..	..
Developed economies: Europe - Économies développées : Europe	..	..	..	..	..	..	..	..
Developed economies: Oceania - Économies développées : Océanie	..	..	..	..	..	..	..	..
Least developed countries - Pays les moins avancés	..	..	..	..	..	..	..	..
Developing economies excluding LDCs - Économies en développement sans les PMA	..	..	..	..	..	..	..	..
Developing economies excluding China - Économies en développement sans la Chine	..	..	..	..	..	..	..	..
25 LEADING IMPORTERS: DEVELOPING AND TRANSITION ECONOMIES / 25 PRINCIPAUX IMPORTATEURS : ÉCONOMIES EN DÉVELOPPEMENT ET EN TRANSITION								
Singapore - Singapour (11)	(e)621	-	-	-	(e)2.1	-	-	-
Saudi Arabia - Arabie saoudite (20)	-	(e)2 197	(e)2 599	(e)2 027	-	(e)2.9	(e)3.3	(e)2.8
Russian Federation - Fédération de Russie (14)	288	2 100	2 530	3 085	(e)1.7	2.9	2.8	2.9
China, Hong Kong SAR - Chine (RAS de Hong Kong) (12)	(e)698	1 673	2 002	-	(e)2.8	3.3	3.5	-
Korea, Republic of - Corée, République de	623	1 460	1 540	1 613	1.9	1.5	1.5	1.5
India - Inde (13)	105	1 166	1 406	(e)1 019	0.5	1.0	1.1	(e)0.8
China - Chine	242	1 137	1 191	1 647	0.7	(e)0.6	(e)0.5	(e)0.6
Malaysia - Malaisie (12)	231	922	1 169	1 294	1.4	2.9	3.1	3.1
Indonesia - Indonésie	_	547	806	717	_	2.1	2.6	2.1
China, Taiwan Province of - Province chinoise de Taiwan	528	454	542	611	2.0	1.2	1.3	1.4
Argentina - Argentine	205	395	459	443	2.2	2.7	2.6	2.4
Thailand - Thaïlande (16)	39	301	402	460	0.3	0.7	0.8	0.9
Venezuela (Bolivarian Rep. of) - Venezuela (Rép. bolivarienne du)	84	369	357	403	1.9	2.8	2.3	2.2
Egypt - Égypte	102	338	355	-	1.4	2.3	2.5	-
Angola	-	362	352	-	-	1.9	1.5	-
Turkey - Turquie	84	270	341	(e)343	0.9	1.4	1.6	(e)1.7
Lebanon - Liban	-	309	310	-	-	2.3	2.4	-
South Africa - Afrique du Sud	83	397	309	302	1.4	2.2	1.6	1.7
United Arab Emirates - Émirats arabes unis	-	-	-	-	-	-	-	-
Qatar	-	365	253	1 386	-	4.2	1.5	5.8
Colombia - Colombie	123	210	240	279	3.7	2.6	2.5	2.6
Serbia - Serbie	_	149	230	214	_	3.7	5.1	5.2
Nigeria - Nigéria	-	286	229	(e)410	-	1.3	0.9	(e)1.8
Kuwait - Koweït (17)	-	99	227	(e)238	-	0.7	1.3	(e)1.2
Congo	8	-	-	-	1.1	-	-	-
15 LEADING IMPORTERS: DEVELOPED ECONOMIES / 15 PRINCIPAUX IMPORTATEURS : ÉCONOMIES DÉVELOPPÉES								
United States - États-Unis	5 926	8 407	8 057	(e)8 280	2.7	2.1	1.9	(e)1.9
Germany - Allemagne	3 143	7 577	7 690	(e)11 499	2.3	2.8	2.6	(e)3.9
United Kingdom - Royaume-Uni	2 825	7 211	7 537	(e)7 446	2.8	4.2	4.2	(e)4.1
Italy - Italie	1 933	6 486	6 584	(e)5 746	3.5	5.9	5.7	(e)5.4
Netherlands - Pays-Bas	1 421	4 086	4 752	(e)4 340	2.7	3.8	3.9	(e)3.6
France	1 146	4 555	4 539	(e)4 761	1.9	2.7	2.4	(e)2.8
Belgium - Belgique (18)	(a)991	3 299	3 495	(e)3 409	(a)2.4	4.0	3.8	(e)3.7
Spain - Espagne	743	2 671	2 823	(e)2 651	2.2	3.0	3.0	(e)3.0
Sweden - Suède	792	2 231	2 428	(e)2 161	3.3	4.7	4.4	(e)3.9
Canada (19)	1 381	2 418	2 359	-	3.1	2.5	2.2	-
Ireland - Irlande	344	1 482	1 496	(e)1 418	1.2	1.4	1.3	(e)1.3
Austria - Autriche	(e)432	1 085	1 168	(e)1 122	(e)2.6	2.9	2.8	(e)2.6
Norway - Norvège	165	1 622	1 108	(e)1 138	1.1	3.8	2.4	(e)2.3
Switzerland - Suisse	885	1 054	1 039	(e)747	6.9	2.9	2.3	(e)1.6
Japan - Japon	1 150	1 025	973	(e)1 176	1.0	0.7	0.6	(e)0.7

For sources and notes, see end of table.

Pour les sources et les notes, se reporter à la fin du tableau.

Country or territory / Pays ou territoires	Exports (4) - Exportations (4)							
	Millions of dollars / Millions de dollars				As % of total services / En % du total des services			
	2000	2010	2011	2012	2000	2010	2011	2012
SELECTED COUNTRY GROUPINGS / **SÉLECTION DE GROUPEMENTS DE PAYS**								
World - Monde	30 200	101 400	110 700	113 000	2.0	2.6	2.6	2.6
Developing economies - Économies en développement	5 400	36 900	41 400	46 400	1.5	3.3	3.3	3.4
Transition economies - Économies en transition	600	5 200	6 200	6 800	2.5	5.0	5.1	5.3
Developed economies - Économies développées	24 200	59 300	63 000	59 800	2.1	2.2	2.1	2.0
Developing economies: Africa - Économies en développement : Afrique	300	1 900	1 800	1 900	0.9	2.1	1.9	1.9
Developing economies: America - Économies en développement : Amérique	300	200	200	200	0.5	0.2	0.1	0.1
Developing economies: Asia - Économies en développement : Asie	4 700	34 600	39 400	44 300	1.8	3.9	3.9	4.1
Developing economies: Oceania - Économies en développement : Océanie	-	100	100	-	-	4.6	-	-
Developed economies: America - Économies développées : Amérique	2 000	3 000	3 500	3 600	0.6	0.5	0.5	0.5
Developed economies: Asia - Économies développées : Asie	6 000	11 500	12 000	12 900	7.1	6.9	6.9	7.4
Developed economies: Europe - Économies développées : Europe	16 100	44 700	47 400	43 300	2.3	2.5	2.3	2.2
Developed economies: Oceania - Économies développées : Océanie	0	100	100	100	0.1	0.2	0.1	0.1
Least developed countries - Pays les moins avancés	(u)100	1 400	1 900	2 000	(u)1.5	5.8	6.4	(u)6.4
Developing economies excluding LDCs - Économies en développement sans les PMA	5 300	35 400	39 500	44 400	1.5	3.3	3.2	3.4
Developing economies excluding China - Économies en développement sans la Chine	4 800	22 400	26 700	34 100	1.5	2.4	2.5	3.0
25 LEADING EXPORTERS: DEVELOPING AND TRANSITION ECONOMIES / **25 PRINCIPAUX EXPORTATEURS : ÉCONOMIES EN DÉVELOPPEMENT ET EN TRANSITION**								
Korea, Republic of - Corée, République de	933	11 977	15 478	21 905	3.0	13.7	16.2	19.8
China - Chine	602	14 495	14 724	12 246	2.0	(e)8.9	(e)8.3	(e)6.4
Russian Federation - Fédération de Russie (14)	170	3 487	4 408	4 751	(e)1.7	7.7	8.0	8.0
Singapore - Singapour (11)	(e)134	1 032	1 543	1 681	(e)0.5	1.1	1.4	1.5
Turkey - Turquie	1 033	1 120	1 245	(e)1 343	5.1	3.2	3.2	(e)3.1
Afghanistan	-	1 057	-	-	-	33.5	-	-
Malaysia - Malaisie (12)	314	1 032	1 103	1 311	2.3	3.3	3.1	3.5
Iran (Islamic Rep. of) - Iran (Rép. islamique d')	-	951	-	-	-	11.5	-	-
India - Inde (13)	502	525	838	(e)933	3.0	0.4	0.6	(e)0.7
Indonesia - Indonésie	—	520	551	863	—	3.1	2.7	3.7
Lebanon - Liban	-	598	535	-	-	3.7	2.7	-
Thailand - Thaïlande (16)	230	472	442	440	1.7	1.4	1.1	0.9
Egypt - Égypte	93	711	395	-	0.9	3.0	2.1	-
Tunisia - Tunisie	50	479	358	-	1.8	8.2	7.5	-
China, Taiwan Province of - Province chinoise de Taiwan	119	355	348	418	0.6	0.9	0.8	0.9
Serbia - Serbie	—	239	307	246	—	5.6	6.0	5.1
Ukraine (12)	38	234	255	304	(e)1.0	1.4	1.4	1.6
Uganda - Ouganda	(e)0	(e)0	(b)247	245	(e)0.0	(e)0.0	(b)14.4	12.3
Turkmenistan - Turkménistan	-	-	-	-	-	-	-	-
Belarus - Bélarus (12)	42	151	226	418	4.2	3.3	4.3	7.1
Croatia - Croatie	199	311	176	(e)85	4.9	2.7	1.4	(e)0.7
China, Hong Kong SAR - Chine (RAS de Hong Kong) (12)	(e)338	145	143	-	(e)0.8	0.1	0.1	-
Algeria - Algérie	-	180	133	-	-	5.0	3.5	-
Azerbaijan - Azerbaïdjan	5	153	113	245	1.9	7.2	4.1	5.7
Uzbekistan - Ouzbékistan	-	-	-	-	-	-	-	-
15 LEADING EXPORTERS: DEVELOPED ECONOMIES / **15 PRINCIPAUX EXPORTATEURS : ÉCONOMIES DÉVELOPPÉES**								
Germany - Allemagne	4 239	11 958	12 248	(e)10 122	5.1	4.9	4.6	(e)3.9
Japan - Japon	5 843	10 637	10 955	(e)11 552	8.4	7.5	7.5	(e)7.9
France	2 861	9 071	9 518	(e)7 961	3.5	4.7	4.2	(e)3.8
Spain - Espagne	589	4 128	4 250	(e)4 799	1.1	3.3	3.0	(e)3.5
United States - États-Unis	1 815	2 645	3 084	-	0.6	0.5	0.5	-
Belgium - Belgique (18)	(a)921	2 682	2 812	(e)2 197	(a)1.9	2.9	2.9	(e)2.3
Netherlands - Pays-Bas	2 589	2 784	2 710	(e)2 797	4.9	2.4	2.0	(e)2.1
United Kingdom - Royaume-Uni	197	2 248	2 648	(e)2 416	0.2	0.8	0.9	(e)0.9
Finland - Finlande	435	1 094	1 947	(e)4 086	5.7	4.1	6.5	(e)13.7
Poland - Pologne	297	1 323	1 611	(e)1 476	2.8	4.0	4.3	(e)3.9
Switzerland - Suisse	-	-	-	-	-	-	-	-
Greece - Grèce	233	(e)707	(e)1 280	..	1.2	(e)1.9	(e)3.2	..
Israel - Israël	182	838	1 004	1 332	1.2	3.4	3.7	4.5
Sweden - Suède	681	840	906	(e)756	3.1	1.3	1.2	(e)1.0
Czech Republic - République tchèque	167	975	854	(e)827	2.4	4.7	3.7	(e)3.8

For sources and notes, see end of table.　　　　Pour les sources et les notes, se reporter à la fin du tableau.

Country or territory Pays ou territoires	Imports (4) - Importations (4)							
	Millions of dollars / Millions de dollars				As % of total services En % du total des services			
	2000	2010	2011	2012	2000	2010	2011	2012
SELECTED COUNTRY GROUPINGS **SÉLECTION DE GROUPEMENTS DE PAYS**								
World - Monde	..	..	..	..	..	..	..	..
Developing economies - Économies en développement	..	..	..	..	..	..	..	..
Transition economies - Économies en transition	..	..	..	..	..	..	..	..
Developed economies - Économies développées	..	..	..	..	..	..	..	..
Developing economies: Africa - Économies en développement : Afrique	..	..	..	..	..	..	..	..
Developing economies: America - Économies en développement : Amérique	..	..	..	..	..	..	..	..
Developing economies: Asia - Économies en développement : Asie	..	..	..	..	..	..	..	..
Developing economies: Oceania - Économies en développement : Océanie	..	..	..	..	..	..	..	..
Developed economies: America - Économies développées : Amérique	..	..	..	..	..	..	..	..
Developed economies: Asia - Économies développées : Asie	..	..	..	..	..	..	..	..
Developed economies: Europe - Économies développées : Europe	..	..	..	..	..	..	..	..
Developed economies: Oceania - Économies développées : Océanie	..	..	..	..	..	..	..	..
Least developed countries - Pays les moins avancés	..	..	..	..	..	..	..	..
Developing economies excluding LDCs - Économies en développement sans les PMA	..	..	..	..	..	..	..	..
Developing economies excluding China - Économies en développement sans la Chine	..	..	..	..	..	..	..	..
25 LEADING IMPORTERS: DEVELOPING AND TRANSITION ECONOMIES **25 PRINCIPAUX IMPORTATEURS : ÉCONOMIES EN DÉVELOPPEMENT ET EN TRANSITION**								
Angola	-	4 643	7 932	-	-	24.8	33.5	-
Russian Federation - Fédération de Russie (14)	406	4 602	5 600	7 424	(e)2.4	6.3	6.3	7.0
Korea, Republic of - Corée, République de	187	2 302	3 795	5 153	0.6	2.4	3.8	4.8
China - Chine	994	5 072	3 728	3 619	2.8	(e)2.6	(e)1.6	(e)1.3
Saudi Arabia - Arabie saoudite (20)	-	3 789	2 578	2 729	-	4.9	3.3	3.7
Algeria - Algérie	-	2 556	1 988	-	-	21.5	15.9	-
Kazakhstan	539	1 666	1 900	(e)2 757	29.1	14.7	17.4	(e)21.7
Malaysia - Malaisie (12)	1 091	1 178	1 350	2 348	6.5	3.7	3.6	5.6
Kuwait - Koweït (17)	26	1 546	1 252	(e)2 045	0.5	10.4	7.1	(e)10.7
India - Inde (13)	127	992	1 132	(e)1 085	0.7	0.8	0.9	(e)0.8
Papua New Guinea - Papouasie-Nouvelle-Guinée	-	676	(e)1 029	(e)1 226	-	24.5	(e)34.5	(e)33.6
Singapore - Singapour (11)	(e)124	515	768	836	(e)0.4	0.5	0.7	0.7
Iran (Islamic Rep. of) - Iran (Rép. islamique d')	-	794	-	-	-	3.4	-	-
Timor-Leste	_	324	629	-	_	31.4	42.4	-
Azerbaijan - Azerbaïdjan	91	325	514	485	18.7	8.5	9.0	6.7
Lebanon - Liban	-	508	498	-	-	3.8	3.8	-
Indonesia - Indonésie	_	592	497	632	_	2.3	1.6	1.9
Ethiopia - Éthiopie	10	361	479	(e)436	2.1	14.2	14.4	(e)11.3
Turkey - Turquie	65	261	407	(e)341	0.7	1.3	1.9	(e)1.7
Belarus - Bélarus (12)	11	163	320	613	2.1	5.7	10.1	16.8
Turkmenistan - Turkménistan	-	-	-	-	-	-	-	-
Thailand - Thaïlande (16)	105	713	308	224	0.7	1.6	0.6	0.4
Tunisia - Tunisie	112	399	308	-	9.2	11.9	9.4	-
China, Macao SAR - Chine (RAS de Macao) (22)	-	149	305	-	-	2.0	3.0	-
Egypt - Égypte	-	386	267	-	-	2.6	1.9	-
15 LEADING IMPORTERS: DEVELOPED ECONOMIES **15 PRINCIPAUX IMPORTATEURS : ÉCONOMIES DÉVELOPPÉES**								
Germany - Allemagne	4 933	7 447	7 783	(e)7 732	3.6	2.8	2.6	(e)2.6
Japan - Japon	4 002	7 883	7 702	(e)7 735	3.5	5.0	4.6	(e)4.4
France	1 528	6 331	6 453	(e)5 312	2.5	3.7	3.4	(e)3.1
Belgium - Belgique (18)	(a)612	2 301	2 543	(e)1 893	(a)1.5	2.8	2.8	(e)2.0
United States - États-Unis	1 326	2 385	2 412	-	0.6	0.6	0.6	-
Netherlands - Pays-Bas	976	2 012	2 176	(e)2 467	1.8	1.9	1.8	(e)2.1
Sweden - Suède	322	1 135	1 849	(e)1 965	1.3	2.4	3.4	(e)3.6
United Kingdom - Royaume-Uni	83	2 004	1 706	(e)1 721	0.1	1.2	0.9	(e)1.0
Spain - Espagne	216	1 792	1 512	(e)1 216	0.6	2.0	1.6	(e)1.4
Finland - Finlande	53	497	1 349	(e)2 954	0.6	1.9	4.5	(e)9.8
Norway - Norvège	31	48	1 086	(e)1 365	0.2	0.1	2.4	(e)2.8
Austria - Autriche	(e)312	897	794	(e)843	(e)1.9	2.4	1.9	(e)2.0
Poland - Pologne	318	710	710	(e)861	3.5	2.4	2.2	(e)2.7
Denmark - Danemark	-	743	592	(e)534	-	1.4	1.0	(e)0.9
Czech Republic - République tchèque	146	623	538	(e)606	2.7	3.7	2.8	(e)3.2

For sources and notes, see end of table.

Pour les sources et les notes, se reporter à la fin du tableau.

5

Country or territory Pays ou territoires	Exports (5) - Exportations (5)							
	Millions of dollars / Millions de dollars				As % of total services En % du total des services			
	2000	2010	2011	2012	2000	2010	2011	2012
SELECTED COUNTRY GROUPINGS **SÉLECTION DE GROUPEMENTS DE PAYS**								
World - Monde	45 700	218 000	247 800	262 700	3.0	5.6	5.7	5.9
Developing economies - Économies en développement	5 800	62 000	71 200	78 300	1.7	5.6	5.7	5.8
Transition economies - Économies en transition	(u)200	2 700	3 600	4 400	(u)0.6	2.6	2.9	3.4
Developed economies - Économies développées	39 700	153 300	173 100	180 000	3.5	5.7	5.8	6.1
Developing economies: Africa - Économies en développement : Afrique	100	1 000	1 200	1 200	0.4	1.1	1.3	1.3
Developing economies: America - Économies en développement : Amérique	400	3 900	4 800	5 600	0.7	3.0	3.1	3.5
Developing economies: Asia - Économies en développement : Asie	5 300	57 100	65 200	71 400	2.1	6.4	6.5	6.6
Developing economies: Oceania - Économies en développement : Océanie	-	0	-	-	-	0.2	-	-
Developed economies: America - Économies développées : Amérique	9 400	20 700	22 500	23 900	2.8	3.3	3.3	3.3
Developed economies: Asia - Économies développées : Asie	5 800	8 800	10 700	12 700	6.8	5.3	6.2	7.2
Developed economies: Europe - Économies développées : Europe	24 000	122 100	137 900	141 600	3.4	6.7	6.8	7.1
Developed economies: Oceania - Économies développées : Océanie	600	1 700	1 900	1 900	2.4	3.0	3.0	2.9
Least developed countries - Pays les moins avancés	(u)100	(u)200	(u)200	(u)300	(u)0.7	(u)0.7	(u)0.8	(u)0.9
Developing economies excluding LDCs - Économies en développement sans les PMA	5 800	61 800	70 900	78 100	1.7	5.7	5.8	5.9
Developing economies excluding China - Économies en développement sans la Chine	5 500	52 700	59 000	63 900	1.7	5.6	5.5	5.5
25 LEADING EXPORTERS: DEVELOPING AND TRANSITION ECONOMIES **25 PRINCIPAUX EXPORTATEURS : ÉCONOMIES EN DÉVELOPPEMENT ET EN TRANSITION**								
India - Inde (13)	(e)4 048	(e)40 236	(e)43 634	(e)47 323	(e)24.3	(e)32.4	(e)31.7	(e)33.5
China - Chine	356	9 256	12 182	14 454	1.2	(e)5.7	(e)6.9	(e)7.6
Philippines (12)	76	1 928	2 381	2 036	2.3	13.7	13.4	11.0
Singapore - Singapour (11)	(e)247	-	-	-	(e)0.9	-	-	-
Argentina - Argentine	147	1 338	1 790	1 826	3.0	9.8	11.5	12.0
Malaysia - Malaisie (12)	82	1 442	1 770	1 990	0.6	4.5	4.9	5.3
Russian Federation - Fédération de Russie (14)	59	1 359	1 753	2 088	(e)0.6	3.0	3.2	3.5
Costa Rica	60	1 217	1 567	(e)1 852	3.1	28.2	31.4	(e)33.2
China, Hong Kong SAR - Chine (RAS de Hong Kong) (12)	(e)60	885	946	-	(e)0.1	0.9	0.8	-
Ukraine (12)	6	429	698	992	(e)0.2	2.6	3.7	5.1
Cuba	-	-	-	-	-	-	-	-
Korea, Republic of - Corée, République de	11	234	426	462	0.0	0.3	0.4	0.4
China, Taiwan Province of - Province chinoise de Taiwan	117	218	388	505	0.6	0.5	0.8	1.0
Morocco - Maroc	-	297	378	-	-	2.4	2.7	-
Sri Lanka	-	265	355	(e)436	-	10.7	11.5	(e)11.5
South Africa - Afrique du Sud	-	290	319	295	-	2.1	2.2	1.9
Belarus - Bélarus (12)	5	223	281	414	0.4	4.9	5.3	7.0
Croatia - Croatie	33	170	244	(e)238	0.8	1.5	1.9	(e)2.0
Pakistan	22	193	240	266	1.6	2.9	4.8	4.1
Brazil - Brésil	34	210	236	596	0.4	0.7	0.6	1.5
Chile - Chili (15)	33	(e)195	(e)230	(e)206	0.8	(e)1.8	(e)1.7	(e)1.6
Indonesia - Indonésie	_	114	207	203	_	0.7	1.0	0.9
Serbia - Serbie	_	172	206	222	_	4.1	4.0	4.6
Uruguay	10	177	177	(e)177	0.8	6.9	5.2	(e)5.5
Egypt - Égypte	23	152	163	-	0.2	0.6	0.9	-
15 LEADING EXPORTERS: DEVELOPED ECONOMIES **15 PRINCIPAUX EXPORTATEURS : ÉCONOMIES DÉVELOPPÉES**								
Ireland - Irlande	5 496	36 937	44 233	(e)46 929	32.5	37.5	39.1	(e)40.5
Germany - Allemagne	3 791	16 539	18 606	(e)19 399	4.6	6.8	7.0	(e)7.4
United States - États-Unis	6 949	13 984	15 501	-	2.4	2.5	2.6	-
United Kingdom - Royaume-Uni	4 335	13 505	14 687	(e)14 403	3.6	5.1	5.0	(e)5.1
Israel - Israël	4 246	7 764	9 529	11 329	27.0	31.9	35.5	38.2
Sweden - Suède	1 200	7 207	8 737	(e)8 062	5.5	11.3	11.7	(e)10.6
Canada (19)	2 428	6 718	6 993	-	6.0	9.1	8.8	-
Spain - Espagne	2 046	6 439	6 698	(e)6 267	3.9	5.2	4.7	(e)4.6
Finland - Finlande	205	6 469	6 687	(e)5 936	2.7	24.0	22.2	(e)20.0
Netherlands - Pays-Bas	1 159	6 302	6 298	(e)6 136	2.2	5.3	4.6	(e)4.6
Belgium - Belgique (18)	(a)1 793	4 017	4 864	(e)5 314	(a)3.6	4.4	5.1	(e)5.5
Switzerland - Suisse	-	-	-	-	-	-	-	-
France	805	3 534	4 190	(e)4 499	1.0	1.8	1.9	(e)2.1
Austria - Autriche	(e)298	2 007	2 594	(e)3 179	(e)1.3	3.7	4.2	(e)5.2
Italy - Italie	442	2 010	2 375	(e)2 558	0.8	2.1	2.2	(e)2.5

For sources and notes, see end of table.   Pour les sources et les notes, se reporter à la fin du tableau.

Country or territory / Pays ou territoires	Imports (5) - Importations (5)							
	Millions of dollars / Millions de dollars				As % of total services / En % du total des services			
	2000	2010	2011	2012	2000	2010	2011	2012
SELECTED COUNTRY GROUPINGS / SÉLECTION DE GROUPEMENTS DE PAYS								
World - Monde	..	..	..	..	..	..	..	..
Developing economies - Économies en développement	..	..	..	..	..	..	..	..
Transition economies - Économies en transition	..	..	..	..	..	..	..	..
Developed economies - Économies développées	..	..	..	..	..	..	..	..
Developing economies: Africa - Économies en développement : Afrique	..	..	..	..	..	..	..	..
Developing economies: America - Économies en développement : Amérique	..	..	..	..	..	..	..	..
Developing economies: Asia - Économies en développement : Asie	..	..	..	..	..	..	..	..
Developing economies: Oceania - Économies en développement : Océanie	..	..	..	..	..	..	..	..
Developed economies: America - Économies développées : Amérique	..	..	..	..	..	..	..	..
Developed economies: Asia - Économies développées : Asie	..	..	..	..	..	..	..	..
Developed economies: Europe - Économies développées : Europe	..	..	..	..	..	..	..	..
Developed economies: Oceania - Économies développées : Océanie	..	..	..	..	..	..	..	..
Least developed countries - Pays les moins avancés	..	..	..	..	..	..	..	..
Developing economies excluding LDCs - Économies en développement sans les PMA	..	..	..	..	..	..	..	..
Developing economies excluding China - Économies en développement sans la Chine	..	..	..	..	..	..	..	..
25 LEADING IMPORTERS: DEVELOPING AND TRANSITION ECONOMIES / 25 PRINCIPAUX IMPORTATEURS : ÉCONOMIES EN DÉVELOPPEMENT ET EN TRANSITION								
Brazil - Brésil	1 145	3 505	4 036	4 447	6.9	5.6	5.3	5.5
China - Chine	265	2 965	3 844	3 843	0.7	(e)1.5	(e)1.6	(e)1.4
Russian Federation - Fédération de Russie (14)	474	1 890	2 433	2 651	(e)2.8	2.6	2.7	2.5
Singapore - Singapour (11)	(e)226	-	-	-	(e)0.8	-	-	-
India - Inde (13)	577	2 531	1 856	(e)2 497	3.0	2.2	1.5	(e)1.9
Saudi Arabia - Arabie saoudite (20)	-	-	-	-	-	-	-	-
Malaysia - Malaisie (12)	201	1 057	1 199	1 453	1.2	3.3	3.2	3.4
Indonesia - Indonésie	_	585	715	726	_	2.2	2.3	2.1
Argentina - Argentine	149	461	591	718	1.6	3.1	3.3	3.8
Korea, Republic of - Corée, République de	92	496	559	480	0.3	0.5	0.6	0.4
China, Hong Kong SAR - Chine (RAS de Hong Kong) (12)	(e)128	564	541	-	(e)0.5	1.1	1.0	-
China, Taiwan Province of - Province chinoise de Taiwan	217	435	479	568	0.8	1.1	1.1	1.3
Chile - Chili (15)	78	(e)356	(e)443	(e)554	1.6	(e)2.7	(e)2.8	(e)3.7
United Arab Emirates - Émirats arabes unis	-	-	-	-	-	-	-	-
Iran (Islamic Rep. of) - Iran (Rép. islamique d')	-	399	-	-	-	1.7	-	-
Ukraine (12)	51	247	296	371	1.7	2.0	2.2	2.6
Congo	-	-	-	-	-	-	-	-
Croatia - Croatie	57	232	258	(e)259	3.1	6.6	7.1	(e)7.0
Colombia - Colombie	46	152	203	193	1.4	1.9	2.1	1.8
South Africa - Afrique du Sud	-	186	201	185	-	1.0	1.0	1.0
Peru - Pérou	-	208	196	-	-	3.4	3.0	-
Philippines (12)	99	109	193	158	1.9	1.0	1.6	1.1
Pakistan	-	168	192	184	-	2.4	2.4	2.3
Nigeria - Nigéria	-	124	165	(e)176	-	0.6	0.7	(e)0.8
Serbia - Serbie	_	188	160	159	_	4.7	3.6	3.8
15 LEADING IMPORTERS: DEVELOPED ECONOMIES / 15 PRINCIPAUX IMPORTATEURS : ÉCONOMIES DÉVELOPPÉES								
United States - États-Unis	6 230	21 094	24 538	-	2.8	5.2	5.7	-
Germany - Allemagne	4 963	14 224	16 331	(e)16 925	3.6	5.3	5.5	(e)5.7
United Kingdom - Royaume-Uni	1 268	6 613	6 398	(e)6 649	1.3	3.9	3.5	(e)3.7
Netherlands - Pays-Bas	1 184	5 331	5 270	(e)5 385	2.2	5.0	4.3	(e)4.5
France	744	4 100	5 202	(e)5 691	1.2	2.4	2.7	(e)3.3
Italy - Italie	914	4 331	4 545	(e)4 600	1.6	3.9	3.9	(e)4.3
Japan - Japon	3 069	3 572	4 218	(e)4 496	2.7	2.3	2.5	(e)2.5
Belgium - Belgique (18)	(a)1 326	2 899	3 656	(e)4 071	(a)3.2	3.5	4.0	(e)4.4
Sweden - Suède	1 078	2 662	3 431	(e)3 851	4.5	5.6	6.2	(e)7.0
Canada (19)	899	2 897	3 184	-	2.0	3.0	3.0	-
Spain - Espagne	1 227	2 825	3 100	(e)2 843	3.7	3.2	3.3	(e)3.2
Denmark - Danemark	-	1 973	2 148	(e)2 014	-	3.7	3.6	(e)3.5
Finland - Finlande	305	2 145	2 131	(e)2 462	3.2	8.1	7.2	(e)8.1
Poland - Pologne	218	1 664	1 929	(e)1 961	2.4	5.6	6.0	(e)6.2
Austria - Autriche	(e)375	1 580	1 761	(e)1 859	(e)2.3	4.3	4.2	(e)4.4

For sources and notes, see end of table.

Pour les sources et les notes, se reporter à la fin du tableau.

Country or territory / Pays ou territoires	Exports (6) - Exportations (6)							
	Millions of dollars / Millions de dollars				As % of total services / En % du total des services			
	2000	2010	2011	2012	2000	2010	2011	2012
SELECTED COUNTRY GROUPINGS **SÉLECTION DE GROUPEMENTS DE PAYS**								
World - Monde	27 700	97 500	98 100	100 300	1.8	2.5	2.3	2.3
Developing economies - Économies en développement	6 800	17 200	19 200	20 100	1.9	1.6	1.5	1.5
Transition economies - Économies en transition	100	800	700	700	0.5	0.7	0.6	0.5
Developed economies - Économies développées	20 800	79 500	78 300	79 500	1.8	3.0	2.6	2.7
Developing economies: Africa - Économies en développement : Afrique	900	1 100	1 200	1 100	2.6	1.2	1.3	1.2
Developing economies: America - Économies en développement : Amérique	2 800	3 500	4 200	4 400	4.5	2.7	2.7	2.7
Developing economies: Asia - Économies en développement : Asie	3 200	12 600	13 700	14 500	1.2	1.4	1.4	1.3
Developing economies: Oceania - Économies en développement : Océanie	0	0	0	-	0.8	0.3	-	-
Developed economies: America - Économies développées : Amérique	5 600	16 500	17 500	18 500	1.7	2.6	2.5	2.6
Developed economies: Asia - Économies développées : Asie	200	1 300	1 700	-400	0.2	0.8	1.0	-0.2
Developed economies: Europe - Économies développées : Europe	14 500	61 500	58 600	60 800	2.1	3.4	2.9	3.1
Developed economies: Oceania - Économies développées : Océanie	500	300	500	500	1.9	0.6	0.7	0.8
Least developed countries - Pays les moins avancés	(u)100	100	200	200	(u)1.2	0.6	0.6	(u)0.6
Developing economies excluding LDCs - Économies en développement sans les PMA	6 800	17 100	19 000	19 900	2.0	1.6	1.6	1.5
Developing economies excluding China - Économies en développement sans la Chine	6 700	15 500	16 200	16 800	2.1	1.6	1.5	1.5
25 LEADING EXPORTERS: DEVELOPING AND TRANSITION ECONOMIES **25 PRINCIPAUX EXPORTATEURS : ÉCONOMIES EN DÉVELOPPEMENT ET EN TRANSITION**								
China - Chine	108	1 727	3 018	3 329	0.4	(e)1.1	(e)1.7	(e)1.7
Singapore - Singapour (11)	(e)559	3 753	2 967	2 983	(e)2.0	4.0	2.7	2.7
India - Inde (13)	257	1 781	2 573	(e)2 228	1.5	1.4	1.9	(e)1.6
Mexico - Mexique	1 799	1 831	2 262	2 215	13.3	12.1	14.8	13.8
Turkey - Turquie	32	719	869	(e)988	0.2	2.1	2.2	(e)2.3
China, Hong Kong SAR - Chine (RAS de Hong Kong) (12)	(e)443	858	849	(e)841	(e)1.1	0.8	0.7	(e)0.7
Korea, Republic of - Corée, République de	68	515	518	495	0.2	0.6	0.5	0.4
China, Taiwan Province of - Province chinoise de Taiwan	607	430	513	595	3.0	1.1	1.1	1.2
Brazil - Brésil	312	416	505	541	3.3	1.3	1.3	1.4
Malaysia - Malaisie (12)	156	331	439	541	1.1	1.0	1.2	1.4
Chile - Chili (15)	76	286	378	393	1.9	2.6	2.9	3.1
Qatar	-	311	368	616	-	10.3	5.0	6.2
Bahrain - Bahreïn	-	906	352	-	-	22.4	11.6	-
Russian Federation - Fédération de Russie (14)	35	429	334	329	(e)0.4	1.0	0.6	0.6
South Africa - Afrique du Sud	451	273	319	296	8.9	1.9	2.2	2.0
Saudi Arabia - Arabie saoudite (20)	-	290	251	362	-	2.7	2.2	3.3
Peru - Pérou	113	166	230	(e)361	7.2	4.5	5.3	(e)7.1
Cuba	-	-	-	-	-	-	-	-
Thailand - Thaïlande (16)	82	67	156	383	0.6	0.2	0.4	0.8
Egypt - Égypte	30	97	151	-	0.3	0.4	0.8	-
Kuwait - Koweït (17)	72	331	142	-	3.9	3.5	1.4	-
Panama	39	123	140	136	1.9	2.0	1.9	1.5
Morocco - Maroc	30	153	133	(e)129	1.0	1.2	0.9	(e)1.0
Botswana	7	4	131	3	2.0	1.5	25.4	1.1
Trinidad and Tobago - Trinité-et-Tobago	46	139	111	-	8.3	15.9	(e,b)1.9	-
15 LEADING EXPORTERS: DEVELOPED ECONOMIES **15 PRINCIPAUX EXPORTATEURS : ÉCONOMIES DÉVELOPPÉES**								
United Kingdom - Royaume-Uni	5 740	23 369	16 358	(e)18 825	4.8	8.7	5.6	(e)6.6
United States - États-Unis	3 631	14 530	15 477	(e)16 626	1.3	2.6	2.5	(e)2.6
Ireland - Irlande	1 126	10 549	11 313	(e)11 042	6.7	10.7	10.0	(e)9.5
Germany - Allemagne	614	5 850	6 393	(e)5 959	0.7	2.4	2.4	(e)2.3
Switzerland - Suisse	1 508	4 928	5 743	(e)5 811	4.9	5.9	6.0	(e)6.3
France	1 329	3 677	5 323	(e)4 273	1.6	1.9	2.4	(e)2.0
Luxembourg	..	3 552	3 151	(e)3 266	..	5.6	4.4	(e)4.7
Italy - Italie	806	2 710	2 575	(e)3 221	1.4	2.8	2.4	(e)3.1
Canada (19)	1 939	1 894	1 980	1 848	4.8	2.6	2.5	2.3
Japan - Japon	173	1 273	1 658	(e)- 378	0.2	0.9	1.1	(e)-0.3
Spain - Espagne	211	1 075	1 371	(e)1 559	0.4	0.9	1.0	(e)1.1
Belgium - Belgique (18)	(a)1 061	1 110	1 207	(e)1 104	(a)2.1	1.2	1.3	(e)1.1
Austria - Autriche	(e)676	1 150	927	(e)1 312	(e)2.9	2.1	1.5	(e)2.1
Sweden - Suède	518	802	911	(e)852	2.4	1.3	1.2	(e)1.1
Netherlands - Pays-Bas	205	625	712	(e)681	0.4	0.5	0.5	(e)0.5

For sources and notes, see end of table.

Pour les sources et les notes, se reporter à la fin du tableau.

Country or territory / Pays ou territoires	Imports (6) - Importations (6)							
	Millions of dollars / Millions de dollars				As % of total services / En % du total des services			
	2000	2010	2011	2012	2000	2010	2011	2012
SELECTED COUNTRY GROUPINGS / SÉLECTION DE GROUPEMENTS DE PAYS								
World - Monde	..	..	..	..	..	..	..	..
Developing economies - Économies en développement	..	..	..	..	..	..	..	..
Transition economies - Économies en transition	..	..	..	..	..	..	..	..
Developed economies - Économies développées	..	..	..	..	..	..	..	..
Developing economies: Africa - Économies en développement : Afrique	..	..	..	..	..	..	..	..
Developing economies: America - Économies en développement : Amérique	..	..	..	..	..	..	..	..
Developing economies: Asia - Économies en développement : Asie	..	..	..	..	..	..	..	..
Developing economies: Oooania - Économies en développement : Océanie	..	..	..	..	..	..	..	..
Developed economies: America - Économies développées : Amérique	..	..	..	..	..	..	..	..
Developed economies: Asia - Économies développées : Asie	..	..	..	..	..	..	..	..
Developed economies: Europe - Économies développées : Europe	..	..	..	..	..	..	..	..
Developed economies: Oceania - Économies développées : Océanie	..	..	..	..	..	..	..	..
Least developed countries - Pays les moins avancés	..	..	..	..	..	..	..	..
Developing economies excluding LDCs - Économies en développement sans les PMA	..	..	..	..	..	..	..	..
Developing economies excluding China - Économies en développement sans la Chine	..	..	..	..	..	..	..	..
25 LEADING IMPORTERS: DEVELOPING AND TRANSITION ECONOMIES / 25 PRINCIPAUX IMPORTATEURS : ÉCONOMIES EN DÉVELOPPEMENT ET EN TRANSITION								
China - Chine	2 471	15 755	19 738	20 600	6.9	(e)8.1	(e)8.3	(e)7.3
India - Inde (13)	813	4 981	6 052	(e)6 260	4.2	4.3	4.9	(e)4.9
Singapore - Singapour (11)	(e)1 537	3 868	4 473	4 473	(e)5.1	4.0	3.9	3.8
Mexico - Mexique	1 359	2 626	4 086	4 086	8.0	10.4	13.9	14.0
Thailand - Thaïlande (16)	801	2 164	2 753	3 050	5.2	4.8	5.3	5.8
Saudi Arabia - Arabie saoudite (20)	249	1 669	1 949	2 300	1.0	2.2	2.5	3.1
Iraq	-	1 771	1 935	-	-	17.9	17.5	-
Brazil - Brésil	317	1 529	1 717	1 535	1.9	2.4	2.3	1.9
Egypt - Égypte	450	1 459	1 476		6.0	9.9	10.5	-
Chile - Chili (15)	192	1 127	1 364	1 084	4.0	8.7	8.7	7.2
Indonesia - Indonésie	_	1 153	1 290	1 096	_	4.4	4.1	3.2
Turkey - Turquie	342	1 188	1 276	(e)1 302	3.8	6.1	6.1	(e)6.3
Russian Federation - Fédération de Russie (14)	412	1 011	1 245	1 288	(e)2.4	1.4	1.4	1.2
China, Hong Kong SAR - Chine (RAS de Hong Kong) (12)	(e)528	1 192	1 193	(e)993	(e)2.1	2.3	2.1	(e)1.7
China, Taiwan Province of - Province chinoise de Taiwan	587	999	1 155	1 293	2.2	2.6	2.7	3.0
Qatar	-	420	1 107	1 014	-	4.8	6.6	4.2
Oman	114	715	759	(e)817	6.5	11.4	10.7	(e)10.3
Argentina - Argentine	200	541	719	408	2.2	3.7	4.0	2.2
Colombia - Colombie	202	576	715	837	6.1	7.1	7.5	7.9
Nigeria - Nigéria	88	503	703	(e)717	2.7	2.4	2.9	(e)3.2
Malaysia - Malaisie (12)	289	559	693	953	1.7	1.7	1.8	2.3
Korea, Republic of - Corée, République de	146	882	686	828	0.4	0.9	0.7	0.8
South Africa - Afrique du Sud	380	527	635	645	6.5	2.9	3.2	3.6
Peru - Pérou	150	491	588	(e)728	6.5	8.1	9.1	(e)9.9
Viet Nam	-	481	567	582	-	4.8	4.8	4.6
15 LEADING IMPORTERS: DEVELOPED ECONOMIES / 15 PRINCIPAUX IMPORTATEURS : ÉCONOMIES DÉVELOPPÉES								
United States - États-Unis	11 284	61 013	56 620	(e)53 340	5.1	15.1	13.2	(e)12.1
Ireland - Irlande	1 458	8 307	8 337	(e)7 573	5.0	7.7	7.2	(e)6.8
Japan - Japon	2 025	6 799	6 806	(e)7 406	1.8	4.3	4.1	(e)4.2
Canada (19)	2 840	4 375	4 728	4 400	6.4	4.5	4.5	4.1
Germany - Allemagne	962	3 960	4 554	(e)3 612	0.7	1.5	1.5	(e)1.2
Italy - Italie	1 088	4 019	4 050	(e)4 104	2.0	3.6	3.5	(e)3.8
United Kingdom - Royaume-Uni	1 091	4 711	3 520	(e)3 460	1.1	2.8	1.9	(e)1.9
France	-302	3 074	3 039	(e)1 534	-0.5	1.8	1.6	(e)0.9
Spain - Espagne	325	1 972	2 063	(e)1 880	1.0	2.2	2.2	(e)2.1
Luxembourg	..	2 091	1 822	(e)1 862	..	5.7	4.4	(e)4.6
Greece - Grèce	207	1 451	1 487	(e)1 175	1.8	7.2	7.7	(e)7.6
Belgium - Belgique (18)	(a)863	1 168	1 305	(e)1 341	(a)2.1	1.4	1.4	(e)1.5
Netherlands - Pays-Bas	557	1 066	1 189	(e)1 148	1.0	1.0	1.0	(e)1.0
Austria - Autriche	(e)85	979	1 070	(e)1 087	(e)0.5	2.6	2.5	(e)2.6
Switzerland - Suisse	74	852	968	(e)1 008	0.6	2.3	2.1	(e)2.2

For sources and notes, see end of table.

Pour les sources et les notes, se reporter à la fin du tableau.

5

Country or territory / Pays ou territoires	Exports (7) - Exportations (7)							
	Millions of dollars / Millions de dollars				As % of total services En % du total des services			
	2000	2010	2011	2012	2000	2010	2011	2012
SELECTED COUNTRY GROUPINGS **SÉLECTION DE GROUPEMENTS DE PAYS**								
World - Monde	97 600	282 300	316 900	303 100	6.4	7.3	7.3	6.8
Developing economies - Économies en développement	13 000	46 900	52 100	51 800	3.7	4.2	4.2	3.8
Transition economies - Économies en transition	200	1 800	1 700	2 000	1.0	1.8	1.4	1.6
Developed economies - Économies développées	84 400	233 600	263 000	249 300	7.4	8.7	8.9	8.4
Developing economies: Africa - Économies en développement : Afrique	1 000	1 900	2 100	2 200	2.9	2.1	2.3	2.2
Developing economies: America - Économies en développement : Amérique	1 000	3 500	4 600	5 100	1.6	2.6	3.0	3.2
Developing economies: Asia - Économies en développement : Asie	11 000	41 500	45 300	44 500	4.3	4.7	4.5	4.1
Developing economies: Oceania - Économies en développement : Océanie	-	0	100	0	-	1.3	-	-
Developed economies: America - Économies développées : Amérique	23 000	73 900	78 000	76 300	7.0	11.7	11.3	10.6
Developed economies: Asia - Économies développées : Asie	3 700	4 800	5 300	5 900	4.4	2.9	3.1	3.3
Developed economies: Europe - Économies développées : Europe	57 100	153 900	178 100	165 300	8.1	8.4	8.7	8.3
Developed economies: Oceania - Économies développées : Océanie	600	1 000	1 500	1 800	2.3	1.8	2.5	2.8
Least developed countries - Pays les moins avancés	(u)100	800	900	1 000	(u)1.7	3.1	3.1	(u)3.3
Developing economies excluding LDCs - Économies en développement sans les PMA	12 900	46 100	51 200	50 800	3.7	4.2	4.2	3.9
Developing economies excluding China - Économies en développement sans la Chine	12 900	45 600	51 300	49 900	4.0	4.8	4.8	4.3
25 LEADING EXPORTERS: DEVELOPING AND TRANSITION ECONOMIES **25 PRINCIPAUX EXPORTATEURS : ÉCONOMIES EN DÉVELOPPEMENT ET EN TRANSITION**								
Singapore - Singapour (11)	(e)1 814	11 900	14 827	14 837	(e)6.4	12.6	13.6	13.2
China, Hong Kong SAR - Chine (RAS de Hong Kong) (12)	(e)4 371	13 140	14 570	(e)14 442	(e)10.8	12.6	12.3	(e)11.7
India - Inde (13)	276	5 834	6 234	(e)5 531	1.7	4.7	4.5	(e)3.9
Korea, Republic of - Corée, République de	705	2 736	3 389	3 192	2.2	3.1	3.6	2.9
Brazil - Brésil	376	2 073	2 662	2 684	4.0	6.5	7.0	6.7
Lebanon - Liban	-	(b)2 076	1 227	-	-	(b)13.0	6.2	-
Russian Federation - Fédération de Russie (14)	100	1 053	1 103	1 312	(e)1.0	2.3	2.0	2.2
China, Taiwan Province of - Province chinoise de Taiwan	805	847	922	936	4.0	2.1	2.0	1.9
South Africa - Afrique du Sud	-	827	901	891	-	5.9	6.1	5.9
China - Chine	78	1 331	849	1 886	0.3	(e)0.8	(e)0.5	(e)1.0
Panama	141	452	658	943	7.0	7.3	9.1	10.6
Afghanistan	-	533	-	-	-	16.9	-	-
Turkey - Turquie	368	490	531	(e)534	1.8	1.4	1.4	(e)1.2
Cuba	-	-	-	-	-	-	-	..
Indonesia - Indonésie	_	332	407	190	_	2.0	2.0	0.8
Chile - Chili (15)	38	(e)60	(e)314	(e)408	0.9	(e)0.6	(e)2.4	(e)3.2
Ukraine (12)	22	475	312	249	(e)0.6	2.9	1.7	1.3
Malaysia - Malaisie (12)	160	106	284	144	1.1	0.3	0.8	0.4
Thailand - Thaïlande (16)	-	188	269	372	-	0.5	0.6	0.8
Algeria - Algérie	-	221	236	-	-	6.2	6.3	-
Viet Nam	-	192	208	150	-	2.6	2.4	1.6
Mauritius - Maurice	21	56	163	137	2.0	2.1	5.0	4.0
Kenya	-	109	159	-	-	2.9	3.9	-
Kuwait - Koweït (17)	18	191	147	-	1.0	2.0	1.4	-
Uruguay	62	121	138	(e)128	4.9	4.7	4.1	(e)4.0
15 LEADING EXPORTERS: DEVELOPED ECONOMIES **15 PRINCIPAUX EXPORTATEURS : ÉCONOMIES DÉVELOPPÉES**								
United States - États-Unis	22 117	70 346	74 055	(e)72 328	7.6	12.7	12.2	(e)11.3
United Kingdom - Royaume-Uni (24)	20 243	53 971	64 953	(e)57 998	16.8	20.2	22.1	(e)20.5
Luxembourg	..	37 620	41 699	(e)39 883	..	59.0	58.6	(e)56.8
Switzerland - Suisse (25)	10 633	15 823	17 017	(e)16 076	34.6	19.0	17.6	(e)17.3
Germany - Allemagne	3 546	12 658	14 648	(e)13 994	4.3	5.2	5.5	(e)5.3
Ireland - Irlande	2 081	8 378	9 168	(e)9 164	12.3	8.5	8.1	(e)7.9
France	1 259	3 322	(b)6 525	(e)5 227	1.6	1.7	(b)2.9	(e)2.5
Spain - Espagne	1 393	4 572	5 289	(e)4 502	2.6	3.7	3.7	(e)3.3
Japan - Japon	2 864	3 606	4 111	(e)4 651	4.1	2.6	2.8	(e)3.2
Belgium - Belgique (18)	(a)13 106	3 349	3 823	(e)3 589	(a)26.3	3.7	4.0	(e)3.7
Canada (19)	879	3 292	3 747	3 767	2.2	4.5	4.7	4.8
Italy - Italie	421	2 559	2 609	(e)2 778	0.7	2.6	2.4	(e)2.7
Norway - Norvège	386	1 375	2 314	(e)2 527	2.2	3.5	5.5	(e)5.8
Netherlands - Pays-Bas	732	1 402	1 568	(e)1 465	1.4	1.2	1.1	(e)1.1
Sweden - Suède	702	1 048	1 519	(e)1 485	3.2	1.6	2.0	(e)1.9

For sources and notes, see end of table.   Pour les sources et les notes, se reporter à la fin du tableau.

Country or territory / Pays ou territoires	Imports (7) - Importations (7)							
	Millions of dollars / Millions de dollars				As % of total services En % du total des services			
	2000	2010	2011	2012	2000	2010	2011	2012
SELECTED COUNTRY GROUPINGS **SÉLECTION DE GROUPEMENTS DE PAYS**								
World - Monde	..	..	..	..	..	..	..	..
Developing economies - Économies en développement	..	..	..	..	..	..	..	..
Transition economies - Économies en transition	..	..	..	..	..	..	..	..
Developed economies - Économies développées	..	..	..	..	..	..	..	..
Developing economies: Africa - Économies en développement : Afrique	..	..	..	..	..	..	..	..
Developing economies: America - Économies en développement : Amérique	..	..	..	..	..	..	..	..
Developing economies: Asia - Économies en développement : Asie	..	..	..	..	..	..	..	..
Developing economies: Oceania - Économies en développement : Océanie	..	..	..	..	..	..	..	..
Developed economies: America - Économies développées : Amérique	..	..	..	..	..	..	..	..
Developed economies: Asia - Économies développées : Asie	..	..	..	..	..	..	..	..
Developed economies: Europe - Économies développées : Europe	..	..	..	..	..	..	..	..
Developed economies: Oceania - Économies développées : Océanie	..	..	..	..	..	..	..	..
Least developed countries - Pays les moins avancés	..	..	..	..	..	..	..	..
Developing economies excluding LDCs - Économies en développement sans les PMA	..	..	..	..	..	..	..	..
Developing economies excluding China - Économies en développement sans la Chine	..	..	..	..	..	..	..	..
25 LEADING IMPORTERS: DEVELOPING AND TRANSITION ECONOMIES **25 PRINCIPAUX IMPORTATEURS : ÉCONOMIES EN DÉVELOPPEMENT ET EN TRANSITION**								
India - Inde (13)	1 277	6 787	8 211	(e)5 434	6.7	5.8	6.6	(e)4.2
China, Hong Kong SAR - Chine (RAS de Hong Kong) (12)	(e)824	3 543	3 882	(e)4 082	(e)3.3	6.9	6.9	(e)7.1
Singapore - Singapour (11)	(e)603	2 569	3 036	3 019	(e)2.0	2.6	2.6	2.6
Brazil - Brésil	670	1 679	1 804	1 975	4.0	2.7	2.4	2.4
Russian Federation - Fédération de Russie (14)	36	1 720	1 744	1 881	(e)0.2	2.3	2.0	1.8
Saudi Arabia - Arabie saoudite (20)	-	1 034	1 619	1 074	-	1.3	2.1	1.5
Turkey - Turquie	671	724	1 221	(e)1 177	7.4	3.7	5.8	(e)5.7
Iraq	-	997	1 096	-	-	10.1	9.9	-
Chile - Chili (15)	222	(e)643	(e)1 086	(e)723	4.6	(e)5.0	(e)6.9	(e)4.8
Ukraine (12)	74	1 086	954	946	2.5	8.6	7.2	6.7
Korea, Republic of - Corée, République de	191	843	894	1 012	0.6	0.9	0.9	0.9
China - Chine	97	1 387	747	1 926	0.3	(e)0.7	(e)0.3	(e)0.7
Indonesia - Indonésie	_	450	581	516	_	1.7	1.9	1.5
Panama	36	319	574	884	3.2	11.7	17.0	22.9
Mexico - Mexique	918	548	452	272	5.4	2.2	1.5	0.9
United Arab Emirates - Émirats arabes unis	-	-	-	-	-	-	-	-
Malaysia - Malaisie (12)	175	332	359	369	1.0	1.0	0.9	0.9
Iran (Islamic Rep. of) - Iran (Rép. islamique d')	-	386	-	-	-	1.6	-	-
Nigeria - Nigéria	-	34	318	(e)430	-	0.2	1.3	(e)1.9
Congo	-	-	-	-	-	-	-	-
Lebanon - Liban	-	(b)1 010	309	-	-	(b)7.5	2.4	-
Angola	-	830	301	-	-	4.4	1.3	-
China, Taiwan Province of - Province chinoise de Taiwan	1 037	197	267	267	3.9	0.5	0.6	0.6
Mauritius - Maurice	21	83	226	137	2.8	4.2	9.1	5.6
Viet Nam	-	195	217	175	-	2.0	1.8	1.4
15 LEADING IMPORTERS: DEVELOPED ECONOMIES **15 PRINCIPAUX IMPORTATEURS : ÉCONOMIES DÉVELOPPÉES**								
Luxembourg	..	19 065	21 399	(e)20 451	..	51.8	51.7	(e)50.5
United States - États-Unis	10 936	14 763	16 207	(e)15 641	5.0	3.6	3.8	(e)3.5
United Kingdom - Royaume-Uni (24)	4 165	9 725	12 295	(e)10 169	4.2	5.7	6.8	(e)5.7
Germany - Allemagne	2 009	7 128	9 502	(e)7 709	1.5	2.7	3.2	(e)2.6
Ireland - Irlande	1 448	5 977	6 635	(e)5 921	5.0	5.6	5.7	(e)5.3
Italy - Italie	541	4 547	5 134	(e)4 975	1.0	4.1	4.4	(e)4.7
Spain - Espagne	1 085	4 659	5 006	(e)5 378	3.3	5.3	5.3	(e)6.0
Canada (19)	1 546	4 536	4 432	4 330	3.5	4.7	4.2	4.1
France	1 458	2 385	(b)3 670	(e)3 540	2.4	1.4	(b)1.9	(e)2.1
Japan - Japon	1 882	3 149	3 346	(e)3 221	1.6	2.0	2.0	(e)1.8
Belgium - Belgique (18)	(a)7 884	1 910	2 285	(e)2 253	(a)18.8	2.3	2.5	(e)2.4
Switzerland - Suisse (25)	783	1 721	1 894	(e)1 687	6.1	4.7	4.2	(e)3.6
Norway - Norvège	585	1 259	1 876	(e)2 087	3.9	2.9	4.1	(e)4.3
Netherlands - Pays-Bas	957	1 579	1 751	(e)1 601	1.8	1.5	1.4	(e)1.3
Australia - Australie (21)	348	591	893	(e)786	1.8	1.2	1.5	(e)1.2

For sources and notes, see end of table.

Pour les sources et les notes, se reporter à la fin du tableau.

Country or territory / Pays ou territoires	Exports (8) - Exportations (8)							
	Millions of dollars / Millions de dollars				As % of total services / En % du total des services			
	2000	2010	2011	2012	2000	2010	2011	2012
SELECTED COUNTRY GROUPINGS / SÉLECTION DE GROUPEMENTS DE PAYS								
World - Monde	92 100	254 700	289 500	289 600	6.1	6.6	6.7	6.5
Developing economies - Économies en développement	2 200	8 100	10 800	10 400	0.6	0.7	0.9	0.8
Transition economies - Économies en transition	200	700	900	1 000	0.9	0.7	0.7	0.7
Developed economies - Économies développées	89 600	245 900	277 900	278 200	7.8	9.2	9.4	9.4
Developing economies: Africa - Économies en développement : Afrique	200	500	400	(u)400	0.7	0.5	0.4	(u)0.4
Developing economies: America - Économies en développement : Amérique	500	1 200	1 500	1 500	0.8	0.9	1.0	0.9
Developing economies: Asia - Économies en développement : Asie	1 500	6 400	8 800	8 400	0.6	0.7	0.9	0.8
Developing economies: Oceania - Économies en développement : Océanie	-	-	-	-	-	-	-	-
Developed economies: America - Économies développées : Amérique	54 100	110 000	123 700	127 900	16.4	17.4	18.0	17.7
Developed economies: Asia - Économies développées : Asie	10 700	27 500	30 200	33 000	12.6	16.6	17.5	18.8
Developed economies: Europe - Économies développées : Europe	24 400	107 300	122 800	116 300	3.5	5.9	6.0	5.8
Developed economies: Oceania - Économies développées : Océanie	400	1 100	1 200	1 100	1.7	2.0	1.9	1.7
Least developed countries - Pays les moins avancés	(u)100	(u)300	(u)200	(u)200	(u)1.0	(u)1.2	(u)0.6	(u)0.6
Developing economies excluding LDCs - Économies en développement sans les PMA	2 200	7 800	10 600	10 200	0.6	0.7	0.9	0.8
Developing economies excluding China - Économies en développement sans la Chine	2 200	7 300	10 000	9 300	0.7	0.8	0.9	0.8
25 LEADING EXPORTERS: DEVELOPING AND TRANSITION ECONOMIES / 25 PRINCIPAUX EXPORTATEURS : ÉCONOMIES EN DÉVELOPPEMENT ET EN TRANSITION								
Korea, Republic of - Corée, République de	688	3 145	4 336	3 436	2.2	3.6	4.6	3.1
Singapore - Singapour (11)	(e)85	976	1 637	1 649	(e)0.3	1.0	1.5	1.5
China, Taiwan Province of - Province chinoise de Taiwan	371	460	838	932	1.9	1.1	1.8	1.9
China - Chine	80	830	743	1 044	0.3	(e)0.5	(e)0.4	(e)0.5
Brazil - Brésil	125	397	591	511	1.3	1.2	1.5	1.3
Russian Federation - Fédération de Russie (14)	91	386	556	664	(e)0.9	0.9	1.0	1.1
China, Hong Kong SAR - Chine (RAS de Hong Kong) (12)	(e)107	400	459	-	(e)0.3	0.4	0.4	-
India - Inde (13)	83	128	302	(e)316	0.5	0.1	0.2	(e)0.2
Paraguay	203	254	297	-	34.0	17.2	15.5	-
Thailand - Thaïlande (16)	9	153	177	241	0.1	0.4	0.4	0.5
Argentina - Argentine	37	145	174	164	0.7	1.1	1.1	1.1
Cuba	-	-	-	-	-	-	-	-
Malaysia - Malaisie (12)	18	99	149	135	0.1	0.3	0.4	0.4
Ukraine (12)	1	132	107	124	(e)0.0	0.8	0.6	0.6
Indonesia - Indonésie	_	60	79	58	_	0.4	0.4	0.3
Chile - Chili (15)	10	64	75	75	0.2	0.6	0.6	0.6
South Africa - Afrique du Sud	49	59	66	67	1.0	0.4	0.4	0.4
Guyana	15	47	-	-	8.7	18.9	-	-
Colombia - Colombie	5	56	59	89	0.3	1.3	1.2	1.7
Serbia - Serbie	_	40	57	36	_	0.9	1.1	0.7
Kenya	7	54	55	-	0.7	1.4	1.3	-
United Republic of Tanzania - République-Unie de Tanzanie	0	-	-	-	0.0	-	-	-
Congo	-	-	-	-	-	-	-	-
Egypt - Égypte	59	-	-	-	0.6	-	-	-
Papua New Guinea - Papouasie-Nouvelle-Guinée	-	-	-	-	-	-	-	-
15 LEADING EXPORTERS: DEVELOPED ECONOMIES / 15 PRINCIPAUX EXPORTATEURS : ÉCONOMIES DÉVELOPPÉES								
United States - États-Unis	51 808	107 165	120 836	(e)124 303	17.9	19.3	19.9	(e)19.4
Netherlands - Pays-Bas	2 155	24 593	30 850	(e)29 632	4.1	20.8	22.3	(e)22.2
Japan - Japon	10 230	26 683	29 058	(e)31 846	14.8	18.9	20.0	(e)21.9
Switzerland - Suisse	2 744	16 546	19 523	-	8.9	19.8	20.2	-
France	2 313	13 132	15 704	(e)12 726	2.9	6.8	7.0	(e)6.0
Germany - Allemagne	2 925	14 746	14 334	(e)13 395	3.5	6.1	5.4	(e)5.1
United Kingdom - Royaume-Uni	8 154	14 165	14 176	(e)11 376	6.8	5.3	4.8	(e)4.0
Sweden - Suède	1 282	5 847	6 231	(e)6 657	5.9	9.2	8.4	(e)8.7
Ireland - Irlande	509	2 903	5 055	(e)4 790	3.0	2.9	4.5	(e)4.1
Italy - Italie	555	3 646	3 691	(e)3 776	1.0	3.7	3.5	(e)3.6
Finland - Finlande	883	2 324	3 224	(e)3 622	11.5	8.6	10.7	(e)12.2
Canada (19)	2 259	2 814	2 911	3 583	5.6	3.8	3.6	4.5
Denmark - Danemark	-	2 207	2 629	(e)2 498	-	3.6	3.9	(e)3.8
Belgium - Belgique (18)	(a)779	2 342	2 579	(e)2 711	(a)1.6	2.6	2.7	(e)2.8
Israel - Israël	496	849	1 100	1 146	3.2	3.5	4.1	3.9

For sources and notes, see end of table.

Pour les sources et les notes, se reporter à la fin du tableau.

Country or territory / Pays ou territoires	Imports (8) - Importations (8)							
	Millions of dollars / Millions de dollars				As % of total services / En % du total des services			
	2000	2010	2011	2012	2000	2010	2011	2012
SELECTED COUNTRY GROUPINGS / **SÉLECTION DE GROUPEMENTS DE PAYS**								
World - Monde	..	..	..	..	..	..	..	..
Developing economies - Économies en développement	..	..	..	..	..	..	..	..
Transition economies - Économies en transition	..	..	..	..	..	..	..	..
Developed economies - Économies développées	..	..	..	..	..	..	..	..
Developing economies: Africa - Économies en développement : Afrique	..	..	..	..	..	..	..	..
Developing economies: America - Économies en développement : Amérique	..	..	..	..	..	..	..	..
Developing economies: Asia - Économies en développement : Asie	..	..	..	..	..	..	..	..
Developing economies: Oceania - Économies en développement : Océanie	..	..	..	..	..	..	..	..
Developed economies: America - Économies développées : Amérique	..	..	..	..	..	..	..	..
Developed economies: Asia - Économies développées : Asie	..	..	..	..	..	..	..	..
Developed economies: Europe - Économies développées : Europe	..	..	..	..	..	..	..	..
Developed economies: Oceania - Économies développées : Océanie	..	..	..	..	..	..	..	..
Least developed countries - Pays les moins avancés	..	..	..	..	..	..	..	..
Developing economies excluding LDCs - Économies en développement sans les PMA	..	..	..	..	..	..	..	..
Developing economies excluding China - Économies en développement sans la Chine	..	..	..	..	..	..	..	..
25 LEADING IMPORTERS: DEVELOPING AND TRANSITION ECONOMIES / **25 PRINCIPAUX IMPORTATEURS : ÉCONOMIES EN DÉVELOPPEMENT ET EN TRANSITION**								
Singapore - Singapour (11)	(e)5 047	14 009	16 391	16 511	(e)16.8	14.3	14.3	14.0
China - Chine	1 281	13 040	14 706	17 749	3.6	(e)6.7	(e)6.2	(e)6.3
Korea, Republic of - Corée, République de	3 221	9 031	7 295	8 387	9.6	9.4	7.2	7.8
Russian Federation - Fédération de Russie (14)	69	4 842	5 830	7 629	(e)0.4	6.6	6.5	7.2
China, Taiwan Province of - Province chinoise de Taiwan	1 834	4 943	5 788	4 549	6.9	13.1	13.8	10.6
Brazil - Brésil	1 415	2 850	3 301	3 666	8.5	4.6	4.3	4.5
Thailand - Thaïlande (16)	710	3 084	3 119	3 611	4.6	6.8	6.0	6.8
Saudi Arabia - Arabie saoudite (20)	-	-	-	-	-	-	-	-
India - Inde (13)	282	2 438	2 820	(e)3 998	1.5	2.1	2.3	(e)3.1
South Africa - Afrique du Sud	246	1 941	2 118	2 017	4.2	10.5	10.8	11.4
China, Hong Kong SAR - Chine (RAS de Hong Kong) (12)	(e)461	1 978	2 009	-	(e)1.9	3.9	3.6	-
Argentina - Argentine	580	1 610	1 919	2 186	6.3	10.9	10.8	11.7
Indonesia - Indonésie	_	1 616	1 788	1 800	_	6.2	5.7	5.3
Malaysia - Malaisie (12)	546	1 316	1 638	1 532	3.3	4.1	4.3	3.6
United Arab Emirates - Émirats arabes unis	-	-	-	-	-	-	-	-
Chile - Chili (15)	297	726	774	849	6.2	5.6	4.9	5.6
Ukraine (12)	663	744	746	727	22.1	5.9	5.6	5.1
Congo	-	-	-	-	-	-	-	-
Turkey - Turquie	173	816	680	(e)742	1.9	4.2	3.2	(e)3.6
Philippines (12)	197	445	442	504	3.8	3.9	3.6	3.5
Colombia - Colombie	74	362	425	499	2.2	4.5	4.5	4.7
Oman	-	-	-	-	-	-	-	-
Venezuela (Bolivarian Rep. of) - Venezuela (Rép. bolivarienne du)	184	340	364	397	4.1	2.6	2.3	2.2
Equatorial Guinea - Guinée équatoriale	-	-	-	-	-	-	-	-
Croatia - Croatie	61	224	272	(e)282	3.3	6.4	7.5	(e)7.6
15 LEADING IMPORTERS: DEVELOPED ECONOMIES / **15 PRINCIPAUX IMPORTATEURS : ÉCONOMIES DÉVELOPPÉES**								
Ireland - Irlande	7 922	37 428	40 621	(e)41 191	27.4	34.9	35.1	(e)36.7
United States - États-Unis	16 606	33 434	36 620	(e)41 992	7.5	8.3	8.5	(e)9.5
Netherlands - Pays-Bas	2 559	20 038	21 697	(e)19 699	4.8	18.9	17.8	(e)16.4
Switzerland - Suisse	1 828	16 591	21 697		14.3	45.5	48.1	
Japan - Japon	11 008	18 774	19 158	(e)19 919	9.6	11.9	11.4	(e)11.3
Germany - Allemagne	5 699	13 220	13 162	(e)12 185	4.1	4.9	4.4	(e)4.1
United Kingdom - Royaume-Uni	6 626	8 489	10 661	(e)8 159	6.7	5.0	5.9	(e)4.5
Canada (19)	3 768	9 731	10 352	10 563	8.5	10.1	9.8	9.9
France	2 047	9 339	9 941	(e)8 691	3.4	5.5	5.2	(e)5.0
Italy - Italie	1 191	7 135	7 206	(e)6 234	2.2	6.5	6.2	(e)5.8
Australia - Australie (21)	1 160	3 422	4 098	(e)4 231	6.1	6.7	6.8	(e)6.6
Spain - Espagne	1 676	2 723	2 780	(e)2 254	5.0	3.1	2.9	(e)2.5
Belgium - Belgique (18)	(a)915	1 887	2 625	(e)2 661	(a)2.2	2.3	2.9	(e)2.9
Poland - Pologne	557	2 242	2 413	(e)2 297	6.2	7.6	7.5	(e)7.3
Denmark - Danemark	-	1 723	1 834	(e)1 838	-	3.2	3.1	(e)3.2

For sources and notes, see end of table.   Pour les sources et les notes, se reporter à la fin du tableau.

Country or territory / Pays ou territoires	Exports (9) - Exportations (9)							
	Millions of dollars / Millions de dollars				As % of total services / En % du total des services			
	2000	2010	2011	2012	2000	2010	2011	2012
SELECTED COUNTRY GROUPINGS / SÉLECTION DE GROUPEMENTS DE PAYS								
World - Monde	325 800	970 000	1 098 600	1 127 200	21.4	25.0	25.4	25.5
Developing economies - Économies en développement	82 000	250 400	296 600	330 400	23.3	22.5	23.7	24.5
Transition economies - Économies en transition	3 300	20 300	24 800	26 400	13.5	19.8	20.3	20.4
Developed economies - Économies développées	240 600	699 300	777 200	770 500	21.0	26.2	26.3	26.1
Developing economies: Africa - Économies en développement : Afrique	5 000	9 900	10 000	10 400	15.1	11.0	10.8	10.7
Developing economies: America - Économies en développement : Amérique	8 400	30 900	42 200	43 800	13.6	23.4	27.4	27.3
Developing economies: Asia - Économies en développement : Asie	68 300	209 300	244 000	275 600	26.7	23.7	24.4	25.4
Developing economies: Oceania - Économies en développement : Océanie	-	-	-	-	-	-	-	-
Developed economies: America - Économies développées : Amérique	56 000	138 100	144 100	152 700	17.0	21.9	20.9	21.2
Developed economies: Asia - Économies développées : Asie	20 600	46 700	49 600	42 100	24.3	28.2	28.8	24.1
Developed economies: Europe - Économies développées : Europe	161 600	506 400	574 500	566 100	22.9	27.8	28.2	28.4
Developed economies: Oceania - Économies développées : Océanie	2 400	8 000	8 900	9 500	9.8	14.3	14.3	15.1
Least developed countries - Pays les moins avancés	(u)1 200	(u)2 900	3 000	(u)3 200	(u)17.2	(u)11.5	10.2	(u)10.2
Developing economies excluding LDCs - Économies en développement sans les PMA	80 800	247 500	293 600	327 200	23.4	22.8	24.0	24.9
Developing economies excluding China - Économies en développement sans la Chine	74 300	198 200	238 400	263 700	23.1	20.9	22.2	22.8
25 LEADING EXPORTERS: DEVELOPING AND TRANSITION ECONOMIES / 25 PRINCIPAUX EXPORTATEURS : ÉCONOMIES EN DÉVELOPPEMENT ET EN TRANSITION								
China - Chine	7 663	52 203	58 270	66 623	25.2	(e)32.2	(e)33.0	(e)34.8
China, Hong Kong SAR - Chine (RAS de Hong Kong) (12)	(e)15 954	35 121	39 573	-	(e)39.5	33.8	33.5	-
India - Inde (13)	-	(e)34 957	(e)39 524	(e)45 009	-	(e)28.2	(e)28.7	(e)31.9
Singapore - Singapour (11)	(e)8 264	19 476	23 469	24 223	(e)28.9	20.6	21.6	21.6
China, Taiwan Province of - Province chinoise de Taiwan	9 692	18 818	21 298	23 014	48.4	46.6	46.4	46.9
Brazil - Brésil	4 568	15 777	19 675	21 276	48.1	49.6	51.5	53.4
Korea, Republic of - Corée, République de	7 200	16 834	18 464	22 880	22.8	19.3	19.4	20.6
Russian Federation - Fédération de Russie (14)	1 740	12 410	15 859	16 846	(e)17.8	27.5	28.7	28.5
Philippines (12)	285	7 600	10 032	10 037	8.4	53.9	56.6	54.3
Lebanon - Liban (26)	-	(b)3 817	8 974	-	-	(b)23.8	45.5	-
Thailand - Thaïlande (16)	2 600	6 582	6 567	7 564	18.7	19.2	15.8	15.3
Malaysia - Malaisie (12)	5 055	4 846	6 497	7 734	36.3	15.3	18.1	20.6
Indonesia - Indonésie (27)	_	4 309	5 789	7 750	_	25.7	28.0	33.5
Argentina - Argentine (28)	324	4 297	5 178	5 168	6.6	31.5	33.2	33.9
Trinidad and Tobago - Trinité-et-Tobago	41	32	(b)4 941	-	7.3	3.6	(e,b)85.0	-
Cuba	-	-	-	-	-	-	-	-
Ukraine (12)	323	2 456	2 772	2 951	(e)8.3	14.9	14.7	15.2
Chile - Chili (15)	602	1 901	2 289	2 303	14.7	17.5	17.4	18.2
Algeria - Algérie	-	1 901	2 130	-	-	53.3	57.0	-
Morocco - Maroc (29)	164	1 994	2 065	(e)2 233	5.4	15.9	14.8	(e)16.5
Serbia - Serbie	_	1 163	1 295	1 290	_	27.5	25.4	26.8
South Africa - Afrique du Sud (30)	472	1 115	1 231	1 131	9.4	8.0	8.3	7.5
Croatia - Croatie	266	1 137	1 218	(e)1 176	6.5	9.8	9.6	(e)9.8
Afghanistan (31)	-	939	-	-	-	29.7	-	-
Turkmenistan - Turkménistan	-	-	-	-	-	-	-	-
15 LEADING EXPORTERS: DEVELOPED ECONOMIES / 15 PRINCIPAUX EXPORTATEURS : ÉCONOMIES DÉVELOPPÉES								
United States - États-Unis	45 569	112 860	117 175	(e)127 248	15.8	20.3	19.3	(e)19.9
United Kingdom - Royaume-Uni	33 957	80 114	89 925	(e)85 491	28.3	30.0	30.6	(e)30.1
Germany - Allemagne	24 223	79 096	88 595	(e)87 165	29.1	32.5	33.5	(e)33.3
France	19 343	60 378	71 820	(e)67 956	24.0	31.4	32.0	(e)32.1
Japan - Japon	17 713	42 472	45 367	(e)37 603	25.6	30.1	31.2	(e)25.8
Netherlands - Pays-Bas	15 642	35 779	42 555	(e)40 687	29.9	30.3	30.8	(e)30.5
Spain - Espagne	8 026	28 843	34 360	(e)33 847	15.3	23.2	24.2	(e)24.8
Belgium - Belgique (18)	(a)10 239	33 658	33 847	(e)36 395	(a)20.6	36.7	35.4	(e)37.6
Ireland - Irlande	3 015	29 337	31 659	(e)32 627	17.9	29.8	28.0	(e)28.1
Italy - Italie	13 725	25 244	28 626	(e)28 811	24.3	25.8	26.8	(e)27.6
Sweden - Suède	7 212	23 936	28 014	(e)29 139	33.4	37.6	37.6	(e)38.1
Canada (19)	10 402	24 783	26 461	24 978	25.9	33.7	33.2	31.5
Switzerland - Suisse (25)	2 476	22 059	25 621	-	8.1	26.4	26.6	-
Austria - Autriche	5 404	14 620	18 115	(e)19 269	23.5	26.8	29.6	(e)31.4
Norway - Norvège	4 014	12 360	13 245	(e)14 073	22.7	31.1	31.2	(e)32.1

For sources and notes, see end of table.

Pour les sources et les notes, se reporter à la fin du tableau.

Country or territory / Pays ou territoires	Imports (9) - Importations (9)							
	Millions of dollars / Millions de dollars				As % of total services / En % du total des services			
	2000	2010	2011	2012	2000	2010	2011	2012
SELECTED COUNTRY GROUPINGS / SÉLECTION DE GROUPEMENTS DE PAYS								
World - Monde	..	..	..	..	..	..	..	..
Developing economies - Économies en développement	..	..	..	..	..	..	..	..
Transition economies - Économies en transition	..	..	..	..	..	..	..	..
Developed economies - Économies développées	..	..	..	..	..	..	..	..
Developing economies: Africa - Économies en développement : Afrique	..	..	..	..	..	..	..	..
Developing economies: America - Économies en développement : Amérique	..	..	..	..	..	..	..	..
Developing economies: Asia - Économies en développement : Asie	..	..	..	..	..	..	..	..
Developing economies: Oceania - Économies en développement : Océanie	..	..	..	..	..	..	..	..
Developed economies: America - Économies développées : Amérique	..	..	..	..	..	..	..	..
Developed economies: Asia - Économies développées : Asie	..	..	..	..	..	..	..	..
Developed economies: Europe - Économies développées : Europe	..	..	..	..	..	..	..	..
Developed economies: Oceania - Économies développées : Océanie	..	..	..	..	..	..	..	..
Least developed countries - Pays les moins avancés	..	..	..	..	..	..	..	..
Developing economies excluding LDCs - Économies en développement sans les PMA	..	..	..	..	..	..	..	..
Developing economies excluding China - Économies en développement sans la Chine	..	..	..	..	..	..	..	..
25 LEADING IMPORTERS: DEVELOPING AND TRANSITION ECONOMIES / 25 PRINCIPAUX IMPORTATEURS : ÉCONOMIES EN DÉVELOPPEMENT ET EN TRANSITION								
China - Chine	6 959	34 310	39 620	42 354	19.3	(e)17.7	(e)16.6	(e)15.1
Korea, Republic of - Corée, République de	10 328	30 422	34 679	38 132	30.8	31.7	34.3	35.2
Singapore - Singapour (11)	(e)4 190	24 124	28 736	29 580	(e)13.9	24.7	25.0	25.1
India - Inde (13)	4 323	25 547	25 458	(e)30 296	22.5	21.8	20.4	(e)23.6
Brazil - Brésil	3 434	20 874	25 367	28 346	20.6	33.3	33.3	35.0
Russian Federation - Fédération de Russie (14)	3 367	15 635	18 565	19 875	(e)20.0	21.3	20.8	18.7
Saudi Arabia - Arabie saoudite (20)	-	8 449	13 589	6 866	-	11.0	17.4	9.4
Thailand - Thaïlande (16)	4 142	10 258	12 692	10 065	26.8	22.8	24.3	19.1
China, Taiwan Province of - Province chinoise de Taiwan	6 348	10 381	12 240	13 038	23.8	27.4	29.1	30.4
China, Hong Kong SAR - Chine (RAS de Hong Kong) (12)	(e)2 726	9 997	10 680	-	(e)11.0	19.5	18.9	-
Angola (32)	1 754	6 470	9 593	-	65.0	34.5	40.5	-
China, Macao SAR - Chine (RAS de Macao) (22)	-	5 134	7 611	-	-	70.3	73.9	-
Malaysia - Malaisie (12)	6 035	6 223	7 545	8 380	36.0	19.3	19.9	19.9
Indonesia - Indonésie (27)	_	5 456	6 493	7 852	_	20.9	20.7	23.2
Nigeria - Nigéria (33)	1 841	4 477	6 021	(e)4 415	55.8	20.9	24.5	(e)19.8
Algeria - Algérie	-	4 849	5 564	-	-	40.7	44.4	-
Lebanon - Liban (26)	-	(b)4 347	5 058	-	-	(b)32.3	39.0	-
Trinidad and Tobago - Trinité-et-Tobago	37	93	(b)4 583	-	9.6	24.0	(e,b)83.3	-
Kazakhstan	447	5 412	4 181	(e)4 414	24.2	47.8	38.3	(e)34.8
Argentina - Argentine (28)	648	2 377	3 161	3 425	7.0	16.0	17.7	18.3
United Arab Emirates - Émirats arabes unis	-	-	-	-	-	-	-	-
Venezuela (Bolivarian Rep. of) - Venezuela (Rép. bolivarienne du) (34)	736	2 307	2 622	2 703	16.6	17.7	16.7	14.9
Colombia - Colombie (35)	289	1 798	2 258	2 201	8.7	22.3	23.8	20.8
South Africa - Afrique du Sud (30)	421	2 133	2 255	1 833	7.2	11.6	11.5	10.4
Chile - Chili (15)	909	1 697	2 189	2 193	18.9	13.1	13.9	14.6
15 LEADING IMPORTERS: DEVELOPED ECONOMIES / 15 PRINCIPAUX IMPORTATEURS : ÉCONOMIES DÉVELOPPÉES								
United States - États-Unis	24 446	67 600	78 192	(e)81 622	11.1	16.7	18.2	(e)18.5
Germany - Allemagne	32 199	66 634	77 657	(e)79 616	23.3	24.9	26.2	(e)27.0
France	15 474	51 988	56 717	(e)53 145	25.4	30.4	29.7	(e)30.8
United Kingdom - Royaume-Uni	16 713	45 969	48 460	(e)50 666	16.8	26.9	26.8	(e)28.2
Ireland - Irlande	12 183	43 634	48 163	(e)46 455	42.1	40.7	41.6	(e)41.4
Japan - Japon	24 296	39 162	45 889	(e)46 509	21.1	24.9	27.4	(e)26.3
Netherlands - Pays-Bas	16 714	32 256	41 246	(e)42 119	31.4	30.4	33.9	(e)35.1
Spain - Espagne	10 100	30 184	33 648	(e)33 198	30.4	34.3	35.6	(e)37.1
Italy - Italie	17 714	27 803	30 531	(e)27 966	32.0	25.2	26.2	(e)26.2
Belgium - Belgique (18)	(a)9 426	26 341	27 711	(e)30 397	(a)22.5	31.9	30.4	(e)32.9
Canada (19)	9 626	18 444	19 974	19 096	21.8	19.1	18.9	18.0
Sweden - Suède	8 029	17 414	19 816	(e)19 043	33.5	36.9	36.1	(e)34.6
Norway - Norvège	3 100	10 908	13 173	(e)14 484	20.7	25.4	28.6	(e)29.5
Finland - Finlande	3 460	10 924	11 345	(e)10 967	36.8	41.0	38.2	(e)36.2
Denmark - Danemark	2 573	8 292	10 451	(e)10 444	12.2	15.5	17.7	(e)18.1

For sources and notes, see end of table.

Pour les sources et les notes, se reporter à la fin du tableau.

5.2 Exports and imports of services by service category
Personal, cultural and recreational services

5.2 Exportations et importations des services par catégories de services
Services personnels, culturels et relatifs aux loisirs

Country or territory / Pays ou territoires	Exports (10) - Exportations (10)							
	Millions of dollars / Millions de dollars				As % of total services / En % du total des services			
	2000	2010	2011	2012	2000	2010	2011	2012
SELECTED COUNTRY GROUPINGS **SÉLECTION DE GROUPEMENTS DE PAYS**								
World - Monde	14 700	31 500	35 900	36 400	1.0	0.8	0.8	0.8
Developing economies - Économies en développement	3 600	5 100	5 900	7 100	1.0	0.5	0.5	0.5
Transition economies - Économies en transition	100	1 200	1 100	1 200	0.2	1.1	0.9	0.9
Developed economies - Économies développées	11 000	25 300	28 900	28 100	1.0	0.9	1.0	1.0
Developing economies: Africa - Économies en développement : Afrique	100	300	400	400	0.2	0.3	0.4	0.4
Developing economies: America - Économies en développement : Amérique	500	900	800	900	0.9	0.7	0.5	0.5
Developing economies: Asia - Économies en développement : Asie	3 000	3 800	4 700	5 800	1.2	0.4	0.5	0.5
Developing economies: Oceania - Économies en développement : Océanie	-	0	0	-	-	0.4	-	-
Developed economies: America - Économies développées : Amérique	1 600	3 200	3 400	3 400	0.5	0.5	0.5	0.5
Developed economies: Asia - Économies développées : Asie	-	-	-	-	-	-	-	-
Developed economies: Europe - Économies développées : Europe	8 000	20 700	24 100	23 200	1.1	1.1	1.2	1.2
Developed economies: Oceania - Économies développées : Océanie	1 200	1 000	1 100	1 200	4.9	1.9	1.8	2.0
Least developed countries - Pays les moins avancés	0	100	100	100	0.2	0.2	0.3	(u)0.4
Developing economies excluding LDCs - Économies en développement sans les PMA	3 600	5 000	5 800	7 000	1.0	0.5	0.5	0.5
Developing economies excluding China - Économies en développement sans la Chine	3 600	4 900	5 800	7 000	1.1	0.5	0.5	0.6
25 LEADING EXPORTERS: DEVELOPING AND TRANSITION ECONOMIES **25 PRINCIPAUX EXPORTATEURS : ÉCONOMIES EN DÉVELOPPEMENT ET EN TRANSITION**								
Turkey - Turquie	2 591	912	1 267	(e)1 220	12.7	2.6	3.3	(e)2.9
Korea, Republic of - Corée, République de	137	637	929	1 253	0.4	0.7	1.0	1.1
Singapore - Singapour (11)	(e)19	505	503	507	(e)0.1	0.5	0.5	0.5
Russian Federation - Fédération de Russie (14)	-	474	493	556	-	1.1	0.9	0.9
China, Hong Kong SAR - Chine (RAS de Hong Kong) (12)	(e)51	426	472	-	(e)0.1	0.4	0.4	-
Argentina - Argentine	18	320	345	335	0.4	2.3	2.2	2.2
India - Inde (13)	-	(e)327	(e)343	(e)770	-	(e)0.3	(e)0.2	(e)0.5
Serbia - Serbie	_	186	198	139	_	4.4	3.9	2.9
Lebanon - Liban	-	(b)202	166	-	-	(b)1.3	0.8	-
Malaysia - Malaisie (12)	33	111	159	175	0.2	0.4	0.4	0.5
Indonesia - Indonésie	_	104	159	210	_	0.6	0.8	0.9
Iran (Islamic Rép. of) - Iran (Rép. islamique d')	-	145	-	-	-	1.8	-	-
China, Taiwan Province of - Province chinoise de Taiwan	26	98	136	154	0.1	0.2	0.3	0.3
China - Chine	11	123	123	126	0.0	(e)0.1	(e)0.1	(e)0.1
Egypt - Égypte	15	99	108	-	0.2	0.4	0.6	-
Kyrgyzstan - Kirghizistan	3	68	94	-	4.4	9.8	8.4	-
Ukraine (12)	3	113	93	119	(e)0.1	0.7	0.5	0.6
Thailand - Thaïlande (16)	-	121	92	83	-	0.4	0.2	0.2
Colombia - Colombie	23	84	86	85	1.1	1.9	1.8	1.6
Cuba	-	-	-	-	-	-	-	-
Ecuador - Équateur	39	66	82	(e)101	4.6	4.5	5.2	(e)5.6
Mexico - Mexique	328	80	80	80	2.4	0.5	0.5	0.5
South Africa - Afrique du Sud	-	67	66	59	-	0.5	0.4	0.4
Philippines (12)	18	41	60	79	0.5	0.3	0.3	0.4
Syrian Arab Republic - République arabe syrienne	-	52	-	-	-	0.7	-	-
15 LEADING EXPORTERS: DEVELOPED ECONOMIES **15 PRINCIPAUX EXPORTATEURS : ÉCONOMIES DÉVELOPPÉES**								
United Kingdom - Royaume-Uni	1 974	3 946	4 610	(e)3 947	1.6	1.5	1.6	(e)1.4
France	1 595	3 540	4 137	(e)4 007	2.0	1.8	1.8	(e)1.9
Luxembourg	..	1 996	2 804	(e)2 974	..	3.1	3.9	(e)4.2
Canada (19)	1 451	2 184	2 474	2 409	3.6	3.0	3.1	3.0
Spain - Espagne	537	1 773	2 173	(e)2 281	1.0	1.4	1.5	(e)1.7
Malta - Malte	0	(e)1 894	(e)2 126	-	0.0	(e)42.1	(e)42.7	-
Hungary - Hongrie	213	1 263	1 324	(e)1 218	3.5	6.5	6.1	(e)6.1
Germany - Allemagne	405	1 106	906	(e)801	0.5	0.5	0.3	(e)0.3
United States - États-Unis	141	1 006	893	-	0.0	0.2	0.1	-
Australia - Australie (21)	1 058	701	874	(e)914	5.3	1.5	1.7	(e)1.7
Netherlands - Pays-Bas	556	699	791	(e)763	1.1	0.6	0.6	(e)0.6
Belgium - Belgique (18)	(a)626	661	748	(e)708	(a)1.3	0.7	0.8	(e)0.7
Sweden - Suède	113	411	621	(e)584	0.5	0.6	0.8	(e)0.8
Denmark - Danemark	-	589	563	(e)589	-	0.9	0.8	(e)0.9
Poland - Pologne	51	308	526	(e)390	0.5	0.9	1.4	(e)1.0

For sources and notes, see end of table.

Pour les sources et les notes, se reporter à la fin du tableau.

5.2 Exports and imports of services by service category
Personal, cultural and recreational services

5.2 Exportations et importations des services par catégories de services
Services personnels, culturels et relatifs aux loisirs

Country or territory / Pays ou territoires	Imports (10) - Importations (10)							
	Millions of dollars / Millions de dollars				As % of total services / En % du total des services			
	2000	2010	2011	2012	2000	2010	2011	2012
SELECTED COUNTRY GROUPINGS **SÉLECTION DE GROUPEMENTS DE PAYS**								
World - Monde	..	..	..	..	..	..	..	..
Developing economies - Économies en développement	..	..	..	..	..	..	..	..
Transition economies - Économies en transition	..	..	..	..	..	..	..	..
Developed economies - Économies développées	..	..	..	..	..	..	..	..
Developing economies: Africa - Économies en développement : Afrique	..	..	..	..	..	..	..	..
Developing economies: America - Économies en développement : Amérique	..	..	..	..	..	..	..	..
Developing economies: Asia - Économies en développement : Asie	..	..	..	..	..	..	..	..
Developing economies: Oceania - Économies en développement : Océanie	..	..	..	..	..	..	..	..
Developed economies: America - Économies développées : Amérique	..	..	..	..	..	..	..	..
Developed economies: Asia - Économies développées : Asie	..	..	..	..	..	..	..	..
Developed economies: Europe - Économies développées : Europe	..	..	..	..	..	..	..	..
Developed economies: Oceania - Économies développées : Océanie	..	..	..	..	..	..	..	..
Least developed countries - Pays les moins avancés	..	..	..	..	..	..	..	..
Developing economies excluding LDCs - Économies en développement sans les PMA	..	..	..	..	..	..	..	..
Developing economies excluding China - Économies en développement sans la Chine								
25 LEADING IMPORTERS: DEVELOPING AND TRANSITION ECONOMIES **25 PRINCIPAUX IMPORTATEURS : ÉCONOMIES EN DÉVELOPPEMENT ET EN TRANSITION**								
Venezuela (Bolivarian Rep. of) - Venezuela (Rép. bolivarienne du)	72	3 262	3 652	3 747	1.6	25.0	23.3	20.6
Qatar	-	-	1 428	1 398	-	-	8.5	5.8
Brazil - Brésil	363	1 271	1 121	1 034	2.2	2.0	1.5	1.3
Russian Federation - Fédération de Russie (14)	-	999	1 059	1 117	-	1.4	1.2	1.1
Korea, Republic of - Corée, République de	160	1 022	1 023	1 167	0.5	1.1	1.0	1.1
Singapore - Singapour (11)	(e)82	472	484	488	(e)0.3	0.5	0.4	0.4
Argentina - Argentine	171	381	460	480	1.9	2.6	2.6	2.6
Saudi Arabia - Arabie saoudite (20)	-	-	-	-	-	-	-	-
China - Chine	37	371	400	564	0.1	(e)0.2	(e)0.2	(e)0.2
Malaysia - Malaisie (12)	70	290	348	599	0.4	0.9	0.9	1.4
India - Inde (13)	-	(e)461	(e)347	(e)555	-	(e)0.4	(e)0.3	(e)0.4
Turkey - Turquie	1 541	259	294	(e)336	17.0	1.3	1.4	(e)1.6
Mexico - Mexique	245	272	272	272	1.4	1.1	0.9	0.9
Iran (Islamic Rep. of) - Iran (Rép. islamique d')	-	322	-	-	-	1.4	-	-
China, Taiwan Province of - Province chinoise de Taiwan	163	215	237	279	0.6	0.6	0.6	0.7
Ukraine (12)	11	221	234	231	0.4	1.7	1.8	1.6
Indonesia - Indonésie	_	133	212	281	_	0.5	0.7	0.8
Ecuador - Équateur	52	168	188	(e)210	4.1	5.6	5.9	(e)6.5
Angola	-	156	184	-	-	0.8	0.8	-
China, Macao SAR - Chine (RAS de Macao) (22)	-	-	-	-	-	-	-	-
United Arab Emirates - Émirats arabes unis	-	-	-	-	-	-	-	-
Lebanon - Liban	-	(b)114	113	-	-	(b)0.8	0.9	-
Croatia - Croatie	30	111	110	(e)85	1.7	3.1	3.0	(e)2.3
Congo	5	-	-	-	0.6	-	-	-
China, Hong Kong SAR - Chine (RAS de Hong Kong) (12)	(e)65	84	94	-	(e)0.3	0.2	0.2	-
15 LEADING IMPORTERS: DEVELOPED ECONOMIES **15 PRINCIPAUX IMPORTATEURS : ÉCONOMIES DÉVELOPPÉES**								
France	1 972	3 424	3 664	(e)3 818	3.2	2.0	1.9	(e)2.2
Germany - Allemagne	3 608	2 783	2 715	(e)2 420	2.6	1.0	0.9	(e)0.8
Canada (19)	1 647	2 123	2 200	2 460	3.7	2.2	2.1	2.3
Luxembourg	..	1 569	2 124	(e)1 831	..	4.3	5.1	(e)4.5
Spain - Espagne	1 422	2 091	2 113	(e)1 942	4.3	2.4	2.2	(e)2.2
Australia - Australie (21)	509	1 267	1 646	(e)1 696	2.7	2.5	2.7	(e)2.7
Norway - Norvège	179	611	1 560	(e)1 546	1.2	1.4	3.4	(e)3.2
Poland - Pologne	140	862	1 080	(e)1 028	1.6	2.9	3.4	(e)3.2
Denmark - Danemark	-	1 069	1 033	(e)962	-	2.0	1.7	(e)1.7
United Kingdom - Royaume-Uni	1 179	1 038	1 025	(e)960	1.2	0.6	0.6	(e)0.5
Austria - Autriche	(e)209	991	1 020	(e)1 041	(e)1.3	2.7	2.4	(e)2.4
Hungary - Hongrie	157	966	1 008	(e)946	3.2	6.2	5.9	(e)6.0
Japan - Japon	1 276	935	977	(e)1 200	1.1	0.6	0.6	(e)0.7
Belgium - Belgique (18)	(a)824	849	891	(e)666	(a)2.0	1.0	1.0	(e)0.7
Netherlands - Pays-Bas	600	701	778	(e)881	1.1	0.7	0.6	(e)0.7

For sources and notes, see next page.

Pour les sources et les notes, se reporter à la page suivante.

5

Sources:

UNCTAD, WTO and ITC secretariats' calculations, based on:
- IMF, *Balance of Payments Statistics*
- Eurostat, online database
- UN/DESA/Statistics Division, *UN Service Trade Statistical Database*
- OECD, *OECD.Stat*
- Other international and national sources

Notes:
- The statistics presented correspond to the concepts and definitions from the IMF *Balance of Payments Manual*, fifth edition (*BPM5*, 1993). For those countries and territories who present their figures according to the Sixth edition of the *Manual* (*BPM6*, 2009), data were adjusted to fit the *BPM5* concepts.

  Estimated data for individual countries are included in geographical regions or economic groupings calculation, but not always shown separately. When possible, the values missing in principal international sources are estimated by using the growth rates derived from the data available in national or other international sources.

  UNCTAD , WTO and ITC may use different definitions for certain country groups ("developed" and "developing" economies, for example). Consequently, some aggregates will be different, although the individual-country underlying data are the same.

  Individual economies are ranked based on both reported and estimated 2011 figures. Non-publishable estimates are indicated by a - sign.

(a) Refers to Belgium-Luxembourg Economic Union.

(1) Covers all transportation services that involve carriage of passengers, movement of goods (freight), rentals with crew, and related supporting services. Excludes freight insurance, which is included with insurance services. Excludes goods procured in ports by non-resident carriers and repairs on transport equipment, which are included in goods.

(2) Includes goods and services acquired from an economy by non-resident travellers during visits shorter than one year.

(3) Consists of postal, courier and telecommunications services between residents and non-residents.

(4) Covers the work performed on construction projects and installations by an enterprise outside the economy of residence of that enterprise.

(5) (1) Computer services consist of hardware and software-related services and data-processing.

  (2) New agency services include the provision of news, photographs and feature articles to the media.

  (3) Other information services cover database services: database conception, data storage and dissemination of data. Direct non-bulk subscriptions to periodicals regardless of means of information transmission also belong to this service category.

(6) Covers all types of insurance, reinsurance and related auxiliary services. Insurance services are estimated or valued by the service charges included in total premiums rather than by total value of the premiums. Negative insurance services exports would indicate that the claims payable to non-residents were higher than the premiums earned from non-residents' insurance payments.

(7) Includes financial intermediation and auxiliary services, except those directly related to life insurance and pension funds (covered under insurance services).

(8) Covers franchising fees, royalties paid for the use of registered trade marks, and other fees paid for authorised use of intangible, non-produced non-financial assets and proprietary rights. Distributive rights with limitations for audiovisual products are not included here.

(9) Includes merchanting and other trade-related services; operational leasing services; and miscellaneous business, professional and technical services (legal, advertising, consulting, accounting, R&D, etc.)

(10) (1) Audiovisual and related services cover the production of motion pictures, video and radio programmes, musical recordings, (and similar) including fees paid to personnel involved. Related limited distribution rights are also covered. Fees paid for sporting, theatrical and similar events belong to this category as well.

  (2) Other personal cultural and recreational services encompass services associated with museums, libraries, archives, and other cultural and sporting activities. Education and health services are covered under this category (excluding, however, the expenses for health and education services paid by travellers, which belong to travel services).

Sources :

Calculs des secrétariats de la CNUCED, de l'OMC et du CCI, sur la base de :
- FMI, *Statistiques de la balance des paiements*
- Eurostat, base de données en ligne
- ONU/DAES/Division des statistiques, *ONU Service Trade Statistical Database*
- OCDE, *OECD.Stat*
- Autres sources internationales et nationales

Notes :
- Les statistiques présentées correspondent aux concepts et définitions *du Manuel de la balance des paiements* du FMI, cinquième édition (*MBP5*, 1993). Pour les pays et territoires qui présentent leur statistiques conformément à la Sixième édition du *Manuel* (*MBP6*, 2009), les données ont été ajustées selon les concepts du *MBP5*.

  Les valeurs estimées pour les pays individuels sont comprises dans les calculs des groupements géographiques ou régionaux, mais elles ne sont pas toujours présentées séparément. Lorsque c'est possible, les données manquantes dans les sources principales sont estimées en utilisant les taux d'évolution dérivés des données disponibles dans les sources nationales ou autres sources internationales.

  La composition de groupements de pays peut être différente pour la CNUCED, l'OMC et le CCI ("pays en développement" et "pays développés", par exemple). Par conséquent, certains agrégats seront différents bien que les données des pays individuels soient les mêmes.

  Les économies individuelles sont classées en fonction des données rapportées et estimées de l'année 2011. Les estimations qui ne sont pas publiables sont indiquées par le signe -.

(a) Se réfère à l'Union économique belgo-luxembourgeoise.

(1) Recouvre tous les services de transport de passagers, l'acheminement des marchandises (fret), la location de moyens de transports avec leur équipage et les services annexes qui s'y rapportent. L'assurance du fret n'est pas comprise. Elle fait partie des services d'assurance. Les achats effectués dans les ports par les transporteurs non résidents, ainsi que les réparations du matériel de transport ne sont pas compris. Ils sont classés dans les biens.

(2) Comprend les biens et services acquis dans une économie par les voyageurs non-résidents au cours d'un séjour inférieur à un an.

(3) Englobe les services postaux (y compris les messageries) et les services de télécommunication, entre résidents et non-résidents.

(4) Recouvre les travaux de construction et d'installation par une entreprise en dehors de l'économie dans laquelle l'entreprise est résidente.

(5) (1) Les services informatiques englobent les services liés aux matériels et logiciels informatiques et les services de traitement de données.

  (2) Les services d'agence de presse incluent la communication d'informations, de photographies et d'articles de fond aux médias.

  (3) Les autres services d'information couvrent les services concernant les bases de données : leur conception, le stockage et la diffusion des données. Les abonnements directs individuels aux périodiques font partie de cette catégorie de services.

(6) Comprend diverses formes d'assurances, réassurances et services auxiliaires connexes. Ces services sont évalués ou estimés au montant des frais de service inclus dans le total des primes perçues, et non au montant total des primes proprement dites. Les valeurs négatives des exportations des services d'assurance signifieraient que les primes à recevoir des non-résidents sont plus faibles que les indemnités de dédommagements à payer aux non-résidents.

(7) Comprend les services d'intermédiation financière et les services auxiliaires, à l'exception de ceux directement liés à l'assurance-vie ou aux fonds de pension (déjà compris dans les services d'assurance).

(8) Recouvre les redevances de franchises et les redevances payées pour l'utilisation des marques déposées, ainsi que les autres redevances et droits de licence liés à l'utilisation légale d'actifs intangibles non produits non financiers et de droits de propriété. Les droits de distribution limitée des produits audiovisuels ne sont pas compris dans cette catégorie.

(9) Y compris le négoce international et les autres services liés au commerce, la location-exploitation et divers services aux entreprises, spécialisés et techniques (juridiques, comptabilité, conseil, publicité, R&D, etc.).

(10) (1) Les services audiovisuels et connexes sont attachés à la production de films cinématographiques, d'émissions de radio et de télévision, d'enregistrements musicaux (et similaires). Les cachets versés au personnel impliqué et les droits limités de distributions figurent également dans cette catégorie, ainsi que les paiements liés aux événements sportifs, théâtraux et spectacles divers.

  (2) Les autres services personnels, culturels et relatifs aux loisirs englobent les services associés aux musées, bibliothèques, archives et autres activités culturelles et sportives. Les services d'éducation et de santé figurent aussi dans cette catégorie. Cependant, ne sont pas comprises les dépenses liées à l'éducation ou à la santé encourues par des voyageurs (et qui figurent sous la catégorie 'voyages').

(11) Starting from 2009, data converted from BPM6 to BPM5 methodology. Data do not include merchanting. Financial services include financial intermediation services indirectly measured (FISIM).

(12) Starting from 2009, data converted from BPM6 to BPM5 methodology.

(13) Starting from 2009, data converted from BPM6 to BPM5 methodology. Imports: Other business services may include transactions belonging to other services categories for 2000-2003. Other business services: figures are estimated by UNCTAD-WTO. They include an estimate for Information Technology Enabled Services (ITES) and Business Process Outsourcing Services (BPO) which are classified under "software" by the Reserve Bank of India (source: RBI, Survey on Computer Software & Information Technology Services Exports, various issues). Computer and information services, and Computer services: Figures are estimated by UNCTAD-WTO. They are estimated based on data reported on computer services by the Reserve Bank of India and exclude estimates for Information Technology Enabled Services (ITES) and Business Process Outsourcing Services (BPO), (source: RBI, Survey on Computer Software & Information Technology Services Exports, various issues), which have been included under other business services.

(14) Starting from 2009, data converted from BPM6 to BPM5 methodology. Imports: Other business services cover personal, cultural and recreational services prior to 2001.

(15) Starting from 2009, data converted from BPM6 to BPM5 methodology. Imports: Other business services may include transactions belonging to other services categories for 2000-2008.

(16) Starting from 2009, data converted from BPM6 to BPM5 methodology. Exports and imports: Other business services cover financial, computer and information services, and personal, cultural and recreational services prior to 2005.

(17) Starting from 2009, data converted from BPM6 to BPM5 methodology. Exports: Other business services may include transactions belonging to other services categories for 2006-2011. Imports: Other business services may include transactions belonging to other services categories for 2008-2011.

(18) Data from 1980 to 2001 inclusive refer to Belgium-Luxembourg Economic Union and from 2002 onwards to Belgium only.

(19) Starting from 2009, data converted from BPM6 to BPM5 methodology. Financial services include financial intermediation services indirectly measured (FISIM).

(20) Starting from 2009, data converted from BPM6 to BPM5 methodology. Exports: Other business services cover other services (except communications services) for 2005-2007. Imports: Other business services cover computer and information services, royalties and licence fees, and personal, cultural and recreational services for 2005-2012.

(21) Starting from 2009, data converted from BPM6 to BPM5 methodology. Financial services include financial intermediation services indirectly measured (FISIM). Imports: Other business services cover construction up to 2008.

(22) Starting from 2009, data converted from BPM6 to BPM5 methodology. Imports: Other business services may include transactions belonging to other services categories for 2002-2011.

(23) Starting from 2009, data converted from BPM6 to BPM5 methodology. Exports: Other business services may include transactions belonging to other services categories for 2001.

(24) Financial services include financial intermediation services indirectly measured (FISIM).

(25) Financial services include financial intermediation services indirectly measured (FISIM). Exports and imports: Other business services may include transactions belonging to other services categories for 2000-2011.

(26) Exports: Other business services may include transactions belonging to other services categories for 2006-2009. Imports: Other business services may include transactions belonging to other services categories for 2002-2009.

(27) Imports: Other business services may include transactions belonging to other services categories for 2003.

(28) Exports: Other business services may include transactions belonging to other services categories for 2001-2007. Imports: Other business services may include transactions belonging to other services categories for 2000-2001.

(29) Exports and imports: Other business services may include transactions belonging to other services categories for 2000-2007.

(11) À partir do 2009, données converties de la présentation MBP6 à la présentation MBP5. Les données ne couvrent pas le négoce international. Les services financiers comprennent les services d'intermédiation financière indirectement mesurés (SIFIM).

(12) À partir de 2009, données converties de la présentation MBP6 à la présentation MBP5.

(13) À partir de 2009, données converties de la présentation MBP6 à la présentation MBP5. Importations: Autres services aux entreprises peuvent couvrir les transactions appartenant aux autres catégories des services pour 2000-2003. Autres services aux entreprises : Estimations de la CNUCED-OMC. Comprennent les estimations des services facilités par la technologie de l'information et les services de l'externalisation des processus métiers classifiés sous "logiciels" par la 'Reserve Bank of India' (source : RBI, Survey on Computer Software & Information Technology Services Exports, différentes éditions). Services d'informatique et d'information, et Services d'informatique : Estimations de la CNUCED-OMC, basées sur les données des services informatiques de la 'Reserve Bank of India'. Elles excluent les estimations des services facilités par la technologie de l'information et les services de l'externalisation des processus métiers, comprises sous la rubrique Autres services aux entreprises (source : RBI, Survey on Computer Software & Information Technology Services Exports, différentes éditions).

(14) À partir de 2009, données converties de la présentation MBP6 à la présentation MBP5. Importations: Autres services aux entreprises couvrent les services personnels, culturels et relatifs aux loisirs avant 2001.

(15) À partir de 2009, données converties de la présentation MBP6 à la présentation MBP5. Importations: Autres services aux entreprises peuvent couvrir les transactions appartenant aux autres catégories des services pour 2000-2008.

(16) À partir de 2009, données converties de la présentation MBP6 à la présentation MBP5. Exportations et importations : Autres services aux entreprises couvrent les services financiers, l'informatique et l'information et les services personnels, culturels et relatifs aux loisirs avant 2005.

(17) À partir de 2009, données converties de la présentation MBP6 à la présentation MBP5. Exportations : Autres services aux entreprises peuvent couvrir les transactions appartenant aux autres catégories des services pour 2006-2011. Importations : Autres services aux entreprises peuvent couvrir les transactions appartenant aux autres catégories des services pour 2008-2011.

(18) Les données de 1980 à 2001 se réfèrent à l'Union économique belgo-luxembourgeoise et à partir de 2002 uniquement à la Belgique.

(19) À partir de 2009, données converties de la présentation MBP6 à la présentation MBP5. Les services financiers comprennent les services d'intermédiation financière indirectement mesurés (SIFIM).

(20) À partir de 2009, données converties de la présentation MBP6 à la présentation MBP5. Exportations : Autres services aux entreprises couvrent toutes les catégories des services, sauf la communication, entre 2005 et 2007. Importations : Autres services aux entreprises couvrent les services d'informatique et d'information, les redevances et droits du licence et les services personnels, culturels et relatifs aux loisirs pour 2005-2012.

(21) À partir de 2009, données converties de la présentation MBP6 à la présentation MBP5. Les services financiers comprennent les services d'intermédiation financière indirectement mesurés (SIFIM). Importations: Autres services aux entreprises couvrent la construction jusqu'à 2008.

(22) À partir de 2009, données converties de la présentation MBP6 à la présentation MBP5. Importations : Autres services aux entreprises peuvent couvrir les transactions appartenant aux autres catégories des services pour 2002-2011.

(23) À partir de 2009, données converties de la présentation MBP6 à la présentation MBP5. Exportations : Autres services aux entreprises peuvent couvrir les transactions appartenant aux autres catégories des services pour 2001.

(24) Les services financiers comprennent les services d'intermédiation financière indirectement mesurés (SIFIM).

(25) Les services financiers comprennent les services d'intermédiation financière indirectement mesurés (SIFIM). Exportations et importations : Autres services aux entreprises peuvent couvrir les transactions appartenant aux autres catégories des services pour 2000-2011.

(26) Exportations : Autres services aux entreprises peuvent couvrir les transactions appartenant aux autres catégories des services pour 2006-2009. Importations : Autres services aux entreprises peuvent couvrir les transactions appartenant aux autres catégories des services pour 2002-2009.

(27) Importations : Autres services aux entreprises peuvent couvrir les transactions appartenant aux autres catégories des services pour 2003.

(28) Exportations : Autres services aux entreprises peuvent couvrir les transactions appartenant aux autres catégories des services pour 2001-2007. Importations : Autres services aux entreprises peuvent couvrir les transactions appartenant aux autres catégories des services pour 2000-2001.

(29) Exportations et importations : Autres services aux entreprises peuvent couvrir les transactions appartenant aux autres catégories des services pour 2000-2007.

5

(30) Exports: Other business services cover construction, financial, computer and information services, and personal, cultural and recreational services prior to 2001. Imports: Other business services cover construction, financial, computer and information services, and personal, cultural and recreational services prior to 2001.

(31) Exports: Other business services may include transactions belonging to other services categories for 2010.

(32) Exports: Other business services may include transactions belonging to other services categories for 2002-2011. Imports: Other business services may include transactions belonging to other services categories for 2000-2003.

(33) Exports: Other business services may include transactions belonging to other services categories for 2000-2007. Imports: Other business services may include transactions belonging to other services categories for 2000-2004.

(34) Imports: Other business services may include transactions belonging to other services categories for 2000-2012.

(35) Imports: Other business services may include transactions belonging to other services categories for 2000-2007.

(30) Exportations : Autres services aux entreprises couvrent la construction, les services financiers, l'informatique et l'information et les services personnels, culturels et relatifs aux loisirs avant 2001. Importations : Autres services aux entreprises couvrent la construction, les services financiers, l'informatique et l'information et les services personnels, culturels et relatifs aux loisirs avant 2001.

(31) Exportations : Autres services aux entreprises peuvent couvrir les transactions appartenant aux autres catégories des services pour 2010.

(32) Exportations : Autres services aux entreprises peuvent couvrir les transactions appartenant aux autres catégories des services pour 2002-2011. Importations : Autres services aux entreprises peuvent couvrir les transactions appartenant aux autres catégories des services pour 2000-2003.

(33) Exportations : Autres services aux entreprises peuvent couvrir les transactions appartenant aux autres catégories des services pour 2000-2007. Importations : Autres services aux entreprises peuvent couvrir les transactions appartenant aux autres catégories des services pour 2000-2004.

(34) Importations : Autres services aux entreprises peuvent couvrir les transactions appartenant aux autres catégories des services pour 2000-2012.

(35) Importations : Autres services aux entreprises peuvent couvrir les transactions appartenant aux autres catégories des services pour 2000-2007.

5.3 World merchant fleet by flag of registration and type of ship of countries and geographical regions

5.3 Flotte marchande mondiale par pavillons d'immatriculation et par types de navires des pays et des régions géographiques

Region, country or territory / Régions pays ou territoires	Year / Année	Total fleet (thousands of DWT) / Flotte totale (milliers de TPL) (1)	As percentage of world total fleet / En pourcentage de la flotte mondiale					As percentage of the country or region total fleet / En pourcentage de la flotte totale du pays ou de la région				
			Oil tankers / Pétroliers	Bulk carriers / Vraquiers	General cargo / Navires de charge classique (2)	Container ships / Porte-conteneurs	Other types / Autres navires	Oil tankers / Pétroliers	Bulk carriers / Vraquiers	General cargo / Navires de charge classique (2)	Container ships / Porte-conteneurs	Other types / Autres navires
WORLD - MONDE	1990	629 976.0	100.0	100.0	100.0	100.0	100.0	37.4	35.5	15.9	3.5	7.6
	2000	793 770.8	100.0	100.0	100.0	100.0	100.0	35.7	34.6	12.8	8.0	9.0
	2010	1276 137.2	100.0	100.0	100.0	100.0	100.0	35.3	35.8	8.5	13.3	7.2
	2013	1628 782.6	100.0	100.0	100.0	100.0	100.0	30.1	42.0	4.9	12.7	10.2
DEVELOPING ECONOMIES - ÉCONOMIES EN DÉVELOPPEMENT (3)	1990	334 184.0	52.2	56.5	54.4	43.1	43.1	36.8	37.8	16.4	2.9	6.2
	2000	487 692.9	56.6	68.5	63.7	58.3	53.0	32.9	38.5	13.3	7.6	7.7
	2010	915 120.5	69.1	77.6	70.0	68.4	63.6	34.0	38.7	8.3	12.6	6.4
	2013	1232 176.9	72.3	81.2	65.5	72.3	71.9	20.0	46.1	4.3	12.1	9.7
TRANSITION ECONOMIES - ÉCONOMIES EN TRANSITION	1990	35 090.0	2.9	4.4	12.4	3.2	11.0	19.2	28.4	35.4	2.0	15.0
	2000	13 598.3	0.9	0.9	5.4	0.7	3.8	18.5	18.0	40.2	3.4	19.9
	2010	12 777.5	0.8	0.4	4.5	0.1	2.1	29.6	15.7	38.5	1.3	14.8
	2013	11 801.4	0.8	0.3	5.2	0.0	1.2	32.0	15.3	35.5	0.7	16.5
DEVELOPED ECONOMIES - ÉCONOMIES DÉVELOPPÉES (3)	1990	260 702.0	45.0	39.1	33.2	53.7	45.8	40.7	33.5	12.8	4.6	8.4
	2000	292 479.6	42.5	30.6	30.9	40.9	43.2	41.1	28.7	10.7	8.9	10.5
	2010	342 619.1	29.8	21.8	23.4	31.4	33.3	39.1	29.0	7.4	15.5	9.0
	2013	380 525.8	26.8	18.5	28.6	27.7	25.1	34.6	33.4	6.0	15.0	11.0
Developing economies: Africa - Économies en développement : Afrique	1990	97 139.0	23.1	12.7	6.1	5.4	14.6	56.0	29.3	6.4	1.2	7.2
	2000	91 552.9	14.7	9.7	6.5	9.5	15.1	45.3	29.2	7.2	6.6	11.8
	2010	150 731.7	14.8	8.0	5.4	20.2	8.4	44.1	24.3	3.9	22.6	5.2
	2013	220 715.9	16.9	10.1	5.4	23.1	10.2	37.5	31.2	2.0	21.6	7.7
Eastern Africa - Afrique orientale	*1990*	*482.0*	*0.0*	*0.0*	*0.2*	*0.1*	*0.1*	*22.2*	*13.7*	*50.4*	*6.0*	*7.5*
	2000	*437.0*	*0.0*	*0.0*	*0.2*	*0.2*	*0.1*	*6.8*	*1.2*	*49.6*	*30.0*	*12.5*
	2010	*1 930.1*	*0.1*	*0.1*	*0.8*	*0.0*	*0.3*	*29.8*	*13.7*	*43.3*	*0.9*	*12.3*
	2013	*10 771.4*	*1.9*	*0.0*	*1.3*	*0.0*	*0.2*	*85.1*	*2.5*	*9.6*	*0.5*	*2.3*
Comoros - Comores	1990	3.0	..	..	0.0	..	..	..	..	100.0	..	..
	2000	1.0	..	..	0.0	..	..	..	..	100.0	..	..
	2010	1 211.8	0.1	0.1	0.5	0.0	0.1	27.3	20.5	42.0	1.4	8.8
	2013	937.5	0.0	0.0	0.6	0.0	0.1	23.2	17.0	48.5	0.5	10.8
Djibouti	2000	4.9	..	..	0.0	..	0.0	..	..	90.8	..	9.2
	2010	0.7	..	..	..	..	0.0	..	..	..	..	100.0
	2013	6.8	0.0	..	0.0	..	0.0	73.8	..	10.5	..	15.7
Eritrea - Érythrée	2010	14.0	0.0	..	0.0	..	0.0	22.7	..	73.3	..	4.0
	2013	13.8	0.0	..	0.0	..	0.0	23.0	..	74.6	..	2.4
Ethiopia (...1991) - Éthiopie (...1991)	1990	94.0	0.0	..	0.1	..	..	2.1	..	96.8	..	..
Ethiopia - Éthiopie	2000	119.7	0.0	..	0.1	..	..	3.0	..	97.0	..	..
	2010	150.0	..	..	0.1	..	..	..	..	100.0	..	..
	2013	223.2	0.0	..	0.2	..	..	18.9	..	81.1	..	..
Kenya	1990	5.0	..	..	..	..	0.0	..	..	..	..	100.0
	2000	19.1	0.0	..	0.0	..	0.0	40.0	..	10.4	..	49.7
	2010	14.0	0.0	..	0.0	..	0.0	54.4	..	3.3	..	42.4
	2013	7.1	0.0	..	..	..	0.0	29.3	..	..	..	70.7
Madagascar	1990	88.0	0.0	..	0.1	..	0.0	8.0	..	80.7	..	11.4
	2000	45.1	0.0	..	0.0	..	0.0	37.5	..	47.5	..	15.0
	2010	30.6	0.0	..	0.0	..	0.0	22.9	..	53.6	..	23.5
	2013	25.8	0.0	..	0.0	..	0.0	22.5	..	60.0	..	17.5
Mauritius - Maurice	1990	216.0	0.0	0.0	0.0	0.1	0.0	42.6	30.6	11.1	13.4	2.3
	2000	189.7	..	0.0	0.0	0.2	0.0	..	2.8	21.4	69.0	6.8
	2010	63.8	..	..	0.0	..	0.1	..	..	18.3	..	81.7
	2013	135.3	0.0	..	..	..	0.0	56.0	..	..	..	44.0
Mozambique	1990	27.0	0.0	..	0.0	..	0.0	7.4	..	66.7	..	25.9
	2000	25.2	..	..	0.0	..	0.0	..	..	49.9	..	50.1
	2010	35.0	..	..	0.0	..	0.0	..	..	30.2	..	69.8
	2013	20.7	..	..	0.0	..	0.0	..	..	71.7	..	28.3
Seychelles	1990	2.0	..	..	0.0	..	..	..	..	100.0	..	..
	2000	22.7	..	..	0.0	..	0.0	..	..	50.9	..	49.1
	2010	288.0	0.0	..	0.1	..	0.0	69.6	..	19.4	..	10.9
	2013	585.2	0.1	..	0.0	..	0.0	90.4	..	0.7	..	9.0

For sources and notes, see end of table.

Pour les sources et les notes, se reporter à la fin du tableau.

5.3 World merchant fleet by flag of registration and type of ship of countries and geographical regions

5.3 Flotte marchande mondiale par pavillons d'immatriculation et par types de navires des pays et des régions géographiques

Region, country or territory / Régions pays ou territoires	Year / Année	Total fleet (thousands of DWT) / Flotte totale (milliers de TPL) (1)	As percentage of world total fleet / En pourcentage de la flotte mondiale					As percentage of the country or region total fleet / En pourcentage de la flotte totale du pays ou de la région				
			Oil tankers / Pétroliers	Bulk carriers / Vraquiers	General cargo / Navires de charge classique (2)	Container ships / Porte-conteneurs	Other types / Autres navires	Oil tankers / Pétroliers	Bulk carriers / Vraquiers	General cargo / Navires de charge classique (2)	Container ships / Porte-conteneurs	Other types / Autres navires
Somalia - Somalie	1990	14.0	..	..	0.0	..	0.0	..	..	71.4	..	28.6
	2000	6.8	0.0	..	0.0	..	0.0	22.6	..	59.5	..	17.9
	2010	5.5	0.0	..	0.0	..	0.0	27.9	..	25.9	..	46.3
	2013	0.6	..	..	0.0	..	0.0	..	..	71.4	..	28.6
Uganda - Ouganda	1990	1.0	..	..	..	..	0.0	..	..	..	..	100.0
	2000	2.7	..	..	0.0	..	..	..	..	100.0	..	..
United Republic of Tanzania - République-Unie de Tanzanie	1990	32.0	0.0	..	0.0	..	0.0	12.5	..	75.0	..	12.5
	2010	116.6	0.0	0.0	0.1	..	0.0	21.3	13.9	60.7	..	4.1
	2013	8 815.5	1.7	0.0	0.4	0.0	0.0	94.1	1.2	4.0	0.6	0.2
Middle Africa - Afrique centrale	*1990*	*285.0*	*0.0*	*..*	*0.2*	*..*	*0.1*	*0.7*	*..*	*82.8*	*..*	*16.5*
	2000	*143.3*	*0.0*	*..*	*0.1*	*0.0*	*0.1*	*4.9*	*..*	*65.6*	*1.0*	*28.5*
	2010	*132.2*	*0.0*	*0.0*	*0.0*	*..*	*0.1*	*11.7*	*5.2*	*32.7*	*..*	*50.3*
	2013	*1 422.7*	*0.0*	*..*	*0.1*	*..*	*0.8*	*1.8*	*..*	*3.5*	*..*	*94.7*
Angola	1990	122.0	0.0	..	0.1	..	0.0	1.6	..	86.9	..	11.5
	2000	69.7	0.0	..	0.0	..	0.0	6.5	..	69.1	..	24.4
	2010	52.2	0.0	..	0.0	..	0.0	15.7	..	29.3	..	55.0
	2013	312.3	0.0	..	0.0	..	0.2	5.2	..	4.3	..	90.6
Cameroon - Cameroun	1990	39.0	..	..	0.0	..	0.0	..	..	92.3	..	7.7
	2000	5.7	..	..	0.0	..	0.0	..	..	5.3	..	94.7
	2010	9.1	..	..	0.0	..	0.0	..	..	28.3	..	71.7
	2013	655.1	..	..	0.0	..	0.4	..	..	0.3	..	99.7
Congo	1990	11.0	..	..	..	..	0.0	..	..	..	..	100.0
	2000	0.7	..	..	..	..	0.0	..	..	..	..	100.0
	2010	0.7	..	..	..	..	0.0	..	..	..	..	100.0
	2013	0.3	..	..	..	..	0.0	..	..	..	..	100.0
Dem. Rep. of the Congo - Rép. dém. du Congo	1990	76.0	..	..	0.1	..	0.0	..	..	80.3	..	19.7
	2010	16.7	0.0	..	0.0	..	0.0	9.8	..	3.6	..	86.6
	2013	10.6	0.0	..	0.0	..	0.0	15.4	..	5.6	..	79.0
Equatorial Guinea - Guinée équatoriale	1990	7.0	..	..	0.0	..	..	..	..	100.0	..	..
	2000	19.4	..	..	0.0	..	0.0	..	..	53.1	..	46.9
	2010	16.9	0.0	..	0.0	..	0.0	23.2	..	13.1	..	63.7
	2013	13.3	0.0	..	0.0	..	0.0	52.7	..	20.8	..	26.4
Gabon	1990	29.0	..	..	0.0	..	0.0	..	..	89.7	..	10.3
	2000	11.6	0.0	..	0.0	..	0.0	6.4	..	61.0	..	32.6
	2010	8.9	0.0	..	0.0	..	0.0	8.4	..	50.6	..	41.0
	2013	404.4	0.0	..	0.0	..	0.2	0.1	..	1.3	..	98.6
Sao Tome and Principe - Sao Tomé-et-Principe	1990	1.0	..	..	..	..	0.0	..	..	..	..	100.0
	2000	36.3	0.0	..	0.0	0.0	0.0	4.8	..	77.6	4.1	13.5
	2010	27.8	0.0	0.0	0.0	..	0.0	3.6	24.8	64.9	..	6.7
	2013	26.7	..	..	0.0	..	0.0	..	..	96.5	..	3.5
Northern Africa - Afrique septentrionale	*1990*	*5 391.0*	*0.7*	*0.4*	*1.4*	*0.0*	*2.9*	*31.0*	*17.5*	*25.7*	*0.2*	*25.6*
	2000	*4 477.3*	*0.4*	*0.5*	*1.1*	*0.1*	*1.3*	*22.5*	*30.1*	*25.1*	*1.0*	*21.3*
	2010	*4 143.9*	*0.4*	*0.2*	*0.4*	*0.1*	*1.0*	*43.2*	*22.0*	*9.8*	*3.2*	*21.9*
	2013	*4 391.8*	*0.3*	*0.2*	*0.4*	*0.1*	*0.9*	*28.9*	*28.5*	*6.9*	*2.7*	*33.1*
Algeria - Algérie	1990	964.0	0.0	0.1	0.3	..	1.0	4.8	16.2	30.7	..	48.3
	2000	1 110.8	0.0	0.1	0.3	..	0.7	4.7	25.9	26.6	..	42.7
	2010	764.6	0.0	0.0	0.1	..	0.5	3.3	26.7	8.4	..	61.6
	2013	739.1	0.0	0.0	0.1	..	0.3	2.3	20.2	8.9	..	68.6
Egypt - Égypte	1990	1 796.0	0.2	0.3	0.7	..	0.2	25.9	31.5	37.4	..	5.3
	2000	2 092.6	0.1	0.4	0.5	0.0	0.2	17.4	49.5	26.0	0.8	6.3
	2010	1 517.9	0.1	0.1	0.2	0.0	0.2	24.7	44.7	16.0	4.2	10.4
	2013	1 722.2	0.1	0.2	0.2	0.0	0.1	14.8	62.4	8.1	3.6	11.0
Libya - Libye	1990	1 463.0	0.5	..	0.1	..	0.6	74.7	..	6.8	..	18.5
	2000	667.1	0.2	..	0.1	..	0.1	80.5	..	13.7	..	5.8
	2010	1 404.9	0.3	..	0.0	..	0.0	95.8	..	2.2	..	2.0
	2013	1 408.0	0.2	..	0.0	..	0.2	70.2	..	0.8	..	29.0

For sources and notes, see end of table.

Pour les sources et les notes, se reporter à la fin du tableau.

5.3 World merchant fleet by flag of registration and type of ship of countries and geographical regions

5.3 Flotte marchande mondiale par pavillons d'immatriculation et par types de navires des pays et des régions géographiques

Region, country or territory / Régions pays ou territoires	Year / Année	Total fleet (thousands of DWT) / Flotte totale (milliers de TPL) (1)	As percentage of world total fleet / En pourcentage de la flotte mondiale					As percentage of the country or region total fleet / En pourcentage de la flotte totale du pays ou de la région				
			Oil tankers / Pétroliers	Bulk carriers / Vraquiers	General cargo / Navires de charge classique (2)	Container ships / Porte-conteneurs	Other types / Autres navires	Oil tankers / Pétroliers	Bulk carriers / Vraquiers	General cargo / Navires de charge classique (2)	Container ships / Porte-conteneurs	Other types / Autres navires
Morocco - Maroc	1990	594.0	0.0	0.1	0.1	0.0	0.6	3.2	27.4	21.7	1.7	46.0
	2000	383.8	0.0	..	0.1	0.0	0.3	5.3	..	29.2	6.6	58.9
	2010	332.0	0.0	..	0.0	0.0	0.2	6.0	..	5.8	20.9	67.3
	2013	127.7	0.0	..	0.0	0.0	0.0	5.5	..	8.6	43.1	42.8
Sudan (...2011) - Soudan (...2011)	1990	127.0	0.0	..	0.1	..	0.0	0.8	..	98.4	..	0.8
	2000	53.2	0.0	..	0.1	..	0.0	2.3	..	96.2	..	1.5
	2010	27.0	..	..	0.0	..	0.0	..	..	95.0	..	5.0
Sudan - Soudan	2013	27.7	..	..	0.0	..	0.0	..	..	94.6	..	5.4
Tunisia - Tunisie	1990	447.0	0.0	0.0	0.1	..	0.6	10.5	13.2	14.8	..	61.5
	2000	169.9	0.0	0.0	0.0	..	0.1	19.1	15.5	17.9	..	47.5
	2010	96.9	0.0	0.0	0.0	..	0.0	24.8	27.2	21.8	..	26.2
	2013	367.0	..	0.0	0.1	..	0.2	..	7.2	13.2	..	79.7
Southern Africa - Afrique australe	*1990*	*352.0*	*0.0*	*..*	*..*	*1.1*	*0.2*	*9.1*	*..*	*..*	*68.2*	*22.7*
	2000	*369.0*	*0.0*	*..*	*0.0*	*0.4*	*0.1*	*1.4*	*..*	*0.0*	*71.1*	*27.4*
	2010	*196.2*	*0.0*	*..*	*0.0*	*0.0*	*0.2*	*4.6*	*..*	*0.9*	*15.1*	*79.4*
	2013	*65.9*	*0.0*	*..*	*0.0*	*..*	*0.0*	*25.7*	*..*	*3.6*	*..*	*70.7*
Namibia - Namibie	2010	70.4	..	..	0.0	..	0.1	..	..	2.2	..	97.8
	2013	3.3	..	..	0.0	..	0.0	..	..	66.3	..	33.7
South Africa - Afrique du Sud	1990	352.0	0.0	..	..	1.1	0.2	9.1	..	..	68.2	22.7
	2000	369.0	0.0	..	0.0	0.4	0.1	1.4	..	0.0	71.1	27.4
	2010	125.9	0.0	..	0.0	0.0	0.1	7.1	..	0.1	23.6	69.2
	2013	62.5	0.0	..	0.0	..	0.0	27.1	..	0.2	..	72.7
Western Africa - Afrique occidentale	*1990*	*90 629.0*	*22.3*	*12.3*	*4.3*	*4.2*	*11.3*	*58.0*	*30.2*	*4.7*	*1.0*	*6.0*
	2000	*86 126.4*	*14.3*	*9.2*	*5.1*	*8.8*	*13.5*	*47.0*	*29.4*	*6.0*	*6.5*	*11.2*
	2010	*144 329.3*	*14.2*	*7.7*	*4.2*	*20.1*	*7.0*	*44.4*	*24.5*	*3.1*	*23.5*	*4.4*
	2013	*204 064.1*	*14.7*	*9.8*	*3.7*	*23.0*	*8.3*	*35.4*	*33.0*	*1.4*	*23.3*	*6.8*
Benin - Bénin	1990	5.0	..	..	0.0	..	0.0	..	..	80.0	..	20.0
	2000	0.2	..	..	..	..	0.0	..	..	..	..	100.0
	2010	0.4	..	..	..	..	0.0	..	..	..	..	100.0
	2013	0.2	..	..	..	..	0.0	..	..	..	..	100.0
Cape Verde - Cap-Vert	1990	26.0	..	..	0.0	..	0.0	..	..	92.3	..	7.7
	2000	24.0	0.0	..	0.0	..	0.0	6.4	..	78.4	..	15.3
	2010	23.5	0.0	..	0.0	..	0.0	26.6	..	48.7	..	24.7
	2013	27.9	0.0	..	0.0	..	0.0	15.0	..	65.6	..	19.4
Côte d'Ivoire	1990	100.0	..	..	0.1	..	0.0	..	..	85.0	..	15.0
	2000	5.9	0.0	..	..	..	0.0	19.9	..	..	..	80.1
	2010	5.1	0.0	..	..	..	0.0	22.8	..	..	..	77.2
	2013	9.9	0.0	..	..	..	0.0	11.8	..	..	..	88.2
Gambia - Gambie	1990	2.0	..	..	..	..	0.0	..	..	..	..	100.0
	2000	1.9	..	..	..	..	0.0	..	..	..	..	100.0
	2010	11.7	0.0	..	0.0	..	0.0	42.7	..	38.4	..	18.9
	2013	3.0	..	..	..	..	0.0	..	..	..	..	100.0
Ghana	1990	114.0	0.0	..	0.1	..	0.1	0.9	..	69.3	..	29.8
	2000	92.1	0.0	0.0	0.0	..	0.1	9.3	0.3	19.2	..	71.1
	2010	84.7	0.0	0.0	0.0	..	0.1	5.4	0.3	20.9	..	73.4
	2013	25.5	0.0	..	0.0	..	0.0	17.4	..	20.8	..	61.8
Guinea - Guinée	1990	3.0	..	..	..	..	0.0	..	..	..	..	100.0
	2000	4.8	..	..	0.0	..	0.0	..	..	6.0	..	94.0
	2010	11.6	..	..	0.0	..	0.0	..	..	2.5	..	97.5
	2013	6.0	..	..	..	..	0.0	..	..	..	..	100.0
Guinea-Bissau - Guinée-Bissau	1990	2.0	..	..	..	..	0.0	..	..	..	..	100.0
	2000	2.2	..	..	0.0	..	0.0	..	..	24.7	..	75.3
	2010	2.2	..	..	0.0	..	0.0	..	..	10.2	..	89.8
	2013	0.6	..	..	0.0	..	..	..	..	100.0	..	..
Liberia - Libéria	1990	89 501.0	22.1	12.3	3.8	4.2	10.9	58.3	30.6	4.2	1.0	5.8
	2000	85 186.9	14.1	9.2	4.9	8.8	13.3	46.8	29.7	5.8	6.6	11.1
	2010	142 121.0	14.0	7.7	3.5	20.0	6.5	44.5	24.8	2.7	23.9	4.2
	2013	198 032.0	14.5	9.8	2.6	22.9	6.3	35.9	33.9	1.0	23.9	5.3

For sources and notes, see end of table.

Pour les sources et les notes, se reporter à la fin du tableau.

5

5.3 World merchant fleet by flag of registration and type of ship of countries and geographical regions

5.3 Flotte marchande mondiale par pavillons d'immatriculation et par types de navires des pays et des régions géographiques

Region, country or territory / Régions pays ou territoires	Year / Année	Total fleet (thousands of DWT) Flotte totale (milliers de TPL) (1)	As percentage of world total fleet / En pourcentage de la flotte mondiale					As percentage of the country or region total fleet / En pourcentage de la flotte totale du pays ou de la région				
			Oil tankers Pétroliers	Bulk carriers Vraquiers	General cargo Navires de charge classique (2)	Container ships Porte-conteneurs	Other types Autres navires	Oil tankers Pétroliers	Bulk carriers Vraquiers	General cargo Navires de charge classique (2)	Container ships Porte-conteneurs	Other types Autres navires
Mauritania - Mauritanie	1990	22.0	..	..	0.0	..	0.0	..	..	18.2	..	81.8
	2000	22.2	..	..	0.0	..	0.0	..	..	3.2	..	96.8
	2010	24.7	..	..	0.0	..	0.0	..	..	3.5	..	96.5
	2013	0.9	..	..	0.0	..	0.0	..	..	78.1	..	21.9
Nigeria - Nigéria	1990	737.0	0.2	..	0.3	..	0.1	59.0	..	35.7	..	5.3
	2000	677.9	0.2	..	0.1	..	0.1	76.6	..	17.0	..	6.4
	2010	989.4	0.2	0.0	0.0	..	0.2	75.8	1.3	1.9	..	20.9
	2013	3 599.8	0.1	0.0	0.0	..	1.9	13.5	0.4	0.4	..	85.7
Saint Helena - Sainte-Hélène	1990	2.0	..	..	..	..	0.0	..	..	..	..	100.0
	2000	0.5	..	..	..	..	0.0	..	..	..	..	100.0
	2010	0.8	..	..	..	..	0.0	..	..	..	..	100.0
Senegal - Sénégal	1990	36.0	..	..	0.0	..	0.0	..	..	47.2	..	52.8
	2000	22.4	..	..	0.0	..	0.0	..	..	9.1	..	90.9
	2010	19.3	0.0	..	0.0	..	0.0	1.4	..	8.0	..	90.5
	2013	5.3	0.0	..	0.0	..	0.0	5.3	..	29.1	..	65.6
Sierra Leone	1990	14.0	0.0	..	0.0	..	0.0	7.1	..	21.4	..	71.4
	2000	11.2	0.0	..	0.0	..	0.0	55.0	..	8.5	..	36.5
	2010	792.2	0.0	0.0	0.5	0.0	0.0	12.9	9.6	70.3	1.4	5.7
	2013	1 520.8	0.1	0.0	0.8	0.1	0.1	16.7	18.4	39.9	16.5	8.4
Togo	1990	65.0	0.0	..	0.0	..	0.1	1.5	..	32.3	..	67.7
	2000	74.4	..	0.0	..	..	0.0	..	99.1	..	..	0.9
	2010	242.8	0.0	0.0	0.1	0.0	0.0	3.3	31.2	57.9	3.4	4.1
	2013	832.2	0.1	0.0	0.3	0.0	0.0	58.2	7.9	27.3	2.9	3.8
Developing economies: America - Économies en développement : Amérique	**1990**	**119 936.0**	**16.4**	**20.2**	**24.0**	**19.3**	**16.2**	**32.2**	**37.6**	**20.1**	**3.6**	**6.4**
	2000	**237 755.2**	**26.8**	**34.5**	**31.6**	**28.8**	**23.7**	**31.9**	**39.8**	**13.5**	**7.7**	**7.1**
	2010	**395 591.2**	**24.8**	**38.9**	**33.7**	**25.6**	**28.6**	**28.2**	**45.0**	**9.2**	**11.0**	**6.7**
	2013	**467 431.3**	**21.1**	**35.0**	**25.0**	**23.2**	**33.9**	**22.2**	**51.2**	**4.3**	**10.3**	**12.1**
Caribbean - Caraïbes	*1990*	*24 104.0*	*5.1*	*2.7*	*4.3*	*1.1*	*3.0*	*49.8*	*25.2*	*18.0*	*1.0*	*5.9*
	2000	*62 854.5*	*9.5*	*5.3*	*13.4*	*6.1*	*5.4*	*42.6*	*23.4*	*21.7*	*6.2*	*6.1*
	2010	*94 721.4*	*8.2*	*4.6*	*15.1*	*5.4*	*12.1*	*39.1*	*22.3*	*17.3*	*9.6*	*11.7*
	2013	*104 423.5*	*7.4*	*3.6*	*10.6*	*4.5*	*15.3*	*34.7*	*23.8*	*8.2*	*8.9*	*24.4*
Anguilla	1990	4.0	..	..	0.0	..	..	..	..	75.0	..	..
	2000	2.0	..	..	0.0	..	..	..	..	100.0	..	..
	2010	0.9	..	..	0.0	..	..	..	..	100.0	..	..
	2013	0.9	..	..	0.0	..	..	..	..	100.0	..	..
Antigua and Barbuda - Antigua-et-Barbuda	1990	696.0	0.0	0.0	0.5	0.3	0.1	12.2	0.7	70.3	11.2	5.6
	2000	4 677.6	0.0	0.1	1.8	3.9	0.1	0.2	6.7	39.2	53.0	0.9
	2010	13 033.6	0.0	0.3	4.0	4.3	0.1	0.2	9.8	33.1	56.0	0.9
	2013	14 141.7	0.0	0.2	6.5	3.4	0.2	0.4	11.1	36.8	49.9	1.8
Aruba	2010	0.1	..	..	..	..	0.0	..	..	..	..	100.0
	2013	0.1	..	..	..	..	0.0	..	..	..	..	100.0
Bahamas	1990	19 228.0	4.8	2.2	1.8	0.4	2.2	59.2	25.3	9.6	0.5	5.4
	2000	44 941.4	8.8	3.2	7.3	1.9	3.9	55.4	19.3	16.5	2.7	6.1
	2010	64 109.1	7.4	2.8	6.0	0.9	10.5	52.2	20.1	10.2	2.4	15.1
	2013	73 702.1	6.9	2.6	1.1	0.9	11.5	46.3	24.1	1.1	2.4	26.0
Barbados - Barbade	1990	8.0	..	..	0.0	..	..	..	..	100.0	..	..
	2000	1 162.0	0.2	0.1	0.2	0.0	0.1	55.0	22.7	13.3	1.5	7.4
	2010	1 181.1	0.1	0.1	0.3	..	0.1	23.9	43.4	27.7	..	5.0
	2013	1 485.1	0.0	0.1	0.4	0.1	0.1	14.8	46.2	20.5	7.2	11.3
British Virgin Islands - Îles Vierges britanniques	1990	5.0	..	..	0.0	..	..	..	..	100.0	..	..
	2000	2.1	..	..	0.0	..	0.0	..	..	68.8	..	31.2
	2010	11.0	..	..	0.0	..	0.0	..	..	5.1	..	94.9
	2013	1.6	..	..	0.0	..	0.0	..	..	60.6	..	39.4
Cayman Islands - Îles Caïmanes	1990	566.0	0.0	0.1	0.2	..	0.2	11.0	33.2	38.9	..	17.0
	2000	1 756.2	0.1	0.3	0.4	0.1	0.3	11.9	52.7	22.1	2.2	11.1
	2010	3 960.6	0.5	0.3	0.3	..	0.4	55.0	29.4	7.4	..	8.2
	2013	4 310.5	0.1	0.2	0.0	..	1.4	12.8	31.7	0.2	..	55.3

For sources and notes, see end of table.

Pour les sources et les notes, se reporter à la fin du tableau.

5.3 World merchant fleet by flag of registration and type of ship of countries and geographical regions

5.3 Flotte marchande mondiale par pavillons d'immatriculation et par types de navires des pays et des régions géographiques

Region, country or territory / Régions pays ou territoires	Year / Année	Total fleet (thousands of DWT) / Flotte totale (milliers de TPL) (1)	As percentage of world total fleet / En pourcentage de la flotte mondiale					As percentage of the country or region total fleet / En pourcentage de la flotte totale du pays ou de la région				
			Oil tankers / Pétroliers	Bulk carriers / Vraquiers	General cargo / Navires de charge classique (2)	Container ships / Porte-conteneurs	Other types / Autres navires	Oil tankers / Pétroliers	Bulk carriers / Vraquiers	General cargo / Navires de charge classique (2)	Container ships / Porte-conteneurs	Other types / Autres navires
Cuba	1990	1 198.0	0.0	0.0	0.8	..	0.3	9.8	8.3	68.1	..	13.8
	2000	156.3	0.0	0.0	0.1	..	0.1	3.0	2.0	53.3	..	41.6
	2010	49.4	0.0	0.0	0.0	..	0.0	2.1	7.0	28.8	..	62.1
	2013	39.7	0.0	..	0.0	..	0.0	2.6	..	79.7	..	17.7
Curaçao	2013	2 137.1	0.0	0.0	0.3	0.0	1.0	7.9	3.4	9.9	0.4	78.4
Dominica - Dominique	1990	5.0	..	..	0.0	..	..	..	..	100.0	..	..
	2000	2.7	..	..	0.0	..	0.0	..	..	79.9	..	20.1
	2010	1 610.4	0.1	0.2	0.1	..	0.0	28.5	62.1	7.1	..	2.3
	2013	2 037.5	0.1	0.2	0.1	..	0.0	30.3	63.9	3.0	..	2.8
Dominican Republic - République dominicaine	1990	68.0	0.0	0.0	0.0	..	..	2.9	27.9	69.1	..	..
	2000	8.4	..	..	0.0	..	0.0	..	..	85.6	..	14.4
	2010	5.6	..	..	0.0	..	0.0	..	..	89.0	..	11.0
	2013	166.2	0.0	..	0.0	..	0.0	89.8	..	9.3	..	0.9
Grenada - Grenade	1990	1.0	..	..	..	..	0.0	..	..	..	..	100.0
	2000	1.0	..	..	0.0	..	..	..	..	100.0	..	..
	2010	1.0	..	..	0.0	..	0.0	..	..	95.5	..	4.5
	2013	1.1	..	..	0.0	..	0.0	..	..	85.6	..	14.4
Haiti - Haïti	2000	1.0	..	..	0.0	..	0.0	..	..	82.3	..	17.7
	2010	1.5	..	..	0.0	..	0.0	..	..	88.9	..	11.1
	2013	0.6	..	..	0.0	..	..	..	..	100.0	..	..
Jamaica - Jamaïque	1990	21.0	0.0	0.0	0.0	0.0	0.0	14.3	19.0	38.1	23.8	4.8
	2000	3.3	0.0	..	..	..	0.0	92.9	..	..	..	7.1
	2010	353.3	..	0.1	0.1	0.0	0.0	..	74.4	15.6	9.9	0.2
	2013	224.0	..	0.0	0.0	0.0	0.0	..	56.9	10.8	31.9	0.4
Montserrat	1990	1.0	..	..	0.0	..	..	..	..	100.0	..	..
Netherlands Antilles - Antilles néerlandaises	2010	1 836.7	0.0	0.0	1.1	0.0	0.3	9.4	8.1	66.7	0.5	15.4
Saint Kitts and Nevis - Saint-Kitts-et-Nevis	1990	1.0	..	..	0.0	..	..	..	..	100.0	..	..
	2000	0.6	..	..	0.0	..	..	..	..	100.0	..	..
	2010	1 219.2	0.0	0.1	0.5	0.0	0.1	10.5	39.3	45.0	0.9	4.3
	2013	1 230.7	0.1	0.1	0.4	0.0	0.1	23.7	30.4	26.2	1.6	18.1
Saint Lucia - Sainte-Lucie	1990	2.0	..	..	0.0	..	..	..	..	100.0	..	..
Saint Vincent and the Grenadines - Saint-Vincent-et-les Grenadines	1990	2 282.0	0.2	0.4	0.9	0.3	0.2	15.6	39.7	38.9	2.7	3.2
	2000	10 131.0	0.4	1.6	3.7	0.3	1.0	10.0	44.4	36.8	1.8	7.0
	2010	7 329.2	0.1	0.7	2.8	0.1	0.5	4.3	46.1	40.7	2.1	6.7
	2013	4 918.7	0.0	0.2	1.9	0.1	0.9	2.1	31.8	30.4	5.1	30.6
Trinidad and Tobago - Trinité-et-Tobago	1990	16.0	..	..	0.0	..	0.0	..	..	37.5	..	62.5
	2000	8.9	0.0	..	0.0	..	0.0	16.6	..	28.9	..	54.5
	2010	18.3	0.0	..	..	..	0.0	22.6	..	..	..	77.4
	2013	25.7	0.0	..	0.0	..	0.0	16.1	..	1.9	..	82.0
Turks and Caicos Islands - Îles Turques et Caïques	1990	2.0	..	..	0.0	..	0.0	..	..	50.0	..	50.0
	2000	0.2	..	..	0.0	..	..	..	..	100.0	..	..
	2010	0.2	..	..	0.0	..	..	..	..	100.0	..	..
	2013	0.3	..	..	0.0	..	0.0	..	..	51.4	..	48.6
Central America - Amérique centrale	*1990*	*78 245.0*	*8.9*	*14.3*	*16.4*	*17.2*	*10.3*	*27.0*	*40.7*	*21.1*	*4.9*	*6.3*
	2000	*164 753.9*	*15.8*	*27.9*	*17.2*	*22.3*	*16.4*	*27.2*	*46.6*	*10.6*	*8.6*	*7.1*
	2010	*292 694.0*	*15.7*	*34.0*	*17.9*	*20.0*	*14.8*	*24.2*	*53.0*	*6.6*	*11.6*	*4.7*
	2013	*355 187.1*	*12.9*	*31.2*	*13.2*	*18.5*	*17.8*	*17.9*	*60.1*	*3.0*	*10.8*	*8.3*
Belize	2000	3 052.4	0.2	0.1	1.7	0.1	0.6	18.8	10.6	55.5	1.8	13.2
	2010	1 451.1	0.0	0.1	0.8	..	0.3	2.2	20.4	61.4	..	16.0
	2013	2 195.7	0.0	0.1	1.4	0.0	0.2	6.8	26.9	50.7	2.0	13.7
Costa Rica	1990	7.0	..	..	0.0	..	0.0	..	..	42.9	..	57.1
	2000	1.2	..	..	..	..	0.0	..	..	..	..	100.0
	2010	0.4	..	..	..	..	0.0	..	..	..	..	100.0
	2013	1.7	..	..	0.0	..	0.0	..	..	79.4	..	20.6
El Salvador	1990	3.0	..	..	..	..	0.0	..	..	..	..	100.0
	2010	1.7	..	..	..	..	0.0	..	..	..	..	100.0

For sources and notes, see end of table.

Pour les sources et les notes, se reporter à la fin du tableau.

5.3 World merchant fleet by flag of registration and type of ship of countries and geographical regions

5.3 Flotte marchande mondiale par pavillons d'immatriculation et par types de navires des pays et des régions géographiques

Region, country or territory / Régions pays ou territoires	Year / Année	Total fleet (thousands of DWT) / Flotte totale (milliers de TPL) (1)	As percentage of world total fleet / En pourcentage de la flotte mondiale					As percentage of the country or region total fleet / En pourcentage de la flotte totale du pays ou de la région				
			Oil tankers / Pétroliers	Bulk carriers / Vraquiers	General cargo / Navires de charge classique (2)	Container ships / Porte-conteneurs	Other types / Autres navires	Oil tankers / Pétroliers	Bulk carriers / Vraquiers	General cargo / Navires de charge classique (2)	Container ships / Porte-conteneurs	Other types / Autres navires
Guatemala	1990	7.0	..	..	0.0	..	0.0	..	..	85.7	..	14.3
	2000	3.8	..	..	..	..	0.0	..	..	..	..	100.0
	2010	2.8	0.0	..	..	..	0.0	33.4	..	..	..	66.6
	2013	1.0	0.0	..	..	..	0.0	93.9	..	..	..	6.1
Honduras	1990	982.0	0.1	0.1	0.6	0.0	0.1	14.1	17.6	62.8	0.9	4.6
	2000	1 520.7	0.1	0.1	0.9	0.0	0.3	15.8	14.6	57.0	0.5	12.1
	2010	702.2	0.0	0.0	0.3	0.0	0.1	26.7	10.1	44.3	0.3	18.5
	2013	645.2	0.0	0.0	0.4	0.0	0.1	24.9	4.4	54.2	0.3	16.1
Mexico - Mexique	1990	1 883.0	0.3	0.2	0.1	0.1	1.4	42.9	18.4	3.3	0.6	34.8
	2000	1 226.6	0.3	..	0.0	..	0.6	62.3	..	2.0	..	35.8
	2010	1 775.7	0.3	0.0	0.0	..	0.6	63.7	5.2	2.0	..	29.1
	2013	1 835.3	0.2	0.0	0.0	..	0.3	57.4	10.6	1.2	..	30.8
Nicaragua	1990	3.0	..	..	0.0	..	..	..	..	100.0	..	..
	2000	2.0	..	..	0.0	..	0.0	..	..	59.4	..	40.6
	2010	2.7	0.0	..	0.0	..	0.0	33.9	..	43.4	..	22.7
	2013	2.6	0.0	..	0.0	..	0.0	35.5	..	45.4	..	19.1
Panama	1990	75 360.0	8.5	14.0	15.7	17.1	8.8	26.7	41.6	21.0	5.1	5.6
	2000	158 947.3	15.3	27.7	14.6	22.2	15.0	27.2	47.9	9.3	8.9	6.7
	2010	288 757.6	15.4	33.9	16.7	20.0	13.9	24.0	53.6	6.3	11.7	4.4
	2013	350 505.6	12.7	31.0	11.4	18.5	17.2	17.7	60.6	2.6	10.9	8.2
South America - Amérique du Sud	*1990*	*17 587.0*	*2.4*	*3.2*	*3.3*	*1.0*	*2.9*	*31.6*	*40.5*	*18.9*	*1.3*	*7.8*
	2000	*10 146.7*	*1.5*	*1.2*	*1.0*	*0.4*	*1.9*	*42.5*	*32.0*	*10.2*	*2.3*	*13.0*
	2010	*8 175.8*	*0.8*	*0.4*	*0.7*	*0.2*	*1.7*	*46.5*	*19.9*	*9.1*	*5.0*	*19.5*
	2013	*7 820.7*	*0.8*	*0.2*	*1.2*	*0.2*	*0.8*	*49.2*	*15.7*	*12.1*	*6.0*	*16.9*
Argentina - Argentine	1990	2 764.0	0.4	0.4	0.8	0.3	0.5	32.6	29.1	27.6	2.6	8.2
	2000	599.3	0.1	0.0	0.1	..	0.3	30.1	8.7	21.9	..	39.3
	2010	980.9	0.1	0.0	0.1	0.0	0.3	54.7	11.7	7.2	1.9	24.6
	2013	532.7	0.1	0.0	0.1	..	0.0	65.9	4.5	14.4	..	15.2
Bolivia (Plurinational State of) - Bolivie (État plurinational de)	1990	16.0	..	..	0.0	..	..	..	..	100.0	..	..
	2000	244.5	0.0	0.0	0.1	0.0	0.0	11.4	35.7	44.1	3.4	5.5
	2010	166.0	0.0	0.0	0.1	..	0.0	14.5	28.7	48.1	..	8.7
	2013	535.9	0.0	0.1	0.1	0.0	0.0	12.4	69.0	16.2	1.2	1.2
Brazil - Brésil	1990	10 063.0	1.4	2.3	1.1	0.5	1.1	32.2	50.6	10.9	1.1	5.2
	2000	6 383.6	1.1	0.9	0.4	0.3	0.3	48.0	39.8	6.1	2.6	3.5
	2010	3 406.8	0.3	0.2	0.3	0.2	0.5	42.4	25.3	8.2	10.5	13.6
	2013	3 232.4	0.3	0.1	0.3	0.2	0.4	48.5	12.3	7.6	12.3	19.2
Chile - Chili	1990	870.0	..	0.2	0.2	..	0.3	..	63.4	22.8	..	13.8
	2000	1 012.0	0.1	0.1	0.1	0.1	0.5	16.4	34.5	12.0	5.0	32.1
	2010	1 095.8	0.1	0.1	0.1	0.0	0.2	36.1	34.8	6.9	1.9	20.3
	2013	803.6	0.1	0.0	0.1	0.0	0.0	49.7	32.6	8.0	4.8	4.9
Colombia - Colombie	1990	546.0	0.0	0.1	0.4	..	0.0	2.7	28.8	65.0	..	3.5
	2000	119.4	0.0	..	0.1	..	0.0	8.3	..	67.7	..	24.1
	2010	109.0	0.0	..	0.0	..	0.1	7.1	..	49.4	..	43.4
	2013	115.1	0.0	..	0.1	..	0.0	8.0	..	53.7	..	38.4
Ecuador - Équateur	1990	531.0	0.1	0.0	0.2	..	0.1	39.4	7.2	47.1	..	6.4
	2000	446.6	0.1	..	0.0	..	0.1	86.3	..	0.8	..	12.9
	2010	400.6	0.1	..	0.0	..	0.1	81.6	..	1.5	..	16.9
	2013	363.9	0.1	..	0.0	..	0.0	94.3	..	1.6	..	4.1
Falkland Islands (Malvinas) - Îles Falkland (Malvinas)	1990	4.0	..	..	..	..	0.0	..	..	..	..	100.0
	2000	31.1	..	..	0.0	..	0.0	..	..	2.0	..	98.0
	2010	34.6	..	..	..	..	0.0	..	..	..	..	100.0
	2013	6.1	..	..	0.0	..	0.0	..	..	16.5	..	83.5
Guyana	1990	11.0	..	..	0.0	..	0.0	..	..	45.5	..	54.5
	2000	12.5	..	..	0.0	..	0.0	..	..	53.8	..	46.2
	2010	41.7	0.0	..	0.0	..	0.0	16.4	..	67.1	..	16.5
	2013	42.3	0.0	..	0.0	..	0.0	19.8	..	46.1	..	34.1
Paraguay	1990	44.0	0.0	..	0.0	..	0.0	2.3	..	59.1	..	38.6
	2000	48.8	0.0	..	0.0	0.0	0.0	18.2	..	73.3	4.5	4.0
	2010	63.3	0.0	..	0.0	0.0	0.0	10.3	..	73.9	13.4	2.4
	2013	56.0	0.0	..	0.1	0.0	0.0	11.4	..	74.5	11.4	2.7

For sources and notes, see end of table.

Pour les sources et les notes, se reporter à la fin du tableau.

5.3 World merchant fleet by flag of registration and type of ship of countries and geographical regions

5.3 Flotte marchande mondiale par pavillons d'immatriculation et par types de navires des pays et des régions géographiques

Region, country or territory / Régions pays ou territoires	Year / Année	Total fleet (thousands of DWT) / Flotte totale (milliers de TPL) (1)	As percentage of world total fleet / En pourcentage de la flotte mondiale					As percentage of the country or region total fleet / En pourcentage de la flotte totale du pays ou de la région				
			Oil tankers / Pétroliers	Bulk carriers / Vraquiers	General cargo / Navires de charge classique (2)	Container ships / Porte-conteneurs	Other types / Autres navires	Oil tankers / Pétroliers	Bulk carriers / Vraquiers	General cargo / Navires de charge classique (2)	Container ships / Porte-conteneurs	Other types / Autres navires
Peru - Pérou	1990	841.0	0.1	0.1	0.2	..	0.1	40.1	25.7	28.2	..	6.1
	2000	267.0	0.0	0.0	0.1	..	0.1	29.7	9.6	30.4	..	30.4
	2010	317.9	0.0	..	0.0	..	0.1	55.7	..	9.3	..	35.0
	2013	403.4	0.1	..	0.0	0.0	0.0	74.9	..	5.2	3.6	16.3
Suriname	1990	15.0	0.0	..	0.0	0.0	0.0	13.3	..	66.7	13.3	6.7
	2000	7.2	0.0	..	0.0	..	0.0	42.1	..	43.8	..	14.2
	2010	5.7	0.0	..	0.0	..	0.0	59.7	..	31.3	..	9.0
	2013	6.5	0.0	..	0.0	..	0.0	40.3	..	48.4	..	3.3
Uruguay	1990	155.0	0.0	..	0.0	0.2	0.1	60.6	..	1.9	21.9	15.5
	2000	38.1	0.0	..	0.0	..	0.0	22.0	..	3.3	..	74.7
	2010	69.9	0.0	0.0	0.0	..	0.0	22.3	4.6	12.4	..	60.6
	2013	43.4	0.0	..	0.0	..	0.0	23.1	..	25.7	..	51.3
Venezuela (Bolivarian Rep. of) - Venezuela (Rép. bolivarienne du)	1990	1 727.0	0.3	0.1	0.4	0.0	0.7	43.9	15.3	21.1	0.2	19.5
	2000	936.7	0.1	0.1	0.1	0.0	0.4	40.1	20.7	8.1	0.1	31.0
	2010	1 483.6	0.2	0.0	0.1	..	0.4	58.0	14.8	4.2	..	22.9
	2013	1 679.3	0.2	0.0	0.4	0.0	0.2	46.6	10.4	18.3	0.4	24.2
Developing economies: Asia - Économies en développement : Asie	**1990**	**115 295.0**	**12.6**	**23.2**	**23.8**	**18.2**	**12.1**	**25.7**	**45.0**	**20.7**	**3.5**	**5.0**
	2000	**156 453.2**	**15.1**	**24.0**	**25.1**	**20.0**	**13.4**	**27.4**	**42.1**	**16.3**	**8.1**	**6.1**
	2010	**285 345.4**	**20.3**	**24.9**	**28.7**	**19.4**	**17.6**	**32.1**	**39.9**	**10.9**	**11.5**	**5.7**
	2013	**397 694.6**	**21.9**	**27.5**	**32.8**	**21.6**	**18.6**	**27.1**	**47.3**	**6.6**	**11.2**	**7.8**
Eastern Asia - Asie orientale	*1990*	*43 401.0*	*2.4*	*10.8*	*9.8*	*9.3*	*3.8*	*12.8*	*55.5*	*22.8*	*4.8*	*4.2*
	2000	*54 642.3*	*2.4*	*11.0*	*9.2*	*9.8*	*3.2*	*12.2*	*55.1*	*17.1*	*11.4*	*4.2*
	2010	*146 890.9*	*7.0*	*17.8*	*11.9*	*10.1*	*4.5*	*21.5*	*55.4*	*8.7*	*11.6*	*2.8*
	2013	*221 307.7*	*8.5*	*19.8*	*12.5*	*12.1*	*5.2*	*18.9*	*61.3*	*4.5*	*11.3*	*3.9*
China - Chine	1990	20 200.0	1.1	3.6	7.7	4.0	1.8	13.2	39.9	38.2	4.5	4.2
	2000	23 701.2	1.2	4.0	6.4	2.6	1.6	14.3	46.8	27.2	7.0	4.7
	2010	45 157.3	2.1	5.0	5.6	3.1	1.7	20.5	51.0	13.4	11.7	3.4
	2013	68 642.4	2.9	5.8	5.6	3.0	2.5	20.5	57.8	6.5	9.1	6.0
China, Hong Kong SAR - Chine (RAS de Hong Kong)	1990	10 337.0	0.6	3.5	0.4	2.1	0.6	13.1	75.2	4.2	4.5	2.8
	2000	13 190.9	0.3	3.6	0.9	2.3	0.1	7.1	73.9	7.2	11.2	0.6
	2010	74 513.5	4.1	9.0	3.5	6.0	1.2	24.9	55.0	5.0	13.6	1.5
	2013	129 805.6	5.3	11.9	3.3	8.0	1.9	20.1	62.7	2.1	12.7	2.4
China, Macao SAR - Chine (RAS de Macao)	2010	2.2	..	..	..	..	0.0	..	..	..	..	100.0
	2013	2.2	..	..	..	..	0.0	..	..	..	..	100.0
China, Taiwan Province of - Province chinoise de Taiwan	2000	8 248.1	0.6	1.6	0.2	3.4	0.1	18.9	51.8	2.4	26.3	0.7
	2010	3 944.1	0.3	0.4	0.1	0.4	0.1	29.0	46.4	4.1	18.0	2.4
	2013	3 486.5	0.0	0.3	0.2	0.4	0.0	6.0	61.1	4.4	26.6	1.9
Korea, Dem. People's Rep. of - Corée, Rép. populaire dém. de	1990	529.0	0.0	0.0	0.4	..	0.0	3.8	20.6	71.6	..	4.0
	2000	846.6	0.0	0.0	0.7	..	0.1	1.4	10.4	80.7	..	7.6
	2010	1 265.6	0.0	0.0	0.8	0.0	0.1	9.3	12.8	71.1	2.5	4.3
	2013	1 007.8	0.0	0.0	1.0	0.0	0.0	9.9	8.1	77.6	1.4	3.0
Korea, Republic of - Corée, République de	1990	12 335.0	0.6	3.6	1.4	3.2	1.3	12.2	65.8	11.0	5.8	5.2
	2000	8 655.5	0.3	1.8	1.1	1.5	1.3	8.9	56.8	12.3	11.0	11.1
	2010	20 818.6	0.5	3.2	1.6	0.5	1.4	11.7	69.7	8.4	4.1	6.2
	2013	17 720.0	0.3	1.8	2.1	0.6	0.8	7.4	68.2	9.6	7.4	7.5
Mongolia - Mongolie	2010	1 189.6	0.0	0.2	0.2	..	0.0	1.6	75.9	21.0	..	1.5
	2013	643.1	0.0	0.0	0.3	0.0	0.0	11.3	43.1	36.6	2.5	6.6
Southern Asia - Asie méridionale	*1990*	*20 524.0*	*3.9*	*3.2*	*3.5*	*..*	*1.4*	*45.3*	*34.6*	*16.9*	*..*	*3.3*
	2000	*18 704.6*	*3.0*	*2.3*	*2.4*	*0.3*	*1.7*	*45.2*	*34.5*	*13.1*	*1.0*	*6.3*
	2010	*18 185.6*	*2.1*	*1.1*	*1.3*	*0.4*	*1.6*	*52.6*	*28.4*	*7.6*	*3.5*	*8.0*
	2013	*20 554.1*	*1.9*	*1.0*	*2.5*	*0.6*	*0.9*	*45.1*	*32.5*	*9.6*	*5.8*	*7.1*
Afghanistan	2013	1.5	..	..	..	..	0.0	..	..	..	..	100.0
Bangladesh	1990	587.0	0.0	..	0.5	..	0.0	14.1	..	83.5	..	2.4
	2000	518.7	0.0	0.0	0.4	..	0.0	19.6	1.7	74.9	..	3.8
	2010	975.3	0.0	0.1	0.3	0.0	0.0	11.4	47.4	33.7	5.0	2.5
	2013	1 655.8	0.0	0.2	0.5	0.0	0.0	4.8	68.7	22.2	2.3	2.0

For sources and notes, see end of table.

Pour les sources et les notes, se reporter à la fin du tableau.

5.3 World merchant fleet by flag of registration and type of ship of countries and geographical regions

5.3 Flotte marchande mondiale par pavillons d'immatriculation et par types de navires des pays et des régions géographiques

Region, country or territory — Régions pays ou territoires	Year Année	Total fleet (thousands of DWT) — Flotte totale (milliers de TPL) (1)	As percentage of world total fleet — En pourcentage de la flotte mondiale					As percentage of the country or region total fleet — En pourcentage de la flotte totale du pays ou de la région				
			Oil tankers Pétroliers	Bulk carriers Vraquiers	General cargo Navires de charge classique (2)	Container ships Porte-conteneurs	Other types Autres navires	Oil tankers Pétroliers	Bulk carriers Vraquiers	General cargo Navires de charge classique (2)	Container ships Porte-conteneurs	Other types Autres navires
India - Inde	1990	10 207.0	1.2	2.3	1.6	..	1.0	28.5	50.9	15.9	..	4.7
	2000	11 209.3	1.7	1.7	0.6	0.2	1.4	43.1	41.3	5.9	1.2	8.6
	2010	14 969.6	2.0	0.9	0.3	0.2	1.3	60.2	27.5	2.4	2.2	7.8
	2013	15 875.7	1.7	0.7	1.0	0.2	0.8	54.0	30.9	5.0	2.2	7.9
Iran (Islamic Rep. of) - Iran (Rép. islamique d')	1990	8 685.0	2.6	0.8	0.6	..	0.3	71.3	20.4	6.5	..	1.8
	2000	6 097.3	1.2	0.6	0.9	0.0	0.2	55.9	26.4	14.8	0.2	2.6
	2010	1 333.3	0.0	0.1	0.3	0.1	0.2	9.0	34.0	22.3	18.9	15.7
	2013	1 965.4	0.1	0.0	0.7	0.4	0.1	13.4	11.1	30.6	39.4	5.6
Maldives	1990	148.0	0.0	0.0	0.1	..	0.0	6.8	48.6	43.2	..	1.4
	2000	132.8	0.0	..	0.1	..	0.0	6.5	..	88.5	..	4.9
	2010	187.5	0.0	0.0	0.1	..	0.0	8.4	0.9	86.0	..	4.7
	2013	123.6	0.0	..	0.1	0.0	0.0	12.3	..	74.3	7.3	6.0
Pakistan	1990	526.0	0.0	..	0.4	..	0.0	17.1	..	80.8	..	2.1
	2000	458.7	0.0	0.0	0.3	0.1	0.0	19.8	11.4	56.8	9.1	2.9
	2010	481.1	0.1	0.0	0.1	..	0.0	58.5	13.7	22.3	..	5.5
	2013	692.9	0.1	0.0	0.0	..	0.0	46.5	46.3	2.6	..	4.5
Sri Lanka	1990	371.0	0.0	0.0	0.3	..	0.0	4.0	14.8	80.1	..	1.1
	2000	287.6	0.0	0.1	0.1	..	0.0	3.5	52.0	42.2	..	2.4
	2010	238.9	0.0	0.0	0.1	..	0.0	10.9	31.5	51.2	..	6.3
	2013	239.2	0.0	0.0	0.1	0.0	0.0	6.2	41.4	39.4	7.0	6.0
South-Eastern Asia - Asie du Sud-Est	*1990*	*35 050.0*	*2.8*	*7.9*	*6.9*	*6.5*	*4.9*	*19.0*	*50.2*	*19.9*	*4.1*	*6.7*
	2000	*62 945.1*	*7.7*	*7.9*	*9.4*	*8.0*	*6.9*	*34.5*	*34.5*	*15.2*	*8.1*	*7.8*
	2010	*101 728.6*	*9.4*	*5.1*	*12.8*	*7.7*	*10.0*	*41.5*	*23.0*	*13.6*	*12.8*	*9.1*
	2013	*135 937.4*	*10.0*	*5.8*	*14.9*	*8.0*	*11.1*	*36.1*	*29.4*	*8.8*	*12.1*	*13.6*
Brunei Darussalam - Brunéi Darussalam	1990	346.0	..	..	0.0	..	0.7	..	..	0.3	..	99.7
	2000	349.6	0.0	..	0.0	..	0.5	0.1	..	0.7	..	99.2
	2010	448.9	0.0	0.0	0.0	..	0.5	0.1	4.5	0.7	..	94.6
	2013	449.3	0.0	..	0.0	..	0.3	1.5	..	1.8	..	96.7
Cambodia - Cambodge	1990	4.0	..	..	0.0	..	0.0	..	..	25.0	..	75.0
	2010	2 517.0	0.0	0.1	1.8	0.0	0.1	2.6	14.6	78.2	0.6	4.0
	2013	2 319.4	0.0	0.0	2.2	0.0	0.1	3.5	13.9	76.7	1.5	4.2
Indonesia (...2002) - Indonésie (...2002)	1990	2 742.0	0.4	0.1	1.2	0.3	0.5	35.2	7.7	45.4	2.7	9.0
	2000	4 153.7	0.5	0.2	1.8	0.1	0.5	32.1	14.8	43.5	1.4	8.2
Indonesia - Indonésie	2010	10 470.7	0.9	0.5	2.7	0.5	0.8	36.9	19.9	28.0	7.9	7.3
	2013	14 267.4	0.8	0.3	4.2	0.8	1.9	27.3	16.1	23.6	11.4	21.6
Lao People's Dem. Rep. - Rép. dém. populaire lao	2010	1.6	..	..	0.0	..	..	..	..	100.0	..	..
	2013	1.6	..	..	0.0	..	..	..	..	100.0	..	..
Malaysia - Malaisie	1990	2 364.0	0.1	0.3	0.7	1.0	1.1	12.0	26.9	29.6	9.8	21.8
	2000	7 577.5	0.6	1.0	0.8	1.3	2.3	21.6	35.3	11.4	10.5	21.3
	2010	10 224.8	1.2	0.1	0.5	0.5	3.3	51.1	4.9	5.8	8.4	29.8
	2013	10 507.7	0.9	0.0	0.5	0.3	2.8	43.7	2.3	4.1	5.6	44.3
Myanmar	1990	907.0	0.0	0.3	0.2	..	0.1	0.4	72.5	23.5	..	3.5
	2000	792.3	0.0	0.2	0.2	0.0	0.0	0.6	63.7	30.8	3.2	1.7
	2010	210.1	0.0	0.0	0.2	..	0.0	2.2	11.3	79.9	..	6.6
	2013	182.4	0.0	..	0.2	..	0.0	2.6	..	89.3	..	8.1
Philippines	1990	15 468.0	0.3	5.5	2.1	0.3	0.3	5.0	79.9	13.7	0.4	1.1
	2000	11 112.0	0.1	3.0	2.0	0.2	0.5	2.1	74.7	18.5	1.4	3.2
	2010	7 032.8	0.2	0.8	1.6	0.2	0.4	11.1	54.6	24.1	5.0	5.2
	2013	6 417.2	0.1	0.6	1.3	0.2	0.4	6.9	61.2	16.5	5.5	10.0
Singapore - Singapour	1990	11 888.0	1.9	1.7	1.7	4.6	2.1	37.6	31.2	14.2	8.6	8.4
	2000	34 635.5	6.2	3.2	2.6	6.1	2.6	50.9	25.0	7.5	11.2	5.4
	2010	61 660.4	6.6	3.2	2.7	6.2	4.4	48.3	23.4	4.7	17.0	6.6
	2013	89 697.4	7.5	4.4	1.8	6.5	4.7	41.1	33.6	1.6	14.9	8.7
Thailand - Thaïlande	1990	805.0	0.1	0.0	0.6	0.2	0.1	16.0	2.1	70.2	6.2	5.5
	2000	3 068.4	0.2	0.3	1.3	0.3	0.2	22.4	25.6	42.7	5.2	4.1
	2010	3 746.8	0.2	0.2	1.2	0.2	0.2	27.7	23.6	34.7	8.4	5.7
	2013	4 811.1	0.3	0.2	0.7	0.1	0.5	33.1	29.8	12.1	6.0	19.0
Timor-Leste	2010	0.3	..	..	..	..	0.0	..	..	..	..	100.0

For sources and notes, see end of table.

Pour les sources et les notes, se reporter à la fin du tableau.

5.3 World merchant fleet by flag of registration and type of ship of countries and geographical regions

5.3 Flotte marchande mondiale par pavillons d'immatriculation et par types de navires des pays et des régions géographiques

Region, country or territory / Régions pays ou territoires	Year / Année	Total fleet (thousands of DWT) / Flotte totale (milliers de TPL) (1)	As percentage of world total fleet / En pourcentage de la flotte mondiale					As percentage of the country or region total fleet / En pourcentage de la flotte totale du pays ou de la région				
			Oil tankers / Pétroliers	Bulk carriers / Vraquiers	General cargo / Navires de charge classique (2)	Container ships / Porte-conteneurs	Other types / Autres navires	Oil tankers / Pétroliers	Bulk carriers / Vraquiers	General cargo / Navires de charge classique (2)	Container ships / Porte-conteneurs	Other types / Autres navires
Viet Nam	1990	526.0	0.0	0.0	0.4	..	0.0	6.5	4.6	85.9	..	3.0
	2000	1 256.1	0.1	0.1	0.7	0.0	0.3	13.5	12.0	54.3	1.3	18.9
	2010	5 415.2	0.3	0.3	2.1	0.1	0.3	27.3	22.6	42.2	3.0	4.8
	2013	7 283.9	0.3	0.2	3.8	0.1	0.5	21.0	22.4	42.4	2.7	11.5
Western Asia - Asie occidentale	*1990*	*16 320.0*	*3.5*	*1.4*	*3.5*	*2.4*	*1.9*	*50.2*	*19.0*	*21.8*	*3.3*	*5.7*
	2000	*20 161.2*	*2.1*	*2.8*	*4.1*	*1.9*	*1.7*	*30.1*	*37.5*	*20.5*	*5.9*	*6.0*
	2010	*10 540.3*	*1.8*	*0.8*	*2.7*	*1.3*	*1.6*	*44.0*	*20.8*	*15.9*	*11.6*	*7.8*
	2013	*19 895.4*	*1.5*	*0.8*	*3.0*	*1.0*	*1.4*	*37.5*	*20.4*	*13.2*	*10.2*	*11.8*
Bahrain - Bahreïn	1990	65.0	0.0	0.0	0.0	..	0.0	3.1	30.8	41.5	..	24.6
	2000	369.8	0.0	0.0	0.1	0.2	0.0	26.2	11.9	26.5	27.0	8.3
	2010	613.4	0.0	0.0	0.0	0.2	0.1	25.2	13.9	0.3	44.2	16.4
	2013	640.2	0.0	0.0	0.0	0.1	0.1	24.1	6.9	0.3	43.7	25.0
Iraq	1990	1 813.0	0.7	..	0.1	..	0.3	85.6	..	7.5	..	6.9
	2000	834.7	0.2	..	0.1	..	0.1	79.0	..	12.6	..	8.4
	2010	180.1	0.0	..	0.1	..	0.1	37.7	..	30.2	..	32.1
	2013	110.4	0.0	..	0.0	..	0.0	25.3	..	28.1	..	46.5
Jordan - Jordanie	1990	48.0	..	0.0	..	..	0.0	..	91.7	..	..	8.3
	2000	59.3	..	0.0	0.0	0.0	0.0	..	56.3	32.1	11.2	0.4
	2010	369.3	0.1	..	0.1	..	0.0	78.5	..	16.1	..	5.4
	2013	60.9	..	..	0.1	..	0.0	..	..	87.7	..	12.3
Kuwait - Koweït	1990	2 887.0	0.8	..	0.5	0.7	0.6	65.9	..	18.8	5.1	10.2
	2000	3 884.4	1.0	0.0	0.3	0.4	0.5	76.2	0.7	7.9	5.8	9.4
	2010	3 856.2	0.7	0.0	0.1	0.2	0.3	83.4	1.0	2.0	7.6	6.0
	2013	4 169.0	0.7	0.0	0.0	0.2	0.1	84.2	1.9	0.2	7.9	5.8
Lebanon - Liban	1990	593.0	0.0	0.1	0.4	0.0	0.0	3.9	26.3	68.1	0.5	1.2
	2000	483.2	0.0	0.1	0.2	0.0	0.0	0.3	52.5	44.7	1.5	1.0
	2010	158.6	0.0	0.0	0.1	..	0.0	0.9	33.9	63.2	..	2.0
	2013	141.6	0.0	0.0	0.1	0.0	0.0	0.6	16.5	76.2	4.6	2.2
Oman	1990	13.0	..	..	0.0	..	0.0	..	..	53.8	..	46.2
	2000	10.9	0.0	..	0.0	..	0.0	4.2	..	27.5	..	68.2
	2010	14.3	0.0	..	0.0	..	0.0	15.5	..	11.5	..	73.0
	2013	14.5	0.0	..	0.0	..	0.0	21.2	..	12.4	..	66.3
Qatar	1990	459.0	0.1	..	0.2	0.4	0.0	43.8	..	32.9	20.0	3.3
	2000	1 154.0	0.2	0.1	0.2	0.3	0.0	40.4	23.4	17.5	17.1	1.5
	2010	1 363.4	0.1	0.0	0.0	0.2	0.3	40.0	8.5	0.0	29.6	21.8
	2013	1 224.2	0.1	0.0	0.0	0.1	0.2	44.6	9.5	0.1	21.7	24.1
Saudi Arabia - Arabie saoudite	1990	3 535.0	1.0	0.1	0.7	0.3	0.5	63.4	8.8	18.6	2.1	7.0
	2000	1 443.0	0.1	..	0.6	0.3	0.3	28.4	..	39.6	15.0	17.1
	2010	2 319.3	0.3	..	0.3	0.1	0.3	65.1	..	12.7	9.5	12.6
	2013	1 420.9	0.1	..	0.3	0.1	0.2	46.4	..	15.1	13.0	25.5
Syrian Arab Republic - République arabe syrienne	1990	102.0	..	..	0.1	..	0.0	..	..	97.1	..	2.9
	2000	679.4	..	0.0	0.6	..	0.0	..	6.5	92.1	..	1.4
	2010	344.2	..	0.0	0.2	0.0	0.0	..	22.4	74.9	2.5	0.3
	2013	169.2	..	0.0	0.2	..	0.0	..	11.2	87.8	..	1.0
Turkey - Turquie	1990	5 477.0	0.6	1.1	1.3	..	0.2	27.0	46.3	24.6	..	2.2
	2000	10 174.2	0.4	2.5	1.7	0.3	0.4	10.4	67.3	17.2	2.1	3.0
	2010	7 878.0	0.4	0.7	1.9	0.3	0.3	21.5	42.6	25.5	7.3	3.1
	2013	10 215.1	0.4	0.8	2.2	0.3	0.2	21.4	51.7	17.5	6.7	2.8
United Arab Emirates - Émirats arabes unis	1990	1 316.0	0.3	0.0	0.2	1.0	0.2	59.4	2.9	14.6	16.6	6.5
	2000	1 042.5	0.1	0.0	0.2	0.4	0.2	39.3	3.5	22.6	21.8	12.8
	2010	1 412.3	0.1	0.0	0.1	0.2	0.2	46.0	8.5	5.8	26.8	12.9
	2013	1 287.2	0.1	0.0	0.1	0.1	0.3	26.5	6.7	6.0	21.1	39.7
Yemen - Yémen	1990	12.0	0.0	..	0.0	..	0.0	25.0	..	33.3	..	41.7
	2000	25.8	0.0	..	0.0	..	0.0	12.3	..	11.9	..	75.8
	2010	31.2	0.0	..	0.0	..	0.0	69.3	..	10.9	..	19.9
	2013	442.1	0.0	..	0.0	..	0.2	6.3	..	0.9	..	92.8

For sources and notes, see end of table.

Pour les sources et les notes, se reporter à la fin du tableau.

5.3 World merchant fleet by flag of registration and type of ship of countries and geographical regions

5.3 Flotte marchande mondiale par pavillons d'immatriculation et par types de navires des pays et des régions géographiques

Region, country or territory / Régions pays ou territoires	Year / Année	Total fleet (thousands of DWT) Flotte totale (milliers de TPL) (1)	As percentage of world total fleet / En pourcentage de la flotte mondiale					As percentage of the country or region total fleet / En pourcentage de la flotte totale du pays ou de la région				
			Oil tankers Pétroliers	Bulk carriers Vraquiers	General cargo Navires de charge classique (2)	Container ships Porte-conteneurs	Other types Autres navires	Oil tankers Pétroliers	Bulk carriers Vraquiers	General cargo Navires de charge classique (2)	Container ships Porte-conteneurs	Other types Autres navires
Developing economies: Oceania - Économies en développement : Océanie (3)	**1990**	**1 814.0**	**0.1**	**0.4**	**0.4**	**0.2**	**0.3**	**15.5**	**48.5**	**24.9**	**2.8**	**8.4**
	2000	**1 931.6**	**0.0**	**0.3**	**0.5**	**0.1**	**0.7**	**1.2**	**44.4**	**25.4**	**1.8**	**27.2**
	2010	**83 461.2**	**9.2**	**5.7**	**2.2**	**3.2**	**8.9**	**49.6**	**31.2**	**2.9**	**6.4**	**9.9**
	2013	**146 335.2**	**12.3**	**8.7**	**2.3**	**4.3**	**9.3**	**41.4**	**40.7**	**1.3**	**6.0**	**10.6**
Cook Islands - Îles Cook	2013	479.3	0.0	0.0	0.2	0.0	0.0	0.1	63.0	30.9	1.2	4.8
Fiji - Fidji	1990	64.0	0.0	..	0.0	..	0.0	10.9	..	71.9	..	17.2
	2000	24.4	0.0	..	0.0	..	0.0	14.8	..	23.6	..	61.6
	2010	17.0	..	..	0.0	..	0.0	..	..	40.0	..	60.0
	2013	15.1	..	..	0.0	..	0.0	..	..	41.8	..	58.2
French Polynesia - Polynésie française	2010	1.1	..	..	0.0	..	..	..	..	100.0	..	..
	2013	10.2	..	..	0.0	..	0.0	..	..	89.2	..	10.8
Guam	2013	0.2	..	..	..	..	0.0	..	..	..	..	100.0
Kiribati	1990	3.0	..	..	0.0	..	..	..	..	100.0	..	..
	2000	4.1	..	..	0.0	..	0.0	..	..	84.0	..	16.0
	2010	828.8	0.0	0.1	0.3	..	0.1	19.7	41.5	33.3	..	5.6
	2013	366.9	0.0	0.0	0.2	0.0	0.1	22.2	12.9	35.7	1.2	28.1
Marshall Islands - Îles Marshall (6)	2010	77 827.4	8.9	5.2	1.4	3.1	8.0	51.3	30.3	2.0	6.8	9.5
	2013	140 015.9	12.1	8.3	1.5	4.2	8.2	42.4	40.7	0.9	6.3	9.7
Micronesia (Federated States of) - Micronésie (États fédérés de)	2010	9.8	..	0.0	0.0	..	0.0	..	3.8	64.8	..	31.5
	2013	7.7	..	..	0.0	..	0.0	..	..	88.8	..	11.2
Nauru	1990	45.0	..	0.0	0.0	..	0.0	..	60.0	42.2	..	2.2
New Caledonia - Nouvelle-Calédonie	2010	2.7	..	..	0.0	..	..	..	..	100.0	..	..
	2013	3.7	..	..	0.0	..	0.0	..	..	93.1	..	6.9
Northern Mariana Islands - Îles Mariannes du Nord	2013	0.1	..	..	..	..	0.0	..	..	..	..	100.0
Papua New Guinea - Papouasie-Nouvelle-Guinée	1990	42.0	0.0	0.0	0.0	..	0.0	4.8	11.9	57.1	..	26.2
	2000	70.9	0.0	..	0.1	..	0.0	3.9	..	77.8	..	18.4
	2010	111.1	0.0	0.0	0.1	..	0.0	2.5	5.7	80.8	..	11.0
	2013	137.9	0.0	..	0.1	0.0	0.0	2.5	..	65.9	20.8	10.9
Samoa	1990	35.0	..	..	0.0	..	0.0	..	..	97.1	..	2.9
	2010	9.8	..	..	0.0	..	0.0	..	..	93.9	..	6.1
	2013	9.8	..	..	0.0	..	0.0	..	..	95.2	..	4.8
Solomon Islands - Îles Salomon	1990	7.0	..	..	0.0	..	0.0	..	..	71.4	..	28.6
	2000	6.9	..	..	0.0	..	0.0	..	..	35.9	..	64.1
	2010	8.0	..	..	0.0	..	0.0	..	..	24.9	..	75.1
	2013	3.2	..	..	0.0	..	0.0	..	..	61.8	..	38.2
Tonga	1990	43.0	..	..	0.0	0.1	0.0	..	..	27.9	69.8	2.3
	2000	29.3	..	..	0.0	..	0.0	..	..	63.1	..	36.9
	2010	77.5	0.0	0.0	0.1	..	0.0	2.1	8.6	77.5	..	11.8
	2013	47.5	0.0	..	0.0	..	0.0	7.2	..	84.6	..	8.1
Tuvalu	1990	1.0	..	..	0.0	..	..	..	..	100.0	..	..
	2000	68.4	..	..	0.0	..	0.1	..	..	37.6	..	62.4
	2010	1 884.1	0.3	0.1	0.1	0.0	0.1	67.3	19.2	7.8	0.8	4.9
	2013	2 351.0	0.2	0.1	0.2	0.0	0.4	47.8	15.4	6.9	0.2	29.7
Vanuatu	1990	1 574.0	0.1	0.4	0.3	0.1	0.3	17.3	53.9	19.5	1.3	8.0
	2000	1 727.7	0.0	0.3	0.4	0.1	0.6	1.0	49.7	21.9	2.0	25.4
	2010	2 683.7	..	0.4	0.2	0.0	0.7	..	65.2	8.9	1.1	24.9
	2013	2 886.7	0.0	0.3	0.0	0.0	0.6	0.2	63.5	1.3	1.0	34.1
Transition economies - Économies en transition	**1990**	**35 090.0**	**2.9**	**4.4**	**12.4**	**3.2**	**11.0**	**19.2**	**28.4**	**35.4**	**2.0**	**15.0**
	2000	**13 598.3**	**0.9**	**0.9**	**5.4**	**0.7**	**3.8**	**18.5**	**18.0**	**40.2**	**3.4**	**19.9**
	2010	**12 777.5**	**0.8**	**0.4**	**4.5**	**0.1**	**2.1**	**29.6**	**15.7**	**38.5**	**1.3**	**14.8**
	2013	**11 801.4**	**0.8**	**0.3**	**5.2**	**0.0**	**1.2**	**32.0**	**15.3**	**35.5**	**0.7**	**16.5**
Albania - Albanie	1990	63.0	..	..	0.1	..	..	..	..	100.0	..	..
	2000	20.1	..	..	0.0	..	0.0	..	..	93.8	..	6.2
	2010	96.8	..	..	0.1	..	0.0	..	..	98.5	..	1.5
	2013	93.0	..	..	0.1	..	0.0	..	..	98.7	..	1.3

For sources and notes, see end of table.

Pour les sources et les notes, se reporter à la fin du tableau.

5.3 World merchant fleet by flag of registration and type of ship of countries and geographical regions

5.3 Flotte marchande mondiale par pavillons d'immatriculation et par types de navires des pays et des régions géographiques

Region, country or territory / Régions pays ou territoires	Year / Année	Total fleet (thousands of DWT) / Flotte totale (milliers de TPL) (1)	As percentage of world total fleet / En pourcentage de la flotte mondiale					As percentage of the country or region total fleet / En pourcentage de la flotte totale du pays ou de la région				
			Oil tankers / Pétroliers	Bulk carriers / Vraquiers	General cargo / Navires de charge classique (2)	Container ships / Porte-conteneurs	Other types / Autres navires	Oil tankers / Pétroliers	Bulk carriers / Vraquiers	General cargo / Navires de charge classique (2)	Container ships / Porte-conteneurs	Other types / Autres navires
Azerbaijan - Azerbaïdjan	2000	507.5	0.1	..	0.1	..	0.2	45.8	..	20.2	..	33.9
	2010	662.6	0.1	..	0.1	..	0.2	53.3	..	18.4	..	28.3
	2013	683.6	0.1	..	0.2	..	0.1	52.0	..	19.2	..	28.9
Belarus - Bélarus	2013	57.8	..	0.0	..	..	0.0	..	95.9	..	..	4.1
Croatia - Croatie	2000	1 227.7	0.0	0.3	0.2	0.2	0.0	1.1	70.7	17.7	8.0	2.5
	2010	2 277.1	0.3	0.2	0.0	..	0.0	54.4	41.6	2.4	..	1.6
	2013	2 269.4	0.2	0.2	0.1	..	0.0	48.1	48.3	1.9	..	1.7
Georgia - Géorgie	2000	183.8	0.0	0.0	0.0	..	0.0	65.3	0.1	24.8	..	9.8
	2010	935.2	0.0	0.0	0.6	0.0	0.0	4.0	22.1	68.2	1.3	4.5
	2013	441.7	0.0	0.0	0.4	0.0	0.0	6.6	13.9	71.1	1.5	6.9
Kazakhstan	2000	4.7	..	..	0.0	..	0.0	..	..	16.6	..	83.4
	2010	91.3	0.0	..	0.0	..	0.0	69.4	..	2.2	..	28.4
	2013	128.3	0.0	..	..	..	0.0	70.8	..	..	..	29.2
Montenegro - Monténégro	2010	6.1	..	..	0.0	..	0.0	..	..	87.7	..	12.3
	2013	77.1	..	0.0	0.0	..	0.0	..	90.8	8.0	..	1.2
Republic of Moldova - République de Moldova	2010	459.8	0.0	0.0	0.3	0.0	0.0	7.1	25.9	64.3	1.2	1.4
	2013	566.3	0.0	0.0	0.5	0.0	0.0	2.8	18.1	72.4	1.8	4.8
Russian Federation - (5) Fédération de Russie	2000	9 950.4	0.7	0.5	4.1	0.5	2.9	20.6	13.2	42.0	3.2	21.0
	2010	7 283.0	0.4	0.1	2.9	0.1	1.5	27.2	8.6	43.5	2.1	18.6
	2013	6 784.4	0.4	0.1	3.5	0.0	0.8	31.1	6.2	41.0	1.0	20.7
SFR of Yugoslavia - RSF de Yougoslavie	1990	5 815.0	0.2	1.5	1.8	0.5	0.1	9.1	57.2	30.9	2.0	0.8
Turkmenistan - Turkménistan	2000	36.5	0.0	0.0	0.0	..	0.0	9.3	18.3	41.6	..	30.8
	2010	61.8	0.0	..	0.0	..	0.0	36.4	..	25.1	..	38.5
	2013	92.3	0.0	..	0.0	..	0.0	44.6	..	11.2	..	44.3
Ukraine	2000	1 667.5	0.0	0.1	0.9	0.1	0.5	5.4	15.9	52.8	2.7	23.1
	2010	903.9	0.0	0.0	0.5	..	0.2	5.8	12.3	58.2	..	23.6
	2013	607.4	0.0	..	0.5	..	0.1	6.7	..	65.8	..	27.5
USSR - URSS	1990	29 212.0	2.6	3.0	10.5	2.7	10.9	21.2	22.7	36.2	2.1	17.9
Developed economies: America - Économies développées : Amérique (3)	**1990**	**31 335.0**	**9.0**	**0.9**	**2.0**	**13.0**	**6.7**	**67.6**	**6.3**	**6.5**	**9.3**	**10.2**
	2000	**37 163.0**	**7.3**	**2.4**	**2.0**	**6.8**	**5.1**	**55.4**	**17.8**	**5.4**	**11.7**	**9.7**
	2010	**26 299.5**	**1.6**	**1.6**	**1.1**	**2.7**	**6.6**	**27.5**	**27.8**	**4.5**	**17.2**	**23.1**
	2013	**28 107.0**	**1.4**	**0.7**	**5.1**	**1.6**	**5.3**	**25.0**	**17.2**	**14.7**	**11.8**	**31.4**
Bermuda - Bermudes	1990	7 625.0	2.8	0.1	0.2	0.1	1.0	86.7	3.6	2.8	0.4	6.4
	2000	10 468.5	1.9	1.3	0.3	0.9	0.8	51.0	35.3	3.0	5.3	5.4
	2010	10 106.6	0.5	0.7	0.1	0.4	4.0	22.3	33.0	1.1	7.0	36.5
	2013	12 378.4	0.5	0.6	0.0	0.3	3.3	18.7	32.4	0.1	4.4	44.4
Canada	1990	756.0	0.1	0.2	0.0	0.0	0.1	34.5	53.2	6.3	0.9	5.0
	2000	1 018.4	0.1	0.1	0.1	0.0	0.5	40.1	16.0	11.6	0.2	32.2
	2010	3 401.1	0.2	0.4	0.1	0.0	0.6	29.6	50.8	2.9	0.5	16.2
	2013	3 371.5	0.2	0.1	1.7	0.0	0.4	30.7	11.0	40.4	0.4	17.5
Greenland - Groenland	2013	3.7	..	..	0.0	..	0.0	..	..	82.8	..	17.2
United States - États-Unis (7)	1990	22 954.0	6.1	0.6	1.8	12.8	5.6	62.4	5.7	7.8	12.5	11.7
	2000	25 676.0	5.2	1.0	1.6	5.9	3.8	57.8	10.8	6.2	14.7	10.5
	2010	12 791.8	0.9	0.5	0.9	2.2	2.0	31.1	17.5	7.6	29.6	14.4
	2013	12 353.4	0.7	0.1	3.4	1.3	1.6	29.7	3.5	22.3	22.4	22.0
Developed economies: Asia - Économies développées : Asie	**1990**	**42 943.0**	**6.1**	**7.7**	**6.4**	**7.7**	**6.7**	**33.2**	**40.3**	**15.0**	**4.0**	**7.5**
	2000	**23 554.9**	**3.2**	**2.4**	**2.7**	**2.5**	**5.3**	**38.2**	**27.8**	**11.4**	**6.6**	**16.0**
	2010	**18 193.3**	**1.1**	**1.4**	**2.3**	**0.4**	**3.8**	**27.7**	**36.3**	**13.7**	**3.3**	**19.0**
	2013	**20 727.3**	**1.0**	**1.3**	**3.5**	**0.2**	**2.1**	**24.2**	**43.5**	**13.6**	**1.9**	**16.8**
Israel - Israël	1990	586.0	0.0	0.0	0.1	1.7	0.0	0.2	8.9	24.7	65.9	0.3
	2000	832.1	0.0	..	0.0	1.3	0.0	0.3	..	0.9	98.3	0.5
	2010	486.1	0.0	..	0.0	0.3	0.0	1.1	..	1.1	96.8	1.0
	2013	318.4	0.0	..	0.0	0.1	0.0	1.5	..	4.5	92.4	1.6

For sources and notes, see end of table.

Pour les sources et les notes, se reporter à la fin du tableau.

5.3 World merchant fleet by flag of registration and type of ship of countries and geographical regions

5.3 Flotte marchande mondiale par pavillons d'immatriculation et par types de navires des pays et des régions géographiques

Region, country or territory Régions pays ou territoires	Year Année	Total fleet (thousands of DWT) Flotte totale (milliers de TPL) (1)	As percentage of world total fleet En pourcentage de la flotte mondiale					As percentage of the country or region total fleet En pourcentage de la flotte totale du pays ou de la région				
			Oil tankers Pétroliers	Bulk carriers Vraquiers	General cargo Navires de charge classique (2)	Container ships Porte-conteneurs	Other types Autres navires	Oil tankers Pétroliers	Bulk carriers Vraquiers	General cargo Navires de charge classique (2)	Container ships Porte-conteneurs	Other types Autres navires
Japan - Japon	1990	42 357.0	6.1	7.7	6.3	6.0	6.7	33.7	40.7	14.8	3.2	7.6
	2000	22 722.9	3.2	2.4	2.6	1.2	5.3	39.6	28.8	11.8	3.3	16.5
	2010	17 707.2	1.1	1.4	2.3	0.1	3.8	28.4	37.3	14.1	0.7	19.5
	2013	20 408.9	1.0	1.3	3.5	0.0	2.1	24.6	44.2	13.7	0.5	17.0
Developed economies: Europe - Économies développées : Europe	1990	182 418.0	29.4	29.6	24.5	32.4	31.5	38.0	36.3	13.5	4.0	8.2
	2000	228 742.9	31.9	25.3	26.2	31.6	31.4	39.4	30.4	11.6	8.8	9.8
	2010	295 627.9	27.0	18.6	19.7	28.4	21.7	41.0	28.7	7.2	16.3	6.8
	2013	329 578.4	24.3	16.5	19.8	25.9	16.8	36.2	34.3	4.8	16.2	8.5
Austria - Autriche	1990	355.0	..	0.1	0.1	..	..	..	69.3	30.7	..	..
	2000	100.3	..	..	0.1	..	..	..	..	100.0	..	..
	2010	11.7	..	..	0.0	..	..	..	..	100.0	..	..
Belgium - Belgique	1990	3 282.0	0.1	0.9	0.1	1.0	1.5	6.3	62.5	3.4	6.6	21.2
	2000	149.5	0.0	..	0.0	..	0.2	4.5	..	0.4	..	95.1
	2010	6 575.1	0.5	0.6	0.1	0.1	1.5	33.0	41.5	2.3	2.0	21.2
	2013	6 912.7	0.4	0.5	0.2	0.1	0.9	27.6	47.4	1.8	1.8	21.4
Bulgaria - Bulgarie	1990	1 956.0	0.2	0.4	0.4	0.1	0.2	23.6	49.5	22.3	0.9	3.7
	2000	1 501.6	0.1	0.3	0.3	0.1	0.1	18.0	54.1	20.8	4.5	2.7
	2010	696.8	0.0	0.1	0.1	0.0	0.0	3.7	66.6	16.8	9.2	3.8
	2013	483.3	0.0	0.1	0.1	..	0.0	2.3	79.3	15.8	..	2.6
Cyprus - Chypre	1990	32 699.0	4.7	7.1	4.9	1.9	0.9	33.9	48.5	14.9	1.3	1.3
	2000	36 669.4	2.4	7.2	5.7	4.6	1.7	18.8	54.1	15.9	7.9	3.4
	2010	31 305.2	2.3	3.0	1.6	2.9	0.9	32.4	43.7	5.6	15.6	2.7
	2013	31 706.1	1.2	2.7	1.7	2.6	0.6	18.5	57.3	4.2	16.7	3.4
Czechoslovakia - Tchécoslovaquie	1990	279.0	..	0.1	0.1	..	0.0	..	54.8	44.8	..	0.4
Denmark - Danemark	1990	6 926.0	1.2	0.3	0.8	5.5	2.8	42.0	8.7	12.0	17.7	19.6
	2000	7 420.8	0.4	0.3	0.8	5.0	2.0	16.1	11.8	10.8	42.5	18.8
	2010	13 813.8	1.2	0.1	0.3	4.0	1.1	38.1	3.7	2.4	48.5	7.2
	2013	13 859.6	1.0	0.0	0.3	3.7	0.5	34.5	2.3	1.9	54.7	6.5
Estonia - Estonie	2000	363.1	0.0	0.0	0.2	..	0.1	3.7	27.8	51.9	..	16.7
	2010	98.7	0.0	..	0.0	..	0.1	12.9	..	15.6	..	71.6
	2013	75.3	0.0	..	0.0	0.0	0.1	21.6	..	20.0	3.9	54.5
Faeroe Islands - Îles Féroé	2013	218.7	0.0	..	0.1	0.0	0.0	23.8	..	32.9	13.8	29.5
Finland - Finlande	1990	838.0	0.1	0.1	0.3	..	0.5	21.4	14.8	35.2	..	28.6
	2000	1 239.5	0.2	0.0	0.4	..	0.3	41.0	10.8	31.2	..	17.0
	2010	1 171.3	0.1	0.0	0.4	0.0	0.1	52.0	0.3	34.2	3.2	10.3
	2013	1 338.3	0.1	0.0	0.5	0.0	0.1	42.5	13.4	31.9	1.0	11.2
France	1990	6 653.0	1.6	0.5	0.6	2.6	1.1	57.3	16.3	9.4	8.8	8.2
	2000	7 292.5	1.6	0.4	0.4	0.8	1.4	60.8	14.0	4.9	7.1	13.2
	2010	8 822.3	1.3	0.1	0.1	1.1	1.0	64.0	3.9	1.0	20.3	10.7
	2013	7 434.7	0.7	0.1	0.2	1.1	0.6	49.2	4.6	1.6	31.5	13.1
Germany - Allemagne	1990	6 778.0	0.1	0.5	2.5	9.1	2.0	4.6	14.9	36.9	29.9	13.8
	2000	7 788.3	0.0	0.0	1.0	9.9	0.5	0.1	0.1	13.6	81.2	4.9
	2010	17 570.2	0.1	0.2	0.5	9.0	0.4	3.2	4.7	3.1	86.9	2.1
	2013	17 128.4	0.1	0.1	0.3	7.3	0.2	3.3	5.0	1.5	88.2	2.0
Gibraltar	1990	5 026.0	1.7	0.3	0.2	..	0.1	80.7	14.0	3.9	..	1.4
	2000	728.5	0.2	0.0	0.0	0.1	0.1	76.0	3.7	4.9	8.6	6.8
	2013	2 829.0	0.1	0.1	0.9	0.3	0.2	23.3	14.4	26.3	22.5	13.4
Greece - Grèce	1990	38 465.0	6.8	8.2	2.9	1.0	2.1	41.6	47.7	7.5	0.6	2.6
	2000	42 532.1	8.9	5.1	0.9	2.2	1.8	58.9	32.7	2.1	3.3	3.0
	2010	67 629.2	9.4	4.7	0.3	1.4	1.2	62.6	31.6	0.5	3.6	1.7
	2013	75 424.0	9.2	3.8	0.4	1.2	0.7	60.0	34.6	0.4	3.2	1.6
Hungary - Hongrie	1990	108.0	..	..	0.1	..	..	..	..	100.0	..	..
	2000	14.9	..	..	0.0	..	..	..	..	100.0	..	..
Iceland - Islande	1990	155.0	0.0	0.0	0.1	..	0.1	0.6	12.3	49.7	..	37.4
	2000	83.6	0.0	0.0	0.0	0.0	0.1	3.2	0.8	3.5	14.8	77.7
	2010	69.4	0.0	0.0	0.0	..	0.1	0.7	0.9	1.0	..	97.4
	2013	10.9	0.0	..	0.0	..	0.0	4.3	..	12.3	..	83.5

For sources and notes, see end of table.

Pour les sources et les notes, se reporter à la fin du tableau.

5.3 World merchant fleet by flag of registration and type of ship of countries and geographical regions

5.3 Flotte marchande mondiale par pavillons d'immatriculation et par types de navires des pays et des régions géographiques

Region, country or territory / Régions pays ou territoires	Year / Année	Total fleet (thousands of DWT) / Flotte totale (milliers de TPL) (1)	As percentage of world total fleet / En pourcentage de la flotte mondiale					As percentage of the country or region total fleet / En pourcentage de la flotte totale du pays ou de la région				
			Oil tankers / Pétroliers	Bulk carriers / Vraquiers	General cargo / Navires de charge classique (2)	Container ships / Porte-conteneurs	Other types / Autres navires	Oil tankers / Pétroliers	Bulk carriers / Vraquiers	General cargo / Navires de charge classique (2)	Container ships / Porte-conteneurs	Other types / Autres navires
Ireland - Irlande	1990	178.0	0.0	..	0.1	0.1	0.1	6.2	..	55.1	14.0	24.7
	2000	154.4	0.0	0.0	0.1	0.0	0.0	0.2	7.9	65.5	4.4	22.0
	2010	196.2	0.0	..	0.1	0.0	0.0	9.4	..	73.9	3.8	12.9
	2013	243.9	0.0	0.0	0.1	..	0.0	0.1	46.2	42.2	..	11.4
Italy - Italie (4)	1990	11 524.0	1.8	1.9	1.2	1.5	2.9	37.7	36.5	10.7	2.9	12.2
	2000	9 768.8	1.0	1.3	0.9	1.0	2.7	28.7	35.8	9.5	6.7	19.4
	2010	17 276.0	1.8	1.1	1.4	0.6	1.6	47.3	29.0	8.8	6.3	8.7
	2013	20 611.8	1.6	1.2	2.0	0.5	1.4	30.2	38.3	7.9	4.7	11.0
Latvia - Lettonie	2000	101.5	0.0	..	0.0	..	0.1	15.1	..	47.0	..	37.9
	2010	180.3	0.0	..	0.0	..	0.1	58.9	..	12.5	..	28.6
	2013	72.4	0.0	..	0.0	..	0.0	12.8	..	29.8	..	57.4
Lithuania - Lituanie	2000	414.6	0.0	0.1	0.2	..	0.1	1.8	38.6	45.8	..	13.8
	2010	364.2	0.0	..	0.3	0.0	0.1	0.4	..	75.2	3.8	20.6
	2013	288.6	0.0	0.0	0.2	0.0	0.0	0.6	32.4	44.7	4.8	17.6
Luxembourg	1990	6.0	0.0	..	..	..	0.0	50.0	..	..	..	50.0
	2000	1 959.6	0.4	0.1	0.1	0.0	1.0	51.0	8.8	2.9	1.2	36.1
	2010	1 099.8	0.1	0.0	0.1	0.1	0.4	23.2	17.5	10.2	17.1	32.0
	2013	1 600.6	0.1	0.0	0.3	0.1	0.5	20.6	6.1	13.7	12.1	47.6
Malta - Malte	1990	5 691.0	1.1	0.9	1.1	0.0	0.3	43.5	35.2	19.0	0.1	2.2
	2000	46 749.4	7.8	6.2	5.3	1.5	1.7	47.4	36.5	11.5	2.0	2.6
	2010	56 156.1	4.6	6.1	3.4	1.7	1.2	36.8	49.4	6.6	5.1	2.0
	2013	68 830.9	5.0	5.0	3.1	2.6	1.5	35.8	49.4	3.6	7.7	3.5
Netherlands - Pays-Bas	1990	4 557.0	0.2	0.2	1.8	2.3	2.4	12.6	12.0	38.7	11.2	25.6
	2000	6 607.3	0.1	0.0	2.8	2.8	2.3	4.0	1.6	42.4	27.0	25.0
	2010	7 252.5	0.1	0.0	3.3	1.1	1.2	9.0	0.7	49.7	25.6	15.0
	2013	8 711.7	0.1	0.1	5.4	0.7	1.1	5.3	9.3	49.5	15.6	20.3
Norway - Norvège	1990	26 568.0	5.5	3.5	1.7	0.3	8.3	48.9	29.6	6.3	0.2	14.9
	2000	35 388.0	6.2	2.6	3.8	0.2	9.8	49.2	19.9	10.8	0.3	19.7
	2010	20 811.2	2.1	0.9	3.1	0.0	4.4	45.0	19.4	15.9	0.0	19.6
	2013	20 974.3	1.5	0.9	0.6	0.0	4.1	35.5	29.2	2.4	0.2	32.7
Poland - Pologne	1990	4 490.0	0.1	1.2	1.4	0.2	0.5	4.9	57.6	31.6	1.0	4.9
	2000	1 855.4	0.0	0.6	0.1	..	0.2	0.4	88.8	3.8	..	6.9
	2010	130.9	0.0	..	0.0	..	0.1	5.7	..	22.7	..	71.6
	2013	75.4	0.0	..	0.0	..	0.0	11.7	..	43.2	..	45.1
Portugal	1990	1 102.0	0.3	0.1	0.1	0.0	0.2	54.8	26.3	9.5	0.9	8.4
	2000	1 630.0	0.3	0.1	0.4	0.1	0.3	44.9	17.6	23.7	2.5	11.3
	2010	1 288.3	0.2	0.0	0.2	0.0	0.2	52.5	11.4	20.1	2.7	13.3
	2013	1 224.6	0.1	0.0	0.3	0.0	0.2	46.1	12.1	16.5	3.3	22.0
Romania - Roumanie	1990	5 711.0	0.4	1.3	1.6	0.1	0.3	18.5	51.1	27.8	0.3	2.3
	2000	1 618.3	0.0	0.2	0.8	0.0	0.2	6.4	32.1	51.3	0.5	9.6
	2010	244.1	0.0	..	0.1	..	0.1	19.3	..	33.6	..	47.1
	2013	148.6	0.0	..	0.1	..	0.0	7.7	..	41.3	..	51.0
Slovakia - Slovaquie	2000	19.5	..	..	0.0	..	..	..	..	100.0	..	..
	2010	192.9	..	0.0	0.2	..	0.0	..	7.9	92.0	..	0.1
	2013	46.1	..	..	0.1	..	0.0	..	..	87.8	..	12.2
Slovenia - Slovénie	2000	0.8	..	..	0.0	..	0.0	..	..	29.9	..	70.1
	2010	0.4	..	..	..	..	0.0	..	..	..	..	100.0
	2013	1.0	..	..	..	..	0.0	..	..	..	..	100.0
Spain - Espagne	1990	6 461.0	1.3	0.8	0.8	0.5	1.6	47.4	27.3	12.0	1.7	11.6
	2000	2 053.0	0.4	0.0	0.3	0.2	0.7	51.1	3.4	14.3	6.6	24.6
	2010	2 554.7	0.2	0.0	0.2	0.1	1.2	40.5	1.4	8.1	6.5	43.5
	2013	2 572.2	0.2	0.0	0.2	0.0	0.8	39.5	0.4	7.7	2.6	49.8
Sweden - Suède	1990	1 995.0	0.1	0.1	0.9	0.3	0.9	14.6	13.7	46.8	3.6	21.3
	2000	1 846.0	0.1	0.0	1.0	..	0.9	8.7	2.4	55.9	..	33.0
	2010	2 206.3	0.1	0.0	1.2	..	0.3	28.0	1.6	57.1	..	13.3
	2013	1 887.2	0.1	0.0	0.9	..	0.4	27.1	1.1	36.4	..	35.3
Switzerland - Suisse	1990	363.0	..	0.1	0.0	..	0.1	..	83.7	9.4	..	6.9
	2000	779.0	..	0.3	0.0	..	0.1	..	91.7	3.6	..	4.7
	2010	1 023.1	0.0	0.1	0.1	0.1	0.0	8.6	61.3	10.3	19.2	0.5
	2013	1 144.4	0.0	0.1	0.1	0.0	0.0	7.0	75.6	9.2	6.9	1.3

For sources and notes, see end of table.

Pour les sources et les notes, se reporter à la fin du tableau.

5.3 World merchant fleet by flag of registration and type of ship of countries and geographical regions

5.3 Flotte marchande mondiale par pavillons d'immatriculation et par types de navires des pays et des régions géographiques

Region, country or territory / Régions pays ou territoires	Year / Année	Total fleet (thousands of DWT) / Flotte totale (milliers de TPL) (1)	As percentage of world total fleet / En pourcentage de la flotte mondiale					As percentage of the country or region total fleet / En pourcentage de la flotte totale du pays ou de la région				
			Oil tankers / Pétroliers	Bulk carriers / Vraquiers	General cargo / Navires de charge classique (2)	Container ships / Porte-conteneurs	Other types / Autres navires	Oil tankers / Pétroliers	Bulk carriers / Vraquiers	General cargo / Navires de charge classique (2)	Container ships / Porte-conteneurs	Other types / Autres navires
United Kingdom - Royaume-Uni	1990	10 252.0	2.0	1.0	0.7	5.9	2.7	46.1	21.8	6.9	12.8	12.4
	2000	11 913.1	2.0	0.5	0.6	3.0	3.3	46.9	11.8	5.5	16.3	19.6
	2010	36 887.2	2.9	1.5	2.5	6.1	4.3	34.9	18.9	7.4	28.0	10.8
	2013	43 723.8	2.6	1.9	1.8	5.7	2.9	29.6	29.1	3.2	27.1	11.0
Developed economies: Oceania - Économies développées : Océanie	1990	4 006.0	0.5	0.9	0.3	0.6	0.9	30.7	48.4	7.0	3.1	10.8
	2000	3 018.8	0.2	0.5	0.1	0.1	1.5	17.6	44.0	2.3	1.6	34.5
	2010	2 498.5	0.1	0.1	0.3	0.0	1.2	19.3	24.0	11.6	0.3	44.8
	2013	2 113.1	0.0	0.0	0.2	0.0	0.9	10.9	9.1	7.3	0.8	71.8
Australia - Australie	1990	3 707.0	0.5	0.8	0.2	0.5	0.8	29.8	51.1	5.3	3.0	10.8
	2000	2 686.2	0.1	0.5	0.1	0.1	1.2	15.2	48.9	2.2	1.8	32.0
	2010	2 171.1	0.1	0.1	0.1	..	1.2	18.1	26.7	6.1	..	49.1
	2013	1 946.9	0.0	0.0	0.2	..	0.9	6.8	9.9	6.8	..	76.5
New Zealand - Nouvelle-Zélande	1990	299.0	0.1	0.0	0.1	0.1	0.1	42.1	14.0	27.8	4.7	11.4
	2000	332.7	0.0	0.0	0.0	..	0.3	37.1	5.1	3.2	..	54.6
	2010	327.4	0.0	0.0	0.1	0.0	0.1	27.2	6.2	47.6	2.5	16.5
	2013	166.2	0.0	..	0.0	0.0	0.0	59.2	..	14.1	10.0	16.7
World n.e.s. - Monde n.d.a.	2010	5 611.0	0.3	0.2	2.1	0.1	1.0	22.5	17.5	40.4	3.5	16.2
	2013	4 278.5	0.2	0.0	0.6	0.0	1.8	18.4	1.0	11.8	0.3	68.5

Sources:

Clarksons Research Services from 2011 onwards and UNCTAD *Review of Maritime Transport* for earlier years.

Notes:

(1) DWT (deadweight ton) is the weight measure of a vessel's carrying capacity. It includes cargo, fuel and stores.

(2) Including passenger/cargo combined.

(3) Year 2002: break in series; from 2002 onwards, ships registered under the flag of the Marshall Islands (developing country) are shown separately; before they were included with the United States of America (developed country).

(4) Including San Marino.

(5) In 1992, includes data for ships of the former USSR not yet registered in the economies that succeeded from the former USSR.

(6) From 2002 onwards, ships registered under the flag of the Marshall Islands are shown separately; before they were included with the United States of America.

(7) Year 2002: break in series; from 2002 onwards, ships registered under the flag of the Marshall Islands are shown separately; before they were included with the United States of America.

Sources :

Clarksons Research Services à partir de 2011 et *Review of Maritime Transport* de la CNUCED pour les années antérieures.

Notes :

(1) TPL (Tonne de port en lourd) : c'est une mesure de poids de la capacité de charge d'un navire. Il inclut la cargaison, le carburant et les magasins.

(2) Y compris les cargos mixtes.

(3) Année 2002 : rupture de série ; les navires immatriculés aux Îles Marshall (pays en développement) sont présentés séparément à partir de 2002 ; avant, ils étaient compris dans les chiffres des États-Unis (pays développé).

(4) Y compris Saint-Marin.

(5) Année 1992 : inclut les données de l'ancienne URSS qui n'ont pas encore été enregistrées dans les différents pays qui lui ont succédé.

(6) Les navires immatriculés aux Îles Marshall sont présentés séparément à partir de 2002 ; avant, ils étaient compris dans les chiffres des États-Unis.

(7) Année 2002 : rupture de série ; les navires immatriculés aux Îles Marshall sont présentés séparément à partir de 2002 ; avant, ils étaient compris dans les chiffres des États-Unis.

6 COMMODITIES

PRODUITS DE BASE

6.1 Annual and quaterly indices of free-market prices of selected primary commodities
2000 = 100

Primary commodity	Level (1) Niveau (1) 2000	1985	1990	1995	2005	2006	2007	2008	2009	2010	2011	2012
ALL COMMODITIES	_	96.2	124.0	137.6	140.4	182.8	206.5	256.0	212.7	(r)256.0	(r)302.0	277.0
All food	_	103.4	121.8	138.9	128.4	149.4	169.2	235.6	215.6	231.6	272.8	269.0
Food and tropical beverages	_	98.8	123.5	135.5	127.0	149.6	162.5	228.2	215.9	227.9	265.6	264.4
Food	_	89.6	125.4	132.3	127.2	151.3	164.1	233.9	219.9	229.6	265.1	270.4
1. Wheat*	119.6	91.4	88.9	139.4	109.2	128.5	209.1	246.0	183.1	210.8	256.5	247.3
2. Wheat	119.2	115.6	114.8	150.0	132.9	168.2	225.9	288.0	197.4	204.0	275.6	275.5
3. Maize	86.8	..	123.9	142.7	103.8	138.6	188.8	237.9	195.9	226.8	332.5	312.9
4. Maize*	90.0	..	121.9	139.0	109.9	136.8	189.0	253.2	191.4	216.8	325.5	334.1
5. Rice	203.8	106.7	140.9	157.8	141.2	149.0	163.1	343.6	289.2	255.8	270.9	284.8
6. Sugar (2)	8.2	49.6	153.4	162.4	120.9	180.6	123.3	156.5	221.9	260.2	317.9	263.4
7. Beef (2)	87.8	111.2	131.5	98.5	135.2	131.9	134.5	138.0	136.3	173.8	208.6	214.1
8. Bananas (2)	19.0	90.7	123.6	104.7	137.4	162.8	161.4	201.1	202.6	210.0	232.6	234.6
9. Pepper	4 341.6	93.0	41.3	87.3	57.1	74.5	109.3	119.9	105.4	139.0	219.3	226.4
10. Soybean meal	199.7	78.7	107.1	105.5	116.5	110.3	160.5	226.2	210.4	196.0	200.9	254.7
11. Fish meal	413.0	67.8	99.8	119.9	172.2	281.9	285.0	274.4	297.7	408.6	372.3	377.3
Tropical beverages	_	179.1	107.6	163.3	125.7	134.1	148.0	178.0	181.5	213.2	270.3	212.3
12. Coffee (2)	102.6	151.9	94.1	154.3	114.0	115.4	123.5	142.1	176.3	218.1	276.6	198.7
13. Coffee (2)	79.9	190.0	103.7	182.7	126.9	128.8	138.6	153.4	139.5	182.5	305.1	214.5
14. Coffee (2)	85.1	171.1	104.7	175.4	134.3	133.9	144.8	162.5	166.5	228.4	321.1	220.4
15. Coffee (2)	42.1	288.2	130.5	301.0	126.7	166.9	209.6	252.4	183.2	199.6	275.4	262.7
16. Coffee* (2)	63.6	209.8	113.3	217.0	131.8	144.8	166.3	192.3	172.0	218.9	305.9	234.4
17. Cocoa (2)	40.3	254.0	143.2	161.5	173.3	179.4	219.9	290.7	325.4	353.0	335.7	269.5
18. Tea (3)	248.1	..	..	71.1	87.2	97.4	85.4	108.6	126.5	125.3	139.5	140.6
Vegetable oilseeds and oils	_	141.2	107.0	167.1	140.6	147.7	225.7	297.8	213.3	261.7	332.8	307.5
19. Soybeans	211.8	106.3	116.5	122.4	129.7	126.8	181.3	246.8	205.9	212.3	255.2	279.2
20. Soybean oil	338.1	169.2	132.3	184.9	161.2	177.1	260.7	372.2	251.0	297.2	384.3	362.7
21. Sunflower oil	391.8	153.7	124.9	176.9	172.9	167.9	260.8	382.5	218.1	274.2	347.2	322.3
22. Groundnut oil	713.7	126.8	135.0	138.8	148.6	135.9	189.4	292.7	165.9	196.7	263.7	339.8
23. Copra	304.8	126.7	75.7	143.9	135.8	132.1	199.3	267.7	157.4	246.0	379.8	243.0
24. Coconut oil	450.3	131.1	74.8	148.7	137.0	134.8	204.1	271.8	161.1	249.5	384.2	246.7
25. Palm kernel oil	443.5	124.3	75.3	152.8	141.4	131.0	200.3	254.7	158.4	267.0	371.6	250.3
26. Palm oil	310.3	161.3	93.4	202.5	136.1	154.2	251.5	305.8	220.1	290.4	362.7	322.1
Agricultural raw materials	_	94.0	128.2	150.4	129.4	146.6	164.2	197.9	163.3	225.7	289.1	222.6
27. Linseed oil	398.4	157.5	177.9	165.0	276.5	168.6	251.3	389.3	246.6	292.0	358.0	314.7
28. Tobacco	2 988.1	87.4	113.7	88.5	93.4	99.4	110.9	120.1	141.8	144.4	149.8	144.0
29. Cotton (2)	83.8	117.6	112.1	133.8	88.0	102.5	..	116.1	105.0	126.9	291.3	137.8
30. Cotton (2)	65.5	108.9	127.9	159.4	89.9	92.8	98.8	111.1	100.4	156.8	244.3	140.3
31. Cotton (2)	57.3	111.8	138.4	176.0	97.6	101.6	111.2	124.7	113.8	180.1	276.6	159.5
32. Cotton* (2)	59.2	101.0	139.5	164.4	91.5	97.0	106.8	120.5	105.8	175.0	258.1	150.4
33. Cotton (2)	108.5	147.9	236.0	..	93.2	126.3	114.8	113.8	106.4	156.9	201.4	139.2
34. Wool	7 335.4	..	..	..	92.4	97.6	132.6	132.0	106.1	139.5	223.4	183.4
35. Wool	2 809.8	..	..	..	188.8	192.4	272.2	252.4	217.6	291.7	430.5	431.6
36. Jute	278.8	204.2	146.5	131.2	135.4	136.3	119.6	167.7	201.0	309.9	228.9	187.1
37. Sisal	782.1	79.2	95.0	97.4	128.0	134.2	130.9	145.4	104.5	142.0	183.0	204.6
38. Sisal	628.7	83.6	113.7	113.0	143.3	150.7	152.4	171.3	122.6	160.6	210.4	236.4
39. Hides (2)	80.2	63.8	115.0	109.9	82.0	86.1	90.0	79.8	55.9	89.7	102.2	103.7
40. Non-coniferous woods*	85.2	..	..	103.6	117.4	131.8	145.5	154.0	154.4	160.7	158.1	153.1
41. Tropical logs (4)	244.6	71.1	140.4	139.4	136.7	130.2	155.7	216.8	172.1	175.2	199.4	184.7
42. Tropical sawnwood* (5)	531.8	51.9	98.6	144.2	103.4	103.4	(b)99.1	115.5	123.5	132.3	141.3	133.3
43. Plywood* (6)	448.5	47.0	79.1	129.9	113.4	132.8	143.9	143.9	125.9	126.9	135.5	136.1
44. Rubber	726.5	..	119.6	226.9	210.9	289.5	319.4	372.7	270.6	492.4	660.0	470.3
45. Rubber (3)	63.6	..	..	231.1	217.1	305.2	334.1	390.6	285.2	542.7	716.2	498.1

For sources and notes, see end of table.

2010		2011				2012				2013		Produits de base
III	IV	I	II	III	IV	I	II	III	IV	I	II	
(r)249.3	(r)290.1	(r)320.6	(r)308.1	(r)305.7	(r)273.6	(r)280.4	(r)274.9	277.6	274.2	273.3	259.2	**TOTAL DES PRODUITS**
228.3	261.5	284.1	271.8	275.9	259.3	261.1	264.3	281.8	269.0	260.3	252.8	Total des produits alimentaires
224.8	254.2	274.6	263.0	270.1	254.5	254.4	257.9	277.3	268.0	257.9	251.6	*Produits alimentaires et boissons tropicales*
225.3	256.7	274.3	260.8	269.7	255.4	257.0	263.6	284.9	276.0	266.2	260.2	*Produits alimentaires*
223.2	249.3	285.3	289.5	250.2	200.9	215.7	213.2	270.3	290.1	296.7	263.3	1. Blé*
226.0	255.4	291.7	292.9	270.5	247.5	248.4	236.6	308.8	308.2	280.0	272.1	2. Blé
234.4	290.1	330.5	353.1	343.5	302.8	304.3	285.1	334.3	327.8	326.6	293.9	3. Maïs
222.2	275.5	320.0	347.4	334.1	300.4	310.7	304.4	367.4	353.7	339.3	326.3	4. Maïs*
242.1	263.9	257.3	248.5	284.5	293.2	272.6	295.2	286.6	284.8	280.1	270.3	5. Riz
238.3	321.7	347.7	291.5	336.8	295.5	292.6	261.0	259.8	240.3	226.7	214.0	6. Sucre (2)
171.2	183.8	211.5	210.9	202.9	209.2	220.0	213.7	206.4	216.1	220.7	207.1	7. Viande de boeuf (2)
219.9	216.7	234.9	240.1	228.1	227.4	249.5	233.7	229.5	225.8	222.3	217.1	8. Bananes (2)
144.9	164.5	184.4	205.2	229.3	258.3	235.6	233.3	216.2	220.6	223.9	219.5	9. Poivre
193.0	213.9	221.1	201.0	200.8	180.6	197.3	244.7	301.7	275.0	255.1	266.4	10. Farine de soja
402.7	390.5	421.3	399.0	345.3	323.4	314.7	358.7	406.0	429.9	452.5	440.9	11. Farine de poisson
220.4	232.9	277.7	283.0	273.6	246.9	231.8	208.2	211.1	198.1	185.6	176.4	*Boissons tropicales*
231.3	234.5	282.8	294.3	278.9	250.5	237.6	197.5	189.8	169.9	162.1	154.1	12. Café (2)
192.7	220.8	293.8	327.5	311.4	287.7	259.8	208.4	205.8	184.0	168.0	157.3	13. Café (2)
250.8	266.8	331.2	342.5	320.1	290.4	261.2	215.2	214.0	191.0	181.9	173.7	14. Café (2)
210.6	227.0	271.5	292.8	276.2	261.0	264.5	269.9	266.9	249.4	259.6	245.6	15. Café (2)
237.5	253.7	311.4	326.1	305.6	280.7	262.3	233.4	231.5	210.4	207.6	197.5	16. Café* (2)
344.6	334.1	376.6	346.2	341.9	278.0	263.7	257.1	281.0	276.1	248.8	260.0	17. Cacao (2)
120.8	137.5	140.9	132.6	144.6	140.0	136.9	137.4	142.0	146.1	128.6	106.5	18. Thé (3)
257.6	322.4	363.6	344.8	323.9	298.8	316.4	317.8	318.3	277.3	280.1	262.3	*Graines oléagineuses et huiles végétales*
213.4	246.4	266.7	262.8	261.2	230.2	244.4	269.9	317.2	285.3	279.5	238.6	19. Fèves de soja
291.0	367.3	398.9	387.8	391.6	359.0	370.7	365.6	372.1	342.4	343.2	316.4	20. Huile de soja
265.8	355.5	369.0	363.9	345.3	310.5	316.7	322.5	330.9	319.1	320.3	311.0	21. Huile de tournesol
182.4	224.7	241.4	256.4	297.1	311.8	..	355.6	347.0	322.0	280.5	260.6	22. Huile d'arachide
252.4	340.6	452.5	440.4	325.2	301.0	306.1	260.3	220.4	185.3	181.6	183.7	23. Coprah
257.3	343.4	460.4	443.3	327.3	305.8	310.9	263.6	224.9	187.3	185.0	186.2	24. Huile de coprah
261.9	365.1	480.5	422.6	301.7	281.8	308.0	280.1	229.9	183.3	185.9	188.6	25. Huile de palmiste
281.9	357.1	403.2	369.7	347.8	330.3	356.7	350.8	320.1	260.8	274.9	274.1	26. Huile de palme
215.9	268.3	314.9	303.4	289.7	248.2	245.9	228.9	204.9	210.7	215.8	202.6	*Matières premières d'origine agricole*
322.9	339.0	380.5	388.0	349.6	313.9	322.8	331.4	303.7	300.8	301.0	328.9	27. Huile de lin
145.0	144.9	146.6	149.5	152.0	151.1	147.3	144.9	140.5	143.2	147.2	147.5	28. Tabac
140.0	..	..	293.1	289.4	..	..	..	141.5	134.1	127.8	128.0	29. Coton (2)
142.6	228.1	310.4	293.5	187.2	166.9	161.1	142.0	130.6	127.7	140.1	143.9	30. Coton (2)
161.3	258.9	352.5	329.7	213.9	189.5	180.8	162.3	149.3	145.4	159.6	164.0	31. Coton (2)
157.1	253.4	349.9	309.1	198.7	174.8	169.6	151.1	142.1	138.5	151.7	156.7	32. Coton* (2)
141.6	219.5	257.2	..	..	164.3	140.9	136.8	139.8	139.3	138.3	147.0	33. Coton (2)
129.1	164.8	222.0	245.4	228.8	197.2	209.2	184.8	166.0	173.5	185.7	158.4	34. Laine
279.7	311.3	393.4	474.5	452.1	401.9	476.2	442.5	405.0	402.5	436.9	390.6	35. Laine
260.6	289.3	271.4	245.1	223.6	175.7	188.9	181.1	187.7	190.7	209.2	221.2	36. Jute
148.3	150.9	162.8	166.2	198.2	204.6	198.2	196.1	212.9	211.0	192.9	191.8	37. Sisal
168.9	172.9	186.6	190.9	230.6	233.3	229.3	228.0	248.2	240.2	221.4	221.4	38. Sisal
90.6	93.7	98.0	109.7	107.1	94.2	96.4	104.7	106.4	107.2	107.2	116.9	39. Peaux (2)
166.5	166.7	158.8	157.0	160.7	156.0	152.8	155.3	154.1	150.4	149.9	160.2	40. Bois non conifères*
174.4	183.5	182.3	201.1	210.8	197.5	189.7	185.2	178.4	185.4	186.6	187.1	41. Grumes tropicales (4)
136.7	136.1	138.6	142.3	144.6	139.7	135.4	134.6	131.8	131.2	131.3	131.4	42. Grumes tropicales sciées* (5)
127.6	129.4	131.2	134.5	138.5	137.7	136.6	136.1	135.4	136.3	131.9	123.4	43. Contre-plaqué* (6)
459.5	614.4	759.7	679.9	661.9	538.5	548.0	490.0	412.5	430.6	439.1	368.4	44. Caoutchouc
501.2	642.1	851.3	787.2	691.0	535.4	572.1	526.2	434.3	459.7	468.6	431.1	45. Caoutchouc (3)

Pour les sources et les notes, se reporter à la fin du tableau.

6

6.1 Annual and quaterly indices of free-market prices of selected primary commodities
2000 = 100

Primary commodity	Level (1) Niveau (1) 2000	1985	1990	1995	2005	2006	2007	2008	2009	2010	2011	2012
Minerals, ores and metals	–	**81.2**	**127.0**	**128.1**	**173.2**	**277.7**	**313.2**	**332.5**	**231.6**	**(r)327.3**	**(r)375.2**	**322.0**
46. Phosphate rock	43.8	76.6	92.6	80.0	96.0	101.1	162.1	789.9	278.1	281.2	422.6	424.9
47. Manganese ore	186.0	74.5	213.1	109.7	175.8	139.7	191.9	758.5	293.8	415.0	324.4	262.1
48. Iron ore (7)	27.7	96.0	111.3	97.4	225.9	268.8	294.4	485.8	348.8	..	..	..
49. Iron ore* (7)	27.5	96.5	109.8	97.4	201.0	256.4	286.1	467.6	396.0	..	..	..
50. Iron ore* (8)	..	..	..	..	..	..	..	..	100.0	183.9	210.1	161.0
51. Aluminium	1 549.2	69.8	105.8	116.6	122.5	165.9	170.3	166.1	107.4	140.2	154.8	130.3
52. Copper	1 813.1	78.2	146.8	161.8	202.9	370.7	392.6	383.6	282.8	415.6	486.6	438.5
53. Copper* (2)	86.8	75.6	140.4	158.4	198.4	361.2	376.5	366.3	276.4	399.9	466.7	421.7
54. Nickel*	8 637.7	56.8	102.6	95.3	170.6	280.7	430.9	244.3	169.6	252.4	265.0	203.0
55. Nickel (2)	397.9	56.8	102.3	98.1	171.2	276.0	424.8	248.1	174.0	262.3	264.1	202.6
56. Lead	454.0	86.1	178.5	138.9	215.0	283.8	568.2	460.2	378.6	473.2	529.0	454.1
57. Lead* (2)	43.6	43.8	103.4	96.3	140.1	178.0	284.2	276.2	199.4	250.0	279.3	262.0
58. Zinc	1 128.1	67.0	134.6	91.4	122.5	290.3	287.4	166.2	146.7	191.5	194.4	172.7
59. Zinc* (2)	55.6	72.6	134.1	95.9	120.7	285.7	277.6	159.9	139.8	183.4	191.0	172.1
60. Tin	5 432.8	221.8	114.8	114.3	135.8	161.5	267.4	340.5	249.6	375.4	480.5	388.5
61. Tin*	5 382.0	221.5	113.1	113.1	136.7	162.9	269.9	341.6	248.9	377.8	486.7	392.6
62. Tungsten (9)	44.9	150.9	103.4	141.2	271.3	369.7	367.4	366.5	334.0	334.0	334.0	334.0
62. Gold* (10)	279.0	113.7	137.4	137.7	159.4	216.6	249.7	312.4	348.7	439.9	562.2	598.1
64. Silver* (11)	499.9	122.9	96.4	103.8	146.8	231.4	268.3	300.1	294.0	404.1	705.4	624.3
MEMO ITEM:												
65. Crude petroleum (12)	28.2	95.6	78.1	59.9	189.1	227.8	252.1	343.8	219.0	280.2	368.3	372.1
66. Unit value index of manufactured goods exports	100.0	70.9	110.9	122.3	119.4	123.5	132.8	139.3	131.5	(r)135.5	(r)147.5	145.5

Sources:

- The prices used in the calculation of the indices shown in this table are extracted from *UNCTADstat* Commodity Price Statistics

Notes:

- The group indices include all commodities shown except for those with an asterisk (*).
- The average annual indices are calculated from monthly data and may not correspond to the average from quarterly data.

(1) Dollars per metric ton (unless otherwise specified).
(2) Cents per pound.
(3) Cents per kilogram.
(4) Dollars per cubic meter.
(5) Pounds per cubic meter.
(6) Cents per sheet.
(7) Cents per Fe unit.
(8) Dollars per dry ton.
(9) Dollars per metric ton unit of WO3.
(10) Dollars per troy ounce.
(11) Cents per troy ounce.
(12) Dollars per barrel.

- For specifications, see next page.

| 2010 | | 2011 | | | | 2012 | | | | 2013 | | Produits de base |
III	IV	I	II	III	IV	I	II	III	IV	I	II	
(r)314.3	(r)366.2	(r)406.5	(r)393.1	(r)382.0	(r)319.4	(r)342.2	(r)322.6	305.8	318.6	332.5	302.9	**Minéraux, minerais et métaux**
285.7	320.0	361.9	417.1	451.4	460.1	447.6	410.0	419.1	422.9	395.4	380.0	46. Phosphate brut
447.0	389.8	376.4	340.6	290.4	290.4	249.0	249.0	276.0	274.2	..	..	47. Minerai de manganèse
..	..	..	..	..	..	..	..	..	..	..	..	48. Minerai de fer (7)
..	..	..	..	..	..	..	..	..	..	..	..	49. Minerai de fer* (7)
172.1	199.2	223.8	220.0	220.2	176.3	177.5	174.7	139.9	151.6	185.7	157.0	50. Minerai de fer* (8)
134.9	151.2	161.3	168.0	154.9	134.8	140.5	127.6	124.1	129.2	129.2	118.4	51. Aluminium
399.5	476.3	532.3	504.7	496.2	413.0	458.2	433.8	425.6	436.2	437.2	409.8	52. Cuivre
385.5	457.9	510.5	484.1	474.5	397.7	441.3	413.8	411.4	420.3	420.6	379.9	53. Cuivre* (2)
245.3	273.3	311.4	281.2	255.4	211.9	227.6	198.5	189.2	196.6	200.3	173.1	54. Nickel*
255.2	273.3	307.2	280.5	258.5	210.0	227.2	197.4	189.1	196.7	199.5	175.8	55. Nickel (2)
447.5	526.2	573.2	563.6	542.4	436.7	461.1	434.3	436.1	485.0	506.4	452.3	56. Plomb
224.3	272.2	278.4	285.0	292.7	261.2	262.0	261.0	261.2	263.9	264.8	262.7	57. Plomb* (2)
178.4	205.1	212.3	199.8	197.3	168.1	179.4	170.9	167.4	172.9	180.2	163.1	58. Zinc
172.4	197.6	205.0	195.9	195.1	168.2	178.0	170.3	167.5	172.7	180.8	166.2	59. Zinc* (2)
378.1	478.5	550.4	532.2	456.2	383.1	422.0	378.5	355.4	397.8	443.6	384.5	60. Étain
379.2	480.3	556.6	540.8	460.1	389.1	426.7	384.0	357.8	401.8	447.3	390.7	61. Étain*
334.0	334.0	334.0	334.0	334.0	334.0	334.0	334.0	334.0	334.0	334.0	334.0	62. Tungstène (9)
439.6	490.1	496.1	539.1	609.3	604.1	606.0	577.3	593.0	616.0	584.3	506.6	63. Or* (10)
380.4	529.8	635.8	770.2	778.1	637.4	654.4	589.9	600.8	652.3	601.3	462.7	64. Argent* (11)
												POUR MÉMOIRE :
267.8	302.8	353.2	390.1	365.2	364.6	398.5	364.6	364.2	361.1	372.4	351.9	65. Pétrole brut (12)
135.0	141.0	144.0	150.0	150.0	146.0	147.0	144.0	(p)144.0	(p)147.0	(p)147.0	..	66. Valeur unitaire des exportations d'articles manufacturés en dollars

Sources :

- Les prix utilisés pour le calcul des indices présentés dans ce tableau sont extraits des statistiques des prix des produits de base de *UNCTADstat*

Notes :

- Les indices agrégés recouvrent tous les produits présentés à l'exception de ceux munis d'un astérisque (*).
- Les indices moyens annuels sont calculés sur la base de données mensuelles et peuvent ne pas correspondre aux moyennes calculées sur la base de données trimestrielles.

(1) Dollars par tonne métrique (sauf mention spéciale).
(2) Cents par livre.
(3) Cents par kilogramme.
(4) Dollars par mètre cube.
(5) Livres par mètre cube.
(6) Cents par feuille.
(7) Cents par unité de Fe.
(8) Dollars par tonne sèche.
(9) Dollars par tonne métrique d'unité de WO3.
(10) Dollars par once troy.
(11) Cents par once troy.
(12) Dollars par baril.

- Pour les spécifications, se reporter à la page suivante.

Specifications	Spécifications

Food

1. Wheat: Argentina, Trigo Pan Upriver, f.o.b.
2. Wheat: United States, no. 2, Hard Red Winter (ordinary), f.o.b. Gulf ports.
3. Maize: Argentina, Rosario, f.o.b.
4. Maize: United States, no. 3 yellow, f.o.b. Gulf ports.
5. Rice: Thailand, white milled, 5 % broken, nominal price quotes, f.o.b. Bangkok.
6. Sugar: Caribbean ports, f.o.b. bulk basis (I.S.A.).
7. Beef: Australia and New-Zealand, frozen and boneless, 85 % visible lean, U.S. import price, f.o.b. port of entry.
8. Bananas: Central America and Ecuador, fresh, U.S. importer's price, f.o.b. U.S. ports.
9. Pepper: Muntok, white, fair average quality (faq) spot. Prior to June 2003, Singapore.
10. Soybean meal: Hamburg, 44/45% protein, f.o.b. ex-mill.
11. Fish meal: Any origin, 64/65% protein, Bremen free carrier price. Prior to March 2006, cost and freight Hamburg.

Tropical beverages

12. Coffee: Colombian mild Arabicas, ex-dock New York (I.C.A.).
13. Coffee: Brazilian and other natural Arabicas, ex-dock New York (I.C.A.).
14. Coffee: Other mild Arabicas, ex-dock New York (I.C.A.).
15. Coffee: Robustas, ex-dock New York (I.C.A.).
16. Coffee: Composite indicator price 1976 (I.C.A.).
17. Cocoa: Average of daily prices, New York/London, 3 months futures (I.C.C.A.).
18. Tea: Best Pekoe Fannings 1, Mombasa auction prices.

Vegetable oils and oilseeds

19. Soybeans: United States, no. 2 yellow, c.i.f. Rotterdam.
20. Soybean oil: Any origin, crude oil, the Netherlands, f.o.b. ex-mill.
21. Sunflower oil: European Union, f.o.b. N.W. European ports.
22. Groundnut oil: Any origin, c.i.f. Rotterdam.
23. Copra: Philippines/Indonesia, bulk, c.i.f. N.W. European ports.
24. Coconut oil: Philippines, c.i.f. Rotterdam.
25. Palm kernel oil: Malaysia, c.i.f. Rotterdam.
26. Palm oil: generally Indonesia, 5% ffa, c.i.f. N.W. European ports.

Agricultural raw materials

27. Linseed oil: Any origin, ex-tank, c.i.f. Rotterdam.
28. Tobacco: Unmanufactured tobacco, US general import price.
29. Cotton: Sudan, Barakat, X4B, CFR Far Eastern quotations. Prior to August 2005, c.i.f. North Europe.
30. Cotton: United States, Memphis/Eastern Midd 1-3/32", c.i.f. North Europe.
31. Cotton: United States; Memphis/Orleans/Texas, Midd 1-3/32", CFR Far Eastern quotations. Prior to June 2005, Memphis/Orleans/Texas, Midd 1-3/32", c.i.f. North Europe.
32. Cotton: Cotton Outlook Index A, Middling 1-3/32", CFR Far Eastern quotations. Prior to August 2004, c.i.f. North Europe.
33. Cotton: Egypt, Giza 88, good + 3/8, CFR Far Eastern quotations. Prior to August 2005, Giza 70, good + 3/8, f.o.b. Alexandria.
34. Wool: fine, 19 micron, Australia.
35. Wool: coarse, 23 micron, Australia.
36. Jute: Bangladesh, Bangladesh White D (BWD), f.o.b. Mongla.
37. Sisal: Tanzania/Kenya, no. 2 & 3 long, f.o.b. Prior to 2007, c.i.f. main European ports.
38. Sisal: Tanzania/Kenya no. 3 & UG, f.o.b. Prior to 2007, c.i.f. main European ports.
39. Hides: US, Chicago packer's heavy native steers over 53lbs., wholesale dealer's price, f.o.b. shipping point.
40. Non-coniferous woods: United Kingdom, import price index 2005=100, dollar equivalent.
41. Tropical logs: Sapele, loyal and marchand, UK import price, f.o.b. plus commission. Prior to June 2000, Cameroon f.o.b.
42. Tropical sawnwood: Malaysia, Meranti Tembaga, select and better, CIF plus commission, UK. Prior to January, 2008, Malaysia, Dark Red Meranti, select and better, c.i.f. French ports.
43. Plywood: Southeast Asia, Lauan, 3-ply, Extra, 91 cm x 182 cm x 4 mm, wholesale price, spot Tokyo.
44. Rubber: TSR 20 New York.
45. Rubber: no. 3 RSS, monthly average of weighted daily future prices, Singapore.

Produits alimentaires

1. Blé : Argentine, Trigo Pan Upriver, f.a.b.
2. Blé : États-Unis, Hard Red Winter, n° 2 (ordinaire), f.a.b. ports du Golfe.
3. Maïs : Argentine, Rosario, f.a.b.
4. Maïs : États-Unis, jaune n° 3, f.a.b. ports du Golfe.
5. Riz : Thaïlande, blanchi, 5 % brisures, prix nominal, f.a.b. Bangkok.
6. Sucre : Ports des Caraïbes, f.a.b. en vrac (A.I.S.).
7. Viande de boeuf : Australie et Nouvelle-Zélande, désossée et congelée, maigres à 85 % visibles, prix à l'importation aux États-Unis, f.a.b. port d'entrée.
8. Bananes : Amérique centrale et Equateur, fraîches, f.a.b. ports des États-Unis.
9. Poivre : Muntok blanc, 'fair average quality' (faq) au comptant. Avant juin 2003, Singapour.
10. Farine de soja : Hambourg, 44/45 % protéines, f.a.b. départ moulin.
11. Farine de poisson : toutes origines, 64/65 % protéines, Brême, prix franco transporteur. Avant mars 2006, coût et fret Hambourg.

Boissons tropicales

12. Café : Arabicas doux colombiens, ex-dock New York (A.I.C.).
13. Café : Brésilien et autres Arabicas naturels, ex-dock New York (A.I.C.).
14. Café : autres Arabicas doux, ex-dock New York (A.I.C.).
15. Café : Robustas, ex-dock New York (A.I.C.).
16. Café : Prix indicatif composite de 1976 (A.I.C.).
17. Cacao : moyenne des cours quotidiens New York/Londres, 3 mois à terme (A.I.C.C.).
18. Thé : Best Pekoe Fannings 1, cours aux enchères à Mombasa.

Huiles végétales et graines oléagineuses

19. Fèves de soja : États-Unis, n° 2 jaune, c.a.f. Rotterdam.
20. Huile de soja : toutes origines, huile brute, f.a.b. Pays-Bas, départ raffinerie.
21. Huile de tournesol : Union européenne, f.a.b. ports de l'Europe du Nord-Ouest.
22. Huile d'arachide : toutes origines, c.a.f. Rotterdam.
23. Coprah : Philippines/Indonésie, en vrac, c.a.f. ports de l'Europe du Nord-Ouest.
24. Huile de coprah : Philippines, c.a.f. Rotterdam.
25. Huile de palmiste : Malaisie, c.a.f. Rotterdam.
26. Huile de palme : généralement Indonésie, 5 % ffa, c.a.f. ports de l'Europe du Nord-Ouest.

Matières premières d'origine agricole

27. Huile de lin : toutes origines, cours du disponible, c.a.f. Rotterdam.
28. Tabac : tabac non fabriqué, prix général à l'importation aux États-Unis.
29. Coton : Soudan, Barakat, classe X4B, cotations coût et fret Extrême Orient. Avant août 2005, c.a.f. Europe septentrionale.
30. Coton : États-Unis, Memphis, oriental Midd 1-3/32", c.a.f. Europe septentrionale.
31. Coton : États-Unis, Memphis/Orléans/Texas, Midd 1-3/32", cotations coût et fret Extrême Orient. Avant juin 2005, Memphis/Orléans/Texas, Midd 1-3/32", c.a.f. Europe septentrionale.
32. Coton : Indice A de "Cotton Outlook", Middling 1-3/32", cotations coût et fret Extrême Orient. Avant août 2005, c.a.f. Europe septentrionale.
33. Coton : Égypte, Giza 88, good + 3/8, cotations coût et fret Extrême Orient. Avant août 2005, Giza 70, good + 3/8, f.a.b. Alexandrie.
34. Laine : fine, 19 microns, Australie.
35. Laine : grossière, 23 microns, Australie.
36. Jute : Bengladesh, Bangladesh White D (BWD), f.a.b. Mongla.
37. Sisal : Tanzanie/Kenya, n° 2 et 3 long, f.a.b. Avant 2007 : c.a.f. principaux ports européens.
38. Sisal : Tanzanie/Kenya, n° 3 et UG, f.a.b. Avant 2007 : c.a.f. principaux ports européens.
39. Peaux : États-Unis, lourdes de bouvillons de plus de 24 kgs, abattus à Chicago, prix de gros, f.a.b. point d'expédition.
40. Bois non conifères : Royaume-Uni, indice des prix à l'importation 2005=100, équivalent dollar.
41. Grumes tropicales : Sapelli, loyal et marchand, prix d'importation au Royaume-Uni, f.a.b plus commission. Avant juin 2000, Cameroun, f.a.b.
42. Grumes tropicales sciées : Meranti Tembaga, Malaisie, select and better, CAF plus commission, Royaume-Uni. Avant janvier 2008, Malaisie, Meranti rouge foncé, select and better, c.a.f. ports français.
43. Contre-plaqué : Asie du Sud-Est, Lauan, 3-feuilles, extra, 91 cm x 182 cm x 4 mm, prix de gros, cours du disponible à Tokyo.
44. Caoutchouc : TSR 20 New York.
45. Caoutchouc : RSS n° 3, moyenne mensuelle des prix quotidiens pondérés à terme, Singapour.

Minerals, ores and metals

46. Phosphate rock: Morocco, 70% BPL, contract f.a.s. Casablanca.
47. Manganese ore: Metallurgical 48/50% Mn content, f.o.b. United Kingdom.
48. Iron ore: Brazilian to Europe, fines, Vale, Itabira, f.o.b.
49. Iron ore: Australian to Japan, fines, Hamersley, f.o.b.
50. Iron ore: China import, fines 62% Fe, spot, CFR, Tianjin port.(2009=100).
51. Aluminium: London Metal Exchange, high grade, cash.
52. Copper: London Metal Exchange, grade A, cash.
53. Copper: United States producer, wire bars, f.o.b. refinery.
54. Nickel: London Metal Exchange, cash.
55. Nickel: New York dealer, 4x4 cathodes, free market.
56. Lead: London Metal Exchange, settlement and cash seller's price in warehouse, excluding duty, range main United Kingdom ports; purity 99 97% Pb,
57. Lead: North America, producer price, refined.
58. Zinc: London Metal Exchange, cash settlement.
59. Zinc: North America, special high grade, daily weighted average, delivered basis.
60. Tin: London Metal Exchange, high grade, cash.
61. Tin: Ex-smelter price, Kuala Lumpur market.
62. Tungsten ore: wolframite and sheelite, c.i.f. European ports, basis minimum 65% WO3. Prior to April 1992, Wolfram.
63. Gold: United Kingdom, 99.5% fine, London afternoon fixing, average of daily rates.
64. Silver: Handy & Harman, 99.9% grade refined, average of daily quotations, New York.

MEMO ITEM:

65. Crude petroleum: Average of United Kingdom Brent, Dubai, and West Texas crude prices, reflecting relatively equal consumption of light, medium and heavy crudes worldwide.
66. Unit value index of manufactured goods exports: Developed economies, sections 5-8 less 68 of the Standard International Trade Classification (SITC), Revision 2.

Minéraux, minerais et métaux

46. Phosphate brut : Maroc, 70 % BPL, f.a.s. Casablanca.
47. Minerai de manganèse : 48/50 % teneur en Mn, f.a.b. Royaume-Uni.
48. Minerai de fer : Brésilien vers l'Europe, minerai fin, Vale, Itabira, f.a.b.
49. Minerai de fer : Australien vers le Japon, minerai fin, Hamersley, f.a.b.
50. Minerai de fer : importé en Chine, fin, 62% Fe, au comptant, coût et fret, port de Tianjin. (2009=100).
51. Aluminium : Bourse des métaux de Londres, haute qualité, cours au comptant.
52. Cuivre : Bourse des métaux de Londres, grade A, comptant.
53. Cuivre : Producteur États-Unis, barres à fil, f.a.b. sortie affinerie.
54. Nickel : Bourse des métaux de Londres, cours au comptant.
55. Nickel : Prix du négociant à New York, cathodes 4x4, marché libre.
56. Plomb : Bourse des métaux de Londres, prix vendeur, à terme et au comptant, à l'entrepôt, droits non acquittés, principaux ports du Royaume-Uni; pureté : 99,97 % Pb.
57. Plomb : Amérique du Nord, prix des producteurs, raffiné.
58. Zinc : Bourse des métaux de Londres, cours de vente au comptant.
59. Zinc : Amérique du Nord, haute qualité spéciale, moyenne pondérée des prix journaliers à la livraison.
60. Étain : Bourse des métaux de Londres, haute qualité, cours au comptant.
61. Étain : Prix départ fonderie, marché de Kuala Lumpur.
62. Minerai de tungstène : wolframite et scheelite, c.a.f. ports européens, minimum 65 % de WO3. Avant avril 1992, Wolfram.
63. Or : Royaume-Uni, 99,5 % fin, cotation de l'après-midi à Londres, moyenne des taux journaliers.
64. Argent : Handy & Harman, 99,9 % raffiné, moyenne des cotations journalières à New York.

POUR MÉMOIRE :

65. Pétrole brut : moyenne des prix du Brent du Royaume-Uni, de Dubaï et du Texas de l'Ouest, correspondant aux parts relatives de la consommation mondiale du brut léger, moyen et lourd.
66. Valeur unitaire des exportations des produits manufacturés : Économies développées, sections 5 à 8 moins 68 de la Classification type pour le commerce international (CTCI), révision 2.

6

Primary commodity	Price instability indices (1) Indices d'instabilité des prix (1)			Price trends (2) (annual average rate of change in percentage) Tendances des prix (2) (taux de variation annuel en pourcentage)						Produits de base
				In current dollars En dollars courants			In constant dollars (3) En dollars constants (3)			
	83-92	93-02	03-12	83-92	93-02	03-12	83-92	93-02	03-12	
ALL COMMODITIES (4)	**9.6**	**8.6**	**10.9**	**1.7**	**-3.3**	**11.4**	**-3.0**	**-3.1**	**8.3**	**TOTAL DES PRODUITS (4)**
All food	**8.7**	**9.4**	**7.6**	**0.3**	**-3.6**	**11.1**	**-4.4**	**-3.3**	**8.0**	**Total des produits alimentaires**
Food and tropical beverages	***9.0***	***8.9***	***7.2***	***0.9***	***-3.5***	***11.2***	***-3.8***	***-3.3***	***8.1***	***Produits alimentaires et boissons tropicales***
Food	*11.1*	*8.8*	*7.5*	*2.4*	*-3.3*	*11.3*	*-2.3*	*-3.1*	*8.2*	*Produits alimentaires*
Wheat, United States	13.2	14.7	14.8	-0.3	-2.7	9.0	-4.9	-2.4	5.9	Blé, États-Unis
Maize, United States	14.4	13.5	15.8	-1.6	-3.0	12.5	-6.3	-2.8	9.4	Maïs, États-Unis
Rice	11.4	13.7	16.5	2.9	-6.8	12.7	-1.8	-6.5	9.6	Riz
Sugar	27.7	17.3	17.7	7.9	-6.2	14.3	3.2	-6.0	11.2	Sucre
Beef	5.6	11.1	8.2	1.6	-1.5	6.5	-3.1	-1.2	3.4	Viande de boeuf
Bananas	16.6	16.5	12.1	3.3	1.8	9.8	-1.4	2.0	6.7	Bananes
Pepper	44.8	39.9	16.1	-8.1	0.6	15.9	-12.7	0.9	12.7	Poivre
Soybean meal	12.8	13.5	15.1	1.5	-2.3	9.3	-3.2	-2.1	6.2	Farine de soja
Fishmeal	15.5	19.1	13.5	3.3	2.7	11.5	-1.4	2.9	8.3	Farine de poisson
Tropical beverages	*11.0*	*21.1*	*8.4*	*-9.4*	*-4.9*	*10.8*	*-14.0*	*-4.6*	*7.7*	*Boissons tropicales*
Coffee, other mild Arabicas	17.3	30.1	13.8	-8.8	-6.4	13.0	-13.4	-6.1	9.9	Café, autres Arabicas doux
Cocoa	9.9	19.3	15.3	-9.3	-0.4	7.8	-13.9	-0.1	4.7	Cacao
Tea	18.3	13.8	7.8	-3.0	0.8	7.3	-7.7	1.0	4.2	Thé
Vegetable oilseeds and oils	**17.5**	**16.1**	**15.5**	**-3.4**	**-4.2**	**10.3**	**-8.1**	**-4.0**	**7.2**	**Graines oléagineuses et huiles végétales**
Soybeans	11.3	10.6	13.4	-0.6	-3.5	9.4	-5.3	-3.3	6.3	Fèves de soja
Soybean oil	18.0	15.7	15.4	-3.0	-4.9	10.2	-7.6	-4.6	7.1	Huile de soja
Sunflower oil	17.5	14.9	18.0	-2.9	-2.4	9.1	-7.6	-2.1	6.0	Huile de tournesol
Groundnut oil	25.5	10.3	20.1	-0.2	-3.3	6.7	-4.9	-3.1	3.5	Huile d'arachide
Copra	29.7	21.4	23.1	-5.4	-4.9	10.9	-10.1	-4.6	7.8	Coprah
Coconut oil	31.8	22.3	22.3	-5.7	-4.4	10.7	-10.4	-4.1	7.6	Huile de coprah
Palm kernel oil	30.2	22.8	22.2	-5.2	-4.6	10.8	-9.8	-4.4	7.6	Huile de palmiste
Palm oil	23.4	23.5	17.8	-5.2	-4.7	11.0	-9.8	-4.5	7.9	Huile de palme
Cotton oil	14.9	11.6	21.6	-1.9	-4.9	5.8	-6.6	-4.7	2.7	Huile de coton
Agricultural raw materials	**6.2**	**8.6**	**9.9**	**2.7**	**-4.1**	**9.3**	**-1.9**	**-3.8**	**6.2**	**Matières premières d'origine agricole**
Linseed oil	26.7	18.0	21.3	-0.3	-2.1	6.8	-5.0	-1.8	3.6	Huile de lin
Tobacco	6.9	7.6	4.7	3.4	0.5	6.7	-1.3	0.7	3.6	Tabac
Cotton, Cotton Outlook Index A	16.5	15.2	20.2	-0.6	-5.9	7.6	-5.3	-5.6	4.5	Coton, Cotton Outlook Indice A
Wool, fine	26.3	15.7	15.0	2.5	2.0	8.3	-2.2	2.2	5.2	Laine fine
Jute	25.7	19.0	18.1	-2.1	-1.1	11.4	-6.8	-0.9	8.1	Jute
Sisal	7.5	11.2	10.5	0.1	1.6	5.8	-4.6	1.9	2.5	Sisal
Hides	14.2	8.4	10.3	6.7	-0.7	1.3	2.0	-0.4	-1.8	Peaux
Non-coniferous woods	6.5	3.7	5.5	7.8	0.7	4.6	3.1	1.0	1.5	Bois non conifères
Tropical logs, Sapele	8.0	7.8	8.8	8.9	-3.8	5.7	4.2	-3.6	2.6	Grumes tropicales, Sapelli
Tropical sawnwood, Meranti	12.8	12.4	5.7	7.5	-3.9	4.4	2.8	-3.7	1.3	Grumes tropicales sciées, Meranti
Plywood	11.0	7.3	8.1	6.8	-5.5	3.2	2.1	-5.3	0.2	Contre-plaqué
Rubber, no. 3 RSS	12.1	23.1	19.1	-1.1	-7.8	14.6	-5.7	-7.5	11.5	Caoutchouc, n° 3 RSS
Minerals, ores and metals	**15.0**	**10.1**	**21.7**	**4.6**	**-2.2**	**13.1**	**-0.1**	**-2.0**	**10.0**	**Minéraux, minerais et métaux**
Phosphate rock	3.5	5.2	41.1	3.6	3.0	21.1	-1.1	3.3	18.0	Phosphate brut
Manganese ore	19.5	5.7	41.7	14.7	-2.3	14.4	10.0	-2.1	11.3	Minerai de manganèse
Iron ore, China spot	7.5	3.4	19.3	1.9	0.6	19.9	-2.8	0.9	16.7	Minerai de fer, au comptant Chine
Aluminium	22.8	11.1	17.7	1.5	0.1	2.8	-3.2	0.4	-0.3	Aluminium
Copper, LME	17.3	14.1	25.9	7.7	-5.0	14.6	2.9	-4.7	11.5	Cuivre, BML
Nickel, LME	30.5	17.8	32.3	9.0	0.5	5.3	4.3	0.7	2.2	Nickel, BML
Lead, LME	16.9	14.4	25.8	5.4	-1.8	14.6	0.7	-1.6	11.5	Plomb, BML
Zinc, LME	20.4	11.2	34.8	7.5	-1.5	7.6	2.8	-1.2	4.5	Zinc, BML
Tin, Kuala Lumpur	15.4	9.5	20.3	-9.2	-2.8	16.7	-13.9	-2.6	13.6	Étain, Kuala Lumpur
Tungsten ore	13.7	18.6	30.2	-4.3	0.9	11.5	-8.9	1.2	8.4	Minerai de tungstène
Gold	9.4	7.5	6.1	-0.5	-3.9	18.2	-5.2	-3.6	15.0	Or
Silver	12.8	7.7	15.1	-9.5	-0.4	20.7	-14.1	-0.1	17.6	Argent
Crude petroleum	20.1	15.3	18.5	-4.6	5.4	12.7	-9.3	5.6	9.6	Pétrole brut

For sources and notes, see next page.

Pour les sources et les notes, se reporter à la page suivante.

Source:

UNCTAD calculations based on *UNCTADstat* Commodity Price Statistics

Notes:

(1) The measure of price instability is

$$1/n\sum_{t=1}^{n}\left[\left(\left|Y(t)-y(t)\right|\right)/y(t)\right]*100$$

where

$Y(t)$ is the observed magnitude of the variable

$y(t)$ is the magnitude estimated by fitting an exponential trend to the observed value

n is the number of observations

Accordingly, instability is measured as the percentage deviation of the variables concerned from their exponential trend levels for a given period.

(2) The growth rate of each period has been calculated using the formula:

$$\log(p)=a+b(t)$$

where

p is the price and t is time

(3) Constant 2000 dollars (current dollars divided by the United Nations unit value index of manufactured goods exported by developed economies).

(4) Excluding petroleum.

The commodities description is detailed at the end of table 6.1.

Source :

Calculs du secrétariat de la CNUCED basés sur les statistiques des prix des produits de base de *UNCTADstat*

Notes :

(1) L'indice d'instabilité des prix est calculé selon

$$1/n\sum_{t=1}^{n}\left[\left(\left|Y(t)-y(t)\right|\right)/y(t)\right]*100$$

où

$Y(t)$ est la valeur observée de la variable

$y(t)$ est la valeur estimée par ajustement à la tendance exponentielle des valeurs observées

n est le nombre d'observations

L'instabilité est le pourcentage de déviation des variables en question par rapport à la ligne de tendance exponentielle pour une période donnée.

(2) Le taux de croissance de chaque période a été calculé selon la formule :

$$\log(p)=a+b(t)$$

où

p est l'indice de prix et t le temps

(3) Dollars constants 2000 (dollar courant divisé par l'index des Nations Unies de la valeur unitaire des exportations des produits manufacturés par les économies développées).

(4) Pétrole exclu.

La description détaillée des produits se trouve à la fin du tableau 6.1.

6

7

INTERNATIONAL FINANCE

FINANCE INTERNATIONALE

**7.1.1 Balance of payments:
Current account net of countries
and geographical regions**

Region, country or territory	Millions of dollars - Millions de dollars							
	1980	1990	2000	2005	2009	2010	2011	2012
DEVELOPING ECONOMIES	28 455	13 190	105 321	465 610	404 065	432 699	462 061	445 871
TRANSITION ECONOMIES	-2 301	-2 482	47 079	83 239	32 519	61 931	101 510	67 976
DEVELOPED ECONOMIES	-78 726	-104 763	-323 815	-508 282	-227 305	-202 238	-262 946	-225 196
Developing economies: Africa	**6 656**	**3 635**	**16 898**	**60 644**	**-32 812**	**3 275**	**-12 801**	**-17 302**
Eastern Africa	*-3 801*	*-3 451*	*-3 274*	*-6 902*	*-12 272*	*-12 693*	*-17 358*	*-23 802*
Burundi	-83	-69	-50	-6	-161	-301	-284	-255
Comoros	-9	-10	0	-29	-42	-31	-55	(e)-32
Djibouti	-	-11	-19	20	-71	50	-172	(e)- 181
Eritrea	–	–	-105	(e)-81	(e)- 101	(e)- 194	(e)- 115	(e)72
Ethiopia (...1991)	-226	-294						
Ethiopia	–	–	13	-1 568	-2 191	-425	-783	(e)-2 437
Kenya	-876	-527	-199	-252	-1 689	-2 369	-3 333	(e)-3 727
Madagascar	-556	-265	-260	-554	-1 947	(e)-1 997	-680	(e)- 782
Malawi	-260	-86	-74	-507	-553	-905	-765	(e)- 155
Mauritius	-117	-119	-37	-324	-655	-1 006	-1 506	-1 175
Mozambique	-367	-415	-764	-761	-1 246	-1 523	-2 996	-5 167
Rwanda	-52	-85	-94	-52	-379	-421	-468	(e)- 786
Seychelles	-16	-13	-43	-174	-82	-190	-226	-219
Uganda	-83	-263	-359	-26	-1 139	-1 752	-2 160	-2 222
United Republic of Tanzania	-521	-559	-428	-1 093	-1 810	-1 960	-3 992	-3 640
Zambia	-516	-594	-662	-600	582	1 206	700	-1
Zimbabwe	-149	-140	(e)- 193	(e)- 897	(e)- 790	(e)- 874	(e)- 523	(e)-2 366
Middle Africa	*-465*	*-1 751*	*1 870*	*6 349*	*-12 569*	*2 305*	*12 754*	*10 300*
Angola	68	-236	796	5 138	-7 572	7 506	13 085	13 851
Cameroon	-445	-551	-218	-493	-1 119	-856	-752	(e)-1 099
Central African Republic	-43	-89	-13	-88	-182	-202	-167	(e)- 135
Chad	12	-46	-213	50	(e)- 288	(e)- 430	(e)- 100	(e)- 488
Congo	-167	-251	648	696	-1 279	(e)-16	(e)995	(e)800
Dem. Rep. of the Congo	-254	-715	86	-389	-1 123	-2 174	-1 281	(e)-2 192
Equatorial Guinea	-21	-19	-196	-511	-1 835	(e)-2 724	(e)-1 596	(e)-2 663
Gabon	384	168	1 001	1 983	907	1 290	2 676	(e)2 324
Sao Tome and Principe	1	-12	-20	-36	-79	-88	-106	-99
Northern Africa	*5 951*	*4 917*	*12 627*	*36 201*	*-3 619*	*17 733*	*4 996*	*16 059*
Algeria	249	1 420	9 142	21 180	401	12 146	19 688	(e)12 269
Egypt	-436	2 327	-971	2 103	-3 349	-4 504	-5 484	-6 972
Libya	8 214	2 201	6 270	14 945	9 381	16 801	1 410	(e)29 372
Morocco	-1 407	-196	-475	1 041	-4 971	-3 925	-8 000	-9 555
Sudan (...2011)	-316	-372	-518	-2 768	-3 846	-680	768	–
Sudan	–	–	–	–	–	–	–	-5 282
Tunisia	-353	-463	-821	-299	-1 234	-2 104	-3 386	-3 773
Southern Africa	*2 947*	*1 676*	*429*	*-6 742*	*-12 621*	*-11 033*	*-14 193*	*-25 491*
Botswana	-151	-19	545	1 562	-708	-192	359	-795
Lesotho	56	65	-71	-17	-50	-440	-520	(e)- 345
Namibia	-	28	192	333	-122	105	-148	-336
South Africa	3 161	1 552	-191	-8 518	-11 327	-10 117	-13 683	-24 069
Swaziland	-130	51	-46	-103	-414	-388	(e)- 201	(e)54
Western Africa	*2 024*	*2 244*	*5 246*	*31 738*	*8 269*	*6 962*	*1 001*	*5 634*
Benin	-36	-18	-81	-226	-649	-530	(e)- 728	(e)- 711
Burkina Faso	-49	-77	-319	-634	-380	-181	(e)- 156	(e)- 827
Cape Verde	4	-4	-58	-41	-247	-223	-304	-209
Côte d'Ivoire	-1 826	-1 214	-241	40	1 618	465	(e)-47	(e)-49
Gambia	-91	24	53	-43	63	56	110	58
Ghana	30	-223	-386	-1 105	-1 897	-2 747	-3 501	(e)-4 921
Guinea	54	-203	-140	-160	-403	-327	-1 161	(e)-1 918
Guinea-Bissau	-61	-45	32	-10	-48	-71	(e)-40	(e)-65
Mali	-124	-221	-255	-438	-655	-1 190	(e)-1 122	(e)- 749
Mauritania	-133	-10	-98	-877	-323	-319	(e)- 313	(e)-1 084
Niger	-276	-236	-104	-312	-1 320	-1 136	(e)-1 484	(e)-1 510
Nigeria	5 178	4 988	7 427	36 529	13 868	14 459	12 554	20 353
Senegal	-386	-363	-332	-676	-854	-600	(e)-1 459	(e)-1 618
Sierra Leone	-165	-69	-112	-105	-327	-493	-1 127	(e)- 787
Togo	-95	-84	-140	-204	-177	-200	(e)- 221	(e)- 330
Developing economies: America	**-29 931**	**-4 028**	**-49 111**	**35 702**	**-29 458**	**-61 941**	**-76 851**	**-102 860**
Caribbean	*-769*	*-3 226*	*-2 791*	*730*	*-4 539*	*-4 880*	*-7 481*	*-7 847*
Anguilla	..	-9	-61	-52	-96	-51	-37	(e)-66

For sources and notes, see end of table.

As percentage of GDP - En pourcentage du PIB (1)								Régions, pays ou territoires
1980	1990	2000	2005	2009	2010	2011	2012	
1.17	0.35	1.51	4.30	2.33	2.08	1.92	1.76	ÉCONOMIES EN DÉVELOPPEMENT
-3.19	-2.84	11.84	7.57	1.82	2.92	3.91	2.47	ÉCONOMIES EN TRANSITION
-0.95	-0.60	-1.30	-1.50	-0.58	-0.50	-0.61	-0.52	ÉCONOMIES DÉVELOPPÉES
1.54	0.74	2.83	6.02	-2.22	0.19	-0.67	-0.85	Économies en développement : Afrique
-7.44	*-5.39*	*-4.80*	*-7.13*	*-7.67*	*-7.50*	*-9.13*	*-10.16*	*Afrique orientale*
-6.27	-4.32	-5.04	-0.51	-8.79	-14.59	-12.12	-10.35	Burundi
-7.21	-4.30	-0.20	-7.37	-7.80	-5.69	-9.06	(e)-5.44	Comores
-	-2.30	-3.41	2.84	-6.78	4.47	-13.39	(e)-12.94	Djibouti
		-14.82	(e)-7.36	(e)-5.42	(e)-9.16	(e)-4.40	(e)2.35	Érythrée
-3.84	-2.52	–						Éthiopie (...1991)
		0.17	-12.76	-7.69	-1.60	-2.59	(e)-5.94	Éthiopie
-9.56	-4.78	-1.58	-1.35	-5.52	-7.36	-9.79	(e)-9.08	Kenya
-17.04	-8.60	-6.72	-11.00	-22.76	(e)-22.87	-6.91	(e)-7.82	Madagascar
-15.23	-3.57	-3.06	-18.39	-11.15	-16.99	-12.82	(e)-3.27	Malawi
-10.10	-4.55	-0.79	-4.99	-7.42	-10.35	-13.32	-10.20	Maurice
-7.60	-13.99	-17.72	-11.56	-12.88	-16.54	-23.36	-34.68	Mozambique
-3.72	-3.29	-5.33	-2.02	-7.21	-7.49	-7.33	(e)-10.85	Rwanda
-8.59	-2.85	-5.63	-18.59	-9.79	-19.74	-22.31	-21.99	Seychelles
-2.78	-6.78	-5.88	-0.26	-6.88	-9.88	-11.21	-9.42	Ouganda
-7.13	-10.20	-4.11	-7.54	-8.21	-8.31	-16.38	-12.64	République-Unie de Tanzanie
-11.97	-15.66	-20.46	-8.25	4.55	7.44	3.64	0.00	Zambie
-2.09	-1.19	(e)-2.56	(e)-14.41	(e)-12.89	(e)-11.76	(e)-5.90	(e)-24.45	Zimbabwe
-1.40	*-4.04*	*5.24*	*7.32*	*-8.20*	*1.34*	*5.98*	*4.50*	*Afrique centrale*
1.26	-2.29	8.98	15.66	-10.03	9.10	12.54	11.74	Angola
-5.02	-4.65	-2.35	-2.97	-4.78	-3.63	-2.85	(e)-4.23	Cameroun
-3.87	-6.19	-1.38	-6.52	-9.19	-10.20	-7.59	(e)-6.25	République centrafricaine
1.34	-2.96	-15.39	0.86	(e)-3.80	(e)-4.82	(e)-0.96	(e)-4.50	Tchad
-9.77	-8.98	20.13	11.43	-15.61	(e)-0.15	(e)7.51	(e)6.38	Congo
-2.58	-7.65	1.63	-5.40	-10.08	-16.48	-7.97	(e)-12.24	Rép. dém. du Congo
-38.17	-14.25	-16.68	-7.09	-18.40	(e)-23.06	(e)-9.89	(e)-15.30	Guinée équatoriale
7.32	2.87	18.24	20.96	5.90	6.87	11.08	(e)9.84	Gabon
0.83	-10.01	-26.68	-29.42	-39.78	-42.24	-41.30	-36.16	Sao Tomé-et-Principe
4.32	*2.67*	*4.85*	*9.78*	*-0.62*	*2.72*	*0.74*	*2.19*	*Afrique septentrionale*
0.59	2.29	16.69	20.52	0.29	7.50	9.91	(e)5.88	Algérie
-2.17	6.47	-1.01	2.23	-1.78	-2.10	-2.37	-2.76	Égypte
21.51	7.08	16.30	32.88	15.96	23.45	4.49	(e)40.11	Libye
-6.69	-0.68	-1.28	1.75	-5.47	-4.32	-7.98	-9.76	Maroc
-4.96	-2.94	-3.95	-7.87	-6.35	-0.98	1.11		Soudan (...2011)
							-9.43	Soudan
-3.66	-3.41	-3.83	-0.93	-2.83	-4.76	-7.31	-8.30	Tunisie
3.47	*1.40*	*0.30*	*-2.51*	*-4.09*	*-2.79*	*-3.19*	*-5.97*	*Afrique australe*
-17.75	-0.52	9.68	15.23	-6.14	-1.29	2.07	-4.41	Botswana
16.05	11.94	-9.27	-1.24	-2.91	-20.20	-21.28	(e)-14.59	Lesotho
-	1.03	4.90	4.59	-1.33	0.92	-1.17	-2.71	Namibie
3.93	1.39	-0.14	-3.45	-4.00	-2.78	-3.35	-6.17	Afrique du Sud
-19.53	4.68	-3.01	-3.97	-13.08	-9.98	(e)-4.91	(e)1.36	Swaziland
1.61	*2.74*	*6.00*	*17.16*	*2.98*	*2.02*	*0.26*	*1.37*	*Afrique occidentale*
-2.60	-0.98	-3.42	-5.19	-9.85	-8.09	(e)-9.97	(e)-9.63	Bénin
-2.52	-2.46	-12.11	-11.61	-4.55	-2.05	(e)-1.55	(e)-8.01	Burkina Faso
3.04	-1.24	-10.76	-4.18	-15.55	-13.52	-16.12	-11.05	Cap-Vert
-17.95	-10.21	-2.26	0.23	7.02	2.02	(e)-0.19	(e)-0.20	Côte d'Ivoire
-17.97	3.42	6.78	-6.89	6.95	5.84	8.97	4.78	Gambie
0.58	-2.24	-4.84	-6.42	-7.25	-8.78	-8.93	(e)-12.50	Ghana
3.63	-6.95	-4.39	-5.46	-7.60	-6.25	-20.89	(e)-31.35	Guinée
-11.90	-7.45	8.63	-1.83	-5.52	-8.66	(e)-4.36	(e)-7.79	Guinée-Bissau
-8.74	-8.81	-9.58	-7.98	-7.31	-12.66	(e)-10.56	(e)-7.50	Mali
-8.91	-0.59	-7.55	-40.14	-11.21	-10.11	(e)-7.05	(e)-25.24	Mauritanie
-10.22	-8.94	-6.03	-9.25	-24.60	-20.03	(e)-23.25	(e)-23.28	Niger
5.56	14.24	16.01	32.54	8.18	6.30	5.12	7.36	Nigéria
-11.86	-5.86	-7.10	-7.76	-6.69	-4.67	(e)-10.10	(e)-11.46	Sénégal
-12.50	-7.97	-13.18	-6.45	-13.52	-19.47	-38.91	(e)-19.96	Sierra Leone
-8.40	-4.72	-10.79	-9.66	-5.59	-6.29	(e)-5.98	(e)-9.05	Togo
-4.06	-0.37	-2.30	1.32	-0.72	-1.22	-1.35	-1.81	Économies en développement : Amérique
-3.35	*-5.30*	*-3.03*	*0.57*	*-2.67*	*-2.73*	*-3.90*	*-3.84*	*Caraïbes*
..	-11.21	-40.49	-22.55	-32.35	-18.51	-12.76	(e)-21.40	Anguilla

Pour les sources et les notes, se reporter à la fin du tableau.

7.1.1 Balance of payments:
Current account net of countries
and geographical regions

Region, country or territory	Millions of dollars - Millions de dollars							
	1980	1990	2000	2005	2009	2010	2011	2012
Antigua and Barbuda	-19	-31	-42	-171	-169	-167	-121	-79
Aruba	..	-158	207	114	182	-437	-246	(e)120
Bahamas	-75	-37	-633	-701	-809	-814	-1 090	-1 467
Barbados	-17	-8	-213	-466	-260	-218	-506	(e)- 255
Curaçao	–	–	–	–	–	–	-830	-879
Dominica	-14	-44	-60	-76	-109	-81	-71	-55
Dominican Republic	-720	-280	-1 027	-473	-2 331	-4 330	-4 499	-4 240
Grenada	0	-46	-88	-193	-197	-203	-204	-214
Haiti	-101	-22	-114	7	-226	-166	-339	-349
Jamaica	-136	-312	-367	-1 071	-1 128	-934	-2 063	-1 905
Montserrat	..	-23	-8	-16	-13	-19	-10	(e)-18
Netherlands Antilles	1	-44	-48	-106	-340	-968	–	–
Saint Kitts and Nevis	-3	-47	-66	-65	-180	-139	-88	-71
Saint Lucia	-33	-57	-95	-129	-137	-203	-244	-184
Saint Vincent and the Grenadines	-9	-24	-24	-102	-197	-208	-199	-216
Sint Maarten (Dutch part)	–	–	–	–	–	–	-3	95
Trinidad and Tobago	357	459	544	3 881	1 633	4 172	2 899	2 070
Central America	*-12 276*	*-8 372*	*-23 207*	*-10 965*	*-9 972*	*-9 507*	*-21 830*	*-22 879*
Belize	-4	15	-162	-151	-83	-46	-20	-28
Costa Rica	-664	-424	-707	-981	-576	-1 281	-2 203	-2 376
El Salvador	34	-152	-431	-622	-312	-576	-1 070	-1 257
Guatemala	-163	-213	-1 050	-1 241	8	-626	-1 599	-1 447
Honduras	-317	-51	-508	-304	-557	-836	-1 498	-1 744
Mexico	-10 422	-7 451	-18 743	-5 861	-7 497	-2 519	-10 347	-11 410
Nicaragua	-411	-305	-936	-784	-776	-859	-1 268	-1 350
Panama, excl. Canal Zone	-329	–	–	–	–	–	–	–
Panama	–	209	-673	-1 022	-178	-2 765	-3 826	-3 267
South America	*-16 886*	*7 569*	*-23 113*	*45 937*	*-14 947*	*-47 554*	*-47 540*	*-72 134*
Argentina	-4 774	4 552	-8 981	5 274	8 338	1 360	-2 397	107
Bolivia (Plurinational State of)	-6	-199	-446	622	814	874	537	2 127
Brazil	-12 831	-3 823	-24 225	13 985	-24 306	-47 273	-52 480	-54 246
Chile	-1 971	-485	-898	1 449	3 518	3 224	-3 283	-9 497
Colombia	-206	542	795	-1 886	-4 964	-8 809	-9 525	-11 415
Ecuador	-642	-360	1 113	474	136	-1 636	-239	-427
Guyana	-129	-161	-82	-96	-231	-155	-372	-395
Paraguay	-277	390	-163	16	484	-66	289	116
Peru	-101	-1 419	-1 546	1 148	-723	-3 782	-3 341	-7 136
Suriname	32	67	32	-144	111	651	251	241
Uruguay	-709	186	-566	42	-382	-753	-1 367	-2 626
Venezuela (Bolivarian Rep. of)	4 728	8 279	11 853	25 053	2 258	8 812	24 387	11 016
Developing economies: Asia	**52 066**	**13 782**	**137 264**	**369 311**	**468 207**	**494 028**	**554 021**	**570 364**
Eastern Asia	*-7 380*	*25 654*	*51 143*	*188 827*	*338 966*	*321 188*	*212 579*	*288 893*
China	286	11 997	20 518	132 378	243 257	237 810	136 097	193 139
China, Hong Kong SAR	-1 432	4 764	6 993	20 181	20 338	14 998	11 944	-
China, Taiwan Province of	-818	10 923	8 899	17 578	42 923	39 872	41 230	49 859
Korea, Republic of	-5 071	-1 390	14 803	18 607	32 791	29 394	26 068	43 139
Mongolia	-346	-640	-70	84	-342	-886	-2 760	-3 362
Southern Asia	*-6 440*	*-9 374*	*6 224*	*513*	*-19 525*	*-28 209*	*-7 829*	*-67 663*
Afghanistan	54	..	..	192	-1 828	-2 688	398	(e)800
Bangladesh	-702	-398	-306	-176	3 556	2 106	-165	2 648
Bhutan	14	-28	-40	-235	-20	-142	-355	(e)- 410
India	-1 785	-7 036	-4 601	-10 284	-26 186	-52 275	-60 038	-91 471
Iran (Islamic Rep. of)	-2 438	327	12 481	15 392	9 477	27 554	(e)59 382	(e)26 765
Maldives	-22	10	-51	-273	-334	-207	-490	(e)- 584
Nepal	-39	-289	-131	153	18	-128	289	577
Pakistan	-866	-1 661	-85	-3 606	-3 993	-1 354	-2 234	-
Sri Lanka	-655	-298	-1 044	-650	-215	-1 075	-4 615	-3 915
South-Eastern Asia	*-6 768*	*-8 961*	*37 558*	*44 856*	*105 955*	*116 881*	*118 978*	*71 834*
Brunei Darussalam	..	2 531	2 998	4 033	3 977	5 623	5 294	(e)8 061
Cambodia	..	-35	-136	-307	-785	-772	-712	-1 208
Indonesia (...2002)	..	-2 988	7 992	–	–	–	–	–
Indonesia	–	–	–	278	10 629	5 144	1 685	-24 074
Lao People's Dem. Rep.	-43	-55	-8	-174	-61	29	-206	-
Malaysia	-266	-870	8 488	19 980	31 801	26 998	33 508	18 638
Myanmar	-350	-431	-210	582	986	1 574	-1 424	(e)-2 232
Philippines	-1 904	-2 695	-2 228	1 980	9 358	8 922	6 970	7 126
Singapore	-1 563	3 122	10 244	26 429	33 482	62 026	65 323	51 437
Thailand	-2 076	-7 281	9 313	-7 647	21 891	9 946	5 918	2 759

For sources and notes, see end of table.

As percentage of GDP - En pourcentage du PIB (1)								Régions, pays ou territoires
1980	1990	2000	2005	2009	2010	2011	2012	
-12.67	-6.88	-5.37	-17.12	-13.93	-14.48	-10.86	-6.76	Antigua-et-Barbuda
..	-20.68	11.06	4.87	7.29	-18.13	-9.19	(e)4.56	Aruba
-4.76	-0.99	-10.00	-9.09	-10.48	-10.48	-14.00	-18.24	Bahamas
-1.65	-0.39	-6.88	-11.92	-5.90	-5.14	-11.73	(e)-5.62	Barbade
			—	—	—	-20.07	-21.23	Curaçao
-20.22	-21.76	-18.44	-21.04	-22.40	-16.91	-14.40	-10.48	Dominique
-8.80	-2.98	-4.34	-1.41	-5.02	-8.49	-8.12	-7.21	République dominicaine
0.36	-20.92	-16.84	-27.59	-25.42	-25.86	-24.78	-25.37	Grenade
-7.29	-0.84	-3.40	0.18	-3.82	-2.73	-5.03	-4.87	Haïti
-4.47	-6.47	-4.08	-9.53	-9.17	-6.94	-13.99	-12.57	Jamaïque
..	-34.13	-20.93	-31.92	-21.08	-33.76	-16.72	(e)-29.55	Montserrat
0.06	-2.22	-1.69	-3.23	-8.57	-23.74		—	Antilles néerlandaises
-4.38	-23.32	-15.90	-12.07	-26.11	-20.58	-12.39	-9.72	Saint-Kitts-et-Nevis
-24.58	-13.71	-13.54	-15.29	-12.87	-17.42	-19.43	-14.40	Sainte-Lucie
-13.26	-10.03	-6.02	-18.53	-29.35	-30.87	-28.91	-30.17	Saint-Vincent-et-les Grenadines
—	—	—	—	—	—	..	11.35	Saint-Martin (partie néerlandaise)
5.72	9.06	6.67	24.29	8.32	20.50	13.23	8.79	Trinité-et-Tobago
-4.88	*-2.62*	*-3.28*	*-1.16*	*-0.98*	*-0.81*	*-1.65*	*-1.69*	*Amérique centrale*
-1.90	3.79	-19.43	-13.56	-6.14	-3.26	-1.35	-1.77	Belize
-10.81	-5.84	-4.43	-4.91	-1.96	-3.54	-5.37	-5.27	Costa Rica
2.89	-3.16	-3.28	-3.64	-1.51	-2.69	-4.64	-5.29	El Salvador
-2.32	-3.12	-6.10	-4.56	0.02	-1.51	-3.41	-2.90	Guatemala
-10.35	-1.41	-7.07	-3.12	-3.93	-5.43	-8.59	-9.26	Honduras
-4.58	-2.59	-2.94	-0.69	-0.85	-0.24	-0.90	-0.97	Mexique
-19.76	-11.10	-23.76	-16.08	-12.49	-13.03	-17.38	-17.20	Nicaragua
-8.11								Panama, sans la zone du canal
—	3.44	-5.79	-6.61	-0.74	-10.40	-12.47	-9.21	Panama
-3.65	*1.07*	*-1.73*	*2.81*	*-0.51*	*-1.28*	*-1.14*	*-1.75*	*Amérique du Sud*
-6.32	3.22	-3.16	2.88	2.70	0.37	-0.53	0.02	Argentine
-0.18	-4.09	-5.32	6.52	4.69	4.45	2.24	7.85	Bolivie (État plurinational de)
-6.71	-1.04	-3.76	1.59	-1.50	-2.21	-2.12	-2.41	Brésil
-6.50	-1.41	-1.16	1.18	2.04	1.49	-1.32	-3.57	Chili
-0.44	0.95	0.80	-1.29	-2.12	-3.08	-2.86	-3.12	Colombie
-5.19	-3.20	6.83	1.28	0.26	-2.82	-0.36	-0.58	Équateur
-13.63	-25.45	-7.23	-7.32	-11.38	-6.85	-14.45	-13.98	Guyana
-7.05	8.38	-2.29	0.21	3.38	-0.36	1.26	0.51	Paraguay
-0.60	-4.85	-2.90	1.45	-0.55	-2.40	-1.85	-3.53	Pérou
2.89	8.89	2.79	-6.55	2.86	14.96	5.45	4.79	Suriname
-6.66	2.01	-2.48	0.24	-1.25	-1.91	-2.93	-5.32	Uruguay
6.84	17.60	10.12	17.22	0.69	2.24	7.72	2.90	Venezuela (Rép. bolivarienne du)
4.13	**0.62**	**3.23**	**5.21**	**4.00**	**3.54**	**3.38**	**3.24**	**Économies en développement : Asie**
-1.67	*2.79*	*2.30*	*5.14*	*5.22*	*4.21*	*2.35*	*2.89*	*Asie orientale*
0.09	2.97	1.72	5.80	4.80	4.00	1.89	2.39	Chine
-4.97	6.20	4.13	11.35	9.72	6.69	4.91	-	Chine (RAS de Hong Kong)
-1.94	6.62	2.73	4.82	11.37	9.27	8.84	10.47	Province chinoise de Taiwan
-7.88	-0.51	2.78	2.20	3.93	2.90	2.34	3.73	Corée, République de
-58.37	-42.45	-6.15	3.34	-7.46	-14.29	-32.22	-33.41	Mongolie
-1.94	*-1.85*	*0.87*	*0.04*	*-0.97*	*-1.14*	*-0.28*	*-2.39*	*Asie méridionale*
1.47	..	..	2.89	-14.54	-16.72	2.10	(e)4.04	Afghanistan
-4.20	-1.41	-0.67	-0.31	3.99	2.11	-0.16	2.41	Bangladesh
11.06	-10.01	-9.04	-28.71	-1.59	-8.97	-20.58	(e)-23.08	Bhoutan
-0.97	-2.15	-0.98	-1.23	-1.96	-3.11	-3.16	-4.92	Inde
-2.65	0.36	12.00	7.49	2.57	6.42	(e)11.38	(e)4.90	Iran (Rép. islamique d')
-26.88	3.88	-6.42	-27.51	-17.19	-9.98	-23.90	(e)-27.59	Maldives
-1.86	-7.65	-2.28	1.85	0.14	-0.79	1.56	3.17	Népal
-3.01	-3.47	-0.12	-3.30	-2.56	-0.78	-1.07	-	Pakistan
-15.33	-3.64	-6.24	-2.66	-0.51	-2.17	-7.80	-6.58	Sri Lanka
-5.81	*-2.44*	*6.11*	*4.81*	*6.90*	*6.13*	*5.38*	*3.07*	*Asie du Sud-Est*
..	71.91	49.96	42.31	37.06	45.45	32.36	(e)48.51	Brunéi Darussalam
..	-2.04	-3.71	-4.87	-7.54	-6.86	-5.55	-8.53	Cambodge
..	-2.38	4.83		—	—	—	—	Indonésie (...2002)
			0.10	1.97	0.73	0.20	-2.74	Indonésie
-13.48	-6.34	-0.51	-6.40	-1.09	0.43	-2.52	—	Rép. dém. populaire lao
-1.01	-1.83	8.70	13.92	15.72	10.94	11.64	6.14	Malaisie
-5.93	-8.34	-2.89	4.88	2.99	3.73	-2.57	(e)-3.86	Myanmar
-5.30	-5.49	-2.75	1.92	5.56	4.47	3.10	2.85	Philippines
-12.97	8.04	10.86	21.07	18.04	27.28	25.14	19.02	Singapour
-6.20	-8.25	7.38	-4.05	7.84	2.92	1.60	0.71	Thaïlande

Pour les sources et les notes, se reporter à la fin du tableau.

**7.1.1 Balance of payments:
Current account net of countries
and geographical regions**

Region, country or territory	Millions of dollars - Millions de dollars							
	1980	1990	2000	2005	2009	2010	2011	2012
Timor-Leste	–	–	–	262	1 285	1 667	2 385	(e)1 914
Viet Nam	-565	-259	1 106	-560	-6 608	-4 276	236	-
Western Asia	*72 653*	*6 462*	*42 339*	*135 115*	*42 810*	*84 168*	*230 293*	*277 300*
Bahrain	184	70	830	1 474	560	770	3 247	(e)4 170
Jordan	374	-227	27	-2 272	-1 244	-1 882	-3 469	-5 604
Kuwait	15 302	3 886	14 672	30 071	28 384	36 958	67 157	79 209
Lebanon	-139	-	-	-2 748	-6 741	-7 587	-4 866	(e)-6 637
Oman	942	1 106	3 129	5 178	-596	5 871	10 263	8 312
Qatar	8 364	-947	4 128	13 301	9 987	23 797	51 978	61 585
Saudi Arabia	41 503	-4 147	14 317	90 061	20 955	66 751	158 545	164 764
State of Palestine	..	..	-990	-1 152	-713	-691	-2 205	(p)-2 815
Syrian Arab Republic	251	1 762	1 061	299	-1 030	-367	-	-
Turkey	-3 408	-2 625	-9 920	-22 088	-13 268	-45 315	-74 916	-47 166
United Arab Emirates	10 089	7 942	16 696	22 367	9 080	7 246	33 313	(e)29 402
Yemen, Arab Republic	-685	–	–	–	–	–	–	–
Yemen, Democratic	-124	–	–	–	–	–	–	–
Yemen	–	739	1 337	624	-2 565	-1 381	-1 029	-
Developing economies: Oceania	**-336**	**-198**	**271**	**-47**	**-1 872**	**-2 664**	**-2 308**	**-4 331**
Fiji	-17	-94	-26	-300	-225	-360	(e)- 363	(e)- 425
French Polynesia	..	..	..	9	-42	153	331	-
Kiribati	2	-9	-2	-17	-24	-21	-43	(e)-12
New Caledonia	..	..	..	-112	-824	-1 426	-1 654	-
Papua New Guinea	-289	-76	351	539	-585	-633	(e)- 296	(e)-2 370
Samoa	-13	9	-4	-25	-8	-67	-78	(e)-68
Solomon Islands	-12	-28	-41	-90	-129	-210	-60	(e)-58
Tonga	-7	6	-12	-21	-54	-15	-17	(e)-20
Tuvalu	..	..	..	5	8	-1	-10	(e)-3
Vanuatu	..	-6	5	-34	10	-84	-116	(e)-52
Transition economies	**-2 301**	**-2 482**	**47 079**	**83 239**	**32 519**	**61 931**	**101 510**	**67 976**
Albania	16	-118	-156	-571	-1 851	-1 353	-1 650	-1 314
Armenia	–	–	-278	-52	-1 369	-1 373	-1 136	-1 052
Azerbaijan	–	–	-168	167	10 175	15 040	17 145	14 977
Belarus	–	–	-338	436	-6 133	-8 280	-5 026	-1 819
Bosnia and Herzegovina	–	–	-396	-1 844	-1 136	-914	-1 729	-1 607
Croatia	–	–	-533	-2 333	-3 041	-483	-505	48
Georgia	–	–	-177	-710	-1 139	-1 196	-1 840	-1 814
Kazakhstan			366	-1 056	-4 114	1 393	12 281	7 716
Kyrgyzstan	–	–	-76	-37	-94	-312	-484	-1 431
Montenegro	–	–	–	–	-1 150	-952	-791	-769
Republic of Moldova	–	–	-98	-226	-447	-449	-790	-511
Russian Federation	–	–	46 839	84 602	50 384	67 452	97 274	71 432
Serbia and Montenegro	–	–	35	-308				
Serbia	–	–	–	–	-2 867	-2 819	-3 834	-4 002
SFR of Yugoslavia	-2 317	-2 364	–	–	–	–	–	–
Tajikistan	–	–	-62	-19	-180	-894	-787	(e)- 146
TFYR of Macedonia	–	–	-103	-152	-633	-191	-313	-374
Turkmenistan	–	–	412	875	-2 981	-2 349	569	(e)579
Ukraine	–	–	1 481	2 531	-1 736	-3 016	-10 233	-14 777
Uzbekistan			-	1 936	(e)833	(e)2 628	(e)3 360	(e)2 839
Developed economies: America	**-3 961**	**-98 716**	**-396 721**	**-724 067**	**-421 337**	**-497 968**	**-514 221**	**-536 512**
Bermuda	..	..	..	..	581	696	681	(e)719
Canada	-6 088	-19 764	19 622	21 714	-40 023	-56 709	-48 978	-62 261
United States	2 127	-78 952	-416 343	-745 780	-381 896	-441 955	-465 923	-474 970
Developed economies: Asia	**-11 621**	**44 242**	**117 604**	**169 884**	**154 931**	**211 088**	**122 317**	**61 286**
Israel	-871	163	-2 056	4 101	7 914	7 172	3 253	850
Japan	-10 750	44 078	119 660	165 783	147 017	203 916	119 064	60 436
Developed economies: Europe	**-57 724**	**-32 888**	**-27 529**	**95 709**	**86 475**	**125 074**	**169 018**	**315 789**
Austria	-3 865	1 166	-1 339	6 645	10 401	12 900	5 673	7 025
Belgium	(a)-4 931	(a)3 627	9 352	7 452	-6 672	9 011	-5 865	-7 750
Bulgaria	954	-1 710	-703	-3 364	-4 329	-707	56	-677
Cyprus	-258	-154	-488	-995	-2 512	-2 266	-835	-1 492
Czechoslovakia	-	-1 227	–	–				
Czech Republic	–	–	-2 690	-1 296	-4 762	-7 806	-5 904	-4 801
Denmark	-2 389	1 372	2 262	11 202	10 551	18 429	18 881	16 757
Estonia	–	–	-299	-1 387	653	556	471	-333
Faeroe Islands	..	..	99	31	-16	135	..	..
Finland	-1 403	-6 962	10 526	6 562	4 202	3 544	-4 026	-4 399

For sources and notes, see end of table.

As percentage of GDP - En pourcentage du PIB (1)								Régions, pays ou territoires
1980	1990	2000	2005	2009	2010	2011	2012	
–	–	–	14.45	39.14	40.36	42.81	(e)27.93	Timor-Leste
-23.60	-4.00	3.55	-1.06	-6.80	-4.02	0.19	-	Viet Nam
19.64	*1.49*	*6.03*	*10.94*	*2.57*	*4.28*	*9.94*	*11.45*	*Asie occidentale*
5.60	1.62	10.34	10.95	2.85	3.51	12.57	(e)15.66	Bahreïn
9.32	-5.65	0.32	-18.05	-5.22	-7.12	-12.03	-17.96	Jordanie
53.33	21.04	38.90	37.22	26.79	29.73	41.73	46.04	Koweït
-3.41	-	-	-12.57	-19.45	-20.44	-12.46	(e)-16.01	Liban
15.06	9.57	16.09	16.75	-1.27	9.91	14.12	10.52	Oman
106.72	-12.87	23.24	29.87	10.21	18.69	29.99	33.70	Qatar
25.22	-3.56	7.60	28.54	5.56	14.64	26.55	25.40	Arabie saoudite
..	..	-23.61	-24.86	-10.60	-8.29	-25.14	(p)-32.10	État de Palestine
1.91	15.81	5.40	1.05	-1.90	-0.61	-	-	République arabe syrienne
-3.69	-1.30	-3.72	-4.57	2.16	-6.20	-9.67	-5.96	Turquie
23.14	15.67	16.00	12.38	3.50	2.55	9.84	(e)8.33	Émirats arabes unis
-42.20	–	–	–	–	–	–	–	Yémen, République arabe du
-34.90	–	–	–	–	–	–	–	Yémen, Démocratique
–	18.36	12.30	3.28	-9.12	-4.76	-3.27	-	Yémen
-7.62	**-3.72**	**4.29**	**-0.22**	**-6.51**	**-8.62**	**-6.34**	**-10.82**	**Économies en développement : Océanie**
-1.44	-6.96	-1.48	-9.97	-7.80	-11.35	(e)-9.53	(e)-10.45	Fidji
..	..	..	0.16	-0.62	2.30	4.60	-	Polynésie française
7.00	-22.27	-3.68	-16.20	-19.04	-14.31	-23.66	(e)-5.97	Kiribati
..	..	..	-1.80	-9.41	-16.11	-16.78	-	Nouvelle-Calédonie
-10.23	-2.30	10.02	11.08	-7.22	-6.52	(e)-2.35	(e)-15.09	Papouasie-Nouvelle-Guinée
-11.52	7.69	-1.81	-5.78	-1.49	-11.20	-11.72	(e)-9.74	Samoa
-8.48	-13.34	-12.11	-21.00	-21.53	-31.10	-7.19	(e)-5.96	Îles Salomon
-8.62	3.57	-6.11	-8.06	-16.61	-4.06	-3.83	(e)-4.11	Tonga
..	..	..	24.29	28.57	-3.75	-28.64	(e)-8.33	Tuvalu
..	-3.57	1.83	-8.66	1.74	-12.25	-14.88	(e)-6.55	Vanuatu
-3.19	**-2.84**	**11.84**	**7.57**	**1.82**	**2.92**	**3.91**	**2.47**	**Économies en transition**
0.72	-5.32	-4.29	-7.00	-15.28	-11.32	-12.69	-10.49	Albanie
–	–	-14.56	-1.06	-15.84	-14.83	-11.21	-10.63	Arménie
–	–	-3.18	1.26	22.97	28.43	27.04	22.27	Azerbaïdjan
–	–	-3.25	1.44	-12.46	-14.99	-9.12	-3.12	Bélarus
–	–	-7.13	-16.85	-6.65	-5.49	-9.59	-9.30	Bosnie-Herzégovine
–	–	-2.48	-5.21	-4.89	-0.81	-0.81	0.08	Croatie
–	–	-5.78	-11.07	-10.58	-10.28	-12.81	-11.48	Géorgie
–	–	2.00	-1.85	-3.57	0.94	6.59	3.86	Kazakhstan
–	–	-5.55	-1.52	-2.00	-6.52	-8.17	-23.14	Kirghizistan
–	–	–	–	-27.78	-23.17	-17.39	-17.72	Monténégro
–	–	-7.62	-7.56	-8.21	-7.73	-11.29	-6.96	République de Moldova
–	–	18.05	11.07	4.12	4.53	5.24	3.61	Fédération de Russie
–	–	0.31	-0.99					Serbie-et-Monténégro
–	–	–	–	-6.27	-6.61	-8.06	-9.66	Serbie
-3.31	-2.78	–	–	–	–	–	–	RSF de Yougoslavie
–	–	-7.20	-0.82	-3.62	-15.85	-12.06	(e)-1.92	Tadjikistan
–	–	-2.87	-2.53	-6.80	-2.04	-3.08	-3.98	LERY de Macédoine
–	–	8.36	6.27	-15.99	-11.74	2.21	(e)1.87	Turkménistan
–	–	4.74	2.94	-1.48	-2.21	-6.19	-8.28	Ukraine
–	–	-	13.45	(e)2.53	(e)6.71	(e)7.38	(e)5.54	Ouzbékistan
-0.13	**-1.55**	**-3.71**	**-5.25**	**-2.75**	**-3.09**	**-3.05**	**-3.07**	**Économies développées : Amérique**
..	..	..	..	10.01	12.07	11.40	(e)12.04	Bermudes
-2.26	-3.39	2.71	1.92	-2.99	-3.60	-2.82	-3.51	Canada
0.08	-1.36	-4.18	-5.90	-2.73	-3.04	-3.09	-3.03	États-Unis
-1.05	**1.40**	**2.42**	**3.61**	**2.96**	**3.70**	**2.00**	**0.99**	**Économies développées : Asie**
-3.67	0.28	-1.65	3.06	4.06	3.30	1.34	0.35	Israël
-0.99	1.42	2.53	3.63	2.92	3.72	2.03	1.02	Japon
-1.46	**-0.43**	**-0.31**	**0.66**	**0.50**	**0.72**	**0.90**	**1.78**	**Économies développées : Europe**
-4.76	0.71	-0.70	2.18	2.71	3.40	1.36	1.76	Autriche
-3.94	1.79	4.02	1.97	-1.41	1.91	-1.14	-1.60	Belgique
8.85	-8.25	-5.45	-11.64	-8.91	-1.48	0.10	-1.33	Bulgarie
-11.58	-2.67	-5.32	-5.89	-10.73	-9.83	-3.34	-6.49	Chypre
-	-2.22	–	–	–	–	–	–	Tchécoslovaquie
–	–	-4.57	-1.00	-2.42	-3.92	-2.72	-2.45	République tchèque
-3.43	1.01	1.41	4.35	3.39	5.91	5.69	5.37	Danemark
–	–	-5.26	-9.97	3.41	2.93	2.13	-1.52	Estonie
..	..	..	..	..	..	..	..	Îles Féroé
-2.65	-5.01	8.64	3.35	1.76	1.50	-1.53	-1.76	Finlande

Pour les sources et les notes, se reporter à la fin du tableau.

7.1.1 Balance of payments:
Current account net of countries
and geographical regions

Region, country or territory	Millions of dollars - Millions de dollars							
	1980	1990	2000	2005	2009	2010	2011	2012
France	-4 208	-9 944	19 674	-10 355	-34 928	-39 961	-54 123	-57 487
Germany, Federal Republic of	-15 656							
Germany	_	46 456	-32 484	140 016	196 623	206 598	224 084	238 356
Greece	-2 209	-3 537	-9 820	-18 336	-35 861	-29 801	-28 677	-7 697
Hungary	-1 102	379	-4 004	-8 234	-245	1 408	1 134	2 176
Iceland	-76	-134	-847	-2 675	-1 428	-1 018	-874	-663
Ireland	-2 132	-361	-356	-7 076	-5 228	2 360	2 481	10 510
Italy	-10 588	-16 479	-5 781	-15 673	-41 917	-72 442	-67 093	-14 891
Latvia	_	_	-371	-2 022	2 220	705	-603	-477
Lithuania	_	_	-675	-1 843	1 384	26	-1 600	-215
Luxembourg	..	..	2 562	4 346	3 590	4 348	4 209	3 262
Malta	39	-56	-480	-524	-610	-396	-14	21
Netherlands	-855	8 089	7 264	47 250	41 219	60 565	84 784	77 793
Norway	1 079	3 992	25 280	50 120	44 396	50 087	63 040	71 753
Poland	-3 417	3 067	-10 343	-7 291	-16 883	-24 000	-24 986	-17 144
Portugal	-1 064	-181	-12 189	-19 803	-25 564	-24 196	-16 657	-3 288
Romania	-2 420	-3 254	-1 355	-8 551	-6 860	-7 253	-8 252	-6 767
Slovakia	_	_	-694	-4 057	-2 260	-3 250	-1 985	2 073
Slovenia			-548	-619	-342	-278	1	1 050
Spain	-5 580	-18 009	-23 185	-83 148	-70 208	-62 199	-55 311	-14 807
Sweden	-4 331	-6 339	10 074	25 143	27 059	31 671	37 876	36 323
Switzerland	-201	6 124	32 830	53 149	36 120	73 462	35 900	85 760
United Kingdom	6 862	-38 811	-38 800	-58 960	-31 318	-75 160	-32 767	-94 183
Developed economies: Oceania	**-5 420**	**-17 401**	**-17 170**	**-49 809**	**-47 374**	**-40 432**	**-40 060**	**-65 759**
Australia	-4 447	-15 948	-14 763	-41 032	-44 212	-35 667	-33 141	-57 140
New Zealand	-973	-1 453	-2 407	-8 777	-3 162	-4 765	-6 920	-8 618

Source:

UNCTAD secretariat calculations based on:

- IMF, *Balance of Payments Statistics*
- Eurostat, online database
- OECD, *OECD.Stat*
- IMF, *World Economic Outlook*
- ECLAC, *CEPALSTAT* database
- Economist Intelligence Unit, *Country Data*
- national sources

Notes:

- Balance-of-payments current account data cover all transactions between residents and non-residents of a reporting economy, involving economic values and mainly concerning goods, services, income and current transfers. In general, the current account balance describes the difference between current receipts and expenditures for internationally traded goods, services and income payments. At the same time, from a national perspective, the current account balance would equal the gap between national savings and domestic investment.

(a) Data from 1980 to 1994 inclusive refer to Belgium-Luxembourg.

(1) Source of GDP data: UNCTAD, based on UN DESA Statistics Division (UNSD).

As percentage of GDP - En pourcentage du PIB (1)								Régions, pays ou territoires
1980	1990	2000	2005	2009	2010	2011	2012	
-0.61	-0.80	1.48	-0.48	-1.33	-1.55	-1.95	-2.20	France
-1.70								Allemagne, Rép. fédérale d'
_	2.71	-1.72	5.06	5.96	6.25	6.22	7.03	Allemagne
-4.08	-3.79	-7.80	-7.64	-11.14	-9.90	-9.59	-3.00	Grèce
-4.41	1.04	-8.63	-7.46	-0.19	1.10	0.82	1.72	Hongrie
-2.29	-2.10	-9.74	-16.42	-11.79	-8.10	-6.23	-4.88	Islande
-9.93	-0.75	-0.37	-3.49	-2.33	1.14	1.12	5.01	Irlande
-2.29	-1.45	-0.52	-0.88	-1.99	-3.52	-3.06	-0.74	Italie
_	_	-4.77	-12.69	8.59	2.92	-2.12	-1.68	Lettonie
_	_	-5.87	-7.06	3.73	0.07	-3.73	-0.51	Lituanie
..	..	12.64	11.54	6.91	8.15	7.07	5.72	Luxembourg
3.10	-2.19	-12.14	-8.75	-7.55	-4.88	-0.16	0.24	Malte
-0.47	2.74	1.09	7.40	5.18	7.77	10.13	10.07	Pays-Bas
1.69	3.39	15.02	16.48	11.85	12.00	12.99	14.44	Norvège
-5.91	4.75	-6.04	-2.40	-3.92	-5.11	-4.86	-3.52	Pologne
-3.28	-0.23	-10.39	-10.32	-10.92	-10.58	-7.01	-1.55	Portugal
-6.64	-8.02	-3.63	-8.62	-4.17	-4.41	-4.35	-3.85	Roumanie
_	_	-3.40	-8.47	-2.59	-3.73	-2.07	2.26	Slovaquie
_	_	-2.74	-1.73	-0.69	-0.59	0.00	2.30	Slovénie
-2.47	-3.46	-4.00	-7.35	-4.82	-4.48	-3.74	-1.10	Espagne
-3.28	-2.59	4.07	6.78	6.67	6.84	7.02	6.92	Suède
-0.18	2.49	12.70	13.68	7.03	13.22	5.38	13.43	Suisse
1.27	-3.83	-2.63	-2.57	-1.43	-3.32	-1.35	-3.87	Royaume-Uni
-2.75	**-4.71**	**-3.70**	**-5.70**	**-4.20**	**-2.83**	**-2.39**	**-3.79**	**Économies développées : Océanie**
-2.56	-4.92	-3.60	-5.40	-4.38	-2.78	-2.19	-3.65	Australie
-4.17	-3.23	-4.48	-7.71	-2.67	-3.33	-4.25	-5.02	Nouvelle-Zélande

Sources :

Calculs du secrétariat de la CNUCED, sur la base de :

- FMI, *Statistiques de la balance des paiements*
- Eurostat, base de données en ligne
- OCDE, *OECD.Stat*
- FMI, *World Economic Outlook*
- ECLAC, *CEPALSTAT*, base de données en ligne
- Economist Intelligence Unit, *Country Data*
- sources nationales

Notes :

- Les données du compte des transactions courantes de la balance des paiements recouvrent toutes les transactions, entre entités résidentes et non-résidentes, portant sur des valeurs économiques, concernant notamment les biens, les services, les revenus et les transferts courants. En général, la balance du compte courant indique la différence entre les recettes et les paiements pour les biens, les services et les revenus faisant partie des transactions internationales. De même, d'une perspective nationale, la balance du compte courant représente l'écart entre les épargnes nationales et l'investissement intérieur.

(a) Les données de 1980 à 1994 se réfèrent à Belgique-Luxembourg.

(1) Source des données du PIB : CNUCED, sur la base des données de ONU DAES Division de statistiques (UNSD).

Economic grouping	Millions of dollars - Millions de dollars							
	1980	1990	2000	2005	2009	2010	2011	2012
DEVELOPING ECONOMIES	28 455	13 190	105 321	465 610	404 065	432 699	462 061	445 871
Developing economies excluding China	28 169	1 193	84 803	333 232	160 808	194 889	325 964	253 461
Developing economies excluding LDCs	34 954	19 122	109 420	472 403	432 948	445 459	472 916	468 793
High-income developing economies	48 359	27 994	57 154	293 138	188 971	229 456	361 932	398 827
Middle-income developing economies	-11 347	-2 157	50 801	164 459	262 696	271 790	181 071	159 956
Low-income developing economies	-8 557	-12 647	-2 633	8 013	-47 602	-68 547	-80 942	-112 912
Heavily indebted poor countries (IMF)	-7 954	-8 157	-7 240	-13 416	-25 058	-23 854	-26 032	-39 320
Landlocked developing countries	-2 716	-2 924	-2 429	-1 538	-8 375	2 852	20 362	8 386
Small island developing States	-444	-493	-983	349	-2 713	-263	-2 977	-5 790
Least developed countries	*-6 500*	*-5 932*	*-4 099*	*-6 793*	*-28 884*	*-12 761*	*-10 854*	*-22 922*
Africa and Haiti	-4 593	-5 378	-4 541	-7 489	-29 208	-12 525	-9 566	-23 425
Asia	-1 876	-497	506	659	-698	-1 402	-3 205	-1 086
Islands	-31	-57	-64	36	1 023	1 166	1 916	1 589
Major petroleum and gas exporters	*92 199*	*24 821*	*100 911*	*279 213*	*95 623*	*227 900*	*451 761*	*456 899*
Africa	13 708	8 374	23 635	77 792	16 078	50 912	46 736	75 845
America	4 728	8 279	11 853	25 053	2 258	8 812	24 387	11 016
Asia	73 763	8 168	65 423	176 369	77 287	168 176	380 638	370 038
Major exporters of manufactured goods	*-21 362*	*13 814*	*60 515*	*221 645*	*418 985*	*418 524*	*309 741*	*353 680*
America	-10 422	-7 451	-18 743	-5 861	-7 497	-2 519	-10 347	-11 410
Asia	-10 940	21 265	79 258	227 506	426 482	421 043	320 088	365 089
Emerging economies	*-39 893*	*-4 122*	*-2 644*	*90 941*	*142 217*	*119 244*	*100 199*	*83 650*
America	-30 099	-8 626	-54 391	15 994	-20 670	-48 991	-71 848	-82 182
Asia	-9 794	4 503	51 747	74 947	162 887	168 235	172 047	165 831
Newly industrialized Asian economies	*-13 130*	*3 585*	*64 504*	*97 385*	*203 211*	*197 299*	*192 646*	*155 003*
First tier	-8 883	17 419	40 938	82 795	129 533	146 289	144 565	150 554
Second tier	-4 246	-13 834	23 565	14 591	73 678	51 010	48 081	4 449
Developing economies: Africa	6 656	3 635	16 898	60 644	-32 812	3 275	-12 801	-17 302
Northern Africa excluding Sudan	6 267	5 289	13 145	38 969	227	18 413	4 228	21 341
Sub-Saharan Africa	390	-1 655	3 753	21 675	-33 039	-15 138	-17 029	-38 642
Sub-Saharan Africa excluding South Africa	-2 772	-3 206	3 943	30 194	-21 712	-5 021	-3 346	-13 845
Developing economies: America	-29 931	-4 028	-49 111	35 702	-29 458	-61 941	-76 851	-102 860
Central America and Greater Caribbean Islands excluding Puerto Rico	-13 233	-11 530	-25 412	-12 153	-13 819	-15 051	-28 559	-29 507
Central America and Greater Caribbean Islands excluding Mexico and Puerto Rico	-2 811	-4 079	-6 669	-6 292	-6 322	-12 532	-18 212	-18 097
South America and Central America	-29 162	-802	-46 321	34 972	-24 919	-57 060	-69 370	-95 013
South America excluding Brazil	-4 055	11 392	1 111	31 952	9 358	-280	4 940	-17 887
Developing economies: Asia	52 066	13 782	137 264	369 311	468 207	494 028	554 021	570 364
Eastern and South-Eastern Asia excluding China	-14 434	4 697	68 183	101 305	201 665	200 259	195 459	167 588
Southern Asia excluding India	-4 655	-2 338	10 825	10 796	6 661	24 066	52 209	23 808

Sources:

For sources and notes, see end of table 7.1.1.

As percentage of GDP - En pourcentage du PIB (1)								Groupements économiques
1980	1990	2000	2005	2009	2010	2011	2012	
1.17	**0.35**	**1.51**	**4.30**	**2.33**	**2.08**	**1.92**	**1.76**	**ÉCONOMIES EN DÉVELOPPEMENT**
1.32	0.03	1.46	3.90	1.31	1.31	1.94	1.47	Économies en développement sans la Chine
1.50	0.52	1.61	4.49	2.58	2.21	2.03	1.91	Économies en développement sans les PMA
3.79	1.34	1.46	5.38	2.62	2.61	3.65	3.97	Économies en développement à revenu élevé
-1.61	-0.19	2.27	4.21	3.38	2.97	1.66	1.33	Économies en développement à revenu intermédiaire
-1.88	-2.06	-0.31	0.55	-2.04	-2.42	-2.53	-3.46	Économies en développement à revenu faible
-7.29	-5.88	-5.18	-5.51	-6.41	-5.60	-5.43	-7.90	Pays pauvres très endettés (FMI)
-5.55	1.16	-1.97	-0.66	-1.91	0.55	3.29	1.22	Pays en développement sans littoral
-2.38	-1.85	-2.28	0.54	-3.42	-0.31	-3.10	-5.58	Petits États insulaires en développement
-6.07	*-4.06*	*-2.34*	*-2.17*	*-5.31*	*-2.11*	*-1.57*	*-3.07*	*Pays les moins avancés*
-6.05	-5.31	-4.58	-3.82	-8.47	-3.35	-2.23	-4.98	Afrique et Haïti
-6.09	-1.13	0.67	0.58	-0.36	-0.63	-1.27	-0.41	Asie
-6.23	-6.35	-5.35	0.98	17.40	16.62	21.43	15.25	Îles
15.60	*5.16*	*13.69*	*21.52*	*4.72*	*9.42*	*16.37*	*15.04*	*Principaux exportateurs de pétrole et de gaz*
7.65	6.05	15.92	26.49	3.64	9.33	8.06	11.21	Afrique
6.84	17.60	10.12	17.22	0.69	2.24	7.72	2.90	Amérique
21.51	2.76	13.87	20.56	6.16	11.37	20.41	18.68	Asie
-2.88	*1.00*	*1.91*	*4.46*	*5.21*	*4.42*	*2.79*	*2.92*	*Principaux exportateurs d'articles manufacturés*
-4.58	-2.59	-2.94	-0.69	-0.85	-0.24	-0.90	-0.97	Amérique
-2.13	1.95	3.12	5.51	5.96	4.99	3.22	3.33	Asie
-5.54	*-0.28*	*-0.09*	*2.41*	*2.85*	*1.93*	*1.43*	*1.20*	*Économies émergentes*
-5.56	-1.00	-3.21	0.76	-0.66	-1.25	-1.59	-1.88	Amérique
-5.48	0.74	4.39	4.50	8.67	7.44	6.88	6.39	Asie
-5.40	*0.42*	*4.05*	*4.36*	*7.27*	*5.82*	*5.05*	*3.89*	*Économies nouvellement industrialisées d'Asie*
-6.02	3.16	3.65	5.47	8.06	7.71	6.93	6.97	Première génération
-4.43	-4.45	5.01	2.02	6.19	3.41	2.78	0.24	Deuxième génération
1.54	**0.74**	**2.83**	**6.02**	**-2.22**	**0.19**	**-0.67**	**-0.85**	**Économies en développement : Afrique**
4.77	3.09	5.31	11.64	0.04	3.16	0.70	3.15	Afrique septentrionale sans le Soudan
0.13	-0.51	1.07	3.23	-3.44	-1.32	-1.31	-2.85	Afrique subsaharienne
-1.25	-1.53	1.82	7.10	-3.21	-0.64	-0.38	-1.45	Afrique subsaharienne sans l'Afrique du Sud
-4.06	**-0.37**	**-2.30**	**1.32**	**-0.72**	**-1.22**	**-1.35**	**-1.81**	**Économies en développement : Amérique**
-5.01	-3.16	-3.29	-1.18	-1.21	-1.14	-1.94	-1.95	Amérique centrale et Grandes Antilles sans Porto Rico
-7.74	-5.28	-4.89	-3.37	-2.43	-4.42	-5.81	-5.36	Amérique centrale et Grandes Antilles sans le Mexique et Porto Rico
-4.08	-0.08	-2.27	1.36	-0.63	-1.17	-1.26	-1.73	Amérique du Sud et Amérique centrale
-1.49	3.35	0.16	4.25	0.72	-0.02	0.29	-0.96	Amérique du Sud sans le Brésil
4.13	**0.62**	**3.23**	**5.21**	**4.00**	**3.54**	**3.38**	**3.24**	**Économies en développement : Asie**
-5.71	0.53	4.15	4.36	6.81	5.59	4.83	3.95	Asie orientale et Asie du Sud-Est sans la Chine
-3.15	-1.30	4.43	2.61	0.97	3.05	5.57	2.43	Asie méridionale sans l'Inde

Sources :

Pour les sources et les notes, se reporter à la fin du tableau 7.1.1.

7

Trade group	Millions of dollars - Millions de dollars							
	1980	1990	2000	2005	2009	2010	2011	2012
AFRICA								
CEMAC	-279	-788	1 009	1 636	-3 796	-2 939	1 055	-1 260
CEPGL	-389	-869	-59	-446	-1 663	-2 896	-2 032	-3 232
COMESA	4 165	1 015	2 739	8 740	-8 568	-155	-15 158	715
EAC	-1 616	-1 503	-1 131	-1 429	-5 177	-6 803	-10 237	-10 629
ECCAS	-600	-1 905	1 725	6 292	-13 109	1 583	12 002	9 259
ECOWAS	2 158	2 254	5 344	32 615	8 592	7 282	1 314	6 717
MRU	-1 937	-1 487	-494	-226	887	-356	-2 335	-2 754
SADC	259	-1 467	-1 151	-6 902	-27 817	-12 950	-12 378	-27 338
UMA	6 570	2 953	14 018	35 990	3 254	22 598	9 399	27 229
WAEMU	-2 853	-2 259	-1 439	-2 460	-2 464	-3 444	-5 256	-5 857
AMERICA								
ANCOM	-955	-1 436	-84	358	-4 738	-13 353	-12 567	-16 850
CACM	-1 522	-1 145	-3 631	-3 931	-2 214	-4 177	-7 638	-8 175
CARICOM	-151	-269	-1 378	506	-1 994	1 470	-2 179	-2 924
FTAA	-33 893	-99 966	-445 226	-688 655	-450 948	-559 014	-590 798	-639 209
LAIA	-27 540	-2 124	-43 174	39 644	-22 665	-53 448	-61 419	-86 791
MERCOSUR	-13 870	9 385	-22 528	44 992	-12 795	-37 046	-31 031	-43 506
NAFTA	-14 383	-106 167	-415 463	-729 927	-429 416	-501 183	-525 248	-548 641
OAS	-33 893	-102 511	-445 922	-688 305	-451 111	-559 129	-590 626	-639 343
OECS	-78	-280	-444	-805	-1 098	-1 071	-975	-903
ASIA								
APTA	-7 970	2 820	29 362	139 701	253 142	215 989	97 141	143 225
ASEAN	-6 768	-8 961	37 558	44 594	104 670	115 214	116 592	69 920
ECO	-6 659	-3 959	3 279	-8 244	-5 975	-6 297	14 714	2 862
GCC	76 385	7 911	53 773	162 451	68 370	141 392	324 503	347 443
SAARC	-4 002	-9 701	-6 257	-14 879	-29 002	-55 763	-67 211	-94 428
EUROPE								
EFTA	801	9 982	57 263	100 594	79 088	122 530	98 065	156 850
EU27	-58 525	-42 869	-84 891	-4 916	7 403	2 408	70 952	158 939
Euro area	-52 710	3 654	-38 286	50 300	30 586	65 094	87 118	227 946
OCEANIA								
MSG	-318	-204	289	115	-928	-1 287	-836	-2 905
INTERREGIONAL								
ACP	-817	-4 924	931	22 394	-37 235	-17 817	-22 124	-46 288
APEC	-46 323	-63 615	-179 100	-292 979	166 659	165 018	-21 617	-135 605
BSEC	-7 067	-11 244	25 645	33 404	-9 168	-10 789	-16 854	632
CIS	–	–	48 408	89 157	44 337	69 840	112 172	77 808

Sources:

For sources and notes, see end of table 7.1.1.

As percentage of GDP - En pourcentage du PIB (1)								Groupements commerciaux
1980	1990	2000	2005	2009	2010	2011	2012	
								AFRIQUE
-1.56	-3.34	4.70	3.51	-5.71	-3.87	1.14	-1.36	CEMAC
-3.10	-6.43	-0.73	-4.10	-9.12	-13.87	-8.20	-11.70	CEPGL
3.65	0.70	1.32	3.35	-1.90	-0.03	-3.00	0.12	COMESA
-7.28	-6.12	-3.55	-3.04	-6.79	-8.38	-11.85	-10.31	CAE
-1.67	-4.01	4.49	6.96	-8.17	0.88	5.41	3.88	CEEAC
1.74	2.80	6.20	17.85	3.12	2.13	0.35	1.65	CEDEAO
-14.92	-9.48	-3.35	-1.04	2.88	-1.16	-7.17	-8.09	UFM
0.20	-0.85	-0.59	-1.93	-5.93	-2.26	-1.88	-4.12	CADC
5.83	2.15	9.16	14.83	0.97	6.08	2.47	6.34	UMA
-12.68	-7.38	-5.45	-5.22	-3.57	-4.90	-6.78	-7.63	UEMOA
								AMÉRIQUE
-1.20	-1.40	-0.05	0.13	-1.09	-2.56	-2.08	-2.52	ANCOM
-7.81	-4.53	-6.33	-4.98	-2.05	-3.45	-5.63	-5.62	MCAC
-0.94	-1.24	-3.80	0.99	-3.21	2.26	-3.14	-4.00	CARICOM
-0.89	-1.35	-3.48	-4.19	-2.33	-2.65	-2.63	-2.77	ZLEA
-3.98	-0.21	-2.15	1.56	-0.58	-1.11	-1.13	-1.61	ALADI
-3.92	1.63	-2.08	3.61	-0.55	-1.24	-0.93	-1.36	MERCOSUR
-0.44	-1.59	-3.67	-4.99	-2.65	-2.93	-2.92	-2.94	ALENA
-0.89	-1.37	-3.48	-4.18	-2.32	-2.64	-2.62	-2.76	OEA
-13.94	-14.98	-13.30	-18.81	-20.88	-20.35	-17.91	-16.05	OECO
								ASIE
-1.38	0.27	1.30	3.45	3.43	2.45	0.93	1.27	ACAP
-5.81	-2.44	6.11	4.80	6.83	6.06	5.29	3.00	ANASE
-3.07	-1.16	0.67	-0.91	-0.44	-0.39	0.79	0.15	ECO
30.05	3.79	14.31	24.40	7.54	13.18	23.71	23.76	CCG
-1.66	-2.34	-1.03	-1.42	-1.76	-2.74	-2.91	-4.12	SAARC
								EUROPE
0.44	2.70	13.15	14.19	8.78	12.43	8.41	13.65	AELE
-1.55	-0.59	-1.00	-0.04	0.05	0.01	0.40	0.96	UE27
-1.85	0.06	-0.61	0.50	0.25	0.54	0.66	1.87	Zone euro
								OCÉANIE
-7.61	-4.06	4.96	1.33	-7.62	-9.04	-4.64	-13.48	MSG
								INTERRÉGIONAUX
-0.25	-1.27	0.21	2.76	-3.24	-1.32	-1.46	-2.93	ACP
-0.90	-0.55	-0.91	-1.14	0.52	0.47	-0.06	-0.33	CEAP
-3.60	-3.13	3.43	1.92	-0.35	-0.36	-0.48	0.02	CEMN
–	–	13.88	8.99	2.73	3.55	4.62	3.00	CEI

Sources :

Pour les sources et les notes, se reporter à la fin du tableau 7.1.1.

Region, country or territory	Inward flows - Flux entrants Millions of dollars							
	1980	1990	2000	2005	2009	2010	2011	2012
WORLD	54 069	207 362	1 413 169	989 618	1 216 475	1 408 537	1 651 511	1 350 926
DEVELOPING ECONOMIES	7 469	34 762	264 543	334 521	530 289	637 063	735 212	702 826
TRANSITION ECONOMIES	24	75	7 038	33 612	72 750	75 056	96 290	87 382
DEVELOPED ECONOMIES	46 576	172 525	1 141 588	621 485	613 436	696 418	820 008	560 718
Developing economies: Africa	400	2 846	9 621	30 913	52 964	43 582	47 598	50 041
Eastern Africa	*197*	*389*	*1 468*	*2 585*	*5 736*	*7 513*	*8 951*	*13 297*
Burundi	5	1	12	1	0	1	3	1
Comoros	0	0	0	1	14	8	23	17
Djibouti	0	0	3	22	100	27	78	100
Eritrea	–	–	28	1	91	91	39	74
Ethiopia (…1991)	1	12						
Ethiopia	–	–	135	265	221	288	627	970
Kenya	79	57	111	21	115	178	335	259
Madagascar	-1	22	83	86	1 066	808	810	895
Malawi	9	23	40	140	49	97	129	129
Mauritius	1	41	277	42	248	430	273	361
Mozambique	4	9	139	108	893	1 018	2 663	5 218
Rwanda	16	8	8	14	119	42	106	160
Seychelles	10	0	24	86	118	160	144	114
Somalia	0	6	0	24	108	112	102	107
Uganda	4	-6	181	380	842	544	894	1 721
United Republic of Tanzania	5	0	282	936	953	1 813	1 229	1 706
Zambia	62	203	122	357	695	1 729	1 108	1 066
Zimbabwe	2	12	23	103	105	166	387	400
Middle Africa	*353*	*-345*	*1 503*	*1 619*	*8 114*	*6 119*	*4 987*	*2 941*
Angola	37	-335	879	-1 304	2 205	-3 227	-3 024	-6 898
Cameroon	130	-113	159	244	740	538	243	507
Central African Republic	5	1	1	10	42	62	37	71
Chad	0	9	115	-99	376	313	282	323
Congo	40	23	162	1 475	1 862	2 211	3 056	2 758
Dem. Rep. of the Congo	110	-14	72	267	664	2 939	1 687	3 312
Equatorial Guinea	0	11	154	769	1 636	2 734	1 975	2 115
Gabon	32	73	-43	242	573	499	696	702
Sao Tome and Principe	0	..	4	16	16	51	35	50
Northern Africa	*152*	*1 155*	*3 250*	*12 236*	*18 224*	*15 709*	*8 496*	*11 502*
Algeria	349	40	280	1 081	2 746	2 264	2 571	1 484
Egypt	548	734	1 235	5 376	6 712	6 386	-483	2 798
Libya	-1 089	159	141	1 038	3 310	1 909	..	..
Morocco	89	165	422	1 654	1 952	1 574	2 568	2 836
Sudan (…2011)	9	-31	392	2 305	1 816	2 064	2 692	–
Sudan	–	–	–	–	–	–	–	2 466
Tunisia	246	89	779	783	1 688	1 513	1 148	1 918
Southern Africa	*132*	*93*	*1 269*	*7 298*	*6 182*	*2 265*	*7 459*	*5 484*
Botswana	112	96	57	279	129	-6	414	293
Lesotho	4	17	32	70	100	114	132	172
Namibia	0	30	186	348	522	793	816	357
South Africa	-10	-78	887	6 647	5 365	1 228	6 004	4 572
Swaziland	26	28	106	-46	66	136	93	90
Western Africa	*-434*	*1 553*	*2 131*	*7 174*	*14 709*	*11 977*	*17 705*	*16 817*
Benin	4	62	60	53	134	177	161	159
Burkina Faso	0	0	23	34	101	35	42	40
Cape Verde	..	0	43	82	119	112	93	71
Côte d'Ivoire	95	48	235	312	377	339	286	478
Gambia	0	14	44	45	40	37	36	79
Ghana	16	15	115	193	2 897	2 527	3 248	3 295
Guinea	1	18	10	105	141	101	956	744
Guinea-Bissau	0	2	1	9	17	33	25	16
Liberia	72	225	21	83	218	450	508	1 354
Mali	2	6	82	224	748	406	556	310
Mauritania	27	7	40	814	-3	131	589	1 204
Niger	49	41	8	30	791	940	1 066	793
Nigeria	-739	1 003	1 310	4 978	8 650	6 099	8 915	7 029
Saint Helena	..	..	-4	0	..	..	..	..
Senegal	14	57	63	45	320	266	338	338
Sierra Leone	-19	32	39	91	110	238	715	740
Togo	43	23	42	77	49	86	171	166

For sources and notes, see end of table.

Outward flows - Flux sortants Millions de dollars								Régions, pays ou territoires
1980	1990	2000	2005	2009	2010	2011	2012	
51 576	241 421	1 240 316	903 764	1 149 776	1 504 928	1 678 035	1 390 956	**MONDE**
3 179	11 838	146 273	139 935	273 401	413 220	422 067	426 082	ÉCONOMIES EN DÉVELOPPEMENT
-	-	3 197	19 422	48 369	61 872	72 880	55 491	ÉCONOMIES EN TRANSITION
48 397	229 583	1 090 846	744 407	828 006	1 029 837	1 183 089	909 383	ÉCONOMIES DÉVELOPPÉES
1 097	659	1 534	2 051	6 281	9 311	5 376	14 296	**Économies en développement : Afrique**
-	-	-	-	-	-	-	-	*Afrique orientale*
..	0	..	..	..	..	..	..	Burundi
..	1	..	..	..	..	..	..	Comores
..	..	..	..	..	..	..	..	Djibouti
–	–	..	..	..	..	..	..	Érythrée
..	..	–	–	–	–	–	–	Éthiopie (...1991)
–	–	..	..	..	..	..	..	Éthiopie
1	0	..	10	46	2	9	16	Kenya
..	1	..	..	..	..	..	..	Madagascar
..	..	-1	3	-1	42	50	50	Malawi
0	1	13	48	37	129	89	89	Maurice
..	..	0	0	-3	1	-3	-9	Mozambique
..	..	..	..	..	..	..	..	Rwanda
4	1	8	33	5	6	8	4	Seychelles
..	..	..	..	..	..	..	..	Somalie
..	..	..	..	..	-4	..	..	Ouganda
..	..	..	..	..	..	..	..	République-Unie de Tanzanie
..	..	..	..	270	1 095	-2	177	Zambie
..	17	8	1	..	43	14	46	Zimbabwe
0	*52*	*33*	*298*	*60*	*1 931*	*2 416*	*3 439*	*Afrique centrale*
..	1	..	219	7	1 340	2 093	2 741	Angola
-8	15	10	-14	-69	503	144	193	Cameroun
0	4	..	..	..	..	..	..	République centrafricaine
0	0	..	..	..	..	..	..	Tchad
0	3	4	..	..	..	..	..	Congo
..	..	-2	13	35	7	91	421	Rép. dém. du Congo
0	0	-4	..	..	..	..	..	Guinée équatoriale
8	29	25	65	87	81	88	85	Gabon
..	..	..	15	0	0	0	1	Sao Tomé-et-Principe
87	*135*	*223*	*289*	*2 588*	*4 847*	*1 582*	*3 134*	*Afrique septentrionale*
34	5	14	-20	215	220	534	-41	Algérie
7	12	51	92	571	1 176	626	211	Égypte
47	105	98	128	1 165	2 722	131	2 509	Libye
0	13	59	77	470	589	179	361	Maroc
..	..	..	..	89	66	84	–	Soudan (...2011)
–	–	–	–	–	–	–	80	Soudan
0	0	1	12	77	74	28	13	Tunisie
766	*39*	*285*	*951*	*1 160*	*-73*	*-257*	*4 323*	*Afrique australe*
2	7	2	56	6	1	-11	-10	Botswana
..	..	..	-1	-2	-2	-4	-37	Lesotho
0	1	3	-13	-3	5	5	-5	Namibie
755	27	271	930	1 151	-76	-257	4 369	Afrique du Sud
9	3	10	-22	7	-1	9	6	Swaziland
-	*412*	*965*	*418*	*2 119*	*1 292*	*1 472*	*3 026*	*Afrique occidentale*
0	0	4	0	31	-18	60	-63	Bénin
0	-1	0	0	8	-4	1	1	Burkina Faso
..	0	..	..	0	0	1	-1	Cap-Vert
..	..	8	..	-9	25	15	26	Côte d'Ivoire
..	..	..	..	..	..	..	..	Gambie
..	..	..	..	7	..	25	1	Ghana
..	0	0	..	..	..	1	3	Guinée
0	0	..	1	0	6	1	1	Guinée-Bissau
236	6	780	437	364	369	372	1 354	Libéria
..	0	4	-1	-1	7	4	4	Mali
..	..	..	2	4	4	4	4	Mauritanie
-4	0	-1	-4	59	-60	9	7	Niger
5	415	169	15	1 542	923	824	1 539	Nigéria
..	..	..	..	..	..	..	..	Sainte-Hélène
2	-10	1	-8	77	2	47	47	Sénégal
..	0	..	-8	0	0	..	..	Sierra Leone
..	..	0	-15	37	37	106	103	Togo

Pour les sources et les notes, se reporter à la fin du tableau.

Region, country or territory	Inward flows - Flux entrants Millions of dollars							
	1980	1990	2000	2005	2009	2010	2011	2012
Developing economies: America	**6 416**	**8 925**	**98 048**	**78 054**	**150 150**	**189 855**	**249 432**	**243 861**
Caribbean	*390*	*827*	*20 521*	*5 725*	*72 243*	*70 021*	*90 102*	*77 725*
Anguilla	..	11	43	119	44	11	38	18
Antigua and Barbuda	20	59	67	238	85	101	68	74
Aruba	..	131	-128	-208	-32	158	468	-140
Bahamas	4	-17	609	1 054	873	1 148	1 533	1 094
Barbados	3	11	55	240	247	290	532	356
British Virgin Islands	-1	18	9 877	-9 090	46 503	49 058	62 725	64 896
Cayman Islands	20	49	7 627	10 221	20 426	15 875	19 836	4 234
Curaçao	–	–	–	–	–	–	69	94
Dominica	0	8	20	32	43	25	14	20
Dominican Republic	93	133	953	1 123	2 165	1 896	2 275	3 610
Grenada	0	13	39	73	104	64	45	33
Haiti	13	8	13	26	38	150	181	179
Jamaica	28	175	469	682	541	228	218	362
Montserrat	0	10	2	6	3	4	2	3
Netherlands Antilles	35	8	-1	42	95	122	–	–
Saint Kitts and Nevis	1	49	99	104	136	119	112	101
Saint Lucia	31	46	58	82	152	127	116	113
Saint Vincent and the Grenadines	1	8	38	41	111	97	86	126
Sint Maarten (Dutch part)	–	–	–	–	–	–	-48	26
Trinidad and Tobago	143	109	680	940	709	549	1 831	2 527
Central America	*2 505*	*3 056*	*20 472*	*28 288*	*21 188*	*27 700*	*29 907*	*21 733*
Belize	0	19	30	155	113	100	99	198
Costa Rica	53	162	409	861	1 347	1 466	2 156	2 265
El Salvador	6	2	173	511	366	117	386	516
Guatemala	111	59	230	508	600	806	1 026	1 207
Honduras	6	44	382	600	509	969	1 014	1 059
Mexico	2 099	2 633	18 282	24 449	16 561	21 372	21 504	12 659
Nicaragua	13	1	267	241	434	508	968	810
Panama, excl. Canal Zone	219	–	–	–	–	–	–	–
Panama	–	136	700	962	1 259	2 363	2 755	3 020
South America	*3 521*	*5 042*	*57 056*	*44 041*	*56 719*	*92 134*	*129 423*	*144 402*
Argentina	678	1 836	10 418	5 265	4 017	7 848	9 882	12 551
Bolivia (Plurinational State of)	47	67	736	-288	423	643	859	1 060
Brazil	1 910	989	32 779	15 066	25 949	48 506	66 660	65 272
Chile	213	661	4 860	7 097	12 887	15 373	22 931	30 323
Colombia	157	500	2 436	10 252	7 137	6 758	13 438	15 823
Ecuador	70	126	-23	493	306	163	639	587
Falkland Islands (Malvinas)	..	0	45	..	..	..	..	..
Guyana	1	8	67	77	208	270	215	231
Paraguay	30	71	100	35	95	228	215	320
Peru	27	41	810	2 579	6 431	8 455	8 233	12 240
Suriname	18	-77	-148	28	-93	-248	70	70
Uruguay	290	42	273	847	1 529	2 289	2 505	2 710
Venezuela (Bolivarian Rep. of)	80	778	4 701	2 589	-2 169	1 849	3 778	3 216
Developing economies: Asia	**532**	**22 658**	**156 581**	**225 004**	**324 688**	**400 687**	**436 150**	**406 770**
Eastern Asia	*939*	*8 820*	*125 490*	*122 778*	*162 523*	*214 604*	*233 818*	*214 804*
China	57	3 487	40 715	72 406	95 000	114 734	123 985	121 080
China, Hong Kong SAR	710	3 275	70 508	40 960	54 274	82 708	96 125	74 584
China, Macao SAR	..	0	-1	1 240	858	2 831	647	1 500
China, Taiwan Province of	166	1 330	4 928	1 625	2 805	2 492	-1 957	3 205
Korea, Dem. People's Rep. of	..	-61	3	50	2	38	56	79
Korea, Republic of	6	789	9 283	6 309	8 961	10 110	10 247	9 904
Mongolia	..	..	54	188	624	1 691	4 715	4 452
Southern Asia	*284*	*213*	*4 864*	*14 429*	*42 438*	*28 726*	*44 231*	*33 511*
Afghanistan	9	0	0	271	76	211	83	94
Bangladesh	9	3	579	845	700	913	1 136	990
Bhutan	0	2	..	6	18	26	10	16
India	79	237	3 588	7 622	35 657	21 125	36 190	25 543
Iran (Islamic Rep. of)	81	-362	194	3 136	3 048	3 648	4 150	4 870
Maldives	0	6	22	73	158	216	256	284
Nepal	0	6	0	2	39	87	95	92
Pakistan	64	278	309	2 201	2 338	2 022	1 327	847
Sri Lanka	43	43	173	272	404	478	981	776

For sources and notes, see end of table.

Outward flows - Flux sortants Millions de dollars								Régions, pays ou territoires
1980	1990	2000	2005	2009	2010	2011	2012	
893	222	50 179	44 337	55 512	119 236	105 154	103 045	**Économies en développement : Amérique**
-	-	*42 449*	*24 598*	*41 668*	*72 742*	*63 261*	*53 972*	*Caraïbes*
..	..	3	1	0	0	0	..	Anguilla
..	..	23	17	4	5	3	3	Antigua-et-Barbuda
..	487	3	-9	1	3	3	3	Aruba
115	0	140	143	216	149	524	367	Bahamas
1	1	1	9	-56	-54	-29	-46	Barbade
0	-2 520	34 459	17 755	35 143	58 717	52 233	42 394	Îles Vierges britanniques
5	282	7 649	6 122	6 311	13 857	9 436	9 938	Îles Caïmanes
–	–	–	–	–	–	-30	-14	Curaçao
..	..	3	13	1	1	0	0	Dominique
..	..	61	21	-32	-23	-25	-27	République dominicaine
..	..	2	3	1	3	3	2	Grenade
..	-8	..	..	..	..	..	..	Haïti
0	37	74	101	61	58	75	17	Jamaïque
..	..	0	1	0	0	0	0	Montserrat
1	2	-3	65	6	18	–	–	Antilles néerlandaises
..	..	3	11	5	3	2	0	Saint-Kitts-et-Nevis
..	..	4	4	6	5	4	3	Sainte-Lucie
..	..	0	1	1	0	0	0	Saint-Vincent-et-les Grenadines
–	–	–	–	–	–	1	-2	Saint-Martin (partie néerlandaise)
..	..	25	341	..	..	1 060	1 332	Trinité-et-Tobago
351	*828*	*-309*	*7 890*	*9 925*	*15 546*	*13 900*	*27 540*	*Amérique centrale*
0	2	6	28	4	3	5	2	Belize
5	2	8	-43	7	25	58	426	Costa Rica
..	..	5	-113	..	..	..	..	El Salvador
2	..	40	38	26	24	17	39	Guatemala
1	-1	7	1	4	-1	18	6	Honduras
3	223	363	6 474	8 464	15 045	12 139	25 597	Mexique
..	..	..	..	..	..	..	..	Nicaragua
341	–	–	–	–	–	–	–	Panama, sans la zone du canal
–	602	-739	1 504	1 419	451	1 664	1 469	Panama
420	*1 112*	*8 040*	*11 849*	*3 920*	*30 948*	*27 993*	*21 533*	*Amérique du Sud*
-110	35	901	1 311	712	965	1 488	1 089	Argentine
1	1	3	3	-3	-29	..	..	Bolivie (État plurinational de)
367	625	2 282	2 517	-10 084	11 588	-1 029	-2 821	Brésil
44	8	3 987	2 135	7 233	9 461	20 373	21 090	Chili
106	16	325	4 662	3 348	6 842	8 280	-248	Colombie
1	3	15	12	43	143	-81	17	Équateur
..	..	..	..	..	..	..	..	Îles Falkland (Malvinas)
..	..	2	..	..	..	..	..	Guyana
..	..	6	6	8	-4	..	..	Paraguay
..	50	..	..	411	266	113	-57	Pérou
..	..	..	..	..	..	-3	1	Suriname
0	0	-1	36	16	-60	-7	2	Uruguay
12	375	521	1 167	2 236	1 776	-1 141	2 460	Venezuela (Rép. bolivarienne du)
1 178	10 943	94 565	93 128	211 525	283 972	310 612	308 159	**Économies en développement : Asie**
150	*9 574*	*82 108*	*58 623*	*137 783*	*206 777*	*212 519*	*214 408*	*Asie orientale*
0	830	916	12 261	56 530	68 811	74 654	84 220	Chine
82	2 448	70 005	33 905	57 940	98 414	95 885	83 985	Chine (RAS de Hong Kong)
..	..	..	60	-11	-441	120	150	Chine (RAS de Macao)
42	5 243	6 701	6 028	5 877	11 574	12 766	13 031	Province chinoise de Taiwan
..	1	6	..	..	..	..	..	Corée, Rép. populaire dém. de
26	1 052	4 482	6 366	17 392	28 357	28 999	32 978	Corée, République de
..	..	..	2	54	62	94	44	Mongolie
-	*10*	*551*	*3 524*	*16 507*	*16 383*	*12 952*	*9 219*	*Asie méridionale*
..	..	..	..	..	..	..	..	Afghanistan
0	1	2	3	29	15	13	53	Bangladesh
..	..	..	..	..	..	..	..	Bhoutan
4	6	514	2 985	16 031	15 933	12 456	8 583	Inde
7	0	22	452	356	346	360	430	Iran (Rép. islamique d')
..	..	..	..	..	..	..	..	Maldives
..	..	..	..	..	..	..	..	Népal
..	2	11	45	71	47	62	73	Pakistan
0	1	2	38	20	43	60	80	Sri Lanka

Pour les sources et les notes, se reporter à la fin du tableau.

7

Region, country or territory	Inward flows - Flux entrants Millions of dollars							
	1980	1990	2000	2005	2009	2010	2011	2012
South-Eastern Asia	*2 636*	*12 821*	*22 641*	*43 300*	*47 810*	*97 898*	*109 044*	*111 336*
Brunei Darussalam	-20	7	550	289	371	626	1 208	850
Cambodia	1	..	149	381	539	783	902	1 557
Indonesia (...2002)	180	1 092	-4 550					
Indonesia	–	–	–	8 336	4 877	13 771	19 241	19 853
Lao People's Dem. Rep.	..	6	34	28	190	279	301	294
Malaysia	934	2 611	3 788	4 065	1 453	9 060	12 198	10 074
Myanmar	0	225	208	235	973	1 285	2 200	2 243
Philippines	114	550	2 240	1 854	1 963	1 298	1 816	2 797
Singapore	1 236	5 575	15 515	18 090	24 939	53 623	55 923	56 651
Thailand	189	2 575	3 410	8 067	4 854	9 147	7 779	8 607
Timor-Leste	–	–	–	1	50	29	47	42
Viet Nam	2	180	1 298	1 954	7 600	8 000	7 430	8 368
Western Asia	*-3 328*	*804*	*3 586*	*44 497*	*71 919*	*59 459*	*49 058*	*47 119*
Bahrain	-418	-183	364	1 049	257	156	781	891
Iraq	2	0	-3	515	1 598	1 396	2 082	2 549
Jordan	34	38	913	1 984	2 413	1 651	1 474	1 403
Kuwait	1	6	16	234	1 114	456	855	1 851
Lebanon	-12	6	964	3 321	4 804	4 280	3 485	3 787
Oman	98	142	83	1 538	1 485	1 243	739	1 514
Qatar	11	5	252	2 500	8 125	4 670	-87	327
Saudi Arabia	-3 192	312	183	12 097	36 458	29 233	16 308	12 182
State of Palestine	..	..	62	47	301	180	214	244
Syrian Arab Republic	0	40	270	583	2 570	1 469	..	..
Turkey	18	684	982	10 031	8 663	9 036	16 047	12 419
United Arab Emirates	98	-116	-506	10 900	4 003	5 500	7 679	9 602
Yemen, Arab Republic	34	–	–	–	–	–	–	–
Yemen	–	-131	6	-302	129	189	-518	349
Developing economies: Oceania	**-**	**333**	**292**	**551**	**2 486**	**2 939**	**2 032**	**2 154**
Cook Islands	..	..	59	6	-6	..	..	..
Fiji	36	84	3	160	142	355	417	268
French Polynesia	..	22	2	8	22	115	123	87
Kiribati	..	0	1	3	3	-7	-2	-2
Marshall Islands	–	1	126	296	555	275	-142	38
Micronesia (Federated States of)	–	..	..	0	1	1	1	1
Nauru	..	1	1	1	1	..	..	..
New Caledonia	2	31	-41	-7	1 182	1 863	1 702	1 588
Niue	..	..	5	..	..	..	..	..
Northern Mariana Islands	–	7	2	-8	0	15	-1	5
Palau	–	1	..	1	1	7	6	5
Papua New Guinea	76	155	98	34	423	29	-309	29
Samoa	0	7	-1	4	10	1	12	22
Solomon Islands	2	10	13	19	120	238	146	69
Tonga	..	0	5	8	0	7	19	7
Vanuatu	5	13	20	28	32	41	58	38
Transition economies	**24**	**75**	**7 038**	**33 612**	**72 750**	**75 056**	**96 290**	**87 382**
Albania	..	..	144	264	996	1 051	1 036	957
Armenia	–	–	104	239	778	570	525	489
Azerbaijan	–	–	130	1 680	473	563	1 467	2 005
Belarus	–	–	119	307	1 877	1 393	4 002	1 442
Bosnia and Herzegovina	–	–	146	351	149	324	380	633
Croatia	–	–	1 051	1 825	3 339	432	1 502	1 251
Georgia	–	–	131	453	659	814	1 048	866
Kazakhstan	–	–	1 283	1 971	13 243	11 551	13 903	14 022
Kyrgyzstan	–	–	-2	43	189	438	694	372
Montenegro	–	–	–	–	1 527	760	558	610
Republic of Moldova	–	–	128	191	145	197	281	159
Russian Federation	–	–	2 714	15 508	36 583	43 168	55 084	51 416
Serbia and Montenegro	–	–	52	2 211			–	–
Serbia	–	–	–	–	2 364	1 813	3 258	650
SFR of Yugoslavia (1)	24	71	–	–	–	–	–	–
Tajikistan	–	–	24	54	16	16	11	290
TFYR of Macedonia	–	–	215	96	201	212	468	135
Turkmenistan	–	–	131	418	4 553	3 631	3 399	3 159
Ukraine	–	–	595	7 808	4 816	6 495	7 207	7 833
USSR (2)	0	4	–	–	–	–	–	–
Uzbekistan	–	–	75	192	842	1 628	1 467	1 094

For sources and notes, see end of table.

Outward flows - Flux sortants Millions de dollars								Régions, pays ou territoires
1980	1990	2000	2005	2009	2010	2011	2012	
-	2 328	8 972	18 529	39 345	47 414	58 957	60 592	**Asie du Sud-Est**
..	0	30	15	9	6	10	8	Brunéi Darussalam
..	..	7	6	19	21	29	31	Cambodge
6	-11	150	—	—	—	—	—	Indonésie (…2002)
—	—	—	3 065	2 249	2 664	7 713	5 423	Indonésie
..	0	4	-6	1	-1	0	-21	Rép. dém. populaire lao
201	129	2 026	3 076	7 784	13 399	15 249	17 115	Malaisie
..	..	..	..	..	..	..	..	Myanmar
86	22	125	189	359	616	539	1 845	Philippines
98	2 034	6 650	11 589	24 051	25 341	26 249	23 080	Singapour
3	154	-20	529	4 172	4 467	8 217	11 911	Thaïlande
—	—	—	—	..	..	..	..	Timor-Leste
..	..	..	65	700	900	950	1 200	Viet Nam
-	-969	2 933	12 452	17 890	13 398	26 184	23 941	**Asie occidentale**
0	25	10	1 135	-1 791	334	894	922	Bahreïn
..	..	..	89	72	125	366	549	Iraq
3	-31	9	163	72	28	31	5	Jordanie
407	-239	-303	5 142	8 584	1 530	8 896	7 562	Koweït
2	-16	108	715	1 126	487	754	611	Liban
..	..	..	234	109	1 498	1 220	1 371	Oman
2	2	18	352	3 215	1 863	6 027	1 840	Qatar
211	-638	1 550	-350	2 177	3 907	3 430	4 402	Arabie saoudite
..	..	213	13	-15	77	-37	-2	État de Palestine
..	3	44	80	..	..	..	..	République arabe syrienne
..	-16	870	1 064	1 553	1 464	2 349	4 073	Turquie
-2	-58	424	3 750	2 723	2 015	2 178	2 536	Émirats arabes unis
..	—	—	—	—	—	—	—	Yémen, République arabe du
—	..	-9	65	66	70	77	71	Yémen
-	-	-	418	84	701	925	-	**Économies en développement : Océanie**
..	..	0	296	13	540	809	454	Îles Cook
2	3	2	10	3	6	1	2	Fidji
..	..	..	16	8	89	28	42	Polynésie française
..	..	0	0	-1	0	..	..	Kiribati
—	..	-15	52	-7	-15	41	13	Îles Marshall
—	..	..	..	..	..	..	..	Micronésie (États fédérés de)
-6	4	..	..	..	..	..	..	Nauru
..	..	2	31	58	76	40	58	Nouvelle-Calédonie
..	..	5	1	0	..	-1	..	Nioué
..	..	..	..	..	0	0	0	Îles Mariannes du Nord
—	-1	-1	-2	..	..	..	..	Palaos
16	8	1	7	4	0	1	..	Papouasie-Nouvelle-Guinée
..	..	..	1	1	..	1	9	Samoa
..	..	0	2	3	2	4	3	Îles Salomon
..	0	..	5	0	2	1	1	Tonga
..	..	..	1	1	1	1	1	Vanuatu
-	-	3 197	19 422	48 369	61 872	72 880	55 491	**Économies en transition**
..	..	..	4	36	6	42	23	Albanie
—	—	..	7	53	8	78	16	Arménie
—	—	1	1 221	326	232	554	1 194	Azerbaïdjan
—	—	0	3	102	51	126	99	Bélarus
—	—	..	0	-95	78	2	36	Bosnie-Herzégovine
—	—	5	239	1 233	-146	30	-99	Croatie
—	—	3	-89	-19	135	147	263	Géorgie
—	—	4	-146	3 159	7 885	4 630	1 582	Kazakhstan
—	—	5	..	0	0	0	0	Kirghizistan
—	—	—	—	46	29	17	27	Monténégro
—	—	0	0	7	4	21	20	République de Moldova
—	—	3 177	17 880	43 281	52 616	66 851	51 058	Fédération de Russie
—	—	2	27	—	—	—	—	Serbie-et-Monténégro
—	—	—	—	67	235	191	75	Serbie
..	..	—	—	—	—	—	—	RSF de Yougoslavie (1)
—	—	..	..	..	..	..	..	Tadjikistan
—	—	-1	3	11	2	0	-8	LERY de Macédoine
—	—	..	..	..	..	..	..	Turkménistan
—	—	1	275	162	736	192	1 206	Ukraine
0	0	—	—	—	—	—	—	URSS (2)
—	—	..	..	..	..	..	..	Ouzbékistan

Pour les sources et les notes, se reporter à la fin du tableau.

Region, country or territory	Inward flows - Flux entrants Millions of dollars							
	1980	1990	2000	2005	2009	2010	2011	2012
Developed economies: America	-	-	380 869	130 508	166 233	227 240	268 214	213 123
Bermuda	..	..	67	44	-71	249	-109	128
Canada	5 807	7 582	66 795	25 692	22 700	29 086	41 386	45 375
United States	16 918	48 422	314 007	104 773	143 604	197 905	226 937	167 620
Developed economies: Asia	287	1 943	15 280	7 594	16 546	4 259	9 325	12 145
Israel	9	137	6 957	4 818	4 607	5 510	11 081	10 414
Japan	278	1 806	8 323	2 775	11 939	-1 251	-1 755	1 731
Developed economies: Europe	21 363	104 414	728 480	506 109	404 791	429 230	472 852	275 580
Austria	239	653	8 501	10 784	9 303	840	11 378	6 315
Belgium (3)	1 545	8 047	88 739	34 370	60 963	85 676	103 280	-1 614
Bulgaria	..	4	1 016	3 920	3 385	1 525	1 827	1 899
Cyprus	85	127	855	1 170	3 472	766	1 372	849
Czechoslovakia	0	165	–	–	–	–	–	–
Czech Republic	–	–	4 985	11 653	2 927	6 141	2 318	10 592
Denmark	104	1 132	33 823	12 871	3 917	-11 540	12 685	2 883
Estonia	–	–	392	2 869	1 840	1 599	257	1 470
Finland	28	787	8 834	4 750	718	7 359	2 668	-1 806
France	3 328	15 629	43 252	84 954	24 219	33 627	38 547	25 093
Germany, Federal Republic of	342	–	–	–	–	–	–	–
Germany	–	2 962	198 277	47 439	22 460	57 428	48 937	6 565
Gibraltar	2	36	138	122	172	165	166	168
Greece	672	1 005	1 108	623	2 436	330	1 143	2 945
Hungary	..	554	2 764	7 709	1 995	2 163	5 757	13 469
Iceland	22	22	171	3 071	86	246	1 108	511
Ireland	286	622	25 779	-31 689	25 715	42 804	11 467	29 318
Italy	577	6 345	13 375	23 291	20 077	9 178	34 324	9 625
Latvia	–	–	413	707	94	380	1 466	988
Lithuania	–	–	379	1 028	-14	800	1 448	835
Luxembourg	..	..	582	6 564	19 946	34 753	22 166	27 878
Malta	27	46	582	676	372	980	413	157
Netherlands	2 005	10 514	63 855	39 047	38 610	-7 366	17 179	-244
Norway	60	1 564	7 090	2 181	16 641	16 824	18 205	12 775
Poland	10	88	9 445	10 293	12 932	13 876	18 911	3 356
Portugal	165	2 902	6 635	3 930	2 706	2 646	11 150	8 916
Romania	0	0	1 057	6 483	4 844	2 940	2 523	2 242
Slovakia	–	–	2 720	3 110	-6	1 770	2 143	2 826
Slovenia	–	–	133	588	-653	359	999	145
Spain	1 493	13 294	39 575	25 020	10 407	39 873	26 816	27 750
Sweden	251	1 971	23 433	11 626	10 033	-64	9 246	13 711
Switzerland	0	5 484	19 255	-951	28 891	32 550	11 817	3 613
United Kingdom	10 123	30 461	121 898	177 901	76 301	50 604	51 137	62 351
Developed economies: Oceania	2 200	10 164	16 959	-22 726	25 867	35 689	69 617	59 870
Australia	1 866	8 479	15 612	-24 246	26 701	35 242	65 297	56 959
New Zealand	334	1 685	1 347	1 519	-834	448	4 320	2 911

Source:

UNCTAD, *FDI/TNC database*

Notes:

- Foreign direct investment (FDI) is defined as an investment involving a long-term relationship and reflecting a lasting interest in and control by a resident entity in one economy (foreign direct investor or parent enterprise) of an enterprise resident in a different economy (FDI enterprise or affiliate enterprise or foreign affiliate). Such investment involves both the initial transaction between the two entities and all subsequent transactions between them and among foreign affiliates.

  FDI inflows and outflows comprise capital provided (either directly or through other related enterprises) by a foreign direct investor to a FDI enterprise, or capital received by a foreign direct investor from a FDI enterprise. FDI includes the three following components: equity capital, reinvested earnings and intra-company loans. Data on FDI flows are presented on net bases (capital transactions' credits less debits between direct investors and their foreign affiliates). Net decreases in assets or net increases in liabilities are recorded as credits, while net increases in assets or net decreases in liabilities are recorded as debits. Hence, FDI flows with a negative sign indicate that at least one of the three components of FDI is negative and not offset by positive amounts of the remaining components. These are called reverse investment or disinvestment.

(1) Data from 1988 to 1991 inclusive refer to Slovenia only, except for the FDI inflows that also cover other Republics of the former SFR Yugoslavia.

(2) Partial data; total USSR territory is not covered.

(3) Data from 1970 to 2001 inclusive refer to Belgium-Luxembourg Economic Union; from 2002 onwards data cover Belgium only.

Outward flows - Flux sortants Millions de dollars								Régions, pays ou territoires
1980	1990	2000	2005	2009	2010	2011	2012	
-	-	187 318	42 939	306 567	339 108	446 168	383 030	Économies développées : Amérique
..	..	14	31	11	-14	-337	222	Bermudes
4 098	5 237	44 678	27 538	39 601	34 723	49 849	53 939	Canada
19 230	30 982	142 626	15 369	266 955	304 399	396 656	328 869	États-Unis
2 382	51 036	34 892	48 727	76 450	64 920	110 910	125 729	Économies développées : Asie
-3	261	3 335	2 946	1 751	8 656	3 309	3 178	Israël
2 385	50 775	31 557	45 781	74 699	56 263	107 601	122 551	Japon
22 156	139 341	863 805	685 168	429 790	598 007	609 201	384 973	Économies développées : Europe
101	1 701	5 509	11 145	10 006	9 994	24 782	16 648	Autriche
196	6 314	86 362	32 658	7 525	43 894	82 492	14 668	Belgique (3)
..	-3	3	310	-95	230	101	227	Bulgarie
..	5	172	550	383	679	846	-1 929	Chypre
0	20	–	–	–	–	–	–	Tchécoslovaquie
–	–	43	-19	949	1 167	-327	1 341	République tchèque
196	1 482	26 549	16 193	6 305	-107	13 299	7 596	Danemark
–	–	61	691	1 547	142	-1 458	886	Estonie
137	2 708	24 030	4 223	5 681	10 167	4 878	4 533	Finlande
3 137	36 233	177 449	114 978	107 130	64 575	59 553	37 197	France
4 699	–	–	–	–	–	–	–	Allemagne, Rép. fédérale d'
–	24 235	56 557	75 893	69 643	121 525	52 168	66 926	Allemagne
..	..	..	..	..	..	..	..	Gibraltar
0	11	2 137	1 468	2 055	1 558	1 772	-39	Grèce
..	..	620	2 179	1 883	1 135	4 693	10 578	Hongrie
0	12	390	7 072	2 292	-2 357	23	-3 318	Islande
..	364	4 629	14 313	26 616	22 348	-4 290	18 966	Irlande
740	7 614	6 686	39 362	21 275	32 655	53 629	30 397	Italie
–	–	12	128	-62	19	62	190	Lettonie
–	–	4	346	198	-6	55	402	Lituanie
..	..	..	9 932	1 522	21 435	9 169	17 273	Luxembourg
..	..	20	-21	65	87	20	-89	Malte
3 847	13 658	75 634	123 072	34 471	68 332	40 900	-3 509	Pays-Bas
253	1 583	9 505	23 678	19 165	23 274	25 362	20 847	Norvège
21	5	17	3 437	4 699	7 226	7 211	-894	Pologne
12	163	8 132	2 111	816	-7 493	14 905	1 915	Portugal
0	18	-13	-31	-88	-20	-33	42	Roumanie
–	–	41	191	904	946	490	-73	Slovaquie
–	–	65	641	260	-211	112	-94	Slovénie
311	3 349	58 213	41 829	13 070	37 844	36 578	-4 869	Espagne
625	14 746	40 907	27 712	25 908	20 178	28 158	33 428	Suède
0	7 176	44 673	51 118	26 378	79 290	47 316	44 313	Suisse
7 881	17 948	235 398	80 009	39 287	39 502	106 673	71 415	Royaume-Uni
531	2 988	4 831	-32 427	15 198	27 802	16 810	15 652	Économies développées : Océanie
460	624	4 221	-31 137	16 233	27 271	14 285	16 141	Australie
71	2 363	610	-1 290	-1 035	530	2 525	-489	Nouvelle-Zélande

Source :

CNUCED, *base de données IED/STN*

Notes :

- L'investissement étranger direct (IED) est un investissement impliquant une relation à long terme et témoignant de l'intérêt durable d'une entité résidant dans un pays (investisseur étranger direct ou société mère) à l'égard d'une entreprise résidant dans un autre pays (entreprise bénéficiaire, entreprise affiliée, ou encore filiale étrangère). Cet investissement englobe à la fois la transaction initiale entre les deux entités et toutes les transactions ultérieures entre elles et entre filiales étrangères.

  Les flux entrants et sortants de l'IED comprennent les capitaux fournis par l'investisseur direct (soit directement, soit par l'intermédiaire d'autres entreprises avec lesquelles il est lié) à l'entreprise d'investissement direct ou les capitaux reçus de cette entreprise par l'investisseur. L'IED est composé des trois catégories suivantes : le capital social, les bénéfices réinvestis et les emprunts intra-compagnie. Les données sur l'IED se présentent sur une base nette (les crédits moins les débits des transactions en capital entre l'investisseur direct et son entreprise apparentée). Les augmentations nettes en passifs et les décroissances nettes en actifs se déclarent comme crédits, tandis que les augmentations nettes en actifs et les décroissances nettes en passifs se déclarent comme débits. Les flux de l'IED précédés d'un signe négatif indiquent qu'au moins une des trois catégories de l'IED est négative et n'est pas contrebalancée par les valeurs positives des autres catégories. Il s'agit alors de désinvestissements ou de réductions d'investissement.

(1)   Les données de 1988 à 1991 se réfèrent seulement à la Slovénie, à l'exception des flux entrants qui comprennent aussi d'autres Républiques de l'ex Yougoslavie (RSF).

(2)   Données partielles : elles ne couvrent pas la totalité du territoire de l'URSS.

(3)   Les données de 1970 à 2001 se réfèrent à l'Union économique belgo-luxembourgeoise ; à partir de 2002 les données couvrent uniquement la Belgique.

7.2.2 Foreign direct investment: Inward and outward flows of economic groupings

Economic grouping	Inward flows - Flux entrants Millions of dollars							
	1980	1990	2000	2005	2009	2010	2011	2012
DEVELOPING ECONOMIES	7 469	34 762	264 543	334 521	530 289	637 063	735 212	702 826
Developing economies excluding China	7 412	31 275	223 828	262 115	435 289	522 329	611 227	581 746
Developing economies excluding LDCs	6 931	34 189	260 407	326 999	512 703	618 312	713 769	677 123
High-income developing economies	4 490	22 555	199 987	184 383	302 025	393 790	451 131	414 775
Middle-income developing economies	2 668	9 519	53 961	123 654	153 645	181 124	200 510	207 447
Low-income developing economies	312	2 689	10 595	26 484	74 618	62 148	83 571	80 604
Heavily indebted poor countries (IMF)	791	831	4 181	9 568	18 193	23 246	27 782	34 701
Landlocked developing countries	384	603	3 955	6 888	26 287	26 836	34 369	34 592
Small island developing States	360	781	2 770	4 337	5 011	4 699	5 636	6 217
Least developed countries	*538*	*574*	*4 136*	*7 522*	*17 586*	*18 751*	*21 443*	*25 703*
Africa and Haiti	478	432	3 124	5 986	14 679	14 619	16 913	19 833
Asia	53	111	975	1 467	2 663	3 772	4 210	5 635
Islands	7	31	37	70	243	361	320	235
Major petroleum and gas exporters	*-4 264*	*1 632*	*7 529*	*39 302*	*70 572*	*55 040*	*43 967*	*37 726*
Africa	-1 442	867	2 609	5 794	16 911	7 045	8 462	1 615
America	80	778	4 701	2 589	-2 169	1 849	3 778	3 216
Asia	-2 902	-13	218	30 920	55 830	46 146	31 726	32 895
Major exporters of manufactured goods	*5 397*	*22 275*	*166 429*	*175 971*	*208 847*	*303 246*	*325 803*	*296 765*
America	2 099	2 633	18 282	24 449	16 561	21 372	21 504	12 659
Asia	3 298	19 641	148 147	151 522	192 286	281 873	304 299	284 105
Emerging economies	*7 458*	*19 040*	*104 074*	*92 612*	*108 857*	*185 987*	*213 397*	*221 486*
America	4 928	6 160	67 149	54 456	65 844	101 555	129 209	133 045
Asia	2 531	12 879	36 924	38 156	43 012	84 432	84 188	88 441
Newly industrialized Asian economies	*3 535*	*17 796*	*105 122*	*89 306*	*104 127*	*182 208*	*201 371*	*185 675*
First tier	2 118	10 968	100 234	66 984	90 979	148 932	160 338	144 344
Second tier	1 417	6 828	4 888	22 322	13 148	33 275	41 034	41 331
Developing economies: Africa	400	2 846	9 621	30 913	52 964	43 582	47 598	50 041
Northern Africa excluding Sudan	144	1 187	2 858	9 932	16 408	13 645	5 805	9 035
Sub-Saharan Africa	257	1 660	6 763	20 981	36 557	29 937	41 794	41 006
Sub-Saharan Africa excluding South Africa	267	1 738	5 876	14 334	31 191	28 708	35 789	36 433
Developing economies: America	6 416	8 925	98 048	78 054	150 150	189 855	249 432	243 861
Central America and Greater Caribbean Islands excluding Puerto Rico	2 639	3 371	21 907	30 119	23 933	29 974	32 581	25 884
Central America and Greater Caribbean Islands excluding Mexico and Puerto Rico	539	738	3 625	5 670	7 372	8 601	11 077	13 225
South America and Central America	6 026	8 098	77 528	72 329	77 908	119 834	159 330	166 136
South America excluding Brazil	1 610	4 053	24 277	28 975	30 771	43 628	62 763	79 130
Developing economies: Asia	532	22 658	156 581	225 004	324 688	400 687	436 150	406 770
Eastern and South-Eastern Asia excluding China	3 518	18 154	107 416	93 672	115 332	197 768	218 877	205 060
Southern Asia excluding India	205	-24	1 276	6 807	6 780	7 601	8 040	7 968

For sources and notes, see end of table 7.2.1.

Outward flows - Flux sortants Millions de dollars								Groupements économiques
1980	1990	2000	2005	2009	2010	2011	2012	
3 179	**11 838**	**146 273**	**139 935**	**273 401**	**413 220**	**422 067**	**426 082**	**ÉCONOMIES EN DÉVELOPPEMENT**
-	11 008	145 358	127 673	216 871	344 409	347 413	341 862	Économies en développement sans la Chine
2 945	11 841	145 487	139 209	272 307	410 220	419 028	421 052	Économies en développement sans les PMA
2 667	10 257	142 624	114 261	184 911	305 273	302 706	304 559	Économies en développement à revenu élevé
261	1 121	2 133	21 967	69 008	87 789	103 550	107 019	Économies en développement à revenu intermédiaire
-	-	-	3 707	19 482	20 158	15 810	14 505	Économies en développement à revenu faible
-	-	-	-	899	2 050	1 028	2 406	Pays pauvres très endettés (FMI)
-	-	-	1 122	3 962	9 279	5 447	3 071	Pays en développement sans littoral
-	-	205	813	287	301	1 789	1 799	Petits États insulaires en développement
-	**-**	**-**	**-**	**1 095**	**2 999**	**-**	**-**	***Pays les moins avancés***
-	-5	-	-	974	2 890	2 914	4 884	Afrique et Haïti
-	-	-	-	-	-	-	-	Asie
..	-	-	18	5	-	-	-	Îles
723	***-32***	***2 512***	***11 177***	***22 400***	***18 265***	***24 918***	***27 898***	***Principaux exportateurs de pétrole et de gaz***
85	525	281	342	2 929	5 206	3 582	6 748	Afrique
12	375	521	1 167	2 236	1 776	-1 141	2 460	Amérique
625	-933	1 710	9 669	17 235	11 284	22 478	18 690	Asie
455	***12 113***	***91 122***	***80 229***	***182 211***	***265 409***	***274 158***	***291 917***	***Principaux exportateurs d'articles manufacturés***
3	223	363	6 474	8 464	15 045	12 139	25 597	Amérique
452	11 889	90 759	73 755	173 747	250 364	262 020	266 320	Asie
673	***9 551***	***27 371***	***40 025***	***66 012***	***120 463***	***124 565***	***143 012***	***Économies émergentes***
303	940	7 532	12 437	6 735	37 324	33 084	44 897	Amérique
370	8 611	19 839	27 589	59 277	83 139	91 480	98 115	Asie
544	***11 070***	***90 119***	***64 748***	***119 825***	***184 833***	***195 618***	***189 368***	***Économies nouvellement industrialisées d'Asie***
248	10 776	87 837	57 889	105 261	163 687	163 899	153 075	Première génération
296	294	2 281	6 859	14 564	21 147	31 718	36 294	Deuxième génération
1 097	**659**	**1 534**	**2 051**	**6 281**	**9 311**	**5 376**	**14 296**	**Économies en développement : Afrique**
87	135	223	289	2 498	4 781	1 498	3 054	Afrique septentrionale sans le Soudan
-	524	-	1 762	3 782	4 530	3 878	11 242	Afrique subsaharienne
-	496	-	832	2 631	4 606	4 135	6 873	Afrique subsaharienne sans l'Afrique du Sud
893	**222**	**50 179**	**44 337**	**55 512**	**119 236**	**105 154**	**103 045**	**Économies en développement : Amérique**
351	857	-174	8 012	9 954	15 581	13 950	27 530	Amérique centrale et Grandes Antilles sans Porto Rico
-	634	-537	1 538	1 489	536	1 811	1 933	Amérique centrale et Grandes Antilles sans le Mexique et Porto Rico
771	1 941	7 731	19 739	13 845	46 493	41 893	49 072	Amérique du Sud et Amérique centrale
54	488	5 759	9 332	14 004	19 360	29 022	24 354	Amérique du Sud sans le Brésil
1 178	**10 943**	**94 565**	**93 128**	**211 525**	**283 972**	**310 612**	**308 159**	**Économies en développement : Asie**
-	11 072	90 165	64 891	120 597	185 380	196 822	190 780	Asie orientale et Asie du Sud-Est sans la Chine
-	-	-	-	-	-	-	-	Asie méridionale sans l'Inde

Pour les sources et les notes, se reporter à la fin du tableau 7.2.1.

7.2.3 Foreign direct investment: Inward and outward flows of trade groups

Trade group	Inward flows - Flux entrants Millions of dollars							
	1980	1990	2000	2005	2009	2010	2011	2012
AFRICA								
CEMAC	206	4	549	2 641	5 229	6 356	6 289	6 477
CEPGL	131	-6	92	281	783	2 982	1 796	3 473
COMESA	-208	1 250	2 992	10 457	16 350	18 003	8 945	14 932
EAC	109	60	593	1 351	2 028	2 578	2 568	3 846
ECCAS	374	-336	1 523	1 634	8 233	6 162	5 096	3 101
ECOWAS	-461	1 547	2 095	6 359	14 712	11 846	17 117	15 612
MRU	148	324	304	590	846	1 129	2 465	3 316
SADC	371	55	3 210	8 117	13 177	8 198	12 865	11 788
UMA	-378	459	1 662	5 370	9 693	7 390	6 876	7 442
WAEMU	208	239	514	783	2 537	2 282	2 646	2 301
AMERICA								
ANCOM	301	734	3 959	13 036	14 297	16 018	23 168	29 709
CACM	188	268	1 460	2 721	3 255	3 865	5 549	5 856
CARICOM	262	428	2 098	3 778	3 269	3 022	5 123	5 486
FTAA	29 088	64 703	461 384	207 429	249 416	351 618	434 666	387 724
LAIA	5 820	7 880	76 074	69 348	74 425	115 847	153 397	159 780
MERCOSUR	3 035	3 783	49 009	23 516	29 843	61 364	83 898	85 129
NAFTA	24 825	58 638	399 084	154 914	182 864	248 363	289 827	225 654
OAS	29 088	64 703	461 384	207 429	249 416	351 618	434 666	387 724
OECS	51	221	10 244	-8 395	47 180	49 606	63 207	65 383
ASIA								
APTA	194	4 565	54 372	87 481	140 912	147 639	172 840	158 587
ASEAN	2 636	12 821	22 641	43 299	47 760	97 870	108 997	111 294
ECO	172	600	3 124	19 997	33 440	32 743	42 548	39 171
GCC	-3 403	166	391	28 318	51 441	41 258	26 275	26 367
SAARC	203	575	4 671	11 293	39 390	25 079	40 081	28 641
EUROPE								
EFTA	82	7 070	26 517	4 300	45 618	49 620	31 130	16 898
EU27	21 279	97 308	701 826	501 687	359 000	379 444	441 557	258 514
Euro area	10 791	62 933	502 612	257 496	242 585	312 621	334 239	146 187
OCEANIA								
MSG	119	263	134	239	717	663	313	404
INTERREGIONAL								
ACP	731	2 484	10 145	26 434	43 320	35 827	49 444	50 614
APEC	31 193	92 935	580 532	324 135	484 092	655 394	777 621	697 236
BSEC	690	1 693	8 110	47 200	66 142	68 502	91 447	83 881
CIS	–	–	5 299	28 411	63 514	69 650	88 040	82 281

For sources and notes, see end of table 7.2.1.

Outward flows - Flux sortants Millions de dollars								Groupements commerciaux
1980	1990	2000	2005	2009	2010	2011	2012	
								AFRIQUE
0	51	35	-	-	-	-	-	CEMAC
..	-	-	-	-	-	-	-	CEPGL
-	141	-	-	2 224	5 283	1 108	3 608	COMESA
-	-	..	-	-	-	-	-	CAE
0	52	-	-	-	-	-	-	CEEAC
-	412	965	416	2 115	1 288	1 467	3 022	CEDEAO
-	6	788	-	354	394	388	1 383	UFM
-	60	311	1 269	1 500	2 591	2 080	7 841	SADC
80	123	172	199	1 932	3 609	877	2 847	UMA
-3	-10	16	-28	203	-4	243	125	UEMOA
								AMÉRIQUE
108	70	343	4 677	3 799	7 222	8 312	-288	ANCOM
8	-	60	-117	37	47	93	472	MCAC
-	-	284	671	243	172	1 644	1 682	CARICOM
24 215	38 190	195 372	63 310	320 607	385 762	490 016	433 533	ZLEA
764	1 938	7 662	19 827	13 803	46 444	41 799	48 598	ALADI
269	1 036	3 711	5 040	-7 115	14 236	-689	730	MERCOSUR
23 332	36 442	187 667	49 381	315 020	354 167	458 644	408 404	ALENA
24 215	38 190	195 372	63 310	320 607	385 762	490 016	433 533	OEA
-	-	34 498	17 805	35 161	58 733	52 245	42 404	OECO
								ASIE
30	1 889	5 920	21 648	90 004	113 158	116 182	125 893	ACAP
-	2 328	8 972	18 529	39 345	47 414	58 957	60 592	ANASE
-	-14	912	-	5 465	9 974	7 956	7 352	ECO
618	-908	1 698	10 263	15 016	11 147	22 645	18 633	CCG
-	-	-	-	-	-	-	-	SAARC
								EUROPE
253	8 770	54 568	81 868	47 835	100 206	72 702	61 842	AELE
21 902	130 571	809 238	603 300	381 955	497 801	536 499	323 131	UE27
13 181	96 354	505 697	473 037	302 972	428 476	376 546	198 806	Zone euro
								OCÉANIE
-	-	4	20	12	9	6	5	MSG
								INTERRÉGIONAUX
-	570	1 650	2 825	4 011	5 216	6 354	13 379	ACP
26 851	102 170	322 284	159 847	632 911	755 125	941 624	893 494	CEAP
-	10	6 178	22 107	47 339	57 205	72 324	58 158	CEMN
–	–	3 188	19 239	47 090	61 532	72 451	55 174	CEI

Pour les sources et les notes, se reporter à la fin du tableau 7.2.1.

7

7.3.1 Migrants' remittances: Receipts of countries and geographical regions

Region, country or territory	Millions of dollars - Millions de dollars							
	1980	1990	2000	2005	2009	2010	2011	2012 (e)
WORLD	**41 734**	**80 682**	**138 610**	**288 812**	**436 879**	**464 449**	**515 425**	**527 727**
DEVELOPING ECONOMIES	18 993	34 522	82 803	188 679	293 845	318 479	355 060	375 017
TRANSITION ECONOMIES	4 102	9 360	6 170	12 262	27 330	28 237	32 583	32 095
DEVELOPED ECONOMIES	18 639	36 801	49 637	87 871	115 704	117 733	127 781	120 615
Developing economies: Africa	**5 862**	**8 864**	**11 486**	**33 410**	**45 461**	**52 126**	**56 092**	**62 437**
Eastern Africa	*158*	*112*	*1 100*	*1 371*	*2 279*	*2 482*	*3 241*	*3 467*
Burundi	..	..	..	0	28	34	45	42
Comoros	2	10	-	-	-	-	-	..
Djibouti	..	..	12	26	32	33	32	32
Eritrea	–	–	3	..	..	..	..	..
Ethiopia (…1991)	(a)12	(a)5						
Ethiopia	–	–	53	174	262	345	513	524
Kenya	13	8	-	425	631	686	934	1 228
Madagascar	0	8	11	11	-	-	-	..
Malawi	..	..	1	23	17	17	17	16
Mauritius	..	..	177	215	211	226	249	247
Mozambique	53	70	37	59	111	132	157	99
Rwanda	3	3	7	21	93	103	171	156
Seychelles	..	8	3	12	16	17	26	26
Somalia	57	..	..	..	..	..	..	..
Uganda	..	..	238	322	778	768	949	977
United Republic of Tanzania	..	..	8	19	40	55	76	75
Zambia	..	..	..	53	41	44	46	46
Zimbabwe	17	1	..	..	..	..	..	..
Middle Africa	*33*	*29*	*51*	*108*	*218*	*162*	*146*	*116*
Angola	..	..	-	-	0	18	0	0
Cameroon	29	23	30	77	192	115	115	109
Central African Republic	0	0	..	..	..	..	..	..
Congo	3	-	10	11	-	-	-	..
Gabon	0	-	6	11	-	-	-	..
Sao Tome and Principe	1	0	0	2	2	6	7	6
Northern Africa	*4 737*	*7 255*	*7 249*	*13 778*	*19 594*	*24 101*	*25 988*	*32 576*
Algeria	406	352	790	2 060	2 059	2 044	1 942	1 843
Egypt	2 696	4 284	2 852	5 017	7 150	12 453	14 324	20 515
Libya	..	..	9	15	-	-	-	..
Morocco	1 054	2 006	2 161	4 590	6 270	6 423	7 256	6 894
Sudan (…2011)	262	62	641	704	2 135	1 100	442	–
Sudan	–	–	–	–	–	–	–	1 126
Tunisia	319	551	796	1 393	1 964	2 063	2 004	2 198
Southern Africa	*443*	*775*	*914*	*1 502*	*1 667*	*1 863*	*1 995*	*1 835*
Botswana	77	86	26	131	110	63	63	55
Lesotho	263	428	478	599	548	610	649	602
Namibia	..	13	9	18	14	16	16	17
South Africa	67	136	344	658	902	1 119	1 212	1 115
Swaziland	35	113	57	95	93	55	55	47
Western Africa	*491*	*693*	*2 172*	*16 650*	*21 703*	*23 518*	*24 722*	*24 443*
Benin	77	101	87	173	150	185	185	179
Burkina Faso	150	140	67	57	111	140	140	130
Cape Verde	40	59	87	137	138	133	178	177
Côte d'Ivoire	32	44	119	163	315	373	373	325
Gambia	-	-	-	59	80	116	91	89
Ghana	1	6	32	99	114	136	152	152
Guinea	..	-	1	42	64	60	78	75
Guinea-Bissau	..	1	-	20	49	46	46	42
Liberia	..	..	..	32	25	31	360	372
Mali	59	107	73	177	454	473	473	444
Mauritania	6	14	-	-	-	-	-	..
Niger	11	14	14	66	102	134	134	122
Nigeria	22	10	1 392	14 640	18 368	19 818	20 619	20 568
Senegal	77	142	233	789	1 350	1 478	1 478	1 367
Sierra Leone	0	0	7	2	47	58	77	79
Togo	10	27	34	193	335	337	337	321

For sources and notes, see end of table.

As percentage of GDP (1) En pourcentage du PIB (1)				As percentage of exports of goods and services (2) En pourcentage des exportations des biens et services (2)				Régions, pays ou territoires
1990	2000	2010	2012 (e)	1990	2000	2010	2012 (e)	
0.40	0.45	0.76	0.78	2.24	1.92	2.64	2.59	**MONDE**
1.02	1.28	1.59	1.58	5.08	4.06	4.81	4.83	ÉCONOMIES EN DÉVELOPPEMENT
11.00	1.63	1.37	1.20	45.26	3.59	4.00	3.39	ÉCONOMIES EN TRANSITION
0.22	0.20	0.30	0.29	1.27	0.99	1.15	1.04	ÉCONOMIES DÉVELOPPÉES
2.10	1.99	3.08	3.40	8.51	6.49	9.09	10.70	**Économies en développement : Afrique**
0.26	*1.95*	*1.56*	*1.75*	*1.89*	*9.41*	*5.56*	*6.42*	*Afrique orientale*
..	..	1.67	1.71	..	..	19.09	17.08	Burundi
4.08	-	-	..	28.55	-	-	..	Comores
..	2.21	2.00	2.25	..	6.36	7.76	7.40	Djibouti
..	0.47	..	..	..	3.36	..	..	Érythrée
0.04	–	–	–	0.87	–	–	–	Éthiopie (...1991)
–	0.66	1.30	1.28	–	5.36	7.43	8.88	Éthiopie
0.07	-	2.13	2.99	0.35	-	7.63	10.60	Kenya
0.26	0.29	-	..	1.67	0.95	-	..	Madagascar
..	0.03	0.31	0.34	..	0.17	1.37	1.18	Malawi
..	3.80	2.33	2.14	..	6.75	4.57	4.06	Maurice
2.37	0.85	1.43	0.67	30.69	5.34	4.50	2.31	Mozambique
0.10	0.37	1.83	2.16	1.84	5.19	16.98	15.40	Rwanda
1.65	0.41	1.80	2.60	3.28	0.66	1.75	2.43	Seychelles
..	..	..	..	..	..	..	..	Somalie
..	3.90	4.33	4.14	..	35.91	22.55	20.36	Ouganda
..	0.08	0.23	0.26	..	0.59	0.86	0.87	République-Unie de Tanzanie
..	..	0.27	0.23	..	..	0.57	0.53	Zambie
0.01	..	..	..	0.04	..	..	..	Zimbabwe
0.12	*0.19*	*0.12*	*0.08*	*0.40*	*0.30*	*0.22*	*0.15*	*Afrique centrale*
..	-	0.02	0.00	..	-	0.03	0.00	Angola
0.19	0.32	0.49	0.42	0.92	1.13	2.03	1.83	Cameroun
0.01	..	..	..	0.04	..	..	..	République centrafricaine
-	0.32	-	..	-	0.39	-	..	Congo
-	0.11	-	..	-	0.17	-	..	Gabon
0.26	0.60	3.07	2.37	3.93	2.80	26.17	21.83	Sao Tomé-et-Principe
4.74	*2.78*	*3.69*	*4.93*	*20.55*	*9.99*	*10.81*	*17.71*	*Afrique septentrionale*
0.57	1.44	1.26	0.88	2.61	3.50	3.37	2.44	Algérie
11.92	2.98	5.80	8.11	43.29	16.91	25.50	42.21	Égypte
..	0.02	-	..	..	0.07	-	..	Libye
6.95	5.84	7.07	7.04	32.16	20.67	21.32	19.81	Maroc
0.49	4.89	1.58		12.40	34.94	9.44		Soudan (...2011)
–	–	–	2.01	–	–	–	41.29	Soudan
4.06	3.71	4.66	4.83	10.59	9.25	9.28	9.89	Tunisie
0.65	*0.63*	*0.47*	*0.43*	*2.49*	*2.13*	*1.66*	*1.49*	*Afrique australe*
2.30	0.47	0.42	0.30	4.27	0.87	1.27	0.87	Botswana
78.56	61.92	28.00	25.45	427.60	177.68	66.42	56.91	Lesotho
0.50	0.24	0.14	0.13	1.10	0.64	0.32	0.34	Namibie
0.12	0.26	0.31	0.29	0.50	0.93	1.12	1.03	Afrique du Sud
10.40	3.73	1.41	1.18	17.15	4.59	2.65	2.20	Swaziland
0.84	*2.48*	*6.80*	*6.00*	*2.82*	*6.62*	*19.72*	*16.69*	*Afrique occidentale*
5.48	3.69	2.81	2.43	27.77	16.48	11.13	10.28	Bénin
4.46	2.56	1.58	1.26	40.00	28.41	7.39	5.32	Burkina Faso
19.20	16.12	8.04	9.33	104.05	59.57	20.83	22.64	Cap-Vert
0.37	1.12	1.63	1.35	1.27	2.73	2.96	2.75	Côte d'Ivoire
-	-	12.02	7.41	-	-	42.76	27.16	Gambie
0.06	0.41	0.43	0.38	0.61	1.33	1.44	0.93	Ghana
-	0.04	1.15	1.22	-	0.16	3.94	4.06	Guinée
0.16	-	5.62	5.09	3.83	-	26.90	29.15	Guinée-Bissau
..	..	2.93	28.79	..	..	7.88	26.76	Libéria
4.26	2.76	5.03	4.45	25.47	11.36	19.38	17.27	Mali
0.84	-	-	..	2.91	-	-	..	Mauritanie
0.53	0.84	2.37	1.89	2.61	4.50	10.57	7.45	Niger
0.03	3.00	8.63	7.43	0.07	6.64	24.83	20.74	Nigéria
2.29	4.99	11.49	9.68	9.78	17.87	46.10	39.12	Sénégal
0.00	0.84	2.27	2.00	0.01	12.96	13.60	6.23	Sierra Leone
1.50	2.65	10.61	8.80	4.05	8.08	25.96	22.61	Togo

Pour les sources et les notes, se reporter à la fin du tableau.

7

Region, country or territory	Millions of dollars - Millions de dollars							
	1980	1990	2000	2005	2009	2010	2011	2012 (e)
Developing economies: America	1 936	5 842	21 074	50 853	58 388	59 050	63 576	62 488
Caribbean	*416*	*786*	*4 355*	*6 709*	*8 295*	*8 694*	*9 394*	*7 697*
Antigua and Barbuda	..	13	21	22	24	24	24	22
Aruba	..	..	8	12	21	16	15	15
Barbados	9	38	115	94	114	82	82	84
Dominica	9	14	16	25	25	26	27	26
Dominican Republic	183	315	1 839	2 719	3 467	3 474	3 682	3 505
Grenada	..	18	46	52	53	53	55	59
Haiti	106	-	578	986	1 376	1 474	1 551	1 625
Jamaica	96	229	892	1 784	1 908	2 044	2 123	2 158
Saint Kitts and Nevis	1	19	27	34	43	52	52	42
Saint Lucia	..	16	26	29	30	32	32	31
Saint Vincent and the Grenadines	..	16	22	26	33	33	34	36
Trinidad and Tobago	6	3	38	92	109	91	91	95
Central America	*1 185*	*3 786*	*10 869*	*31 867*	*33 711*	*34 282*	*36 554*	*37 164*
Belize	..	18	26	46	80	80	77	83
Costa Rica	4	12	136	420	513	552	541	522
El Salvador	49	366	1 765	3 030	3 405	3 449	3 667	3 965
Guatemala	26	119	596	3 067	4 019	4 232	4 508	4 922
Honduras	2	63	484	1 818	2 512	2 655	2 875	2 971
Mexico	1 039	3 098	7 525	22 742	22 076	22 080	23 588	23 219
Nicaragua	..	..	320	616	770	825	914	1 010
Panama, excl. Canal Zone	65	—	—	—	—	—	—	—
Panama	—	110	16	130	336	410	384	472
South America	*336*	*1 269*	*5 850*	*12 276*	*16 382*	*16 073*	*17 627*	*17 627*
Argentina	56	-	86	432	621	639	690	573
Bolivia (Plurinational State of)	1	5	127	346	1 069	953	1 049	1 019
Brazil	111	573	1 649	3 540	4 234	4 000	4 793	4 936
Chile	..	0	13	13	4	3	3	3
Colombia	106	495	1 610	3 346	4 180	4 058	4 205	4 110
Ecuador	-	51	1 322	2 460	2 742	2 599	2 681	2 682
Guyana	..	..	27	201	267	373	373	397
Paraguay	52	34	278	269	619	664	893	872
Peru	..	87	718	1 440	2 409	2 534	2 697	2 808
Suriname	6	1	-	4	5	4	4	4
Uruguay	..	..	..	77	101	103	102	99
Venezuela (Bolivarian Rep. of)	..	1	17	148	131	143	138	126
Developing economies: Asia	11 157	19 708	50 100	103 067	188 380	205 727	233 708	248 420
Eastern Asia	*1 139*	*2 645*	*10 101*	*31 374*	*58 570*	*62 225*	*73 120*	*72 074*
China	-	196	4 822	23 478	47 930	52 269	61 365	60 246
China, Hong Kong SAR	..	..	136	297	348	340	357	377
China, Macao SAR	..	..	..	588	725	114	114	121
Korea, Republic of	563	2 413	4 858	6 509	8 913	8 725	10 391	11 042
Mongolia	..	..	12	180	200	277	279	288
Southern Asia	*5 295*	*6 771*	*17 742*	*34 956*	*76 368*	*83 853*	*98 557*	*110 520*
Afghanistan	..	..	..	..	233	462	462	445
Bangladesh	339	779	1 968	4 315	10 521	10 850	12 068	14 060
Bhutan	..	..	..	..	5	8	10	10
India	2 757	2 384	12 883	22 125	49 468	54 035	63 011	69 350
Iran (Islamic Rep. of)	..	-	536	1 032	1 072	1 181	1 330	1 376
Maldives	..	2	2	2	5	3	3	3
Nepal	..	..	111	1 212	2 986	3 469	4 217	4 953
Pakistan	2 048	2 006	1 075	4 280	8 717	9 690	12 263	14 010
Sri Lanka	152	401	1 166	1 991	3 363	4 155	5 193	6 312
South-Eastern Asia	*1 050*	*2 806*	*11 754*	*24 770*	*36 912*	*41 761*	*44 264*	*47 995*
Cambodia	..	..	121	200	335	318	245	257
Indonesia (...2002)	..	(a)166	(a)1 190	—	—	—	—	—
Indonesia	—	—	—	5 420	6 793	6 916	6 924	7 207
Lao People's Dem. Rep.	..	11	1	1	38	42	110	117
Malaysia	-	185	342	1 117	1 131	1 102	1 198	1 272
Myanmar	..	6	102	129	54	115	127	566
Philippines	626	1 465	6 961	13 566	19 765	21 427	23 065	24 453
Thailand	383	973	1 697	1 187	2 776	3 580	3 994	4 124
Viet Nam	..	..	1 340	3 150	6 020	8 260	8 600	10 000
Western Asia	*3 673*	*7 485*	*10 504*	*11 966*	*16 530*	*17 888*	*17 767*	*17 831*
Iraq	..	..	..	711	152	177	386	381
Jordan	794	499	1 845	2 500	3 597	3 641	3 453	3 643

For sources and notes, see end of table.

As percentage of GDP (1) En pourcentage du PIB (1)				As percentage of exports of goods and services (2) En pourcentage des exportations des biens et services (2)				Régions, pays ou territoires
1990	2000	2010	2012 (e)	1990	2000	2010	2012 (e)	
0.54	1.00	1.17	1.12	3.35	4.91	5.74	4.92	Économies en développement : Amérique
1.39	5.07	5.08	6.57	4.91	14.14	16.45	16.53	Caraïbes
2.78	2.62	2.08	1.86	3.63	4.17	4.57	3.92	Antigua-et-Barbuda
..	0.42	0.66	0.57	..	0.22	0.87	0.48	Aruba
1.88	3.71	1.93	1.86	4.34	8.88	3.96	3.61	Barbade
6.96	5.03	5.45	4.99	15.56	11.28	15.46	15.10	Dominique
3.35	7.77	6.81	5.96	17.19	20.51	29.17	24.09	République dominicaine
8.13	8.86	6.82	6.92	19.31	19.67	31.79	31.67	Grenade
-	17.21	24.24	22.68	-	114.75	183.68	151.26	Haïti
4.74	9.90	15.18	14.24	10.32	24.85	51.03	48.81	Jamaïque
0.58	6.51	7.70	5.74	23.41	18.07	26.01	18.09	Saint-Kitts-et-Nevis
3.87	3.78	2.71	2.42	5.72	7.02	5.02	5.38	Sainte-Lucie
6.65	5.66	4.93	4.98	12.01	12.53	18.13	18.22	Saint-Vincent et les Grenadines
0.07	0.47	0.45	0.40	0.15	0.79	0.75	0.50	Trinité-et-Tobago
1.19	1.54	2.91	2.74	6.41	5.22	9.14	7.95	Amérique centrale
4.55	3.18	5.68	5.31	7.54	6.08	9.59	7.94	Belize
0.17	0.85	1.52	1.16	0.61	1.75	3.99	3.06	Costa Rica
7.63	13.44	16.10	16.68	37.64	48.21	62.12	58.60	El Salvador
1.74	3.47	10.24	9.86	7.57	15.44	39.09	39.20	Guatemala
1.73	6.73	17.24	15.78	6.09	12.57	37.47	33.00	Honduras
1.08	1.18	2.14	1.98	6.35	4.18	7.03	5.98	Mexique
..	8.13	12.51	12.86	..	29.04	22.08	18.91	Nicaragua
—	—	—	—	—	—	—	—	Panama, sans la zone du canal
1.81	0.14	1.54	1.33	2.47	0.21	2.17	1.70	Panama
0.18	0.45	0.43	0.43	1.28	3.08	2.68	2.33	Amérique du Sud
-	0.03	0.17	0.12	-	0.28	0.78	0.59	Argentine
0.09	1.51	4.85	3.76	0.47	8.63	13.93	8.45	Bolivie (État plurinational de)
0.16	0.26	0.19	0.22	1.63	2.55	1.71	1.74	Brésil
0.00	0.02	0.00	0.00	0.00	0.06	0.00	0.00	Chili
0.87	1.61	1.42	1.12	5.70	10.19	8.96	6.15	Colombie
0.45	8.12	4.48	3.65	1.56	22.39	13.25	10.13	Équateur
..	2.40	16.51	14.05	..	4.06	32.94	23.00	Guyana
0.73	3.92	3.62	3.83	1.34	9.51	6.64	7.43	Paraguay
0.30	1.35	1.61	1.39	2.11	8.43	6.45	5.53	Pérou
0.07	-	0.10	0.07	0.06	-	0.18	0.13	Suriname
..	..	0.26	0.20	..	..	0.97	0.75	Uruguay
0.00	0.01	0.04	0.03	0.01	0.05	0.21	0.13	Venezuela (Rép. bolivarienne du)
1.04	1.32	1.55	1.53	4.94	3.50	4.10	4.21	Économies en développement : Asie
0.31	0.45	0.81	0.75	1.29	1.12	2.00	2.04	Asie orientale
0.05	0.40	0.88	0.74	0.34	1.72	3.00	2.68	Chine
..	0.08	0.15	0.15	..	0.06	0.07	0.07	Chine (RAS de Hong Kong)
..	..	0.40	0.28	..	..	0.38	0.26	Chine (RAS de Macao)
0.89	0.91	0.86	0.96	3.25	2.32	1.59	1.66	Corée, République de
..	1.06	4.46	2.86	..	1.96	8.15	5.61	Mongolie
1.35	2.49	3.40	3.90	12.53	15.34	15.59	18.70	Asie méridionale
..	..	2.87	2.25	..	..	7.70	6.78	Afghanistan
2.77	4.33	10.88	12.79	37.74	27.27	50.11	52.03	Bangladesh
..	..	0.52	0.55	..	..	1.35	1.41	Bhoutan
0.73	2.75	3.22	3.73	10.40	21.50	15.44	16.06	Inde
-	0.52	0.28	0.25	-	1.77	1.01	1.81	Iran (Rép. islamique d')
0.67	0.27	0.15	0.14	0.95	0.48	0.16	0.13	Maldives
..	1.95	21.26	27.20	..	8.70	220.43	256.75	Népal
4.19	1.51	5.58	6.32	29.35	10.62	34.53	44.84	Pakistan
4.88	6.97	8.39	10.62	17.48	18.28	37.43	46.55	Sri Lanka
0.89	2.29	2.51	2.35	2.72	3.59	5.27	5.00	Asie du Sud-Est
..	3.29	2.83	1.81	..	6.60	5.73	3.00	Cambodge
0.13	0.72	—	—	0.57	1.69	—	—	Indonésie (…2002)
—	—	0.98	0.82	—	—	3.96	3.41	Indonésie
1.26	0.04	0.62	1.27	10.64	0.13	1.85	4.69	Rép. dém. populaire lao
0.39	0.35	0.45	0.42	0.57	0.30	0.48	0.48	Malaisie
0.11	1.40	0.27	0.98	1.87	4.84	1.43	6.62	Myanmar
2.98	8.59	10.74	9.77	12.82	17.09	33.04	37.72	Philippines
1.10	1.35	1.05	1.06	3.33	2.08	1.58	1.50	Thaïlande
..	4.30	7.76	7.11	..	7.81	10.36	8.06	Viet Nam
3.17	3.04	1.18	0.97	20.74	12.65	3.11	2.17	Asie occidentale
..	..	0.16	0.26	..	..	0.32	0.41	Iraq
12.42	21.81	13.78	11.68	19.88	52.14	28.83	26.85	Jordanie

Pour les sources et les notes, se reporter à la fin du tableau.

7

Region, country or territory	Millions of dollars - Millions de dollars							
	1980	1990	2000	2005	2009	2010	2011	2012 (e)
Lebanon	..	-	-	4 924	7 558	7 653	7 531	7 472
Oman	35	39	39	39	39	39	39	39
Saudi Arabia	..	..	..	94	214	236	244	245
State of Palestine	..	..	1 010	705	1 210	1 545	1 545	1 545
Syrian Arab Republic	774	385	180	823	1 550	2 079	2 079	2 079
Turkey	2 071	3 246	4 560	887	1 050	993	1 087	940
Yemen		1 498	1 288	1 283	1 160	1 526	1 404	1 487
Developing economies: Oceania	**38**	**108**	**142**	**1 350**	**1 617**	**1 576**	**1 685**	**1 672**
Fiji	5	22	44	185	154	158	158	165
French Polynesia	..	..	..	557	728	700	755	755
Kiribati	2	5	-	-	-	-	-	..
New Caledonia	..	..	..	512	509	492	519	519
Papua New Guinea	5	5	7	7	12	11	11	9
Samoa	19	43	-	1	119	122	139	128
Solomon Islands	..	..	4	7	2	2	2	2
Tonga	-	24	..	69	72	72	72	74
Vanuatu	..	8	35	5	11	12	22	19
Transition economies	**4 102**	**9 360**	**6 170**	**12 262**	**27 330**	**28 237**	**32 583**	**32 095**
Albania	..	..	598	1 290	1 318	1 156	1 162	1 035
Armenia	—	—	87	498	769	996	1 295	1 449
Azerbaijan	—	—	57	693	1 274	1 432	1 915	1 804
Belarus	—	—	139	255	589	589	697	655
Bosnia and Herzegovina	—	—	1 607	2 043	2 133	1 824	1 959	1 863
Croatia	—	—	641	711	1 271	1 287	1 378	1 389
Georgia	..	—	209	346	714	806	1 110	1 061
Kazakhstan	—	—	122	178	261	291	240	162
Kyrgyzstan	—	—	9	322	991	1 275	1 724	2 024
Montenegro	—	—	—	—	302	301	343	327
Republic of Moldova	—	—	179	920	1 211	1 363	1 612	1 770
Russian Federation	—	—	1 275	3 012	5 359	5 264	5 667	5 169
Serbia	—	—	—	—	3 936	3 351	3 272	2 754
Tajikistan	—	—	..	467	1 748	2 306	3 060	3 739
TFYR of Macedonia	—	—	81	227	381	388	434	393
Ukraine	—	—	33	595	5 073	5 607	6 716	6 500
Developed economies: America	**80**	**1 170**	**4 395**	**4 795**	**6 521**	**6 633**	**6 793**	**5 879**
Bermuda	..	..	..	..	1 345	1 356	1 356	1 356
United States	80	1 170	4 395	4 795	5 176	5 277	5 437	4 523
Developed economies: Asia	**561**	**1 225**	**1 774**	**1 930**	**3 043**	**3 214**	**4 007**	**4 029**
Israel	421	812	400	850	1 267	1 411	1 709	1 300
Japan	140	-	1 374	1 080	1 776	1 802	2 298	2 728
Developed economies: Europe	**17 110**	**31 274**	**41 328**	**77 417**	**104 171**	**105 442**	**114 505**	**108 203**
Austria	245	635	1 805	2 608	3 100	2 990	3 137	2 912
Belgium	-	-	-	7 242	10 442	10 296	10 975	10 023
Bulgaria	..	..	58	1 613	1 592	1 333	1 483	1 376
Cyprus	94	79	64	189	150	142	131	110
Czech Republic	—	—	297	1 528	2 077	2 066	1 849	2 003
Denmark	..	..	667	867	1 219	1 206	1 273	1 222
Estonia	—	—	4	264	306	320	407	394
Faeroe Islands	..	..	43	80	139	146	146	146
Finland	106	63	473	693	875	848	889	853
France	1 440	4 035	8 610	11 945	16 202	16 896	19 483	19 451
Germany, Federal Republic of	2 380	—	—	—	—	—	—	—
Germany	—	4 876	3 644	6 933	12 489	12 969	14 886	13 655
Greece	1 119	1 817	2 194	1 220	2 020	1 499	1 186	618
Hungary	..	..	281	1 931	2 137	2 162	2 441	2 188
Iceland	2	62	88	88	23	25	27	35
Ireland	..	286	252	513	573	658	755	742
Italy	4 013	5 075	1 937	2 397	5 221	6 803	7 025	7 226
Latvia	—	—	72	381	591	614	695	732
Lithuania	—	—	50	534	1 239	1 674	1 956	1 387
Luxembourg	..	..	579	1 268	1 632	1 639	1 756	1 642
Malta	35	58	20	34	53	36	37	33
Netherlands	604	709	1 157	2 197	1 918	1 959	1 943	1 764
Norway	102	158	270	505	631	680	765	756
Poland	..	..	1 496	6 482	8 126	7 575	7 641	6 913
Portugal	2 968	4 479	3 495	3 101	3 585	3 599	3 836	3 895
Romania	..	..	96	4 733	4 952	3 952	3 890	3 669

For sources and notes, see end of table.

As percentage of GDP (1) En pourcentage du PIB (1)				As percentage of exports of goods and services (2) En pourcentage des exportations des biens et services (2)				Régions, pays ou territoires
1990	2000	2010	2012 (e)	1990	2000	2010	2012 (e)	
-	-	20.61	18.02	-	-	35.62	23.85	Liban
0.34	0.20	0.07	0.05	0.71	0.33	0.10	0.07	Oman
..	..	0.05	0.04	..	..	0.09	0.06	Arabie saoudite
..	24.07	18.55	17.62	..	99.74	103.23	96.72	État de Palestine
3.45	0.92	3.44	3.83	7.65	2.63	10.60	17.46	République arabe syrienne
1.60	1.71	0.14	0.12	15.43	8.88	0.64	0.46	Turquie
37.24	11.86	5.26	4.43	100.57	32.13	16.48	17.81	Yémen
2.10	**2.32**	**5.10**	**4.20**	**4.52**	**3.87**	**13.59**	**12.65**	**Économies en développement : Océanie**
1.62	2.55	4.98	4.05	2.64	4.54	9.65	7.58	Fidji
..	..	10.48	10.49	..	..	66.43	63.52	Polynésie française
12.47	-	-	..	46.39	-	-	..	Kiribati
..	..	5.55	5.26	..	..	25.05	26.91	Nouvelle-Calédonie
0.17	0.21	0.11	0.06	0.09	0.31	0.18	0.13	Papouasie-Nouvelle-Guinée
38.26	-	20.49	18.34	96.24	-	71.28	64.58	Samoa
..	1.28	0.25	0.23	..	3.56	0.51	0.35	Îles Salomon
14.78	..	19.16	15.38	62.59	..	151.39	104.25	Tonga
4.74	12.74	1.72	2.45	11.11	22.08	3.59	5.19	Vanuatu
11.00	**1.63**	**1.37**	**1.20**	**45.26**	**3.59**	**4.00**	**3.39**	**Économies en transition**
..	16.42	9.67	8.26	..	84.98	29.98	25.38	Albanie
–	4.58	10.75	14.64	–	19.58	51.41	58.46	Arménie
–	1.08	2.71	2.68	–	2.70	5.01	4.89	Azerbaïdjan
–	1.34	1.07	1.12	–	1.82	1.97	1.25	Bélarus
–	28.94	10.96	10.78	–	101.74	30.11	29.47	Bosnie-Herzégovine
–	2.98	2.16	2.43	–	7.42	5.46	5.66	Croatie
–	6.85	6.93	6.72	–	24.38	19.85	17.56	Géorgie
–	0.67	0.20	0.08	–	1.18	0.44	0.17	Kazakhstan
–	0.65	26.60	32.73	–	1.54	51.60	63.07	Kirghizistan
–	–	7.32	7.54	–	–	20.58	19.53	Monténégro
–	13.86	23.46	24.11	–	27.85	59.52	55.95	République de Moldova
–	0.49	0.35	0.26	–	1.11	1.18	0.87	Fédération de Russie
–	–	7.85	6.65	–	–	23.19	16.70	Serbie
–	..	40.87	49.25	–	..	290.81	258.04	Tadjikistan
–	2.26	4.15	4.18	–	4.94	9.13	7.79	LERY de Macédoine
–	0.11	4.11	3.64	–	0.17	8.15	7.29	Ukraine
0.02	**0.04**	**0.05**	**0.04**	**0.22**	**0.41**	**0.36**	**0.27**	**Économies développées : Amérique**
..	..	23.53	22.71	..	..	95.78	97.21	Bermudes
0.02	0.04	0.04	0.03	0.22	0.41	0.29	0.21	États-Unis
0.04	**0.04**	**0.06**	**0.07**	**0.36**	**0.31**	**0.34**	**0.40**	**Économies développées : Asie**
1.41	0.32	0.65	0.54	4.69	0.86	1.75	1.43	Israël
-	0.03	0.03	0.05	-	0.26	0.21	0.30	Japon
0.43	**0.46**	**0.61**	**0.61**	**1.59**	**1.27**	**1.47**	**1.34**	**Économies développées : Europe**
0.39	0.94	0.79	0.73	1.00	2.06	1.48	1.30	Autriche
-	-	2.18	2.07	-	-	2.77	2.46	Belgique
..	0.45	2.79	2.70	..	0.83	4.89	4.05	Bulgarie
1.36	0.70	0.62	0.48	2.66	1.28	1.50	1.12	Chypre
–	0.50	1.04	1.02	–	0.83	1.53	1.30	République tchèque
..	0.42	0.39	0.39	..	0.90	0.77	0.72	Danemark
–	0.07	1.69	1.81	–	0.08	1.98	1.83	Estonie
..	..	..	..	..	8.10	14.40	12.86	Îles Féroé
0.05	0.39	0.36	0.34	0.20	0.88	0.88	0.83	Finlande
0.32	0.65	0.66	0.75	1.46	2.28	2.38	2.51	France
–	–	–	–	–	–	–	–	Allemagne, Rép. fédérale d'
0.28	0.19	0.39	0.40	1.03	0.58	0.82	0.77	Allemagne
1.95	1.74	0.50	0.24	13.96	7.42	2.48	0.99	Grèce
..	0.61	1.69	1.73	..	0.80	1.95	1.85	Hongrie
0.98	1.01	0.20	0.26	2.90	2.97	0.35	0.43	Islande
0.59	0.26	0.32	0.35	1.07	0.28	0.32	0.33	Irlande
0.45	0.18	0.33	0.36	2.31	0.65	1.25	1.19	Italie
–	0.93	2.55	2.58	–	2.22	4.80	4.26	Lettonie
–	0.43	4.58	3.29	–	0.97	6.74	3.90	Lituanie
..	2.85	3.07	2.88	..	6.70	2.04	1.90	Luxembourg
2.29	0.50	0.45	0.39	2.99	0.56	0.45	0.37	Malte
0.24	0.30	0.25	0.23	0.45	0.45	0.33	0.26	Pays-Bas
0.13	0.16	0.16	0.15	0.34	0.35	0.40	0.37	Norvège
..	0.87	1.61	1.42	..	3.22	3.82	3.06	Pologne
5.77	2.98	1.57	1.83	20.78	10.24	4.94	4.69	Portugal
..	0.26	2.40	2.08	..	0.79	6.78	5.42	Roumanie

Pour les sources et les notes, se reporter à la fin du tableau.

Region, country or territory	Millions of dollars - Millions de dollars							
	1980	1990	2000	2005	2009	2010	2011	2012 (e)
Slovakia	–	–	18	946	1 671	1 591	1 753	1 622
Slovenia	–	–	205	264	277	309	433	536
Spain	2 188	2 186	4 859	7 961	10 372	10 538	11 543	10 133
Sweden	66	153	438	673	652	688	776	722
Switzerland	609	924	1 119	1 924	2 655	2 829	3 307	3 116
United Kingdom	..	2 099	3 614	6 302	7 252	7 399	8 078	8 332
Developed economies: Oceania	**888**	**3 131**	**2 139**	**3 729**	**1 968**	**2 444**	**2 476**	**2 503**
Australia	632	2 370	1 903	2 990	1 340	1 601	1 601	1 620
New Zealand	256	762	236	739	628	843	875	883

Sources:

UNCTAD secretariat calculations, based on:

- World Bank, *Migration and Remittances*

Notes:

- Migrants' remittances data cover: workers' remittances, compensation of employees and migrants' transfers.

(1)   GDP data source: *UNCTADstat*.

(2)   Exports and imports of goods and services data are based on IMF, *Balance of Payments Statistics*.

As percentage of GDP (1) En pourcentage du PIB (1)				As percentage of exports of goods and services (2) En pourcentage des exportations des biens et services (2)				Régions, pays ou territoires
1990	2000	2010	2012 (e)	1990	2000	2010	2012 (e)	
–	0.09	1.83	1.77	–	0.13	2.28	1.84	Slovaquie
–	1.03	0.66	1.17	–	1.92	1.00	1.57	Slovénie
0.42	0.84	0.76	0.75	2.61	2.89	2.76	2.34	Espagne
0.06	0.18	0.15	0.14	0.22	0.40	0.31	0.29	Suède
0.38	0.43	0.51	0.49	0.94	0.89	0.83	0.77	Suisse
0.21	0.24	0.33	0.34	0.88	0.89	1.09	1.10	Royaume-Uni
0.85	**0.46**	**0.17**	**0.14**	**5.09**	**2.10**	**0.81**	**0.70**	**Économies développées : Océanie**
0.73	0.46	0.12	0.10	4.75	2.27	0.61	0.52	Australie
1.69	0.44	0.59	0.51	6.52	1.33	2.06	1.85	Nouvelle-Zélande

Sources :

Calculs du secrétariat de la CNUCED, basés sur :

- Banque Mondiale, *Migration and Remittances*

Notes :

- Les envois de fonds des migrants couvrent : les envois de fonds des travailleurs, la rémunération des employés et les transferts des migrants.

(1) Source de données du PIB : *UNCTADstat*.

(2) Les données sur les exportations et importations des biens et services se basent sur les *Statistiques de la balance des paiements* du FMI.

7

Economic grouping	Millions of dollars - Millions de dollars							
	1980	1990	2000	2005	2009	2010	2011	2012 (e)
DEVELOPING ECONOMIES	18 993	34 522	82 803	188 679	293 845	318 479	355 060	375 017
Developing economies excluding China	18 417	34 326	77 981	165 201	245 916	266 210	293 695	314 772
Developing economies excluding LDCs	17 477	30 950	76 496	176 892	270 124	293 725	328 164	344 424
High-income developing economies	4 160	11 949	22 146	44 811	51 468	50 747	55 100	54 581
Middle-income developing economies	8 413	14 570	36 704	85 808	134 040	149 022	165 866	172 859
Low-income developing economies	6 420	8 002	23 953	58 060	108 338	118 710	134 094	147 577
Heavily indebted poor countries (IMF)	962	938	3 282	7 327	13 155	13 065	13 727	14 343
Landlocked developing countries	683	945	2 078	7 031	14 419	16 711	20 555	22 208
Small island developing States	200	552	1 628	2 819	3 106	3 219	3 406	3 408
Least developed countries	*1 516*	*3 571*	*6 307*	*11 787*	*23 721*	*24 754*	*26 896*	*30 593*
Africa and Haiti	1 154	1 211	2 613	4 614	8 234	7 801	8 063	8 541
Asia	339	2 294	3 590	7 139	15 331	16 790	18 643	21 895
Islands	23	66	103	33	156	163	191	157
Major petroleum and gas exporters	*463*	*1 602*	*2 787*	*18 746*	*22 051*	*23 674*	*24 717*	*24 579*
Africa	428	362	2 195	16 722	20 443	21 898	22 580	22 412
America	..	1	17	148	131	143	138	126
Asia	35	1 239	575	1 876	1 477	1 633	1 999	2 041
Major exporters of manufactured goods	*2 602*	*6 901*	*19 653*	*55 652*	*83 628*	*88 597*	*101 507*	*100 279*
America	1 039	3 098	7 525	22 742	22 076	22 080	23 588	23 219
Asia	1 563	3 803	12 128	32 911	61 552	66 517	77 918	77 060
Emerging economies	*2 193*	*7 389*	*17 162*	*37 303*	*42 618*	*43 164*	*47 968*	*47 976*
America	1 206	3 781	9 991	28 167	29 344	29 256	31 772	31 539
Asia	987	3 607	7 171	9 136	13 275	13 908	16 196	16 437
Newly industrialized Asian economies	*1 613*	*5 238*	*15 458*	*28 418*	*40 180*	*42 590*	*46 542*	*48 475*
First tier	563	2 449	5 267	7 129	9 715	9 565	11 361	11 419
Second tier	1 050	2 789	10 190	21 290	30 465	33 026	35 181	37 056
Developing economies: Africa	5 862	8 864	11 486	33 410	45 461	52 126	56 092	62 437
Northern Africa excluding Sudan	4 474	7 193	6 608	13 075	17 458	23 001	25 546	31 450
Sub-Saharan Africa	1 388	1 671	4 878	20 335	28 002	29 125	30 546	30 987
Sub-Saharan Africa excluding South Africa	1 320	1 536	4 535	19 677	27 100	28 006	29 333	29 872
Developing economies: America	1 936	5 842	21 074	50 853	58 388	59 050	63 576	62 488
Central America and Greater Caribbean Islands excluding Puerto Rico	1 570	4 407	14 878	38 157	41 489	42 505	45 511	44 452
Central America and Greater Caribbean Islands excluding Mexico and Puerto Rico	531	1 309	7 353	15 415	19 413	20 425	21 922	21 234
South America and Central America	1 521	5 055	16 719	44 143	50 093	50 356	54 181	54 791
South America excluding Brazil	225	696	4 200	8 736	12 147	12 073	12 834	12 691
Developing economies: Asia	11 157	19 708	50 100	103 067	188 380	205 727	233 708	248 420
Eastern and South-Eastern Asia excluding China	1 613	5 255	17 033	32 666	47 552	51 716	56 018	59 824
Southern Asia excluding India	2 538	4 388	4 858	12 831	26 900	29 818	35 546	41 170

For sources and notes, see end of table 7.3.1.

As percentage of GDP (1) En pourcentage du PIB (1)				As percentage of exports of goods and services (2) En pourcentage des exportations des biens et services (2)				Groupements économiques
1990	2000	2010	2012 (e)	1990	2000	2010	2012 (e)	
1.02	**1.28**	**1.59**	**1.58**	**5.08**	**4.06**	**4.81**	**4.83**	**ÉCONOMIES EN DÉVELOPPEMENT**
1.15	1.47	1.88	2.01	5.51	4.43	5.45	5.71	Économies en développement sans la Chine
0.94	1.21	1.50	1.49	4.64	3.82	4.55	4.55	Économies en développement sans les PMA
0.69	0.65	0.63	0.64	3.14	1.81	1.65	1.61	Économies en développement à revenu élevé
1.33	1.64	1.63	1.45	6.32	5.56	5.34	5.07	Économies en développement à revenu intermédiaire
1.40	2.93	4.09	4.43	11.55	15.53	15.76	15.37	Économies en développement à revenu faible
0.86	2.56	3.26	3.28	5.00	10.23	10.82	11.40	Pays pauvres très endettés (FMI)
1.79	2.33	3.81	3.92	8.67	6.82	9.94	9.70	Pays en développement sans littoral
2.74	4.45	4.38	3.87	5.94	8.00	8.62	7.08	Petits États insulaires en développement
3.47	*3.89*	*4.40*	*4.63*	*28.61*	*16.24*	*14.81*	*15.77*	*Pays les moins avancés*
1.89	3.03	2.32	2.17	14.52	12.18	7.02	6.64	Afrique et Haïti
6.01	4.81	7.53	8.28	57.75	21.19	30.55	34.12	Asie
9.63	8.72	5.71	5.71	38.60	23.49	17.10	12.62	Îles
0.65	*0.72*	*1.19*	*1.02*	*2.22*	*1.98*	*3.03*	*2.54*	*Principaux exportateurs de pétrole et de gaz*
0.37	1.48	4.01	3.71	1.29	3.43	9.08	9.15	Afrique
0.00	0.01	0.04	0.03	0.01	0.05	0.21	0.13	Amérique
1.21	0.47	0.15	0.14	4.91	1.37	0.35	0.33	Asie
0.55	*0.64*	*0.96*	*0.88*	*2.18*	*1.54*	*2.30*	*2.28*	*Principaux exportateurs d'articles manufacturés*
1.08	1.18	2.14	1.98	6.35	4.18	7.03	5.98	Amérique
0.39	0.50	0.81	0.76	1.42	1.10	1.88	1.92	Asie
0.52	*0.62*	*0.73*	*0.77*	*2.29*	*1.94*	*2.08*	*2.27*	*Économies émergentes*
0.44	0.59	0.75	0.72	3.34	3.25	3.90	3.47	Amérique
0.63	0.66	0.68	0.89	1.72	1.25	1.05	1.36	Asie
0.70	*1.03*	*1.35*	*1.50*	*2.09*	*1.66*	*2.10*	*2.38*	*Économies nouvellement industrialisées d'Asie*
0.56	0.51	0.57	0.81	1.65	0.84	0.72	0.93	Première génération
0.90	2.17	2.21	2.03	2.72	3.34	4.74	4.53	Deuxième génération
2.10	**1.99**	**3.08**	**3.40**	**8.51**	**6.49**	**9.09**	**10.70**	**Économies en développement : Afrique**
5.13	2.67	3.94	5.20	20.67	9.35	10.89	17.36	Afrique septentrionale sans le Soudan
0.59	1.48	2.63	2.51	2.41	4.59	8.03	7.70	Afrique subsaharienne
0.90	2.32	3.77	3.55	3.64	6.54	10.66	10.17	Afrique subsaharienne sans l'Afrique du Sud
0.54	**1.00**	**1.17**	**1.12**	**3.35**	**4.91**	**5.74**	**4.92**	**Économies en développement : Amérique**
1.22	1.92	3.23	3.09	6.36	6.59	10.44	9.12	Amérique centrale et Grandes Antilles sans Porto Rico
1.76	5.39	7.20	8.05	6.38	16.03	22.00	21.33	Amérique centrale et Grandes Antilles sans le Mexique et Porto Rico
0.50	0.83	1.03	1.00	3.19	4.20	5.16	4.48	Amérique du Sud et Amérique centrale
0.21	0.63	0.77	0.68	1.08	3.36	3.30	2.69	Amérique du Sud sans le Brésil
1.04	**1.32**	**1.55**	**1.53**	**4.94**	**3.50**	**4.10**	**4.21**	**Économies en développement : Asie**
0.70	1.10	1.54	1.70	2.09	1.79	2.40	2.68	Asie orientale et Asie du Sud-Est sans la Chine
2.50	1.99	3.78	4.21	14.10	8.72	15.87	25.86	Asie méridionale sans l'Inde

Pour les sources et les notes, se reporter à la fin du tableau 7.3.1.

7

Region, country or territory	Millions of dollars - Millions de dollars							
	1980	1990	2000	2005	2008	2009	2010	2011
WORLD	30 246	67 941	117 657	198 841	320 241	312 421	312 662	341 503
DEVELOPING ECONOMIES	11 607	19 572	33 141	55 575	88 429	95 460	94 516	101 028
TRANSITION ECONOMIES	..	..	1 890	10 249	31 893	23 604	24 074	28 937
DEVELOPED ECONOMIES	18 639	48 369	82 626	133 018	199 918	193 357	194 072	211 538
Developing economies: Africa	4 660	3 407	3 078	4 408	5 920	6 381	6 831	5 793
Eastern Africa	*317*	*127*	*657*	*510*	*835*	*892*	*773*	*796*
Burundi	..	6	2	0	0	1	6	7
Comoros	2	4	..	..	..	..	..	..
Djibouti	..	..	2	5	5	6	12	13
Eritrea	–	–	1	..	..	..	..	..
Ethiopia (...1991)	1	-	–	–	–	–	–	–
Ethiopia	–	–	13	16	21	27	66	19
Kenya	13	7	-	56	64	61	19	26
Madagascar	31	18	12	21	-	-	-	..
Malawi	0	0	0	7	11	13	15	18
Mauritius	2	1	1	11	14	12	13	11
Mozambique	25	25	156	24	48	66	70	45
Rwanda	22	21	28	35	70	71	76	103
Seychelles	..	10	10	10	12	21	21	20
Uganda	4	..	353	197	381	480	324	348
United Republic of Tanzania	..	..	20	33	48	47	62	116
Zambia	82	18	24	94	139	66	68	70
Zimbabwe	135	16	..	..	..	..	..	..
Middle Africa	*308*	*539*	*411*	*523*	*1 019*	*956*	*871*	*619*
Angola	..	150	266	215	669	716	714	564
Cameroon	102	111	30	56	62	137	54	54
Central African Republic	20	36	..	..	..	..	..	..
Chad	4	39	..	..	..	..	..	..
Congo	39	55	37	66	-	-	-	..
Gabon	144	147	78	186	-	..	..	..
Sao Tome and Principe	0	0	1	0	0	1	1	1
Northern Africa	*1 370*	*534*	*556*	*1 055*	*1 308*	*1 736*	*2 018*	*1 106*
Algeria	165	31	..	27	27	46	28	71
Egypt	..	27	32	57	241	255	305	293
Libya	1 052	446	463	914	964	1 361	1 609	650
Morocco	77	16	29	40	58	61	62	71
Sudan (...2011)	53	2	4	2	2	0	1	2
Tunisia	22	13	27	16	16	13	13	19
Southern Africa	*1 051*	*1 352*	*873*	*1 218*	*1 332*	*1 296*	*1 532*	*1 628*
Botswana	26	119	147	129	145	106	96	96
Lesotho	..	..	10	6	5	5	19	31
Namibia	..	30	9	19	43	16	33	46
South Africa	1 017	1 199	685	1 055	1 133	1 158	1 372	1 443
Swaziland	9	4	21	8	7	11	12	12
Western Africa	*1 614*	*855*	*582*	*1 100*	*1 426*	*1 500*	*1 637*	*1 644*
Benin	2	21	9	40	88	76	78	78
Burkina Faso	52	81	45	84	100	99	112	112
Cape Verde	..	2	0	5	10	12	8	9
Côte d'Ivoire	786	471	390	597	756	743	726	726
Gambia	-	..	..	1	3	8	58	33
Ghana	9	4	6	-	-	-	-	..
Guinea	..	20	27	60	56	45	43	43
Guinea-Bissau	..	12	-	5	17	20	20	20
Liberia	32	..	..	0	0	1	1	1
Mali	19	45	26	69	105	167	176	176
Mauritania	33	31	..	..	..	..	..	..
Niger	53	66	12	29	22	25	72	72
Nigeria	523	9	1	68	58	47	48	76
Senegal	91	79	55	98	144	174	216	216
Sierra Leone	2	0	..	2	3	3	11	21
Togo	9	13	7	35	58	72	63	63

For sources and notes, see end of table.

As percentage of GDP (1) En pourcentage du PIB (1)				As percentage of imports of goods and services (2) En pourcentage des importations des biens et services (2)				Régions, pays ou territoires
1990	2000	2010	2011	1990	2000	2010	2011	
0.35	0.39	0.53	0.52	1.97	1.69	1.86	1.72	MONDE
0.75	0.63	0.51	0.47	3.81	2.09	1.62	1.45	ÉCONOMIES EN DÉVELOPPEMENT
..	0.52	1.17	1.14	..	1.59	4.13	3.89	ÉCONOMIES EN TRANSITION
0.29	0.34	0.50	0.51	1.64	1.57	1.87	1.75	ÉCONOMIES DÉVELOPPÉES
0.72	0.59	0.41	0.33	2.95	2.11	1.20	0.94	Économies en développement : Afrique
0.23	1.09	0.49	0.47	0.96	3.58	1.19	1.03	*Afrique orientale*
0.36	0.25	0.28	0.31	1.83	1.64	0.95	0.93	Burundi
1.82	..	..	..	4.97	..	..	..	Comores
..	0.32	1.03	1.00	..	0.63	2.36	1.91	Djibouti
—	0.19	..	..	—	0.26	..	..	Érythrée
-	-	—	—	-	—	—	—	Éthiopie (...1991)
—	0.15	0.25	0.06	—	0.77	0.67	0.16	Éthiopie
0.07	-	0.06	0.08	0.27	-	0.14	0.16	Kenya
0.57	0.31	-	..	2.16	0.78	-	..	Madagascar
0.00	0.02	0.28	0.29	0.01	0.07	0.60	0.62	Malawi
0.02	0.01	0.14	0.10	0.03	0.02	0.22	0.15	Maurice
0.86	3.62	0.76	0.35	2.55	10.47	1.45	0.65	Mozambique
0.83	1.58	1.35	1.61	6.05	6.62	4.64	4.70	Rwanda
2.15	1.32	2.14	2.02	3.97	2.01	1.77	1.57	Seychelles
..	5.79	1.83	1.80	..	25.06	5.24	4.68	Ouganda
..	0.19	0.26	0.47	..	0.99	0.68	0.96	République-Unie de Tanzanie
0.46	0.74	0.42	0.37	0.92	1.84	1.21	0.92	Zambie
0.14	..	..	..	0.82	..	..	..	Zimbabwe
1.59	1.53	0.74	0.47	5.46	3.69	1.71	1.22	*Afrique centrale*
1.46	3.01	0.87	0.54	4.43	4.64	2.02	1.29	Angola
0.94	0.32	0.23	0.21	4.48	1.20	0.85	0.80	Cameroun
2.50	..	..	..	8.77	..	..	..	République centrafricaine
2.53	..	..	..	7.98	..	..	..	Tchad
1.98	1.13	-	..	4.33	3.06	-	..	Congo
2.52	1.41	..	..	8.13	4.69	..	..	Gabon
0.07	0.83	0.30	0.23	0.41	1.67	0.52	0.41	Sao Tomé-et-Principe
0.29	0.27	0.31	0.16	1.12	1.07	0.93	0.50	*Afrique septentrionale*
0.05	..	0.02	0.04	0.31	..	0.06	0.12	Algérie
0.07	0.03	0.14	0.13	0.19	0.14	0.51	0.48	Égypte
1.43	1.20	2.25	2.07	4.97	9.22	5.24	4.16	Libye
0.06	0.08	0.07	0.07	0.21	0.23	0.15	0.14	Maroc
0.02	0.03	0.00	0.00	0.24	0.22	0.01	0.02	Soudan (...2011)
0.09	0.13	0.03	0.04	0.21	0.29	0.05	0.07	Tunisie
1.13	0.60	0.39	0.37	5.33	2.21	1.31	1.17	*Afrique australe*
3.20	2.62	0.65	0.56	5.98	6.35	1.54	1.21	Botswana
..	1.34	0.89	1.26	..	0.99	0.80	1.14	Lesotho
1.11	0.23	0.28	0.36	1.88	0.55	0.58	0.73	Namibie
1.07	0.52	0.38	0.35	5.71	2.07	1.37	1.21	Afrique du Sud
0.38	1.36	0.30	0.29	0.54	1.44	0.45	0.43	Swaziland
1.05	0.69	0.48	0.49	4.45	2.29	1.40	1.30	*Afrique occidentale*
1.12	0.38	1.19	1.07	4.56	1.25	3.41	3.17	Bénin
2.58	1.69	1.27	1.11	10.66	6.77	4.37	3.36	Burkina Faso
0.59	0.09	0.48	0.46	1.23	0.14	0.71	0.63	Cap-Vert
3.96	3.65	3.16	3.01	13.68	10.74	6.73	7.73	Côte d'Ivoire
..	..	6.04	2.72	..	..	18.22	9.14	Gambie
0.04	0.08	-	..	0.26	0.18	-	..	Ghana
0.70	0.84	0.83	0.77	2.14	3.09	2.41	1.61	Guinée
1.91	-	2.40	2.15	13.18	-	6.57	5.80	Guinée-Bissau
..	..	0.11	0.07	..	..	0.06	0.02	Libéria
1.81	0.99	1.87	1.66	5.47	2.84	4.69	4.58	Mali
1.92	..	..	..	6.01	..	..	..	Mauritanie
2.52	0.69	1.27	1.13	9.13	2.61	2.57	2.30	Niger
0.03	0.00	0.02	0.03	0.13	0.01	0.07	0.09	Nigéria
1.28	1.17	1.68	1.50	4.32	3.15	4.16	3.60	Sénégal
0.01	..	0.42	0.71	0.03	..	1.02	1.09	Sierra Leone
0.75	0.52	1.98	1.70	1.59	1.12	3.43	2.98	Togo

Pour les sources et les notes, se reporter à la fin du tableau.

7

Region, country or territory	Millions of dollars - Millions de dollars							
	1980	1990	2000	2005	2008	2009	2010	2011
Developing economies: America	1 083	1 140	2 238	2 640	4 647	4 421	5 323	5 678
Caribbean	209	143	432	845	917	804	809	891
Antigua and Barbuda	..	6	2	2	2	2	2	2
Aruba	..	..	49	70	86	77	71	70
Bahamas	42	46	73	144	83	71	92	125
Barbados	1	6	19	41	39	37	35	35
Dominica	..	2	0	0	0	0	0	0
Dominican Republic	..	..	19	25	35	27	33	35
Grenada	3	1	3	3	4	4	3	4
Haiti	54	..	11	60	117	135	167	240
Jamaica	35	27	179	410	419	312	323	361
Saint Kitts and Nevis	2	7	7	8	6	6	6	6
Saint Lucia	..	4	3	4	4	4	5	5
Saint Vincent and the Grenadines	..	3	6	6	7	7	7	8
Trinidad and Tobago	31	22	..	..	..	..	..	..
Central America	71	45	260	384	579	783	853	882
Belize	..	7	11	20	29	23	23	24
Costa Rica	..	..	142	209	269	239	271	304
El Salvador	9	3	20	24	19	21	23	28
Guatemala	11	14	56	42	26	22	21	24
Honduras	..	..	9	0	37	27	27	33
Mexico	11	..	..	..	..	..	..	..
Nicaragua	2	..	..	..	1	1	1	1
Panama, excl. Canal Zone	37	–	–	–	–	–	–	–
Panama	–	22	22	88	198	450	486	468
South America	804	951	1 547	1 411	3 151	2 834	3 661	3 905
Argentina	36	-	268	314	630	767	1 040	1 131
Bolivia (Plurinational State of)	2	8	37	67	106	103	102	117
Brazil	152	12	366	498	1 191	1 003	1 198	1 344
Chile	70	7	16	16	6	6	5	5
Colombia	39	44	219	56	88	92	112	117
Ecuador	67	2	6	54	66	95	136	148
Guyana	..	..	27	55	77	91	133	133
Paraguay	2	..	..	..	..	..	..	..
Peru	..	75	275	129	133	85	122	117
Suriname	18	8	2	10	8	5	1	3
Uruguay	..	..	..	2	5	6	7	7
Venezuela (Bolivarian Rep. of)	418	701	331	211	842	581	805	782
Developing economies: Asia	5 821	14 937	27 696	48 262	77 325	84 098	81 702	88 896
Eastern Asia	58	1 033	6 502	13 921	18 627	15 699	16 052	18 965
China	..	5	790	3 123	6 349	4 444	1 754	3 566
China, Hong Kong SAR	..	..	225	348	393	413	483	549
China, Macao SAR	..	..	..	227	960	693	565	565
Korea, Republic of	58	1 028	3 653	8 769	9 114	8 648	11 366	11 865
Mongolia	..	..	3	40	172	83	169	336
Southern Asia	31	114	575	1 749	4 691	3 937	5 092	5 239
Afghanistan	..	..	..	..	190	340	355	355
Bangladesh	0	..	4	5	14	8	9	12
Bhutan	..	..	..	..	61	54	63	98
India	29	106	486	1 348	3 812	2 891	3 888	3 888
Maldives	0	8	46	70	219	190	189	217
Nepal	..	..	17	66	5	12	32	39
Pakistan	1	1	2	3	-	8	9	28
Sri Lanka	..	..	20	257	385	435	545	601
South-Eastern Asia	66	434	738	7 452	9 493	12 556	7 807	8 365
Brunei Darussalam	..	..	..	376	420	445	445	445
Cambodia	..	..	104	184	230	215	258	234
Indonesia	–	–	–	1 179	1 971	2 702	2 840	3 164
Lao People's Dem. Rep.	..	..	0	1	9	22	19	76
Malaysia	19	230	599	5 679	6 786	6 529	1 754	1 970
Myanmar	..	..	14	19	-	-	-	..
Philippines	12	5	21	15	44	54	62	79
Thailand	35	199	..	..	..	2 558	2 397	2 397
Western Asia	5 667	13 356	19 881	25 140	44 513	51 905	52 751	56 328
Bahrain	330	332	1 013	1 223	1 774	1 391	1 642	2 050
Iraq	..	..	..	83	31	27	48	253
Jordan	154	71	197	349	472	502	495	439

For sources and notes, see end of table.

As percentage of GDP (1) En pourcentage du PIB (1)				As percentage of imports of goods and services (2) En pourcentage des importations des biens et services (2)				Régions, pays ou territoires
1990	2000	2010	2011	1990	2000	2010	2011	
0.16	**0.16**	**0.14**	**0.13**	**1.32**	**0.93**	**0.79**	**0.68**	**Économies en développement : Amérique**
0.74	*0.81*	*0.86*	*0.92*	*1.54*	*1.51*	*1.89*	*1.87*	*Caraïbes*
1.40	0.20	0.18	0.18	1.85	0.31	0.30	0.31	Antigua-et-Barbuda
..	2.60	2.94	2.62	..	1.51	3.46	1.04	Aruba
1.25	1.15	1.18	1.61	2.81	2.41	2.43	2.94	Bahamas
0.31	0.62	0.82	0.81	0.71	1.26	1.55	1.51	Barbade
0.81	0.04	0.04	0.04	1.21	0.07	0.06	0.07	Dominique
..	0.08	0.06	0.06	..	0.18	0.18	0.18	République dominicaine
0.58	0.63	0.43	0.43	0.93	1.06	0.89	0.90	Grenade
..	0.33	2.75	3.57	..	0.80	4.09	5.78	Haïti
0.55	1.99	2.40	2.45	1.12	4.05	5.00	4.61	Jamaïque
3.46	1.80	0.86	0.85	5.27	3.01	1.72	1.93	Saint-Kitts-et-Nevis
1.07	0.48	0.40	0.38	1.39	0.75	0.60	0.59	Sainte-Lucie
1.40	1.44	1.11	1.09	2.16	2.86	1.92	1.95	Saint-Vincent-et-les Grenadines
0.43	..	..	..	1.51	..	..	..	Trinité-et-Tobago
0.25	*0.39*	*0.57*	*0.53*	*0.57*	*0.81*	*1.13*	*0.95*	*Amérique centrale*
1.76	1.27	1.65	1.64	2.88	1.75	2.85	2.54	Belize
..	0.89	0.75	0.74	..	1.95	1.84	1.76	Costa Rica
0.06	0.15	0.11	0.12	0.17	0.35	0.25	0.26	El Salvador
0.20	0.32	0.05	0.05	0.75	1.00	0.14	0.14	Guatemala
..	0.13	0.18	0.19	..	0.20	0.27	0.26	Honduras
..	..	..	..	..	..	..	..	Mexique
..	..	0.02	0.02	..	..	0.02	0.02	Nicaragua
–	–	–	–	–	–	–	–	Panama, sans la zone du canal
0.36	0.19	1.83	1.52	0.52	0.27	2.44	1.78	Panama
0.14	*0.12*	*0.10*	*0.09*	*1.38*	*0.85*	*0.66*	*0.56*	*Amérique du Sud*
-	0.09	0.28	0.25	-	0.81	1.51	1.28	Argentine
0.16	0.44	0.52	0.49	0.71	1.78	1.65	1.33	Bolivie (État plurinational de)
0.00	0.06	0.06	0.05	0.04	0.51	0.49	0.44	Brésil
0.02	0.02	0.00	0.00	0.08	0.07	0.01	0.01	Chili
0.08	0.22	0.04	0.04	0.64	1.52	0.24	0.19	Colombie
0.02	0.04	0.23	0.22	0.08	0.12	0.60	0.56	Équateur
..	2.41	5.90	5.18	..	3.69	8.12	6.46	Guyana
..	..	..	..	..	..	..	..	Paraguay
0.26	0.52	0.08	0.06	1.84	2.85	0.35	0.27	Pérou
1.12	0.16	0.03	0.06	1.00	0.39	0.07	0.12	Suriname
..	..	0.02	0.02	..	..	0.07	0.06	Uruguay
1.49	0.28	0.20	0.25	7.42	1.55	1.56	1.25	Venezuela (Rép. bolivarienne du)
1.07	**0.83**	**0.63**	**0.59**	**4.84**	**2.32**	**1.79**	**1.62**	**Économies en développement : Asie**
0.15	*0.29*	*0.21*	*0.21*	*0.84*	*0.77*	*0.57*	*0.56*	*Asie orientale*
0.00	0.07	0.03	0.05	0.01	0.31	0.12	0.19	Chine
..	0.13	0.22	0.23	..	0.10	0.11	0.11	Chine (RAS de Hong Kong)
..	..	2.00	1.55	..	..	4.07	2.94	Chine (RAS de Macao)
0.38	0.68	1.12	1.06	1.34	1.89	2.20	1.91	Corée, République de
..	0.26	2.73	3.93	..	0.39	4.37	4.43	Mongolie
0.03	*0.09*	*0.25*	*0.23*	*0.29*	*0.55*	*0.94*	*0.78*	*Asie méridionale*
..	..	2.21	1.87	..	..	3.40	3.33	Afghanistan
..	0.01	0.01	0.01	..	0.05	0.03	0.03	Bangladesh
..	..	3.99	5.69	..	..	6.78	7.54	Bhoutan
0.03	0.10	0.23	0.20	0.36	0.67	0.89	0.72	Inde
3.24	5.78	9.12	10.59	5.16	10.26	11.19	9.58	Maldives
..	0.29	0.20	0.21	..	0.93	0.55	0.61	Népal
0.00	0.00	0.01	0.01	0.01	0.02	0.02	0.06	Pakistan
..	0.12	1.10	1.02	..	0.24	3.58	2.70	Sri Lanka
0.23	*0.39*	*0.50*	*0.47*	*0.53*	*0.50*	*1.22*	*1.11*	*Asie du Sud-Est*
..	..	3.60	2.72	..	..	11.25	12.82	Brunéi Darussalam
..	2.83	2.30	1.82	..	4.59	4.01	2.91	Cambodge
..	..	0.40	0.37	..	..	1.86	1.60	Indonésie
–	0.03	0.29	0.92	–	0.08	0.83	2.75	Rép. dém. populaire lao
0.48	0.61	0.71	0.68	0.72	0.63	0.93	0.91	Malaisie
..	0.19	-	..	..	0.56	-	..	Myanmar
0.01	0.03	0.03	0.04	0.04	0.04	0.08	0.12	Philippines
0.22	..	0.70	0.65	0.55	..	1.16	0.94	Thaïlande
8.40	*6.70*	*3.17*	*2.92*	*20.83*	*21.25*	*9.16*	*8.34*	*Asie occidentale*
7.74	12.62	7.49	7.94	8.31	19.73	12.54	14.76	Bahreïn
..	..	0.04	0.21	..	..	0.10	0.49	Iraq
1.75	2.33	1.87	1.52	1.98	3.41	2.71	2.06	Jordanie

Pour les sources et les notes, se reporter à la fin du tableau.

Region, country or territory	Millions of dollars - Millions de dollars							
	1980	1990	2000	2005	2008	2009	2010	2011
Kuwait	692	770	1 734	2 648	10 323	11 749	11 770	11 770
Lebanon	..	..	..	4 012	4 366	5 749	4 749	4 820
Oman	397	856	1 451	2 257	5 181	5 316	5 704	7 215
Saudi Arabia	4 094	11 221	15 390	14 315	21 697	26 470	27 069	28 475
State of Palestine	..	..	6	8	9	8	19	19
Syrian Arab Republic	..	..	29	40	212	214	749	749
Turkey	..	..	..	96	111	141	168	205
Yemen	–	106	61	109	337	337	338	333
Developing economies: Oceania	**42**	**88**	**128**	**265**	**537**	**561**	**659**	**660**
Fiji	10	22	26	34	44	22	23	23
French Polynesia	..	..	..	47	69	64	71	56
Kiribati	3	1	..	..	..	..	..	..
New Caledonia	..	..	..	28	68	92	83	92
Papua New Guinea	28	43	18	128	328	323	401	401
Samoa	..	3	-	11	9	8	7	9
Solomon Islands	..	6	6	2	3	39	62	67
Tonga	-	1	..	12	14	9	9	9
Vanuatu	..	12	73	3	3	3	3	4
Transition economies	**..**	**..**	**1 890**	**10 249**	**31 893**	**23 604**	**24 074**	**28 937**
Albania	..	..	..	7	16	10	24	21
Armenia	–	–	5	152	185	145	157	161
Azerbaijan	–	–	101	269	593	652	961	1 284
Belarus	–	–	58	95	141	112	104	88
Bosnia and Herzegovina	–	–	2	40	69	61	54	56
Croatia	–	–	44	100	194	174	167	159
Georgia	–	–	25	29	47	32	50	71
Kazakhstan	–	–	440	2 000	3 559	3 058	3 020	3 544
Kyrgyzstan	–	–	45	125	198	186	297	337
Montenegro	–	–	–	–	27	26	28	35
Republic of Moldova	–	–	46	68	115	104	120	100
Russian Federation	–	–	1 099	7 008	26 323	18 779	18 796	22 730
Serbia	–	–	–	–	140	91	70	93
Tajikistan	–	–	..	145	199	124	180	201
TFYR of Macedonia	–	–	14	16	33	26	23	24
Ukraine	–	–	10	34	54	25	24	31
Developed economies: America	**1 360**	**11 850**	**34 397**	**46 293**	**54 581**	**51 825**	**51 799**	**51 794**
Bermuda	..	..	..	..	182	187	202	202
United States	1 360	11 850	34 397	46 293	54 399	51 639	51 597	51 592
Developed economies: Asia	**251**	**2 041**	**6 422**	**3 487**	**8 293**	**7 489**	**8 140**	**9 045**
Israel	31	850	3 255	2 206	3 550	3 421	3 666	4 274
Japan	220	-	3 167	1 281	4 743	4 068	4 474	4 771
Developed economies: Europe	**16 573**	**33 437**	**40 295**	**79 873**	**132 700**	**129 916**	**129 209**	**145 511**
Austria	334	320	1 298	2 567	3 505	3 279	3 590	4 047
Belgium	-	-	-	2 754	4 048	4 238	4 152	4 574
Bulgaria	..	..	26	35	162	101	25	26
Cyprus	9	12	63	273	562	393	392	481
Czech Republic	–	–	605	1 187	3 359	2 768	2 304	2 312
Denmark	..	..	662	1 488	3 977	3 425	2 851	3 153
Estonia	–	–	3	50	98	78	94	86
Faeroe Islands	..	..	6	18	41	31	31	31
Finland	15	16	100	266	457	454	517	542
France	5 070	6 949	3 769	4 182	6 452	14 071	14 451	14 769
Germany, Federal Republic of	5 819		–	–	–	–	–	–
Germany	–	6 856	9 042	13 148	15 701	16 171	15 058	16 677
Greece	59	122	545	902	1 912	1 843	1 932	1 941
Hungary	..	..	86	915	1 536	1 229	1 159	1 209
Iceland	6	25	31	65	56	34	13	12
Ireland	..	165	181	1 535	2 779	2 638	2 354	2 381
Italy	428	3 764	2 582	7 622	13 058	12 868	11 580	13 017
Latvia	–	–	7	20	58	46	43	47
Lithuania	–	–	38	47	652	680	553	1 028
Luxembourg	..	..	2 720	6 573	10 839	10 562	10 343	11 399
Malta	8	25	14	33	56	51	52	53
Netherlands	970	1 393	3 122	5 928	14 914	10 526	9 462	10 974
Norway	110	295	1 060	2 174	4 750	4 174	4 118	4 427
Poland	..	..	311	756	1 775	1 388	1 575	1 981
Portugal	33	77	455	1 306	1 410	1 459	1 406	1 571

For sources and notes, see end of table.

As percentage of GDP (1) En pourcentage du PIB (1)				As percentage of imports of goods and services (2) En pourcentage des importations des biens et services (2)				Régions, pays ou territoires
1990	2000	2010	2011	1990	2000	2010	2011	
4.17	4.60	9.47	7.31	10.74	15.25	33.60	29.65	Koweït
..	..	12.79	12.35	..	..	15.24	14.67	Liban
7.40	7.46	9.63	9.93	25.60	22.85	23.60	25.26	Oman
9.62	8.17	5.94	4.77	25.57	29.08	15.54	14.38	Arabie saoudite
..	0.14	0.22	0.21	..	0.18	0.34	0.29	État de Palestine
..	0.15	1.24	1.17	..	0.54	3.86	3.92	République arabe syrienne
..	..	0.02	0.03	..	..	0.09	0.08	Turquie
2.64	0.56	1.17	1.06	4.90	1.84	3.06	3.17	Yémen
1.65	**2.11**	**2.14**	**1.82**	**3.06**	**3.87**	**3.96**	**3.54**	**Économies en développement : Océanie**
1.59	1.48	0.71	0.59	2.40	2.32	1.10	0.92	Fidji
..	..	1.06	0.78	..	..	3.03	2.39	Polynésie française
3.22	..	..	..	2.86	..	..	..	Kiribati
..	..	0.94	0.93	..	..	1.88	1.89	Nouvelle-Calédonie
1.30	0.53	4.14	3.19	2.83	1.04	6.39	5.52	Papouasie-Nouvelle-Guinée
2.72	-	1.21	1.41	3.21	-	1.99	2.38	Samoa
2.77	1.91	9.13	7.95	3.70	3.92	11.26	10.89	Îles Salomon
0.75	..	2.49	2.05	1.64	..	4.58	3.73	Tonga
7.18	26.71	0.45	0.45	12.05	49.39	0.75	0.78	Vanuatu
..	**0.52**	**1.17**	**1.14**	**..**	**1.59**	**4.13**	**3.89**	**Économies en transition**
..	..	0.20	0.16	..	..	0.38	0.29	Albanie
–	0.25	1.69	1.59	–	0.49	3.72	3.36	Arménie
–	1.91	1.82	2.02	–	4.99	9.08	8.08	Azerbaïdjan
–	0.56	0.19	0.16	–	0.72	0.28	0.18	Bélarus
–	0.04	0.32	0.31	–	0.06	0.55	0.49	Bosnie-Herzégovine
–	0.20	0.28	0.25	–	0.46	0.71	0.61	Croatie
–	0.82	0.43	0.50	–	1.90	0.82	0.89	Géorgie
–	2.41	2.04	1.90	–	4.91	6.83	6.80	Kazakhstan
–	3.31	6.19	5.70	–	6.93	7.60	6.65	Kirghizistan
–	–	0.67	0.76	–	–	1.06	1.19	Monténégro
–	3.57	2.06	1.43	–	4.73	2.62	1.66	République de Moldova
–	0.42	1.26	1.22	–	1.78	5.81	5.46	Fédération de Russie
–	–	0.16	0.20	–	–	0.31	0.35	Serbie
–	..	3.19	3.08	–	..	4.68	4.16	Tadjikistan
–	0.40	0.24	0.24	–	0.62	0.37	0.31	LERY de Macédoine
–	0.03	0.02	0.02	–	0.06	0.03	0.03	Ukraine
0.20	**0.35**	**0.36**	**0.34**	**1.92**	**2.37**	**2.21**	**1.94**	**Économies développées : Amérique**
..	..	3.51	3.39	..	..	10.10	10.73	Bermudes
0.20	0.35	0.36	0.34	1.92	2.37	2.21	1.94	États-Unis
0.06	**0.13**	**0.14**	**0.15**	**0.64**	**1.27**	**0.93**	**0.85**	**Économies développées : Asie**
1.47	2.61	1.69	1.76	4.20	6.96	4.83	4.67	Israël
-	0.07	0.08	0.08	-	0.69	0.56	0.49	Japon
0.46	**0.45**	**0.75**	**0.78**	**1.72**	**1.26**	**1.87**	**1.81**	**Économies développées : Europe**
0.19	0.68	0.95	0.97	0.52	1.52	1.90	1.79	Autriche
-	-	0.88	0.89	-	-	1.13	1.05	Belgique
..	0.20	0.05	0.05	..	0.34	0.09	0.07	Bulgarie
0.21	0.68	1.70	1.92	0.38	1.22	3.58	4.10	Chypre
–	1.03	1.16	1.07	–	1.61	1.80	1.54	République tchèque
..	0.41	0.91	0.95	..	1.03	2.06	1.98	Danemark
–	0.05	0.50	0.39	–	0.06	0.64	0.41	Estonie
..	..	..	..	..	0.94	2.80	2.31	Îles Féroé
0.01	0.08	0.22	0.21	0.05	0.24	0.56	0.49	Finlande
0.56	0.28	0.56	0.53	2.54	1.04	1.90	1.67	France
–	–	–	–	–	–	–	–	Allemagne, Rép. fédérale d'
0.40	0.48	0.46	0.46	1.60	1.44	1.08	1.01	Allemagne
0.13	0.43	0.64	0.65	0.62	1.31	2.41	2.27	Grèce
..	0.19	0.91	0.87	..	0.23	1.13	1.03	Hongrie
0.39	0.36	0.10	0.09	1.19	0.87	0.22	0.17	Islande
0.34	0.19	1.14	1.08	0.67	0.23	1.39	1.30	Irlande
0.33	0.23	0.56	0.59	1.72	0.90	1.98	1.96	Italie
–	0.08	0.18	0.17	–	0.17	0.33	0.27	Lettonie
–	0.33	1.51	2.40	–	0.65	2.17	2.99	Lituanie
..	13.42	19.39	19.15	..	24.60	17.59	16.75	Luxembourg
0.97	0.35	0.64	0.59	1.09	0.35	0.66	0.61	Malte
0.47	0.81	1.21	1.31	0.94	1.29	1.79	1.81	Pays-Bas
0.25	0.63	0.99	0.91	0.76	2.14	3.51	3.22	Norvège
..	0.18	0.34	0.39	..	0.54	0.76	0.82	Pologne
0.10	0.39	0.61	0.66	0.28	0.96	1.57	1.65	Portugal

Pour les sources et les notes, se reporter à la fin du tableau.

Region, country or territory	Millions of dollars - Millions de dollars							
	1980	1990	2000	2005	2008	2009	2010	2011
Romania	..	..	6	33	664	305	360	363
Slovakia	–	–	8	39	144	138	70	70
Slovenia	–	–	29	94	380	195	153	166
Spain	11	254	2 486	8 136	14 826	12 751	12 244	12 904
Sweden	83	654	539	537	742	787	695	1 233
Switzerland	2 339	8 168	7 591	13 311	19 150	19 834	24 193	30 779
United Kingdom	..	2 034	2 044	3 877	4 637	3 400	3 439	3 256
Developed economies: Oceania	**455**	**1 041**	**1 512**	**3 365**	**4 343**	**4 126**	**4 925**	**5 189**
Australia	304	674	1 053	2 375	3 049	3 173	3 776	3 776
New Zealand	151	367	459	991	1 295	953	1 149	1 413

Sources:

UNCTAD secretariat calculations, based on:

- World Bank, *Migration and Remittances*

- Other national sources

Notes:

-    Migrants' remittances data cover: workers' remittances, compensation of employees and migrants' transfers.

(1)   GDP data source: *UNCTADstat*.

(2)   Exports and imports of goods and services data are based on IMF *Balance Of Payments Statistics*.

As percentage of GDP (1) En pourcentage du PIB (1)				As percentage of imports of goods and services (2) En pourcentage des importations des biens et services (2)				Régions, pays ou territoires
1990	2000	2010	2011	1990	2000	2010	2011	
..	0.02	0.22	0.19	..	0.04	0.53	0.44	Roumanie
_	0.04	0.08	0.07	_	0.05	0.10	0.08	Slovaquie
_	0.15	0.32	0.33	_	0.26	0.50	0.47	Slovénie
0.05	0.43	0.88	0.87	0.25	1.34	3.00	2.80	Espagne
0.27	0.22	0.15	0.23	0.93	0.56	0.36	0.53	Suède
3.33	2.94	4.35	4.61	8.70	7.19	8.57	8.43	Suisse
0.20	0.14	0.15	0.13	0.77	0.47	0.47	0.40	Royaume-Uni
0.28	**0.33**	**0.35**	**0.31**	**1.61**	**1.44**	**1.72**	**1.48**	**Économies développées : Océanie**
0.21	0.26	0.29	0.25	1.27	1.20	1.53	1.25	Australie
0.81	0.85	0.80	0.87	3.13	2.65	2.96	3.04	Nouvelle-Zélande

Sources:

Calculs du secrétariat de la CNUCED, basés sur :

- Banque Mondiale, *Migration and Remittances*

- Autres sources nationales

Notes :

-    Les envois de fonds des migrants couvrent : les envois de fonds des travailleurs, la rémunération des employés et les transferts des migrants.

(1)   Source de données du PIB : *UNCTADstat.*

(2)   Les données sur les exportations et importations des biens et services se basent sur les *Statistiques de la balance des paiements* du FMI.

Economic grouping	Millions of dollars - Millions de dollars							
	1980	1990	2000	2005	2008	2009	2010	2011
DEVELOPING ECONOMIES	**11 607**	**19 572**	**33 141**	**55 575**	**88 429**	**95 460**	**94 516**	**101 028**
Developing economies excluding China	11 607	19 567	32 351	52 452	82 081	91 016	92 762	97 462
Developing economies excluding LDCs	11 010	18 754	31 768	54 034	85 403	92 043	90 864	97 391
High-income developing economies	8 673	17 311	28 647	45 432	68 842	75 157	74 793	78 676
Middle-income developing economies	712	842	2 497	6 485	12 178	13 424	11 659	13 937
Low-income developing economies	2 223	1 419	1 997	3 658	7 409	6 879	8 065	8 414
Heavily indebted poor countries (IMF)	1 534	1 189	1 347	1 762	2 790	3 171	3 233	3 222
Landlocked developing countries	431	460	1 390	3 625	6 431	5 983	6 541	7 737
Small island developing States	159	238	479	905	1 221	1 084	1 210	1 316
Least developed countries	*597*	*818*	*1 373*	*1 541*	*3 026*	*3 417*	*3 652*	*3 636*
Africa and Haiti	592	685	1 089	1 140	2 133	2 346	2 472	2 410
Asia	0	106	200	384	879	1 020	1 108	1 147
Islands	4	27	84	16	14	51	73	80
Major petroleum and gas exporters	*7 341*	*14 184*	*19 637*	*20 737*	*39 792*	*46 313*	*47 795*	*49 856*
Africa	1 740	636	730	1 224	1 719	2 170	2 399	1 361
America	418	701	331	211	842	581	805	782
Asia	5 183	12 847	18 576	19 302	37 232	43 562	44 591	47 713
Major exporters of manufactured goods	*123*	*1 462*	*7 098*	*19 332*	*24 281*	*24 010*	*19 469*	*22 431*
America	11	..	..	..	..	..	..	..
Asia	112	1 462	7 098	19 332	24 281	24 010	19 469	22 431
Emerging economies	*381*	*1 645*	*7 007*	*16 818*	*19 499*	*21 013*	*19 597*	*20 912*
America	269	188	925	957	1 960	1 861	2 365	2 596
Asia	112	1 457	6 083	15 861	17 539	19 152	17 232	18 316
Newly industrialized Asian economies	*124*	*1 462*	*6 329*	*17 403*	*19 948*	*22 321*	*20 617*	*22 108*
First tier	58	1 028	5 709	10 530	11 147	10 479	13 563	14 497
Second tier	66	434	620	6 873	8 801	11 842	7 053	7 611
Developing economies: Africa	4 660	3 407	3 078	4 408	5 920	6 381	6 831	5 793
Northern Africa excluding Sudan	1 317	532	551	1 054	1 306	1 736	2 017	1 105
Sub-Saharan Africa	3 344	2 875	2 527	3 354	4 614	4 645	4 814	4 688
Sub-Saharan Africa excluding South Africa	2 327	1 676	1 842	2 298	3 482	3 487	3 442	3 246
Developing economies: America	1 083	1 140	2 238	2 640	4 647	4 421	5 323	5 678
Central America and Greater Caribbean Islands excluding Puerto Rico	160	72	469	878	1 150	1 257	1 375	1 519
Central America and Greater Caribbean Islands excluding Mexico and Puerto Rico	149	72	469	878	1 150	1 257	1 375	1 519
South America and Central America	875	997	1 807	1 795	3 730	3 617	4 514	4 787
South America excluding Brazil	652	939	1 181	913	1 960	1 831	2 463	2 561
Developing economies: Asia	5 821	14 937	27 696	48 262	77 325	84 098	81 702	88 896
Eastern and South-Eastern Asia excluding China	124	1 462	6 450	18 250	21 772	23 811	22 105	23 764
Southern Asia excluding India	1	9	89	401	879	1 047	1 203	1 350

For sources and notes, see end of table 7.4.1.

As percentage of GDP (1) En pourcentage du PIB (1)				As percentage of imports of goods and services (2) En pourcentage des importations des biens et services (2)				Groupements économiques
1990	2000	2010	2011	1990	2000	2010	2011	
0.75	0.63	0.51	0.47	3.81	2.09	1.62	1.45	ÉCONOMIES EN DÉVELOPPEMENT
0.89	0.79	0.74	0.69	4.19	2.43	2.16	1.93	Économies en développement sans la Chine
0.74	0.62	0.50	0.47	3.81	2.07	1.62	1.45	Économies en développement sans les PMA
1.40	1.05	1.05	0.99	6.47	2.91	2.89	2.59	Économies en développement à revenu élevé
0.10	0.14	0.13	0.14	0.50	0.56	0.48	0.47	Économies en développement à revenu intermédiaire
0.26	0.25	0.29	0.28	1.82	1.29	1.00	0.89	Économies en développement à revenu faible
1.08	1.08	0.81	0.84	4.73	3.48	2.07	2.11	Pays pauvres très endettés (FMI)
0.84	1.61	1.55	1.54	3.42	4.15	4.25	4.07	Pays en développement sans littoral
0.89	1.39	2.01	1.95	1.03	2.63	3.42	3.20	Petits États insulaires en développement
0.99	0.84	0.65	0.64	3.85	2.85	1.88	1.64	Pays les moins avancés
0.88	1.24	0.74	0.65	3.69	3.94	2.04	1.69	Afrique et Haïti
2.64	0.27	0.50	0.58	4.90	1.00	1.55	1.48	Asie
3.02	9.20	3.36	3.16	5.30	17.99	5.03	4.98	Îles
4.27	4.30	2.83	2.70	15.22	17.11	9.25	8.54	Principaux exportateurs de pétrole et de gaz
0.46	0.78	0.44	0.23	2.17	3.21	1.30	0.67	Afrique
1.49	0.28	0.20	0.25	7.42	1.55	1.56	1.25	Amérique
8.76	7.56	5.94	5.00	23.62	26.29	15.89	15.01	Asie
0.18	0.31	0.24	0.23	0.77	0.76	0.61	0.59	Principaux exportateurs d'articles manufacturés
..	..	..	..	..	..	..	..	Amérique
0.18	0.31	0.24	0.23	0.77	0.76	0.61	0.59	Asie
0.17	0.35	0.40	0.37	0.85	1.19	1.21	1.08	Économies émergentes
0.03	0.09	0.08	0.08	0.39	0.67	0.57	0.50	Amérique
0.36	0.64	0.85	0.82	1.01	1.35	1.44	1.30	Asie
0.32	0.52	0.65	0.62	0.92	0.86	1.10	1.00	Économies nouvellement industrialisées d'Asie
0.38	0.56	0.81	0.79	1.34	0.96	1.08	0.99	Première génération
0.23	0.35	0.47	0.44	0.53	0.43	1.13	1.03	Deuxième génération
0.72	0.59	0.41	0.33	2.95	2.11	1.20	0.94	Économies en développement : Afrique
0.31	0.29	0.35	0.18	1.13	1.11	0.98	0.53	Afrique septentrionale sans le Soudan
0.95	0.77	0.44	0.41	4.20	2.62	1.33	1.16	Afrique subsaharienne
0.88	0.94	0.48	0.44	3.53	2.91	1.32	1.14	Afrique subsaharienne sans l'Afrique du Sud
0.16	0.16	0.14	0.13	1.32	0.93	0.79	0.68	Économies en développement : Amérique
0.31	0.46	0.63	0.62	0.70	0.97	1.33	1.22	Amérique centrale et Grandes Antilles sans Porto Rico
0.31	0.46	0.63	0.62	0.70	0.97	1.33	1.22	Amérique centrale et Grandes Antilles sans le Mexique et Porto Rico
0.14	0.13	0.12	0.11	1.30	0.85	0.71	0.61	Amérique du Sud et Amérique centrale
0.29	0.18	0.16	0.15	2.30	1.09	0.79	0.65	Amérique du Sud sans le Brésil
1.07	0.83	0.63	0.59	4.84	2.32	1.79	1.62	Économies en développement : Asie
0.32	0.53	0.68	0.65	0.92	0.87	1.15	1.06	Asie orientale et Asie du Sud-Est sans la Chine
0.02	0.06	0.34	0.32	0.09	0.28	1.16	1.06	Asie méridionale sans l'Inde

Pour les sources et les notes, se reporter à la fin du tableau 7.4.1.

7

Region, country or territory	Total reserves including gold (1) - Réserves totales, y compris l'or (1) Millions of dollars - Millions de dollars							
	1980	1990	2000	2005	2009	2010	2011	2012
DEVELOPING ECONOMIES	177 117	330 903	1 057 607	2 693 789	5 946 630	6 782 471	7 449 895	7 938 272
Developing economies: Africa	36 550	27 978	79 903	220 395	474 698	490 135	506 801	544 527
Eastern Africa	*1 788*	*2 326*	*6 017*	*10 735*	*21 590*	*24 082*	*25 103*	*28 798*
Burundi	95	106	34	100	322	331	294	307
Comoros	6	30	43	86	150	145	155	(e)179
Djibouti	-	94	68	89	242	249	244	249
Eritrea			27	28	90	114	115	(e)181
Ethiopia (...1991)	94	25						
Ethiopia			316	1 043	1 781	(e)2 766	(e)3 100	(e)3 169
Kenya	495	209	898	1 799	3 849	4 320	4 264	5 711
Madagascar	9	92	285	481	1 135	1 172	1 279	1 191
Malawi	69	138	244	160	150	308	198	224
Mauritius	92	741	900	1 343	2 186	2 449	2 589	2 843
Mozambique	-	232	726	1 059	2 103	2 163	2 473	2 776
Rwanda	196	44	191	406	743	813	1 050	(e)1 035
Seychelles	18	17	44	56	191	236	290	319
Somalia	26	..	..	..	..	..	..	..
Uganda	3	44	808	1 344	2 994	2 706	2 617	3 169
United Republic of Tanzania	20	193	974	2 049	3 470	3 905	3 726	4 053
Zambia	88	194	245	560	1 892	2 094	2 324	3 042
Zimbabwe	229	168	214	(e)133	(e)291	(e)312	(e)383	(e)350
Middle Africa	*2 344*	*2 401*	*2 187*	*8 176*	*28 321*	*34 084*	*42 970*	*49 579*
Angola	-	-	1 198	3 197	13 664	19 749	26 477	30 983
Cameroon	190	27	213	951	3 676	3 643	3 199	3 381
Central African Republic	55	119	134	140	211	181	155	158
Chad	6	128	111	226	617	632	968	(e)1 076
Congo	86	6	223	732	3 806	4 447	5 641	5 550
Dem. Rep. of the Congo	217	224	83	131	1 035	1 300	1 268	1 633
Equatorial Guinea	-	1	23	2 102	3 252	2 346	3 054	4 397
Gabon	108	274	191	669	1 993	1 736	2 157	2 352
Sao Tome and Principe	1	0	12	27	67	49	51	52
Northern Africa	*19 482*	*12 721*	*44 993*	*139 591*	*315 712*	*329 711*	*330 483*	*345 537*
Algeria	4 022	981	12 278	56 582	149 347	162 915	183 122	191 597
Egypt	1 155	2 805	13 228	20 731	32 386	33 743	15 046	11 758
Libya	13 228	6 018	12 672	39 739	98 979	99 895	104 999	(e)117 227
Morocco	430	2 102	4 855	16 223	22 836	22 651	19 564	16 394
Sudan (...2011)	49	11	138	1 869	1 094	1 036	295	
Sudan								193
Tunisia	598	804	1 821	4 448	11 069	9 471	7 457	8 369
Southern Africa	*1 811*	*4 912*	*13 700*	*26 163*	*48 089*	*49 741*	*54 235*	*55 349*
Botswana	334	3 331	6 318	6 309	8 704	7 885	8 082	7 628
Lesotho	50	72	418	519	(e)918	(e)1 012	(e)955	(e)1 023
Namibia	..	80	260	312	2 051	1 696	1 787	1 746
South Africa	1 268	1 212	6 352	18 779	35 458	38 392	42 811	44 212
Swaziland	159	216	352	244	959	756	601	741
Western Africa	*11 125*	*5 618*	*13 007*	*35 731*	*60 986*	*52 516*	*54 011*	*65 263*
Benin	9	65	459	655	1 230	1 200	887	713
Burkina Faso	69	301	243	438	1 296	1 068	957	1 025
Cape Verde	42	77	28	174	398	382	339	376
Côte d'Ivoire	22	6	674	1 367	3 267	3 624	4 316	3 928
Gambia	6	55	109	98	224	202	223	236
Ghana	192	231	245	1 767	3 402	4 778	5 498	5 383
Guinea	-	-	151	95	111	134	112	(e)189
Guinea-Bissau	-	18	67	80	169	156	220	165
Liberia	5	-	0	25	372	466	513	500
Mali	15	191	382	854	1 604	1 344	1 379	1 341
Mauritania	140	55	47	65	226	272	485	950
Niger	126	223	81	251	656	760	673	1 015
Nigeria	10 265	3 899	9 942	28 314	44 800	34 956	35 249	46 442
Senegal	9	12	388	1 186	2 123	2 047	1 946	2 082
Sierra Leone	31	5	49	171	405	409	439	478
Togo	78	354	141	192	703	715	774	442
Developing economies: America	40 316	49 202	157 762	258 662	553 794	638 014	744 569	804 175
Caribbean	*3 445*	*1 712*	*5 471*	*14 210*	*23 640*	*25 614*	*27 083*	*26 085*
Anguilla	..	7	20	40	37	40	38	40
Antigua and Barbuda	8	28	64	127	128	137	148	159

For sources and notes, see end of table.

7.5.1 Réserves internationales des économies en développement par pays et régions géographiques

Annual change in reserves (millions of dollars) Variations annuelles des réserves (millions de dollars)				Number of months of imports (2) Nombre de mois d'importations (2)								Régions, pays ou territoires
2005	2010	2011	2012	1980	1990	2000	2005	2009	2010	2011	2012	
517 207	835 841	666 985	488 480	4.4	5.0	6.7	9.5	15.4	13.6	12.2	12.5	ÉCONOMIES EN DÉVELOPPEMENT
54 097	15 437	16 667	37 828	4.6	3.6	7.4	10.3	13.9	12.4	10.8	10.8	Économies en développement : Afrique
-458	2 492	1 021	3 695	2.0	2.2	4.4	4.2	5.0	4.9	4.1	4.3	Afrique orientale
34	9	-37	13	6.8	5.5	2.7	4.5	9.6	7.8	4.7	4.7	Burundi
-18	-5	10	(e)23	2.6	6.9	12.0	10.4	8.6	7.5	6.7	(e)7.1	Comores
-5	7	-5	5	-	5.2	3.9	3.9	6.4	8.0	5.7	5.1	Djibouti
-7	24	1	(e)66	_	_	0.7	0.7	1.8	2.0	1.5	(e)2.3	Érythrée
_	_	_	_	1.6	0.3	_	_	_	_	_	_	Éthiopie (…1991)
-454	(e)985	(e)334	(e)69	_	_	3.0	3.1	2.8	(e)3.9	(e)4.2	(e)3.2	Éthiopie
280	471	-56	1 447	2.8	1.1	3.5	3.7	4.5	4.3	3.5	4.2	Kenya
-22	36	108	-88	0.2	1.7	3.1	3.4	4.3	5.6	5.3	4.7	Madagascar
31	158	-110	26	1.9	2.9	5.5	1.0	0.0	1.7	1.0	1.1	Malawi
-266	263	141	254	1.8	5.5	4.9	5.1	7.0	6.7	6.0	6.6	Maurice
-76	60	310	303	-	3.2	7.5	5.3	6.7	5.6	4.7	4.9	Mozambique
91	70	237	(e)-15	9.0	1.9	10.7	11.3	6.8	6.8	7.1	(e)6.2	Rwanda
22	45	55	28	2.2	1.1	1.5	1.0	2.9	4.3	4.6	4.8	Seychelles
..	..	..	..	0.7	..	..	..	..	..	..	..	Somalie
36	-288	-89	551	0.1	1.8	6.3	7.9	8.5	7.0	5.6	6.4	Ouganda
-247	434	-179	327	0.2	1.7	7.7	7.5	6.8	6.2	4.3	4.4	République-Unie de Tanzanie
223	202	230	718	1.0	1.9	3.3	2.6	5.9	4.7	3.9	4.6	Zambie
(e)-79	(e)21	(e)71	(e)-32	2.0	1.1	1.4	(e)0.7	(e)1.2	(e)1.0	(e)1.0	(e)1.0	Zimbabwe
3 834	5 763	8 886	6 609	4.8	4.1	3.5	5.2	7.7	9.8	10.3	10.7	Afrique centrale
1 823	6 085	6 728	4 505	-	-	4.7	4.6	7.2	14.2	15.7	15.5	Angola
120	-33	-444	182	1.4	0.2	1.7	4.2	9.9	8.5	5.9	5.7	Cameroun
-9	-29	-27	3	8.2	9.3	13.7	9.6	9.4	7.2	6.0	5.9	République centrafricaine
4	15	336	(e)108	0.9	3.1	4.2	2.9	3.7	3.2	4.3	(e)5.0	Tchad
612	641	1 194	-92	1.8	0.1	5.7	6.7	15.8	13.3	13.0	12.8	Congo
-105	264	-32	365	1.7	1.5	1.4	0.6	3.2	3.5	2.8	3.2	Rép. dém. du Congo
1 158	-906	707	1 343	-	0.1	0.5	19.3	7.5	4.9	6.1	8.8	Guinée équatoriale
225	-257	421	194	1.9	3.6	2.4	5.5	9.6	7.0	7.0	7.2	Gabon
7	-17	2	0	0.7	0.0	4.7	6.4	7.7	5.3	4.7	4.4	Sao Tomé-et-Principe
34 035	13 999	772	15 156	7.4	4.1	11.0	18.7	23.9	22.1	20.7	19.1	Afrique septentrionale
13 033	13 568	20 207	8 475	4.6	1.2	16.1	33.4	45.6	48.3	46.5	49.1	Algérie
6 325	1 357	-18 697	-3 288	2.9	3.7	10.9	11.1	8.6	7.7	3.1	2.0	Égypte
13 799	916	5 104	(e)12 228	23.4	13.5	40.7	78.4	92.4	67.8	157.5	(e)61.2	Libye
-152	-185	-3 087	-3 171	1.2	3.6	5.1	9.4	8.3	7.7	5.3	4.4	Maroc
531	-58	-741	_	0.4	0.2	1.1	3.3	1.4	1.2	0.4	_	Soudan (…2011)
			..	_	_	_	_	_	_	_	0.3	Soudan
500	-1 598	-2 014	912	2.0	1.8	2.6	4.1	7.0	5.1	3.7	4.1	Tunisie
5 973	1 652	4 494	1 114	1.0	2.6	4.7	4.4	6.6	5.4	4.7	4.7	Afrique australe
648	-819	197	-454	5.8	20.5	36.4	24.0	22.1	16.7	13.3	11.4	Botswana
18	(e)95	(e)-58	(e)68	1.4	1.3	6.2	4.4	(e)6.0	(e)5.3	(e)4.6	(e)4.7	Lesotho
-33	-355	91	-41	..	0.8	2.0	1.5	4.9	3.7	3.4	3.1	Namibie
5 421	2 934	4 420	1 401	0.8	0.8	2.6	3.6	5.7	4.9	4.2	4.3	Afrique du Sud
-80	-203	-156	140	3.0	3.9	4.0	1.5	6.5	4.6	3.7	4.6	Swaziland
10 711	-8 469	1 494	11 252	5.1	4.6	7.4	9.5	10.7	7.4	6.1	7.3	Afrique occidentale
20	-30	-313	-175	0.3	3.0	9.0	7.7	7.1	7.0	4.8	3.9	Bénin
-221	-228	-111	68	2.3	6.7	4.8	4.2	8.3	6.3	4.8	3.9	Burkina Faso
34	-16	-44	37	7.5	6.8	1.5	4.8	6.7	6.2	4.3	5.9	Cap-Vert
-313	358	692	-388	0.1	0.0	3.3	2.8	5.6	5.5	7.7	4.8	Côte d'Ivoire
15	-23	22	13	0.4	3.5	7.0	4.5	8.9	8.5	7.8	7.5	Gambie
125	1 377	720	-116	2.0	2.3	1.0	4.0	5.1	5.2	4.1	3.6	Ghana
-15	24	-23	(e)77	-	2.6	3.0	1.4	1.3	1.1	0.6	(e)1.0	Guinée
8	-12	64	-55	-	2.6	13.5	7.8	10.0	9.5	10.2	7.9	Guinée-Bissau
7	94	47	-14	0.1	-	0.0	1.0	8.1	7.9	5.9	5.6	Libéria
3	-260	34	-37	0.4	3.8	5.7	6.6	7.7	4.7	4.9	5.5	Mali
31	46	213	465	5.9	3.0	1.2	0.5	1.8	1.7	2.4	4.1	Mauritanie
1	105	-87	341	2.6	6.9	2.5	3.2	3.6	3.7	3.0	4.2	Niger
11 321	-9 844	292	11 193	7.4	8.3	13.7	16.4	15.9	9.5	7.6	10.9	Nigéria
-182	-76	-102	136	0.1	0.1	3.0	4.1	5.4	5.1	4.0	3.9	Sénégal
45	4	30	39	0.9	0.4	4.0	5.9	9.3	6.4	3.1	3.3	Sierra Leone
-166	12	59	-333	1.7	7.3	3.0	2.2	5.6	5.4	5.2	2.9	Togo
35 401	84 220	106 116	59 606	4.1	4.7	4.9	5.8	9.6	8.6	8.2	8.5	Économies en développement : Amérique
3 774	1 974	1 029	-998	2.0	1.2	2.2	4.4	6.1	5.9	5.2	4.9	Caraïbes
5	2	-2	2	..	..	2.6	3.7	2.7	3.0	2.9	3.2	Anguilla
7	9	11	11	1.1	1.3	1.9	3.0	2.9	3.3	3.8	3.7	Antigua-et-Barbuda

Pour les sources et les notes, se reporter à la fin du tableau.

Region, country or territory	Total reserves including gold (1) - Réserves totales, y compris l'or (1) Millions of dollars - Millions de dollars							
	1980	1990	2000	2005	2009	2010	2011	2012
Aruba	..	103	213	279	584	574	542	608
Bahamas	92	158	350	586	1 010	1 044	1 070	847
Barbados	79	118	473	603	871	834	813	(e)785
Cuba	..	(e)198	(e)543	(e)2 393	(e)3 893	(e)4 093	(e)4 393	(e)4 693
Dominica	5	14	29	49	75	76	81	94
Dominican Republic	208	62	628	1 934	3 564	3 858	4 090	3 549
Grenada	13	18	58	94	129	119	121	118
Haiti	17	4	182	133	789	1 335	1 195	1 285
Jamaica	105	(e)168	1 054	2 170	2 076	2 501	2 282	1 981
Montserrat	..	10	10	14	14	17	25	31
Saint Kitts and Nevis	..	16	45	72	136	169	244	262
Saint Lucia	8	45	79	116	175	206	213	230
Saint Vincent and the Grenadines	7	26	55	70	88	113	90	110
Trinidad and Tobago	2 783	495	1 389	4 964	9 181	9 609	10 409	9 798
Central America	*4 116*	*11 728*	*43 037*	*86 124*	*118 431*	*140 539*	*164 126*	*184 617*
Belize	13	70	123	71	214	218	237	290
Costa Rica	149	521	1 318	2 313	4 066	4 627	4 756	6 857
El Salvador	101	438	1 794	1 739	2 882	2 582	2 165	2 819
Guatemala	468	292	1 756	3 675	4 976	5 649	5 847	6 337
Honduras	151	41	1 314	2 328	2 088	2 672	2 751	2 496
Mexico	3 052	9 909	35 520	74 060	99 604	120 277	144 174	160 628
Nicaragua	65	113	489	728	1 573	1 799	1 892	1 887
Panama, excl. Canal Zone	117	–	–	–	–	–	–	–
Panama	–	344	723	1 211	3 028	2 714	2 304	(e)3 303
South America	*32 756*	*35 762*	*109 254*	*158 327*	*411 723*	*471 861*	*553 360*	*593 473*
Argentina (3)	6 915	4 803	25 148	27 267	46 190	49 829	43 333	40 027
Bolivia (Plurinational State of)	140	211	969	1 373	7 634	8 195	9 984	11 733
Brazil	5 853	7 668	32 531	53 299	237 424	287 114	350 415	369 682
Chile	3 199	6 161	15 038	16 930	25 284	27 817	41 932	41 637
Colombia	4 955	4 659	8 931	14 803	24 760	27 778	31 404	36 462
Ecuador	1 031	861	985	1 757	2 920	1 480	1 710	1 125
Guyana	13	29	305	252	631	782	802	864
Paraguay	763	663	764	1 297	3 840	4 138	4 951	4 571
Peru	2 042	1 150	8 424	13 655	32 074	42 708	47 266	62 360
Suriname	192	24	75	127	600	605	712	889
Uruguay	537	643	2 528	3 074	8 029	7 644	10 289	13 591
Venezuela (Bolivarian Rep. of)	7 116	8 891	13 555	24 493	22 339	13 771	10 562	10 533
Developing economies: Asia	**99 596**	**252 901**	**818 969**	**2 213 349**	**4 914 393**	**5 649 770**	**6 192 461**	**6 583 642**
Eastern Asia	*13 441*	*143 242*	*483 419*	*1 418 060*	*3 312 233*	*3 836 739*	*4 216 848*	*4 397 994*
China	3 117	30 219	168 857	822 479	2 417 911	2 867 905	3 204 615	3 332 949
China, Hong Kong SAR	(e)5 041	24 579	107 545	124 247	255 772	268 652	285 299	317 254
China, Macao SAR	..	521	3 323	6 689	18 350	23 726	34 026	16 600
China, Taiwan Province of	2 345	73 115	107 360	253 971	348 946	382 739	386 277	403 901
Korea, Republic of	2 938	14 809	96 150	210 340	269 958	291 515	304 349	323 353
Mongolia	..	..	183	333	1 296	2 200	2 281	3 937
Southern Asia	*19 546*	*9 587*	*56 683*	*197 283*	*381 254*	*391 580*	*391 622*	*381 718*
Afghanistan	414	314	-	-	3 540	4 212	5 306	6 020
Bangladesh	302	633	1 491	2 773	10 225	10 588	8 533	12 055
Bhutan	-	89	318	467	891	1 002	790	(e)830
India	7 327	2 053	38 427	132 500	266 166	276 243	272 249	271 551
Iran (Islamic Rep. of)	10 417	5 351	(e)12 426	(e)45 459	(e)81 309	(e)75 060	(e)79 860	(e)69 860
Maldives	1	24	123	189	276	364	349	318
Nepal	190	303	952	1 505	2 761	2 925	3 631	-
Pakistan	577	393	1 609	10 138	11 434	14 457	14 639	10 353
Sri Lanka	248	426	1 054	2 658	4 653	6 728	6 265	(e)7 100
South-Eastern Asia	*21 461*	*60 508*	*187 248*	*297 858*	*548 267*	*670 963*	*739 496*	*792 195*
Brunei Darussalam	..	..	408	492	1 357	1 563	2 490	3 321
Cambodia	..	..	520	973	2 873	3 277	3 471	4 289
Indonesia (...2002)	5 499	7 614	28 643	–	–	–	–	–
Indonesia	–	–	–	33 296	63 692	93 035	106 665	108 965
Lao People's Dem. Rep.	..	2	139	234	609	703	757	(e)771
Malaysia	4 491	9 871	28 383	69 916	95 496	104 947	131 843	137 847
Myanmar	272	325	234	782	5 265	5 729	7 016	(e)5 751
Philippines	2 932	1 068	13 420	16 174	39 056	55 630	67 565	73 812
Singapore	6 567	27 790	79 961	115 960	187 591	225 504	237 528	259 094
Thailand	1 671	13 428	32 124	50 826	135 631	167 703	167 653	173 591
Timor-Leste	–	–	–	153	250	406	462	884
Viet Nam	-	409	3 417	9 051	16 447	12 467	14 046	(e)23 871

For sources and notes, see end of table.

Annual change in reserves (millions of dollars) / Variations annuelles des réserves (millions de dollars)				Number of months of imports (2) / Nombre de mois d'importations (2)								Régions, pays ou territoires
2005	2010	2011	2012	1980	1990	2000	2005	2009	2010	2011	2012	
-22	-10	-32	66	..	2.3	3.1	3.2	6.4	6.8	5.4	5.8	Aruba
-88	34	26	-223	0.1	1.7	2.0	3.0	4.8	4.8	4.3	2.9	Bahamas
24	-38	-21	(e)-27	1.8	2.0	4.9	4.5	7.2	6.4	5.4	(e)5.3	Barbade
(e)500	(e)200	(e)300	(e)300	..	(e)0.5	(e)1.3	(e)3.6	(e)4.9	(e)4.3	(e)3.7	(e)3.9	Cuba
7	1	5	13	1.3	1.5	2.4	3.6	4.0	4.2	4.5	5.6	Dominique
1 135	295	232	-541	1.3	0.2	0.8	2.4	3.5	3.0	2.8	2.4	République dominicaine
-27	-10	2	-2	3.1	2.0	2.9	3.4	5.5	4.5	4.4	4.2	Grenade
19	546	-140	90	0.5	0.1	2.1	1.1	4.5	5.1	4.7	5.5	Haïti
323	425	-219	-301	1.1	(e)1.0	3.8	5.5	4.9	5.7	4.1	3.5	Jamaïque
0	3	8	6	..	2.7	5.8	5.6	5.8	6.9	8.9	10.7	Montserrat
-7	32	75	18	..	1.8	2.8	4.1	5.5	7.5	11.9	13.7	Saint-Kitts-et-Nevis
-16	31	7	16	0.8	2.0	2.7	2.9	4.0	3.7	3.7	3.9	Sainte-Lucie
-5	25	-23	21	1.5	2.3	4.1	3.5	3.2	4.0	3.2	3.8	Saint-Vincent-et-les Grenadines
1 792	428	800	-612	10.5	5.4	5.0	10.5	15.8	17.8	13.1	12.5	Trinité-et-Tobago
11 520	*22 108*	*23 587*	*20 491*	*1.7*	*2.7*	*2.5*	*3.8*	*4.8*	*4.5*	*4.4*	*4.7*	**Amérique centrale**
23	4	19	53	1.0	4.0	2.8	1.4	3.8	3.7	3.4	3.2	Belize
391	561	129	2 101	1.2	3.1	2.5	2.8	4.3	4.1	3.5	4.7	Costa Rica
-38	-299	-417	654	1.3	4.2	4.4	3.1	4.7	3.7	2.6	3.3	El Salvador
237	673	198	490	3.5	2.1	4.1	4.2	5.2	4.9	4.2	4.5	Guatemala
357	584	79	-255	1.8	0.5	4.0	4.3	3.4	3.6	3.0	2.7	Honduras
9 911	20 673	23 897	16 454	1.7	2.7	2.4	3.9	4.4	4.7	4.8	5.1	Mexique
60	226	93	-5	0.9	2.1	3.3	3.3	5.4	5.2	4.4	3.9	Nicaragua
				1.0	–	–	–	–	–	–	–	Panama, sans la zone du canal
580	-314	-411	(e)999	–	2.7	2.6	1.5	2.6	1.9	1.3	(e)1.7	Panama
20 107	*60 138*	*81 499*	*40 113*	*5.9*	*7.6*	*8.7*	*8.7*	*14.2*	*12.2*	*11.3*	*11.8*	**Amérique du Sud**
8 286	3 639	-6 495	-3 306	7.9	14.1	12.0	11.4	14.3	10.6	7.0	7.0	Argentine (3)
451	561	1 789	1 749	2.5	3.7	6.4	7.0	20.2	18.3	15.6	17.4	Bolivie (État plurinational de)
779	49 690	63 301	19 267	2.8	4.1	6.7	8.2	21.3	18.0	17.7	19.0	Brésil
935	2 533	14 115	-296	6.6	9.3	9.8	6.2	7.1	5.6	6.7	6.3	Chili
1 392	3 018	3 626	5 058	12.5	10.0	9.3	8.4	9.0	8.2	6.9	7.5	Colombie
641	-1 439	229	-584	5.5	5.5	3.2	2.0	2.3	0.9	0.8	0.5	Équateur
20	151	20	62	0.4	1.1	6.4	3.8	6.5	6.7	5.4	5.6	Guyana
129	298	813	-380	14.9	5.9	4.1	4.2	6.6	4.9	4.8	4.8	Paraguay
1 418	10 634	4 558	15 094	9.5	5.2	13.6	13.1	17.6	17.0	14.9	17.6	Pérou
-3	6	107	177	4.6	0.6	1.7	1.5	5.2	5.2	5.2	6.5	Suriname
566	-385	2 645	3 302	3.8	5.7	8.8	9.5	14.0	10.6	11.5	14.0	Uruguay
5 493	-8 569	-3 209	-29	7.2	14.5	10.0	12.2	6.5	4.2	2.6	2.1	Venezuela (Rép. bolivarienne du)
427 784	**735 377**	**542 691**	**391 181**	**4.4**	**5.3**	**7.1**	**10.2**	**16.7**	**14.7**	**13.1**	**13.4**	**Économies en développement : Asie**
231 838	*524 506*	*380 109*	*181 146*	*1.9*	*6.5*	*7.8*	*12.1*	*21.3*	*18.2*	*16.5*	*16.6*	**Asie orientale**
206 931	449 994	336 710	128 334	1.9	6.8	9.0	15.0	28.8	24.6	22.1	22.0	Chine
704	12 880	16 647	31 955	(e)2.6	3.5	6.0	5.0	8.7	7.3	6.7	6.9	Chine (RAS de Hong Kong)
1 253	5 376	10 300	-17 426	..	4.1	15.2	17.8	46.3	50.6	51.5	21.9	Chine (RAS de Macao)
11 494	33 793	3 538	17 624	1.4	16.0	9.2	16.7	24.0	18.3	16.5	17.9	Province chinoise de Taiwan
11 319	21 558	12 833	19 004	1.6	2.5	7.2	9.7	10.0	8.2	7.0	7.5	Corée, République de
138	904	81	1 655	..	..	3.6	3.4	7.3	8.1	4.1	7.0	Mongolie
18 529	*10 326*	*42*	*-9 904*	*6.1*	*2.0*	*7.2*	*10.0*	*12.0*	*9.3*	*7.3*	*7.0*	**Asie méridionale**
-	672	1 094	714	5.9	4.0	-	-	12.7	9.8	10.0	11.7	Afghanistan
-406	363	-2 055	3 522	1.4	2.1	2.0	2.4	5.6	4.6	2.8	4.2	Bangladesh
69	111	-212	(e)40	-	13.1	21.8	14.5	20.2	14.1	9.0	(e)9.8	Bhoutan
5 281	10 077	-3 993	-699	5.9	1.0	8.9	11.1	12.4	9.5	7.0	6.7	Inde
(e)12 500	(e)-6 249	(e)4 800	(e)-10 000	10.2	3.5	(e)10.7	(e)13.6	(e)19.2	(e)13.8	(e)15.5	(e)14.8	Iran (Rép. islamique d')
-17	89	-16	-30	0.4	2.1	3.8	3.0	3.4	4.0	2.9	2.5	Maldives
35	164	706	-	6.6	5.8	7.3	7.9	7.6	6.8	7.5	-	Népal
225	3 024	182	-4 286	1.3	0.6	1.8	4.8	4.3	4.6	4.0	2.8	Pakistan
517	2 075	-463	(e)835	1.5	1.9	2.0	3.6	5.6	6.0	3.7	(e)4.5	Sri Lanka
12 525	*122 696*	*68 532*	*52 699*	*4.0*	*4.5*	*5.9*	*5.9*	*9.0*	*8.4*	*7.7*	*7.8*	**Asie du Sud-Est**
3	206	927	831	..	..	4.4	4.0	6.7	7.6	10.2	11.6	Brunéi Darussalam
8	404	195	818	..	..	3.2	3.0	5.9	5.8	4.5	4.7	Cambodge
				6.1	4.2	7.9						Indonésie (...2002)
-1 825	29 342	13 630	2 300	–	–	–	5.3	8.1	8.2	7.3	6.9	Indonésie
11	95	54	(e)14	..	0.1	3.1	3.2	5.0	4.1	3.8	(e)3.4	Rép. dém. populaire lao
3 972	9 451	26 897	6 004	5.0	4.0	4.2	7.3	9.3	7.7	8.4	8.4	Malaisie
98	465	1 287	(e)-1 265	9.1	14.5	1.2	4.9	14.5	14.4	9.3	(e)6.3	Myanmar
2 671	16 573	11 935	6 247	4.2	1.0	4.3	3.9	10.2	11.4	12.7	13.6	Philippines
3 593	37 912	12 024	21 566	3.3	5.5	7.1	7.0	9.2	8.7	7.8	8.2	Singapour
2 015	32 072	-50	5 937	2.2	4.9	6.2	5.2	12.2	11.0	8.8	8.4	Thaïlande
-29	156	55	422	–	–	–	16.9	10.2	16.4	16.3	28.7	Timor-Leste
2 009	-3 981	1 579	(e)9 825	-	1.8	2.6	3.0	2.8	1.8	1.6	(e)2.5	Viet Nam

Pour les sources et les notes, se reporter à la fin du tableau.

Region, country or territory	Total reserves including gold (1) - Réserves totales, y compris l'or (1) Millions of dollars - Millions de dollars							
	1980	1990	2000	2005	2009	2010	2011	2012
Western Asia	*45 147*	*39 564*	*91 619*	*300 148*	*672 639*	*750 488*	*844 496*	*1 011 736*
Bahrain	960	1 242	1 571	1 982	3 853	5 097	4 553	(e)4 853
Iraq	-	-	7 882	12 114	44 138	50 367	60 754	68 785
Jordan (4)	1 188	886	3 350	5 271	11 712	13 079	11 489	(e)8 321
Kuwait	4 042	2 078	7 198	8 990	20 407	21 373	25 932	29 022
Lebanon	2 000	1 119	6 364	12 348	29 609	32 011	34 236	37 682
Oman	591	1 687	2 393	4 358	12 203	13 024	14 365	14 400
Qatar	365	673	1 159	4 543	18 392	30 642	16 220	32 542
Saudi Arabia (5)	23 640	11 897	19 795	(b)155 259	410 263	445 281	541 235	657 023
State of Palestine	..	..	..	..	498	532	498	664
Syrian Arab Republic (6)	374	1 730	(e)2 805	17 388	17 443	19 510	(e)14 833	(e)4 774
Turkey	1 245	6 253	22 659	50 766	71 078	80 914	78 660	100 565
United Arab Emirates	2 040	4 624	13 541	21 010	26 104	32 785	37 269	47 035
Yemen, Arab Republic	1 283	–	–	–	–	–	–	–
Yemen, Democratic	236	–	–	–	–	–	–	–
Yemen	–	425	2 903	6 118	6 930	5 871	4 452	6 070
Developing economies: Oceania	**655**	**823**	**974**	**1 383**	**3 745**	**4 552**	**6 063**	**5 929**
Fiji	168	261	412	321	569	719	832	920
Micronesia (Federated States of)	–	..	113	50	56	56	75	77
Papua New Guinea	426	406	290	721	2 564	3 036	4 260	3 934
Samoa	3	69	64	82	166	209	167	169
Solomon Islands	30	18	32	95	146	266	412	469
Tonga	14	31	25	47	96	105	143	152
Vanuatu	-	38	39	67	149	161	174	(e)208

Sources:

UNCTAD secretariat calculations, based on:

- IMF, *International Financial Statistics*

- World Bank, *Global Development Finance*

- IMF, *World Economic Outlook*

- Economist Intelligence Unit, *Country Data*

- Other national sources

Notes:

(1)   End of year position.

(2)   Reserve stock of the year, divided by the average monthly imports of the current year. Data on imports are based on figures shown in table 1.1.1.

(3)   Year 1985, break in series.

(4)   Year 1993, break in series.

(5)   Year 1996, break in series. Year 2005, break in series: prior to 2005, data exclude Saudi Arabian Monetary Agency investments and deposits abroad.

(6)   Year 2005, break in series.

Annual change in reserves (millions of dollars) Variations annuelles des réserves (millions de dollars)				Number of months of imports (2) Nombre de mois d'importations (2)								Régions, pays ou territoires
2005	2010	2011	2012	1980	1990	2000	2005	2009	2010	2011	2012	
164 891	*77 849*	*94 008*	*167 240*	*6.6*	*5.6*	*6.5*	*9.9*	*14.5*	*14.0*	*12.8*	*14.6*	*Asie occidentale*
34	1 243	-544	(e)301	3.3	4.0	4.1	2.5	4.6	5.0	4.3	(e)3.9	Bahreïn
4 279	6 229	10 387	8 030	-	-	8.6	6.2	13.8	13.8	14.9	14.5	Iraq
-18	1 367	-1 590	(e)-3 169	5.9	4.1	8.7	6.0	9.9	10.1	7.3	(e)4.8	Jordanie (4)
610	967	4 558	3 091	7.4	6.3	12.1	6.8	12.3	11.3	12.0	13.4	Koweït
113	2 402	2 225	3 446	6.6	5.3	12.3	15.4	21.4	20.8	19.8	20.6	Liban
761	821	1 341	35	4.1	7.2	5.6	5.8	8.2	7.8	7.2	6.0	Oman
1 145	12 251	-14 422	16 322	3.1	4.8	4.3	5.4	8.9	15.8	6.5	10.8	Qatar
(b)127 718	35 018	95 954	115 788	9.4	5.9	7.9	(b)31.3	51.5	50.0	49.3	54.7	Arabie saoudite (5)
..	34	-34	166	..	..	..	..	1.7	1.6	1.3	1.6	État de Palestine
(e)12 425	2 067	(e)-4 677	(e)-10 059	1.1	8.7	(e)8.8	19.2	13.6	13.3	(e)10.5	(e)7.3	République arabe syrienne (6)
14 894	9 836	-2 254	21 905	1.9	3.4	5.0	5.2	6.1	5.2	3.9	5.1	Turquie
2 480	6 681	4 484	9 766	2.8	5.0	4.6	3.0	2.1	2.4	2.2	2.6	Émirats arabes unis
–	–	–	–	8.3	–	–	–	–	–	–	–	Yémen, République arabe du
–	–	–	–	1.9	–	–	–	–	–	–	–	Yémen, Démocratique
450	-1 067	-1 419	1 619	–	3.2	15.0	13.7	9.1	7.6	5.3	6.1	Yémen
-74	**807**	**1 511**	**-134**	**3.9**	**4.5**	**4.8**	**4.0**	**7.8**	**7.7**	**8.4**	**7.5**	**Économies en développement : Océanie**
-162	150	113	88	3.6	4.2	6.0	2.4	4.7	4.8	4.2	4.5	Fidji
-5	0	19	2	–	..	12.7	4.6	3.9	3.9	5.0	4.4	Micronésie (États fédérés de)
85	472	1 224	-326	4.3	4.4	3.0	5.0	9.6	9.2	10.6	8.6	Papouasie-Nouvelle-Guinée
-4	44	-43	2	0.5	10.3	8.5	4.1	8.6	8.1	5.8	5.9	Samoa
15	120	146	57	4.0	2.3	4.2	6.1	6.5	7.9	10.6	11.3	Îles Salomon
-8	9	39	9	4.4	6.1	4.3	4.7	7.9	7.9	8.9	8.7	Tonga
5	13	12	(e)34	-	4.7	5.4	5.4	6.1	6.8	6.9	(e)8.4	Vanuatu

Sources :

Calculs du secrétariat de la CNUCED, basés sur :

- FMI, *Statistiques financières internationales*
- Banque mondiale, *Global Development Finance*
- FMI, *World Economic Outlook*
- Economist Intelligence Unit, *Country Data*
- Autres sources nationales

Notes :

(1)   Position en fin d'année.

(2)   Montant des réserves de l'année, divisé par la moyenne mensuelle des importations de l'année en cours. Les données des importations se basent sur les chiffres présentés dans le tableau 1.1.1.

(3)   Année 1985, rupture de série.

(4)   Année 1993, rupture de série.

(5)   Année 1996, rupture de série. Année 2005, rupture de série : avant 2005 les données ne comprennent pas les investissements et les dépôts en devises de l'Agence monétaire de l'Arabie Saudite à l'étranger.

(6)   Année 2005, rupture de série.

7

Economic grouping	Total reserves including gold (1) - Réserves totales, y compris l'or (1) Millions of dollars - Millions de dollars							
	1980	1990	2000	2005	2009	2010	2011	2012
DEVELOPING ECONOMIES	177 117	330 903	1 057 607	2 693 789	5 946 630	6 782 471	7 449 895	7 938 272
Developing economies excluding China	174 000	300 685	888 750	1 871 310	3 528 719	3 914 565	4 245 280	4 605 323
Developing economies excluding LDCs	170 672	323 911	1 042 257	2 659 087	5 866 979	6 693 937	7 354 123	7 827 620
High-income developing economies	101 387	232 071	653 736	1 320 097	2 379 425	2 640 333	2 921 153	3 224 303
Middle-income developing economies	44 050	78 791	325 863	1 145 325	3 104 069	3 667 070	4 042 881	4 194 328
Low-income developing economies	31 680	20 041	78 008	228 367	463 136	475 068	485 861	519 641
Heavily indebted poor countries (IMF)	3 104	3 970	11 384	25 042	57 380	63 979	69 261	74 097
Landlocked developing countries	3 166	6 884	20 434	37 492	105 772	115 636	129 178	135 671
Small island developing States	3 917	2 797	5 719	12 263	21 131	23 391	25 770	25 283
Least developed countries	*6 445*	*6 992*	*15 350*	*34 702*	*79 651*	*88 534*	*95 772*	*110 652*
Africa and Haiti	3 624	4 748	8 321	19 745	45 622	52 989	60 395	69 276
Asia	2 766	2 091	6 839	14 447	33 101	34 308	33 956	39 417
Islands	54	154	190	510	927	1 238	1 421	1 960
Major petroleum and gas exporters	*84 569*	*54 668*	*114 040*	*404 058*	*941 945*	*999 820*	*1 136 045*	*1 315 448*
Africa	29 175	12 518	36 091	127 832	306 790	317 516	349 847	386 248
America	7 116	8 891	13 555	24 493	22 339	13 771	10 562	10 533
Asia	48 279	33 260	64 394	251 733	612 815	668 534	775 636	918 667
Major exporters of manufactured goods	*29 222*	*203 720*	*655 901*	*1 721 800*	*3 810 909*	*4 429 243*	*4 861 738*	*5 108 616*
America	3 052	9 909	35 520	74 060	99 604	120 277	144 174	160 628
Asia	26 170	193 811	620 381	1 647 740	3 711 305	4 308 965	4 717 564	4 947 988
Emerging economies	*39 073*	*168 704*	*460 640*	*886 224*	*1 478 197*	*1 700 152*	*1 854 770*	*1 972 118*
America	21 061	29 691	116 661	185 211	440 575	527 745	627 120	674 333
Asia	18 012	139 013	343 979	701 013	1 037 622	1 172 408	1 227 650	1 297 785
Newly industrialized Asian economies	*31 483*	*172 275*	*493 587*	*874 731*	*1 396 142*	*1 589 724*	*1 687 179*	*1 797 816*
First tier	16 891	140 293	391 017	704 519	1 062 267	1 168 410	1 213 453	1 303 602
Second tier	14 593	31 982	102 570	170 212	333 876	421 314	473 726	494 214
Developing economies: Africa	36 550	27 978	79 903	220 395	474 698	490 135	506 801	544 527
Northern Africa excluding Sudan	19 433	12 710	44 855	137 723	314 618	328 675	330 188	345 344
Sub-Saharan Africa	17 117	15 268	35 048	82 673	160 080	161 460	176 613	199 182
Sub-Saharan Africa excluding South Africa	15 849	14 056	28 696	63 894	124 622	123 069	133 802	154 970
Developing economies: America	40 316	49 202	157 762	258 662	553 794	638 014	744 569	804 175
Central America and Greater Caribbean Islands excluding Puerto Rico	4 446	12 160	45 443	92 754	128 752	152 326	176 085	196 124
Central America and Greater Caribbean Islands excluding Mexico and Puerto Rico	1 394	2 252	9 923	18 694	29 147	32 049	31 911	35 496
South America and Central America	36 872	47 490	152 291	244 452	530 154	612 400	717 487	778 090
South America excluding Brazil	26 903	28 094	76 724	105 028	174 300	184 747	202 946	223 792
Developing economies: Asia	99 596	252 901	818 969	2 213 349	4 914 393	5 649 770	6 192 461	6 583 642
Eastern and South-Eastern Asia excluding China	31 785	173 531	501 810	893 439	1 442 589	1 639 797	1 751 728	1 857 239
Southern Asia excluding India	12 219	7 533	18 256	64 783	115 089	115 337	119 373	110 167

Sources:
UNCTAD secretariat calculations, based on:
- IMF, *International Financial Statistics*
- World Bank, *Global Development Finance*
- IMF, *World Economic Outlook*
- Economist Intelligence Unit, *Country Data*
- Other national sources

Notes:

(1) End of year position.

(2) Reserve stock of the year, divided by the average monthly imports of the current year. Data on imports are based on figures shown in table 1.1.1.

7.5.2 Réserves internationales des économies en développement par groupements économiques

Annual change in reserves (millions of dollars) Variations annuelles des réserves (millions de dollars)				Number of months of imports (2) Nombre de mois d'importations (2)								Groupements économiques
2005	2010	2011	2012	1980	1990	2000	2005	2009	2010	2011	2012	
517 207	835 841	666 985	488 480	4.4	5.0	6.7	9.5	15.4	13.6	12.2	12.5	ÉCONOMIES EN DÉVELOPPEMENT
310 276	385 846	330 275	360 146	4.5	4.9	6.3	8.2	11.7	10.2	9.1	9.5	Économies en développement sans la Chine
514 055	826 958	659 746	473 498	4.5	5.1	6.7	9.6	15.7	13.8	12.4	12.7	Économies en développement sans les PMA
229 834	260 908	280 381	303 150	4.2	5.6	6.3	8.4	12.1	10.6	9.8	10.4	Économies en développement à revenu élevé
263 879	563 000	375 811	151 447	4.6	4.5	7.7	11.8	22.1	19.6	17.5	17.4	Économies en développement à revenu intermédiaire
23 495	11 932	10 793	33 883	4.7	3.0	6.2	7.8	9.4	7.6	6.1	6.2	Économies en développement à revenu faible
1 339	6 599	5 283	4 938	1.5	2.0	3.8	4.1	6.1	5.8	5.2	5.1	Pays pauvres très endettés (FMI)
2 216	9 864	13 542	6 493	3.7	5.6	6.7	6.0	9.7	9.2	8.4	8.0	Pays en développement sans littoral
1 668	2 260	2 378	-487	3.0	3.3	4.0	5.7	8.2	8.6	7.6	7.2	Petits États insulaires en développement
3 153	8 883	7 239	14 982	3.1	3.3	4.3	4.8	6.3	6.3	5.6	6.0	*Pays les moins avancés*
2 585	7 366	7 407	8 983	2.6	3.2	4.2	4.4	5.5	6.0	5.9	6.2	Afrique et Haïti
591	1 206	-352	5 461	4.4	3.4	4.3	5.6	7.8	6.7	5.1	5.6	Asie
-24	310	184	538	2.4	5.4	6.6	7.4	7.9	9.0	9.1	12.1	Îles
194 961	57 875	136 225	179 404	8.7	6.7	9.3	15.1	20.6	19.8	19.3	20.4	*Principaux exportateurs de pétrole et de gaz*
39 975	10 725	32 332	36 401	9.9	6.7	17.6	27.6	33.9	32.0	31.9	32.0	Afrique
5 493	-8 569	-3 209	-29	7.2	14.5	10.0	12.2	6.5	4.2	2.6	2.1	Amérique
149 493	55 718	107 102	143 032	8.3	5.8	7.3	12.5	18.5	17.9	17.7	19.4	Asie
249 938	618 334	432 496	246 878	2.3	5.7	6.6	10.0	17.6	15.3	13.9	14.0	*Principaux exportateurs d'articles manufacturés*
9 911	20 673	23 897	16 454	1.7	2.7	2.4	3.9	4.9	4.7	4.8	5.1	Amérique
240 027	597 661	408 599	230 424	2.4	6.0	7.3	10.8	18.9	16.3	14.7	14.9	Asie
53 722	221 955	154 618	117 348	3.1	6.2	6.4	8.5	12.0	10.3	9.4	9.8	*Économies émergentes*
21 330	87 170	99 376	47 213	3.8	4.4	4.8	5.9	11.0	9.8	9.6	10.1	Amérique
32 392	134 786	55 242	70 135	2.5	6.7	7.1	9.6	12.4	10.5	9.3	9.6	Asie
33 941	193 582	97 454	110 637	2.9	5.6	6.8	8.1	11.2	9.7	8.7	8.9	*Économies nouvellement industrialisées d'Asie*
27 109	106 143	45 043	90 149	2.3	6.2	7.2	9.0	11.6	9.8	8.7	9.1	Première génération
6 832	87 439	52 412	20 488	4.5	4.0	5.5	5.7	10.1	9.3	8.7	8.5	Deuxième génération
54 097	15 437	16 667	37 828	4.6	3.6	7.4	10.3	13.9	12.4	10.8	10.8	Économies en développement : Afrique
33 505	14 057	1 514	15 156	7.8	4.1	11.3	19.9	25.3	23.4	21.7	19.9	Afrique septentrionale sans le Soudan
20 592	1 380	15 153	22 671	3.1	3.2	5.1	5.7	7.4	6.3	5.6	6.1	Afrique subsaharienne
15 171	-1 554	10 733	21 271	4.2	4.3	6.6	6.9	8.0	7.0	6.3	6.8	Afrique subsaharienne sans l'Afrique du Sud
35 401	84 220	106 116	59 606	4.1	4.7	4.9	5.8	9.6	8.6	8.2	8.5	Économies en développement : Amérique
13 497	23 575	23 759	20 039	1.6	2.4	2.4	3.7	4.7	4.4	4.4	4.6	Amérique centrale et Grandes Antilles sans Porto Rico
3 586	2 902	-137	3 585	1.5	1.5	2.7	3.2	4.1	3.8	3.1	3.3	Amérique centrale et Grandes Antilles sans le Mexique et Porto Rico
31 627	82 246	105 087	60 604	4.6	5.3	5.1	5.9	9.9	8.7	8.4	8.7	Amérique du Sud et Amérique centrale
19 328	10 447	18 199	20 846	7.8	10.0	10.1	8.9	9.8	8.1	7.0	7.3	Amérique du Sud sans le Brésil
427 784	735 377	542 691	391 181	4.4	5.3	7.1	10.2	16.7	14.7	13.1	13.4	Économies en développement : Asie
37 432	197 207	111 932	105 511	2.9	5.6	6.7	7.9	10.9	9.5	8.5	8.6	Asie orientale et Asie du Sud-Est sans la Chine
13 248	249	4 035	-9 206	6.2	2.7	5.1	8.3	11.2	8.8	8.1	7.8	Asie méridionale sans l'Inde

Sources :
Calculs du secrétariat de la CNUCED, basés sur :
- FMI, *Statistiques financières internationales*
- Banque mondiale, *Global Development Finance*
- FMI, *World Economic Outlook*
- Economist Intelligence Unit, *Country Data*
- Autres sources nationales

Notes :

(1) Position en fin d'année.

(2) Montant des réserves de l'année, divisé par la moyenne mensuelle des importations de l'année en cours. Les données des importations se basent sur les chiffres présentés dans le tableau 1.1.1.

Region, country or territory / Régions, pays ou territoires	Year / Année	Total official net (1) / Total secteur officiel net (1)	Total ODA Net (2) / APD totale nette (2)			Total OOF Net (3) / Flux AASP nets (3)		
			Total donors (4) / Tous donneurs (4)	of which: / dont :		Total donors / Tous donneurs	of which: / dont :	
				DAC bilateral donors / Donneurs bilatéraux du CAD	Multilateral donors / Donneurs multilatéraux		DAC bilateral donors / Donneurs bilatéraux du CAD	Multilateral donors / Donneurs multilatéraux
		Millions of dollars / Millions de dollars						
WORLD - MONDE	1990	76 565.4	58 487.9	38 416.5	12 606.8	18 077.6	7 958.7	10 146.8
	2000	53 427.0	49 672.8	36 102.6	12 679.4	3 754.3	-4 995.0	8 749.2
	2005	112 341.3	108 448.5	82 777.9	22 746.2	3 892.8	2 994.0	504.5
	2011	163 017.2	139 452.9	92 865.5	38 725.7	23 564.3	8 931.7	14 620.9
DEVELOPING ECONOMIES - ÉCONOMIES EN DÉVELOPPEMENT (5)	1990	75 021.6	56 851.6	36 816.6	12 576.6	18 170.0	8 065.1	10 128.2
	2000	48 057.8	45 009.2	33 328.9	10 902.5	3 048.6	-5 196.4	8 245.0
	2005	106 428.0	103 155.3	79 457.5	21 142.8	3 272.7	2 806.0	439.1
	2011	151 035.4	131 832.4	89 824.8	34 639.6	19 203.1	7 834.3	11 367.1
TRANSITION ECONOMIES - ÉCONOMIES EN TRANSITION	1990	72.4	177.9	165.5	12.4	-105.6	-83.7	-17.2
	2000	5 249.7	4 581.5	2 751.9	1 715.8	668.1	203.3	464.8
	2005	5 913.2	5 293.2	3 320.4	1 603.3	620.1	188.0	65.4
	2011	11 981.8	7 620.5	3 040.7	4 086.0	4 361.2	1 097.4	3 253.7
DEVELOPED ECONOMIES - ÉCONOMIES DÉVELOPPÉES	1990	1 471.4	1 458.4	1 434.3	17.8	13.1	-22.8	35.9
	2000	119.5	82.1	21.9	61.1	37.5	-1.9	39.4
Developing economies: Africa - Économies en développement : Afrique	1990	29 077.5	26 127.6	15 767.9	6 124.3	2 949.9	850.9	1 950.3
	2000	14 088.1	15 363.0	10 297.2	4 708.3	-1 274.8	-343.5	-931.4
	2005	35 322.9	35 632.0	24 438.1	10 742.4	-309.0	-487.8	178.8
	2011	54 209.8	50 649.8	31 573.8	18 416.2	3 560.1	-998.7	4 557.2
Eastern Africa - Afrique orientale	*1990*	*8 318.8*	*8 166.2*	*5 110.7*	*2 706.0*	*152.6*	*137.0*	*11.9*
	2000	*6 484.1*	*6 588.0*	*4 195.6*	*2 326.4*	*-103.9*	*-38.1*	*-65.8*
	2005	*10 999.6*	*11 385.6*	*6 790.4*	*4 546.8*	*-386.1*	*-297.4*	*-88.7*
	2011	*19 507.3*	*18 581.9*	*11 706.2*	*6 695.8*	*925.4*	*528.6*	*396.8*
Burundi	1990	259.1	262.6	157.6	104.7	-3.4	1.0	-4.4
	2000	93.1	93.1	40.9	52.2	0.0	0.0	0.0
	2005	364.0	364.0	180.5	183.4	0.0	0.0	0.0
	2011	579.0	579.0	273.1	305.3	0.0	0.0	0.0
Comoros - Comores	1990	45.0	44.9	30.6	14.0	0.1	0.1	0.0
	2000	18.7	18.7	10.8	7.7	0.0	0.0	0.0
	2005	22.8	22.8	15.1	7.7	0.0	0.0	0.0
	2011	50.7	51.6	28.2	22.5	-0.8	-0.8	0.0
Djibouti	1990	207.0	207.0	88.3	17.3	-0.1	-0.1	0.0
	2000	72.1	72.1	42.2	19.7	0.0	0.0	0.0
	2005	74.1	74.1	53.7	21.4	0.0	0.0	0.0
	2011	146.5	141.6	89.4	45.6	4.9	1.3	3.6
Eritrea - Érythrée	2000	177.1	177.0	112.0	54.7	0.0	0.0	0.0
	2005	349.2	349.2	226.0	127.1	0.0	0.0	0.0
	2011	135.1	135.1	33.5	97.4	0.0	0.0	0.0
Ethiopia (…1991) - Éthiopie (…1991)	1990	1 011.7	1 013.8	509.8	431.7	-2.0	-2.3	0.3
Ethiopia - Éthiopie	2000	668.4	687.2	380.0	291.5	-18.8	-1.0	-17.9
	2005	1 818.1	1 927.8	1 187.6	714.0	-109.7	-69.3	-40.4
	2011	3 686.1	3 532.4	1 975.8	1 540.7	153.8	-0.9	154.7
Kenya	1990	1 141.3	1 181.3	735.2	441.6	-40.0	15.4	-55.4
	2000	478.9	512.7	292.4	211.4	-33.8	-4.9	-29.0
	2005	779.4	759.2	521.2	229.7	20.2	16.6	3.6
	2011	2 928.3	2 484.3	1 563.5	913.4	444.0	311.2	132.8
Madagascar	1990	411.9	397.0	268.2	129.9	14.9	11.2	3.2
	2000	314.7	320.2	138.7	182.6	-5.5	1.4	-6.9
	2005	786.2	913.0	497.7	415.8	-126.9	-126.5	-0.4
	2011	658.5	441.3	227.5	210.1	217.2	201.6	15.6

For sources and notes, see end of table.

Pour les sources et les notes, se reporter à la fin du tableau.

Region, country or territory / Régions, pays ou territoires	Year / Année	Total official net (1) / Total secteur officiel net (1)	Total ODA Net (2) / APD totale nette (2)			Total OOF Net (3) / Flux AASP nets (3)		
			Total donors (4) / Tous donneurs (4)	of which: / dont :		Total donors / Tous donneurs	of which: / dont :	
				DAC bilateral donors / Donneurs bilatéraux du CAD	Multilateral donors / Donneurs multilatéraux		DAC bilateral donors / Donneurs bilatéraux du CAD	Multilateral donors / Donneurs multilatéraux
				Millions of dollars / Millions de dollars				
Malawi	1990	486.3	500.4	216.2	283.6	-14.1	-5.8	-8.3
	2000	443.7	446.1	270.3	170.7	-2.4	-0.1	-2.3
	2005	570.8	573.4	327.7	246.5	-2.6	0.1	-2.6
	2011	792.8	804.3	450.2	354.9	-11.5	-1.2	-10.3
Mauritius - Maurice	1990	107.2	88.3	75.7	11.9	18.9	16.2	2.7
	2000	-18.1	20.2	12.4	7.2	-38.3	-20.7	-17.5
	2005	18.5	34.6	21.5	10.4	-16.1	-1.8	-14.3
	2011	254.9	182.7	113.5	70.8	72.3	0.0	72.3
Mozambique	1990	999.4	997.5	750.3	246.9	1.9	3.3	-1.5
	2000	1 072.7	906.2	624.7	282.7	166.5	105.2	61.2
	2005	1 279.4	1 297.2	761.9	535.3	-17.8	-21.1	3.3
	2011	2 119.0	2 070.8	1 701.0	367.8	48.2	74.1	-25.9
Rwanda	1990	286.9	287.9	183.2	94.5	-1.0	-0.1	-0.9
	2000	323.5	321.5	175.4	145.9	2.1	2.2	-0.2
	2005	572.0	577.4	281.4	295.6	-5.4	-5.4	0.0
	2011	1 283.9	1 262.2	590.9	662.3	21.7	7.0	14.6
Seychelles	1990	37.4	35.6	32.7	3.0	1.9	-0.8	-0.4
	2000	19.3	23.1	3.3	8.2	-3.8	-0.7	-3.1
	2005	15.5	16.7	7.9	6.6	-1.3	0.0	-1.3
	2011	22.0	20.9	6.6	9.1	1.1	0.0	1.1
Somalia - Somalie	1990	513.6	514.8	269.6	139.8	-1.2	-0.8	-0.4
	2000	102.2	102.2	56.4	44.4	0.0	0.0	0.0
	2005	240.2	240.2	145.1	91.8	0.0	0.0	0.0
	2011	1 095.8	1 095.6	754.6	230.3	0.1	0.1	0.0
Uganda - Ouganda	1990	665.2	663.1	244.4	376.1	2.1	9.4	-7.3
	2000	809.7	853.3	578.2	269.2	-43.6	-46.3	2.8
	2005	1 189.3	1 192.2	692.4	499.3	-2.8	-0.1	-2.7
	2011	1 623.7	1 582.4	994.5	585.3	41.3	5.7	35.6
United Republic of Tanzania - République-Unie de Tanzanie	1990	1 163.1	1 163.2	844.1	315.8	-0.1	28.2	-28.2
	2000	1 091.0	1 063.9	779.0	286.6	27.1	32.0	-4.9
	2005	1 491.4	1 499.1	860.8	629.0	-7.7	-7.8	0.1
	2011	2 383.5	2 435.8	1 661.7	766.6	-52.3	-61.0	8.7
Zambia - Zambie	1990	540.8	474.8	408.9	65.9	66.0	47.2	18.8
	2000	674.5	794.7	486.3	308.1	-120.1	-104.4	-15.8
	2005	1 067.8	1 172.1	823.0	347.4	-104.3	-79.2	-25.1
	2011	1 030.8	1 046.4	702.2	338.4	-15.5	-9.5	-6.0
Zimbabwe	1990	443.0	334.3	295.9	29.3	108.7	14.9	93.8
	2000	142.4	175.6	192.7	-16.3	-33.2	-0.9	-32.3
	2005	361.0	372.7	186.9	185.8	-11.7	-2.9	-8.9
	2011	716.6	715.5	540.0	175.5	1.1	1.1	0.0
Middle Africa - Afrique centrale	*1990*	*3 591.1*	*2 628.2*	*1 821.6*	*725.4*	*963.0*	*678.6*	*284.4*
	2000	*969.9*	*1 162.5*	*667.9*	*498.5*	*-192.6*	*-52.5*	*-140.2*
	2005	*4 993.7*	*4 740.1*	*3 214.7*	*1 517.7*	*253.6*	*521.0*	*-267.4*
	2011	*5 525.6*	*7 510.8*	*5 347.8*	*2 161.3*	*-1 985.2*	*-2 074.2*	*89.0*
Angola	1990	343.5	265.8	163.2	100.8	77.7	76.2	1.5
	2000	256.3	302.2	197.7	107.1	-45.9	-23.3	-22.6
	2005	406.7	414.6	248.0	167.4	-7.9	-6.3	-1.6
	2011	232.7	199.9	119.7	80.1	32.7	24.3	8.5
Cameroon - Cameroun	1990	607.2	444.4	339.1	107.9	162.8	75.1	87.7
	2000	306.1	376.7	213.7	165.9	-70.6	9.4	-80.0
	2005	321.8	413.9	332.2	79.4	-92.2	-35.5	-56.7
	2011	598.4	611.0	326.7	284.2	-12.6	-40.6	28.0
Central African Republic - République centrafricaine	1990	251.6	248.9	99.9	146.7	2.8	3.9	-1.1
	2000	74.0	75.3	53.1	22.4	-1.3	-1.3	0.0
	2005	88.9	88.9	60.5	28.0	0.0	0.0	0.0
	2011	273.9	271.6	108.3	163.0	2.2	-0.9	3.2

For sources and notes, see end of table.

Pour les sources et les notes, se reporter à la fin du tableau.

7

Region, country or territory / Régions, pays ou territoires	Year / Année	Total official net (1) Total secteur officiel net (1)	Total ODA Net (2) APD totale nette (2)			Total OOF Net (3) Flux AASP nets (3)		
			Total donors (4) Tous donneurs (4)	DAC bilateral donors Donneurs bilatéraux du CAD	Multilateral donors Donneurs multilatéraux	Total donors Tous donneurs	DAC bilateral donors Donneurs bilatéraux du CAD	Multilateral donors Donneurs multilatéraux
		Millions of dollars / Millions de dollars						
Chad - Tchad	1990	310.5	310.6	183.3	125.0	-0.1	-0.1	0.0
	2000	130.4	131.3	53.5	76.1	-0.9	-0.9	0.0
	2005	379.9	384.5	161.8	214.0	-4.6	-0.2	-4.4
	2011	483.6	468.4	247.8	221.2	15.2	-3.6	18.8
Congo	1990	226.3	217.2	202.0	15.2	9.1	13.2	-4.1
	2000	16.4	32.0	23.0	9.0	-15.6	-12.4	-3.2
	2005	1 855.7	1 425.5	1 344.0	81.5	430.2	458.7	-28.5
	2011	204.3	259.8	175.0	84.3	-55.5	-47.1	-8.5
Dem. Rep. of the Congo - Rép. dém. du Congo	1990	1 419.7	895.8	632.7	185.9	523.9	380.6	143.3
	2000	173.7	177.1	102.7	74.3	-3.4	0.0	-3.4
	2005	1 810.3	1 881.7	990.5	893.5	-71.5	60.2	-131.7
	2011	3 469.5	5 532.5	4 249.2	1 283.6	-2 063.0	-1 977.7	-85.2
Equatorial Guinea - Guinée équatoriale	1990	60.8	60.2	43.6	16.5	0.6	0.0	0.6
	2000	20.2	21.3	18.2	3.3	-1.1	-0.7	-0.4
	2005	54.0	38.1	29.8	9.2	15.9	15.9	0.0
	2011	48.1	24.2	21.6	2.6	23.9	23.2	0.7
Gabon	1990	317.5	131.2	126.9	4.4	186.3	129.7	56.5
	2000	-42.1	11.7	-11.6	23.3	-53.7	-23.2	-30.5
	2005	44.0	60.4	29.5	30.9	-16.4	28.1	-44.6
	2011	140.8	68.6	61.6	5.5	72.2	-51.8	124.0
Sao Tome and Principe - Sao Tomé-et-Principe	1990	54.1	54.1	31.0	23.1	0.0	0.0	0.0
	2000	34.9	34.9	17.7	17.2	0.0	0.0	0.0
	2005	32.4	32.4	18.4	14.0	0.0	0.0	0.0
	2011	74.4	74.8	37.9	36.9	-0.4	0.0	-0.4
Northern Africa - Afrique septentrionale	*1990*	*9 063.3*	*8 887.1*	*4 501.3*	*653.2*	*176.2*	*-949.7*	*977.3*
	2000	*2 081.0*	*2 451.0*	*1 751.0*	*428.0*	*-370.0*	*91.4*	*-461.4*
	2005	*4 177.0*	*4 325.1*	*2 963.2*	*1 045.0*	*-148.1*	*-786.4*	*638.3*
	2011	*6 857.4*	*4 719.4*	*2 817.0*	*1 582.4*	*2 138.1*	*-201.2*	*2 337.6*
Algeria - Algérie	1990	875.6	331.7	102.2	21.5	543.9	114.2	283.3
	2000	-41.8	199.6	65.7	62.7	-241.4	-143.4	-98.0
	2005	-1 159.9	346.6	266.8	68.5	-1 506.5	-813.4	-693.1
	2011	10.5	196.6	117.6	78.7	-186.1	-185.2	-0.8
Egypt - Égypte	1990	4 793.4	6 065.2	3 163.1	76.2	-1 271.8	-1 234.0	-37.6
	2000	1 410.5	1 370.6	1 139.6	134.2	39.9	220.0	-180.0
	2005	2 101.8	1 034.2	667.3	240.3	1 067.6	131.6	936.0
	2011	928.4	412.2	229.8	71.9	516.2	34.6	481.6
Libya - Libye	1990	8.3	8.3	7.7	0.7	0.0	0.0	0.0
	2005	23.8	23.8	16.8	3.1	0.0	0.0	0.0
	2011	639.8	642.2	464.2	58.7	-2.4	-2.4	0.0
Morocco - Maroc	1990	1 889.2	1 241.1	595.4	91.5	648.1	164.5	486.2
	2000	291.4	434.4	293.1	129.8	-143.0	-47.3	-95.7
	2005	1 070.7	732.3	288.5	313.3	338.4	-47.2	385.6
	2011	2 385.3	1 427.4	841.8	560.9	958.0	-12.1	970.1
Sudan (...2011) - Soudan (...2011)	1990	845.7	848.2	420.0	385.2	-2.6	2.7	-5.2
	2000	215.2	224.7	90.3	30.7	-9.5	-9.1	-0.4
	2005	1 852.0	1 825.8	1 455.7	318.7	26.2	0.1	26.2
	2011	1 209.9	1 122.8	672.8	401.7	87.0	0.0	85.4
Tunisia - Tunisie	1990	651.1	392.5	212.9	78.1	258.5	2.9	250.7
	2000	205.7	221.7	162.3	70.6	-16.0	71.2	-87.2
	2005	288.6	362.4	268.2	101.2	-73.8	-57.5	-16.3
	2011	1 683.5	918.3	490.8	410.5	765.3	-36.1	801.3

For sources and notes, see end of table.   Pour les sources et les notes, se reporter à la fin du tableau.

Region, country or territory / Régions, pays ou territoires	Year / Année	Total official net (1) / Total secteur officiel net (1)	Total ODA Net (2) / APD totale nette (2) Total donors (4) / Tous donneurs (4)	of which: / dont : DAC bilateral donors / Donneurs bilatéraux du CAD	of which: / dont : Multilateral donors / Donneurs multilatéraux	Total OOF Net (3) / Flux AASP nets (3) Total donors / Tous donneurs	of which: / dont : DAC bilateral donors / Donneurs bilatéraux du CAD	of which: / dont : Multilateral donors / Donneurs multilatéraux
					Millions of dollars / Millions de dollars			
Southern Africa - Afrique australe	*1990*	*460.8*	*457.6*	*281.9*	*177.8*	*3.2*	*-2.2*	*5.4*
	2000	*842.3*	*719.1*	*501.4*	*219.5*	*123.2*	*-83.6*	*206.8*
	2005	*1 033.9*	*977.5*	*646.8*	*331.3*	*56.4*	*-114.8*	*171.2*
	2011	*3 807.0*	*2 176.7*	*1 567.4*	*592.1*	*1 630.4*	*263.6*	*1 366.8*
Botswana	1990	167.4	145.2	121.2	25.8	22.2	4.6	17.6
	2000	34.2	30.6	23.5	0.0	3.6	23.1	-19.5
	2005	63.9	48.0	30.0	19.8	15.9	2.0	13.9
	2011	716.7	120.6	90.0	22.5	596.1	0.0	596.1
Lesotho	1990	139.7	139.1	85.2	54.3	0.5	-1.5	2.0
	2000	47.1	36.7	21.8	16.1	10.4	-8.2	18.6
	2005	58.7	67.5	39.9	28.6	-8.8	-0.5	-8.3
	2011	288.4	259.3	142.3	114.0	29.2	0.0	29.2
Namibia - Namibie	1990	119.6	119.6	39.4	80.3	0.0	0.0	0.0
	2000	154.0	152.3	97.9	54.5	1.6	-0.5	2.1
	2005	142.0	125.1	89.9	33.0	16.9	-3.1	20.0
	2011	272.0	274.5	234.0	39.1	-2.5	0.0	-2.5
South Africa - Afrique du Sud	2000	591.2	486.4	355.5	130.8	104.8	-94.5	199.3
	2005	732.3	690.2	466.0	223.5	42.1	-113.2	155.2
	2011	2 418.3	1 397.5	1 034.1	362.4	1 020.8	263.6	757.2
Swaziland	1990	34.1	53.6	36.1	17.4	-19.5	-5.3	-14.2
	2000	15.9	13.1	2.8	10.2	2.8	-3.5	6.2
	2005	37.0	46.7	21.0	26.3	-9.6	0.0	-9.6
	2011	111.6	124.9	66.9	54.1	-13.2	0.0	-13.2
Western Africa - Afrique occidentale	*1990*	*6 724.3*	*5 085.8*	*3 212.0*	*1 808.8*	*1 638.5*	*981.3*	*660.7*
	2000	*2 678.4*	*3 411.0*	*2 333.6*	*1 065.0*	*-732.6*	*-267.6*	*-465.0*
	2005	*11 761.9*	*11 975.5*	*9 023.3*	*2 895.8*	*-213.5*	*104.1*	*-317.7*
	2011	*13 215.2*	*12 563.2*	*6 675.1*	*5 845.6*	*652.0*	*404.9*	*247.1*
Benin - Bénin	1990	294.8	266.9	125.7	141.5	27.9	26.2	1.7
	2000	232.5	243.5	190.5	54.0	-11.0	-11.0	0.0
	2005	346.3	346.9	207.7	139.7	-0.7	-0.3	-0.3
	2011	669.3	672.4	425.3	247.5	-3.1	-2.1	-1.0
Burkina Faso	1990	328.0	326.5	238.7	76.5	1.4	1.3	0.1
	2000	174.3	179.8	227.8	-51.8	-5.5	-3.5	-2.0
	2005	694.3	693.4	338.8	346.7	1.0	-0.3	1.2
	2011	993.7	995.7	467.1	526.7	-1.9	0.0	-1.9
Cape Verde - Cap-Vert	1990	103.9	105.3	75.9	29.0	-1.4	-0.2	-1.1
	2000	92.2	93.7	69.7	24.4	-1.6	-0.1	-1.4
	2005	168.9	162.2	104.1	55.7	6.6	0.0	6.6
	2011	344.5	250.8	221.1	30.5	93.7	16.8	76.9
Côte d'Ivoire	1990	1 121.9	686.4	530.6	155.8	435.5	134.2	301.3
	2000	275.7	350.6	250.1	99.9	-74.9	17.8	-92.7
	2005	75.1	91.2	129.4	-38.5	-16.1	-10.0	-6.1
	2011	1 381.2	1 436.1	722.2	711.2	-54.8	-21.7	-33.1
Gambia - Gambie	1990	105.3	97.3	56.9	39.9	8.0	8.5	-0.5
	2000	49.0	49.6	14.6	32.6	-0.7	0.0	-0.7
	2005	60.5	60.5	14.8	45.4	0.0	0.0	0.0
	2011	142.4	134.4	36.5	96.3	8.0	0.0	8.0
Ghana	1990	716.4	559.7	264.9	293.7	156.6	26.4	130.2
	2000	581.4	598.2	375.6	219.2	-16.8	8.6	-25.3
	2005	1 118.7	1 150.7	615.3	529.2	-32.0	-14.1	-17.9
	2011	1 964.0	1 800.0	901.5	898.2	164.0	151.2	12.8
Guinea - Guinée	1990	300.4	291.6	139.0	148.4	8.8	19.6	-10.8
	2000	141.5	152.9	92.8	57.5	-11.4	-1.4	-10.0
	2005	189.6	198.2	126.1	60.5	-8.6	-0.3	-8.3
	2011	194.2	201.2	82.5	117.7	-7.0	0.0	-7.0

For sources and notes, see end of table.

Pour les sources et les notes, se reporter à la fin du tableau.

Region, country or territory / Régions, pays ou territoires	Year / Année	Total official net (1) / Total secteur officiel net (1)	Total ODA Net (2) / APD totale nette (2)			Total OOF Net (3) / Flux AASP nets (3)		
			Total donors (4) / Tous donneurs (4)	of which: / dont :		Total donors / Tous donneurs	of which: / dont :	
				DAC bilateral donors / Donneurs bilatéraux du CAD	Multilateral donors / Donneurs multilatéraux		DAC bilateral donors / Donneurs bilatéraux du CAD	Multilateral donors / Donneurs multilatéraux
					Millions of dollars / Millions de dollars			
Guinea-Bissau - Guinée-Bissau	1990	125.0	126.4	75.4	51.0	-1.3	0.0	-1.3
	2000	81.1	81.1	41.6	39.5	0.0	0.1	-0.1
	2005	65.9	66.0	26.8	39.2	-0.1	-0.1	0.0
	2011	111.5	118.8	52.3	66.3	-7.3	-7.3	0.0
Liberia - Libéria	1990	66.5	113.7	42.3	69.2	-47.3	-12.5	-34.8
	2000	69.1	67.4	23.8	43.6	1.6	-1.9	3.5
	2005	221.8	222.5	144.1	78.4	-0.7	0.0	-0.7
	2011	770.3	765.5	522.5	242.8	4.8	1.8	3.0
Mali	1990	480.3	479.2	312.5	151.1	1.1	1.9	-0.8
	2000	271.6	288.0	299.8	-10.6	-16.4	-6.9	-9.5
	2005	716.3	721.3	370.9	326.3	-5.1	-4.1	-1.0
	2011	1 278.0	1 270.1	782.0	485.0	7.9	10.1	-2.2
Mauritania - Mauritanie	1990	224.9	236.2	106.4	105.1	-11.3	0.8	-12.1
	2000	219.3	223.5	82.5	138.2	-4.2	6.8	-11.0
	2005	188.1	188.7	105.4	81.3	-0.6	0.0	-0.6
	2011	436.9	381.1	130.8	238.1	55.9	9.2	46.7
Niger	1990	392.9	387.6	254.6	129.4	5.3	6.7	-1.4
	2000	184.8	209.1	105.8	102.6	-24.3	-24.3	0.0
	2005	513.9	522.2	254.6	265.3	-8.2	-5.8	-2.4
	2011	624.9	646.0	302.4	338.1	-21.0	-19.3	-1.8
Nigeria - Nigéria	1990	1 307.7	255.1	181.7	73.4	1 052.6	739.4	313.2
	2000	-390.6	173.7	84.4	89.1	-564.3	-260.5	-303.8
	2005	6 308.6	6 408.8	5 930.8	477.4	-100.2	154.8	-255.0
	2011	2 257.0	1 776.7	856.0	919.5	480.3	318.6	161.7
Saint Helena - Sainte-Hélène	1990	24.7	24.7	23.3	1.4	0.0	0.0	0.0
	2000	18.7	18.7	18.4	0.3	0.0	0.0	0.0
	2005	22.6	22.6	22.5	0.1	0.0	0.0	0.0
	2011	83.9	83.9	79.3	4.7	0.0	0.0	0.0
Senegal - Sénégal	1990	823.8	811.7	589.2	220.1	12.0	31.1	-15.6
	2000	425.2	431.2	288.5	145.6	-6.0	9.2	-15.2
	2005	653.0	698.0	444.1	254.3	-45.0	-15.0	-29.9
	2011	1 008.4	1 049.3	589.7	451.1	-40.9	-30.7	-10.2
Sierra Leone	1990	55.1	59.3	39.9	19.3	-4.3	-3.4	-0.9
	2000	178.8	180.6	115.6	65.0	-1.8	-0.9	-0.9
	2005	338.7	339.9	129.3	211.3	-1.2	0.0	-1.1
	2011	431.1	424.2	175.7	243.5	6.9	9.8	-2.9
Togo	1990	252.8	258.2	155.0	103.9	-5.4	1.3	-6.7
	2000	74.0	69.6	52.0	16.2	4.5	0.4	4.1
	2005	79.7	82.5	58.8	23.4	-2.9	-0.6	-2.3
	2011	523.8	557.2	328.2	228.6	-33.4	-31.5	-1.9
Developing economies: Africa n.e.s. - Économies en développement : Afrique n.d.a. (6)	*1990*	*919.3*	*902.8*	*840.4*	*53.1*	*16.5*	*5.8*	*10.6*
	2000	*1 032.5*	*1 031.4*	*847.7*	*170.9*	*1.1*	*6.9*	*-5.8*
	2005	*2 356.9*	*2 228.2*	*1 799.7*	*405.8*	*128.8*	*85.6*	*43.1*
	2011	*5 297.3*	*5 097.8*	*3 460.3*	*1 539.1*	*199.5*	*79.6*	*119.9*
Developing economies: America - Économies en développement : Amérique	**1990**	**13 525.1**	**5 190.4**	**4 146.4**	**1 032.0**	**8 334.7**	**3 729.7**	**4 634.3**
	2000	**10 364.7**	**4 837.7**	**3 858.9**	**940.8**	**5 527.0**	**-1 012.2**	**6 539.2**
	2005	**3 452.5**	**6 707.9**	**4 866.7**	**1 827.7**	**-3 255.4**	**-1 589.2**	**-1 666.3**
	2011	**14 528.6**	**11 537.7**	**7 750.4**	**3 697.5**	**2 990.8**	**3 655.8**	**-665.0**
Caribbean - Caraïbes	*1990*	*1 015.6*	*809.2*	*624.6*	*180.0*	*206.4*	*93.9*	*130.5*
	2000	*570.5*	*418.7*	*279.2*	*121.1*	*151.8*	*-88.9*	*240.6*
	2005	*858.5*	*769.5*	*517.9*	*240.8*	*89.0*	*43.9*	*45.1*
	2011	*3 115.0*	*2 230.3*	*1 503.7*	*724.1*	*884.7*	*291.0*	*593.8*
Anguilla	1990	3.9	3.8	2.4	1.4	0.1	0.0	0.1
	2000	7.7	3.5	3.8	-0.3	4.2	0.0	4.2
	2005	3.7	4.0	4.3	-0.3	-0.3	0.0	-0.3
	2011	-0.9	0.3	0.4	-0.1	-1.2	0.0	-1.2

For sources and notes, see end of table.

Pour les sources et les notes, se reporter à la fin du tableau.

Region, country or territory / Régions, pays ou territoires	Year / Année	Total official net (1) / Total secteur officiel net (1)	Total ODA Net (2) / APD totale nette (2)			Total OOF Net (3) / Flux AASP nets (3)		
			Total donors (4) / Tous donneurs (4)	of which: / dont :		Total donors / Tous donneurs	of which: / dont :	
				DAC bilateral donors / Donneurs bilatéraux du CAD	Multilateral donors / Donneurs multilatéraux		DAC bilateral donors / Donneurs bilatéraux du CAD	Multilateral donors / Donneurs multilatéraux
		Millions of dollars / Millions de dollars						
Antigua and Barbuda - Antigua-et-Barbuda	1990	-2.7	4.6	2.9	1.7	-7.3	-7.3	0.0
	2000	9.9	9.8	3.7	1.1	0.1	0.0	0.1
	2005	7.1	7.8	7.0	0.2	-0.7	-0.6	-0.2
	2011	48.2	14.8	11.1	3.7	33.4	17.8	15.6
Aruba	1990	30.0	30.0	28.9	1.1	0.0	0.0	0.0
Bahamas	1990	30.6	3.2	0.4	1.8	27.4	-0.6	28.0
Barbados - Barbade	1990	21.4	2.6	1.4	1.2	18.8	10.7	8.1
	2000	13.1	0.2	1.0	-0.8	12.8	3.1	9.7
	2005	-2.8	-1.8	6.1	-7.9	-1.0	5.8	-6.8
British Virgin Islands - Îles Vierges britanniques	1990	9.4	5.6	3.0	2.5	3.9	1.6	2.3
Cayman Islands - Îles Caïmanes	1990	11.9	3.0	2.1	0.9	8.9	2.4	6.5
Cuba	1990	60.1	51.8	33.6	17.2	8.3	8.3	0.0
	2000	47.5	44.0	30.8	12.8	3.5	3.5	0.0
	2005	109.0	88.4	68.1	18.9	20.6	20.6	0.0
	2011	84.3	83.4	60.0	22.8	0.8	1.5	-0.7
Dominica - Dominique	1990	19.4	19.6	10.8	8.4	-0.3	-0.4	0.1
	2000	18.5	15.2	5.9	6.4	3.3	-0.1	3.4
	2005	24.2	21.1	4.6	10.8	3.1	0.0	3.1
	2011	27.7	24.4	8.1	16.8	3.3	0.0	3.3
Dominican Republic - République dominicaine	1990	136.4	101.7	72.7	27.8	34.7	1.4	33.3
	2000	72.9	56.0	44.7	11.3	16.9	-36.3	53.1
	2005	264.1	80.6	55.8	24.8	183.5	40.5	143.0
	2011	680.5	223.7	187.5	36.1	456.7	162.4	294.3
Grenada - Grenade	1990	12.9	13.8	5.0	8.7	-0.9	-1.1	0.2
	2000	19.9	16.5	9.9	3.2	3.4	-0.2	3.6
	2005	61.6	52.5	26.1	24.6	9.1	0.0	9.1
	2011	6.8	12.0	9.3	3.7	-5.2	-3.0	-2.3
Haiti - Haïti	1990	166.9	167.4	117.1	50.1	-0.5	-0.1	-0.4
	2000	206.7	207.8	153.9	53.9	-1.1	-1.1	0.0
	2005	425.5	425.6	284.0	141.6	-0.1	-0.1	0.0
	2011	1 742.9	1 712.4	1 184.3	526.1	30.5	29.7	0.8
Jamaica - Jamaïque	1990	325.3	270.6	251.9	18.9	54.7	55.4	17.3
	2000	128.8	8.6	-26.3	28.5	120.2	-19.9	140.1
	2005	-56.7	39.6	11.6	24.8	-96.3	-5.8	-90.5
	2011	408.9	43.8	-6.7	52.7	365.1	66.6	298.5
Montserrat	1990	8.3	8.4	7.8	0.5	-0.1	0.0	-0.1
	2000	30.9	30.9	30.9	0.1	-0.1	0.0	-0.1
	2005	27.6	27.8	27.0	0.9	-0.2	0.0	-0.2
	2011	46.6	46.6	44.5	2.2	0.0	0.0	0.0
Netherlands Antilles - Antilles néerlandaises	1990	50.1	58.0	53.0	5.0	-7.9	-10.9	3.0
Saint Kitts and Nevis - Saint-Kitts-et-Nevis	1990	8.2	8.1	5.0	2.9	0.1	0.0	0.1
	2000	6.0	3.9	0.1	4.1	2.1	-1.3	3.3
	2005	1.7	2.5	1.8	1.8	-0.8	-2.0	1.2
	2011	28.8	15.8	1.5	14.9	13.1	15.9	-2.8
Saint Lucia - Sainte-Lucie	1990	15.8	12.3	6.2	5.8	3.5	-0.4	3.9
	2000	13.5	11.0	7.1	4.4	2.5	0.0	2.5
	2005	11.5	10.5	6.6	4.5	1.0	0.0	1.0
	2011	26.0	35.3	2.7	27.9	-9.3	0.0	-9.3
Saint Vincent and the Grenadines - Saint-Vincent-et-les Grenadines	1990	15.4	15.4	5.2	9.7	0.0	0.0	0.0
	2000	9.7	6.2	3.8	1.1	3.5	0.0	3.5
	2005	10.5	7.7	5.8	2.4	2.8	0.0	2.8
	2011	15.3	17.8	1.0	17.5	-2.5	0.0	-2.5
Trinidad and Tobago - Trinité-et-Tobago	1990	80.8	17.8	6.1	11.7	63.0	34.8	28.2
	2000	-21.6	-1.5	4.4	-5.9	-20.1	-36.7	16.5
	2005	-34.3	-2.0	6.1	-8.1	-32.3	-14.7	-17.6

For sources and notes, see end of table.

Pour les sources et les notes, se reporter à la fin du tableau.

Region, country or territory / Régions, pays ou territoires	Year / Année	Total official net (1) / Total secteur officiel net (1)	Total ODA Net (2) / APD totale nette (2)			Total OOF Net (3) / Flux AASP nets (3)		
			Total donors (4) / Tous donneurs (4)	of which: / dont :		Total donors / Tous donneurs	of which: / dont :	
				DAC bilateral donors / Donneurs bilatéraux du CAD	Multilateral donors / Donneurs multilatéraux		DAC bilateral donors / Donneurs bilatéraux du CAD	Multilateral donors / Donneurs multilatéraux
			Millions of dollars / Millions de dollars					
Turks and Caicos Islands - Îles Turques et Caïques	1990	11.6	11.6	8.9	2.8	0.0	0.0	0.0
	2000	7.3	6.7	5.6	1.1	0.6	0.0	0.6
	2005	5.8	5.2	3.1	2.1	0.6	0.0	0.6
Central America - Amérique centrale	*1990*	*6 613.6*	*1 839.6*	*1 599.5*	*234.1*	*4 774.0*	*2 028.6*	*2 751.0*
	2000	*1 723.2*	*1 433.3*	*1 011.7*	*414.7*	*289.9*	*-740.0*	*1 029.9*
	2005	*1 389.7*	*2 159.6*	*1 566.3*	*594.9*	*-769.9*	*-423.2*	*-346.7*
	2011	*7 469.7*	*3 126.5*	*2 008.4*	*1 040.0*	*4 343.2*	*1 578.8*	*2 764.4*
Belize	1990	38.5	30.3	18.8	11.3	8.1	4.1	4.1
	2000	31.8	14.7	2.9	11.2	17.2	3.5	13.7
	2005	10.8	12.2	7.5	5.6	-1.3	-0.1	-1.2
	2011	28.9	28.3	6.4	22.0	0.6	-1.8	2.3
Costa Rica	1990	237.7	227.0	206.6	19.1	10.8	21.1	-10.3
	2000	-39.6	9.6	17.5	-8.4	-49.2	-26.9	-22.3
	2005	-102.6	25.8	25.5	0.2	-128.4	7.1	-135.5
	2011	217.3	38.4	31.3	6.7	178.9	35.4	143.5
El Salvador	1990	308.3	347.3	312.0	34.3	-39.0	-0.9	-38.1
	2000	283.4	179.7	172.4	6.8	103.7	-13.5	117.2
	2005	323.3	204.5	164.9	39.2	118.9	-14.6	133.4
	2011	454.8	280.8	249.5	31.0	174.0	-23.6	197.6
Guatemala	1990	221.5	201.4	149.5	50.5	20.1	6.2	13.9
	2000	321.2	263.1	230.5	32.3	58.0	6.7	51.4
	2005	251.7	256.6	220.7	35.8	-4.9	-5.5	0.6
	2011	448.3	391.8	289.0	102.2	56.5	-4.9	61.4
Honduras	1990	433.3	448.5	383.5	64.0	-15.2	-0.7	-14.6
	2000	396.1	448.3	310.7	133.1	-52.2	19.5	-71.7
	2005	510.2	690.1	458.1	234.1	-179.9	-82.9	-97.0
	2011	642.5	624.1	161.0	461.7	18.4	77.6	-59.1
Mexico - Mexique	1990	5 024.2	156.3	144.8	11.5	4 868.0	2 035.6	2 837.9
	2000	74.1	-57.8	-68.3	10.0	131.9	-710.7	842.6
	2005	-204.2	180.5	161.3	18.7	-384.7	-209.3	-175.4
	2011	4 386.3	958.2	847.2	109.5	3 428.1	1 138.8	2 289.3
Nicaragua	1990	326.6	329.6	288.5	41.1	-2.9	-1.8	-1.1
	2000	552.1	560.4	326.1	234.1	-8.3	-6.2	-2.0
	2005	636.7	763.4	510.5	252.7	-126.7	-115.0	-11.7
	2011	730.4	695.0	333.4	287.9	35.4	-0.3	35.7
Panama	1990	23.5	99.3	96.0	2.4	-75.8	-35.0	-40.8
	2000	104.0	15.4	19.8	-4.5	88.7	-12.4	101.1
	2005	-36.3	26.7	17.9	8.8	-63.0	-3.1	-59.9
	2011	561.2	109.9	90.6	19.1	451.2	357.5	93.7
South America - Amérique du Sud	*1990*	*5 246.4*	*2 030.9*	*1 569.5*	*460.0*	*3 215.5*	*1 607.5*	*1 613.8*
	2000	*6 917.9*	*1 868.6*	*1 565.3*	*290.6*	*5 049.3*	*-184.8*	*5 234.2*
	2005	*250.2*	*2 756.0*	*2 097.6*	*654.0*	*-2 505.8*	*-1 209.8*	*-1 296.0*
	2011	*2 521.4*	*3 992.9*	*3 023.9*	*962.1*	*-1 471.6*	*2 587.8*	*-4 059.3*
Argentina - Argentine	1990	903.8	168.7	166.2	2.6	735.1	411.9	323.2
	2000	677.1	52.5	43.6	1.4	624.6	-553.4	1 178.0
	2005	-435.7	96.2	78.0	18.8	-531.9	-106.3	-425.6
	2011	578.3	83.7	60.1	23.3	494.5	-35.1	529.6
Bolivia (Plurinational State of) - Bolivie (État plurinational de)	1990	576.2	545.4	364.7	180.7	30.8	10.4	20.4
	2000	445.9	481.7	336.3	145.4	-35.8	-25.4	-10.4
	2005	618.9	643.1	441.8	201.3	-24.1	-30.1	5.9
	2011	573.2	728.7	429.1	299.5	-155.5	-87.6	-67.8
Brazil - Brésil	1990	526.5	151.1	142.1	9.0	375.5	715.7	-334.5
	2000	4 097.7	231.4	222.5	7.3	3 866.3	430.9	3 435.4
	2005	175.0	243.1	174.5	67.4	-68.1	-425.9	357.8
	2011	-3 067.1	826.5	647.9	176.8	-3 893.6	1 339.2	-5 232.8

For sources and notes, see end of table.   Pour les sources et les notes, se reporter à la fin du tableau.

Region, country or territory / Régions, pays ou territoires	Year / Année	Total official net (1) / Total secteur officiel net (1)	Total ODA Net (2) / APD totale nette (2) Total donors (4) / Tous donneurs (4)	of which: / dont : DAC bilateral donors / Donneurs bilatéraux du CAD	of which: / dont : Multilateral donors / Donneurs multilatéraux	Total OOF Net (3) / Flux AASP nets (3) Total donors / Tous donneurs	of which: / dont : DAC bilateral donors / Donneurs bilatéraux du CAD	of which: / dont : Multilateral donors / Donneurs multilatéraux
				Millions of dollars / Millions de dollars				
Chile - Chili	1990	787.2	103.5	83.4	20.2	683.7	207.9	475.8
	2000	-207.6	48.9	41.0	7.3	-256.5	-175.6	-80.8
	2005	28.6	167.3	91.9	75.1	-138.8	50.7	-189.5
	2011	526.8	161.4	57.1	103.8	365.4	431.3	-66.0
Colombia - Colombie	1990	-1.5	88.5	86.7	1.9	-90.0	-93.2	3.2
	2000	-24.9	185.9	178.5	6.8	-210.9	-276.9	66.0
	2005	-245.6	620.5	572.2	47.7	-866.1	-119.6	-746.5
	2011	1 399.8	1 024.5	930.6	93.0	375.3	17.8	357.6
Ecuador - Équateur	1990	352.6	159.3	122.2	36.7	193.3	112.7	80.6
	2000	226.4	146.1	138.0	7.9	80.3	-28.4	108.7
	2005	45.5	225.8	192.2	33.4	-180.3	-68.7	-111.7
	2011	413.7	162.6	128.5	33.3	251.1	-5.5	256.6
Falkland Islands (Malvinas) - Îles Falkland (Malvinas)	1990	1.8	1.8	1.8	..	0.0	0.0	..
Guyana	1990	221.5	168.3	35.8	132.5	53.2	72.0	-18.8
	2000	103.9	115.8	51.9	64.0	-11.9	-0.7	-11.2
	2005	152.4	149.9	40.1	109.8	2.5	0.0	2.5
	2011	158.3	158.5	70.4	88.1	-0.2	0.0	-0.2
Paraguay	1990	29.4	57.2	47.6	8.6	-27.8	1.6	-29.4
	2000	202.0	81.6	73.1	8.2	120.5	8.3	112.2
	2005	45.3	50.7	57.4	-6.8	-5.3	-3.9	-1.4
	2011	180.8	93.7	42.8	50.6	87.2	15.2	72.0
Peru - Pérou	1990	398.3	397.1	350.4	46.7	1.2	-2.0	3.2
	2000	1 111.9	396.8	374.5	21.7	715.1	513.2	201.9
	2005	229.7	450.5	391.9	57.0	-220.8	-399.6	178.8
	2011	520.2	599.2	558.6	39.9	-79.0	279.4	-358.4
Suriname	1990	64.3	61.1	51.2	10.0	3.1	-0.9	4.0
	2000	36.2	34.3	29.2	5.2	1.8	0.0	1.8
	2005	42.7	44.2	33.6	10.6	-1.5	-0.6	-0.8
	2011	199.0	94.6	67.2	27.4	104.4	31.4	73.1
Uruguay	1990	86.6	52.4	41.7	10.7	34.2	1.1	33.1
	2000	198.7	17.4	15.4	1.3	181.3	2.0	179.2
	2005	62.5	14.4	3.0	11.0	48.1	4.2	43.9
	2011	200.6	15.1	1.1	13.0	185.5	39.8	145.7
Venezuela (Bolivarian Rep. of) - Venezuela (Rép. bolivarienne du)	1990	1 299.5	76.4	75.8	0.6	1 223.2	170.3	1 052.9
	2000	50.6	76.1	61.3	14.1	-25.5	-78.8	53.3
	2005	-469.1	50.3	21.1	28.8	-519.4	-110.0	-409.4
	2011	837.7	44.5	30.6	13.6	793.3	561.9	231.4
Developing economies: America n.e.s. - Économies en développement : Amérique n.d.a.(6)	*1990*	*649.5*	*510.7*	*352.8*	*157.9*	*138.8*	*-0.2*	*139.1*
	2000	*1 153.2*	*1 117.1*	*1 002.7*	*114.4*	*36.1*	*1.5*	*34.5*
	2005	*954.2*	*1 022.9*	*684.9*	*337.9*	*-68.7*	*0.0*	*-68.7*
	2011	*1 422.5*	*2 188.0*	*1 214.5*	*971.2*	*-765.5*	*-801.7*	*36.2*
Developing economies: Asia - Économies en développement : Asie	**1990**	**24 710.4**	**18 299.4**	**10 546.2**	**4 600.1**	**6 411.1**	**3 072.7**	**3 481.1**
	2000	**13 501.6**	**15 042.5**	**10 386.2**	**4 146.7**	**-1 541.0**	**-4 175.8**	**2 634.8**
	2005	**51 817.9**	**45 403.9**	**37 272.1**	**6 702.9**	**6 414.0**	**4 514.8**	**1 871.6**
	2011	**46 936.8**	**38 465.9**	**22 881.3**	**9 740.6**	**8 470.9**	**1 030.7**	**7 440.2**
Eastern Asia - Asie orientale	*1990*	*2 881.4*	*2 179.9*	*1 553.4*	*605.2*	*701.6*	*662.3*	*39.3*
	2000	*1 451.7*	*2 002.0*	*1 450.9*	*546.7*	*-550.3*	*-2 189.4*	*1 639.1*
	2005	*2 400.5*	*2 121.5*	*1 859.6*	*175.6*	*279.1*	*-961.1*	*1 240.2*
	2011	*1 435.3*	*-202.6*	*773.0*	*-993.8*	*1 637.9*	*362.6*	*1 275.3*
China - Chine	1990	3 296.5	2 032.4	1 465.5	570.1	1 264.1	835.9	428.2
	2000	1 160.6	1 711.8	1 271.2	440.3	-551.2	-2 190.2	1 639.1
	2005	2 092.5	1 814.3	1 685.6	79.9	278.2	-962.0	1 240.2
	2011	887.1	-660.9	480.9	-1 129.6	1 548.0	301.5	1 246.5
China, Hong Kong SAR - Chine (RAS de Hong Kong)	1990	31.4	38.2	19.5	18.7	-6.8	-6.8	0.0
China, Macao SAR - Chine (RAS de Macao)	1990	0.2	0.2	0.1	0.1	0.0	0.0	0.0
China, Taiwan Province of - Province chinoise de Taiwan	1990	24.6	36.3	6.4	..	-11.7	-3.1	-8.6

For sources and notes, see end of table.

Pour les sources et les notes, se reporter à la fin du tableau.

7.6.1   Official financial flows from
bilateral and multilateral sources
by country and geographical region

7.6.1   Flux financiers publics bilatéraux
et multilatéraux par pays et régions
géographiques

Region, country or territory / Régions, pays ou territoires	Year / Année	Total official net (1) / Total secteur officiel net (1)	Total ODA Net (2) / APD totale nette (2)			Total OOF Net (3) / Flux AASP nets (3)		
			Total donors (4) / Tous donneurs (4)	of which: / dont :		Total donors / Tous donneurs	of which: / dont :	
				DAC bilateral donors / Donneurs bilatéraux du CAD	Multilateral donors / Donneurs multilatéraux		DAC bilateral donors / Donneurs bilatéraux du CAD	Multilateral donors / Donneurs multilatéraux
				Millions of dollars / Millions de dollars				
Korea, Dem. People's Rep. of -	1990	6.9	7.7	0.9	6.9	-0.9	-0.9	0.0
Corée, Rép. populaire dém. de	2000	74.2	73.3	26.9	46.4	0.9	0.9	0.0
	2005	88.2	87.6	39.6	42.2	0.6	0.6	0.0
	2011	159.6	118.5	40.5	50.5	41.1	41.1	0.0
Korea, Republic of - Corée, République de	1990	-491.2	52.0	54.8	2.7	-543.2	-162.9	-380.3
Mongolia - Mongolie	1990	13.1	13.1	6.4	6.7	0.0	0.0	0.0
	2000	217.0	217.0	152.8	60.1	0.0	0.0	0.0
	2005	219.8	219.6	134.4	53.5	0.2	0.3	0.0
	2011	388.7	339.8	251.6	85.3	48.8	20.0	28.9
Southern Asia - Asie méridionale	*1990*	*7 892.6*	*6 064.8*	*3 318.8*	*2 741.1*	*1 827.9*	*174.5*	*1 654.6*
	2000	*3 371.7*	*4 247.8*	*2 480.5*	*1 744.6*	*-876.1*	*-662.2*	*-213.9*
	2005	*11 837.1*	*9 507.0*	*5 802.1*	*3 467.1*	*2 330.1*	*651.2*	*1 651.3*
	2011	*18 372.0*	*16 732.8*	*12 552.6*	*3 666.3*	*1 639.2*	*-651.4*	*2 290.6*
Afghanistan	1990	121.7	121.7	100.4	22.7	0.0	0.0	0.0
	2000	136.0	136.0	87.6	47.8	0.0	0.0	0.0
	2005	2 892.6	2 837.6	2 180.2	603.9	54.9	12.9	42.0
	2011	6 812.8	6 710.9	5 764.5	738.0	102.0	57.8	44.2
Bangladesh	1990	2 112.4	2 092.8	1 103.3	999.8	19.7	21.9	-2.2
	2000	1 172.1	1 172.8	623.1	519.9	-0.7	-5.3	4.6
	2005	1 459.8	1 318.9	580.3	735.1	140.9	-12.8	153.7
	2011	1 644.8	1 497.8	1 080.2	421.1	147.1	-52.3	199.3
Bhutan - Bhoutan	1990	46.0	46.0	20.1	26.7	0.0	0.0	0.0
	2000	53.0	53.1	33.8	19.8	-0.1	-0.1	0.0
	2005	94.9	90.1	57.2	33.3	4.8	4.4	0.4
	2011	156.1	143.9	71.6	71.9	12.2	-1.5	13.7
India - Inde	1990	2 900.2	1 398.9	751.9	644.6	1 501.2	252.9	1 248.3
	2000	1 153.4	1 372.8	650.5	734.0	-219.4	51.6	-271.0
	2005	2 964.8	1 875.8	863.1	1 003.3	1 089.0	-166.7	1 255.7
	2011	5 561.1	3 221.1	2 037.1	1 182.3	2 340.0	700.6	1 639.4
Iran (Islamic Rep. of) - Iran (Rép. islamique d')	1990	-94.4	106.5	34.8	35.7	-200.9	-133.9	-67.0
	2000	-586.5	129.9	112.8	16.9	-716.4	-756.8	40.4
	2005	982.1	109.0	77.4	27.0	873.1	831.4	41.8
	2011	-1 267.6	101.7	68.6	20.9	-1 369.3	-1 432.6	63.3
Maldives	1990	24.9	20.9	11.6	9.9	4.1	4.1	0.0
	2000	16.2	19.2	13.3	7.1	-3.0	-1.8	-1.2
	2005	118.8	75.8	42.8	22.5	43.0	-1.1	44.0
	2011	32.6	46.0	21.1	19.5	-13.4	3.2	-16.6
Nepal - Népal	1990	432.1	422.8	239.0	181.5	9.3	0.0	9.2
	2000	409.1	386.1	233.6	151.3	23.0	2.7	20.2
	2005	416.3	424.1	347.3	77.1	-7.9	-0.6	-7.2
	2011	884.1	892.3	489.7	402.2	-8.2	0.4	-8.6
Pakistan	1990	1 631.4	1 126.9	653.8	492.3	504.5	31.2	474.7
	2000	766.0	702.7	475.5	224.3	63.3	74.7	-11.4
	2005	1 684.9	1 614.6	793.8	685.2	70.3	-22.4	65.1
	2011	3 745.4	3 508.6	2 635.7	591.6	236.8	36.2	200.6
Sri Lanka	1990	718.3	728.3	404.0	328.0	-10.0	-1.6	-8.5
	2000	252.4	275.2	250.4	23.5	-22.8	-27.2	4.4
	2005	1 223.1	1 161.2	859.9	279.8	61.9	6.2	55.8
	2011	802.6	610.6	384.2	218.8	192.1	36.9	155.2
South-Eastern Asia - Asie du Sud-Est	*1990*	*7 777.3*	*4 783.1*	*4 086.8*	*677.7*	*2 994.1*	*1 561.3*	*1 456.8*
	2000	*4 310.6*	*5 661.7*	*4 767.8*	*894.6*	*-1 351.0*	*-1 685.8*	*334.8*
	2005	*4 722.5*	*6 040.2*	*4 650.3*	*1 315.1*	*-1 317.7*	*-218.3*	*-1 099.5*
	2011	*8 040.2*	*5 540.2*	*3 042.6*	*2 462.2*	*2 500.0*	*966.9*	*1 533.2*
Brunei Darussalam - Brunéi Darussalam	1990	-4.5	3.9	3.7	0.1	-8.4	-8.4	0.0

For sources and notes, see end of table.

Pour les sources et les notes, se reporter à la fin du tableau.

Region, country or territory / Régions, pays ou territoires	Year / Année	Total official net (1) / Total secteur officiel net (1)	Total ODA Net (2) / APD totale nette (2)			Total OOF Net (3) / Flux AASP nets (3)		
			Total donors (4) / Tous donneurs (4)	of which: / dont :		Total donors / Tous donneurs	of which: / dont :	
				DAC bilateral donors / Donneurs bilatéraux du CAD	Multilateral donors / Donneurs multilatéraux		DAC bilateral donors / Donneurs bilatéraux du CAD	Multilateral donors / Donneurs multilatéraux
		Millions of dollars / Millions de dollars						
Cambodia - Cambodge	1990	41.3	41.3	28.5	12.8	0.0	0.0	0.0
	2000	395.3	395.7	248.6	147.0	-0.4	-0.4	0.0
	2005	550.9	535.6	364.3	171.2	15.3	2.3	13.0
	2011	809.5	792.3	491.9	291.6	17.3	13.6	3.7
Indonesia (...2002) - Indonésie (...2002)	1990	3 255.5	1 716.0	1 520.7	171.4	1 539.6	534.3	1 029.3
	2000	2 965.9	1 884.3	1 760.1	121.4	1 081.6	360.4	721.2
Indonesia - Indonésie	2005	863.7	2 534.0	2 261.1	214.2	-1 670.3	-1 346.9	-323.4
	2011	432.0	414.6	123.9	294.5	17.4	-189.1	206.5
Lao People's Dem. Rep. - Rép. dém. populaire lao	1990	149.1	149.1	51.2	96.9	0.0	0.0	0.0
	2000	280.3	280.6	195.5	84.9	-0.4	-0.5	0.2
	2005	361.5	301.9	168.6	132.7	59.6	10.2	49.4
	2011	393.5	396.7	264.3	114.6	-3.2	-2.4	-0.8
Malaysia - Malaisie	1990	538.5	468.5	458.7	13.3	70.1	-6.3	76.4
	2000	-117.3	45.7	43.5	3.3	-163.0	-89.1	-73.9
	2005	-542.4	26.2	18.5	5.5	-568.5	-423.8	-144.7
	2011	448.0	30.6	17.9	12.3	417.4	399.5	17.9
Myanmar	1990	184.0	160.8	83.1	77.7	23.2	23.6	-0.4
	2000	125.8	105.6	68.9	36.6	20.2	20.2	0.0
	2005	116.9	144.8	85.8	59.0	-27.9	-27.9	0.0
	2011	373.3	374.2	273.1	101.7	-0.9	-0.9	0.0
Philippines	1990	2 176.9	1 270.6	1 102.2	167.3	906.3	411.7	494.6
	2000	353.3	571.7	505.1	66.3	-218.4	-20.3	-198.1
	2005	-191.5	567.1	532.6	30.1	-758.6	-574.6	-184.1
	2011	636.4	-191.8	-229.5	38.3	828.3	122.7	705.6
Singapore - Singapour	1990	152.1	-3.1	-3.2	0.1	155.2	193.2	-38.1
Thailand - Thaïlande	1990	1 103.8	795.6	734.0	65.7	308.2	413.2	-104.9
	2000	-1 246.6	696.6	683.6	15.8	-1 943.2	-1 783.5	-159.7
	2005	1 340.8	-167.7	-210.4	37.0	1 508.4	2 000.7	-492.3
	2011	72.4	-155.3	-199.2	43.5	227.7	161.2	66.5
Timor-Leste	2005	185.8	184.8	160.4	24.3	1.1	1.1	0.0
	2011	271.8	283.8	243.4	40.1	-11.9	-11.9	0.0
Viet Nam	1990	180.6	180.6	107.9	72.5	0.0	0.2	-0.1
	2000	1 553.9	1 681.4	1 262.5	419.1	-127.5	-172.5	45.1
	2005	2 036.7	1 913.5	1 269.5	641.0	123.3	140.7	-17.4
	2011	4 603.2	3 595.2	2 056.8	1 525.4	1 008.0	474.2	533.8
Western Asia - Asie occidentale	*1990*	*5 064.2*	*4 176.7*	*1 349.8*	*203.4*	*887.5*	*674.6*	*330.4*
	2000	*3 734.0*	*2 498.3*	*1 255.7*	*834.1*	*1 235.7*	*352.7*	*883.0*
	2005	*29 856.3*	*24 818.7*	*23 294.9*	*1 295.7*	*5 037.7*	*4 960.5*	*77.1*
	2011	*12 096.7*	*9 799.3*	*4 882.8*	*4 318.7*	*2 297.4*	*16.5*	*2 280.9*
Bahrain - Bahreïn	1990	136.7	137.5	1.9	2.3	-0.8	-0.8	0.0
	2000	60.2	60.4	1.6	-0.1	-0.2	-0.2	0.0
Iraq	1990	700.0	63.1	-8.6	16.3	636.9	642.3	-5.4
	2000	101.8	101.8	84.1	15.4	0.0	0.0	0.0
	2005	27 256.4	22 057.1	21 981.9	49.3	5 199.3	5 199.3	0.0
	2011	2 222.5	1 904.1	1 802.8	69.0	318.5	118.5	200.0
Jordan - Jordanie	1990	1 145.7	951.7	435.0	25.0	194.1	126.1	75.5
	2000	552.5	552.7	385.1	167.7	-0.2	-21.4	21.2
	2005	787.0	708.5	441.7	138.9	78.6	26.4	52.2
	2011	1 004.1	977.8	471.2	257.5	26.3	49.7	-23.5
Kuwait - Koweït	1990	12.9	12.9	2.2	3.5	0.0	0.0	0.0
Lebanon - Liban	1990	263.2	285.7	64.9	39.0	-22.5	-13.6	-8.9
	2000	268.8	200.0	93.8	90.9	68.8	2.8	66.0
	2005	182.8	230.5	129.8	102.7	-47.7	-2.7	-45.0
	2011	342.6	471.9	260.8	180.1	-129.2	-70.6	-58.6

For sources and notes, see end of table.

Pour les sources et les notes, se reporter à la fin du tableau.

Region, country or territory / Régions, pays ou territoires	Year / Année	Total official net (1) / Total secteur officiel net (1)	Total ODA Net (2) / APD totale nette (2)			Total OOF Net (3) / Flux AASP nets (3)		
			Total donors (4) / Tous donneurs (4)	DAC bilateral donors / Donneurs bilatéraux du CAD	Multilateral donors / Donneurs multilatéraux	Total donors / Tous donneurs	DAC bilateral donors / Donneurs bilatéraux du CAD	Multilateral donors / Donneurs multilatéraux
				Millions of dollars / Millions de dollars				
Oman	1990	64.7	68.2	11.4	2.2	-3.5	6.0	-9.6
	2000	84.6	79.7	9.2	1.7	5.0	9.7	-4.7
	2005	263.8	19.0	3.7	0.7	244.7	191.0	53.8
Qatar	1990	2.9	3.0	1.3	0.2	0.0	0.0	0.0
Saudi Arabia - Arabie saoudite	1990	14.1	14.7	12.8	1.7	-0.6	-0.6	0.0
	2000	48.1	22.0	18.0	2.1	26.1	26.1	0.0
	2005	-34.7	25.1	13.2	1.2	-59.8	-109.5	49.7
State of Palestine - État de Palestine	2000	729.8	684.5	307.7	226.1	45.3	-0.1	45.4
	2005	1 015.2	1 015.7	570.9	398.4	-0.5	0.2	-0.8
	2011	2 449.5	2 442.0	1 561.6	797.6	7.6	11.3	-3.7
Syrian Arab Republic - République arabe syrienne	1990	873.7	882.8	69.4	34.2	-9.1	0.5	-10.3
	2000	486.8	158.9	97.4	38.1	327.9	342.1	-14.2
	2005	101.7	70.2	5.9	65.5	31.4	-17.5	48.9
	2011	341.5	334.5	77.6	120.2	7.0	-30.1	37.0
Turkey - Turquie	1990	1 393.9	1 303.9	587.9	-16.2	90.0	-88.5	289.1
	2000	1 082.4	326.9	99.1	190.3	755.5	-6.2	761.6
	2005	-11.1	396.0	-9.3	407.4	-407.1	-326.7	-80.5
	2011	5 285.4	3 193.0	396.3	2 803.3	2 092.4	-37.6	2 130.0
United Arab Emirates - Émirats arabes unis	1990	3.8	3.5	2.8	0.7	0.3	0.3	0.0
Yemen - Yémen	1990	452.6	449.8	168.8	94.5	2.8	2.8	0.0
	2000	318.9	311.3	159.8	101.9	7.6	0.0	7.7
	2005	295.3	296.5	157.3	131.7	-1.2	0.0	-1.2
	2011	451.1	476.1	312.4	90.9	-25.0	-24.8	-0.3
Developing economies: Asia n.e.s. - Économies en développement : Asie n.d.a. (6)	*1990*	*1 094.9*	*1 094.9*	*237.5*	*372.6*	*0.0*	*0.0*	*0.0*
	2000	*633.6*	*632.8*	*431.4*	*126.7*	*0.7*	*8.9*	*-8.2*
	2005	*3 001.5*	*2 916.6*	*1 665.3*	*449.4*	*84.9*	*82.4*	*2.5*
	2011	*6 992.7*	*6 596.3*	*1 630.4*	*287.2*	*396.4*	*336.2*	*60.2*
Developing economies: Oceania - Économies en développement : Océanie	**1990**	**1 495.0**	**1 372.5**	**1 215.0**	**154.6**	**122.5**	**60.0**	**62.5**
	2000	**886.8**	**815.9**	**712.5**	**102.2**	**70.9**	**68.4**	**2.4**
	2005	**1 157.7**	**1 160.6**	**974.4**	**184.9**	**-2.8**	**-11.3**	**8.5**
	2011	**4 076.8**	**2 222.7**	**1 979.9**	**239.4**	**1 854.1**	**1 859.8**	**-5.7**
Cook Islands - Îles Cook	1990	11.4	12.1	10.1	2.0	-0.8	-0.8	0.0
	2000	4.2	4.3	3.4	0.9	-0.2	-0.2	0.0
	2005	7.4	7.8	7.0	0.8	-0.3	-0.3	0.0
	2011	30.6	25.4	20.8	4.6	5.2	-0.4	5.6
Fiji - Fidji	1990	34.9	49.6	43.5	5.6	-14.7	-0.4	-14.3
	2000	22.8	29.1	28.9	0.2	-6.3	-0.1	-6.2
	2005	76.4	66.1	39.2	27.0	10.2	2.2	8.1
	2011	96.9	75.3	64.4	10.5	21.6	6.6	15.0
French Polynesia - Polynésie française	1990	304.0	259.7	258.0	1.7	44.3	44.7	-0.4
Kiribati	1990	20.2	20.2	17.7	2.5	0.0	0.0	0.0
	2000	17.9	17.9	14.8	3.1	0.0	0.0	0.0
	2005	28.2	28.0	21.4	6.6	0.2	0.2	0.0
	2011	64.5	63.6	59.2	4.5	0.9	0.9	0.0
Marshall Islands - Îles Marshall	2000	57.2	57.2	47.1	10.1	0.0	0.0	0.0
	2005	56.7	56.8	55.8	1.0	-0.1	0.0	-0.1
	2011	81.9	82.3	84.2	-1.9	-0.4	0.0	-0.4
Micronesia (Federated States of) - Micronésie (États fédérés de)	2000	101.4	101.5	96.6	4.9	-0.1	-0.1	0.0
	2005	106.8	106.6	104.4	2.2	0.3	0.3	0.0
	2011	136.5	133.9	129.0	4.8	2.6	0.5	2.1
Nauru	1990	0.2	0.2	0.2	..	0.0	0.0	..
	2000	4.0	4.0	3.9	0.1	0.0	0.0	0.0
	2005	9.5	9.3	9.0	0.2	0.2	0.2	0.0
	2011	37.6	37.5	37.3	0.2	0.1	0.4	-0.4
New Caledonia - Nouvelle-Calédonie	1990	325.8	302.4	300.2	2.2	23.4	24.0	-0.6

For sources and notes, see end of table.

Pour les sources et les notes, se reporter à la fin du tableau.

Region, country or territory / Régions, pays ou territoires	Year / Année	Total official net (1) / Total secteur officiel net (1)	Total ODA Net (2) / APD totale nette (2)			Total OOF Net (3) / Flux AASP nets (3)		
			Total donors (4) / Tous donneurs (4)	of which: / dont :		Total donors / Tous donneurs	of which: / dont :	
				DAC bilateral donors / Donneurs bilatéraux du CAD	Multilateral donors / Donneurs multilatéraux		DAC bilateral donors / Donneurs bilatéraux du CAD	Multilateral donors / Donneurs multilatéraux
			Millions of dollars / Millions de dollars					
Niue - Nioué	1990	7.2	7.2	7.0	0.2	0.0	0.0	0.0
	2000	3.2	3.2	3.0	0.2	0.0	0.0	0.0
	2005	21.1	21.1	20.1	1.0	0.0	0.0	0.0
	2011	20.9	20.9	19.8	1.1	0.0	0.0	0.0
Northern Mariana Islands - Îles Mariannes du Nord	1990	63.1	63.1	61.9	1.2	0.0	0.0	0.0
Palau - Palaos	2000	37.7	39.1	39.0	0.2	-1.5	-1.5	0.0
	2005	21.6	23.7	23.4	0.3	-2.1	-2.1	0.0
	2011	34.0	27.6	24.0	3.6	6.4	0.0	6.4
Papua New Guinea - Papouasie-Nouvelle-Guinée	1990	474.9	412.4	320.2	90.8	62.5	-15.3	77.8
	2000	357.0	275.2	270.4	4.9	81.9	72.7	9.2
	2005	263.9	266.9	244.9	22.4	-3.0	-3.6	0.6
	2011	2 209.7	610.7	557.5	53.2	1 599.0	1 621.2	-22.3
Samoa	1990	47.4	47.6	27.8	19.5	-0.1	-0.1	0.0
	2000	27.5	27.1	18.2	9.0	0.4	0.3	0.1
	2005	44.0	43.6	30.1	13.5	0.4	0.5	-0.1
	2011	101.0	99.7	61.4	38.3	1.3	1.3	0.0
Solomon Islands - Îles Salomon	1990	46.2	45.7	31.1	14.2	0.5	0.5	0.0
	2000	69.5	68.3	20.8	46.2	1.2	1.2	0.0
	2005	186.8	198.5	172.3	26.1	-11.7	-11.7	0.0
	2011	341.7	333.8	299.2	35.0	7.9	15.4	-7.4
Tokelau - Tokélaou	1990	4.8	4.8	4.4	0.4	0.0	0.0	0.0
	2000	3.5	3.5	3.4	0.1	0.0	0.0	0.0
	2005	16.0	16.0	15.9	0.1	0.0	0.0	0.0
	2011	20.0	20.0	19.9	0.1	0.0	0.0	0.0
Tonga	1990	29.6	29.8	24.2	5.4	-0.2	-0.2	0.0
	2000	18.9	18.8	14.9	4.0	0.0	0.0	0.0
	2005	32.4	32.0	24.8	7.2	0.4	0.4	0.0
	2011	94.4	93.7	66.8	26.8	0.8	0.8	0.0
Tuvalu	1990	5.1	5.1	4.8	0.3	0.0	0.0	0.0
	2000	4.0	4.0	3.8	0.2	0.0	0.0	0.0
	2005	9.2	9.2	5.9	3.3	0.0	0.0	0.0
	2011	42.6	42.6	28.4	11.0	0.0	0.0	0.0
Vanuatu	1990	54.1	49.5	42.1	7.5	4.6	4.6	0.0
	2000	45.2	45.8	28.3	17.5	-0.7	0.0	-0.7
	2005	40.3	39.5	33.4	6.1	0.8	0.8	0.0
	2011	92.4	91.1	90.3	0.7	1.3	1.3	0.0
Wallis and Futuna Islands - Îles Wallis-et-Futuna	1990	3.9	0.9	0.0	0.9	3.0	3.0	0.0
	2000	53.3	52.1	52.1	0.0	1.2	1.2	0.0
	2005	69.0	72.0	71.7	0.4	-3.0	-3.0	0.0
	2011	128.9	130.1	122.6	7.6	-1.3	-1.3	0.0
Developing economies: Oceania n.e.s. - Économies en développement : Océanie n.d.a. (6)	*1990*	*62.4*	*62.4*	*61.9*	*0.1*	*0.0*	*0.0*	*0.0*
	2000	*59.5*	*64.7*	*64.0*	*0.7*	*-5.2*	*-5.2*	*0.0*
	2005	*168.5*	*163.7*	*95.1*	*66.9*	*4.9*	*4.9*	*0.0*
	2011	*543.4*	*334.7*	*295.2*	*39.5*	*208.7*	*213.1*	*-4.4*
Developing economies n.e.s. - Économies en développement n.d.a.(6)	*1990*	*6 213.6*	*5 861.7*	*5 141.0*	*665.6*	*351.9*	*351.9*	*0.0*
	2000	*9 216.6*	*8 950.0*	*8 074.1*	*1 004.5*	*266.6*	*266.6*	*0.0*
	2005	*14 677.0*	*14 251.0*	*11 906.2*	*1 685.0*	*426.0*	*379.5*	*46.5*
	2011	*31 283.4*	*28 956.2*	*25 639.4*	*2 545.9*	*2 327.2*	*2 286.7*	*40.4*
Transition economies - Économies en transition	**1990**	**72.4**	**177.9**	**165.5**	**12.4**	**-105.6**	**-83.7**	**-17.2**
	2000	**5 249.7**	**4 581.5**	**2 751.9**	**1 715.8**	**668.1**	**203.3**	**464.8**
	2005	**5 913.2**	**5 293.2**	**3 320.4**	**1 603.3**	**620.1**	**188.0**	**65.4**
	2011	**11 981.8**	**7 620.5**	**3 040.7**	**4 086.0**	**4 361.2**	**1 097.4**	**3 253.7**
Albania - Albanie	1990	11.1	11.1	9.0	2.0	0.0	0.0	0.0
	2000	316.4	317.9	141.9	175.0	-1.5	-1.1	-0.4
	2005	426.5	319.1	178.7	131.7	107.3	10.3	74.3
	2011	537.3	348.8	206.6	138.0	188.5	4.9	185.3

For sources and notes, see end of table.   Pour les sources et les notes, se reporter à la fin du tableau.

Region, country or territory / Régions, pays ou territoires	Year / Année	Total official net (1) / Total secteur officiel net (1)	Total ODA Net (2) / APD totale nette (2)			Total OOF Net (3) / Flux AASP nets (3)		
			Total donors (4) / Tous donneurs (4)	of which: / dont :		Total donors / Tous donneurs	of which: / dont :	
				DAC bilateral donors / Donneurs bilatéraux du CAD	Multilateral donors / Donneurs multilatéraux		DAC bilateral donors / Donneurs bilatéraux du CAD	Multilateral donors / Donneurs multilatéraux
		Millions of dollars / Millions de dollars						
Armenia - Arménie	2000	232.8	215.9	139.4	75.6	16.9	2.5	14.4
	2005	159.8	170.3	126.9	43.1	-10.6	0.0	-10.6
	2011	495.4	378.2	164.7	205.6	117.2	-4.1	121.3
Azerbaijan - Azerbaïdjan	2000	204.8	139.1	70.7	60.2	65.7	42.4	23.3
	2005	332.1	216.5	95.6	91.9	115.6	71.6	3.1
	2011	782.7	292.2	176.0	89.5	490.5	34.0	456.5
Belarus - Bélarus	2005	72.5	57.8	35.0	13.2	14.7	0.2	5.3
	2011	194.9	125.8	68.1	33.5	69.1	23.0	17.1
Bosnia and Herzegovina - Bosnie-Herzégovine	2000	775.9	737.9	453.3	266.2	37.9	18.5	19.5
	2005	578.2	548.5	267.1	241.1	29.7	-0.7	30.4
	2011	598.8	623.7	253.0	325.9	-24.9	-6.7	-18.3
Croatia - Croatie	2000	154.9	65.5	42.7	22.7	89.4	-18.1	107.5
	2005	250.9	123.5	62.7	57.6	127.5	-11.7	139.2
Georgia - Géorgie	2000	230.9	169.2	120.4	42.9	61.8	2.5	59.3
	2005	378.8	292.1	183.9	99.7	86.7	1.0	23.5
	2011	934.1	590.0	315.9	258.5	344.1	124.9	223.2
Kazakhstan	2000	277.7	189.2	160.7	14.4	88.5	-12.1	100.6
	2005	-362.4	228.9	150.3	25.4	-591.2	172.7	-860.5
	2011	1 397.2	213.3	32.1	47.3	1 183.9	115.6	1 080.7
Kyrgyzstan - Kirghizistan	2000	211.5	214.7	91.9	111.6	-3.2	0.0	-3.2
	2005	329.3	267.9	125.8	84.1	61.5	-0.4	7.2
	2011	572.8	522.9	176.2	261.5	49.9	-0.2	50.1
Montenegro - Monténégro	2011	150.1	124.4	26.5	88.3	25.6	-14.1	40.5
Republic of Moldova - République de Moldova	2000	121.3	122.5	61.6	51.1	-1.2	-2.4	1.2
	2005	138.6	169.1	85.1	76.5	-30.5	0.0	-40.7
	2011	509.1	469.3	105.4	338.2	39.8	-3.9	43.7
Serbia and Montenegro - Serbie-et-Monténégro	2000	1 132.5	1 134.3	592.9	540.2	-1.8	-1.8	0.0
	2005	1 371.4	1 070.2	773.4	260.8	301.1	97.3	203.8
Serbia - Serbie	2011	2 016.7	1 377.6	253.4	1 099.1	639.1	62.8	576.3
SFR of Yugoslavia - RSF de Yougoslavie	1990	0.0	0.0	..	..	0.0	..	..
Tajikistan - Tadjikistan	2000	124.3	123.5	38.2	84.8	0.7	0.0	0.7
	2005	274.9	251.5	105.1	134.6	23.4	0.0	8.9
	2011	363.4	354.5	152.4	190.1	8.9	-0.3	9.2
TFYR of Macedonia - LERY de Macédoine	2000	269.4	250.2	111.0	138.7	19.2	-5.9	25.1
	2005	277.8	227.3	165.8	54.6	50.5	-17.3	67.9
	2011	266.3	192.6	74.2	109.2	73.7	-2.3	76.0
Turkmenistan - Turkménistan	2000	196.9	35.3	9.9	5.7	161.6	138.0	23.6
	2005	26.7	30.4	11.9	7.0	-3.7	-28.5	-12.3
	2011	302.5	38.4	12.3	12.0	264.1	174.1	90.0
Ukraine	2005	792.2	411.7	240.7	138.3	380.5	-50.0	430.5
	2011	1 109.3	810.7	487.0	292.0	298.6	-24.0	322.6
Uzbekistan - Ouzbékistan	2000	324.2	185.8	152.2	16.9	138.5	40.0	98.4
	2005	187.8	169.8	123.9	32.6	18.0	-58.8	58.3
	2011	106.3	214.6	51.5	150.7	-108.3	-77.9	-30.4
Transition economies n.e.s. - Économies en transition n.d.a.(6)	*1990*	*61.3*	*166.8*	*156.5*	*10.3*	*-105.6*	*-83.7*	*-17.2*
	2000	*676.3*	*680.6*	*565.3*	*110.0*	*-4.4*	*0.8*	*-5.2*
	2005	*678.0*	*738.6*	*588.5*	*111.2*	*-60.6*	*2.3*	*-62.9*
	2011	*1 644.8*	*943.5*	*485.5*	*446.8*	*701.3*	*691.6*	*9.7*
Developed economies: America - Économies développées : Amérique	**1990**	**51.0**	**42.2**	**42.1**	**0.1**	**8.8**	**8.8**	**0.0**
Bermuda - Bermudes	1990	51.0	42.2	42.1	0.1	8.8	8.8	0.0
Developed economies: Asia - Économies développées : Asie	**1990**	**1 351.1**	**1 371.9**	**1 370.7**	**1.2**	**-20.8**	**-47.1**	**26.2**
Israel - Israël	1990	1 351.1	1 371.9	1 370.7	1.2	-20.8	-47.1	26.2

For sources and notes, see end of table.

Pour les sources et les notes, se reporter à la fin du tableau.

Region, country or territory / Régions, pays ou territoires	Year / Année	Total official net (1) / Total secteur officiel net (1)	Total ODA Net (2) / APD totale nette (2)			Total OOF Net (3) / Flux AASP nets (3)		
			Total donors (4) / Tous donneurs (4)	of which: / dont :		Total donors / Tous donneurs	of which: / dont :	
				DAC bilateral donors / Donneurs bilatéraux du CAD	Multilateral donors / Donneurs multilatéraux		DAC bilateral donors / Donneurs bilatéraux du CAD	Multilateral donors / Donneurs multilatéraux
		Millions of dollars / Millions de dollars						
Developed economies: Europe - Économies développées : Europe	**1990**	**69.4**	**44.3**	**21.6**	**16.5**	**25.1**	**15.4**	**9.7**
	2000	**119.5**	**82.1**	**21.9**	**61.1**	**37.5**	**-1.9**	**39.4**
Cyprus - Chypre	1990	42.4	38.4	18.5	14.8	4.0	3.1	1.0
Gibraltar	1990	-0.8	0.6	0.6	..	-1.3	-1.3	..
Malta - Malte	1990	27.7	5.3	2.5	1.8	22.4	13.7	8.7
	2000	19.6	21.2	21.2	0.9	-1.6	-0.6	-1.1
Slovenia - Slovénie	2000	99.9	60.8	0.6	60.1	39.1	-1.4	40.5

Sources:
- OECD, *OECD.Stat Extracts*

Notes:

(1) Total Official Flows: The sum of Official Development Assistance (ODA) and Other Official Flows (OOF) represents the total net disbursements by the official sector at large to the recipient country.

(2) The Total Official Development Assistance (ODA) includes grants or loans to countries and territories on the DAC List of Developing Countries which are:
- undertaken by the official sector;
- with promotion of economic development and welfare as the main objective;
- at concessional financial terms (if a loan, have a grant element of at least 25%).

(3) The Other Official Flows (OOF) are transactions by the official sector whose main objective is other than development motivated, or, if development motivated, whose grant element is below the 25% threshold which would make them eligible to be recorded as ODA. The main classes of transactions included here are official export credits, official sector equity and portfolio investment, and debt reorganisation undertaken by the official sector at non-concessional terms (irrespective of the nature or the identity of the original creditor).

(4) Total Donors is the sum of the three following donor types:
- DAC Bilateral Donors: The Development Assistance Committee (DAC) is the Committee of the OECD which deals with development co-operation matters. It consists of 23 Member countries.
- Multilateral Donors (i.e. AfDB, IBRD, IMF, UNDP).
- Other Bilateral Donors: the Non-DAC Bilateral Donors (i.e Hungary, Lithuania, Turkey)

(5) Developing economies is the sum of:
- Developing economies: Africa
- Developing economies: America
- Developing economies: Asia
- Developing economies: Oceania
- Developing economies n.e.s.

(6) "n.e.s." refers to Unallocated or Unspecified economies, i.e. a group of recipient economies and not an individual recipient economy.

Sources :
- OCDE, *OECD.Stat Extracts*

Notes :

(1) Apports totaux du secteur public : il s'agit du total de l'aide publique au développement (APD) et des autres apports du secteur public (AASP). Cet agrégat correspond aux versements nets effectués par le secteur public dans son ensemble aux pays bénéficiaires considérés.

(2) Par aide publique au développement (APD), on entend l'ensemble des apports de ressources qui sont fournis aux pays en développement et aux institutions multilatérales par des organismes officiels, y compris les collectivités locales, ou par leurs agents d'exécution et qui, considérés au niveau de chaque opération, répondent aux critères suivants :
a) être dispensés dans le but essentiel de favoriser le développement économique et l'amélioration du niveau de vie dans les pays en développement ; et
b) revêtir un caractère de faveur et comporter un élément de libéralité d'au moins 25%.

(3) Autres apports du secteur public (AASP) : il s'agit des opérations du secteur public dont le but essentiel est autre que le développement ou qui, tout en visant à favoriser le développement, sont assorties d'un élément de libéralité inférieur au seuil de 25 pour cent à partir duquel elles auraient pu être notifiées comme de l'APD. Les principales catégories d'opérations couvertes dans les AASP sont les crédits publics à l'exportation, les prises de participation et les investissements de portefeuille du secteur public et le réaménagement de la dette effectué par le secteur public aux conditions du marché (et ce, quelle que soit la nature ou l'identité du créancier initial).

(4) Tous Donneurs est la somme des 3 types de donneurs suivants :
- Donneurs Bilatéraux du CAD : Le Comité d'aide au développement (CAD) est la principale instance chargée, à l'OCDE, des questions relatives à la coopération avec les pays en développement. Le CAD regroupe 23 pays membres.
- Donneurs Multilatéraux (i.e. BAfD, BIRD, FMI, PNUD).
- Autres Donneurs Biletéraux : les Donneurs Bilatéraux non-membres du CAD (i.e. Hongrie, Lituanie, Turquie).

(5) Économies en développement est la somme de :
- Économies en développement : Afrique
- Économies en développement : Amérique
- Économies en développement : Asie
- Économies en développement : Océanie
- Économies en développement n.d.a.

(6) "n.d.a." se réfère à des économies "Non ventilées" ou "Non spécifiées", c-à-d un groupe d' économies bénéficiaires et non pas une économie bénéficiaire individuelle.

7

7.6.2 Official financial flows from bilateral and multilateral sources to developing economies by economic grouping

7.6.2 Flux financiers publics bilatéraux et multilatéraux à destination des économies en développement par groupements économiques

Economic grouping / Groupements économiques	Year / Année	Total official net (1) / Total secteur officiel net (1)	Total ODA Net (2) / APD totale nette (2) — Total donors (4) / Tous donneurs (4)	of which / dont : DAC bilateral donors / Donneurs bilatéraux du CAD	Multilateral donors / Donneurs multilatéraux	Total OOF Net (3) / Flux AASP nets (3) — Total donors / Tous donneurs	of which / dont : DAC bilateral donors / Donneurs bilatéraux du CAD	Multilateral donors / Donneurs multilatéraux
					Millions of dollars / Millions de dollars			
DEVELOPING ECONOMIES - ÉCONOMIES EN DÉVELOPPEMENT (5)	1990	75 021.6	56 851.6	36 816.6	12 576.6	18 170.0	8 065.1	10 128.2
	2000	48 057.8	45 009.2	33 328.9	10 902.5	3 048.6	-5 196.4	8 245.0
	2005	106 428.0	103 155.3	79 457.5	21 142.8	3 272.7	2 806.0	439.1
	2011	151 035.4	131 832.4	89 824.8	34 639.6	19 203.1	7 834.3	11 367.1
Developing economies excluding China - Économies en développement sans la Chine	1990	62 785.5	46 386.7	28 717.6	10 757.1	16 398.8	6 871.7	9 550.3
	2000	34 801.9	31 501.3	21 637.8	9 045.0	3 300.5	-3 284.9	6 585.4
	2005	83 177.4	80 758.8	61 620.7	18 117.9	2 418.6	3 215.6	-824.6
	2011	104 609.1	89 320.3	57 104.1	30 386.4	15 288.9	5 419.0	9 868.3
Developing economies excluding LDCs - Économies en développement sans les PMA	1990	48 737.8	31 795.3	20 382.4	5 207.5	16 942.6	7 020.1	9 942.9
	2000	23 786.9	20 965.0	15 233.2	5 151.0	2 821.9	-5 404.3	8 226.1
	2005	59 585.8	56 618.6	47 379.1	8 372.9	2 967.2	2 540.9	398.7
	2011	62 463.7	44 400.8	27 894.0	15 257.4	18 062.9	7 472.4	10 590.5
High-income developing economies - Économies en développement à revenu élevé	1990	12 771.4	4 792.8	3 377.2	280.1	7 978.6	3 683.7	4 413.6
	2000	7 146.3	1 870.3	1 141.0	513.5	5 276.0	-1 335.3	6 611.4
	2005	-4.9	2 600.8	1 479.6	1 082.5	-2 605.8	-1 547.1	-1 058.7
	2011	14 841.6	8 630.6	4 375.6	4 088.8	6 211.0	4 423.2	1 787.8
Middle-income developing economies - Économies en développement à revenu intermédiaire	1990	24 985.7	20 516.5	12 862.5	2 635.1	4 469.2	1 503.1	2 866.3
	2000	11 112.3	12 611.1	9 902.2	2 350.3	-1 498.8	-3 883.3	2 384.5
	2005	16 371.8	16 905.4	12 906.3	3 370.6	-533.6	-1 038.3	504.7
	2011	19 282.0	13 958.4	9 596.9	3 715.7	5 323.5	-612.7	5 936.2
Low-income developing economies - Économies en développement à revenu faible	1990	28 325.0	23 109.8	13 943.3	8 412.1	5 215.2	2 520.9	2 698.5
	2000	17 703.8	18 731.7	11 865.8	6 621.5	-1 027.9	-256.5	-771.5
	2005	68 903.1	63 066.9	48 920.4	13 744.7	5 836.2	4 838.9	969.7
	2011	71 372.6	66 070.3	43 612.5	21 452.3	5 302.3	1 910.0	3 390.7
Heavily indebted poor countries (IMF) - Pays pauvres très endettés (FMI)	1990	17 232.1	15 820.6	10 011.9	5 387.8	1 411.5	888.5	525.9
	2000	11 538.9	11 911.1	7 634.2	4 121.3	-372.2	-46.2	-326.1
	2005	26 590.3	27 072.6	17 242.7	9 627.9	-482.3	-91.7	-390.6
	2011	42 942.8	44 459.2	28 672.3	15 248.4	-1 516.3	-1 708.2	190.3
Landlocked developing countries - Pays en développement sans littoral	1990	7 165.1	6 982.8	4 176.8	2 635.9	182.3	87.9	94.4
	2000	7 793.7	7 447.6	4 859.9	2 470.5	346.2	11.6	334.6
	2005	14 509.9	15 050.6	9 334.1	5 371.7	-540.7	-33.2	-780.1
	2011	28 668.8	25 660.6	15 991.7	9 053.0	3 008.2	225.2	2 795.4
Small island developing States - Petits États insulaires en développement	1990	1 612.1	1 376.9	1 064.1	307.6	235.2	99.5	150.5
	2000	1 123.9	967.7	723.4	214.3	156.2	-5.8	162.0
	2005	1 461.1	1 547.3	1 210.5	310.1	-86.2	-31.8	-54.4
	2011	4 945.7	2 766.0	2 200.5	553.0	2 179.8	1 752.9	426.9
Least developed countries - Pays les moins avancés	*1990*	*17 344.1*	*16 623.8*	*9 800.7*	*6 119.8*	*720.3*	*687.6*	*35.6*
	2000	*12 175.6*	*12 248.1*	*7 675.7*	*4 334.2*	*-72.5*	*-70.8*	*-1.7*
	2005	*25 684.2*	*25 954.5*	*15 927.2*	*9 824.9*	*-270.3*	*-287.4*	*17.0*
	2011	*43 032.5*	*44 258.6*	*29 691.1*	*13 999.4*	*-1 226.1*	*-1 751.9*	*524.2*
Africa and Haiti - Afrique et Haïti	1990	13 532.9	12 872.5	7 821.2	4 526.1	660.3	634.4	28.9
	2000	9 067.4	9 190.1	5 910.6	3 124.1	-122.7	-88.9	-33.8
	2005	18 946.6	19 446.3	11 529.3	7 779.3	-499.7	-266.8	-232.9
	2011	30 468.2	31 933.7	20 095.5	11 578.3	-1 465.6	-1 747.9	280.7
Asia - Asie	1990	3 539.3	3 484.3	1 794.4	1 512.6	55.0	48.2	6.7
	2000	2 890.5	2 841.3	1 650.9	1 109.2	49.2	16.5	32.7
	2005	6 188.1	5 949.6	3 940.9	1 944.0	238.6	-11.5	250.1
	2011	11 525.3	11 284.0	8 747.5	2 232.1	241.3	-10.0	251.2
Islands - Îles	1990	272.0	267.0	185.1	81.1	5.0	5.0	0.0
	2000	217.6	216.7	114.3	100.9	0.9	1.5	-0.6
	2005	549.5	558.7	457.0	101.6	-9.2	-9.1	-0.1
	2011	1 039.1	1 040.8	848.0	189.0	-1.8	6.0	-7.8

For sources and notes, see end of table.

Pour les sources et les notes, se reporter à la fin du tableau.

7.6.2 Official financial flows from bilateral and multilateral sources to developing economies by economic grouping

7.6.2 Flux financiers publics bilatéraux et multilatéraux à destination des économies en développement par groupements économiques

Economic grouping / Groupements économiques	Year / Année	Total official net (1) / Total secteur officiel net (1)	Total ODA Net (2) / APD totale nette (2) Total donors (4) / Tous donneurs (4)	of which: / dont : DAC bilateral donors / Donneurs bilatéraux du CAD	Multilateral donors / Donneurs multilatéraux	Total OOF Net (3) / Flux AASP nets (3) Total donors / Tous donneurs	of which: / dont : DAC bilateral donors / Donneurs bilatéraux du CAD	Multilateral donors / Donneurs multilatéraux
					Millions of dollars / Millions de dollars			
Major petroleum and gas exporters - *Principaux exportateurs de pétrole et de gaz*	*1990*	*4 538.6*	*1 209.0*	*587.2*	*257.2*	*3 329.6*	*1 614.4*	*1 568.9*
	2000	*-477.5*	*1 084.9*	*633.2*	*309.0*	*-1 562.4*	*-1 226.9*	*-335.4*
	2005	*33 577.7*	*29 454.3*	*28 559.6*	*823.3*	*4 123.4*	*5 337.3*	*-1 213.8*
	2011	*4 932.6*	*4 865.6*	*3 459.5*	*1 240.5*	*67.0*	*-597.0*	*664.0*
Africa - Afrique	1990	2 535.1	860.8	454.8	196.3	1 674.2	929.9	597.9
	2000	-176.1	675.5	347.7	258.8	-851.6	-427.2	-424.4
	2005	5 579.2	7 193.8	6 462.4	716.3	-1 614.5	-664.9	-949.6
	2011	3 140.0	2 815.3	1 557.5	1 137.0	324.6	155.3	169.3
America - Amérique	1990	1 299.5	76.4	75.8	0.6	1 223.2	170.3	1 052.9
	2000	50.6	76.1	61.3	14.1	-25.5	-78.8	53.3
	2005	-469.1	50.3	21.1	28.8	-519.4	-110.0	-409.4
	2011	837.7	44.5	30.6	13.6	793.3	561.9	231.4
Asia - Asie	1990	704.0	271.8	56.7	60.3	432.2	514.2	-82.0
	2000	-352.0	333.3	224.1	36.1	-685.3	-721.0	35.7
	2005	28 467.6	22 210.2	22 076.2	78.1	6 257.4	6 112.1	145.3
	2011	954.9	2 005.8	1 871.5	90.0	-1 050.9	-1 314.2	263.3
Major exporters of manufactured goods - *Principaux exportateurs d'articles manufacturés*	*1990*	*9 679.9*	*3 576.1*	*2 880.3*	*682.1*	*6 103.9*	*3 298.9*	*2 810.5*
	2000	*-129.2*	*2 396.3*	*1 930.0*	*469.4*	*-2 525.5*	*-4 773.5*	*2 248.1*
	2005	*2 686.7*	*1 853.3*	*1 655.0*	*141.1*	*833.5*	*405.6*	*427.9*
	2011	*5 793.8*	*172.7*	*1 146.9*	*-964.3*	*5 621.1*	*2 001.0*	*3 620.1*
America - Amérique	1990	5 024.2	156.3	144.8	11.5	4 868.0	2 035.6	2 837.9
	2000	74.1	-57.8	-68.3	10.0	131.9	-710.7	842.6
	2005	-204.2	180.5	161.3	18.7	-384.7	-209.3	-175.4
	2011	4 386.3	958.2	847.2	109.5	3 428.1	1 138.8	2 289.3
Asia - Asie	1990	4 655.7	3 419.8	2 735.5	670.6	1 235.9	1 263.3	-27.4
	2000	-203.3	2 454.1	1 998.3	459.4	-2 657.3	-4 062.8	1 405.5
	2005	2 890.9	1 672.8	1 493.7	122.4	1 218.1	614.8	603.3
	2011	1 407.5	-785.5	299.7	-1 073.8	2 193.0	862.2	1 330.8
Emerging economies - *Économies émergentes*	*1990*	*8 967.9*	*2 326.0*	*2 137.4*	*171.6*	*6 642.0*	*3 803.2*	*2 850.1*
	2000	*4 389.4*	*1 414.1*	*1 340.5*	*66.9*	*2 975.3*	*-2 368.3*	*5 343.6*
	2005	*591.7*	*996.0*	*705.7*	*279.5*	*-404.4*	*486.4*	*-890.8*
	2011	*3 464.9*	*2 504.4*	*1 989.6*	*509.2*	*960.5*	*3 714.4*	*-2 753.9*
America - Amérique	1990	7 640.1	976.7	886.8	89.9	6 663.4	3 369.1	3 305.7
	2000	5 753.2	671.8	613.4	47.8	5 081.4	-495.7	5 577.1
	2005	-206.7	1 137.6	897.6	237.0	-1 344.3	-1 090.5	-253.8
	2011	2 944.5	2 629.0	2 170.8	453.3	315.5	3 153.7	-2 838.2
Asia - Asie	1990	1 327.8	1 349.3	1 250.6	81.7	-21.5	434.1	-455.6
	2000	-1 363.9	742.3	727.1	19.2	-2 106.2	-1 872.6	-233.6
	2005	798.4	-141.5	-191.9	42.5	939.9	1 576.9	-637.0
	2011	520.4	-124.6	-181.2	55.9	645.1	560.7	84.3
Newly industrialized Asian economies - *Économies nouvellement industrialisées d'Asie*	*1990*	*6 791.6*	*4 374.1*	*3 893.0*	*439.1*	*2 417.6*	*1 373.3*	*1 068.3*
	2000	*1 955.3*	*3 198.3*	*2 992.2*	*206.9*	*-1 243.0*	*-1 532.5*	*289.5*
	2005	*1 470.6*	*2 959.6*	*2 601.8*	*286.9*	*-1 489.0*	*-344.6*	*-1 144.4*
	2011	*1 588.9*	*98.1*	*-286.8*	*388.7*	*1 490.7*	*494.3*	*996.5*
First tier - Première génération	1990	-283.1	123.4	77.5	21.5	-406.5	20.5	-427.0
Second tier - Deuxième génération	1990	7 074.8	4 250.7	3 815.5	417.7	2 824.1	1 352.8	1 495.3
	2000	1 955.3	3 198.3	2 992.2	206.9	-1 243.0	-1 532.5	289.5
	2005	1 470.6	2 959.6	2 601.8	286.9	-1 489.0	-344.6	-1 144.4
	2011	1 588.9	98.1	-286.8	388.7	1 490.7	494.3	996.5

For sources and notes, see end of table.

Pour les sources et les notes, se reporter à la fin du tableau.

7.6.2 Official financial flows from bilateral and multilateral sources to developing economies by economic grouping

7.6.2 Flux financiers publics bilatéraux et multilatéraux à destination des économies en développement par groupements économiques

Economic grouping / Groupements économiques	Year / Année	Total official net (1) / Total secteur officiel net (1)	Total ODA Net (2) / APD totale nette (2) — Total donors (4) / Tous donneurs (4)	Total ODA Net (2) of which / dont : DAC bilateral donors / Donneurs bilatéraux du CAD	Total ODA Net (2) of which / dont : Multilateral donors / Donneurs multilatéraux	Total OOF Net (3) / Flux AASP nets (3) — Total donors / Tous donneurs	Total OOF Net (3) of which / dont : DAC bilateral donors / Donneurs bilatéraux du CAD	Total OOF Net (3) of which / dont : Multilateral donors / Donneurs multilatéraux
		Millions of dollars / Millions de dollars						
Developing economies: Africa - Économies en développement : Afrique	1990	29 077.5	26 127.6	15 767.9	6 124.3	2 949.9	850.9	1 950.3
	2000	14 088.1	15 363.0	10 297.2	4 708.3	-1 274.8	-343.5	-931.4
	2005	35 322.9	35 632.0	24 438.1	10 742.4	-309.0	-487.8	178.8
	2011	54 209.8	50 649.8	31 573.8	18 416.2	3 560.1	-998.7	4 557.2
Northern Africa excluding Sudan - Afrique septentrionale sans le Soudan	1990	8 217.6	8 038.8	4 081.3	268.0	178.7	-952.3	982.5
	2000	1 865.8	2 226.3	1 660.7	397.3	-360.5	100.5	-461.0
	2005	2 325.0	2 499.3	1 507.5	726.4	-174.4	-786.5	612.1
	2011	5 647.6	3 596.5	2 144.2	1 180.6	2 051.0	-201.2	2 252.2
Sub-Saharan Africa - Afrique subsaharienne	1990	19 940.7	17 186.0	10 846.2	5 803.2	2 754.7	1 797.4	957.1
	2000	11 189.9	12 105.2	7 788.8	4 140.0	-915.4	-450.8	-464.6
	2005	30 641.1	30 904.5	21 130.9	9 610.2	-263.4	213.0	-476.4
	2011	43 265.0	41 955.4	25 969.3	15 696.5	1 309.6	-877.1	2 185.1
Sub-Saharan Africa excluding South Africa - Afrique subsaharienne sans l'Afrique du Sud	1990	19 940.7	17 186.0	10 846.2	5 803.2	2 754.7	1 797.4	957.1
	2000	10 598.7	11 618.9	7 433.4	4 009.2	-1 020.2	-356.2	-663.9
	2005	29 908.8	30 214.3	20 664.9	9 386.7	-305.5	326.2	-631.6
	2011	40 846.7	40 557.9	24 935.2	15 334.1	288.8	-1 140.7	1 427.9
Developing economies: America - Économies en développement : Amérique	1990	13 525.1	5 190.4	4 146.4	1 032.0	8 334.7	3 729.7	4 634.3
	2000	10 364.7	4 837.7	3 858.9	940.8	5 527.0	-1 012.2	6 539.2
	2005	3 452.5	6 707.9	4 866.7	1 827.7	-3 255.4	-1 589.2	-1 666.3
	2011	14 528.6	11 537.7	7 750.4	3 697.5	2 990.8	3 655.8	-665.0
Central America and Greater Caribbean Islands excluding Puerto Rico - Amérique centrale et Grandes Antilles sans Porto Rico	1990	7 302.3	2 431.1	2 074.9	348.1	4 871.2	2 093.5	2 801.2
	2000	2 179.0	1 749.7	1 214.7	521.3	429.4	-793.8	1 223.1
	2005	2 131.7	2 793.8	1 985.7	804.9	-662.2	-367.9	-294.2
	2011	10 386.2	5 189.9	3 433.5	1 677.7	5 196.3	1 839.0	3 357.3
Central America and Greater Caribbean Islands excluding Mexico and Puerto Rico - Amérique centrale et Grandes Antilles sans le Mexique et Porto Rico	1990	2 278.0	2 274.8	1 930.2	336.6	3.2	57.9	-36.7
	2000	2 104.9	1 807.4	1 283.0	511.3	297.5	-83.1	380.5
	2005	2 335.9	2 613.3	1 824.4	786.2	-277.5	-158.6	-118.9
	2011	5 999.9	4 231.7	2 586.3	1 568.2	1 768.2	700.2	1 068.0
South America and Central America - Amérique du Sud et Amérique centrale	1990	11 860.0	3 870.5	3 169.0	694.1	7 989.5	3 636.0	4 364.7
	2000	8 641.1	3 301.9	2 577.0	705.3	5 339.2	-924.9	6 264.1
	2005	1 639.8	4 915.6	3 663.9	1 248.9	-3 275.7	-1 633.1	-1 642.7
	2011	9 991.1	7 119.5	5 032.3	2 002.2	2 871.6	4 166.6	-1 295.0
South America excluding Brazil - Amérique du Sud sans le Brésil	1990	4 719.9	1 879.9	1 427.4	451.0	2 840.0	891.8	1 948.2
	2000	2 820.2	1 637.2	1 342.8	283.3	1 183.0	-615.7	1 798.7
	2005	75.2	2 512.9	1 923.1	586.6	-2 437.7	-783.9	-1 653.8
	2011	5 588.5	3 166.5	2 376.0	785.4	2 422.0	1 248.6	1 173.5
Developing economies: Asia - Économies en développement : Asie	1990	24 710.4	18 299.4	10 546.2	4 600.1	6 411.1	3 072.7	3 481.1
	2000	13 501.6	15 042.5	10 386.2	4 146.7	-1 541.0	-4 175.8	2 634.8
	2005	51 817.9	45 403.9	37 272.1	6 702.9	6 414.0	4 514.8	1 871.6
	2011	46 936.8	38 465.9	22 881.3	9 740.6	8 470.9	1 030.7	7 440.2
Eastern and South-Eastern Asia excluding China - Asie orientale et Asie du Sud-Est sans la Chine	1990	7 362.2	4 930.6	4 174.8	712.8	2 431.6	1 387.7	1 067.9
	2000	4 601.8	5 951.9	4 947.5	1 001.0	-1 350.2	-1 684.9	334.8
	2005	5 030.5	6 347.3	4 824.3	1 410.8	-1 316.9	-217.4	-1 099.5
	2011	8 588.5	5 998.5	3 334.7	2 598.1	2 590.0	1 028.0	1 562.0
Southern Asia excluding India - Asie méridionale sans l'Inde	1990	4 992.5	4 665.9	2 566.9	2 096.5	326.6	-78.4	406.3
	2000	2 218.3	2 874.9	1 830.0	1 010.6	-656.7	-713.8	57.1
	2005	8 872.4	7 631.3	4 939.0	2 463.8	1 241.1	817.9	395.6
	2011	12 810.9	13 511.6	10 515.4	2 483.9	-700.8	-1 352.0	651.2

For sources and notes, see next page.

Pour les sources et les notes, se reporter à la page suivante.

7.6.2 Official financial flows from bilateral and multilateral sources to developing economies by economic grouping

7.6.2 Flux financiers publics bilatéraux et multilatéraux à destination des économies en développement par groupements économiques

Source:
OECD, *OECD.Stat Extracts*

Notes:

- The groupings presented in this table do not include "n.e.s." recipient countries.

(1) Total Official Flows: The sum of Official Development Assistance (ODA) and Other Official Flows (OOF) represents the total net disbursements by the official sector at large to the recipient country.

(2) The Total Official Development Assistance (ODA) includes grants or loans to countries and territories on the DAC List of Developing Countries which are:
- undertaken by the official sector;
- with promotion of economic development and welfare as the main objective;
- at concessional financial terms (if a loan, have a grant element of at least 25%).

(3) The Other Official Flows (OOF) are transactions by the official sector whose main objective is other than development motivated, or, if development motivated, whose grant element is below the 25% threshold which would make them eligible to be recorded as ODA. The main classes of transactions included here are official export credits, official sector equity and portfolio investment, and debt reorganisation undertaken by the official sector at non-concessional terms (irrespective of the nature or the identity of the original creditor).

(4) Total Donors is the sum of the three following donor types:
- DAC Bilateral Donors: The Development Assistance Committee (DAC) is the Committee of the OECD which deals with development co-operation matters. It consists of 23 Member countries.
- Multilateral Donors (i.e. AfDB, IBRD, IMF, UNDP).
- Other Bilateral Donors: the Non-DAC Bilateral Donors (i.e Hungary, Lithuania, Turkey)

(5) Developing economies is the sum of:
- Developing economies: Africa
- Developing economies: America
- Developing economies: Asia
- Developing economies: Oceania
- Developing economies n.e.s.

Source :
OCDE, *OECD.Stat Extracts*

Notes :

- Les groupements présentés dans ce tableau n'incluent pas les pays bénéficiaires "n.d.a.".

(1) Apports totaux du secteur public : il s'agit du total de l'aide publique au développement (APD) et des autres apports du secteur public (AASP). Cet agrégat correspond aux versements nets effectués par le secteur public dans son ensemble aux pays bénéficiaires considérés.

(2) Par aide publique au développement (APD), on entend l'ensemble des apports de ressources qui sont fournis aux pays en développement et aux institutions multilatérales par des organismes officiels, y compris les collectivités locales, ou par leurs agents d'exécution et qui, considérés au niveau de chaque opération, répondent aux critères suivants :
a) être dispensés dans le but essentiel de favoriser le développement économique et l'amélioration du niveau de vie dans les pays en développement ; et
b) revêtir un caractère de faveur et comporter un élément de libéralité d'au moins 25%.

(3) Autres apports du secteur public (AASP) : il s'agit des opérations du secteur public dont le but essentiel est autre que le développement ou qui, tout en visant à favoriser le développement, sont assorties d'un élément de libéralité inférieur au seuil de 25 pour cent à partir duquel elles auraient pu être notifiées comme de l'APD. Les principales catégories d'opérations couvertes dans les AASP sont les crédits publics à l'exportation, les prises de participation et les investissements de portefeuille du secteur public et le réaménagement de la dette effectué par le secteur public aux conditions du marché (et ce, quelle que soit la nature ou l'identité du créancier initial).

(4) Tous Donneurs est la somme des 3 types de donneurs suivants :
- Donneurs Bilatéraux du CAD : Le Comité d'aide au développement (CAD) est la principale instance chargée, à l'OCDE, des questions relatives à la coopération avec les pays en développement. Le CAD regroupe 23 pays membres.
- Donneurs Multilatéraux (i.e. BAfD, BIRD, FMI, PNUD).
- Autres Donneurs Bilatéraux : les Donneurs Bilatéraux non-membres du CAD (i.e. Hongrie, Lituanie, Turquie).

(5) Économies en développement est la somme de :
- Économies en développement : Afrique
- Économies en développement : Amérique
- Économies en développement : Asie
- Économies en développement : Océanie
- Économies en développement n.d.a.

	Total long-term debt (1) / Dette totale à long terme (1)	Public and publicly guaranteed debt (2) / Dette publique et garantie par l'état (2)									Private non-guaranteed debt (5) / Dette privée non garantie (5)
		Total creditors / Total créanciers	Official creditors (3) / Créanciers publics (3)					Private creditors (4) / Créanciers privés (4)			
			Total	Bilateral / Bilatéraux			Multilateral / Multilatéraux	Total	Bonds / Obligations	Commercial banks / Banques commerciales	
				Total	DAC / CAD	OPEC / OPEP					
	Millions of dollars / Millions de dollars										
1980											
Debt outstanding	366 377	309 125	140 815	96 767	68 531	13 743	44 048	168 310	12 676	109 472	57 252
Disbursements (6)	85 197	67 517	24 024	15 602	10 439	2 479	8 422	43 493	1 573	28 407	17 680
Debt service (7)	62 006	46 475	10 436	6 779	4 946	872	3 657	36 038	1 404	24 897	15 531
Principal repayments	34 609	24 935	5 655	4 184	2 930	525	1 471	19 279	500	12 141	9 675
Interest payments	27 397	21 540	4 781	2 595	2 016	347	2 186	16 759	904	12 756	5 857
Net transfers on debt (8)	23 190	21 042	13 588	8 823	5 493	1 606	4 765	7 454	169	3 510	2 148
1990											
Dette totale	961 787	905 658	505 210	308 920	209 326	18 380	196 290	400 448	97 364	196 392	56 129
Décaissements (6)	95 678	79 625	45 284	19 141	16 306	572	26 143	34 340	3 862	13 507	16 053
Service de la dette (7)	105 496	95 232	39 018	17 759	13 423	1 123	21 259	56 214	8 389	29 113	10 264
Remboursement du principal	60 772	54 704	21 827	10 562	7 544	871	11 265	32 876	4 367	15 145	6 069
Paiement des intérêts	44 724	40 529	17 191	7 197	5 879	253	9 994	23 337	4 022	13 969	4 195
Transfers nets (8)	-9 818	-15 608	6 266	1 382	2 883	-551	4 884	-21 874	-4 527	-15 607	5 789
2000											
Debt outstanding	1 580 318	1 131 745	649 857	346 221	252 514	13 870	303 636	481 888	299 930	121 577	448 573
Disbursements (6)	214 222	130 015	47 973	16 462	13 898	456	31 511	82 042	54 851	16 962	84 207
Debt service (7)	276 330	156 226	66 929	31 697	24 777	791	35 232	89 298	44 857	31 120	120 103
Principal repayments	189 524	97 883	43 324	22 106	16 896	624	21 218	54 560	21 920	22 624	91 640
Interest payments	86 806	58 343	23 605	9 591	7 881	167	14 014	34 738	22 936	8 495	28 463
Net transfers on debt (8)	-62 108	-26 211	-18 956	-15 235	-10 879	-335	-3 721	-7 255	9 994	-14 158	-35 897
2005											
Dette totale	1 614 310	1 152 961	642 334	298 835	244 638	13 187	343 499	510 627	365 404	108 003	461 349
Décaissements (6)	266 624	124 647	41 980	11 072	7 749	845	30 908	82 667	58 862	20 327	141 978
Service de la dette (7)	290 290	168 619	68 388	35 347	30 658	866	33 041	100 231	65 415	25 901	121 672
Remboursement du principal	220 014	114 899	47 935	24 452	21 039	729	23 483	66 963	37 972	21 377	105 116
Paiement des intérêts	70 276	53 720	20 452	10 895	9 619	138	9 557	33 268	27 443	4 524	16 556
Transfers nets (8)	-23 666	-43 972	-26 408	-24 275	-22 909	-22	-2 133	-17 564	-6 553	-5 574	20 306
2008											
Debt outstanding	1 966 507	1 213 442	653 697	294 072	224 618	15 542	359 625	559 745	418 454	115 635	753 065
Disbursements (6)	355 721	144 601	62 106	18 899	10 681	2 145	43 206	82 495	59 156	21 012	211 120
Debt service (7)	339 397	165 610	62 129	27 269	23 443	843	34 860	103 481	75 822	19 487	173 787
Principal repayments	256 493	114 434	45 104	21 218	18 399	664	23 886	69 330	47 666	15 032	142 058
Interest payments	82 904	51 176	17 025	6 051	5 044	179	10 974	34 151	28 157	4 455	31 729
Net transfers on debt (8)	16 324	-21 009	-23	-8 370	-12 761	1 302	8 347	-20 986	-16 667	1 525	37 333
2009											
Dette totale	2 045 234	1 285 567	705 588	307 687	222 787	16 235	397 901	579 979	440 779	110 266	759 668
Décaissements (6)	338 408	170 876	85 770	24 801	11 188	1 503	60 970	85 106	62 372	16 471	167 532
Service de la dette (7)	338 123	145 440	57 738	25 649	21 543	924	32 089	87 702	52 187	27 399	192 683
Remboursement du principal	262 135	98 132	42 468	19 752	16 891	708	22 716	55 664	25 352	23 312	164 003
Paiement des intérêts	75 988	47 308	15 270	5 897	4 652	216	9 373	32 039	26 836	4 088	28 680
Transfers nets (8)	285	25 437	28 033	-848	-10 355	579	28 881	-2 596	10 185	-10 929	-25 151
2010											
Debt outstanding	2 265 031	1 378 694	746 632	313 270	218 855	16 210	433 361	632 062	487 773	116 117	886 338
Disbursements (6)	465 627	214 960	95 389	31 925	12 240	1 891	63 464	119 571	82 353	27 589	250 667
Debt service (7)	349 752	146 966	60 055	28 885	21 948	1 318	31 170	86 911	57 669	20 463	202 786
Principal repayments	268 345	98 652	44 942	21 745	17 433	1 055	23 197	53 710	28 513	17 508	169 693
Interest payments	81 407	48 314	15 113	7 140	4 515	263	7 973	33 201	29 157	2 955	33 093
Net transfers on debt (8)	115 875	115 875	67 994	35 334	3 040	-9 708	32 294	32 660	24 684	7 126	47 881
2011											
Dette totale	2 479 374	1 455 455	771 384	322 905	217 843	17 444	448 480	684 071	536 551	119 663	1 023 919
Décaissements (6)	490 250	186 353	78 572	29 092	12 210	2 136	49 481	107 781	76 813	25 067	303 896
Service de la dette (7)	380 371	163 682	68 502	29 181	20 901	880	39 321	95 180	62 074	24 841	216 689
Remboursement du principal	285 760	111 606	53 292	22 331	16 687	638	30 961	58 314	29 232	21 738	174 154
Paiement des intérêts	94 612	52 077	15 210	6 851	4 214	242	8 360	36 867	32 842	3 103	42 535
Transfers nets (8)	109 878	22 671	10 070	-90	-8 691	1 257	10 160	12 601	14 739	226	87 207

For sources and notes, see end of table 7.7.G.

Pour les sources et les notes, se reporter à la fin du tableau 7.7.G.

7.7.B External long-term debt by lending source
Developing economies:
Africa

7.7.B Dette extérieure à long terme par catégories de prêt
Économies en développement :
Afrique

	Total long-term debt (1) / Dette totale à long terme (1)	Total creditors / Total créanciers	Public and publicly guaranteed debt (2) / Dette publique et garantie par l'état (2)								Private non-guaranteed debt (5) / Dette privée non garantie (5)
			Official creditors (3) / Créanciers publics (3)					Private creditors (4) / Créanciers privés (4)			
			Total	Bilateral / Bilatéraux			Multilateral / Multilatéraux	Total	Bonds / Obligations	Commercial banks / Banques commerciales	
				Total	DAC CAD	OPEC OPEP					
	Millions of dollars / Millions de dollars										
1980											
Debt outstanding	90 299	85 137	47 338	35 672	20 855	7 813	11 666	37 799	1 357	16 435	5 162
Disbursments (6)	19 421	17 985	7 888	5 721	4 001	1 265	2 166	10 098	119	3 922	1 436
Debt service (7)	11 561	10 354	2 529	1 773	1 237	276	756	7 826	141	3 922	1 207
Principal repayments	6 512	5 000	1 249	932	627	96	317	4 557	57	1 995	706
Interest payments	5 049	4 548	1 280	841	610	180	439	3 269	84	1 928	501
Net transfers on debt (8)	7 861	7 631	5 359	3 949	2 764	989	1 410	2 272	-22	0	230
1990											
Dette totale	235 385	228 691	157 999	107 383	77 559	11 464	50 616	70 692	1 721	24 622	6 694
Décaissements (6)	21 528	20 809	12 158	5 502	4 701	204	6 656	8 651	0	1 032	719
Service de la dette (7)	23 034	21 957	9 982	5 725	4 755	294	4 257	11 975	231	3 782	1 078
Remboursement du principal	14 680	14 038	5 402	3 013	2 521	210	2 389	8 636	108	2 517	643
Paiement des intérêts	8 354	7 919	4 580	2 712	2 234	84	1 868	3 339	123	1 265	435
Transfers nets (8)	-1 507	-1 148	2 176	-223	-54	-90	2 399	-3 324	-231	-2 750	-359
2000											
Debt outstanding	250 432	235 878	196 044	123 715	78 686	9 354	72 329	39 834	10 630	15 351	14 554
Disbursments (6)	14 637	11 357	6 533	1 726	1 300	271	4 806	4 824	765	2 514	3 280
Debt service (7)	22 259	20 179	11 329	6 221	4 418	340	5 108	8 850	1 580	4 155	2 080
Principal repayments	15 327	13 748	6 953	3 712	2 454	256	3 241	6 795	903	3 425	1 578
Interest payments	6 933	6 431	4 376	2 509	1 965	84	1 867	2 055	677	730	502
Net transfers on debt (8)	-7 622	-8 822	-4 797	-4 495	-3 118	-69	-301	-4 026	-815	-1 641	1 200
2005											
Dette totale	263 846	245 298	192 666	100 926	82 027	8 793	91 740	52 632	22 166	22 002	18 548
Décaissements (6)	23 099	19 158	10 123	2 327	1 102	477	7 795	9 036	1 499	6 912	3 940
Service de la dette (7)	32 247	30 528	20 976	15 041	13 654	489	5 935	9 552	2 485	5 035	1 719
Remboursement du principal	21 725	20 557	13 132	8 738	7 572	413	4 394	7 426	1 268	4 463	1 168
Paiement des intérêts	10 522	9 971	7 844	6 303	6 081	77	1 541	2 127	1 217	572	551
Transfers nets (8)	-9 149	-11 370	-10 853	-12 714	-12 551	-12	1 860	-516	-986	1 876	2 221
2008											
Debt outstanding	232 006	202 269	151 203	78 439	55 421	9 962	72 764	51 066	23 952	21 745	29 736
Disbursments (6)	21 145	18 538	12 915	5 081	2 152	656	7 834	5 623	0	5 162	2 607
Debt service (7)	23 099	18 936	11 265	5 478	4 263	410	5 787	7 671	2 829	3 524	4 164
Principal repayments	16 740	13 349	7 948	4 023	3 132	313	3 925	5 401	1 479	2 826	3 392
Interest payments	6 359	5 587	3 317	1 456	1 131	97	1 861	2 270	1 350	698	772
Net transfers on debt (8)	-1 954	-397	1 650	-397	-2 111	246	2 047	-2 048	-2 829	1 638	-1 556
2009											
Dette totale	256 077	220 350	164 012	83 593	58 001	9 978	80 420	56 337	28 257	22 214	35 727
Décaissements (6)	28 282	24 701	17 446	5 927	2 112	483	11 518	7 255	2 200	3 736	3 581
Service de la dette (7)	21 412	17 865	10 305	5 169	3 750	446	5 137	7 560	1 952	4 664	3 547
Remboursement du principal	15 513	12 723	7 230	3 800	2 787	342	3 430	5 494	563	4 137	2 790
Paiement des intérêts	5 898	5 141	3 075	1 369	963	103	1 706	2 066	1 389	527	757
Transfers nets (8)	6 871	6 836	7 141	759	-1 637	38	6 382	-304	248	-928	34
2010											
Debt outstanding	279 097	232 352	163 398	78 270	46 255	9 839	85 128	68 954	42 615	20 623	46 745
Disbursments (6)	33 545	29 451	21 334	9 513	1 896	743	11 821	8 117	4 827	2 377	4 095
Debt service (7)	21 685	16 785	9 970	5 546	4 045	514	4 424	6 815	2 019	4 016	4 899
Principal repayments	14 852	11 585	7 170	4 110	3 021	398	3 059	4 416	23	3 714	3 266
Interest payments	6 833	5 200	2 800	1 436	1 023	116	1 365	2 399	1 996	301	1 633
Net transfers on debt (8)	11 860	12 665	11 364	3 967	-2 148	229	7 397	1 302	2 808	-1 639	-805
2011											
Dette totale	305 017	250 762	172 198	80 324	45 329	10 202	91 874	78 565	48 463	23 594	54 255
Décaissements (6)	37 358	31 142	20 780	8 442	2 539	665	12 339	10 361	4 510	5 491	6 217
Service de la dette (7)	24 808	19 110	10 920	5 954	3 859	430	4 967	8 189	3 860	3 611	5 698
Remboursement du principal	17 440	13 407	8 196	4 720	3 066	300	3 476	5 211	1 301	3 287	4 033
Paiement des intérêts	7 368	5 702	2 724	1 233	793	129	1 491	2 978	2 559	323	1 665
Transfers nets (8)	12 550	12 032	9 860	2 488	-1 319	236	7 372	2 172	650	1 880	518

For sources and notes, see end of table 7.7.G.

Pour les sources et les notes, se reporter à la fin du tableau 7.7.G.

7.7.C External long-term debt by lending source
Developing economies:
America

7.7.C Dette extérieure à long terme par catégories de prêt
Économies en développement :
Amérique

	Total long-term debt (1) / Dette totale à long terme (1)	Public and publicly guaranteed debt (2) / Dette publique et garantie par l'état (2)									Private non-guaranteed debt (5) / Dette privée non garantie (5)
		Total creditors / Total créanciers	Official creditors (3) / Créanciers publics (3)					Private creditors (4) / Créanciers privés (4)			
			Total	Bilateral / Bilatéraux			Multilateral / Multilatéraux	Total	Bonds / Obligations	Commercial banks / Banques commerciales	
				Total	DAC / CAD	OPEC / OPEP					
	Millions of dollars / Millions de dollars										
1980											
Debt outstanding	172 968	130 521	31 057	16 929	12 991	1 240	14 128	99 464	9 599	76 682	42 447
Disbursments (6)	43 969	31 009	6 423	3 462	2 230	506	2 961	24 586	1 219	19 937	12 960
Debt service (7)	38 537	27 148	3 910	2 196	1 695	111	1 714	23 238	1 128	18 776	11 389
Principal repayments	21 175	14 215	2 134	1 421	1 110	48	713	12 081	401	9 332	6 960
Interest payments	17 362	12 933	1 776	775	585	63	1 001	11 157	727	9 444	4 429
Net transfers on debt (8)	5 432	3 861	2 513	1 266	535	395	1 247	1 348	92	1 161	1 571
1990											
Dette totale	352 866	327 848	121 469	61 499	48 108	1 742	59 970	206 378	75 976	101 883	25 018
Décaissements (6)	27 731	23 033	13 183	4 198	3 245	211	8 986	9 850	1 938	4 803	4 698
Service de la dette (7)	36 600	32 124	11 950	3 075	2 368	182	8 875	20 174	4 406	11 917	4 476
Remboursement du principal	18 470	16 255	6 453	1 702	1 215	133	4 751	9 803	2 008	5 219	2 215
Paiement des intérêts	18 130	15 869	5 498	1 373	1 153	49	4 124	10 371	2 398	6 698	2 261
Transfers nets (8)	-8 869	-9 091	1 233	1 123	876	29	110	-10 324	-2 468	-7 113	222
2000											
Debt outstanding	637 963	396 415	140 217	46 736	36 466	833	93 481	256 198	216 334	31 404	241 548
Disbursments (6)	116 375	58 478	16 225	2 837	2 223	39	13 388	42 252	35 022	6 484	57 898
Debt service (7)	148 896	72 892	25 399	9 173	8 182	114	16 226	47 493	35 430	9 649	76 004
Principal repayments	100 924	42 934	16 907	6 988	6 438	80	9 920	26 027	17 488	6 935	57 990
Interest payments	47 973	29 958	8 492	2 186	1 744	34	6 306	21 466	17 942	2 715	18 015
Net transfers on debt (8)	-32 521	-14 415	-9 174	-6 336	-5 960	-75	-2 838	-5 241	-408	-3 166	-18 106
2005											
Dette totale	600 647	420 845	134 394	30 916	25 159	430	103 477	286 451	243 601	38 460	179 802
Décaissements (6)	98 533	57 702	12 879	2 342	1 904	140	10 537	44 823	38 150	6 169	40 830
Service de la dette (7)	113 077	67 692	22 132	6 819	5 898	47	15 312	45 561	35 685	8 892	45 384
Remboursement du principal	79 748	42 872	16 592	5 700	5 101	39	10 892	26 280	18 231	7 265	36 877
Paiement des intérêts	33 329	24 821	5 540	1 120	797	7	4 420	19 281	17 454	1 627	8 508
Transfers nets (8)	-14 544	-9 990	-9 252	-4 477	-3 994	94	-4 775	-738	2 466	-2 724	-4 554
2008											
Debt outstanding	694 302	440 437	131 109	29 359	22 281	2 327	101 750	309 328	264 510	41 440	253 865
Disbursments (6)	131 620	63 744	19 554	3 640	1 243	1 040	15 914	44 191	36 212	7 819	67 876
Debt service (7)	132 171	72 850	18 306	3 171	2 634	54	15 135	54 544	46 075	7 579	59 320
Principal repayments	93 452	47 704	12 860	2 374	2 013	37	10 486	34 844	28 127	6 084	45 748
Interest payments	38 719	25 146	5 446	797	621	18	4 649	19 700	17 948	1 495	13 573
Net transfers on debt (8)	-550	-9 106	1 248	469	-1 390	986	779	-10 354	-9 863	241	8 555
2009											
Dette totale	711 624	457 777	149 548	34 236	22 785	2 887	115 313	308 229	268 111	35 942	253 847
Décaissements (6)	140 340	73 491	31 020	6 822	2 103	640	24 197	42 472	37 371	4 436	66 849
Service de la dette (7)	130 054	62 489	18 420	4 504	3 701	159	13 916	44 068	29 760	12 820	67 566
Remboursement du principal	93 172	39 191	13 522	3 690	3 149	118	9 832	25 669	13 377	11 101	53 981
Paiement des intérêts	36 883	23 298	4 898	814	551	40	4 084	18 399	16 383	1 718	13 585
Transfers nets (8)	10 286	11 003	12 599	2 318	-1 598	481	10 281	-1 596	7 611	-8 384	-717
2010											
Debt outstanding	838 669	502 672	171 072	38 889	22 354	3 202	132 183	331 600	287 321	38 970	335 997
Disbursments (6)	203 354	93 345	36 345	8 538	2 385	789	27 807	57 000	43 223	11 315	110 009
Debt service (7)	130 778	63 397	19 049	5 104	3 935	206	13 945	44 348	35 042	7 721	67 381
Principal repayments	91 423	39 874	14 364	4 173	3 519	153	10 191	25 509	17 534	6 643	51 549
Interest payments	39 354	23 523	4 685	930	416	52	3 754	18 839	17 507	1 078	15 831
Net transfers on debt (8)	72 576	29 948	17 296	3 434	-1 550	584	13 862	12 652	8 181	3 594	42 629
2011											
Dette totale	969 034	538 403	174 479	41 134	22 207	3 916	133 345	363 923	318 188	40 728	430 631
Décaissements (6)	226 057	81 259	23 008	5 681	2 119	1 065	17 327	58 250	47 453	9 899	144 799
Service de la dette (7)	147 991	71 700	23 308	4 183	2 671	135	19 125	48 392	36 038	10 802	76 291
Remboursement du principal	103 551	45 816	18 517	3 179	2 267	80	15 338	27 299	16 419	9 572	57 735
Paiement des intérêts	44 440	25 884	4 791	1 004	404	56	3 787	21 092	19 619	1 230	18 556
Transfers nets (8)	78 066	9 559	-300	1 498	-552	929	-1 797	9 858	11 416	-903	68 508

For sources and notes, see end of table 7.7.G.

Pour les sources et les notes, se reporter à la fin du tableau 7.7.G.

7.7.D External long-term debt by lending source
Developing economies:
Asia

7.7.D Dette extérieure à long terme par catégories de prêt
Économies en développement :
Asie

	Total long-term debt (1) / Dette totale à long terme (1)	Public and publicly guaranteed debt (2) / Dette publique et garantie par l'état (2)									Private non-guaranteed debt (5) / Dette privée non garantie (5)
		Total creditors / Total créanciers	Official creditors (3) / Créanciers publics (3)					Private creditors (4) / Créanciers privés (4)			
			Total	Bilateral / Bilatéraux			Multilateral / Multilatéraux	Total	Bonds / Obligations	Commercial banks / Banques commerciales	
				Total	DAC CAD	OPEC OPEP					
Millions of dollars / Millions de dollars											
1980											
Debt outstanding	102 144	92 704	62 024	44 030	34 561	4 687	17 993	30 681	1 629	16 101	9 439
Disbursments (6)	21 561	18 293	9 599	6 379	4 170	704	3 219	8 694	235	4 442	3 268
Debt service (7)	11 759	8 886	3 971	2 797	2 002	485	1 174	4 914	118	2 164	2 874
Principal repayments	6 837	4 869	2 261	1 824	1 185	380	437	2 608	33	797	1 968
Interest payments	4 922	4 017	1 710	974	817	105	737	2 307	85	1 307	906
Net transfers on debt (8)	9 802	9 407	5 627	3 582	2 168	219	2 046	3 780	118	2 278	394
1990											
Dette totale	370 418	347 034	224 149	139 592	83 247	5 164	84 557	122 885	19 628	69 557	23 384
Décaissements (6)	45 737	35 458	19 665	9 382	8 304	157	10 282	15 793	1 923	7 651	10 279
Service de la dette (7)	45 197	40 785	16 923	8 913	6 256	646	8 010	23 862	3 749	13 239	4 411
Remboursement du principal	27 149	24 160	9 874	5 822	3 783	527	4 053	14 285	2 251	7 271	2 989
Paiement des intérêts	18 048	16 626	7 049	3 091	2 473	119	3 958	9 577	1 498	5 968	1 422
Transfers nets (8)	540	-5 327	2 742	469	2 048	-490	2 272	-8 069	-1 826	-5 588	5 868
2000											
Debt outstanding	689 429	497 429	311 636	175 073	136 798	3 673	136 563	185 793	72 966	74 767	192 000
Disbursments (6)	82 918	59 924	24 972	11 754	10 241	143	13 219	34 952	19 063	7 950	22 993
Debt service (7)	104 928	62 946	30 016	16 231	12 116	336	13 785	32 930	7 847	17 302	41 982
Principal repayments	73 109	41 057	19 340	11 357	7 961	288	7 983	21 717	3 529	12 255	32 052
Interest payments	31 819	21 889	10 676	4 874	4 155	48	5 801	11 213	4 318	5 047	9 930
Net transfers on debt (8)	-22 010	-3 021	-5 043	-4 477	-1 875	-192	-566	2 022	11 217	-9 351	-18 989
2005											
Dette totale	747 515	484 905	313 412	166 455	137 052	3 957	146 957	171 492	99 637	47 532	262 610
Décaissements (6)	144 624	47 706	18 899	6 399	4 739	227	12 500	28 807	19 212	7 247	96 917
Service de la dette (7)	144 695	70 212	25 120	13 419	11 047	330	11 700	45 092	27 245	11 957	74 483
Remboursement du principal	118 335	51 333	18 099	9 965	8 320	276	8 134	33 234	18 473	9 633	67 002
Paiement des intérêts	26 361	18 879	7 021	3 454	2 726	53	3 567	11 858	8 772	2 324	7 482
Transfers nets (8)	-72	-22 506	-6 220	-7 020	-6 308	-102	800	-16 285	-8 033	-4 710	22 434
2008											
Debt outstanding	1 038 108	568 786	369 631	185 782	146 596	3 251	183 849	199 155	129 841	52 447	469 321
Disbursments (6)	202 771	62 235	29 553	10 138	7 286	449	19 416	32 682	22 943	8 031	140 536
Debt service (7)	183 855	73 573	32 325	18 501	16 436	377	13 823	41 249	26 909	8 384	110 282
Principal repayments	146 086	53 188	24 109	14 719	13 156	313	9 390	29 079	18 060	6 122	92 898
Interest payments	37 769	20 385	8 216	3 783	3 280	64	4 433	12 170	8 849	2 263	17 383
Net transfers on debt (8)	18 916	-11 338	-2 771	-8 364	-9 150	72	5 592	-8 567	-3 965	-353	30 255
2009											
Dette totale	1 075 325	605 472	390 247	189 338	141 706	3 368	200 909	215 225	144 261	52 106	469 853
Décaissements (6)	169 259	72 582	37 203	11 998	6 972	380	25 205	35 378	22 801	8 299	96 678
Service de la dette (7)	186 070	64 953	28 897	15 939	14 062	319	12 958	36 056	20 465	9 916	121 117
Remboursement du principal	152 912	46 127	21 633	12 237	10 932	247	9 396	24 494	11 411	8 074	106 786
Paiement des intérêts	33 158	18 826	7 264	3 702	3 131	72	3 562	11 562	9 054	1 842	14 332
Transfers nets (8)	-16 811	7 629	8 307	-3 941	-7 091	61	12 248	-678	2 337	-1 617	-24 440
2010											
Debt outstanding	1 141 573	641 571	410 247	195 487	149 934	3 167	214 760	231 325	157 688	56 521	500 002
Disbursments (6)	225 542	91 976	37 522	13 788	7 953	358	23 734	54 454	34 303	13 896	133 566
Debt service (7)	196 445	66 648	30 919	18 197	13 938	598	12 723	35 729	20 598	8 725	129 797
Principal repayments	161 278	47 095	23 319	13 437	10 870	504	9 882	23 777	10 956	7 149	114 182
Interest payments	35 167	19 552	7 600	4 760	3 068	94	2 840	11 952	9 642	1 576	15 615
Net transfers on debt (8)	29 097	25 328	6 603	-4 409	-5 985	-239	11 012	18 725	13 705	5 171	3 769
2011											
Dette totale	1 192 632	663 936	422 630	200 659	149 997	3 325	221 971	241 306	169 650	55 338	528 696
Décaissements (6)	218 421	73 460	34 540	14 799	7 539	406	19 741	38 920	24 600	9 677	144 961
Service de la dette (7)	206 208	72 555	34 136	18 994	14 334	314	15 142	38 419	22 004	10 428	133 653
Remboursement du principal	163 519	52 119	26 473	14 398	11 325	257	12 075	25 645	11 363	8 879	111 401
Paiement des intérêts	42 689	20 436	7 663	4 596	3 009	57	3 067	12 774	10 642	1 549	22 253
Transfers nets (8)	12 213	905	404	-4 195	-6 795	92	4 599	501	2 596	-750	11 308

For sources and notes, see end of table 7.7.G.

Pour les sources et les notes, se reporter à la fin du tableau 7.7.G.

7.7.E External long-term debt by lending source
Developing economies: Oceania

7.7.E Dette extérieure à long terme par catégories de prêt
Économies en développement : Océanie

	Total long-term debt (1) / Dette totale à long terme (1)	Public and publicly guaranteed debt (2) / Dette publique et garantie par l'état (2)									Private non-guaranteed debt (5) / Dette privée non garantie (5)
		Total creditors / Total créanciers	Official creditors (3) / Créanciers publics (3)					Private creditors (4) / Créanciers privés (4)			
			Total	Bilateral / Bilatéraux			Multilateral / Multilatéraux	Total	Bonds / Obligations	Commercial banks / Banques commerciales	
				Total	DAC CAD	OPEC OPEP					
1980											
Debt outstanding	966	763	396	136	123	3	261	367	92	254	204
Disbursments (6)	245	230	115	40	37	3	75	115	0	106	15
Debt service (7)	149	87	27	13	12	0	14	61	17	35	62
Principal repayments	86	46	12	7	7	0	4	34	10	17	40
Interest payments	64	42	15	6	5	0	9	27	8	18	22
Net transfers on debt (8)	96	143	89	27	26	3	62	54	-17	71	-47
1990											
Dette totale	3 118	2 085	1 593	447	412	10	1 146	493	39	330	1 033
Décaissements (6)	682	325	279	59	57	0	219	46	0	21	358
Service de la dette (7)	665	366	163	47	44	0	116	203	3	175	299
Remboursement du principal	473	251	99	26	25	0	73	152	0	137	222
Paiement des intérêts	193	115	65	21	19	0	44	50	3	38	77
Transfers nets (8)	17	-42	115	12	13	0	103	-157	-3	-155	59
2000											
Debt outstanding	2 494	2 023	1 959	697	564	10	1 263	64	0	54	471
Disbursments (6)	291	256	243	145	134	2	98	13	0	13	35
Debt service (7)	246	209	184	71	60	1	113	25	0	13	37
Principal repayments	164	144	124	50	43	1	74	20	0	10	21
Interest payments	82	65	61	21	17	0	40	5	0	3	16
Net transfers on debt (8)	45	47	58	74	74	1	-16	-11	0	0	-2
2005											
Dette totale	2 302	1 913	1 862	537	400	7	1 324	52	0	8	389
Décaissements (6)	369	80	78	3	3	0	75	1	0	0	290
Service de la dette (7)	271	186	160	67	59	1	93	26	0	17	85
Remboursement du principal	206	137	113	50	45	1	64	23	0	15	69
Paiement des intérêts	65	49	47	17	14	0	29	2	0	1	16
Transfers nets (8)	99	-106	-82	-64	-56	-1	-18	-25	0	-17	205
2008											
Debt outstanding	2 091	1 949	1 754	492	320	3	1 262	195	150	4	142
Disbursments (6)	184	83	83	41	0	0	43	0	0	0	101
Debt service (7)	272	251	233	119	110	2	115	17	10	1	21
Principal repayments	215	194	187	103	98	2	85	6	0	0	21
Interest payments	57	57	46	16	12	0	30	11	10	0	0
Net transfers on debt (8)	-88	-168	-150	-78	-110	-2	-72	-17	-10	-1	80
2009											
Dette totale	2 209	1 968	1 780	521	296	2	1 260	188	150	3	241
Décaissements (6)	527	102	102	53	1	0	49	1	0	0	424
Service de la dette (7)	587	133	115	38	30	1	78	18	10	0	453
Remboursement du principal	538	91	84	26	22	1	58	7	0	0	447
Paiement des intérêts	49	43	32	12	8	0	20	11	10	0	6
Transfers nets (8)	-60	-31	-14	15	-29	-1	-29	-17	-10	0	-29
2010											
Debt outstanding	5 693	2 099	1 915	624	313	2	1 291	184	150	3	3 594
Disbursments (6)	3 186	189	189	87	6	0	102	0	0	0	2 997
Debt service (7)	845	136	117	39	30	1	79	19	10	0	709
Principal repayments	793	97	90	25	22	0	65	8	0	0	695
Interest payments	52	39	27	14	8	0	14	11	10	0	14
Net transfers on debt (8)	2 341	53	72	48	-24	-1	24	-18	-10	0	2 288
2011											
Dette totale	12 691	2 354	2 077	787	310	1	1 290	277	250	3	10 337
Décaissements (6)	8 413	493	243	170	13	0	73	250	250	0	7 920
Service de la dette (7)	1 365	318	138	50	37	1	87	180	172	0	1 047
Remboursement du principal	1 249	264	106	33	29	0	73	158	150	0	986
Paiement des intérêts	115	54	32	17	8	0	15	22	22	0	61
Transfers nets (8)	7 049	176	106	120	-24	-1	-14	70	78	0	6 873

Millions of dollars / Millions de dollars

For sources and notes, see end of table 7.7.G.

Pour les sources et les notes, se reporter à la fin du tableau 7.7.G.

7.7.F **External long-term debt by lending source**
Developing economies:
Major petroleum and gas exporters

7.7.F **Dette extérieure à long terme par catégories de prêt**
Économies en développement :
Principaux exportateurs de pétrole et de gaz

	Total long-term debt (1) Dette totale à long terme (1)	Public and publicly guaranteed debt (2) Dette publique et garantie par l'état (2)									Private non-guaranteed debt (5) Dette privée non garantie (5)
		Total creditors Total créanciers	Official creditors (3) / Créanciers publics (3)					Private creditors (4) Créanciers privés (4)			
			Total	Bilateral / Bilatéraux			Multilateral Multilatéraux	Total	Bonds Obligations	Commercial banks Banques commerciales	
				Total	DAC CAD	OPEC OPEP					
	Millions of dollars / Millions de dollars										
1980											
Debt outstanding	41 301	37 023	6 340	4 589	3 670	264	1 751	30 683	1 671	17 356	4 278
Disbursments (6)	10 318	7 861	830	683	613	7	147	7 031	305	3 748	2 456
Debt service (7)	10 371	8 611	847	529	448	13	318	7 764	133	4 552	1 760
Principal repayments	6 451	5 039	510	337	271	11	173	4 529	28	2 320	1 412
Interest payments	3 920	3 572	337	193	177	2	145	3 235	106	2 232	348
Net transfers on debt (8)	-54	-750	-18	154	165	-6	-171	-732	172	-804	696
1990											
Dette totale	98 584	94 543	27 197	19 493	16 065	238	7 704	67 346	21 064	14 847	4 041
Décaissements (6)	11 296	11 296	3 814	1 569	1 255	14	2 245	7 482	599	249	0
Service de la dette (7)	17 859	17 267	3 918	2 793	2 265	36	1 125	13 349	509	6 043	592
Remboursement du principal	10 653	10 464	2 188	1 520	1 348	27	669	8 276	269	2 803	188
Paiement des intérêts	7 206	6 803	1 730	1 273	917	9	456	5 073	240	3 240	403
Transfers nets (8)	-6 563	-5 971	-104	-1 224	-1 010	-22	1 120	-5 867	90	-5 794	-592
2000											
Debt outstanding	100 344	93 997	54 634	43 167	16 840	500	11 467	39 363	18 268	9 667	6 347
Disbursments (6)	6 227	6 227	2 248	1 198	619	10	1 051	3 979	462	1 946	0
Debt service (7)	15 827	14 551	6 852	4 786	1 854	81	2 066	7 699	2 545	2 524	1 276
Principal repayments	10 608	9 918	4 636	3 388	989	49	1 248	5 282	1 119	2 027	690
Interest payments	5 219	4 633	2 216	1 398	864	32	819	2 417	1 426	497	586
Net transfers on debt (8)	-9 600	-8 324	-4 604	-3 588	-1 234	-71	-1 015	-3 720	-2 083	-578	-1 276
2005											
Dette totale	91 423	86 856	39 156	30 598	27 632	609	8 558	47 700	24 988	13 351	4 568
Décaissements (6)	15 283	14 820	2 190	1 076	232	25	1 113	12 630	6 143	5 026	463
Service de la dette (7)	23 871	22 581	14 073	11 354	10 619	114	2 719	8 508	2 144	3 807	1 290
Remboursement du principal	14 714	13 799	8 269	6 017	5 395	103	2 253	5 529	226	3 158	916
Paiement des intérêts	9 157	8 783	5 804	5 337	5 224	11	467	2 979	1 917	649	374
Transfers nets (8)	-8 589	-7 761	-11 883	-10 277	-10 387	-89	-1 606	4 122	3 999	1 219	-827
2008											
Debt outstanding	63 255	58 501	15 608	8 680	3 131	532	6 928	42 894	23 353	13 991	4 754
Disbursments (6)	11 992	10 935	2 625	1 510	251	47	1 115	8 309	4 000	3 894	1 057
Debt service (7)	11 449	10 624	2 393	1 254	547	98	1 139	8 231	3 301	2 839	825
Principal repayments	7 401	6 958	1 818	944	428	91	874	5 140	1 295	2 102	444
Interest payments	4 048	3 666	575	310	119	7	265	3 091	2 005	738	382
Net transfers on debt (8)	543	311	232	256	-296	-51	-24	79	699	1 055	232
2009											
Dette totale	67 656	63 364	17 299	9 332	2 912	509	7 967	46 065	28 360	13 241	4 292
Décaissements (6)	10 739	10 615	2 971	1 516	132	13	1 455	7 644	4 992	2 473	123
Service de la dette (7)	10 876	9 982	2 082	1 270	501	42	812	7 900	2 024	4 401	895
Remboursement du principal	7 238	6 716	1 577	970	421	36	607	5 139	0	3 846	522
Paiement des intérêts	3 639	3 266	505	300	80	6	205	2 761	2 024	555	373
Transfers nets (8)	-138	634	889	246	-370	-28	643	-256	2 968	-1 928	-771
2010											
Debt outstanding	70 474	66 447	22 022	11 981	2 499	485	10 041	44 425	29 762	10 807	4 028
Disbursments (6)	10 031	10 030	6 567	3 779	33	16	2 788	3 463	3 000	167	2
Debt service (7)	9 179	8 365	1 893	1 172	483	46	721	6 472	2 530	2 939	815
Principal repayments	5 621	5 138	1 461	932	424	41	529	3 677	119	2 641	484
Interest payments	3 558	3 227	432	239	59	5	193	2 795	2 411	297	331
Net transfers on debt (8)	852	1 665	4 674	2 607	-450	-30	2 067	-3 009	470	-2 772	-813
2011											
Dette totale	79 220	74 782	25 038	13 405	2 055	465	11 634	49 744	36 279	10 353	4 438
Décaissements (6)	16 414	15 914	5 544	3 081	51	19	2 463	10 370	7 710	2 504	500
Service de la dette (7)	11 219	10 778	2 856	1 852	539	43	1 003	7 923	3 924	3 133	441
Remboursement du principal	7 381	7 260	2 438	1 642	484	38	796	4 822	1 186	2 838	121
Paiement des intérêts	3 838	3 518	417	211	56	4	207	3 101	2 737	295	320
Transfers nets (8)	5 195	5 135	2 688	1 228	-488	-24	1 459	2 448	3 786	-629	60

For sources and notes, see end of table 7.7.G.

Pour les sources et les notes, se reporter à la fin du tableau 7.7.G.

7.7.G External long-term debt by lending source
Developing economies:
Major manufactured goods exporters

7.7.G Dette extérieure à long terme par catégories de prêt
Économies en développement :
Principaux exportateurs d'articles manufacturés

	Total long-term debt (1) / Dette totale à long terme (1)	Total creditors / Total créanciers	Public and publicly guaranteed debt (2) / Dette publique et garantie par l'état (2)								Private non-guaranteed debt (5) / Dette privée non garantie (5)
			Official creditors (3) / Créanciers publics (3)					Private creditors (4) / Créanciers (4)			
			Total	Bilateral / Bilatéraux			Multilateral / Multilatéraux	Total	Bonds / Obligations	Commercial banks / Banques commerciales	
				Total	DAC CAD	OPEC OPEP					
							Millions of dollars / Millions de dollars				
1980											
Debt outstanding	56 620	46 369	8 539	3 613	3 507	34	4 926	37 830	3 576	29 887	10 251
Disbursments (6)	18 180	14 001	2 159	1 163	1 125	18	996	11 841	330	8 900	4 179
Debt service (7)	12 208	9 638	1 023	440	437	1	583	8 615	417	7 301	2 570
Principal repayments	6 500	4 921	488	278	278	0	211	4 433	134	3 675	1 578
Interest payments	5 708	4 716	535	163	159	1	372	4 181	283	3 626	992
Net transfers on debt (8)	5 972	4 363	1 136	723	688	17	413	3 227	-87	1 599	1 609
1990											
Dette totale	160 518	145 541	49 609	23 667	20 974	305	25 942	95 932	50 354	25 561	14 976
Décaissements (6)	27 963	21 726	9 655	4 315	3 558	8	5 340	12 071	1 252	5 966	6 237
Service de la dette (7)	22 974	20 613	5 873	2 303	2 067	41	3 571	14 740	4 054	6 560	2 360
Remboursement du principal	12 291	11 034	3 290	1 379	1 241	28	1 911	7 744	2 115	2 981	1 257
Paiement des intérêts	10 683	9 580	2 583	924	826	13	1 659	6 996	1 938	3 579	1 103
Transfers nets (8)	4 989	1 113	3 782	2 012	1 491	-33	1 769	-2 669	-2 802	-594	3 877
2000											
Debt outstanding	362 728	225 528	97 037	47 301	41 965	204	49 736	128 491	77 530	23 308	137 201
Disbursments (6)	61 808	29 919	12 267	5 599	4 639	59	6 669	17 651	9 277	2 354	31 889
Debt service (7)	95 100	46 397	15 369	8 008	6 853	102	7 361	31 027	16 283	8 463	48 704
Principal repayments	71 114	31 599	10 162	6 044	5 129	91	4 118	21 436	10 072	6 822	39 515
Interest payments	23 986	14 798	5 207	1 964	1 724	11	3 243	9 591	6 211	1 641	9 188
Net transfers on debt (8)	-33 292	-16 478	-3 102	-2 409	-2 214	-43	-693	-13 376	-7 006	-6 109	-16 815
2005											
Dette totale	356 885	239 205	85 615	40 949	31 553	79	44 666	153 590	110 989	27 329	117 680
Décaissements (6)	80 211	31 823	5 894	1 858	1 601	1	4 036	25 929	19 243	5 177	48 388
Service de la dette (7)	85 377	41 319	10 253	4 838	4 477	6	5 414	31 066	20 329	7 080	44 058
Remboursement du principal	69 783	29 894	7 482	3 620	3 442	3	3 863	22 412	12 747	6 437	39 888
Paiement des intérêts	15 594	11 424	2 770	1 219	1 036	3	1 552	8 654	7 582	643	4 170
Transfers nets (8)	-5 166	-9 496	-4 359	-2 981	-2 876	-6	-1 378	-5 137	-1 086	-1 903	4 330
2008											
Debt outstanding	444 831	257 297	87 887	45 910	26 740	28	41 976	169 410	128 114	30 656	187 535
Disbursments (6)	89 121	32 735	6 827	1 328	303	0	5 499	25 909	18 748	5 536	56 386
Debt service (7)	87 848	36 545	8 026	3 821	3 769	16	4 205	28 519	20 364	3 959	51 302
Principal repayments	69 795	25 401	5 910	3 137	3 108	14	2 773	19 491	12 576	3 447	44 394
Interest payments	18 052	11 144	2 116	684	661	2	1 432	9 029	7 788	512	6 908
Net transfers on debt (8)	1 273	-3 810	-1 199	-2 493	-3 466	-16	1 293	-2 611	-1 616	1 577	5 084
2009											
Dette totale	433 421	250 229	100 002	49 179	25 591	17	50 823	150 227	110 852	25 611	183 192
Décaissements (6)	77 605	39 162	12 006	1 904	1 250	0	10 102	27 156	20 235	3 215	38 443
Service de la dette (7)	90 981	33 881	7 788	3 690	3 619	11	4 098	26 093	14 749	6 546	57 099
Remboursement du principal	76 248	24 661	5 911	3 025	2 972	10	2 886	18 751	8 624	5 819	51 586
Paiement des intérêts	14 733	9 220	1 878	665	647	1	1 212	7 342	6 125	727	5 513
Transfers nets (8)	-13 376	5 280	4 217	-1 787	-2 369	-11	6 004	1 063	5 485	-3 331	-18 657
2010											
Debt outstanding	480 436	277 902	102 801	45 824	25 091	11	56 977	175 101	131 695	29 629	202 534
Disbursments (6)	122 904	59 001	10 902	3 366	1 641	0	7 535	48 099	29 508	11 456	63 903
Debt service (7)	89 347	36 240	10 195	6 565	4 542	7	3 631	26 044	13 851	6 156	53 107
Principal repayments	71 950	26 522	7 515	4 948	3 928	6	2 567	19 007	7 699	5 666	45 428
Interest payments	17 397	9 717	2 680	1 616	614	1	1 064	7 037	6 152	490	7 679
Net transfers on debt (8)	33 557	22 761	707	-3 198	-2 901	-7	3 905	22 055	15 656	5 300	10 795
2011											
Dette totale	511 124	300 693	105 130	46 799	23 519	8	58 331	195 563	155 622	26 152	210 431
Décaissements (6)	113 012	53 437	11 516	5 033	1 393	0	6 482	41 921	33 585	2 961	59 576
Service de la dette (7)	107 433	41 901	12 210	6 234	4 223	4	5 976	29 691	16 858	6 928	65 532
Remboursement du principal	85 949	30 564	9 446	4 741	3 647	3	4 705	21 119	9 156	6 481	55 385
Paiement des intérêts	21 484	11 337	2 765	1 494	575	0	1 271	8 572	7 702	447	10 147
Transfers nets (8)	5 579	11 535	-695	-1 201	-2 829	-4	506	12 230	16 727	-3 967	-5 956

For sources and notes, see next page.   Pour les sources et les notes, se reporter à la page suivante.

7.7.G External long-term debt by lending source
Developing economies:
Major manufactured goods exporters

7.7.G Dette extérieure à long terme par catégories de prêt
Économies en développement :
Principaux exportateurs d'articles manufacturés

Source:
World Bank, *Global Development Finance*

Source :
Banque mondiale, *Global Development Finance*

Notes:

(1) Long-term debt is defined as debt that has an original or extended maturity of more than one year and that is owed to nonresidents and repayable in foreign currency, goods, or services.
Long-term debt has three components:
-"Public debt";
-"Publicly guaranteed debt";
-"Private nonguaranteed debt".
In this table, "Public debt" and "Publicly guaranteed debt" are aggregated.

(2) "Public debt" is an obligation of a public debtor, including the national government, a political subdivision (or an agency of either), and autonomous public bodies.
"Publicly guaranteed debt" is an external obligation of a private debtor that is guaranteed for repayment by a public entity.
In this table, "Public debt" and "Publicly guaranteed debt" are aggregated.
Data of "Public and publicly guaranteed debt" is shown by type of creditor: official creditors and private creditors.

(3) "Public and publicly guaranteed debt" from official creditors includes loans from governments (referred to as bilateral creditors) and loans from international organizations (referred to as multilateral creditors).
Government loans include loans from governments and their agencies (including central banks), loans from autonomous bodies, and direct loans from official export credit agencies.
Loans from international organizations include loans and credits from the World Bank, regional development banks, and other multilateral and intergovernmental agencies. Excluded are loans from funds administered by an international organization on behalf of a single donor government; these are classified as loans from governments.

(4) "Public and publicly guaranteed debt" from private creditors includes:
- "Bonds" that are either publicly issued or privately placed;
- "Commercial bank loans" from private banks and other private financial institutions;
- "Other private credits" from manufacturers, exporters, and other suppliers of goods, and bank credits covered by a guarantee of an export credit agency.

(5) Private nonguaranteed long-term debt outstanding and disbursed is an obligation of a private debtor that is not guaranteed for repayment by a public entity.

(6) Disbursements on long-term debt are drawings on loan commitments during the year specified.

(7) Long-term debt service payments are the sum of principal repayments and interest payments in the year specified.

(8) Net transfers on long-term debt are "disbursements" minus "debt service payments".

Notes :

(1) La dette à long terme a une durée de remboursement (d'origine ou différée) supérieure à une année, et son amortissement est dû, en monnaies convertibles ou en nature, à des créanciers non-résidents.
La dette à long terme a trois composantes :
- "Dette publique" ;
- "Dette garantie par l'État" ;
- "Dette du secteur privé non garantie".
Dans ce tableau, la "dette publique" et la "dette garantie par l'État" sont agrégées.

(2) La "dette publique" est une dette contractée par le secteur public, y compris le gouvernement, une entité politique et d'autres organismes publics autonomes.
La "dette garantie par l'État" est une dette contractée par le secteur privé, dont l'amortissement est garanti par une entité publique.
Dans ce tableau, "dette publique" et "dette garantie par l'État" sont agrégées.
Les données de la "dette publique et garantie par l'État" sont indiquées par types de créanciers : créanciers publics et créanciers privés.

(3) La "dette publique et garantie par l'État" octroyée par les créanciers publics inclut les prêts des gouvernements (appelés créditeurs bilatéraux) et les prêts des organisations internationales (appelées créditeurs multilatéraux).
Les prêts des gouvernements incluent les prêts des gouvernements et des organismes publics (y compris les banques centrales), les prêts provenant d'entités autonomes et les prêts octroyés directement par des organismes publics de crédits à l'exportation.
Les prêts des organisations internationales incluent les prêts et les crédits de la Banque mondiale, des banques régionales de développement, et d'autres organismes multilatéraux et intergouvernementaux. Ne sont pas compris les prêts provenant des fonds administrés par une organisation internationale, pour le compte d'un gouvernement ; ceux-ci sont classés sous la rubrique des prêts des gouvernements.

(4) La "dette publique et garantie par l'État" octroyée par les créanciers privés comprend :
- "Obligations" qui sont soit des émissions publiques, soit des placements privés ;
- "Prêts des banques commerciales" octroyés par des banques privées et par d'autres entités financières ;
- "Autres crédits privés" provenant du secteur manufacturier, du secteur des exportations, et d'autres fournisseurs de biens, ainsi que des crédits bancaires couverts par un organisme de crédits à l'exportation.

(5) La dette du secteur privé non-garantie encourue et décaissée, est une dette contractée par le secteur privé, dont l'amortissement n'est pas garanti par une entité publique.

(6) Les décaissements de la dette à long terme sont les tirages sur les engagements de la dette effectués au cours de l'année spécifiée.

(7) Les paiements du service de la dette à long terme sont la somme du remboursement du principal et du paiement des intérêts, effectués au cours de l'année spécifiée.

(8) Les transferts nets sont les "décaissements" moins les "paiements du service de la dette".

8 | DEVELOPMENT INDICATORS

INDICATEURS DU DÉVELOPPEMENT

8.1.1 Nominal gross domestic product: Total and per capita of countries and geographical regions

Region, country or territory	Total gross domestic product (1) / Produit intérieur brut total (1) Millions of dollars / Millions de dollars							
	1980	1990	2000	2005	2009	2010	2011	2012 (e)
WORLD	11 903 792	22 274 225	32 370 841	45 849 262	58 193 951	63 580 799	70 201 920	71 435 240
DEVELOPING ECONOMIES	2 570 539	3 862 899	7 037 652	10 894 061	17 469 323	20 957 174	24 204 766	25 561 043
TRANSITION ECONOMIES	1 012 216	863 143	397 600	1 099 288	1 785 371	2 120 611	2 599 062	2 753 025
DEVELOPED ECONOMIES	8 321 038	17 548 183	24 935 589	33 855 913	38 939 256	40 503 014	43 398 092	43 121 172
Developing economies: Africa	434 114	494 952	599 205	1 009 905	1 482 671	1 736 610	1 905 456	2 037 067
Eastern Africa	*51 672*	*65 005*	*70 324*	*99 056*	*161 996*	*170 208*	*191 286*	*235 408*
Burundi	1 332	1 608	995	1 117	1 833	2 063	2 340	2 464
Comoros	124	244	202	387	535	543	610	595
Djibouti	301	457	556	709	1 049	1 129	1 283	1 400
Eritrea	–	–	706	1 098	1 857	2 117	2 609	3 078
Ethiopia (...1991)	5 889	11 658						
Ethiopia	–	–	8 111	12 286	28 477	26 575	30 247	41 010
Kenya	9 165	11 035	12 604	18 739	30 600	32 181	34 059	41 038
Madagascar	3 265	3 080	3 878	5 039	8 552	8 733	9 844	10 004
Malawi	1 705	2 414	2 402	2 755	4 963	5 327	5 966	4 758
Mauritius	1 160	2 619	4 663	6 489	8 824	9 714	11 313	11 515
Mozambique	4 826	2 969	4 310	6 579	9 674	9 209	12 823	14 901
Rwanda	1 401	2 574	1 772	2 581	5 253	5 625	6 377	7 243
Seychelles	182	455	763	937	841	963	1 014	996
Somalia	571	994	2 052	2 316	2 012	1 071	1 067	-
Uganda	2 979	3 885	6 099	10 040	16 554	17 735	19 271	23 575
United Republic of Tanzania	7 310	5 480	10 424	14 492	22 034	23 587	24 378	28 787
Zambia	4 315	3 795	3 239	7 271	12 805	16 201	19 219	20 177
Zimbabwe	7 148	11 738	7 549	6 223	6 133	7 433	8 865	9 678
Middle Africa	*33 209*	*43 365*	*35 674*	*86 688*	*153 326*	*171 797*	*213 238*	*228 708*
Angola	5 390	10 297	8 858	32 811	75 492	82 513	104 332	117 966
Cameroon	8 869	11 846	9 287	16 588	23 381	23 619	26 410	25 995
Central African Republic	1 112	1 441	915	1 350	1 982	1 986	2 196	2 163
Chad	919	1 542	1 385	5 873	7 580	8 919	10 450	10 830
Congo	1 706	2 799	3 220	6 087	8 196	10 775	13 240	12 538
Dem. Rep. of the Congo	9 837	9 350	5 267	7 191	11 147	13 190	16 069	17 910
Equatorial Guinea	54	133	1 177	7 206	9 968	11 816	16 139	17 407
Gabon	5 240	5 838	5 487	9 459	15 382	18 771	24 146	23 624
Sao Tome and Principe	82	120	77	123	198	207	256	275
Northern Africa	*137 692*	*184 002*	*260 532*	*370 085*	*579 860*	*652 982*	*677 055*	*734 355*
Algeria	42 348	61 891	54 790	103 198	138 123	161 986	198 735	208 750
Egypt	20 119	35 939	95 684	94 456	187 978	214 623	231 222	252 947
Libya	38 186	31 088	38 471	45 451	58 762	71 654	31 373	73 238
Morocco (2)	21 030	28 855	37 022	59 524	90 907	90 803	100 257	97 935
Sudan (...2011)	6 365	12 645	13 092	35 183	60 562	69 665	69 136	–
Tunisia	9 645	13 584	21 473	32 272	43 528	44 252	46 332	45 470
Southern Africa	*84 942*	*120 038*	*144 715*	*268 521*	*308 611*	*395 946*	*444 739*	*427 032*
Botswana	851	3 715	5 633	10 256	11 537	14 905	17 328	18 018
Lesotho	351	545	771	1 368	1 711	2 179	2 443	2 365
Namibia	2 532	2 679	3 909	7 261	9 183	11 447	12 641	12 408
South Africa	80 544	112 014	132 878	247 052	283 012	363 523	408 237	390 282
Swaziland	664	1 085	1 524	2 584	3 167	3 892	4 090	3 959
Western Africa	*126 599*	*82 543*	*87 960*	*185 556*	*278 878*	*345 676*	*379 138*	*411 566*
Benin	1 374	1 845	2 359	4 358	6 585	6 558	7 295	7 385
Burkina Faso	1 933	3 133	2 633	5 463	8 348	8 831	10 095	10 324
Cape Verde	142	308	539	972	1 587	1 648	1 889	1 894
Côte d'Ivoire	10 176	11 893	10 682	17 085	23 043	22 947	24 102	23 994
Gambia	504	707	783	630	907	963	1 225	1 205
Ghana	5 204	9 983	7 985	17 198	26 169	31 305	39 200	39 360
Guinea	1 487	2 920	3 192	2 935	5 310	5 233	5 558	6 120
Guinea-Bissau	513	608	371	573	862	817	914	829
Liberia	765	487	528	608	1 024	1 074	1 147	1 293
Mali	1 423	2 510	2 655	5 486	8 964	9 400	10 623	9 983
Mauritania	1 496	1 623	1 294	2 184	2 881	3 156	4 443	4 294
Niger	2 697	2 638	1 727	3 369	5 365	5 672	6 381	6 485
Nigeria	93 181	35 026	46 386	112 248	169 481	229 508	245 229	276 696
Senegal	3 254	6 205	4 680	8 708	12 769	12 858	14 448	14 117
Sierra Leone	1 319	870	852	1 628	2 419	2 533	2 897	3 941
Togo	1 131	1 787	1 294	2 110	3 163	3 173	3 695	3 646

For sources and notes, see end of table.

Per capita gross domestic product / Produit intérieur brut par habitant Dollars								Régions, pays ou territoires
1980	1990	2000	2005	2009	2010	2011	2012 (e)	
2 684	4 214	5 307	7 073	8 567	9 253	10 068	10 132	MONDE
781	950	1 458	2 101	3 193	3 780	4 292	4 474	ÉCONOMIES EN DÉVELOPPEMENT
3 496	2 738	1 303	3 643	5 903	7 002	8 572	9 068	ÉCONOMIES EN TRANSITION
9 722	19 370	25 781	34 003	38 215	39 540	42 157	41 694	ÉCONOMIES DÉVELOPPÉES
900	780	740	1 110	1 486	1 701	1 825	1 907	Économies en développement : Afrique
361	*338*	*281*	*348*	*515*	*527*	*577*	*672*	*Afrique orientale*
322	287	156	154	224	246	273	282	Burundi
376	557	359	602	748	740	809	769	Comores
885	813	759	877	1 203	1 271	1 417	1 517	Djibouti
		193	245	364	403	482	552	Érythrée
155	226	–	–	–	–	–	–	Éthiopie (…1991)
		124	165	351	320	357	474	Éthiopie
563	471	403	526	775	794	819	960	Kenya
379	273	252	282	425	422	462	456	Madagascar
273	257	214	215	344	357	388	300	Malawi
1 203	2 472	3 899	5 163	6 832	7 477	8 659	8 765	Maurice
397	219	237	317	423	394	536	609	Mozambique
271	362	219	281	509	529	583	643	Rwanda
2 895	6 403	9 693	11 214	9 774	11 131	11 675	11 426	Seychelles
89	151	277	277	221	115	112	-	Somalie
235	220	252	353	511	531	558	662	Ouganda
391	215	306	373	506	526	527	604	République-Unie de Tanzanie
747	483	317	634	1 006	1 238	1 426	1 453	Zambie
981	1 121	603	495	492	591	695	744	Zimbabwe
622	*605*	*371*	*781*	*1 242*	*1 356*	*1 641*	*1 715*	*Afrique centrale*
706	996	636	1 990	4 069	4 324	5 318	5 851	Angola
974	972	592	945	1 219	1 205	1 319	1 270	Cameroun
489	491	247	336	459	451	489	473	République centrafricaine
202	256	168	600	693	794	907	915	Tchad
949	1 172	1 027	1 723	2 079	2 665	3 198	2 962	Congo
364	257	106	125	174	200	237	257	Rép. dém. du Congo
244	356	2 263	11 856	14 635	16 871	22 409	23 508	Guinée équatoriale
7 677	6 284	4 442	6 901	10 411	12 469	15 738	15 106	Gabon
869	1 036	545	808	1 218	1 254	1 519	1 598	Sao Tomé-et-Principe
1 219	*1 261*	*1 482*	*1 932*	*2 823*	*3 125*	*3 187*	*3 571*	*Afrique septentrionale*
2 251	2 446	1 794	3 138	3 952	4 567	5 523	5 721	Algérie
448	632	1 414	1 273	2 358	2 646	2 801	3 013	Égypte
12 467	7 172	7 354	7 878	9 383	11 275	4 885	11 321	Libye
1 075	1 164	1 286	1 959	2 874	2 842	3 107	3 004	Maroc (2)
317	477	383	916	1 426	1 600	1 549	–	Soudan (…2011)
1 494	1 653	2 271	3 256	4 200	4 222	4 373	4 248	Tunisie
2 574	*2 852*	*2 813*	*4 889*	*5 387*	*6 853*	*7 640*	*7 288*	*Afrique australe*
854	2 688	3 204	5 468	5 822	7 427	8 533	8 776	Botswana
268	332	393	662	796	1 004	1 114	1 067	Lesotho
2 500	1 894	2 062	3 491	4 096	5 013	5 439	5 248	Namibie
2 770	3 044	2 969	5 169	5 689	7 251	8 090	7 692	Afrique du Sud
1 100	1 257	1 433	2 339	2 711	3 281	3 399	3 244	Swaziland
906	*452*	*373*	*694*	*941*	*1 136*	*1 214*	*1 285*	*Afrique occidentale*
381	387	362	571	766	741	802	790	Bénin
268	336	214	385	522	536	595	591	Burkina Faso
474	885	1 233	2 055	3 228	3 323	3 773	3 748	Cap-Vert
1 197	950	644	948	1 191	1 163	1 196	1 165	Côte d'Ivoire
800	732	604	419	539	557	689	660	Gambie
476	675	417	795	1 098	1 283	1 570	1 541	Ghana
337	507	383	325	544	524	544	584	Guinée
615	598	299	419	581	539	591	525	Guinée-Bissau
398	229	185	191	267	269	278	305	Libéria
196	289	235	416	601	612	671	612	Mali
985	813	490	717	853	912	1 254	1 185	Mauritanie
459	339	158	259	358	366	397	390	Niger
1 233	359	375	803	1 097	1 449	1 509	1 661	Nigéria
601	857	492	801	1 055	1 034	1 132	1 077	Sénégal
417	219	206	316	422	432	483	643	Sierra Leone
424	487	270	390	536	526	600	580	Togo

Pour les sources et les notes, se reporter à la fin du tableau.

8

Region, country or territory	Total gross domestic product (1) / Produit intérieur brut total (1) Millions of dollars / Millions de dollars							
	1980	1990	2000	2005	2009	2010	2011	2012 (e)
Developing economies: America	757 366	1 090 505	2 135 871	2 709 270	4 104 166	5 073 122	5 690 157	5 691 558
Caribbean	*43 449*	*62 048*	*95 578*	*133 096*	*175 221*	*183 927*	*197 031*	*210 021*
Anguilla	12	76	151	231	296	274	288	307
Antigua and Barbuda	148	450	788	1 002	1 214	1 154	1 118	1 162
Aruba	297	765	1 873	2 331	2 502	2 409	2 677	2 625
Bahamas	1 581	3 700	6 328	7 706	7 717	7 771	7 788	8 043
Barbados	1 016	2 020	3 098	3 908	4 397	4 245	4 313	4 530
British Virgin Islands	54	146	751	870	876	894	916	-
Cayman Islands	173	930	2 277	3 042	3 314	3 191	3 268	-
Cuba	19 913	28 645	30 565	42 644	62 079	64 328	68 715	74 089
Curaçao	–	–	–	–	–	–	4 138	-
Dominica	71	200	324	362	488	482	496	524
Dominican Republic	8 178	9 385	23 655	33 431	46 475	50 980	55 433	58 848
Grenada	75	221	523	701	776	784	825	845
Haiti	1 384	2 614	3 358	3 807	5 929	6 079	6 731	7 166
Jamaica	3 045	4 822	9 005	11 239	12 289	13 458	14 746	15 156
Montserrat	24	67	37	50	60	58	62	-
Netherlands Antilles	943	1 980	2 857	3 277	3 966	4 078	–	–
Saint Kitts and Nevis	61	201	416	536	690	673	712	728
Saint Lucia	135	416	700	847	1 062	1 164	1 254	1 280
Saint Vincent and the Grenadines	70	235	397	551	672	675	688	715
Trinidad and Tobago	6 236	5 068	8 154	15 982	19 623	20 352	21 907	23 541
Turks and Caicos Islands	32	106	319	579	796	878	955	-
Central America	*251 392*	*319 756*	*706 585*	*941 573*	*1 013 781*	*1 180 076*	*1 323 060*	*1 355 906*
Belize	195	405	832	1 115	1 349	1 401	1 474	1 558
Costa Rica	6 139	7 254	15 947	19 965	29 383	36 218	41 007	45 079
El Salvador	1 173	4 801	13 134	17 094	20 661	21 428	23 054	23 773
Guatemala	7 024	6 820	17 196	27 211	37 734	41 341	46 898	49 919
Honduras	3 061	3 637	7 187	9 757	14 176	15 400	17 447	18 833
Mexico	227 664	288 013	636 731	846 095	880 103	1 031 109	1 155 206	1 173 435
Nicaragua	2 082	2 749	3 938	4 872	6 214	6 591	7 297	7 851
Panama, excl. Canal Zone (3)	4 054				–	–		
Panama	–	6 077	11 621	15 465	24 163	26 590	30 677	35 458
South America	*462 525*	*708 701*	*1 333 708*	*1 634 601*	*2 915 163*	*3 709 118*	*4 170 067*	*4 125 631*
Argentina	75 515	141 353	284 346	183 196	308 740	370 263	448 165	477 036
Bolivia (Plurinational State of)	3 502	4 868	8 398	9 549	17 340	19 650	23 949	27 086
Brazil	191 125	368 234	644 729	882 044	1 620 165	2 143 035	2 476 651	2 253 728
Chile	30 336	34 481	77 383	123 056	172 591	216 309	248 592	265 939
Colombia	47 204	56 925	99 876	146 566	233 822	286 398	333 185	366 115
Ecuador	12 351	11 248	16 283	36 942	52 022	57 978	66 381	73 427
Guyana	943	632	1 137	1 315	2 026	2 259	2 577	2 823
Paraguay	3 931	4 653	7 095	7 473	14 295	18 331	22 890	22 731
Peru	16 739	29 280	53 336	79 389	130 355	157 324	180 464	202 201
Suriname	1 089	752	1 157	2 193	3 892	4 350	4 610	5 033
Uruguay	10 642	9 239	22 823	17 363	30 497	39 412	46 710	49 395
Venezuela (Bolivarian Rep. of)	69 147	47 036	117 146	145 513	329 419	393 808	315 893	380 118
Developing economies: Asia	1 371 782	2 265 966	4 288 815	7 152 922	11 852 831	14 115 534	16 571 659	17 791 279
Eastern Asia	*453 401*	*936 146*	*2 239 682*	*3 698 502*	*6 528 340*	*7 667 321*	*9 087 137*	*10 048 867*
China	306 520	404 494	1 192 836	2 283 671	5 069 470	5 951 462	7 203 784	8 094 362
China, Hong Kong SAR	28 818	76 890	169 121	177 772	209 310	224 176	243 302	257 288
China, Macao SAR	982	3 174	6 433	11 791	21 312	28 270	36 428	42 672
China, Taiwan Province of	42 225	164 974	326 162	364 849	377 568	430 184	466 424	476 419
Korea, Dem. People's Rep. of	9 879	14 702	10 608	13 031	12 035	12 139	12 385	-
Korea, Republic of	64 385	270 405	533 385	844 866	834 060	1 014 890	1 116 247	1 155 679
Mongolia	592	1 507	1 137	2 523	4 584	6 201	8 567	10 063
Southern Asia	*332 408*	*510 044*	*715 812*	*1 251 025*	*2 017 521*	*2 466 315*	*2 834 902*	*2 836 400*
Afghanistan	3 642	3 622	3 532	6 622	12 573	16 078	18 949	19 810
Bangladesh	16 729	28 137	45 470	57 628	89 050	99 689	106 200	109 911
Bhutan	131	279	439	819	1 265	1 585	1 725	1 776
India	184 760	326 795	467 788	837 499	1 334 018	1 678 297	1 897 608	1 857 547
Iran (Islamic Rep. of)	91 943	91 036	104 016	205 586	368 146	428 960	521 835	545 720
Maldives	83	254	802	992	1 942	2 076	2 050	2 117
Nepal	2 089	3 780	5 730	8 259	12 744	16 317	18 501	18 213
Pakistan	28 757	47 937	71 319	109 213	155 716	173 764	208 860	221 848
Sri Lanka	4 273	8 204	16 717	24 406	42 066	49 550	59 175	59 457

For sources and notes, see end of table.

Per capita gross domestic product / Produit intérieur brut par habitant Dollars								Régions, pays ou territoires
1980	1990	2000	2005	2009	2010	2011	2012 (e)	
2 114	2 487	4 135	4 907	7 093	8 670	9 618	9 514	Économies en développement : Amérique
1 688	*2 080*	*2 836*	*3 755*	*4 783*	*4 982*	*5 304*	*5 603*	*Caraïbes*
1 817	9 111	13 605	17 005	19 631	17 817	18 408	19 293	Anguilla
2 112	7 238	10 143	11 940	13 830	13 006	12 480	12 837	Antigua-et-Barbuda
4 940	12 308	20 754	23 080	23 467	22 416	24 753	24 173	Aruba
7 506	14 447	21 258	24 130	22 807	22 665	22 431	22 897	Bahamas
4 083	7 782	11 582	14 448	16 120	15 531	15 744	16 502	Barbade
4 919	8 876	36 617	39 565	38 095	38 460	38 972	-	Îles Vierges britanniques
10 272	35 699	56 658	58 195	59 429	56 751	57 610	-	Îles Caïmanes
2 029	2 710	2 753	3 789	5 512	5 714	6 106	6 586	Cuba
						28 683	-	Curaçao
939	2 821	4 656	5 246	7 181	7 107	7 322	7 751	Dominique
1 411	1 304	2 753	3 609	4 744	5 135	5 512	5 779	République dominicaine
841	2 298	5 154	6 819	7 450	7 600	7 868	8 027	Grenade
243	367	388	407	601	608	665	699	Haïti
1 428	2 039	3 488	4 191	4 500	4 910	5 360	5 489	Jamaïque
2 034	6 265	7 492	8 858	10 218	9 725	10 396	-	Montserrat
5 444	10 393	15 890	17 622	20 029	20 321	–	–	Antilles néerlandaises
1 407	4 945	9 037	10 906	13 328	12 850	13 424	13 562	Saint-Kitts-et-Nevis
1 151	3 014	4 455	5 125	6 160	6 677	7 124	7 201	Sainte-Lucie
698	2 187	3 684	5 070	6 153	6 172	6 291	6 541	Saint-Vincent-et-les Grenadines
5 784	4 169	6 311	12 150	14 684	15 171	16 272	17 425	Trinité-et-Tobago
4 276	9 171	16 926	18 953	21 347	22 898	24 363	-	Îles Turques et Caïques
2 739	*2 823*	*5 213*	*6 476*	*6 594*	*7 570*	*8 373*	*8 466*	*Amérique centrale*
1 354	2 131	3 320	3 968	4 416	4 496	4 636	4 803	Belize
2 620	2 363	4 069	4 633	6 400	7 774	8 676	9 404	Costa Rica
252	900	2 211	2 825	3 354	3 460	3 702	3 795	El Salvador
998	764	1 530	2 140	2 689	2 873	3 178	3 298	Guatemala
844	744	1 156	1 418	1 903	2 026	2 250	2 380	Honduras
3 310	3 416	6 370	7 946	7 856	9 091	10 063	10 103	Mexique
642	667	776	898	1 088	1 139	1 243	1 318	Nicaragua
2 076	–	–	–	–	–	–	–	Panama, sans la zone du canal (3)
–	2 515	3 931	4 776	6 980	7 561	8 590	9 782	Panama
1 921	*2 399*	*3 841*	*4 403*	*7 509*	*9 454*	*10 519*	*10 300*	*Amérique du Sud*
2 684	4 330	7 699	4 736	7 706	9 162	10 994	11 601	Argentine
654	731	1 011	1 044	1 774	1 979	2 374	2 643	Bolivie (État plurinational de)
1 570	2 461	3 696	4 743	8 384	10 993	12 594	11 362	Brésil
2 714	2 615	5 018	7 549	10 179	12 640	14 395	15 263	Chili
1 756	1 714	2 512	3 405	5 122	6 186	7 100	7 699	Colombie
1 552	1 096	1 319	2 751	3 648	4 008	4 526	4 940	Équateur
1 214	872	1 550	1 763	2 690	2 994	3 408	3 726	Guyana
1 230	1 096	1 328	1 267	2 254	2 840	3 485	3 401	Paraguay
968	1 350	2 062	2 881	4 532	5 411	6 138	6 800	Pérou
2 978	1 847	2 478	4 392	7 487	8 292	8 708	9 422	Suriname
3 651	2 972	6 876	5 226	9 084	11 699	13 819	14 565	Uruguay
4 599	2 389	4 811	5 457	11 550	13 589	10 731	12 717	Venezuela (Rép. bolivarienne du)
561	759	1 228	1 926	3 050	3 593	4 149	4 408	Économies en développement : Asie
434	*769*	*1 662*	*2 664*	*4 606*	*5 384*	*6 249*	*6 880*	*Asie orientale*
317	360	957	1 777	3 864	4 515	5 346	5 980	Chine
5 703	13 271	24 932	26 105	29 953	31 784	34 161	35 752	Chine (RAS de Hong Kong)
3 986	8 824	14 896	24 493	40 121	51 999	65 551	75 200	Chine (RAS de Macao)
2 393	8 135	14 702	16 051	16 357	18 590	20 072	20 438	Province chinoise de Taiwan
573	730	463	549	497	499	506	-	Corée, Rép. populaire dém. de
1 719	6 291	11 598	17 959	17 389	21 063	23 067	23 785	Corée, République de
350	687	471	991	1 690	2 250	3 060	3 538	Mongolie
352	*426*	*490*	*789*	*1 201*	*1 447*	*1 640*	*1 618*	*Asie méridionale*
257	278	155	240	411	512	586	593	Afghanistan
207	267	351	410	606	670	706	721	Bangladesh
304	499	769	1 242	1 772	2 183	2 336	2 366	Bhoutan
264	374	444	735	1 105	1 370	1 528	1 476	Inde
2 383	1 659	1 592	2 948	5 034	5 799	6 977	7 217	Iran (Rép. islamique d')
527	1 157	2 933	3 362	6 230	6 570	6 405	6 529	Maldives
139	198	235	303	433	545	607	587	Népal
357	429	493	688	913	1 001	1 182	1 233	Pakistan
283	473	892	1 230	2 035	2 375	2 812	2 801	Sri Lanka

Pour les sources et les notes, se reporter à la fin du tableau.

Region, country or territory	Total gross domestic product (1) / Produit intérieur brut total (1) Millions of dollars / Millions de dollars							
	1980	1990	2000	2005	2009	2010	2011	2012 (e)
South-Eastern Asia	**202 535**	**367 243**	**614 262**	**931 727**	**1 535 107**	**1 906 026**	**2 210 958**	**2 338 693**
Brunei Darussalam	5 587	3 520	6 001	9 531	10 733	12 371	16 360	16 619
Cambodia	769	1 698	3 667	6 293	10 402	11 242	12 830	14 160
Indonesia (...2002)	79 636	125 720	165 415					
Indonesia	–	–	–	285 869	539 580	708 027	846 834	878 425
Lao People's Dem. Rep.	318	866	1 665	2 717	5 585	6 744	8 196	9 194
Malaysia	26 458	47 565	97 584	143 534	202 257	246 823	287 934	303 488
Myanmar	5 905	5 172	7 275	11 931	32 946	42 207	55 320	57 764
Philippines	35 954	49 095	81 026	103 072	168 335	199 591	224 754	250 269
Singapore	12 046	38 835	94 308	125 429	185 638	227 382	259 850	270 462
Thailand	33 467	88 299	126 148	188 620	279 168	341 084	369 709	390 855
Timor-Leste	–	–	–	1 814	3 283	4 130	5 572	6 852
Viet Nam	2 396	6 472	31 173	52 917	97 180	106 427	123 600	140 605
Western Asia	**383 438**	**452 534**	**719 059**	**1 271 668**	**1 771 862**	**2 075 873**	**2 438 662**	**2 567 319**
Bahrain	3 292	4 293	8 028	13 459	19 621	21 930	25 825	26 635
Iraq	12 458	17 043	16 900	36 268	103 188	110 693	122 750	144 501
Jordan	4 013	4 020	8 461	12 589	23 820	26 425	28 840	31 197
Kuwait	28 691	18 471	37 718	80 798	105 968	124 331	160 916	172 042
Lebanon	4 074	2 812	16 679	21 861	34 650	37 124	39 039	41 453
Oman	6 256	11 556	19 450	30 905	46 865	59 228	72 680	79 038
Qatar	7 838	7 360	17 760	44 530	97 798	127 332	173 320	182 757
Saudi Arabia	164 540	116 622	188 442	315 583	376 692	455 922	597 086	648 599
State of Palestine	1 074	1 936	4 195	4 634	6 720	8 331	8 769	-
Syrian Arab Republic	13 146	11 150	19 666	28 397	54 112	60 465	64 273	54 334
Turkey	92 477	202 546	266 560	482 986	614 570	731 144	774 983	791 356
United Arab Emirates	43 599	50 701	104 337	180 617	259 734	283 916	338 690	353 084
Yemen, Arab Republic	1 624	–	–	–	–	–	–	–
Yemen, Democratic	356	–	–	–	–	–	–	–
Yemen	–	4 023	10 865	19 041	28 124	29 031	31 492	33 556
Developing economies: Oceania	**7 276**	**11 475**	**13 761**	**21 965**	**29 656**	**31 908**	**37 494**	**41 139**
Cook Islands	22	59	92	183	207	241	275	-
Fiji	1 215	1 351	1 723	3 007	2 882	3 173	3 813	4 069
French Polynesia	1 381	3 181	3 444	5 463	6 816	6 675	7 198	-
Kiribati	35	41	67	106	124	146	182	193
Marshall Islands	–	79	108	139	165	177	189	208
Micronesia (Federated States of)	–	158	234	250	280	297	318	334
Nauru	36	49	21	26	54	63	72	-
New Caledonia	1 182	2 529	3 412	6 236	8 756	8 855	9 859	-
Pacific Islands (Trust Territory)	118	–	–	–	–	–	–	–
Palau	–	77	120	145	204	212	229	-
Papua New Guinea	2 823	3 286	3 499	4 866	8 105	9 707	12 586	15 712
Samoa	112	112	231	435	522	596	667	700
Solomon Islands	144	208	338	429	598	676	838	979
Tonga	79	162	189	264	326	373	453	483
Tuvalu	4	10	12	22	27	32	37	. 37
Vanuatu	125	173	272	393	590	683	778	791
Transition economies	**1 012 216**	**863 143**	**397 600**	**1 099 288**	**1 785 371**	**2 120 611**	**2 599 062**	**2 753 025**
Albania	2 219	2 222	3 640	8 159	12 119	11 954	13 000	12 532
Armenia	–	–	1 912	4 900	8 648	9 260	10 138	9 903
Azerbaijan	–	–	5 273	13 245	44 292	52 906	63 404	67 255
Belarus	–	–	10 418	30 210	49 209	55 221	55 136	58 389
Bosnia and Herzegovina	–	–	5 553	10 948	17 083	16 647	18 037	17 278
Croatia	–	–	21 518	44 821	62 202	59 472	62 493	57 139
Georgia	–	–	3 058	6 411	10 767	11 638	14 367	15 792
Kazakhstan	–	–	18 292	57 124	115 309	148 047	186 427	199 899
Kyrgyzstan	–	–	1 370	2 460	4 690	4 794	5 919	6 183
Montenegro	–	–	–	–	4 141	4 111	4 550	4 339
Republic of Moldova	–	–	1 288	2 988	5 439	5 812	7 000	7 344
Russian Federation	–	–	259 446	764 016	1 222 646	1 487 516	1 857 770	1 977 996
Serbia and Montenegro	–	–	11 431	31 223				
Serbia	–	–	–	–	45 685	42 659	47 588	41 420
SFR of Yugoslavia	69 959	85 112	–	–	–	–	–	–
Tajikistan	–	–	861	2 312	4 979	5 642	6 523	7 593
TFYR of Macedonia	–	–	3 587	5 987	9 314	9 339	10 165	9 407
Turkmenistan	–	–	4 932	13 946	18 651	20 001	25 742	30 933
Ukraine	–	–	31 262	86 142	117 227	136 419	165 245	178 361
USSR	940 038	775 810	–	–	–	–	–	–
Uzbekistan	–	–	13 759	14 396	32 971	39 173	45 558	51 262

For sources and notes, see end of table.

Per capita gross domestic product / Produit intérieur brut par habitant Dollars								Régions, pays ou territoires
1980	1990	2000	2005	2009	2010	2011	2012 (e)	
564	*825*	*1 173*	*1 664*	*2 616*	*3 212*	*3 685*	*3 855*	**Asie du Sud-Est**
29 513	13 963	18 351	26 249	27 391	31 010	39 483	39 418	Brunéi Darussalam
118	178	295	471	744	795	897	978	Cambodge
526	679	772						Indonésie (...2002)
–	–	–	1 258	2 273	2 952	3 495	3 589	Indonésie
98	206	313	472	914	1 088	1 303	1 442	Rép. dém. populaire lao
1 913	2 612	4 168	5 499	7 237	8 691	9 977	10 350	Malaisie
180	132	162	258	692	880	1 144	1 186	Myanmar
764	797	1 048	1 205	1 836	2 140	2 370	2 594	Philippines
4 989	12 874	24 063	29 402	37 536	44 704	50 087	51 455	Singapour
705	1 547	1 997	2 828	4 063	4 934	5 318	5 592	Thaïlande
			1 795	2 985	3 674	4 829	5 772	Timor-Leste
44	96	396	636	1 118	1 211	1 392	1 567	Viet Nam
4 007	*3 561*	*4 453*	*6 990*	*8 772*	*10 036*	*11 533*	*11 895*	**Asie occidentale**
9 197	8 710	12 579	18 569	16 776	17 379	19 512	19 592	Bahreïn
906	981	708	1 326	3 358	3 495	3 758	4 287	Iraq
1 746	1 177	1 753	2 357	3 953	4 271	4 556	4 831	Jordanie
20 836	8 848	19 434	35 688	40 044	45 430	57 102	59 498	Koweït
1 458	954	4 457	5 394	8 256	8 781	9 165	9 659	Liban
5 296	6 186	8 590	12 721	17 280	21 286	25 536	27 217	Oman
35 371	15 537	30 053	54 240	61 210	72 397	92 682	94 265	Qatar
16 787	7 226	9 401	13 127	14 051	16 610	21 262	22 595	Arabie saoudite
711	930	1 311	1 303	1 710	2 062	2 112	-	État de Palestine
1 476	905	1 230	1 536	2 698	2 962	3 095	2 573	République arabe syrienne
2 097	3 742	4 189	7 088	8 554	10 050	10 524	10 621	Turquie
42 903	28 033	34 395	44 385	37 432	37 797	42 921	43 559	Émirats arabes unis
272	–	–	–	–	–	–	–	Yémen, République arabe du
148	–	–	–	–	–	–	–	Yémen, Démocratique
–	337	613	922	1 206	1 207	1 270	1 312	Yémen
1 468	*1 842*	*1 762*	*2 531*	*3 143*	*3 313*	*3 817*	*4 108*	**Économies en développement : Océanie**
1 276	3 330	5 139	9 409	10 247	11 895	13 478	-	Îles Cook
1 913	1 854	2 122	3 655	3 381	3 687	4 391	4 646	Fidji
9 138	16 282	14 492	21 434	25 463	24 654	26 290	-	Polynésie française
631	574	795	1 148	1 266	1 468	1 803	1 882	Kiribati
–	1 666	2 067	2 678	3 089	3 281	3 448	3 736	Îles Marshall
–	1 639	2 181	2 285	2 528	2 678	2 855	2 977	Micronésie (États fédérés de)
4 775	5 377	2 099	2 600	5 312	6 182	6 954	-	Nauru
8 302	14 906	16 095	26 987	35 463	35 298	38 690		Nouvelle-Calédonie
889								Îles du Pacifique (Territoire sous tutelle des)
–	5 096	6 252	7 267	10 008	10 348	11 096	-	Palaos
878	790	651	798	1 209	1 415	1 794	2 191	Papouasie-Nouvelle-Guinée
723	695	1 308	2 415	2 862	3 255	3 629	3 790	Samoa
626	672	827	914	1 140	1 255	1 529	1 745	Îles Salomon
848	1 703	1 933	2 617	3 154	3 587	4 335	4 609	Tonga
534	1 059	1 302	2 289	2 720	3 259	3 713	3 795	Tuvalu
1 083	1 181	1 470	1 862	2 525	2 851	3 168	3 141	Vanuatu
3 496	*2 738*	*1 303*	*3 643*	*5 903*	*7 002*	*8 572*	*9 068*	**Économies en transition**
831	675	1 185	2 597	3 796	3 731	4 042	3 883	Albanie
–	–	621	1 598	2 803	2 995	3 270	3 185	Arménie
–	–	650	1 542	4 885	5 758	6 813	7 139	Azerbaïdjan
–	–	1 036	3 075	5 107	5 755	5 768	6 128	Bélarus
–	–	1 503	2 896	4 534	4 427	4 807	4 615	Bosnie-Herzégovine
–	–	4 776	10 090	14 102	13 506	14 217	13 023	Croatie
–	–	644	1 432	2 462	2 674	3 319	3 669	Géorgie
–	–	1 223	3 765	7 279	9 238	11 503	12 203	Kazakhstan
–	–	277	488	890	899	1 098	1 135	Kirghizistan
–	–			6 569	6 510	7 196	6 857	Monténégro
–	–	314	793	1 510	1 627	1 975	2 087	République de Moldova
–	–	1 768	5 311	8 546	10 405	13 006	13 861	Fédération de Russie
–	–	1 062	2 978					Serbie-et-Monténégro
–	–	–	–	4 637	4 328	4 829	4 207	Serbie
3 263	3 727	–	–	–	–	–	–	RSF de Yougoslavie
–	–	139	358	734	820	935	1 073	Tadjikistan
–	–	1 785	2 937	4 528	4 532	4 925	4 551	LERY de Macédoine
–	–	1 096	2 937	3 745	3 967	5 042	5 983	Turkménistan
–	–	639	1 836	2 564	3 002	3 657	3 969	Ukraine
3 542	2 684							URSS
–	–	555	555	1 215	1 427	1 641	1 826	Ouzbékistan

Pour les sources et les notes, se reporter à la fin du tableau.

8

8.1.1 Nominal gross domestic product: Total and per capita of countries and geographical regions

Region, country or territory	Total gross domestic product (1) / Produit intérieur brut total (1) Millions of dollars / Millions de dollars							
	1980	1990	2000	2005	2009	2010	2011	2012 (e)
Developed economies: America	**3 053 716**	**6 372 859**	**10 697 452**	**13 790 732**	**15 341 099**	**16 103 148**	**16 838 077**	**17 480 025**
Bermuda	902	2 035	3 480	4 868	5 806	5 765	5 973	-
Canada	268 889	582 735	724 914	1 133 757	1 337 577	1 577 040	1 736 869	1 773 288
Greenland	468	1 002	1 050	1 650	2 268	2 186	2 439	-
United States	2 783 456	5 787 087	9 968 008	12 650 457	13 995 447	14 518 157	15 092 796	15 698 325
Developed economies: Asia	**1 110 702**	**3 161 461**	**4 856 093**	**4 705 835**	**5 230 007**	**5 705 869**	**6 113 277**	**6 177 227**
Israel	23 714	57 763	124 894	133 968	194 865	217 445	242 920	240 024
Japan	1 086 988	3 103 698	4 731 199	4 571 867	5 035 142	5 488 424	5 870 357	5 937 203
Developed economies: Europe	**3 959 822**	**7 644 467**	**8 918 429**	**14 485 837**	**17 240 860**	**17 267 557**	**18 768 488**	**17 727 813**
Andorra	546	1 259	1 387	3 133	3 658	3 422	3 577	-
Austria	81 212	164 757	192 071	304 984	383 627	379 311	418 031	398 214
Belgium	125 288	202 830	232 672	377 351	473 404	471 660	514 122	484 185
Bulgaria	10 778	20 726	12 904	28 894	48 569	47 727	53 514	50 943
Cyprus	2 230	5 777	9 174	16 902	23 413	23 053	24 994	22 987
Czechoslovakia	47 822	55 198						
Czech Republic	–	–	58 803	130 066	197 187	198 947	217 077	195 971
Denmark	69 709	135 839	160 082	257 676	311 114	311 989	332 019	311 966
Estonia	–	–	5 680	13 903	19 127	18 981	22 175	21 835
Finland	53 011	138 891	121 794	195 778	239 383	236 802	263 247	249 729
France	691 724	1 246 616	1 328 991	2 140 836	2 625 240	2 571 225	2 781 435	2 610 779
Germany, Federal Republic of (4)	919 651	–	–	–	–	–	–	–
Germany	–	1 714 447	1 886 400	2 766 254	3 298 634	3 306 028	3 604 061	3 391 480
Greece	54 205	93 347	125 934	240 076	321 795	301 065	299 001	256 722
Hungary	25 009	36 500	46 386	110 322	126 663	127 967	138 714	126 785
Iceland	3 331	6 373	8 697	16 286	12 113	12 569	14 026	13 604
Ireland	21 474	48 226	97 452	202 752	224 042	207 255	221 022	209 702
Italy	462 048	1 138 979	1 104 009	1 786 275	2 111 147	2 056 941	2 195 937	2 012 823
Latvia	–	–	7 776	15 938	25 854	24 099	28 480	28 386
Lithuania	–	–	11 501	26 100	37 050	36 574	42 872	42 129
Luxembourg	5 969	12 670	20 270	37 659	51 945	53 330	59 528	56 990
Malta	1 250	2 547	3 957	5 981	8 072	8 110	8 887	8 463
Netherlands	180 777	294 869	385 074	638 471	796 333	779 742	836 823	772 182
Norway	63 714	117 623	168 288	304 060	374 757	417 465	485 416	496 769
Poland	57 828	64 550	171 276	303 912	430 912	469 799	514 115	487 528
Portugal	32 457	77 668	117 299	191 848	234 084	228 688	237 586	212 265
Romania	36 432	40 550	37 305	99 173	164 344	164 436	189 776	175 985
San Marino	326	804	1 102	1 959	2 188	1 976	2 046	1 894
Slovakia	–	–	20 403	47 896	87 234	87 072	96 000	91 729
Slovenia	–	–	19 982	35 718	49 394	47 159	50 284	45 586
Spain	225 984	520 938	580 345	1 130 799	1 455 956	1 389 166	1 478 206	1 350 907
Sweden	132 065	244 415	247 259	370 580	405 783	463 062	539 387	524 873
Switzerland	113 066	245 451	258 520	388 413	513 975	555 841	666 947	638 408
United Kingdom	541 917	1 012 617	1 475 637	2 295 843	2 183 862	2 266 094	2 429 184	2 432 416
Developed economies: Oceania	**196 798**	**369 396**	**463 615**	**873 510**	**1 127 290**	**1 426 440**	**1 678 250**	**1 736 106**
Australia	173 465	324 407	409 835	759 697	1 008 728	1 283 352	1 515 468	1 564 566
New Zealand	23 332	44 989	53 780	113 813	118 562	143 088	162 783	171 540

Source:

UNCTAD secretariat calculations, based on UN DESA Statistics Division, *National Accounts Main Aggregates Database*

Notes:

(1) GDP by expenditure, in current prices and current exchange rates.

(2) Including Western Sahara.

(3) Data refer to Panama, including Canal zone.

(4) Data refer to the former Federal Republic of Germany and the former Democratic Republic of Germany.

Per capita gross domestic product / Produit intérieur brut par habitant Dollars								Régions, pays ou territoires
1980	1990	2000	2005	2009	2010	2011	2012 (e)	
11 848	**22 378**	**33 724**	**41 399**	**44 422**	**46 223**	**47 916**	**49 317**	Économies développées : Amérique
16 096	34 032	55 388	75 910	89 602	88 766	91 780	-	Bermudes
10 968	21 037	23 638	35 119	39 720	46 361	50 565	51 141	Canada
9 322	18 034	18 686	28 856	39 583	38 154	42 575	-	Groenland
11 940	22 520	34 802	42 068	44 922	46 201	47 620	49 112	États-Unis
9 282	**24 942**	**36 863**	**35 383**	**39 085**	**42 596**	**45 601**	**46 054**	Économies développées : Asie
6 331	12 836	20 764	20 284	26 837	29 312	32 123	31 194	Israël
9 377	25 388	37 633	36 172	39 787	43 374	46 407	46 959	Japon
8 596	**16 131**	**18 008**	**28 684**	**33 570**	**33 504**	**36 307**	**34 204**	Économies développées : Europe
14 630	23 856	21 459	40 228	43 718	40 324	41 517	-	Andorre
10 758	21 479	23 995	37 048	45 835	45 190	49 686	47 244	Autriche
12 723	20 387	22 866	36 234	44 400	44 031	47 807	44 883	Belgique
1 216	2 350	1 612	3 734	6 439	6 368	7 187	6 886	Bulgarie
4 384	9 971	13 227	22 298	29 277	28 483	31 070	28 530	Chypre
3 141	3 545	_	_	_	_	_	_	Tchécoslovaquie
_	_	5 741	12 726	18 888	18 960	20 607	18 548	République tchèque
13 607	26 423	29 981	47 546	56 311	56 213	59 581	55 781	Danemark
_	_	4 144	10 330	14 257	14 153	16 542	16 298	Estonie
11 091	27 854	23 542	37 331	44 815	44 142	48 887	46 224	Finlande
12 546	21 414	21 859	34 051	40 762	39 700	42 710	39 874	France
11 747	_	_	_	_	_	_	_	Allemagne, Rép. fédérale d' (4)
_	21 675	22 907	33 514	40 029	40 169	43 865	41 364	Allemagne
5 621	9 187	11 462	21 468	28 411	26 504	26 251	22 482	Grèce
2 338	3 518	4 543	10 937	12 663	12 818	13 919	12 743	Hongrie
14 601	25 012	30 928	54 884	38 388	39 263	43 240	41 439	Islande
6 283	13 657	25 620	48 761	50 778	46 367	48 836	45 792	Irlande
8 218	20 041	19 373	30 446	35 041	33 970	36 124	33 016	Italie
_	_	3 260	6 913	11 433	10 701	12 697	12 703	Lettonie
_	_	3 286	7 641	11 089	11 004	12 962	12 796	Lituanie
16 391	33 236	46 544	82 370	104 384	105 095	115 377	108 893	Luxembourg
3 827	6 931	9 958	14 613	19 441	19 471	21 269	20 187	Malte
12 832	19 801	24 275	39 157	48 090	46 936	50 215	46 199	Pays-Bas
15 595	27 732	37 473	65 767	77 525	85 492	98 565	100 145	Norvège
1 625	1 696	4 472	7 963	11 266	12 274	13 424	12 724	Pologne
3 317	7 825	11 348	18 196	21 965	21 422	22 226	19 839	Portugal
1 641	1 747	1 681	4 555	7 631	7 653	8 853	8 228	Roumanie
15 245	33 320	40 883	64 664	69 767	62 674	64 480	59 296	Saint-Marin
_	_	3 775	8 844	16 001	15 941	17 545	16 738	Slovaquie
_	_	10 064	17 840	24 404	23 235	24 709	22 346	Slovénie
6 027	13 395	14 405	26 058	31 902	30 149	31 820	28 883	Espagne
15 891	28 557	27 907	41 042	43 581	49 369	57 134	55 277	Suède
17 866	36 620	35 902	52 138	67 125	72 184	86 191	82 160	Suisse
9 592	17 634	24 970	37 991	35 288	36 390	38 771	38 588	Royaume-Uni
11 021	**18 024**	**20 138**	**35 599**	**42 985**	**53 552**	**62 111**	**63 408**	Économies développées : Océanie
11 792	18 975	21 385	37 234	46 056	57 631	67 039	68 266	Australie
7 414	13 240	13 940	27 530	27 428	32 757	36 874	38 451	Nouvelle-Zélande

Source :

Calculs du secrétariat de la CNUCED, basés sur ONU DAES Division de statistique, *National Accounts Main Aggregates Database*

Notes :

(1) PIB par dépenses, aux prix et taux de change courants.

(2) Y compris le Sahara occidental.

(3) Les données se réfèrent au Panama, incluant la zone du canal.

(4) Les données se réfèrent à l'ex-République Fédérale d'Allemagne et l'ex-République Démocratique d'Allemagne.

8

Economic grouping	Total gross domestic product (1) / Produit intérieur brut total (1) Millions of dollars / Millions de dollars							
	1980	1990	2000	2005	2009	2010	2011	2012 (e)
DEVELOPING ECONOMIES	2 570 539	3 862 899	7 037 652	10 894 061	17 469 323	20 957 174	24 204 766	25 561 043
Developing economies excluding China	2 264 018	3 458 404	5 844 816	8 610 391	12 399 853	15 005 71.1	17 000 982	17 453 561
Developing economies excluding LDCs	2 461 148	3 711 603	6 856 075	10 577 920	16 922 724	20 351 279	23 510 973	24 813 210
High-income developing economies	1 285 738	2 099 705	3 927 826	5 462 056	7 244 595	8 838 177	9 950 500	10 105 182
Middle-income developing economies	804 363	1 112 437	2 239 588	3 910 906	7 770 852	9 165 863	10 921 382	12 029 690
Low-income developing economies	480 438	650 756	870 238	1 521 099	2 453 876	2 953 134	3 332 884	3 426 172
Heavily indebted poor countries (IMF)	110 497	143 772	146 017	246 613	393 661	427 725	481 479	499 931
Landlocked developing countries	48 923	73 852	126 680	233 344	437 352	516 622	619 544	684 805
Small island developing States	18 901	27 039	43 594	64 631	80 016	86 175	96 713	104 578
Least developed countries	*109 391*	*151 296*	*181 577*	*316 141*	*546 599*	*605 895*	*693 793*	*747 833*
Africa and Haiti	77 202	102 813	101 735	199 122	348 032	375 988	431 639	473 027
Asia	31 563	47 575	78 643	113 309	192 690	222 892	253 213	264 384
Islands	626	908	1 199	3 710	5 878	7 014	8 940	10 421
Major petroleum and gas exporters	*603 576*	*498 129*	*754 276*	*1 333 509*	*2 129 669*	*2 529 850*	*2 882 837*	*3 182 508*
Africa	179 104	138 302	148 505	293 709	441 858	545 661	579 669	676 649
America	69 147	47 036	117 146	145 513	329 419	393 808	315 893	380 118
Asia	355 325	312 790	488 624	894 287	1 358 392	1 590 382	1 987 276	2 125 740
Major exporters of manufactured goods	*741 583*	*1 379 476*	*3 176 275*	*4 974 835*	*8 037 575*	*9 467 109*	*11 102 455*	*12 121 988*
America	227 664	288 013	636 731	846 095	880 103	1 031 109	1 155 206	1 173 435
Asia	513 919	1 091 463	2 539 544	4 128 740	7 157 472	8 436 000	9 947 250	10 948 553
Emerging economies	*719 960*	*1 471 441*	*2 874 111*	*3 781 077*	*4 990 646*	*6 178 403*	*7 009 242*	*6 969 241*
America	541 379	861 362	1 696 524	2 113 780	3 111 954	3 918 041	4 509 078	4 372 338
Asia	178 581	610 079	1 177 587	1 667 298	1 878 692	2 260 362	2 500 164	2 596 904
Newly industrialized Asian economies	*322 989*	*861 784*	*1 593 148*	*2 234 010*	*2 795 917*	*3 392 156*	*3 815 053*	*3 982 885*
First tier	147 474	551 104	1 122 976	1 512 915	1 606 576	1 896 632	2 085 823	2 159 848
Second tier	175 515	310 680	470 172	721 095	1 189 340	1 495 524	1 729 230	1 823 037
Developing economies: Africa	434 114	494 952	599 205	1 009 905	1 482 671	1 736 610	1 905 456	2 037 067
Northern Africa excluding Sudan	131 327	171 357	247 440	334 902	519 298	583 318	607 919	678 339
Sub-Saharan Africa	302 787	323 596	351 765	675 003	963 373	1 153 292	1 297 536	1 358 728
Sub-Saharan Africa excluding South Africa	222 243	211 582	218 887	427 952	680 361	789 769	889 300	955 325
Developing economies: America	757 366	1 090 505	2 135 871	2 709 270	4 104 166	5 073 122	5 690 157	5 691 558
Central America and Greater Caribbean Islands excluding Puerto Rico	283 913	365 222	773 169	1 032 694	1 140 554	1 314 922	1 468 685	1 511 164
Central America and Greater Caribbean Islands excluding Mexico and Puerto Rico	56 249	77 209	136 438	186 600	260 451	283 813	313 480	337 730
South America and Central America	713 917	1 028 458	2 040 293	2 576 174	3 928 944	4 889 195	5 493 127	5 481 537
South America excluding Brazil	271 400	340 467	688 979	752 557	1 294 998	1 566 083	1 693 416	1 871 903
Developing economies: Asia	1 371 782	2 265 966	4 288 815	7 152 922	11 852 831	14 115 534	16 571 659	17 791 279
Eastern and South-Eastern Asia excluding China	349 416	898 894	1 661 107	2 346 558	2 993 977	3 621 885	4 094 311	4 293 198
Southern Asia excluding India	147 647	183 249	248 024	413 526	683 503	788 018	937 294	978 853

Source:

UNCTAD secretariat calculations, based on UN DESA Statistics Division, *National Accounts Main Aggregates Database*

Notes:

(1) GDP by expenditure, in current prices and current exchange rates.

8.1.2 Produit intérieur brut nominal : total et par habitant des groupements économiques

Per capita gross domestic product / Produit intérieur brut par habitant Dollars								Groupements économiques
1980	1990	2000	2005	2009	2010	2011	2012 (e)	
781	950	1 458	2 101	3 193	3 780	4 292	4 474	ÉCONOMIES EN DÉVELOPPEMENT
974	1 177	1 632	2 208	2 981	3 551	3 961	4 013	Économies en développement sans la Chine
850	1 044	1 646	2 382	3 633	4 319	4 910	5 124	Économies en développement sans les PMA
3 007	3 986	6 353	8 257	10 393	12 530	13 952	14 021	Économies en développement à revenu élevé
544	628	1 114	1 856	3 565	4 171	4 880	5 334	Économies en développement à revenu intermédiaire
347	368	396	629	946	1 118	1 240	1 252	Économies en développement à revenu faible
395	395	302	447	644	682	748	769	Pays pauvres très endettés (FMI)
321	373	382	632	1 089	1 259	1 477	1 559	Pays en développement sans littoral
1 763	2 127	2 901	3 746	4 365	4 631	5 122	5 457	Petits États insulaires en développement
278	297	275	424	671	728	815	859	Pays les moins avancés
334	337	253	433	679	715	799	853	Afrique et Haïti
196	235	305	401	645	735	823	845	Asie
634	725	765	1 340	1 942	2 266	2 825	3 214	Îles
3 245	1 978	2 396	3 785	5 498	6 385	7 120	7 697	Principaux exportateurs de pétrole et de gaz
1 705	1 006	857	1 506	2 062	2 488	2 582	2 945	Afrique
4 599	2 389	4 811	5 457	11 550	13 589	10 731	12 717	Amérique
5 390	3 306	4 174	6 841	9 396	10 754	13 163	13 816	Asie
640	1 017	2 100	3 179	5 013	5 871	6 751	7 332	Principaux exportateurs d'articles manufacturés
3 310	3 416	6 370	7 946	7 856	9 091	10 063	10 103	Amérique
472	858	1 798	2 831	4 799	5 627	6 502	7 123	Asie
1 968	3 321	5 622	6 978	8 853	10 860	12 210	12 034	Économies émergentes
2 191	2 857	4 812	5 637	7 958	9 920	11 304	10 855	Amérique
1 503	4 310	7 422	9 993	10 882	12 995	14 271	14 724	Asie
1 002	2 187	3 486	4 592	5 496	6 598	7 344	7 589	Économies nouvellement industrialisées d'Asie
2 357	7 647	14 237	18 713	19 361	22 724	24 849	25 605	Première génération
676	965	1 243	1 778	2 793	3 473	3 970	4 139	Deuxième génération
900	780	740	1 110	1 486	1 701	1 825	1 907	Économies en développement : Afrique
1 414	1 434	1 747	2 187	3 187	3 527	3 623	3 985	Afrique septentrionale sans le Soudan
778	628	526	892	1 154	1 348	1 480	1 513	Afrique subsaharienne
617	443	351	604	867	981	1 077	1 141	Afrique subsaharienne sans l'Afrique du Sud
2 114	2 487	4 135	4 907	7 093	8 670	9 618	9 514	Économies en développement : Amérique
2 464	2 599	4 644	5 804	6 086	6 928	7 641	7 765	Amérique centrale et Grandes Antilles sans Porto Rico
1 211	1 374	2 051	2 612	3 456	3 716	4 050	4 304	Amérique centrale et Grandes Antilles sans le Mexique et Porto Rico
2 147	2 516	4 226	4 986	7 250	8 919	9 907	9 776	Amérique du Sud et Amérique centrale
2 279	2 335	3 986	4 062	6 642	7 935	8 476	9 258	Amérique du Sud sans le Brésil
561	759	1 228	1 926	3 050	3 593	4 149	4 408	Économies en développement : Asie
797	1 674	2 660	3 538	4 325	5 178	5 794	6 016	Asie orientale et Asie du Sud-Est sans la Chine
604	569	610	930	1 447	1 643	1 925	1 979	Asie méridionale sans l'Inde

Source :

Calculs du secrétariat de la CNUCED, basés sur ONU DAES Division de statistique, *National Accounts Main Aggregates Database*

Notes :

(1) PIB par dépenses, aux prix et taux de change courants.

8

8.2.1 Annual average growth rates of total and per capita real gross domestic product of countries and geographical regions

Region, country or territory	Total real gross domestic product (1) / Produit intérieur brut réel total (1) Percentage / En pourcentage										
	80 -89	92 -00	00 -10	04 -07	05 -12 (e)	08 -12 (e)	2005	2009	2010	2011	2012 (e)
WORLD	3.3	3.1	2.8	3.9	2.0	2.0	3.5	-2.1	4.0	2.7	2.2
DEVELOPING ECONOMIES	3.5	4.8	6.1	7.5	5.7	5.5	6.8	2.7	7.7	5.8	4.7
TRANSITION ECONOMIES	3.4	-2.4	5.7	7.9	3.2	1.9	6.5	-6.5	4.4	4.5	3.1
DEVELOPED ECONOMIES	3.2	2.9	1.6	2.6	0.6	0.6	2.4	-3.7	2.5	1.4	1.2
Developing economies: Africa	1.8	3.1	5.3	5.9	4.2	3.4	5.9	2.8	4.8	1.0	5.3
Eastern Africa	2.6	3.4	5.4	6.4	6.7	7.3	6.1	5.4	6.9	6.4	11.3
Burundi	4.3	-2.9	4.4	4.3	6.1	4.0	0.9	3.5	3.9	4.2	4.4
Comoros	3.0	1.1	1.9	1.9	1.6	2.1	4.2	1.8	2.1	2.2	2.5
Djibouti	0.4	1.0	5.0	7.5	5.4	4.4	3.2	5.0	3.5	4.8	4.7
Eritrea	_	5.7	0.2	0.8	1.1	5.3	2.6	3.9	2.2	8.7	6.5
Ethiopia (...1991)	1.7										
Ethiopia	_	5.3	8.9	11.3	10.6	10.3	11.8	8.8	12.6	11.2	7.0
Kenya	4.3	2.5	4.4	6.4	4.3	4.5	5.9	2.7	5.8	4.4	4.5
Madagascar	0.8	2.8	3.4	5.3	2.2	0.2	4.6	-4.1	0.4	1.6	2.3
Malawi	2.0	3.4	5.7	5.7	7.4	6.6	3.3	8.9	6.7	4.5	7.5
Mauritius	6.2	5.1	4.2	4.2	4.4	3.8	1.8	3.3	4.1	4.1	3.1
Mozambique	-1.5	8.7	7.8	8.2	7.0	6.9	8.4	6.3	6.8	7.1	7.5
Rwanda	2.1	3.0	8.0	8.7	8.2	7.6	9.3	6.2	7.2	8.6	7.9
Seychelles	3.7	4.8	2.7	8.9	4.2	4.4	8.0	0.5	6.7	4.9	4.0
Somalia	1.7	-1.6	2.9	2.6	2.6	2.6	3.0	2.6	2.6	2.6	2.6
Uganda	3.0	7.6	7.5	8.2	6.5	4.9	10.0	4.2	6.3	4.1	4.6
United Republic of Tanzania	2.4	4.0	7.0	7.0	6.8	6.6	7.3	6.0	7.0	6.4	6.8
Zambia	1.4	0.8	5.6	5.9	6.3	6.5	5.2	6.1	7.1	6.6	5.8
Zimbabwe	3.3	1.7	-2.1	-3.6	4.7	9.9	-4.1	16.9	9.6	10.3	3.1
Middle Africa	2.5	2.9	8.3	10.7	6.6	4.5	10.8	2.7	4.4	4.6	6.2
Angola	3.6	5.0	13.0	20.5	9.3	4.2	20.5	2.4	3.5	3.9	7.5
Cameroon	1.5	3.6	3.2	3.0	3.2	3.5	2.3	1.9	3.2	4.1	4.5
Central African Republic	1.2	2.5	1.3	3.3	2.9	3.0	2.4	1.7	3.0	3.3	3.8
Chad	6.7	3.0	8.7	2.4	4.4	7.4	7.9	4.1	14.6	3.6	6.2
Congo	4.0	1.2	4.4	4.2	5.2	6.2	7.6	7.5	8.7	4.5	3.7
Dem. Rep. of the Congo	2.2	-3.6	5.5	6.4	5.7	5.9	7.8	2.8	7.2	6.9	5.8
Equatorial Guinea	2.3	28.5	16.6	11.5	8.5	4.0	8.9	4.6	-0.8	7.1	6.3
Gabon	0.5	2.1	1.8	2.3	3.0	4.2	5.6	-0.4	5.6	5.8	4.7
Sao Tome and Principe	-1.2	1.7	5.6	6.4	5.9	4.8	3.1	4.8	4.5	4.9	5.0
Northern Africa	2.9	3.3	4.9	5.3	2.9	1.2	5.5	3.8	4.5	-5.8	4.5
Algeria	2.9	2.5	3.9	3.2	2.7	2.9	5.1	2.4	3.3	2.9	2.8
Egypt	7.7	4.8	5.1	6.2	5.0	3.3	4.5	4.6	5.2	1.8	1.6
Libya	-3.4	0.8	5.2	7.3	-5.3	-12.6	10.3	-0.7	4.2	-61.3	100.7
Morocco (2)	4.2	2.9	4.9	4.8	4.4	3.8	3.0	4.8	3.7	4.1	2.5
Sudan (...2011)	2.2	5.9	6.7	7.0	_	_	9.0	10.0	8.6	-3.9	_
Tunisia	3.2	4.7	4.7	5.3	3.4	1.7	4.0	3.1	3.5	-1.5	2.4
Southern Africa	1.5	2.9	3.9	5.4	2.8	2.1	5.0	-1.6	3.1	3.2	2.6
Botswana	11.3	7.2	4.1	4.0	3.1	3.6	1.7	-4.8	7.0	5.7	4.2
Lesotho	3.7	3.7	3.7	4.0	4.5	4.3	2.7	2.9	5.6	4.2	4.0
Namibia	1.0	3.7	5.1	5.2	4.0	3.7	2.5	-0.7	6.6	3.6	4.0
South Africa	1.4	2.7	3.9	5.5	2.8	2.0	5.3	-1.5	2.9	3.1	2.5
Swaziland	6.1	3.2	2.5	3.1	2.0	1.4	2.5	1.2	1.9	1.3	1.0
Western Africa	-0.5	3.1	6.6	5.5	6.0	6.3	5.8	5.5	6.8	6.5	6.1
Benin	3.4	5.3	3.8	3.7	3.6	2.9	2.9	2.7	2.6	3.1	3.4
Burkina Faso	2.6	6.0	5.9	6.3	5.3	5.7	8.7	3.0	7.9	5.1	6.0
Cape Verde	5.6	7.9	6.3	8.6	5.9	4.8	6.5	3.6	5.4	5.0	4.8
Côte d'Ivoire	1.1	4.1	1.1	1.3	1.8	1.5	1.7	3.8	3.0	-4.7	7.0
Gambia	3.4	3.0	3.8	1.8	4.8	4.5	-0.9	6.3	6.1	5.5	-1.0
Ghana	2.6	4.3	5.7	5.6	7.6	8.9	6.2	4.7	6.6	15.1	7.4
Guinea	3.0	4.6	2.4	1.8	2.4	2.6	3.0	-0.1	1.9	4.2	4.0
Guinea-Bissau	2.8	-0.5	2.9	3.6	3.9	3.2	4.0	7.9	1.6	4.3	-0.5
Liberia	-0.4	16.7	2.0	9.5	8.4	7.9	5.3	7.8	7.3	8.2	8.4
Mali	3.8	4.4	5.3	5.2	3.8	2.6	6.1	4.5	5.8	2.7	-4.0
Mauritania	1.4	2.9	5.5	10.5	3.7	4.2	9.0	0.1	5.6	5.1	4.8
Niger	-1.9	3.6	4.5	5.5	5.0	4.8	7.4	-0.7	8.2	2.3	9.1
Nigeria	-2.3	2.3	8.6	6.3	6.9	7.2	6.5	6.9	7.8	7.4	6.4
Senegal	3.2	4.1	4.2	4.1	3.4	3.3	5.6	2.1	4.1	2.8	3.9
Sierra Leone	2.5	-9.5	7.9	5.4	6.6	8.2	4.3	3.2	5.3	6.0	22.0
Togo	1.3	3.1	2.4	2.6	3.4	4.1	1.2	3.4	4.0	4.9	4.0

For sources and notes, see end-of table.

8.2.1 Taux de croissance annuels moyens du produit intérieur brut réel total et par habitant des pays et des régions géographiques

Per capita real gross domestic product (1) / Produit intérieur brut réel par habitant (1) Percentage / En pourcentage											Régions, pays ou territoires
80 -89	92 -00	00 -10	04 -07	05 -12 (e)	08 -12 (e)	2005	2009	2010	2011	2012 (e)	
1.5	1.7	1.6	2.7	0.8	0.8	2.3	-3.2	2.8	1.2	1.1	**MONDE**
1.3	3.0	4.6	6.0	4.3	4.0	5.4	1.3	6.3	4.0	3.3	ÉCONOMIES EN DÉVELOPPEMENT
2.5	-2.3	5.8	7.9	3.1	1.8	6.7	-6.7	4.3	4.4	3.0	ÉCONOMIES EN TRANSITION
2.6	2.3	1.0	2.0	0.1	0.1	1.8	-4.3	2.0	0.9	0.7	ÉCONOMIES DÉVELOPPÉES
-1.0	0.7	2.9	3.5	1.8	1.0	3.5	0.4	2.5	-1.2	2.9	Économies en développement : Afrique
-0.4	0.7	2.8	3.8	3.7	4.0	3.5	2.7	4.2	3.6	5.2	*Afrique orientale*
1.0	-3.8	1.5	1.2	3.2	1.5	-2.0	0.6	1.3	1.9	2.3	Burundi
0.1	-1.5	-0.8	-0.8	-1.1	-0.5	1.5	-0.9	-0.6	-0.4	-0.1	Comores
-4.5	-1.7	3.0	5.5	3.5	2.5	1.3	3.0	1.6	2.9	2.7	Djibouti
	3.8	-3.4	-2.7	-2.0	2.2	-1.3	0.8	-0.8	5.5	3.3	Érythrée
-1.4	–	–	–	–	–	–	–	–		–	Éthiopie (…1991)
	2.2	6.4	8.8	8.2	7.9	9.2	6.5	10.2	8.8	4.8	Éthiopie
0.5	-0.3	1.7	3.7	1.7	1.8	3.2	0.1	3.0	1.6	1.7	Kenya
-1.8	-0.4	0.3	2.2	-0.7	-2.6	1.5	-6.9	-2.4	-1.3	-0.5	Madagascar
-2.2	1.4	2.8	2.7	4.2	3.3	0.5	5.6	3.4	1.3	4.1	Malawi
5.3	3.9	3.3	3.4	3.8	3.2	0.9	2.7	3.5	3.5	2.5	Maurice
-2.5	5.5	5.2	5.5	4.6	4.5	5.7	3.9	4.3	4.7	5.1	Mozambique
-1.6	-0.7	5.3	6.0	5.1	4.4	7.0	3.1	4.1	5.4	4.8	Rwanda
2.4	3.7	1.7	7.9	3.6	3.9	6.9	-0.1	6.2	4.5	3.7	Seychelles
1.8	-3.2	0.5	0.4	0.3	0.2	0.7	0.4	0.3	0.1	0.1	Somalie
-0.4	4.3	4.1	4.8	3.1	1.6	6.5	0.9	2.9	0.8	1.4	Ouganda
-0.7	1.2	4.1	4.1	3.7	3.4	4.4	3.0	3.9	3.2	3.6	République-Unie de Tanzanie
-1.7	-1.8	3.0	3.3	3.5	3.5	2.7	3.2	4.1	3.5	2.7	Zambie
-0.5	0.1	-2.1	-3.3	4.3	8.7	-3.9	16.7	8.8	8.8	1.0	Zimbabwe
-0.5	0.1	5.4	7.7	3.9 (e)	1.8 (e)	7.7	0.0	1.7	2.0	3.5	*Afrique centrale*
0.4	2.0	9.5	16.8	6.2	1.3	16.6	-0.5	0.6	1.0	4.6	Angola
-1.4	1.1	1.0	0.7	0.9	1.3	0.0	-0.3	1.0	1.9	2.3	Cameroun
-1.4	0.2	-0.4	1.6	1.0	1.0	0.7	-0.2	1.1	1.3	1.8	République centrafricaine
3.8	-0.2	5.4	-0.6	1.6	4.6	4.5	1.4	11.6	0.9	3.5	Tchad
1.0	-1.6	1.8	1.5	2.5	3.6	5.0	4.6	6.0	2.0	1.4	Congo
-0.8	-6.3	2.5	3.4	2.9	3.1	4.7	0.0	4.3	4.1	3.0	Rép. dém. du Congo
-3.4	24.4	13.2	8.3	5.5	1.2	5.7	1.7	-3.5	4.1	3.4	Guinée équatoriale
-2.6	-0.7	-0.2	0.4	1.1	2.3	3.6	-2.2	3.6	3.8	2.7	Gabon
-3.2	-0.2	3.9	4.8	4.1	2.9	1.5	3.1	2.7	3.0	3.0	Sao Tomé-et-Principe
0.2	1.5	3.1	3.5	1.6	0.4	3.7	2.0	2.8	-7.4	7.9	*Afrique septentrionale*
-0.1	0.7	2.3	1.7	1.2	1.4	3.5	0.9	1.8	1.4	1.3	Algérie
5.2	3.0	3.2	4.3	3.2	1.5	2.6	2.8	3.3	0.0	-0.1	Égypte
-6.9	-1.0	3.1	5.0	-6.9	-13.7	8.1	2.5	2.7	-61.7	99.2	Libye
1.7	1.5	3.8	3.7	3.3	2.8	1.9	3.7	2.6	3.1	1.5	Maroc (2)
-0.6	3.3	4.2	4.4	–	–	6.5	7.2	6.0	-6.2	–	Soudan (…2011)
0.7	3.3	3.7	4.2	2.2	0.6	3.0	2.0	2.4	-2.5	1.3	Tunisie
-0.9	1.0	2.7	4.2	1.9	1.3	3.8	-2.5	2.3	2.5	1.9	*Afrique australe*
7.7	4.7	2.7	2.6	1.7	2.3	0.5	-6.1	5.7	4.5	3.1	Botswana
1.4	1.8	2.7	3.0	3.4	3.2	1.8	1.8	4.5	3.1	2.9	Lesotho
-2.3	0.8	3.2	3.3	2.1	1.8	0.7	-2.6	4.7	1.8	2.2	Namibie
-1.0	0.9	2.7	4.3	1.9	1.3	4.0	-2.4	2.1	2.5	1.9	Afrique du Sud
2.3	1.1	1.4	2.0	0.6	-0.1	1.6	-0.3	0.3	-0.2	-0.4	Swaziland
-3.1	0.5	3.9	2.8	3.3	3.6	3.1	2.9	4.1	3.8	3.4	*Afrique occidentale*
0.6	2.2	0.7	0.6	0.6	0.0	-0.3	-0.3	-0.3	0.3	0.6	Bénin
0.0	3.1	2.8	3.2	2.3	2.6	5.5	-0.1	4.8	2.0	2.9	Burkina Faso
4.0	5.5	5.0	7.4	5.0	3.9	5.1	2.7	4.5	4.1	3.8	Cap-Vert
-2.8	1.4	-0.6	-0.4	-0.1	-0.5	0.1	1.9	1.0	-6.7	4.7	Côte d'Ivoire
-1.0	0.1	0.8	-1.1	1.9	1.7	-3.7	3.4	3.2	2.6	-3.6	Gambie
-0.5	1.7	3.2	3.1	5.1	6.3	3.6	2.2	4.1	12.5	5.0	Ghana
0.5	1.5	0.6	0.0	0.3	0.3	1.3	-2.2	-0.3	1.8	1.4	Guinée
0.9	-2.4	0.8	1.5	1.7	1.1	2.0	5.7	-0.5	2.2	-2.6	Guinée-Bissau
-1.7	11.5	-1.4	5.3	3.9	4.0	2.3	2.8	3.0	4.7	5.4	Libéria
2.0	1.6	2.1	2.0	0.7	-0.5	2.9	1.3	2.6	-0.4	-6.8	Mali
-1.4	0.0	2.7	7.6	1.2	1.7	6.0	-2.3	3.1	2.7	2.4	Mauritanie
-4.6	0.1	0.9	1.8	1.3	1.1	3.7	-4.2	4.5	-1.3	5.3	Niger
-4.8	-0.1	6.0	3.7	4.2	4.6	3.9	4.3	5.2	4.7	3.7	Nigéria
0.2	1.4	1.4	1.4	0.7	0.6	2.8	-0.6	1.4	0.1	1.2	Sénégal
0.0	-9.9	4.2	1.9	4.1	5.9	0.3	0.9	3.0	3.7	19.4	Sierra Leone
-2.0	0.2	0.1	0.3	1.2	2.0	-1.0	1.2	1.8	2.7	1.9	Togo

Pour les sources et les notes, se reporter à la fin du tableau.

8

8.2.1 Annual average growth rates of total and per capita real gross domestic product of countries and geographical regions

Region, country or territory	Total real gross domestic product (1) / Produit intérieur brut réel total (1) Percentage / En pourcentage										
	80 -89	92 -00	00 -10	04 -07	05 -12 (e)	08 -12 (e)	2005	2009	2010	2011	2012 (e)
Developing economies: America	**1.8**	**3.1**	**3.6**	**5.3**	**3.5**	**3.2**	**4.6**	**-1.9**	**5.9**	**4.3**	**3.0**
Caribbean	*2.6*	*3.6*	*4.6*	*7.7*	*3.2*	*2.1*	*7.6*	*0.0*	*2.9*	*2.5*	*2.5*
Anguilla	7.7	5.2	6.1	16.0	-0.7	-3.5	13.1	-18.3	-3.7	4.0	2.1
Antigua and Barbuda	6.9	3.7	3.8	10.1	-2.1	-6.2	6.1	-11.9	-7.9	-5.0	0.9
Aruba	11.0	4.7	0.0	1.2	-1.7	-1.1	1.2	-6.9	-5.7	8.9	-2.5
Bahamas	4.5	4.6	0.6	2.5	-0.5	0.0	3.4	-4.9	0.2	1.6	2.5
Barbados	1.7	3.0	1.5	4.0	0.2	-0.4	4.0	-4.1	0.2	0.6	0.9
British Virgin Islands	5.9	14.8	1.8	4.9	2.7	3.4	14.3	4.3	4.5	2.5	2.4
Cayman Islands	8.9	8.1	1.5	4.7	-1.1	-2.0	6.5	-7.8	-3.3	1.1	1.5
Cuba	4.0	2.2	6.1	10.3	4.1	2.4	11.2	1.4	2.4	2.7	3.0
Curaçao											3.0
Dominica	5.2	2.0	3.2	3.4	3.0	1.0	-0.5	-0.9	2.1	0.5	2.0
Dominican Republic	3.0	6.3	5.6	9.6	6.0	5.1	9.3	3.5	7.8	4.5	3.8
Grenada	5.4	5.2	1.4	4.0	-0.6	-1.2	12.0	-6.8	0.4	0.0	0.4
Haiti	0.1	1.1	0.6	2.4	1.3	1.0	1.8	2.9	-5.4	5.6	2.5
Jamaica	1.5	0.3	1.0	1.8	-0.4	-0.6	0.9	-3.1	-1.4	1.5	-0.2
Montserrat	2.8	-11.2	2.1	2.7	1.1	-0.2	3.2	0.4	-3.8	1.8	2.0
Netherlands Antilles	-0.9	0.8	1.5	2.1			1.1	-0.5	0.0		
Saint Kitts and Nevis	6.0	4.9	2.9	5.4	-0.3	-2.3	9.9	-6.8	-2.4	0.0	-0.8
Saint Lucia	7.7	2.7	3.2	4.5	1.8	0.7	8.5	0.1	0.4	1.3	0.9
Saint Vincent and the Grenadines	6.2	3.2	3.3	5.4	0.7	-0.9	2.0	-2.2	-2.8	0.1	1.5
Trinidad and Tobago	-3.7	5.9	6.6	8.5	1.8	-0.2	6.2	-3.5	2.5	-1.4	1.0
Turks and Caicos Islands	10.7	9.2	8.7	14.3	4.3	1.8	14.4	-11.1	7.5	6.1	1.1
Central America	*0.8*	*3.3*	*2.4*	*4.2*	*2.0*	*2.4*	*3.4*	*-5.4*	*5.2*	*4.0*	*4.0*
Belize	3.8	4.6	4.0	3.2	2.3	2.4	3.1	0.0	2.7	2.4	4.2
Costa Rica	2.8	5.0	4.9	7.7	3.9	3.3	5.9	-1.0	4.7	4.2	4.5
El Salvador	0.3	4.2	2.2	3.8	1.1	0.5	3.6	-3.1	1.4	1.5	1.6
Guatemala	0.4	4.1	3.6	5.0	3.4	2.8	3.3	0.5	2.9	3.9	3.3
Honduras	2.7	2.9	4.6	6.3	3.0	2.2	6.1	-2.1	2.8	3.6	3.5
Mexico	0.8	3.3	2.1	4.0	1.7	2.3	3.3	-6.0	5.3	3.9	3.9
Nicaragua	-1.7	4.6	3.1	4.0	2.9	3.2	4.3	-1.5	4.5	4.7	4.0
Panama		4.2	7.0	9.2	8.7	8.3	7.2	3.9	7.6	10.6	10.5
South America	*2.2*	*2.9*	*4.3*	*5.8*	*4.3*	*3.7*	*5.1*	*-0.2*	*6.5*	*4.5*	*2.5*
Argentina	-0.2	3.0	5.6	8.7	6.3	5.9	9.2	0.9	9.2	8.9	1.9
Bolivia (Plurinational State of)	-0.7	4.0	4.1	4.6	4.7	4.4	4.4	3.4	4.1	5.2	4.7
Brazil	3.1	2.9	3.7	4.4	3.8	3.1	3.2	-0.3	7.5	2.7	0.9
Chile	2.5	5.7	4.5	5.7	4.0	4.5	6.2	-1.0	6.1	6.0	5.6
Colombia	3.5	2.4	4.5	6.2	4.4	4.2	4.7	1.7	4.0	5.9	4.4
Ecuador	1.9	1.9	4.6	4.2	4.2	4.4	5.7	0.4	3.6	7.8	4.8
Guyana	-3.2	4.6	2.2	3.0	3.8	3.9	-2.0	3.3	3.6	4.6	3.8
Paraguay	2.5	1.7	3.8	4.6	4.5	4.3	2.9	-3.8	15.0	3.8	-1.8
Peru	0.4	4.8	6.1	7.8	6.8	6.1	6.8	0.9	8.8	6.9	6.2
Suriname	1.0	1.4	5.0	5.0	4.2	3.9	3.9	3.0	4.1	4.5	3.6
Uruguay	0.7	2.8	3.6	5.8	5.7	5.6	7.5	2.4	8.9	5.7	3.8
Venezuela (Bolivarian Rep. of)	0.6	0.9	4.7	9.7	3.0	1.1	10.3	-3.2	-1.5	4.0	5.1
Developing economies: Asia	**5.3**	**5.9**	**7.1**	**8.5**	**6.7**	**6.5**	**7.8**	**4.3**	**8.7**	**6.8**	**5.1**
Eastern Asia	*9.7*	*7.6*	*8.3*	*9.9*	*8.0*	*7.5*	*8.6*	*5.9*	*9.5*	*7.6*	*6.0*
China	10.8	9.9	10.8	12.7	10.3	9.2	11.3	9.2	10.3	9.2	7.8
China, Hong Kong SAR	7.3	2.8	4.6	6.8	3.4	3.3	7.1	-2.6	7.0	5.0	1.4
China, Macao SAR	7.4	0.6	12.1	12.6	12.4	16.3	8.5	1.7	27.0	20.7	10.0
China, Taiwan Province of	7.8	5.7	4.1	5.4	3.6	4.2	4.7	-1.8	10.7	4.0	1.3
Korea, Dem. People's Rep. of	2.7	-2.3	1.2	0.3	0.2	0.1	3.8	-0.9	-0.5	-0.1	2.5
Korea, Republic of	10.1	5.8	4.1	4.8	3.4	3.4	4.0	0.3	6.3	3.6	2.0
Mongolia	6.3	3.0	7.2	8.7	8.0	9.1	7.3	-1.3	6.4	17.3	12.5
Southern Asia	*4.6*	*5.3*	*7.1*	*8.5*	*6.5*	*6.3*	*8.2*	*7.0*	*8.3*	*5.8*	*3.3*
Afghanistan	-1.0	-2.2	11.7	11.4	8.6	7.4	9.9	17.2	3.2	5.7	7.0
Bangladesh	3.7	4.9	5.9	6.4	6.2	6.2	6.0	5.7	6.1	6.7	6.2
Bhutan	10.4	6.1	8.5	10.1	8.8	8.2	7.1	6.7	11.8	5.9	8.0
India	5.7	6.3	7.8	9.4	7.4	7.3	9.3	8.2	9.6	6.9	4.0
Iran (Islamic Rep. of)	1.5	3.3	5.5	6.5	3.7	2.7	5.3	4.0	5.9	2.0	-1.9
Maldives	11.9	8.2	7.2	7.7	6.6	3.7 *	-8.7	-4.7	5.7	7.5	4.0
Nepal	4.6	4.9	3.9	3.4	4.5	4.4	3.1	4.5	4.8	3.9	4.2
Pakistan	6.4	3.4	5.0	6.5	3.7	3.5	7.7	3.6	3.5	3.0	4.0
Sri Lanka	4.1	5.3	5.7	7.0	6.5	6.9	6.2	3.5	8.0	8.3	6.5
South-Eastern Asia	*4.7*	*4.2*	*5.4*	*6.2*	*5.0*	*5.1*	*5.7*	*1.4*	*8.0*	*4.5*	*5.4*
Brunei Darussalam	-2.5	1.7	1.2	1.9	0.6	1.3	0.4	-1.8	2.6	2.2	1.2
Cambodia	6.6	6.5	8.7	11.3	6.1	5.1	13.3	0.1	6.0	7.1	6.0

For sources and notes, see end of table.

426

Per capita real gross domestic product (1) / Produit intérieur brut réel par habitant (1) Percentage / En pourcentage											Régions, pays ou territoires
80 -89	92 -00	00 -10	04 -07	05 -12 (e)	08 -12 (e)	2005	2009	2010	2011	2012 (e)	
-0.3	1.4	2.4	4.0	2.3	2.1	3.3	-3.0	4.7	3.1	1.8	**Économies en développement : Amérique**
1.1	*2.4*	*3.6*	*6.8*	*2.4*	*1.4*	*6.6*	*-0.8*	*2.1*	*1.9*	*1.8*	*Caraïbes*
5.7	2.6	2.6	12.4	-2.9	-5.4	9.0	-20.0	-5.6	2.1	0.4	Anguilla
8.4	1.2	2.4	8.8	-3.2	-7.1	4.8	-12.8	-8.9	-6.0	-0.1	Antigua-et-Barbuda
10.8	1.3	-1.7	-0.5	-2.7	-1.8	-0.8	-7.8	-6.4	8.2	-2.9	Aruba
2.4	3.1	-0.8	1.0	-1.8	-1.2	1.9	-6.2	-1.1	0.4	1.3	Bahamas
1.3	2.7	1.3	3.8	-0.1	-0.6	3.8	-4.3	0.0	0.4	0.7	Barbade
1.5	12.4	0.5	3.6	1.5	2.3	12.9	3.2	3.4	1.3	1.4	Îles Vierges britanniques
4.4	3.7	-1.9	1.8	-2.3	-2.8	2.4	-8.6	-4.2	0.2	0.6	Îles Caïmanes
3.3	1.8	6.0	10.2	4.1	2.5	11.0	1.5	2.4	2.7	3.0	Cuba
										2.1	Curaçao
5.9	2.3	3.5	3.7	3.3	1.2	-0.2	-0.6	2.3	0.7	2.0	Dominique
0.8	4.5	4.1	8.0	4.6	3.7	7.7	2.1	6.3	3.1	2.5	République dominicaine
4.2	4.7	1.1	3.7	-0.9	-1.6	11.7	-7.1	0.0	0.4	0.0	Grenade
-2.2	-0.8	-0.9	1.0	0.0	-0.3	0.3	1.5	-6.6	4.2	1.2	Haïti
0.4	-0.7	0.4	1.3	-0.8	-1.0	0.3	-3.5	-1.8	1.1	-0.6	Jamaïque
4.0	-1.5	-0.6	-0.4	0.1	-0.9	-1.9	0.1	-4.5	0.8	1.1	Montserrat
-1.9	1.7	0.3	0.7			-0.2	-2.0	-1.3			Antilles néerlandaises
6.7	3.5	1.5	4.1	-1.5	-3.5	8.5	-8.0	-3.7	-1.3	-2.0	Saint-Kitts-et-Nevis
6.0	1.3	2.2	3.4	0.8	-0.3	7.4	-0.9	-0.6	0.3	-0.1	Sainte-Lucie
5.5	3.2	3.1	5.3	0.6	-1.0	1.8	-2.3	-2.8	0.1	1.5	Saint-Vincent-et-les Grenadines
-5.0	5.3	6.2	8.1	1.4	-0.6	5.8	-3.9	2.1	-1.7	0.7	Trinité-et-Tobago
6.0	4.7	1.1	6.9	0.5	-0.7	5.6	-14.2	4.4	3.9	-0.4	Îles Turques et Caïques
-1.3	*1.5*	*0.9*	*2.8*	*0.6*	*1.0*	*2.0*	*-6.7*	*3.7*	*2.6*	*2.6*	*Amérique centrale*
0.9	1.8	1.7	1.0	0.3	0.3	0.8	-2.0	0.7	0.3	2.2	Belize
0.0	2.5	3.1	5.9	2.4	1.8	4.1	-2.5	3.1	2.7	3.1	Costa Rica
-1.0	3.3	1.8	3.4	0.6	0.0	3.2	-3.6	0.8	0.9	1.0	El Salvador
-2.0	1.8	1.1	2.5	0.8	0.2	0.7	-1.9	0.4	1.3	0.7	Guatemala
-0.4	0.5	2.5	4.2	1.0	0.1	4.0	-4.1	0.7	1.6	1.4	Honduras
-1.2	1.5	0.9	2.7	0.5	1.0	2.0	-7.2	4.0	2.7	2.7	Mexique
-4.0	2.5	1.8	2.7	1.5	1.8	3.0	-2.8	3.1	3.2	2.5	Nicaragua
	2.1	5.2	7.3	7.0	6.6	5.3	2.2	5.9	8.9	8.9	Panama
0.1	*1.3*	*3.0*	*4.5*	*3.2*	*2.6*	*3.8*	*-1.3*	*5.4*	*3.4*	*1.4*	*Amérique du Sud*
-1.7	1.7	4.6	7.8	5.4	5.0	8.2	0.0	8.2	7.9	1.0	Argentine
-2.9	1.8	2.2	2.8	3.0	2.8	2.6	1.7	2.5	3.5	3.0	Bolivie (État plurinational de)
0.9	1.3	2.6	3.3	2.9	2.3	2.0	-1.2	6.6	1.8	0.0	Brésil
0.9	4.1	3.4	4.6	3.0	3.5	5.1	-2.0	5.1	5.0	4.7	Chili
1.3	0.6	2.9	4.6	2.9	2.8	3.1	0.2	2.6	4.5	3.1	Colombie
-0.7	0.2	3.0	2.6	2.7	3.0	4.0	-1.1	2.1	6.3	3.4	Équateur
-2.4	4.4	1.9	2.7	3.6	3.7	-2.3	3.1	3.4	4.4	3.6	Guyana
-0.4	-0.6	1.9	2.7	2.7	2.5	0.9	-5.5	13.0	2.0	-3.5	Paraguay
-1.9	3.0	4.9	6.6	5.7	4.9	5.6	-0.2	7.6	5.7	5.0	Pérou
0.0	0.0	3.7	3.8	3.2	3.0	2.7	2.1	3.2	3.6	2.7	Suriname
0.1	2.1	3.5	5.7	5.4	5.2	7.4	2.1	8.5	5.3	3.5	Uruguay
-2.1	-1.2	2.9	7.8	1.4	-0.5	8.4	-4.8	-3.1	2.3	3.5	Venezuela (Rép. bolivarienne du)
3.2	4.3	5.9	7.3	5.5	5.2	6.6	3.2	7.5	5.1	4.0	**Économies en développement : Asie**
8.0	*6.6*	*7.7*	*9.3*	*7.3*	*6.5*	*8.0*	*5.4*	*9.0*	*5.4*	*5.6*	*Asie orientale*
9.1	8.9	10.2	12.1	9.5	8.2	10.7	8.7	9.8	6.8	7.3	Chine
5.9	1.0	4.3	6.5	2.6	2.3	7.0	-3.5	6.1	4.0	0.4	Chine (RAS de Hong Kong)
3.2	-1.0	9.5	9.9	9.8	13.7	6.0	-0.7	24.1	18.1	7.7	Chine (RAS de Macao)
6.3	4.8	3.6	3.2	3.2	3.9	4.3	-2.1	10.4	3.6	0.9	Province chinoise de Taiwan
1.1	-3.5	0.6	-0.2	-0.3	-0.3	3.1	-1.4	-0.9	-0.5	2.1	Corée, Rép. populaire dém. de
8.6	5.1	3.6	4.3	2.9	3.0	3.5	-0.2	5.8	3.2	1.6	Corée, République de
3.4	2.2	5.8	7.1	6.3	7.4	5.9	-2.9	4.7	15.4	10.8	Mongolie
2.2	*3.3*	*5.4*	*6.8*	*4.9*	*4.8*	*6.5*	*5.5*	*6.7*	*4.3*	*1.9*	*Asie méridionale*
0.9	-6.6	8.2	8.2	5.7	4.4	6.2	14.4	0.5	2.6	3.7	Afghanistan
1.0	2.8	4.5	5.0	5.0	5.0	4.5	4.6	4.9	5.4	4.9	Bangladesh
7.3	5.4	6.0	7.6	6.8	6.4	4.4	4.9	9.9	4.1	6.2	Bhoutan
3.3	4.4	6.2	7.8	5.9	5.9	7.7	6.7	8.0	5.4	2.6	Inde
-2.1	1.6	4.2	5.2	2.5	1.6	4.0	2.7	4.7	0.9	-3.0	Iran (Rép. islamique d')
8.1	6.0	5.6	6.2	5.2	2.3	-10.0	-6.0	4.3	6.1	2.6	Maldives
2.1	2.3	1.8	1.4	2.6	2.5	1.0	2.7	3.0	2.1	2.4	Népal
2.9	0.7	3.2	4.6	1.8	1.6	5.8	1.7	1.7	1.1	2.1	Pakistan
2.6	4.6	4.5	5.8	5.5	5.9	5.0	2.6	7.0	7.3	5.6	Sri Lanka
2.5	*2.5*	*4.1*	*4.9*	*3.8*	*3.9*	*4.4*	*0.3*	*6.8*	*3.3*	*4.2*	*Asie du Sud-Est*
-5.3	-0.8	-0.8	-0.1	-1.6	-1.1	-1.6	-3.6	0.8	-1.6	-0.5	Brunéi Darussalam
2.4	3.9	7.3	10.0	4.9	3.9	11.9	-1.0	4.8	5.8	4.7	Cambodge

Pour les sources et les notes, se reporter à la fin du tableau.

8

8.2.1 Annual average growth rates of total and per capita real gross domestic product of countries and geographical regions

Region, country or territory	Total real gross domestic product (1) / Produit intérieur brut réel total (1) Percentage / En pourcentage										
	80 -89	92 -00	00 -10	04 -07	05 -12 (e)	08 -12 (e)	2005	2009	2010	2011	2012 (e)
Indonesia (…2002)	5.7	2.9	–	–	–	–	–	–	–	–	–
Indonesia	–	–	–	5.8	5.9	6.0	5.7	4.6	6.2	6.5	6.2
Lao People's Dem. Rep.	4.9	6.5	7.2	7.8	7.9	7.9	6.8	7.5	8.1	8.0	7.9
Malaysia	4.9	6.1	5.0	5.7	4.4	4.4	5.3	-1.5	7.2	5.1	5.6
Myanmar	0.9	7.2	12.3	12.9	9.7	7.8	13.6	10.6	10.4	5.5	5.0
Philippines	0.5	3.7	4.9	5.5	4.8	4.9	4.8	1.1	7.6	3.7	6.6
Singapore	6.7	6.7	6.0	8.4	5.4	5.8	7.4	-1.0	14.8	4.9	1.3
Thailand	7.0	2.7	4.6	4.9	3.1	3.3	4.2	-1.1	7.5	0.1	6.4
Timor-Leste	–	–	–	37.2	6.6	3.1	54.3	-7.0	-1.5	10.6	10.0
Viet Nam	5.6	7.8	7.5	8.4	6.5	5.9	8.4	5.3	6.8	5.9	5.0
Western Asia	*1.1*	*4.0*	*5.0*	*6.2*	*4.1*	*4.6*	*6.8*	*-1.7*	*7.0*	*7.0*	*3.8*
Bahrain	-0.7	3.7	6.3	7.5	4.8	3.1	7.9	3.1	4.5	2.2	2.5
Iraq	0.9	16.8	4.2	5.7	6.3	7.2	4.4	5.8	5.9	8.6	8.5
Jordan	2.0	3.8	6.8	8.1	5.2	3.1	8.1	5.5	2.3	2.6	2.9
Kuwait	1.1	3.8	6.8	8.3	3.7	4.1	10.6	-7.8	7.9	8.2	5.0
Lebanon	1.6	3.4	5.0	3.0	6.1	4.6	0.7	9.0	7.0	1.5	1.7
Oman	8.2	3.7	4.9	5.4	6.5	5.2	4.0	1.1	8.1	5.5	4.5
Qatar	1.1	8.5	13.9	17.9	15.5	12.6	7.5	12.0	16.7	13.5	6.2
Saudi Arabia	-2.2	1.8	3.7	3.5	3.8	5.0	5.6	0.1	5.1	7.1	6.8
State of Palestine	2.8	8.1	4.2	1.9	6.6	8.5	8.6	7.4	9.8	9.9	5.4
Syrian Arab Republic	0.9	5.3	5.1	5.6	2.1	-1.7	6.2	5.9	3.4	-2.0	-15.0
Turkey	5.3	3.8	4.7	6.7	3.3	4.6	8.4	-4.8	9.2	8.5	2.2
United Arab Emirates	-2.9	6.3	4.8	6.3	1.9	1.3	4.9	-4.8	1.3	4.2	3.2
Yemen, Arab Republic	5.1	–	–	–	–	–	–	–	–	–	–
Yemen, Democratic	2.4	–	–	–	–	–	–	–	–	–	–
Yemen	–	8.9	4.8	4.4	2.2	0.0	5.1	4.3	7.8	-10.5	1.0
Developing economies: Oceania	3.8	1.9	2.9	3.3	3.3	3.7	3.4	2.3	3.5	4.4	4.2
Cook Islands	4.9	0.7	1.0	1.6	0.0	1.4	-1.1	-3.6	0.2	3.4	5.4
Fiji	1.3	3.1	1.4	2.1	0.3	0.6	5.4	-1.3	-0.2	2.0	1.8
French Polynesia	5.9	1.8	1.9	1.5	1.7	1.7	1.3	1.6	1.6	1.6	2.1
Kiribati	0.8	4.2	1.2	1.1	1.0	1.0	0.0	-2.3	-0.4	3.0	3.5
Marshall Islands	–	-1.0	2.5	1.4	2.3	3.8	2.0	-1.3	5.2	5.0	5.0
Micronesia (Federated States of)	–	0.6	-0.2	0.0	0.2	1.5	2.1	0.7	3.1	1.0	0.8
Nauru	-1.0	-9.6	-1.9	-14.5	5.7	-2.0	-9.8	-18.2	0.0	4.0	4.0
New Caledonia	4.6	1.4	3.6	4.6	3.1	3.0	3.6	2.4	3.5	3.4	2.2
Palau	–	3.2	1.9	3.5	1.7	2.1	5.5	2.9	2.0	1.8	2.0
Papua New Guinea	2.3	2.0	4.0	4.2	7.0	8.0	3.9	6.1	7.6	8.9	9.4
Samoa	1.1	3.5	2.9	3.5	0.6	1.1	5.3	-1.4	1.8	1.4	2.1
Solomon Islands	1.8	1.7	4.8	7.3	4.8	5.4	12.8	-4.7	7.0	10.7	6.0
Tonga	4.6	2.1	0.8	-1.2	1.2	3.0	2.4	2.9	2.7	4.7	1.1
Tuvalu	6.6	4.1	0.7	2.8	1.3	0.1	-4.1	-1.7	-0.5	1.0	1.4
Vanuatu	6.0	2.9	4.0	6.5	4.6	3.5	5.2	3.5	2.2	4.3	4.2
Transition economies	3.4	-2.4	5.7	7.9	3.2	1.9	6.5	-6.5	4.4	4.5	3.1
Albania	1.9	6.3	5.6	5.7	4.3	2.7	5.8	3.3	3.9	2.0	1.2
Armenia	–	4.4	9.4	13.6	2.8	0.4	13.9	-14.1	2.2	4.7	7.1
Azerbaijan	–	-2.1	17.1	29.2	10.8	3.8	26.4	9.3	5.0	0.1	2.2
Belarus	–	0.6	8.0	9.4	6.1	4.2	9.4	0.2	7.7	5.3	1.5
Bosnia and Herzegovina	–	22.2	4.8	6.6	2.1	0.2	8.0	-2.9	0.7	1.7	0.2
Croatia	–	3.6	3.1	4.8	-0.3	-2.2	4.3	-6.9	-1.4	0.0	-1.9
Georgia	–	1.2	6.9	10.3	4.7	4.3	9.6	-3.8	6.3	7.0	6.1
Kazakhstan	–	-2.5	8.3	9.7	5.7	5.6	9.7	1.2	7.3	7.5	5.0
Kyrgyzstan	–	-0.8	4.5	3.7	4.1	1.9	-0.2	2.9	-0.5	5.7	-0.9
Montenegro	–	–	–	–	–	0.4	–	-5.7	2.5	2.5	0.3
Republic of Moldova	–	-6.4	5.3	5.0	3.2	2.9	7.5	-6.0	7.1	6.4	0.6
Russian Federation	–	-2.6	5.4	7.7	2.9	1.6	6.4	-7.8	4.3	4.3	3.4
Serbia and Montenegro	–	-0.2	–	4.9	–	–	5.1	–	–	–	–
Serbia	–	–	–	–	–	0.3	–	-2.7	1.4	2.2	-0.9
SFR of Yugoslavia	1.0	–	–	–	–	–	–	–	–	–	–
Tajikistan	–	-6.8	8.1	7.0	6.6	6.5	6.7	4.0	6.5	7.4	7.5
TFYR of Macedonia	–	1.3	3.3	5.2	2.7	1.2	4.4	-0.9	1.8	3.0	-0.3
Turkmenistan	–	-1.0	8.5	12.0	11.0	10.6	13.0	6.1	9.2	14.7	11.1
Ukraine	–	-7.9	4.8	6.1	0.5	-0.4	2.7	-14.8	4.1	5.2	0.2
USSR	3.8	–	–	–	–	–	–	–	–	–	–
Uzbekistan	–	1.6	7.2	7.9	8.5	8.3	7.0	8.1	8.5	8.3	8.2
Developed economies: America	3.6	3.9	1.8	2.5	0.7	1.1	3.0	-3.1	2.4	1.8	2.2
Bermuda	1.5	3.7	1.9	3.7	-0.3	-1.6	2.0	-4.8	-1.9	0.6	-1.0
Canada	3.3	3.7	2.0	2.7	1.2	1.5	3.0	-2.8	3.2	2.5	1.8
Greenland	2.4	3.2	2.6	4.4	2.3	1.8	3.7	1.4	1.2	2.6	2.0
United States	3.7	3.9	1.7	2.5	0.7	1.0	3.1	-3.1	2.4	1.8	2.2

For sources and notes, see end of table.

428

Per capita real gross domestic product (1) / Produit intérieur brut réel par habitant (1) Percentage / En pourcentage											Régions, pays ou territoires
80 -89	92 -00	00 -10	04 -07	05 -12 (e)	08 -12 (e)	2005	2009	2010	2011	2012 (e)	
3.5	1.4	–	–	–	–	–	–	–	–	–	Indonésie (…2002)
–	–	–	4.6	4.8	4.9	4.4	3.5	5.1	5.4	5.2	Indonésie
2.2	4.1	5.6	6.2	6.3	6.4	5.2	5.9	6.6	6.5	6.4	Rép. dém. populaire lao
2.0	3.5	3.0	3.8	2.7	2.8	3.3	-3.1	5.4	3.4	3.9	Malaisie
-0.9	5.8	11.7	12.2	8.9	7.0	13.0	9.8	9.6	4.6	4.2	Myanmar
-2.2	1.4	3.0	3.6	3.0	3.2	2.8	-0.5	5.8	2.0	4.8	Philippines
4.3	4.0	3.2	4.9	2.2	3.3	4.7	-4.5	11.6	2.8	0.0	Singapour
5.0	1.7	3.6	4.0	2.4	2.7	3.2	-1.8	6.9	-0.5	5.8	Thaïlande
–	–	–	33.4	4.3	0.6	48.8	-8.7	-3.7	7.8	6.9	Timor-Leste
3.3	6.2	6.3	7.2	5.3	4.7	7.3	4.2	5.6	4.8	3.9	Viet Nam
-1.8	*1.7*	*2.4*	*3.5*	*1.6*	*2.2*	*4.1*	*-4.1*	*4.5*	*4.7*	*1.7*	*Asie occidentale*
-3.7	1.0	-1.3	-3.4	-4.6	-3.2	0.0	-7.2	-3.1	-2.6	-0.2	Bahreïn
-1.4	13.1	1.3	2.8	3.2	4.0	1.6	2.7	2.7	5.3	5.2	Iraq
-1.9	0.9	4.2	5.1	2.3	0.6	5.5	2.4	-0.4	0.3	0.9	Jordanie
-3.6	3.3	0.2	4.4	0.1	0.8	7.0	-11.2	4.4	5.1	2.3	Koweït
1.2	1.1	3.7	1.8	5.2	3.9	-0.7	8.2	6.2	0.7	0.9	Liban
3.3	2.5	2.6	2.8	3.7	2.7	1.8	-1.7	5.4	3.1	2.4	Oman
-6.9	5.8	1.0	-0.3	1.8	3.8	-6.4	-2.2	6.0	6.7	2.5	Qatar
-7.2	0.0	0.4	0.3	1.2	2.6	1.9	-2.3	2.7	4.6	4.5	Arabie saoudite
-0.3	3.5	1.8	-0.4	3.8	5.5	6.4	4.6	6.9	6.9	2.5	État de Palestine
-2.4	2.7	2.6	3.1	0.2	-3.4	3.5	4.0	1.6	-3.7	-16.4	République arabe syrienne
3.1	2.2	3.3	5.2	2.0	3.3	7.0	-6.0	7.8	7.2	1.0	Turquie
-8.2	0.9	-5.0	-6.7	-7.9	-5.2	-5.7	-14.8	-6.4	-0.8	0.5	Émirats arabes unis
2.2	–	–	–	–	–	–	–	–	–	–	Yémen, République arabe du
-3.5	–	–	–	–	–	–	–	–	–	–	Yémen, Démocratique
–	5.0	1.7	1.3	-0.8	-3.0	2.0	1.2	4.6	-13.2	-2.0	Yémen
1.4	*-0.4*	*0.7*	*1.1*	*1.2*	*1.6*	*1.3*	*0.2*	*1.4*	*2.3*	*2.2*	*Économies en développement : Océanie*
4.8	0.8	-0.4	0.2	-0.8	0.8	-2.8	-4.2	-0.4	2.8	4.8	Îles Cook
-0.2	2.0	0.8	1.4	-0.6	-0.3	5.0	-2.3	-1.2	1.1	0.9	Fidji
3.2	-0.1	0.6	0.2	0.5	0.6	0.0	0.4	0.4	0.5	1.0	Polynésie française
-2.0	2.6	-0.5	-0.5	-0.6	-0.6	-1.7	-3.8	-2.0	1.4	1.9	Kiribati
–	-1.7	2.2	1.0	1.3	2.4	1.9	-2.3	4.0	3.5	3.3	Îles Marshall
–	0.0	-0.5	-0.3	-0.2	1.1	1.6	0.4	2.8	0.6	0.3	Micronésie (États fédérés de)
-3.0	-10.2	-2.1	-14.6	5.3	-2.5	-10.0	-18.4	-0.4	3.5	3.4	Nauru
2.9	-0.9	1.9	2.9	1.4	1.4	1.9	0.7	1.8	1.8	0.7	Nouvelle-Calédonie
–	0.8	1.2	2.9	1.1	1.5	5.0	2.3	1.4	1.1	1.3	Palaos
-0.4	-0.6	1.5	1.7	4.5	5.6	1.4	3.7	5.1	6.5	7.0	Papouasie-Nouvelle-Guinée
0.8	2.5	2.5	3.2	0.2	0.7	5.0	-1.8	1.5	0.9	1.6	Samoa
-1.2	-1.1	2.0	4.4	2.1	3.0	9.8	-7.3	4.2	8.7	3.6	Îles Salomon
4.4	1.8	0.2	-1.8	0.7	2.5	1.7	2.3	2.2	4.2	0.7	Tonga
5.3	3.7	0.3	2.4	1.0	-0.1	-4.6	-1.9	-0.7	0.8	1.2	Tuvalu
3.6	0.7	1.3	3.7	2.1	1.0	2.5	0.9	-0.3	1.8	1.7	Vanuatu
2.5	*-2.3*	*5.8*	*7.9*	*3.1*	*1.8*	*6.7*	*-6.7*	*4.3*	*4.4*	*3.0*	*Économies en transition*
-0.4	7.2	5.1	5.2	3.9	2.3	5.2	2.9	3.6	1.6	0.8	Albanie
–	5.9	9.3	13.4	2.6	0.1	13.7	-14.3	2.0	4.4	6.8	Arménie
–	-3.1	15.6	27.5	9.3	2.4	24.9	7.8	3.7	-1.2	1.0	Azerbaïdjan
–	0.9	8.5	9.9	6.6	4.6	10.0	0.6	8.2	5.7	1.8	Bélarus
–	22.8	4.7	6.6	2.3	0.4	8.0	-2.7	0.9	1.9	0.4	Bosnie-Herzégovine
–	3.9	3.3	5.0	-0.1	-2.1	4.5	-6.8	-1.2	0.2	-1.7	Croatie
–	2.7	7.8	11.2	5.3	4.9	10.6	-3.3	6.8	7.5	6.7	Géorgie
–	-1.2	7.5	8.7	4.5	4.4	8.8	0.0	6.0	6.3	3.9	Kazakhstan
–	-2.1	3.7	2.9	2.9	0.8	-0.7	1.6	-1.7	4.5	-1.9	Kirghizistan
–	–	–	–	0.2	–	–	-5.8	2.3	2.4	0.2	Monténégro
–	-5.6	6.8	6.5	4.2	3.7	9.2	-5.1	8.0	7.3	1.4	République de Moldova
–	-2.5	5.7	8.0	3.0	1.7	6.7	-7.8	4.4	4.4	3.5	Fédération de Russie
–	-0.5	–	5.1	–	–	5.5	–	–	–	–	Serbie-et-Monténégro
–	–	–	–	–	0.3	–	-2.8	1.4	2.2	-0.8	Serbie
0.4	–	–	–	–	–	–	–	–	–	–	RSF de Yougoslavie
–	-8.1	6.9	5.8	5.2	5.0	5.7	2.6	5.1	5.9	6.0	Tadjikistan
–	0.8	3.1	4.9	2.5	1.0	4.1	-1.1	1.6	2.9	-0.4	LERY de Macédoine
–	-2.8	7.3	10.7	9.7	9.2	11.8	4.8	7.9	13.3	9.7	Turkménistan
–	-7.2	5.6	6.9	1.1	0.2	3.5	-14.2	4.8	5.8	0.8	Ukraine
2.8	–	–	–	–	–	–	–	–	–	–	URSS
–	-0.2	6.1	6.8	7.3	7.1	6.0	6.8	7.2	7.1	7.0	Ouzbékistan
2.6	*2.8*	*0.8*	*1.6*	*-0.2*	*0.2*	*2.1*	*-3.9*	*1.5*	*1.0*	*1.3*	*Économies développées : Amérique*
0.9	3.3	1.5	3.4	-0.5	-1.8	1.6	-5.0	-2.1	0.3	-1.2	Bermudes
2.1	2.7	0.9	1.6	0.2	0.5	1.9	-3.8	2.2	1.5	0.8	Canada
1.2	3.1	2.4	4.3	2.3	1.8	3.5	1.4	1.2	2.6	2.0	Groenland
2.7	2.8	0.8	1.6	-0.2	0.2	2.1	-3.9	1.5	0.9	1.3	États-Unis

Pour les sources et les notes, se reporter à la fin du tableau.

8

8.2.1 Annual average growth rates of total and per capita real gross domestic product of countries and geographical regions

Region, country or territory	Total real gross domestic product (1) / Produit intérieur brut réel total (1) Percentage / En pourcentage										
	80 -89	92 -00	00 -10	04 -07	05 -12 (e)	08 -12 (e)	2005	2009	2010	2011	2012 (e)
Developed economies: Asia	**4.4**	**1.0**	**0.9**	**1.8**	**0.1**	**0.4**	**1.4**	**-5.3**	**4.4**	**-0.6**	**2.0**
Israel	3.4	5.2	3.6	5.4	3.9	3.6	4.9	0.8	4.8	4.7	3.1
Japan	4.5	0.9	0.8	1.7	0.0	0.3	1.3	-5.5	4.4	-0.7	2.0
Developed economies: Europe	**2.4**	**2.6**	**1.6**	**2.9**	**0.5**	**0.2**	**2.1**	**-4.2**	**2.1**	**1.5**	**-0.2**
Andorra	2.9	3.9	3.2	3.9	-2.5	-3.2	6.4	-5.1	-3.4	-2.8	-1.6
Austria	2.0	2.7	1.8	3.3	1.2	0.8	2.4	-3.8	2.1	2.7	0.8
Belgium	1.9	2.5	1.6	2.5	0.9	0.6	1.8	-2.8	2.4	1.8	-0.2
Bulgaria	4.1	-0.8	4.8	6.4	1.8	-0.4	6.4	-5.5	0.4	1.7	0.8
Cyprus	6.1	4.5	3.1	4.3	1.4	-0.3	3.9	-1.9	1.3	0.5	-2.4
Czechoslovakia	2.1	–	–	–	–	–	–	–	–	–	–
Czech Republic	–	–	4.0	6.6	1.6	0.1	6.8	-4.5	2.5	1.9	-1.3
Denmark	2.6	3.0	0.9	2.6	-0.5	-0.7	2.4	-5.8	1.3	0.8	-0.6
Estonia	–	3.8	4.3	8.9	0.2	1.0	8.9	-14.1	3.3	8.3	3.2
Finland	3.3	4.1	2.1	4.2	0.4	0.0	2.9	-8.5	3.3	2.7	-0.2
France	2.2	2.2	1.3	2.2	0.4	0.4	1.8	-3.2	1.7	1.7	0.0
Germany, Federal Republic of (3)	2.0	–	–	–	–	–	–	–	–	–	–
Germany	–	1.6	1.1	2.7	1.2	1.2	0.7	-5.1	4.2	3.0	0.7
Greece	0.7	2.6	2.6	3.8	-2.0	-5.1	2.3	-3.2	-3.5	-6.9	-6.4
Hungary	1.6	2.3	2.2	2.8	-0.5	-0.9	4.0	-6.8	1.3	1.6	-1.7
Iceland	3.2	3.8	3.2	5.8	-0.1	-1.5	7.2	-6.6	-4.0	2.6	1.6
Ireland	2.1	9.0	3.1	5.6	-0.1	-0.8	5.9	-5.5	-0.8	1.4	0.7
Italy	2.5	1.8	0.5	1.7	-0.7	-0.9	0.9	-5.5	1.8	0.4	-2.4
Latvia	–	3.0	4.8	10.4	-1.1	-1.5	10.1	-17.7	-0.9	5.5	5.6
Lithuania	–	1.4	5.2	8.4	0.8	-0.3	7.8	-14.8	1.5	5.9	3.6
Luxembourg	5.0	4.7	3.2	5.6	1.1	0.2	5.4	-5.3	2.7	1.6	0.2
Malta	3.2	5.1	1.9	3.5	1.8	0.9	3.7	-2.7	2.3	2.1	0.8
Netherlands	2.2	3.6	1.6	3.1	0.8	-0.1	2.0	-3.7	1.6	1.0	-0.9
Norway	3.1	4.0	1.7	2.6	0.9	0.9	2.6	-1.7	0.7	1.4	3.2
Poland	2.3	5.7	4.3	5.6	4.2	3.2	3.6	1.6	3.9	4.3	2.0
Portugal	2.9	3.5	0.7	1.5	-0.4	-1.3	0.8	-2.9	1.4	-1.7	-3.2
Romania	2.0	1.0	4.9	6.3	1.6	-1.1	4.2	-6.6	-1.6	2.5	0.3
San Marino	2.5	6.7	0.8	3.3	-3.9	-5.5	2.3	-12.8	-5.2	-2.6	-2.6
Slovakia	–	–	5.4	8.5	3.6	1.6	6.7	-4.9	4.2	3.3	2.0
Slovenia	–	4.3	3.3	5.6	0.6	-1.5	4.0	-7.8	1.2	0.6	-2.3
Spain	2.9	3.2	2.4	3.7	0.1	-1.0	3.6	-3.7	-0.3	0.4	-1.4
Sweden	2.5	3.1	2.3	3.7	1.5	2.2	3.2	-5.0	6.6	3.9	0.8
Switzerland	2.1	1.5	2.0	3.5	1.8	1.3	2.7	-2.0	3.1	1.9	1.0
United Kingdom	3.3	3.3	1.9	3.0	0.2	0.0	2.8	-4.0	1.8	0.8	0.2
Developed economies: Oceania	**3.5**	**4.0**	**3.0**	**3.4**	**2.4**	**2.6**	**3.1**	**2.2**	**1.7**	**3.1**	**3.3**
Australia	3.6	4.1	3.1	3.6	2.7	2.7	3.0	2.3	1.9	3.4	3.4
New Zealand	2.3	3.6	2.4	2.7	0.9	1.2	3.2	0.9	0.2	1.1	3.0

Source:

UNCTAD secretariat calculations, based on UN DESA Statistics Division, *National Accounts Main Aggregates Database*

Notes:

(1)   Growth rates are based on gross domestic product at constant 2005 US dollars.

(2)   Including Western Sahara.

(3)   Data refer to the former Federal Republic of Germany and the former Democratic Republic of Germany.

8.2.1 Taux de croissance annuels moyens du produit intérieur brut réel total et par habitant des pays et des régions géographiques

Per capita real gross domestic product (1) / Produit intérieur brut réel par habitant (1) Percentage / En pourcentage											Régions, pays ou territoires
80 -89	92 -00	00 -10	04 -07	05 -12 (e)	08 -12 (e)	2005	2009	2010	2011	2012 (e)	
3.8	**0.7**	**0.7**	**1.7**	**0.0**	**0.4**	**1.2**	**-5.4**	**4.3**	**-0.6**	**2.0**	**Économies développées : Asie**
1.7	2.3	1.4	3.0	1.6	1.6	2.8	-1.5	2.6	2.7	1.3	Israël
3.9	0.7	0.8	1.7	0.0	0.4	1.2	-5.5	4.4	-0.7	2.1	Japon
2.2	**2.4**	**1.2**	**2.5**	**0.2**	**-0.1**	**1.7**	**-4.6**	**1.8**	**1.2**	**-0.5**	**Économies développées : Europe**
-0.7	2.8	0.3	1.3	-4.0	-4.6	2.8	-6.3	-4.8	-4.3	-3.1	Andorre
1.9	2.4	1.3	2.8	0.8	0.5	1.8	-4.1	1.8	2.5	0.6	Autriche
1.8	2.3	1.1	1.9	0.4	0.2	1.2	-3.3	1.9	1.4	-0.5	Belgique
4.0	0.1	5.5	7.1	2.5	0.3	7.0	-4.9	1.0	2.3	1.4	Bulgarie
4.9	2.9	1.4	2.2	0.5	-0.7	1.0	-2.7	0.1	1.1	-2.6	Chypre
1.9	–										Tchécoslovaquie
		3.7	6.2	1.1	-0.3	6.6	-5.1	2.0	1.5	-1.6	République tchèque
2.6	2.5	0.5	2.1	-1.0	-1.1	2.1	-6.3	0.8	0.4	-1.0	Danemark
	5.2	4.5	9.1	0.2	1.0	9.1	-14.0	3.4	8.3	3.3	Estonie
2.9	3.8	1.7	3.8	0.0	-0.4	2.6	-9.0	2.9	2.4	-0.5	Finlande
1.6	1.8	0.6	1.6	-0.1	-0.2	1.1	-3.7	1.1	1.1	-0.5	France
2.0											Allemagne, Rép. fédérale d' (3)
	1.3	1.0	2.7	1.3	1.4	0.7	-5.0	4.3	3.2	0.9	Allemagne
0.3	1.9	2.3	3.5	-2.3	-5.3	2.0	-3.5	-3.8	-7.2	-6.6	Grèce
2.0	2.5	2.4	3.0	-0.3	-0.7	4.2	-6.6	1.5	1.8	-1.5	Hongrie
2.1	2.8	1.8	4.4	-1.6	-2.9	5.9	-8.0	-5.4	1.2	0.4	Islande
1.7	8.1	1.5	3.8	-1.5	-2.0	4.0	-6.7	-2.0	0.2	-0.5	Irlande
2.4	1.8	-0.2	1.0	-1.2	-1.4	0.2	-6.1	1.3	0.0	-2.7	Italie
	4.2	5.4	11.0	-0.6	-1.1	10.8	-17.4	-0.5	5.9	6.0	Lettonie
	2.1	5.8	9.0	1.3	0.2	8.3	-14.4	2.1	6.4	4.1	Lituanie
4.7	3.2	1.6	3.7	-0.9	-1.6	4.0	-7.4	0.7	-0.1	-1.2	Luxembourg
1.9	4.3	1.4	3.1	1.5	0.6	3.1	-3.0	2.0	1.7	0.5	Malte
1.6	2.9	1.1	2.7	0.4	-0.5	1.5	-4.0	1.3	0.7	-1.2	Pays-Bas
2.7	3.4	0.9	1.6	-0.2	0.0	1.8	-2.8	-0.3	0.6	2.5	Norvège
1.5	5.7	4.3	5.6	4.1	3.1	3.6	1.5	3.8	4.3	2.0	Pologne
2.7	3.0	0.3	1.2	-0.6	-1.5	0.4	-3.1	1.2	-1.8	-3.3	Portugal
1.6	1.5	5.2	6.6	1.8	-0.8	4.5	-6.3	-1.4	2.7	0.5	Roumanie
1.3	5.7	-0.8	1.8	-4.5	-6.0	0.4	-13.2	-5.7	-3.2	-3.2	Saint-Marin
		5.3	8.3	3.4	1.4	6.6	-5.1	4.0	3.2	1.8	Slovaquie
	4.0	3.0	5.4	0.3	-1.8	3.8	-8.1	1.0	0.3	-2.5	Slovénie
2.5	2.9	1.0	2.3	-0.9	-1.9	2.0	-4.8	-1.3	-0.4	-2.1	Espagne
2.3	2.9	1.7	3.0	0.7	1.5	2.6	-5.8	5.8	3.2	0.2	Suède
1.5	0.9	1.3	2.8	1.1	0.8	2.0	-2.6	2.5	1.4	0.6	Suisse
3.1	3.0	1.4	2.4	-0.4	-0.6	2.2	-4.6	1.2	0.1	-0.4	Royaume-Uni
2.0	**2.8**	**1.5**	**1.8**	**0.8**	**1.0**	**1.6**	**0.5**	**0.1**	**1.7**	**2.0**	**Économies développées : Océanie**
2.1	2.9	1.6	1.9	0.9	1.1	1.5	0.5	0.2	1.9	2.0	Australie
1.6	2.4	1.1	1.5	-0.2	0.1	1.8	-0.1	-0.8	0.0	1.9	Nouvelle-Zélande

Source :.

Calculs du secrétariat de la CNUCED, basés sur ONU DAES Division de statistique, *National Accounts Main Aggregates Database*

Notes :

(1) Les taux de croissance sont basés sur le produit intérieur brut aux prix constants en dollars des États-Unis de 2005.

(2) Y compris le Sahara occidental.

(3) Les données se réfèrent à l'ex-République Fédérale d'Allemagne et l'ex-République Démocratique d'Allemagne.

8

Region, country or territory	Total real gross domestic product (1) / Produit intérieur brut réel total (1) Percentage / En pourcentage										
	80 - 89	92 - 00	00 - 10	04 - 07	05 - 12 (e)	08 - 12 (e)	2005	2009	2010	2011	2012 (e)
DEVELOPING ECONOMIES	**3.5**	**4.8**	**6.1**	**7.5**	**5.7**	**5.5**	**6.8**	**2.7**	**7.7**	**5.8**	**4.7**
Developing economies excluding China	2.9	3.9	4.8	6.1	4.3	4.2	5.7	0.6	6.8	4.5	3.4
Developing economies excluding LDCs	3.6	4.8	6.0	7.4	5.7	5.5	6.8	2.6	7.8	5.8	4.7
High-income developing economies	2.7	3.8	4.1	5.5	3.5	3.5	5.1	-1.8	6.8	4.3	3.1
Middle-income developing economies	5.6	6.3	8.5	10.0	8.2	7.4	8.8	6.7	8.6	7.3	6.4
Low-income developing economies	3.6	5.3	7.0	8.0	6.6	6.5	8.1	6.9	8.1	6.0	4.4
Heavily indebted poor countries (IMF)	1.6	3.5	5.3	5.7	4.9	4.4	6.2	5.0	6.1	4.1	1.8
Landlocked developing countries	2.4	1.1	7.2	8.7	6.8	6.4	8.2	3.8	7.2	6.6	7.6
Small island developing States	1.5	3.4	3.9	5.7	2.0	1.3	4.8	-2.1	1.8	2.3	2.7
Least developed countries	*2.5*	*4.4*	*7.3*	*8.4*	*6.2*	*5.0*	*8.6*	*5.2*	*6.1*	*3.8*	*4.8*
Africa and Haiti	2.2	3.9	7.4	8.9	6.3	4.8	9.3	4.8	6.0	3.7	4.5
Asia	3.2	5.4	6.7	7.2	6.1	5.5	7.0	6.4	6.7	3.7	5.3
Islands	2.4	2.3	15.6	19.8	5.0	3.1	25.2	-4.3	0.4	8.1	7.5
Major petroleum and gas exporters	*-0.4*	*3.1*	*5.5*	*6.7*	*4.3*	*3.8*	*6.7*	*0.7*	*4.9*	*3.5*	*5.5*
Africa	0.0	2.3	6.9	7.0	4.4	3.1	8.0	3.7	5.2	-4.2	10.8
America	0.6	0.9	4.7	9.7	3.0	1.1	10.3	-3.2	-1.5	4.0	5.1
Asia	-0.7	3.9	5.2	6.1	4.4	4.4	5.8	0.4	5.9	6.0	4.0
Major exporters of manufactured goods	*6.1*	*6.4*	*7.0*	*8.5*	*6.8*	*6.5*	*7.4*	*3.6*	*8.9*	*6.8*	*5.6*
America	0.8	3.3	2.1	4.0	1.7	2.3	3.3	-6.0	5.3	3.9	3.9
Asia	9.3	7.3	8.0	9.5	7.7	7.2	8.3	5.3	9.5	7.2	5.9
Emerging economies	*3.5*	*4.1*	*3.8*	*5.0*	*3.5*	*3.5*	*4.2*	*-1.6*	*7.4*	*3.9*	*2.6*
America	1.7	3.2	3.4	4.8	3.4	3.3	4.0	-2.4	6.8	4.2	2.6
Asia	8.4	5.5	4.4	5.3	3.7	3.9	4.5	-0.6	8.1	3.6	2.6
Newly industrialized Asian economies	*7.2*	*4.8*	*4.5*	*5.5*	*4.0*	*4.2*	*4.9*	*0.0*	*7.8*	*4.1*	*3.2*
First tier	8.8	5.5	4.3	5.5	3.6	3.8	4.8	-0.7	8.2	4.0	1.7
Second tier	4.7	3.6	5.0	5.5	4.7	4.8	5.1	1.4	6.9	4.2	6.2
Developing economies: Africa	**1.8**	**3.1**	**5.3**	**5.9**	**4.2**	**3.4**	**5.9**	**2.8**	**4.8**	**1.0**	**5.3**
Northern Africa excluding Sudan	2.9	3.1	4.7	5.1	3.0	1.4	5.1	3.2	4.1	-6.0	7.6
Sub-Saharan Africa	1.3	3.2	5.6	6.3	4.8	4.3	6.3	2.6	5.2	4.4	4.3
Sub-Saharan Africa excluding South Africa	1.3	3.5	6.6	6.8	5.8	5.2	6.9	4.8	6.4	5.1	3.8
Developing economies: America	**1.8**	**3.1**	**3.6**	**5.3**	**3.5**	**3.2**	**4.6**	**-1.9**	**5.9**	**4.3**	**3.0**
Central America and Greater Caribbean Islands excluding Puerto Rico	1.0	3.3	2.6	4.6	2.2	2.5	3.9	-4.7	5.0	4.0	3.9
Central America and Greater Caribbean Islands excluding Mexico and Puerto Rico	2.2	3.7	4.7	7.3	4.1	3.4	6.7	0.8	3.9	4.1	3.9
South America and Central America	1.7	3.1	3.6	5.2	3.5	3.3	4.5	-2.0	6.0	4.3	3.0
South America excluding Brazil	1.1	2.9	4.9	7.4	4.9	4.3	7.4	-0.1	5.3	6.5	4.2
Developing economies: Asia	**5.3**	**5.9**	**7.1**	**8.5**	**6.7**	**6.5**	**7.8**	**4.3**	**8.7**	**6.8**	**5.1**
Eastern and South-Eastern Asia excluding China	7.0	4.8	4.7	5.6	4.1	4.3	5.0	0.2	7.8	4.3	3.3
Southern Asia excluding India	3.1	3.6	5.5	6.5	4.4	3.8	6.0	4.3	5.4	3.4	1.7

Source:

UNCTAD secretariat calculations, based on UN DESA Statistics Division, *National Accounts Main Aggregates Database*

Notes:

(1) Growth rates are based on gross domestic product at constant 2005 U.S. dollars.

8.2.2 Taux de croissance annuels moyens du produit intérieur brut réel total et par habitant des groupements économiques

Per capita real gross domestic product (1) / Produit intérieur brut réel par habitant (1) Percentage / En pourcentage											Régions, pays ou territoires
80 - 89	92 - 00	00 - 10	04 - 07	05 - 12 (e)	08 - 12 (e)	2005	2009	2010	2011	2012 (e)	
1.3	3.0	4.6	6.0	4.3	4.0	5.4	1.3	6.3	4.0	3.3	ÉCONOMIES EN DÉVELOPPEMENT
0.5	2.0	3.1	4.3	2.7	2.6	4.0	-1.0	5.1	2.9	2.1	Économies en développement sans la Chine
1.4	3.2	4.7	6.1	4.4	4.2	5.5	1.4	6.5	4.1	3.5	Économies en développement sans les PMA
0.5	2.2	2.7	4.1	2.3	2.4	3.7	-3.0	5.5	3.1	2.1	Économies en développement à revenu élevé
3.7	5.0	7.5	9.0	7.1	6.2	7.8	5.8	7.7	5.4	5.6	Économies en développement à revenu intermédiaire
1.1	3.1	5.0	6.1	4.7	4.6	6.1	5.1	6.2	4.1	2.6	Économies en développement à revenu faible
-1.0	0.6	2.6	3.0	2.4	2.1	3.5	2.3	3.4	1.4	0.8	Pays pauvres très endettés (FMI)
-0.2	-1.2	4.9	6.5	4.3	3.6	6.0	1.6	4.9	4.3	2.8	Pays en développement sans littoral
-0.3	1.6	1.7	4.0	0.5	-0.2	3.1	-3.5	0.3	0.8	1.2	Petits États insulaires en développement
-0.1	1.8	4.8	6.0	3.9	2.7	6.1	3.0	3.8	1.5	2.5	*Pays les moins avancés*
-0.6	1.1	4.6	6.0	3.5	2.0	6.3	2.0	3.2	1.0	1.8	Afrique et Haïti
0.8	3.0	5.0	5.5	4.6	3.9	5.3	5.0	5.2	2.1	3.7	Asie
-0.1	0.1	7.5	16.9	2.7	0.8	21.8	-6.3	-1.8	5.7	4.9	Îles
-3.4	0.9	3.1	4.2	1.9	1.5	4.3	-1.6	2.6	1.2	3.3	*Principaux exportateurs de pétrole et de gaz*
-2.7	0.0	4.4	4.5	2.0	0.7	5.4	1.3	2.8	-6.4	8.2	Afrique
-2.1	-1.2	2.9	7.8	1.4	-0.5	8.4	-4.8	-3.1	2.3	3.5	Amérique
-4.4	1.7	2.8	3.5	2.0	2.2	3.3	-2.0	3.5	3.9	2.0	Asie
4.4	5.3	6.3	7.9	5.9	5.5	6.7	3.0	8.3	4.7	5.1	*Principaux exportateurs d'articles manufacturés*
-1.2	1.5	0.9	2.7	0.5	1.0	2.0	-7.2	4.0	2.7	2.7	Amérique
7.6	6.3	7.3	8.8	6.9	6.2	7.6	4.7	8.9	5.0	5.4	Asie
1.5	2.7	2.7	3.9	2.5	2.6	3.1	-2.5	6.4	3.0	1.7	*Économies émergentes*
-0.3	1.7	2.2	3.7	2.3	2.3	2.8	-3.4	5.8	3.1	1.6	Amérique
6.5	4.3	3.4	4.3	2.9	3.1	3.5	-1.4	7.3	2.8	1.9	Asie
5.1	3.3	3.3	4.3	2.9	3.1	3.6	-1.0	6.6	3.0	2.1	*Économies nouvellement industrialisées d'Asie*
7.2	4.5	3.7	4.9	3.0	3.2	4.2	-1.3	7.6	3.4	1.2	Première génération
2.5	1.9	3.6	4.2	3.5	3.7	3.7	0.3	5.7	3.0	5.0	Deuxième génération
-1.0	0.7	2.9	3.5	1.8	1.0	3.5	0.4	2.5	-1.2	2.9	Économies en développement : Afrique
0.3	1.5	3.1	3.5	1.4	-0.1	3.5	1.6	2.5	-7.4	6.0	Afrique septentrionale sans le Soudan
-1.5	0.5	3.0	3.7	2.3	1.7	3.7	0.1	2.7	1.9	1.8	Afrique subsaharienne
-1.5	0.8	3.9	4.1	3.2	2.8	4.2	2.2	3.7	2.4	2.4	Afrique subsaharienne sans l'Afrique du Sud
-0.3	1.4	2.4	4.0	2.3	2.1	3.3	-3.0	4.7	3.1	1.8	Économies en développement : Amérique
-0.9	1.6	1.3	3.3	0.9	1.2	2.5	-5.9	3.7	2.7	2.6	Amérique centrale et Grandes Antilles sans Porto Rico
0.3	2.0	3.2	5.9	2.7	2.0	5.2	-0.5	2.5	2.8	2.5	Amérique centrale et Grandes Antilles sans le Mexique et Porto Rico
-0.4	1.4	2.3	3.9	2.3	2.1	3.1	-3.1	4.8	3.2	1.8	Amérique du Sud et Amérique centrale
-0.9	1.2	3.5	6.0	3.6	3.1	6.0	-1.3	4.0	5.2	3.0	Amérique du Sud sans le Brésil
3.2	4.3	5.9	7.3	5.5	5.2	6.6	3.2	7.5	5.1	4.0	Économies en développement : Asie
4.8	3.3	3.5	4.5	3.0	3.2	3.9	-0.8	6.7	3.2	2.3	Asie orientale et Asie du Sud-Est sans la Chine
0.3	1.3	3.8	4.9	2.8	2.3	4.3	2.8	3.8	1.9	0.1	Asie méridionale sans l'Inde

Source :

Calculs du secrétariat de la CNUCED, basés sur ONU DAES Division de statistique, *National Accounts Main Aggregates Database*

Notes :

(1) Les taux de croissance sont basés sur le produit intérieur brut aux prix constants en dollars des États-Unis de 2005.

8

8.3.1 Nominal gross domestic product by type of expenditure and by kind of economic activity of countries and geographical regions

8.3.1 Produit intérieur brut nominal par catégories de dépenses et par branches d'activité économique des pays et des régions géographiques

Region, country or territory / Régions, pays ou territoires	Year / Année	Total GDP / PIB total	Final consumption / Consommation finale — Government / Administration publique	Final consumption — Household / Ménages	Gross capital formation / Formation brute de capital	Exports / Exportations — Of goods and services / Des biens et services	Less imports / Moins les importations — Of goods and services	Agriculture (3)	Industry (4) — Total	Industry (4) — Manufacturing / Activités de fabrication	Services (5)
									Percentage / En pourcentage		
WORLD - MONDE	2000	100.0	16.3	61.2	22.4	24.8	24.7	3.5	28.9	17.2	67.5
	2005	100.0	17.1	60.2	22.3	28.4	28.0	3.4	28.8	17.0	67.8
	2010	100.0	18.0	58.5	22.7	30.0	29.1	4.2	29.4	16.8	66.4
	2011	100.0	17.6	58.1	23.4	32.0	31.1	4.4	30.1	16.9	65.6
DEVELOPING ECONOMIES - ÉCONOMIES EN DÉVELOPPEMENT	2000	100.0	14.0	58.4	24.9	34.9	32.3	10.1	36.2	15.3	53.6
	2005	100.0	13.5	54.6	27.1	40.8	36.1	9.4	38.9	21.0	51.7
	2010	100.0	14.1	51.3	31.8	36.3	33.6	9.4	38.9	21.3	51.6
	2011	100.0	13.9	50.5	32.5	38.0	35.1	9.4	39.5	21.2	51.0
TRANSITION ECONOMIES - ÉCONOMIES EN TRANSITION	2000	100.0	16.2	52.7	19.3	45.0	32.9	10.3	37.4	21.2	52.3
	2005	100.0	16.8	53.0	22.2	38.9	30.3	6.9	37.1	18.3	56.0
	2010	100.0	17.9	54.1	23.5	34.3	28.5	5.4	35.8	15.2	58.7
	2011	100.0	17.1	52.4	24.8	36.6	29.6	5.7	37.0	16.0	57.3
DEVELOPED ECONOMIES - ÉCONOMIES DÉVELOPPÉES	2000	100.0	16.9	62.1	21.8	21.6	22.4	1.6	26.7	17.7	71.7
	2005	100.0	18.3	62.3	20.7	24.1	25.4	1.4	25.2	15.7	73.3
	2010	100.0	20.0	62.5	17.9	26.5	26.9	1.4	24.1	14.6	74.5
	2011	100.0	19.7	62.6	18.3	28.4	29.0	1.4	24.4	14.6	74.2
Developing economies: Africa - Économies en développement : Afrique	2000	100.0	15.2	63.2	17.5	31.3	27.1	15.2	35.7	12.8	49.1
	2005	100.0	14.6	61.5	18.9	36.2	31.1	15.3	39.0	11.3	45.7
	2010	100.0	15.8	60.0	22.1	34.7	32.8	16.2	37.5	9.8	46.3
	2011	100.0	16.6	59.1	21.8	37.1	35.2	16.3	37.0	9.6	46.8
Eastern Africa - Afrique orientale	2000	100.0	15.3	74.6	19.1	22.2	30.8	30.9	18.8	10.6	50.4
	2005	100.0	15.6	76.4	20.4	25.1	37.7	28.3	21.8	9.8	49.8
	2010	100.0	14.9	76.0	22.9	27.0	40.3	27.5	21.7	9.8	50.8
	2011	100.0	15.3	76.0	23.1	28.6	42.9	27.8	21.9	9.7	50.4
Burundi	2000	100.0	8.1	89.1	13.2	4.2	15.1	40.5	18.8	13.2	40.7
	2005	100.0	14.5	90.0	18.3	6.2	28.9	43.0	18.5	13.0	38.6
	2010	100.0	42.5	78.3	22.4	9.9	53.0	36.0	21.9	13.2	42.1
	2011	100.0	34.9	84.3	22.4	7.8	49.4	36.4	22.7	14.1	40.9
Comoros - Comores	2000	100.0	11.7	94.0	10.1	16.7	32.5	47.7	11.3	4.5	41.0
	2005	100.0	13.5	98.7	9.3	14.3	35.8	48.5	10.5	4.1	41.0
	2010	100.0	14.6	106.7	14.3	14.7	50.6	48.7	10.5	4.1	40.8
	2011	100.0	13.9	104.9	16.9	15.0	51.3	48.9	10.5	4.1	40.6
Djibouti	2000	100.0	25.6	81.2	12.2	43.8	63.3	3.5	15.2	2.6	81.3
	2005	100.0	25.0	79.8	19.3	46.3	70.4	3.6	16.2	2.6	80.2
	2010	100.0	21.3	83.4	19.1	38.0	61.8	3.8	21.1	2.5	75.2
	2011	100.0	20.8	83.8	18.9	36.8	60.3	3.8	20.1	2.4	76.0
Eritrea - Érythrée	2000	100.0	54.8	71.7	22.0	9.7	58.2	15.1	23.0	11.2	61.9
	2005	100.0	35.2	93.2	20.3	6.2	54.9	24.2	21.9	7.3	53.9
	2010	100.0	23.9	85.4	9.3	4.8	23.3	19.1	23.1	6.0	57.8
	2011	100.0	21.1	77.7	10.0	14.4	23.1	17.0	24.1	6.1	58.9
Ethiopia - Éthiopie	2000	100.0	17.9	73.1	20.3	12.0	23.9	49.4	12.2	5.5	38.4
	2005	100.0	12.4	81.7	23.8	15.1	35.5	46.4	12.9	4.7	40.8
	2010	100.0	8.6	86.2	24.7	13.6	33.0	46.4	10.2	3.9	43.4
	2011	100.0	8.1	83.1	25.5	16.8	31.8	46.0	10.5	3.5	43.5
Kenya	2000	100.0	15.3	78.1	17.6	22.3	30.5	32.8	17.3	11.5	49.9
	2005	100.0	17.4	75.4	16.9	27.9	37.0	27.0	18.9	11.7	54.1
	2010	100.0	17.6	77.8	19.8	27.8	40.1	24.8	18.3	11.2	56.9
	2011	100.0	17.8	77.7	20.9	28.7	45.4	27.4	16.9	10.6	55.7
Madagascar	2000	100.0	7.9	83.5	16.2	31.1	38.7	28.9	15.9	12.2	55.2
	2005	100.0	9.0	86.2	22.2	28.2	45.6	28.1	18.6	14.4	53.3
	2010	100.0	10.6	88.3	18.8	24.1	41.8	28.0	19.9	14.5	51.2
	2011	100.0	10.2	89.5	14.5	26.7	40.9	28.1	19.9	14.6	52.3

For sources and notes, see end of table.

Pour les sources et les notes, se reporter à la fin du tableau.

8.3.1 Nominal gross domestic product by type of expenditure and by kind of economic activity of countries and geographical regions

8.3.1 Produit intérieur brut nominal par catégories de dépenses et par branches d'activité économique des pays et des régions géographiques

Region, country or territory / Régions, pays ou territoires	Year / Année	Total GDP / PIB total	GDP by type of expenditure (1) / PIB par catégories de dépenses (1)					GDP by kind of economic activity (2) / PIB par branches d'activité économique (2)			
			Final consumption / Consommation finale		Gross capital formation / Formation brute de capital	Exports / Exportations	Less imports / Moins les importations	Agri-culture (3)	Industry (4) / Industrie (4)		Services (5)
			Government / Administration publique	Household / Ménages	Formation brute de capital	Of goods and services / Des biens et services			Total	Manu-facturing / Activités de fabrication	
			Percentage / En pourcentage								
Malawi	2000	100.0	8.5	78.6	20.0	21.8	28.8	35.5	18.4	11.5	46.0
	2005	100.0	10.8	94.6	22.7	24.0	52.2	31.1	16.2	8.7	52.7
	2010	100.0	10.0	86.4	24.8	23.3	44.8	30.0	16.4	10.4	53.6
	2011	100.0	10.7	82.3	13.5	23.8	30.5	20.0	16.5	10.5	53.6
Mauritius - Maurice	2000	100.0	14.3	59.9	26.0	61.1	61.2	6.5	29.6	22.5	63.9
	2005	100.0	14.5	68.0	22.7	59.0	64.2	5.7	26.6	19.2	67.8
	2010	100.0	13.9	73.7	23.7	52.5	63.8	3.6	27.2	18.3	69.2
	2011	100.0	13.6	74.1	25.2	53.5	66.3	3.7	26.5	18.1	69.8
Mozambique	2000	100.0	11.5	80.1	33.5	12.7	37.8	23.6	24.1	12.0	52.3
	2005	100.0	13.0	83.3	17.9	30.5	44.4	26.4	24.8	15.1	48.9
	2010	100.0	13.1	82.7	13.4	25.2	34.4	30.2	21.9	12.9	47.8
	2011	100.0	13.7	85.9	14.7	18.0	30.8	29.2	22.9	13.9	47.9
Rwanda	2000	100.0	17.6	83.1	14.2	6.1	21.8	39.2	15.2	7.4	45.6
	2005	100.0	18.2	79.8	15.8	11.4	25.2	40.9	15.0	7.5	44.1
	2010	100.0	16.0	83.6	21.0	10.0	30.6	34.3	15.9	7.1	49.7
	2011	100.0	15.2	82.5	21.4	13.4	32.5	34.0	17.4	7.0	48.6
Seychelles	2000	100.0	42.2	36.7	27.6	75.5	81.9	4.5	18.9	12.5	76.6
	2005	100.0	33.9	52.3	35.1	76.8	98.1	3.8	19.1	10.2	77.1
	2010	100.0	27.5	53.6	36.7	103.0	120.8	2.7	15.8	8.8	81.5
	2011	100.0	29.4	55.2	35.4	107.7	127.8	2.8	16.1	8.9	81.1
Somalia - Somalie	2000	100.0	8.6	72.3	20.5	0.3	1.7	60.2	7.3	2.5	32.5
	2005	100.0	8.7	72.4	20.3	0.3	1.7	60.1	7.3	2.5	32.6
	2010	100.0	8.7	72.7	19.9	0.3	1.7	60.2	7.4	2.5	32.5
	2011	100.0	8.7	72.6	20.0	0.3	1.7	60.2	7.4	2.5	32.5
Uganda - Ouganda	2000	100.0	14.6	77.6	19.0	10.9	22.2	28.5	22.4	7.5	49.1
	2005	100.0	13.7	74.9	21.6	15.2	25.3	25.5	24.4	7.3	50.1
	2010	100.0	9.6	82.9	22.3	19.6	34.4	22.4	25.2	8.1	52.4
	2011	100.0	9.2	83.3	22.4	19.6	34.5	23.5	25.4	8.0	51.1
United Republic of Tanzania - République-Unie de Tanzanie	2000	100.0	11.7	78.3	16.7	13.4	20.1	33.0	18.9	9.2	48.1
	2005	100.0	17.6	66.3	24.9	20.8	29.7	31.3	22.3	8.5	46.3
	2010	100.0	16.1	62.6	31.7	27.8	38.6	28.0	24.1	9.6	47.9
	2011	100.0	16.6	60.8	32.9	33.7	44.1	28.8	23.4	9.1	47.8
Zambia - Zambie	2000	100.0	9.5	82.1	18.7	21.1	31.4	21.0	23.8	10.8	55.2
	2005	100.0	20.2	63.3	28.3	23.4	35.3	21.4	29.0	10.9	49.7
	2010	100.0	16.4	49.1	22.6	46.7	34.9	19.7	35.9	8.8	44.5
	2011	100.0	20.6	45.4	24.9	46.0	37.0	19.0	37.7	8.4	43.4
Zimbabwe	2000	100.0	24.3	59.9	13.6	38.2	35.9	23.1	19.2	13.6	57.8
	2005	100.0	15.2	92.2	1.5	33.5	42.5	12.3	41.9	6.5	45.9
	2010	100.0	30.1	79.4	24.3	36.2	70.0	17.7	35.1	17.8	47.2
	2011	100.0	32.6	98.1	25.6	40.1	96.4	15.5	36.0	17.9	48.5
Middle Africa - Afrique centrale	*2000*	*100.0*	*17.3*	*54.1*	*15.6*	*48.1*	*34.9*	*19.0*	*50.1*	*8.1*	*30.8*
	2005	*100.0*	*17.4*	*41.9*	*15.8*	*63.4*	*38.4*	*14.1*	*59.5*	*6.6*	*26.4*
	2010	*100.0*	*17.3*	*43.0*	*24.4*	*57.9*	*42.3*	*13.9*	*57.3*	*6.7*	*28.8*
	2011	*100.0*	*18.7*	*38.3*	*23.9*	*59.3*	*43.3*	*13.1*	*59.1*	*6.5*	*27.8*
Angola	2000	100.0	34.1	39.5	11.7	67.5	52.8	5.8	72.8	3.0	21.4
	2005	100.0	27.9	31.0	8.7	86.0	53.6	7.5	73.0	3.5	19.4
	2010	100.0	24.1	40.7	16.1	62.2	43.1	10.1	61.5	6.3	28.4
	2011	100.0	24.1	35.5	16.1	70.5	46.3	9.5	63.6	6.1	26.9
Cameroon - Cameroun	2000	100.0	9.5	70.2	16.7	23.3	19.7	22.0	35.8	20.7	42.3
	2005	100.0	10.0	72.0	19.1	20.5	21.5	20.4	31.8	18.5	47.8
	2010	100.0	11.6	75.0	19.0	17.4	23.0	23.3	29.7	16.1	47.0
	2011	100.0	12.0	73.1	22.0	18.1	23.9	23.3	30.1	16.2	46.6

For sources and notes, see end of table.

Pour les sources et les notes, se reporter à la fin du tableau.

8.3.1 Nominal gross domestic product by type of expenditure and by kind of economic activity of countries and geographical regions

8.3.1 Produit intérieur brut nominal par catégories de dépenses et par branches d'activité économique des pays et des régions géographiques

Region, country or territory / Régions, pays ou territoires	Year / Année	Total GDP / PIB total	GDP by type of expenditure (1) / PIB par catégories de dépenses (1)					GDP by kind of economic activity (2) / PIB par branches d'activité économique (2)			
			Final consumption / Consommation finale		Gross capital formation / Formation brute de capital	Exports / Exportations	Less imports / Moins les importations	Agriculture (3)	Industry (4) / Industrie (4)		Services (5)
			Government / Administration publique	Household / Ménages	Formation brute de capital	Of goods and services / Des biens et services			Total	Manufacturing / Activités de fabrication	
			Percentage / En pourcentage								
Central African Republic - République centrafricaine	2000	100.0	16.3	77.6	11.1	20.4	25.3	52.1	14.6	6.2	33.3
	2005	100.0	10.4	88.1	9.8	13.2	21.5	54.9	14.3	6.4	30.8
	2010	100.0	8.2	89.8	14.1	10.4	22.6	54.2	13.8	6.7	32.0
	2011	100.0	6.2	90.1	14.9	10.8	22.0	54.5	13.9	6.6	31.6
Chad - Tchad	2000	100.0	39.4	65.8	17.5	20.0	42.7	42.3	11.3	9.1	46.4
	2005	100.0	21.0	24.9	25.1	54.5	25.5	21.3	53.8	5.8	24.9
	2010	100.0	23.7	27.8	27.7	45.1	24.4	21.9	48.5	6.3	29.5
	2011	100.0	20.1	27.5	19.1	51.4	21.7	17.9	53.9	5.8	28.2
Congo	2000	100.0	11.1	27.7	19.7	81.8	40.3	5.4	73.9	3.6	20.7
	2005	100.0	10.1	27.3	24.5	79.2	41.2	4.6	73.4	4.1	22.0
	2010	100.0	9.1	29.2	44.9	78.4	61.6	4.2	75.0	4.1	20.8
	2011	100.0	8.5	24.8	54.8	80.9	62.4	4.6	73.0	4.5	22.4
Dem. Rep. of the Congo - Rép. dém. du Congo	2000	100.0	6.5	88.3	3.5	22.4	20.7	49.7	20.2	4.8	30.2
	2005	100.0	11.4	86.9	13.9	33.6	45.2	48.4	22.6	5.4	29.0
	2010	100.0	9.7	71.5	26.4	68.4	76.7	45.0	23.1	5.4	32.0
	2011	100.0	12.7	64.5	27.5	66.1	73.1	44.8	23.1	5.4	32.1
Equatorial Guinea - Guinée équatoriale	2000	100.0	4.9	19.0	61.9	105.2	90.9	8.3	88.1	0.2	3.7
	2005	100.0	3.1	7.6	21.7	98.5	31.0	2.6	94.4	0.1	3.0
	2010	100.0	4.5	7.4	70.6	89.4	69.1	2.6	94.3	0.2	3.1
	2011	100.0	4.3	7.5	50.8	91.2	55.3	2.6	94.2	0.2	3.2
Gabon	2000	100.0	14.3	33.1	19.0	63.6	28.8	4.3	59.7	3.7	36.0
	2005	100.0	12.7	31.5	20.7	59.1	24.0	3.8	63.0	4.9	33.2
	2010	100.0	10.4	24.7	24.4	62.3	21.1	2.6	71.1	3.7	26.3
	2011	100.0	22.2	21.9	25.8	26.4	24.7	2.8	68.5	4.6	28.6
Sao Tome and Principe - Sao Tomé-et-Principe	2000	100.0	31.6	92.4	35.8	35.1	95.0	20.0	17.3	7.7	62.6
	2005	100.0	13.0	94.9	21.8	13.0	42.8	18.4	16.4	7.0	65.2
	2010	100.0	14.3	115.3	21.1	9.4	60.0	17.6	18.9	7.1	63.5
	2011	100.0	15.0	111.0	20.9	7.8	55.6	17.5	19.0	7.2	63.5
Northern Africa - Afrique septentrionale	*2000*	*100.0*	*14.2*	*61.9*	*19.7*	*29.0*	*24.9*	*12.6*	*38.7*	*12.7*	*48.7*
	2005	*100.0*	*12.7*	*54.2*	*23.3*	*40.5*	*30.6*	*12.3*	*45.1*	*10.8*	*42.6*
	2010	*100.0*	*13.9*	*56.7*	*26.4*	*33.8*	*30.8*	*13.1*	*42.3*	*11.1*	*44.6*
	2011	*100.0*	*15.3*	*58.3*	*25.2*	*32.6*	*31.2*	*13.7*	*39.9*	*11.0*	*46.4*
Algeria - Algérie	2000	100.0	13.6	41.6	23.6	42.1	20.8	8.8	56.7	6.0	34.5
	2005	100.0	11.5	33.8	31.7	47.2	24.1	7.9	59.8	4.5	32.3
	2010	100.0	18.0	34.5	40.4	38.3	31.1	8.6	51.1	4.0	40.3
	2011	100.0	16.6	35.5	33.1	44.4	29.0	8.2	53.3	4.1	38.5
Egypt - Égypte	2000	100.0	11.1	76.8	17.7	19.1	24.7	13.8	33.3	18.0	52.9
	2005	100.0	11.1	72.9	17.6	31.3	32.9	14.4	36.9	17.3	48.8
	2010	100.0	11.2	74.6	19.5	21.3	26.6	14.0	37.5	16.9	48.5
	2011	100.0	11.3	75.5	17.1	20.6	24.5	14.5	37.6	16.5	47.9
Libya - Libye	2000	100.0	20.6	46.4	13.0	35.2	15.3	6.5	47.6	5.4	45.9
	2005	100.0	12.0	32.4	8.9	72.5	25.8	2.2	75.7	4.7	22.2
	2010	100.0	12.5	36.1	9.6	68.7	26.9	2.5	73.8	5.6	23.7
	2011	100.0	42.5	34.2	13.6	52.6	42.9	1.9	50.2	2.2	47.9
Morocco - Maroc (6)	2000	100.0	18.4	61.4	25.5	28.0	33.4	14.2	27.7	17.5	58.1
	2005	100.0	19.4	57.5	28.8	32.3	37.9	14.0	26.9	15.8	59.1
	2010	100.0	17.5	57.3	35.1	33.0	42.9	14.7	28.3	15.0	57.1
	2011	100.0	17.6	59.4	35.5	34.4	46.8	14.7	28.1	14.6	57.2
Sudan (...2011) - Soudan (...2011)	2000	100.0	5.5	86.0	11.5	14.6	17.6	37.1	17.3	5.7	45.6
	2005	100.0	6.5	79.3	24.7	14.0	24.5	34.5	21.7	7.8	43.7
	2010	100.0	7.5	70.2	21.7	17.1	16.4	34.6	22.9	8.2	42.5
	2011	100.0	7.4	71.0	20.6	16.4	15.3	34.6	25.5	8.0	39.9

For sources and notes, see end of table.

Pour les sources et les notes, se reporter à la fin du tableau.

8.3.1 Nominal gross domestic product by type of expenditure and by kind of economic activity of countries and geographical regions

8.3.1 Produit intérieur brut nominal par catégories de dépenses et par branches d'activité économique des pays et des régions géographiques

Region, country or territory / Régions, pays ou territoires	Year / Année	Total GDP / PIB total	GDP by type of expenditure (1) / PIB par catégories de dépenses (1)					GDP by kind of economic activity (2) / PIB par branches d'activité économique (2)			
			Final consumption / Consommation finale		Gross capital formation / Formation brute de capital	Exports / Exportations	Less imports / Moins les importations	Agri-culture (3)	Industry (4) / Industrie (4)		Services (5)
			Government / Administration publique	Household / Ménages	Formation brute de capital	Of goods and services / Des biens et services	Moins les importations		Total	Manu-facturing / Activités de fabrication	
			Percentage / En pourcentage								
Tunisia - Tunisie	2000	100.0	16.7	60.6	25.9	39.7	42.9	11.1	29.8	18.1	59.1
	2005	100.0	16.9	61.8	21.7	44.9	45.3	10.0	28.8	17.0	61.3
	2010	100.0	16.6	62.7	26.1	48.7	54.0	7.9	31.7	17.7	60.4
	2011	100.0	18.0	65.2	23.9	40.0	66.6	8.4	32.0	18.3	59.7
Southern Africa - Afrique australe	*2000*	*100.0*	*18.7*	*62.6*	*16.5*	*29.7*	*27.3*	*3.6*	*32.6*	*18.4*	*63.8*
	2005	*100.0*	*19.6*	*62.3*	*18.3*	*29.3*	*29.5*	*3.0*	*32.0*	*17.9*	*65.0*
	2010	*100.0*	*21.7*	*59.0*	*19.9*	*28.5*	*29.6*	*2.7*	*31.3*	*13.7*	*66.0*
	2011	*100.0*	*21.6*	*58.4*	*20.5*	*30.2*	*31.7*	*2.7*	*31.5*	*13.3*	*65.8*
Botswana	2000	100.0	25.4	33.4	31.8	53.3	41.2	2.7	52.6	4.5	44.7
	2005	100.0	22.4	36.6	26.3	51.2	34.5	1.8	50.6	3.7	47.6
	2010	100.0	20.9	42.2	29.5	33.0	40.0	2.5	45.2	4.0	52.3
	2011	100.0	20.2	45.9	31.3	39.1	44.3	2.5	46.1	4.2	51.4
Lesotho	2000	100.0	35.4	123.0	43.5	34.8	134.7	11.9	30.4	13.6	57.7
	2005	100.0	36.7	109.7	22.0	48.9	120.9	8.9	32.8	19.2	58.2
	2010	100.0	37.2	103.0	28.0	43.8	113.9	8.4	31.2	12.6	60.3
	2011	100.0	31.7	96.1	34.3	46.8	112.4	7.8	34.0	17.2	58.1
Namibia - Namibie	2000	100.0	23.5	60.8	17.1	40.9	44.5	11.6	27.5	12.6	60.9
	2005	100.0	19.3	57.9	19.7	40.4	40.3	11.2	28.8	13.4	60.0
	2010	100.0	25.6	54.5	26.0	47.2	51.8	9.2	34.8	15.0	55.9
	2011	100.0	28.8	54.0	30.0	47.9	59.2	9.2	34.7	14.4	56.1
South Africa - Afrique du Sud	2000	100.0	18.1	63.4	15.7	27.9	24.9	3.3	31.8	19.0	64.9
	2005	100.0	19.5	63.1	18.0	27.4	27.9	2.7	31.2	18.5	66.2
	2010	100.0	21.5	59.2	19.4	27.3	27.5	2.4	30.4	13.8	67.2
	2011	100.0	21.5	58.6	19.7	28.8	29.4	2.4	30.6	13.4	67.0
Swaziland	2000	100.0	18.2	77.3	18.1	74.3	88.0	12.0	43.1	37.9	44.9
	2005	100.0	15.2	73.9	15.0	87.1	91.2	8.6	43.7	38.0	47.7
	2010	100.0	14.1	90.9	9.7	53.0	67.7	7.3	45.5	41.7	47.2
	2011	100.0	14.9	83.7	9.3	64.6	72.5	7.0	44.9	41.2	48.1
Western Africa - Afrique occidentale	*2000*	*100.0*	*11.2*	*62.8*	*12.1*	*41.1*	*27.0*	*27.8*	*38.4*	*7.9*	*33.8*
	2005	*100.0*	*9.2*	*76.0*	*11.5*	*30.8*	*27.3*	*32.1*	*35.2*	*6.1*	*32.7*
	2010	*100.0*	*12.7*	*67.9*	*15.0*	*35.9*	*31.9*	*32.6*	*32.6*	*4.6*	*34.8*
	2011	*100.0*	*12.7*	*64.7*	*15.4*	*45.3*	*38.0*	*32.1*	*32.6*	*4.7*	*35.3*
Benin - Bénin	2000	100.0	12.6	73.1	18.7	25.4	29.7	37.8	14.0	8.9	48.2
	2005	100.0	12.0	76.8	18.2	21.6	28.5	35.2	14.5	8.6	50.2
	2010	100.0	11.9	76.6	21.0	15.1	24.6	35.4	14.4	8.4	50.2
	2011	100.0	12.1	75.7	21.6	14.6	24.0	35.6	14.7	8.6	49.7
Burkina Faso	2000	100.0	20.7	74.7	20.1	9.5	25.0	32.8	21.5	13.2	45.6
	2005	100.0	19.8	72.2	24.1	9.7	25.8	38.8	17.9	11.6	43.3
	2010	100.0	17.5	60.6	28.3	18.3	24.5	34.8	25.3	8.9	39.8
	2011	100.0	18.0	69.5	26.0	20.7	31.3	35.0	27.9	9.2	37.0
Cape Verde - Cap-Vert	2000	100.0	18.9	82.8	30.7	24.8	57.3	14.0	16.3	5.4	69.7
	2005	100.0	21.5	81.3	36.0	18.8	57.6	9.9	17.1	4.0	73.0
	2010	100.0	20.4	68.9	47.1	19.0	57.3	11.2	17.6	3.5	71.2
	2011	100.0	16.3	75.9	45.5	21.2	61.0	9.5	17.9	3.6	72.6
Côte d'Ivoire	2000	100.0	15.5	67.2	11.3	39.8	33.8	24.8	27.4	22.5	47.8
	2005	100.0	10.6	71.3	11.3	49.9	43.1	25.6	24.2	17.0	50.1
	2010	100.0	14.2	65.5	9.6	49.0	38.3	28.5	25.5	15.7	46.0
	2011	100.0	12.6	62.8	8.8	49.0	34.0	28.1	25.9	15.6	46.0
Gambia - Gambie	2000	100.0	17.6	74.8	17.3	47.7	57.4	23.8	14.4	6.6	61.7
	2005	100.0	7.0	82.5	32.8	6.8	35.4	28.7	13.6	7.1	57.7
	2010	100.0	7.7	73.2	30.2	10.0	24.6	32.1	11.3	4.9	56.6
	2011	100.0	8.1	82.8	30.7	6.8	28.4	31.3	13.8	5.5	54.9

For sources and notes, see end of table.

Pour les sources et les notes, se reporter à la fin du tableau.

8

8.3.1 Nominal gross domestic product by type of expenditure and by kind of economic activity of countries and geographical regions

8.3.1 Produit intérieur brut nominal par catégories de dépenses et par branches d'activité économique des pays et des régions géographiques

Region, country or territory / Régions, pays ou territoires	Year / Année	Total GDP / PIB total	GDP by type of expenditure (1) / PIB par catégories de dépenses (1)					GDP by kind of economic activity (2) / PIB par branches d'activité économique (2)			
			Final consumption / Consommation finale		Gross capital formation / Formation brute de capital	Exports / Exportations	Less imports / Moins les importations	Agriculture (3)	Industry (4) / Industrie (4)		Services (5)
			Government / Administration publique	Household / Ménages		Of goods and services / Des biens et services			Total	Manufacturing / Activités de fabrication	
			Percentage / En pourcentage								
Ghana	2000	100.0	10.9	83.0	17.1	31.1	42.3	30.7	21.2	11.1	48.1
	2005	100.0	9.9	86.9	20.6	22.9	38.6	31.8	20.3	10.4	47.9
	2010	100.0	11.2	76.3	22.4	25.3	38.4	29.8	19.1	6.8	51.1
	2011	100.0	9.5	77.9	26.2	39.3	52.8	25.6	25.9	6.7	48.5
Guinea - Guinée	2000	100.0	10.2	59.1	36.7	17.9	18.6	22.7	32.7	3.0	44.6
	2005	100.0	9.5	65.5	28.2	32.1	35.3	24.3	34.8	6.4	40.9
	2010	100.0	16.8	55.8	32.6	29.3	34.4	26.0	34.5	6.1	39.5
	2011	100.0	15.5	51.5	45.1	32.2	37.2	24.5	35.4	6.0	40.1
Guinea-Bissau - Guinée-Bissau	2000	100.0	14.0	94.6	11.3	31.8	51.6	58.1	12.5	9.7	29.4
	2005	100.0	15.3	90.4	6.6	15.8	28.1	44.5	14.2	12.6	41.3
	2010	100.0	9.5	88.5	7.3	18.1	29.3	45.3	13.3	12.5	41.4
	2011	100.0	9.4	85.3	8.9	19.1	29.1	45.3	13.2	12.4	41.5
Liberia - Libéria	2000	100.0	13.5	80.6	7.5	26.5	28.1	70.4	0.6	0.3	28.9
	2005	100.0	11.1	86.4	16.4	37.9	51.9	69.6	9.7	5.7	20.6
	2010	100.0	13.3	113.4	19.5	32.8	78.9	70.7	11.4	5.8	18.0
	2011	100.0	12.8	112.6	19.3	32.6	77.3	70.7	11.4	5.8	17.9
Mali	2000	100.0	16.4	73.4	20.2	22.8	32.7	36.3	20.9	7.2	42.9
	2005	100.0	16.9	68.9	22.0	25.0	32.9	37.5	24.0	9.8	38.5
	2010	100.0	16.9	60.8	24.5	23.7	26.0	40.5	20.1	5.4	39.4
	2011	100.0	17.1	61.8	22.9	25.0	26.8	39.0	22.1	6.4	38.9
Mauritania - Mauritanie	2000	100.0	20.2	74.5	20.6	30.0	45.3	35.9	27.4	11.1	36.7
	2005	100.0	25.2	65.1	61.5	30.7	82.5	29.8	32.4	9.0	37.8
	2010	100.0	25.2	70.4	18.3	61.1	75.0	23.9	37.2	6.5	38.9
	2011	100.0	15.1	69.1	25.9	74.1	84.2	23.7	38.5	6.5	37.9
Niger	2000	100.0	18.3	73.9	15.6	18.6	26.4	41.2	12.8	6.4	46.1
	2005	100.0	15.8	73.5	23.1	18.7	31.1	45.5	11.8	5.9	42.7
	2010	100.0	14.8	70.6	35.9	20.4	41.7	45.1	15.5	5.2	39.4
	2011	100.0	16.7	73.2	32.1	22.7	44.7	42.7	16.1	5.3	41.2
Nigeria - Nigéria	2000	100.0	8.3	52.5	7.0	51.7	19.7	26.0	52.2	3.7	21.8
	2005	100.0	6.8	75.2	5.5	31.7	19.1	32.8	43.5	2.8	23.7
	2010	100.0	12.0	66.2	11.6	39.1	29.0	33.1	37.9	2.4	29.1
	2011	100.0	12.5	60.5	11.1	51.3	35.3	33.3	36.9	2.4	29.8
Senegal - Sénégal	2000	100.0	12.6	76.2	20.5	27.9	37.2	19.1	23.2	14.7	57.6
	2005	100.0	13.0	77.9	24.5	27.0	42.4	16.8	23.6	15.1	59.6
	2010	100.0	14.6	78.5	22.6	24.2	39.8	17.4	23.7	14.0	58.9
	2011	100.0	16.3	78.9	22.2	23.3	40.5	16.8	23.3	14.0	59.8
Sierra Leone	2000	100.0	14.3	98.9	6.9	18.1	39.3	48.8	9.6	3.4	41.6
	2005	100.0	10.0	90.4	11.4	17.8	29.7	51.7	11.8	2.6	36.5
	2010	100.0	10.6	82.9	24.5	17.1	35.1	56.2	8.1	2.3	35.7
	2011	100.0	10.2	86.8	40.8	16.5	54.4	56.7	8.3	2.3	35.1
Togo	2000	100.0	14.5	83.5	15.8	32.7	46.5	37.8	19.7	9.2	42.4
	2005	100.0	13.5	98.7	16.9	39.7	68.8	43.3	19.0	9.5	37.6
	2010	100.0	12.1	85.8	18.9	40.9	57.6	46.1	18.2	8.7	35.7
	2011	100.0	11.8	84.8	19.4	40.9	56.9	46.9	18.4	8.3	34.7

For sources and notes, see end of table.

Pour les sources et les notes, se reporter à la fin du tableau.

8.3.1 Nominal gross domestic product by type of expenditure and by kind of economic activity of countries and geographical regions

8.3.1 Produit intérieur brut nominal par catégories de dépenses et par branches d'activité économique des pays et des régions géographiques

Region, country or territory / Régions, pays ou territoires	Year / Année	Total GDP / PIB total	GDP by type of expenditure (1) / PIB par catégories de dépenses (1)					GDP by kind of economic activity (2) / PIB par branches d'activité économique (2)			
			Final consumption / Consommation finale		Gross capital formation / Formation brute de capital	Exports / Exportations / Of goods and services / Des biens et services	Less imports / Moins les importations	Agriculture (3)	Industry (4) / Industrie (4)		Services (5)
			Government / Administration publique	Household / Ménages					Total	Manufacturing / Activités de fabrication	
						Percentage / En pourcentage					
Developing economies: America - Économies en développement : Amérique	2000	100.0	14.4	65.6	21.2	20.5	21.5	5.6	31.8	18.6	62.7
	2005	100.0	14.5	63.0	20.3	24.9	22.8	5.5	33.5	17.9	61.0
	2010	100.0	16.5	61.6	21.7	21.2	21.0	5.6	32.7	16.2	61.7
	2011	100.0	16.4	61.6	22.1	22.2	22.3	5.7	32.4	15.7	61.9
Caribbean - Caraïbes	2000	100.0	17.3	67.4	19.6	35.2	39.4	6.4	28.3	15.7	65.3
	2005	100.0	18.2	63.7	19.2	36.4	37.4	5.1	27.4	13.2	67.5
	2010	100.0	19.9	67.4	15.9	31.6	34.7	4.9	27.0	14.0	68.1
	2011	100.0	20.8	67.2	16.7	32.0	36.7	4.8	28.0	14.5	67.1
Anguilla	2000	100.0	13.0	88.4	35.0	46.1	82.4	2.3	17.3	3.3	80.5
	2005	100.0	11.4	81.3	32.0	49.2	73.9	2.7	19.3	3.0	78.0
	2010	100.0	20.3	82.0	24.2	45.3	71.7	2.0	15.3	2.7	82.7
	2011	100.0	17.6	79.1	26.0	45.5	68.3	2.2	13.3	2.5	84.5
Antigua and Barbuda - Antigua-et-Barbuda	2000	100.0	17.5	54.0	29.4	62.9	63.8	1.8	16.0	1.9	82.1
	2005	100.0	16.5	67.9	29.3	54.4	68.1	2.0	16.8	2.1	81.2
	2010	100.0	17.1	60.2	36.3	45.4	58.9	2.1	21.9	2.2	76.0
	2011	100.0	17.3	62.8	29.5	48.0	57.6	2.4	19.2	1.9	78.4
Aruba	2000	100.0	21.4	49.4	25.5	74.4	70.7	0.4	16.3	4.0	83.3
	2005	100.0	23.1	52.7	33.6	68.5	77.9	0.4	19.6	3.8	80.0
	2010	100.0	26.3	60.0	28.7	61.4	76.4	0.4	19.6	4.0	80.0
	2011	100.0	26.4	58.9	28.7	68.9	82.8	0.4	19.1	4.0	80.4
Bahamas	2000	100.0	10.8	63.8	27.9	44.4	46.8	2.7	16.7	5.3	80.5
	2005	100.0	11.3	66.2	25.3	45.2	48.0	2.1	14.6	4.3	83.4
	2010	100.0	14.9	69.1	24.6	41.5	50.1	2.1	14.2	3.3	83.7
	2011	100.0	15.0	70.7	27.4	43.4	56.5	2.0	14.9	3.6	83.1
Barbados - Barbade	2000	100.0	13.4	73.5	17.9	42.7	46.7	2.3	18.1	9.0	79.6
	2005	100.0	16.3	73.9	19.0	43.8	51.6	1.8	18.2	8.4	80.0
	2010	100.0	19.7	71.3	14.2	45.8	50.7	1.6	15.5	7.0	82.9
	2011	100.0	19.2	74.3	14.8	47.1	54.5	1.5	15.5	6.8	83.1
British Virgin Islands - Îles Vierges britanniques	2000	100.0	10.5	40.5	23.2	104.4	78.6	1.2	11.9	3.5	86.8
	2005	100.0	9.2	37.1	22.4	108.8	77.7	1.1	11.9	3.1	87.1
	2010	100.0	8.6	35.3	22.0	111.3	77.2	1.0	10.0	3.0	89.0
	2011	100.0	8.5	35.0	21.9	111.5	77.1	1.0	11.0	2.9	88.0
Cayman Islands - Îles Caïmanes	2000	100.0	14.6	63.3	22.4	61.9	61.1	0.2	9.2	0.8	90.5
	2005	100.0	14.6	63.4	22.4	61.9	61.3	0.2	9.1	0.8	90.7
	2010	100.0	14.6	63.4	22.4	61.9	61.3	0.3	7.7	0.8	92.0
	2011	100.0	14.6	63.4	22.4	61.9	61.3	0.3	8.2	0.8	91.5
Cuba	2000	100.0	29.6	60.7	12.5	14.1	16.9	8.4	27.9	17.7	63.7
	2005	100.0	33.6	52.9	10.8	21.0	18.3	5.6	19.4	9.5	75.0
	2010	100.0	34.8	50.3	10.4	22.2	17.7	5.0	20.5	10.6	74.5
	2011	100.0	37.9	49.2	12.2	20.0	19.1	5.0	20.5	10.7	74.5
Curaçao	2011	100.0	16.8	64.7	35.9	78.6	96.0	0.7	15.8	6.5	83.6
Dominica - Dominique	2000	100.0	18.8	72.6	20.5	44.5	56.4	13.3	17.5	7.6	69.3
	2005	100.0	15.6	82.7	20.2	35.8	54.2	13.2	15.0	4.6	71.9
	2010	100.0	17.0	78.7	21.6	38.8	56.1	13.6	14.4	2.8	72.0
	2011	100.0	17.3	79.1	22.4	37.4	56.2	14.6	14.8	2.6	70.6
Dominican Republic - République dominicaine	2000	100.0	7.8	77.8	23.3	37.0	45.9	7.0	34.6	25.2	58.4
	2005	100.0	6.7	82.3	16.5	30.0	35.5	7.2	31.1	22.2	61.7
	2010	100.0	7.7	86.6	16.5	23.0	33.8	6.0	31.0	23.3	63.0
	2011	100.0	7.4	86.6	16.4	24.9	35.3	5.8	32.0	23.8	62.2
Grenada - Grenade	2000	100.0	11.7	64.9	37.7	45.0	59.3	5.9	20.4	5.2	73.7
	2005	100.0	13.0	76.4	46.0	21.3	56.6	3.4	26.1	3.3	70.5
	2010	100.0	16.4	89.3	21.2	21.4	48.3	5.1	16.8	4.4	78.0
	2011	100.0	16.2	88.3	20.3	21.4	46.1	5.5	16.6	4.5	77.9

For sources and notes, see end of table.

Pour les sources et les notes, se reporter à la fin du tableau.

8

8.3.1 Nominal gross domestic product by type of expenditure and by kind of economic activity of countries and geographical regions

8.3.1 Produit intérieur brut nominal par catégories de dépenses et par branches d'activité économique des pays et des régions géographiques

Region, country or territory / Régions, pays ou territoires	Year / Année	Total GDP / PIB total	GDP by type of expenditure (1) / PIB par catégories de dépenses (1)					GDP by kind of economic activity (2) / PIB par branches d'activité économique (2)			
			Final consumption / Consommation finale		Gross capital formation / Formation brute de capital	Exports / Exportations	Less imports / Moins les importations	Agriculture (3)	Industry (4) / Industrie (4)		Services (5)
			Government / Administration publique	Household / Ménages		Of goods and services / Des biens et services			Total	Manufacturing / Activités de fabrication	
			Percentage / En pourcentage								
Haiti - Haïti	2000	100.0	9.0	99.6	14.3	13.8	35.9	23.5	32.0	10.0	44.6
	2005	100.0	8.3	109.7	14.3	15.3	46.1	22.4	32.9	10.1	44.8
	2010	100.0	9.5	135.4	13.3	13.4	66.9	20.9	33.6	8.6	45.4
	2011	100.0	8.7	123.2	14.6	14.9	59.2	19.9	35.3	9.5	44.8
Jamaica - Jamaïque	2000	100.0	14.0	74.5	23.5	38.8	50.7	6.7	24.3	10.1	68.9
	2005	100.0	14.2	78.8	26.9	35.3	55.2	5.7	23.9	8.4	70.4
	2010	100.0	15.8	80.3	20.0	31.0	47.1	5.9	20.5	8.6	73.6
	2011	100.0	15.6	83.7	21.0	30.5	51.0	6.1	21.2	8.9	72.7
Montserrat	2000	100.0	48.0	74.1	43.8	46.9	112.8	1.3	17.3	1.3	81.4
	2005	100.0	46.7	92.7	31.8	33.6	104.7	0.9	16.5	1.5	82.7
	2010	100.0	47.6	79.9	25.7	21.2	74.4	1.0	12.4	1.3	86.5
	2011	100.0	44.5	72.2	30.6	21.1	68.5	1.3	13.8	1.4	85.0
Netherlands Antilles - Antilles néerlandaises	2000	100.0	22.8	53.6	27.2	73.2	76.8	0.7	16.2	6.8	83.1
	2005	100.0	16.6	60.4	29.9	75.8	82.6	0.8	15.6	5.2	83.7
	2010	100.0	17.0	64.6	35.4	78.0	95.0	0.6	15.7	6.3	83.7
Saint Kitts and Nevis - Saint-Kitts-et-Nevis	2000	100.0	11.0	59.3	56.3	36.7	63.5	1.7	29.9	7.8	68.4
	2005	100.0	10.7	57.9	46.2	42.2	56.9	2.0	25.9	7.5	72.1
	2010	100.0	11.4	72.1	38.8	31.2	53.5	1.6	23.6	6.2	74.8
	2011	100.0	11.1	72.9	35.2	32.4	51.3	1.5	24.3	6.6	74.2
Saint Lucia - Sainte-Lucie	2000	100.0	18.7	61.4	29.8	53.8	63.7	6.9	18.8	4.6	74.2
	2005	100.0	19.1	57.3	31.9	62.0	70.2	3.7	20.4	5.6	76.0
	2010	100.0	16.5	60.2	34.5	51.0	62.2	3.2	16.2	3.8	80.6
	2011	100.0	16.5	69.7	35.4	45.9	67.5	3.3	16.4	3.7	80.2
Saint Vincent and the Grenadines - Saint-Vincent-et-les Grenadines	2000	100.0	16.4	65.4	23.3	45.1	50.3	8.4	19.4	5.7	72.1
	2005	100.0	15.7	74.1	26.6	36.4	52.8	6.2	18.6	5.8	75.2
	2010	100.0	19.9	84.7	25.9	27.2	57.7	7.1	19.2	5.6	73.7
	2011	100.0	16.3	87.4	25.4	27.1	56.2	6.3	19.4	5.7	74.4
Trinidad and Tobago - Trinité-et-Tobago	2000	100.0	12.0	57.4	16.8	59.2	45.3	1.2	44.8	16.9	53.9
	2005	100.0	11.6	31.4	30.2	65.8	39.0	0.5	56.7	21.3	42.8
	2010	100.0	13.7	46.2	15.3	57.9	33.1	0.6	52.7	19.3	46.7
	2011	100.0	13.9	46.3	15.3	63.3	38.7	0.5	56.2	20.1	43.3
Turks and Caicos Islands - Îles Turques et Caïques	2000	100.0	15.2	30.8	26.3	78.5	50.8	1.5	15.6	3.5	82.9
	2005	100.0	17.2	50.3	38.7	56.6	62.7	1.2	19.7	2.2	79.1
	2010	100.0	17.8	54.0	45.9	62.0	79.7	0.6	18.4	1.6	81.1
	2011	100.0	17.9	53.5	45.4	61.7	78.6	0.5	17.5	1.6	82.0
Central America - Amérique centrale	*2000*	*100.0*	*10.8*	*66.1*	*26.0*	*29.7*	*32.1*	*4.8*	*34.4*	*21.1*	*60.8*
	2005	*100.0*	*10.8*	*67.8*	*23.8*	*28.7*	*31.2*	*4.1*	*33.4*	*18.6*	*62.6*
	2010	*100.0*	*12.1*	*67.1*	*23.1*	*31.8*	*33.9*	*4.3*	*33.3*	*18.0*	*62.4*
	2011	*100.0*	*11.8*	*66.3*	*24.3*	*33.2*	*35.6*	*4.2*	*34.8*	*18.0*	*61.0*
Belize	2000	100.0	12.9	74.0	31.7	53.0	73.7	16.4	20.7	10.6	63.0
	2005	100.0	14.5	71.6	19.5	54.6	62.7	14.5	16.5	8.6	69.0
	2010	100.0	16.6	63.8	18.0	59.4	57.8	11.8	20.9	12.9	67.3
	2011	100.0	17.0	61.4	19.0	63.2	60.7	11.9	21.1	13.1	67.1
Costa Rica	2000	100.0	13.3	67.0	16.9	48.6	45.8	9.1	31.0	24.5	59.9
	2005	100.0	13.8	67.3	24.3	48.5	54.0	8.6	27.8	20.7	63.6
	2010	100.0	17.7	64.5	20.1	38.1	40.3	6.8	25.0	16.6	68.2
	2011	100.0	18.1	65.2	21.3	37.5	42.0	6.9	26.1	17.6	67.0
El Salvador	2000	100.0	10.2	87.9	16.9	27.4	42.4	10.0	30.3	23.6	59.7
	2005	100.0	9.6	92.8	16.1	25.6	44.2	10.2	28.7	22.2	61.1
	2010	100.0	10.7	93.2	13.3	25.9	43.2	12.1	25.9	19.6	62.1
	2011	100.0	11.1	94.0	14.2	28.1	47.3	12.2	26.0	19.4	61.8

For sources and notes, see end of table.

Pour les sources et les notes, se reporter à la fin du tableau.

8.3.1 Nominal gross domestic product by type of expenditure and by kind of economic activity of countries and geographical regions

8.3.1 Produit intérieur brut nominal par catégories de dépenses et par branches d'activité économique des pays et des régions géographiques

Region, country or territory / Régions, pays ou territoires	Year / Année	Total GDP / PIB total	GDP by type of expenditure (1) / PIB par catégories de dépenses (1)					GDP by kind of economic activity (2) / PIB par branches d'activité économique (2)			
			Final consumption / Consommation finale		Gross capital formation / Formation brute de capital	Exports / Exportations	Less imports / Moins les importations	Agriculture (3)	Industry (4) / Industrie (4)		Services (5)
			Government / Administration publique	Household / Ménages		Of goods and services / Des biens et services			Total	Manufacturing / Activités de fabrication	
			Percentage / En pourcentage								
Guatemala	2000	100.0	9.3	82.5	19.7	30.3	41.3	14.9	28.7	21.0	56.4
	2005	100.0	8.5	87.7	19.7	25.1	41.0	13.1	28.6	19.7	58.3
	2010	100.0	10.5	86.1	13.9	25.8	36.3	11.3	28.0	19.3	60.7
	2011	100.0	10.5	00.0	13.6	27.1	37.9	11.0	29.0	19.6	60.0
Honduras	2000	100.0	13.4	70.8	28.3	54.0	66.4	15.2	31.1	21.7	53.7
	2005	100.0	15.5	75.3	27.6	59.0	77.5	13.1	27.6	20.1	59.3
	2010	100.0	18.2	79.6	23.0	43.9	64.6	11.8	25.1	17.4	63.1
	2011	100.0	16.5	77.7	27.0	47.6	68.8	13.7	25.9	18.2	60.4
Mexico - Mexique	2000	100.0	10.6	65.1	26.6	28.2	30.0	4.1	35.1	21.2	60.9
	2005	100.0	10.7	66.6	24.1	27.2	28.6	3.3	34.1	18.7	62.5
	2010	100.0	11.8	65.8	23.7	30.4	31.6	3.5	34.6	18.3	61.9
	2011	100.0	11.4	65.0	24.8	31.7	32.9	3.4	36.1	18.2	60.5
Nicaragua	2000	100.0	17.2	79.0	31.0	23.9	51.1	20.1	27.2	16.4	52.7
	2005	100.0	18.8	80.8	30.1	29.0	58.6	18.2	28.1	17.7	53.8
	2010	100.0	17.6	83.6	25.8	42.6	69.7	19.7	28.1	18.8	52.1
	2011	100.0	17.8	83.0	31.5	45.9	78.1	20.5	29.6	19.5	49.9
Panama	2000	100.0	13.2	59.9	24.1	72.6	69.8	7.0	18.5	9.7	74.5
	2005	100.0	13.2	62.1	18.4	75.5	69.1	6.8	16.3	7.2	76.9
	2010	100.0	13.5	58.1	26.0	77.0	74.6	4.3	16.6	5.7	79.0
	2011	100.0	15.9	55.4	28.9	85.8	86.4	4.8	17.1	6.1	78.1
South America - Amérique du Sud	*2000*	*100.0*	*16.2*	*65.3*	*18.7*	*14.5*	*14.6*	*5.9*	*30.5*	*17.3*	*63.6*
	2005	*100.0*	*16.3*	*60.2*	*18.4*	*21.8*	*16.8*	*6.4*	*34.2*	*17.7*	*59.4*
	2010	*100.0*	*17.8*	*59.6*	*21.5*	*17.4*	*16.2*	*6.1*	*32.7*	*15.7*	*61.1*
	2011	*100.0*	*17.6*	*59.8*	*21.7*	*18.3*	*17.4*	*6.3*	*31.7*	*15.0*	*62.0*
Argentina - Argentine	2000	100.0	13.8	69.3	17.5	11.0	11.6	5.0	27.6	17.5	67.4
	2005	100.0	11.9	61.3	20.9	25.1	19.2	9.4	35.6	23.2	55.0
	2010	100.0	14.9	57.3	24.5	21.7	18.4	10.0	30.9	20.5	59.1
	2011	100.0	15.1	56.4	26.2	21.8	19.5	10.6	30.8	20.6	58.5
Bolivia (Plurinational State of) - Bolivie (État plurinational de)	2000	100.0	14.5	76.4	18.1	18.3	27.3	14.3	28.3	14.6	57.4
	2005	100.0	16.0	66.3	14.3	35.5	32.1	13.9	30.9	13.7	55.2
	2010	100.0	13.8	62.3	17.0	41.2	34.3	12.4	35.8	13.4	51.8
	2011	100.0	13.8	60.9	19.6	44.1	38.4	12.0	37.4	12.7	50.6
Brazil - Brésil	2000	100.0	19.2	64.3	18.3	10.0	11.7	5.6	27.7	17.2	66.7
	2005	100.0	19.9	60.3	16.2	15.1	11.5	5.7	29.3	18.1	65.0
	2010	100.0	21.1	59.6	20.2	10.9	11.9	5.3	28.1	16.2	66.6
	2011	100.0	20.7	60.3	19.7	11.9	12.6	5.5	27.5	14.6	67.0
Chile - Chili	2000	100.0	12.1	63.6	22.6	30.7	28.9	5.2	37.6	19.6	57.3
	2005	100.0	10.6	58.9	22.0	40.3	31.8	4.1	40.3	15.4	55.6
	2010	100.0	12.0	58.3	23.5	38.1	31.9	3.4	39.5	11.7	57.0
	2011	100.0	11.8	60.2	24.6	38.1	34.7	3.4	39.1	11.9	57.5
Colombia - Colombie	2000	100.0	16.5	69.5	14.9	15.9	16.8	8.9	29.4	15.0	61.6
	2005	100.0	15.7	66.0	20.2	16.8	18.8	8.4	32.8	15.4	58.8
	2010	100.0	16.7	63.4	22.0	15.9	18.0	7.1	35.0	14.1	57.9
	2011	100.0	16.0	61.7	23.5	19.0	20.1	7.0	37.6	13.9	55.5
Ecuador - Équateur	2000	100.0	9.6	63.6	21.3	36.2	30.8	10.8	40.9	18.8	48.3
	2005	100.0	11.2	66.3	23.6	30.9	32.0	6.9	36.6	11.4	56.5
	2010	100.0	11.7	67.8	26.2	32.9	38.6	6.8	37.8	11.1	55.4
	2011	100.0	11.6	63.3	29.0	36.1	40.0	6.8	38.6	11.6	54.6
Guyana	2000	100.0	17.3	62.0	24.1	40.0	51.5	27.7	32.6	6.6	39.7
	2005	100.0	16.9	91.4	20.3	53.7	75.8	25.7	28.7	7.4	45.6
	2010	100.0	15.1	87.4	25.4	50.1	78.0	17.6	34.5	6.6	47.9
	2011	100.0	15.9	93.4	21.6	55.0	85.0	17.9	33.8	6.8	48.2

For sources and notes, see end of table.

Pour les sources et les notes, se reporter à la fin du tableau.

8

8.3.1 Nominal gross domestic product by type of expenditure and by kind of economic activity of countries and geographical regions

8.3.1 Produit intérieur brut nominal par catégories de dépenses et par branches d'activité économique des pays et des régions géographiques

Region, country or territory / Régions, pays ou territoires	Year / Année	Total GDP / PIB total	GDP by type of expenditure (1) / PIB par catégories de dépenses (1)					GDP by kind of economic activity (2) / PIB par branches d'activité économique (2)			
			Final consumption / Consommation finale		Gross capital formation / Formation brute de capital	Exports / Exportations	Less imports / Moins les importations	Agriculture (3)	Industry (4) / Industrie (4)		Services (5)
			Government / Administration publique	Household / Ménages		Of goods and services / Des biens et services			Total	Manufacturing / Activités de fabrication	
			Percentage / En pourcentage								
Paraguay	2000	100.0	12.7	79.2	18.8	38.1	48.8	18.5	24.8	17.2	56.7
	2005	100.0	10.9	74.5	19.9	50.2	55.5	23.2	22.7	15.2	54.1
	2010	100.0	11.4	77.3	17.7	51.6	58.1	24.9	22.8	13.7	52.3
	2011	100.0	12.1	74.9	19.3	56.1	62.7	24.1	22.8	13.9	53.1
Peru - Pérou	2000	100.0	10.6	71.2	20.2	16.0	18.0	8.5	29.9	15.8	61.6
	2005	100.0	10.1	66.1	17.9	25.1	19.2	7.2	34.3	16.4	58.5
	2010	100.0	9.5	60.7	26.4	25.4	22.0	6.8	35.9	14.4	57.3
	2011	100.0	9.2	59.6	27.0	28.4	24.2	7.1	35.4	14.8	57.5
Suriname	2000	100.0	14.3	57.6	43.1	49.2	60.0	20.6	27.0	18.7	52.4
	2005	100.0	12.3	53.7	45.6	51.3	59.3	11.3	37.4	23.5	51.3
	2010	100.0	13.4	36.1	36.4	52.8	38.6	10.7	37.6	22.7	51.7
	2011	100.0	12.5	35.3	38.8	60.1	43.0	10.5	39.3	24.0	50.3
Uruguay	2000	100.0	12.4	76.5	14.5	16.7	20.0	6.4	23.6	13.4	70.0
	2005	100.0	10.9	69.4	17.7	30.4	28.5	9.8	26.6	16.6	63.6
	2010	100.0	12.9	67.7	18.6	26.8	26.0	8.9	25.6	13.4	65.5
	2011	100.0	13.0	67.9	19.4	27.1	27.3	9.5	24.3	12.6	66.2
Venezuela (Bolivarian Rep. of) - Venezuela (Rép. bolivarienne du)	2000	100.0	12.4	51.7	24.2	29.7	18.1	4.1	48.4	19.3	47.5
	2005	100.0	11.1	46.8	23.0	39.7	20.5	4.0	56.9	16.2	39.2
	2010	100.0	11.2	55.9	22.0	28.5	17.6	5.7	51.0	13.6	43.4
	2011	100.0	11.3	54.9	22.7	30.4	19.3	5.3	49.0	14.4	45.7
Developing economies: Asia - Économies en développement : Asie	2000	100.0	13.7	54.0	27.7	42.5	38.3	11.6	38.5	14.1	49.9
	2005	100.0	12.9	50.4	30.9	47.5	41.8	9.9	40.9	23.5	49.2
	2010	100.0	13.0	46.5	36.6	41.9	38.1	9.9	41.2	24.4	48.9
	2011	100.0	12.8	45.7	37.3	43.5	39.5	9.8	42.1	24.2	48.1
Eastern Asia - Asie orientale	2000	100.0	14.0	51.0	31.9	40.5	37.8	9.8	39.6	10.4	50.6
	2005	100.0	13.6	45.3	35.8	47.7	42.6	8.7	41.9	29.4	49.4
	2010	100.0	13.3	39.3	43.3	40.8	36.8	8.4	43.7	30.9	47.9
	2011	100.0	13.2	39.2	44.4	41.7	38.0	8.6	44.0	30.8	47.4
China - Chine	2000	100.0	15.9	46.4	35.3	23.4	21.0	15.1	45.9	..	39.0
	2005	100.0	14.1	39.0	41.6	36.6	31.2	12.1	47.4	32.5	40.5
	2010	100.0	13.2	34.9	48.0	29.3	25.5	10.1	46.7	32.5	43.2
	2011	100.0	13.1	35.0	49.2	30.6	27.1	10.1	46.8	32.2	43.1
China, Hong Kong SAR - Chine (RAS de Hong Kong)	2000	100.0	9.1	59.0	27.5	143.3	138.8	0.1	12.7	4.8	87.2
	2005	100.0	8.8	58.2	20.6	198.7	186.3	0.1	8.8	2.9	91.2
	2010	100.0	8.5	62.7	23.4	223.1	217.7	0.1	7.1	1.8	92.9
	2011	100.0	8.3	65.2	22.9	229.7	226.0	0.0	7.0	1.7	92.9
China, Macao SAR - Chine (RAS de Macao)	2000	100.0	13.2	45.3	10.9	97.7	67.1	..	14.7	9.6	85.3
	2005	100.0	10.1	31.1	26.5	94.6	62.3	..	15.2	4.3	84.8
	2010	100.0	8.1	22.7	13.3	106.3	50.4	..	7.4	0.9	92.6
	2011	100.0	7.4	20.7	13.2	112.4	53.6	..	12.0	1.5	88.0
China, Taiwan Province of - Province chinoise de Taiwan	2000	100.0	13.4	58.8	25.7	52.9	50.8	2.1	31.5	25.4	66.4
	2005	100.0	12.5	60.4	22.7	62.5	58.1	1.7	32.2	27.3	66.1
	2010	100.0	12.1	58.0	22.8	73.5	66.5	1.7	32.1	26.8	66.2
	2011	100.0	12.3	59.7	21.1	75.8	68.9	1.8	30.4	25.6	67.8
Korea, Dem. People's Rep. of - Corée, Rép. populaire dém. de	2000	100.0	..	..	..	4.2	10.0	30.4	37.1	17.7	32.5
	2005	100.0	..	..	..	6.0	11.1	25.0	42.8	19.0	32.2
	2010	100.0	..	..	..	5.9	11.1	20.8	48.2	21.9	31.0
	2011	100.0	..	..	..	5.9	11.1	21.1	47.1	22.2	31.7
Korea, Republic of - Corée, République de	2000	100.0	12.0	54.8	30.6	38.6	35.7	4.6	38.6	28.3	56.8
	2005	100.0	13.9	53.8	29.7	39.3	36.6	3.3	38.3	27.5	58.4
	2010	100.0	15.2	52.6	29.5	52.3	49.7	2.6	39.3	30.3	58.0
	2011	100.0	15.4	52.9	29.5	56.2	54.1	2.7	39.7	31.2	57.6

For sources and notes, see end of table.

Pour les sources et les notes, se reporter à la fin du tableau.

8.3.1 Nominal gross domestic product by type of expenditure and by kind of economic activity of countries and geographical regions

8.3.1 Produit intérieur brut nominal par catégories de dépenses et par branches d'activité économique des pays et des régions géographiques

Region, country or territory / Régions, pays ou territoires	Year / Année	Total GDP / PIB total	GDP by type of expenditure (1) / PIB par catégories de dépenses (1)					GDP by kind of economic activity (2) / PIB par branches d'activité économique (2)			
			Final consumption / Consommation finale		Gross capital formation / Formation brute de capital	Exports / Exportations	Less imports / Moins les importations	Agriculture (3)	Industry (4) / Industrie (4)		Services (5)
			Government / Administration publique	Household / Ménages	Formation brute de capital	Of goods and services / Des biens et services			Total	Manufacturing / Activités de fabrication	
			Percentage / En pourcentage								
Mongolia - Mongolie	2000	100.0	14.7	75.7	29.0	54.0	67.9	30.9	25.0	7.6	44.1
	2005	100.0	11.3	56.0	37.5	58.8	63.6	22.1	36.2	6.4	41.7
	2010	100.0	13.1	54.3	40.8	54.7	62.4	16.2	37.5	7.3	46.3
	2011	100.0	13.2	51.5	58.4	63.4	86.0	19.1	34.9	7.2	45.9
Southern Asia - Asie méridionale	*2000*	*100.0*	*11.9*	*63.8*	*24.7*	*15.5*	*16.3*	*22.3*	*27.5*	*15.3*	*50.2*
	2005	*100.0*	*11.0*	*58.7*	*31.6*	*21.5*	*23.0*	*17.3*	*31.0*	*15.2*	*51.7*
	2010	*100.0*	*11.3*	*56.9*	*34.6*	*22.6*	*25.6*	*16.5*	*29.8*	*14.7*	*53.7*
	2011	*100.0*	*11.3*	*56.9*	*34.0*	*24.2*	*27.9*	*16.2*	*29.3*	*14.1*	*54.5*
Afghanistan	2000	100.0	8.6	119.1	12.2	34.7	74.5	57.0	23.2	16.8	19.8
	2005	100.0	10.0	115.7	21.8	26.0	73.6	36.6	26.9	16.7	36.5
	2010	100.0	11.5	97.4	17.5	9.8	43.9	29.6	21.9	13.0	48.5
	2011	100.0	10.9	97.7	15.1	8.8	38.8	30.6	23.8	14.8	45.6
Bangladesh	2000	100.0	4.6	77.5	23.0	14.0	19.2	25.5	25.3	15.2	49.2
	2005	100.0	5.5	74.4	24.5	16.6	23.0	20.1	27.2	16.5	52.6
	2010	100.0	5.4	74.5	24.4	18.4	25.0	18.6	28.5	17.9	53.0
	2011	100.0	5.5	74.9	24.7	23.1	31.6	18.4	28.6	18.2	53.0
Bhutan - Bhoutan	2000	100.0	21.9	47.7	48.2	29.0	53.5	27.4	36.0	8.4	36.6
	2005	100.0	21.9	40.4	49.9	39.1	62.8	23.2	37.3	7.4	39.5
	2010	100.0	20.0	41.7	52.3	39.8	58.4	17.5	44.6	9.1	37.9
	2011	100.0	20.7	43.1	54.1	41.2	60.4	18.4	44.1	8.7	37.5
India - Inde	2000	100.0	12.6	63.7	24.2	13.2	14.2	23.2	26.4	15.8	50.4
	2005	100.0	10.9	58.3	34.3	19.3	22.0	18.7	28.3	15.6	53.0
	2010	100.0	11.9	56.5	35.8	22.8	26.9	17.6	27.3	14.7	55.1
	2011	100.0	11.7	56.0	35.5	24.6	29.8	17.2	26.4	13.9	56.4
Iran (Islamic Rep. of) - Iran (Rép. islamique d')	2000	100.0	13.8	46.4	33.4	22.1	17.0	13.4	36.2	13.2	50.5
	2005	100.0	14.3	42.7	30.2	33.3	23.9	9.0	44.5	11.3	46.5
	2010	100.0	11.1	40.8	41.2	27.6	20.7	9.7	41.8	12.9	48.5
	2011	100.0	11.7	42.1	39.6	27.9	21.3	9.4	41.4	11.9	49.2
Maldives	2000	100.0	22.9	32.9	26.3	89.5	71.6	5.2	11.9	4.8	82.9
	2005	100.0	41.6	30.4	61.1	67.0	100.1	7.5	14.8	6.3	77.7
	2010	100.0	38.9	26.2	56.7	76.5	98.3	3.8	15.2	4.2	81.0
	2011	100.0	39.7	25.6	57.5	76.2	99.1	3.5	15.7	4.6	80.9
Nepal - Népal	2000	100.0	7.4	79.8	22.5	23.5	34.3	37.7	17.3	9.2	45.0
	2005	100.0	8.9	79.5	26.5	14.6	29.5	35.2	17.1	7.9	47.7
	2010	100.0	10.0	78.5	38.3	9.6	36.4	35.4	15.1	6.3	49.5
	2011	100.0	9.6	81.8	32.5	8.9	32.8	37.2	14.9	6.2	47.9
Pakistan	2000	100.0	8.6	75.4	17.2	13.4	14.7	25.9	23.3	14.7	50.7
	2005	100.0	7.8	76.9	19.1	15.7	19.6	21.5	27.1	18.6	51.4
	2010	100.0	8.0	82.3	15.6	13.6	19.4	21.2	25.4	17.7	53.4
	2011	100.0	7.9	84.1	13.1	14.2	19.2	21.6	24.9	18.6	53.4
Sri Lanka	2000	100.0	13.7	70.9	25.6	38.2	48.4	17.6	29.9	19.5	52.5
	2005	100.0	13.1	69.0	26.1	32.3	41.3	11.8	30.2	19.5	58.0
	2010	100.0	15.6	65.8	27.4	21.7	30.8	12.8	29.4	18.0	57.8
	2011	100.0	14.8	69.8	29.9	23.1	37.6	12.1	29.9	18.2	58.0
South-Eastern Asia - Asie du Sud-Est	*2000*	*100.0*	*10.1*	*55.7*	*24.8*	*82.8*	*73.6*	*11.5*	*39.8*	*26.6*	*48.7*
	2005	*100.0*	*10.2*	*57.2*	*24.9*	*83.1*	*75.1*	*10.8*	*41.1*	*26.6*	*48.1*
	2010	*100.0*	*10.8*	*54.7*	*27.4*	*67.1*	*60.1*	*12.7*	*40.6*	*24.7*	*46.8*
	2011	*100.0*	*10.8*	*54.3*	*27.4*	*67.2*	*61.6*	*13.1*	*40.0*	*23.9*	*46.9*
Brunei Darussalam - Brunéi Darussalam	2000	100.0	25.8	24.8	13.1	67.3	35.8	1.0	63.7	15.4	35.3
	2005	100.0	18.4	22.5	11.4	70.2	27.3	0.9	71.6	12.3	27.5
	2010	100.0	22.4	23.2	15.9	81.4	32.9	0.8	66.8	12.1	32.4
	2011	100.0	17.3	19.9	13.4	81.3	29.1	0.6	71.7	11.8	27.7

For sources and notes, see end of table.

Pour les sources et les notes, se reporter à la fin du tableau.

8

8.3.1 Nominal gross domestic product by type of expenditure and by kind of economic activity of countries and geographical regions

8.3.1 Produit intérieur brut nominal par catégories de dépenses et par branches d'activité économique des pays et des régions géographiques

Region, country or territory / Régions, pays ou territoires	Year / Année	Total GDP / PIB total	GDP by type of expenditure (1) / PIB par catégories de dépenses (1)					GDP by kind of economic activity (2) / PIB par branches d'activité économique (2)			
			Final consumption / Consommation finale		Gross capital formation / Formation brute de capital	Exports / Exportations	Less imports / Moins les importations	Agriculture (3)	Industry (4) / Industrie (4)		Services (5)
			Government / Administration publique	Household / Ménages	Formation brute de capital	Of goods and services / Des biens et services			Total	Manufacturing / Activités de fabrication	
			Percentage / En pourcentage								
Cambodia - Cambodge	2000	100.0	5.2	88.8	17.5	49.8	61.8	37.8	23.0	16.9	39.1
	2005	100.0	5.8	84.3	18.5	64.1	72.7	32.4	26.4	18.8	41.2
	2010	100.0	6.3	81.3	17.4	54.1	59.5	36.0	23.3	15.6	40.7
	2011	100.0	6.0	82.9	17.1	54.1	59.5	36.7	23.5	16.1	39.8
Indonesia (...2002) - Indonésie (...2002)	2000	100.0	6.6	61.6	22.3	40.9	30.5	15.6	45.9	27.7	38.5
Indonesia - Indonésie	2005	100.0	8.1	64.4	25.1	34.1	29.9	13.1	46.5	27.4	40.3
	2010	100.0	9.0	56.6	32.6	24.6	22.9	15.3	47.0	24.8	37.6
	2011	100.0	9.0	54.6	32.8	26.3	24.9	14.7	47.2	24.3	38.1
Lao People's Dem. Rep. - Rép. dém. populaire lao	2000	100.0	6.7	93.5	13.9	30.0	44.1	43.5	18.7	7.8	37.8
	2005	100.0	8.2	69.9	36.3	25.8	39.0	36.3	23.2	8.5	40.5
	2010	100.0	12.4	59.9	27.3	24.5	24.9	29.7	28.9	10.1	41.4
	2011	100.0	11.5	63.2	31.1	22.8	28.8	28.4	28.2	9.6	43.4
Malaysia - Malaisie	2000	100.0	9.4	43.1	30.1	115.2	96.7	8.5	45.1	28.7	46.4
	2005	100.0	11.5	44.2	22.4	112.9	91.0	8.4	46.9	27.9	44.7
	2010	100.0	12.2	47.5	23.1	93.7	76.6	10.5	41.5	24.8	48.0
	2011	100.0	13.0	47.5	23.6	91.6	75.7	12.0	40.7	24.6	47.3
Myanmar	2000	100.0	18.9	68.7	12.4	0.5	0.6	57.2	9.7	7.2	33.1
	2005	100.0	10.4	76.5	13.2	0.2	0.1	46.7	17.5	12.8	35.8
	2010	100.0	9.0	69.4	22.7	0.1	0.1	36.4	26.0	19.5	37.6
	2011	100.0	10.3	70.2	19.3	0.1	0.1	38.2	24.4	18.1	37.4
Philippines	2000	100.0	11.4	72.2	18.4	51.4	53.4	14.0	34.5	24.5	51.6
	2005	100.0	9.0	75.0	21.6	46.1	51.7	12.7	33.8	24.1	53.5
	2010	100.0	9.7	71.6	20.5	34.8	36.6	12.3	32.6	21.4	55.1
	2011	100.0	9.4	73.4	21.8	31.2	36.2	12.8	31.5	21.1	55.7
Singapore - Singapour	2000	100.0	10.9	41.9	33.2	192.3	179.5	0.1	34.5	26.9	65.4
	2005	100.0	10.5	40.1	20.0	229.7	200.3	0.1	31.6	26.8	68.3
	2010	100.0	10.5	38.4	22.1	207.2	178.7	0.0	27.9	22.1	72.1
	2011	100.0	10.3	39.4	22.4	209.0	182.3	0.0	26.6	20.9	73.4
Thailand - Thaïlande	2000	100.0	13.5	54.0	22.3	65.0	56.6	8.5	36.9	28.6	54.6
	2005	100.0	13.7	55.9	30.5	68.6	69.7	9.2	38.8	29.9	52.0
	2010	100.0	15.4	52.1	24.9	66.7	60.4	10.9	40.1	31.5	49.0
	2011	100.0	15.7	52.8	25.5	72.0	68.5	11.6	38.4	29.9	50.0
Timor-Leste	2005	100.0	11.6	21.4	4.8	82.5	20.4	7.1	78.2	0.7	14.7
	2010	100.0	23.4	14.7	14.1	95.4	47.5	4.5	81.2	0.7	14.3
	2011	100.0	22.5	14.9	11.2	95.5	44.3	4.6	82.0	0.6	13.4
Viet Nam	2000	100.0	6.4	66.5	29.6	55.0	57.5	24.5	36.7	18.6	38.7
	2005	100.0	6.2	63.5	35.6	69.0	73.2	21.0	41.0	20.6	38.0
	2010	100.0	6.5	66.5	38.9	77.5	87.8	20.6	41.1	19.7	38.3
	2011	100.0	6.5	64.3	32.6	74.6	86.5	22.0	40.3	19.4	37.7
Western Asia - Asie occidentale	*2000*	*100.0*	*17.5*	*52.5*	*20.1*	*41.3*	*31.5*	*6.8*	*44.5*	*13.5*	*48.7*
	2005	*100.0*	*14.9*	*52.3*	*20.4*	*46.4*	*34.0*	*5.8*	*47.2*	*12.4*	*47.0*
	2010	*100.0*	*16.2*	*53.2*	*22.8*	*45.9*	*38.1*	*5.0*	*45.9*	*11.4*	*49.1*
	2011	*100.0*	*14.7*	*49.0*	*23.3*	*51.4*	*38.2*	*4.4*	*51.1*	*11.2*	*44.5*
Bahrain - Bahreïn	2000	100.0	17.4	44.5	12.6	89.5	63.9	0.7	40.0	10.5	59.3
	2005	100.0	15.7	36.7	24.5	99.5	76.4	0.4	39.1	11.0	60.5
	2010	100.0	15.0	34.2	29.0	81.5	59.7	0.4	42.9	14.3	56.7
	2011	100.0	12.7	37.1	24.4	76.6	50.8	0.4	46.3	16.0	53.4
Iraq	2000	100.0	14.7	16.8	36.2	93.9	61.6	4.6	84.6	0.9	10.8
	2005	100.0	27.5	51.7	30.5	74.9	84.6	6.9	63.3	1.3	29.9
	2010	100.0	25.0	55.6	12.0	50.0	42.6	5.3	55.6	2.3	39.1
	2011	100.0	20.3	52.3	15.9	53.1	35.9	4.8	56.6	2.2	38.7

For sources and notes, see end of table.

Pour les sources et les notes, se reporter à la fin du tableau.

8.3.1 Nominal gross domestic product by type of expenditure and by kind of economic activity of countries and geographical regions

8.3.1 Produit intérieur brut nominal par catégories de dépenses et par branches d'activité économique des pays et des régions géographiques

Region, country or territory / Régions, pays ou territoires	Year / Année	Total GDP / PIB total	GDP by type of expenditure (1) / PIB par catégories de dépenses (1)					GDP by kind of economic activity (2) / PIB par branches d'activité économique (2)			
			Final consumption / Consommation finale		Gross capital formation / Formation brute de capital	Exports / Exportations / Of goods and services / Des biens et services	Less imports / Moins les importations /	Agriculture (3)	Industry (4) / Industrie (4)		Services (5)
			Government / Administration publique	Household / Ménages					Total	Manufacturing / Activités de fabrication	
			Percentage / En pourcentage								
Jordan - Jordanie	2000	100.0	23.7	80.6	22.4	41.8	68.5	2.3	24.4	14.8	73.3
	2005	100.0	19.5	87.8	34.1	52.7	94.2	3.0	26.9	16.6	70.1
	2010	100.0	20.4	77.1	24.9	46.1	68.5	3.2	29.1	18.2	67.6
	2011	100.0	19.8	82.7	20.0	41.2	71.4	3.2	29.6	18.4	67.3
Kuwait - Koweït	2000	100.0	21.5	41.5	10.7	56.5	30.1	0.3	57.2	6.7	42.5
	2005	100.0	15.7	32.2	16.4	64.0	28.3	0.3	60.2	7.0	39.5
	2010	100.0	16.7	30.4	19.1	60.1	26.3	0.2	57.5	5.1	42.4
	2011	100.0	15.1	22.8	15.6	71.1	24.6	0.2	67.4	4.5	32.4
Lebanon - Liban	2000	100.0	17.6	85.6	20.3	13.6	37.1	6.4	20.9	12.0	72.7
	2005	100.0	15.1	84.2	21.9	21.4	42.6	5.3	17.9	10.7	76.8
	2010	100.0	14.3	79.8	33.9	22.2	50.2	4.7	19.7	7.2	75.5
	2011	100.0	12.7	87.9	31.4	21.7	51.0	5.2	19.2	7.5	75.6
Oman	2000	100.0	21.5	35.2	15.4	53.9	26.0	2.0	58.5	5.7	39.4
	2005	100.0	20.9	30.6	21.1	58.6	31.2	1.5	62.3	8.3	36.2
	2010	100.0	17.9	33.9	24.9	56.3	32.8	1.2	62.4	10.6	36.4
	2011	100.0	16.1	32.7	26.8	56.4	31.3	1.0	66.0	10.1	32.9
Qatar	2000	100.0	19.7	15.2	20.2	67.3	22.3	0.4	69.5	5.3	30.1
	2005	100.0	14.3	16.0	34.3	65.1	29.7	0.1	73.8	9.8	26.0
	2010	100.0	12.1	15.9	34.2	61.1	23.3	0.1	67.0	10.5	32.9
	2011	100.0	9.7	17.6	29.2	61.7	19.9	0.1	71.0	9.8	28.9
Saudi Arabia - Arabie saoudite	2000	100.0	26.0	36.5	18.7	43.7	24.9	4.9	53.6	9.6	41.5
	2005	100.0	22.2	26.5	18.2	60.9	27.8	3.2	62.9	9.3	33.9
	2010	100.0	23.1	35.0	22.6	57.4	38.2	2.5	62.2	10.1	35.4
	2011	100.0	19.7	29.4	21.1	63.0	33.2	2.0	68.0	10.1	30.1
State of Palestine - État de Palestine	2000	100.0	26.5	94.5	33.8	16.6	71.4	11.3	25.7	13.1	63.0
	2005	100.0	18.0	103.1	27.5	13.2	61.8	6.5	27.4	15.3	66.1
	2010	100.0	24.5	98.7	18.5	13.8	55.5	6.0	19.8	11.9	74.2
	2011	100.0	24.5	94.8	16.9	11.6	47.8	6.0	20.1	11.6	73.9
Syrian Arab Republic - République arabe syrienne	2000	100.0	12.4	63.4	17.3	36.1	29.2	24.7	33.3	1.5	41.9
	2005	100.0	13.7	65.9	18.4	41.0	39.1	20.3	31.2	2.5	48.5
	2010	100.0	12.4	60.6	26.7	32.7	32.3	19.7	30.7	4.8	49.6
	2011	100.0	14.4	59.7	27.7	30.0	31.5	20.4	30.7	4.6	48.8
Turkey - Turquie	2000	100.0	11.7	70.5	20.8	20.1	23.1	10.8	30.0	21.4	59.2
	2005	100.0	11.8	71.7	20.0	21.9	25.4	10.6	28.0	19.6	61.3
	2010	100.0	14.3	71.7	19.5	21.2	26.8	9.5	26.4	17.6	64.1
	2011	100.0	13.9	71.2	23.8	23.7	32.6	9.0	27.5	18.3	63.5
United Arab Emirates - Émirats arabes unis	2000	100.0	15.4	43.5	23.2	73.7	55.8	2.2	51.4	12.8	46.4
	2005	100.0	6.9	58.3	19.2	67.6	52.0	1.4	53.8	10.3	44.8
	2010	100.0	8.6	55.2	29.6	79.3	72.8	0.9	51.4	8.5	47.7
	2011	100.0	7.5	51.5	28.3	86.9	74.3	0.8	56.7	7.7	42.5
Yemen - Yémen	2000	100.0	13.0	60.3	20.3	36.7	30.3	12.2	42.0	5.3	45.7
	2005	100.0	11.4	57.4	26.7	36.0	31.5	9.6	43.8	5.8	46.6
	2010	100.0	13.2	76.9	15.8	32.1	37.9	12.1	34.4	8.0	53.4
	2011	100.0	13.9	77.8	7.4	31.7	32.6	11.3	37.3	7.0	51.5
Developing economies: Oceania - Économies en développement : Océanie	2000	100.0	19.3	67.3	20.5	38.0	45.9	15.3	25.2	10.0	59.4
	2005	100.0	18.1	71.9	21.4	36.2	49.4	12.9	25.4	10.0	61.6
	2010	100.0	17.5	74.9	24.2	36.0	53.8	14.0	28.9	9.6	57.1
	2011	100.0	18.2	79.0	23.5	36.1	58.3	15.0	28.8	9.1	56.2
Cook Islands - Îles Cook	2000	100.0	34.2	42.4	13.8	83.8	74.2	10.3	8.3	3.5	81.4
	2005	100.0	35.0	40.3	13.1	73.8	62.3	6.9	9.6	3.9	83.5
	2010	100.0	31.8	47.3	15.4	82.8	77.4	4.9	9.1	3.4	86.0
	2011	100.0	32.3	47.0	15.3	81.5	76.2	4.9	9.4	3.5	85.8

For sources and notes, see end of table.

Pour les sources et les notes, se reporter à la fin du tableau.

8

8.3.1 Nominal gross domestic product by type of expenditure and by kind of economic activity of countries and geographical regions

8.3.1 Produit intérieur brut nominal par catégories de dépenses et par branches d'activité économique des pays et des régions géographiques

Region, country or territory / Régions, pays ou territoires	Year / Année	Total GDP / PIB total	GDP by type of expenditure (1) / PIB par catégories de dépenses (1)					GDP by kind of economic activity (2) / PIB par branches d'activité économique (2)			
			Final consumption / Consommation finale		Gross capital formation / Formation brute de capital	Exports / Exportations	Less imports / Moins les importations	Agriculture (3)	Industry (4) / Industrie (4)		Services (5)
			Government / Administration publique	Household / Ménages		Of goods and services / Des biens et services			Total	Manufacturing / Activités de fabrication	
			Percentage / En pourcentage								
Fiji - Fidji	2000	100.0	16.9	72.6	18.3	56.1	63.8	16.3	19.2	14.7	64.5
	2005	100.0	15.6	80.3	17.1	49.7	62.6	14.1	19.2	14.2	66.8
	2010	100.0	12.4	80.6	18.9	52.8	64.7	11.6	21.7	15.8	66.7
	2011	100.0	12.4	80.3	19.1	52.6	64.8	12.8	20.1	15.0	67.1
French Polynesia - Polynésie française	2000	100.0	8.2	87.0	15.5	17.6	32.8	3.9	16.3	7.5	79.8
	2005	100.0	6.2	96.2	17.2	12.0	39.3	2.6	14.8	6.5	82.6
	2010	100.0	7.3	94.7	17.3	12.3	38.9	2.4	14.3	6.3	83.3
	2011	100.0	7.5	94.4	17.3	12.4	38.9	2.4	14.3	6.3	83.3
Kiribati	2000	100.0	29.6	76.9	33.4	6.9	46.8	22.0	11.6	4.9	66.4
	2005	100.0	42.1	109.5	47.5	14.3	113.4	24.2	6.7	4.5	69.2
	2010	100.0	38.1	99.0	42.9	10.9	90.9	25.8	8.5	5.3	65.7
	2011	100.0	37.6	97.8	42.4	13.0	90.8	25.8	8.5	5.3	65.7
Marshall Islands - Îles Marshall	2000	100.0	54.1	91.1	56.8	12.4	114.5	10.0	19.2	4.6	70.9
	2005	100.0	54.1	91.1	56.8	12.4	114.5	9.0	9.2	2.2	81.8
	2010	100.0	54.1	91.1	56.8	12.4	114.5	15.0	12.5	1.9	72.5
	2011	100.0	54.1	91.1	56.8	12.4	114.5	12.7	12.6	1.8	74.7
Micronesia (Federated States of) - Micronésie (États fédérés de)	2000	100.0	71.5	71.5	32.1	17.9	71.2	25.5	8.7	1.7	65.8
	2005	100.0	73.8	73.8	33.2	16.7	74.9	24.1	5.7	0.6	70.2
	2010	100.0	73.6	73.6	33.1	22.3	80.2	26.0	8.0	0.5	66.0
	2011	100.0	74.1	74.1	33.3	21.1	79.9	26.6	6.4	0.5	67.0
Nauru	2000	100.0	29.6	76.9	33.4	6.9	46.8	7.1	7.7	4.5	85.2
	2005	100.0	42.1	109.5	47.5	14.3	113.4	7.8	-6.5	3.5	98.7
	2010	100.0	38.1	99.0	42.9	10.9	90.9	6.2	35.6	13.3	58.2
	2011	100.0	37.6	97.8	42.4	13.0	90.8	5.2	41.6	17.5	53.2
New Caledonia - Nouvelle-Calédonie	2000	100.0	26.8	65.1	22.9	22.8	37.6	2.4	26.0	14.9	71.6
	2005	100.0	25.6	63.6	29.8	21.5	40.4	1.7	26.6	16.0	71.7
	2010	100.0	24.5	60.7	39.2	20.5	44.9	1.6	29.4	16.3	69.0
	2011	100.0	25.0	62.0	39.7	18.2	44.9	1.6	27.7	13.9	70.6
Palau - Palaos	2000	100.0	41.9	125.5	29.0	9.6	106.1	3.9	15.3	1.4	80.8
	2005	100.0	34.6	52.5	16.5	77.6	81.2	3.2	19.2	0.4	77.6
	2010	100.0	34.6	49.5	21.3	71.1	76.5	3.2	20.9	0.4	75.9
	2011	100.0	34.6	48.9	22.3	69.8	75.6	3.2	21.2	0.3	75.6
Papua New Guinea - Papouasie-Nouvelle-Guinée	2000	100.0	16.6	44.6	21.9	66.2	49.2	35.2	40.7	7.4	24.1
	2005	100.0	16.1	48.0	17.5	74.5	56.1	34.0	44.3	6.3	21.7
	2010	100.0	15.1	72.6	14.9	59.9	62.6	31.5	45.1	5.8	23.4
	2011	100.0	17.0	85.5	14.5	57.3	74.3	31.1	43.9	6.8	25.0
Samoa	2000	100.0	24.0	85.2	14.2	30.6	53.9	16.7	26.8	15.0	56.6
	2005	100.0	22.4	91.6	10.4	29.9	54.3	12.3	30.5	15.5	57.2
	2010	100.0	20.3	92.9	9.0	30.8	53.0	9.7	27.4	9.5	62.9
	2011	100.0	20.0	93.1	9.0	31.1	53.1	9.9	26.7	8.2	63.4
Solomon Islands - Îles Salomon	2000	100.0	31.8	48.5	19.6	59.1	59.1	34.7	12.7	8.0	52.6
	2005	100.0	38.4	64.5	17.2	32.9	52.0	30.4	7.5	5.2	62.1
	2010	100.0	33.2	66.6	37.4	46.4	78.6	28.3	10.0	5.9	61.6
	2011	100.0	30.5	55.8	21.0	54.2	70.0	28.9	10.3	5.9	60.8
Tonga	2000	100.0	18.1	91.7	20.7	15.3	46.7	22.1	20.7	10.2	57.2
	2005	100.0	15.2	100.7	22.2	17.6	57.7	20.0	18.9	8.3	61.1
	2010	100.0	18.1	98.2	30.1	13.2	58.0	18.3	20.0	6.8	61.7
	2011	100.0	17.1	90.9	37.9	17.9	60.8	18.9	22.0	6.5	59.1
Tuvalu	2000	100.0	147.1	5.6	11.7	2.1	66.5	17.3	13.1	1.4	69.7
	2005	100.0	73.3	28.6	62.6	1.6	66.2	21.2	8.4	0.9	70.4
	2010	100.0	70.7	24.5	53.6	1.7	50.5	22.1	9.3	0.9	68.6
	2011	100.0	70.1	23.7	51.8	1.7	47.4	22.3	9.4	0.9	68.2

For sources and notes, see end of table.

Pour les sources et les notes, se reporter à la fin du tableau.

8.3.1 Nominal gross domestic product by type of expenditure and by kind of economic activity of countries and geographical regions

8.3.1 Produit intérieur brut nominal par catégories de dépenses et par branches d'activité économique des pays et des régions géographiques

Region, country or territory / Régions, pays ou territoires	Year / Année	Total GDP / PIB total	GDP by type of expenditure (1) / PIB par catégories de dépenses (1)					GDP by kind of economic activity (2) / PIB par branches d'activité économique (2)			
			Final consumption / Consommation finale		Gross capital formation / Formation brute de capital	Exports / Exportations	Less imports / Moins les importations	Agriculture (3)	Industry (4) / Industrie (4)		Services (5)
			Government / Administration publique	Household / Ménages		Of goods and services / Des biens et services			Total	Manufacturing / Activités de fabrication	
			Percentage / En pourcentage								
Vanuatu	2000	100.0	15.5	66.4	25.8	39.5	47.7	25.2	12.3	5.0	62.5
	2005	100.0	13.3	70.4	20.4	52.4	57.2	23.8	8.5	4.3	67.7
	2010	100.0	15.6	62.2	34.1	49.9	61.0	21.5	10.8	3.3	67.7
	2011	100.0	15.6	62.2	34.1	49.9	61.0	21.5	10.8	3.3	67.7
Transition economies - Économies en transition	**2000**	**100.0**	**16.2**	**52.7**	**19.3**	**45.0**	**32.9**	**10.3**	**37.4**	**21.2**	**52.3**
	2005	**100.0**	**16.8**	**53.0**	**22.2**	**38.9**	**30.3**	**6.9**	**37.1**	**18.3**	**56.0**
	2010	**100.0**	**17.9**	**54.1**	**23.5**	**34.3**	**28.5**	**5.4**	**35.8**	**15.2**	**58.7**
	2011	**100.0**	**17.1**	**52.4**	**24.8**	**36.6**	**29.6**	**5.7**	**37.0**	**16.0**	**57.3**
Albania - Albanie	2000	100.0	9.5	76.6	31.7	17.9	38.1	25.5	16.1	4.8	58.5
	2005	100.0	10.9	78.0	37.0	22.8	47.5	20.6	24.4	6.6	55.0
	2010	100.0	10.3	78.5	32.3	31.9	53.0	20.3	22.1	7.8	57.6
	2011	100.0	9.9	80.8	31.2	33.4	55.8	19.3	23.6	7.7	57.1
Armenia - Arménie	2000	100.0	11.8	97.1	18.6	23.4	50.5	25.1	38.3	18.2	36.5
	2005	100.0	10.6	75.5	30.5	28.8	43.2	20.6	44.7	14.6	34.6
	2010	100.0	13.1	82.0	32.9	20.8	45.3	18.8	36.1	10.7	45.1
	2011	100.0	13.7	82.9	27.9	23.7	47.3	22.1	31.7	10.9	46.2
Azerbaijan - Azerbaïdjan	2000	100.0	15.2	64.4	20.7	40.2	38.4	17.0	45.1	5.6	37.9
	2005	100.0	10.4	42.1	41.5	62.9	52.9	9.8	63.2	7.0	27.0
	2010	100.0	10.9	39.4	18.1	54.3	20.7	5.9	64.0	5.1	30.1
	2011	100.0	9.5	39.1	19.9	58.7	25.0	5.8	66.1	4.7	28.1
Belarus - Bélarus	2000	100.0	19.5	56.9	25.4	64.7	68.2	14.0	41.7	27.8	44.3
	2005	100.0	20.8	52.0	28.5	59.8	59.1	9.8	43.4	29.1	46.8
	2010	100.0	16.8	54.5	41.2	54.3	67.9	10.2	40.8	26.6	49.0
	2011	100.0	15.1	51.6	36.3	87.9	90.0	9.6	42.7	30.8	47.7
Bosnia and Herzegovina - Bosnie-Herzégovine	2000	100.0	20.8	98.2	27.5	28.5	75.1	10.9	27.0	12.0	62.1
	2005	100.0	22.2	96.9	27.9	32.4	73.4	10.1	25.5	12.1	64.4
	2010	100.0	23.5	89.8	22.0	37.4	59.1	8.3	25.9	13.1	65.8
	2011	100.0	24.0	91.5	21.9	40.8	64.4	8.6	26.5	13.1	64.9
Croatia - Croatie	2000	100.0	22.4	61.8	18.9	41.7	44.8	6.5	29.2	19.9	64.3
	2005	100.0	19.0	60.2	27.0	42.3	48.6	5.0	29.2	17.1	65.8
	2010	100.0	19.9	58.9	21.7	39.4	39.9	5.0	26.8	15.8	68.2
	2011	100.0	19.9	59.1	21.1	41.8	41.9	5.1	26.5	16.2	68.4
Georgia - Géorgie	2000	100.0	8.5	90.5	26.6	23.0	39.7	21.7	22.1	12.9	56.1
	2005	100.0	17.3	66.9	33.5	33.7	51.6	16.5	26.5	13.5	57.0
	2010	100.0	21.1	74.9	21.6	35.0	52.8	8.3	22.0	12.0	69.8
	2011	100.0	18.3	74.2	25.6	36.5	55.1	9.2	23.2	13.1	67.5
Kazakhstan	2000	100.0	12.1	61.9	18.1	56.6	49.1	8.6	40.1	17.5	51.3
	2005	100.0	11.2	49.9	31.0	53.5	44.7	6.6	39.2	12.5	54.2
	2010	100.0	10.8	45.4	25.4	44.0	29.2	4.7	41.9	11.7	53.4
	2011	100.0	10.8	43.2	22.4	49.9	28.0	5.4	40.3	12.0	54.3
Kyrgyzstan - Kirghizistan	2000	100.0	20.0	65.7	20.0	41.8	47.6	36.6	31.3	19.4	32.1
	2005	100.0	17.5	84.5	16.4	38.3	56.8	31.3	22.0	14.1	46.7
	2010	100.0	18.1	84.6	27.4	51.6	81.7	18.8	28.2	18.2	53.1
	2011	100.0	18.5	84.1	25.3	57.2	85.5	19.7	27.9	18.3	52.4
Montenegro - Monténégro	2010	100.0	23.4	82.2	22.8	34.7	63.1	9.2	19.5	5.4	71.3
	2011	100.0	20.5	84.7	19.3	39.4	64.3	9.5	20.2	6.0	70.3
Republic of Moldova - République de Moldova	2000	100.0	14.7	88.4	23.9	49.6	76.6	28.3	21.2	15.8	50.6
	2005	100.0	16.4	93.4	30.8	51.2	91.9	19.1	22.2	15.5	58.7
	2010	100.0	22.2	93.6	23.5	39.2	78.5	14.1	19.5	12.4	66.4
	2011	100.0	20.3	96.4	24.5	45.0	86.2	14.4	20.2	13.1	65.5
Russian Federation - Fédération de Russie	2000	100.0	15.3	46.2	18.7	44.1	24.1	6.8	39.4	22.3	53.8
	2005	100.0	16.9	49.9	20.1	35.2	21.5	5.0	38.1	18.3	57.0
	2010	100.0	18.7	52.5	22.8	30.0	21.7	4.0	35.4	15.0	60.6
	2011	100.0	17.9	50.3	25.0	31.1	22.3	4.3	37.0	16.0	58.7

For sources and notes, see end of table.

Pour les sources et les notes, se reporter à la fin du tableau.

8

8.3.1 Nominal gross domestic product by type of expenditure and by kind of economic activity of countries and geographical regions

8.3.1 Produit intérieur brut nominal par catégories de dépenses et par branches d'activité économique des pays et des régions géographiques

Region, country or territory / Régions, pays ou territoires	Year / Année	Total GDP / PIB total	GDP by type of expenditure (1) / PIB par catégories de dépenses (1)					GDP by kind of economic activity (2) / PIB par branches d'activité économique (2)			
			Final consumption / Consommation finale		Gross capital formation / Formation brute de capital	Exports / Exportations	Less imports / Moins les importations	Agriculture (3)	Industry (4) / Industrie (4)		Services (5)
			Government / Administration publique	Household / Ménages		Of goods and services / Des biens et services			Total	Manufacturing / Activités de fabrication	
			Percentage / En pourcentage								
Serbia and Montenegro - Serbie-et-Monténégro	2000	100.0	22.0	81.2	12.1	14.5	29.8	22.3	30.3	21.8	47.4
	2005	100.0	20.2	77.9	23.3	27.3	48.8	12.2	27.4	16.8	60.4
Serbia - Serbie	2010	100.0	19.3	81.6	19.2	33.7	53.8	10.4	27.0	15.5	62.6
	2011	100.0	19.2	80.0	20.7	34.5	54.8	10.9	27.5	15.8	61.7
Tajikistan - Tadjikistan	2000	100.0	11.6	87.7	9.4	92.4	100.2	27.3	38.4	36.1	34.3
	2005	100.0	14.6	81.1	11.6	54.3	72.8	23.8	30.7	25.6	45.6
	2010	100.0	11.3	84.7	23.8	26.8	59.0	21.8	27.9	16.4	50.3
	2011	100.0	13.1	91.8	25.0	28.2	72.9	21.6	27.6	16.1	50.7
TFYR of Macedonia - LERY de Macédoine	2000	100.0	18.2	74.4	22.3	48.6	63.5	11.7	32.9	20.2	55.4
	2005	100.0	18.4	77.3	21.3	44.1	61.1	12.3	28.2	17.4	59.5
	2010	100.0	19.1	74.1	25.5	46.6	65.3	12.2	27.0	16.7	60.8
	2011	100.0	18.4	76.2	25.4	56.0	76.1	12.3	28.3	16.6	59.4
Turkmenistan - Turkménistan	2000	100.0	14.2	36.5	34.7	95.5	80.9	22.9	41.8	35.0	35.2
	2005	100.0	13.2	46.6	22.9	65.0	47.8	18.8	37.6	31.1	43.6
	2010	100.0	11.1	33.2	58.6	51.7	54.6	12.0	54.0	45.0	34.0
	2011	100.0	9.7	43.6	46.9	55.6	51.9	12.0	54.0	44.9	34.0
Ukraine	2000	100.0	18.6	56.6	19.7	62.4	57.4	16.8	37.6	21.3	45.5
	2005	100.0	18.2	58.3	22.6	51.5	50.6	10.3	34.4	21.9	55.3
	2010	100.0	20.3	64.1	18.5	50.7	53.7	8.3	29.2	15.8	62.6
	2011	100.0	18.1	65.8	21.5	53.8	59.2	9.2	30.5	15.8	60.3
Uzbekistan - Ouzbékistan	2000	100.0	18.7	61.9	19.6	24.6	21.5	34.9	22.8	13.2	42.3
	2005	100.0	17.6	46.7	26.5	37.9	28.7	29.5	29.1	19.8	41.4
	2010	100.0	17.6	51.9	26.5	31.5	30.9	19.5	35.4	23.9	45.1
	2011	100.0	18.0	51.8	26.7	32.6	33.6	20.1	33.1	22.4	46.8
Developed economies: America - Économies développées : Amérique	**2000**	**100.0**	**14.6**	**68.0**	**20.5**	**13.8**	**16.9**	**1.0**	**23.7**	**15.7**	**75.2**
	2005	**100.0**	**16.0**	**68.8**	**20.1**	**13.1**	**17.9**	**1.1**	**22.7**	**13.9**	**76.3**
	2010	**100.0**	**18.2**	**69.5**	**15.5**	**14.8**	**18.1**	**1.2**	**21.0**	**12.9**	**77.8**
	2011	**100.0**	**17.7**	**70.0**	**15.7**	**16.1**	**19.5**	**1.1**	**21.3**	**12.6**	**77.5**
Bermuda - Bermudes	2000	100.0	10.9	53.9	20.1	46.8	40.9	0.7	11.0	2.4	88.4
	2005	100.0	20.6	75.2	20.6	37.2	53.6	0.8	9.7	1.6	89.5
	2010	100.0	19.9	74.0	19.8	41.2	54.9	0.7	7.2	1.3	92.0
	2011	100.0	19.9	74.2	19.8	41.2	55.0	0.7	8.3	1.4	91.0
Canada	2000	100.0	18.6	55.4	20.2	45.6	39.8	2.3	33.2	19.2	64.5
	2005	100.0	18.9	55.2	22.1	37.8	34.1	1.8	32.4	15.0	65.8
	2010	100.0	21.8	57.9	22.2	29.4	31.3	1.8	30.6	10.9	67.6
	2011	100.0	21.4	57.2	22.8	31.2	32.4	1.7	30.9	10.9	67.4
Greenland - Groenland	2000	100.0	50.9	48.8	23.2	37.0	60.0	10.5	15.2	6.0	74.3
	2005	100.0	52.5	52.7	24.0	36.9	66.0	10.2	15.2	6.3	74.5
	2010	100.0	53.8	51.1	55.1	27.9	88.0	8.8	16.1	5.8	75.1
	2011	100.0	54.3	49.8	47.3	28.2	79.6	9.1	16.3	6.2	74.6
United States - États-Unis	2000	100.0	14.3	68.9	20.6	11.5	15.2	1.0	23.1	15.5	76.0
	2005	100.0	15.7	70.0	19.9	10.9	16.5	1.0	21.9	13.9	77.1
	2010	100.0	17.8	70.8	14.8	13.2	16.6	1.1	20.1	13.1	78.8
	2011	100.0	17.3	71.5	14.9	14.4	18.0	1.1	20.3	12.8	78.6
Developed economies: Asia - Économies développées : Asie	**2000**	**100.0**	**17.2**	**56.5**	**25.0**	**11.6**	**10.1**	**1.5**	**31.1**	**21.4**	**67.4**
	2005	**100.0**	**18.6**	**57.7**	**22.4**	**15.1**	**13.8**	**1.2**	**28.0**	**19.8**	**70.8**
	2010	**100.0**	**19.9**	**59.2**	**19.6**	**16.0**	**14.8**	**1.2**	**27.2**	**19.4**	**71.6**
	2011	**100.0**	**20.8**	**60.2**	**19.8**	**16.1**	**17.0**	**1.2**	**26.8**	**18.9**	**72.0**
Israel - Israël	2000	100.0	25.8	53.9	20.5	37.3	37.5	1.7	24.7	17.3	73.6
	2005	100.0	25.7	55.8	18.9	42.7	43.1	2.1	21.2	15.0	76.7
	2010	100.0	23.9	58.2	16.0	36.9	34.9	1.9	20.6	14.1	77.4
	2011	100.0	23.9	58.3	18.7	36.9	37.8	2.0	21.0	14.4	77.0

For sources and notes, see end of table.

Pour les sources et les notes, se reporter à la fin du tableau.

8.3.1 Nominal gross domestic product by type of expenditure and by kind of economic activity of countries and geographical regions

8.3.1 Produit intérieur brut nominal par catégories de dépenses et par branches d'activité économique des pays et des régions géographiques

Region, country or territory / Régions, pays ou territoires	Year / Année	Total GDP / PIB total	GDP by type of expenditure (1) / PIB par catégories de dépenses (1)					GDP by kind of economic activity (2) / PIB par branches d'activité économique (2)			
			Final consumption / Consommation finale		Gross capital formation / Formation brute de capital	Exports / Exportations	Less imports / Moins les importations	Agriculture (3) / Agriculture (3)	Industry (4) / Industrie (4)		Services (5)
			Government / Administration publique	Household / Ménages		Of goods and services / Des biens et services			Total	Manufacturing / Activités de fabrication	
			Percentage / En pourcentage								
Japan - Japon	2000	100.0	16.9	56.5	25.1	10.9	9.4	1.5	31.3	21.5	67.2
	2005	100.0	18.4	57.8	22.5	14.3	12.9	1.2	28.1	19.9	70.6
	2010	100.0	19.8	59.2	19.8	15.2	14.0	1.2	27.5	19.5	71.4
	2011	100.0	20.6	60.3	19.9	15.2	16.1	1.2	27.0	19.1	71.8
Developed economies: Europe - Économies développées : Europe	**2000**	**100.0**	**19.5**	**58.4**	**21.4**	**36.4**	**35.7**	**2.2**	**28.2**	**18.4**	**69.6**
	2005	**100.0**	**20.5**	**57.9**	**20.4**	**37.6**	**36.4**	**1.8**	**26.8**	**16.4**	**71.4**
	2010	**100.0**	**21.8**	**57.7**	**18.9**	**41.1**	**39.6**	**1.6**	**25.8**	**15.1**	**72.6**
	2011	**100.0**	**21.3**	**57.5**	**19.3**	**43.9**	**42.0**	**1.7**	**26.2**	**15.5**	**72.1**
Andorra - Andorre	2000	100.0	17.1	59.7	26.3	29.1	32.2	0.5	17.8	4.5	81.7
	2005	100.0	18.0	57.8	29.5	25.7	30.9	0.4	17.9	4.1	81.7
	2010	100.0	21.4	58.0	22.8	27.2	29.4	0.5	15.2	4.2	84.3
	2011	100.0	20.9	58.3	21.5	30.3	31.1	0.6	14.0	4.1	85.5
Austria - Autriche	2000	100.0	19.0	54.9	24.5	46.2	44.5	1.9	31.4	20.1	66.7
	2005	100.0	18.4	55.0	22.7	53.8	49.9	1.5	30.2	19.2	68.3
	2010	100.0	19.4	54.7	21.6	54.1	49.9	1.5	28.7	18.4	69.8
	2011	100.0	18.8	54.4	23.2	57.3	54.0	1.6	29.3	18.7	69.0
Belgium - Belgique	2000	100.0	21.3	53.2	22.6	78.1	75.2	1.3	27.2	18.7	71.5
	2005	100.0	22.7	51.5	21.9	78.7	74.7	0.8	24.4	16.6	74.9
	2010	100.0	24.3	52.9	20.6	79.9	77.6	0.8	22.5	13.8	76.7
	2011	100.0	24.4	52.6	21.8	84.3	83.1	0.7	22.7	13.8	76.6
Bulgaria - Bulgarie	2000	100.0	19.0	68.4	18.0	50.5	55.8	12.6	26.3	14.1	61.1
	2005	100.0	18.3	69.2	27.6	40.5	55.6	8.5	29.2	16.6	62.3
	2010	100.0	16.2	62.8	22.9	57.4	59.3	4.9	29.4	14.5	65.6
	2011	100.0	15.5	60.7	23.1	66.5	65.8	5.6	31.1	16.9	63.2
Cyprus - Chypre	2000	100.0	16.2	65.1	17.8	56.1	55.2	3.8	20.9	9.7	75.3
	2005	100.0	18.0	64.8	19.8	48.6	51.2	2.9	22.2	8.4	74.9
	2010	100.0	20.0	66.4	19.8	42.0	48.2	2.4	18.3	6.3	79.3
	2011	100.0	20.1	66.5	16.5	42.8	45.9	2.3	16.9	6.1	80.8
Czech Republic - République tchèque	2000	100.0	20.3	51.9	29.9	60.9	63.1	3.6	37.5	25.9	58.9
	2005	100.0	21.4	49.3	26.5	64.4	61.7	2.6	38.0	25.5	59.5
	2010	100.0	21.3	50.7	24.9	66.5	63.3	1.7	36.9	22.9	61.4
	2011	100.0	20.6	50.8	24.6	72.5	68.5	2.2	37.0	23.8	60.9
Denmark - Danemark	2000	100.0	25.1	47.7	21.2	46.5	40.5	2.5	26.6	15.4	70.9
	2005	100.0	26.0	48.2	20.8	49.0	44.1	1.3	25.4	13.5	73.2
	2010	100.0	29.1	48.5	17.2	50.3	45.1	1.3	22.2	11.5	76.5
	2011	100.0	28.6	48.5	17.5	53.8	48.4	1.4	22.3	10.9	76.3
Estonia - Estonie	2000	100.0	19.8	55.5	28.4	84.6	88.2	4.8	27.6	17.0	67.7
	2005	100.0	17.2	55.5	33.8	77.7	84.2	3.5	29.7	16.5	66.8
	2010	100.0	20.9	52.4	20.3	79.4	72.7	3.3	28.4	16.0	68.3
	2011	100.0	19.5	51.1	24.8	91.5	87.6	3.6	30.0	17.3	66.4
Finland - Finlande	2000	100.0	20.6	49.4	20.9	43.6	34.4	3.5	34.4	25.6	62.1
	2005	100.0	22.5	51.5	21.8	41.8	37.7	2.8	32.1	22.5	65.1
	2010	100.0	24.7	55.5	18.5	40.3	39.0	2.9	28.2	17.4	68.9
	2011	100.0	24.3	55.5	20.9	40.7	41.4	2.9	27.8	17.3	69.4
France	2000	100.0	22.9	56.2	19.9	28.8	27.8	2.5	22.8	15.2	74.7
	2005	100.0	23.8	56.9	20.0	26.4	27.0	2.0	20.9	12.6	77.1
	2010	100.0	24.9	58.0	19.3	25.6	27.7	1.8	18.9	10.3	79.3
	2011	100.0	24.5	57.7	20.6	27.0	29.8	1.8	18.7	10.1	79.5
Germany - Allemagne	2000	100.0	19.0	58.4	22.3	33.4	33.1	1.1	30.5	22.3	68.4
	2005	100.0	18.8	58.8	17.3	41.3	36.1	0.8	29.3	22.0	69.9
	2010	100.0	19.5	57.4	17.5	47.0	41.4	0.8	29.7	21.5	69.5
	2011	100.0	19.3	57.4	18.3	50.2	45.1	0.9	30.8	22.6	68.3

For sources and notes, see end of table.

Pour les sources et les notes, se reporter à la fin du tableau.

8

8.3.1 Nominal gross domestic product by type of expenditure and by kind of economic activity of countries and geographical regions

8.3.1 Produit intérieur brut nominal par catégories de dépenses et par branches d'activité économique des pays et des régions géographiques

Region, country or territory / Régions, pays ou territoires	Year / Année	Total GDP / PIB total	GDP by type of expenditure (1) / PIB par catégories de dépenses (1)					GDP by kind of economic activity (2) / PIB par branches d'activité économique (2)			
			Final consumption / Consommation finale		Gross capital formation / Formation brute de capital	Exports / Exportations	Less imports / Moins les importations	Agriculture (3)	Industry (4) / Industrie (4)		Services (5)
			Government / Administration publique	Household / Ménages		Of goods and services / Des biens et services			Total	Manufacturing / Activités de fabrication	
			Percentage / En pourcentage								
Greece - Grèce	2000	100.0	18.9	69.9	25.3	25.7	39.6	6.6	21.0	11.1	72.5
	2005	100.0	18.1	69.8	21.4	23.2	32.5	4.9	19.7	9.5	75.4
	2010	100.0	18.2	74.5	16.2	21.5	30.4	3.1	18.8	10.0	78.0
	2011	100.0	17.5	75.5	14.5	24.0	31.5	3.1	18.0	9.9	78.9
Hungary - Hongrie	2000	100.0	21.5	54.9	27.1	74.6	78.1	5.9	32.5	22.9	61.7
	2005	100.0	22.6	55.0	24.5	65.9	68.1	4.4	31.5	22.3	64.1
	2010	100.0	21.9	52.9	18.7	86.9	80.4	3.5	30.7	22.0	65.8
	2011	100.0	20.8	53.0	19.5	91.3	84.6	4.5	31.1	22.9	64.4
Iceland - Islande	2000	100.0	23.4	60.6	23.2	33.6	40.9	8.5	26.5	13.2	65.1
	2005	100.0	24.6	59.4	28.2	31.7	44.0	5.8	25.0	10.3	69.2
	2010	100.0	25.9	51.4	12.5	56.3	46.2	7.9	23.7	14.3	68.4
	2011	100.0	25.3	51.9	14.2	59.3	50.8	7.0	24.6	13.3	68.3
Ireland - Irlande	2000	100.0	14.7	48.0	23.9	97.4	84.1	3.4	40.8	32.3	55.8
	2005	100.0	16.3	45.7	27.2	81.3	69.6	1.8	34.1	23.0	64.1
	2010	100.0	19.2	49.9	11.6	100.8	82.0	1.7	30.9	25.8	67.4
	2011	100.0	18.4	46.5	10.3	104.9	82.9	2.3	31.0	25.9	66.7
Italy - Italie	2000	100.0	18.3	59.9	20.8	26.8	25.8	2.8	27.7	20.1	69.5
	2005	100.0	20.1	59.0	20.9	25.9	25.9	2.2	26.5	17.8	71.3
	2010	100.0	21.1	60.6	20.3	26.6	28.5	1.9	25.1	16.1	73.0
	2011	100.0	20.5	61.3	19.7	28.8	30.3	2.0	24.7	16.0	73.3
Latvia - Lettonie	2000	100.0	20.9	63.0	23.1	41.9	49.0	4.5	25.4	14.4	70.0
	2005	100.0	17.8	63.1	33.6	48.2	62.6	3.9	23.1	12.9	72.9
	2010	100.0	18.4	63.1	19.8	53.6	54.9	5.0	23.9	13.3	71.1
	2011	100.0	16.1	61.9	26.8	58.8	63.6	5.1	24.7	14.1	70.2
Lithuania - Lituanie	2000	100.0	22.6	65.2	18.5	44.5	50.8	6.3	29.6	18.8	64.1
	2005	100.0	18.6	64.9	23.6	57.3	64.4	4.8	32.7	20.1	62.5
	2010	100.0	20.4	63.8	17.8	68.0	70.0	3.3	29.4	19.0	67.3
	2011	100.0	18.9	63.4	20.5	77.6	80.4	3.5	31.3	20.6	65.2
Luxembourg	2000	100.0	15.1	40.7	23.2	150.0	129.0	0.7	18.4	11.3	81.0
	2005	100.0	16.5	35.5	22.5	155.8	130.3	0.4	16.6	9.2	82.9
	2010	100.0	16.6	33.5	18.7	165.0	133.8	0.3	12.8	6.1	86.9
	2011	100.0	16.5	33.3	20.7	164.7	135.2	0.3	13.3	6.9	86.4
Malta - Malte	2000	100.0	18.2	64.4	25.3	90.6	98.4	2.3	28.5	22.4	69.1
	2005	100.0	19.5	65.5	18.1	76.8	79.9	2.6	21.6	16.0	75.7
	2010	100.0	21.1	61.6	15.9	95.3	93.9	1.9	19.9	13.4	78.3
	2011	100.0	21.1	61.4	12.5	98.0	93.1	1.9	20.3	14.1	77.8
Netherlands - Pays-Bas	2000	100.0	22.0	50.4	22.0	70.1	64.5	2.5	24.8	14.6	72.7
	2005	100.0	23.7	48.8	19.0	69.6	61.1	1.9	24.1	13.5	73.9
	2010	100.0	28.4	45.5	18.0	78.2	70.1	1.8	24.1	12.4	74.1
	2011	100.0	27.9	45.0	18.1	83.0	74.1	1.6	24.8	12.9	73.6
Norway - Norvège	2000	100.0	19.3	43.2	20.4	46.5	29.4	2.1	41.7	9.8	56.2
	2005	100.0	19.7	42.6	21.5	44.1	27.8	1.6	42.8	9.0	55.6
	2010	100.0	22.0	43.1	22.4	41.1	28.8	1.7	39.4	7.8	58.8
	2011	100.0	21.5	41.5	23.2	42.1	28.3	1.5	42.3	7.7	56.3
Poland - Pologne	2000	100.0	17.4	64.1	24.8	27.1	33.5	4.9	31.1	17.2	64.0
	2005	100.0	18.1	63.4	19.3	37.1	37.8	4.6	30.8	17.8	64.6
	2010	100.0	18.9	61.3	21.0	42.2	43.4	3.7	32.2	16.8	64.1
	2011	100.0	18.0	61.2	21.9	45.2	46.4	4.0	33.1	17.6	62.9
Portugal	2000	100.0	19.0	63.6	28.4	28.9	39.9	3.6	28.5	17.1	67.9
	2005	100.0	21.1	64.7	23.5	27.7	37.1	2.7	25.5	14.6	71.8
	2010	100.0	21.6	66.0	19.6	31.0	38.2	2.2	23.3	12.7	74.5
	2011	100.0	20.1	66.3	17.5	35.5	39.3	2.1	23.3	13.1	74.5

For sources and notes, see end of table.

Pour les sources et les notes, se reporter à la fin du tableau.

8.3.1 Nominal gross domestic product by type of expenditure and by kind of economic activity of countries and geographical regions

8.3.1 Produit intérieur brut nominal par catégories de dépenses et par branches d'activité économique des pays et des régions géographiques

Region, country or territory / Régions, pays ou territoires	Year / Année	Total GDP / PIB total	GDP by type of expenditure (1) / PIB par catégories de dépenses (1)					GDP by kind of economic activity (2) / PIB par branches d'activité économique (2)			
			Final consumption / Consommation finale		Gross capital formation / Formation brute de capital	Exports / Exportations	Less imports / Moins les importations	Agriculture (3)	Industry (4) / Industrie (4)		Services (5)
			Government / Administration publique	Household / Ménages		Of goods and services / Des biens et services			Total	Manufacturing / Activités de fabrication	
						Percentage / En pourcentage					
Romania - Roumanie	2000	100.0	17.5	68.5	19.4	32.8	38.1	12.1	34.4	23.4	53.6
	2005	100.0	17.4	69.5	23.3	33.1	43.2	9.5	35.5	24.0	55.0
	2010	100.0	16.4	64.0	24.8	35.5	40.7	6.7	39.6	24.1	53.8
	2011	100.0	14.4	62.0	20.8	38.3	43.5	7.4	41.0	25.1	51.6
San Marino - Saint-Marin	2000	100.0	11.1	38.3	34.8	205.0	190.4	0.1	35.9	32.4	64.1
	2005	100.0	12.9	30.1	38.4	194.7	179.2	0.1	32.9	28.8	67.0
	2010	100.0	16.0	32.1	24.1	196.1	168.3	0.1	32.8	28.4	67.2
	2011	100.0	14.8	31.7	28.0	210.5	184.9	0.1	32.6	28.2	67.3
Slovakia - Slovaquie	2000	100.0	20.1	56.5	26.0	70.4	73.0	4.5	36.1	23.9	59.4
	2005	100.0	18.3	57.5	28.9	76.3	80.9	3.6	36.3	23.3	60.1
	2010	100.0	19.4	58.5	23.4	81.2	82.6	3.1	40.2	23.6	56.7
	2011	100.0	18.1	57.5	21.8	89.1	86.5	3.2	41.9	25.9	54.9
Slovenia - Slovénie	2000	100.0	18.7	57.3	27.4	53.7	57.2	3.4	34.7	24.4	61.9
	2005	100.0	19.0	54.3	27.2	62.2	62.6	2.6	33.7	23.0	63.6
	2010	100.0	20.7	57.2	21.1	66.0	65.0	2.5	29.9	19.2	67.7
	2011	100.0	20.8	57.8	20.1	72.4	71.2	2.6	30.5	20.3	66.9
Spain - Espagne	2000	100.0	17.1	59.7	26.3	29.1	32.2	4.2	31.1	17.9	64.7
	2005	100.0	18.0	57.8	29.5	25.7	30.9	3.1	31.8	15.3	65.1
	2010	100.0	21.4	58.0	22.8	27.2	29.4	2.6	27.1	13.0	70.3
	2011	100.0	20.9	58.3	21.5	30.3	31.1	2.5	27.0	13.5	70.5
Sweden - Suède	2000	100.0	25.8	49.2	18.6	46.5	40.2	2.0	28.5	21.3	69.5
	2005	100.0	26.2	48.2	17.7	48.4	40.6	1.2	27.9	19.3	70.9
	2010	100.0	26.7	48.5	18.7	49.5	43.3	1.7	26.9	17.0	71.4
	2011	100.0	26.4	47.8	19.6	49.9	43.7	1.8	26.8	16.8	71.4
Switzerland - Suisse	2000	100.0	11.1	60.6	23.3	45.4	40.4	1.3	26.5	17.9	72.2
	2005	100.0	11.6	59.9	21.9	47.6	40.9	1.0	26.4	18.6	72.6
	2010	100.0	11.0	57.8	20.0	51.7	40.5	0.8	26.2	18.4	73.0
	2011	100.0	11.1	57.4	20.8	51.2	40.4	0.8	26.2	18.4	73.0
United Kingdom - Royaume-Uni	2000	100.0	18.7	65.5	17.7	27.7	29.6	1.0	27.0	15.6	71.9
	2005	100.0	21.2	64.6	16.9	27.0	29.8	0.6	23.7	11.9	75.7
	2010	100.0	22.8	64.2	15.1	30.5	32.7	0.6	22.9	10.7	76.5
	2011	100.0	22.4	64.3	14.9	32.5	34.1	0.7	23.2	10.8	76.2
Developed economies: Oceania - Économies développées : Océanie	**2000**	**100.0**	**17.6**	**59.2**	**22.9**	**23.6**	**23.2**	**4.4**	**26.1**	**12.8**	**69.5**
	2005	**100.0**	**17.4**	**56.9**	**27.3**	**20.7**	**22.3**	**3.2**	**28.1**	**11.8**	**68.7**
	2010	**100.0**	**18.1**	**54.3**	**25.9**	**22.2**	**20.6**	**3.1**	**27.5**	**8.8**	**69.4**
	2011	**100.0**	**17.9**	**54.8**	**27.1**	**22.4**	**22.0**	**2.9**	**27.8**	**9.3**	**69.3**
Australia - Australie	2000	100.0	17.6	59.1	23.1	22.1	21.9	3.8	26.2	12.3	70.0
	2005	100.0	17.3	56.5	27.8	19.7	21.2	3.0	28.4	11.2	68.6
	2010	100.0	17.9	53.8	26.7	21.3	19.8	2.8	27.8	8.3	69.4
	2011	100.0	17.7	54.2	28.0	21.6	21.2	2.5	28.1	8.9	69.4
New Zealand - Nouvelle-Zélande	2000	100.0	17.2	59.8	21.2	35.0	33.2	8.4	25.5	16.7	66.1
	2005	100.0	18.0	59.6	24.5	27.4	29.5	4.9	25.9	15.7	69.1
	2010	100.0	20.1	59.2	19.2	29.9	28.4	6.2	25.1	13.2	68.7
	2011	100.0	20.2	59.9	19.0	30.3	29.4	6.0	25.1	13.2	68.9

For sources and notes, see next page.

Pour les sources et les notes, se reporter à la page suivante.

8.3.1 Nominal gross domestic product by type of expenditure and by kind of economic activity of countries and geographical regions

8.3.1 Produit intérieur brut nominal par catégories de dépenses et par branches d'activité économique des pays et des régions géographiques

Source:
UNCTAD secretariat calculations, based on UN DESA Statistics Division, *National Accounts Main Aggregates Database*

Notes:

- Data in this table are shown as percentage of GDP / Value added at current prices in US Dollars.

- For countries' notes on GDP / Value added breakdown, see: http://unstats.un.org/unsd/snaama/downloads/Download-GDPcurrent-USD-countries.xls

(1) The breakdown in shares by type of expenditure is shown as percentage of GDP. The breakdown in shares of GDP might not add-up to 100 percent due to statistical discrepancies.

(2) The breakdown in shares by kind of economic activity is shown as percentage of total value added.

(3) Includes agriculture, hunting, forestry and fishing (ISIC Revision 3 divisions 01-05).

(4) Includes mining and quarrying, manufacturing, electricity, gas and water supply, and construction (ISIC Revision 3 divisions 10-45).

(5) Include all other economic activities (ISIC Revision 3 divisions 50-99).

(6) Including Western Sahara.

Source :
Calculs du secrétariat de la CNUCED, basés sur ONU DAES Division de statistique, *National Accounts Main Aggregates Database*

Notes :

- Les données de ce tableau sont indiquées en pourcentage du PIB / Valeur ajoutée aux prix courants en dollars des États-Unis.

- Pour les notes des pays sur la ventilation du PIB / Valeur ajoutée, se référer à : http://unstats.un.org/unsd/snaama/downloads/Download-GDPcurrent-USD-countries.xls

(1) La ventilation par catégories de dépense est calculée en pourcentage du PIB. La somme des pourcentages du PIB ventilé peut ne pas être égale à 100 à cause des écarts statistiques.

(2) La ventilation par branches d'activité économique est calculée en pourcentage de la valeur ajoutée totale.

(3) Inclut l'agriculture, la chasse, la sylviculture et la pêche (CITI Révision 3 divisions 01-05).

(4) Inclut les activités extractives, les activités de fabrication, la production et distribution d'électricité, de gaz et d'eau et la construction (CITI Révision 3 divisions 10-45).

(5) Incluent toutes les autres activités économiques (CITI Révision 3 divisions 50-99).

(6) Y compris le Sahara occidental.

8.3.2 Nominal gross domestic product by type of expenditure and by kind of economic activity of economic groupings

8.3.2 Produit intérieur brut nominal par catégories de dépenses et par branches d'activité économique des groupements économiques

Economic grouping / Groupements économiques	Year / Année	Total GDP / PIB total	GDP by type of expenditure (1) / PIB par catégories de dépenses (1)					GDP by kind of economic activity (2) / PIB par branches d'activité économique (2)			
			Final consumption / Consommation finale		Gross capital formation / Formation brute de capital	Exports / Exportations	Less imports / Moins les importations	Agriculture (3)	Industry (4) / Industrie (4)		Services (5)
			Government / Administration publique	Household / Ménages		Of goods and services / Des biens et services			Total	Manufacturing / Activités de fabrication	
			Percentage / En pourcentage								
DEVELOPING ECONOMIES - ÉCONOMIES EN DÉVELOPPEMENT	2000	100.0	14.0	58.4	24.9	34.9	32.3	10.1	36.2	15.3	53.6
	2005	100.0	13.5	54.6	27.1	40.8	36.1	9.4	38.9	21.0	51.7
	2010	100.0	14.1	51.3	31.8	36.3	33.6	9.4	38.9	21.3	51.6
	2011	100.0	13.9	50.5	32.5	38.0	35.1	9.4	39.5	21.2	51.0
Developing economies excluding China - Économies en développement sans la Chine	2000	100.0	13.7	60.8	22.7	37.2	34.6	9.0	34.2	18.6	56.8
	2005	100.0	13.3	58.8	23.3	41.9	37.4	8.6	36.6	17.8	54.8
	2010	100.0	14.4	57.8	25.3	39.1	36.8	9.2	35.7	16.6	55.1
	2011	100.0	14.3	57.1	25.4	41.2	38.5	9.1	36.2	16.2	54.7
Developing economies excluding LDCs - Économies en développement sans les PMA	2000	100.0	14.1	57.9	25.0	35.2	32.4	9.5	36.5	15.4	53.9
	2005	100.0	13.5	54.2	27.3	41.1	36.2	8.9	39.1	21.4	52.0
	2010	100.0	14.2	50.8	32.0	36.5	33.6	9.0	39.2	21.6	51.9
	2011	100.0	14.0	50.1	32.8	38.2	35.1	9.0	39.7	21.5	51.3
High-income developing economies - Économies en développement à revenu élevé	2000	100.0	14.3	59.0	23.3	41.4	37.9	4.5	34.7	19.4	60.7
	2005	100.0	14.1	56.7	21.8	47.8	40.4	4.2	37.3	18.8	58.5
	2010	100.0	15.8	56.3	23.0	45.5	40.6	4.3	36.3	17.3	59.5
	2011	100.0	15.6	55.5	23.2	47.7	42.3	4.2	37.1	16.9	58.6
Middle-income developing economies - Économies en développement à revenu intermédiaire	2000	100.0	14.5	54.3	28.9	29.1	26.9	13.7	41.7	8.9	44.6
	2005	100.0	13.7	47.9	34.4	37.5	33.5	11.5	44.2	26.7	44.3
	2010	100.0	13.2	42.9	41.1	30.5	27.7	10.5	44.3	27.6	45.2
	2011	100.0	13.1	42.5	42.1	31.8	29.2	10.5	44.6	27.4	44.9
Low-income developing economies - Économies en développement à revenu faible	2000	100.0	11.4	65.9	21.3	20.5	20.6	25.4	28.6	13.7	46.0
	2005	100.0	10.6	64.5	27.7	24.1	27.5	22.0	30.5	13.6	47.5
	2010	100.0	11.8	62.7	28.9	26.8	30.6	20.9	29.6	12.8	49.6
	2011	100.0	11.6	62.0	28.4	29.2	33.0	20.8	29.1	12.5	50.2
Heavily indebted poor countries (IMF) - Pays pauvres très endettés (FMI)	2000	100.0	12.6	77.3	17.9	24.0	31.9	30.7	23.7	11.5	45.6
	2005	100.0	12.5	76.0	21.7	27.0	37.2	29.5	25.1	10.8	45.3
	2010	100.0	12.5	72.7	22.4	28.3	36.4	29.1	25.3	9.6	45.6
	2011	100.0	12.4	71.9	23.3	30.9	38.4	28.5	27.0	9.7	44.5
Landlocked developing countries - Pays en développement sans littoral	2000	100.0	15.8	70.0	20.0	35.3	40.7	25.6	28.1	13.6	46.3
	2005	100.0	14.1	62.4	25.8	41.2	43.2	20.0	33.7	12.7	46.3
	2010	100.0	13.3	58.2	25.8	37.1	36.4	16.4	36.7	12.2	46.9
	2011	100.0	13.1	57.7	24.7	41.4	38.0	16.3	36.9	12.2	46.8
Small island developing States - Petits États insulaires en développement	2000	100.0	15.1	63.5	23.3	50.8	52.6	8.2	27.5	11.2	64.4
	2005	100.0	15.1	58.8	25.8	53.0	52.5	7.1	33.3	11.7	59.6
	2010	100.0	16.7	63.8	21.1	50.7	52.3	7.7	33.8	10.6	58.6
	2011	100.0	16.8	66.4	21.0	52.6	56.8	8.2	35.4	10.8	56.3
Least developed countries - Pays les moins avancés	*2000*	*100.0*	*11.6*	*76.3*	*19.1*	*21.5*	*28.4*	*31.1*	*25.0*	*9.8*	*43.9*
	2005	*100.0*	*12.5*	*69.3*	*21.6*	*30.3*	*34.2*	*26.4*	*31.8*	*9.6*	*41.7*
	2010	*100.0*	*12.5*	*67.9*	*23.3*	*29.1*	*33.2*	*25.5*	*31.8*	*10.3*	*42.7*
	2011	*100.0*	*12.9*	*66.3*	*22.0*	*32.4*	*34.3*	*25.2*	*33.6*	*10.2*	*41.2*
Africa and Haiti - Afrique et Haïti	2000	100.0	14.5	75.7	17.7	22.8	30.6	31.9	25.0	7.6	43.1
	2005	100.0	15.2	66.5	20.6	34.8	37.2	27.8	33.7	7.5	38.5
	2010	100.0	14.8	63.9	23.3	35.1	37.0	26.5	34.0	7.5	39.4
	2011	100.0	15.2	61.1	22.6	39.5	38.3	25.4	36.8	7.3	37.8
Asia - Asie	2000	100.0	7.6	77.1	20.8	19.6	25.3	30.0	25.3	12.6	44.7
	2005	100.0	7.7	74.8	23.8	21.5	28.9	24.3	28.2	13.5	47.5
	2010	100.0	8.2	75.5	23.4	17.6	26.1	24.3	27.2	15.3	48.4
	2011	100.0	8.6	76.3	21.3	18.7	27.0	25.4	27.3	15.2	47.3
Islands - Îles	2000	100.0	24.3	71.2	20.1	37.0	52.7	29.5	15.5	7.9	55.0
	2005	100.0	17.6	52.9	11.1	55.5	37.2	17.5	45.6	4.0	36.9
	2010	100.0	22.9	42.9	18.8	69.8	53.8	13.3	54.1	2.7	32.7
	2011	100.0	22.2	39.3	15.4	72.8	50.6	12.6	56.8	2.4	30.6

For sources and notes, see end of table 8.3.1.

Pour les sources et les notes, se reporter à la fin du tableau 8.3.1.

8

8.3.2 Nominal gross domestic product by type of expenditure and by kind of economic activity of economic groupings

8.3.2 Produit intérieur brut nominal par catégories de dépenses et par branches d'activité économique des groupements économiques

Economic grouping / Groupements économiques	Year / Année	Total GDP / PIB total	GDP by type of expenditure (1) / PIB par catégories de dépenses (1)					GDP by kind of economic activity (2) / PIB par branches d'activité économique (2)			
			Final consumption / Consommation finale		Gross capital formation / Formation brute de capital	Exports / Exportations / Of goods and services / Des biens et services	Less imports / Moins les importations	Agriculture (3)	Industry (4) / Industrie (4)		Services (5)
			Government / Administration publique	Household / Ménages					Total	Manufacturing / Activités de fabrication	
			Percentage / En pourcentage								
Major petroleum and gas exporters - Principaux exportateurs de pétrole et de gaz	*2000*	*100.0*	*17.8*	*42.4*	*21.4*	*45.5*	*27.3*	*6.8*	*51.8*	*10.5*	*41.5*
	2005	*100.0*	*14.8*	*41.2*	*21.0*	*53.4*	*30.9*	*6.6*	*57.3*	*8.8*	*36.1*
	2010	*100.0*	*15.1*	*44.2*	*26.0*	*47.9*	*33.2*	*7.2*	*53.0*	*8.9*	*39.8*
	2011	*100.0*	*14.6*	*40.4*	*25.3*	*53.6*	*33.6*	*6.7*	*55.5*	*8.6*	*37.8*
Africa - Afrique	2000	100.0	15.0	46.1	15.0	44.8	20.9	13.2	53.8	5.0	33.0
	2005	100.0	11.6	49.1	15.6	49.5	25.7	16.3	57.8	3.8	25.9
	2010	100.0	15.7	49.0	20.6	46.2	31.5	18.0	50.6	3.9	31.4
	2011	100.0	17.6	46.0	19.7	52.5	35.6	18.6	48.0	3.6	33.3
America - Amérique	2000	100.0	12.4	51.7	24.2	29.7	18.1	4.1	48.4	19.3	47.5
	2005	100.0	11.1	46.8	23.0	39.7	20.5	4.0	56.9	16.2	39.2
	2010	100.0	11.2	55.9	22.0	28.5	17.6	5.7	51.0	13.6	43.4
	2011	100.0	11.3	54.9	22.7	30.4	19.3	5.3	49.0	14.4	45.7
Asia - Asie	2000	100.0	20.0	39.0	22.7	49.5	31.4	5.4	51.9	10.1	42.7
	2005	100.0	16.5	37.8	22.4	56.9	34.3	3.9	57.2	9.3	38.9
	2010	100.0	15.8	39.7	28.9	53.2	37.6	3.9	54.3	9.6	41.8
	2011	100.0	14.2	36.5	27.3	57.5	35.3	3.6	58.5	9.1	38.0
Major exporters of manufactured goods - Principaux exportateurs d'articles manufacturés	*2000*	*100.0*	*13.1*	*53.6*	*30.6*	*45.8*	*43.1*	*8.2*	*38.6*	*14.3*	*53.1*
	2005	*100.0*	*13.0*	*49.3*	*33.0*	*51.4*	*46.6*	*7.5*	*40.4*	*27.5*	*52.1*
	2010	*100.0*	*13.1*	*42.9*	*39.6*	*45.8*	*41.5*	*7.8*	*42.2*	*29.3*	*49.9*
	2011	*100.0*	*13.0*	*42.7*	*40.9*	*46.7*	*42.8*	*8.1*	*42.6*	*29.2*	*49.3*
America - Amérique	2000	100.0	10.6	65.1	26.6	28.2	30.0	4.1	35.1	21.2	60.9
	2005	100.0	10.7	66.6	24.1	27.2	28.6	3.3	34.1	18.7	62.5
	2010	100.0	11.8	65.8	23.7	30.4	31.6	3.5	34.6	18.3	61.9
	2011	100.0	11.4	65.0	24.8	31.7	32.9	3.4	36.1	18.2	60.5
Asia - Asie	2000	100.0	13.7	50.7	31.6	50.2	46.3	9.3	39.6	12.6	51.2
	2005	100.0	13.5	45.7	34.8	56.4	50.3	8.4	41.7	29.4	49.9
	2010	100.0	13.3	40.1	41.5	47.7	42.7	8.4	43.2	30.6	48.5
	2011	100.0	13.2	40.1	42.7	48.4	43.9	8.6	43.4	30.4	48.0
Emerging economies - Économies émergentes	*2000*	*100.0*	*13.5*	*60.8*	*24.4*	*36.9*	*35.6*	*4.7*	*33.4*	*22.4*	*61.9*
	2005	*100.0*	*13.9*	*58.9*	*23.1*	*42.8*	*38.8*	*4.5*	*34.7*	*22.7*	*60.8*
	2010	*100.0*	*15.9*	*57.6*	*23.5*	*40.9*	*38.0*	*4.9*	*33.4*	*21.2*	*61.7*
	2011	*100.0*	*15.8*	*57.9*	*23.5*	*42.2*	*39.7*	*5.1*	*33.2*	*20.5*	*61.7*
America - Amérique	2000	100.0	14.5	65.6	21.5	18.1	19.6	5.0	31.1	18.9	63.9
	2005	100.0	14.6	63.0	20.2	22.7	20.5	5.0	32.7	18.6	62.3
	2010	100.0	17.1	61.0	22.0	19.1	19.2	5.2	31.2	16.9	63.6
	2011	100.0	16.8	61.1	22.2	20.0	20.2	5.3	31.3	16.1	63.4
Asia - Asie	2000	100.0	12.2	53.8	28.5	64.0	58.7	4.3	36.6	27.4	59.1
	2005	100.0	13.1	53.6	26.9	68.3	62.0	3.9	37.2	27.8	58.9
	2010	100.0	13.8	51.6	26.1	78.6	70.4	4.4	37.1	28.3	58.5
	2011	100.0	14.1	52.1	25.9	82.1	74.8	4.8	36.5	28.0	58.7
Newly industrialized Asian economies - Économies nouvellement industrialisées d'Asie	*2000*	*100.0*	*11.3*	*56.1*	*27.2*	*69.4*	*64.0*	*5.6*	*34.9*	*24.9*	*59.4*
	2005	*100.0*	*11.9*	*56.4*	*25.9*	*73.3*	*67.3*	*5.2*	*36.0*	*25.5*	*58.8*
	2010	*100.0*	*12.2*	*54.5*	*27.0*	*74.3*	*68.3*	*7.0*	*37.0*	*25.4*	*56.0*
	2011	*100.0*	*12.3*	*54.8*	*27.0*	*76.1*	*71.1*	*7.3*	*36.7*	*25.0*	*56.0*
First tier - Première génération	2000	100.0	11.9	55.5	28.9	71.4	67.7	2.8	32.0	23.6	65.2
	2005	100.0	12.7	54.8	26.1	79.4	72.9	2.2	32.5	24.4	65.3
	2010	100.0	13.1	53.3	26.4	95.9	88.8	1.8	32.2	24.9	66.0
	2011	100.0	13.3	53.2	25.9	99.8	93.5	1.8	31.9	25.0	66.3
Second tier - Deuxième génération	2000	100.0	9.9	57.6	23.2	64.6	55.2	11.9	41.4	27.6	46.7
	2005	100.0	10.4	59.7	25.5	60.5	55.6	11.1	42.8	27.7	46.1
	2010	100.0	11.1	56.1	27.7	47.0	42.2	13.1	42.6	25.9	44.3
	2011	100.0	11.2	55.5	28.3	47.6	44.1	13.4	42.2	25.1	44.5

For sources and notes, see end of table 8.3.1.

Pour les sources et les notes, se reporter à la fin du tableau 8.3.1.

8.3.2 Nominal gross domestic product by type of expenditure and by kind of economic activity of economic groupings

8.3.2 Produit intérieur brut nominal par catégories de dépenses et par branches d'activité économique des groupements économiques

Economic grouping / Groupements économiques	Year / Année	Total GDP / PIB total	GDP by type of expenditure (1) / PIB par catégories de dépenses (1)					GDP by kind of economic activity (2) / PIB par branches d'activité économique (2)			
			Final consumption / Consommation finale		Gross capital formation / Formation brute de capital	Exports / Exportations	Less imports / Moins les importations	Agriculture (3)	Industry (4) / Industrie (4)		Services (5)
			Government / Administration publique	Household / Ménages		Of goods and services / Des biens et services			Total	Manufacturing / Activités de fabrication	
			Percentage / En pourcentage								
Developing economies: Africa - Économies en développement : Afrique	2000	100.0	15.2	63.2	17.5	31.3	27.1	15.2	35.7	12.8	49.1
	2005	100.0	14.6	61.5	18.9	36.2	31.1	15.3	39.0	11.3	45.7
	2010	100.0	15.8	60.0	22.1	34.7	32.8	16.2	37.5	9.8	46.3
	2011	100.0	16.6	59.1	21.8	37.1	35.2	16.3	37.0	9.6	46.8
Northern Africa excluding Sudan - Afrique septentrionale sans le Soudan	2000	100.0	14.7	60.6	20.2	29.8	25.3	11.3	39.9	13.1	48.9
	2005	100.0	13.4	51.5	23.1	43.3	31.3	10.0	47.5	11.1	42.5
	2010	100.0	14.6	55.1	27.0	35.7	32.5	10.5	44.7	11.5	44.8
	2011	100.0	16.2	56.9	25.7	34.4	33.0	11.3	41.6	11.4	47.1
Sub-Saharan Africa - Afrique subsaharienne	2000	100.0	15.5	65.1	15.6	32.4	28.3	18.1	32.6	12.6	49.3
	2005	100.0	15.2	66.4	16.7	32.7	31.0	18.1	34.5	11.3	47.4
	2010	100.0	16.5	62.5	19.7	34.2	32.9	19.2	33.7	8.9	47.0
	2011	100.0	16.8	60.2	20.0	38.4	36.2	18.7	34.8	8.7	46.6
Sub-Saharan Africa excluding South Africa - Afrique subsaharienne sans l'Afrique du Sud	2000	100.0	13.9	66.1	15.6	35.1	30.4	26.8	33.1	8.9	40.1
	2005	100.0	12.7	68.3	16.0	35.7	32.8	26.5	36.3	7.4	37.2
	2010	100.0	14.1	64.0	19.8	37.3	35.4	26.5	35.2	6.8	38.3
	2011	100.0	14.7	60.9	20.1	42.8	39.4	25.7	36.5	6.7	37.7
Developing economies: America - Économies en développement : Amérique	2000	100.0	14.4	65.6	21.2	20.5	21.5	5.6	31.8	18.6	62.7
	2005	100.0	14.5	63.0	20.3	24.9	22.8	5.5	33.5	17.9	61.0
	2010	100.0	16.5	61.6	21.7	21.2	21.0	5.6	32.7	16.2	61.7
	2011	100.0	16.4	61.6	22.1	22.2	22.3	5.7	32.4	15.7	61.9
Central America and Greater Caribbean Islands excluding Puerto Rico - Amérique centrale et Grandes Antilles sans Porto Rico	2000	100.0	11.4	66.5	25.3	29.4	32.1	5.1	34.0	21.0	60.9
	2005	100.0	11.7	67.9	23.1	28.5	31.1	4.3	32.7	18.3	63.0
	2010	100.0	13.0	67.4	22.1	30.9	33.4	4.5	32.6	17.8	63.0
	2011	100.0	12.9	66.7	23.4	32.2	35.1	4.4	34.0	17.8	61.6
Central America and Greater Caribbean Islands excluding Mexico and Puerto Rico - Amérique centrale et Grandes Antilles sans le Mexique et Porto Rico	2000	100.0	15.2	72.7	19.5	34.7	42.0	10.1	28.9	19.6	60.9
	2005	100.0	16.0	73.9	18.2	34.2	42.3	9.1	25.7	16.4	65.2
	2010	100.0	17.5	73.5	16.5	32.4	39.8	8.1	25.0	15.7	67.0
	2011	100.0	18.2	73.0	17.9	34.0	43.1	8.2	25.7	16.2	66.2
South America and Central America - Amérique du Sud et Amérique centrale	2000	100.0	14.3	65.5	21.2	19.8	20.7	5.5	31.9	18.7	62.6
	2005	100.0	14.3	63.0	20.4	24.4	22.1	5.5	33.9	18.1	60.6
	2010	100.0	16.4	61.4	21.9	20.8	20.5	5.7	32.9	16.3	61.5
	2011	100.0	16.2	61.3	22.3	21.9	21.8	5.8	32.5	15.7	61.7
South America excluding Brazil - Amérique du Sud sans le Brésil	2000	100.0	13.4	66.1	19.1	18.7	17.3	6.2	32.9	17.4	60.9
	2005	100.0	12.1	60.2	21.1	29.7	23.0	7.2	39.5	17.4	53.3
	2010	100.0	13.1	59.5	23.2	26.3	22.1	7.2	38.6	15.0	54.2
	2011	100.0	13.2	59.0	24.6	27.6	24.4	7.5	37.4	15.4	55.1
Developing economies: Asia - Économies en développement : Asie	2000	100.0	13.7	54.0	27.7	42.5	38.3	11.6	38.5	14.1	49.9
	2005	100.0	12.9	50.4	30.9	47.5	41.8	9.9	40.9	23.5	49.2
	2010	100.0	13.0	46.5	36.6	41.9	38.1	9.9	41.2	24.4	48.9
	2011	100.0	12.8	45.7	37.3	43.5	39.5	9.8	42.1	24.2	48.1
Eastern and South-Eastern Asia excluding China - Asie orientale et Asie du Sud-Est sans la Chine	2000	100.0	11.2	56.0	26.9	68.4	63.1	6.5	34.9	24.5	58.6
	2005	100.0	11.7	56.1	25.9	72.5	66.6	6.0	36.1	25.0	57.9
	2010	100.0	12.0	54.6	27.0	73.4	67.4	7.9	37.0	24.8	55.2
	2011	100.0	12.0	54.7	26.8	75.0	70.0	8.3	36.7	24.4	55.0
Southern Asia excluding India - Asie méridionale sans l'Inde	2000	100.0	10.4	63.9	25.8	19.7	20.3	20.6	29.5	14.3	49.9
	2005	100.0	11.2	59.6	26.1	25.8	24.8	14.8	36.0	14.3	49.2
	2010	100.0	10.0	57.7	32.1	22.4	22.7	14.3	34.9	14.7	50.8
	2011	100.0	10.4	58.8	30.8	23.3	23.9	14.1	34.8	14.4	51.0

For sources and notes, see end of table 8.3.1.

Pour les sources et les notes, se reporter à la fin du tableau 8.3.1.

Region, country or territory Régions, pays ou territoires	Year Année	Population		Total labour force Main-d'œuvre totale		Agriculture labour force Main-d'œuvre dans l'agriculture	
		Total (thousands) Total (milliers)	Urban population (% of total population) Population urbaine (en % de la population totale)	Total (thousands) Total (milliers)	Female labour (% of total labour force) Main-d'œuvre féminine (en % de la main-d'œuvre totale)	Total (thousands) Total (milliers)	Female labour (% of total agriculture labour force) Main-d'œuvre féminine (en % de la main-d'œuvre totale dans l'agriculture)
		(1)	(2)	(3)	(4)	(5)	(6)
WORLD - MONDE	**1990**	**5 320 817**	**42.9**	**2 375 048**	**39.3**	**1 146 816**	**41.6**
	2000	**6 127 700**	**46.7**	**2 796 254**	**39.9**	**1 236 175**	**42.1**
	2010	**6 916 183**	**51.5**	**3 276 145**	**40.6**	**1 307 071**	**42.6**
	2012	**7 080 072**	**52.3**	**3 366 449**	**40.7**	**1 316 391**	**42.7**
DEVELOPING ECONOMIES - ÉCONOMIES EN DÉVELOPPEMENT	1990	4 075 547	34.7	1 768 280	37.9	1 086 867	41.7
	2000	4 828 704	40.0	2 159 799	38.5	1 192 669	42.3
	2010	5 559 482	45.9	2 566 384	38.4	1 272 876	42.9
	2012	5 712 287	47.0	2 652 747	38.3	1 283 871	42.9
TRANSITION ECONOMIES - ÉCONOMIES EN TRANSITION	1990	315 797	63.9	153 486	47.4	29 389	40.2
	2000	305 443	63.3	144 092	47.5	21 316	35.8
	2010	304 577	63.2	151 578	47.5	18 235	33.2
	2012	305 307	63.4	152 752	47.5	17 581	32.7
DEVELOPED ECONOMIES - ÉCONOMIES DÉVELOPPÉES	1990	909 240	73.2	437 127	42.5	30 560	38.8
	2000	971 618	75.3	476 930	44.1	22 190	37.5
	2010	1 028 979	78.9	510 467	45.2	15 960	36.3
	2012	1 038 765	79.5	514 901	45.2	14 939	36.2
Developing economies: Africa - Économies en développement : Afrique	**1990**	**629 284**	**32.2**	**227 627**	**39.9**	**144 596**	**45.9**
	2000	**807 419**	**35.6**	**302 119**	**41.5**	**177 263**	**47.1**
	2010	**1 030 035**	**38.8**	**397 233**	**42.5**	**214 508**	**48.4**
	2012	**1 082 443**	**39.4**	**419 826**	**42.5**	**222 939**	**48.6**
Eastern Africa - Afrique orientale	*1990*	*191 919*	*17.6*	*83 428*	*47.9*	*68 513*	*50.2*
	2000	*252 463*	*20.3*	*110 102*	*48.0*	*88 608*	*51.0*
	2010	*331 605*	*22.7*	*148 140*	*48.5*	*112 616*	*51.3*
	2012	*361 619*	*23.1*	*160 630*	*48.0*	*118 189*	*51.3*
Burundi	1990	5 606	6.3	2 809	52.5	2 546	55.7
	2000	6 674	7.9	2 915	53.2	2 754	56.5
	2010	9 233	9.7	4 314	52.1	3 741	56.0
	2012	9 850	9.9	4 543	51.9	3 852	56.0
Comoros - Comores	1990	413	29.6	126	25.6	135	50.4
	2000	528	29.9	179	28.0	171	50.9
	2010	683	30.1	243	30.2	222	51.8
	2012	718	30.3	257	30.6	234	52.1
Djibouti	1990	590	72.1	147	29.5	182	46.2
	2000	723	77.5	209	32.4	233	46.4
	2010	834	82.0	292	34.9	285	46.3
	2012	860	82.8	310	35.3	297	46.5
Eritrea - Érythrée	2000	3 939	16.4	1 661	47.3	1 090	44.0
	2010	5 741	19.1	2 596	48.6	1 547	43.6
	2012	6 131	19.8	2 767	48.6	1 634	43.5
Ethiopia (...1991) - Éthiopie (...1991)	1990	51 315	12.9	22 957	45.2	18 086	42.3
Ethiopia - Éthiopie	2000	66 024	14.6	28 972	45.2	24 049	44.3
	2010	87 095	16.0	40 787	47.2	31 657	45.5
	2012	91 729	16.3	43 517	47.3	33 142	45.4
Kenya	1990	23 446	16.7	8 997	47.2	7 846	49.4
	2000	31 285	19.9	11 857	46.8	10 757	49.4
	2010	40 909	23.3	15 461	46.5	13 220	48.7
	2012	43 178	24.1	16 449	46.4	13 770	48.6
Madagascar	1990	11 546	23.0	5 373	48.4	4 029	54.2
	2000	15 745	26.5	7 299	48.7	5 243	53.7
	2010	21 080	31.4	10 147	48.9	7 255	53.5
	2012	22 294	32.7	10 848	48.9	7 731	53.4
Malawi	1990	9 447	11.5	3 945	50.7	3 377	55.7
	2000	11 321	14.5	4 816	49.7	3 907	57.1
	2010	15 014	15.4	6 710	51.5	4 909	58.9
	2012	15 906	15.8	7 134	51.2	5 221	59.3

For sources and notes, see end of table.

Pour les sources et les notes, se reporter à la fin du tableau.

Region, country or territory Régions, pays ou territoires	Year Année	Population		Total labour force Main-d'œuvre totale		Agriculture labour force Main-d'œuvre dans l'agriculture	
		Total (thousands) Total (milliers)	Urban population (% of total population) Population urbaine (en % de la population totale)	Total (thousands) Total (milliers)	Female labour (% of total labour force) Main-d'œuvre féminine (en % de la main-d'œuvre totale)	Total (thousands) Total (milliers)	Female labour (% of total agriculture labour force) Main-d'œuvre féminine (en % de la main-d'œuvre totale dans l'agriculture)
		(1)	(2)	(3)	(4)	(5)	(6)
Mauritius - Maurice	1990	1 056	44.1	444	31.8	75	28.0
	2000	1 185	43.1	532	34.5	63	25.4
	2010	1 231	44.1	603	37.7	48	25.0
	2012	1 240	44.3	619	38.1	45	24.4
Mozambique	1990	13 568	21.1	6 019	55.5	5 209	62.2
	2000	18 276	29.0	8 726	56.1	7 092	64.3
	2010	23 967	30.2	11 078	53.5	8 674	65.2
	2012	25 203	30.5	11 619	53.2	9 047	65.3
Rwanda	1990	7 215	5.3	3 222	51.1	2 824	53.9
	2000	8 396	13.3	3 799	52.3	3 242	55.9
	2010	10 837	18.4	5 228	51.8	4 360	56.4
	2012	11 458	19.1	5 529	51.7	4 618	56.4
Seychelles	1990	69	50.4	..	..	25	52.0
	2000	80	49.7	..	..	28	50.0
	2010	91	50.5	..	..	30	50.0
	2012	92	51.0	..	..	30	50.0
Somalia - Somalie	1990	6 322	31.0	2 060	31.9	1 875	44.4
	2000	7 385	33.3	2 348	32.8	2 048	45.3
	2010	9 636	36.1	2 926	33.6	2 440	45.9
	2012	10 195	36.7	3 069	33.8	2 545	46.0
South Sudan - Sud Soudan (7)	2012	10 838	17.9	3 359	28.9	..	..
Uganda - Ouganda	1990	17 535	11.2	7 550	50.8	6 665	49.6
	2000	24 276	12.1	10 133	50.0	8 420	50.1
	2010	33 987	14.9	13 419	49.3	11 016	49.6
	2012	36 346	15.7	14 306	49.2	11 621	49.5
United Republic of Tanzania - République-Unie de Tanzanie	1990	25 485	18.9	12 246	49.8	10 554	54.0
	2000	34 021	22.3	16 709	49.7	13 557	54.3
	2010	44 973	26.2	22 137	49.8	16 879	54.9
	2012	47 783	27.1	23 423	49.7	17 805	55.0
Zambia - Zambie	1990	7 845	39.5	3 402	46.8	2 215	47.5
	2000	10 101	35.1	4 475	47.2	2 685	47.1
	2010	13 217	38.3	5 579	46.1	3 215	46.3
	2012	14 075	39.0	5 866	46.0	3 388	46.1
Zimbabwe	1990	10 462	29.0	4 131	46.3	2 870	54.8
	2000	12 504	33.8	5 470	46.4	3 269	54.4
	2010	13 077	36.7	6 620	49.3	3 118	52.4
	2012	13 724	37.1	7 015	49.2	3 209	52.1
Middle Africa - *Afrique centrale*	*1990*	*70 000*	*33.2*	*27 167*	*46.8*	*19 582*	*50.4*
	2000	*93 751*	*37.1*	*36 817*	*48.3*	*23 998*	*49.7*
	2010	*124 978*	*41.5*	*49 787*	*47.9*	*28 772*	*50.7*
	2012	*132 093*	*42.4*	*52 914*	*47.9*	*29 688*	*50.9*
Angola	1990	10 334	37.1	3 844	47.6	3 323	53.3
	2000	13 925	49.0	5 199	48.4	4 337	53.1
	2010	19 549	57.0	7 109	45.9	5 878	54.8
	2012	20 821	58.1	7 612	45.9	6 193	55.2
Cameroon - Cameroun	1990	12 070	40.0	4 493	41.8	3 086	48.1
	2000	15 928	44.8	6 199	45.1	3 482	48.1
	2010	20 624	49.0	8 211	45.6	3 569	47.4
	2012	21 700	49.7	8 663	45.7	3 574	47.1
Central African Republic - République centrafricaine	1990	2 913	37.1	1 301	45.7	1 038	50.0
	2000	3 638	38.3	1 679	46.4	1 189	50.4
	2010	4 350	39.3	2 064	47.1	1 254	49.8
	2012	4 525	39.7	2 165	47.1	1 275	49.6

For sources and notes, see end of table.

Pour les sources et les notes, se reporter à la fin du tableau.

Region, country or territory Régions, pays ou territoires	Year Année	Population		Total labour force Main-d'œuvre totale		Agriculture labour force Main-d'œuvre dans l'agriculture	
		Total (thousands) Total (milliers)	Urban population (% of total population) Population urbaine (en % de la population totale)	Total (thousands) Total (milliers)	Female labour (% of total labour force) Main-d'œuvre féminine (en % de la main-d'œuvre totale)	Total (thousands) Total (milliers)	Female labour (% of total agriculture labour force) Main-d'œuvre féminine (en % de la main-d'œuvre totale dans l'agriculture)
		(1)	(2)	(3)	(4)	(5)	(6)
Chad - Tchad	1990	5 952	21.0	2 363	45.3	1 889	45.5
	2000	8 301	21.3	3 215	45.5	2 418	51.6
	2010	11 721	20.8	4 425	45.2	2 962	56.9
	2012	12 448	20.8	4 683	45.2	3 032	57.4
Congo	1990	2 383	54.5	891	45.5	447	59.1
	2000	3 126	58.9	1 251	48.0	501	58.7
	2010	4 112	62.2	1 693	48.6	524	56.3
	2012	4 337	62.6	1 781	48.6	527	55.8
Dem. Rep. of the Congo - Rép. dém. du Congo	1990	34 911	28.9	13 694	48.7	9 460	50.9
	2000	46 949	31.0	18 525	50.1	11 694	48.2
	2010	62 191	35.8	25 270	49.9	14 194	48.6
	2012	65 705	36.9	26 934	49.8	14 684	48.8
Equatorial Guinea - Guinée équatoriale	1990	374	34.7	201	45.1	108	38.9
	2000	518	39.0	260	44.3	142	41.5
	2010	696	39.6	369	44.7	176	42.0
	2012	736	39.9	391	44.8	184	42.4
Gabon	1990	947	67.9	344	45.1	207	50.2
	2000	1 226	80.7	444	45.6	207	48.3
	2010	1 556	83.0	587	46.4	183	45.4
	2012	1 633	82.9	623	46.5	185	47.6
Sao Tome and Principe - Sao Tomé-et-Principe	1990	117	43.2	35	33.4	24	41.7
	2000	139	54.0	45	35.2	28	42.9
	2010	178	57.5	59	37.2	32	50.0
	2012	188	57.9	63	37.5	34	50.0
Northern Africa - Afrique septentrionale	*1990*	*145 636*	*44.5*	*42 285*	*23.5*	*17 638*	*35.8*
	2000	*175 984*	*47.3*	*54 479*	*22.9*	*19 564*	*39.5*
	2010	*209 561*	*49.6*	*70 050*	*24.7*	*20 886*	*42.9*
	2012	*206 499*	*51.6*	*69 947*	*24.8*	*20 993*	*43.3*
Algeria - Algérie	1990	26 240	50.2	6 032	11.8	1 907	49.8
	2000	31 719	58.5	8 802	13.7	2 718	51.6
	2010	37 063	68.9	11 207	16.9	3 175	52.7
	2012	38 482	70.0	11 727	17.3	3 194	52.8
Egypt - Égypte	1990	56 337	43.9	16 842	26.5	6 495	37.5
	2000	66 137	43.8	20 085	21.4	6 339	36.2
	2010	78 076	45.1	27 076	24.2	6 620	40.4
	2012	80 722	45.4	28 397	24.5	6 569	40.6
Libya - Libye	1990	4 260	77.1	1 166	17.7	127	41.7
	2000	5 176	77.1	1 801	26.1	103	60.2
	2010	6 041	81.6	2 381	28.0	71	70.4
	2012	6 155	81.9	2 360	28.6	64	73.4
Morocco - Maroc	1990	24 675	48.6	7 867	25.3	3 264	35.6
	2000	28 710	53.5	10 206	27.9	3 372	43.2
	2010	31 642	57.2	11 375	27.1	3 009	47.7
	2012	32 521	57.5	11 755	27.6	2 935	49.0
Sudan (...2011) - Soudan (...2011)	1990	25 773	25.8	7 863	26.0	5 151	28.7
	2000	34 383	29.2	10 326	27.8	6 223	35.8
	2010	45 593	28.3	13 991	28.7	7 124	39.5
Sudan - Soudan (7)	2012	37 195	31.4	11 532	28.9	7 336	40.1
Tunisia - Tunisie	1990	8 135	58.5	2 448	21.6	652	34.2
	2000	9 553	62.8	3 151	24.9	756	34.7
	2010	10 632	65.2	3 801	26.9	805	33.0
	2012	10 875	65.5	3 940	27.1	809	32.6

For sources and notes, see end of table.

Pour les sources et les notes, se reporter à la fin du tableau.

Region, country or territory Régions, pays ou territoires	Year Année	Population		Total labour force Main-d'œuvre totale		Agriculture labour force Main-d'œuvre dans l'agriculture	
		Total (thousands) Total (milliers)	Urban population (% of total population) Population urbaine (en % de la population totale)	Total (thousands) Total (milliers)	Female labour (% of total labour force) Main-d'œuvre féminine (en % de la main-d'œuvre totale)	Total (thousands) Total (milliers)	Female labour (% of total agriculture labour force) Main-d'œuvre féminine (en % de la main-d'œuvre totale dans l'agriculture)
		(1)	(2)	(3)	(4)	(5)	(6)
Western Sahara - Sahara occidental	1990	217	87.7	68	14.6	42	47.6
	2000	306	86.5	109	17.8	53	50.9
	2010	515	84.3	219	23.3	82	53.7
	2012	549	84.8	237	23.7	86	54.7
Southern Africa - Afrique australe	*1990*	*42 053*	*48.9*	*12 816*	*36.7*	*2 479*	*40.5*
	2000	*51 420*	*53.8*	*18 132*	*43.6*	*2 512*	*41.4*
	2010	*58 803*	*57.4*	*21 481*	*43.2*	*2 272*	*42.2*
	2012	*59 932*	*58.0*	*22 171*	*43.1*	*2 223*	*42.4*
Botswana	1990	1 384	41.9	561	46.6	206	45.6
	2000	1 755	53.3	817	46.9	281	53.0
	2010	1 969	62.1	1 036	46.3	317	56.5
	2012	2 004	63.8	1 073	46.2	326	57.1
Lesotho	1990	1 598	14.3	682	49.6	301	67.1
	2000	1 856	21.1	848	49.1	348	67.0
	2010	2 009	29.0	894	46.0	362	65.7
	2012	2 052	30.6	929	45.7	368	65.2
Namibia - Namibie	1990	1 415	27.6	444	44.5	219	48.9
	2000	1 898	32.3	639	44.4	253	45.5
	2010	2 179	39.6	929	46.3	267	43.8
	2012	2 259	40.8	981	46.3	271	43.2
South Africa - Afrique du Sud	1990	36 793	52.0	10 878	35.0	1 614	31.7
	2000	44 846	56.8	15 497	43.1	1 482	30.7
	2010	51 452	60.0	18 208	42.8	1 188	29.4
	2012	52 386	60.5	18 753	42.7	1 121	29.1
Swaziland	1990	863	22.9	251	41.7	139	64.0
	2000	1 064	22.6	331	40.3	148	58.8
	2010	1 193	21.2	414	39.6	138	54.3
	2012	1 231	21.0	435	39.5	137	53.3
Western Africa - Afrique occidentale	*1990*	*179 675*	*33.7*	*61 930*	*37.9*	*36 384*	*40.5*
	2000	*233 803*	*38.8*	*82 588*	*41.6*	*42 581*	*41.3*
	2010	*305 088*	*44.2*	*107 773*	*43.0*	*49 962*	*43.2*
	2012	*322 300*	*45.2*	*114 163*	*43.0*	*51 846*	*43.5*
Benin - Bénin	1990	5 001	32.9	1 850	42.5	1 095	41.1
	2000	6 949	36.0	2 559	46.5	1 384	42.2
	2010	9 510	41.2	3 616	47.6	1 601	40.7
	2012	10 051	42.4	3 847	47.7	1 630	40.6
Burkina Faso	1990	8 811	14.6	4 084	48.5	3 742	48.5
	2000	11 608	18.9	5 500	48.2	4 982	48.2
	2010	15 540	27.2	7 548	47.6	6 909	48.1
	2012	16 460	29.0	8 016	47.5	7 394	48.1
Cape Verde - Cap-Vert	1990	352	43.6	117	36.9	34	38.2
	2000	442	52.8	163	38.1	35	37.1
	2010	488	62.9	224	38.4	32	40.6
	2012	494	64.8	237	38.7	31	38.7
Côte d'Ivoire	1990	12 116	40.7	4 607	30.1	2 686	35.6
	2000	16 131	44.8	6 384	35.1	2 946	36.5
	2010	18 977	52.6	7 792	37.4	2 814	36.1
	2012	19 840	54.0	8 235	37.8	2 811	36.0
Gambia - Gambie	1990	917	40.4	399	44.8	351	50.7
	2000	1 229	51.5	544	47.0	461	51.6
	2010	1 681	58.3	752	47.9	605	53.6
	2012	1 791	58.9	801	48.0	640	53.9
Ghana	1990	14 629	36.9	5 899	48.4	3 585	45.2
	2000	18 825	44.7	8 426	48.1	4 785	43.9
	2010	24 263	51.5	10 372	47.6	6 075	44.1
	2012	25 366	52.9	10 972	47.5	6 394	44.1

For sources and notes, see end of table.

Pour les sources et les notes, se reporter à la fin du tableau.

Region, country or territory Régions, pays ou territoires	Year Année	Population		Total labour force Main-d'œuvre totale		Agriculture labour force Main-d'œuvre dans l'agriculture	
		Total (thousands) Total (milliers)	Urban population (% of total population) Population urbaine (en % de la population totale)	Total (thousands) Total (milliers)	Female labour (% of total labour force) Main-d'œuvre féminine (en % de la main-d'œuvre totale)	Total (thousands) Total (milliers)	Female labour (% of total agriculture labour force) Main-d'œuvre féminine (en % de la main-d'œuvre totale dans l'agriculture)
		(1)	(2)	(3)	(4)	(5)	(6)
Guinea - Guinée	1990	6 020	26.8	2 282	45.1	2 372	49.6
	2000	8 746	29.6	3 294	44.6	3 320	49.6
	2010	10 876	32.1	4 090	45.2	3 832	49.7
	2012	11 451	32.9	4 330	45.3	3 999	49.8
Guinea-Bissau - Guinée-Bissau	1990	1 017	28.1	396	44.5	338	45.3
	2000	1 273	34.9	498	45.5	391	45.5
	2010	1 587	41.3	649	47.3	447	45.4
	2012	1 664	42.4	681	47.3	463	45.6
Liberia - Libéria	1990	2 103	59.8	694	47.2	568	45.6
	2000	2 892	43.6	963	49.1	712	44.9
	2010	3 958	48.2	1 375	47.7	913	44.0
	2012	4 190	49.2	1 474	47.5	952	43.8
Mali	1990	7 964	25.4	2 328	38.8	1 953	36.2
	2000	10 261	30.9	3 058	37.5	2 376	36.3
	2010	13 986	37.7	4 296	35.4	3 049	37.2
	2012	14 854	39.1	4 593	35.2	3 198	36.9
Mauritania - Mauritanie	1990	2 024	39.1	521	19.9	435	48.3
	2000	2 708	39.0	761	23.3	570	50.9
	2010	3 609	39.5	1 116	26.6	745	54.2
	2012	3 796	39.8	1 183	26.8	782	55.1
Niger	1990	7 754	15.4	2 285	22.6	2 247	36.5
	2000	10 990	16.1	3 526	30.9	3 099	35.4
	2010	15 894	17.2	5 114	31.2	4 237	36.4
	2012	17 157	17.5	5 500	31.3	4 525	36.6
Nigeria - Nigéria	1990	95 617	36.0	30 564	34.5	12 689	34.2
	2000	122 877	42.6	39 254	40.1	12 443	35.2
	2010	159 708	48.6	50 245	42.9	12 267	39.2
	2012	168 834	49.6	53 095	42.7	12 293	40.3
Saint Helena - Sainte-Hélène	1990	6	42.6	..	..	1	..
	2000	5	39.9	..	..	1	..
	2010	4	38.3	..	..	1	..
	2012	4	38.0	..	..	1	..
Senegal - Sénégal	1990	7 514	37.5	2 897	41.5	2 296	45.6
	2000	9 862	38.9	3 948	43.0	2 929	46.1
	2010	12 951	40.6	5 384	43.9	3 821	47.4
	2012	13 726	40.9	5 720	43.9	4 047	47.7
Sierra Leone	1990	4 043	32.5	1 516	50.3	1 083	59.2
	2000	4 140	35.9	1 560	53.2	1 041	57.7
	2010	5 752	39.7	2 262	50.7	1 326	61.6
	2012	5 979	40.6	2 374	50.5	1 360	62.1
Togo	1990	3 788	27.7	1 490	45.1	909	38.1
	2000	4 865	32.4	2 150	49.0	1 106	39.4
	2010	6 306	35.9	2 938	50.5	1 288	41.2
	2012	6 643	36.4	3 107	50.4	1 326	41.7
Developing economies: America - Économies en développement : Amérique	1990	440 721	69.9	170 320	33.7	42 460	16.8
	2000	521 398	74.6	225 581	38.3	43 453	19.5
	2010	591 285	77.9	279 453	41.2	41 502	20.9
	2012	604 869	78.4	289 983	41.5	40 819	21.0
Caribbean - *Caraïbes*	*1990*	*29 897*	*52.7*	*11 955*	*37.4*	*3 653*	*24.0*
	2000	*33 720*	*56.6*	*13 747*	*39.6*	*3 657*	*24.0*
	2010	*36 949*	*62.5*	*16 408*	*41.8*	*3 667*	*24.4*
	2012	*37 523*	*63.5*	*16 864*	*42.0*	*3 663*	*24.5*
Anguilla	1990	8	100.0	..	..	1	..
	2000	11	100.0	..	..	1	..
	2010	14	100.0	..	..	1	..
	2012	14	100.0	..	..	1	..

For sources and notes, see end of table.

Pour les sources et les notes, se reporter à la fin du tableau.

Region, country or territory / Régions, pays ou territoires	Year / Année	Population		Total labour force / Main-d'œuvre totale		Agriculture labour force / Main-d'œuvre dans l'agriculture	
		Total (thousands) / Total (milliers)	Urban population (% of total population) / Population urbaine (en % de la population totale)	Total (thousands) / Total (milliers)	Female labour (% of total labour force) / Main-d'œuvre féminine (en % de la main-d'œuvre totale)	Total (thousands) / Total (milliers)	Female labour (% of total agriculture labour force) / Main-d'œuvre féminine (en % de la main-d'œuvre totale dans l'agriculture)
		(1)	(2)	(3)	(4)	(5)	(6)
Antigua and Barbuda - Antigua-et-Barbuda	1990	62	35.6	..	..	7	28.6
	2000	78	32.1	..	..	7	28.6
	2010	87	30.4	..	..	8	25.0
	2012	89	30.3	..	..	8	25.0
Aruba	1990	62	50.3	..	..	7	28.6
	2000	91	46.4	..	..	9	22.2
	2010	102	49.5	..	..	9	22.2
	2012	102	49.8	..	..	9	22.2
Bahamas	1990	256	79.8	125	45.9	6	16.7
	2000	298	82.0	148	48.8	5	20.0
	2010	360	80.0	197	48.3	5	..
	2012	372	79.8	204	48.3	4	..
Barbados - Barbade	1990	259	32.7	136	46.8	9	44.4
	2000	267	38.4	145	46.5	7	42.9
	2010	280	42.8	159	46.7	4	50.0
	2012	283	43.6	161	46.7	4	50.0
Bonaire, Sint Eustatius and Saba - Bonaire, Saint-Eustache et Saba (8)	2012	19	..	10	49.8	..	..
British Virgin Islands - Îles Vierges britanniques	1990	16	..	..	..	2	..
	2000	21	..	..	..	2	..
	2010	27	..	..	..	2	50.0
	2012	..	..	..	..	2	50.0
Cayman Islands - Îles Caïmanes	1990	25	100.0	..	..	3	33.3
	2000	42	96.4	..	..	4	25.0
	2010	56	100.0	..	..	5	20.0
	2012	58	99.4	..	..	5	20.0
Cuba	1990	10 601	73.2	4 363	32.6	833	14.9
	2000	11 138	75.4	4 697	35.0	733	17.6
	2010	11 282	75.1	5 270	38.0	586	17.7
	2012	11 271	75.0	5 320	38.3	562	18.5
Curaçao (8)	2012	155	100.0	73	49.8	..	..
Dominica - Dominique	1990	71	67.7	..	..	8	25.0
	2000	70	67.2	..	..	7	28.6
	2010	71	63.8	..	..	6	16.7
	2012	72	63.5	..	..	6	16.7
Dominican Republic - République dominicaine	1990	7 245	54.8	2 848	34.0	621	8.9
	2000	8 663	61.2	3 537	36.6	547	19.7
	2010	10 017	68.5	4 432	39.4	457	31.3
	2012	10 277	69.6	4 595	39.7	438	33.1
Grenada - Grenade	1990	96	33.4	..	..	10	30.0
	2000	102	36.0	..	..	10	20.0
	2010	105	38.7	..	..	9	22.2
	2012	105	39.4	..	..	9	22.2
Haiti - Haïti	1990	7 110	28.6	2 713	44.0	1 787	33.0
	2000	8 578	35.9	3 242	46.5	1 994	27.1
	2010	9 896	52.5	4 163	47.0	2 277	24.6
	2012	10 174	55.2	4 356	47.1	2 323	24.1
Jamaica - Jamaïque	1990	2 365	49.4	1 133	46.3	275	27.3
	2000	2 582	51.8	1 187	44.3	248	27.4
	2010	2 741	52.0	1 240	45.1	214	27.6
	2012	2 769	52.0	1 264	45.2	210	27.6
Montserrat	1990	11	12.5	..	..	1	..
	2000	5	11.0	..	..	..	..
	2010	5	16.9	..	..	1	..
	2012	5	17.2	..	..	1	..

For sources and notes, see end of table.

Pour les sources et les notes, se reporter à la fin du tableau.

Region, country or territory / Régions, pays ou territoires	Year / Année	Population		Total labour force / Main-d'œuvre totale		Agriculture labour force / Main-d'œuvre dans l'agriculture	
		Total (thousands) / Total (milliers)	Urban population (% of total population) / Population urbaine (en % de la population totale)	Total (thousands) / Total (milliers)	Female labour (% of total labour force) / Main-d'œuvre féminine (en % de la main-d'œuvre totale)	Total (thousands) / Total (milliers)	Female labour (% of total agriculture labour force) / Main-d'œuvre féminine (en % de la main-d'œuvre totale dans l'agriculture)
		(1)	(2)	(3)	(4)	(5)	(6)
Netherlands Antilles - Antilles néerlandaises	1990	188	86.6	83	43.8	1	..
	2000	178	91.1	83	48.4	..	..
	2010	208	90.0	100	49.7	..	..
Saint Kitts and Nevis - Saint-Kitts-et-Nevis	1990	41	34.5	..	..	4	25.0
	2000	46	33.2	..	..	4	25.0
	2010	52	32.0	..	..	5	20.0
	2012	54	32.1	..	..	5	20.0
Saint Lucia - Sainte-Lucie	1990	138	29.3	58	45.0	15	26.7
	2000	157	28.0	73	47.0	16	25.0
	2010	177	18.0	91	47.2	17	23.5
	2012	181	16.5	94	47.3	17	23.5
Saint Vincent and the Grenadines - Saint-Vincent-et-les Grenadines	1990	108	41.4	42	36.0	12	25.0
	2000	108	45.2	48	38.4	11	27.3
	2010	109	48.9	54	41.0	11	27.3
	2012	109	49.7	55	41.3	11	27.3
Sint Maarten (Dutch part) - Saint-Martin (partie néerlandaise) (8)	2012	44	..	20	49.8	..	..
Trinidad and Tobago - Trinité-et-Tobago	1990	1 222	8.5	455	35.2	50	18.0
	2000	1 268	11.0	586	39.9	50	18.0
	2010	1 328	13.6	701	43.3	47	17.0
	2012	1 337	14.1	712	43.4	45	17.8
Turks and Caicos Islands - Îles Turques et Caïques	1990	12	74.3	..	..	1	..
	2000	19	84.5	..	..	2	..
	2010	31	100.0	..	..	3	33.3
	2012	32	100.0	..	..	3	33.3
Central America - Amérique centrale	*1990*	*115 106*	*63.9*	*40 464*	*30.2*	*12 217*	*11.5*
	2000	*139 596*	*66.8*	*53 574*	*33.4*	*12 545*	*11.6*
	2010	*160 546*	*70.0*	*67 215*	*36.8*	*12 173*	*11.9*
	2012	*165 087*	*70.5*	*70 334*	*37.1*	*12 031*	*11.9*
Belize	1990	188	48.1	63	31.2	18	5.6
	2000	239	50.0	91	32.6	25	4.0
	2010	309	45.4	131	37.5	31	3.2
	2012	324	44.5	140	37.8	32	3.1
Costa Rica	1990	3 079	50.5	1 158	27.6	307	7.2
	2000	3 930	58.9	1 600	30.8	326	9.8
	2010	4 670	64.0	2 192	36.3	322	12.7
	2012	4 805	65.0	2 300	36.7	317	13.2
El Salvador	1990	5 344	49.1	1 890	35.4	655	9.0
	2000	5 959	58.7	2 218	39.6	661	8.3
	2010	6 218	64.0	2 594	41.5	590	9.3
	2012	6 297	64.9	2 687	41.9	577	9.5
Guatemala	1990	8 890	41.3	3 133	31.6	1 488	7.3
	2000	11 204	45.3	3 969	34.6	1 492	7.2
	2010	14 342	49.5	5 680	38.1	2 061	9.9
	2012	15 083	50.4	6 077	38.3	2 148	9.8
Honduras	1990	4 904	40.3	1 590	28.1	672	18.2
	2000	6 236	45.3	2 363	34.2	735	21.6
	2010	7 621	51.4	2 988	34.1	665	20.8
	2012	7 936	52.6	3 182	34.5	662	21.0
Mexico - Mexique	1990	86 077	70.0	30 395	29.9	8 439	12.4
	2000	103 874	71.9	40 256	33.0	8 658	12.3
	2010	117 886	74.9	49 605	36.5	7 905	12.3
	2012	120 847	75.4	51 717	36.9	7 708	12.3

For sources and notes, see end of table.

Pour les sources et les notes, se reporter à la fin du tableau.

Region, country or territory Régions, pays ou territoires	Year Année	Population		Total labour force Main-d'œuvre totale		Agriculture labour force Main-d'œuvre dans l'agriculture	
		Total (thousands) Total (milliers)	Urban population (% of total population) Population urbaine (en % de la population totale)	Total (thousands) Total (milliers)	Female labour (% of total labour force) Main-d'œuvre féminine (en % de la main-d'œuvre totale)	Total (thousands) Total (milliers)	Female labour (% of total agriculture labour force) Main-d'œuvre féminine (en % de la main-d'œuvre totale dans l'agriculture)
		(1)	(2)	(3)	(4)	(5)	(6)
Nicaragua	1990	4 138	52.1	1 308	30.3	391	10.0
	2000	5 101	54.4	1 797	32.5	390	7.7
	2010	5 822	56.9	2 376	37.9	351	7.7
	2012	5 992	57.5	2 510	38.3	343	7.9
Panama	1990	2 487	52.0	926	32.6	247	3.6
	2000	3 055	63.7	1 281	35.4	258	3.9
	2010	3 678	71.3	1 649	37.3	248	3.6
	2012	3 802	72.3	1 720	37.6	244	3.3
South America - *Amérique du Sud*	*1990*	*295 718*	*74.0*	*117 901*	*34.5*	*26 590*	*18.2*
	2000	*348 081*	*79.5*	*158 259*	*39.9*	*27 251*	*22.5*
	2010	*393 790*	*82.5*	*195 830*	*42.6*	*25 662*	*24.6*
	2012	*402 259*	*83.0*	*202 785*	*42.9*	*25 125*	*24.8*
Argentina - Argentine	1990	32 625	87.0	13 304	36.1	1 458	6.7
	2000	36 903	90.2	15 408	38.1	1 458	9.9
	2010	40 374	92.4	18 366	40.2	1 405	10.7
	2012	41 087	92.7	18 904	40.5	1 388	10.8
Bolivia (Plurinational State of) - Bolivie (État plurinational de)	1990	6 794	54.5	2 600	39.0	1 190	34.8
	2000	8 495	60.5	3 529	43.2	1 560	40.7
	2010	10 157	64.9	4 585	44.8	1 973	41.9
	2012	10 496	65.7	4 819	45.0	2 056	41.8
Brazil - Brésil	1990	149 648	73.9	62 657	35.1	14 062	18.5
	2000	174 505	81.2	83 762	41.2	13 325	23.4
	2010	195 210	84.2	101 601	43.6	11 049	24.5
	2012	198 656	84.8	104 717	43.9	10 478	24.5
Chile - Chili	1990	13 214	83.1	4 999	30.5	934	9.7
	2000	15 454	85.8	6 087	33.1	962	11.5
	2010	17 151	88.7	8 032	39.6	964	14.2
	2012	17 465	89.2	8 289	39.9	957	14.7
Colombia - Colombie	1990	33 307	68.1	11 362	30.0	3 342	18.6
	2000	39 898	71.8	17 269	38.7	3 584	22.6
	2010	46 445	74.8	22 143	42.4	3 529	24.8
	2012	47 704	75.3	23 136	42.9	3 484	25.0
Ecuador - Équateur	1990	10 124	55.8	3 862	31.9	1 117	14.7
	2000	12 533	59.4	5 391	37.4	1 210	20.2
	2010	15 001	64.5	6 857	39.7	1 228	24.8
	2012	15 492	65.3	7 197	40.2	1 219	25.4
Falkland Islands (Malvinas) - Îles Falkland (Malvinas)	1990	2	75.3	..	..	..	..
	2000	3	67.6	..	..	..	..
	2010	3	73.6	..	..	..	..
	2012	3	74.6	..	..	..	..
Guyana	1990	725	29.6	281	31.4	58	12.1
	2000	744	28.3	285	32.6	55	10.9
	2010	786	27.2	302	34.7	50	8.0
	2012	795	27.1	314	35.5	49	8.2
Paraguay	1990	4 250	48.6	1 802	36.7	576	8.3
	2000	5 350	55.3	2 281	36.7	715	8.1
	2010	6 460	61.3	3 088	39.7	831	7.7
	2012	6 687	62.4	3 249	40.2	851	7.5
Peru - Pérou	1990	21 772	68.6	8 273	37.4	2 773	26.1
	2000	26 000	72.7	11 968	41.2	3 344	28.2
	2010	29 263	76.4	15 481	44.5	3 692	31.3
	2012	29 988	76.9	16 084	44.8	3 728	31.7
Suriname	1990	407	60.0	157	37.3	29	27.6
	2000	467	64.9	166	35.1	30	26.7
	2010	525	69.3	204	37.1	33	24.2
	2012	535	70.1	211	37.5	33	24.2

For sources and notes, see end of table.   Pour les sources et les notes, se reporter à la fin du tableau.

8

Region, country or territory Régions, pays ou territoires	Year Année	Population		Total labour force Main-d'œuvre totale		Agriculture labour force Main-d'œuvre dans l'agriculture	
		Total (thousands) Total (milliers)	Urban population (% of total population) Population urbaine (en % de la population totale)	Total (thousands) Total (milliers)	Female labour (% of total labour force) Main-d'œuvre féminine (en % de la main-d'œuvre totale)	Total (thousands) Total (milliers)	Female labour (% of total agriculture labour force) Main-d'œuvre féminine (en % de la main-d'œuvre totale dans l'agriculture)
		(1)	(2)	(3)	(4)	(5)	(6)
Uruguay	1990	3 110	88.9	1 392	39.0	184	10.9
	2000	3 321	91.3	1 586	43.1	197	12.7
	2010	3 372	92.4	1 708	44.5	186	14.0
	2012	3 395	92.5	1 736	44.7	184	14.1
Venezuela (Bolivarian Rep. of) -	1990	19 741	84.0	7 213	31.5	867	4.2
Venezuela (Rép. bolivarienne du)	2000	24 408	89.7	10 527	37.2	811	5.4
	2010	29 043	93.1	13 463	39.4	722	6.4
	2012	29 955	93.5	14 130	39.8	698	6.4
Developing economies: Asia - Économies en développement : Asie	1990	2 999 068	30.0	1 367 866	38.1	898 011	42.2
	2000	3 491 781	35.9	1 628 874	37.9	969 780	42.4
	2010	3 928 277	43.1	1 885 572	37.1	1 014 276	42.6
	2012	4 014 712	44.4	1 938 604	37.0	1 017 422	42.5
Eastern Asia - Asie orientale	1990	1 236 934	29.7	687 487	44.4	489 840	47.2
	2000	1 358 911	39.0	773 268	44.7	510 620	47.8
	2010	1 443 073	51.4	851 089	44.4	505 536	47.9
	2012	1 461 333	53.7	862 931	44.3	500 419	47.9
China - Chine (9)	1990	1 145 150	26.4	649 073	44.6	482 507	47.2
	2000	1 258 244	36.2	728 129	45.0	504 849	47.9
	2010	1 336 659	49.4	801 588	44.6	500 977	48.0
	2012	1 353 749	51.9	812 345	44.5	496 081	47.9
China, Hong Kong SAR - Chine (RAS de Hong Kong)	1990	5 794	99.5	2 892	36.5	..	..
	2000	6 835	99.2	3 410	41.9	..	..
	2010	7 050	100.0	3 689	46.0	..	..
	2012	7 148	100.0	3 774	46.2	..	..
China, Macao SAR - Chine (RAS de Macao)	1990	360	99.8	155	40.5	..	..
	2000	432	100.0	217	45.3	..	..
	2010	535	100.0	337	48.8	..	..
	2012	557	100.0	356	48.8	..	..
China, Taiwan Province of - Province chinoise de Taiwan (10)	1990	20 279	66.1	3 220	18.4	..	..
	2000	22 185	69.1	4 825	20.2	..	..
	2010	23 162	73.0	5 452	15.2	..	..
	2012	23 316	73.3	5 803	15.6	..	..
Korea, Dem. People's Rep. of - Corée, Rép. populaire dém. de	1990	20 194	58.2	12 192	48.1	3 618	45.2
	2000	22 840	59.6	13 565	47.5	3 328	45.3
	2010	24 501	59.8	14 575	47.7	3 065	46.4
	2012	24 763	59.9	14 797	47.6	2 990	46.4
Korea, Republic of - Corée, République de	1990	42 972	73.9	19 207	39.7	3 470	44.1
	2000	45 977	79.6	22 175	40.5	2 206	44.0
	2010	48 454	82.5	24 265	41.3	1 274	43.4
	2012	49 003	82.8	24 618	41.4	1 132	43.2
Mongolia - Mongolie	1990	2 184	57.3	748	46.6	245	44.1
	2000	2 397	57.5	946	46.8	237	45.1
	2010	2 713	68.6	1 183	46.4	220	47.7
	2012	2 796	70.7	1 238	46.5	216	48.1
Southern Asia - Asie méridionale	1990	1 191 647	26.5	441 093	27.5	274 258	33.0
	2000	1 447 851	29.2	554 268	27.9	313 156	33.5
	2010	1 681 407	32.7	663 247	26.8	355 387	34.8
	2012	1 726 444	33.4	690 407	26.9	363 089	35.0
Afghanistan	1990	11 731	20.2	3 459	14.9	2 804	28.6
	2000	20 595	22.8	5 745	13.3	4 485	29.0
	2010	28 398	25.7	8 270	15.2	6 046	32.1
	2012	29 825	26.7	8 923	15.6	6 405	32.8
Bangladesh	1990	107 386	19.4	45 675	39.4	30 773	44.9
	2000	132 383	23.1	57 288	37.5	31 757	45.0
	2010	151 125	27.4	72 274	39.9	32 100	50.9
	2012	154 695	28.4	75 643	40.2	31 845	51.9

For sources and notes, see end of table.

Pour les sources et les notes, se reporter à la fin du tableau.

Region, country or territory Régions, pays ou territoires	Year Année	Population		Total labour force Main-d'œuvre totale		Agriculture labour force Main-d'œuvre dans l'agriculture	
		Total (thousands) Total (milliers)	Urban population (% of total population) Population urbaine (en % de la population totale)	Total (thousands) Total (milliers)	Female labour (% of total labour force) Main-d'œuvre féminine (en % de la main-d'œuvre totale)	Total (thousands) Total (milliers)	Female labour (% of total agriculture labour force) Main-d'œuvre féminine (en % de la main-d'œuvre totale dans l'agriculture)
		(1)	(2)	(3)	(4)	(5)	(6)
Bhutan - Bhoutan	1990	536	17.1	206	37.1	166	22.9
	2000	564	25.7	228	39.5	169	23.1
	2010	717	35.2	365	42.5	311	34.4
	2012	742	36.8	387	42.4	329	35.0
India - Inde	1990	868 891	25.7	330 509	27.4	210 181	32.4
	2000	1 042 262	28.0	409 206	27.9	239 959	32.4
	2010	1 205 625	31.4	472 580	25.3	269 740	32.4
	2012	1 236 687	32.2	489 839	25.3	275 633	32.5
Iran (Islamic Rep. of) - Iran (Rép. islamique d')	1990	56 362	54.8	13 329	10.8	5 040	27.2
	2000	65 911	63.5	18 491	16.0	5 761	39.2
	2010	74 462	68.5	25 226	17.9	6 553	46.5
	2012	76 424	68.5	26 472	18.3	6 558	48.2
Maldives	1990	216	26.3	58	19.4	20	15.0
	2000	273	27.8	89	33.8	21	28.6
	2010	326	38.8	153	41.8	23	39.1
	2012	338	40.6	162	42.2	22	40.9
Nepal - Népal	1990	18 111	9.3	9 379	46.9	6 653	39.4
	2000	23 184	14.1	12 352	49.0	8 677	44.1
	2010	26 846	18.6	16 034	49.2	12 066	48.1
	2012	27 474	19.5	16 973	49.2	12 755	48.5
Pakistan	1990	111 091	30.8	31 717	12.8	15 044	16.3
	2000	143 832	33.3	43 036	15.3	18 712	22.9
	2010	173 149	36.0	59 739	20.7	24 520	30.1
	2012	179 160	36.7	63 225	21.1	25 498	31.3
Sri Lanka	1990	17 324	17.2	6 761	31.5	3 577	38.0
	2000	18 846	15.6	7 833	33.1	3 615	34.1
	2010	20 759	15.1	8 607	32.2	4 028	37.2
	2012	21 098	15.2	8 783	32.5	4 044	37.4
South-Eastern Asia - Asie du Sud-Est	*1990*	*443 735*	*31.7*	*200 255*	*42.8*	*119 013*	*43.2*
	2000	*524 410*	*38.1*	*251 831*	*42.0*	*131 986*	*42.5*
	2010	*597 097*	*43.8*	*302 270*	*42.4*	*139 939*	*42.4*
	2012	*611 117*	*44.9*	*312 353*	*42.5*	*140 716*	*42.4*
Brunei Darussalam - Brunéi Darussalam	1990	257	..	105	31.7	2	50.0
	2000	332	..	154	40.7	1	..
	2010	401	..	195	42.0	1	..
	2012	..	..	203	42.1	..	..
Cambodia - Cambodge	1990	9 057	16.4	4 321	52.6	3 138	55.7
	2000	12 223	18.9	5 773	51.2	4 028	53.5
	2010	14 365	19.5	7 973	49.8	4 966	51.3
	2012	14 865	19.6	8 312	49.6	5 091	51.0
Indonesia (...2002) - Indonésie (...2002)	1990	179 385	31.5	76 784	38.6	43 171	39.4
	2000	209 792	42.8	99 691	37.6	48 669	39.1
Indonesia - Indonésie	2010	240 676	49.8	118 023	38.2	49 513	39.4
	2012	246 864	51.0	121 706	38.4	49 442	39.6
Lao People's Dem. Rep. - Rép. dém. populaire lao	1990	4 245	15.2	1 924	49.7	1 486	51.3
	2000	5 388	21.7	2 459	49.9	1 865	52.0
	2010	6 396	32.1	3 169	49.8	2 368	52.3
	2012	6 646	33.9	3 332	49.6	2 480	52.1
Malaysia - Malaisie	1990	18 211	49.8	7 124	34.3	1 933	32.1
	2000	23 421	62.0	9 890	34.7	1 849	26.3
	2010	28 276	72.3	11 977	35.8	1 612	21.0
	2012	29 240	73.7	12 480	36.0	1 557	20.2

For sources and notes, see end of table.

Pour les sources et les notes, se reporter à la fin du tableau.

8

Region, country or territory Régions, pays ou territoires	Year Année	Population		Total labour force Main-d'œuvre totale		Agriculture labour force Main-d'œuvre dans l'agriculture	
		Total (thousands) Total (milliers)	Urban population (% of total population) Population urbaine (en % de la population totale)	Total (thousands) Total (milliers)	Female labour (% of total labour force) Main-d'œuvre féminine (en % de la main-d'œuvre totale)	Total (thousands) Total (milliers)	Female labour (% of total agriculture labour force) Main-d'œuvre féminine (en % de la main-d'œuvre totale dans l'agriculture)
		(1)	(2)	(3)	(4)	(5)	(6)
Myanmar	1990	42 123	22.9	19 003	48.4	14 482	47.3
	2000	48 453	25.3	24 151	48.3	17 125	47.3
	2010	51 931	29.6	27 971	48.9	18 788	47.8
	2012	52 797	30.6	28 752	48.8	19 143	47.9
Philippines	1990	61 949	48.3	23 724	36.6	10 844	24.4
	2000	77 652	47.8	30 971	37.4	12 405	24.1
	2010	93 444	48.6	38 719	38.8	13 404	24.2
	2012	96 707	48.9	40 691	39.0	13 542	24.2
Singapore - Singapour	1990	3 016	100.0	1 539	39.1	6	16.7
	2000	3 918	100.0	2 012	40.7	3	..
	2010	5 079	100.0	2 809	42.3	2	..
	2012	5 303	99.1	2 917	42.4	2	..
Thailand - Thaïlande	1990	56 583	29.7	32 486	47.4	21 272	48.0
	2000	62 343	31.5	34 824	46.1	20 089	46.4
	2010	66 402	35.1	39 404	45.7	19 302	45.1
	2012	66 785	36.0	40 130	45.8	18 877	44.8
Timor-Leste	2010	1 079	29.1	343	33.3	352	44.9
	2012	1 114	30.6	367	33.4	374	44.9
Viet Nam	1990	68 910	19.7	33 244	49.6	22 679	50.7
	2000	80 888	23.7	41 906	49.1	25 952	50.1
	2010	89 047	30.0	51 687	48.5	29 631	49.1
	2012	90 796	31.3	53 464	48.4	30 208	48.9
Western Asia - Asie occidentale	*1990*	*126 752*	*60.7*	*39 031*	*22.7*	*14 900*	*41.4*
	2000	*160 608*	*64.0*	*49 508*	*22.0*	*14 018*	*43.5*
	2010	*206 700*	*67.5*	*68 966*	*22.1*	*13 414*	*47.9*
	2012	*215 819*	*68.4*	*72 913*	*22.3*	*13 198*	*48.7*
Bahrain - Bahreïn	1990	496	87.6	214	17.0	4	..
	2000	668	84.4	302	21.4	3	..
	2010	1 252	89.3	711	19.3	4	..
	2012	1 318	91.5	763	19.4	4	..
Iraq	1990	17 518	69.1	3 712	14.2	626	34.8
	2000	23 801	68.0	5 437	15.9	535	42.8
	2010	30 962	68.1	7 452	17.6	436	50.7
	2012	32 778	68.3	8 061	17.9	425	52.0
Jordan - Jordanie	1990	3 358	73.5	708	10.7	102	37.3
	2000	4 767	80.8	1 212	14.3	118	50.0
	2010	6 455	79.1	1 589	18.1	114	61.4
	2012	7 009	76.4	1 728	18.3	110	63.6
Kuwait - Koweït	1990	2 060	99.3	786	26.9	9	..
	2000	1 906	99.9	962	25.1	11	..
	2010	2 992	89.9	1 357	23.9	14	..
	2012	3 250	87.4	1 439	24.0	15	..
Lebanon - Liban	1990	2 703	90.7	786	21.1	69	31.9
	2000	3 235	99.5	1 140	22.9	48	33.3
	2010	4 341	84.9	1 454	25.5	28	32.1
	2012	4 647	80.7	1 503	25.7	25	32.0
Oman	1990	1 810	68.2	558	12.9	256	6.6
	2000	2 193	73.9	787	17.1	293	6.8
	2010	2 803	72.7	1 216	17.9	318	6.9
	2012	3 314	64.6	1 312	17.7	322	6.8
Qatar	1990	477	92.2	274	14.4	7	..
	2000	594	95.9	332	15.6	4	..
	2010	1 750	99.2	1 315	12.4	8	..
	2012	2 051	93.6	1 430	12.1	8	..

For sources and notes, see end of table.   Pour les sources et les notes, se reporter à la fin du tableau.

Region, country or territory / Régions, pays ou territoires	Year / Année	Population		Total labour force / Main-d'œuvre totale		Agriculture labour force / Main-d'œuvre dans l'agriculture	
		Total (thousands) / Total (milliers)	Urban population (% of total population) / Population urbaine (en % de la population totale)	Total (thousands) / Total (milliers)	Female labour (% of total labour force) / Main-d'œuvre féminine (en % de la main-d'œuvre totale)	Total (thousands) / Total (milliers)	Female labour (% of total agriculture labour force) / Main-d'œuvre féminine (en % de la main-d'œuvre totale dans l'agriculture)
		(1)	(2)	(3)	(4)	(5)	(6)
Saudi Arabia - Arabie saoudite	1990	16 206	76.3	4 998	10.7	966	6.9
	2000	20 145	79.5	5 963	14.8	659	6.5
	2010	27 258	82.7	9 557	14.8	515	5.6
	2012	28 288	83.7	10 079	15.6	470	5.5
State of Palestine - État de Palestine	1990	2 081	67.9	425	12.5	128	61.7
	2000	3 205	71.8	656	13.4	125	66.4
	2010	4 013	74.6	947	17.9	110	72.7
	2012	4 219	75.5	1 029	18.6	108	74.1
Syrian Arab Republic - République arabe syrienne	1990	12 452	48.4	3 220	18.4	954	41.7
	2000	16 371	50.7	4 825	20.2	1 116	49.1
	2010	21 533	52.8	5 452	15.2	1 337	60.7
	2012	21 890	54.5	5 806	15.6	1 344	62.5
Turkey - Turquie	1990	53 995	59.4	19 951	30.0	10 355	47.8
	2000	63 174	65.2	21 960	26.9	9 131	48.7
	2010	72 138	71.1	26 531	28.7	8 067	52.6
	2012	73 997	73.0	27 413	28.7	7 855	53.5
United Arab Emirates - Émirats arabes unis	1990	1 806	79.1	905	9.7	73	..
	2000	3 026	80.4	1 718	12.0	87	..
	2010	8 442	74.8	4 927	14.8	148	..
	2012	9 206	74.5	5 329	14.9	144	..
Yemen - Yémen	1990	11 790	21.2	2 497	18.9	1 351	27.8
	2000	17 523	26.6	4 212	24.0	1 888	34.3
	2010	22 763	33.5	6 459	25.9	2 315	40.3
	2012	23 852	35.3	7 019	26.2	2 368	40.6
Developing economies: Oceania - Économies en développement : Océanie	**1990**	**6 475**	**23.7**	**2 468**	**43.8**	**1 800**	**48.1**
	2000	**8 106**	**22.8**	**3 225**	**45.3**	**2 173**	**50.3**
	2010	**9 886**	**21.8**	**4 127**	**45.4**	**2 590**	**51.9**
	2012	**10 263**	**21.8**	**4 335**	**45.4**	**2 691**	**52.1**
American Samoa - Samoa américaines	1990	47	81.0	..	..	7	28.6
	2000	58	88.9	..	..	8	37.5
	2010	56	100.0	..	..	8	37.5
	2012	55	100.0	..	..	7	42.9
Cook Islands - Îles Cook	1990	18	57.7	..	..	3	33.3
	2000	18	65.2	..	..	2	50.0
	2010	20	73.3	..	..	2	50.0
	2012	21	73.8	..	..	2	50.0
Fiji - Fidji	1990	728	41.6	253	25.5	116	16.4
	2000	812	47.9	311	32.9	125	20.8
	2010	861	51.8	365	32.4	126	21.4
	2012	875	52.7	372	32.5	128	21.9
French Polynesia - Polynésie française	1990	198	55.0	78	37.4	33	36.4
	2000	237	52.5	94	39.4	34	35.3
	2010	268	51.9	117	40.5	33	36.4
	2012	274	51.9	120	40.7	32	37.5
Guam	1990	130	93.2	61	35.4	20	25.0
	2000	155	93.0	68	38.5	19	26.3
	2010	159	100.0	79	38.6	20	25.0
	2012	163	100.0	82	38.7	20	25.0
Kiribati	1990	71	35.4	..	..	10	30.0
	2000	83	43.6	..	..	10	30.0
	2010	98	44.6	..	..	11	27.3
	2012	101	44.8	..	..	11	27.3
Marshall Islands - Îles Marshall	1990	47	65.0	..	..	..	..
	2000	52	68.3	..	..	6	33.3
	2010	52	73.7	..	..	6	33.3
	2012	53	76.5	..	..	6	33.3

For sources and notes, see end of table.

Pour les sources et les notes, se reporter à la fin du tableau.

Region, country or territory / Régions, pays ou territoires	Year / Année	Population		Total labour force / Main-d'œuvre totale		Agriculture labour force / Main-d'œuvre dans l'agriculture	
		Total (thousands) / Total (milliers) (1)	Urban population (% of total population) / Population urbaine (en % de la population totale) (2)	Total (thousands) / Total (milliers) (3)	Female labour (% of total labour force) / Main-d'œuvre féminine (en % de la main-d'œuvre totale) (4)	Total (thousands) / Total (milliers) (5)	Female labour (% of total agriculture labour force) / Main-d'œuvre féminine (en % de la main-d'œuvre totale dans l'agriculture) (6)
Micronesia (Federated States of) - Micronésie (États fédérés de)	1990	96	25.8	..	..	..	..
	2000	107	22.3	..	..	13	23.1
	2010	104	24.1	..	..	12	25.0
	2012	103	24.6	..	..	12	25.0
Nauru	1990	9	100.0	..	..	1	..
	2000	10	100.0	..	..	1	..
	2010	10	100.0	..	..	1	..
	2012	10	100.0	..	..	1	..
New Caledonia - Nouvelle-Calédonie	1990	169	59.9	68	37.6	30	40.0
	2000	210	62.4	90	40.1	32	40.6
	2010	246	63.0	108	40.9	32	40.6
	2012	253	62.9	112	41.1	32	37.5
Niue - Nioué	1990	2	30.9	..	..	..	..
	2000	2	33.1	..	..	..	..
	2010	1	37.5	..	..	..	..
	2012	1	38.4	..	..	..	..
Northern Mariana Islands - Îles Mariannes du Nord	1990	44	89.7	..	..	..	..
	2000	68	90.2	..	..	8	25.0
	2010	54	100.0	..	..	7	28.6
	2012	53	100.0	..	..	7	28.6
Palau - Palaos	1990	15	69.6	..	..	..	..
	2000	19	70.0	..	..	2	50.0
	2010	20	83.4	..	..	2	50.0
	2012	21	85.1	..	..	2	50.0
Papua New Guinea - Papouasie-Nouvelle-Guinée	1990	4 158	15.0	1 740	48.1	1 421	52.4
	2000	5 379	13.2	2 319	48.5	1 725	54.4
	2010	6 859	12.4	3 025	48.3	2 110	55.5
	2012	7 167	12.5	3 194	48.3	2 202	55.7
Samoa	1990	163	21.0	56	31.9	24	29.2
	2000	175	22.2	65	33.0	22	31.8
	2010	186	19.8	69	34.3	18	33.3
	2012	189	19.2	71	34.3	18	33.3
Solomon Islands - Îles Salomon	1990	312	..	110	39.2	90	45.6
	2000	412	..	158	38.9	118	45.8
	2010	526	..	217	38.5	151	46.4
	2012	548	..	231	38.5	159	46.5
Tokelau - Tokélaou	1990	2	..	..	..	..	..
	2000	2	..	..	..	..	..
	2010	1	..	..	..	..	..
	2012	1	..	..	..	..	..
Tonga	1990	95	22.7	32	32.3	12	25.0
	2000	98	23.0	37	40.1	12	41.7
	2010	104	23.4	42	42.7	11	45.5
	2012	105	23.5	42	42.7	11	36.4
Tuvalu	1990	9	40.7	..	..	1	..
	2000	9	46.1	..	..	1	..
	2010	10	50.1	..	..	1	..
	2012	10	51.0	..	..	1	..
Vanuatu	1990	147	18.7	69	46.2	30	50.0
	2000	185	21.7	83	44.7	33	48.5
	2010	236	24.9	105	42.9	38	47.4
	2012	247	25.7	111	42.9	39	46.2

For sources and notes, see end of table.

Pour les sources et les notes, se reporter à la fin du tableau.

Region, country or territory Régions, pays ou territoires	Year Année	Population		Total labour force Main-d'œuvre totale		Agriculture labour force Main-d'œuvre dans l'agriculture	
		Total (thousands) Total (milliers)	Urban population (% of total population) Population urbaine (en % de la population totale)	Total (thousands) Total (milliers)	Female labour (% of total labour force) Main-d'œuvre féminine (en % de la main-d'œuvre totale)	Total (thousands) Total (milliers)	Female labour (% of total agriculture labour force) Main-d'œuvre féminine (en % de la main-d'œuvre totale dans l'agriculture)
		(1)	(2)	(3)	(4)	(5)	(6)
Wallis and Futuna Islands - Îles Wallis-et-Futuna	1990	14	..	..	..	2	50.0
	2000	14	..	..	..	2	50.0
	2010	14	..	..	..	1	100.0
	2012	13	..	..	..	1	100.0
Transition economies - Économies en transition	**1990**	**315 797**	**63.9**	**153 486**	**47.4**	**29 389**	**40.2**
	2000	**305 443**	**63.3**	**144 092**	**47.5**	**21 316**	**35.8**
	2010	**304 577**	**63.2**	**151 578**	**47.5**	**18 235**	**33.2**
	2012	**305 307**	**63.4**	**152 752**	**47.5**	**17 581**	**32.7**
Albania - Albanie	1990	3 447	34.8	1 415	40.4	921	47.6
	2000	3 305	38.8	1 331	41.7	620	44.4
	2010	3 150	53.2	1 496	41.6	614	42.5
	2012	3 162	55.6	1 526	41.5	604	42.1
Armenia - Arménie	2000	3 076	64.7	1 472	48.8	174	23.0
	2010	2 963	66.8	1 438	46.5	148	16.2
	2012	2 969	67.1	1 466	46.4	143	15.4
Azerbaijan - Azerbaïdjan	2000	8 118	51.3	3 573	47.0	972	54.4
	2010	9 095	53.9	4 676	49.0	1 085	53.4
	2012	9 309	54.5	4 854	48.8	1 091	52.9
Belarus - Bélarus	2000	9 981	70.5	4 768	48.9	636	25.3
	2010	9 491	75.4	4 530	48.9	434	18.7
	2012	9 405	76.4	4 537	48.9	400	17.5
Bosnia and Herzegovina - Bosnie-Herzégovine	2000	3 834	41.4	1 332	39.0	100	60.0
	2010	3 846	46.7	1 478	40.0	44	59.1
	2012	3 834	47.6	1 484	39.9	37	59.5
Croatia - Croatie	2000	4 475	56.0	2 005	44.2	170	35.3
	2010	4 338	58.4	1 964	46.0	84	29.8
	2012	4 307	59.2	1 963	45.9	73	28.8
Georgia - Géorgie	2000	4 744	52.7	2 357	46.2	472	39.6
	2010	4 389	52.3	2 322	47.0	354	36.2
	2012	4 358	52.3	2 321	47.0	336	35.1
Kazakhstan	2000	14 576	57.2	7 585	49.1	1 321	29.1
	2010	15 921	54.1	8 625	49.4	1 192	24.2
	2012	16 271	53.8	8 790	49.3	1 168	23.2
Kyrgyzstan - Kirghizistan	2000	4 955	35.3	2 090	44.7	543	35.2
	2010	5 334	35.3	2 476	42.7	510	29.8
	2012	5 474	35.2	2 562	42.7	504	29.0
Montenegro - Monténégro	2010	620	64.3	..	..	39	38.5
	2012	621	64.7	..	..	36	36.1
Republic of Moldova - République de Moldova	2000	4 107	44.6	1 857	49.7	390	34.4
	2010	3 573	46.9	1 221	49.2	200	30.0
	2012	3 514	48.5	1 234	49.3	181	28.7
Russian Federation - Fédération de Russie	2000	146 763	73.3	73 524	48.6	7 648	28.9
	2010	143 618	73.3	76 185	48.8	6 251	24.6
	2012	143 170	73.7	76 123	48.9	5 944	23.6
Serbia and Montenegro - Serbie-et-Monténégro	2000	10 884	52.7	4 758	45.0	1 007	44.0
Serbia - Serbie	2010	9 647	57.2	4 433	43.2	617	38.1
	2012	9 553	58.5	4 473	43.3	563	36.9
SFR of Yugoslavia - RSF de Yougoslavie	1990	23 684	47.8	10 231	43.9	911	49.0
Tajikistan - Tadjikistan	2000	6 186	26.4	2 374	44.1	610	52.8
	2010	7 627	23.9	2 847	45.2	773	53.2
	2012	8 009	23.5	2 987	45.3	783	53.3

For sources and notes, see end of table.

Pour les sources et les notes, se reporter à la fin du tableau.

8

Region, country or territory / Régions, pays ou territoires	Year / Année	Population		Total labour force / Main-d'œuvre totale		Agriculture labour force / Main-d'œuvre dans l'agriculture	
		Total (thousands) Total (milliers)	Urban population (% of total population) Population urbaine (en % de la population totale)	Total (thousands) Total (milliers)	Female labour (% of total labour force) Main-d'œuvre féminine (en % de la main-d'œuvre totale)	Total (thousands) Total (milliers)	Female labour (% of total agriculture labour force) Main-d'œuvre féminine (en % de la main-d'œuvre totale dans l'agriculture)
		(1)	(2)	(3)	(4)	(5)	(6)
TFYR of Macedonia - LERY de Macédoine	2000	2 052	58.1	831	38.8	107	36.4
	2010	2 102	58.0	946	38.5	68	32.4
	2012	2 106	58.3	961	38.7	62	30.6
Turkmenistan - Turkménistan	2000	4 501	45.9	1 735	40.6	627	52.2
	2010	5 042	48.4	2 164	39.3	705	53.2
	2012	5 173	49.0	2 256	39.2	721	53.3
Ukraine	2000	49 057	66.9	23 259	49.2	3 295	33.0
	2010	46 050	67.8	22 999	49.3	2 412	27.4
	2012	45 530	68.2	22 903	49.4	2 256	26.3
USSR - URSS	1990	288 666	65.6	141 840	47.8	27 557	39.6
Uzbekistan - Ouzbékistan	2000	24 829	37.3	9 243	40.6	2 624	45.5
	2010	27 769	35.8	11 780	39.8	2 705	43.5
	2012	28 541	35.6	12 312	39.7	2 679	43.0
Developed economies: America - Économies développées : Amérique	**1990**	**285 907**	**75.1**	**144 627**	**44.6**	**4 263**	**22.6**
	2000	**319 323**	**78.8**	**163 523**	**45.8**	**3 515**	**25.8**
	2010	**350 317**	**81.7**	**176 863**	**46.2**	**2 867**	**28.9**
	2012	**356 272**	**82.2**	**179 840**	**46.2**	**2 746**	**29.5**
Bermuda - Bermudes	1990	60	100.0	..	..	1	..
	2000	63	100.0	..	..	1	..
	2010	65	100.0	..	..	1	..
	2012	65	100.0	..	..	1	..
Canada	1990	27 658	76.7	14 669	44.1	495	32.1
	2000	30 697	79.4	16 206	45.7	382	41.9
	2010	34 126	80.3	18 930	47.1	332	52.4
	2012	34 838	80.4	19 310	47.1	320	54.7
Greenland - Groenland	1990	56	79.6	..	..	1	..
	2000	56	81.6	..	..	1	..
	2010	57	85.5	..	..	..	..
	2012	57	85.7	..	..	..	..
Saint Pierre and Miquelon - Saint-Pierre-et-Miquelon	1990	6	88.9	..	..	..	..
	2000	6	89.1	..	..	..	..
	2010	6	90.6	..	..	..	..
	2012	6	90.8	..	..	..	..
United States - États-Unis	1990	258 128	74.9	129 958	44.7	3 766	21.3
	2000	288 500	78.7	147 317	45.8	3 131	23.9
	2010	316 063	81.9	157 933	46.1	2 534	25.8
	2012	321 306	82.4	160 530	46.1	2 425	26.2
Developed economies: Asia - Économies développées : Asie	**1990**	**126 748**	**77.8**	**64 860**	**40.7**	**4 678**	**46.2**
	2000	**131 728**	**79.2**	**69 349**	**40.8**	**2 773**	**42.3**
	2010	**134 773**	**90.1**	**69 284**	**42.6**	**1 469**	**39.7**
	2012	**134 894**	**91.4**	**68 879**	**42.7**	**1 287**	**39.2**
Israel - Israël	1990	4 499	90.4	1 603	40.4	65	21.5
	2000	6 014	91.2	2 343	45.8	61	23.0
	2010	7 420	91.8	3 094	47.1	51	21.6
	2012	7 644	92.6	3 201	47.0	49	20.4
Japan - Japon	1990	122 249	77.3	63 257	40.7	4 613	46.5
	2000	125 715	78.7	67 006	40.6	2 712	42.7
	2010	127 353	90.0	66 190	42.4	1 418	40.3
	2012	127 250	91.3	65 678	42.5	1 238	39.9
Developed economies: Europe - Économies développées : Europe	**1990**	**476 090**	**70.3**	**217 474**	**41.6**	**20 978**	**40.8**
	2000	**497 449**	**71.4**	**232 496**	**43.8**	**15 285**	**39.3**
	2010	**517 116**	**73.6**	**250 149**	**45.1**	**10 981**	**37.5**
	2012	**520 089**	**74.0**	**251 640**	**45.2**	**10 261**	**37.2**

For sources and notes, see end of table.

Pour les sources et les notes, se reporter à la fin du tableau.

Region, country or territory / Régions, pays ou territoires	Year / Année	Population		Total labour force / Main-d'œuvre totale		Agriculture labour force / Main-d'œuvre dans l'agriculture	
		Total (thousands) / Total (milliers)	Urban population (% of total population) / Population urbaine (en % de la population totale)	Total (thousands) / Total (milliers)	Female labour (% of total labour force) / Main-d'œuvre féminine (en % de la main-d'œuvre totale)	Total (thousands) / Total (milliers)	Female labour (% of total agriculture labour force) / Main-d'œuvre féminine (en % de la main-d'œuvre totale dans l'agriculture)
		(1)	(2)	(3)	(4)	(5)	(6)
Andorra - Andorre	1990	55	91.7	..	..	3	33.3
	2000	65	91.3	..	..	2	50.0
	2010	78	95.7	..	..	2	50.0
	2012	78	96.8	..	..	2	50.0
Austria - Autriche	1990	7 670	65.8	3 524	40.9	274	47.1
	2000	8 020	65.7	3 860	43.5	199	46.7
	2010	8 402	67.4	4 337	45.9	144	45.8
	2012	8 464	67.6	4 364	46.0	134	45.5
Belgium - Belgique	1990	9 978	96.1	3 924	39.0	..	..
	2000	10 268	96.2	4 402	43.0	79	29.1
	2010	10 941	95.4	4 810	45.3	59	32.2
	2012	11 060	95.1	4 834	45.5	55	32.7
Bulgaria - Bulgarie	1990	8 821	66.4	4 128	47.9	572	47.0
	2000	8 001	68.9	3 535	47.1	228	37.7
	2010	7 389	73.6	3 491	46.8	124	30.6
	2012	7 278	74.9	3 458	46.8	107	29.9
Cyprus - Chypre (11)	1990	767	66.8	344	38.1	50	42.0
	2000	943	68.6	445	40.7	38	42.1
	2010	1 104	70.3	584	43.6	30	36.7
	2012	1 129	70.7	604	43.5	28	35.7
Czechoslovakia - Tchécoslovaquie	1990	15 604	68.7	7 467	45.2	985	36.8
Czech Republic - République tchèque	2000	10 250	73.9	5 155	44.4	431	29.0
	2010	10 554	73.0	5 277	43.3	327	23.2
	2012	10 660	72.7	5 329	43.5	309	22.3
Denmark - Danemark	1990	5 140	84.9	2 912	46.1	162	24.1
	2000	5 338	85.1	2 863	46.6	108	24.1
	2010	5 551	86.8	2 941	47.1	75	24.0
	2012	5 598	87.0	2 953	47.2	70	24.3
Estonia - Estonie	2000	1 366	69.6	657	48.7	76	30.3
	2010	1 299	71.7	699	50.4	61	26.2
	2012	1 291	72.2	701	50.2	58	25.9
Faeroe Islands - Îles Féroé	1990	48	30.3	..	..	1	..
	2000	46	35.8	..	..	1	..
	2010	50	40.2	..	..	1	..
	2012	50	41.0	..	..	1	..
Finland - Finlande	1990	4 987	79.4	2 615	47.1	218	35.3
	2000	5 176	82.1	2 613	47.4	143	35.0
	2010	5 368	83.5	2 696	47.8	98	35.7
	2012	5 408	83.7	2 693	47.8	90	35.6
France	1990	58 439	74.2	25 094	43.3	1 414	34.8
	2000	61 105	77.0	26 474	45.5	913	34.2
	2010	65 407	84.8	28 918	47.1	598	32.9
	2012	66 165	85.8	29 088	47.2	544	32.7
Germany - Allemagne	1990	80 487	71.9	37 155	40.7	1 557	41.7
	2000	83 512	72.0	40 445	43.7	1 016	39.7
	2010	83 017	73.2	42 465	45.6	661	36.9
	2012	82 800	73.3	42 283	45.6	604	36.3
Gibraltar	1990	27	100.0	..	..	2	50.0
	2000	27	100.0	..	..	1	..
	2010	29	100.0	..	..	1	..
	2012	29	100.0	..	..	1	..
Greece - Grèce	1990	10 161	58.8	4 185	36.1	963	45.4
	2000	10 987	59.7	4 897	39.2	826	49.6
	2010	11 110	62.6	5 293	41.5	637	52.7
	2012	11 125	63.3	5 348	41.8	596	53.2

For sources and notes, see end of table.

Pour les sources et les notes, se reporter à la fin du tableau.

471

Region, country or territory / Régions, pays ou territoires	Year / Année	Population		Total labour force Main-d'œuvre totale		Agriculture labour force Main-d'œuvre dans l'agriculture	
		Total (thousands) Total (milliers)	Urban population (% of total population) Population urbaine (en % de la population totale)	Total (thousands) Total (milliers)	Female labour (% of total labour force) Main-d'œuvre féminine (en % de la main-d'œuvre totale)	Total (thousands) Total (milliers)	Female labour (% of total agriculture labour force) Main-d'œuvre féminine (en % de la main-d'œuvre totale dans l'agriculture)
		(1)	(2)	(3)	(4)	(5)	(6)
Holy See - Saint-Siège	1990	1	100.0	..	..	..	..
	2000	1	100.0	..	..	..	..
	2010	1	100.0	..	..	..	..
	2012	1	100.0	..	..	..	..
Hungary - Hongrie	1990	10 385	65.8	4 540	44.5	701	31.0
	2000	10 224	64.5	4 178	44.7	452	26.3
	2010	10 015	68.8	4 312	46.0	322	22.7
	2012	9 976	69.8	4 304	46.0	299	21.7
Iceland - Islande	1990	255	90.7	143	45.4	15	20.0
	2000	281	92.4	166	46.8	13	15.4
	2010	318	94.2	189	47.3	12	16.7
	2012	326	94.5	195	47.2	11	9.1
Ireland - Irlande	1990	3 531	56.9	1 360	34.2	186	8.1
	2000	3 804	59.1	1 757	40.6	166	8.4
	2010	4 468	61.9	2 124	43.7	149	7.4
	2012	4 576	62.5	2 179	43.7	143	7.0
Italy - Italie	1990	56 832	66.7	23 830	36.4	2 068	38.9
	2000	56 986	67.2	23 312	38.6	1 250	40.9
	2010	60 509	68.3	25 151	40.3	845	45.0
	2012	60 885	68.6	25 391	40.3	774	45.9
Latvia - Lettonie	2000	2 371	68.5	1 095	48.1	132	31.8
	2010	2 091	72.9	1 163	50.0	113	25.7
	2012	2 060	73.4	1 174	49.8	108	24.1
Lithuania - Lituanie	2000	3 498	67.0	1 685	49.5	204	28.9
	2010	3 068	72.6	1 648	50.3	126	23.0
	2012	3 028	73.1	1 655	50.2	116	21.6
Luxembourg	1990	382	80.8	160	34.7	..	..
	2000	436	83.6	189	39.7	4	25.0
	2010	508	85.1	238	43.4	3	33.3
	2012	524	85.6	247	43.8	3	33.3
Malta - Malte	1990	375	88.5	143	26.7	3	..
	2000	408	90.1	159	30.4	3	..
	2010	425	92.8	181	34.7	2	..
	2012	428	93.1	183	35.1	2	..
Netherlands - Pays-Bas	1990	14 890	68.7	6 860	38.9	314	28.7
	2000	15 860	76.8	8 131	43.1	269	33.1
	2010	16 615	82.7	8 860	45.7	213	36.6
	2012	16 714	83.6	8 918	45.7	202	37.1
Norway - Norvège	1990	4 240	72.0	2 169	44.6	139	27.3
	2000	4 492	76.1	2 376	46.4	110	33.6
	2010	4 891	79.0	2 613	46.9	88	39.8
	2012	4 994	79.1	2 664	47.0	85	41.2
Poland - Pologne	1990	38 150	61.1	18 069	45.5	4 956	45.5
	2000	38 351	61.6	17 302	45.8	3 763	41.3
	2010	38 199	61.1	18 230	45.1	2 960	36.2
	2012	38 211	61.0	18 235	45.1	2 807	35.2
Portugal	1990	9 899	48.0	4 782	42.8	857	50.6
	2000	10 306	54.6	5 277	45.4	678	58.0
	2010	10 590	61.0	5 614	47.4	515	63.7
	2012	10 604	62.2	5 654	47.4	500	66.0
Romania - Roumanie	1990	23 372	52.8	10 529	44.7	2 603	53.7
	2000	22 388	52.5	11 704	46.6	1 739	48.8
	2010	21 861	51.9	10 208	44.7	868	43.3
	2012	21 755	51.9	10 303	45.0	777	42.2

For sources and notes, see end of table.

Pour les sources et les notes, se reporter à la fin du tableau.

Region, country or territory / Régions, pays ou territoires	Year / Année	Population		Total labour force / Main-d'œuvre totale		Agriculture labour force / Main-d'œuvre dans l'agriculture	
		Total (thousands) / Total (milliers)	Urban population (% of total population) / Population urbaine (en % de la population totale)	Total (thousands) / Total (milliers)	Female labour (% of total labour force) / Main-d'œuvre féminine (en % de la main-d'œuvre totale)	Total (thousands) / Total (milliers)	Female labour (% of total agriculture labour force) / Main-d'œuvre féminine (en % de la main-d'œuvre totale dans l'agriculture)
		(1)	(2)	(3)	(4)	(5)	(6)
San Marino - Saint-Marin	1990	24	90.4	..	..	1	100.0
	2000	27	93.4	..	..	1	..
	2010	31	96.1	..	..	1	..
	2012	31	96.2	..	..	1	..
Slovakia - Slovaquie	2000	5 388	56.4	2 598	45.6	240	28.3
	2010	5 433	55.1	2 742	44.6	197	21.8
	2012	5 446	55.0	2 773	44.8	188	20.7
Slovenia - Slovénie	2000	1 990	50.6	960	46.3	19	47.4
	2010	2 054	49.4	1 031	46.4	7	42.9
	2012	2 068	49.2	1 032	46.3	6	33.3
Spain - Espagne	1990	38 883	75.4	15 825	34.4	1 890	30.3
	2000	40 283	76.3	18 209	39.5	1 339	34.8
	2010	46 182	77.1	23 235	44.3	1 015	37.6
	2012	46 755	77.6	23 513	44.3	934	38.0
Sweden - Suède	1990	8 559	83.1	4 687	47.7	209	28.7
	2000	8 872	83.9	4 545	47.1	146	31.5
	2010	9 382	85.0	4 990	47.0	115	35.7
	2012	9 511	85.2	5 043	47.1	109	36.7
Switzerland - Suisse	1990	6 703	72.9	3 756	42.8	196	31.1
	2000	7 199	73.1	3 990	44.3	167	38.3
	2010	7 867	71.8	4 404	45.8	137	43.1
	2012	8 034	71.1	4 431	46.0	134	44.8
United Kingdom - Royaume-Uni	1990	57 425	78.0	29 273	43.3	639	20.3
	2000	59 177	78.4	29 517	45.3	529	22.9
	2010	62 310	79.3	31 707	45.9	475	24.8
	2012	63 030	79.6	32 093	46.0	463	25.3
Developed economies: Oceania - Économies développées : Océanie	**1990**	**20 495**	**85.3**	**10 166**	**41.6**	**641**	**29.3**
	2000	**23 117**	**86.6**	**11 562**	**44.0**	**617**	**35.7**
	2010	**26 773**	**88.1**	**14 172**	**45.5**	**643**	**41.8**
	2012	**27 510**	**88.4**	**14 543**	**45.6**	**645**	**43.3**
Australia - Australie	1990	17 097	85.4	8 505	41.3	470	28.9
	2000	19 259	86.7	9 631	43.8	442	36.7
	2010	22 404	88.5	11 822	45.3	457	44.6
	2012	23 050	88.8	12 140	45.4	458	46.3
New Zealand - Nouvelle-Zélande	1990	3 398	84.7	1 660	43.2	171	30.4
	2000	3 858	85.7	1 932	45.2	175	33.1
	2010	4 368	86.2	2 350	46.8	186	34.9
	2012	4 460	86.3	2 403	46.8	187	35.8

For sources and notes, see next page.

Pour les sources et les notes, se reporter à la page suivante.

Sources:
- UN DESA Population Division, *World Population Prospects: The 2012 Revision*
- UN DESA Population Division, *World Urbanisation Prospects: The 2011 Revision*
- ILO, *LABORSTA*
- FAO, *FAOSTAT*
- Other national sources

Notes:

- Labour force data are derived from activity rates that were based on population estimates and projections of World Population Prospects: The 2010 Revision.

(1) Total population: de facto population in a country, area or region as of 1 July of the year indicated. Figures are presented in thousands.

(2) Urban population as percentage of total population: population living in areas classified as urban according to the criteria used by each area or country. Data refer to 1st July of the year indicated.

(3) Total labour force: comprises all persons (both sexes) of age 15 and above.

(4) Female labour force as percentage of total labour force: comprises all females of age 15 and above.

(5) Total labour force in agriculture: is that part (male and female) of the total labour force engaged or seeking work in agriculture, hunting, fishing or forestry.

(6) Female labour force as percentage of total agriculture labour force: is that part (female) of the total labour force engaged or seeking work in agriculture, hunting, fishing or forestry.

(7) As from 2012, UNCTAD estimates.

(8) As from 2011, UNCTAD estimates.

(9) Agriculture labour force: includes China, Hong Kong SAR, China, Macao SAR and Taiwan, Province of China; Total labour force: includes Taiwan, Province of China only.

(10) National source.

(11) Population data refer to Republic of Cyprus and labour data refer to Cyprus Island.

Sources :
- ONU DAES Division de la population, *Perspectives de la population mondiale : La révision de 2012*
- ONU DAES Division de la population, *Perspectives de l'urbanisation mondiale : La révision de 2011*
- BIT, *LABORSTA*
- FAO, *FAOSTAT*
- Autres sources nationales

Notes :

- Les données de la main-d'œuvre sont dérivées des taux d'activité qui sont basés sur des estimations et projections du *Perspectives de la population mondiale : La révision de 2010*.

(1) Population totale : de facto population d'un pays ou d'une région au 1er juillet de l'année indiquée. Les chiffres sont présentés en milliers.

(2) Population urbaine en pourcentage de la population totale : la population au 1er juillet vivant dans une région classée comme urbaine selon les critères définis par une région ou un pays.

(3) Main-d'œuvre totale : toutes les personnes (hommes et femmes) de 15 ans et plus.

(4) Main-d'œuvre féminine en pourcentage de la main d'œuvre totale : toutes les personnes de sexe féminin de 15 ans et plus.

(5) Main-d'œuvre totale dans l'agriculture : la part (hommes et femmes) du total de la main-d'œuvre qui travaille ou cherche du travail dans l'agriculture, la chasse, la pêche ou la sylviculture.

(6) Main-d'œuvre totale féminine en pourcentage du total de la main-d'œuvre dans l'agriculture : la part (femmes) du total de la main-d'œuvre qui travaille ou cherche du travail dans l'agriculture, la chasse, la pêche ou la sylviculture.

(7) A partir de 2012, estimations de la CNUCED.

(8) A partir de 2011, estimations de la CNUCED.

(9) La main d'œuvre agricole inclut : Chine (RAS de Hong Kong), Chine (RAS de Macao) et Province chinoise de Taiwan. La main d'œuvre totale inclut uniquement Province chinoise de Taiwan.

(10) Source nationale.

(11) Les données de la population se réfèrent à la République de Chypre et les données de la main-d'oeuvre se réfèrent à l'île de Chypre.

Economic grouping / Groupements économiques	Year / Année	Population		Total labour force / Main-d'œuvre totale		Agriculture labour force / Main-d'œuvre agricole	
		Total (thousands) Total (milliers)	Urban population (% of total population) Population urbaine (en % de la population totale)	Total (thousands) Total (milliers)	Female labour (% of total labour force) Main-d'œuvre féminine (en % de la main-d'œuvre totale)	Total (thousands) Total (milliers)	Female labour (% of total agriculture labour force) Main-d'œuvre féminine (en % de la main-d'œuvre agricole totale)
		(1)	(2)	(3)	(4)	(5)	(6)
DEVELOPING ECONOMIES - ÉCONOMIES EN DÉVELOPPEMENT	1990	4 075 547	34.7	1 768 280	37.9	1 086 867	41.7
	2000	4 828 704	40.0	2 159 799	38.5	1 192 669	42.3
	2010	5 559 482	45.9	2 566 384	38.4	1 272 876	42.9
	2012	5 712 287	47.0	2 652 747	38.3	1 283 871	42.9
Developing economies excluding China - Économies en développement sans la Chine	1990	2 930 397	37.9	1 119 207	34.0	604 360	37.3
	2000	3 570 460	41.4	1 431 670	35.1	687 820	38.2
	2010	4 222 823	44.8	1 764 796	35.5	771 899	39.5
	2012	4 347 701	45.6	1 837 043	35.6	787 790	39.8
Developing economies excluding LDCs - Économies en développement sans les PMA	1990	3 566 945	36.6	1 558 285	37.1	927 692	40.9
	2000	4 166 306	42.6	1 883 339	37.7	997 256	41.3
	2010	4 720 676	49.1	2 200 196	37.3	1 034 113	41.4
	2012	4 834 191	50.4	2 265 792	37.3	1 035 973	41.4
High-income developing economies - Économies en développement à revenu élevé	1990	528 506	70.7	199 453	32.8	46 240	26.0
	2000	621 805	75.7	257 041	36.3	42 836	26.7
	2010	712 192	79.1	317 198	37.8	37 042	27.3
	2012	728 772	79.7	328 392	38.0	35 695	27.5
Middle-income developing economies - Économies en développement à revenu intermédiaire	1990	1 786 615	32.6	890 025	41.9	598 350	45.3
	2000	2 018 002	41.2	1 037 171	42.0	630 798	45.8
	2010	2 215 938	51.3	1 180 660	41.8	632 506	46.0
	2012	2 257 730	53.1	1 206 213	41.8	627 617	46.0
Low-income developing economies - Économies en développement à revenu faible	1990	1 760 209	25.9	678 733	34.1	442 235	38.6
	2000	2 188 591	28.8	865 479	34.8	518 982	39.3
	2010	2 630 838	32.5	1 068 307	34.7	603 246	40.5
	2012	2 725 236	33.3	1 117 905	34.8	620 473	40.7
Heavily indebted poor countries (IMF) - Pays pauvres très endettés (FMI)	1990	359 517	24.9	143 551	43.8	109 172	46.4
	2000	479 379	27.8	193 408	44.5	139 114	47.1
	2010	631 801	30.9	260 865	45.0	174 598	48.0
	2012	655 972	31.8	273 633	45.2	182 659	48.1
Landlocked developing countries - Pays en développement sans littoral	1990	194 512	18.6	81 990	44.6	63 218	44.8
	2000	327 144	26.4	137 856	44.6	88 243	45.6
	2010	410 235	27.8	181 313	45.0	112 445	46.6
	2012	440 690	27.9	195 006	44.7	117 730	46.7
Small island developing States - Petits États insulaires en développement	1990	12 692	29.6	4 989	41.9	2 414	44.1
	2000	14 964	29.8	6 169	43.0	2 779	46.7
	2010	18 455	29.4	7 890	43.5	3 552	48.6
	2012	18 985	29.5	8 214	43.6	3 679	48.9
Least developed countries - Pays les moins avancés	*1990*	*508 602*	*21.0*	*209 995*	*43.9*	*159 175*	*46.6*
	2000	*662 398*	*24.2*	*276 460*	*43.8*	*195 413*	*47.3*
	2010	*838 807*	*27.9*	*366 188*	*44.4*	*238 763*	*49.0*
	2012	*878 096*	*28.7*	*386 955*	*44.5*	*247 898*	*49.2*
Africa and Haiti - Afrique et Haïti	1990	302 392	22.2	123 134	45.6	98 008	47.9
	2000	400 552	25.2	163 721	46.2	125 036	48.7
	2010	533 269	28.3	222 638	46.4	158 978	49.5
	2012	564 085	29.0	236 516	46.4	166 612	49.6
Asia - Asie	1990	204 979	19.2	86 464	41.5	60 853	44.4
	2000	260 314	22.7	112 209	40.3	69 994	44.8
	2010	302 541	27.1	142 514	41.4	78 960	48.0
	2012	310 896	28.1	149 341	41.5	80 416	48.4
Islands - Îles (7)	1990	1 232	21.4	397	34.5	314	45.9
	2000	1 532	23.0	530	35.1	383	46.7
	2010	2 997	25.6	1 035	34.9	825	46.8
	2012	3 115	26.2	1 098	35.1	870	46.9

For sources and notes, see end of table.

Pour les sources et les notes, se reporter à la fin du tableau.

Economic grouping / Groupements économiques	Year / Année	Population		Total labour force / Main-d'œuvre totale		Agriculture labour force / Main-d'œuvre agricole	
		Total (thousands) / Total (milliers)	Urban population (% of total population) / Population urbaine (en % de la population totale)	Total (thousands) / Total (milliers)	Female labour (% of total labour force) / Main-d'œuvre féminine (en % de la main-d'œuvre totale)	Total (thousands) / Total (milliers)	Female labour (% of total agriculture labour force) / Main-d'œuvre féminine (en % de la main-d'œuvre agricole totale)
		(1)	(2)	(3)	(4)	(5)	(6)
Major petroleum and gas exporters - *Principaux exportateurs de pétrole et de gaz*	*1990*	*252 430*	*52.2*	*73 379*	*25.2*	*25 890*	*34.1*
	2000	*315 680*	*58.4*	*99 273*	*29.4*	*27 762*	*38.7*
	2010	*400 072*	*63.4*	*135 453*	*30.5*	*30 105*	*43.6*
	2012	*419 556*	*63.9*	*143 045*	*30.7*	*30 384*	*44.7*
Africa - Afrique	1990	136 451	40.1	41 606	31.9	18 046	39.4
	2000	173 697	47.1	55 056	36.2	19 601	41.5
	2010	222 360	53.6	70 941	38.6	21 391	45.6
	2012	234 291	54.6	74 794	38.6	21 744	46.5
America - Amérique	1990	19 741	84.0	7 213	31.5	867	4.2
	2000	24 408	89.7	10 527	37.2	811	5.4
	2010	29 043	93.1	13 463	39.4	722	6.4
	2012	29 955	93.5	14 130	39.8	698	6.4
Asia - Asie	1990	96 238	62.9	24 560	11.9	6 977	24.0
	2000	117 576	68.5	33 690	15.8	7 350	34.7
	2010	148 669	72.2	51 049	17.0	7 992	41.5
	2012	155 311	72.2	54 122	17.4	7 942	43.2
Major exporters of manufactured goods - *Principaux exportateurs d'articles manufacturés*	*1990*	*1 378 082*	*32.1*	*745 935*	*43.8*	*517 627*	*46.6*
	2000	*1 526 797*	*41.1*	*845 522*	*44.1*	*537 654*	*47.1*
	2010	*1 632 968*	*52.7*	*938 790*	*43.9*	*531 072*	*47.2*
	2012	*1 655 392*	*54.9*	*953 784*	*43.8*	*525 357*	*47.2*
America - Amérique	1990	86 077	70.0	30 395	29.9	8 439	12.4
	2000	103 874	71.9	40 256	33.0	8 658	12.3
	2010	117 886	74.9	49 605	36.5	7 905	12.3
	2012	120 847	75.4	51 717	36.9	7 708	12.3
Asia - Asie	1990	1 292 005	29.6	715 540	44.4	509 188	47.2
	2000	1 422 923	38.8	805 266	44.6	528 996	47.7
	2010	1 515 082	51.0	889 185	44.3	523 167	47.8
	2012	1 534 544	53.3	902 067	44.2	517 649	47.7
Emerging economies - Économies émergentes	*1990*	*444 398*	*67.3*	*183 203*	*36.6*	*54 347*	*31.2*
	2000	*514 580*	*72.2*	*231 207*	*39.3*	*51 894*	*31.1*
	2010	*571 257*	*75.9*	*276 993*	*41.3*	*47 205*	*31.2*
	2012	*581 690*	*76.5*	*285 659*	*41.5*	*45 827*	*31.1*
America - Amérique	1990	303 336	74.2	119 628	33.8	27 666	16.5
	2000	356 736	79.0	157 481	38.5	27 747	19.4
	2010	399 884	81.9	193 086	41.4	25 015	20.5
	2012	408 043	82.4	199 712	41.7	24 259	20.6
Asia - Asie	1990	141 061	52.5	63 575	41.9	26 681	46.3
	2000	157 844	57.0	73 726	41.0	24 147	44.6
	2010	171 373	61.7	83 907	40.9	22 190	43.2
	2012	173 647	62.5	85 947	41.0	21 568	42.9
Newly industrialized Asian economies - *Économies nouvellement industrialisées d'Asie*	*1990*	*388 189*	*42.8*	*166 976*	*39.5*	*80 696*	*39.7*
	2000	*452 123*	*49.5*	*207 799*	*38.9*	*85 221*	*38.5*
	2010	*512 543*	*54.2*	*244 339*	*39.4*	*85 107*	*38.0*
	2012	*524 366*	*55.1*	*252 119*	*39.5*	*84 552*	*38.0*
First tier - Première génération	1990	72 062	74.8	26 858	36.7	3 476	44.1
	2000	78 915	79.4	32 422	37.6	2 209	44.0
	2010	83 744	82.4	36 215	37.9	1 276	43.3
	2012	84 770	82.7	37 112	37.9	1 134	43.1
Second tier - Deuxième génération	1990	316 127	35.5	140 118	40.1	77 220	39.5
	2000	373 208	43.2	175 377	39.1	83 012	38.3
	2010	428 799	48.7	208 124	39.6	83 831	37.9
	2012	439 596	49.8	215 007	39.7	83 418	37.9

For sources and notes, see end of table.　　　　　　　　　　Pour les sources et les notes, se reporter à la fin du tableau.

Economic grouping / Groupements économiques	Year / Année	Population Total (thousands) / Total (milliers) (1)	Population Urban population (% of total population) / Population urbaine (en % de la population totale) (2)	Total labour force / Main-d'œuvre totale Total (thousands) / Total (milliers) (3)	Total labour force Female labour (% of total labour force) / Main-d'œuvre féminine (en % de la main-d'œuvre totale) (4)	Agriculture labour force / Main-d'œuvre agricole Total (thousands) / Total (milliers) (5)	Agriculture labour force Female labour (% of total agriculture labour force) / Main-d'œuvre féminine (en % de la main-d'œuvre agricole totale) (6)
Developing economies: Africa - Économies en développement : Afrique	1990	629 284	32.2	227 627	39.9	144 596	45.9
	2000	807 419	35.6	302 119	41.5	177 263	47.1
	2010	1 030 035	38.8	397 233	42.5	214 508	48.4
	2012	1 082 443	39.4	419 826	42.5	222 939	48.6
Northern Africa excluding Sudan - Afrique septentrionale sans le Soudan	1990	119 646	48.4	34 354	23.0	12 445	38.7
	2000	141 295	51.6	44 045	21.8	13 288	41.2
	2010	163 453	55.5	55 840	23.7	13 680	44.6
	2012	168 754	56.0	58 178	24.0	13 571	45.0
Sub-Saharan Africa - Afrique subsaharienne	1990	509 421	28.4	193 204	42.9	132 109	46.6
	2000	665 819	32.2	257 965	44.9	163 922	47.6
	2010	866 067	35.6	341 173	45.5	200 746	48.7
	2012	913 139	36.3	361 410	45.5	209 282	48.8
Sub-Saharan Africa excluding South Africa - Afrique subsaharienne sans l'Afrique du Sud	1990	472 844	26.6	182 395	43.4	130 537	46.7
	2000	621 278	30.5	242 577	45.0	162 493	47.7
	2010	815 129	34.1	323 185	45.7	199 640	48.8
	2012	850 465	35.1	339 536	45.8	208 247	48.9
Developing economies: America - Économies en développement : Amérique	1990	440 721	69.9	170 320	33.7	42 460	16.8
	2000	521 398	74.6	225 581	38.3	43 453	19.5
	2010	591 285	77.9	279 453	41.2	41 502	20.9
	2012	604 869	78.4	289 983	41.5	40 819	21.0
Central America and Greater Caribbean Islands excluding Puerto Rico - Amérique centrale et Grandes Antilles sans Porto Rico	1990	142 427	62.1	51 521	31.7	15 733	14.3
	2000	170 558	65.3	66 238	34.5	16 067	14.3
	2010	194 482	69.0	82 321	37.7	15 707	14.7
	2012	199 577	69.7	85 870	38.0	15 564	14.8
Central America and Greater Caribbean Islands excluding Mexico and Puerto Rico - Amérique centrale et Grandes Antilles sans le Mexique et Porto Rico	1990	56 350	50.2	21 126	34.3	7 294	16.5
	2000	66 685	55.0	25 982	36.9	7 409	16.7
	2010	76 596	60.1	32 716	39.4	7 802	17.2
	2012	78 730	61.0	34 152	39.7	7 856	17.2
South America and Central America - Amérique du Sud et Amérique centrale	1990	410 824	71.2	158 365	33.4	38 807	16.1
	2000	487 678	75.9	211 834	38.2	39 796	19.1
	2010	554 336	78.9	263 045	41.1	37 835	20.5
	2012	567 346	79.4	273 119	41.4	37 156	20.6
South America excluding Brazil - Amérique du Sud sans le Brésil	1990	146 070	74.1	55 244	33.8	12 528	17.8
	2000	173 577	77.8	74 497	38.4	13 926	21.7
	2010	198 579	80.9	94 228	41.5	14 613	24.6
	2012	203 603	81.3	98 068	41.9	14 647	25.0
Developing economies: Asia - Économies en développement : Asie	1990	2 999 068	30.0	1 367 866	38.1	898 011	42.2
	2000	3 491 781	35.9	1 628 874	37.9	969 780	42.4
	2010	3 928 277	43.1	1 885 572	37.1	1 014 276	42.6
	2012	4 014 712	44.4	1 938 604	37.0	1 017 422	42.5
Eastern and South-Eastern Asia excluding China - Asie orientale et Asie du Sud-Est sans la Chine	1990	535 519	38.3	238 669	42.4	126 346	43.3
	2000	625 077	43.8	296 969	41.8	137 757	42.6
	2010	703 511	48.6	351 771	42.2	144 498	42.5
	2012	718 700	49.6	362 939	42.2	145 054	42.5
Southern Asia excluding India - Asie méridionale sans l'Inde	1990	322 757	28.9	110 584	27.7	64 077	35.1
	2000	405 589	32.4	145 063	27.9	73 197	37.2
	2010	475 782	35.9	190 667	30.3	85 647	42.2
	2012	489 757	36.5	200 568	30.6	87 456	43.0

For sources and notes, see next page.

Pour les sources et les notes, se reporter à la page suivante.

8

Source:

Data in this table are based on figures in table 8.4.1

Notes: ·

(1)   Total population: de facto population in a country, area or region as of 1 July of the year indicated. Figures are presented in thousands.

(2)   Urban population as percentage of total population: population living in areas classified as urban according to the criteria used by each area or country. Data refer to 1st July of the year indicated.

(3)   Total labour force: comprises all persons (both sexes) of age 15 and above.

(4)   Female labour force as percentage of total labour force: comprises all females of age 15 and above.

(5)   Total labour force in agriculture: is that part (male and female) of the total labour force engaged or seeking work in agriculture, hunting, fishing or forestry.

(6)   Female labour force as percentage of total agriculture labour force: is that part (female) of the total labour force engaged or seeking work in agriculture, hunting, fishing or forestry.

(7)   2003: Break in the series.

Sources :

Les données dans ce tableau ont été calculées d'après les chiffres du tableau 8.4.1

Notes :

(1)   Population totale : de facto population d'un pays ou d'une région au 1er juillet de l'année indiquée. Les chiffres sont présentés en milliers.

(2)   Population urbaine en pourcentage de la population totale : la population au 1er juillet vivant dans une région classée comme urbaine selon les critères définis par une région ou un pays.

(3)   Main-d'œuvre totale : toutes les personnes (hommes et femmes) de 15 ans et plus.

(4)   Main-d'œuvre féminine en pourcentage de la main d'œuvre totale : toutes les personnes de sexe féminin de 15 ans et plus.

(5)   Main-d'œuvre totale dans l'agriculture : la part (hommes et femmes) du total de la main-d'œuvre qui travaille ou cherche du travail dans l'agriculture, la chasse, la pêche ou la sylviculture.

(6)   Main-d'œuvre totale féminine en pourcentage du total de la main-d'œuvre dans l'agriculture : la part (femmes) du total de la main-d'œuvre qui travaille ou cherche du travail dans l'agriculture, la chasse, la pêche ou la sylviculture.

(7)   2003 : Rupture dans la série.